AUGUSTANA UNIVERSITY COLLEGE
LIBRARY

A Preponderance of Power

Stanford Nuclear Age Series

General Editor, Martin Sherwin

ADVISORY BOARD   Barton J. Bernstein, David Holloway, and Wolfgang K.H. Panofsky

MELVYN P. LEFFLER

A Preponderance of

POWER

National Security,

the Truman Administration,

and the Cold War

 Stanford University Press, Stanford, California

Stanford University Press
Stanford, California
© 1992 by the Board of Trustees of the
Leland Stanford Junior University
Printed in the United States of America

CIP data appear at the end of the book

Published with the assistance of the
National Endowment for the Humanities

E
813
.L45
1992

70629

For Mollie and Louis Leffler
and for Sarah and Elliot

לְדֹר וָדֹר

From Generation to Generation

AUGUSTANA UNIVERSITY COLLEGE
LIBRARY

Preface and Acknowledgments

In the United States the cold war shaped our political culture, our institutions, and our national priorities. Abroad, it influenced the destinies of people everywhere. It divided Europe, split Germany, and engulfed the Third World. It led to a feverish arms race and massive sales of military equipment to poor nations. For at least four decades it left the world in a chronic state of tension where a miscalculation could trigger nuclear holocaust.

When I began research on this book in the summer of 1979, the cold war was entering a dangerous new stage. But then a dramatic sequence of events took place. Mikhail Gorbachev assumed power in the Soviet Union. He loosened the reins of internal repression and entered into serious arms control talks. Within a couple of years, he allowed East European satellites to gravitate out of the Soviet orbit, cut Russian troops and armaments in Central Europe, and began retrenching from positions in the Third World. More spectacularly, Gorbachev permitted the East Germans to undergo their own revolution, pull down the Berlin Wall, and unite with West Germany. Almost overnight the geopolitical and ideological competition of the cold war appeared to end.

And as it did, historians of U.S. foreign policy have had to rethink many fundamental assumptions and critical issues. What did contemporary developments mean for our understanding of the origins of the cold war? Of course, recent events did not alter the facts of history. We still had the documents, oral histories, and memoirs that illuminated the goals, motives, and fears of U.S. officials; these did not change. But what needed reappraisal was our judgment of policymakers' perceptions, actions, and tactics.

In the view of many observers, the cold warriors of the 1940's and 1950's seem more prescient than ever before. They had always insisted that a relentless policy of containment would force the Soviets to rethink their foreign policy, modify their ideology, and restructure their social system. And they prophesied that, when Soviet attitudes and policies shifted, the cold war would end.

But the dramatic changes of the Gorbachev era have also invited inquiries of a different sort. Had opportunities been lost? Might changes have come earlier? Were Soviet goals insatiably expansionist and dictated by rigid ideological imperatives? Or did U.S. policies help cause, widen, and prolong a competition that otherwise might have evolved in different ways?

In the past several years, Soviet and U.S. historians have been meeting to discuss the origins of the cold war. Thanks to the sponsorship of the Tufts University Nuclear Age History and Humanities Center, the Soviet Foreign Ministry, the Soviet Institute for the USA and Canada, the U.S. Institute for Peace, and Princeton University's John Foster Dulles Program, I have attended four such meetings. The polemics are gone, and serious inquiry has been the norm. Soviet scholars want to study their past. They are particularly eager to examine the cold war. In their view it exacted a far heavier toll upon them than upon Americans, since it helped to perpetuate the neo-Stalinist system they endured for decades.

To underscore the importance that Soviet reformers attach to such matters, Foreign Minister Eduard Shevardnadze invited a group of historians to meet with him in June 1990. In solemn, carefully measured tones he urged us to conduct our studies with objectivity. The cold war, he insisted, wasted lives and money. Science and technology were put to destructive uses. We all had illusions; we all made mistakes; we all lost. Historians, he went on, had an obligation to sharpen understanding of the past and to shape public opinion. Our children and grandchildren, he said, deserve a better future, and they will not have it unless we can overcome our mutual fears, learn the lessons of the past, and focus on the common human values that bind us together rather than on the class and national interests that divide us.

Shevardnadze's message was inspiring, but the dialogue between the historians was not quite so fruitful. Soviet historians still work under a major handicap; they do not have anything approaching free access to the documents. The individuals we met with, of course, were a privileged group, and many of them had seen selected files from the Foreign Ministry records. In the future an archives law, just passed, may make materials available in a more formal, systematic, and equitable manner. But Soviet historians concede that, even under the most auspicious political circumstances, conditions will not change quickly. And even when they do, the results may not live up to expectations. The documents that have become available thus far do not illuminate the thinking and deliberations of the leading men in the Kremlin; they are mostly instructions to foreign embassies and dispatches from ambassadors abroad. Stalin's aims and motives remain as enigmatic as ever. Despite the revelations about the purges and collectivization, despite the open inquiry into the Nazi-Soviet pact of 1939 and the Katyn forest massacre of 1940, scant new evidence has appeared thus far about his diplomacy in the late 1940's and early 1950's.

Nevertheless, Soviet historians are not reluctant to discuss Stalin's role in the making of the cold war. They have no desire to conceal the brutality of his regime and they denounce his domestic policies. But when some U.S. scholars sought to pin the blame for the cold war on his shoulders, few of the Soviet historians concurred. They freely admit that he erred repeatedly, but they insist that Truman did as well. They emphasize, moreover, that Stalin had reason to fear the American atomic monopoly. Yet, notwithstanding this apprehension, they believe that at least initially he wanted to cooperate with the United States.

It is difficult to evaluate these assertions. Western students of Soviet foreign policy are themselves debating these issues, but they, too, labor under the handicap of inadequate source materials and must draw inferences from very limited evidence.[1] In this book, rather than dwell on Soviet aims and motives that remain unknowable, I have chosen to focus on the U.S. side of the cold war equation.

My aim is to answer questions of enduring interest: Did the United States want to cooperate with or contain the Soviet Union at the end of World War II? What were the most important factors shaping American policy? Who were the most influential men making decisions? To what extent were they motivated by economic, strategic, ideological, bureaucratic, or political considerations? Why did the cold war spread to the Third World? Why did Soviet-U.S. competition develop into a feverish arms race? Was the United States responsible for the cold war, and, if so, in what ways? Overall, was U.S. policy wise or foolish?

I am the beneficiary of a massive declassification of documents that has gone on in the United States during the past ten to fifteen years. Before the late 1970's, writers on the cold war relied on an extensive memoir literature, some private manuscripts, and selective State Department files. Now we have access to the files of the Army, Navy, and Air Force, the Joint Chiefs of Staff, the Department of Defense, the Bureau of the Budget, and some intelligence agencies as well as to a vastly larger number of manuscript collections and State Department records. Other historians have used these records to explore specialized topics and discrete chronological periods, but I believe I am the first to try to marshal this evidence in behalf of an overall analysis of national security policy during the Truman years.

My emphasis is on grand strategy. Grand strategy describes the process by which officials identified vital national security interests and charted the political, economic, military, and diplomatic moves necessary for their realization. Truman administration officials believed in the importance of an open international economy and a favorable balance of power. But they encountered formidable challenges. I spend a good deal of time examining their perception of threat and analyzing their assessment of Soviet intentions and capabilities. To safeguard American security, they believed the United States had to help rebuild Western Europe, co-opt German and Japanese power, and promote orderly decolonization in the Third World. These tasks demanded considerable risk-taking. And risk-taking required a belief in one's superior military power. The significance of my approach, therefore, rests in the linkages I draw between threat assessment and foreign policy behavior, between economics and geopolitics, between action in the industrial core of Eurasia and initiatives in the underdeveloped periphery, and between military capabilities and diplomatic risk-taking. I would not have been able to draw these linkages without the work of political psychologists, economists, and sociologists who have been studying the relationships between threat perception, deterrence, and security and who have been illuminating the dynamics of dependency and hegemony in the world political economy.[2]

Nor would this book have been possible without the help of many historians who have written articles, essays, and monographs of greater and greater erudition and sophistication. I have benefited enormously from their study of the Soviet-U.S. confrontation in Eastern Europe, from their assessments of U.S. policies in China and Southeast Asia, and from their analyses of reconstruction policies in Western Europe.[3] As my intent is to blend military history with diplomacy and occupation history with foreign economic policy, I have also been dependent on their thoughtful accounts of the strategic arms race and their incisive studies of U.S. occupation regimes in Germany, Japan, and Korea.[4] In fact, one of the goals of this book is to synthesize this body of monographic work.

One of the most interesting questions raised by the recent literature on the cold war is the extent to which U.S. policy was influenced by other nations. The British, some historians now say, were even more eager than the Americans to contain the Soviet Union. Winston Churchill, not Truman, was the archetypical cold warrior; Ernest Bevin, not George Marshall or Dean Acheson, was the real founder of the Atlantic alliance. European reconstruction, some argue, sprang not from the Marshall Plan but from European initiatives. Beyond Western Europe, as well, U.S. policy was often shaped by the fears, demands, and pressures of prospective allies. Geir Lundestad, the insightful Norwegian historian, has coined the phrase "empire by invitation" to describe these developments and to explain the evolution of America's global posture.[5]

This historical scholarship has influenced my thinking. Foreign governments conveyed their hopes and fears to American diplomats and policymakers. Officials in London, Paris, Bonn, Tokyo, Ankara, Manila, and elsewhere had their own objectives. Sometimes their goals converged with U.S. aims; sometimes they did not. Although this book does not pretend to be an international history of the cold war and I do not examine the actions of other governments in any depth, I am concerned with assessing their impact on policy formulation in the United States.

Policymakers in Washington realized they could not preserve a favorable correlation of forces vis-à-vis the Soviet Union without accommodating the needs of local governments, regional powers, and foreign elites. The United States could not dictate policy; weaker allies retained considerable leverage. Their very weakness was sometimes a source of strength because officials in Washington feared, often mistakenly, that foreign governments might veer toward neutrality, succumb to leftist pressures, adopt statist practices, or look to the Kremlin for help against regional foes or domestic adversaries.

Some foreign requests for guarantees and assistance were not new. After World War I the British and French had sought American commitments and government loans. Similarly, the Germans had maneuvered for U.S. support of their efforts to reduce reparations and achieve territorial revision and equality of armaments.[6] What differentiated the two postwar eras was the degree to which U.S. officials chose to involve themselves in such controversies. Because of the lessons of the past, the threats they perceived, and the new ways in which they defined vital interests, Truman administration officials had reason to make sacrifices and assume responsibilities that their predecessors had eschewed. They also had unprecedented wealth and power to exert their influence.

Democratic allies and authoritarian friends assented to U.S. leadership of the non-Communist world because they found it beneficial to do so. They often received money, arms, and guarantees that they could use to stabilize their countries, promote economic growth, and counter domestic foes and regional enemies as well as to defy the Kremlin. They often participated in defining the terms and elaborating the tactics that were used by U.S. policymakers to wage the cold war. American officials, however, set their own goals, focusing their attention on reviving productivity in the industrial core nations of Eurasia, incorporating Western Europe, West Germany, and Japan into a U.S.-managed alliance, and integrating core and periphery. If they failed to achieve these objectives, they thought Soviet power would grow and American preponderance would be compromised. And if such things should happen, they believed the physical safety of the United States would be imperiled, its economic interests threatened, and its free institutions and marketplace economy endangered. The United States, as Dean Acheson liked to say, might survive but it would not be the country he loved.[7]

■

I have been working on this book for almost a dozen years. Many people and institutions have helped me. First and foremost have been my wife, Phyllis, and my children, Sarah and Elliot. As I have approached the completion of this book, they have cheered me on, commenting on my exquisite timing, waiting as I did for the tumultuous events of recent years to unfold before finishing my analysis! Actually, my children have grown up with this book, and one of the unintended benefits of having worked on it so long has been to hear them ask more and more penetrating questions about its findings and purpose.

Many organizations have supported my research and writing. Fellowships from the Woodrow Wilson Center, the American Council of Learned Societies, and the Harry S. Truman Institute enabled me to complete much of the research. Timely grants from the Vanderbilt University Research Council also helped. I was a Council on Foreign Relations Fellow in 1980–81, and the experiences I had working in the Pentagon as a result of that opportunity provided me with a much better grasp of how the government functions. In 1984–85 the Lehrman Foundation afforded me a wonderful forum to discuss some of the ideas that make up the early chapters of the book. Subsequently, the Center for Advanced Study at the University of Virginia gave me the released time to complete the volume.

As everyone who works on the cold war knows, the records are voluminous. I am deeply indebted to many archivists. Particularly helpful were Dennis Bilger at the Truman Library; Sally Marks, Ron Swerczek, and Steve Tilly at the National Archives; and Martha Crawley, Leslie Grover, and Dean Allard at the Naval Historical Center. But most of all I want to thank Wilbert Mahoney, who worked patiently with me for many years in the modern military branch of the National Archives. Each time I appeared and pressed for more indexes and more records, I sensed Will's exasperation. But he never ceased to assist me, and without his aid I would never have gotten through the materials that were indispensable to the writing of this book.

As I grappled with the issues and events that make up this volume, I benefited greatly from the work and assistance of many graduate students. Cecilia Stiles Cornell shared her knowledge of James Forrestal with me; Peter Hahn illuminated the strategic role of Egypt in Anglo-American relations; Doug Flamming helped me think about the impact of geopolitics on postwar U.S. foreign policy; Mary DeCredico did some valuable research on Persian Gulf oil; Nick Cullather patiently explained the significance of the Philippines in the East Asian policy of the United States; Carey Goodman explored the attitudes of business organizations and associations during the first postwar recession; and Laura Belmonte looked at the reactions of the popular media to Stalinist repression. I owe a special thanks to James Lewis, who made sense out of my index cards and helped put together my bibliography.

Once I began putting my ideas on paper, I received wonderfully constructive criticism from scholars working on related issues. Sam Walker began reading drafts of my early chapters in 1984 and has prodded me forward ever since. David Painter exchanged notes with me on Middle Eastern oil questions, phoned me repeatedly with references to new books and articles, and encouraged me to think ever more deeply about the relationships between national strategy and political economy. Bill Burr did much the same, sending me documents and probing my writings with insightful questions. Bob McMahon spent a year in Charlottesville in 1987–88, read my manuscript with painstaking care, and gave me invaluable substantive and organizational suggestions. At an even later stage, Marty Sherwin, Richard Immerman, and Michael Hogan reviewed the book and offered much constructive advice.

There are others who made this book possible. John Arthur offered endless encouragement. Lewis Bateman helped with some wonderful stylistic suggestions. Liz Safly made each visit to the Truman Library a pleasant experience. Kiddy

Moore, Ella Wood, Lottie McCauley, and Kathleen Miller typed and corrected draft after draft with enormous patience and good cheer. And the late Henry Blumenthal bequeathed to me the research materials he was collecting for another volume in his series of books on Franco-American relations.

Finally, I want to express a word of appreciation to mentors, friends, and colleagues who have been so important over the years. Gerd Korman was the first to introduce me to a serious study of history, and although I forgot to mention him in my first book, I shan't make the same mistake again. Marvin Zahniser, John Burnham, and Mary Young were teachers whose friendship and advice I still deeply cherish. Sam McSeveney, Bob Isherwood, Keith Davies, Paul Conkin, Holger Herwig, Susan Wiltshire, Raj Menon, John Oneal, Harry Ransom, and Elizabeth and Lew Perry provided intellectual sustenance and companionship during some very good and some very tough times at Vanderbilt. And to my current colleagues at Virginia, I salute you all for creating such a congenial place to work.

Contents

Maps

Abbreviations

CCP	Chinese Communist Party
CEEC	Committee on European Economic Cooperation
CIA	Central Intelligence Agency
EAM	Greek National Liberation Front
ECA	Economic Cooperation Administration
EDC	European Defense Community
EPU	European Payments Union
ERP	European Recovery Program
GATT	General Agreement on Tariffs and Trade
ITO	International Trade Organization
JCS	Joint Chiefs of Staff
KKE	Greek Communist Party
KMT	Kuomintang Party (Nationalist; China)
KPD	German Communist Party
MRP	Mouvement républicain populaire (France)
NATO	North Atlantic Treaty Organization
NME	National Military Establishment
NSC	National Security Council
NSRB	National Security Resources Board
OEEC	Organization of European Economic Cooperation
SED	Socialist Unity Party (Germany)
SPD	Social Democratic Party (Germany)
SWNCC	State-War-Navy Coordinating Committee
UMT	Universal Military Training

A Preponderance of Power

Introduction

So much suffering; such fleeting hope. World War II wrought devastation and destruction on an unprecedented scale. Man's brutality and inhumanity reached new heights. Fifty million people perished. Along with the battlefield casualties there was genocide, disease, starvation. Urban centers were bombed, civilians were deported, innocent people were massacred. The war came to a stunning end with atomic blasts over Hiroshima and Nagasaki, instantly killing over a hundred thousand people in the two cities.[1]

Although the survivors yearned for a better future, the process of reconstruction would be painful, wrenching, and disillusioning. Much of Europe and important parts of Asia were wastelands. Many of the world's greatest cities—Berlin, Warsaw, Vienna, Leningrad, Tokyo—had been reduced to rubble. Tens of millions of people had no shelter. Millions more were on the road, returning home from battlefields and forced labor camps; equal numbers, usually ethnic minorities, were seeking new homes after being expelled from the countries of their birth.[2]

Hunger reigned. Everywhere farm lands had been despoiled, cattle slaughtered, herds dispersed, and draft animals killed. Many of the dikes along China's Yellow River had been blown up. Water covered 540,000 acres of the Dutch countryside. In Poland almost three-fourths of the horses and two-thirds of the cattle were gone. In the Ukraine most of the villages had been razed, hundreds of thousands of farms burned, half of all the tractors destroyed, and most of the livestock killed. Famine wracked parts of China and Russia. Millions died from diseases—cholera, tuberculosis, plague, smallpox, and malaria—that ravaged undernourished and weakened bodies.[3] For Europe as a whole, food production in 1945–46 was less than two-thirds of its prewar total; as late as 1948–49 rice production in Asia had still not reached the levels of the mid-1930's.[4]

Transportation facilities were wrecked. Demolished bridges and sunken vessels clogged river traffic on the Rhine and the Danube as well as on hundreds of other inland waterways and canals. Railroad roadbeds were ruined and rolling stock destroyed. Ports were bombed and coastal shipping sunk. In 1945 less than a quarter of the aid that Yugoslavia needed could be imported and transported; in 1946 only a third of Poland's railroads operated normally.[5]

Given the magnitude of the devastation, the recuperative forces were most impressive. Governments and peoples immediately turned their efforts to reconstruction. Notwithstanding the food and fuel shortages, industries in most countries (but not Germany and Japan) soon produced as many goods as they had before the war. But people's hopes and expectations far exceeded the realities they encountered. They wanted more than their governments were able to deliver. In Western Europe, for example, even the meager improvements appeared ephemeral as frigid temperatures in the winter of 1947 exhausted fuel supplies and as inadequate rainfall shriveled crops and intensified the need for imported grain.[6]

Conditions in the United States were of a different sort. Almost 400,000 American soldiers died in World War II and another million were wounded. But the American people did not experience the suffering, the hardship, the profound upheaval that beset most of humanity during the early 1940's. The United States emerged from the conflict richer and stronger than it had ever been before. While the mines, fields, and factories of Eurasia were flooded, ravaged, and bombed, American manufacturing and agricultural production attained new peaks. National income soared. At the end of the war the United States had two-thirds of the world's gold reserves and three-fourths of its invested capital. More than half of the entire world's manufacturing capacity was located in the United States, and the nation was turning out more than a third of all goods produced around the world. It owned half the world's supply of shipping and was the world's largest exporter of goods and services. The gross national product of the United States was three times Soviet Russia's and more than five times Great Britain's.[7]

America's enormously productive economy bestowed upon the country great military power. During the war the United States developed the capability to turn out almost 100,000 planes a year and 30,000 tanks. In 1943 its factories produced $37.5 billion worth of armaments (compared to $13.9 billion in Soviet Russia, $11.1 billion in Britain, $13.8 billion in Germany, and $4.5 billion in Japan). Its strategic air force was unrivaled. Its navy dominated the seas. Its aircraft carriers and marine divisions enabled it to project its power across the oceans. It held a monopoly over humanity's most intimidating weapon, the atomic bomb. The United States had preponderant power.[8]

As Paul Kennedy shows in his masterly book, American preponderance inhered in its economic strength and technological prowess. For centuries these factors had been the keys to relative power in the international system.[9] U.S. policymakers were altogether cognizant that their country's national security resided in its relative economic and technological superiority over any potential adversary. Power inhered in a nation's control over or access to industrial infrastructure, raw materials, skilled labor, and critical bases. In 1945 the United States held a uniquely preeminent position. For many officials, businessmen, and publicists, victory confirmed the superiority of American values: individual liberty, representative government, free enterprise, private property, and a marketplace economy. Given their country's overwhelming power, they now expected to refashion the world in America's image and create the American century. They intended to promote world peace and foster international stability at the same time that they safeguarded national security, perpetuated American power, and further augmented American prosperity.[10] It was a wonderful image. Yet even before the guns fell silent, the exhilaration of victory was marred by omnipresent fears that America's relative power would soon erode, its security would be endangered, and its prosperity would prove fleeting.

Fears and Threats

As World War II drew to a close, U.S. officials worried about the growing strength of the Soviet Union. The Kremlin had proven itself a valiant and courageous ally. Soviet armies, totaling almost fourteen million troops, had turned the tide of battle at Stalingrad. Beginning in 1943 Soviet soldiers counterattacked. Withstanding incalculable hardship, they drove Nazi forces out of Russian territory, across Eastern Europe and the Balkans, and back into Germany. The Kremlin was not easy to deal with. Nevertheless, America's most important military leaders, like Chief of Staff George C. Marshall and General Dwight D. Eisenhower, considered the Soviets reliable on essential military issues. Like President Franklin D. Roosevelt, they aspired for a cooperative relationship with the Kremlin in the postwar world. Yet they were also attuned to disconcerting realities: to Soviet secrecy, territorial aggrandizement, and brutality. Much of this could be explained away in terms of the bestiality of the war on the eastern front, the difficulties of command, control, and logistics, the centuries of ethnic distrust and hatred, and the understandable Soviet desire for security in the future. But the great imponderable was whether the Kremlin wanted more than just security.[11]

The Soviets had overwhelming power on the Eurasian land mass. Germany and Japan were defeated and occupied. France was humiliated, Britain weakened, China engulfed in civil war. Meanwhile, Soviet Russia had annexed strategic strips of Finland, the Baltic provinces of Estonia, Latvia, and Lithuania, small parts of eastern Prussia, a third of prewar Poland, and critical chunks of territory in Ruthenia, Moldavia, and Bessarabia. (See Map 1.) At the Yalta Conference in February 1945, Roosevelt had acceded to Soviet reannexation of the Kurile Islands and southern Sakhalin as well as to the reaffirmation of Russian privileges and concessions on the Manchurian railroads and in Dairen and Port Arthur. Soviet military officers dominated the Allied Control Commissions in Germany's defeated East European

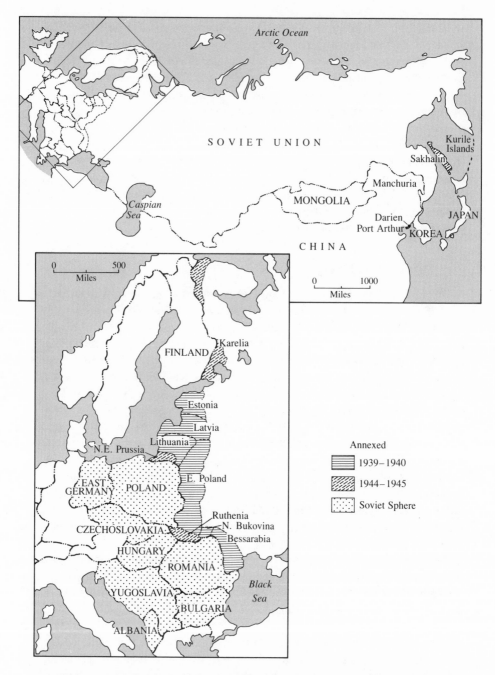

Arctic Ocean

SOVIET UNION

Kurile
Islands
Sakhalin

Caspian
Sea

MONGOLIA

Manchuria

Darien
Port Arthur

JAPAN

KOREA

CHINA

0   1000
Miles

0   500
Miles

FINLAND

Karelia

Estonia

Latvia

Lithuania

N.E. Prussia

E. Poland

EAST
GERMANY

POLAND

Ruthenia

CZECHOSLOVAKIA

N. Bukovina

Bessarabia

HUNGARY

ROMANIA

YUGOSLAVIA

Black
Sea

BULGARIA

ALBANIA

Annexed

1939–1940

1944–1945

Soviet Sphere

1. The Soviet Union in Eurasia at the End of World War II. Adapted from Woodford
McClellan, *Russia: A History of the Soviet Period*, 2nd ed. (Englewood Cliffs, N.J.:
Prentice Hall, 1990), p. 199.

satellites: Hungary, Bulgaria, Romania, and Finland. Russian troops were spread across the liberated countries of Czechoslovakia and Poland, and Soviet military lines of communication to Austria and Germany ran through most of East and East-Central Europe, affording the Kremlin enormous potential influence over the future of this region should it choose to exercise that influence. And there were disturbing signs that it would, including the imposition of pro-Soviet governments, the support of indigenous Communist parties, the extraction of reparation payments, and the confiscation of war booty. Surveying the world scene in the spring of 1944, Admiral William Leahy, the president's chief of staff, remarked that the "outstanding fact to be noted is the recent phenomenal development of heretofore latent Russian military and economic strength—a development which seems certain to prove epochal in its bearing on future politico-military international relationships, and which has yet to reach the full scope attainable with Russian resources." [12]

Worries there were, but at the time of Roosevelt's death American officials did *not* regard the Soviet Union as an enemy and were *not* frightened by Soviet military prowess. Soviet power paled next to that of the United States. The Soviet Union had considerable potential strength, but its existing capabilities were severely circumscribed. After World War II the Soviet Union was an exhausted, devastated nation. American diplomats and military attachés in Moscow could not travel freely, but they could still discern the monumental toll that the war had taken. In early 1947 the Kremlin published the war damage that Soviet Russia had experienced at the hands of Nazi Germany. No one disputed the figures. They confirmed a story of plunder, rapacity, cruelty, and suffering that challenged one's imagination. They compellingly described a country with a herculean task of reconstruction ahead of it.

The German invaders had destroyed over 1,700 cities and towns and more than 70,000 villages and hamlets. They demolished more than six million buildings and over 31,000 industrial enterprises. They wrecked 61 of the largest power stations, 1,100 coal pits, and more than 3,000 oil wells. They dismantled 40,000 miles of railroad track, blew up 56,000 miles of main road, and ruined 90,000 bridges. The Germans ransacked the countryside, destroying tens of thousands of collective farms and machine and tractor stations. They stole and slaughtered 17 million head of cattle, 20 million hogs, 27 million sheep and goats, 110 million poultry, and 7 million horses. More than 20 million Soviet lives were lost in the war, engendering massive bereavement, creating significant shortages in the labor supply, and establishing demographic trends that would last for more than a generation. [13]

U.S. embassy officials in Moscow knew the toll the war had taken. Compared to the United States the Soviets were weak. This realization dramatically affected the thinking of George F. Kennan, certain as he was that the Kremlin would defer to American strength. [14] Similarly, Michael Forrestal, son of Navy Secretary James V. Forrestal, went to Moscow as a naval attaché in April 1947. Young, energetic, curious, and impressionable, he remonstrated against Soviet surveillance and traveled whenever and wherever he could. He was awed by the poverty, devastation, and stoicism of the Russian people. Although they accepted their government, they could not be aroused to go to war. They respected U.S. technological prowess and they would not challenge it. "As for life here," wrote Michael Forrestal, "I don't remember the depression in the states, but the standard of living and mental attitude brought about by the worst depression must be a kind of paradise unimaginable in comparison to official prosperity here." [15]

The Soviet Union would become a formidable competitor of the United States only if it could capture or co-opt the industrial infrastructure, natural resources, and skilled labor of more advanced countries. The men in the Kremlin would not opt voluntarily to use military force to achieve their objectives. If they did so, they would provoke war with the United States because American officials would never permit the Soviet Union to assimilate the human and material resources of Western Europe or Japan. If the Russians should launch a premeditated attack, they would pay for their transitory success in the protracted war that would ensue. Eventually, America's enormously superior warmaking economy and its strategic air power would prevail. In the 1940's, after all, the Soviets had no long-range air force, no atomic bomb, no surface fleet. Military officials and civilian policymakers might fret about the specter of another Pearl Harbor, but the truth of the matter was that in the early postwar years the only conceivable adversary of the United States had no capacity to attack American territory and had no ability to inflict damage on the American economy.[16]

U.S. officials, therefore, did not expect Soviet military aggression. But they were frightened that the men in the Kremlin might capitalize on developments they did not cause but that could redound to their long-term advantage. Throughout the war years the political left had gathered momentum. As people withstood the travail of the conflict, they expected their governments to lead them forward to a better future. They would not tolerate the restoration of the old order. They would not passively accept another depression. They expected their governments to protect them from the vagaries of business fluctuations, the avarice of capitalists, and the occasional disasters of the natural world. This was their due for the sacrifices they had endured and the hardships they had overcome. Moreover, their vision of the future embraced more than democratic political reforms; they wanted a more just and equitable social and economic order. Throughout Europe, east and west, people demanded land reform, nationalization, and social welfare.[17] "They have suffered so much," said Assistant Secretary of State Dean G. Acheson, "and they believe so deeply that governments can take some action which will alleviate their sufferings, that they will demand that the whole business of state control and state interference shall be pushed further and further." [18]

Amidst the recrudescence of Europe's left, Communist strength looked increasingly formidable. In many countries, the Communists overcame the opprobrium that had fallen upon them when the Kremlin signed the infamous Molotov-Ribbentrop pact with Germany in 1939. After the Nazi attack on Soviet territory in June 1941, Communist partisans came to play an important role in resistance movements. At the same time the courage and achievements of Soviet armies in defeating the bulk of Nazi strength imparted a new image to the Soviet Union. Notwithstanding the ravages and pillage of Russian armies, particularly in defeated Axis countries, many Europeans now saw the Kremlin as liberator. In many countries Communist leaders appeared as heroes of the resistance, proponents of socioeconomic reform, and champions of their nations' self-interest.[19]

Communist membership soared. The Belgian party grew from 9,000 in 1939 to 100,000 in November 1945; in Holland from 10,000 in 1938 to 53,000 in 1946; in Greece from 17,000 in 1935 to 70,000 in 1945; in Italy from 5,000 in 1943 to 1,700,000 at the end of 1945; in Czechoslovakia from 28,000 in May 1945 to 750,000 in September 1945; in Hungary from a few hundred in 1942 to 100,000 in December 1945. In France, Italy, and Finland the Communist vote was already 20 percent of the electorate in 1945; in Belgium, Denmark, Norway, Holland, and Sweden, it was close to 10 percent. These percentages were all the more impressive because of the fractious nature of multiparty politics in most European countries.[20]

U.S. policymakers viewed these developments with trepidation. They were altogether aware of the great appeal of Communist ideology to demoralized peoples who had suffered greatly in depression and war and who faced new hardships and shortages during the difficult reconstruction process. Many of these peoples had become disillusioned with bourgeois middle-of-the-road parties that had failed to meet their needs in the past. Yet American officials regarded Communist parties everywhere as tools of the Kremlin. Initially they were uncertain if Moscow was or was not encouraging local Communists to seize power. But this was not of decisive importance. Policymakers in Washington assumed that wherever and however Communists gained power, they would pursue policies that directly or indirectly served the purposes of the Soviet government.[21]

Apprehensions about Communist takeovers in Western Europe were accentuated by what U.S. officials observed to be happening in Eastern Europe. Almost immediately the Kremlin signed bilateral economic treaties with Romania, Hungary, Bulgaria, and Poland that reoriented their trade eastward. These agreements underscored the Kremlin's efforts to co-opt valuable East European resources and use them to hasten Russia's economic recovery and augment her military strength. Traditionally, Eastern Europe provided Western Europe and especially Germany with grain, meat, wood and pulp, hides, skins, coal, coke, and oil. These products were among those commodities most desperately needed in France, Belgium, Italy, and the western zones of Germany.[22] Their absence intensified the dollar shortage in Western Europe as these countries had to turn to the United States for supplies. The shortage of foodstuffs and raw materials exacerbated conditions on which local Communists capitalized. If these Communists (in France, Italy, or elsewhere) gained or seized power, not only might they, too, sign bilateral economic pacts with the Kremlin but they might also offer the Soviet Union air transit rights, communication facilities, or base privileges.

The commercial policies of the Soviet Union in Eastern Europe were an exaggerated form of the restricted economic arrangements that so agitated U.S. officials. European nations had to import far more than they could export. Governments, therefore, carefully controlled foreign trade. In 1947 nearly two-thirds of Western Europe's trade was organized bilaterally, particularly through exchange controls, quantitative restrictions, and barter arrangements.[23] The maze of state regulations contradicted the multilateral, open patterns of international commercial and financial transactions that American officials deemed imperative for the preservation of a full-employment economy in the United States and for the maintenance of international peace and prosperity.[24]

Bilateral arrangements, moreover, could divide the world into closed trading blocs. In the 1930's totalitarian governments like Germany and Japan had employed such arrangements to maximize their access to critical raw materials and to support their rearmament programs. After the war, U.S. officials worried that the proliferation of bilateral accords might tempt Western nations to compete destructively with one another while the Kremlin used these same devices to lure vulnerable governments into its orbit. Communist parties in Western Europe would find bilateral agreements particularly appealing because they could be coupled with internal price controls and state economic planning. Increases in government expenditures and wage hikes could take place without exposing domestic producers and home markets to the vagaries of international competition. There were, then, complex and intricate interrelationships between the ways nations organized their internal economies, the mechanisms by which they conducted foreign trade, and prospective correlations of power in the international system.[25]

As time elapsed, U.S. officials also grew increasingly fearful about the future orientation of Germany and Japan. They were not so worried about the specter of communism in these countries, although this concern also was present, as they were frightened by the prospective renaissance of virulent nationalism or the development of independent neutralism. Of course, so long as occupation authorities were in charge, these threats were manageable. But once political life got under way, the pressures to end the occupation gathered momentum. American officials worried that nationalists or neutralists would capture widespread support, challenge the status quo, and maneuver between the great powers. Worse yet, they might ally themselves with the Kremlin, believing that the emerging Eastern bloc offered trade and political benefits that the United States and the West could not match.[26]

In the view of U.S. officials, key centers of industrial power, like Western Europe, Germany, and Japan, could remain independent of the Soviet orbit only if they maintained viable trade relationships within the so-called free world. These countries, therefore, had to reduce their dependence on the United States for food and raw materials and overcome their mammoth shortage of dollars. They had to find alternate sources of supplies in colonial or underdeveloped regions, revive some of their investment income from these areas, and compete more effectively there and in the United States. But once many of the colonies had suffered so much destruction during the war and were so engulfed in civil conflict, they no longer enjoyed a surplus in their trade with the United States and no longer earned dollars to funnel back to Britain, France, and Holland. Nevertheless, West European countries tightened their trade relationships with their colonies even while many of the latter clamored for their independence.[27]

In the late 1940's, U.S. officials feared that revolutionary upheaval and xenophobic nationalism might turn Third World countries against the West, drive them into the Soviet camp, and jeopardize efforts to recreate a viable international economy. Because economic relationships and standards of living shaped geopolitical relationships and correlations of power, American policymakers wanted to co-opt nationalist movements in the Third World. Yet the unrest and turmoil in many underdeveloped countries accelerated and the appeal of Communist ideology to nationalist leaders grew. From Southeast Asia to the Middle East and to North Africa, Indonesians, Vietnamese, Iranians, Egyptians, Moroccans, and Tunisians clamored for the right to determine their own future or to gain control of their own resources or to expel the formal or informal remnants of the colonial past.[28]

In 1949 and 1950, new developments reinforced older fears. The Chinese Communists' seizure of power, their intervention in the Korean conflict, and their aspirations for leadership in Southeast Asia portended immense new problems for the United States and its advanced industrial allies. The threat was magnified by the Soviets' acquisition of atomic capabilities and their continued conventional superiority in Europe. Soviet atomic capabilities, if joined to the development of a strategic air force, meant that the American people and the American economy would be vulnerable to attack. The industrial infrastructure of the United States, the source of America's overwhelming power, could be crippled. The United States, therefore, might hesitate to use its atomic arsenal against the Soviet Union. If American atomic capabilities were neutralized, the Kremlin would have an easier task of overrunning Europe and assimilating its industrial potential. These scenarios struck fear in U.S. policymakers, circumscribed their response to China's intervention in Korea, and made them even more dubious about their ability to take risks to counter mounting revolutionary nationalism on the periphery.

The Soviet possession of the atomic bomb symbolized that U.S. strategic superiority might be at an end, that its warmaking capabilities would be at risk, and that the fundamental source of its superior power was no longer impregnable. Seeing these eventualities, American officials might doubt their own will, their allies might reassess their own alignments, and their friends in the Third World might reappraise their own allegiances or capitulate to their revolutionary nationalist foes. The Kremlin, then, would gain new opportunities to make inroads into the Third World, to gain leverage among the advanced industrial nations, and to splinter the emerging Western alliance structure. In sum, Soviet Russia might gradually co-opt new sources of strength for itself, augment its power, erode that of its adversaries, and overcome American preponderance.[29]

Economics, Power, and National Security

This brief discussion of fears and threats, which will be elaborated upon in the chapters to follow, illuminates the extent to which U.S. officials defined their national security in terms of correlations of power. American power depended on the country's magnificently productive economic machine, its technological prowess, and its capacity to use strategic air power to inflict great damage on the economy of any enemy. Adversaries would be able to threaten U.S. security only if they could undermine the American economy, attack it militarily, or develop comparable or superior industrial warmaking capabilities. These eventualities were most likely to occur if the Soviet Union gained direct or indirect control over the industrial infrastructure and skilled labor of advanced nations or if the Kremlin developed its own strategic air force, atomic bomb, and forward bases.

From the perspective of postwar Washington, a viable international economy was the surest way to defend the health of core industrial nations and to protect friendly governments from internal disorders and nationalist impulses that might impel them to gravitate eastward. American officials believed that they had to relieve the problems besetting the industrial democracies of Western Europe, integrate former enemies like Germany and Japan into the international economy, and insure that all these industrial core nations could find markets and raw materials in the underdeveloped periphery of the Third World. If they failed in these tasks, the correlation of power in the international system would be transformed. The Soviet Union would grow stronger, the United States weaker.[30]

This mode of thinking about national security was influenced by the rising popularity of geopolitics in the late 1930's and 1940's. In a world beleaguered by totalitarian regimes and ravished by global conflict, power became a central organizing concept for understanding behavior in the international system. Political philosophers, economists, and journalists as well as international relations experts and government officials believed that totalitarian states sought to monopolize internal power and to expand their external power. They did so by organizing their economies for warfighting purposes. Geopolitics sought to explain how nations mobilized their capabilities, acquired additional resources, and combined them with new forms of transport and weaponry for the pursuit of power politics. The Nazis popularized geopolitics. During the war the widespread appearance of maps in U.S. newspapers and magazines helped to disseminate popular notions of geopolitics.[31]

Realistic statesmen had to be aware of correlations of power based on configurations of geopolitical influence and trade.[32] If an adversary gained control of Eurasia, Walter Lippmann reminded Americans in 1943, the United States would face a desperate situation.[33] At the time it was not clear to Lippmann and to most commentators whether Stalinist Russia would behave as an aggressive totalitarian power in the postwar world. But those who were certain of the Kremlin's malevolent intentions attributed to Stalin a fixed political ambition to dominate Eurasia. Soviet power, wrote James Burnham, flowed outward from the Eurasian heartland and lapped "the shores of the Atlantic, the Yellow and China Seas, the Mediterranean, and the Persian Gulf."[34]

Most illustrative of American thinking about national security at the end of the war was a Brookings Institution study in 1945 authored by a number of the nation's most prominent experts on international relations: Frederick S. Dunn, Edward M. Earle, William T. R. Fox, Grayson L. Kirk, David N. Rowe, Harold Sprout, and Arnold Wolfers. They concluded that it was essential to prevent any one power or coalition of powers from gaining control of Eurasia. The United States would not be able to withstand attack from an adversary who had subdued the whole of Europe or Eurasia. Like Lippmann, they aspired for good relations with Soviet Russia. Still, they insisted that the United States must not rely on assumptions about the Kremlin's good intentions. "In all the world only Soviet Russia and the ex-enemy powers are capable of forming nuclei around which an anti-American coalition could form to threaten the security of the United States." The indefinite westward movement of the Soviet Union, they added, must not be permitted "whether it occurs by formal annexation, political coup, or progressive subversion."[35]

Military planners got hold of this study, deeming it so important that they classified it as an official Joint Chiefs of Staff (JCS) document.[36] The ideas expressed in it accurately reflected U.S. strategic thinking in the early postwar years. So much excellent writing has been focused on the development of American air power that it is often overlooked that military officials and their civilian superiors in the Pentagon operated from assumptions that attributed primacy to geopolitical configurations of power and to warmaking capabilities.[37] Military planners assumed that if war erupted it would be protracted; the side that had the superior industrial and technological capabilities would prevail. In peacetime, therefore, it was essential to thwart the Kremlin from gaining indirect control of critical industrial infrastructure, skilled labor, raw materials, and forward bases. The United States had to retain allies across the oceans, particularly in England, France, Germany, and Japan. "The potential military strength of the Old World [Europe, Asia, and Africa]," argued the JCS, "in terms of manpower and in terms of war-making capacity is enormously greater than that of [the Western Hemisphere]."[38]

These attitudes were especially pervasive in the Army. While writers usually dwell on the rivalries between the Air Force and the Navy when they seek to elucidate the threads of America's postwar defense posture, the Army probably had greater importance in shaping overall national security strategy in the early postwar years. The Army, after all, had occupational responsibility in Germany and Japan as well as Austria and Korea. Army officers in the Civil Affairs Division and the

Operations Division (later Plans and Operations) and their civilian superiors like Howard C. Petersen and William H. Draper as well as proconsuls abroad like Generals Lucius Du Bignon Clay and Douglas MacArthur realized that their policies would shape overall correlations of power in the international system. They recognized, for example, that the Ruhr/Rhine industrial complex must not be allowed to support the military potential of a future adversary whether it be Germany or Russia or a combination of the two. Instead the region's resources had to be used to expedite recovery in Western Europe, undermine the appeal of local Communists, and bar the Kremlin from gaining preponderance in Europe.[39]

Subsequently, the most important National Security Council (NSC) papers of the Truman administration incorporated a geostrategic vision. National security was interpreted in terms of correlations of power. Power was defined in terms of the control of resources, industrial infrastructure, and overseas bases. In the autumn of 1948, NSC 20/4 became the first comprehensive strategy study to be adopted as national policy. "Soviet domination of the potential power of Eurasia," it emphasized, "whether achieved by armed aggression or by political and subversive means, would be strategically and politically unacceptable to the United States."[40]

The Central Intelligence Agency (CIA), formally established in 1947, used the same criteria when it identified threats and assessed vital interests. According to the CIA, nations could not become powerful if they did not have adequate supplies of mechanical energy (coal, water power, or petroleum), raw materials for basic industries, skilled technicians, experienced managers, and a sophisticated social structure accustomed to producing surpluses beyond consumption for military purposes. The task of American policymakers, the CIA advised, was to keep "the still widely dispersed power resources of Europe and Asia from being drawn together into a single Soviet power structure with a uniformly communist social organization." Winning the loyalties of peoples on the periphery was part of a "sociological" security dilemma whose solution would thwart Communist inroads and Soviet efforts to gain domination over the "Eurasian littoral."[41]

The highest civilian officials in the United States shared this geopolitical perspective. They defined security in terms of correlations of power. When Dean Acheson became secretary of state in 1949, he used this framework of analysis to tackle the most important issues he encountered, including those decisions relating to the atomic stockpile and the hydrogen bomb. "The loss of Western Europe," he said, "or of important parts of Asia or the Middle East would be a transfer of potential from West to East, which, depending on the area, might have the gravest consequences in the long run."[42] But perhaps no one articulated these views better than did President Harry S. Truman. "Our own national security," he emphasized in his annual message to Congress in January 1951, "is deeply involved with that of the other free nations. . . . If Western Europe were to fall to Soviet Russia it would double the Soviet supply of coal and triple the Soviet supply of steel. If the free nations of Asia and Africa should fall to Soviet Russia, we would lose the sources of many of our most vital raw materials, including uranium, which is the basis of our atomic power. And Soviet command of the manpower of the free nations of Europe and Asia would confront us with military forces which we could never hope to equal." [43]

National security, however, meant more than defending territory. Truman, Acheson, and their advisers repeatedly emphasized that the Soviet Union did not have to attack the United States to undermine its security. "If Communism is allowed to absorb the free nations," said the president, "then we would be isolated from our sources of supply and detached from our friends. Then we would have to take defense measures which might really bankrupt our economy, and change our way of life so that we couldn't recognize it as American any longer." In other words, Soviet/Communist domination of the preponderant resources of Eurasia would force the United States to alter its political and economic system. The U.S. government would have to restructure the nation's domestic economy, regiment its foreign trade, and monitor its domestic foes. "It would require," stressed Truman, "a stringent and comprehensive system of allocation and rationing in order to husband our smaller resources. It would require us to become a garrison state, and to impose upon ourselves a system of centralized regimentation unlike anything we have ever known." [44]

These possibilities were anathema to Truman and his advisers. Defending the nation's core values, its organizing ideology, and its free political and economic institutions was vital to national security.[45] The war resurrected faith in the capacity of the capitalist system to serve the welfare of the American people. For most Americans the record of totalitarian barbarity during the 1930's and 1940's discredited statist formulations of the good society. Instead of redistribution, Truman's supporters preferred productivity and abundance. Instead of planning, controls, and regulations, they preferred fiscal and monetary management. Instead of restructuring power in a capitalist society, they preferred to safeguard personal freedom and to focus attention on civil rights.[46] The good society was one that circumscribed the role of government in the nation's political economy; the good society was one that attributed primacy to the protection of civil liberties and individual rights. Yet that good society would be difficult to sustain either in a world divided by trade blocs or, worse yet, in a world dominated by the Kremlin's power.

These considerations inspired U.S. officials to configure an external environment compatible with their domestic vision of a good society. They were driven less by a desire to help others than by an ideological conviction that their own political economy of freedom would be jeopardized if a totalitarian foe became too powerful. If additional critical resources and industrial infrastructure fell within the grasp of the Kremlin or were subject to autarkic practices, the United States would have to protect itself by increasing military spending or regimenting its domestic economy. And if such contingencies materialized, domestic freedoms would be imperiled because there was no way to separate the economic from the political realms of governmental activity.[47] Time and again, Acheson reiterated that his aim was "to foster an environment in which our national life and individual freedom can survive and prosper." [48]

Economic interests often reinforced geostrategic imperatives and ideological predilections. During the war there was a vast growth in the overall influence of large corporations and high-technology companies in the U.S. economy. International bankers, corporate chief executives, and Wall Street and Washington lawyers like Robert Lovett, John J. McCloy, Ferdinand Eberstadt, Charles E. Wilson, Paul H. Nitze, James Forrestal, W. Averell Harriman, and Acheson assumed important positions in the State, War, Navy, and other departments. They were particularly aware of the relationships between foreign markets, American exports, and business profitability.[49] Their concerns about correlations of power, however, far exceeded their apprehensions about the well-being of the American economy. The latter surprised everyone by its durability and vigor. Tough choices between economic and strategic goals, however, rarely proved necessary. Because they defined power in terms of control over or access to resources, U.S. officials could usually pursue economic and strategic objectives in tandem.[50]

Organizational imperatives, like economic interests, often buttressed geostrategic and ideological pressures but were not the mainspring behind national security policies. Service rivalries were intense. The Air Force and Navy had much to gain by exaggerating foreign threats and squeezing additional military expenditures out of an administration that initially believed it could pursue its national security objectives without engaging in extravagant defense spending.[51] But the basic outlook of military officers resembled that of civilians in the Pentagon and at Foggy Bottom. Controlling industrial infrastructure, natural resources, and skilled labor or denying them to a prospective adversary were keys to power relationships. So were the possession of strategic air power, atomic bombs, and overseas bases that could be used to strike the adversary's mobilization base or to retard his efforts to seize additional resources. Military officers, of course, wanted to modernize their equipment, augment their forces-in-being, and balance American commitments and military capabilities.[52] Yet they often defined interests more narrowly than did civilians and were usually less inclined to use force on the periphery than were their colleagues at the State Department. Indeed, once the Soviets acquired their own atomic capabilities and showed a greater willingness to take risks, State Department officials like Acheson and Nitze became far more vociferous advocates of military expenditures and of intervention in Third World areas than were military officers.[53]

Partisan politics hardened attitudes toward the Soviet Union, solidified anti-Communist sentiment, and influenced particular policies but did not shape the basic contours of national security thinking. During the war public attitudes toward the Soviet Union had become much more friendly. But even while Soviet armies were fighting the bulk of Nazi forces, even while millions of Soviet soldiers were dying on battlefields, and even while Roosevelt, Stalin, and Churchill were meeting at summit conferences and declaring their loyalty to one another, almost a third of all Americans still distrusted the Soviet Union. Most polls showed that fewer than half of all Americans expected cooperation to persist into the postwar period. In other words, the American people retained a strong residue of animosity and suspicion toward the Bolshevik motherland.[54]

Public attitudes may have been malleable, but after Roosevelt's death policymakers did little to cultivate friendly feelings among the American people toward the Soviet Union.[55] During 1945 and 1946 Truman and his advisers clearly feared that Republicans could exploit anti-Communism for their political advantage.[56] Democrats, however, distrusted the Soviets and the Communists as much as did their political opponents. Liberal anticommunism was as fierce as the conservative variety, although the former differentiated a little more carefully between Communists and other leftists.[57]

What distinguished the Democratic administration was its ability to translate its suspicions of the Soviet Union into action when circumstances demanded. Although Truman's style of leadership was to grant wide decisionmaking authority to his foreign policy advisers, the president and his aides all shared the conviction that, even while the United States faced grave dangers, it also possessed unprecedented strength. If it used that strength wisely to prevent a potential adversary from gaining leverage over additional power centers, the nation's preeminence would remain unchallenged. Republicans might argue that countries like China were as important as Western Europe, but they never posed an alternative vision of national security interests. So long as the president preached indiscriminate anti-Communism, he was politically vulnerable whenever and wherever the Communists seized or won power. Republican criticisms, in turn, reinforced the administration's determination to avoid future losses.[58]

The Strategy of Preponderance

At the end of the war, U.S. officials did not think that they were engaged in a zero-sum game of power politics with the Soviet Union. They wanted to cooperate with the Kremlin. But they harbored a distrust sufficiently profound to require terms of cooperation compatible with vital American interests. Truman said it pointedly when he emphasized that the United States had to have its way 85 percent of the time. Senator Arthur H. Vandenberg, the Republican spokesman on foreign policy, was a little more categorical: "I think our two antipathetical systems can dwell in the world together—but only on a basis which establishes the fact that we mean what we say when we say it."[59]

Within a year, events transformed these suspicious attitudes into what became known as the containment policy. Did containment mean preponderance? Initially it meant preponderance only in a defensive sense: Soviet-directed world communism had to be thwarted lest the Kremlin gain control over the preponderant resources of

Eurasia and seek to dominate the world.[60] At the end of the war, U.S. officials certainly had no desire to retain substantial military forces overseas, to incur strategic commitments, or to supplant British, French, and Dutch political influence in large parts of the Third World (except perhaps in some oil-producing countries like Saudi Arabia).[61]

Policymakers in Washington preferred an economic approach. They sought to create an open world economy conducive to the free movement of goods, capital, and technology. They wanted to break down England's sterling bloc, create convertible currencies, and establish the conditions for nondiscriminatory trade. During 1944 and 1945, Roosevelt, Truman, and their advisers placed a great deal of stress on creating the International Monetary Fund and the World Bank. These instruments would foster world peace and international prosperity.[62]

U.S. officials were ready to assume Britain's former role as financial hegemon. They recognized the connections between the economic and political spheres. If they stymied the diffusion of bilateral and autarkic practices, they would prevent artificial acquisitions of economic resources that could be used to build up military strength. Loans also might be used to extract political as well as economic concessions. In a world free of barriers to the movement of goods and capital, moreover, the private sector could serve as an instrument, albeit not a docile one, of state policy. Oil corporations, for example, while pursuing their own interests and generating growth in host countries, might help ensure American control over the most important raw material. If the United States managed an open world economy, it could be a more peaceful place and everyone would benefit. But the position of preponderance that the United States inherited as a result of the war would remain intact.[63]

Truman and his advisers were not naive. "We must face the fact," the president told Congress in one of his first postwar addresses, "that peace must be built upon power, as well as upon good will and good deeds." Truman wanted to inaugurate universal military training, establish an overseas base system, and maintain a monopoly over atomic weapons. "Until we are sure that our peace machinery is functioning adequately, we must relentlessly preserve our superiority on land and sea and in the air." [64] Strategic air power, financial hegemony, and economic predominance were thought sufficient to thwart any prospective Soviet drive for preponderance.

Truman and his advisers miscalculated. Britain was weaker than they thought; European financial problems more intractable; German and Japanese economic woes more deep-seated; revolutionary nationalism more virulent; Soviet actions more ominous; and American demobilization more rapid. In 1947 and 1948 U.S. officials responded with new policies focusing on massive economic assistance and limited military aid. With equal effectiveness and more sophistication, the Truman administration used the private sector to fashion new sets of corporatist arrangements in Europe, arrangements that endeavored to mitigate social conflict, forestall

Communist political victories, and foster economic growth. The overall purpose was to revive production in Western Europe, western Germany, and Japan and to integrate these areas into an American-led orbit before they could gravitate to the East.[65]

U.S. policymakers and intelligence analysts understood that the Kremlin might react negatively and take countermeasures. They believed, however, that Russian retaliatory measures would be limited. Soviet leaders would not go to war with the United States. The forces-in-being of the United States might be small but America's strategic superiority, atomic monopoly, and warmaking capabilities supported the risk-taking that inhered in the reconstruction of the industrial core of Eurasia. "As long as we can outproduce the world, can control the sea and can strike inland with the atomic bomb," James Forrestal noted in his diary in 1947, "we can assume certain risks otherwise unacceptable." [66]

By reviving the German and Japanese economies, the United States was restoring their latent military capabilities. America's former allies in World War II looked with great trepidation on the revitalization of their former enemies. There were no assurances that Germany and Japan would become peaceful democracies; past history suggested the contrary. Moreover, the specter of independent German and Japanese power might provoke the Kremlin to take preemptive military action. To allay Allied apprehensions about these different contingencies, the United States was willing to offer military guarantees. By joining alliances first in the Atlantic and then in the Pacific, and by endorsing French plans for a European coal and steel community and a European defense community, the Truman administration tried to mold multilateral political agreements and supranational institutions for the purpose of luring industrial core areas into an American-led community. Given Britain's determination to remain independent of a federated Europe, the North Atlantic Treaty Organization (NATO) served as a particularly useful mechanism to integrate Western Europe and England into an orbit amenable to American leadership. Neither an integrated Europe nor a united Germany nor an independent Japan must be permitted to emerge as a third force or a neutral bloc. Neutralism, said Acheson, "is a shortcut to suicide." [67]

In order to align Western Europe, West Germany, and Japan permanently with the United States, American officials were convinced that they had to narrow the dollar gap and help their industrial allies sell their goods, earn dollars, and purchase foodstuffs and raw materials in the underdeveloped periphery.[68] Linking core and periphery in the face of revolutionary nationalism was a daunting task. But American officials thought it could be managed. Eschewing responsibilities for the United States in the Third World, they tried to convince the British, French, and Dutch to co-opt nationalist movements by acknowledging the rights of colonial peoples to determine their own future and to establish their own governments. Policymakers in Washington insisted that decolonization could occur without endangering Western interests. Strategic requirements could be accommodated; bases obtained; investments and trade safeguarded. For American officials their own policies toward the Philippines set the model. Mutually beneficial relationships could be established by working with entrenched elites and even with emerging military modernizers. Metropolitan governments simply had to be wise enough to cede the formal levers of power and to make symbolic gestures before Communists wrapped themselves in the mantle of nationalism and monopolized it.[69]

As circumstances changed and threats mounted, U.S. tactics shifted but the overall goal remained the same. The periphery had to be held or the Eurasian industrial core would be weakened. To simplify, Japan needed Southeast Asia; Western Europe needed the Middle East; and the American rearmament effort required raw materials from throughout the Third World. The Truman administration first offered limited amounts of technical and economic assistance and then larger and larger amounts of military aid. In Indochina, it came to finance a substantial part of the French struggle against Ho Chi Minh's Communist Viet Minh. But as French efforts in Indochina faltered and British policies in Iran and Egypt foundered, Truman, Acheson, and their advisers thought the United States should prepare mobile forces for intervention in Third World areas.[70]

The Korean War accelerated changes in American tactics. When Chinese troops crossed the Yalu River in the fall of 1950, U.S. policymakers did not retaliate for fear they might precipitate an escalatory cycle they could not control. The lesson was clear. The United States must be able to check enemy counteraction and, if deterrence failed, dominate the escalatory process. Hurriedly, the Truman administration proceeded to enlarge the atomic stockpile, develop the hydrogen bomb, rearm Germany, and strengthen NATO's conventional forces. Overwhelming strategic superiority was required to maintain the atomic umbrella under which the United States could support its friends, utilize covert actions, deploy its own mobile forces, and conduct conventional bombing raids in limited war situations. As the atomic monopoly had provided the psychological backdrop for the implementation of the Marshall Plan and the creation of the Federal Republic of Germany, strategic superiority still remained essential for inspiring American risk-taking on the periphery, deterring the adversary's countermeasures, and preserving Allied support and solidarity.[71]

All these tactics aimed to achieve a hierarchy of objectives: "strength at the center; strength at the periphery; the retraction of Soviet power and a change in the Soviet system." The United States, American officials believed, should not risk war in order to break up the Soviet empire, or to drive a wedge between the Kremlin and its satellites, or to overthrow incumbent Communist regimes. But if the United States was successful at creating strength at the center and binding core and periphery, the West's attraction would be magnetic. The satellites would be pulled westward; German unification might occur on American terms; the Communist bloc could unravel. By containing Communist gains and Soviet expansion, American officials hoped to perpetuate American preponderance. The "United States and the

Soviet Union," said Acheson's Policy Planning Staff, "are engaged in a struggle for preponderant power. . . . [T]o seek less than preponderant power would be to opt for defeat. Preponderant power must be the object of U.S. policy." [72]

Preponderance did not mean domination. It meant creating a world environment hospitable to U.S. interests and values; it meant developing the capabilities to overcome threats and challenges; it meant mobilizing the strength to reduce Soviet influence on its own periphery; it meant undermining the appeal of communism; it meant fashioning the institutional techniques and mechanisms to manage the free world; and it meant establishing a configuration of power and a military posture so that if war erupted, the United States would prevail. If adversaries saw the handwriting on the wall, they would defer to American wishes. The United States, said Paul Nitze in mid-1952, could "gain preponderant power." [73]

Lessons of the Past

Images of the past cast their influence on American perceptions, tactics, and goals. Most of the civilians who were to make America's cold war policies—Acheson, Forrestal, Lovett, Draper, Harriman, McCloy, and Robert P. Patterson—were born in the 1880's and 1890's. As young men they watched Woodrow Wilson try to remake the world at Versailles and suffer repudiation at home. Many of them enjoyed lucrative careers in investment banking and law during the interwar years. From their comfortable affluence they observed the domestic travail of the Depression and the onslaught of Nazi aggression and Japanese militarism. The image of appeasement at Munich seared itself in their memories. In 1940 and 1941 they gravitated from the private sector to public service.[74]

When World War II approached its final stages, their intent was not to lose the peace as Wilson had done. They shared many Wilsonian goals. They regarded the United Nations as a symbol of great importance. Men like Acheson did not think that it would preserve the peace, but they did believe that membership in the United Nations would signal the end of the political isolation of the interwar years.[75] In 1919 the strife among the victorious allies had underscored their selfishness, triggered American revulsion, and culminated in the defeat of the League of Nations. Hence Truman, Roosevelt, and their advisers wished to avoid a premature rift with the Soviet Union in the spring of 1945. But they hoped that ratification of the U.N. charter would establish a pattern of international collaboration that could then be used to contain the Soviet Union should the Kremlin prove to be a destructive force in the postwar world.[76]

To avert isolationism, the Democrats had learned that bipartisanship was essential. Wilson had underestimated his political foes and had treated Congress contemptuously. His heirs were determined to see that these errors did not recur. Republicans and senators would be consulted; they would be asked to attend the key conferences; they would have the chance to contribute to agreements and treaties.[77]

Wisened by the experiences of the 1920's and 1930's, Truman administration officials also desired to play a more constructive role in international economic affairs. During the war years, for example, Acheson testified frequently on the lend-lease agreements. He never failed to emphasize the importance of lower tariffs, increased trade, and nondiscrimination. When peace returned, the United States would have to play a more responsible role as a creditor nation. It would have to exert leadership in the formation of the International Monetary Fund and the World Bank; it would have to enlarge the lending powers of the Export-Import Bank; it would have to avoid a new wrangle over war debts; and it would have to mobilize the private sector in behalf of international stabilization.[78]

According to Harley Notter, the State Department official in charge of planning, these commercial and financial initiatives also were "indispensable to postwar security."[79] The bilateralism and autarky of the 1930's contracted trade, intensified commercial rivalries, and allowed totalitarian governments to acquire the materiel and resources to wage war.[80] In his testimony on the Bretton Woods agreements in June 1945, Acheson vividly described how Germany had organized a system that turned Europe inward upon itself "and with perfectly amazing skill had made that system work and work so effectively that the Germans were able to fight all the rest of the world and support reasonably well the peoples of Europe." Acheson feared that the deplorable conditions that beset postwar Europe might again force that continent to turn inward, with incalculable consequences for the peace of the world and for American safety.[81] Multilateral trade was a mechanism to stymie trade alliances that not only could erode American prosperity but could also foster configurations of power that endangered American security. The unrestricted flow of capital and goods would tend to bind other nations to the United States. If necessary, their resources might then be used to bolster the military strength of the free world.[82]

Many of the top civilian officials who molded the Truman administration's foreign policies had been intimately familiar with American financial diplomacy and international economic developments in the interwar years.[83] Their knowledge of events in Weimar Germany profoundly influenced their policies. As after World War I, they believed that European stability depended on German reconstruction. But they had learned that the raw materials and industrial resources of the Ruhr and Rhine must not remain in German hands alone, where they had been used to support the German war machine. German coal and steel had to be co-opted for the benefit of all Western Europe through the imposition of international controls or the development of supranational mechanisms.[84] Moreover, prompt action was imperative because Acheson, McCloy, and their associates always sensed the precariousness of the democratic experiment in postwar Germany. If concessions were not made to democratic leaders like Konrad Adenauer, if German autonomy were not restored to moderates, Germany would fall once again into the hands of virulent nationalists. Whether they be on the right or the left, they would insist on even more extreme concessions and would be willing to turn toward the Kremlin for help. The

Rapallo and Molotov-Ribbentrop agreements resonated in the memories of U.S. officials, who were aware that both Weimar and Nazi Germany had been willing to play a Russian card when it served German interests.[85]

Whereas concessions to German democrats made sense, appeasement of a totalitarian foe must never be contemplated. So long as they hoped to secure favorable agreements, Truman and his advisers were willing to deal with Stalin.[86] But when the Soviet government refused to accept free elections in Poland, Bulgaria, and Romania, rebuffed the Baruch Plan for the control of atomic energy, rejected American blueprints for postwar Germany, probed for weak spots in the Eastern Mediterranean and the Near East, and appeared ready to capitalize on prospective Communist successes in Greece, Italy, and France, U.S. officials concluded that they had to take unilateral actions to build situations of strength. Appeasing an adversary who might be intent on world domination made no sense. The lessons of Munich and of the recent war were fresh in their minds. Free men had allowed the Nazis to militarize the Rhineland, annex Austria, and seize Czechoslovakia, had acquiesced to the Japanese conquest of Manchuria and the invasion of China, and had permitted Axis domination of much of Eurasia. Truman would not make the same mistakes again.[87]

The men who advised Truman were the same people who had gathered around Roosevelt to prepare the United States for conflict. For Acheson, Forrestal, Lovett, Patterson, McCloy, Harriman, Nitze, and many other officials, the events of 1940 altered their careers and shaped their thinking. Their wartime work in the government on mobilization, procurement, lend-lease, and commercial warfare underscored the relationships between economic resources and military capabilities.[88] They saw how industrial strength bestowed military power, how geographical conquest enhanced aggressive purposes. According to Acheson, the Nazi "New Order" and the Japanese "Co-Prosperity Sphere" "meant that the resources and the population of neighboring countries have been turned entirely to the ends of the enemy and have been spent with utter ruthlessness."[89]

In 1940 the immediate challenge for policymakers was to determine whether U.S. political and economic interests could be protected if Eurasia were dominated by the Axis powers. The results of their wide-ranging studies left a lasting impression. The American economy, if properly managed and regulated, might adjust. But the American free enterprise system would be altered radically; the political economy would be transformed; the role of the government would become omnipresent; and political freedom would be jeopardized. U.S. officials believed that domination of the European marketplace afforded Germany great leverage over the countries in the southern cone of South America, countries that traditionally sold their grain, meat, and raw materials to European purchasers. Argentina, Chile, Brazil, and Uruguay might cave in to Nazi pressure and fall within the Nazi orbit.[90] More worrisome still, because Europe remained the major market for American goods, Roosevelt's advisers and American businessmen had to consider how they would bargain with the Nazis should Hitler win the war and consolidate his hold over the continent. Because the German government carefully regulated trade for political and strategic purposes, the U.S. government might have to take over the export sector and organize the producers of the Western Hemisphere and the British empire (if it survived) into powerful cartels capable of negotiating on equal terms with Axis counterparts.[91]

Such schemes were anathema to Roosevelt. "The logic of such implications," said the president, "would lead us to embark upon a course of action which would subject our producers, consumers, and foreign traders, and ultimately the entire nation, to the regimentation of a totalitarian system. For it is naive to imagine that we could adopt a totalitarian control of our foreign trade and at the same time escape totalitarian regimentation of our internal economy."[92] With great fervor, Roosevelt insisted that the United States could not become "a lone island in a world dominated by the philosophy of force. Such an island represents to me—the nightmare of a people lodged in prison, handcuffed, hungry, and fed through the bars from day to day by the contemptuous, unpitying masters of other continents." The dictatorships, Roosevelt thought, "wanted to segregate us to such an extent that we will become vulnerable to a final attack when they get ready to make it."[93] His aid to the allies was inspired by his recognition that Axis domination of Eurasia would demand a reconfiguration of the U.S. and Western Hemisphere economies, unprecedented governmental interference in the private marketplace, a huge increment in defense expenditures, and eternal vigilance against internal subversion from fifth columnists and external threats from totalitarian foes. In such a context, personal freedoms and individual liberties might not survive.[94]

Roosevelt and his advisers forswore coexistence and accommodation with the Axis powers. They suspected that Hitler would not be satisfied with domination of Europe and believed that Japan would not comply with any agreements regarding China and Southeast Asia. They were aware of the advantages that would accrue to the Nazi military machine if German forces took Dakar, endangered the bulge of Brazil, and controlled the Atlantic. They were attuned to and perhaps even exaggerated the potential of fifth columnists in Brazil and Argentina. Even if the Nazis had no immediate ability to attack the United States, as most experts agreed, the task was to prevent Germany from gaining the time and opportunity to develop those capabilities.[95]

The physical safety of the United States required that Hitler be defeated before he had the capacity to assimilate the resources of Europe, acquire bases in Northwest Africa, take over the British fleet, or gain sustained access to the petroleum of the Caucasus and the Near East or the breadbasket of the Ukraine. Time was not necessarily on the side of the United States unless Germany's enemies remained in the conflict, wearing down German energies and complicating Nazi efforts to absorb the new resources falling within their orbit. For with the defeat of each nation and the co-optation of others, Germany was gaining the raw materials and developing the potential for unprecedented military-industrial strength. From France, Germany could secure iron ore, railway equipment, cast-iron pipe, and machinery; from Bohemia and Moravia, it obtained arms, chemicals, and iron and steel plants; from Poland, it could get coal, zinc, timber, and meat; from Belgium, iron, steel, industrial equipment, and railway supplies; from Romania, petroleum; from Hungary, bauxite; and from Yugoslavia, copper and chrome. And as Germany vanquished its enemies, it also gained extended leverage over neutrals like Sweden and Switzerland. Germany was gaining strength, not losing it.[96] Unless Great Britain and the Soviet Union could be given the wherewithal to persevere in the struggle and to shun a compromise peace, U.S. officials had every reason to think that the nation's physical safety as well as its political institutions and economic welfare would be endangered.[97]

Policymakers grasped that modern warfare demanded huge resources. Roosevelt and his chiefs of staff assigned priority to defeating Germany because Germany appeared on the brink of defeating Britain, penetrating Latin America, and integrating the raw materials and granaries of the Near East, Eastern Europe, and North Africa with the industrial infrastructure, technological knowhow, and skilled labor of northwestern Europe and Scandinavia. The Japanese gambled on attacking Pearl Harbor because they hoped that a successful assault would provide the time to consolidate their hold over the natural resources of Southeast Asia. With their strength enormously augmented, they hoped to convince Americans that it was not worthwhile to contest Japanese supremacy in East Asia. Japanese assessments of American psychology were terribly flawed. But their capacity to wage war for a protracted period of time was abetted by their previous imperial acquisitions, the integration of Manchuria, Korea, and Taiwan into the Japanese economic orbit, and the growth of Japanese heavy industry in the 1930's, a development made possible, at least in part, by previous successful aggression and aggrandizement.[98]

For U.S. officials, the most decisive and lasting legacy of the wartime experience was that potential adversaries must never again be allowed to gain control of the resources of Eurasia through autarkical economic practices, political subversion, and/or military aggression. The acquisition of such resources allowed potential foes to augment their military capabilities, encouraged them to penetrate the Western Hemisphere, tempted them to attack the United States, and enabled them to wage a protracted struggle. Postwar peace and stability had to be constructed on the foundation of nonaggression, self-determination, equal access to raw materials, and nondiscriminatory trade.[99] When these principles were violated, nations used military power and autarkical practices to accrue strength disproportionate to their size and stature, dysfunctional to the international system, and dangerous to the physical security of the United States. Faced with such realities, American officials had to contemplate substantial changes in the political economy of the United States, including huge defense expenditures, increments in the powers of the federal government, infringements on free-market mechanisms, and curtailment of individual liberties.

Axis aggression and military successes in 1940 and 1941 demonstrated that the traditional principles of self-determination and the open door, principles that heretofore had been geared to American economic needs and ideological inclinations, now had profound implications for the national security, physical safety, and political economy of the United States. Once this fusion of geopolitical, economic, ideological, and strategic considerations occurred, traditional foreign policy goals were transformed into national security imperatives. The self-imposed restraints on political commitments, military guarantees, and the use of force eroded. The economic costs of global embroilments, which had heretofore constrained American strategic obligations abroad, now became less salient than their alleged geopolitical and military benefits. Roosevelt's advisers were prepared to use their acquired wisdom to help Truman mobilize U.S. power to overcome the threats and dangers of the postwar world.

Ambivalence, Disorganization, and the East European Litmus Test, 1945

O n the afternoon of 12 April 1945, a somber group of officials gathered at the White House to receive the news that Franklin Delano Roosevelt had died. The new president, Harry S. Truman, talked to them briefly, expressed his grief, and asked for their help. His aim, he said, was to carry out his predecessor's policies.[1]

But what of these policies? Throughout the war Roosevelt had tried to establish a basis for harmonious Soviet-U.S. relations. But in the closing weeks of his life he grew distraught over Soviet actions in Poland and Romania. He was genuinely outraged by Stalin's insinuations that the United States was maneuvering for a secret peace with Germany. Yet he never abandoned his hope for postwar cooperation.[2] What Roosevelt would have done after the Axis powers capitulated must remain a matter of conjecture. How the availability of atomic weapons would have influenced his diplomacy is unknowable.

Truman faced uncharted waters. Insecure and uncertain, he sought help from advisers and friends, but they, too, were divided. The rift was not simply between hawks and doves, between champions of the Riga and Yalta axioms: within the minds of most officials and within the offices of most agencies of the U.S. government, the impulse to cooperate with the Kremlin clashed with the penchant to contain Soviet influence.[3] American policymakers were uncertain of Soviet intentions. They exhorted the Kremlin to permit free elections, representative government, and nondiscriminatory trade in the areas occupied by Soviet armies. They monitored Soviet behavior closely in Eastern Europe because they thought it would help to illuminate overall Soviet aims and objectives. Yet they equivocated about the meaning of Soviet actions and vacillated about what they should do. Truman in fact personified the ambivalence that prevailed throughout his administration.

Rather quickly, however, the impulse to compete with and contain the Soviet Union triumphed over the desire to maintain Allied solidarity. How and why this process occurred will be the subject of this chapter. The emphasis here will be on high policy—that is, on the perceptions of top U.S. officials, their assessments of Soviet intentions and capabilities, and their diplomacy at summit and foreign ministerial meetings. Chapter Two will cover the same chronological span and look more closely at the decisions made on specific issues, regional matters, and country affairs. It will become clear that, even while American policymakers beckoned for cooperation, it was cooperation of a special sort, based on American terms and compatible with American national security interests. Chapters One and Two, therefore, must be seen as opposite sides of the same coin.

Truman and His Advisers

The new president was a simple, straightforward, unpretentious man. Reared in small-town Missouri and proud of his roots, he had an abiding faith in America's moral superiority and ultimate righteousness. He had fought in World War I, floundered in business, and succeeded beyond his wildest dreams in politics. In 1934 he was elected to the U.S. Senate. During World War II he gained considerable notoriety as the chairman of the Special Committee to Investigate the National Defense Program. In this capacity he acquired a great deal of knowledge about procurement, mobilization, defense organization, and budgetary matters. In 1944 Roosevelt chose him as his running mate.

There was little affinity between the two men, and Roosevelt never confided in him. When the president died, Truman knew little about his diplomacy. Nor did he know much about the elaborate planning that had taken place at the middle levels of the Washington bureaucracy and that had the support of the highest officials in the State, War, Navy, and Treasury departments as well as the backing of the Joint Chiefs of Staff (JCS).[4]

Yet Truman's unrefined ideas were not out of harmony with the basic contours of planning within the Roosevelt administration. Based on a superficial understanding of history and an instinctive appreciation of the lessons of the past, Truman blended a parochial nationalism with a pragmatic internationalism. Isolationism had been a mistake; collective security was imperative; a new international organization was necessary. But, like Roosevelt, he believed that the great powers would have to control the new organization "in the name of all and for the welfare of all." Truman, in other words, was a realist. Nations, he emphasized, had always been motivated "by the international struggle for power." Collective security and an international police force would help preserve the peace. But they were no substitute for American preparedness, adequate defense expenditures, universal military training, and scientific research. "The surest guarantee that no nation will dare again to attack us," he told Congress in October 1945, "is to remain strong in the only kind of strength an aggressor understands—military power." Truman's "internationalism" was always fused with an instinctive appreciation of the importance of force and power in world affairs.[5]

The new president's views on international economic affairs also comported with the basic outlines of State and Treasury Department thinking. Peace and prosperity depended on the end of political nationalism, economic imperialism, and commercial autarky. The country would enjoy full employment if trade barriers were reduced, monetary systems stabilized, and world resources jointly developed. Truman wanted the United States to lead the world into an unprecedented era of productive peace.[6] But enlightened leadership was not to be confused with naiveté. Greedy European nations would not dupe the United States into financing their reparation payments, as they had after World War I.[7]

On inheriting the presidency, Truman was woefully ignorant of the great issues of wartime strategy and diplomacy. For knowledge of these developments he consulted with Admiral William D. Leahy, Secretary of the Navy James V. Forrestal, Secretary of War Henry L. Stimson, Army Chief of Staff George C. Marshall, and Chief of Naval Operations Ernest J. King. More than anyone else, however, Truman turned to James F. Byrnes, the former congressman, senator, Supreme Court justice, and wartime director of mobilization. During 1943 and 1944 Byrnes had exerted tremendous control over the domestic economy and had served almost as an assistant president. When spurned by Roosevelt as a vice presidential candidate in 1944, Byrnes decided to return to his native South Carolina. But before doing so, he agreed to accompany Roosevelt to Yalta. As the Crimean conference drew to a close, Byrnes raced back to Washington and became the administration's foremost proponent of the Yalta accords. The historian Robert Messer has shown how, after Roosevelt died, Truman looked to Byrnes for an understanding of these agreements and for perspective on interallied relationships. The South Carolinian was a familiar and friendly figure from Truman's early Senate days, and his stature in the domestic polity made him an attractive confidant.[8]

Truman's dependence on Byrnes illuminated the considerable disarray in policy-making circles. Roosevelt had had no structured means of reaching decisions. Interdepartmental coordination was informal and haphazard. During the war, the influence of the State Department had fallen dramatically as it was torn by internal strife and as its leaders were eclipsed by the influence and prestige accorded to military officers and civilian defense officials. When Cordell Hull retired in late 1944, Roosevelt appointed Edward R. Stettinius, Jr., as secretary of state. Previously, Stettinius had been president of United States Steel, head of the War Resources Board, and undersecretary of state. He was keenly aware of the relative ineffectiveness of the State Department and of the poor coordination of political-military affairs.

Stettinius knew that Roosevelt would be his own secretary of state. Stettinius's principal mandate was to negotiate the charter for the United Nations at the forthcoming San Francisco conference. Nevertheless, he sought to revive the prestige and influence of the State Department. He made key personnel changes, such as bringing in William L. Clayton as assistant secretary for economic affairs and transferring Dean Acheson to legislative matters. He elevated conservative foreign service officers like Joseph C. Grew and James C. Dunn to policymaking positions. He appointed Charles Bohlen as a liaison officer between the State Department and the White House; Bohlen was an able Kremlinologist and well known to Roosevelt and his entourage for his translating work at the wartime summit conferences. Stettinius also pressed for the establishment of an interagency committee to deal with matters of high policy. At his behest, the State-War-Navy Coordinating Committee (SWNCC) began functioning in late 1944 on the assistant secretary level. Furthermore, after Roosevelt's death Stettinius arranged for weekly meetings of the secretaries of state, navy, and war. Even when Stettinius was out of Washington, as he often was in the spring of 1945, Undersecretary Grew met every Tuesday with Forrestal and Stimson. Grew also briefed Truman daily, and sometimes several times a day, on key diplomatic developments.[9]

But try as he might, Stettinius was unable to gain the confidence of Stimson and Forrestal. They complained of the maladministration, incompetence, and shortsightedness of State Department officials.[10] Truman came quickly to share these feelings. He listened carefully to the views of W. Averell Harriman, the U.S. ambassador to the Soviet Union. Otherwise, he often voiced contempt for the "striped-pants" boys at Foggy Bottom. Stettinius, he said, was "as dumb as they come." He resolved to designate Byrnes as his secretary of state as soon as Stettinius completed his work at the San Francisco conference.[11]

Given the State Department's shrunken stature, the influence of the War Department rose. As World War II approached its final stages, Stimson and his aides were in a position to wield considerable authority. First, the Manhattan Project fell within their purview. Stimson's knowledge of the atomic bomb exceeded that of anyone else in high decisionmaking circles. It was Stimson who familiarized both Truman and Byrnes with the prospective use of the bomb and its concomitant ramifications for postwar strategy and diplomacy.[12] A second critical factor affecting the War Department's influence was its forthcoming role in postwar occupation policy in Germany, Austria, Japan, and Korea. Since 1943, the Civil Affairs Division of the Army had been making preparations for the post-surrender period. The Army's responsibility for implementing occupation policy and for preserving order afforded it significant opportunity to influence, if not to dictate, the overall pattern of U.S. postwar relations with most former enemy states.[13]

The War Department's standing in administration circles was also a function of Stimson's personal prestige and General Marshall's great stature.[14] Stimson's experience in government went back to the administration of William Howard Taft and included a four-year stint as secretary of state under Herbert C. Hoover. In 1945, Stimson was 77 years old. He needed a nap almost every day and frequently flew to his Long Island estate for weekend rests. Nevertheless, he clearly grasped the big issues and commanded attention when he addressed them. Truman felt uneasy with Stimson but respected him and trusted his advice. Although the secretary's lagging energy undermined his effectiveness, he put together a group of impressive assistants, including John J. McCloy, Robert A. Lovett, and Robert P. Patterson. Their interests and influence stretched well beyond the Army's traditional domains. McCloy and Lovett had especially close ties with the international investment community in New York, and they were greatly interested in postwar reconstruction policy abroad.

As assistant secretary of war, McCloy drew on the expertise and relied on the staff work of an extremely talented group of officers within the Strategy and Policy Group of the Army's Operations Division. These men, including Brigadier General George A. Lincoln, Colonel Charles H. Bonesteel, Colonel Dean Rusk, and Colonel James McCormack, Jr., were all former Rhodes scholars who possessed a substantial interest in the interlocking nature of political-military affairs. By early 1945, they were preparing scores of papers on such issues as Soviet-U.S. relations, Indochina, the Dardanelles, and the United Nations. Their work was thoughtful and incisive. McCloy worked as closely with them as Stimson worked harmoniously with General Marshall.[15]

Secretary of the Navy Forrestal's stature in policymaking circles did not rival that of Stimson. Whereas Stimson capitalized on his experience with foreign policy issues over four decades, Forrestal was a newcomer to matters of high policy. He had made a fortune on Wall Street in the interwar years and had become president of the investment banking firm Dillon, Read, and Company. He joined the White House staff as an administrative assistant to the president in 1939, dabbled in Latin American affairs, quickly became bored, and welcomed the move to the Navy Department, where he served with distinction as undersecretary for most of the war. In their initial private meetings, Truman and Forrestal usually discussed organizational problems. But when Forrestal turned his attention to policy issues, he endorsed the views of Stimson and McCloy. Like them, he vigorously supported the acquisition of overseas bases, grasped the interdependent nature of the world economy, and opposed Secretary of the Treasury Henry Morgenthau's plan for the pastoralization of Germany. Unlike Stimson, however, Forrestal had a strained relationship with some top naval officers who disliked civilian authority and who resisted the centralization of decisionmaking around the secretary.[16]

Aside from the War and Navy departments, the JCS assumed considerable prestige during the war. The JCS, as an institutional mechanism, arose as a wartime expedient to facilitate cooperation with the British. Together with their British counterparts, the JCS formed the Combined Chiefs of Staff. The JCS offered advice to the president on matters of grand strategy and Allied relationships as well as on concerns pertaining to munitions, shipping, manpower, and research.[17] Admiral Leahy, former chief of naval operations and ambassador to Vichy France, presided over JCS meetings, maintained liaison with the chief executive, and served as the latter's chief of staff. During Truman's first months in office, Leahy was constantly by his side. Leahy was a crusty old conservative, suspicious of allies as well as adversaries. Like Marshall, however, he was acutely conscious of the political ramifications of military initiatives. He championed close consultation between the White House, the Pentagon, and the State Department. He kept on good terms with some of the civilians on Truman's staff and worked closely with Samuel Rosenman and Clark Clifford.[18]

During the war, the JCS established a labyrinthine structure of committees. The most important was the Joint Strategic Survey Committee, which provided advice on both long-range planning and ongoing strategic developments. After the war the influence of the Joint Planning Staff grew significantly. Planners, like General Lincoln, also constituted critical links between the JCS and the military services they represented.[19]

The entire JCS structure remained inaccessible to outsiders. The chiefs jealously guarded their wartime access to the president and hoped to perpetuate it after the conflict. They established no formal procedures for informing the secretaries of the Army and Navy of their work. There were only a few institutionalized contacts between the JCS and the State Department. Once the SWNCC began functioning, it sometimes served as a conduit for studies relating the interests of the State Department and the JCS. But interdepartmental as well as civilian-military coordination did not develop easily, and overlapping jurisdictions and competing bureaucracies complicated the implementation of policy.[20]

Roosevelt had been able to sit at the pinnacle of this diffuse structure and use it to suit his administrative style. His successor viewed the setup as a morass. Truman did not know how to deal with the conflicting advice that came to him. Orderly procedures for studying options and integrating economic, political, and strategic recommendations did not exist. With little knowledge on which to draw, the new president tended to agree with whomever he was talking to. Because he was insecure and fearful of displaying his own ignorance, he hesitated to discuss his views and rarely thought through a problem aloud. Almost everyone commented on his snap judgments. He conveyed a sense of authority, but at the expense of thoughtful and consistent policy.[21]

Thinking About the Soviets

The combination of an unstructured decisionmaking process and an ill-informed president magnified the problems of defining U.S. relations with the Soviet Union. Truman and his advisers felt a deep ambivalence about the emergence of Soviet power. On the one hand, they felt that wartime cooperation had to be perpetuated if peace and security were to be achieved. On the other hand, they believed that they had to monitor Soviet behavior lest another totalitarian behemoth seek control of countries, bases, resources, and labor that might someday allow it to endanger American security and jeopardize the peace of the world.

State Department officials expressed the gravest reservations about Roosevelt's efforts to accommodate the Kremlin and compromise outstanding differences. As U.S. foreign service officers returned to their posts throughout Eastern Europe, they decried Soviet actions and influence. Many of these men had been trained in the foreign service during the interwar years in an atmosphere and program that encouraged anti-Bolshevik attitudes. Some of these diplomats, like Bohlen, George F. Kennan, Loy W. Henderson, and Elbridge Durbrow, had been posted in Moscow during the trials, purges, and murders of the late 1930's and had been appalled by the oppression and barbarism of Stalinist rule. On the higher rungs of the foreign service, anti-Communist attitudes came naturally to men from upper-class and conservative social backgrounds. The exigencies of war and a few signs of Russian accommodation had checked their crusading fervor. But as Soviet armies moved through Eastern Europe, the diplomats' suspicions of Bolshevik intentions and their fears of Russian power were rekindled. They called for action. Secretary of State Stettinius expressed their views at cabinet meetings. Upon Roosevelt's death, Harriman, the U.S. ambassador in Moscow, rushed to Washington to alert the new president to the Soviet menace.[22]

State Department officials were not alone. General John R. Deane, the head of the U.S. military mission in Moscow, complained bitterly about Russian arrogance. American military officers assigned to the Allied Control Commissions in Hungary, Romania, and Bulgaria also deplored Russian unilateral actions. Increasingly, Deane wanted to restrict military cooperation to matters of vital importance and to insist on safeguarding U.S. interests. Although senior officers on the Joint Strategic Survey Committee expressed apprehension that Deane's ideas would jeopardize Allied unity, the JCS disregarded their advice and approved his recommendations.[23]

The proponents of toughness believed that the United States possessed the power to set the terms for a harmonious relationship with the Russians. When Harriman returned from Moscow in mid-April 1945, he told the president that Soviet leaders wanted to dominate Eastern Europe and penetrate Western Europe. In Harriman's view they had to be stopped immediately. They were weak; their transportation network was inadequate; their work force was impoverished. After the war they would focus on reconstruction, solicit American aid, and avoid conflict. The United States, therefore, had a unique opportunity to exercise financial leverage. Of course, it had to be done adroitly. Harriman did not want to practice a form of coercive diplomacy that would exacerbate the anxieties of the men in the Kremlin and provide them with an excuse to fill the vacuums of power that surrounded them. But the Russians had to be informed that they would not receive American financial aid if they tried to dominate Eastern Europe.[24] When top policymakers met at the White House on 23 April, they endorsed Harriman's position. "The time has arrived," Leahy noted in his diary, "to take a strong American attitude toward the Soviets."[25]

Truman heeded this advice. The Russians, he thought, "needed us more than we needed them." He brusquely told the Soviet foreign minister, V. M. Molotov, that the Kremlin had to comply with its wartime agreements, get rid of the Communist

(Lublin) government in Poland, and establish one that was genuinely representative of the Polish people.[26] In late April and early May, Truman and his advisers then assumed a defiant posture on a number of key issues. When the San Francisco conference opened, they tried to prevent the Lublin Poles from being admitted into the United Nations; when the European war ended, they abruptly suspended lend lease deliveries to the Soviet Union; and when Communist Yugoslavia tried to seize Trieste, they interceded with Stalin and even pondered the use of force.[27]

By mid-May, an open rift with the Soviet Union appeared likely. Truman, however, did not want a break. He sought a cooperative relationship based on Soviet restraint and consistent with U.S. interests. The question was how to bring this about. He went along with the recommendations of Harriman, Stettinius, Grew, Leahy, Deane, and Forrestal because their advice coincided with his instincts. If the United States demonstrated toughness, the Soviets would back down. Toughness, moreover, might defuse the criticism of potential foes in Congress, like Republican Senator Arthur Vandenberg, whose support was needed for a host of legislative enactments.[28] But when the Soviets stood their ground, the president had to reassess his approach. "Did I do wrong?" he asked Joseph Davies in a long, private conversation at the White House.[29]

Davies was a wealthy lawyer and prominent Democrat. He had been ambassador to the Soviet Union in the late 1930's and was renowned for his sympathetic attitude toward Soviet foreign policy. Truman felt relaxed with Davies, dined at his house, attended his card games, and invited him frequently for cruises on the presidential yacht. No other person at the time, except perhaps Byrnes, had such long and intimate conversations with the president on Soviet-U.S. relations. Truman, moreover, permitted Davies to have unlimited access to the highly classified dispatches and telegrams in the president's map room.[30]

Davies urged the president to be patient with the Soviets. They were terribly difficult to deal with, but their anxieties were not surprising. Western nations, Davies told Truman, had fought against the Bolsheviks in 1918 and 1919, isolated them in the 1920's, and rebuffed their overtures in the 1930's. Twice devastated by German invasions within a single generation, the Russians naturally insisted on a friendly Poland and a safe periphery. They could not stake their security on untried collective agreements. But if their suspicions were allayed, their interests in Eastern Europe accommodated, and their rudeness handled with patience, Davies believed that a positive relationship could be established along the lines that Roosevelt had intended. The Russians, he added, were complying with their understanding of the Yalta accords. The British and Americans were trying to escape their true meaning.[31]

According to Davies, Truman listened intently to everything he said. The president probably suspected that Davies' opinions about the wartime agreements were partially true. When Truman read the minutes of the Yalta Conference, he was amazed at their ambiguity. Notwithstanding his categorical assertions about the meaning of the Yalta language on Poland, Truman knew that Leahy and others possessed doubts about the American interpretation.[32] Moreover, during May 1945, Byrnes came to realize that his own views, which he had disseminated to the media and Congress, were deeply flawed. Byrnes had left the Crimea before the final resolution of matters pertaining to Poland, Germany, and the Far East. As he slowly gathered information on these issues in private discussions with Roosevelt's other advisers, who themselves had only a piecemeal knowledge of the various provisions, Byrnes recognized that the Soviet interpretation of the Yalta accords was a credible one. Roosevelt, in fact, had conceded a sphere of influence to the Russians in Eastern Europe, although he hoped that Stalin would abide by democratic forms. On 6 June, Byrnes acknowledged to Davies that "there was no justification under the spirit or letter of the [Yalta] agreement" for insisting on an entirely new government in Poland. Byrnes conveyed these views to Truman, whose respect for Byrnes mounted, even while the latter radically altered his interpretation of the meaning of Yalta.[33]

During these weeks Stimson grew alarmed with the State Department's handling of Soviet-U.S. relations. He listened to Harriman's warnings about Soviet intentions and did not dismiss them. But he thought it a mistake to challenge Russia on its own periphery. If the United States and the Soviet Union acted prudently, he mused in his diary, there was no need for their "orbits" to "clash geographically."[34]

Yet Stimson's personal feelings reflected the ambivalence in policymaking circles during the spring of 1945. While advising the inexperienced president and the hawkish State Department to move cautiously, Stimson wanted to work out relations with the Soviets in ways that fully protected American interests. The time for toughness would come when the United States successfully tested and used the atomic bomb. "We really held all the cards," he told Marshall on 14 May. "I called it a royal straight flush and we mustn't be a fool about the way we play it. They [the Russians] can't get along without our help and industries and we have coming into action a weapon which will be unique. Now the thing is not to get into unnecessary quarrels by talking too much . . . ; let our actions speak for themselves."[35]

Truman recorded in his own diary that Stimson had very sound ideas on Russia.[36] The president saw no need either to hurry to a new conference or to gang up with the British against the Russians.[37] At the end of May he sent Harry Hopkins, Roosevelt's confidant and occasional envoy, to Moscow to patch up Soviet-U.S. relations. Learning that the Soviet understanding of the Yalta provision on Poland was not unreasonable, Truman accepted a modest reorganization of the Polish Lublin government. In turn, he was grateful when Stalin altered his country's position on the procedural veto in the U.N. Security Council, a dispute that had stymied progress at the San Francisco conference. These mutual concessions suggested the possibility of accommodation and on terms that were not incompatible with vital U.S. interests.[38]

The East European Litmus Test

Although Truman could not ignore the intent of Yalta regarding the composition of the provisional government of Poland, he still distrusted Soviet aims. He wanted to remove the "Soviet blackout" in Eastern Europe and was "unalterably opposed" to the police governments in Hungary, Bulgaria, and Romania.[39] But he knew that he could not eliminate Soviet predominance in countries that were occupied by Soviet armies.[40] The Kremlin's policies in Eastern Europe and the Balkans, however, could serve as a clue to Soviet intentions elsewhere. If the Russians imposed governments on occupied countries, curtailed basic freedoms, barred elections, and prohibited equal trade and investment, Soviet leaders would be indicating their contempt for the Atlantic Charter and the Yalta Declaration on Liberated Europe. If they abrogated their commitments, they would fail the litmus test of their intentions and would prove their nefarious ambitions.[41]

The application of the litmus test did not mean that Truman was eager to jeopardize Soviet-U.S. relations. Much could be gained by preserving amicable ties with the Kremlin. Soviet intervention in the Far Eastern war might save American lives and insure the unconditional surrender of Japan. Likewise, Soviet-U.S. collaboration in Asia might help stabilize conditions in China. And, finally, Soviet-U.S. harmony was necessary for the smooth functioning of the United Nations, the development of collective security mechanisms, the control of Germany, and the preservation of peace around the globe. Truman recognized that preemptive action to thwart Soviet ambitions in Eastern Europe, an area of peripheral interest to the United States, might unnecessarily exacerbate Soviet-U.S. relations and jeopardize more important American priorities elsewhere.[42]

Truman's dilemma was to restrain Soviet ambitions in Eastern Europe yet maintain a cooperative relationship consistent with American interests. The president believed, as did Stimson and Byrnes, that American leverage would be enhanced once Soviet leaders had witnessed the power of the atomic bomb. Most scholars now agree that Truman did not authorize its use in order to intimidate the men in the Kremlin, but he was fully conscious of its diplomatic ramifications and eager to reap its anticipated benefits.[43] But the president did not wish to rely solely on the leverage afforded by atomic weapons. He wanted to build upon the rapport produced by Hopkins's talks in Moscow. Consequently, he and Byrnes instructed the State Department to examine the advantages of a treaty guaranteeing the demilitarization of Germany. If Soviet policies in Eastern Europe were truly impelled by suspicions of the West and fears of a revived Germany, then a demilitarization treaty might allay Russian apprehensions and at the same time promote more freedom and openness in Eastern Europe.[44]

Officials in the State Department and the Pentagon recognized that the Soviet Union had "special security interests in certain neighboring countries."[45] Nevertheless, they wanted the Kremlin to reconcile these strategic considerations with

American interests and principles. Believing that Eastern Europe's food and raw materials were needed in Western Europe, U.S. policymakers ridiculed the discriminatory commercial treaties that the Kremlin was imposing. They also maintained that the governments of Hungary, Romania, and Bulgaria should not be recognized until they were reorganized. Peace treaties should not be signed until free elections took place and nondiscriminatory trade was permitted. Media access, free elections, and open trade, they hoped, might sustain some American influence in Eastern Europe even if the United States lacked the means to contest Soviet predominance.[46]

It is hard to make sense out of this preoccupation with Eastern Europe unless it is realized that policymakers did not see events in Eastern Europe as discrete from events in other parts of the world. The precedents of statism, bilateralism, discrimination, and autarky that were being established through Soviet fiat in Eastern Europe threatened to be duplicated elsewhere—not by Soviet action but as a result of the social, political, and financial reverberations produced by fifteen years of depression and war. U.S. officials feared a return to the conditions of the 1930's, when economic autarky perpetuated international depression, enhanced German and Japanese strength, and contributed to the outbreak of war. They worried that the compartmentalization of the world economy into Soviet and British blocs might again circumscribe the sphere of American trade, lead to economic stagnation, and jeopardize a full-employment economy. Even more ominously, the Kremlin might use bilateral commercial agreements and joint stock companies to foster its economic growth and military power. Capitalizing on the prevailing chaos and economic dislocation, the Russians might lure additional countries into their orbit. They would seek to enhance their influence, improve their strategic position, and augment their ability to mobilize resources and labor to wage war. Someday, far in the future, the Kremlin might gain sufficient strength to contest America's preponderant position in the international system.[47]

Soviet actions in Eastern Europe, therefore, and socioeconomic strife elsewhere, although two distinct phenomena, became blurred together in often fuzzy and inchoate but nevertheless significant ways. American fears of autarky and revolution in other regions accentuated American apprehensions about Soviet behavior in Eastern Europe. Soviet actions were contradictory and the Kremlin's intentions were not clear. But no one in U.S. policymaking circles doubted the volatility of the international environment and the opportunities it presented to Soviet leaders should they make a determined effort to capitalize on the ferment and unrest.[48] In April 1945, for example, McCloy returned from a trip to Europe and told Stimson that the situation in Germany was "worse than anything probably that ever happened in the world." Stimson jotted in his diary that he "had anticipated the chaos, but the details of it were appalling." [49]

Less than two months later, Assistant Secretary of State Acheson presented an equally vivid and horrifying account of the international situation to the Senate Committee on Banking and Currency: "There is a situation in the world, very clearly

illustrated in Europe, and also true in the Far East, which threatens the very foundations, the whole fabric of world organization which we have known in our lifetime
and which our fathers and grandfathers knew." In liberated Europe "you find that the
railway systems have ceased to operate; that power systems have ceased to operate;
the financial systems are destroyed. Ownership of property is in terrific confusion.
Management of property is in confusion." Not since the eighth century when the
Muslims split the world in two had conditions been so serious. The industrial and
social life of Europe had "come to a complete and total standstill." Unless action
was taken, Europe would turn in on itself using bilateral agreements, exchange
controls, multiple currencies, and tactics of economic warfare. And Acheson reminded his listeners that these techniques were used by the Nazis to consolidate
their hold over Europe and to mobilize its resources to fight the rest of the world.
Now again, the situation was "one of unparalleled seriousness, in which the whole
fabric of social life might go to pieces unless the most energetic steps are taken on
all fronts." [50]

Acheson never mentioned Russia in his testimony. Russia was not to blame
for the conditions he described. Indeed, Acheson was pleading for U.S. participation in the International Monetary Fund and the World Bank. In the spring and
summer of 1945 the Truman administration put tremendous effort into getting Congress to accept its international economic program. In quick succession Acheson,
Clayton, Morgenthau, and other administration spokesmen appeared before congressional committees and pleaded for the extension and expansion of reciprocal
trade legislation, additional lending authority for the Export-Import Bank, and repeal of the Johnson Act prohibiting private American loans to nations like Britain
and France that had defaulted on their World War I debts. The underlying rationale
was stated and restated: a chaotic world needed American supplies and capital; a
full-employment domestic economy depended on reconstructed markets overseas; a
free enterprise system at home required open trade and the convertibility of foreign
currencies; and a secure America needed peace, stability, and prosperity abroad.[51]

The imponderables that lay ahead were enormous. The Soviets appeared to
be penetrating Eastern Europe and co-opting its resources. Economic dislocation
and political trends presented additional opportunities for the Kremlin to spread its
influence beyond Eastern Europe. Whether they would want to or try to was uncertain. But equally uncertain was the efficacy of the new economic institutions that
the United States was fashioning to cope with the underlying sources of instability.
Military planners and intelligence analysts recognized that failure to improve the
economic conditions might impel "some of the nations of Western Europe to enter
voluntarily the Soviet orbit." [52] And if they did, the worldwide balance of power
would be altered. Prudence, therefore, dictated that the Truman administration seek
to dilute Soviet predominance in Eastern Europe and to deter the expansion of
Soviet Russia beyond it. What happened within its existing orbit, moreover, might
reveal much about the Kremlin's future intentions.

The Potsdam Conference and the Atomic Bomb

Prudence would be Truman's watchword as he approached his first meeting with Churchill and Stalin. The president dreaded the upcoming summit. "How I hate this trip," he confided in his diary. "But I have to make it . . . and we must win." He was pleased to have Byrnes, now formally designated secretary of state, going along with him. He also felt that he could rely on Leahy. These men he could trust for their good judgment and for their tough, hard-nosed approach to international relations.[53]

Truman's continued ambivalence, however, was reflected by the fact that he also encouraged Joseph Davies to serve as a principal adviser. When Davies joined the president and secretary of state in Berlin on 15 July 1945, he immediately feared that State Department officials had poisoned their minds with anti-Soviet propaganda as they had crossed the ocean. Davies was so distraught that he volunteered to leave if Truman felt he could be of no use. In a "moving" heart-to-heart talk, Truman reassured Davies that the latter's fears were unfounded. "Joe, I want you to understand that I am trying my best to save peace and to follow out Roosevelt's plan. It is a hard job. Jim Byrnes knows that too. . . . We are counting on you. I want you at my elbow at the conference table." [54]

Notwithstanding his desire to cooperate with Russia, the president's priorities were to bring about the rapid defeat of Japan, save American lives, and circumscribe Soviet gains in East Asia. In his first meeting with Stalin, Truman was happy to ascertain that the Russians would enter the Far Eastern war and adhere to their Yalta pledge to support the Chinese Nationalists. "I've gotten what I came for," Truman wrote his wife.[55] But as he learned of the successful test of the atomic bomb, his views on Soviet participation in the Pacific war rapidly evolved. The information from New Mexico, Truman told Davies on 16 July, took "a great load off my mind." Two days later he learned that the Japanese were making peace overtures. The "Japs," he wrote, "will fold up before Russia comes in. I am sure they will when Manhattan appears over their homeland." After being "tremendously pepped up" by more news of the atomic test, Truman asked Stimson if Russian intervention in the Far Eastern war were needed. The secretary said it was not.[56]

Truman and Byrnes now hoped "to outmaneuver Stalin on China" and to end the war in the Pacific before the Russians intervened.[57] Admiral Leahy thought such efforts were naive. So did Marshall. Although they agreed that Russian aid was no longer required to defeat Japan, they believed that efforts to outsmart the Russians would fail to check Soviet gains in Northeast Asia and would exacerbate Soviet suspicions.[58] To the extent that Truman and Byrnes contemplated this preemptive strategy, they were revealing how the impulses to contain and deter the Kremlin were wrestling with and gaining ascendancy over the incentives to cooperate and reassure.

At Potsdam the president's overall policies were geared toward the economic stabilization of Western Europe and the dilution of Soviet influence in Eastern Europe.[59] Yet once Truman worked out his initial understanding with Stalin on the Far East and received news of the atomic bomb, he let Byrnes handle most of the technical negotiations regarding German reparations, the Polish border, and the peace terms for Germany's former satellites. Byrnes modulated U.S. demands for free elections in Eastern Europe and for more effective control commissions. He did not persistently press for nondiscriminatory trade and open waterways. He acquiesced to Poland's incorporation of parts of prewar Germany (pending a final peace treaty). In these ways, he believed he was accommodating Soviet interests in a region of vital concern to the Kremlin. But he would neither recognize Soviet-imposed governments in Romania and Bulgaria nor permit the growth of Soviet power beyond its existing sphere in Eastern Europe. Although he complained bitterly about Russian stubbornness, he did not lose hope. The atomic bomb, he believed, "had given us great power, and . . . in the last analysis, it would control." [60]

Truman grew bored as Molotov and Byrnes sparred with one another. He admired Byrnes's tenacity, but the president wanted to go home. He was satisfied with the establishment of the Council of Foreign Ministers as an ongoing institutional arrangement for the negotiation of the peace treaties. Other matters could be deferred until he observed the Russian reaction to the atomic bomb. Meanwhile, he planned to remain tough. Stalin "doesn't know it but I have an ace in the hole and another one showing—so unless he has threes or two pair (and I know he has not) we are sitting all right." Writing in his own diary, Stimson found himself amazed at the "differences of psychology which now exist since the successful test." [61]

On 31 July and 1 August, final agreements were hammered out. Truman, Byrnes, and Leahy immediately set sail for the United States. While they crossed the ocean, a mushroom cloud appeared over Hiroshima and the atomic age was ushered in. A second atomic bomb fell on Nagasaki on 9 August; the Russians declared war and marched into Manchuria; and the Japanese inquired about surrender terms. Back in Washington, the president and his advisers slightly altered the unconditional surrender formula and did not insist on the Japanese emperor's abdication. Writing in his diary, Stimson acknowledged that they wanted the war to end "before the Russians could put in any substantial claim to occupy and help rule [the Japanese mainland]." On 14 August, fighting ceased. On 2 September, the Japanese formally surrendered.[62]

Byrnes Takes Command

While Americans celebrated victory, Truman turned his attention to domestic affairs. Not interested in the details of foreign policy, he gave Byrnes full authority to handle the nation's diplomacy. The secretary of state eagerly grasped the reins of power. Byrnes was confident he could exert leverage over the Russians and establish a basis for cooperation consistent with American goals. The atomic bomb, he told Stimson and McCloy, was "a great weapon" that could be used as an "implied threat" during his forthcoming talks with Molotov. Yet for all his confidence in the bomb, Byrnes never systematically pondered how its military strength could be translated into diplomatic leverage.[63]

Not surprisingly, then, Byrnes grew frustrated at the London meeting of foreign ministers in September 1945 when Molotov mocked the bomb and defied U.S. power. The Soviet foreign minister requested a trusteeship in Tripolitania and wrangled incessantly with the British Labour government's foreign secretary, Ernest Bevin. Molotov refused to reorganize the Bulgarian and Romanian governments and sought to guarantee Soviet predominance in the Balkans.[64] He also infuriated Byrnes by his procedural moves, trying as he did to exclude the Chinese and French foreign ministers from discussions of the peace treaties with Germany's former satellites.[65]

But Byrnes also felt considerable ambivalence. He knew that Molotov's procedural maneuvers had a sound legal basis in the Potsdam Protocol. He could see that the Russian foreign minister was ready to overcome the procedural impasse and defer the trusteeship question if the United States would recognize the Bulgarian and Romanian governments. Aware of Soviet security concerns, Byrnes did not contest the Russian demand for "friendly" neighbors and broached the possibility of a German demilitarization treaty. He even intimated that he might recognize the Romanian and Bulgarian governments if the Kremlin made some token changes in their composition, permitted free elections, and accepted open trade. But when the time came to compromise, neither he nor Molotov would budge.[66]

The deadlock at London caused dismay in the United States. Journalists stressed the deterioration of relations among the big three allies. Some commentators dwelled on the Kremlin's nefarious behavior in Eastern Europe, and Molotov was portrayed as truculent and intransigent. But the State Department's daily assessments of media opinion showed no groundswell of sentiment for a get-tough policy. Indeed a major theme of press comment was the need to repair Soviet-U.S. relations. With the war over, however, most Americans were turning their attention away from international affairs. In late October, only 7 percent of the people polled rated world peace as the number one problem facing the country. Jobs and labor strife were their foremost concerns.[67]

Byrnes returned from London perturbed and indecisive. Although he was not criticized in the press, the secretary had taken sole responsibility for the talks with Russia, and he felt a personal and a political need to make them a success. He blamed the Soviets for the impasse. But he could not ignore the blatant contradiction between American attempts to lock the Kremlin out of Japan and seeking to open the door for greater American influence in Eastern Europe. He also realized that atomic diplomacy and financial leverage had not wrought concessions from Moscow. So he now decided to take a different approach and to reassure the Soviets. With the help of Charles Bohlen, he prepared a major address. On 31 October the secretary of state declared that the United States would not intervene in the countries bordering on Russian territory and would "never join any groups in those countries in hostile intrigue against the Soviet Union." [68]

But Byrnes's willingness to accommodate Soviet strategic interests was still conditioned on the Kremlin's acceptance of liberal economic and political principles. He protested the Soviet economic agreements with Hungary, called for nondiscriminatory trade, and suggested a tripartite economic commission for that country. He made aid to Poland contingent on free elections, refused to acknowledge the legitimacy of the Bulgarian elections in November, and advised Truman not to withdraw U.S. troops from Czechoslovakia until the Russians also departed. He sent Mark Ethridge as a special representative to examine political conditions in the Balkans. Meanwhile, he decided to withhold action on any loan to the Kremlin until Soviet leaders loosened their control over Eastern Europe, adhered to the open door, and opened their own country to American journalists and observers. Through diplomatic overtures, nonrecognition, and financial leverage, Byrnes hoped to achieve some relaxation of Soviet control over Eastern Europe.[69]

Byrnes's diplomacy evoked much criticism within the administration. Part of it was for substantive reasons. His rhetoric and action constituted less forceful action than most American diplomats in Eastern Europe demanded.[70] But much of it was personal. Byrnes's desire to monopolize policy offended almost everyone. At Potsdam, his secrecy and uncollegiality agitated Stimson and McCloy. Harriman felt slighted. Stettinius, now the U.S. representative to the United Nations, found himself ignored. During the August discussions over Japanese surrender terms, Byrnes clashed with Leahy, tried to exclude him from the policy process, and engendered his lasting enmity. Byrnes was no more inclined to consult with the professional diplomats in the State Department. He forced out Undersecretary Grew and brought in his own trusted aides, Donald Russell and Benjamin V. Cohen. Byrnes asked Acheson to be his undersecretary but never worked closely with him or won his loyalty. The secretary scorned many of his subordinates and refused to file daily reports to Foggy Bottom when he was away. He eschewed orderly procedure and systematic preparation. Byrnes thought he could rely on his own instincts, insights, and shrewdness to achieve diplomatic success. He was wrong.[71]

Administrative Disorganization

The result was a further disintegration of the policymaking process. At the end of September, McCloy met Stettinius in London and lamented conditions in Washington. Everything, he said, was in a state of chaos. There was no planning, no cooperation, no high purpose.[72]

Part of this situation was the result of developments within the War Department. Much to Truman's chagrin, Stimson decided to retire. Almost immediately, McCloy and Lovett announced their resignations. Marshall, too, was eager to depart once the war was over. Truman named Undersecretary Robert P. Patterson to succeed Stimson; Dwight D. Eisenhower replaced Marshall; and at the end of 1945 Howard C. Petersen and Stuart Symington moved into the positions vacated by McCloy and Lovett.

The new team faced difficult challenges. In addition to supervising the demobilization of the wartime army, they were charged with implementing occupation policies. This task required an enormous amount of interdepartmental coordination and was particularly tough because of the constant friction between strong-minded commanders in the field and sensitive foreign service officers. Patterson and Petersen sought to establish viable working relationships with the men at the State Department. They also had to clarify responsibilities with powerful proconsuls like Generals Lucius D. Clay in Germany, Mark W. Clark in Austria, Douglas MacArthur in Japan, and John R. Hodge in Korea. Most difficult of all was the fact that, while they retrenched and demobilized, they had to muster the financial and human resources to preserve stability and avoid famine in occupied areas.[73]

The squabbles between occupation authorities, the War Department, and the State Department were a microcosm of larger difficulties besetting Washington's policymaking community in the aftermath of war. In general, officials in the Pentagon believed that the nation's force structure, strategic concepts, military policies, and overseas base requirements had to uphold national objectives. But try as they might, they were unable to ascertain how the White House and the State Department were defining vital interests and security goals. They, therefore, drew up their own objectives.

According to the JCS planners, the territorial integrity of the United States and its possessions had to be protected. So, too, the territory of other Western Hemisphere nations and that of the Philippines. In addition, the United States had to have sufficient forces to support the United Nations and to insure that the defeated enemy states complied with the peace. Furthermore, the United States had to have the military capabilities to advance its political, economic, and social well-being and to maintain itself in the best possible position relative to potential adversaries. What was evident, as the historian Michael Sherry has stressed, was that there were no longer any geographical limitations on the exercise of American power. These goals, moreover, were as ambiguous and uninstructive as they were expansionist and globalist.[74]

Military planners desired to establish a policy of "active defense." When it became evident that aggression was imminent, they wanted civilian officials to make decisions promptly and to order U.S. forces to strike the first blow. There must never be another Pearl Harbor. Consequently, the United States had to possess an intelligence apparatus capable of forewarning of hostile intentions, an overseas base system designed to project American power, and superior air forces.[75]

These recommendations were based on the lessons of the past rather than a penetrating look at the future. The planners knew it. They tried to discern the shape of the postwar world. They foresaw great instability arising from territorial adjustments, decolonization, and social upheaval. In this volatile international environment they hoped to preserve the wartime coalition, but they did not think military policy should be premised on its continuation. "The undefined character of Russian aspirations, the background of mutual suspicion" demanded vigilance.[76]

Although the planners sought no rift with the Kremlin, their pessimistic portrayal of likely postwar scenarios aroused the ire of General Marshall, Assistant Secretary McCloy, and General Lincoln. They told the planners to revise their study. The final paper, however, was still more ambiguous. It stressed that American military policies should be designed to preserve stability in the international system and to maintain the United States in the most favorable position relative to potential enemies. The implications of these generalizations for the configuration of U.S. forces were left obscure. The JCS sent the paper to the SWNCC to flesh out the views of the State Department.[77]

Just a few days later, however, after the deadlock between Byrnes and Molotov at the September foreign ministers' meeting, the JCS reviewed another study. This report focused on Soviet demands and suggested that prudence dictated a worst-case analysis of the Kremlin's intentions. It "may conceivably" be argued that the Soviets were "pushing toward a domination of Europe, comparable with that which inspired the Germans, and toward control of the Eastern Mediterranean, the Persian Gulf, Northern China, and Korea." If there were to be any limit to Russian expansion, it was essential to ascertain where the line could and should be drawn. The chiefs of staff instructed their subordinates to probe these questions more thoroughly. They wanted to reconcile the views of the Pentagon with those of the State Department before submitting a final study to the president.[78]

In October, the JCS took one additional step toward inviting closer civilian-military cooperation. They proposed that the president appoint a special board to assess the nation's security imperatives. Aware that their own studies failed to grapple with the ramifications of the atomic bomb, they wanted a thorough examination of the impact of new technological developments on the nation's defense posture. They also recognized that the economic requirements of total war demanded greater integration of civilian and military plans. Leahy drafted a letter to Truman requesting an expert commission composed of both civilians and military personnel.[79]

No one was more supportive of these attempts to coordinate policy than Secretary of the Navy Forrestal. While dedicated to fostering the organizational interests of the Navy, he was nevertheless the leading proponent of efforts to integrate economic, political, and military policies at the highest levels of the government. He strongly supported the JCS proposal for a wide-ranging study of national security requirements. He also endorsed a reorganization plan worked out by Ferdinand Eberstadt, his close friend, former banking partner, and wartime head of the Munitions Board. The Eberstadt plan called for the establishment of a National Security

Council and a National Security Resources Board. Forrestal and Eberstadt wanted to overcome the gaps revealed during the war between "foreign and military policy, between strategic planning and its logistic implementation, and between the military and civilian agencies responsible for industrial mobilization."[80]

Secretary of War Patterson was less than enthusiastic about these organizational initiatives. Like Forrestal and the JCS, however, Patterson believed that decision-making processes had to be improved in order to coordinate political-military policy. He was gravely worried that rapid demobilization might affect occupation objectives. On 1 November, he sent Byrnes a list of questions designed to underscore the close linkages between military strength and policy objectives. At the existing rate of demobilization, Patterson warned, the armed forces would decline from 8 million men in August 1945 to 1.6 million in April 1946; by September 1946 every soldier currently overseas might be discharged. Did not these figures dictate that the pace of demobilization should be slowed?[81]

State Department officials seemed indifferent to these overtures. On 13 November, more than six weeks after the JCS submitted their study on overall military policy, the topic came up for discussion at the secretary of state's staff committee. No one attending this meeting spoke approvingly of the report.[82] Their objections were justified: the JCS study did not define interests clearly, did not enumerate priorities, did not shrewdly calculate other nations' intentions and capabilities, and did not offer an insightful examination of the international environment. But it did provide a potential framework for grappling with fundamental variables and for linking diplomatic, political, and military policies had State Department officials been willing to do so.

But they were not. Their penchant for ducking the tough questions was apparent when Byrnes responded to Patterson's letter on demobilization. Noting that neither 200,000 nor 400,000 troops in Europe would suffice to achieve political goals, the secretary of state vacuously remarked that "The important thing is that our country must have sufficient military strength at home and abroad to give evidence of a determination to back up the policies of our Government anywhere they may be necessary." But what were the policies that needed to be supported? When Army officials sought this information, Byrnes was unable to provide them with a definition of minimum interests, for example, in the Far East, from which the United States could not retreat.[83]

Byrnes did continue to meet regularly with Patterson and Forrestal. His relations with these men were not as strained as they were with most other officials. For the most part, however, the three secretaries focused on immediate issues and had little time to discuss long-term planning. Byrnes agreed that political and military issues were interrelated, that forces-in-being were necessary to support the conduct of diplomacy. But he did not instruct key subordinates to collaborate with military planners on such matters. He did not express any opposition when Truman vetoed the idea of a presidential board to assess overall national security requirements.

He did not raise any questions when the president indicated in December that the peacetime military budget could not exceed $6 billion.[84]

The paucity of long-range, interdepartmental, civil-military planning was accompanied by the well-known rift between the Army and Navy over proposals to unify the armed services in a single department of defense. In October and November, the differences were voiced publicly before the Senate Military Affairs Committee. Army officials, like Patterson and Marshall, strongly advocated unification in order to reduce costs, enhance efficiency, eliminate duplication, and insure preparedness. Forrestal, Leahy, and the admirals staunchly opposed unification. They disputed its beneficial effects, claimed that the new department would be unmanageable, and argued that competition was constructive—not destructive. They clearly feared that naval interests would be submerged in a new department, especially if the Air Force received coequal status and joined with the Army against the Navy.[85]

The Army-Navy feud made it difficult for the Pentagon to prepare any coordinated plan for the postwar military structure. The Army Air Forces wanted independence and 70 air groups. The Navy demanded a fleet of aircraft carriers, full integration of its air arm, 50,000 officers, 550,000 enlisted men, and 110,000 Marines. General Marshall, on the eve of his retirement, lamented the unrealistic requests of each of the services. He still championed universal military training (UMT) as the clearest manifestation of the nation's readiness to assume its new worldwide obligations. Yet support for UMT was eroding as each of the services pushed its own organizationally driven demands.[86]

Officials at the White House scorned the rivalries and clashes in the Pentagon. Budget Director Harold Smith asked the JCS for a review of the overall peacetime requirements of the armed services in light of the new responsibilities facing the United States and the advances in technology and weapons. But when the results proved so meager and the administrative disarray so glaring, nothing much was done. Policymaking floundered.[87]

Ambivalence and Acrimony

Truman was dismayed by the absence of cohesion within his official circle. During the fall of 1945, domestic problems proliferated. The president faced mounting labor strife and spiraling inflation, and he thought the Republicans would exploit these issues. On 23 October he noted in his diary, "The Congress is balking; labor has gone crazy; management is not far from insane in selfishness. My Cabinet, at least some of them, have Potomac fever. There are more prima donnas per square foot in public life here than in all the opera companies ever to exist." [88]

Truman grew especially disillusioned with Byrnes. He wanted to concentrate on domestic affairs while Byrnes handled foreign relations, but Byrnes's actions engendered too much acrimony. Truman increasingly resented his secretary of state's independent pronouncements on foreign policy. On 8 December, Truman took Davies aside for a chat on the presidential yacht and called Byrnes a "conniver." When the president asked him to keep the secretary in line, Davies rightly concluded that Byrnes would soon be "through." [89]

As the secretary of state's enemies sensed Truman's growing disaffection, they maneuvered to destroy whatever influence Byrnes still possessed. Secretary of Commerce Henry Wallace moved from the left, Admiral Leahy from the right. Wallace sneered at Byrnes's knowledge and urged the president to take command of the nation's diplomacy. As Byrnes's ambivalence between containing and reassuring the Kremlin tilted toward the latter, Leahy tried to provide a corrective. In late October he proposed to Rosenman that they write a major foreign policy speech that the chief executive could deliver at the Navy Day celebration scheduled for 27 October 1945. The speech was modeled after Woodrow Wilson's fourteen points and designed to attract wide attention abroad. Domestically, its purpose was to force "our diplomatic appeasers to pay closer attention to the vital interests of America." [90]

On 27 October almost six million Americans stood along the banks of the Hudson River, lined Fifth Avenue, and crowded into Central Park in New York City. Forty-seven of the nation's warships were anchored along seven miles of the Hudson. Overhead, 1,200 Navy fighters and bombers roared through the sky. Truman reviewed the fleet, commissioned a new aircraft carrier, and heralded the nation's wartime triumph.[91] The president used the occasion to articulate the basic tenets of U.S. foreign policy. Truman eschewed any American self-interest and forswore any new territory. He championed democracy, self-government, and national sovereignty. He warned against territorial changes that took place without the consent of the governed. He advocated freedom of the seas, open trade, unhindered access to raw materials, and global economic cooperation. And he heralded both the United Nations and Pan-Americanism.[92]

The noteworthy aspect of Truman's Navy Day speech and of several other presidential addresses in the autumn of 1945 was the emphasis on power. The United States, Truman declared, had superior military power and intended to preserve it. The nation would continue to hold the atomic bomb as a "sacred trust" for all mankind. Its air and naval forces would control the seas, dominate the skies, enforce the peace, stifle aggression, support the United Nations, and safeguard U.S. interests. Its overseas bases would provide defense in depth and project power across the oceans. Its laboratories would turn out the most advanced weapons. Its young men would have a year of UMT. Just as courts had to have marshals and county governments had to have sheriffs, the United States had to have UMT in order to create a stable world order conducive to American security.[93]

"Our military policy," Truman went on to tell Congress in December 1945, "should be completely consistent with our foreign policy." The president called for unification of the armed services and a Department of National Defense. He maintained that a full national security program required the integration of strategic planning, budget-making, intelligence assessment, industrial mobilization, and raw material stockpiling. Unprecedented cooperation was called for between the War and Navy departments and the rest of the government.[94]

Truman's actions, however, hardly accorded with his rhetoric. He disregarded Forrestal's proposals to effectuate political-military cooperation, he rejected Leahy's desire for a special presidential board to study national security imperatives, and he spurned Wallace's advice that he take control of the policy process. Notwithstanding his talk about the utility of power, he did not even know how many bombs were in the atomic arsenal. He did little to slow down the demobilization momentum. In fact, he told his budget officers to scrutinize military requests and to eliminate all the fat. His projected $6 billion defense budget was incomparably greater than any prewar appropriation, but small in relation to the objectives he mouthed.[95]

For Truman, domestic affairs were of primary importance in 1945. Public and congressional demands to bring the boys home were irresistible. Inflationary pressures and fiscal considerations commanded his attention. The domestic situation, he told Byrnes, had to be stabilized before the United States could exert itself effectively in international affairs.[96]

And the ambivalence remained. To some aides, he spoke apprehensively of Soviet aims in the Near East and lamented that Russia might replace Japan as the dominant power in East Asia. On the other hand, he reassured Wallace that he understood Soviet security needs in the Balkans and wanted to preserve Soviet-U.S. amity. He rejected Leahy's advice to withhold all information on atomic energy, and he supported Byrnes's desire to reactivate talks with the Russians and British in Moscow. Even in his Navy Day speech, he beckoned for cooperation that would be consistent with American interests and principles. As the political scientist Deborah Larson has shown, Truman was not eager for a rift. He wavered in one direction, then moved in another. Foreign relations, he admitted, baffled him.[97]

Truman's ambivalent feelings mirrored the uncertainties and contradictions that persisted within his administration. A few top officials, like Leahy and Forrestal, had decided that Soviet Russia could not be trusted and that it was ideologically inspired. Communist influence was spreading everywhere; therefore, it was too risky to make any concessions. Some influential men, like General Lincoln in the War Department and Senator Vandenberg, shared this perspective.[98] But many prominent defense officials disagreed. Generals Marshall, Eisenhower, and Clay retained vivid memories of wartime collaboration. They got along well with Soviet military leaders, and they thought the Soviets would focus on domestic reconstruction. Seeing the complexity of Russian motivations, they were reluctant to accept a breakdown in Soviet-U.S. relations.[99]

Military planners and intelligence analysts now spent more and more time and energy pondering Soviet intentions and capabilities. They studied the strategic considerations and historical ambitions shaping Soviet policies. They recognized the malleability of Soviet ideology. In their view Soviet behavior would be affected by the complex interaction of domestic influences within the Soviet Union, local and regional circumstances in problem spots around the world, and the Kremlin's perception of the aims and abilities of the United States and Great Britain. American military planners and intelligence analysts took note of the wartime devastation experienced by the Soviet Union and acknowledged the huge task of economic reconstruction that lay ahead; yet they also feared that the Soviets would harness the resources of satellite states in Eastern Europe and of other Communist countries to abet the Russian rehabilitation process. They stressed the strategic weakness of the Soviet air force, the relative impotence of the Soviet navy, and the inability of the Soviet Union to attack U.S. territory; yet they also worried that, if war should erupt, Soviet armies would be able to conquer most of Western Europe and the Middle East as well as parts of Northeast Asia. They believed the Soviet Union would seek to avoid war for five, ten, or fifteen years; yet they placed little confidence in the United Nations and believed that the United States had to remain militarily prepared to safeguard vital interests and to take timely action to thwart any prospective attack.[100]

The same uncertainties remained in the State Department. Most foreign service officers in Moscow and in Soviet-occupied territory were outraged by Soviet actions, pleaded for bolder American initiatives, and abandoned hope for Soviet-U.S. cooperation. Yet a few professional American diplomats posted in Washington, like Charles Bohlen, Geroid T. Robinson, and Cloyce K. Huston, continued to look for ways to satisfy Soviet security imperatives in Eastern Europe without sacrificing U.S. interests and ideals. Bohlen worked closely with Byrnes and, therefore, his views are of special interest. On the one hand, he deplored the Soviet intrusion into the economic and political affairs of East European countries. On the other hand, he did not want "to deny to the Soviet Union the legitimate prerogatives of a great power in regard to smaller countries" in close geographic propinquity. The historian Eduard Mark has shown that Bohlen tried to resolve these contradictory impulses by championing the idea of an open sphere of influence wherein Soviet security requirements would be reconciled with the preservation of open trade and democratic freedoms. Harriman, too, did not give up hope of reaching an accommodation with the Kremlin. After he visited Stalin in the Crimea in late October 1945, he came away encouraged. Stalin, Harriman concluded, wanted to cooperate "but is inordinately suspicious of our every move." At the top rungs of the State Department, Dean Acheson and Benjamin Cohen were not unreceptive to such explanations. They, too, had not forsaken cooperation, if Russian fears could be allayed without compromising major U.S. interests.[101]

Inspired by a desire to establish a working relationship with the Kremlin, Byrnes arranged for a meeting of the British, American, and Soviet foreign ministers in Moscow in December 1945. He hoped to avoid the impasse that paralyzed progress at the September meeting in London. Yet once again he failed to build support for his ideas with influential legislators, important members of the administration, and British officials who were eager to find common ground with the United States. Byrnes now was willing to recognize the existing regimes in Romania and Bulgaria provided the Russians accepted token changes in these governments and permitted free elections. He also wanted to use the prospect of international control of atomic weapons to reassure the Soviets and lure them into a more cooperative mindset. Byrnes was fairly successful. Unlike London, the Moscow meeting ended with a formal agreement and on a hopeful note. Byrnes returned to Washington moderately satisfied with what he had accomplished.[102]

Yet Byrnes's performance in Moscow evoked nasty backbiting from his enemies.[103] Much of this criticism was unfounded. On matters relating to East Asia, the Near East, and the Eastern Mediterranean, Byrnes made no significant concessions. With regard to atomic energy, Byrnes did not get all he wanted. But he gave little away and secured Soviet support of a U.N. commission on atomic energy. His major concession was to relax the American position on reshaping the Bulgarian and Romanian governments.[104] He did this because he now wanted to hasten progress toward the conclusion of peace treaties with Germany's ex-satellites. The Soviets would then be obligated to withdraw most of their troops from the Balkans, thereby removing a potential threat to Turkey and establishing the possibility of an open sphere in Eastern Europe. Of course, there were no guarantees that the Soviets would abide by an open sphere. Byrnes himself was only minimally hopeful. Yet under existing conditions there was no other realistic means of moderating Soviet domination.[105]

Byrnes's foes were uninterested in the logic of his case. Influential senators, like Vandenberg, Democratic leader Tom Connally, and Chairman of the Joint Committee on Atomic Energy Brien McMahon, were outraged by the secretary of state's failure to solicit their advice on the international control of atomic energy. They complained bitterly to the president; so, too, did Leahy. Truman himself was largely at fault because he had made no effort to clarify his own position on most of the issues. But the president's delinquence was not to make Byrnes's predicament any easier.[106]

When Byrnes returned from Moscow, Truman was vexed. Byrnes had not quieted his potential opponents; indeed his arbitrary actions fueled their animus and created more headaches for the president. Nor had the secretary cleared his public statements with the White House. Worse yet, he had withheld Mark Ethridge's report on conditions in Romania and Bulgaria for almost a month. When Truman read it, he was incensed. In a famous memorandum he vented his frustration: "I'm tired [of] babying the Soviets." The president wanted the Romanian and Bulgarian governments radically changed, Soviet actions in Iran condemned, and Russian designs on Turkey checked. Truman called for the creation of strong central governments in China and Korea. There must be no more talk of compromise, he insisted.[107]

Clearly, the president was resolving his ambivalence in favor of a tougher policy toward the Kremlin. He regarded Soviet actions as opportunistic, arbitrary, and outrageous. According to Truman's way of thinking, ongoing Soviet behavior formed part of a continuum with czarist Russia's expansionist past. The lessons of recent history, moreover, instructed that totalitarian nations, if allowed to gather strength, could threaten the United States. For Truman, the United States represented innocence, integrity, and morality; its adversaries were sullied, deceitful, and evil. Although he disliked all foreigners, the Soviets now became the particular target of his venom because they alone had the potential to capitalize on their wartime gains, exploit postwar vacuums of power, and endanger U.S. security. Furthermore, their actions spawned controversy within the United States, even within his own administration, and distracted his attention from the domestic issues on which he preferred to focus. Psychologically, then, there were powerful inducements of a predispositional and motivational nature to incline Truman to sort out different images of the Soviets, disregard elements of their self-restraint, and dwell on the more ominous aspects of their behavior. As the new year began, he told Byrnes to shape up and toe the line. "Unless Russia is faced with an iron fist and strong language another war is in the making." [108]

Fear, Power, and U.S. Policy Toward Eastern Europe

The Truman administration first clashed with the Soviet Union in Eastern Europe. American officials reproached the Russians for their repressive actions, especially in Bulgaria, Romania, Hungary, and Poland. Even some of the most accommodating policymakers in Washington, like Byrnes and Bohlen, wanted Stalin to accept an open sphere. Soviet security concerns, they insisted, could be reconciled with the principles of nondiscriminatory trade and popular elections. Their attitudes were naive.

Germany had come perilously close to crushing and dismembering Soviet Russia. Stalin and his comrades had almost seen their system of government destroyed, their power eradicated, their revolution overturned. Within their lifetimes most Russians had experienced two German invasions, and Stalin expected Russia's traditional foe to rise again. He would not relinquish an unprecedented opportunity to consolidate Russia's position in Eastern Europe. Poland, Stalin emphasized, had repeatedly served as a gateway for German armies. "Neither the British nor American people experienced such German invasions which were a horrible thing to endure and the results of which were not easily forgotten." Nor would the Soviet dictator forget that Hungarian troops had reached the Don and that Romanian divisions had fought along the Volga. Bulgaria had not been a belligerent, Stalin admitted, but had still assisted German submarine, naval, and air action in the Black Sea.[109]

American proponents of an open sphere retorted, of course, that they had no desire to place unfriendly governments on Russia's periphery.[110] But Byrnes and Bohlen did not indicate what they would do or how they would react if free elections in Poland, Romania, or Hungary generated an anti-Russian leadership that objected to a Soviet-imposed treaty structure or that welcomed a substantial U.S., British, French, or German presence. If such contingencies arose, and historical experience suggested their likelihood, could an open sphere be reconciled with Soviet security anxieties? Truman administration officials simply pretended that such eventualities were unlikely to occur. Paying scant attention to the asymmetrical nature of Soviet and American motivations in Eastern Europe, they naively expected Stalin to do likewise.[111]

American claims, however, were as disingenuous as they were naive. American support of an open sphere was designed, at least in part, to circumscribe the very predominance that Americans sometimes said they were willing to accept. Harriman, for example, knew that if his interpretation of the Yalta provisions were accepted, the Lublin Polish regime would eventually be undermined. He assumed that, with the exception of Bulgaria, 70–80 percent of the people of Eastern Europe would vote for anti-Russian and anti-Communist leaders. Even in Bulgaria, a nation historically friendly to Russia, free elections, according to the American minister, would enhance Western influence.[112] Likewise, U.S. opposition to the Kremlin's economic treaties was motivated not by a parochial, material self-interest but by the realization that open trade and the free flow of capital would promote a "far reaching," "enduring," and "healthy American influence" in Eastern Europe.[113] Whatever the intentions of Byrnes and Bohlen, the Russians had reason to "suspect and fear," as more than one American intelligence report maintained, "that the Anglo-American allies . . . do not intend to recognize permanently the Soviet claim of a paramount security interest in the Balkans." [114]

The alternative, as Davies and Wallace suggested, was to accede to Soviet predominance on Russia's periphery and to stop hassling the Kremlin about it. But few policymakers contemplated a policy of reassurance; the risks were too great. Ethridge warned Byrnes that "to concede a limited Soviet sphere of influence even in this area of strategic importance to the USSR might be to invite its extension to other areas." [115] Eastern Europe itself was not vital to the United States. But "it must be admitted," concluded the JCS, "that control over strategic points within these states and over their resources would represent a significant addition to the war potential of an adjacent great power." [116]

The Soviet Union's capabilities would grow further if the Kremlin used its influence in Eastern Europe and the Balkans to push through the Turkish straits, exploit unrest in Western Europe, or spur the proliferation of discriminatory commercial treaties and statist economic policies. If such developments materialized, the sphere of U.S. economic opportunity would shrink. Worse yet, the economic and strategic power of a potential ideological foe would grow. Atomic weapons, wrote Bohlen and Robinson, might supplant the importance of security zones. But, then again, they might not. And American diplomats were as aware as military officers that if Russia should enlarge its security zone and achieve control of Europe, it would gain enormous resources as well as advanced strategic positions. With these additional economic, technological, and military assets, Soviet power could someday threaten the United States.[117] Hence most State Department officials agreed with Ethridge's insistence on holding free elections and establishing representative governments in Romania and Bulgaria. So did Truman. Byrnes and Bohlen were willing to postpone these demands in the short run in order to hasten the withdrawal of Soviet troops and achieve the same goals in the long run.[118]

Most American officials were resolving their ambivalent attitudes toward the Soviet Union by defining cooperation in terms of voluntary Soviet self-restraint in Eastern Europe. This approach blended American self-interest and ideology. It was motivated by fear and power: fear that worldwide conditions might circumscribe U.S. influence and tempt another totalitarian state to co-opt resources and labor that could eventually threaten the strategic and economic interests of the United States; power in the knowledge that in the short run the United States had the capabilities, if it could generate the will, to thwart those very long-term developments it feared. Fear and power—not unrelenting Soviet pressure, not humanitarian impulses, not domestic political considerations, not British influence—were the key factors shaping American policies toward the Kremlin.

This interpretation does not deny that Soviet leaders forced unpopular and repressive governments on Poland, Romania, and Bulgaria; that Soviet commissars imposed unfair economic agreements even on friendly governments like the Lublin Poles; and that Soviet armies lived off the land, ravished the countryside, brutalized the people, and seized parts of the industrial infrastructure of former enemy states. Although these developments influenced American attitudes toward the Soviet Union, they did not decisively shape American policies. For most Americans these events took place in countries far away where democratic institutions never had flourished, in an area of indirect interest to the United States, and in a region of admittedly vital importance to the Kremlin. Moreover, amidst the ominous evidence of Soviet expansion, there were also auspicious signs. Free elections were held in Budapest and then throughout Hungary; Soviet troops were withdrawn from Czechoslovakia; a representative government was installed in Austria. "It is by no means certain," emphasized Bohlen and Robinson, "that Soviet intentions are set irrevocably in the pattern of expansion facilitated by revolution." Many JCS studies echoed this view.[119]

The fears that plagued the policymaking community in Washington did not emanate from an unrelieved sequence of hostile Soviet measures. Soviet actions were mixed. But Truman's advisers, like the president himself, riveted their attention on the more portentous elements of Soviet behavior and dismissed the more favorable signs. Students of perception like Robert Jervis and Richard Ned Lebow suggest that such cognitive tendencies are commonplace. American officials, like leaders everywhere, are prone to overdramatize their nation's vulnerability and to exaggerate unfavorable developments in the international balance of power. At the end of 1945 these officials interpreted their environment in light of their own needs, fears, and interests. Their apprehensions were largely the result of worldwide conditions—socioeconomic instability, political upheaval, vacuums of power, decolonization—occurring against a backdrop of depression, aggression, and war, whose lessons militated against the acceptance of closed blocs and the reassurance of potential adversaries, especially totalitarian ones.[120]

Humanitarian impulses also were a minor influence on U.S. policy. Principles were espoused because they served American interests and because they accorded with American ideological predilections and not because top officials felt a strong sense of empathy with the peoples under former Nazi rule and potential Soviet tutelage. American diplomats and military officers in Eastern Europe were often repelled by acts of oppression, frustrated by their own impotence, and angered by the restrictions placed on their mobility.[121] But in Washington, top officials—Truman, Byrnes, Leahy, Forrestal, Patterson, Davies, Grew, Dunn, Lincoln—rarely thought about the personal travail caused by war, dislocation, and great power competition. At Potsdam, of course, U.S. participants were horrified by the devastation they witnessed. But once home again in safe, comfortable, unspoiled America, policymakers for the most part treated notions of self-determination and open trade as tools and levers to be used to constrain potential foes, influence prospective allies, palliate domestic constituencies, and safeguard long-term interests. Suffering had to be relieved and hope restored in order to quell the potential for revolution. Rarely does a sense of real compassion and/or moral fervor emerge from the documents and diaries of high officials. These men were concerned primarily with power and self-interest, not with real people facing real problems in the world that had just gone through fifteen years of economic strife, Stalinist terror, and Nazi genocide.[122]

Perhaps nothing better illustrates this moral obtuseness than the way top U.S. officials felt about Stalin. Who could doubt his barbarism? Although the full dimensions of the Gulag were not known, the trials, purges, and murders of the 1930's were a matter of public record. Yet far from worrying about their inability to satisfy Stalin's paranoia, American officialdom had great hope for Stalin in 1945. He appeared frank and willing to compromise. Truman liked him. "I can deal with Stalin," the president jotted in his diary. "He is honest—but smart as hell." Lest one think these were the views of a naive American politician, it should be remembered that crusty, tough-nosed Admiral Leahy had some of the same feelings. And so did Eisenhower, Harriman, and Byrnes. Stalin might be insulting at times, but he could be dealt with because he seemed responsive to American power and capable of demonstrating some self-restraint on the Soviet periphery. What went on in Russia, Truman declared, was the Russians' business. The president was fighting for U.S. interests, and Uncle Joe seemed to be the man with whom one could deal. The obstreperous, intransigent, taciturn Molotov was an ogre to most American officials. Truman, among others, frequently voiced concern for Stalin's health; it would be a "real catastrophe" should he die. If "it were possible to see him [Stalin] more frequently," Harriman claimed, "many of our difficulties would be overcome." [123]

If humanitarian impulses played only a small role in shaping U.S. policy toward Soviet Russia in 1945, so, too, did public opinion and domestic politics. American attitudes toward Russia, as measured by pollsters, soured during the latter months of 1945. When asked, people seemed less hopeful of preserving the wartime alliance and more skeptical of Soviet intentions. But there was no popular clamor for a tough, affirmative policy. Most people, again as measured by the polls, cared little about foreign policy. They were, for example, no more opposed to a large loan to Russia than to Britain.[124] Sensing this disposition, policymakers frequently sought to find means to "educate" the people. Harriman met with journalists and alerted them to the difficulties that were arising between the wartime allies. State Department officials wanted journalistic access to Eastern Europe, not because they were being pressured to make this demand but because they desired to mobilize public support for the administration's predetermined policy to establish an open sphere and constrain Soviet power.[125]

Although some leading Republicans, like Vandenberg, and ethnic groups, like the Poles, exerted pressure on the administration, their influence was important but not decisive. When Truman desired, he compromised. Without any serious political reverberations, he recognized the Lublin Poles. The legislative impact was also inconsequential; Congress proceeded to enact the administration's entire legislative package in the international field, including support for the United Nations, the International Monetary Fund, the extension of unconditional reciprocity, and the huge increment in Export-Import Bank funding. "We have a law a day," quipped Acheson.[126] Truman's foreign policies, ambiguous though they were, were not the target of public criticism in the autumn of 1945. And organized pressure groups, as monitored by the State Department, showed no discernible desire for a more belligerent U.S. stand toward the Soviet Union.[127]

Nor did partisan considerations dictate a tough policy at the foreign ministers' meetings. John Foster Dulles, the leading Republican spokesman on international affairs who served on the U.S. delegation to the London conference, possessed much of the same ambivalence that characterized Byrnes's thinking. On some issues in the fall of 1945, Dulles appeared to be even more flexible and openminded than did Byrnes.[128] In their diaries, both Davies and Wallace noted the onset of powerful forces calling for a tougher posture toward the Russians. Many of these forces, however, were within the administration.[129]

The protests from outside official circles surfaced most clearly when Byrnes failed to consult influential legislators. Vandenberg and other leading senators were opposed to Byrnes's atomic energy proposals. Even if he had consulted more extensively and fully, he might not have altered their minds, since there was widespread public opposition to sharing scientific knowledge with foreign governments.[130] But

Byrnes's overall performance at the Moscow conference evoked more praise than criticism in the media. Initially, he was reprimanded not by the political opposition, not by public opinion, and not by the press, but by his own colleagues and chief executive. Although mistrustful of the Soviets, the public was not opposed to intelligent concessions if the United States got something in return.[131] It was a matter of leadership, and the administration was not providing any.

The British, of course, were even more distrustful of the Russians than were American officials. In recent years Fraser Harbutt and Henry Ryan, among other scholars, have ably illuminated how much Churchill and Bevin wanted to harness U.S. strength in support of British interests against the prospective challenge from the Soviet Union. American officials, they show, remained wary of British maneuvers lest it appear to the Russians that the Anglo-Saxons were ganging up against them.[132] By the summer of 1945, however, British attention was turning to the Middle East and Eastern Mediterranean. However grudgingly, the British were willing to accept Soviet predominance in Eastern Europe. It was the Americans, not the British, who made the more sustained, if not wholehearted, effort to dilute the preponderant Soviet position in Eastern Europe.[133]

Fear inspired American officials to prod the Kremlin to accept an open sphere. Soviet leaders, they thought, could live with the strategic imponderables inherent in the conditions of open trade and free elections in Eastern Europe. If the Russians accepted these imponderables, the basis for a cooperative relationship with the United States would emerge. If they considered these imponderables too threatening to their political control, if they found them ideologically intolerable, and if they insisted on a closed sphere and failed the litmus test of their intentions, then the Truman administration would *not* challenge Soviet domination in Eastern Europe directly. Instead American officials would seek to mobilize U.S. power to contain Soviet influence and Communist penetration elsewhere. And despite all the disorganization and ambivalence beleaguering the American policymaking process, there was, as will become apparent, a great deal of consensus about the nature of vital American interests. These interests, moreover, encompassed much of the globe, except Eastern Europe.

Global Security, 1945

While monitoring Soviet behavior in Eastern Europe, U.S. officials looked with trepidation upon developments around the globe. They saw danger almost everywhere. The Soviets were not responsible for most of these threats, but they had the potential of capitalizing on them. Prudence dictated that U.S. officials tackle these problems before the Kremlin had the opportunity to spread its influence and its power across the Eurasian land mass; prudence also dictated that the United States plan to wage war effectively should it ever become necessary to do so.

By surveying American policies in different regions of the globe and by looking at American plans for developing overseas bases and for sharing atomic energy, this chapter will show how U.S. officials sought to perpetuate their nation's preponderant position in the international system. They did not seek a rift with the Kremlin. But, uncertain of Soviet motives and apprehensive about the formation of closed blocs, they sought to establish a postwar order that comported with America's values, fostered its interests, and safeguarded its security.

Initially, U.S. policymakers made little effort to define priorities among their national security objectives. Moreover, they had enormous difficulty mobilizing resources and designing tactics capable of achieving their goals. At home businessmen yearned to be free of price controls; labor unions struck for higher wages; Republicans pressed for smaller budgets and lower taxes; parents and wives clamored for their sons and husbands to come home. These domestic considerations placed constraints on the pursuit of national security goals. In an administration that still lacked able leadership and effective coordinating machinery, American policy looked rudderless. Beneath the surface, however, there was more purposefulness, if less achievement, than usually thought.[1]

Overseas Bases and U.S. Air Power

In 1943 defense officials began studying the question of overseas bases. Taking note of the many imponderables affecting postwar Allied unity and keenly sensitive to the reconstruction problems that lay ahead, military planners redefined the U.S. strategic perimeter and insisted on preserving hegemony over the Pacific and Atlantic oceans. The Joint Chiefs of Staff (JCS) concluded that the United States required bases to insure American strategic domination of the Western Hemisphere and the Far East. In January 1944 President Roosevelt approved the JCS base studies and sent them to the State Department for action.[2]

When the Japanese were about to surrender in September 1945, Undersecretary of State Joseph C. Grew and Assistant Secretary of State William L. Clayton asked military planners to reevaluate their base requirements. Tough decisions had to be made because U.S. wartime rights to many overseas bases would expire within six months.[3] After extensive discussion, the JCS defined a set of primary, secondary, and minor base sites. The primary areas stretched to the western shores of the Pacific (the Philippines, the Bonins, and the southwestern Alaska–Aleutian region), encompassed the polar air routes (Newfoundland and Iceland), and projected U.S. power into the Eastern Atlantic (the Azores) as well as the Caribbean and the Panama Canal zone. Dozens of additional sites were denoted as secondary and minor base areas.[4] (See Map 2.)

In elaborate studies and numerous memoranda, planners laid out their rationale for this extensive base system. The attack on Pearl Harbor, the use of strategic bombing, and the development of atomic weapons had generated an enormous sense of vulnerability and called for defense in depth. Military officials assumed that potential adversaries would seek to bomb the American homeland in order to deny the United States the time for industrial mobilization. Overseas bases would enable the United States to interdict an attack from *any* source far from American shores. Defense in depth encompassed a system of outlying bases that would encircle the Western Hemisphere and reach the west coast of Africa, the perimeter of Asia, and the shores of the Arctic.[5]

Overseas bases would also permit the United States to project its power in peacetime and to punish an aggressor in wartime. In designating bases in the Pacific, for example, Army and Navy officers underscored their utility for quelling prospective unrest in Northeast and Southeast Asia and for maintaining access to critical raw materials.[6] More important, however, military planners and their scientific advisers regarded overseas bases, especially along the polar air routes, as indispensable to attack the vital regions of an enemy should war seem imminent. Although budgetary constraints and international circumstances might militate against immediate base development, the idea was to identify appropriate locations so that negotiations for long-term rights could take place when circumstances seemed most propitious. General Leslie Groves, wartime director of the Manhattan Project, urged colleagues

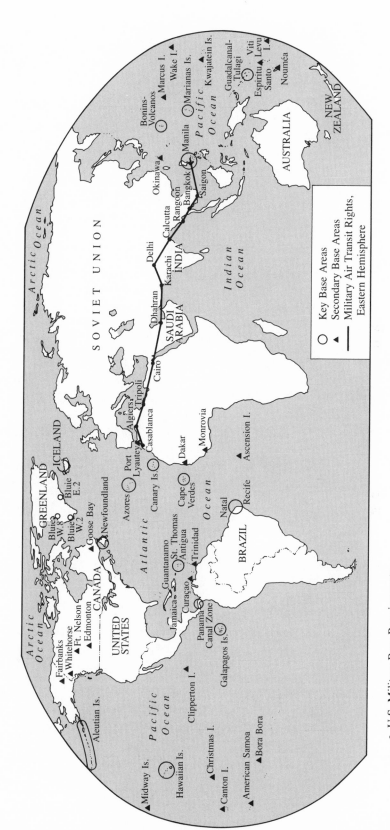

2. U.S. Military Base Requirements

to secure base rights immediately, when there was no direct threat to the United States, "and plan not for ten years but 50–100 years ahead." [7]

Aside from bases, policymakers were eager to obtain military air transit and landing rights. They wanted such rights at key airfields in North Africa, the Middle East, India, and Southeast Asia. They delineated a route from Casablanca through Algiers, Tripoli, Cairo, Dhahran, Karachi, Delhi, Calcutta, Rangoon, Bangkok, and Saigon to Manila. Military air transit rights along the North Africa–India route, said the JCS, "were most desirable in order to provide access and familiarity with bases from which offensive and defensive action might be conducted in the event of a major war." In order to maintain these airfields in a state of readiness, the U.S. government wanted private airlines to locate their peacetime operations in areas designated essential to military air transit rights.[8] The connections, therefore, between civilian and military air power were very close. A "strong United States air transport system," Assistant Secretary of War John McCloy wrote the State Department, "international in scope and readily adapted to military use, is vital to our air power and future national security." [9]

Officials regarded overseas bases as one of the keys to retaining U.S. strategic air superiority and its world leadership role. "I cannot over-emphasize the importance that I place on this entire base problem," Assistant Secretary Robert Lovett wrote his top Army Air Force generals.[10] He was not alone. Navy Secretary James Forrestal conceived of the postwar Navy as a mobile, striking force for which overseas bases were essential. Secretary of War Robert Patterson viewed U.S. bases in the Philippines as springboards for projecting American influence into Southeast Asia. McCloy wanted bases in Iceland in order to dominate the polar air routes. Significantly, McCloy, Henry Stimson, and George Marshall, while not eager to break with Soviet Russia, shared a similar view of overseas bases with Forrestal and Admiral William Leahy, who from the outset were more suspicious of Soviet intentions. These high-level policymakers knew they would not receive the funding to establish all the bases enumerated in the JCS studies. Yet they agreed on the utility of overseas bases in wartime and peacetime. At the end of October 1945, Patterson and Forrestal approved the JCS plans. They submitted them to Secretary of State James Byrnes, hoping his subordinates would soon begin appropriate discussions with foreign governments.[11]

State Department officials, of course, were more attuned to the diplomatic complications that inhered in the negotiation of base rights. They would also have liked to reconcile American strategic imperatives in the Pacific with the trusteeship ideal incorporated into the U.N. charter. But in talks with Forrestal and Patterson, Byrnes did not object to the key features of overseas base planning. In early November, he asked British foreign secretary Ernest Bevin for his help in negotiating U.S. base rights in Iceland and the Azores. Byrnes also wanted to arrange a deal whereby the British and U.S. governments extended to one another the military air transit rights that they secured through agreements with North African, Middle Eastern, and Asian nations. Byrnes was especially interested in prospective bases in Calcutta and Karachi.[12] At the same time his subordinates took the lead in pushing for the construction of an airport at Dhahran, Saudi Arabia, where the United States would have military rights.[13]

President Truman not only approved the Dhahran airfield but consistently reassured Forrestal, Stimson, and their military planners that he agreed with their objectives in the Pacific and Atlantic. After attending the Potsdam conference and witnessing the devastation wrought by strategic bombing, he told the American people that the United States would acquire all the bases that his military advisers deemed imperative. Truman shared the common view that superior air power and overseas bases would play a decisive role in preserving stability, deterring aggression, and punishing transgressors.[14] In August 1945 he even asked the Russians to grant the United States air base rights in the Kuriles. When Stalin bluntly rebuffed the overture, Truman quickly retreated.[15] His demand was not intended as an anti-Soviet initiative. It simply reflected the expansive conception of U.S. security objectives that was embodied in the overseas base planning that went on at the end of the war—even while the president was declaring a desire to cooperate with Soviet Russia.

The Western Hemisphere

Within the Western Hemisphere, U.S. strategic predominance had to be inviolate. Canadian and Latin American raw materials and foodstuffs were indispensable to waging war. Their airfields were critical to controlling the surrounding oceans and the Panama Canal. In the future, from bases in Newfoundland and Labrador, the United States hoped to be able to launch attacks across the polar air routes. It was necessary, therefore, to excise all foreign political and military influence from North and South America. In Latin America, moreover, the United States had to maintain linkages with powerful elites and military establishments. With their help, stability would be maintained in wartime, thereby assuring U.S. access to the region's vital resources.[16]

The initial problem facing U.S. officials was to reconcile their traditional attachment to the Monroe Doctrine with their support of the new principle of collective security. They did not want European or Asian powers to establish a presence in the Western Hemisphere under the guise of enforcing measures mandated by an international organization. At the San Francisco conference in May 1945, the American delegates resolved this dilemma by charging the inter-American system with the responsibility to implement U.N. actions in the Western Hemisphere. Truman supported this approach. Like most of his advisers, he believed that Western Hemisphere states should work together without interference from nations across the oceans. But language had to be artfully crafted so that the U.S. government would not be barred from intervening outside of the Americas if it chose to do so in behalf of collective security.[17]

Strategic predominance, however, meant much more than the preservation of

AUGUSTANA UNIVERSITY COLLEGE
LIBRARY

the Monroe Doctrine. Army officers believed that in the 1930's foreign military missions had enhanced Axis influence and jeopardized U.S. security. After the war, they strongly opposed British, French, and Swedish attempts to sell military items to Latin American governments.[18] At the same time, intelligence officers warned of growing Communist influence. There was "grave unrest, socially, politically, and economically." "These conditions," warned the Joint War Plans Committee, "offer a tempting and fertile field for ideological and economic penetration by potential enemies of the United States." [19] To counter such threats, defense officials vigorously supported the establishment of close ties with Latin American military establishments. When regional officers in the State Department objected to military aid, which they claimed would dissipate Latin American financial resources and encourage political strife, they were overruled by Byrnes and Undersecretary of State Dean Acheson, who deferred to the views of Patterson, Forrestal, and the JCS.[20]

During 1945, bilateral talks went on with Latin American states. Military missions were established almost everywhere, and Latin American officers continued attending U.S. military schools. Plans were discussed for the transfer of arms under the Surplus Property Act. Interim arrangements for the provision of limited military aid were made, pending passage of the Inter-American Military Cooperation Act. Although Congress did not pass the legislation, Truman endorsed this approach. The overriding strategic goal, Patterson subsequently explained, was to have "a stable, secure, and friendly flank to the South, not confused by enemy penetration—political, economic, or military." Neither Byrnes nor his subordinates ever contested this objective, however strongly they might occasionally dispute tactics.[21]

Containment Before Kennan

U.S. officials regarded the establishment of a favorable configuration of power in Europe and Asia as even more important than overseas bases and a strategic sphere of influence in the Western Hemisphere. In May 1945 William J. Donovan, director of the Office of Strategic Services, submitted a long memorandum to President Truman. Donovan's analysts, like those elsewhere in the government, were uncertain of Soviet intentions. But certain realities were indisputable. "Russian armies have overrun Eastern Europe and are at the gates of Berlin. . . . It is clear that in all of the neighboring states Russia will, at a minimum, insist on governments 'friendly' to her." Beyond its immediate periphery, the Kremlin faced a Europe "racked by war and suffering widespread misery." In this environment, the Soviets had "a strong drawing card in the proletarian philosophy of Communism." The United States and its prospective allies had "no political or social philosophy equally dynamic or alluring." The situation in Asia was no more auspicious: "Once Japan is defeated, the position of Russia in Asia will be strengthened enormously." There was little hope that China could balance Russian power. In fact, "if we adopt a hands-off policy, Russia may very well succeed in organizing China as an effective ally of Moscow." The inescapable conclusion was that Russia would pose an enormous threat to the United States should it "succeed in uniting the resources of Europe and Asia under her sway. Within a generation Russia could probably then outbuild us in every phase of military production." [22]

The United States, however, need not despair. According to Donovan's memorandum, the Russians would seek to avoid war for at least ten to fifteen years. If in the interval the United States took "clear, firm, and thoroughly non-provocative" action, it could check Russian expansion and balance Russian power. Donovan's analysts called upon the United States to support popular and progressive forces in Central Europe, Western Europe, and the Mediterranean. At the same time the Office of Strategic Services recommended that the Truman administration foster democratic, independent regimes in China and Japan and balance Soviet influence in those countries. Elsewhere in Asia the United States should do nothing to weaken the European democracies. Indeed, "our interest in developing a balance to Russia should lead us in the opposite direction." [23]

Donovan's memorandum did *not* constitute a blueprint for American action. Nevertheless, it beautifully captured the geopolitical concerns of U.S. officials and illuminated the global scale of American interests. In subsequent months other U.S. officials and agencies would restate the same apprehensions and lay out their own recommendations for thwarting the rise of Communist influence and checking the spread of Soviet power. Containment was the policy of the United States before George Kennan's famous long telegram arrived from Moscow in February 1946.

The British Loan and an Open World

U.S. officials regarded British strength as critically important to American security interests. Acheson and Grew, Stimson and Forrestal, the State Department and the JCS expected the British to play a decisive role upholding the balance of power and checking Russian influence. However much Roosevelt might humor Stalin at the expense of Churchill, however often British and U.S. business interests sparred with one another, and however critical the American public was of British power politics, U.S. policymakers never doubted the conjunction of British and American strategic interests. State Department officials railed against British spheres of influence and economic blocs but were wary of undermining British security interests in vital areas like Western Europe and the Middle East. In peacetime the State Department presupposed a "global entente," and in wartime the Pentagon postulated an Anglo-American alliance. [24]

The convergence of security interests, however, did not mean that Anglo-American relations were without friction. The United States would not cease its competition for markets, raw materials, and aviation routes. It shared little information on atomic weapons. Nor would it assume British military responsibilities and financial burdens in places like Western Europe and the Middle East where the British traditionally played a leading role. U.S. officials initially exaggerated British strength, carped at British imperial practices, and worried that London might engender unnecessary acrimony with the Soviet Union. Truman and Byrnes, like Roosevelt before them, did not want the Anglo-Saxon powers to gang up on the Russians. They wanted the British to eschew economic blocs, refrain from power politics, and practice a wise, discreet, and effective form of containment.[25]

In turn, the British grumbled at American actions. Although their own policies and attitudes toward the Kremlin were equally indecisive, they were frustrated by the ambivalence and disorganization that afflicted U.S. diplomacy. Russian power loomed as a challenge almost everywhere, and the empire was in disarray. The British could ill afford the risks and costs that Washington assigned to them. Their resources appeared pitifully small in relation to their commitments and aspirations. The English needed the United States: they wanted a privileged place in American diplomacy, and they wanted to perpetuate some form of alliance. In their view, shared values, traditions, language, and interests dictated a special relationship. Ernest Bevin, the Labour government's foreign secretary, sought this relationship as much as did Churchill. Accordingly, Bevin deeply resented Byrnes's independent actions. Could not the Truman administration realize that Anglo-American interests were mutual and interdependent?[26]

U.S. officials did realize it. What London was objecting to, in the view of the State Department, was that Americans desired future cooperation to be on American terms.[27] Most of all, policymakers in Washington wanted the British to reform their imperial practices, dissolve the sterling bloc, accept full convertibility of the pound into dollars, and adhere to the principles of open and nondiscriminatory trade. They did not appreciate the crunch that the British would face in trying to preserve a balance of power in Europe and the Middle East while attempting to meet U.S. demands for free convertibility, colonial reform, and the unimpeded movement of capital and goods. In brief, Americans sympathized with Britain's strategic and geopolitical goals, sought to modify its commercial and imperial practices, and misjudged its postwar capabilities.[28]

This misjudgment was apparent at the time of Japan's surrender, when Truman decided to terminate lend-lease assistance. Fred M. Vinson, Truman's new secretary of the treasury, and Dean Acheson argued that lend-lease should be continued because Britain and Western Europe desperately required postwar aid. Without it, communism would spread and U.S. interests would be jeopardized. But the president believed Congress might rebel if he reneged on past promises to cease this assistance at the end of the war. This decision, as historians George Herring and Randall Woods have emphasized, reflected a substantial underestimation of Britain's postwar financial requirements.[29]

Yet the administration did immediately enter into negotiations for a sizable postwar loan. The British had lost about 25 percent of their prewar wealth, had contracted about $14 billion in sterling debt, and had seen the volume of their exports decline by about two-thirds.[30] They desperately needed aid. U.S. officials were willing to help, provided the English ended imperial preferences, stopped their discrimination against American goods, and allowed sterling to be converted freely into dollars after one year. Once London accepted these conditions, Vinson, Acheson, and Clayton extended a $3.75 billion loan at 2 percent interest. Under certain conditions the interest could be waived and the principal need not be repaid for 50 years. At the same time, the United States canceled the $20 billion on the lend lease account and sold over $6 billion worth of surplus property and equipment for $650 million.[31]

Truman administration officials stressed that the deal was essential to sustain U.S. exports and to gain Britain's adherence to an open world. If sterling were not freely convertible to dollars, Britain's creditors would feel constrained to buy most of their goods within the sterling bloc and the American economy would suffer. U.S. officials believed that foreign markets were essential to absorb the huge output that American manufacturers and farmers had become accustomed to producing during the war.[32] If economic blocs were not broken down, Acheson and Clayton insisted that international trade would stagnate, state regulations would proliferate, and free enterprise would suffer. "We believe passionately," Acheson stated, that the dissemination of free enterprise abroad was essential to its preservation at home.[33]

More than jobs and profits was at stake. In Acheson's view, a feeble, impoverished Britain would accentuate worldwide economic dislocation, encourage Communist advances, and weaken America's own position in the international system.[34] On the other hand, a strong Britain, committed to the idea of an open world, would maximize U.S. power because it would allow American goods and capital to flow everywhere. The open door meant a huge infusion of American influence wherever it was ajar. But it was not intended to vitiate British power. The loan itself, although much too small, was to help sustain Britain's global posture while weaning it to a multilateral world order that comported with U.S. goals. Subsequently, when this proved impossible, U.S. officials placed British wishes and American geopolitical imperatives above free convertibility. In 1945, however, U.S. officials hoped that the loan would overcome Britain's financial weaknesses, create an open world, and buttress interlocking Anglo-American security interests.

Germany and Western Europe

Nothing was more important to these overlapping strategic interests than a favorable balance of power in the Old World. Yet in the aftermath of war this balance was immediately endangered by the specter of economic and social chaos. In April 1945, McCloy returned from a European trip and presented an almost apocalyptic account of conditions. "There is a complete economic, social and political collapse going on in Central Europe, the extent of which is unparalleled in history." France and Belgium were potential stabilizing factors, but "without some reestablishment of their economic life they too can very well be torn apart by the collapse now in effect over Middle Europe." As additional reports filtered into the War Department, Stimson alerted Truman to the impending catastrophe. There will be "pestilence and famine in Central Europe next winter," he told the president on 16 May. "This is likely to be followed by political revolution and Communistic infiltration." Truman took heed. "To a great extent," he wrote the heads of U.S. war agencies, "the future permanent peace of Europe depends upon the restoration of the economy of these liberated countries. . . . A chaotic and hungry Europe is not a fertile ground in which stable, democratic and friendly governments can be reared." [35]

From the perspective of U.S. officials, Communist parties, under the control of or susceptible to the influence of the Kremlin, would capitalize on the unrest. Under-secretary of State Grew strongly held this conviction. During May and June 1945 he briefed the president on a daily basis. On 27 June he gave the president a long report on the international Communist movement. He urged Truman to read it carefully prior to the forthcoming Potsdam conference. "Europe today," the study concluded, constitutes a breeding ground for "spontaneous class hatred to be channeled by a skillful agitator." [36]

Far more significant than this report, however, was the one written by Dr. C. J. Potter and Lord Hyndley on the coal situation in northwestern Europe. "Unless immediate and drastic steps are taken," they concluded, "there will occur in North-west Europe and the Mediterranean next winter a coal famine of such severity as to destroy all semblance of law and order, and thus delay any chance of reasonable stability." Byrnes, Grew, and Clayton fully shared this view.[37] After consulting with them, Truman wrote Churchill: "From all the reports which reach me I believe that without immediate concentration on the production of German coal we will have turmoil and unrest in the very areas of Western Europe on which the whole stability of the continent depends." [38]

Truman's letter reveals the emphasis that U.S. officials immediately placed on Germany as a source of coal for the stabilization and reconstruction of Western Europe. Indeed, Stimson and McCloy chose General Lucius Clay as military governor because of his experiences with matters of allocation, industrial management, and production. Notwithstanding JCS 1067, which authorized him to be concerned with the German economy only insofar as was necessary to prevent disease and unrest, Clay immediately turned his attention to reviving coal production. This task, he realized, required him to solve transportation problems, alleviate food shortages, and establish currency stability. "The successful large-scale mining of coal," Clay wrote McCloy before the Potsdam conference, "means some restoration of the German economy, and some industrial activity to support coal mining." [39]

Substantial amounts of food, clothing, timber, and machinery had to be brought into the western zones of Germany in order to resuscitate coal production in the British-controlled Ruhr as well as to revive light industry in the American zone in southwestern Germany. These goods would be costly. It was hoped that they could be secured from eastern Germany. Therefore, U.S. officials stressed the economic unification of Germany, but they could not wait. Grew and Clayton urged Stimson and McCloy to purchase the necessary food, cranes, and coal-mining machinery immediately. War Department officials questioned whether they had the authority to spend money except to avert disease and unrest. On the eve of Truman's departure for Potsdam, top policymakers gathered together to resolve this dilemma. They concluded that the sums necessary to pay for these imports should be a first charge on all German exports from current production and from stocks on hand.[40] In other words, money received from German sales abroad should be used to pay for imports rather than for anything else.

Byrnes explained these conclusions and their implications to Truman as the two men voyaged across the ocean to meet Churchill and Stalin. Truman liked Byrnes's tough-minded approach. His "able and conniving" secretary of state had a "keen mind" and a sharp eye to protect American interests. Knowing that legislative pressures would make it difficult for him to allow lend-lease to be used for reconstruction purposes, Truman looked for other means to preserve stability in Western Europe. German resources could be used toward this end. The president was delighted to learn that Edwin Pauley, the U.S. reparations agent in Moscow, was already pressing Kremlin officials to reduce German reparations.[41]

The American preoccupation with coal production had profound implications for Soviet-U.S. relations. Not only would the amount of reparations going to Soviet Russia have to be scaled down from the figure of $10 billion tentatively agreed on at Yalta as a basis for discussion, but in addition the Kremlin might have to defer reparations until the coal industry was revived and until the imports necessary for the coal industry's rehabilitation were paid for with German exports. State Department officials hoped Soviet leaders would understand the exigencies that prompted these decisions. General Clay himself strongly desired to cooperate with Soviet officials.[42] No one wanted to create a rift in Soviet-U.S. relations, but priorities were priorities.

On 26 July Truman directed General Eisenhower, commander of U.S. troops in Europe, to make the production and export of 25 million tons of coal from western Germany by April 1946 the number-one priority of occupation policy (except for protecting the health and safety of the troops). Eisenhower was ordered to secure the engineering equipment, feed the miners, and maximize production. Truman warned that, without this coal, liberated Europe faced the grave danger of political and economic chaos. The export of the coal was to take precedence over its use for industrial purposes inside Germany. This priority would cause great suffering, the president acknowledged, and might even provoke violence in Germany. Western Europe, however, had to have the coal. Truman hoped the Soviets would collaborate and undertake similar policies for the export of coal from eastern Germany. But Truman's directive to Eisenhower was not contingent on Soviet agreement.[43]

The importance of the Ruhr for Western Europe's stabilization and rehabilitation

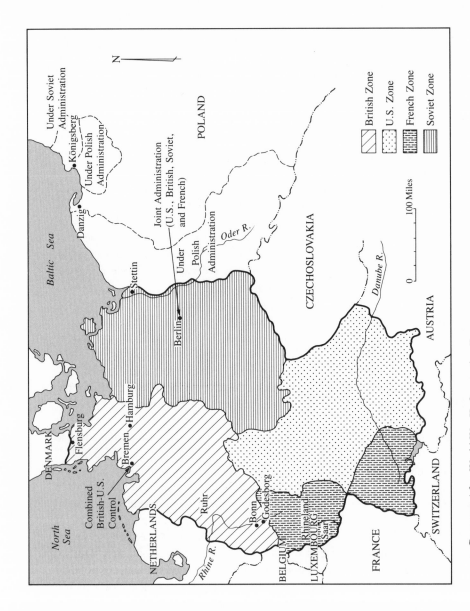

3. Germany After World War II: Occupation Zones

British Zone

U.S. Zone

French Zone

Soviet Zone

Under Soviet
Administration

Königsberg

Under Polish
Administration

Baltic Sea

Danzig

POLAND

Stettin

Joint Administration
(U.S., British, Soviet,
and French)

Under
Polish
Administration

Oder R.

0   100 Miles

Berlin

Danube R.

CZECHOSLOVAKIA

Hamburg

AUSTRIA

North
Sea

DENMARK

Flensburg

Combined
British-U.S.
Control

Bremen

Ruhr

NETHERLANDS

Rhine R.

Bonn

Godesborg

BELGIUM

Rhineland

LUXEMBOURG

Saar

FRANCE

SWITZERLAND

also impelled U.S. officials to reassess earlier proposals to separate the Ruhr from the rest of Germany, pastoralize it, or place it under international supervision. These actions might serve to circumscribe Germany's future warmaking capabilities. But on the eve of Potsdam, the State Department and the JCS submitted briefing papers arguing against any schemes for separation and internationalization. "Under present circumstances an extension of Soviet power and influence into the heart of Western Europe through the device of [international] trusteeship would manifestly be open to grave doubt." Russia had already been "left as the sole great power on the Continent—a position unique in modern history." Nothing should be done that might further enhance that power.[44]

A few officials still argued for internationalization or pastoralization. But for the most part their influence was on the wane, as symbolized by the resignation of Treasury Secretary Henry Morgenthau. Rather than reassure the Russians through the internationalization of the Ruhr, Truman and Byrnes were more inclined to consider a treaty guaranteeing the demilitarization of Germany.[45] Stimson's and McCloy's views were in the ascendancy. Proposals to sever the Ruhr and the Rhineland, they argued in a ten-page memorandum, must be rejected lest they create another irredentist movement, impair Germany's peacetime economy, or drive Germany "toward the east in her economic affiliations and outlook."[46]

Byrnes's negotiating posture at Potsdam comported with evolving U.S. goals. Byrnes explained that conditions in the western zones were much worse than anticipated and the damage much more extensive. He argued that reparations must come primarily from each power's zone of occupation; imports must be a first charge on exports; the Ruhr must not be internationalized; and German economic unity must be preserved. Stalin, Molotov, and Deputy Foreign Minister Andrei Vishinsky accused the West of retreating from Yalta, repudiating promises to allow Soviet participation in the internationalization of the Ruhr, and denying the Kremlin access to the Ruhr's steel, coal, and metallurgy. But with equal fervor, Truman and Byrnes retorted that the Soviets had reneged on their promises to hold free elections in Eastern Europe, had seized huge amounts of reparations from their zone in eastern Germany, and had unilaterally transferred parts of Germany east of the Oder-Neisse to Poland.[47] (See Map 3.)

Eventually, an agreement was reached. The Soviets could have up to 25 percent of the total equipment deemed available for reparations from the Ruhr. Fifteen percent would be in exchange for food, coal, potash, timber, and other products from eastern Germany. But since no fixed figure for reparations was agreed on, the percentage agreement was meaningless. The final accords, with their concomitant stress on German democratization, disarmament, and economic unification, somewhat obfuscated matters and left room for prolonged negotiations over production levels, interzonal transfers, and reparation payments. But certain fundamentals were clear. The United States and the United Kingdom had retained Western control of Germany's industrial heartland. Its productive resources were to be geared to a minimum standard of living in Germany, the coal requirements of Western Europe, and the financial exigencies of Western occupation powers.[48]

■

Following Potsdam, General Charles de Gaulle, France's premier, and Foreign Minister Georges Bidault visited Washington and voiced their misgivings. Since the French had not participated in the conference, they felt no obligation to adhere to a unified administration of the German economy. They believed that their security depended on German dismemberment, international control of the Ruhr, and the containment of Soviet influence. They sought to sever the Saar, Ruhr, and Rhine from the rest of Germany; they were determined to seize as much coal and rolling stock as they could from their own zone of occupation; and they worried that central administration of the German economy would be a ruse under which the Soviets would penetrate the western parts of Germany. De Gaulle voiced grave fears about the revival of German power and the absorption of German strength into a Soviet orbit.[49]

For months thereafter U.S. officials listened to French reservations, protestations, and recommendations. They understood France's security dilemma. They grasped France's need for almost a million tons of German coal per month. They realized that France's purchases of fuel and food from the United States created an unmanageable trade deficit. They were willing to commit $550 million in Export-Import funds to finance the continuation of lend-lease shipments. But they still continued to question the economic benefits that would be derived from French plans to dismember Germany, and they discouraged any international control of the Ruhr that implied Soviet participation. Fundamentally, State Department officials offered no real long-term solution to France's financial and strategic problems. The demilitarization treaty had little appeal. The French, Eisenhower noted, continued to be "terrified at the thought of a unified Germany, no matter how much it is weakened nor how long occupation might obtain." [50]

The Russians, no less than the French, worried about Germany's long-term revival. Germany "will recover, and very quickly," Stalin maintained. "Give them twelve to fifteen years and they'll be on their feet again." [51] Meanwhile, his own policies in Germany were contradictory. On the one hand, Soviet military authorities helped the German Communists (KPD) capture control of the labor unions and many local governments. On the other hand, Soviet officials antagonized German opinion and undermined the KPD by awarding German territory to Poland and dismantling German factories for transshipment to the Soviet Union. Inside their own zone, the Russians quickly began to restore industrial production, carried out land reform, shattered the influence of the old elite, formed joint stock corporations, and placed large industrial, transport, and financial institutions in the hands of the state. All of this was done in the name of national regeneration rather than socialist revolution. Most property and the means of production remained in private hands.

Stalin's lieutenants feuded incessantly over German policy. Stalin himself did not really know whether he wanted to dominate his own zone or make a stab to control all of Germany, whether he wanted the KPD to dominate the ruling coalition of a bourgeois democratic republic or whether he desired a revolutionary dictatorship.[52]

Stalin's actions were tempered by his realization that the industrial core of Germany still remained beyond his grasp and could again be mobilized either independently or as part of a Western coalition to threaten Soviet security. Moreover, he and Molotov wanted reparations from the western zones of Germany. If they could get their hands on the metallurgical equipment, machine tools, and chemical installations of the Ruhr and the Rhineland, they might be able to expedite Russian reconstruction as well as circumscribe Germany's military potential. When Soviet requests to participate in the international control of the Ruhr were rebuffed, Molotov warned against any attempts to absorb Germany's industrial prowess into a Western bloc.[53]

Clay found the French far more intractable than the Soviets. French resistance to his efforts to eliminate transportation and production bottlenecks greatly complicated his task as military governor. The economy in the U.S. zone was in shambles: the production of metals was 5 percent of capacity; chemical production was even lower; labor shortages were omnipresent; and 60 percent of the population was on a substandard diet. Nor were conditions any better in the British zone: coal production languished, and the goal of exporting 25 million tons by April was totally unrealizable. Clay feared mass starvation, runaway inflation, and total economic paralysis.[54] Expert studies detailed the deplorable conditions in Germany, the disruption of industry, the terrible housing shortage, and the inadequate diet.[55] When Robert Murphy, Clay's political adviser, visited Washington in November, he told Leahy that millions of Germans might die from famine during the forthcoming winter.[56]

Increasingly, Clay and his colleagues in the War Department questioned the wisdom of using German coal primarily to meet the needs of other liberated countries in Western Europe. Before leaving office, Lovett asked the State-War-Navy Coordinating Committee (SWNCC) to reconsider whether the economic rehabilitation of all Europe might be expedited by using a larger proportion of coal in Germany. McCloy thought it would. Alluding to the potential for revolution throughout "Middle Europe," McCloy emphasized that "We have an enormous investment in Germany and we are playing for very large stakes. . . . We have to make a more deliberate attempt to restore their economy . . . and we must get at it soon." General John Hilldring, director of the Army's Civil Affairs Division, concurred. Along with Clay, he wanted to exert more pressure on the French. Secretary Patterson wrote Byrnes on 10 December 1945 that the French must be forced to accept the central administration of transportation, finance, communications, and foreign trade.[57]

State Department officials hesitated. In October 1945 elections had been held in France: the Communists won 26 percent of the popular vote and emerged as the principal party. De Gaulle organized a new government, including the Communists, but denied them control of the most important ministries.[58] Nevertheless, Byrnes and his subordinates worried that, if the United States tried to elicit concessions from the French, the Communists would exploit the issue for their own political gain and enhance their influence still further. Although the Communists had renounced revolution, eschewed work stoppages, and pronounced their loyalty to the national reconstruction effort, U.S. ambassador Jefferson Caffery in Paris and his State Department colleagues in Washington never doubted that they were at the beck and call of Stalin. Caffery, Truman noted in his diary, was "scared stiff" of communism.[59] In November, H. Freeman Matthews, chief of the division of West European affairs, admitted to Clay that no pressure was being exerted on the French government. Matthews and his fellow foreign service officers believed that the imperatives of French political life and the needs of liberated countries in Western Europe must take priority over the exigencies of internal German developments and the unlikely prospects of Soviet-U.S. cooperation.[60]

The different tactical priorities of State and War Department officials sometimes obscured the similarity of goals. Everyone agreed that the emasculation of Germany's war potential did not obviate the importance of reviving its coal mines and its peacetime industries, the output of which could be used for the benefit of all Western Europe. Everyone agreed that economic conditions had to be improved in France, Germany, and elsewhere in order to offset the appeal of local Communists. And, everyone agreed that the Russians must not be allowed to harness German economic potential, as embodied in the Ruhr/Rhine industrial complex, for the aggrandizement of Soviet power. Within these parameters, State and War Department officials clashed over the allocation of coal and the distribution of reparations. The diplomats were more sensitive to political developments in France; the occupation authorities more attuned to socioeconomic dislocation in Germany. The men at Foggy Bottom blamed the Russians for the negotiating impasse; Army officials excused the Russians and assailed the French. Clay still believed in the prospects of Soviet-U.S. cooperation; most foreign service officers were by now quite dubious. But even Clay's concept of cooperation presupposed Soviet acceptance of fundamental American objectives.

Truman did nothing to resolve the controversies. It is misleading to state, as some historians have recently done, that his major goal was to cut occupation costs and withdraw U.S. troops.[61] This interpretation confuses means and ends. The president's major objectives in Western Europe were to promote stability and contain the spread of Communist influence and Soviet power. Upon returning from Potsdam, he told the American people:

Europe today is hungry. I am not talking about Germans. I am talking about . . . the people of Western Europe. Many of them lack clothes and fuel and shelter and raw materials. They lack the means to restore their cities and their factories. As the winter comes on their distress will increase. Unless we do what we can to help, we may lose next winter what we won at such terrible cost last spring. Desperate men are liable to destroy the structure of their society to find in the wreckage some substitute for hope. If we let Europe go cold and hungry, we may lose some of the foundations of order on which the hope for worldwide peace must rest.[62]

Truman was willing to offer aid, relief, and loans, but not enough to meet the dire emergency, or to satisfy the pleas of allied governments, or to establish the preconditions for a multilateral commercial order.[63] Because the president did not regard the revival of German military power as an immediate danger, he focused on restoring German coal production, promoting German economic unity, and curtailing reparation transfers. In so doing his aim was to assist West European reconstruction and to contain indigenous communism without imposing too high a burden on U.S. taxpayers and without incurring additional political-military responsibilities. His means were not commensurate with his goals. His means disappointed many allies. Eventually, his means would change. But his goals were clear from the outset.[64]

Italy, Greece, and the Eastern Mediterranean

The fear of economic chaos, revolutionary activity, and Soviet gains that inspired U.S. policies in Western Europe also played the decisive role in shaping American attitudes toward the Mediterranean. (See Map 4.) Even before German troops formally surrendered in northern Italy, American civilian and military officials warned of impending anarchy and radical transformation. Rear Admiral Ellery W. Stone, the U.S. commissioner in Italy, informed Washington that the ground "is fertile for the rapid growth of the seeds of an anarchical movement fostered by Moscow to bring Italy within the sphere of Russian influence." Undersecretary of State Grew concurred. "The problem is immediate," he wrote Truman on 18 June 1945. "Anarchy may result from the present economic distress and political unrest." Not only might Italy be absorbed into the Soviet orbit, but it might be lost as a strategic stronghold in the Mediterranean. There is "no doubt," concluded an interagency report, "that the Italian mainland in the hands of any great power would present a threat to U.S. strategic interests, particularly the line of communications to the Near East outlets of the Saudi-Arabian oil fields." [65]

U.S. officials wanted Italy to become a stable, democratic, non-Communist friend of the United States. They hoped to stimulate private investment, economic recovery, and political stability. Since Italy's surrender in 1943, the American and British governments had not permitted the Soviet Union to exert any significant influence in the Allied Control Commission. At Potsdam and subsequent foreign ministers' meetings, Truman and Byrnes championed Italy's cause. They worked hard to lighten its reparations burden, safeguard its territorial interests, gain its admission into the United Nations, and relax the harsh armistice terms. Inside Italy, U.S. diplomats and military officials sought to reduce the influence of the Italian Communists. Wrongly believing that the Communists were simply serving the inter-

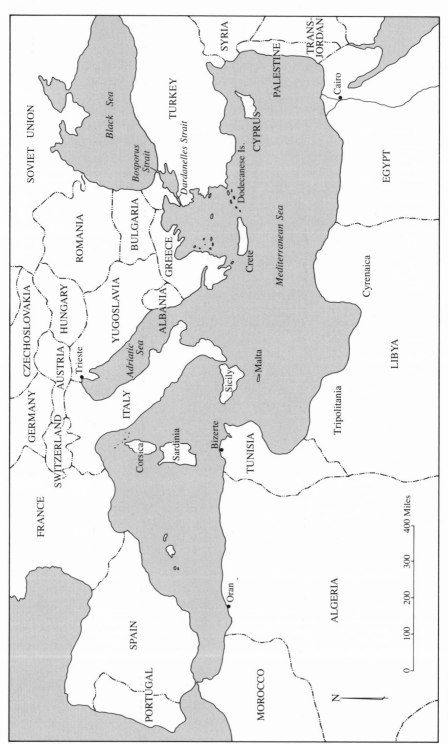

4. The Mediterranean Area, 1945–46

ests of the Kremlin, the Americans looked to establish a partnership with political forces in the center or moderate left of the Italian political spectrum.[66]

If their diplomatic and economic assistance failed to foster stability and recovery, U.S. officials wanted the non-Communist political forces they supported to have the ability to maintain order. Both Stone and Grew, as well as Alexander C. Kirk, the U.S. ambassador in Italy, urged that token American forces be retained in Italy.[67] An ad hoc committee of the SWNCC called for the removal of restrictive military clauses so that the Italian government would have sufficient forces, advised by an American military mission, to insure internal security. The overriding goal was "to strengthen Italy economically and politically so that she can withstand the forces that threaten to sweep her into a new totalitarianism and thence into an international political alignment diametrically opposed to American interests." [68]

U.S. objectives in Italy were clear, but finding appropriate tactics proved elusive and frustrating. The Soviets made a peace treaty with Italy contingent on the conclusion of agreements with Soviet-controlled governments in Romania and Bulgaria.[69] The Soviet Union also demanded reparations from Italy. While peace negotiations and armistice revision stalled, the social and political turmoil persisted. Some economic recovery occurred, but not nearly enough to eliminate widespread unemployment or to quell the political ambitions of the Communists. By the end of 1945, credits provided by U.S. forces and assistance extended by the U.N. Relief and Rehabilitation Administration began to dry up. Yet there were insufficient raw materials to sustain an industrial recovery, and private credits and foreign investments did not flow into Italy. Acheson and Clayton greatly underestimated the outside financial support Italy needed to regenerate its economy. By the end of 1945, they turned to the Export-Import Bank for help, but there were many conflicting demands on the bank's resources. Financial constraints and diplomatic crosscurrents impeded the achievement of security objectives in Italy.[70]

■

The situation was even more alarming in Greece. When Nazi armies withdrew they left a devastated country, a ruined economy, and a divided nation. The British immediately sought to restore order, contain the Greek left, and revive the economy. But violence erupted in late 1944, and British forces had to repress a Communist-led insurrection. Thereafter, rightist elements consolidated power and wreaked revenge upon the left.[71]

Ambassador Lincoln MacVeagh reported on developments in Greece. He described the complexity of the situation to Washington officials, and he emphasized the economic paralysis, traditional Balkan rivalries, and sociopolitical fissures tearing the country asunder. The Communists had played an important role in the resistance. EAM, the key resistance group, included both Communists and non-Communists. They were determined to prevent a royalist restoration, and they had considerable support, perhaps a third of the population. Although they had been temporarily checked by the British, their potential political influence appeared enhanced by Soviet occupation of the rest of the Balkans and by the Communist triumph in neighboring Yugoslavia. Yet as careful as MacVeagh was to scrutinize the linkages between the Kremlin and the Greek Communists (KKE), he found little evidence of assistance from Moscow. The Greek left, he wrote in March 1945, "waited in vain for Russia to support them in their revolt." [72]

But such conclusions did not quell American anxieties. As 1945 progressed, conditions in Greece worsened. The British could not handle the situation. For their part, English officials recognized their own limited financial resources and military capabilities. They sought U.S. support.[73] Policymakers in Washington remonstrated against the selfishness and incompetence of their British allies. They faulted Churchill for supporting the right wing and for ignoring moderate and centrist alternatives. But however much they wished to distance the United States from the United Kingdom, they could not escape the fundamental convergence of their mutual desire to contain the radical left and the growth of Soviet influence.[74]

As soon as the European war ended in May, State Department officials called for a reorientation of U.S. policy. Acknowledging that the Greek situation was causing "grave concern," Grew and Charles Merriam, chief of the State Department's Near East Division, called for an injection of American influence into the Eastern Mediterranean. In June, they decided that the United States should participate in the supervision of Greek elections under the auspices of the Yalta Declaration on Liberated Europe. In the autumn, they agreed that the United States had to provide economic aid and offer technical assistance. In December, they agreed in principle to a $25 million Export-Import Bank loan. During the same month the cruiser USS *Providence* visited Greek ports to show the flag and demonstrate American concern.[75]

The impetus to take action resulted from the impending collapse of the Greek economy and the prospects of renewed civil war. Prices were soaring; the currency was becoming worthless. Salaried and wage-earning classes could hardly afford to buy food. Eggs were $17 a dozen, cheese $11 a pound.[76] Acheson, Byrnes, and Truman feared chaos. Byrnes wrote the president that "A weak, chaotic Greece is a constant temptation to aggressive actions by its northern neighbors." Truman, too, favored assistance. In fact, he advised the State Department to tone down its insistence on internal reform.[77]

U.S. policymakers were caught in a bind. They were unable to find competent, reliable, and moderate allies inside Greece who could garner significant popular support. For the short run the British presence stymied a radical takeover, but London appeared to lack the political savvy and the financial resources to provide long-term solutions. The United States might have withdrawn from the situation, especially since a joint Anglo-American intelligence assessment was concluding that the Soviet Union was not lending moral or material support to its Balkan allies for an attack on Greece.[78]

Nevertheless, Truman administration officials believed they could not risk a leftist takeover. Once in power, whether or not aided by the Kremlin, the Greek Communists might provide the Soviets with a presence in the Eastern Mediterranean and endanger U.S. national security. Although as yet American policymakers had not devised any effective way of achieving their goal, they were determined to prevent such a contingency from arising.

■

The threat from the indigenous left, however, was not the only danger in the Mediterranean. In May 1945, Yugoslav Communist leader Josip Broz Tito's Fourth Army consolidated its hold over most of Venezia Giulia and arrived in Trieste on the Adriatic Sea. At the very same time New Zealand troops under Field Marshal Sir Harold Alexander moved into this area, which for decades had been a point of dispute between Italy and Yugoslavia. Ambassador Kirk in Italy and Grew in Washington urged the president to resist Tito's efforts to seize Trieste. "Russia," Grew told Truman on 10 May, "was undoubtedly behind Tito's move with a view to utilize Trieste as a Russian port in the future." [79]

Truman ordered Eisenhower to make a show of force to coincide with the State Department's submission of notes to Stalin and Tito. The president wanted the Yugoslavs to withdraw from Trieste and accept a territorial settlement at a future peace conference. Tito received little support in the Kremlin and backed down. He pulled his troops out of Trieste and accepted a temporary demarcation line. [80]

The episode was illustrative of U.S. policymaking. Truman and his advisers realized that they could not push Tito's forces out of the entire disputed area, much as they could not force Soviet troops out of Eastern Europe. Without causing a rift in Soviet-U.S. relations, they nevertheless wanted to uphold the principle of self--determination, control a strategic port area, and circumscribe Soviet influence in Central Europe, the Adriatic, and the Eastern Mediterranean. As in many other places, they discounted the nationalist impulses behind Tito's actions and interpreted a regional dispute in terms of the global configuration of power. Disdaining appeasement, they felt that toughness would bring results. State Department officials were far more inclined to threaten and use force than their military counterparts. Yet no one, and certainly not the president, was eager for a conflict. [81]

■

Similar attitudes influenced the U.S. response to Soviet requests for a trusteeship over Tripolitania. This area in North Africa, bordering on the Mediterranean, had formed part of the Italian empire and was now in British hands awaiting final resolution of territorial issues in an Italian peace treaty. At the San Francisco conference, Stettinius had inadvertently intimated that the Russians might have a trusteeship somewhere. Molotov raised the issue anew at the London foreign ministers' meeting in September 1945. Should not the Soviets, he inquired, have a base in the Mediter-

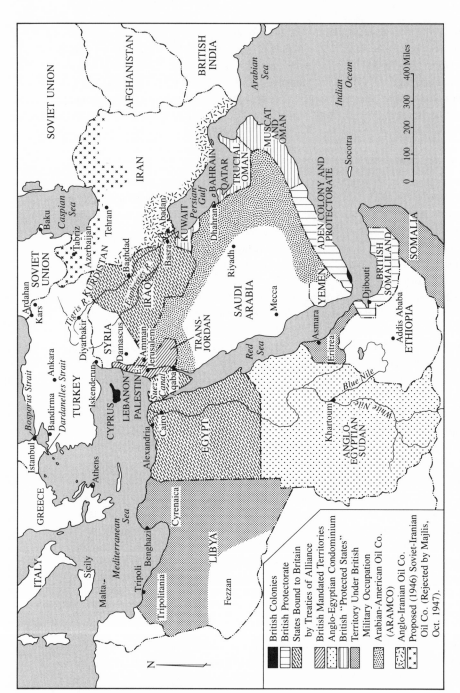

5. The Middle East, 1945–46. Adapted from Wm. Roger Louis, *The British Empire in the Middle East, 1945–1951* (Oxford: Clarendon, 1984), pp. xviii–xix.

Legend:

- British Colonies
- British Protectorate
- States Bound to Britain by Treaties of Alliance
- British Mandated Territories
- Anglo-Egyptian Condominium
- British "Protected States"
- Territory Under British Military Occupation
- Arabian-American Oil Co. (ARAMCO)
- Anglo-Iranian Oil Co.
- Proposed (1946) Soviet-Iranian Oil Co. (Rejected by Majlis, Oct. 1947).

ranean to service their merchant fleet? The British fumed. Byrnes, however, took
the Soviet request for what it was: a negotiating probe designed to elicit tradeoffs on
more important matters. With tact and firmness, Byrnes rebuffed Molotov's overture and submitted an alternate proposal. The Soviet foreign minister readily backed
off. He did not dispute Bevin's soliloquy on the importance of the Mediterranean
to British strategic interests. Instead, Molotov parried with an important strategic
concern of his own: how about a base for the Soviet Union in the Turkish straits? [82]

Turkey, Iran, and the Middle East

The prospect of Soviet aggrandizement in Asia Minor and the Middle East posed a
major threat to the United Kingdom. (See Map 5.) The British had extensive petroleum interests in the Persian Gulf, owned the largest refinery in the world at Abadan,
controlled the oil fields in southern Iran, maintained airfields in Transjordan, Iraq,
and Cyprus, stationed troops in Aden, Sudan, Eritrea, and Somalia, and possessed
a huge military base complex at Suez. The latter stretched from the Mediterranean
to the Red Sea and west towards Cairo. It included roads, harbors, railways, supply
depots, garrisons, ammunition dumps, repair facilities, and numerous airfields. In
1945 there were more than 200,000 troops at the Cairo-Suez base, and close to
100,000 soldiers would remain during the next few years. For reasons of prestige,
trade, finance, and geopolitics, the postwar Labour government of Clement Attlee
and Ernest Bevin wanted to retain Britain's presence in the Middle East. Wm. Roger
Louis, the renowned historian of the British empire, has written that the Labour
government wanted to convert the British approach "from formal rule and alliances
to an informal basis of equal partnership and influence. . . . The purpose of this
transformation was the perpetuation of Britain as a great 'world power.' " [83]

Military officials shaped postwar British policy in the Middle East. They refused
to relinquish their position there. They regarded the base at Cairo-Suez as indispensable: it was the key to guarding imperial communications and transportation
routes; it was the backbone of Britain's ability to project power and maintain access
to Middle East oil fields; and, most important of all, it was essential to their plans
for waging war successfully against the Soviet Union should it become necessary to
do so. From the base at Cairo-Suez, British and (it was hoped) U.S. planes could
strike the petroleum refineries and industrial strongholds of the Soviet Union. No
other area in the world, except for the United Kingdom itself, was considered more
important than the Middle East. According to Britain's overall strategic plan, "The
primary task of the Army, apart from the manning of antiaircraft defences . . . in
the United Kingdom," was "to ensure the security of our Middle East base." [84]

The United States supported Britain's political-military presence in the Middle
East. No matter how much the two Anglo-Saxon nations might compete for oil con-
cessions, markets, and investment opportunities, U.S. policymakers relied on the
British to uphold their common strategic interests in this part of the world. This be-

came altogether apparent on the eve of the Potsdam conference in July 1945 when State Department officials asked their counterparts in the Pentagon to assess Soviet policy toward Turkey. Although the Soviets had not submitted an ultimatum and had not engaged in any threats or intimidation, Byrnes and Grew were worried that the Kremlin's renunciation of its treaty of friendship with Turkey and its requests for frontier rectifications and for base rights in the Dardanelles region posed problems "for the security of the entire Mediterranean." [85]

Surprisingly, U.S. military officials were divided on what should be done. The senior Army and Air Force officers on the Joint Strategic Survey Committee argued in favor of concessions to the Soviet Union. They desired to avoid a rupture in relations with the Kremlin, feared unilateral Soviet moves to achieve its goals, and recoiled at the hypocrisy of the American position. If the Russians should demand "base rights in the Dardanelles-Aegean area," they argued, "it would appear inconsistent for us to oppose them while ourselves asking base rights in areas remote from our shores, such as Iceland, the Azores, and the more distant Pacific Islands." [86]

Logical as this argument was, the JCS decided—and the State Department agreed—that Russia must not be permitted to have a base in the Dardanelles region. Army planners under General Lincoln laid out an elaborate rationale for denying the Soviets a military presence in the Turkish straits: if the Russians established themselves there, it was believed they would then seek additional bases in the Aegean and Mediterranean seas because the Dardanelles could not be protected from modern air power without them. Step by step, the Kremlin might envelop additional areas of Asia Minor, jeopardize British control of the Mediterranean, achieve a preponderant position on the Eurasian land mass, and challenge the United States for world supremacy. Army officers boldly faced the hypocrisy of their position and came to terms with it:

To argue that it is necessary to preserve a unilateral military control by the U.S. or Britain over Panama or Gibraltar and yet deny a similar control to Russia at the Dardanelles may seem open to the criticism of being illogical. It is, however, a logical illogicality. Neither the United States nor the British Empire can by the greatest stretch of the imagination be accused of expansionist or aggressive ambitions. . . . Russia, however, has not as yet proven that she is entirely without expansionistic ambitions. . . . She is inextricably, almost mystically, related to the ideology of Communism which superficially at least can be associated with a rising tide all over the world wherein the common man aspires to higher and wider horizons. Russia must be sorely tempted to combine her strength with her ideology to expand her influence over the earth. Her actions in the past few years give us no assured bases for supposing she has not flirted with the thought.[87]

At Potsdam and in subsequent diplomatic exchanges, the United States refused to contemplate anything but moderate alterations in the Montreux Convention governing rights of passage through the Turkish straits.[88] Although Soviet troop movements exacerbated concerns about Russian adventurism in the area, and although Truman worried that the Russians might seize the Dardanelles, U.S. intelligence analysts reported that the Russians were withdrawing their forces from Southeastern Europe and were not likely to launch an attack.[89] "The U.S.S.R.," George Kennan wrote from Moscow in October 1945, "has remained remarkably inactive with regard to Turkey." [90]

■

American anxieties about Turkey and the entire Middle Eastern region were accentuated by Soviet behavior in Iran. In the fall of 1945 the Kremlin supported separatist movements in Azerbaijan and Kurdistan. Russian troops, still in Iran under the terms of a wartime agreement, prevented Iranian soldiers from crushing provincial uprisings in these two northern provinces. When the U.S. and British governments protested Soviet actions and called upon the Kremlin to withdraw its forces from Iran by 1 March 1946, as it was obligated to do, Stalin and Molotov equivocated.[91] At the Moscow conference in December 1945, Byrnes did not press this matter as vigorously as did Bevin. Realizing that he had little leverage in an area already occupied by Soviet troops, the U.S. secretary of state was prepared to wait and see if the Soviets would comply with their promise to depart.[92]

South of Iran's northern provinces, however, Byrnes was more hopeful of containing Soviet influence. The United States already had two military missions in Iran: one of them served the army, the other the imperial gendarmerie. In September, Undersecretary Acheson reassured Wallace Murray, the U.S. ambassador in Tehran, that the two military missions would remain. They were relatively popular and helped to preserve internal stability in a country that was beleaguered by tribal unrest in the south and separatist movements in the north. The young shah, Mohammad Reza Pahlavi, was weak, and he relied on these U.S. advisers for help against his domestic rivals as well as for assistance against Iran's traditional great power predators.[93] By sustaining the work of these military missions and by maneuvering to keep military supplies flowing to Iran, Byrnes sought to retain some American leverage in that country.[94]

Of course, these measures would not suffice to thwart Soviet expansion should the Kremlin try either to seize a warm-water port on the Persian Gulf or to grab the southern Iranian oil fields. Yet Soviet intentions were unclear. Stalin claimed that he was concerned with protecting his own petroleum facilities at Baku and was fearful that Iranian unrest would spill across his borders.[95] State Department officials scoffed at these explanations. The United States, they retorted, had no direct interest in northern Iran and had no desire to endanger Russian interests.[96]

What the Americans wanted to do was to create a buffer zone between the Soviet Union and the rich oil fields of the Persian Gulf. World War II had underscored the importance of petroleum as a strategic asset as well as an economic resource. Since the late 1930's American corporations, with the help of the U.S. government, had been consolidating their control over Saudi Arabian oil. U.S. defense officials wanted to increase the use of Middle Eastern oil in order to preserve Western Hemisphere petroleum reserves so that the latter would be available in plentiful quantity in case of another war. Saudi Arabian oil, the State Department emphasized to President Truman, constituted "a stupendous source of strategic power, and one of the greatest material prizes in world history." [97]

Acheson pleaded the State Department's case for a $100 million discretionary fund to promote U.S. political and strategic interests in the region. The Middle East, insisted the State Department, "because of its resources and geographic position . . . should be in the hands of a people following the paths of democratic civilization rather than those of Eastern dictatorships." As British power was beginning to falter, the United States had to be able to project its own influence. Nowhere could the money be put to better use, Acheson claimed, than Saudi Arabia where the king was facing a financial crunch and domestic opposition. [98]

Budgetary and political pressures in the United States militated against the development of such a fund in 1945. Nevertheless, Truman and Byrnes authorized Army appropriations for the construction of an airfield in Saudi Arabia. They also approved a military mission to that nation and set aside $25 million in Export-Import Bank funds for the Saudi government. At the same time, U.S. officials expected ARAMCO, the U.S. oil corporation, to increase production and to pay larger royalties to King Ibn Sa'ūd. These measures were intended to satisfy the needs of the Saudi crown and protect American influence in that critical country. The airfield would also help to safeguard strategic air and sea routes and underscore American interest in the entire region. [99] Ibn Sa'ūd, of course, was hardly a representative of "democratic civilization," but with him the United States hoped to establish a partnership that would enable the U.S. government and Saudi crown to pursue their own respective and often overlapping interests.

Although these initiatives were limited, they provide a backdrop for interpreting Soviet actions in Iran in 1945. Stalin's seemingly lame allusion to Baku may have revealed his real concern about the vulnerability of Russian oil fields and petroleum refineries. As the Soviets knew, the British and French had planned to attack the Caucasian oil fields from the south when the Russians had been allied with the Nazis in 1940. [100] After World War II, British and U.S. military officials immediately began to devise plans to bomb these targets in any future conflict. [101] Stalin needed no special insight or privileged information to discern what might happen in case hostilities erupted. The existence of the huge British complex at Cairo-Suez, the U.S. solicitation of aviation rights throughout the region, and the prospective construction of military airstrips at Dhahran made it entirely prudent for him to be concerned with defense in depth along his southern frontier. [102]

Russian intervention in northern Iran was neither legal nor moral. But the Kremlin's actions, as Richard Cottam and Mark Lytle have recently argued, appear to have been prompted by strategic and defensive calculations rather than by offensive ones. [103] The Soviets no less than the Americans and the British had to think about configurations of power and plans for future war should the great alliance fall apart.

If at the end of the war the Soviets were probing to enhance their position in the Middle East, which they were, then the Americans, too, were marking off areas of vital interest, identifying the convergence of Anglo-American strategic interests, and calculating their prospective enemy's vulnerabilities as well as their own requirements. These actions did not mean that Washington or Moscow or London sought or even expected a showdown. Each government was probably acting defensively, but the cumulative effect, as the political scientist Fred Lawson correctly argues, was to trigger a spiraling crisis of misperception and mistrust.[104]

China

In East Asia as well as the Middle East, the Kremlin wanted to excise the influence of potential adversaries along its periphery while the United States sought to contain the expansion of Soviet power. Their incipient rivalry was fueled by China's weakness. For decades Chiang Kai-shek's Nationalist forces had been battling the Chinese Communists. During the war the Japanese had driven Chiang's Kuomintang Party (KMT) to the southwest while Mao Tse-tung's Communist Party (CCP) consolidated its strength in the rural northwest. The Nationalists and the Communists knew that, once Japan surrendered, enormous vacuums of power would exist in the rich provinces of Manchuria and in the populous and urban northeast. They looked to Washington and Moscow for assistance as they planned to race into these areas.[105]

At Yalta in February 1945, Roosevelt and Stalin struck a secret deal regarding the Far East. If the Soviets attacked Japan within two or three months after Germany surrendered, Roosevelt would allow the Soviets to annex southern Sakhalin and the Kuriles, establish a naval base at Port Arthur, and recover Russia's pre-1904 rights in Manchuria, including its "preeminent interests" in the region's two key railroads and the port of Dairen. Chiang would need to be consulted on these matters, but Roosevelt agreed to obtain his concurrence. For his part, Stalin acknowledged Chinese sovereignty over Manchuria and promised to conclude a pact of friendship with Chiang's government.[106] (See Map 6.)

Aside from W. Averell Harriman, the U.S. ambassador to the Soviet Union, no American official knew the precise language or the exact nature of Roosevelt's territorial concessions at Yalta. Many policymakers, however, were aware that the Soviet leader renounced assistance to the Chinese Communists. Thereafter, the Roosevelt administration threw its support behind Chiang. State Department officials realized his government was undemocratic, corrupt, and incompetent. They wanted him to undertake reforms in order to enhance his popularity. Moreover, they advised him to recognize the legal status of the CCP in order to avert civil war. In return, the CCP would be asked to dissolve its local governments and its military formations. The Communists would have to observe the laws and decrees of a united, coalition government in which they would have a minority status.[107] It was hoped that the

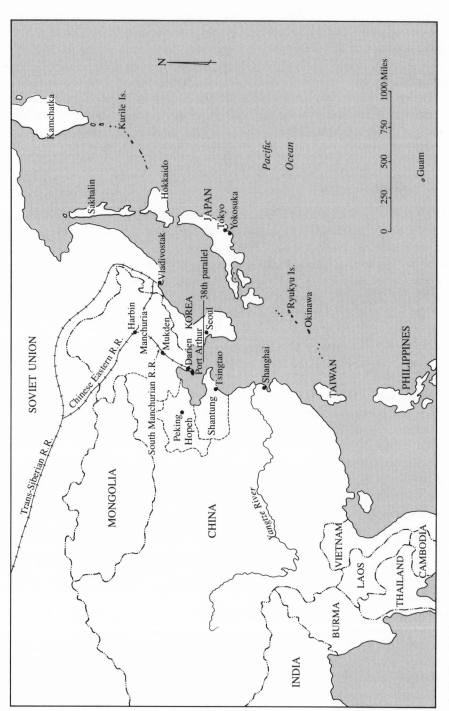

6. Northeast Asia, 1945–46

Soviets would agree to this approach and exert appropriate pressure on the CCP. In an April meeting in Moscow with Patrick J. Hurley, the U.S. ambassador to China, Stalin reemphasized that he would not support the Communist rebels.[108]

Nevertheless, Soviet actions in Eastern Europe triggered grave misgivings about Soviet intentions in Northeast Asia. In May, Grew, Leahy, Forrestal, Stimson, McCloy, and Harriman voiced regret over the prospective aggrandizement of Russian power, especially in Manchuria. Harriman and Grew wanted to reexamine the secret Yalta agreement on the Far East. Stimson and McCloy insisted that they bide their time. Until the new atomic weapon proved its utility, they believed it was unwise to forsake Soviet assistance that might still be needed to save American lives in the Pacific war.[109]

Stimson, however, was more sympathetic with Grew's desire to relax the unconditional surrender formula for Japan. If the Japanese gave up before the Russians intervened, the Kremlin might not be able to lay claim to its Yalta prizes. As attractive as this idea was from the perspective of the international chess table, Truman and Byrnes worried that any modification of the unconditional surrender principle might inflame American public opinion.[110] The challenge was to find a means of containing the Soviets without alienating them and without antagonizing domestic constituencies.

When they met at Potsdam, Stalin immediately told Truman and Byrnes that he would declare war on Japan by the middle of August provided he could work out a satisfactory agreement with Chinese Nationalist foreign minister T. V. Soong. Stalin blamed the Chinese for the stalemate in their talks. Soong, he said, refused to recognize Soviet "preeminent interests" on the Manchurian railroads and in Port Arthur. Stalin insisted that the Soviets were complying with the terms of the secret Yalta agreement and were defining their rights narrowly. He also reiterated that he would not aid the Chinese Communists. Truman said little to encourage Soviet intervention in the Far Eastern war. Instead he pressed Stalin to honor the open door in Dairen.[111] When Stalin raised no objections, Truman was delighted. "I can deal with Stalin," he jotted in his diary. In his first encounter with the Soviet leader, Truman thought he had clinched Soviet support for Chiang and Soviet respect for the open door as well as Soviet assistance against Japan, should it still be wanted.[112]

But as news reached Potsdam of the tremendous success of the atomic test in New Mexico, Truman and Byrnes decided that Soviet participation in the Pacific war was not needed. U.S. military officers no longer displayed any real desire for Soviet intervention.[113] On 23 July, Stimson told the president that "with our new weapon we would not need the assistance of the Russians to conquer Japan." [114] Thereupon, Byrnes decided to exclude the Soviets from the surrender ultimatum to Japan.[115] At the same time, Truman deflected Molotov's request for a public invitation to enter the Far Eastern war. Instead the president told Stalin that he would issue an invitation after a Sino-Soviet treaty had been signed.[116] "It is quite clear,"

Churchill noted, "that the United States do not at the present time desire Russian participation in the war against Japan." [117]

Nor did the Americans want to honor their Yalta pledges in East Asia. By dropping the atomic bomb, they hoped to speed Japan's defeat, save American lives, and contain Soviet influence. Consequently, Stalin faced some tough decisions. If he waited for a settlement with Soong, the war might end without achieving his Yalta gains in Northeast Asia. He realized the Americans would have little reason to fulfill their promises if the Kremlin did not intervene. Moreover, he could see that his negotiating leverage with Soong would be maximized if Soviet troops attacked the Japanese and opened communications with the Chinese Communists. On 8 August the Kremlin declared war on Japan. The following morning Soviet armies marched into Manchuria as their diplomats sat down at the bargaining table with Soong in Moscow. [118]

Soviet actions did not surprise U.S. officials. They now sought to hasten Japan's surrender by modifying the unconditional surrender formula and permitting the retention of the Japanese emperor system. At a meeting on 10 August, Truman and Stimson both acknowledged that their aim was to end the war promptly before the Russians penetrated too deeply into China. Lying to his cabinet, the president denied that the Soviets were entitled to any gains in Manchuria. [119] The following day the JCS sent orders to U.S. military commanders to seize Dairen if they could get there before the Soviets. A week later these instructions were retracted when it was acknowledged that rapid Soviet advances endangered the deployment of U.S. Marines. [120]

Meanwhile, in Moscow Harriman worked tenaciously to bolster Soong's negotiating leverage. He contested Stalin's desires for Soviet administration of Dairen and for its inclusion in a military zone, he insisted on respect for the open-door policy, and he denounced Soviet seizures of Japanese-owned factories in Manchuria. Although he was pleased that Stalin did not insist on stationing troops in Manchuria or placing guards along the railroad lines, as had been the right of the czarist government prior to 1904, Harriman nevertheless challenged Stalin's proposal for preponderant Soviet control of Manchuria's key railroads. The Sino-Soviet agreement that was initialed on 14 August was far more satisfactory than might have been expected from the ambiguous Yalta language. Stalin recognized Chiang, acknowledged Chinese sovereignty over Manchuria, and promised to hand over liberated areas to Nationalist authorities. [121]

■

After the Sino-Soviet treaty was signed and the Japanese surrendered, U.S. officials sought to monitor Russian compliance with their promises. Policymakers in Washington feared that the Japanese would surrender to Soviet military officers and the latter would relinquish Japanese arms to the Chinese Communists, who would then be able to establish their control over Manchuria and northern China. The result would be that much of Northeast Asia would fall within the Kremlin's orbit and augment its future industrial and military power, much as domination of Manchuria and Korea had added to Japan's strength. To thwart the prospect of Soviet/CCP domination, Truman instructed Japanese forces outside of Manchuria to surrender only to Nationalist commanders and not to Chinese Communist authorities. Washington also ordered General Albert Wedemeyer to airlift and sealift Chiang's best divisions to Japanese-occupied areas as rapidly as possible.[122]

Wedemeyer immediately alerted Washington in the most unequivocal terms that, despite the proclamation of U.S. noninvolvement in China's civil war, his aid to Chiang would be construed, and correctly construed, as an anti-Communist measure. Unless informed to the contrary, he was assuming that this accorded with Washington's objectives. "I want to do everything within my power," he wrote on 19 August, "to preclude loss of advantages we now enjoy in Far East and to insure that favorable conditions are created for accomplishment of ultimate U.S. political and economic objectives." [123]

Wedemeyer was correctly interpreting the drift of opinion in Washington. Within the SWNCC, Air Force and Army generals advocated postwar military assistance to China. They foresaw a prolonged civil war. They wanted the United States to assist Chiang in creating a stable, unified China friendly to the United States, but they worried that Chiang and Stalin might work out a deal at the expense of American interests. They wanted to send military advisers to the Nationalist government, extend military assistance, and transport Chiang's troops to northern China and Manchuria. "A measure of security for the United States," they also noted, would be obtained by the presence of a modern, well-equipped air force on the flank of the Soviet Union. A few days later General Marshall told Madame Chiang that the United States would try to transfer surplus transport planes to her husband's forces in order to enhance the mobility of Nationalist troops.[124]

Civilian officials concurred. On 3 September, Byrnes urged Truman to support a military mission for China. The secretary of state, like his military colleagues, wanted to make sure that Chiang looked to the United States for military assistance. After Byrnes left for the London foreign ministers' conference, Acheson wrote Truman that he, Stimson, and Forrestal supported military assistance and a military mission for China. They wanted to complete the 39-division program, transfer naval craft, and equip an air force, the size and composition of which was still undetermined. The next day, 14 September, Truman met with Soong and endorsed the broad outlines of this plan.[125]

A few days later, the first contingents of 50,000 U.S. Marines arrived in Hopeh and Shantung provinces. The function of these Marines, Acheson later explained, was to occupy the principal seaports, guard the key railroad lines, protect the critical coal mines, and thereby help to revive the industrial life of China. Rather than deport the Japanese troops, the official history of the Marines points out that enemy forces were initially used to hold key communication and transportation routes while the Nationalists consolidated their hold over the region.[126] These *initial* actions, it should be stressed, were prompted neither by allusions to Soviet aid to the CCP nor by claims that the Soviets were violating the Yalta accords on the Far East.[127] Nor were they the result of any substantial public or congressional support for Chiang.[128] On the contrary, the U.S. actions were designed by the leading members of the Truman administration to contain Soviet/CCP influence in Northeast Asia. Without these initiatives, Steven Levine has written, Communist authorities would have easily taken control of the critical northeastern provinces of China.[129]

In October, however, news began filtering into Washington that the Soviets were supporting the CCP. In several Manchurian cities Soviet forces disregarded Chinese Nationalist representatives and Soviet commanders handed over Japanese arms to the CCP. Russian troops seized Japanese factories, dismantled them, and shipped them to the Soviet Union. Chiang appealed to Wedemeyer for more help; he wanted the United States to move Nationalist troops directly into areas of Manchuria occupied by the Russians and now infiltrated by large numbers of CCP insurgents.[130]

Wedemeyer had grave misgivings. The Chinese Communists were already enraged by American support to Chiang. The lives of U.S. Marines, therefore, would be further endangered. Noting the total hypocrisy of declaring noninvolvement in the domestic conflict while transporting Nationalist armies to Manchuria and northern China, Wedemeyer insisted on new instructions before acceding to Chiang's most recent request. Wedemeyer advised that U.S. officials consider the wisdom of a four-power (U.S.-British-Chinese-Soviet) trusteeship over Manchuria and Korea.[131]

Throughout November, Chinese developments commanded the attention of the highest American officials in Washington. At the end of the month Truman focused his own attention on the matter when Patrick Hurley resigned as ambassador and blamed Communist sympathizers in the State Department for encouraging Communist resistance to his own unification efforts in China. Policymakers feared that their attempt to thwart Soviet/CCP domination of Manchuria was about to fail. Stalin appeared to be reneging on his Yalta promise to forsake support of the CCP and to collaborate with Chiang. Having fought the Pacific war in order to prevent Japanese domination of Chinese resources and labor, Patterson and Forrestal despaired over the prospect of seeing these resources, especially the raw materials of Manchuria, fall into the Soviet orbit. At a cabinet meeting on 27 November, Truman remonstrated against Soviet seizures of Manchurian factories. He insisted that the United States take a strong stand lest Russia succeed Japan as the preponderant power in the Far East.[132]

The president decided that the Nationalist government's influence had to prevail over all of China, including Manchuria. He asked General Marshall to succeed Hurley. Marshall's mission would be to arrange a truce between the CCP and the KMT, to establish a coalition government with the Nationalists in control, to insure Chinese Nationalist domination over all Manchuria, and to remove Russian troops from that region. Foreseeing that Chiang might be intractable on matters of internal political reform, Marshall wanted Truman to understand that the United States would still have to support him. If the United States withdrew its assistance from the Nationalist government, Marshall told Truman, Byrnes, and Leahy, "there would follow the tragic consequences of a divided China and of a probable Russian resumption of power in Manchuria, the combined effect of this resulting in the defeat or loss of the major purpose of our war in the Pacific." [133] Accordingly, Wedemeyer's directive was rewritten, instructing him to assist the movement of Nationalist troops to Manchuria and implicitly acknowledging that such aid might have "incidental" effects on the internal conflict. [134] Simultaneously, the Truman administration moved ahead with plans to train the postwar Chinese air forces, provide military advisers and military assistance, and relieve Chinese shipping problems. [135]

Like most top officials in the Truman administration, except perhaps Byrnes, Marshall assumed that CCP advances in Manchuria would lead to the accretion of Soviet power. Truman himself expressed displeasure with Byrnes's lackluster support of Chiang and clearly preferred the unequivocal approach insisted on by Marshall. [136] But by the time the wartime chief of staff arrived in China, the links between the Kremlin and the Chinese Communists appeared very hazy. In Marshall's first talk with Chiang, the Chinese leader denounced Soviet support of the CCP yet acknowledged that, since mid-November, Soviet policy had been cooperative. Chiang admitted that he was glad that Soviet troops would remain in Manchuria until February; his own forces could not assume immediate control of this region. [137] Information coming into Washington confirmed that Soviet military authorities were now collaborating with Nationalist commanders and severing contacts with the CCP. [138]

While Marshall was conversing with Chiang, Byrnes was in Moscow meeting with Molotov and Bevin. China was not the focus of their talks, but the issue kept intruding on their deliberations. Repeatedly, Molotov and Stalin defended Soviet actions. They claimed they were violating neither the Yalta accords nor the Sino-Soviet treaty. Russian forces, they said, had been withdrawn from southern Manchuria and remained in northern Manchuria at Chiang's request. They were agitated by the injection of U.S. troops into northern China. The Soviet foreign minister challenged Byrnes to a mutual withdrawal of Soviet and U.S. forces from all of China. In his talk with Stalin, Byrnes defended American policy. Stalin did not press the matter, yet requested that he be informed about U.S. intentions. [139]

The Soviets were playing a double game. They were not prepared to sever all links with the CCP, and they provided assistance that enabled the Communists to ensconce themselves in northern Manchuria. But at the same time they distrusted Mao and were prepared to work with Chiang. Their main objective was to remove America's preponderant influence in postwar China, an influence that had appeared so evident throughout the war. If the grand coalition should disintegrate, or, worse yet, if war should erupt, Stalin realized that from northern China, Manchuria, or Mongolia the Americans might try to cut the Trans-Siberian railroad and dismember the Kremlin's Far Eastern provinces.[140]

Truman, of course, had no desire to undermine the existing Soviet empire. But since the Soviets were demonstrating their desire to dominate Eastern Europe, prudence dictated that the United States seek to thwart additional Russian advances in Northeast Asia. American officials wanted to help Chiang establish control over all of China, including Manchuria. Truman knew little about Chinese politics, but nevertheless he favored a strong, democratic China friendly to the United States.[141] In pursuit of their goals, American officials thought about repudiating Yalta's Far East provisions; sought to preempt Soviet intervention in the Far Eastern war; encouraged Soong to chisel away at Soviet "preeminent interests" in Manchuria; and utilized U.S. Marines, military advisers, and military assistance to aid Chiang's postwar consolidation of power. American officials did not deny that the Kremlin had legitimate strategic imperatives in Northeast Asia. However, they were skeptical of the Kremlin's good intentions and hence demanded that the Soviet leaders accept risks on their strategic frontiers with China—risks that U.S. officials would never have accepted for themselves in Mexico or Canada, for example.

Korea

In Korea, as in Manchuria and northern China, the United States was eager to contain Soviet influence. Throughout the war the State Department's Far Eastern office had given considerable attention to Korea and fully supported Roosevelt's trusteeship idea. Without some form of four-power trusteeship, the Soviet Union might dominate Korea. The Russians would then strengthen the economic resources of the Soviet Far East and "occupy a dominating strategic position in relation both to China and to Japan." At Yalta, Stalin readily agreed to a trusteeship for Korea so long as it did not encompass occupation by foreign troops.[142]

The successful testing of the atomic bomb encouraged Truman and Byrnes to think that they might outmaneuver the Soviets in Korea as well as Manchuria. The historian James Matray has described how, at Potsdam, U.S. officials tried to avoid precise discussions about the application of a trusteeship to Korea. Momentarily, Truman and Byrnes thought they might end the war before Stalin could send his troops across the Siberian border. General Marshall urged MacArthur to be ready to deploy American forces quickly to Korea should the Japanese surrender.[143]

Stalin was not to be outsmarted. He would not allow the Soviet Union to be excluded from a role in postwar Korea, a peninsula that bordered strategically on his own maritime provinces, that possessed warm-water ports, and that the Japanese had seized from Russian control 40 years before. As soon as the Kremlin declared war on Japan, Soviet troops crossed into Korea as well as Manchuria. Stalin, however, readily agreed that Americans might arrange for the surrender of Japanese forces in the southern part of the peninsula. Byrnes instructed the SWNCC to come up with a viable demarcation line as far north as possible. Colonels Dean Rusk and Charles Bonesteel proposed the 38th parallel, a division the Soviets immediately accepted notwithstanding their ability to seize all of Korea.[144]

Inside Korea, the situation was explosive. In his brilliant and comprehensive account of the origins of the Korean War, Bruce Cumings has underscored the popularity of the left. In the south, without any aid from the Kremlin, the Communists may have been the single most important political force. People's committees sprang up everywhere. They were popular expressions of the Korean people's desire for political and economic liberation after 40 years of oppressive Japanese rule. These committees clamored for reform. They excoriated Koreans who had collaborated with the Japanese, they championed independence, and they detested the idea of trusteeship. Most Koreans supported the newly formed Committee for the Preparation of Korean Independence, which was in the hands of the moderate left-winger, Yo Un-hyong.[145]

Taking over his occupation command, General John Hodge was totally unprepared for the situation he faced. He moved swiftly to grapple with the threat of indigenous revolution. In his first report to Washington, Hodge's State Department political adviser, H. Merrell Benninghoff, wrote that "southern Korea can best be described as a powder keg ready to explode at the application of a spark." [146] Fearing the Communists in the south would seize power and collaborate with the Kremlin, Hodge decided to align himself with conservative groups and indigenous elites. He enthusiastically welcomed Syngman Rhee, the aged and bitterly anti-Soviet Korean nationalist, back to the country. To keep order, he relied on Koreans who had worked for the Japanese national police. He also began to plan for a separate southern administration and for separate defense forces.[147] General Hodge, like occupation authorities elsewhere, was responding to local circumstances, dire economic conditions, impending chaos, and the potential aggrandizement of Soviet power. McCloy defended Hodge, explaining to Dean Acheson that if the general did not utilize Koreans who had collaborated with the Japanese, he might not be able to stymie a Communist takeover in the south.[148]

Some State Department officials were appalled by Hodge's actions. They, too, feared the revolutionary ardor and nationalist aspirations of the Korean masses. But they also wanted to get the Soviets out of northern Korea, and they believed that Hodge's actions would lead to the permanent division of the peninsula. In the fall of 1945 they revived the trusteeship idea as the most efficacious means of uniting the country and reducing Soviet influence. At the Moscow conference in December, Byrnes proposed it to Molotov. The Soviet foreign minister thought it over, submitted a counterproposal, and the two men easily reached agreement. Koreans in the south, however, instantaneously raged against the accord, and Hodge had nothing but contempt for it. Truman did not much like it either. Immediately, Byrnes began to backtrack.[149]

Tactical differences between the State Department in Washington and occupation authorities in Korea should not obscure their shared desire to contain indigenous revolution and Soviet power in Northeast Asia. U.S. policymakers, however, had not devised a strategy or mobilized the means to achieve their goals. Ultimately, Hodge's strategy would prevail. He was on the scene and could immediately influence events. He also grasped that the Korean right constituted a strong, determined, indigenous constituency that would never accept trusteeship.[150] If U.S. officials were to accomplish their objectives, they would learn that they had to reconcile their goals and iron out their tactics with prospective local clients.

Japan

In Japan, the situation was less complicated because U.S. officials were firmly in control of the entire country and because the Japanese were more compliant. The United States sought to demilitarize Japan, democratize its sociopolitical structure, reform its economy, integrate it into a multilateral commercial order, and insure its long-term friendship. To achieve these objectives, U.S. policymakers wanted to exclude the influence of all foreign governments, and most particularly that of the Soviet Union. State, War, and Navy Department officials agreed that there must be a unified administration of Japan. Soviet requests to govern a zone of their own, as in Germany, were brusquely rebuffed.[151]

In September 1945, General MacArthur, supreme commander of Allied powers, assumed his occupation duties. He found the Japanese eager to cooperate. They were defeated, humiliated, powerless. Their country was in shambles. In Japan's 66 largest cities, over 40 percent of the buildings were destroyed. Fifteen million Japanese were homeless. Industrial production was a third of what it had been in the mid-1930's. Japan's merchant fleet was destroyed and its commerce was now paralyzed. Prices soared; unemployment spread; prostitution and the black market flourished; food was scarce. By the end of 1945 the economy approached collapse.[152]

Notwithstanding the devastation that surrounded him, MacArthur faced the future with confidence. He was even more determined than U.S. officials in Washington to make the occupation an American show. MacArthur brooked no interference from anyone, but he treated the Soviet mission in Tokyo with particular contempt. When the chief Soviet representative showed up for appointments, he was not infrequently told that he had the wrong date. His plane would be kept circling above Haneda airport for a protracted period of time before clearance for landing was given. He was arrested for reckless driving. MacArthur told him that if a single Russian soldier entered Japan without permission, the entire Russian mission would be thrown into jail. Stalin protested that his representative was treated like "a mere piece of furniture." MacArthur's preeminent biographer agrees with Stalin's judgment.[153]

At the September meeting of the Council of Foreign Ministers, Molotov complained about the pace of MacArthur's demilitarization and demobilization practices. He asked for the establishment of an Allied Control Council, consisting of representatives of the United States, United Kingdom, China, and Soviet Russia. Byrnes, however, did not even want to place Japan on the agenda of the London conference, let alone make any concessions.[154] A few weeks later, when Harriman visited the Crimea to meet with Stalin, the Soviet leader ridiculed U.S. policies. He did not contest American predominance in Japan. He simply insisted on the right to participate in a control commission that resembled the one in Romania.[155]

Harriman urged Washington to make concessions. He pointed out that, for two generations, Japan "has been a constant menace to Russian security in the Far East." Harriman believed that Stalin would settle for a face-saving formula.[156] In Washington, Acheson agreed with Harriman. It was embarrassing to deny the Soviets a status equivalent to the one the Americans had in Romania, a position that the United States still considered entirely inadequate. But MacArthur did not wish to dilute American power, and Admiral Leahy strongly supported his views. Current conditions in Japan, Leahy told Byrnes and Truman, were ideal for the spread of communism. If Japan were sovietized, it would mean that the war in the Pacific had been lost.[157]

In December, a compromise was worked out. An eleven-nation Far East Commission was established as well as a quadripartite Allied Council for Japan. The former was headquartered in Washington; the latter in Tokyo. The former had limited policy authority; the latter was purely advisory. When Molotov haggled for still greater concessions, Byrnes reminded Harriman that the United States would accept no language that constrained the authority and actions of the supreme commander (MacArthur). Byrnes's intention, like Truman's, was to guarantee U.S. security by insuring long-term American domination of Japan.[158] So long as the Soviets (and the other World War II allies) were ready to accept the substance of this arrangement, Byrnes was prepared to make symbolic concessions.

Once the basic institutional structures were established, top officials in Washington left the details of occupation policy to MacArthur. MacArthur scorned the advice of his State Department advisers and ignored the suggestions of the expert commissions that regularly trekked across the Pacific to study problems. The supreme commander introduced a host of liberal reforms and a new democratic constitution. He implemented widespread land reform. He called for the breakup of Japan's great industrial concentrations. For the most part, however, he worked through established Japanese government institutions and relied on Japanese bureaucrats to implement his decrees. Japanese elites struggled to co-opt the occupation, preserve their traditions, and safeguard their economic positions. Until 1947 Truman, Byrnes, Forrestal, and Patterson rarely paid attention to developments in Japan. Having established a monopoly of American power, they could focus their attention on priorities elsewhere.[159]

Southeast Asia

In Southeast Asia, as in Korea, U.S. aspirations collided with the forces of revolution and nationalism. Japan's conquests had severed British, French, and Dutch control over their colonies. Facing defeat, the Japanese relinquished power to Asians. In the Dutch East Indies, Indonesian leaders like Sukarno and Mohammed Hatta immediately declared independence. In Indochina, Ho Chi Minh's Viet Minh, an umbrella organization dominated by Communists, spread its influence from the north to the south. In a country where millions were dying of starvation, Ho's Communists capitalized on their promise to bring relief and reform. There, too, as soon as the Japanese surrendered, Ho announced the formation of the Democratic Republic of Vietnam.[160]

U.S. policymakers recognized that war and Japanese occupation had shattered imperial ties and inspired nationalist movements. In principle, they staunchly supported self-determination. In practice, they molded principles to accommodate geopolitical, strategic, economic, and diplomatic priorities. Under relentless pressure from Churchill, even Roosevelt had retreated from his staunch advocacy of trusteeship. He had grudgingly accepted the restoration of French sovereignty in Indochina and conditionally authorized the return of French forces.[161]

After Roosevelt's death, the proponents of trusteeship and self-determination were without an influential leader. Pentagon officials, like Lovett, pushed the State Department to resolve the ambiguities that inhered in the American approach to Southeast Asia.[162] Truman had no real interest in the issue and left it to his subordinates. Experts in the Office of Far Eastern Affairs like Abbot Low Moffat took up Roosevelt's mantle. They believed that American prestige in the region was great. But if the United States bowed to the desires of its European allies and compromised the principles of the Atlantic Charter, it would not be able to escape the opprobrium that would be heaped upon all Western powers. Moffat and his colleagues believed that a pan-Asian movement directed against the entire Occident could take hold. The Communists could capitalize on it.[163]

Logical as were the arguments of the small group of Asian experts, the views of high-ranking, conservative, European-oriented foreign service officers prevailed. Grew, James C. Dunn, and H. Freeman Matthews took charge of policy and were supported by civilian and military officials at the Pentagon. They did not want to weaken France, Britain, or Holland or to alienate their governments lest they be lost as allies in the prospective struggle against Soviet expansionism. The principle of self-government, therefore, had to be tailored to fit the economic and strategic needs of Britain, France, Holland, and the United States.[164] At Potsdam, Truman agreed that Britain's Southeast Asia Command could arrange the surrender of Japanese troops below the 16th parallel in Indochina and throughout Southeast Asia. The Nationalist Chinese would take charge of handling the Japanese in northern Indochina. In making these decisions, American officials removed the United States from direct involvement in the colonial-nationalist struggle but implicitly identified their country with the restoration of the old order.[165]

When Japan did surrender in mid-August, the nationalist movements in Indochina and Indonesia looked to the United States for assistance. In Vietnam, in particular, Ho Chi Minh and his allies, many of whom had cooperated with U.S. intelligence officers, pleaded for the Americans to withhold aid from the French and to prevent the Chinese from looting and pillaging. Intelligence reports coming to the White House emphasized Ho's popularity, his left-wing orientation, his movement's organizational capabilities, and his friendliness toward the United States. Ho modeled his declaration of independence after the American declaration. He appealed directly to President Truman for support, but his letters went unanswered.[166]

The British facilitated the return of the French to Indochina and the Dutch to the East Indies. In some areas the Europeans initially relied heavily on the Japanese to preserve order. Nevertheless, violence flared, and negotiations between nationalist leaders and their former rulers began. The French and the Dutch promised reforms, but their intentions were unclear and their word distrusted.[167]

The Asianists in the Department of State criticized U.S. policy. Their clout was on the rise once Grew resigned in August, Acheson became undersecretary, and John Carter Vincent took over the Office of Far Eastern Affairs. The Far East experts recognized that Communists led the nationalist movement in Indochina, but they found no evidence that Ho and his supporters were "under the guidance of the USSR, China, the Japanese, or any other external influence." They were gratified when the administration gave no direct assistance to the French, Dutch, and British. However, they were painfully aware that U.S. lend-lease aid provided the guns, ammunition, ships, and planes to repress nationalist forces. Although American insignia were removed from weapons and materiel, nationalists everywhere identified the United States with the restoration of colonial rule. Vincent and his colleagues lamented that the United States was compromising its ideals, sacrificing its prestige, and disillusioning domestic public opinion. In a general way they wanted the administration to press the Europeans to eschew the use of force and negotiate in good faith with the nationalist leaders. If the French and Dutch followed their advice, their efforts would be rewarded. "The Indies and Indochina," wrote Rupert Emerson, "will need Western political and economic assistance for a long period to come, and would be likely to seek it from states with which they have had long association if that association is regarded as being friendly in character." [168]

The Europeanists who still molded the basic contours of America's Southeast Asia policy grasped the wisdom of Emerson's analysis. They identified U.S. security interests with the well-being of the West European democracies, and they did not want to see Western influence excised from Southeast Asia. In peacetime, the region was an important supplier of raw materials and an important source of investment earnings to Europeans. In wartime, the area's resources, harbors, and food had proven indispensable to the adversary. Grew, Dunn, and Matthews, therefore, could not be indifferent to the nationalist aspirations that were emerging in Asia. They wanted to encourage the peoples of Southeast Asia to develop "autonomous, democratic self-rule in close, willing association with major Western powers. . . . If this policy is not followed, the millions who live in that area may well embrace ideologies contrary to our own—or ultimately develop a pan-Asiatic movement against the Western world." [169] The preferred policy, in the words of the Office of Strategic Services, was to "encourage the liberalization of the [colonial] regimes in order the better to maintain them, and to check Soviet influence in the stimulation of the colonial revolt." [170] There was, however, little evidence that the Kremlin was fomenting revolt; Stalin displayed hardly any interest in developments in Southeast Asia.[171] But U.S. officials never doubted that if European influence were expunged from the area, the Soviets would benefit, if only because it would further weaken West European economies and governments.[172]

Orderly decolonization was the key to co-opting nationalist movements, preserving Western influence in Southeast Asia, and promoting American security interests. U.S. officials wanted European governments to emulate the policies that the United States was following in the Philippines. America's Asian colony would be granted its independence in 1946, but the United States was negotiating base privileges and economic arrangements that would preserve American influence and safeguard American interests. Extensive ties were being reestablished with members of the prewar Filipino elite, even with many of those men who had collaborated with the Japanese. The Europeans had the responsibility to forge similar relationships with moderate nationalists in their own colonies.[173]

The United States would monitor developments carefully. Washington had no desire to assume responsibility for the region, but neither did it want to see Southeast Asia relinquished from friendly hands into the grasp of an adversary, whether it be the Kremlin or some unidentifiable pan-Asian movement. Officials in the offices of European and Far Eastern affairs were not disputing whether the retention of Southeast Asia within a Western orbit was a security interest of the United States; they were debating tactics and priorities.

The Atomic Monopoly

As U.S. officials moved to contain Soviet influence and buttress the position of the West European democracies, they pondered the meaning, significance, and utility of atomic weapons. The atomic bomb, Harriman wrote Byrnes, offset the power of the Red Army, rekindled Russian insecurity, and created a siege mentality. Stimson also believed that, if atomic weapons were kept "rather ostentatiously on our hip," Soviet-U.S. relations might be irretrievably embittered. He pressed Truman to open discussions with the Russians on atomic weapons. Patterson and Acheson supported Stimson. In their view the Soviets were certain to develop the bomb, perhaps in four or five years, so if efforts were not made immediately to exchange scientific information and develop some form of international control of atomic energy, an ominous atomic arms race would occur. They agreed with Stimson that secrecy would exacerbate Soviet-U.S. relations and diminish chances of resolving other vital issues.[174]

Forrestal and other cabinet members disagreed with this approach, as did Leahy and the JCS. They feared any demarche to the Soviets. They believed that U.S. urban and industrial areas were especially vulnerable to atomic attack. The Soviet Union, with its closed society, dictatorial rule, and "oriental" mind, was apt to use the bomb in a surprise attack once it had such a weapon at its disposal.[175]

Truman decided to follow the advice proffered by Stimson, Acheson, and Patterson. After Secretary of State Byrnes realized at the London foreign ministers' conference that the bomb could not be used easily as a club to elicit concessions, he became the leading proponent of international control. But such control had to be on terms that did not jeopardize the U.S. monopoly. The real secret of the bomb, as Acheson, Patterson, and presidential scientific adviser Vannevar Bush argued, rested in American engineering and manufacturing know-how rather than in theoretical knowledge. Truman made it clear from the outset that he did not intend to share this technological information.[176]

When Truman met with the prime ministers of Canada and Britain in mid-November 1945, the president introduced the U.S. approach to international control. The first step would be an exchange of basic scientific information. No sharing of industrial applications would take place before "effective, reciprocal, and enforceable safeguards" were devised. The three heads of government supported the creation of a U.N. commission. International control would take place by stages; the successful completion of one stage would constitute the indispensable prerequisite to the next stage.[177] Before the United States would relinquish its atomic monopoly, the U.S. government demanded effective international control over the development of atomic energy in other nations.

Preparing for the Moscow conference in December, Byrnes contemplated deviating from this approach in order to win Soviet goodwill and to make headway in other areas. Officials in the Pentagon objected. So did Senators Vandenberg and Brien McMahon, chairman of the Joint Committee on Atomic Energy. Their influence was decisive. They went to the White House and protested to Truman. They insisted that Russia open itself up and permit inspection. Acheson assured the senators that Byrnes contemplated nothing more than exchanges of theoretical knowledge, and Truman emphasized that he would never disclose information regarding the bomb until safeguards and inspection methods had been arranged.[178]

The president wanted to perpetuate America's atomic monopoly, at least until the raw materials and production capabilities of other nations were put under effective international control.[179] This viewpoint, however, did not dictate a rapid buildup of the nation's atomic arsenal. During 1945 and 1946 there were only a handful of bombs in the U.S. stockpile. The JCS was uncertain about the role of atomic weapons in postwar strategy. The president himself said he did not know how many weapons existed.[180]

Still, the bomb conveyed an enormous sense of power. U.S. officials realized that, so long as they possessed it and others did not, they were in a truly unique position. The bomb cast enormous shadows over the international system. As will become apparent in the chapters that follow, nations who possessed it could afford to take risks that others could not. Consequently, it was not at all surprising that the Soviets moved swiftly to break the American monopoly. The Kremlin, Acheson emphasized in September, "must and will exert every energy to restore the loss of power which this discovery has produced." Indeed Stalin had already ordered an acceleration of the Russian atomic program. No great nation could do otherwise. The British, too, realized that their influence in international affairs would erode and their interests become more vulnerable if they were dependent on the Americans. In the autumn of 1945, they moved ahead with their own atomic energy program.[181]

Security and Cooperation

Buoyed by their economic preponderance, strategic superiority, and atomic monopoly, U.S. officials had no desire, no intention, and no need to enter into an arms race. No one expected the Soviets to engage in conflict, at least not in the short run. Top civilian officials and military planners in the United States and Great Britain agreed that the Soviet Union was too backward economically, too badly hurt by the Nazis, and too demoralized to contemplate war for a long time.[182] During late 1945, moreover, intelligence reports indicated that Soviet forces were rapidly demobilizing.[183]

It is true, of course, that Americans were demobilizing even more swiftly. One ought not conclude from this fact that American power was a "hollow threat." [184] Certainly U.S. officials at the time, no matter how much they remonstrated about demobilization, did not think that it was hollow. If, for example, the unimaginable had occurred and war had erupted, the United States had thousands of strategic bombers with which to strike the Soviet Union. The raids could be launched from hundreds of airfields and bases that were still in American hands or under American supervision in late 1945. Even if Soviet armies overran Western Europe, they would annex an area that was entirely dependent on external sources of food and fuel. In its existing state and under conditions of actual conflict, Western Europe could not add significantly to Soviet war capabilities. Still unable to inflict damage on the United States, the Soviets would be the target of merciless air raids. The people of Dresden and Tokyo knew that atomic bombs were not the only weapons that wrought devastation and horror. If war persisted, however, those new weapons, too, would rain upon the Soviet Union in ever increasing numbers. The United States, after all, had the knowledge, wherewithal, and ability to make the bombs. The Soviets did not.[185]

The Soviet threat would become formidable only if the Kremlin co-opted Japanese or German power, capitalized on the strength of European Communist parties, and exploited revolutionary nationalist unrest in Asia. U.S. officials, therefore, realized that their security interests stretched across the globe and required a favorable configuration of power on the Eurasian land mass. They wanted to resist Soviet expansion in Western Europe, the Middle East, and Northeast Asia. They wanted control over western Germany and all of Japan. They wanted to contain the Communist left in France, Italy, Greece, Korea, and China. They wanted to modify traditional imperial practices, co-opt the forces of revolutionary nationalism, and insure Western control of the underdeveloped world. Should these efforts falter, they also wanted to be able to project U.S. power and defend in depth. Hence they needed overseas bases, hegemony over the sea and air approaches to the Western Hemisphere, and strategic predominance in North and South America.

There were few divisions between American policymakers over U.S. national security objectives. State Department views did not differ significantly from those in the War or Navy departments. Nor were there important cleavages over goals between military officers and civilian authorities in the Pentagon. Disputes were emerging, but they focused on tactics and priorities, not objectives. A most noteworthy development pertained to the apprehension of strategic planners that goals were exceeding capabilities. So extensive were American interests that military planners wanted to know which were vital, which were worth fighting for, which necessitated the insertion of military forces. They explicitly alluded not to European appeasement practices in the 1930's but to America's Far East policies in 1940–41, when in their view civilian policymakers defined vital interests beyond American capabilities, thereby inviting a surprise attack on Pearl Harbor. The major danger of war inhered in the volatility of the international environment and in the penchant of civilian officials to define U.S. interests too broadly.[186]

Domestic considerations engendered the gap between means and ends. Americans wanted to bring their boys home, cut taxes, and focus on internal priorities. Truman wanted to achieve U.S. security objectives on the cheap. He did not want Americans to bear the indirect burden of reparation transfers; he did not want to station U.S. troops in Europe indefinitely; and he did not want to become embroiled in European efforts to restore their colonial authority. Ideally, he wanted others to bear the costs and undertake the policies that would prove compatible with American security needs. Let Russia, for example, wait to receive reparations until German coal resuscitated the European economy. Let Britain shoulder the costs of restoring financial and commercial multilateralism. Let Britain, too, bear the military burden of containing Russian influence in areas that traditionally fell within England's primary interest—for example, in Western Europe and the Middle East. Let the West Europeans reform their empires, co-opt the nationalist movements, and preserve Southeast Asia for the well-being of the Western world. Wherever it could, the United States preferred to stay in the background, buttressing the efforts of others rather than incurring primary responsibilities of its own. If others could not do the job, however, the United States would fill the void both financially and militarily. So although American loans and assistance were not sufficient to meet European wishes, they sufficed to get prospective allies through the difficult transition from war to peace. Although the United States demobilized rapidly, the Truman administration found enough men to make a show of force in Trieste, to insert troops into Korea, to deploy Marines to northern China, to control the occupation of Japan, and to maintain order in the U.S. zones in Germany and Austria.

U.S. officials wanted peace and cooperation. The only caveat was that peace and cooperation had to be on terms that comported with their security objectives. Cooperation, yes—provided that the Soviets not interfere with U.S. base requirements or seek bases of their own in the Dardanelles, the Dodecanese, or Tripolitania. Cooperation, yes—provided that the Soviets accept American domination of Japan and Western control of the Ruhr/Rhine industrial complex. Cooperation—provided that the Kremlin not support the Communists in Greece, Italy, and France and that it restrain Tito in Venezia Giulia; provided that the Soviets evacuate their troops from Manchuria, cooperate with Chiang, and accept the temporary presence of U.S. Marines in north China; provided that the Soviets withdraw from northern Iran and acquiesce to British predominance in the Persian Gulf and American influence in Saudi Arabia; and provided that the Soviets permit international control of their atomic energy facilities prior to American relinquishment of its atomic monopoly. Not only cooperation but perhaps even assistance, provided that the Soviets open up Eastern Europe, allow self-government, and assent to Western trade and investment.

U.S. policymakers would not have characterized their diplomacy in this manner. They perceived their actions as prudent and restrained efforts to apply the geopolitical and strategic lessons of World War II and the economic and financial lessons of the interwar years. The president and his advisers expected the men in the Kremlin to interpret American behavior as Americans intended it. They were unwilling, however, to accept Soviet explanations of Russian behavior, even when the latter's actions resembled those of the United States, for example, in their pursuit of bases. As Stimson's Army planners so aptly put it, this was a "logical illogicality" based on Americans' perception of their own innocence and on their penchant to universalize the benefits of their own security requirements.[187]

As is often the case with many nations, U.S. officials were unable to see the extent to which the position and power of their own country made it a potential menace to others.[188] The Soviets, still seeking to maintain friendly ties (on their terms) with the United States, regarded American (and British) actions as potentially dangerous. The United States, after all, was establishing a military presence in Northeast Asia, ensconcing itself in Saudi Arabia, supporting the British in Iran, intervening in the Adriatic (Trieste), asserting a substantial influence in Germany, negotiating for base rights and air transit privileges far from American shores, and maneuvering to maintain its atomic monopoly as long as possible. The Americans might have had no evil intent, but their actions could seriously endanger the well-being of the Soviet Union should relations deteriorate, should Soviet reconstruction plans falter, or should the immense vacuums of power that surrounded Russia be filled by the recovery of old enemies or by the emergence of new forces hostile to the Kremlin. "Our victory in the war," Nikita Khrushchev remembered, "did not stop him [Stalin] from trembling inside." In contrast, Soviet leaders viewed their own actions, beyond the periphery of their armies of occupation, as restrained. After all, they advised West European Communists to forgo revolutionary action, bowed to the American reparations plan for Germany, cautioned Tito to restrain himself, recognized Chiang's government in China, welcomed the Americans into South Korea, and acceded to U.S. domination of Japan. Their actions in Eastern Europe, so unnerving to the Americans, were regarded by themselves as entirely necessary and justifiable based on the lessons they had learned from their own recent and horrifying experiences.[189]

Neither the Americans nor the Soviets sought to harm the other in 1945. But each side, in pursuit of its security interests, took steps that aroused the other's apprehensions. Moreover, the protests that each country's actions evoked from the other fueled the cycle of distrust as neither could comprehend the fears of the other, perceiving its own actions as defensive. Herein rests the classic security dilemma. Postulating a state of international anarchy—and, given world conditions in 1945, this was much more than a theoretical construct—the security dilemma assumes that each country's quest for security raises the anxieties of a prospective adversary, provokes countermeasures, and results in less security for everyone.[190]

It is not easy to see how the Americans and Soviets (and British) could have escaped from the security dilemma after World War II. But in view of the over-whelming power of the United States and in view of the relative restraint exhibited by the Kremlin *outside its immediate periphery*, U.S. officials might have displayed more tolerance for risk. The terms laid out by the Truman administration for a cooperative relationship were clearly skewed to sustain America's preponderant position in the international system. Seeing ominous portents in Eastern Europe, uncertain of Soviet intentions elsewhere, and recollecting the lessons of appeasement in the 1930's, U.S. officials did not want to repeat the mistakes of the recent past or compromise vital security interests. Conscious of their superior power, they sought to overcome a frightening set of systemic developments (and an exasperating matrix of domestic constraints). Apart from Eastern Europe, they chose to contain and deter the Russians rather than to reassure and placate them, thereby accentuating possibilities for a spiraling cycle of mistrust. Although their calculations were prudent, they were not necessarily wise, if, as seems likely, Soviet aims were more limited than many U.S. and British officials suspected.

The Cold War Begins,
January-November 1946

I n early 1946, U.S. officials defined the Soviet Union as the enemy. Faced with intractable problems abroad and exasperating constraints at home, they grew worried and angry. Rather than dwell on the vacuums of power in Germany and Japan, rather than focus on the popular desire for reform and recovery throughout Europe, rather than emphasize the indigenous sources of civil strife in Asia, and rather than identify with revolutionary nationalism in the Third World, they latched onto an interpretation of international developments that placed blame and responsibility on the Kremlin. It soon became commonplace to charge that Stalin and his comrades sought world domination. George F. Kennan, the American chargé d'affaires in Moscow, did this in his famous "long telegram"; State Department and Pentagon analysts did this in their strategic guidelines for U.S. war plans; and Clark Clifford and George Elsey, Truman's White House aides, did the same in writing their secret report on Soviet foreign policy.[1]

As this chapter will illustrate, Truman welcomed this mode of thinking.[2] By simplifying the threat, depicting the world in bipolar terms, and naming the Soviet Union as an ideological enemy, the president and his advisers found it easier to resolve the ambiguities in the international situation and to take the necessary steps to enhance U.S. security interests. Domestically, sharp images and tough rhetoric quieted allegations of appeasement from political opponents and helped to mobilize congressional and public backing for measures and expenditures that otherwise might not have been forthcoming. Internationally, once top officials identified the Kremlin as a totalitarian foe akin to Nazi Germany, they felt more leeway and greater incentive to launch the initiatives that were designed to thwart the growth of Soviet power in peacetime and to overwhelm it in wartime, should the latter prove necessary.

Systemic Concerns

It is hard to overstate how portentous the international situation appeared to U.S. officials in early 1946. International economic problems proliferated. Turmoil and unrest grew. Communist support mounted. When Undersecretary of State Acheson testified in behalf of the British loan on 6 March, he painted a bleak picture: "The commercial and financial situation of the world is worse than any of us thought a year ago it would be. Destruction is more complete, hunger more acute, exhaustion more widespread than anyone then realized. What might have become passed off as prophecies have become stark facts." [3]

Lest such statements be dismissed as the necessary hyperbole to win Senate approval of the Anglo-American financial agreement, one should keep in mind that the same language was used in secret memoranda among top officials and in their conversations with one another. At cabinet meetings, policymakers talked of the desperate food situation in Western Europe and Japan. "No greater problem faces the world than to prevent . . . widespread starvation in Europe," Navy Secretary Forrestal wrote the president. Unless the United States shipped more grain and meat abroad, Acheson warned Truman, "general disorder and political upheaval" will occur and "mass starvation will undoubtedly develop." "More people," the president acknowledged, "face starvation and even actual death . . . than in any war year and perhaps more than in all the war years combined." [4]

In areas of the greatest importance, conditions worsened and problems abounded. In Germany, General Clay became bogged down in intractable talks over the level of industry, reparations, and economic unification. While the military governors deliberated, the food situation turned desperate. Rations were cut to 1,000 calories per day in the British zone and to 1,160 in the U.S. zone, barely enough to keep people alive, let alone to prevent disease and unrest. "The seriousness of this situation cannot be overemphasized," Clay informed Washington.[5]

Worse yet, the German Communists sought to capitalize on the discontent. In February they began championing German unification. Assured of Soviet backing in the eastern zone, they maneuvered for support in the western zones. Clay feared they would achieve much success. So did Robert Murphy, Clay's State Department political adviser. The Soviets, Murphy informed his superiors at Foggy Bottom, were scheming to gain the confidence of the German people and to establish the basis for "a close affiliation between a new German Reich and the USSR." "We cannot allow this to go on," H. Freeman Matthews wrote the secretary of state.[6]

But, in fact, State Department officials had to continue to react carefully to events in Germany because of developments in France. In January, General de Gaulle resigned, transforming the political situation in that country. The three parties—the Communists, the Socialists, and the Mouvement républicain populaire (MRP)—divided nineteen ministries among themselves. The Communists took six of them.[7] Their march to power seemed more likely than ever before. British foreign secretary Ernest Bevin lamented "the imminent Sovietization of France and the extension of Russian power to the channel."[8] Jefferson Caffery, the U.S. ambassador in Paris, was not quite so pessimistic, but he, too, reported that the average Frenchman was cold, hungry, and disillusioned. Without additional financial assistance, the situation could unravel in ominous ways. Undersecretary of State Clayton agreed, noting it would be a political "catastrophe" to oppose a loan.[9] Fears of a Communist coup even filtered into the White House, where top U.S. officials monitored developments inside France with special care.[10]

Along the periphery of the industrial core, conditions were not much more auspicious. In North Africa, there were nationalist rumblings. In Egypt, mobs attacked the British embassy and demanded England's evacuation of the Cairo-Suez base. In Palestine, Arabs and Jews clashed when Zionists championed increased immigration and an independent state. In Southeast Asia, the French and Dutch were locked in a series of fruitless negotiations with Vietnamese and Indonesian nationalists. In Korea, rightist groups forced the Americans to backtrack on the idea of trusteeship and clamored for independence. In China, General Marshall experienced some dramatic initial successes, arranging a cease-fire between the Communists and the Nationalists and establishing a framework for political dialogue and governmental reform. But when he returned to Washington to consult with the president and when the Soviets finally began to withdraw from northern Manchuria in mid-March, fighting erupted once again.

These developments within the international system presented the Kremlin with tempting opportunities. Whether Stalin would seek to capitalize on them was uncertain. He stood above the factional wrangling in the Kremlin, and more than anyone else he determined the course of Soviet behavior. Domestically, he was a man of monstrous cruelty. But in the conduct of diplomacy, Stalin was more circumspect. He was devious yet cautious, opportunistic yet prudent, ideological yet pragmatic. He saw immense possibilities for Soviet aggrandizement occasioned by the vacuums of power left by the war; yet he also recognized potential threats and the many imponderables that lay ahead. He assumed that cyclical economic setbacks and imperialist rivalries would weaken the capitalist West. Yet he grasped that, for the indefinite future, the correlations of strength were incalculably in America's favor. Provocative action on his part, moreover, might accentuate American suspicions, trigger the security dilemma, and ensconce American power on his immediate periphery: in southern Korea, northern China, Japan, Iran or Turkey, and, of course, western Germany. In contrast, restraint might encourage American withdrawal from the perimeter of the Soviet Union, elicit American financial aid, foster the collection of reparations, expedite domestic recovery, and perhaps even permit the Soviets to maneuver their way diplomatically and economically into western Germany, Manchuria, and Iran. In other words, Stalin could see that Soviet self-interest might be reconcilable with an entente or detente with the United States.

Much would depend on the terms of cooperation, on developments abroad, on the domestic requirements of his regime, and on the dynamics of the internal wrangling and machinations of his lieutenants.[11]

On 9 February 1946, Stalin delivered a celebrated public address. World War II, Stalin said, had its origins in the economic troubles of monopoly capitalism. Periodic crises and struggles for markets, raw materials, and investment opportunities divided the capitalist world into hostile camps. War followed. In these passages, Stalin departed sharply from his wartime disavowal of ideological cant. But then he went on to say that World War II was unique: it was an antifascist war from the very beginning. For the people of the Soviet Union, moreover, "this war was the most cruel and hard of all wars ever experienced in the history of our motherland." Yet "we, together with our allies, were the victors." The war, therefore, meant "that the Soviet social system" had "proved its complete vitality." These expansive introductory remarks enabled Stalin to present a long defense of his policies in the 1920's and 1930's. He emphasized that rapid industrialization and collectivization created the economic infrastructure enabling Soviet Russia to defeat Nazi aggression. He concluded with a few paragraphs outlining future plans. Devastated areas would be reconstructed, prewar levels of production would be restored, and a great leap forward in industrial output would occur. Special attention would be focused on producing goods for mass consumption and on raising living standards. For the long term, he intended to triple overall production, to accelerate the output of iron ore, steel, coal, and oil, and to promote the advancement of science so that it would "surpass" the achievements in foreign lands. "Only under such conditions will our country be insured against any eventuality." It would take at least three five-year plans, maybe more.[12]

Neither Stalin's speech nor his actions were as threatening as some U.S. officials thought they were.[13] But for policymakers already predisposed to fear the worst, the ideological tone of the address confirmed that Stalin would, if he could, exploit systemic developments, vacuums of power, and the popularity of local Communist parties to serve the Kremlin's selfish interests. Signs of Soviet aggressiveness, therefore, achieved a heightened salience, and conflicting evidence was dismissed.[14] There certainly was much to worry about. In Poland, Romania, and Hungary, small and unpopular Communist minorities were consolidating their power and were receiving military aid, officer training, and strategic guarantees from the Soviet government. In Manchuria, Russian troops did not leave on the first of February, as Stalin had indicated they would, and Soviet diplomats pressed Chiang Kai-shek to accept joint ownership of Manchurian mines and industries. Much the same occurred in northern Iran, where Soviet forces continued to support autonomous movements and where Stalin himself demanded oil concessions. When the Iranians protested at the first meeting of the U.N. General Assembly, Soviet foreign minister Molotov turned against the British, whom he held responsible for Iran's defiant behavior, and assailed their imperialist policies. Not only did the Soviets rupture the appearance of great power cooperation in the United Nations, but they also isolated themselves from the reality of international economic cooperation. Their rejection of the Bretton Woods agreements illustrated their penchant for a national-istic, independent, and autarkic course of economic development. If all this was not enough to dispel notions of Soviet goodwill, the Canadian government exposed the Russians' atomic spy ring in mid-February, raising profound questions about their intentions.[15]

Domestic Problems

Systemic disintegration and Soviet opportunism sent shock waves through Washing-ton. In turn, administrative disarray and domestic constraints compounded policy-makers' sense of danger. Officials in Washington could not sort out priorities among their foreign policy goals and could not choose between domestic and international objectives. The president failed to organize his administration effectively: his ad-visers bickered among themselves, antagonized influential legislators, and forfeited leadership to powerful proconsuls abroad. Their inability to close the gap between the means and ends of U.S. foreign policy engendered widespread criticism and created opportunities for partisan attacks and internal divisions.

After Secretary of State Byrnes returned from the Moscow conference, his in-fluence with Truman was never quite the same. The historian Robert Messer has vividly described how Byrnes stayed on as secretary of state for another year but no longer had the same freedom to maneuver as he had been given during the summer and fall of 1945. Truman seized command, but he exercised little leadership. He had neither the time nor the inclination to focus on foreign policy developments; instead, he turned his attention to prices, wages, and budgetary problems. Nobody on his White House staff was equipped to fill the void; nobody was assigned respon-sibility to coordinate political-military policies. Clark Clifford gradually stepped in. But he was then a novice in matters of foreign and defense policies, and at first he relied considerably on Admiral William Leahy's advice.[16]

Byrnes grasped the changing situation. If his critics thought he had been too compromising, he was ready to take a harder line.[17] Almost immediately, however, he departed for London for the opening session of the United Nations. The day-to-day business of foreign policy was left in the hands of Acheson. The undersecretary of state, however, was aware of the personal rift between Truman and Byrnes and moved cautiously. His own subordinates, Acheson knew, were demoralized by Byrnes's contempt for professional diplomats and by Ambassador Patrick Hurley's allegations that foreign service officers with Communist leanings had undermined his policies in China. Acheson's own credibility was shaken when he denied pub-licly that the Kuriles had been handed over to the Soviet Union at Yalta, only to be corrected by Soviet release of the relevant portion of the secret Far East protocol. He was frustrated even more by the deeply ingrained regionalism within the State

Department. This parochialism stymied overall planning, intelligence gathering, and priority setting at a time when foreign service officers themselves could not agree on how to deal with the Kremlin's actions in Eastern Europe.[18]

Decisionmaking responsibility, therefore, lodged itself in the field, where Mac-Arthur in Japan, Clay in Germany, Hodge in Korea, and Marshall in China played critical roles. Although Marshall sometimes relied on Acheson, and Clay on Byrnes, all these generals distrusted the foreign service officers who staffed the middle echelons of the State Department. For support and encouragement, they looked to civilian leaders in the War Department and to their fellow officers in the Army's Plans and Operations and Civil Affairs divisions. In the absence of strong leadership from the top, the division of responsibility between proconsuls abroad, the State Department, and the War Department remained a serious impediment to effective decisionmaking. Recognizing this problem, Acheson lured General John Hilldring to Foggy Bottom to become assistant secretary of state for occupation affairs. But the problem persisted.[19]

Interdepartmental coordination remained unsatisfactory and engendered acrimony. On the lower levels of the bureaucracy, there were extensive day-to-day contacts between branches of the Army and particular offices within the State Department. But no one was really pleased with the quality of military-civilian collaboration.[20] Army, Navy, and Air Force planners continued to ridicule the State Department's apparent indifference to the gulf between U.S. goals and capabilities. "It is imperative," insisted Admiral M. B. Gardner, "that the political authorities state definitely at which point the military will have to support their national policies." [21] But when Pentagon officials reviewed a comprehensive, 106-page State Department report on the nation's foreign policy, their concerns were not allayed. Forrestal, Assistant Secretary of the Navy John L. Sullivan, and Assistant Secretary of War Howard C. Petersen reproached the State Department for taking a piecemeal approach, focusing too much on individual countries, and giving insufficient attention to the Soviet Union. They wanted a more unified and cohesive assessment that clearly defined goals, delineated priorities, and elucidated means.[22]

Defense officials, however, were not able to get their own house in order. In early 1946 interservice rivalries over the unification of the armed services and the establishment of an independent air force escalated. Forrestal and Secretary of War Patterson could not overcome their differences. The Navy simply would not accept a tightly unified defense department and a single chief of staff that jeopardized its autonomy. Army Air Force generals felt betrayed that they could not implement their plans for a force structure of 70 groups. Truman summoned the Pentagon's civilian and military leaders to the White House at the end of February and ordered them to resolve their disputes and follow his lead. But they did not.[23]

At top-level meetings, Forrestal and Patterson lamented the pace of demobilization. Far from disagreeing, Byrnes and Acheson said the erosion of U.S. military strength was undermining their foreign policy. Truman concurred.[24] But he did nothing to alter the basic trends. He was committed to reducing the deficit, balancing the budget, and stifling inflation at a time when his national security objectives required ever larger monetary commitments for relief and recovery abroad as well as for prudent defense expenditures at home. He pleaded with the Congress to approve the $3.75 billion loan to Britain and to expand the lending authority of the Export-Import Bank by another $1.25 billion. But the legislative branch acted slowly.[25]

The Republicans smelled victory in the approaching 1946 congressional elections. Hurley's allegations, evidence of atomic espionage, and news of Roosevelt's secret dealings at Yalta put the administration on the defensive. Secretary of State Byrnes continued to exacerbate partisan wounds by failing to consult sufficiently with Republican leaders like John Foster Dulles and Arthur Vandenberg. Vandenberg had deep anti-Soviet feelings from the outset, stimulated in part by the East European ethnic makeup of his home state, Michigan. Republican leaders were tempted to assail the Truman administration and to denounce the Soviet Union without assuming any responsibility for constructive solutions. Indeed, many Republicans demanded further cuts in expenditures and taxes that would exacerbate the gap between means and ends. But consistency was not an obligation of an opposition party out of power. On 27 February, Vandenberg rose in the Senate and delivered a major address. What is Russia up to now? he asked.[26]

Truman felt beleaguered. Foreign countries needed additional assistance, but the Congress would not allot it; the Joint Chiefs of Staff (JCS) demanded more money, but the Budget Bureau could not find it; the civilian secretaries pleaded for a slowdown in demobilization, but the public would not tolerate it. Truman was harassed by Republican partisans, intransigent unions, and selfish corporations. He could not stop prices from spiraling and workers from striking. He was irritated with Byrnes, irked by Forrestal, and angered by the rivalries between the military services. At the end of February, Harold Smith, the president's budget director, found Truman completely bogged down, exasperated with his staff arrangements, and unable to cope with mounting problems and conflicting goals.[27]

Identifying the Enemy

Truman and Vandenberg were ahead of public opinion. When queried, the number of people saying that the United States could trust Russia declined from an all-time high of 55 percent in March 1945 to 35 percent in March 1946.[28] But most Americans were not concerned with international affairs. In October 1945 only 7 percent of the people considered foreign problems to be of vital importance. This figure rose to 21 percent in February 1946 and then fell back to 11 percent in June.[29]

Public attitudes were shaped by elite opinion. Despite occasional congressional and senatorial denunciations of Soviet behavior, and despite the entrenched suspicions about the Kremlin's intentions, the elite was not yet ready to acknowledge the disintegration of the great wartime coalition. The public-attitudes branch of the State Department monitored editorials in 125 newspapers, assessed the articles of leading columnists, reviewed the statements of political leaders, and studied the resolutions of private religious, philanthropic, and economic organizations. Prior to Vandenberg's speech of 27 February, elite attitudes toward Russia were divided. Joseph and Stewart Alsop, Constantine Brown, and Dorothy Thompson advocated a firm policy, but they acknowledged that the public might not want it. Even the reports on Stalin's election speech in early February did not evoke a widespread outcry for a tougher stand. Ann McCormick, Eric Sevareid, Bill Costello, and the *Washington Post* called it disturbing; *Time* magazine labeled it the most "warlike pronouncement uttered by any statesman since V-J day." But other reactions were much more restrained. The *New York Herald Tribune*, the *Christian Science Monitor*, the *Kansas City Star*, the *Des Moines Register*, and the *St. Louis Post-Dispatch* (among others) contested Walter Lippmann's claim that the speech portended an armaments race. The editors of *Business Week* re-read Stalin's remarks and found little that was alarming. Stalin's speech, they concluded, was no more threatening than Truman's Navy Day address the previous October.[30]

Truman and his advisers wanted to mold elite opinion and shape public attitudes.[31] The favorable response to Vandenberg's strong statement of 27 February confirmed suspicions that the Republicans might be willing and able to use foreign policy issues for partisan advantage.[32] More fundamentally, however, officials in the Truman administration were profoundly worried about prospective changes in the international system. They were concerned about the spread of bilateral trade agreements and autarkical practices among friends and foes. They were apprehensive that the Export-Import Bank would not have sufficient funds to aid needy countries like France, Italy, Greece, and Saudi Arabia. The officials were disheartened by the criticism directed at the British loan agreement. And, most of all, they were frightened by famine conditions, power vacuums, Communist political gains, and Soviet probes.[33]

On the day of Vandenberg's speech, Truman told Byrnes to stiffen up and make no concessions to the Russians. The president wanted his secretary of state to speak out in behalf of the administration's objectives and to parry the senator's implicit criticism of official policy. Byrnes did so the following day.[34] Yet even before Vandenberg's speech and Byrnes's rejoinder, Truman and his advisers sought ways to cohere their own thinking, gain the initiative, mold public opinion, and garner funds from a recalcitrant Congress.

Winston Churchill's visit to the United States provided the administration with an opportunity to launch a public relations and diplomatic offensive. On 10 February the former British prime minister spent several hours at the White House discussing his forthcoming address at Westminster College in Fulton, Missouri. With the president sitting by his side, Churchill planned to warn the world against Soviet intentions and to make a plea for Anglo-American military collaboration.

The president was altogether pleased. Churchill was undoubtedly the most popular foreigner in America. Despite a good deal of Anglophobic feeling in the United States, no one could better frame the issues and orient the debate than the eloquent orator from across the Atlantic. The president, Leahy recorded in his diary, wanted very much to toughen American policy.[35]

So did George Kennan, the chargé d'affaires in the U.S. embassy in Moscow. Kennan was one of the most astute Kremlinologists in the foreign service. He had been in Russia in the mid-1930's and had witnessed the horror of Stalin's purges and the dismal aftermath of agricultural collectivization. He returned to Moscow in 1945 and grew distraught as his cables were ignored. He believed that U.S. policy lacked direction and purposefulness. So disconsolate was Kennan that he was planning retirement. When asked by his superiors in the State Department to evaluate recent Soviet policy, he tackled the assignment with gusto, perhaps seeing it as his last, best effort to influence Washington.[36]

Kennan's 8,000-word telegram of 22 February was a reiteration of many of the points he had been arguing for quite some time. But now he integrated them into a comprehensive critique of Soviet foreign policy. What was particularly significant was his contention that one could not negotiate with or placate Soviet rulers. Motivated by traditional Russian insecurities and influenced by Marxist-Leninist dogma, Soviet leaders exploited the themes of capitalist encirclement and foreign hostility in order to justify and preserve their totalitarian rule at home. The Kremlin would seek to expand everywhere, taking advantage of all opportunities and exploiting every weakness and vulnerability in the West. But while Soviet leaders were impervious to the logic of reason, they were responsive to manifestations of force. Hence American officials need not despair. Fundamentally, Soviet Russia was weak; its rulers would retreat when faced with determination. The U.S. government, therefore, had to mobilize its energies, plan intelligently, educate its citizenry, tackle key problems, and confront the future with courage.[37]

Kennan's analysis was appealing because it provided a unifying theme to U.S. foreign policy. Rather than tackle deep-seated problems in disparate parts of the globe, Kennan urged policymakers to view Soviet Russia as their enemy and to approach all other issues from the viewpoint of competition with the Kremlin. Moreover, Kennan disavowed all legitimacy to Soviet policies and portrayed Russian fears and insecurities as irrational. Policymakers need not agonize over the problems of accommodating legitimate Soviet interests; there were none. Policymakers need not scrutinize avenues for compromise; it was futile. Policymakers need not be dismayed by Soviet power; the Kremlin was a paper tiger. "I was conscious," he wrote a year later, "of the weakness of the Russian position, of the slenderness of the means with which they operated, of the ease with which they could be held and pushed back."[38]

Kennan said very little about U.S. objectives, tactics, and capabilities. His "long telegram" was an analysis of Soviet policy based on a psychological/ideological interpretation of Russian motivations. His message was that Stalinist Russia was a totalitarian regime bent on expansion. He prescribed little, said nothing about priorities, and scarcely mentioned American interests, except the need to contain Soviet power.[39]

Kennan's telegram circulated widely throughout the government. During the last days of February, Harriman showed it to Forrestal. The secretary of the Navy had been brooding over Soviet actions and pondering Soviet motives for quite some time. For Forrestal, Kennan's message forever engraved the Nazi totalitarian image onto Soviet foreign policy. Forrestal distributed many copies of Kennan's telegram to friends and subordinates.[40] At the same time, State Department officials showed it to planners in the War Department and urged that it be scrutinized by the Army's top brass.[41] Everywhere it was greeted with enthusiasm. Kennan's unambiguous appraisal of Soviet intentions and motives, his didactic tone, and his self-confident belief in the West's potential superiority and the Kremlin's inherent weaknesses commanded attention.

Less than two weeks after Kennan's telegram was received in Washington, Churchill said publicly what the professional diplomat wrote privately. Over Eurasia hovered Soviet power, bent on totalitarian expansion. "From Stettin in the Baltic to Trieste in the Adriatic, an iron curtain has descended across the continent." Almost everywhere Communist parties endangered "Christian civilization." Police governments squashed true democracy. Churchill, however, went further than Kennan. He boldly called for an Anglo-Saxon military alliance, for joint strategic planning, for a sharing of overseas bases, and for standardization of weapons.[42]

Churchill's speech had a profound impact at home and abroad. Like Kennan, he simplified the threat, framed it in ideological terms, and merged the specter of Soviet expansionism and Communist subversion. He did not dwell on the problems of relief, recovery, reconversion, and revolutionary nationalism. These problems loomed large only because they could be exploited by a nefarious state intent on extinguishing freedom and gaining hegemony. Americans reacted negatively to Churchill's call for a military alliance. However, his warning of a totalitarian menace intent on geopolitical domination resonated deeply in their psyches. Had he not been right about Nazi Germany? Was it not prudent to stop a totalitarian foe before the enemy gained control of resources, industrial infrastructure, and forward bases that might make it unbeatable?[43]

Churchill's speech, according to the historian Fraser Harbutt, accomplished precisely what the administration wanted: it accelerated a widespread hostility to the Soviet Union. Changing perceptions of the Kremlin permitted Truman and his advisers to go on the offensive. It relieved them of the need to reconcile their geopolitical and economic goals with the security imperatives of the Soviet Union. It enabled them to exploit the shadows of a Red menace to push the British loan through Congress. It undergirded their mounting efforts to ship food and fuel to the occupied areas. Most of all, it strengthened their determination to contain Soviet power on the Russian periphery. On the very day that Churchill delivered his address at Westminster College, the State Department sent notes to the Kremlin demanding explanations for its behavior in Manchuria, Eastern Europe, and Iran.[44] This diplomatic offensive was a response to the overwhelming sense of vulnerability—strategic vulnerability abroad and political vulnerability at home—that Truman and his advisers felt.[45]

■

Iran became the great focal point. Russian troop movements appeared ominous. Soviet forces were only 40 miles from Tehran; the Communist Tudeh Party was growing more strident; and the new Iranian prime minister, Ahmad Qavam, was showing signs of accommodation. U.S. officials grew ever more nervous. Yet Qavam was a wily, experienced politician. He wanted to get the Russians out of his country, not to humiliate them. When the Soviets forswore any intent to use an oil concession as a guise to maintain security forces in Iran, Qavam accepted the formation of a binational corporation to develop oil in the north. The deal was contingent on ratification by the Majlis, the Iranian parliament. Nevertheless, by the end of March 1946, Russian troops began withdrawing; by early May they were all gone. Iranian forces, advised by U.S. brigadier general Norman Schwarzkopf, quickly consolidated their hold over the entire northern area evacuated by the Russians, except for Azerbaijan.[46]

U.S. officials were not altogether pleased by the actions of the Iranian government. Byrnes was eager to press for an unconditional withdrawal of Soviet troops and to bring the matter before the Security Council of the United Nations. He wanted to give it to the Russians "with both barrels." George V. Allen, the U.S. ambassador to Iran, also believed that Qavam had conceded too much. The Americans worried that the settlement might prove porous, that the Soviet Union might find some way to gain influence. But U.S. officials could achieve what they wanted only if they collaborated with indigenous leaders. For the moment, they settled for a Soviet withdrawal from northern Iran. Thereafter, Allen established an extremely cordial relationship with the shah, Mohammad Reza Pahlavi, whose anti-Soviet instincts coincided with his own. They played tennis on Saturday afternoons and dined together on Mondays. As James Bill, the Iranian expert, has written, the shah needed U.S. support in the maelstrom of Iranian politics as much as the United States wanted Iranian resistance to the demands of its new enemy, the Soviet Union.[47]

Thinking About War

The Iranian crisis had extremely important ramifications. Throughout its early stages, newspaper headlines conjured up images of war and columnists wrote of the possibility of grave confrontations.[48] When Secretary of Commerce Henry Wallace dined with Acheson and Charles Bohlen in the middle of the crisis, he gathered the impression that they were willing to run the risk of war, betting that the Russians would back down. Actually, State Department officials were wary of military embroilment.[49] Nonetheless, their tough posture bred results. Kennan seemed to be right; the Soviets retreated when confronted with strength.[50]

U.S. officials were aware that considerable risk-taking inhered in this type of offensive diplomacy. Bluffing was dangerous, Forrestal told Byrnes. The secretary of state knew it. Byrnes again remonstrated over the decline of U.S. military capabilities.[51] Moreover, he now acknowledged the need for greater interagency coordination. He asked the JCS to assess critical areas in the Near East and Africa, and he agreed to the formation of a new subcommittee of the State-War-Navy Coordinating Committee (SWNCC). Its exclusive focus was to be the Soviet Union. Prudence dictated that the administration develop a better grasp of the enemy's peacetime intentions and military capabilities. The three secretaries appointed some of their most talented and experienced subordinates to this subcommittee: Byrnes appointed Bohlen; Patterson designated General John R. Deane; and Forrestal nominated Admiral Forrest Sherman.[52]

The new SWNCC subcommittee formally adopted Kennan's analysis. "The United States," Bohlen, Deane, and Sherman concluded, "must accept the fact that it is confronted with the threat of an expanding totalitarian state which continues to believe and act on the belief that the world is divided into two irreconcilably hostile camps, i.e. Soviet and non-Soviet." Russian policies were not dictated by security considerations or strategic imperatives. Soviet suspicions were deliberately contrived. They could not be allayed because their "source lies within the borders of the Soviet Union." The United States had to "use the best methods at its disposal [especially propaganda and economic aid] to check the actual physical extension of Soviet power beyond its present limits."[53]

Bohlen, Sherman, and Deane did not dwell on Soviet military capabilities. The Kremlin did not want war. The Russians wanted time to expedite reconstruction at home. Yet the danger existed that the Soviets might misinterpret American military weakness. They might seek to extend their influence to areas that jeopardized the vital interests of the United States or Great Britain. Some reconstitution of American military capabilities, therefore, was necessary. Modest rearmament offered several advantages: it would alert the Kremlin to the dangerous consequences of its ambitions; it might permit the United States to resist Soviet expansion in areas of American choosing; and it could help to protect countries that would be strategically essential if full-scale war should erupt.[54]

As a result of the Iranian crisis, the specter of war through miscalculation became more pronounced. Neither top defense officials like Eisenhower nor their military planners thought the Soviets would launch a premeditated attack on Western Europe. But the collision of Anglo-Soviet security interests in the Middle East, the volatile situation in Venezia Giulia, and the prospect of Communist revolution in France might ignite a full-scale conflict. Accidental war might occur, too, if the State Department continued to seize the initiative as it had in Iran.[55]

Prodded by Eisenhower and Leahy, the planners accelerated their initial attempts to outline what the United States should do in case an unexpected conflict erupted. In mid-April, the JCS approved a memorandum for the president summarizing prospective Soviet advances and necessary U.S. countermoves. The JCS expected the Soviets to be able to overrun most of Europe and large parts of the Middle East. Planners called for the withdrawal of U.S. troops from Europe but hoped to hold a lodgment somewhere on the continent. In the Middle East, they wanted to thwart Soviet forces moving across the mountains and deserts toward the Mediterranean. In East Asia, they aimed to pull U.S. troops out of Korea and then deny the Yellow Sea and the Sea of Japan to the enemy.[56]

Building upon the rudimentary concepts outlined in the fall of 1945, planners reiterated that the United States should use its strategic air power to destroy the Soviet will to resist. Initially, the principal task was to cripple the enemy's industrial capabilities. "The industrial heart of the U.S.S.R. lies in that area generally west of the Urals and north of the Caspian and Black Seas." Most critical to the Soviet military effort were the areas around Moscow, the Caucasus, Ploesti (Romania), the Urals, Stalingrad, and Kharkov. "Occupation or neutralization of these areas would create conditions leading to the defeat of the U.S.S.R. It would denude the field armies of the vital support necessary for them to continue effective organized resistance." [57]

The strategic air attack, however, had to be concentrated. Air Force planners studied various targets. The most enticing were the Soviet steel, petroleum, and aviation industries, the transportation infrastructure, the electric power network, and the most advanced weapons factories and assembly plants. Among these objectives, however, there was no doubt that the petroleum targets would prove to be the most remunerative. After the bombing raids were under way, planners advocated "the seizure of the Caucasus and the opening of the Dardanelles in preparation for a subsequent offensive into other Soviet vital areas." [58]

Contingency war planning underscored the convergence of U.S. and British strategic interests. When Byrnes requested a JCS study of Turkey, he instructed military planners to consider the possible identity of security interests between the two Anglo-Saxon countries. Britain should fight, retorted the Joint Planning Staff, if the Soviets "penetrate Turkey." Furthermore, the United States should enter the war on Britain's side as early as possible. It was not in American interests, concluded the JCS, to permit the defeat or disintegration of the British empire. If this should happen, "the military potential of the United States together with the military potential of any allies . . . would then be unable to match that of an expanded Soviet Union." [59]

Access to British bases in the United Kingdom and the Middle East was of particular importance to defense officials. In June 1946, the three chiefs of staff—

Eisenhower, Carl Spaatz, and Chester Nimitz—agreed that American planners should consult informally with their British counterparts on the concepts being developed in U.S. plans for global war with the Soviet Union—code-named PINCHER—and on the need for British bases. Such consultation had to be undertaken in the utmost secrecy. Everything would be done by word of mouth; nothing would be put on paper; and if there were leaks, the planners agreed to deny everything. Air Force chief of staff Carl Spaatz visited Britain, met with his British counterpart, and requested permission in case of emergency to use British bases for atomic bomb missions. Lord Tedder agreed to have five Royal Air Force bases made ready for B-29 bombers. Soon thereafter, the first tentative steps were taken toward the construction of assembly buildings and loading pits at the designated bases.[60]

If war should erupt in the near future, the Middle East was more important than any other region in Eurasia. The first Air Force plan for the strategic air offensive placed enormous stress on the utility of airfields in the Cairo-Suez area. From British-controlled airstrips in Egypt, U.S. bombers could strike more key cities and petroleum refineries in the Soviet Union and Romania than from any other prospective base on the globe. Three heavy bomber groups would be deployed to Cairo airfields within the first 120 days of conflict. Because atomic capabilities were limited, the attacks would be of a conventional nature. Planners hoped that the strategic air offensive would force the Russians to capitulate. But if it did not, planners reaffirmed that an assault into the vital war-materiel-producing areas of Russia through the Eastern Mediterranean and Persian Gulf was more promising than a land trek across Europe. A frontal assault against the bulk of Soviet military strength in the heart of Europe might appeal to prospective friends in the Old World but would leave U.S. forces remote from Soviet core industrial areas and would prove militarily unsound.[61] In the summer of 1946 Admiral Richard Conolly, commander of U.S. forces in the Eastern Atlantic and Mediterranean, first requested use of British bases at Cairo-Suez should hostilities flare.[62]

All of America's contingency plans presupposed U.S. control of the air and sea lanes across the Atlantic and Pacific oceans as well as domination of the polar air routes. For these tasks, overseas bases were imperative.[63] The JCS and the State Department agreed that U.S. troops could not withdraw from critical locations. An agreement was negotiated with the Portuguese permitting use of the airfield on Terceira Island in the Azores. Americans would remain to care for the aircraft and to protect weather installations, navigational aids, and warning devices. Diplomats negotiated a similar arrangement with the Icelandic government, allowing military personnel to service aircraft and repair equipment so long as they stayed out of uniform. In North Africa, too, the JCS kept several hundred enlisted men and officers at Port Lyautey. They stayed to guard runways and a communications installation that was considered "vitally important" for American naval activities in the Mediterranean. And in the Pacific, Truman decided to retain American possession of Okinawa and to uphold U.S. military requirements in the former Japanese mandated islands. Fiscal stringency forced retrenchment elsewhere, but the Navy began discussing the possibility of postwar bases in Japan, especially at Yokosuka.[64]

The strategic thinking that accompanied the Iranian crisis and the planning for overseas bases did *not* mean that U.S. officials were contemplating war. They were not. The United States was only beginning to organize the Strategic Air Command. There was no effort to accelerate the development of an atomic arsenal. There was no joint planning with the British chiefs of staff, although the Combined Chiefs of Staff stayed in existence. There was no agreed-on war plan.[65] War could arise from miscalculation, but the chances were still remote.

Prudence nevertheless dictated that Pentagon planners think seriously about what they would do if war erupted. Defense officials wanted civilians to grasp the broad contours of their military thinking and to keep it in mind as they conducted their diplomacy. If appropriate political arrangements were entered into in peacetime, the burdens of military leaders would be eased in wartime. According to the JCS, these "political arrangements might include at the minimum, neutrality of, and at the maximum, alliances with Italy, Spain, France, Denmark, the Low Countries and Scandinavian countries; friendly relations with the Arabian Trans-Jordan and the Levant areas; military collaboration with Turkey; a quiescent if not openly allied Japan; and a China, which at the minimum is a friendly neutral." [66]

The Baruch Plan

Of critical importance to the Pentagon were the administration's plans for the international control of atomic energy. After Byrnes returned from the Moscow conference, he asked Acheson to take charge of this complex issue. Acheson, in turn, named a group of consultants, headed by David E. Lilienthal, chairman of the Tennessee Valley Authority. In mid-March 1946, after two months of arduous labor, the Acheson-Lilienthal report was completed and submitted to Byrnes. Simply stated, the report called for the creation of an international agency, the Atomic Development Authority (ADA). The ADA would control all supplies of uranium and thorium, manage the production of all fissionable products, and conduct all research in atomic explosives. In order to enhance the possibility of working out a common approach with the Russians, many matters were left open to negotiation. The report did not specify when the ADA would begin each of its functions. It did not dwell on the ADA's inspection activities or provide for sanctions in case of violations. Nor did it stipulate when the United States would disseminate vital information to the ADA or when it would halt its own manufacturing and stockpiling of atomic weapons.[67]

Truman appointed Bernard M. Baruch to head the U.S. delegation to the U.N. Atomic Energy Commission and to translate the report into policy. Baruch had made a fortune in the stock market, had led the War Industries Board during World War I, and had spent a long life cultivating senators and influential Democratic officeholders. The president chose Baruch to mute Senate criticism of any proposals to control atomic energy. Personally, Truman did not like him. Baruch, he ruminated, "wants to run the world, the moon and maybe Jupiter." On substantive matters, however, Baruch and Truman were not far apart.[68]

In 1946 Baruch was 75 years old. Infirm and partially deaf, he nevertheless wanted to leave his imprint on the Acheson-Lilienthal plan. He selected his own assistants, but the Acheson-Lilienthal group regarded them as competitors and interlopers. A destructive rivalry ensued. Baruch's aides, feeling spurned by the State Department and the latter's scientific advisers, looked to military officials for assistance.[69]

Army, Navy, and Air Force officers initially acknowledged that the Acheson-Lilienthal plan was conceptually ingenious and innovative. But they worried about its ambiguities, predicted Soviet opposition, and feared prolonged negotiations, at the start of which the Russians would demand the destruction of existing atomic weapons. In 1946 the rapid departure of scientific and technical personnel placed the U.S. atomic program in disarray. But military officials saw these problems as temporary phenomena. Although jockeying among themselves for interservice advantage, they all believed that the country was on the threshold of amazing technological progress. At their request, Truman approved a series of atomic tests, scheduled for July, after which rapid engineering breakthroughs were expected. The chiefs of staff did not want the talks on international control to interfere with American testing, production, and stockpiling. They did not want to relinquish information or close down atomic plants until it was apparent that the Russians were adhering to their agreements. Eisenhower, Spaatz, Thomas Blandy, and other officers met with Baruch on 15 April and emphasized these views. He was entirely sympathetic.[70]

During May and early June, Baruch frequently consulted with U.S. military officers in New York and Washington. They kept urging him to proceed cautiously. The plan that Baruch presented to the United Nations on 14 June was heavily influenced by this military advice. The core of the Acheson-Lilienthal report was not discarded, but its character was transformed by the heavy emphasis on inspection, enforcement, and sanctions. For almost a month, Acheson and Lilienthal knew that Baruch was heading in this direction. Acheson insisted that the new priorities would guarantee a breakdown in negotiations. But on the critical issues of enforcement and sanctions, Truman supported Baruch. We "should not under any circumstances," emphasized the president, "throw away our gun until we are sure the rest of the world cannot arm against us."[71]

During the summer and autumn of 1946, disarmament talks at the United Nations immediately deadlocked. Molotov called for the destruction of bombs and production facilities while Baruch reiterated America's insistence on safeguards and sanctions. Probably nothing could have avoided the impasse. Stalin was not interested in striking a deal. Acheson was correct, however, when he stated that the American orientation guaranteed failure. According to the most able students of these initial attempts at arms control, Baruch explicitly designed his plan to per-petuate the U.S. atomic monopoly.[72] Hoping to ward off competitors, Truman and Patterson also rejected British requests for U.S. assistance in building an atomic plant in Great Britain.[73]

The atomic monopoly and strategic air power, along with America's superior industrial warmaking capabilities, bestowed on the United States its margin of mili-tary superiority over the adversary. Leahy, Nimitz, and other officers believed that the one fact which "puts us in a position of paramount military power is the atomic bomb." [74] Truman wanted to retain that superiority. According to some intelligence analysts, the Russians could develop their own bomb in three or four years.[75] In the interval, U.S. officials believed they could use their unique advantage to help con-figure the international environment in ways that insured American preponderance. "Our monopoly of the bomb," said General Spaatz, "even though it is transitory, may well prove to be a critical factor in our efforts to achieve first a stabilized con-dition and eventually a lasting peace." [76] In fact, Spaatz and many of his fellow officers in the Pentagon were already worrying that the margin of military superi-ority should be even greater if the United States were to grapple with the enemy in far-off places like Iran. Nevertheless, most civilians believed that, if the United States acted with determination, its industrial superiority along with its strategic air power and atomic monopoly would suffice to undergird American diplomacy in Europe, the Middle East, and Asia. The Soviets, as Kennan insisted, would push but not fight.

Winning the Peace: Western Germany and Western Europe

The primary task was to win the peace rather than to ponder the intricacies of war. In the aftermath of the Iranian crisis, the Truman administration seized the diplo-matic offensive in many critical areas. In April, Byrnes went off to the Paris meeting of foreign ministers intending to be tough "from Korea to Timbuktoo." The men who accompanied Byrnes, including some previous critics like Senator Vanden-berg, now noted the secretary of state's "masterful" intransigence.[77] Rather than spar with Molotov over Eastern Europe where the United States had no leverage, Byrnes sought to salvage a viable peace treaty for Italy and focused more and more of his attention on Germany.

In the spring of 1946, the economy in the three western zones of Germany was creeping forward and constraining recovery throughout Western Europe. The stumbling block was coal production in the British-controlled Ruhr. Before World War II, 40 percent of Europe's hard-coal output came from the Ruhr. Almost 30 percent of the Ruhr's 128 million metric tons was sent to other countries, principally in Western Europe. Yet in 1946 Ruhr coal production was only 40 percent of its prewar levels. Shipments abroad were even lower. In July 1945 Truman had called for the export of 25 million tons; in April 1946 Murphy reported that only about a third of the target was being met. The slow growth of coal production stymied other sectors of the German economy. German industrial production was about 30 percent and steel output about 14 percent of 1938 levels.[78]

The industrial stagnation in the Ruhr symbolized the economic and political travail that afflicted Germany in early 1946. The people of the western zones were hungry, demoralized, and defeated. They did not know whether their country would be united, whether the Americans would withdraw, whether the French would achieve dismemberment, or whether the British would have the wherewithal to re-suscitate the Ruhr. They saw the bickering and floundering of the Western allies and compared it to the more vigorous recovery and political activism in the Soviet zone. There, the German Communists (KPD) publicly called for unification, social reform, and political democracy. Privately, the KPD received enormous support from Soviet occupation authorities and pressured the Social Democrats to join them in the formation of the Socialist Unity Party (SED). Most observers were impressed with the potential appeal of the SED; most despaired over the prospects for German democracy.[79] Carl Schorske, for example, a brilliant young historian, conducted a special study for the prestigious New York Council on Foreign Relations. Dwell-ing on the revival of class antagonisms, the disillusionment of former Nazis, the disgruntlement of rural farmers, and the despair of German migrants from Poland, Czechoslovakia, and eastern Germany, he stressed the "peculiarly explosive" situa-tion.[80]

In the American zone, General Clay sought to counter the appeal of the left and to promote recovery. His top economic aides slowed down decartelization; his advisers on labor policy favored right-wing, anti-Soviet union leaders. His actions engendered much criticism in the United States.[81]

The State Department was deeply divided on what to do. Kennan, Murphy, and H. Freeman Matthews wanted the United States to integrate western Germany into Western Europe. From their perspective, the Soviets had already split Europe in half and were maneuvering for additional gains. Central economic organs would play into their hands and give them leverage in the western zones.[82] Acheson, Clayton, and their economic advisers waffled. They agreed with much of Kennan's analy-sis—they had already been thinking of merging the British and American zones—but they were not quite ready to rupture Soviet-U.S. relations and abandon eastern Germany and Eastern Europe. They did not want to yield western Germany's access to desperately needed raw materials and foodstuffs in the Soviet sphere. Nor did they think it desirable for the United States to incur the responsibility for the division of Germany and Europe. In early May, Acheson and Hilldring advised Byrnes to smoke out the Russians and test their loyalty to the economic unification principles of Potsdam.[83]

Byrnes vacillated. At the meeting of foreign ministers in Paris, he called for the appointment of special deputies to examine the German situation. He did not want to force a showdown over Germany while the peace treaties for Hungary, Romania,

Bulgaria, and Italy were still being framed. So he again floated the idea of a treaty guaranteeing the disarmament and demilitarization of Germany. If the French and Russians were assured that the United States would not turn its back on European political affairs, Byrnes hoped they would be willing to act more generously. But he did not simply offer carrots; he wielded a club. In May, he supported Clay's decision to halt reparation transfers until agreement was reached on economic unification.[84]

Clay's abrupt action, as John Gimbel has argued, was directed at Paris more than Moscow. Clay was infuriated with the French. In March they adopted the Monnet Plan for the modernization of the French economy. The emphasis on rapid growth intensified their appetite for German coal. They demanded control of the Saar coal mines, and they wanted twenty million tons annually from the Ruhr, but they did not want to pay in dollars. They wanted French business to conquer the markets traditionally supplied by the Germans. The economic emasculation of Germany, of course, also was driven by French strategic imperatives. French foreign minister Georges Bidault reiterated that the security of France necessitated detachment of the Ruhr, severance of the Rhineland, and administrative decentralization of the rest of Germany. Bidault's tough posture was popular. His party, the MRP, needed votes to stymie Communist gains and maintain its own position in the tripartite coalition.[85]

War Department officials in Washington were as exasperated with the French as was Clay. The situation, they insisted, was fraught with political-military peril. They prodded the State Department to take some definitive action. The "national security" of the United States, Patterson wrote Byrnes on 10 June 1946, required the industrial revival of the Ruhr and the Rhineland and the use of German resources for the stabilization of Western Europe. Fearful that the Ruhr/Rhine industrial complex might someday sustain a formidable enemy, the secretary of war nevertheless opposed its separation from the rest of Germany. Dismemberment might cause an irredentist movement or be exploited by the German Communists. The War Department's top echelon was much influenced by the memoranda of the talented young colonel Charles Bonesteel. He supported some form of supranational control of the Ruhr's economic resources, a control that excluded Russia, emphasized productivity, and contemplated the integration of the German and French economies. If such experimentation was not tried, Bonesteel argued, economic paralysis and political chaos would facilitate the "communist engulfment of western Europe." The Ruhr might then be "deliberately rebuilt against us by an unscrupulous Communist super-state." Although Secretary Patterson was not quite ready to champion international control, he urged Byrnes to devise demilitarization machinery and to merge the British and American zones.[86]

The British were more than willing. Foreign Secretary Bevin was determined to keep the Russians out of the Ruhr. He disapproved of mechanisms for international control because he believed the Kremlin would use them as a subterfuge to gain preponderance over the most critical industrial infrastructure in the whole of Western Europe. The specter of a Germany controlled by Communists or dominated by the

Soviets imperiled the security of the United Kingdom. Like the Americans, Bevin wanted to use the resources of the Ruhr to abet the economic reconstruction of all Europe. His every move, however, was affected by Britain's crumbling financial position. He needed U.S. money to feed the miners and revive production in the Ruhr. He was uncertain whether the Americans were ready for a break with the Soviets. He looked for opportunities to juxtapose responsibility for the division of Germany onto the Kremlin.[87]

Bevin's opportunity arose when, at the close of another round of the Council of Foreign Ministers, Molotov challenged Western policies in Germany. On 9 and 10 July, the Soviet foreign minister ridiculed Byrnes's four-power demilitarization proposal. He supported German retention of the Ruhr and requested Russian participation in its international control. He chastised the Americans for cutting off reparations. The Soviets now wanted reparations from current production and were ready to approve increases in the German level of industry. The Kremlin seemed to be saying that German economic recovery and political unification could prove compatible with Soviet security needs if there were adequate control machinery. This strategy also directly benefited the German Communists, who were laboring to win the hearts and minds of the German people in the western zones.[88]

Byrnes was incensed by Molotov's stand. In the American view, the Russians were posturing as the supporters of a revived, united, and peaceful Germany and maneuvering for a direct role in the Ruhr. Byrnes feared the political appeal of the Soviet position and dreaded the prospect of an eventual Soviet-German coalition. When Bevin reached out to the United States, the American secretary of state immediately responded. Bevin and Byrnes instructed their subordinates to fuse the British and American zones into Bizonia. Some students of European history now regard this initiative as the first conscious move toward the division of Europe.[89] If the French and the Russians accepted Anglo-American terms, they would be welcome. Otherwise, the Anglo-Saxons would go their own way. The United States would assume a share of British costs in the Ruhr and gain some control over its economy. Boosting coal production, U.S. officials believed, was the most important contribution they could make to Europe's economic stabilization.[90]

Given the volatility of the situation, General Clay wanted to issue a statement outlining America's policy on Germany. He deemed it imperative to mobilize greater German support for his policies, especially for the financial reforms he was preparing to enact. Although these initiatives were necessary to curb inflation and foster production, they were certain to cause real short-term hardship. If the Germans were to endure the immediate sacrifices, they had to be convinced that eventually they would have the opportunity for political self-government, economic advancement, and international respectability. According to Clay, they also had to be reassured that, if they cooperated with him, they would never be abandoned to the Communists or the Soviets. And to boost their morale and their attachment to the West, Germans also had to be told that the United States opposed the detachment of the Ruhr and the Rhineland. When State Department officials objected to his policy statement and questioned aspects of his financial program, Clay threatened to quit.[91]

Byrnes invited Clay to Paris and sought to mollify him. The two men had worked closely together during the war, were good friends, and shared a common disdain for the professional bureaucrats at Foggy Bottom. When Byrnes promised to visit Germany and proclaim the policy that Clay so much desired, the general was tremendously cheered. On 6 September, before an assembly of German officials in Stuttgart and flanked by Senators Vandenberg and Connally, Byrnes outlined U.S. policy. Genuflecting before the terms of the Potsdam agreement, he stressed the importance of unified financial and economic policies. But the secretary of state also expressed dissatisfaction with the performance of the Allied Control Council, said nothing that was incompatible with the contemplated merger of the British and American zones, and insisted that U.S. troops would not leave Germany until American goals were achieved: "I want no misunderstanding. We will not shirk our duty. We are not withdrawing. We are staying here." Germany, Byrnes said, must retain sovereignty over the Ruhr and the Rhineland. It was entitled to an average European standard of living, and it must have the right to export goods in order to be self-sustaining. As John Backer has written, the tone of U.S. policy had changed. Priming the German economy, which Clay had been trying to do for over a year, was now a professed American priority.[92]

U.S. goals were to promote the recovery of Western Europe, check Soviet influence, thwart Communist gains, and lower occupation costs. New tactics were taking shape. The Truman administration was willing to finance Bizonia, retain troops in Germany, guarantee a demilitarization treaty, and divide Germany. "Bizonia," Charles Maier has recently written, "meant that henceforth Americans envisaged a Western economic and a Western geopolitical entity as their preeminent concern." They could not achieve their objectives without the support of the British, Germans, French, and other Europeans. In some cases, their goals converged; in others, U.S. officials structured incentives designed to lure wavering allies into their orbit. By offering to take over a share of Britain's costs in its zone of occupation, the United States assumed the position of primacy in fashioning a West European orbit amenable to American leadership.[93] For hesitant Germans, Byrnes and Clay tried to reassure them with promises of assistance and support. Clay was loath to intrude directly into German politics, but he realized that he would not enlist German backing for his policies if he did not promise to improve their economic lot, restore their political autonomy, and revive their national dignity.[94]

Most difficult of all were the French, who viewed Germany's revival as an economic and strategic threat. If the United States pressed too hard upon the French, the Communist Party (PCF) would exploit the issue domestically and American gains in Germany might be offset by losses in France. Although the PCF had been set back in the constitutional referendum in May, it was still a powerful force in French political life. For this very reason influential sectors of the French elite, as the historian Irwin Wall has shown, looked for assistance abroad to defeat their

Communist political foes at home.[95] Most of the French, moreover, recognized that they depended on the United States to finance their reconstruction efforts.[96] If the American suspension of reparations hurt the French, which it did, its sting was mitigated somewhat by the $650 million credit that the Export-Import Bank approved in May and by Byrnes's promises that France would eventually be a beneficiary of the larger German coal output.[97] Tactfully, too, the U.S. secretary of state tried to allay Bidault's worries by illuminating the significance of the demilitarization treaty and by emphasizing that U.S. forces would remain in Europe to protect France and monitor German behavior.[98] The French, of course, were not yet won over, but important tactics were being forged.

Identification of the Soviet Union as the enemy eased U.S. policymaking. Most obviously, the deterioration of relations meant that credits set aside for a possible loan to Russia could be used elsewhere.[99] The specter of a totalitarian threat, moreover, persuaded wavering legislators to approve the British loan. This rationale might be used again as Truman administration officials realized that additional money would be needed to relieve the food situation in Bizonia and to finance the import of additional raw materials without which German industrial production could not become self-sustaining.[100]

But most of all, the breakdown of Soviet-U.S. relations released policymakers from the insoluble dilemmas they faced when they tried to restore western Germany and Western Europe without offending the Kremlin. Meeting the legitimate and conflicting financial and strategic needs of so many claimants, both former allies and former enemies, was more than the United States could bear, the American people would finance, or Truman administration officials could design. Fear of the Kremlin's potential power should it gain leverage in Germany or should the Communists take control of France made it necessary to make tough choices. Reconstructing Western Europe and integrating western Germany were more important than catering to Soviet demands for reparations or allaying its concerns about its security. So cognitive dissonance was reduced and choices made easier by attributing to the Russians the most malevolent of motives and the most sinister of goals and by denying that their grievances had any legitimacy.[101]

When faced with great peril from abroad and political embarrassment at home, U.S. policymakers, like officials in other times and places, chose to deter and contain rather than reassure the enemy.[102] The Soviets, Truman and his advisers reckoned, might be alienated but U.S. security would be enhanced by ensconcing Europe's industrial heartland into an American-led orbit. Benefits seemed to outweigh costs, notwithstanding the spiraling cycle of distrust.

Winning the Peace: The Eastern Mediterranean and the Middle East

U.S. policymakers were equally concerned with thwarting Soviet influence in the Middle East and the Eastern Mediterranean. This goal, in fact, weighed heavily on

Byrnes's mind as he prepared to negotiate the Italian and Balkan peace treaties. In March and April 1946 the secretary of state asked the JCS to assess the strategic importance of the Turkish straits, Tripolitania, Eritrea, and Italian Somaliland.[103]

As the JCS worked on these tasks, General George Lincoln, the Army's principal planner, established very close relations with Benjamin V. Cohen, Byrnes's most trusted adviser. Lincoln was a member of Byrnes's delegation in Paris and spent much of his time explaining the strategic implications of Russian diplomatic overtures. The Soviet Union, Lincoln told Cohen, must not be permitted to gain a foothold in the Dodecanese and Tripolitania.[104] If war should erupt, any Soviet presence in the Eastern Mediterranean or North Africa would jeopardize the strategic bombing offensive against the Soviet homeland. In fact, the Soviets had to be kept completely out of Africa lest they maneuver to influence emerging nationalist ferment or seek to gain control of uranium deposits. Even in places like Eritrea and Somaliland, the JCS insisted, concessions would be "fatal" because these locations could serve as bases for long-range bombers to operate over the Persian Gulf and for British control of the Indian Ocean.[105]

If Britain retrenched from the Middle East or the Eastern Mediterranean without offering assistance to indigenous armed forces or without providing guarantees to deter external aggression, U.S. officials felt that their own nation's security would be endangered. Yet they did not want to assume formal political-military responsibilities in the region. The situation in Palestine is instructive. Bevin wanted the United States to help preserve order. On the advice of the JCS, however, Truman refused to send troops even though he had endorsed the influx of 100,000 Holocaust survivors. In effect, Truman wanted to win Jewish votes at home without antagonizing Arab nations or dissipating U.S. military strength. Recognizing the expediency of his own position, he knew why Bevin was so infuriated with the American attitude. Truman did not seek to erode British influence. Like his advisers, Truman was conscious of the great importance of Middle Eastern petroleum deposits, and he did not want the Russians to capitalize on Anglo-American friction in Palestine.[106]

To help safeguard their common interests, U.S. officials wanted the British to accommodate the forces of nationalism in the Middle East. After the February riots in Cairo, Byrnes asked if they had been inspired by the Communists. Although the answer from the embassy was reassuring, policymakers in Washington hoped the British would move quickly and make prudent compromises in order to safeguard continued Anglo-American access to Egyptian airfields in wartime situations.[107]

Bevin was ready to negotiate a deal with Egyptian prime minister Ismail Sidky. In early May he asked the Egyptians to permit British air defense and maintenance forces to remain in peacetime and to grant the right of immediate reentry for British air force units and combat troops in wartime. But Sidky would not agree to these terms. Thereupon Bevin requested Byrnes's support, and the secretary of state complied. In a formal letter, the U.S. government told the Egyptians that the British were striking an appropriate balance between the sovereignty of Egypt and the strategic interests of the West. When this demarche did nothing to break the Anglo-Egyptian diplomatic deadlock, Byrnes decided not to press the matter lest he jeopardize America's future influence with the Egyptian government.[108]

■

The prospective devolution of British power in the Eastern Mediterranean accelerated U.S. efforts to prevent the Kremlin and its surrogates from filling the emerging vacuum. This attitude was apparent in Byrnes's approach to the Italian peace treaty. He, more than Bevin, took the lead in championing Italian interests. He continued to press for a lenient reparations settlement. He parried Russian requests for trusteeship rights in the former Italian colonies, and he insisted that the Dodecanese be returned to Greece. Most important of all, he supported Italian claims to territory in Venezia Giulia and adamantly resisted Tito's efforts to gain Trieste.[109]

Tensions remained acute in this key Adriatic port. Anglo-American military officials tried to keep order, but rumors abounded of imminent hostilities.[110] At a meeting with his top civilian and military advisers on 27 February, Truman expressed considerable apprehension over the situation in Venezia Giulia. Forrestal suggested that the United States send a strong naval force to the Mediterranean. The president agreed that the battleship USS *Missouri*, which had already been designated to return the body of the deceased Turkish ambassador to Istanbul, should be well escorted and should illuminate American concern with the entire region. During the following week Patterson became increasingly worried about the capacity of Anglo-American forces to resist a Yugoslav attack. Insisting that Tito was Stalin's proxy, Forrestal, too, emphasized that the area had to be defended.[111]

Although demobilization at home and naval requirements in East Asia made it impossible to deploy a large task force to the Eastern Mediterranean, Byrnes dug in his diplomatic heels. He told Molotov that the United States would never cede Trieste to Tito. The Soviet foreign minister decided to compromise. He accepted a proposal to make Trieste a free port under U.N. tutelage. Tito protested, but to no avail. In early August, however, his forces shot down two U.S. planes flying over Yugoslav airspace.[112]

■

Tensions, therefore, were high when the Soviet government asked Turkey to alter the rules governing ship movements through the Dardanelles. The Russians maintained that the existing regulations had not protected their interests during World War II. They wanted to get together with the other Black Sea powers, formulate a new set of rules, and establish a joint defense of the straits. The Soviet diplomatic note, a copy of which was handed to Acheson while Byrnes was still in Paris, triggered a whirlwind of action at the highest levels of the Truman administration.[113]

U.S. policymakers agreed that Soviet proposals were a ploy to secure bases in

Turkey, take it over, and then gain control of Greece, the Middle East, and the Eastern Mediterranean. Once having sealed off these areas from the Western world, the Soviets would maneuver to achieve their goals in China and India. The time had come, a State Department memorandum declared, "when we must decide that we shall resist with all means at our disposal." [114] At a meeting with the president on 15 August, Acheson, Forrestal, Army Undersecretary Kenneth Royall, and the chiefs of staff outlined the diplomatic and military steps they were contemplating. They would communicate their misgivings to the Russians, urge the Turks to stand firm, and insist that a new regime for the straits must not be framed by the Black Sea powers alone. They would send their newest aircraft carrier to the Eastern Mediterranean and inform the American people of the seriousness of the situation. Acheson and Forrestal talked as if they were prepared to fight. Eisenhower tactfully questioned whether the president grasped the significance of their actions. Truman surprised his visitors by pulling out a map of the Middle East. Describing the strategic value of the region, he stressed that the Soviet Union must not be permitted by force or by threats of force to seize control of the Dardanelles and Turkey. [115]

Actually, the allusions to force were contrived. Elbridge Durbrow, Kennan's replacement in Moscow, did not think the Kremlin would move aggressively against Turkey. Nor did most other U.S. diplomats, military planners, and intelligence analysts. Moreover, reports from Istanbul suggested that the Turks were relieved rather than alarmed by the note. The director of central intelligence informed the president that there were "no indications of any unusual troop concentrations, troop movements, or supply build-ups which would normally precede offensive military action." [116]

American fears did not stem from aggressive Soviet moves against Turkey. The Soviets had done little more than send a diplomatic note. [117] The real problem was that there loomed gaping vacuums of power in this part of the world. In Palestine, the British were beleaguered by the militant actions of the Hagana, the Irgun, and the Stern Gang; in Egypt, the British were threatened with expulsion from the Suez base; in South Asia, they faced an aroused nationalism, which meant that their Indian Army could no longer be used to quell unrest in the Middle East; in Paris, their demands for a trusteeship in Cyrenaica were rebuffed by Molotov; and, in London, Churchill's attack on Bevin's policies focused attention on the impending collapse of the entire British empire. [118]

But while British power foundered, the American desire for access to the airfields and petroleum resources of the Middle East mounted. In fact, Turkey's geopolitical importance was directly related to the evolution of U.S. strategic concepts. On 27 July, Secretary of War Patterson emphasized to President Truman that it was important to have "cushions of distance . . . between Soviet areas and areas vital to us." On 15 August, the very day Truman approved a tough response to the Soviet note, military planners completed a study, code-named GRIDDLE, that called for "every practicable measure . . . to permit the utilization of Turkey as a base for

Allied operations in the event of war with the USSR." The Turks could slow down a Soviet advance toward Cairo-Suez, thereby affording time for the United States to inaugurate the strategic air offensive. Likewise, if the Soviets could be denied control of the Dardanelles, their submarines might be bottled up in the Black Sea, thereby insuring much safer lines of communication for Allied forces traversing the Eastern Mediterranean. If wartime developments permitted, Turkish airfields might even be used to launch raids against vital petroleum areas within the Soviet Union and Romania. At the very least, fighter aircraft, stationed in Turkey, might protect Allied bombers as they ventured into Soviet territory from the bases at Cairo-Suez.[119]

The JCS now wanted to provide Turkey with economic and military assistance. This aid would encourage Turkey to reject Soviet political overtures in peacetime and to resist Soviet military advances in wartime. Turkey needed arms, aircraft, and fuel storage facilities. Military planners prodded State Department officials to approve such assistance, and the JCS pushed the idea with Forrestal and Patterson. The secretary of war worried that this step might unnecessarily provoke the Russians. But Undersecretary of State Clayton endorsed the JCS position and recommended it to Byrnes in Paris.[120] After deliberating on the proposal and talking to Bevin, the secretary of state decided that Britain should continue to offer military aid and the United States should give economic assistance. If, however, the British lacked the appropriate military hardware, the U.S. government would offer the equipment to London for transfer to the Turks.[121]

Turkey was an attractive partner for the United States in the Middle East. Turks were united in their opposition to Russian overtures and demands, and they were eager for American aid. In contrast to Egypt, where there was little sense of threat and strong nationalist impulses, and in contrast to Palestine, where Arab-Jewish conflict threatened to engulf any foreign power, the United States could establish a strategic relationship with Turkey that served the needs of both nations. The deployment of U.S. naval forces to Mediterranean waters and the decision to offer assistance adumbrated the new tactical approach of the Truman administration to shore up Western power in the Eastern Mediterranean.

■

At the same time, U.S. officials could not ignore the deteriorating situation in Greece. In the immediate aftermath of the straits crisis, military planners were especially eager to lend assistance to Greece as well as to Turkey. On 6 September, Colonel James McCormack gave Loy Henderson, director of the State Department's Office of Near Eastern and African Affairs, a memorandum outlining U.S. security interests in Greece. Greece, like Turkey, served as a barrier between the Soviet Union and the Mediterranean. Yet Greece was threatened by territorial disputes, frontier incidents, and domestic disorder engineered by a well-organized and armed Communist minority. "If the fall of the Greek government should result in the emergence of a communist Greece, Soviet encirclement of Turkey will have been enhanced, and Soviet prospects for entering the eastern Mediterranean will have greatly increased." Moreover, there would be "unfavorable repercussions in all those areas where political sympathies are balanced precariously in favor of the West, and against Soviet communism." Since British troops might soon withdraw from Greece and since the country was foundering economically, it was imperative for the United States to offer the Greek government much greater diplomatic, financial, and economic assistance.[122]

McCormack worked tirelessly to expedite his memorandum through the Washington bureaucracy. Collaborating with Henderson, he won the approval of the SWNCC and the JCS. On 12 September, Clayton urged Byrnes to revise State Department policy and to approve the sale of military equipment to Greece, Turkey, and Iran. The Soviet Union, Clayton charged, sought hegemony in the Near East. While Soviet agents were sponsoring insurrectionary activity inside Greece, the Kremlin was building up the armed forces of Bulgaria, Yugoslavia, and Albania and using them to intimidate the Greek government.[123]

This assessment distorted the complexity of developments in the region. Clayton was well informed by reports coming into Washington that right-wing officials bore substantial responsibility for the turmoil in Greece. The government had failed to foster economic recovery. Instead it tried to suppress the Communist Party, discredit all its opponents, and conduct a plebiscite on whether or not to retain the monarchy. Law and order, wrote Ambassador MacVeagh, was largely in the hands of "unscrupulous reactionaries with restoration aims." [124]

On the other hand, the allegations that the Kremlin's Balkan satellites were lending assistance to the guerrilla movement inside Greece were partly correct. Some Greek Communists crossed into Yugoslav and Albanian territory seeking refuge, succor, and arms. But there was little evidence that the Soviets were fomenting trouble. Bulgaria, the Balkan country indisputably under Soviet control, was showing marked restraint toward its southern neighbor. The Americans did not know it, but Tito was operating independently. What they did know was that Albania was defending itself against Greek territorial claims. The root of the problem, wrote the U.S. ambassador in Tirana, "inescapably lies in unfounded Greek claims to southern Albania which have been pressed with increasing aggressiveness for more than two years." [125]

U.S. officials simply intuited that Soviet complicity existed. Even if the Kremlin were innocent, it was of no real significance. The acquisition of power by the Greek Communists was unacceptable whether it came about as a result of Balkan rivalries, indigenous unrest, or internal political maneuverings. It was assumed that, once in power, Greek Communists would provide the Kremlin with a strategic toehold in the Mediterranean. Such a development simply could not be allowed.[126]

To thwart the rise of the Communist insurgency before it developed into a full-scale civil war, Byrnes welcomed the idea of assistance to Greece as well as to

Turkey. Such aid needed to be accompanied by substantial economic and political reforms. But suspecting that change would not come quickly, U.S. officials discouraged the withdrawal of British troops. They hoped the British would provide military aid while the United States concentrated on economic assistance. When the Export-Import Bank failed to provide additional credits, State Department officials started to work on an aid package they could submit to Congress.[127]

Greece and Turkey are our outposts, Byrnes declared at a meeting with Forrestal and Patterson on 18 December 1946.[128] The stage was set for the Truman Doctrine.

Winning the Peace: China

As the Truman administration became more deeply embroiled in Western Europe and the Middle East, it reduced its involvement in China. Did this mean that U.S. officials were reassessing their security interests in Asia? The United States, of course, remained in control of Japan. As for Korea, Truman himself insisted that the United States must stay for the indefinite future.[129] And with regard to Southeast Asia, policymakers bided time, waiting to see the outcome of the talks between Ho Chi Minh and the French and between Sukarno and Mohammed Hatta and the Dutch. In China, however, the Truman administration pulled out most of the U.S. Marines, cut its military assistance, and distanced itself from Chiang Kai-shek. What was the meaning of these developments?

Marshall went to China in December 1945 with the hope of excising Soviet power from Manchuria and diminishing the influence of the Chinese Communists (CCP). The great fear of the Truman administration was that the Russians would ensconce themselves in Manchuria, northern China, and Korea, integrate the resources of this region with the Soviet Far East, and establish a power complex in East Asia that resembled the one that the Japanese had created in the 1930's.[130] Consequently, from the moment Marshall arrived in China, he insisted that Chiang must have the right to reassert Chinese control over Manchuria. He wanted the Russians out. And like his nominal superiors in Washington, Marshall opposed Soviet attempts to form joint economic companies with the Chinese in Manchuria. When the Soviets remained after the 1 February 1946 deadline, the United States protested. After Russian troops withdrew in the spring, Marshall's aim was to insure that they did not return under any pretext.[131]

The former Army chief of staff was equally determined to dilute the influence of the Chinese Communists. He offered them the right to participate legally in Chinese political life and to have a minority status in Chinese administrative structures. He was impressed by the readiness of Chou En-lai to compromise and arrange a cease-fire. He saw rather little evidence of Soviet aid to the CCP, and he was aware of the potential for serious rifts. Personally, his relations with Chou were impeccably correct and altogether statesmanlike. Fundamentally, however, Marshall distrusted the Chinese Communists. Like U.S. officials in Washington, he believed in their ideological kinship to Moscow. He had no doubt that they were real Marxist-Leninists. He suspected that if they controlled Manchuria, they would link it to the Soviet economy. According to U.S. officials, "The resulting self-sufficiency of the U.S.S.R. in the Far East would, taken together with her western industries, place under the control of the Soviet Union the greatest agglomeration of power in the history of the world. China without Manchuria would be no effective counter-poise to maintain the balance of power in the Far East." [132]

The United States, therefore, had real incentive to expedite the movement of Chiang's troops into Manchuria. The Truman administration gave Chiang over $800 million in postwar lend-lease funds, a figure that exceeded the total sum extended to China to fight the Japanese. This money was used to help transport, supply, and train Chinese troops.[133] In August 1946 the Americans also negotiated a surplus property deal with the Nationalists and transferred to them over $500 million worth of nonmilitary supplies.[134] Meanwhile, a military advisory group was formed and began operating in China. Although it was not nearly as large as the one the Pentagon wanted, it included about 750 Army and 165 Navy officers.[135] And during the first half of 1946, U.S. Marines had continued to protect the mining and transport of coal to key cities.[136] The Chinese Communists bitterly resented this assistance to the Nationalists.[137] Chiang himself acknowledged that, without Marshall's support and American logistical assistance, he could never have attempted to reassert his control over Manchuria.[138]

For Marshall, however, the relationship with Chiang remained not an object but an instrument of U.S. policy. As elsewhere, the United States had to have indigenous allies if it were to accomplish its goals. The Americans needed Chinese leaders who were amenable to American influence, capable of establishing stability, and intent on circumscribing Russian power. Marshall's irritation with Chiang mounted during the spring and summer of 1946 precisely because the KMT leader was taking action that contravened U.S. wishes. Chiang insisted on achieving his objectives through military force. He resisted the political, institutional, and administrative reforms that Marshall deemed crucial for the maintenance of order, the dilution of Communist influence, and the exclusion of Russian power.[139]

In mid-summer, Marshall started to curtail American military assistance. He wanted to force Chiang to abandon his military initiatives. He was certain that the Communists could not be defeated militarily. A protracted civil war played into their hands, engendering the misery and dislocation that they capitalized on politically. Chiang's military actions, Marshall believed, would bankrupt the government and ruin the economy.[140]

Marshall came to the conclusion that U.S. assistance was not inducing Chiang to take the constructive steps that he deemed necessary to co-opt the opposition, muster grass-roots support, and establish stability. In his view, therefore, it made sense to reduce America's indirect involvement in the Chinese civil war and remove any incentive the Soviets might have to reassert their authority in Manchuria.

Japanese troops had been repatriated, and there was no longer any excuse for the retention of U.S. Marines. If the Soviets seized on their presence to justify their own meddling, the main purpose of American policy would be defeated.[141]

In Washington, defense officials strongly objected to Marshall's change of tactics. Forrestal visited China in July and spoke to Marshall as well as to other U.S. diplomats and military officers. The secretary of the Navy came away convinced that Russia was seeking to dominate Northeast Asia. He considered Marshall's advice well-intentioned but wrong-headed.[142] Army officials agreed with Forrestal. "Our exclusion from China," they maintained, "would probably result, within the next generation, in an expansion of Soviet influence over the manpower, raw materials, and industrial potential of Manchuria and China. The United States and the world might then be faced in the China Sea and southward with a Soviet power analogous to that of the Japanese in 1941, but with the difference that the Soviets could be perhaps overwhelmingly strong in Europe and the Middle East as well." Analysts in the Navy reviewed these conclusions carefully in early September 1946 and concurred.[143]

In interagency discussions, however, State Department officials strongly supported Marshall's desire to withhold aid. Byrnes was in Paris, focusing little attention on China. Acheson listened to and followed the advice of John Carter Vincent. The director of the Office of Far Eastern Affairs was exasperated by Chiang's violations of Marshall's cease-fire. U.S. military aid, he thought, was encouraging military solutions that would eventually backfire. If this assistance were suspended, Chiang would have to rein in the reactionaries, undertake economic and political reforms, and win the support of the Chinese masses. Since the CCP could not be defeated militarily, Vincent's aim was to co-opt and dilute rather than vanquish the Communist opposition.

Vincent, however, shared the same goals as defense officials. According to Vincent, the primary task of U.S. policy was to prevent China's absorption into a Russian orbit. He backed Marshall because he believed that if the Nationalists acceded to his recommendations, the Kremlin would find it very difficult to intervene. On the other hand, if Chiang ignored Marshall's advice and relied on force, he would drive the CCP into the hands of the Russians. The suspension of aid, Vincent insisted, posed no immediate risks to the Nationalists. He told Acheson that their string of military victories in the summer of 1946 placed them in a strong position, at least for the short run. Even if Chiang ignored American desires, Vincent did not want to reach out to the Communists and recognize their belligerency. In other words, withholding assistance did not mean renunciation of U.S. efforts to contain the Russians and the Communists. It meant a more subtle, flexible policy in which American leverage was maximized. The United States, Vincent reiterated, must not disengage from China.[144]

Acheson's most trusted subordinate in China, Walton Butterworth, agreed with Vincent. The perpetuation of military strife, he wrote, played into the hands of the

Kremlin. If the civil war persisted, China would be split and Soviet influence in the north would predominate. This development "would constitute a threat to the national security of the United States. It is, therefore, of primary importance that the United States remain in China." Like Vincent, Butterworth contended that by reducing assistance the United States would maximize its leverage and force Chiang to become a more cooperative partner. "Should it become apparent at any time that the Soviet Union is giving effective assistance to the Communists, it would, of course, then become necessary to reconsider our position and set our course of action accordingly." [145]

The president paid scant attention to Chinese matters and followed where Marshall and the State Department led.[146] By the fall of 1946, Marshall was infuriated with Chiang Kai-shek. In the American general's view, Chiang had been co-opted by the reactionary elements within the KMT. Marshall spoke to liberal opponents of Chiang, hoping they would unite their weak and disparate factions and constitute a serious non-Communist alternative that the United States could support. He also hoped that time might chasten Chiang. As the Nationalist military offensive faltered and Chiang realized his dependence on American assistance, he might become more amenable to American wishes. One way or another, Marshall grasped that the United States could not achieve its goals without reliable Chinese allies. In this regard he was quite prescient. He also assumed that Republican successes in the 1946 congressional elections would restrict funding for overseas purposes and force the administration to choose priorities. China, he thought, might be an apt place to economize because too much military assistance would draw in the Soviets and defeat American purposes.[147]

The object of U.S. policy was still to stymie Soviet gains, contain Communist influence, and promote a unified, stable China friendly to the United States. The means remained as elusive as ever. Unlike the situation in Western Europe and the Middle East, the reduction of aid, at least for the immediate future, appeared most likely to achieve American goals. Neither Marshall nor anyone else in the administration was prepared to abandon China or the rest of Asia to the adversary. Like most analysts, however, Marshall (in 1946) grossly underestimated CCP capabilities and misjudged the amount of time he had available.[148]

The Clifford-Elsey Report and the Question of Russia

As U.S. officials encountered serious obstacles almost everywhere around the globe, the president grew more angry. His popularity at home was sagging; inflation was spiraling; his party's prospects in the forthcoming congressional elections were sinking. On 12 July, sitting in the White House over a drink with his closest aides, Truman poured out his frustrations. He told Clark Clifford and George Elsey that he was tired of being pushed around. The Soviets, he declared, were chiseling on their agreements. He instructed Clifford to prepare a statement outlining Soviet violations of previous accords. It made no sense to sign new agreements if the Soviets were not complying with the old ones.[149]

Clifford had come to the White House as an assistant to James K. Vardaman, a crony of the president's who was then serving as Truman's naval aide. Within a year Clifford took Vardaman's job and then became the president's special counsel. As Clifford rose in influence, Elsey, a still more junior naval aide with a Harvard master's degree in history, often served as his assistant.[150] When Clifford assigned Elsey the task of drafting the indictment of the Soviet compliance record, Elsey saw it as an opportunity to conduct an overall assessment of U.S. relations with the Soviet Union. Elsey and Clifford drafted a careful set of questions and invited input from the State, War, and Navy departments, the JCS, the Central Intelligence Group, the attorney general, and the reparations expert, Edwin Pauley.[151]

The Clifford-Elsey report was the first comprehensive interdepartmental effort to assess Soviet intentions and capabilities, analyze the Kremlin's motivations, evaluate Russian behavior, and prescribe American measures. It is illustrative of the poor state of decisionmaking that there were no established procedures for coordinated analyses, that Truman had not asked for one, and that Clifford and Elsey, with little background in this area, took on the assignment themselves. It is also illuminating that they made such a special effort to solicit the views of defense officials. They distrusted Byrnes and knew that Truman wanted advice from outside the State Department.[152]

The report painted an ominous picture. The Kremlin was projecting "the effective range of Soviet military power well into areas which the United States regards as vital to its security." Stalin was maintaining the Red Army, building up reserves, improving mobilization procedures, mechanizing ground divisions, integrating tank and infantry units, and enhancing mobility. The Soviets were lengthening airfields, utilizing German submarines, working on atomic and biological weapons, and rapidly developing their overall air and naval power. They were violating the principle of self-determination in Eastern Europe and illegally demanding reparations in kind from Germany. They were penetrating Iran and jeopardizing American access to Middle Eastern oil. They were conspiring with the Chinese Communists and making more difficult the achievement of U.S. objectives in China. In sum, they were seeking "to weaken the position and to destroy the prestige of the United States in Europe, Asia, and South America." [153]

According to Clifford and Elsey, the Soviet Union sought world domination. Russian leaders no longer faced any external threat, so they must be responding to domestic political necessities. They used the theme of capitalist encirclement as a ruse to guarantee their totalitarian oppression at home. They were motivated by the "Marxian theory of ultimate destruction of capitalist states by communist states." Given their existing relative weaknesses, however, they acted opportunistically. They avoided direct clashes yet sought to fill every vacuum.[154]

In writing their prescriptive chapter, Elsey and Clifford were influenced by the

JCS, Forrestal, and Patterson. The United States could not permit any further increments of Soviet power lest the preponderant resources and human capital of Eurasia fall under the Kremlin's control. The United States had not just waged a war against the Axis coalition in order to permit a new behemoth to dominate the Eurasian land mass. In the bipolar world that then existed, the Soviets were incomparably weaker than the Americans. They must not be allowed to capitalize on economic malaise, intracapitalist rivalries, Communist popularity, and nationalist upheavals to enhance their long-term capabilities. If they did, they would gain the capacity to compete with and/or struggle against the United States.

Clifford and Elsey recommended that the United States revitalize its military capabilities, upgrade its atomic arsenal, prepare its overseas bases, and mobilize its economic and financial resources to "assist all democratic countries which are in any way menaced or endangered by the U.S.S.R." Western Europe and the Middle East must remain outside the Soviet sphere. In East Asia, it was essential to have "a unified and economically stable China, a reconstructed and democratic Japan, and a unified and independent Korea." The United States had to "ensure Philippine prosperity" and "assist in the peaceful solution, along non-communist lines, of the political problems of southeast Asia and India." Virtually everywhere, the United States had to project its power and revive the open door in order to establish vigorous non-Communist economies tied to the United States and resistant to the political, economic, and strategic penetration of the Soviet Union.[155]

To what extent did the Clifford-Elsey report accurately assess Soviet behavior, explain Russian motivations, and portray Soviet intentions? Although it is possible to retrace Soviet actions, it is impossible to state Soviet goals and motives with any degree of certainty. Despite *glasnost*, Soviet archives for the postwar years remain closed to most researchers. At best, even favored Soviet historians are handed a small sample of documents by self-interested officials or sympathetic archivists.[156] Western scholars try to glean Soviet intentions and motivations from the publications of *Pravda*, *Izvestiia*, and other published materials as well as from the occasional intimate statements that Stalin and his comrades made to foreign diplomats and Communist leaders. Whether these statements, often contradictory and self-serving, should be taken at face value remains questionable. Nevertheless, they are the best source materials that are available. Students of Soviet foreign policy have used them in imaginative ways to penetrate behind the walls of the Kremlin. Using their findings and U.S. documents, we can try to make a few tentative judgments about Clifford's and Elsey's conclusions.

The impetus to write the Clifford-Elsey report sprang from the conviction that the Soviets consistently violated their agreements. Yet the evidence garnered by Elsey illustrated that reality was far more complex than the White House had assumed. The JCS, for example, acknowledged that the Soviet Union usually adhered to its wartime military accords. Clay emphasized that the Soviets had not violated the agreements regarding Germany; he said that differences arose primarily over interpretations of ambiguous language. Patterson concurred. Even Acheson submitted a long State Department analysis that avoided categorical charges of outright Soviet violations of the letter of agreements. As a result, the authors of the final report acknowledged that "it is difficult to adduce direct evidence of literal violations." [157] With this caveat, they then proceeded with their damning indictment of the Soviet compliance record.

Clifford and Elsey ignored actions that might have injected hues of gray into their black-and-white characterization of Soviet foreign policy. They neglected to mention that the Kremlin made no objection to the entry of U.S. troops into South Korea, pretty much accepted American domination of postwar Japan, and only feebly protested the American military presence in northern China.[158] They were uninterested in the fact that Soviet armies had withdrawn from Manchuria and that there was scant evidence of any ongoing Soviet assistance to the CCP.[159] They overlooked the free elections that were held in Hungary and Czechoslovakia and the relatively representative governments that were established in Austria and Finland. They disregarded the intelligence reports detailing the partial withdrawal of Soviet armies from occupied areas, the large-scale demobilization of Russian troops within the Soviet Union, and the departure of Russian forces from northern Norway and from Bornholm.[160] They failed to acknowledge that Stalin discouraged insurrectionary activity in Europe, offered no leadership to Communist revolutionaries in Southeast Asia, failed to exploit opportunities in Arab lands, and straddled sides between the Nationalists and Communists in China.[161]

Double standards and self-deception repeatedly crept into the Clifford-Elsey report. Truman's advisers did not ask how America's own questionable record of compliance affected Soviet behavior.[162] They did not acknowledge that Clay and other War Department officials consistently identified France, not Russia, as the principal source of U.S. problems in Germany.[163] They suspected that any Soviet interest in German unification masked the Kremlin's quest to gain leverage over all of Germany, but they conveniently dismissed the American desire to dilute Soviet influence in the east and to orient all of Germany to the West.[164] Likewise, Clifford and Elsey pointed to the retention of Russian troops in Iran as irrefutable proof of the Soviet desire to dominate Iran and gain control of Middle Eastern oil. They did not say (and may not have known) that, at the very time they were writing their report, State Department officials and military planners were contending that U.S. troops must remain beyond the stipulated deadlines for their withdrawal in Iceland, the Azores, Panama, the Galapagos, and other locations in order to augment American bargaining leverage for postwar base and military transit rights.[165]

Clifford and Elsey also presented a totally misleading rendition of Soviet capabilities. Army intelligence, for example, estimated that it would take the Soviet Union fifteen years to overcome manpower losses, ten years to correct the deficiency in technicians, five to ten years to build a strategic air force, fifteen to twenty-five years to construct a navy, ten years to make the railway network suitable for military purposes, and three to ten years to develop atomic capabilities. Likewise, it was estimated that it would take ten years to eliminate opposition in occupied countries, fifteen to twenty years to overcome the communications, shipping, and economic weaknesses of the Soviet Far East, and an unspecified number of years to reduce the vulnerability of Soviet petroleum, transport, and industrial facilities to long-range bombing.[166] These weaknesses, so central to any objective appraisal of Soviet policies, never found their way into the Clifford-Elsey report.

To emphasize these points is not to whitewash Soviet behavior. Aid from the Kremlin was making it increasingly possible for Communists in Romania, Bulgaria, and Poland to consolidate their control. Russian power hovered over Hungary and Czechoslovakia despite the free elections. The Soviets were maneuvering for influence throughout Germany. They probed in Manchuria and Iran. They condemned British imperialism. They hoped nationalist uprisings would erode Western control of important Third World areas in Asia, Africa, and the Middle East. They sought to modernize their military arsenal and were working feverishly to develop their own atomic weapons.[167]

But did these actions amount to a quest for world domination? Clifford and Elsey thought so, although they did not define what they meant by the term. They equated any growth of Soviet influence as signaling a Soviet desire for domination.[168] They did not explain why the Soviets should seek world domination. If, in fact, they needed an outside threat to justify their totalitarian rule at home, as may have been the case, did this mean that they necessarily sought world domination?

For Clifford and Elsey their conclusion was dictated by the importance they attributed to the role of ideology in the making of Soviet foreign policy. For them and other officials in the administration, Stalin's speech of 9 February 1946 had proven this point. Yet Kennan's long telegram, on which Clifford and Elsey relied, never included a close textual analysis of the Soviet leader's address. That speech, as many recent students of Soviet foreign policy have pointed out, was quite moderate. Stalin did not speak of capitalist encirclement; he did not discuss the inevitability of capitalist-communist conflict; he did not dwell on the importance of developing an industrial-military infrastructure at the expense of consumer goods. Moreover, during subsequent months, though he vilified Churchill for the latter's own vitriolic rhetoric, Stalin repeatedly emphasized his belief in coexistence (even while he may have hoped and believed that economic disarray in the West might insure the eventual triumph of communism or the expansion of Soviet power).[169] It is interesting to note that both Philip Mosely and John Hazard, the scholars whom Kennan deemed best qualified to assess the role of ideology in Soviet foreign policy, discounted its decisiveness. They especially stressed that Marxist-Leninist doctrine did not dictate the inevitability of war between the United States and the Soviet Union, thereby undermining one of the fundamental tenets of the Clifford-Elsey report.[170]

Still, Clifford, Elsey, and their colleagues could not believe that security imperatives motivated Soviet policy. Germany and Japan were defeated. According to U.S. officials, the Kremlin had nothing to fear. Such statements were incredibly disingenuous because all the nations of Europe and Asia, as well as the United States, were basing their policies, at least in part, on the probable resurgence of German and Japanese power. No one could predict confidently the prospective configuration of internal German and Japanese politics, and no one could be certain of their future places in the international system. Indeed, the very fluidity of postwar international politics encouraged nations to try to take advantage of German and Japanese powerlessness to advance their long-term security and economic interests. The Russians, of course, had not only suffered the most but were also in the best position to insure their future security against their prospective adversaries.

But could not the rulers in the Kremlin realize that the United States posed no threat and would help to guarantee German and Japanese demilitarization? Americans regarded their own motives as pure, and they irrationally expected the Soviets to see them in the same manner.[171] The American people, wrote Bohlen, did not believe that the Soviets feared aggression: "No possible combination of powers could conceivably be a threat to the Soviet Union without the active support of the United States." And, in Bohlen's view, the whole history of the United States demonstrated that the country would never "lend itself to any such aggressive action." When General Walter Bedell Smith, the new U.S. ambassador to Moscow, spoke to Stalin, he repeated these ideas. Did the Soviets really think that the United States would attack Russia?[172]

Such questions missed the point. No one expected war to occur from a premeditated attack. Conflict would erupt from miscalculation as powerful nations strove to enhance their security and maximize their interests. In this respect, the Clifford-Elsey report made no allowance for and gave no legitimacy to Soviet threat perception. However safe Americans thought the Soviet Union was, the Kremlin had to be concerned with the potential revival of Germany and Japan as well as with the possibility of a rupture of relations with the United States and Great Britain. Once before the Germans had been defeated, disarmed, and demilitarized; once before there had been promises, guarantees, and international commitments. And they all had amounted to nothing. Germany had conquered most of Europe, devastated the Soviet Union, and almost shattered Communist rule. Japan dominated much of Northeast Asia, skirmished with the Russians on the Manchurian border, pondered full-scale war, and then headed south to gobble up all of Southeast Asia. For the Soviets (as for most Asians and Europeans), these facts were not history lessons; they were the central experiences of their lifetimes.[173]

Moreover, Soviet officials did not regard American behavior as innocuously as did officials in Washington. The Soviets observed mixed signals. They saw the United States rapidly demobilizing and cutting expenditures. But they also perceived the United States negotiating for overseas bases, conducting a new round of atomic tests, maintaining 170 active airfields in overseas locations, and developing jet fighters and attack planes as well as the intercontinental bomber, the B-36.[174] The

Kremlin heard Americans calling for the control of atomic weapons. The Baruch Plan, however, initially envisioned controls over Russian raw materials and processing plants and left the United States with an indefinite monopoly of this most powerful weapon. The Soviets listened to American proposals for the long-term demilitarization of Germany and Japan. Yet they also realized that U.S. officials were deferring reparation payments, paying attention to rehabilitation, retreating from decartelization, and collaborating with traditionally conservative and anti-Soviet groups. The Soviets saw opportunities in the western zones of Germany should the United States withdraw. But the Kremlin also sensed a potential danger emanating from the prospective formation of a Western bloc or the reestablishment of independent German strength.[175] The Soviets welcomed American acknowledgments of the need for friendly governments on Russian borders. Yet wherever Americans could exert influence—for example, in Turkey, Iran, southern Korea, and Japan—they observed that the United States supported groups or governments and encouraged actions that were antipathetic to Russian security needs. And whereas Americans denied the existence of an alliance with Great Britain, Stalin suspected that one existed and made inquiries about informal Anglo-American military collaboration.[176]

The United States might not want war, but it was not overlooking its security interests. If war should erupt by miscalculation, the Americans wanted to have allies, bases, and materiel to win a decisive victory. The Russians knew that in comparison with the United States their power, especially their economic power, was meager. Even their dominating position in Eurasia was a result of the war and not a consequence of the inner vitality of their system. Despite his rhetoric, did not Stalin know this? Did he not sense that even in Eurasia, Russian strength would erode as recovery took place? "How he quivered!" Khrushchev subsequently reflected about his tyrannical boss. "He was afraid of war. He knew that we were weaker than the United States." [177]

Clifford and Elsey's report was silent on such matters, as it was on all the formidable problems facing Soviet leaders. There was famine in the workers' paradise. There were uprisings in the Ukraine, Lithuania, and Belorussia. There were the monumental problems of internal reconstruction and domestic political purification. There were widespread executions and massive deportations of returning soldiers, repatriated prisoners, and suspect minorities. There were bitter rivalries between competing bureaucracies. There was constant, unremitting infighting among Stalin's top lieutenants. As they struggled for power, disputes flared over industrial dismantling in Germany and Manchuria, over reparations and occupation policy, over support for insurrectionary activity abroad, and over levels of expenditures for defense, heavy industry, and consumer goods. Russian leaders had as much trouble sorting out priorities and choosing tactics as did officials in Washington and London. Their foreign policy strategies were as closely tied to their factional rivalries and organizational imperatives as they were to their assessments of revolutionary opportunities abroad or to their appraisals of the security interests of the Soviet Union.[178]

But little of this, of course, found its way into the Clifford-Elsey report. An objective appraisal of Soviet policy would have underscored its defensive and offensive components, its strategic and ideological inputs, its cooperative and competitive thrusts. But Clifford and Elsey were not writing an objective assessment of Soviet foreign policy; they were preparing a brief to justify U.S. actions, past and future. For them, the specter of Soviet expansionism and adventurism overshadowed the evidence of Soviet restraint and vacillation. Indeed the latter were obscured by the very fact that Soviet moderation in Germany, Japan, Western Europe, and much of the Third World did not translate into easy successes for the United States and its democratic friends. In all these areas, fundamental problems remained and vacuums persisted. U.S. officials were uncertain whether they could mobilize the resources to overcome the shortages of food and fuel in the industrial core countries of Eurasia. They were uncertain whether they could combat autarkical forces, promote recovery, and defeat the left in Western Europe. They were uncertain whether the English, French, and Dutch had the ability to co-opt their rebellious colonies on the periphery. They were worried that the political forces that would arise in Germany and Japan might eventually orient their countries toward the Soviet Union if the Kremlin appeared capable of meeting their interests.

The task of Clifford and Elsey was to cohere the disparate threads of policy, to bring about a consensus within the administration, and to mobilize top officials for the difficult initiatives that lay ahead. For them, it was not important to sort out cause and consequence. Whether or not the Soviets were responsible for many of the ongoing portentous developments, they could nevertheless capitalize on them. And if they did, they would co-opt enormously important resources, industrial infrastructure, skilled labor, and bases. As Elsey's handwritten notes indicate and Clifford's reflections confirm, the president had given them a rough idea of what he believed, and it was up to them to make the case. Clifford's intent was to present a clear, unequivocal report. Truman, he later reflected, liked things in black and white.[179]

Policymakers throughout the administration knew what Clifford wanted. He personally brought the list of questions to each agency. Leahy, for example, submitted Clifford's questions to the Joint Strategic Survey Committee, which, in turn, gave the inquiries to an interagency working group comprised of intelligence analysts from the Army, Navy, Air Force, and State Department. This report was then revised at a higher level and the section on Soviet military weaknesses was deleted before the overall assessment was submitted to the White House.[180] Patterson's response was written by members of the Plans and Operations Division under the guidance of its director, General Lauris Norstad. His aim was to reconcile the Army's answers with those of the JCS and to respond to Clifford's questions "in reasonable detail without ambiguity." Norstad knew that the prevailing aim of policy was to put the squeeze on Russia. He wanted Patterson to reaffirm this orientation and to call for prudent rearmament. Forrestal did the same.[181]

If Clifford and Elsey could muster agreement within the administration, action could then be taken to protect American interests. Given international systemic conditions, the vacuums of power, and the worldwide food and fuel shortages, it was simply too risky to try to reassure the Russians. If critical areas opted out of the U.S.-sponsored liberal capitalist, multilateral world order, and if at the same time the Soviets turned out to be as nefarious as most U.S. officials now assumed, the Truman administration would have committed an egregious error. It behooved the leaders of a great power, and the United States was unquestionably the greatest one on earth, to safeguard their nation's security. If, in so doing, they clashed with the interests of an adversary, so be it. At present, the adversary was comparatively weak. Corrective measures now would insure that when it got stronger, it would still be confronted with preponderant power. Even if in the process of building strength the adversary was turned into an implacable foe, it would be unable to defy the existing correlations of power.

The information in the Clifford-Elsey report, if used adroitly, might help generate a consensus at home. Critics on the left could be shown that it was impossible to allay Soviet fears or satisfy its grievances. Partisans on the right would have the rug pulled out from under them as the Democratic administration displayed its courage and determination. Republicans would not be able to say that Truman was soft on communism. Indeed, the Republicans might be leveraged into a position where they would have to generate the funds to support the program of toughness on which they all supposedly agreed.

The Clifford-Elsey report simplified international realities, distorted Soviet behavior, and probably misread Soviet motivations and intentions. But the authors were no fools. They wanted to parry their domestic critics and insure against worst-case scenarios. Only a few years before, the United States had permitted prospective foes to gather strength; only a few years before, the U.S. government had been slow to set limits on totalitarian aggrandizement. Now the international configuration of power was even less auspicious than in the 1930's. But American strength was incomparably greater. Why take chances?

The Cold War Consensus

The lone dissenter in high administration circles was Henry A. Wallace, the former secretary of agriculture, vice president, and current secretary of commerce. Wallace was the hero of American liberals. He worried terribly about recurrent depression and longed mightily for an open world. Russian friendship, he believed, was a necessary component of this international order. Throughout 1946 Wallace grew increasingly unhappy with the get-tough policy of the administration. He believed that American actions regarding bases and atomic energy could be construed in the Kremlin as threatening legitimate Soviet security imperatives. Wallace wanted the United States to make more of an attempt to accommodate Russian strategic interests in Eastern Europe. When he presented these views to the president in July, Wallace found Truman sympathetic but also equivocal and contradictory. The president maintained that he was not anti-Russian. Yet Elsey wanted to use his report to "indoctrinate" the secretary of commerce about the "facts of life" concerning Russia.[182]

Wallace decided to present his views publicly in a major speech at Madison Square Garden on 12 September. The address was a plea for reasonable compromise and a warning that toughness would beget toughness. Wallace championed a spheres-of-influence approach, denounced British imperialism, and heaped scorn upon Republican isolationists who bedecked themselves as hard-nosed realists. The commerce secretary had shown a copy of the speech to Truman. Not wanting to alienate the liberal wing of the Democratic Party and busy with other matters, the president had perused it quickly and given his assent.[183]

Even before Wallace delivered his speech, State Department officials realized it would have a devastating impact on Byrnes's negotiating posture in Paris. They tried but failed to excise the part of the address emphasizing the president's concurrence. When Byrnes learned of Wallace's remarks, he was infuriated. On 19 September, he threatened to resign. The next day Truman fired Wallace.[184]

The circumstances surrounding Wallace's speech attest to the procedural disarray within the Truman administration. It was personally embarrassing and politically costly for the president to fire him. Immediately thereafter, Truman ordered Clifford to retrieve all copies of his report and to lock them in the White House safe. The president feared that leaks would lend credibility to Wallace's accusations and fuel liberal dissent.[185]

Nevertheless, the controversy catalyzed a consensus around the administration's foreign policies. Wallace's speech triggered an enormous amount of press commentary. The commerce secretary was said to have presented a fundamental alternative to the tough line being pursued by Byrnes. The media elite now overwhelmingly supported the approach identified with the secretary of state. When Truman fired Wallace, he was praised for resolving the discordant signals and for choosing the correct substantive program.[186]

The president had no choice if he wanted to preserve bipartisan support of his foreign policy. Senator Vandenberg interpreted Wallace's speech as an attack on the tough policy with which he had associated himself. Since February he had been collaborating with Byrnes, attending the Paris meetings of foreign ministers and the Paris Peace Conference, and defending the administration's policies in the Senate. If Truman had not dismissed Wallace, then Vandenberg's cooperation would have ceased. But there was never any question where Truman and his advisers stood. They were determined to stand tough and stop "babying" the Soviets.[187]

Among top officials in the administration and Republican leaders, there was a consensus about the direction of U.S. policy. The views of Truman and Governor Thomas Dewey of New York, Byrnes and Vandenberg, and Forrestal and John Foster Dulles pretty much coincided.[188] The Democrats took a terrible drubbing in the November 1946 congressional elections, but foreign policy played practically no role in the defeat of the president's party. Republicans capitalized on inflation, strikes, and shortages. Some members of the GOP accused their opponents of Communist sympathies, but they rarely criticized the administration's diplomacy. The two parties, said Republican senator Robert Taft, stood almost together on the question of foreign policy.[189]

By the autumn of 1946, there was general agreement in the United States that the Kremlin was an ideological enemy with no legitimate fears or grievances. Most people were willing to follow the administration in the direction that it wanted to lead. So long as the Truman administration practiced containment and deterrence, so long as it rejected a policy of reassurance and accommodation, it could do pretty much as it liked.[190] The cold war had begun.

Soviet and U.S. troops meet in Germany, May 1945. Photo courtesy George C. Marshall Research Foundation.

President Truman and Secretary of State James Byrnes study the issues during the transatlantic crossing to the Potsdam conference, July 1945. Photo courtesy Marshall Foundation.

President Truman, Secretary of State Byrnes, and Admiral William Leahy view the ruins of the Reichschancellery in Berlin, July 1945. Photo courtesy Harry S. Truman Library.

President Truman and Secretary of State Byrnes visit Marshal Joseph Stalin at the latter's residence at the Potsdam conference. On the balcony in the foreground are Byrnes, Truman, Stalin, and Soviet foreign minister V. M. Molotov. Photo courtesy Truman Library.

Ho Chi Minh and the French minister of colonies, Marius Moutet, in July 1946. A satisfactory deal could not be struck. Photo courtesy National Archives and AP/Wide World Photos.

At left: General George C. Marshall visiting Chairman Mao Tse-tung's headquarters during Marshall's mission to China, 1946. Photo courtesy Marshall Foundation.

At right: President Truman congratulates General Marshall upon becoming secretary of state, January 1947. Former secretary of state James Byrnes looks on. Photo courtesy Marshall Foundation.

Atomic tests at Bikini Island, July 1946. The atomic monopoly helped to cast the shadows of U.S. power around the globe. Photo courtesy Truman Library.

President Truman, Undersecretary of State Robert Lovett, and State Department officials George F. Kennan and Charles E. Bohlen meeting at the White House, 1947. When George Marshall took over the State Department, he relied heavily on the advice of these three men. Photo courtesy Truman Library and United Press International.

British foreign minister Ernest Bevin, U.S. secretary of state George Marshall, Soviet foreign minister V. M. Molotov, and French foreign minister Georges Bidault at the Moscow conference in March 1947. These four statesmen met for many weeks in Moscow and then in London but did not reach any agreement. Photo courtesy Marshall Foundation and AP/Wide World Photos.

Germany's postwar devastation: corrugated iron barracks as emergency housing for the homeless. Photo courtesy Marshall Foundation.

Rebuilding Germany's coal mines was a high priority of U.S. reconstruction policy in Europe after World War II. Photo courtesy Marshall Foundation.

Secretary of Defense James V. Forrestal and President of Columbia University Dwight D. Eisenhower, 1948. Even after Eisenhower retired from his job as Army chief of staff, Forrestal continued to seek his assistance in helping to resolve the disputes between the armed services. Photo courtesy Eisenhower Library.

The Joint Chiefs of Staff in 1949: Admiral Forrest Sherman, General Omar Bradley, General Hoyt Vandenberg, and General J. Lawton Collins. While fighting with one another over the budgets, missions, and roles of their services, the chiefs of staff shared with their civilian colleagues a global view of U.S. security interests. Photo courtesy Marshall Foundation.

Below: President Truman and the Shah of Iran, November 1949. The Shah sought unlimited aid; the United States gave him just enough to keep Iran oriented toward the West. *At right*: Truman and the Iranian nationalist Mohammed Musaddiq, 1951. The Americans feared his radicalism and tried to strike a deal, but they preferred working with the Shah. Photos courtesy Truman Library; National Park Service–Abbie Rowe.

U.S. secretary of state Dean Acheson, British foreign minister Ernest Bevin, and French foreign minister Robert Schuman, December 1950. These three men developed an extraordinary respect for one another. Photo courtesy Marshall Foundation.

Top officials constantly trekked across the Pacific to visit General Douglas MacArthur. He meets with (*top left*) Undersecretary of the Army William Draper, March 1948; (*top right*) John Foster Dulles, June 1950; (*bottom left*) W. Averell Harriman, August 1950; and (*bottom right*) President Truman in Guam, October 1950. Draper and Harriman photos courtesy Marshall Foundation; Dulles and Truman photos courtesy Truman Library.

At right: Secretary of State Acheson and Japanese prime minister Yoshida Shigeru at the San Francisco conference, September 1951. The treaty between the two countries ended the occupation of Japan, provided for the retention of U.S. troops there, and helped co-opt postwar Japan into the U.S. orbit. Photo courtesy National Archives.

At left: General MacArthur and his entourage get an aerial view of the Yalu River as U.N. troops begin the "final offensive," November 24, 1950. *Below*: Four days later, Secretary of State Dean Acheson and Secretary of Defense George Marshall converse at the White House. The strain is evident on their faces as they cope with the massive Chinese intervention in Korea. Photos courtesy Marshall Foundation; latter photo also courtesy AP/Wide World Photos.

At right: Secretary of State Acheson and German chancellor Konrad Adenauer in May 1952 after signing the contractual agreements designed to restore German sovereignty and to keep Germany within a Western orbit. Photo courtesy National Archives and United Press International.

At left: General Dwight Eisenhower, Supreme Allied Commander, Europe, inspecting NATO troops in Germany, April 1951. Photo courtesy Eisenhower Library.

Below: President Truman inspecting tanks at the Aberdeen Military Proving Grounds, February 1951. During the Korean War the U.S. aim was to produce 35,000 tanks per year. Photo courtesy National Archives.

Russians on parade with banners of Joseph Stalin, Moscow, 1951. Photo courtesy National
Archives.

4 ∎

From the Truman Doctrine
to the National Security Act,
November 1946-July 1947

The Republicans were exhilarated with the election returns of November. Gaining 56 seats in the House and 13 in the Senate, they controlled both houses of Congress for the first time since the 1920's. As Truman's popularity rating fell to 32 percent, presidential aspirants like Thomas Dewey, Robert A. Taft, and Arthur Vandenberg savored the prospect of winning the White House in 1948.[1]

The Republicans who flocked to Congress had campaigned for tax cuts and reductions in government expenditures. Although they occasionally ranted against communism and shared the administration's fear of Soviet power, they had no inclination to incur the costs or to assume the commitments that would translate their rhetoric into reality. Many of them, like Kenneth Wherry of Nebraska and James Kem of Missouri, either ran small businesses or represented business constituencies geared to local and regional markets. They had little interest in lowering tariffs or promoting multilateral trade. They appeared to be economic nationalists and political isolationists.[2]

Truman and his advisers were gravely worried that, despite the consensus over goals, their political opponents would cut defense expenditures, occupation appropriations, and foreign assistance. Lamenting the approaching "shadow of Congress," Navy Secretary Forrestal ruminated that "we want full employment, high wages, low prices, reduced taxes, a balanced budget, a strong Army and Navy, a high export trade and at the same time protection for domestic industries." But "when the chips are down and the heat is on for the final decision," Forrestal predicted, "the winner will be the balanced budget and lower taxes."[3]

This prospect was frightening. Officials knew that more, not less, money would be needed to allay unrest abroad and preserve stability. Frigid temperatures and heavy snows during the winter of 1946–47 set back recovery in Europe, intensified Britain's financial problems, and accentuated food and fuel shortages everywhere.

Systemic problems and vacuums of power loomed larger than ever. New initiatives were imperative, and they came quickly in the form of the Truman Doctrine, the European Recovery Program, and the National Security Act.

Faced with a set of daunting problems abroad and the need to secure congressional support at home, Truman turned to George C. Marshall for help. In January 1947 he announced that Marshall would become his secretary of state. Still not wanting to handle the details of foreign policy, Truman sought someone he could rely on to take charge of the nation's diplomacy, sort out priorities, reconcile means and ends, and mobilize a bipartisan consensus. James Byrnes had flubbed his opportunity. But Marshall had a marvelous capacity to inspire loyalty in his subordinates, make decisions, and think long term. Although he was no longer at the top of his ability, his stature was great and his reputation for integrity enormous. From the moment he returned from China, Marshall sought to reassure Republican leaders that he had no political ambitions of his own and would not use foreign policy for the partisan advantage of the Democratic Party. At the same time he moved immediately to impose order and clarify the chain of command within the State Department. He decided to establish a Policy Planning Staff under the directorship of George Kennan. He also insisted that all divisional recommendations go through the office of the undersecretary of state. As a result, Dean Acheson agreed to stay on the job for another six months. For the first time, moreover, Acheson now had substantial decisionmaking power.[4]

Marshall turned his own attention to mastering the many difficult problems that lay ahead. While in China, he had given little thought to matters elsewhere. Now his subordinates showered him with briefing books. There was much to learn in very little time. He was scheduled to leave for Moscow in early March for another meeting of the Council of Foreign Ministers, at which time German problems would head the agenda.[5] Before Marshall left, however, there was a dramatic new development. And it could not be solved without Republican support.

The Eastern Mediterranean, the Middle East, and the Truman Doctrine

On 21 February, the British informed Washington that given their financial woes they could not sustain their assistance to Greece and Turkey. They wanted to pull their troops out of Greece and terminate their military aid to both countries.[6]

It was a historic moment, but there were no agonizing reappraisals in Washington. Eighteen months before, around the time of the Potsdam conference, U.S. officials had decided to oppose a greater Soviet presence in the Turkish straits, the Eastern Mediterranean, and the Middle East.[7] Thereafter, they pressured the Russians to withdraw from Iran and tried to stiffen Turkish resistance to Soviet diplomatic overtures.[8] During 1946 they also resolved to prolong the Anglo-American military administration in Trieste.[9] And in late 1946, they pressed Iranian prime minister Qavam to excise Communist Tudeh members from his government and to consolidate the shah's control over Azerbaijan.[10]

If the British could not contain the Soviets in the Eastern Mediterranean, the United States would have to do so. Neither Acheson nor William Clayton, the number-three man in the State Department, had any doubt whatsoever about this point. "The reins of world leadership," Clayton noted, "are fast slipping from Britain's competent but now very weak hands. These reins will be picked up either by the United States or by Russia. If by Russia, there will almost certainly be war in the next decade or so, with the odds against us. If by the United States, war can almost certainly be prevented." [11]

The specific fear was that the Greek Communists (KKE) would gain power and align Greece with the Soviet Union. The success of the Communists in Greece might have a bandwagon effect throughout Europe. Truman's recapitulation of his thinking in his *Memoirs* closely paralleled Kennan's contemporaneous arguments in behalf of assistance to Greece. The president declared:

If we were to turn our back on the world, areas such as Greece, weakened and divided as a result of the war, would fall into the Soviet orbit without much effort on the part of the Russians. The success of Russia in such areas and our avowed lack of interest would lead to the growth of domestic Communist parties in such European countries as France and Italy, where they were already significant threats. Inaction . . . could only result in handing to the Russians vast areas of the globe now denied to them.[12]

As Truman's words suggest, Soviet actions were not the source of the problem. The Russians did not have to do much (and were not doing much) to benefit from developments in Greece. Military planners and State Department analysts knew that the problems beleaguering Greece were primarily political and psychological. The British presence had bolstered conservative forces. Should the British depart, the momentum would shift to the left. Communist successes in Greece, moreover, would have profound consequences elsewhere: France and Italy might go Communist; the U.S. position in North Africa and the Iberian Peninsula would be imperiled; and non-Communist parties throughout northwestern Europe would lose hope. At the end of this ominous sequence, Kennan noted, "the military-economic potential of the area of the world which we had abandoned to hostile forces would be several times greater than that of the area which would be left to us." [13]

This scenario deeply troubled Pentagon officials. Forrestal worried that if the Russians gained a presence in the Eastern Mediterranean they would have the ability to cut the flow of critical raw materials to the West. European governments, lacking enough coal to sustain recovery, needed access to Middle Eastern oil. Denied petroleum and other critical resources, Europe would founder and go Communist.[14]

It was taken for granted that Turkey as well as Greece would receive American help. Yet as Acheson worked on the draft legislation, he found it difficult to justify assistance to Turkey. Turkey did not need aid for relief or reconstruction, nor was it wracked by financial instability or internal unrest. It was not under any real pressure from the Kremlin.[15] Nevertheless, U.S. officials decided that Turkey must receive assistance. Greece is on the "flank," conceded Forrestal, but if Turkey falls into the Soviet orbit "you have an impossible military situation." [16]

According to the Joint Chiefs of Staff (JCS), should Russia dominate Turkey, the transportation routes through the Eastern Mediterranean would be severed and the entire Middle East would fall within the Soviet orbit. Army Chief of Staff Dwight Eisenhower emphasized that, if the United States could not traverse the Mediterranean, it would be denied access to Middle Eastern airfields from which to launch strategic air operations in wartime. Admiral Chester Nimitz, the chief of naval operations, agreed. But he believed that Eisenhower was thinking too narrowly about the advantages to the United States. The Mediterranean, said Forrest Sherman, the vice chief of naval operations, should be conceived as "a highway" for the projection of military power "deep into the heart of the land mass of Eurasia and Africa." [17]

Kennan subsequently claimed that the Pentagon deftly inserted military aid for Turkey into legislation initially designed as a political and economic program for Greece. This contention grossly simplifies the bureaucratic process and ignores the strategic thinking that had been evolving since the end of the war. Loy Henderson, director of the State Department's Office of Near Eastern and African Affairs, spoke forcefully in behalf of aid to Turkey. Kennan objected, believing that military assistance would be provocative. Acheson, however, supported Henderson. At a critical interagency meeting on 12 March, when Secretary of War Robert Patterson argued in behalf of an exclusively economic program for Turkey, both Acheson and Henderson made the case for military assistance. Subsequently, State Department officials tried to handle the strategic dimension very delicately in testimony before Congress. Joseph Jones, a key State Department participant in these meetings, nevertheless observed, "The strategic importance of Turkey ranked high in discussions within the executive branch and in discussions with congressional leaders." Indeed, the president himself was fully apprised of these strategic ramifications.[18]

■

The task of convincing Congress and the American people to support aid for Greece and Turkey would be difficult. Throughout the autumn of 1946 and the early winter of 1947, the Russians had seemed conciliatory. Stalin issued moderate statements to correspondents, and Molotov made some important concessions. The Soviets did not obstruct U.N. action on Greece, nor did they react aggressively to Qavam's move into Azerbaijan.[19]

Columnists, commentators, and editors discussed a softening of the Soviet position. In early January, *Newsweek*, *U.S. News*, and *Business Week* speculated optimistically about the future of Soviet-U.S. relations. For a while, allusions to Soviet probes virtually disappeared. There was certainly trouble in many places, but little of it could be attributed directly to the Soviet Union. Briefly, Americans grew more hopeful. There was still considerable distrust of the Kremlin, but State Department analysts of public opinion conceded that "Satisfaction with Big Three cooperation has increased, reversing a trend in progress since September 1945." [20]

Congress seemed no more eager to take positive action than did the American people. The Republican victory resurrected the specter of economic nationalism and political isolationism. Among the entering class of Republican senators were John Bricker from Ohio, Joseph McCarthy from Wisconsin, Zales Ecton from Montana, Arthur H. Watkins from Utah, and Henry Dworshak from Idaho. As the political sociologist Lynn Eden has shown, these men joined the ranks of other isolationist-leaning Republicans from the midwestern and mountain states who had been elected since 1938. Their concerns with overseas developments were limited; their willingness to incur shortages or postpone tax reductions was nonexistent. They were still committed to America first, and their antipathy to foreign entanglements and financial sacrifices was pronounced.[21]

Policymakers dwelled on the constraints posed by public and congressional attitudes. Clayton said the American people had to be "shocked" into action; John Hickerson, deputy director of the State Department's Office of European Affairs, used the term "electrify." On 27 February, when Truman, Marshall, and Acheson met with congressional leaders, Acheson politely interrupted Marshall's presentation and described the situation in apocalyptic terms. A Russian "breakthrough," he warned, "might open three continents to Soviet penetration. . . . The Soviet Union was playing one of the greatest gambles in history at minimal cost. . . . We and we alone were in a position to break up the play." When he finished, there was a long silence. Finally Senator Vandenberg solemnly declared, "Mr. President, if you will say that to the Congress and the country, I will support you and I believe that most of its members will do the same." [22]

But Truman was not convinced. He maintained that the administration faced the greatest selling job in U.S. history. A special committee, including Acheson, Forrestal, and Patterson, took charge of the public-information campaign. Officials expended enormous energy preparing Truman's address to Congress. The president wanted "no hedging in this speech. . . . It had to be clear and free of hesitation or double talk." Acheson met repeatedly with leading reporters; Forrestal called his business acquaintances and talked to owners of newspapers and radio stations; the State Department's Office of Public Affairs launched a full-scale public relations blitz. Finally, on 12 March, the president appeared before a joint session of Congress and requested $400 million for aid to Greece and Turkey. A "fateful hour" had arrived; nations "must choose between alternate ways of life. . . . If we falter in our leadership," Truman declared, "we may endanger the peace of the world." [23]

The media instantly hailed the Truman Doctrine as a "historic landmark in American foreign policy"; Truman's decision to resist aggressive communism was deemed no less significant than the Monroe Doctrine and the decision to oppose

Hitler.[24] The president dramatized the situation to transform public attitudes and win support for a new initiative. Heretofore neither Congress nor the American people had been eager to embark on costly programs to contain Soviet power. Though critical of Russia, most Americans were content with the existing "firm" policy. As Truman and his advisers sensed, most Americans simply did not attribute great significance to problems of foreign affairs.[25]

Truman had to reshape these attitudes. By seizing the initiative, utilizing ideological language, embarking on a crusade, and placing the prestige of the presidency and the country at risk over the issue of aid to Greece and Turkey, he elicited support from a wary Congress. Some senators questioned the administration's case for aid to Turkey; others lamented Truman's disregard of the United Nations. Few, however, could resist the president's tactics. "We are confronted," Vandenberg acknowledged, "with the fundamental fact that if we desert the President of the United States at [this] moment we cease to have any influence in the world forever." Republican senator Henry Cabot Lodge from Massachusetts agreed. Repudiating the president, he said, would be like throwing the flag on the ground and stomping on it.[26]

The debate was protracted, but the administration won. On 22 April the Senate approved, voting 67–23. The House acted on 8 May, and there the vote was 287–107. Although the Republicans controlled both houses, there would be no resurgence of isolationism. Indeed, isolationism remained only a minority strand within the Republican Party. Now almost exclusively rooted in the midwestern and mountain states, isolationism could still influence the size and configuration of administration programs, but it could not masquerade as a policy alternative.[27]

Most people followed the administration's lead. Official rhetoric sometimes conjured up images of war when no such threat existed. But despite the hyperbole, it is important to realize that the fears were real. Truman and his advisers believed that British retrenchment, political instability, and economic dislocation afforded the Soviets opportunities to expand into the Eastern Mediterranean and Middle East, thereby gathering strength that would enable them to challenge the United States in still more important areas. Underlying the ideological crusade were deeply rooted geopolitical convictions that defined national self-interest in terms of correlations of power based on the control of critical resources, bases, and industrial infrastructure. Newspaper editors, sharing these same assumptions, supported the Truman Doctrine because of their concern with prospective shifts in the balance of power. The ideological fervor, however, was important: by defining the enemy as inveterately hostile, it eliminated the prospect for compromise and accommodation; it also helped bring former isolationists into the interventionist camp, thereby creating the climate for yet additional measures.[28]

Priorities

During the hearings, senators had asked searching questions about the global implications and financial costs of the Truman Doctrine. Acheson and Clayton denied that the administration was launching an indiscriminate program of assistance. "I do not think," Clayton told Senator Walter George, "that it would be wise to draw any conclusions . . . that this is just the first step in a great, big program of relief." Greece and Turkey, he insisted, "are the only two critical, really critical, situations that I know of at the moment." [29]

Clayton was dissembling. Top policymakers knew that aid to Greece and Turkey was only the first step in shoring up U.S. interests around the world. At the end of their meeting on 26 February, Marshall, Acheson, Forrestal, and Patterson agreed that "the Greek and Turkish problems were only part of a critical world situation . . . and that attention must be given to the problem as a whole." The draft legislation that Acheson submitted to the president was carefully framed "to cover other countries should analogous situations develop." "This is only the beginning," Truman told the cabinet on 7 March.[30]

But policymakers had to determine priorities, because American resources would be stretched to the breaking point. Assistance programs would fuel inflation. During the last six months of 1946, wholesale prices jumped 24 percent; the consumer price index climbed 15 percent. In March, Edwin G. Nourse, chairman of the newly established Council of Economic Advisers, warned the president of the dangers to the economy.[31] It was imperative to determine which countries most needed assistance, whether aid should be economic or military, and whether foreign assistance should take precedence over domestic rearmament.

For several months, Army officials had been pressing for interagency studies of priorities for military assistance. Tough choices had to be made between programs for Latin America, China, the Philippines, Iran, Greece, and Turkey. In addition, the needs of Germany and Japan were growing, and a grant of $600 million to Korea over three years had been proposed. Assistant Secretary of War Howard Petersen doubted the nation could support all these obligations. Our goals, he wrote Patterson, "are out of balance with our means." Eisenhower, too, bemoaned the gap between resources and "our great bag of commitments." [32]

Patterson and Forrestal, therefore, responded positively when Acheson proposed that they set up a special State-War-Navy Coordinating Committee (SWNCC) subcommittee to devise a comprehensive assistance program. After working throughout April, the subcommittee recommended long-term programs of economic and military assistance. "It is important to maintain in friendly hands areas which contain or protect sources of metals, oil, and other national resources, which contain strategic objectives, . . . which contain a substantial industrial potential, which possess manpower and organized military forces in important quantities, or which [would] . . . enable the United States to exert a greater influence for world stability, security, and peace." The urgency of the situation was the criterion for determining priorities; Greece, Turkey, Iran, Italy, Korea, France, Austria, and Hungary headed the SWNCC list of countries most needing assistance.[33]

Meanwhile, the JCS conducted its own far more sophisticated and practical study of priorities. The JCS identified areas most urgently in need of assistance and most important to national security. The JCS categorically recommended that aid go first to Britain, France, and Germany. Next in importance were Italy, Greece, Turkey, Austria, and Japan. At the bottom of the list were Korea, China, and the Philippines. The message was unequivocal: nothing would be more detrimental to U.S. security than "the conquest or communization" of Britain or France. But these countries could not withstand a Soviet assault on their own; they would need Germany aligned with them. The JCS stressed that "the complete resurgence of German industry, particularly coal mining, is essential for the economic recovery of France—whose security is inseparable from the combined security of the United States, Canada, and Great Britain. The economic revival of Germany is therefore of primary importance from the viewpoint of United States security."[34]

The JCS emphasis on Britain, France, and Germany resembled Kennan's thinking. Kennan, who was about to take charge of the Policy Planning Staff, wanted to concentrate on Western Europe. Herein resided the industrial infrastructure that the Soviets must not be permitted to co-opt. He worried that a Communist triumph in Greece might be replicated in France; he worried even more about the future of Germany. "The only really dangerous thing in my mind is the possibility that the technical skills of the Germans might be combined with the physical resources of Russia." That combination was not likely to arise, but if it ever should come about, "then there would have come into existence an aggregate of economic and military industrial power which ought to make every one of us sit up and take notice damn fast."[35]

■

State Department and Pentagon officials agreed not only on the overriding importance of Western Europe but also that economic assistance should have priority over military aid. This conclusion became clear in the weeks following the submission of the initial SWNCC report. The rearmament subcommittee, for example, presented a study derogating the efficacy of military aid. The War Department Intelligence Staff pointed out that Britain did not need military assistance and that France required it only to consolidate its hold over its colonies. Military assistance was recommended only for a few countries, like Greece and the Philippines, where it could be used by governments friendly to the United States to preserve internal order. In most cases, economic aid was likely to prove much more efficacious in countries beleaguered by strong Communist parties.[36]

Some military men questioned whether domestic rearmament should not take priority over foreign assistance.[37] The Atomic Energy Commission had warned the president of "serious weaknesses" in the defense program. There were only a few atomic bombs (probably thirteen) in the stockpile; military personnel were not fully trained to assemble them; testing was inadequate; and supplies of raw materials were below expectations.[38] At the same time, inflation was eroding aircraft procurement, and overseas base construction was only creeping along.[39] Although plans were made and measures were taken to overcome some of these problems, the steps did not allay anxieties about the contraction of American strategic air power and the inadequacy of the American base system.[40]

Dismayed as they were about the size of appropriations and eager as they were to foster the organizational interests of their services, the most influential men in the Pentagon continued to accord a higher priority to reconstruction than to rearmament. Like Kennan and Marshall, they believed that the major threat to U.S. security stemmed from prevailing economic dislocation and social upheaval. "In the necessary delicate apportioning of our available resources," wrote Petersen, "the time element permits emphasis on strengthening the economic dikes against Soviet communism rather than upon preparing for a possible eventual, but not yet inevitable war."[41]

Rearmament remained subordinate to reconstruction because defense analysts did not expect Soviet aggression. The Russians were too weak economically to risk war with the United States, at least in the short run. Ferdinand Eberstadt, former director of the Army-Navy Munitions Board, studied Soviet economic statistics and reported to Forrestal, "None but mad men . . . would undertake war against us." After visiting the Soviet Union at the end of 1946, British field marshal Bernard Law Montgomery wrote Eisenhower that the Russians are "very, very tired. Devastation in Russia is appalling and the country is in no fit state to go to war." Eisenhower concurred. So did Walter Bedell Smith, Eisenhower's wartime chief of staff, who estimated that the Soviets would not be able to engage in a major military conflict for ten to fifteen years.[42]

Strategic planners worked on their war plans but emphasized that these were merely theoretical exercises.[43] They were not awed by Soviet military strength. They were aware that the Russians were continuing to demobilize at home and to withdraw significant numbers of troops from Korea, Austria, Hungary, Romania, Poland, and Germany.[44] They did not think that Soviet capabilities had increased much during the preceding twelve months, and they did not expect them to grow significantly during the next couple of years. They concluded that the Kremlin would avoid "any serious risk of war with the United States for some years to come." Although Army intelligence analysts still believed that Soviet armies would have no difficulty overrunning Western Europe, the Kremlin's capacity to wage war effectively against the United States was limited "because of the lack of a sufficiently powerful economic system, of mass destruction weapons, of a long-range bomber force, and of a deep sea Navy."[45]

There was, then, substantial consensus about U.S. priorities in early 1947. Military planners, intelligence analysts, and defense officials frequently met with Kennan during these months and found themselves in agreement with much that he had to say. In his view, military preparations and the conduct of diplomacy were intimately related. Preparedness was a great deterrent to war. The United States needed to have in existence a highly mobile force composed of Army, Air Force, and Navy units. They had to be equipped with the most modern weapons in order to seize advanced strategic bases from which long-range bombers could operate against the Soviet Union. The United States, Kennan stressed, should be able to render a quick, sharp punch in any part of the world. If a major war erupted, American air forces should "smash the war-making potential of Russia to hell." [46]

But there was no reason to pour a disproportionate share of resources into defense. In fact, there was time to learn more about Soviet strengths and weaknesses. While military spending was constrained, intelligence expenditures soared. At the end of the war, Truman had disbanded the Office of Strategic Services. In early 1946, however, he had created the Central Intelligence Group (CIG) to coordinate, evaluate, and disseminate intelligence from other agencies. It depended on the Army, Navy, Air Force, and State Department for data, money, and personnel. In June 1946, Hoyt Vandenberg took over the organization. He was a dynamic, three-star Air Force general with superb political connections, related as he was to the Republican senator from Michigan. Vandenberg inherited an agency with only a few hundred professional and clerical personnel. Frustrated by clashes with the existing intelligence agencies and convinced that parochial bureaucratic interests were undermining an important governmental function, he secured permission for the CIG to collect and analyze (not just collate) intelligence data. He expanded the analysis section of the CIG from 29 to 300. He took over the Army's Strategic Services Unit, thereby acquiring overseas personnel and field stations as well as codes and communications equipment. He established the Office of Special Operations for espionage and counterespionage. When Secretary of War Patterson championed covert psychological operations in late 1946 and when the SWNCC formed a subcommittee to establish policy for clandestine activities in April 1947, Vandenberg savored the opportunity for the CIG to assume operational control. By mid-1947, when Vandenberg resigned to become vice chief of staff of the Air Force, the CIG had expanded more than six-fold. He left behind an agency with over 1,800 men and women, a third of whom were overseas. Plans were afoot to hire another 1,200 people.[47]

Civilian and military officials supported CIG growth because they agreed that the priority task was to win the political and psychological contest with the Soviets. Kennan, for example, insisted that if Communist momentum was slowed, people would desert western Communist parties in droves. "I think you might see a general crumbling of Russian influence and prestige which could carry beyond those countries themselves, beyond the satellite countries, and into the heart of the Soviet

Union itself." If, then, the United States did not waste its strength, if it acted wisely and focused on priorities, containment could eventually translate into liberation.[48]

The German Enigma and the Moscow Conference

Almost all U.S. officials agreed that there was no issue of greater importance than Germany. The stultifying economy of the western zones continued to constrain recovery throughout Western Europe. During the first quarter of 1947, German textile production was 21.5 percent of its 1938 level; iron and steel production 19.5 percent; chemical production 22.3 percent; hard-coal production 41 percent; and overall industrial production 24 percent. German imports and exports were less than 20 percent of their levels in 1938 and constituted the principal reason for the laggard recovery in intra-European trade. Even when the terrible winter of 1947 accentuated the importance of German coal for the rest of Europe, German coal exports still hovered around 20 percent of their prewar levels.[49]

From the American perspective, the situation was intolerable. No one wanted to continue subsidizing the German economy. The Republican control of Congress, moreover, intensified the pressure to cut costs and remedy the situation. A report by former president Herbert C. Hoover in late February 1947 won wide approval. Discounting any possibility of severing the Ruhr, Hoover claimed that German industry must be rehabilitated, that certain industries must be taken off the prohibited list, and that German reparations must be subordinated to the larger goals of West European stabilization and U.S. tax reduction. Most Americans now deemed the revival of German peacetime industries more important than unifying the western and eastern zones. In other words, unification took a backseat to recovery.[50]

When Marshall became secretary of state in January, he immediately focused on the German problem. Briefing him for the forthcoming Moscow meeting of the Council of Foreign Ministers, his aides insisted that his principal goal was "a Germany . . . integrated into Europe." Yet Marshall had to move cautiously, because an independent, autonomous Germany could use its control of the resources of the Ruhr to reap major political concessions from other European governments. No one could predict the orientation of a future German government. This uncertainty made it imperative to insure that the new German government be decentralized and that mechanisms be devised for international control of the Ruhr. But under no circumstance should the Russians be permitted to influence economic developments in the Ruhr or to maneuver for political advantage throughout the western zones. Although economic unification would aid German recovery and was a goal worth pursuing, it was not important enough to justify concessions to the Soviets. Priorities were priorities. And there was no more important priority than reviving the production of western Germany and using it to win the loyalty of the German people and to satisfy the economic and political needs of other West European governments.[51]

The advice emanating from the War Department in Washington was quite similar. By now Colonel Charles Bonesteel was the key adviser on German matters to Secretary Patterson and Assistant Secretary Petersen. "The fundamental problem," Bonesteel wrote, "is to achieve a free and independent Germany under adequate safeguards." A divided Germany would have "catastrophic consequences and would create an ever present threat to peace. However, a unified Germany wholly dominated by or genuinely aligned with the Soviets could . . . be an even greater threat." Bonesteel warned against piecemeal concessions that would provide the Kremlin with opportunities to gain influence or absorb German power. Bonesteel's superiors endorsed these views and sent them to John Hilldring at the State Department. The young colonel then joined Marshall's delegation to the Moscow conference.[52]

Marshall also invited John Foster Dulles to accompany him to Moscow. Vandenberg could not get away from his Senate duties and Marshall wanted to sustain bipartisan support of the administration's policies. Dulles agreed to go. He had strong views on the German problem that had evolved from almost three decades of experience with West European economic and financial affairs. Dulles stressed that "German economic potential . . . should be fully developed and integrated into western Europe," but without the risk of giving "economic mastery to the Germans." The Republican spokesman had little confidence in the Germans and even less trust in the Russians. Once the Germans began to recover, Dulles assumed that they "will almost certainly be dominated by a spirit of revenge and ambition to recover a great power status." They would be tempted to align themselves with the Soviets. Already there was plentiful evidence that the Kremlin was taking over east German industry and reorienting it to serve the Soviet economy. If the Western powers allowed the Soviet Union to receive reparations in kind or to participate in the control of the Ruhr, the Kremlin's leverage would be extended into the industrial heartland of Western Europe. The Ruhr, after all, was the fundamental source of Europe's war-manufacturing potential. Dulles warned Marshall "that the economy of Central Europe, including Scandinavia, was being integrated into and drained into that of the Soviet Union, and that if this tendency extended on into Western Europe, western civilization and personal freedom, as we had known it, would be impossible." [53]

With this advice reverberating in his mind, Marshall set out for the Moscow conference in early March. On his way he stopped in Paris. He knew the French would still resist U.S. efforts to revive the German economy and to establish a provisional German government. The French were infuriated that the Anglo-American bizonal arrangement had reduced German coal shipments to France. French production had nearly recovered, but the escalating cost of raw materials, the diminution of foreign exchange reserves, and the shortage of coal posed significant hurdles, especially in view of the frigid winter temperatures and the spiraling inflation that was eroding the real income of French workers. The Communists had done very well again in the fall elections, and Socialist premier Leon Blum held only precarious control of the tripartite coalition. Blum needed money, coal, and strategic guarantees. When he resigned in January 1947, French premier Paul Ramadier and foreign minister Georges Bidault continued the negotiations for a security treaty with the British, the Treaty of Dunkirk. Yet this agreement was primarily a symbolic gesture, reflecting British foreign secretary Ernest Bevin's fear that French unhappiness with Anglo-American policy in Germany might drive the French into the arms of the Kremlin.[54]

In Paris and again in Moscow, Marshall listened courteously to the usual French demands for coal and security. With remarkable sensitivity and great sincerity, Marshall recapitulated his own experiences in France during the last years of World War I. No one outside of France, Marshall said, grasped French apprehensions and suffering better than he did. The United States would not repudiate its allies this time. He stressed the utility of the four-power pact guaranteeing Germany's demilitarization. The proposed treaty represented a transformation in U.S. policy, a long-term pledge to keep Germany disarmed and to enhance European security. Hoping to lure the French into an agreement to fuse their zone in Germany with Bizonia—the combined British and American zones—Marshall also indicated that the French could have a say in the distribution of Ruhr coal.[55]

When he got to Moscow, Marshall also tried to sell the demilitarization pact to the Russians. Molotov, however, questioned its benefits. He was much more concerned with obtaining reparations from current German production to fuel Russian recovery. This issue became the major stumbling block at the conference. If the United States agreed to this demand and to Soviet participation in the control of the Ruhr, Molotov indicated that he would accept an upward revision in the level of German industry as well as economic unification of the four zones.[56]

Although the bleakness of Russian life lent credibility to Molotov's arguments, the U.S. delegates had no desire to accommodate the Soviet position. They feared that reparations from current production would tie the western zones of Germany to the Soviet economy. Moreover, if the Russians participated in the supervision of the Ruhr, they could meddle in West European economic affairs and add to the costs of the U.S. occupation. Likewise, if the United States accepted a more centralized structure for the German provisional government, the German Communists might well increase their influence. The American delegates contended that the Potsdam accords forbade reparations from current production. But Marshall was uncomfortable with this argument. Not only did the British disagree, but even some U.S. officials doubted its veracity.[57]

Faced with a deadlock, Marshall summoned General Lucius Clay to Moscow. Clay told the other American delegates that the Russians were negotiating from weakness. He advocated flexibility. Whereas Dulles, Bonesteel, and Smith hesitated to take risks lest they lose all of Germany, Clay wanted to contest for eastern Germany and to project U.S. influence into Eastern Europe. Shrewd bargaining, Clay insisted, was the key to success. He wanted Marshall to consider reparations from current production. The Kremlin, however, would have to augment the level of German industrial production, provide the raw materials (without cost) for the production of reparations, and defer the collection of reparations until Germany experienced an export-import balance.[58]

Dulles and Clay fumed at one another's positions. Marshall wavered. Clay, he knew, had enormous experience, but Dulles's support would be critical at home when the administration requested additional funding from the Republican-dominated Congress.[59] The matter was still unresolved when a cable arrived from Truman and Acheson. Unhappy about a deal involving reparations from current production, they insisted that reparations, even in limited quantities, would be permissible only after German import needs were fulfilled and West European priorities were met. Recognizing these conditions as too restrictive to permit agreement, Marshall decided to focus the conference's attention on the four-power demilitarization pact and the Austrian treaty. But Molotov refused to abandon his quest for a satisfactory reparations agreement.[60]

Marshall grew increasingly frustrated. By the middle of April he was eager to return to Washington. On the 15th, he had a long interview with Stalin at the Kremlin. During the initial proceedings of the conference, he had not wanted to bother the Soviet leader. But now Marshall was chagrined by the lack of progress; the conferees were deadlocked on the demilitarization issue. Immediate zonal fusion, he told Stalin, was imperative to alleviate the burden on U.S. taxpayers and to avert economic disaster in Germany. Although he hoped for the resumption of wartime cooperation, Marshall said he would inform the president that the Russians appeared to have little desire to reach an accord.

Stalin was conciliatory. He stressed Russian fears of a revived and powerful Germany, yet he opposed dismemberment because he worried about German irredentism. Stalin said he, too, favored German economic unity, but unlike the Anglo-Saxon powers, Soviet Russia could not afford to forgo reparations. Minimizing the differences among the allies, Stalin emphasized that compromises were still possible on the key issues. Patient, painstaking negotiations would produce satisfactory results.[61]

Patience was one quality that Marshall and Bevin no longer possessed. Although Stalin's reparation demands were not excessive, the Americans and the British wanted a quick agreement on their own terms.[62] The situation in the western zones of Germany was worsening every day. Major food riots erupted, and even the 1,550-calories ration was imperiled by growing shortages. Clay remonstrated over the "rapid penetration of communism," and his political adviser, Robert Murphy, said he had not seen German morale so low since the days of Germany's capitulation.[63]

In Moscow, Marshall and Bevin spent more and more time privately discussing their own plans for the improvement of administrative arrangements in Bizonia and for raising the level of industry. Marshall also met with Bidault to elicit France's compliance with new measures to integrate a revived Germany into a Western orbit.

When the Council of Foreign Ministers finally adjourned on 25 April, Marshall was relieved. On his return to Washington, he stopped in Berlin to instruct Clay to renew his efforts to resolve Anglo-American differences in Bizonia and to accelerate production in the Ruhr. These matters were now more important than effecting quadripartite economic unity.[64]

Marshall returned to Washington determined to seize the initiative. His first task was to expedite food shipments to Bizonia. He pleaded with the secretary of agriculture to procure additional wheat for the western zones in order to stave off economic and social chaos. Although Clay felt that neither the State nor the War Department was sufficiently alert to the problems he was encountering, no one in Washington disputed his contention that famine stalked Bizonia. Rations were down to 1,200 calories. Without additional food, they feared they would lose "the great struggle . . . to prevent [Germany] going communistic."[65]

More food was necessary to raise coal production. The daily output of 215,000 tons was far below anticipated levels. Miners were hungry; they had no incentive to work; there was nothing to buy. Absenteeism was high, productivity low. The shortfall in coal production constrained overall industrial output in Germany and was increasingly restraining recovery in neighboring countries, especially France. When Kennan finally took the helm of the Policy Planning Staff in May, his first priority was boosting coal production in the Ruhr. There was nothing original about this approach. For months, Clay and Petersen had been insisting that coal and food were the indispensable prerequisites to economic recovery throughout Western Europe. But the consensus over goals did not make it easier to achieve the objective. Improved productivity in the Ruhr depended on providing the miners with food, consumer goods, and housing, on the supply of new machinery and steel equipment, and, finally, on better management of the Ruhr economy in general and the coal mines in particular.[66]

This latter issue aroused more controversy than any other. Since April, Clay had been expressing virulent opposition to British plans to socialize German industry and to introduce a centralized and planned economy. He maintained that British efforts directly aided the German Social Democrats (SPD). He wanted a strategy that would stifle the influence of the SPD and foster free enterprise. State Department officials questioned Clay's tactics. They especially feared that the German Communists would profit politically if occupation authorities openly forbade socialization and sought to dictate the future of Germany's economy.[67]

The issue came up repeatedly at meetings of the secretaries of state, war, and Navy. Patterson and Forrestal vehemently opposed British socialization plans. Forrestal saw the issue in ideological terms and insisted that the Truman administration should express its unequivocal disapproval to the highest British officials. Ideology was secondary to the leaders of the War Department; their overriding goal was production. Economic and social reform must not be allowed to interfere with output. Patterson and Petersen pressed their views relentlessly upon Marshall. The secretary of state still worried about the political repercussions inside Germany, but he was persuaded by officials in the War Department to take action. At the end of June, admitting that British management of the coal mines was pathetic, he said that future aid would not be forthcoming unless he was convinced that the Labour government could solve the problem. He wanted socialization postponed for five years. He called for an Anglo-American coal conference, at which time he would press these matters with vigor.[68]

Boosting coal production was only part of the larger task of raising German industrial production. When he returned from Moscow, Marshall agreed that the level of industry set by the four powers in March 1946 had to be revised upward. The German population was larger than expected. Germany was unable to export soft goods in the quantities previously predicted, certainly not enough to pay for required imports. Most important, the levels established in 1946 prevented Germany from producing the goods that were needed for recovery by other European countries. Steel quotas, for example, were ridiculously low. Moreover, some industries had to be taken off the prohibited list. Prospective changes would eventually enable Germany to enjoy a standard of living above the average of European countries. Admittedly, these revisions would depart from the Potsdam agreement. Nevertheless, there did not seem to be any alternative if priorities in Western Europe were to be achieved. So the State Department recommended that the United States seek approval from the British and French and act without the compliance of the Soviets. The War Department concurred.[69]

The State Department also wanted Germany to participate fully in the preparation of a comprehensive recovery plan. Patterson and Petersen worried, however, that recommendations to aid overall European recovery might necessitate increased expenditures in Germany, at least in the short run. They wanted to insure that funds would be available to cover these increased costs. This matter would cause interdepartmental friction in the future. On 3 July, however, Marshall, Patterson, and Forrestal had no difficulty reaching agreement: "It is assumed that Germany must cooperate fully in any effective European plan, and that the economic revival of Europe depends in considerable part on a recovery in German production—in coal, in food, steel, fertilizer, etc., and on efficient use of such European resources as the Rhine River."[70]

A week later a new directive was sent to General Clay. The State and War departments had spent months working on it. Designed for public consumption as well as for policy guidance, it set forth U.S. priorities very nicely. World peace depended on the stability and prosperity of Europe, and "an orderly and prosperous Europe requires the economic contributions of a stable and productive Germany."[71] The accelerated efforts to alleviate the food shortages, raise production in the Ruhr coal mines, boost the level of industry, work out zonal arrangements with the British, and lure the French into a trizonal agreement were all designed to overcome western

Germany's economic paralysis and to bind it to the European Recovery Program that the secretary of state had just announced.

The Marshall Plan and Its Motivations

The initiatives in Germany, of course, formed only part of the effort to promote Western Europe's economic reconstruction. When Marshall returned from the Moscow conference, he told a nationwide radio audience that action was imperative.[72] Marshall and his most important aides were particularly alarmed by developments in France and Italy. In April the French appealed for large shipments of grain and cereals. Claiming that conditions were worse than during the Nazi occupation, they were about to reduce the bread ration to its lowest level. After meeting with French agricultural officials in Geneva, Undersecretary Clayton implored Acheson to get the president to expedite food shipments.[73] Writing from Rome, Ambassador James C. Dunn also pleaded for action: "All the indications we receive . . . show that the Communists are consistently gaining ground and that our policy to assist the development of a free and democratic Italy is losing ground." [74]

Notwithstanding the high prices and short supplies in the United States, Marshall struggled to meet these requests. On 7 May the secretary of state informed the French embassy that additional grain would be shipped during the next few months. Two days later, the World Bank approved a $250 million loan for the modernization of the French steel industry, the improvement of the transport system, and the procurement of critical raw materials. More needed to be done, Marshall admitted to the French ambassador, but emergency demands elsewhere imposed limits.[75] Kennan, for example, wanted to give Italy $350 million in emergency relief funds. Marshall did not think the United States could be this generous. He told the Italian ambassador that Italy might receive a $100 million credit from the Export-Import Bank, $60 million in repatriated assets, and an unspecified sum in the form of post–U.N. Relief and Rehabilitation Administration relief (pending legislative approval).[76]

These emergency relief measures were imbued with political overtones. Acheson announced that nations fighting to preserve their independence and democratic institutions would receive priority treatment. This declaration, along with the Truman Doctrine, encouraged moderate Italian and French leaders to exclude Communists from their coalitions. In the U.S. view, the Communist parties of France, Italy, and Belgium demanded wage increases, supported strikes, and fought redistributive battles that diverted attention and energy from productivity gains and economic expansion. When stagnation ensued, they then profited politically. The United States had previously urged Iranian prime minister Qavam to sever his relations with representatives of the Tudeh Party as a condition for aid. Likewise, assistance to Greece had been accompanied by warnings to form a broad coalition, exclusive of the Greek Communists. In early May, French Socialist premier Ramadier reshuffled his coalition and tried to rule without the Communists. The split was by no means irrevocable, yet the U.S. ambassador in Paris, Jefferson Caffery, tried to make it so. "I told Ramadier," he jotted in his diary, "no Communists in gov. or else." The same type of pressure was exerted upon Christian Democratic leaders in Italy. In Washington and Rome, Secretary Marshall and Ambassador Dunn maintained that emergency U.S. assistance would be predicated on the exclusion of Communists from the government.[77]

U.S. officials hoped to promote coalitions that would be amenable to American leadership and capable of mobilizing support for reconstruction programs that required short-term sacrifices for long-term gains. They wanted European countries to boost their productivity and efficiency, compete effectively in international markets, and find sources of supply outside the Western Hemisphere. If these countries succeeded, they would cut their deficits, overcome the dollar gap, free themselves of U.S. subsidies, and be able to adopt multilateral trade arrangements. Acheson, Clayton, and their associates knew that it would take several years to achieve these goals. In the interval, European governments would need to hold down wages, curb inflation, constrain domestic consumption, cap welfare programs, balance budgets, and stabilize currencies. As Ambassador Dunn noted, such conditions could not be met with the Communists in government; theirs were inflationary policies, and they undermined the confidence of bankers and businessmen.[78]

The Truman administration did *not* force changes in the political regimes of West European countries. Instead, U.S. officials structured incentives and invited symbiotic relationships with European parties that saw their own self-interest served by informal alliances with the United States.[79] Policymakers in Washington understood that prospective partners across the ocean had to satisfy domestic constituencies if they were to be able to stay in power and align their nations permanently with the United States. Tension would always exist between their domestic needs and America's international goals. During the difficult transition ahead, however, this friction might be eased by the generous provision of long-term aid.

By the middle of May, then, the circumstances were ripe for the Truman administration to launch a comprehensive recovery program for Europe. Few informed Americans disputed the need for it. In the American press there was widespread speculation only about its magnitude and design.[80] Kennan's Policy Planning Staff sought to establish the administration's criteria. An assistance program had to be premised on new forms of economic cooperation among the European countries themselves and had to allow them to assume part of the initiative. European countries had to be self-supporting at the program's conclusion, which would be four or five years hence. Communists must not be permitted to sabotage its goals.[81]

These generalizations did not amount to much, and a great deal of floundering remained until Undersecretary Clayton returned from Europe and pressed for immediate action. In a famous memorandum to Acheson on 27 May, he acknowledged that he had underestimated the problems besetting the European economy: "Europe is steadily deteriorating. . . . Millions of people in the cities are slowly starving. . . . Without further and substantial aid from the United States, economic, social, and political disintegration will overwhelm Europe. . . . Aside from the awful implications which this would have for the future peace and security of the world, the immediate effects on our domestic economy would be disastrous." Clayton envisioned a three-year assistance program amounting to about $6–7 billion a year.[82]

One week later, Secretary of State Marshall delivered his famous address at Harvard. Without specifying the magnitude or duration of the program, he invited European governments to seize the initiative. Should they design a satisfactory plan, the United States would help to fund it.[83] This promise became known as the Marshall Plan.

■

The Marshall Plan was one of the great initiatives in postwar international relations, and it is worth taking a little time to identify the motivations that lay behind it, explicate their mutually reinforcing nature, and sort out the concerns that were most salient. The provocative British economic historian Alan Milward has argued that the Marshall Plan was not really necessary, that most West European countries were already experiencing substantial recovery, and that with relatively minor adjustments they could have overcome the payments crisis of 1947. His analysis merits careful attention.[84]

It is true, for example, that most West European countries, aside from Germany, were nearing or surpassing their prewar industrial production figures by late 1946. However, this remarkable progress was made possible by the food and fuel received from the Western Hemisphere, especially from the United States. Compared to the prewar years, Western Europe in 1947 was importing $3 billion more from North and Central America and $3.7 billion less from the rest of the world. In fact, more than 45 percent of Western Europe's imports came from the United States, and most of it was paid for with American financial assistance. In 1946 Europe imported goods amounting to $4.4 billion from the United States, yet European exports to the United States equaled only $900 million, leaving a merchandise deficit of $3.5 billion and a total payments deficit of $4.2 billion. In early 1947 those figures worsened, buffeted by the skyrocketing cost of American grain and raw materials. When U.S. lending slackened in late 1946 and early 1947, European reserves began dwindling rapidly. Governments felt impelled to cut their purchases of food and fuel, thereby threatening to choke off the recovery of industrial output and to precipitate massive unrest.[85]

European governments, as Milward insists, might have shifted priorities, made adjustments, negotiated a new set of bilateral deals, and adopted more modest goals.[86] But most of them did not think they could do so. They foresaw the possibility of having to reduce total imports by 50 percent, imports from America by 80 percent. In 1947, for example, 40 percent of West European countries' total consumption of bread grains, aluminum, and cotton came from the Western Hemisphere; 30 percent of their lead, petroleum, and zinc; 15 percent of their fats and oils; 10 percent of their meat and solid fuel. West European countries—soon to form the Committee on European Economic Cooperation (CEEC)—believed that "a catastrophe would develop" if the flow of these goods from the American continent ceased. Life in Europe "would become increasingly unstable and uncertain; industries [would] grind to a halt for lack of material and fuel, and the food supply of Europe [would] diminish and begin to disappear." [87]

U.S. officials held the same convictions. They saw no way that West European governments could overcome their dollar gap without precipitating serious economic dislocation, engendering political upheaval, or negotiating bilateral agreements and autarkic arrangements. Brief as the economic setbacks might be, local Communists would capitalize on them. If Communists won or seized power, they would probably take their countries into the Soviet orbit, signing bilateral agreements and other accords that would work to the advantage of the Kremlin. If the French Communists, for example, gained power, the SWNCC ad hoc committee on foreign aid predicted that France would become "the western bastion of an inherently hostile continental system." Ambassador Caffery foresaw even worse consequences: the triumph of French communism, he said, not only would make the American position in Germany precarious but would also facilitate Soviet penetration of all of Western Europe, Africa, the Mediterranean, and the Middle East.[88]

In light of these considerations, the economic motivations behind the Marshall Plan were secondary. However, they were not unimportant. Clayton predicted domestic economic contraction if massive aid was not extended to Europe. Acheson, Forrestal, Secretary of Commerce Averell Harriman, and Secretary of the Treasury John Snyder also talked about the impact of falling exports on the U.S. economy.[89] These expressions, and many more like them, need to be weighed against other evidence. The specially appointed presidential committee on foreign aid under Harriman emphasized that it was "nonsense" to think that "we need to export our goods and services as free gifts to insure our own prosperity." [90] Harriman was rebutting Communist propaganda that the Marshall Plan was self-interested. Rhetorical though it was, his response illuminated the widespread view that the health of the U.S. economy did not depend on foreign markets. In its study of foreign aid, the Council of Economic Advisers stressed, "It is a mistake to suppose that we are dependent upon the current size of the export surplus to preserve our prosperity." The council believed that exports were only one of many factors, and clearly not the most important one, that contributed to American economic well-being.[91] The statistical evidence for this reasoning was persuasive. As a percentage of gross national product, exports amounted to 4.9 percent in 1946 and 6.6 percent in 1947 (substantially below their post–World War I levels). The U.S. export surplus to Europe constituted only about 2 percent of gross national product.[92] Exports of cars as a percentage of total production was about 7 percent; chemicals, 6 percent; coal, about 9 percent; electrical machinery, about 7 percent; petroleum, 2.5 percent; rolled steel products, about 10 percent; wearing apparel, 2 percent; agricultural machinery, 16 percent; meat and dairy products, about 5 percent; food fats, 14 percent; canned fruit, 6 percent; and wheat, about 45 percent.[93]

Although Marshall Plan aid to Europe would help sustain these exports, it would also contribute to inflation in the United States. Inflation was seen as the greatest short-term threat to the nation's economic health. The fiscal situation in the United States improved significantly in the spring of 1947, but there was still a shortage of goods in relation to demand. On the very day Marshall delivered his address at Harvard, Truman conceded that "foreign aid programs add to our economic problems at home."[94] Rising prices, if not checked, would erode domestic purchasing power and could lead to a depression, not immediately, but in a year or two. The president and Treasury Secretary Snyder reemphasized the importance of a conservative fiscal policy and a balanced budget.[95] Because he was so concerned about inflationary pressures and so fearful of Republican criticism, the president commissioned three studies of the prospective economic consequences of the Marshall Plan. A prime purpose was to demonstrate that the economy was strong enough to withstand the inflationary shocks that a large assistance program would have on such critical commodities as grain, meat, steel, coal, and fertilizer.[96]

Truman administration officials were certain that the Marshall Plan would have a long-term beneficial effect on exports, but inflationary, fiscal, and political considerations would have delayed or prevented its announcement if not for the decisive impact of geopolitical and ideological factors. U.S. policymakers believed that their most fundamental political and economic institutions were endangered by events in Western Europe. Clayton and his assistants would not have disagreed with Milward's contention that European statesmen could have chosen alternative paths; indeed, Clayton's great fear was that they would. If the configuration of political regimes altered even slightly, European governments might choose solutions incompatible with U.S. interests. Accordingly, throughout the spring of 1947 Clayton negotiated painstakingly with Republican leaders at home to relax tariffs and encourage imports while he worked indefatigably at Geneva to convince foreign statesmen to adopt a new charter of international trade, incorporating the principles of multilateralism and open, nondiscriminatory commerce.[97]

The issues were deemed so important that the president was persuaded to deliver a major speech on the topic. Domestic support had to be mobilized behind the administration's efforts to rid the world of all forms of commercial restrictions. At Baylor University on 6 March 1947, President Truman warned that there would be no peace and no prosperity if nations did not cooperate to reduce the impediments to international trade. Political and economic developments, he emphasized, were indivisible, but even more important were the basic freedoms that Americans so cherished—freedom of speech, of worship, of free enterprise. They, too, were indivisible, for wherever free enterprise flourished, societies were more inclined to value other freedoms as well. Yet the future of free enterprise in the world was jeopardized by the devastation wrought by war and the daunting task of reconstruction. Nations had to import food, fuel, and capital equipment. They could not sell enough to pay for these imports. Hence they increasingly controlled their imports, discriminated against countries whose currencies they did not possess, and felt compelled to regiment their domestic economies in order to conserve scarce resources. The trend was taking on formidable dimensions. Much of the world, Truman lamented, was heading toward central planning. The United States, he explained, would come under pressure to adopt the same devices in order to fight for markets and raw materials. The government "would shortly find itself in the business of allocating foreign goods among importers and foreign markets among exporters and telling every trader what he could buy or sell, and how much, and when, and where. . . . It is not the American way. It is not the way to peace." [98]

As European governments grappled to control trade and direct scarce resources into areas of priority, they adopted techniques that appeared to have far-reaching ramifications for U.S. national security and for the structure of the U.S. political economy. Domestic systems could not remain insulated from patterns of international commerce. Officials were convinced that regimented trade abroad would eventually jeopardize economic and political freedom at home. The Harriman committee on the European Recovery Program posed the issue most directly:

The deterioration of the European economy . . . would force European countries to resort to trade by government monopoly—not only for economic but for political ends. The United States would almost inevitably have to follow suit. The resulting system of state controls, at first relating to foreign trade, would soon have to be extended into the domestic economy to an extent that would endanger the survival of the American system of free enterprise. [99]

Geopolitical considerations provided the connecting tissue between foreign economic distress and the prospective decay of liberal capitalism at home. Communist parties would feel most comfortable with domestic regimes that set priorities, regimented trade, and controlled economic transactions. They would look to Moscow and sign bilateral trade agreements with the Kremlin. The Soviets would respond eagerly, seeing such mechanisms as instruments to gain leverage over critical resources. The Communist parties of Western Europe, said the Harriman committee, were loyal allies of the Soviet Union:

If the countries of middle-western and Mediterranean Europe sink under the burden of despair and become Communist, Scandinavia will fall into the same camp. The strategically and economically vital North African and middle-eastern areas will follow. This transfer of Western Europe, the second greatest industrial area in the world, and of the essential regions which must inevitably follow such a lead, would radically change the American position. If it should prove that a weakened United Kingdom could not resist so powerful a current, the shift would be cataclysmic. [100]

The resulting shift in power would force the United States to alter its priorities, regiment its trade, boost defense expenditures, and clamp down on potential fifth columnists. If Britain had to retrench further or if financial pressures impelled it to choose its own independent road to recovery, these trends would have to be accelerated. "National security," said the Harriman committee, would compel the "swift and complete conversion [of the United States] to a military footing." Sweeping new constraints might have to be placed on "our economic and political life, perhaps extending to our very form of government." [101]

U.S. officials in the spring of 1947 saw themselves faced with an unprecedented crisis. No one feared Soviet military aggression. But the long-term balance of power seemed imperiled by the exchange crisis in Europe, imminent economic disarray, the prospective proliferation of autarkical arrangements, and the anticipated capacity of European Communist parties to capitalize on these circumstances. If the United States did not respond, the Soviets would reap the advantages. Autarky and discrimination would permit the Kremlin to manipulate artificial mechanisms to build up its own strength, acquire access to critical resources, expedite Soviet reconstruction, and establish relationships with potentially powerful allies. If these developments occurred, Kennan warned that the "traditional concept of U.S. security," postulating "a reasonable number of free [European] states subservient to no great power," would be "invalidated" and "a basic revision of the whole concept of our international position" would have to take place. According to the JCS, there would be no alternative because without "the support of some of the countries of the Old World . . . our military strength [would] be overshadowed by that of our enemies." [102]

In June 1947 the United States launched the Marshall Plan to arrest an impending shift in the correlation of power between the United States and the Soviet Union. The Truman administration was struggling to preserve an open international economic system. Such a system, U.S. officials assumed, would benefit everyone and most certainly would foster American influence and power. It would also help the United States establish linkages with European elites, bind European economies to the American economy, and gain access to overseas markets and raw materials.

If nothing were done, the repercussions would be harrowing. The United States, said Kennan, would face a Europe that "would be no less hostile to us, and no less dangerous to us, than would have been the European 'New Order' of Hitler's dreams." He went on to say that it was his "deep conviction" and that "of everyone who has served our Government in the European area in recent years, that the dimensions of the deterioration would be great enough to require not only a major and costly readjustment of our political-military strategy but also changes in our domestic life." [103] At risk, then, were not merely economic interests but also vital security considerations that were inextricably linked to fundamental belief systems. This was so because it was assumed that adverse changes in the political regimes of European countries and in the European balance of power would force modifications in free-market mechanisms, reshape U.S. political institutions, and erode the nation's fundamental liberties.

Holding the Periphery

The announcement of the Marshall Plan indicated that the economic recovery of Western Europe, including western Germany, had become the number-one priority of the Truman administration. This orientation did not mean that officials disregarded other areas.[104] On the contrary, the European Recovery Program, along with other strategic and ideological considerations, heightened interest in peripheral regions and broadened the purview of U.S. national security concerns.

The core of the European economic crisis in 1947 was the dollar gap. West European countries had too few dollars to pay for essential foodstuffs and raw materials from the United States. European leaders believed they could not solve their payments problems simply by increasing their production and creating a large free-trade area in the Old World. The dollar gap, the CEEC acknowledged, was "a world problem" that could not be overcome without "the closest possible economic association with countries outside Europe" from which Marshall Plan countries received most of their essential imports.[105] European countries had to save dollars by developing alternative sources of supply outside of North America. They also had to earn dollars by increasing exports to the United States or to countries that had a favorable balance of trade with the United States.

All these solutions placed heavy stress on the overseas colonies and territories of the European powers as well as on other raw-material-producing areas in the Third World. Europe's overseas possessions appeared better able to close the dollar gap than did European countries themselves. During the late 1940's the colonies of the United Kingdom, the Netherlands, and Portugal, for example, usually exported more to the United States than did their metropolises. Moreover, the United States was expected to have more need for the raw materials coming from Europe's Third World dependencies than for the manufactured goods from the Old World itself.[106] If Third World nations could have a net surplus in their merchandise trade with the United States, and if European manufacturers could compete effectively to earn these Third World dollars, a portion of the dollar gap could be overcome. Moreover, if these Third World areas could produce more of the goods that Europe was importing from the United States, then the European recipients of Marshall Plan aid could reduce their imports from the United States and save additional dollars. Britain, France, and the Netherlands, therefore, devised ambitious schemes to augment the production and export of raw materials and foodstuffs in those parts of the Third World over which they still exercised considerable influence.[107]

U.S. officials recognized the importance of integrating the industrial core of Europe (and of Japan) with the underdeveloped periphery in Asia and Africa. Europe's dependent overseas territories were included by definition in the bilateral agreements that the United States signed with each European recipient of assistance. Over the next few years, hundreds of millions of dollars in Marshall Plan aid went directly or indirectly to the colonies of West European countries.[108] At the time of the inception of the Marshall Plan, the Harriman committee stressed the importance of increasing food supplies from tropical areas and of augmenting oil production in the Middle East; Colonel Bonesteel and his superiors in the War Department attributed great significance to increasing Africa's agricultural output; and military intelligence analysts dwelled on the advisability of developing petroleum reserves in Southeast Asia. All of these recommendations were spurred by the realization that the food and fuel of Eastern Europe were no longer available to Western Europe at prewar levels.[109]

■

Marshall Plan expenditures in Europe's overseas dependencies, of course, were small in comparison to the amounts allocated to the Old World itself. They constitute only one indication of how recognition of the core-periphery relationship influenced U.S. policies toward Third World areas like Southeast Asia. In the spring and summer of 1947, for example, the protracted talks between the Dutch and Indonesian nationalists collapsed. Violence flared, and the Dutch resorted to military action. Robert McMahon, the historian who has studied these events most closely, has shown how top U.S. officials subtly aligned the United States on the side of the Dutch. The Southeast Asia experts in the State Department and intelligence analysts in the Pentagon scorned the use of military force, knowing it would be ineffective and would delay the rehabilitation of the Indonesian economy. Moreover, they recognized that moderate leaders spearheaded the Indonesian nationalist movement. Nevertheless, even these more enlightened American experts wanted Sukarno and Hatta to accept Dutch sovereignty, at least temporarily.[110]

Secretary of State Marshall and his advisers in the Office of European Affairs looked upon nationalist leaders in Southeast Asia as politically immature, diplomatically inexperienced, and ideologically unreliable. Indonesian nationalism might be tinged with pan-Asianism or totalitarianism. It could assume an anti-Western character. And such an outcome would be intolerable because Holland, Western Europe, and the United States required access to Indonesian markets and raw materials. The best solution was for the Dutch to permit Indonesian self-government and for the Indonesians to submit themselves voluntarily to Dutch tutelage. The United States would be willing to mediate such a settlement but would not compel the Dutch to sacrifice their economic presence and political influence in a region deemed critical to Holland's commercial and financial viability, to Western Europe's economic rehabilitation, and to America's strategic well-being.[111]

In Indochina, U.S. policy was as much influenced by ideology as it was by France's domestic economic and political needs. The State Department's Southeast Asia experts and some military intelligence analysts grasped the overwhelming popularity of the nationalist movement. In contrast to the situation in Indonesia, however, the Vietnamese nationalist movement continued to be led by a Communist, Ho Chi Minh. Mid-level officials in the State, War, and Navy departments acknowledged that Ho still expressed friendly sentiments toward the United States, remained aloof from the diplomatic struggle between Washington and Moscow, and assumed a position of neutrality in the Chinese civil war. The Kremlin gave such scant support (even of a rhetorical nature) to the Viet Minh that it was unclear whether Soviet leaders considered the Communist leadership of Vietnam a "dependable instrument." [112] Nevertheless, when fighting had erupted between the Viet Minh and the French in the autumn of 1946, the Truman administration had placed itself squarely on the side of the French.

The question was how best to retain French influence in Indochina. Neither military analysts nor foreign service officers favored a military solution.[113] The French could not win a clear victory, and an outright struggle to preserve France's imperial control would play into the hands of Communist leaders and pan-Asian spokesmen. France should understand, however, that the Truman administration would not adopt a policy of neutrality. Acheson and Marshall stressed that Ho, a Communist, could not be trusted. The United States conceived of itself as being "essentially in the same boat as French, also as British and Dutch. We cannot conceive setbacks to long-range interests [of] France which would not also be setbacks [to] our own." Policymakers in Washington worried that the relinquishment of European control would lead to indigenous racial, religious, and political strife, to virulent "anti-Western Pan-Asiatic tendencies," or to Communist domination. "We consider as best safeguard against these eventualities a continued close association between newly-autonomous peoples and powers which have been long responsible [for] their welfare." [114]

The encouragement of reform and gradual self-government constituted sage yet inadequate advice. U.S. officials did not explain how moderate concessions might enable non-Communist nationalists to outmaneuver their foes within the Viet Minh coalition. Nor did Marshall and Acheson demonstrate how French interests could be reconciled with Vietnamese self-government. It was not at all clear that Indochinese peoples would choose to continue their association with their former colonial masters. Unlike the United States, the French (and the Dutch) had neither the financial leverage nor the military and economic power to keep former dependencies within their own orbit. Even if the Vietnamese did not gravitate toward the Kremlin, they might orient themselves toward the United States, which from the French perspective was not desirable. Rather than upset the volatile political situation in France by delving into such divisive issues, U.S. officials opted to avoid the tough tactical questions. They offered the French the same platitudinous and self-serving yet indisputably correct advice that they gave to the Dutch. They argued that it was wise to make concessions in order to co-opt nationalist ferment, avoid military strife, raise production levels, and restore exports. Indochina and Indonesia might then be kept within the Western camp, to make their contribution to Western Europe's economic recovery.

■

No one claimed that retaining southern Korea in an American orbit was important to Western Europe's recovery. In fact, top civilian officials in the War Department wanted to withdraw. The economic situation in southern Korea was so bad, the political turmoil so great, and the recalcitrance of conservative nationalists so fierce that both Secretary Patterson and Assistant Secretary Petersen believed that Soviet domination was inevitable. If Korea were strategically unimportant to the United States in time of global war, as the JCS claimed, Patterson and Petersen thought it best to concentrate elsewhere. They dismissed General Lincoln's contention that withdrawal would endanger U.S. interests in Japan and compromise U.S. prestige throughout Asia.[115]

Their views, however, did not prevail. The administration's determination to hold the periphery in Northeast Asia was as strong as it was in the case of Southeast Asia. Marshall did not favor withdrawal. He disputed Patterson's claims that Korea had no economic or strategic value. He agreed with Army and Air Force generals, like Lincoln and Norstad, who believed that Korean independence would help prevent the Soviet Union from deepening its defensive positions, "outflanking" Japan, and "dominating" Manchuria. Marshall convinced Patterson to go along with his desire for a one-year authorization request of $215 million for Korea.[116] Soviet leaders, made aware of U.S. determination to offer economic assistance, might be convinced that the United States would not abandon southern Korea. If so, they might be more responsive to renewed American diplomatic efforts to unite the two zones.[117]

To the surprise of State Department officials, the Kremlin agreed to reopen unification talks during the Moscow foreign ministers' conference. The men at Foggy Bottom proceeded on a two-track basis. On the one hand, they hoped to achieve unification on terms that would permit non-Communist forces to compete for political ascendancy throughout the Korean peninsula. If, on the other hand, the Soviet government continued to insist on excluding vast numbers of anti-Russian conservatives from the political process, the State Department would prepare to establish an independent government in the south.[118]

The Americans knew, however, that the Kremlin might propose a mutual withdrawal of Soviet and U.S. forces. Large numbers of Soviet troops were leaving the peninsula. War and State Department officials wanted to pull U.S. soldiers out of Korea, but they feared that their allies in the south would not be able to resist a north Korean attack. Southern leftists would rise up and collaborate with their northern brethren. Eisenhower asked the JCS to make plans for a U.S. response should the Soviets withdraw and should northern Korea attack. He thought that General Douglas MacArthur should use whatever means he had available to insure internal order and to retain American authority.[119]

Although Korea was admittedly a tertiary strategic interest in time of global war, the State Department, the other chiefs of staff, and the president shared Eisenhower's view that the United States should not walk away from southern Korea. Wary of overcommitting American power, they were nevertheless inclined to increase U.S. economic assistance and to lend military aid to an independent south Korean government. Seeing themselves locked in a global struggle with the Soviets, they ruminated about falling dominoes and a bandwagon psychology should they relinquish any part of the Third World periphery. To maintain U.S. credibility, historians William Stueck and James Matray have correctly argued, the administration felt it had to hold southern Korea.[120]

■

Nor would U.S. officials disengage from China. Whereas in the case of Korea the top civilians in the War Department were the strongest proponents of withdrawal, in the case of China the State Department's China experts assumed this role. In neither situation did the champions of disengagement win a clear-cut victory. In the spring of 1947, Director of the Office of Far Eastern Affairs John Carter Vincent and his assistants, observing the growing strife among Kuomintang (KMT) officials and the mounting ineptitude of Nationalist generals, argued that U.S. aid to an unreformed KMT would have no benefit. It would only drain American resources and drive the Chinese Communist Party (CCP) into the arms of the Kremlin.[121]

Top defense officials strongly disagreed. Patterson, Forrestal, and the JCS insisted that the Chinese Communists already were "tools of Soviet policy." Patterson told Marshall that the United States could not "accept with equanimity the military collapse of the Nationalist government." According to the JCS, Soviet dominance over Asia, Western Europe, or both "would constitute a major threat" to U.S. security.[122]

Navy and Army intelligence analysts did not believe that the CCP was receiving much support from the Kremlin. Nor did they think that the Communists could soon seize all of China. On these points they concurred with Vincent.[123] But Forrestal, Patterson, and their most influential military strategists assumed that Communist triumphs in northern China, Manchuria, and Shantung would enable the Kremlin to gain indirect control over critical resources and ports. The Kremlin, too, wanted to link its industrial core with a compliant periphery. Admiral Charles M. Cooke, commander of U.S. naval forces in the western Pacific, cogently summarized the strategic calculations:

If the Soviet position in the [Russian] maritime provinces is not integrated to the industrial and agricultural support of Manchuria, not supported by the strategic reinforcement of warm water ports of Port Arthur, Dairen, and northern Korea, and is forced to continue to be dependent upon a line of supplies over the trans-Siberian railway, the maritime province position continues to be a source of weakness and vulnerability to Russia. . . .

If, however, Soviet eastern Asia becomes self-sufficient . . . , Soviet Asia can then become an element of strength in the over-all Soviet power structure. . . .

If it is extended to include Korea and broadened to include Manchuria and possibly Hopei and Shantung, it appears probable that the . . . balance of power has been moved from the side of the democratic powers to that of Soviet Russia and her satellites.[124]

Marshall understood such strategic thinking. His disillusionment with Chiang Kai-shek did not mean that he was prepared to accede to a Communist victory. In February he told the Senate Foreign Relations Committee that he no longer supported a coalition government. Nor would he press Chiang to compromise with the Communists. In Marshall's view, the latter shared the Kremlin's goals and ideology. Gradually during the spring of 1947 he resumed limited assistance to Chiang's Nationalist armies. He decided that 7,000 tons of U.S. ammunition should be left at depots near Tientsin and Tsingtao for Nationalist forces. He endorsed the transfer to the Chinese government of almost 300 ships and naval craft, and he ordered the rapid completion of a portion of the assistance program for the Chinese air force. He resolved that spare parts should be supplied for Chinese combat planes and that 130 million rounds of ammunition should be delivered to Chiang's forces. He also repealed the ban on export permits for military supply shipments to China.[125]

Defense officials pressed Marshall to do more. They wanted to send additional assistance and to monitor its distribution because so much of it was siphoned off to the Communists. Precisely how far Forrestal, Patterson, and the JCS wanted to go is unclear because they, too, regarded China as a lower priority than Western Europe and the Eastern Mediterranean. They believed, however, that the Chinese Communists could quickly translate their military triumphs into political victories, from which the Kremlin would derive significant economic and strategic advantages.[126]

Vincent and Acheson hotly contested this view. They did not think that the Communists could convert battlefield successes into political gains. Nor was it clear to Vincent that the Soviets would benefit from a CCP victory. The Chinese Communists might act independently of the Kremlin, and even if they did not, China was so poor and so weak that the country was likely to be a liability rather than an asset to the Soviet Union. Nevertheless, Vincent and Acheson were not willing to take big risks. They advised Marshall to resume military aid to the Nationalists so long as it was recognized that the goal was to avoid a Nationalist defeat. Ultimate victory, in their view, still depended on political and economic reforms.[127]

Marshall, caught between the views of his subordinates in the State Department and those of his former colleagues in the Pentagon, saw no clear solutions. He deemed JCS pleas for substantial assistance unrealistic. Like the president, Marshall wanted to avoid "pouring sand in a rat hole." China was not as important as priorities in Western Europe and the Eastern Mediterranean. Moreover, despite

Nationalist setbacks, their position did not yet appear hopeless. Too much assistance might push the CCP into the arms of the Kremlin and encourage the Russians to reverse their current policy of nonintervention. He did not want to lift the pressure upon the KMT to undertake far-reaching political and economic reforms. In his view, what the Nationalists lacked was high morale, capable commanders, and popular support.[128]

On the other hand, Marshall did not want to abandon the northeast Asian periphery to the Chinese Communists. After consulting with the president, he decided to send General Albert Wedemeyer to assess Nationalist requirements and prospects. There was relatively little popular and legislative support for Chiang in mid-1947. But Wedemeyer's appointment would satisfy a few influential congressional skeptics who questioned the efficacy of aid to Western Europe, Greece, and Turkey when China was so beleaguered. Wedemeyer had been Chiang's chief of staff at the end of the war and was a renowned friend of China's. He was more likely than anyone else to influence Chiang to effect reforms and to prepare the groundwork for additional aid. At the very least, his mission would buy time for the administration to sort out priorities, assess resources, and calculate requirements in both Europe and Asia.[129]

Influenced by defense officials and concerned with strategic and geopolitical considerations, Truman and Marshall were not willing to write China off in mid-1947. But neither were they prepared to squander scarce resources on an unreliable ally.

■

In the western Pacific as well, European priorities and budgetary constraints shaped U.S. tactics and constricted U.S. ambitions but did not alter U.S. desires to establish and maintain governments friendly to American interests. Army officials, for example, reconsidered their base requirements and troop deployments to the Philippines. Strategically, they were no longer critical. The Russians could not threaten the Philippines, and Soviet territory in Asia could be attacked from bases elsewhere. Politically, moreover, the negotiations over base rights aroused Philippine nationalist sentiment and created problems for the pro-U.S. government of Manuel Roxas. Given the strategic realities and the political liabilities, Patterson and Eisenhower saw no reason to spend scarce Army funds on Philippine bases. In late 1946 they told the State Department that they wanted to remove U.S. troops and saw no real need for peacetime bases.[130]

Officials were not renouncing their desire to retain the Philippines in the U.S. orbit. The Navy, for example, was not quite so willing to accommodate Philippine nationalist sensibilities; anchorage rights in the Philippines remained critical to U.S. control of the southwestern Pacific. Notwithstanding the reduced requirements, the United States still insisted on a treaty providing sixteen active and seven reserve bases. The U.S. Navy secured complete control over the town of Olongapo near Subic Bay, and the Philippine government promised not to offer base privileges to any other government without American permission.[131] When in the course of the negotiations some Filipinos opposed U.S. demands, the State Department threatened to withhold military assistance. Only after the Philippine government approved the base agreement did the Truman administration sanction limited aid and send a few military advisers.[132]

None of this should be construed to mean that U.S. officials imposed their desires on an unwilling Philippine government. Quite to the contrary, Roxas wanted U.S. strategic guarantees, a base deal, and military aid. Both governments saw a convergence of interests. The Filipino elite needed economic aid, favored access to American markets (which they received), and U.S. military help repressing the Huk rebellion. Everything in the Philippines was done on a more limited scale than originally anticipated by U.S. officials, but the base deal, military aid package, and trade arrangements illustrated that the Truman administration would not permit the western Pacific to slip out of its reach while it focused on European priorities.[133]

■

Meanwhile, the JCS launched a new assessment of its overseas base requirements in the spring of 1947. Although funding was inadequate, planners reaffirmed the importance of the primary base areas emphasized in the autumn of 1945, including Hawaii, the Marianas, Panama, the Azores, and Iceland. Most critical were the bases needed for air assault against Soviet Russia and for control of the Mediterranean. Despite growing doubts about the utility of the polar air routes, Greenland's significance as a primary base loomed ever larger as uncertainties persisted over long-term arrangements in the Azores and Iceland. So too did the importance of Okinawa grow as strategists focused attention on Northeast Asia and as Air Force commanders found it easy and profitable to operate in the Far East. And although Dhahran in Saudi Arabia did not receive any special emphasis in the comprehensive studies of base requirements, its airport was being constructed under the aegis of the U.S. Air Transport Command and its potential was fully recognized. From Dhahran, American planes could strike petroleum targets in the Caucasus, command invasion routes between Russia and the Near East, and protect the oil reserves of the Persian Gulf. The Strategic Air Command, in fact, sent squadrons to Dhahran (among other places) for 30-day training rotations. And for the control of the Mediterranean, the United States entered into secret talks with the French government for rights at Casablanca and Port Lyautey.[134]

■

The quest for base rights in North Africa accentuated U.S. concerns about developments in that region. It was in the spring and summer of 1947 that the United States first conveyed its worries to the French government about the simmering discontent and emerging nationalism. Although foreign service and consular officials acknowledged the need for economic development and progressive steps toward autonomy, no one supported independence, not even the area specialists at Foggy Bottom. Accordingly, the State Department instructed Ambassador Caffery to alert the French government to the importance of preemptive reforms. Early concessions would temper nationalist impulses, undermine the machinations of the Communists, and establish linkages with North African elites. U.S. officials did not want to agitate the French, did not want to intrude in North African affairs, and did not want to incur new responsibilities. But because of the strategic importance of North Africa in wartime and its economic value to France in peacetime, American diplomatic initiatives in the region grew accordingly.[135]

■

Holding the underdeveloped periphery within the Western Hemisphere was also deemed to be of critical importance. In peacetime, Latin American and Canadian grain, meat, and raw materials were essential for West European rehabilitation; in wartime, their resources were considered indispensable to the U.S. war machine.[136] European priorities, however, meant that no funds were available for economic aid. Truman insisted that Latin America should rely on private capital.[137]

The administration would bind Latin America to a U.S. orbit by the use of military aid and the inter-American security (Rio) treaty. Army officials wanted to reintroduce the Inter-American Military Cooperation Act to Congress. General Matthew Ridgway, chairman of the Inter-American Defense Board, strongly advocated passage to standardize armament, equipment, and training throughout the hemisphere and to insure Latin American support in times of emergency.[138] When Acheson opposed military aid to Latin America lest it increase the region's economic burdens and undermine its political stability, Patterson and Forrestal protested. "The Western Hemisphere," said Eisenhower, "will in all probability be the main basis of our war potential." Marshall agreed. In his first meeting with Patterson and Forrestal after his return from Moscow, the secretary of state overruled his subordinates.[139]

Thereafter, the administration resubmitted legislation to Congress authorizing military aid to Latin America. The principal aim was to establish linkages with military elites in the region. Most Latin American governments, argued the JCS, depended on the military for stability. "Contact with Latin American military men would in reality mean contact with very strong domestic political leaders." If the United States did not grant military aid, Forrestal warned, other foreign governments would eagerly fill the void. But if Latin American governments relied, for example, on the United States for training, Latin American military officers would flow through U.S. service schools and U.S. military missions south of the border would grow and prosper. "Thus," said Patterson, "will our ideals and ways of life be nurtured . . . , to the eventual exclusion of totalitarianism and other foreign ideologies." [140]

The fear of communism also played a key role in formulating the provisions of the Rio Treaty. Since the spring of 1945, State, War, and Navy Department officials had agreed on the need for a reciprocal treaty of military assistance, the first in American history.[141] Many Latin American nations wanted to make distinctions between aggression emanating from inside and that from outside the hemisphere. Marshall strongly opposed these efforts. He wanted the treaty to provide a legal basis for U.S. action in case of internal unrest, intrigue, and espionage. He worried more about domestic subversion than about an external attack. He wanted to thwart revolutions "inspired and abetted by a non-American state." So, too, did the JCS.[142]

By collaborating with increasingly anti-Communist military elites and by signing the Rio Treaty, the Truman administration was seeking to lock Latin America within a U.S. orbit. Although the treaty did not obligate nations to resort to armed force to deter aggression, this loophole eased passage through the Senate and was of no real strategic consequence to U.S. officials. What the United States needed was assurance that adversaries would not have access to Latin American bases and resources. Under the Rio Treaty, all the signatories were obligated to suspend political and economic relations with an aggressor should two-thirds of them vote in favor of it. The State Department deemed this a real advance in international cooperation, since it meant that the operation of the treaty could not be stymied by the nonconcurrence of a small minority.[143]

■

During the spring and summer of 1947, U.S. interest in the periphery grew. The Marshall Plan defined U.S. priorities in Western Europe, but the Truman administration became ever more involved in events around the globe. Officials believed they were locked in a global struggle with Soviet-directed world communism. New initiatives were dictated by the growing awareness of Britain's declining power and Europe's multiplying economic problems. The United States had to revitalize the world capitalist system. Otherwise, European governments might opt for autarky, European elites might resort to nationalist credos, and European peoples might choose radical solutions. By offering financial assistance and linking core and periphery, the United States hoped to sustain European imports, expedite the recovery of European production, and insure long-term European financial solvency and commercial viability.[144]

Of course, the initiatives were of a different nature in different places because the saliency of the threat differed and because the value of the locale varied. But problems everywhere were vested with national security implications and required some sort of U.S. response. If the Soviets gained control over the periphery through the success of Communist parties, for example, in Manchuria, northern China, Korea, and Indochina, their strength would grow and their leverage over the capitalist democracies would mount. Likewise, if revolutionary nationalist movements succeeded, the West European democracies would suffer as they lost markets and raw materials so vital for their economic and political stability and for their capacity to participate in a multilateral commercial order.

From the U.S. perspective, war still seemed most unlikely. The Kremlin would not want to attack the West until Soviet power equaled that of its major adversary. But as the United States and the Soviet Union maneuvered to co-opt additional resources and countries for their respective spheres, war could erupt through miscalculation. This contingency was improbable but not impossible. It, too, reinforced U.S. interest in the periphery because, if war occurred and the Soviets overran Western Europe, the United States would need access to bases in the Middle East, North Africa, and the western Pacific. The United States would also need the resources of Canada, Latin America, and Southeast Asia. Narrow strategic calculations, therefore, reinforced the geopolitical, economic, and ideological factors that dictated America's global concerns even while it readied to pour most of its resources into Western Europe.

Procedures

The new initiatives and the sheer complexity of U.S. stabilization efforts made it necessary to reform and enhance the policymaking machinery of the Truman administration. During the spring and summer of 1947, new decisionmaking procedures, institutional arrangements, and personnel were introduced into the executive branch. Most important was the elevation of the State Department to a position of primacy. Truman's appointment of Marshall as secretary of state in January had given the department great stature; the former Army chief of staff commanded almost everyone's respect. Moreover, his designation ended the tension between Byrnes, on the one hand, and Truman and Leahy, on the other. The president revered Marshall. The general's rank and experience also forced powerful proconsuls abroad and directors of government agencies at home to pay greater heed, if not obeisance, to State Department wishes. Marshall's emphasis on bolstering prospective allies through economic aid and enhancing their resistance to internal subversion (rather than external aggression) also encouraged defense officials to go along with these priorities.[145]

Equally important was Marshall's impact on State Department personnel and procedures. Unlike Byrnes, he insisted on orderly processes and systematic planning. He trusted subordinates, picked them carefully, gave them authority, and listened to their views. Aware of his own declining energy, he chose Robert Lovett for the key post of undersecretary of state. Lovett was scheduled to replace Acheson at the end of June. For months the two men worked together on an orderly succession. Lovett, who was the assistant secretary of war for air during World War II, had devoted his entire professional life to finance and air power. He had contacts throughout the aviation industry and the respect of Air Force officers; he was also a close friend of Stuart Symington's, the civilian head of the Air Force. Even more important, Lovett was intimately acquainted with Forrestal from their years on Wall Street as well as from their wartime experiences in Washington. Forrestal talked frequently to Lovett on the phone, solicited his views on both substantive issues and personnel matters, and not infrequently joined him for dinner. Lovett was equally familiar with Harriman, the secretary of commerce. Indeed, Lovett's father had worked for Harriman's father and had become president of the latter's railroad interests. Lovett was an inspired choice, if Marshall's goals were to enhance interagency cooperation, reconcile economic and geopolitical views, and mitigate suspicion between defense officials and foreign service officers. One of Lovett's first decisions was to bring the talented Colonel Bonesteel from the War Department to Foggy Bottom to serve as a key assistant.[146]

Equally inspired was Marshall's choice of Kennan to head the Policy Planning Staff. The "long telegram" of February 1946 had earned Kennan a reputation as the nation's foremost expert on Soviet Russia. He spent most of 1946 at the National War College, where for the first time he gave systematic thought to the relationships between political objectives and military forces and where he developed a strategic-political doctrine that matched the geopolitical thinking of civilian and military defense officials. The contacts Kennan made at the National War College, together with his firm conviction that the United States was engaged in an ideological conflict with a tenacious but weak adversary, made him well known and popular in military circles even before he assumed his influential post in the State Department. Kennan was respected in the Pentagon because he appreciated the political and military aspects of diplomatic problems. There was no keener mind in Washington, General Lincoln wrote in March 1947.[147]

For a short time Kennan was one of the most important policymakers in Washington. He put together a small and able staff and worked closely with Lovett and Marshall. As he turned his attention from one issue to another, Kennan consulted with area specialists and pondered the options. He then went off to the Library of Congress where he had a small office and where he wrote a series of brilliant policy papers. Kennan was reluctant to revise these papers once they were completed. His intractability, political insensitivity, and bureaucratic ineptness caused his influence to wane almost as quickly as it had risen. Yet even as his policy recommendations were increasingly shunned after mid-1948, his colleagues continued to respect him for his knowledge of the Soviet Union, his provocative ideas, his analytic reasoning, and his lucid prose.[148]

■

The appointments of Marshall and Lovett, former defense officials, to head the State Department came at a propitious time because in July 1947 Congress passed the National Security Act. This legislation created a host of new agencies, including the National Security Council (NSC), the National Security Resources Board (NSRB), and the Central Intelligence Agency (CIA). The NSC and the NSRB were primarily the brainchildren of Forrestal and Eberstadt. They believed that merging the services into a single department of defense was less important than enhancing coordination between political and military agencies. Forrestal never ceased insisting on the importance of integrating defense and foreign policy, of matching military capabilities with diplomatic commitments, and of reconciling the costs of defense with the needs of the domestic economy. From their wartime experiences, Forrestal and Eberstadt grasped the importance of correlating logistics with strategy and of integrating war planning with resource capabilities. Marshall and Lovett fully sympathized with these efforts.[149]

More suspicious were Truman's closest aides in the White House. Clark Clifford, George Elsey, and James Webb, director of the Budget Bureau, viewed the NSC and the NSRB with misgivings, fearing that these agencies might lead to military dominance of decisionmaking processes and to larger defense appropriations. Webb, in particular, was a skillful and entrepreneurial bureaucrat who broadened the purview and powers of the Budget Bureau as he lent assistance to the president in pursuit of his fiscal goals and domestic programs. Along with Clifford, Webb worked tirelessly to place control of the NSC in the White House and the State Department. He sought to preserve the president's powers and to maintain his leverage over the military budget.[150] Forrestal acquiesced to these efforts because he had great confidence in Marshall, Lovett, and Kennan, because he was a fiscal conservative himself, and because he was sincerely concerned with military-political coordination rather than military domination of the decisionmaking processes.[151]

The NSC became firmly rooted as a coordinating rather than a decisionmaking body. Truman insisted on it. Sidney Souers, a successful Missouri businessman who served in naval intelligence during World War II and who briefly directed the Central Intelligence Group during its first few months, became the first executive secretary of the NSC. Souers, a trusted confidant of the president's, briefed Truman every morning, reviewed intelligence, presented policy options emanating from the departments, and acted as an intermediary between the NSC and the chief executive. The NSC had no real staff, relying on mid-level officers in the departments to draft reports and on higher-level policymakers, called "consultants," to revise them before final consideration by the NSC itself.[152]

The National Security Act also created the National Military Establishment (NME), headed by the secretary of defense. The NME consisted of three autonomous executive departments, the Army, Navy, and Air Force, and several staff and coordinating bodies, including the War Council, the Munitions Board, and the Research and Development Board. Although the secretary of defense was designated the principal assistant to the president on national security matters, his authority and power were carefully delimited as was the size of his staff. The secretary of defense was charged with responsibility for establishing general policies and programs for the NME, eliminating duplication in procurement, transportation, health, research, and other matters, and coordinating budget estimates. The secretaries of the Army, Navy, and Air Force, however, retained cabinet stature. They possessed direct access to the president and could report their differences to him.[153]

Truman appointed Forrestal as the first secretary of defense after Patterson turned down the job. Forrestal had been most responsible for circumscribing the powers of the secretary of defense. He had struggled to preserve the authority and stature of the service secretaries and had opposed efforts to create a general staff (instead of the JCS). He believed in confederation and coordination rather than unification. He wanted to safeguard the interests of the Navy, but he also worried about the dangers of overcentralization. He was convinced that substantial benefits accrued from diversity, competition, and morale-boosting tradition. The president and his staff warned Forrestal not to emasculate his own ability to control the services.[154]

Forrestal approached his new job with both trepidation and optimism. He chose three young, hard-working, and extremely competent assistants: Wilfrid McNeil to handle budgetary matters; Marx Leva to oversee legal and legislative issues; and John (Jack) Ohly to coordinate substantive questions with other agencies and departments. The small staff and lack of military advisers did not initially bother Forrestal. His administrative style had always emphasized cooperation, and he believed he had good working relationships with Clark Clifford, William Leahy, and Sidney Souers at the White House. Moreover, John Sullivan, the new secretary of the Navy, had served as Forrestal's assistant secretary and undersecretary. Stuart Symington, the first secretary of the independent Air Force, had been a friend for many years. Kenneth Royall, who had moved from undersecretary to secretary of the Army upon Patterson's resignation, was also a familiar figure. And William Draper, the new undersecretary of the Army and Lucius Clay's former economic adviser, had been Forrestal's banking partner at Dillon, Read. Below the civilian leaders of the services, Forrestal knew the chiefs of staff and their top assistants from his long experience in Washington. He was especially fortunate to have General Alfred Gruenther, an extremely talented individual, become the first director of the Joint Staff, a group of officers from the three services tasked to do the staff work for the JCS. Gruenther was designated the principal JCS contact with Forrestal and with Souers.[155]

Forrestal expected that service rivalries would diminish now that he accepted an independent Air Force and at the same time safeguarded the Navy's control over the Marines and its stake in aviation. In fact, he hired Jack Ohly, Patterson's former aide, to allay Army and Air Force suspicions that he was loading his new office with Navy people like McNeil and Leva. The new secretary of defense also hoped to capitalize on Eisenhower's tact and discretion by using the Army chief of staff to mediate whatever differences might arise between the Navy and Air Force over roles, missions, and budgets. Underestimating the intensity of organizational feuds, Forrestal believed that periodic meetings with the three chiefs of staff away from Washington would free them of bureaucratic pressures and bring about reasonable compromises.[156]

The emphasis on compromise and conciliation was especially pressing as the agencies dealing with national security matters proliferated. A program as vast as the Marshall Plan required input from the Treasury Department and the Council of Economic Advisers as well as a substantial administrative apparatus of its own. Republicans doubted that existing government bureaucracies could administer the economic program, so Truman decided to create a new organization, the Economic Cooperation Administration (ECA). Supposedly staffed by apolitical, expert businessmen, the ECA, as the historian Michael Hogan has shown, created new sets of linkages between the public and private sectors and experimented with new forms of coordinating mechanisms.[157]

Because the Marshall Plan and other initiatives required annual appropriations, the administration had to forge closer ties with influential legislators. Truman put Paul G. Hoffman, a prominent automobile executive and progressive businessman, in charge of the ECA at home and named Harriman its special representative abroad; the president considered them indispensable for winning support for the Marshall Plan. When Harriman established his special committee to assess the European Recovery Program, he worked closely with Senator Vandenberg. On the latter's recommendation, Harriman invited prominent Republicans and conservative Democrats like Robert LaFollette and Owen D. Young to draft important sections of the final report.[158] Lovett, too, courted Vandenberg with frequent visits to his home in Georgetown and endless rounds of consultation.[159] Marshall would not pander to anyone, but he benefited from the fact that the Michigan senator came to have a warm personal regard for him.[160] Forrestal did not have to work so closely with Vandenberg, but he, too, believed in bipartisanship, found it easy to collaborate with Republicans as well as Democrats, and capitalized on the close ties he had established with congressmen and senators since he first came to Washington in 1940.[161]

■

Despite the commanding presence of Marshall and the extensive personal friendships that knit officials in the administration together, despite the new coordinating mechanisms and the bipartisan ties, conflicts persisted and new ones emerged. Institutional jealousies abounded. The State Department still protested the Army's role in occupation affairs.[162] The feuding between the Navy and Air Force intensified.[163] The Keynesian-oriented ECA and the fiscally more conservative Treasury Department were often at loggerheads.[164] The Budget Bureau and the Defense Department fought over appropriations.[165] The Atomic Energy Commission and the JCS sparred over the control, financing, quality, and magnitude of the nation's atomic stockpile.[166]

Organizational weaknesses compounded institutional jealousies. The secretary of defense did not have enough power to control the services and lacked the expert staff to handle the issues that flooded his office. These problems were exacerbated by the dearth of coordinating mechanisms between the JCS and the NSC and between the JCS and the State Department. The State Department complained that interdepartmental coordination with the newly created NME was too decentralized. Despite the creation of the NSC, procedures had still not been formalized to study overall national security strategy, to relate means and ends, to assess costs, resources, and programs, and to correlate appraisals of the adversary's intentions and capabilities with estimates of the nation's own vital requirements. Indeed, the State Department opposed such comprehensive assessments.[167]

Many related flaws were apparent in the problems besetting the CIA at its inception. Its mandate was vague; its authority blurred. It reported to the NSC and depended on it for funding. Its first director, Admiral Roscoe Hillenkoetter, was neither a strong leader nor savvy in the ways of Washington's bureaucratic life. The intelligence agencies in the State Department and the armed services moved quickly to constrict the CIA's range and authority. It bogged down churning out daily intelligence for the mid-level bureaucrats rather than focusing on broad estimates of the adversary's strength. This orientation was especially unfortunate because the series of papers it did produce for the NSC showed that its analysts understood well the intersection of economic, political, and military considerations, nationalist impulses, and Soviet vulnerabilities. At the behest of the State and Defense departments, however, the CIA soon became deeply immersed in covert, espionage, and paramilitary activities.[168]

At the apex of the national security bureaucracy, of course, sat the president. He displayed remarkably little interest in the new coordinating mechanisms. At the opening meeting of the NSC, he offered only platitudinous comments. Until the Korean War, he rarely attended NSC sessions and almost never gave any guidance on specific issues.[169] Nor did he show much concern about the problems besetting the intelligence community. In general, Truman did not intervene much in the affairs of his subordinates. His aloofness and support made him much beloved by many of his cabinet officers, but this management style complicated the task of policy coordination.[170] As departments and agencies generated more initiatives, commitments outran capabilities.

European Priorities, Global Commitments, and U.S. Politics

However interesting they are, the institutional rivalries should not be exaggerated. Many policy disputes involved tough judgment calls over complicated issues. Likewise, the problems bedeviling the policymaking process adumbrated the difficulties every future administration would face. More striking than the rifts within the administration were the remarkably similar beliefs, goals, and priorities that knit its top officials together. Those views were best expressed in the famous anonymous article signed "X," but written by Kennan, that appeared in the prestigious journal *Foreign Affairs* in July 1947. Kennan emphasized the ideological and psychological sources of Soviet motivations, described Soviet ambitions as unlimited, and disparaged the possibility of resolving differences through negotiation. He called for a policy of containment, of "adroit and vigilant application of counter-force at a series of constantly shifting geographical and political points, corresponding to the shifts and manoeuvres of Soviet policy." Kennan certainly believed in European priorities and was not inclined to spend much money on the periphery.[171] Still, his aim was to check Communist expansionism, thwart Soviet attempts to gain control of additional resources, and maintain a global balance of power favorable to the United States.[172]

Kennan later lamented not having adequately emphasized the political nature of the struggle.[173] In the summer of 1947, however, Kennan's colleagues in the government, if not his public audience, recognized that he was addressing a political, not a military, challenge. All concurred with Kennan that the Soviet Union was militarily much weaker than the United States. All agreed that the Soviets could capitalize on economic dislocation, social unrest, political turmoil, and revolutionary nationalist upheaval. All recognized the economic interdependence of the modern world and of economic and military power. All believed that an open multilateral trading system would foster U.S. interests, enhance U.S. power, promote political liberty and free enterprise abroad as well as at home, and generate worldwide prosperity. All were inspired by the importance of the enterprise that lay before them. They were locked in a terrific struggle with an adversary who possessed an appealing ideology, a tough and experienced leadership, and a totalitarian system.[174] If the United States were to win, U.S. officials had to revive the world capitalist system, rebuild the industrial workshops of Europe and Asia, integrate them with sources of raw materials and foodstuffs on the periphery, and keep them in an American orbit. They would have to spend extravagant amounts of money, take daring diplomatic initiatives, and project enough determination and power to back them up. Should they falter or should war erupt accidentally, they had to be prepared to undertake the strategic steps that would guarantee ultimate victory. Limited resources demanded a definition of priorities, but policymakers never doubted that U.S. security interests existed almost everywhere.

All of this emerged with remarkable clarity during a long evening's discussion at the Council on Foreign Relations in New York on 12 May 1947. Lovett was preparing for his new job as undersecretary of state. He wanted to discuss matters in an intimate setting with a small group of knowledgeable associates. They examined U.S. interests in Latin America and in the western Pacific as well as occupation duties in Germany and Japan. They talked about the requirements for offensive bases in Iceland, England, and the Middle East. They examined the prospects for civil war and Communist accessions to power in France and Spain. They stressed the need to control raw materials. Lovett was confounded by the immensity of U.S. interests compared with the scarcity of available resources. He was advised not to distinguish between interests over which the United States should or should not fight; Soviet expansion had to be prevented in all quarters. Clear priorities included the Western Hemisphere, Greenland, Iceland, the United Kingdom, the West European rimland, and Japan. But notwithstanding these priorities, initiatives everywhere, except perhaps Korea, had to be contemplated. After almost five hours of conversation, these wise men of foreign affairs agreed that there would be a severe and persistent competition of ideologies.[175]

Lovett talked little about Eastern Europe and even less about ultimate victory over the Soviet adversary. Kennan was not so inhibited. In his article in *Foreign Affairs* and in his speeches at the National War College, he expressed his desire to undermine Soviet rule in Eastern Europe and to bring about changes in the Soviet Union itself. The Kremlin's domination might prove ephemeral and its system vulnerable. If Soviet designs were frustrated, the system would have to change or crumble. Kennan's priorities focused on Western Europe, and his favored instruments were economic, political, and psychological. Yet his conception of national security encompassed Italy and Greece as well as France and Germany; it included overseas bases in North Africa as well as the western Pacific; and it encompassed markets, raw materials, and investment outlets for America's industrial allies in Southeast Asia as well as in Africa and Latin America. His ambitions stretched beyond the short-term desire to contain Soviet power and rebuild Western Europe; his vision focused on the erosion of Soviet influence in Eastern Europe, the transformation of Soviet behavior in the international system, and the possible overthrow of the Communist dictatorship itself.[176]

The globalism in Kennan's thinking comported well with the administration's political needs. Waging a worldwide struggle against totalitarian communism was something the American people could understand and support. Stymieing a Soviet quest to rule the world was a goal that Republicans could not contest.[177] In the future Kennan would increasingly scorn the indiscriminate actions and military orientation of U.S. policy. Even then he disliked the rhetorical flourishes in the Truman Doctrine.[178] But most of these rancorous disputes lay in the future. In mid-1947, Kennan and his colleagues agreed that their most important task was to launch the Marshall Plan and co-opt western Germany. They had to defeat Communist efforts and the Kremlin's hopes to lure Western Europe into the Soviet orbit. Afterwards, they could then turn their attention to other goals.

The Marshall Plan, Germany, and the European Cold War, June 1947-June 1948

Threw he Truman Doctrine, the Marshall Plan, and the decisions to boost German industrial production and to integrate western Germany into Western Europe were daring initiatives. They provoked diverse reactions from friends as well as foes. Foreign governments had to make agonizing decisions regarding the growth of German power, the importance of German steel production in Europe's future, and the quantity and type of reparation payments. The British, Russians, and French maneuvered both to take advantage of unprecedented opportunities and to protect themselves.

Their reactions, in turn, impelled U.S. policymakers to undertake yet additional countermeasures. During the first half of 1948, the Truman administration decided to support Bevin's Western Union, to offer military aid to West European governments, to engage in coordinated strategic planning, and to associate the United States with an Atlantic security alliance. U.S. policymakers recognized that these countermeasures could provoke the Kremlin rather than deter it. Prudence, therefore, demanded some increases in American defense expenditures and military readiness. But prudence, significantly, did not entail any willingness to negotiate with the Soviets over outstanding differences. U.S. officials increasingly believed that they had enough power to support their diplomatic risk-taking. Despite the escalating crises, they wagered that the Soviets would not go to war, that this was their unique opportunity to thwart Soviet gains and redress the European balance of power.

Bevin and the British

British foreign secretary Ernest Bevin immediately grasped the lifeline that Marshall extended in his Harvard speech on 5 June 1947. He informed the Americans that he would seek to organize a European response and moved quickly to consult with French foreign minister Georges Bidault. Bevin realized that here was an opportunity to harness America's financial prowess and generosity for the welfare of Great Britain, the rehabilitation of Europe, and the containment of Soviet power. Britain's financial resources were declining rapidly, and the costs of basic foodstuffs and raw materials were climbing. If European officials did not move quickly to avail themselves of Marshall's offer, they would have to cut back imports, endanger their economic programs, and risk domestic upheaval.

Bevin was eager to exclude the Russians. He believed, as did Marshall, that the Kremlin sought to capitalize on rather than to cure the economic crisis. Yet he shrewdly recognized that any overt move to exclude the Soviets would endanger the participation of countries with large Communist parties, like France and Italy, as well as those trapped within the confines of the Soviet sphere, like Hungary and Czechoslovakia. For Bevin, one attraction of the American offer was that it could be used to lure parts of Eastern Europe away from Soviet domination. Indeed this was one of the first points he emphasized to Undersecretary of State William Clayton when they met in London for a series of talks during the last week of June.[1]

But for Bevin, Marshall's offer was irresistible. Committed to full employment, nationalization, and the welfare state, Bevin also wished to retain Britain's presence in the Middle East and Eastern Mediterranean, invigorate its role in an expanded commonwealth, and exert its influence on the continent. The Labour government, of course, did not have the money to do this. Marshall's offer provided an extraordinary opportunity to get England through the critical transition period, at the end of which Bevin hoped Britain's successful rehabilitation would support a social welfare state at home and a prominent position abroad.

This vision presupposed U.S. acceptance of Labour's policies. Bevin skillfully and tenaciously sought to carve out a special place for Britain in America's European program. In a sense, Britain's weakness was Bevin's leverage. He recognized that U.S. officials wanted to use Britain's bases, infrastructure, diplomatic clout, military capabilities, and global presence in the struggle against Soviet communism, and replacing the British would cost the Americans more than sustaining the British. So from the outset of his talks with Clayton, Bevin sought to gain for Britain an intermediary position between the recipients of Marshall Plan aid and the United States. He opposed any schemes for the full integration of European economies, realizing that they might endanger Britain's economic ties with the commonwealth and circumscribe Labour's domestic reforms.[2]

Of course, he did not always succeed, and where he did succeed (for example, in staving off integration schemes) he was not always wise. Bevin, like other European leaders, had to make tough choices and accept compromises in return for Marshall aid. Bevin abandoned his socialization schemes for the Ruhr coal mines. He did not achieve a favored position for the United Kingdom in the European Recovery Program (ERP). He acquiesced to long-term multilateralism, which, although postponed, nevertheless limited Britain's global economic influence and domestic options. But these concessions were rather meager. Bevin gained much of what he wanted because British and U.S. officials defined their national security interests in much the same way. For the British and Americans alike, the expansion of Soviet Communist power now constituted the number-one security danger. And Marshall's offer constituted the principal means of combatting that danger.

Molotov and the Russians

On 17 and 18 June 1947, Bevin and Bidault met in Paris to discuss Marshall's speech. Although neither desired Soviet participation in a European recovery plan, Bidault convinced Bevin that it was a political necessity for the French to make a gesture to include the Kremlin. After having ousted the Communists from his coalition, Socialist premier Paul Ramadier was governing with a precarious majority. If the Russians were excluded, the Communists would denounce him for alienating the Soviet Union and dividing Europe. The Gaullist right as well as the Communist left would attack Ramadier at the first sign that he was appeasing Germany, compromising French interests, or sacrificing national well-being for U.S. dollars. Bidault nevertheless promised Bevin that France would not accept Soviet demands or tolerate Soviet delays. They then issued an invitation to V. M. Molotov to consult with them in Paris during the last days of June.[3]

The Soviet foreign minister arrived in the French capital on 27 June with a huge contingent of experts, suggesting a willingness to engage in serious economic discussions. British and French officials alike acknowledged Molotov's unusual affability in the opening stages of the talks. Yet Molotov raised two sensitive issues. Warning that the Marshall Plan would infringe on the sovereignty of recipient nations, he urged that European nations should individually calculate their needs and collectively submit their requirements to the United States. Second, he inquired how the ERP would influence Germany's level of industry and reparation payments. Bevin and Bidault sought to avoid the German question, so divisive even among the West Europeans. Instead, they told Molotov that the United States required a comprehensive plan, not a list of national requirements, that American demands for statistics and cooperation were innocuous, and that European squabbling might mean the forfeiture of American generosity. Prodded by U.S. ambassador Jefferson Caffery, the British and French did not respond sympathetically to Kremlin concerns. They emphasized that they would not postpone their own joint response to Washington if Soviet Russia proved recalcitrant. After communicating with Moscow, Molotov became more shrill, gave the anticipated Russian *nyet* to French proposals, and warned that unilateral Western action might lead to the division of Europe rather than to its rehabilitation.[4]

U.S. and British officials assumed that Molotov wanted to sabotage the Marshall Plan. In their view the Soviets would have no reason to fear American intentions unless they wanted to capitalize on the crisis to gain a preponderant position in Europe. Already they had consolidated their hold over Poland, Bulgaria, and Romania. In Hungary, moreover, they had just forced Ferenc Nagy, the non-Communist premier, to resign. After Molotov left Paris, the Kremlin forbade East European countries from participating in the ERP and instructed Communist parties in the West to launch a vitriolic campaign against the Marshall Plan. The Russians also condemned the United States for seeking to co-opt a revived Germany into a Western, anti-Soviet bloc. Walter Bedell Smith, the U.S. ambassador in Moscow, said the Soviets' actions constituted "nothing less than a declaration of war" for the control of Europe.[5]

Smith exaggerated. Molotov was not alone in worrying about the Marshall Plan's potential to infringe on national sovereignty. Bevin, for example, worried about the impact of the plan's integrationist thrust on domestic programs and commonwealth ties. Bidault agonized over its potential for derailing the Monnet Plan and placing German recovery ahead of France's rehabilitation. When representatives of the sixteen European countries outside of the Soviet orbit met and formed the Committee on European Economic Cooperation (CEEC), they simply added up their national requirements, much as Molotov said they should. Hence West European reactions shared certain similarities with the Soviet position. The difference was that in their cost-benefit analysis Western statesmen saw that they had more to gain than to lose. U.S. dollars would cover their payment deficits for food and fuel and sustain their welfare measures at home while enabling them to withstand Soviet pressures in Europe and pursue their traditional foreign policy interests in Asia and Africa. They also realized that without American aid they might have to accept deflationary policies and internecine strife that were more dangerous than their dependence on U.S. dollars.[6]

The Soviets were inclined to make their calculations in a different way. Stalin and his comrades did not worry that payment deficits might accelerate autarkic tendencies and eventually jeopardize economic and political freedoms. They concluded that the costs of the Marshall Plan exceeded prospective benefits. They feared that they would have to open up their account books, acknowledge their economic weakness, forgo reparations, and risk being subjected to additional pressure. Although they needed American credits, they could not be certain how much aid they would receive; they could only have suspected that most of it would go to Western Europe. Nor could they see how the plan would advance their foreign policy or national security goals; it appeared to revive Germany's strength, dilute Soviet influence in Eastern Europe, and undermine Communist strength in Western Europe.[7]

Stalin and Molotov had reason to be suspicious. Clayton told Bevin that Soviet Russia would have to alter its policies toward Europe if it were to receive aid. Even if Russia were permitted to participate, Clayton and George Kennan believed that its principal role would be to serve as a donor of raw materials in order to expedite Western Europe's rehabilitation. Only in the latter stages of the program might

Russia be considered entitled to reconstruction credits. Likewise, U.S. officials assumed that, in return for American assistance, East European economies would have to be freed from Soviet domination and reoriented westward.[8] Increases in the production of Polish coal, for example, might be promoted, but for sale to the West, not to Russia.[9] Although hardly anyone intended to use American aid to break the Kremlin's political stranglehold on eastern Germany, most policymakers did envision the Marshall Plan as a device to integrate the western zones of Germany in a viable Western economic orbit that would serve as a magnet to east Germans and East Europeans as well as constitute a counterpoise to Soviet power.[10]

U.S. officials recognized that they were confronting the Kremlin with unpalatable choices. National self-interest, Kennan realized, would probably force the Russians to clamp down on Eastern Europe. Although this was regrettable, it was not unacceptable. Kennan hoped that the Soviets would overreach themselves, sour relations with satellite governments, and create conditions for the future disintegration of the Soviet empire.[11] Anticipating Communist denunciations of the Marshall Plan in France and Italy, Kennan also expected such actions would weaken their influence and redound to America's advantage. "Events of past weeks," he wrote Marshall in late July 1947, constitute "the greatest blow to European Communism since termination of hostilities."[12]

The Soviet response to the Marshall Plan was harsh but calibrated; it was no declaration of war. Stalin saw his periphery being probed (in Turkey as well as in Eastern Europe), his fiercest enemy (Germany) revived, and his foreign supporters imprisoned (as in Greece) or excised from government coalitions (as in Italy and France).[13] He reacted defensively. Most scholars now agree that his aim was to consolidate Soviet power within his orbit rather than to seek new gains in the West. In Eastern Europe, he acted brutishly and unwisely. But beyond his own sphere, he remained cautious.[14] In Germany, for example, the Soviets opposed the increase in the bizonal level of industry, but they wanted to avoid a split.[15] In France and Italy, the Communists assailed the Marshall Plan, but rather than seek to overthrow their governments, they wanted to reenter them.[16]

Kennan and Bohlen, the most astute Kremlinologists within the Truman administration, saw nothing surprising in Soviet actions. Their advice was to keep up the pressure, to move relentlessly forward, to thwart the rise of indigenous communism, and to co-opt German power before economic circumstances and political imponderables decisively shifted the balance of power in favor of the Soviet Union.[17] What they did not fully expect was the tenacity of the French opposition to Germany's revival. For the Kremlin was not alone in fearing that Germany might reemerge as a formidable force in European affairs.

Bidault and the French

The French faced agonizing choices. They desperately needed U.S. dollars to buy critical foodstuffs and raw materials. A year before the French government had adopted the Monnet Plan to foster rapid economic modernization. The French wanted to supplant the Germans in key industries, especially steel. If they succeeded, not only would the standard of living in France be augmented and redistributive struggles be quelled, but French security would be enhanced. To implement the Monnet Plan, however, France desperately needed coal. France imported huge amounts of bituminous coal from the United States; these purchases, along with those of American grain, drained away dollars. Without assistance, the Ramadier ministry might have to cut imports and modify its ambitious economic program. The Marshall Plan offered a way out.[18]

Yet the U.S. initiative posed new dangers. American aid for a European recovery plan was conditional, requiring the inclusion of the western zones of Germany and acceptance of the new level of industry for Germany, including 10.7 million tons of steel.[19] Although the French were eager to increase coal production in the Ruhr, they wanted the additional output for themselves. They opposed U.S. plans to return the coal mines to German owners, and they wanted some control over the distribution of German coal. They ridiculed the new level of industry because it meant that increments in Ruhr coal production would be used, at least in part, to revive German steel, metallurgical, and chemical production. Despite the appeal of long-term American assistance, no French government could ignore the portentous economic and strategic ramifications of a revived Germany.[20]

Inside France, moreover, rumors of the impending Anglo-American decision to revive German industry precipitated an avalanche of criticism. The Communist left and the Gaullist right charged that French recovery was being sacrificed to achieve Germany's renewal. Bidault, Jean Monnet, and Henri Bonnet, the French ambassador in Washington, begged the Americans and the British to postpone their announcement of the change in Germany's level of production. They explained that it would add credence to Communists' vitriolic denunciations of the Marshall Plan and endanger France's ability to cooperate. Desirous of abetting the CEEC talks that Bidault was then hosting in Paris, the State Department in mid-July instructed General Lucius Clay not to publicize the new bizonal agreement on Germany's industrial output.[21]

On 3 August, however, Kenneth Royall, the new secretary of the Army, announced that the United States, if it so chose, could boost the German level of industry without consulting France. The French public was outraged and the government beleaguered. Bonnet implored Undersecretary of State Robert Lovett for a better understanding of Bidault's precarious political position. On 8 August came a most ominous report from Ambassador Caffery: "All work of technical committees of Conference on European Economic Cooperation responsible for steel, coal, and coke has come to a stop because the French are reluctant to participate." [22]

Royall's public statement infuriated Lovett and Marshall, not because they objected to his views but because he had been recklessly indiscreet. The State Department agreed that German industry had to be augmented. No satisfactory program for reconstructing Europe and restoring the balance of power could emerge if Germany's output was not increased and integrated with that of other participants in the CEEC. But because France's collaboration in the ERP was by no means assured, insensitivity to the political and strategic concerns of the French government could prove as disastrous to Europe's future as any retrogression on the German level of industry. France's reaction accentuated the need to reconcile Germany's rehabilitation with France's strategic and economic imperatives. Otherwise, Marshall's initiative might founder, German reconstruction might be thwarted, and the worst of all possible outcomes might eventuate: "a Germany controlled by the Soviet Union with German military potential utilized in alliance with the Soviet." [23]

The Worsening Crisis

By August, the hope inspired by Marshall's speech was waning. Assistance seemed more imperative than ever, but worldwide supplies could not meet demand. The U.S. corn crop and the Canadian wheat crop were below expectations. Other shortages threatened to drive prices higher, intensifying the demands on European dollar reserves. European governments might not be able to await passage of the Marshall Plan before exhausting their resources, abandoning multilateralism, opting for autarky, cutting back rations, and risking political upheaval. At interdepartmental meetings and cabinet sessions, Marshall, Lovett, Kennan, Forrestal, Royall, and Clark Clifford wondered whether the Old World could survive the coming winter. President Truman often presided at these meetings, said little, and offered few ideas. He prodded his subordinates to find ways to handle the emergency. He would follow their lead. [24]

The most chronic and fundamental problem, in the opinion of U.S. officials, was their inability to bring about a rapid increase in German coal production. Thwarting British socialization schemes and returning the coal mines to German managers (under an Anglo-American control commission) would not suffice. After visiting Germany in July and August, both Secretary of Commerce Averell Harriman and Secretary of Agriculture Clinton Anderson explained to the president and to the cabinet that increasing coal production depended on increasing the availability of food. Farmers, however, had little incentive to produce and sell because of the shortage of consumer goods and the depreciation of the reichsmark. Hence financial and currency reforms were indispensable. [25]

Because there was no quick fix to the food and coal crisis inside Germany, the western sectors required additional imports of grain even to maintain the inadequate ration of 1,550 calories. Yet augmenting imports was doubly costly for the United States, since the British were no longer able to handle the financial burden. A new agreement afforded the United States greater economic leverage over bizonal economic affairs but escalated its financial responsibilities at a time when additional appropriations were by no means assured. "Interrupted relief shipments," Army Secretary Royall warned President Truman, "would reduce the populations of the occupied countries to a starvation level." The resulting strife would play into the hands of the Kremlin and might drive all of Germany eastward.[26]

If the seemingly incurable state of German coal production remained a constant variable in the European crisis, the dramatic deterioration of Britain's financial situation injected an alarming new dimension. After restoring the convertibility of sterling in mid-July, the Bank of England experienced an unprecedented drain of dollars. Unless emergency action was taken, Britain might act unilaterally to suspend convertibility, husband its few remaining dollars, resort to additional bilateral arrangements, and accelerate the trend toward autarky.[27] The prospect was ominous. Britain might dismantle its defense and imperial commitments. European nations might follow Britain's example. New vacuums of power might be created.[28]

Dissatisfaction with the progress of the CEEC deliberations in Paris intensified. Lovett had taken charge of guiding the European response to Marshall's overture. On 14 August he telegrammed Clayton and Caffery that too little attention was being focused on self-help and mutual aid, which Marshall had stressed in his Harvard speech. The CEEC countries were simply submitting sixteen shopping lists to the United States. Worse yet, they had shown little inclination to share scarce commodities or direct industrial output into mutually beneficial fields. Nor had they indicated any serious intention to reduce exchange controls, lower tariffs, or stabilize finances. Most worrisome was the absence of any signs that, at the end of four or five years of aid, Europe would be able to function without American assistance. Increasingly agitated, Lovett sent Kennan and Bonesteel to help U.S. diplomats who were engaged in extensive consultations with the executive committee of the CEEC.[29]

When Kennan returned to the United States, his report was filled with the most dire warnings. The economic situation of Britain was "deteriorating with terrifying rapidity." Lamenting the "unforeseeable effects in other areas of the world," Kennan emphasized that Britain's position was "tragic to a point that challenges description." Intelligence assessments and diplomatic reports from U.S. embassies in Rome, Paris, and Athens suggested that conditions were no better in those countries. France and Italy were running out of dollars, cutting back purchases of critical raw materials, and anticipating production slowdowns and mounting unemployment. Additional cuts in basic rations might precipitate strikes, food riots, and perhaps Communist insurrection. The interdepartmental committee on the Marshall Plan concluded that the United States had "to provide Europe with food and fuel this winter if the major European countries are to remain sufficiently strong that the basis will survive upon which to erect the Marshall Plan in its long-term sense."[30]

U.S. officials doubted that the Italian, French, and Greek governments could survive. According to intelligence and diplomatic reports, Greece's neighbors had stepped up their aid to the Greek insurgents in response to the Truman Doctrine, and the Greek government was tottering.[31] The CIA estimated that a swift economic collapse might catapult the French or Italian Communists to power.[32] The political center seemed to be collapsing, as when in the October municipal elections in

France the Gaullist right and Communist left won over 70 percent of the vote. The resurgence of a strong right-wing movement seemed only to increase the likelihood of internecine strife and civil war.[33]

The Kremlin heightened the crisis by summoning leading Communists to a conference in Poland. Attending the meeting in late September were representatives from the Communist parties of the Soviet Union, Poland, Yugoslavia, Hungary, Romania, Bulgaria, Czechoslovakia, France, and Italy. Soviet leaders A. A. Zhadanov and G. M. Malenkov denounced U.S. imperialism, ridiculed the popular front tactics of the Italian and French Communists, and called for the establishment of the Cominform, the Information Bureau of Communist Parties. They ordered forceful, strident opposition to the Marshall Plan in Western Europe. The proceedings were secret, but some of the results soon became apparent. In Western Europe the Communist parties stepped up their opposition, encouraged strikes, and engaged in violent street demonstrations. In Eastern Europe the Hungarians forced scores of non-Communist politicians into exile and called for unification of working-class parties. In Czechoslovakia the Communists began scheming to seize power.[34]

Nothing they saw surprised Kennan and Charles Bohlen, now the State Department's counselor. In their view, the Soviet decision to form the Cominform was a "quite logical development . . . in the face of increasing American determination to assist the free nations of the world both economically and politically." "Subject to a squeeze play," said Kennan, the Communists were making a last-gasp effort to undermine the ERP before it became a reality. By striking, rioting, and excoriating U.S. intentions to enslave the economies of Western Europe, Communists hoped to cause political paralysis and force their reentry into government coalitions. Stalin grasped that a major turning point was at hand. The United States, insisted Kennan, must not falter.[35]

If the United States did not act vigorously, the French, Italian, or Greek Communists might win power legally or seize it violently. If U.S. officials equivocated, the Germans would grow more aggrieved and look eastward to ameliorate their economic plight and solve their political dilemmas. The "greatest potential danger to U.S. security," the CIA emphasized, "lies . . . in the possibility of the economic collapse of Western Europe and of the consequent accession to power of elements subservient to the Kremlin."[36]

Many agencies of the U.S. government pondered the repercussions of Communist parties' coming to power and came to similar conclusions. Communists would prove resistant to American plans and would seek closer ties with the Kremlin. If, for example, the Greek insurgents triumphed, the JCS maintained that "forces friendly to, if not under the domination of, the USSR would be on the Mediterranean and in a position to interdict shipping through that sea route." If Italy, Turkey, and Iran oriented themselves eastward, access to Middle Eastern oil "would be jeopardized." The Policy Planning Staff estimate of the consequences of a Communist takeover of northern Italy was similar. Moreover, Communist successes in

France would provide the Soviet Union with access to French airfields, ports, and roads and would allow the Kremlin to establish bases in North Africa, from which it could interdict shipping in the Atlantic and launch attacks on the United States. But most of all, a Communist triumph would mean that France would become the western bastion of an inherently hostile "continental system" dominated by the Kremlin.[37]

The fear that the Soviet Union would gain indirect control over European resources, skilled labor, industrial infrastructure, and military bases constituted the national security nightmare of U.S. policymakers. The expectation was that Communist regimes not only would sign bilateral economic treaties along the pattern of Russia's East European satellites but would also offer air and naval facilities that would enhance Soviet warmaking capabilities enormously. Marshall, for example, stressed that if the great industrial and economic capabilities of Western Europe and western Germany were to fall within the orbit of the Soviet Union, its industrial-military capabilities would be augmented substantially. The European balance of power, for which the United States had waged two world wars, would be shattered, and the Soviet Union would emerge as a formidable global adversary of the United States.[38]

If local Communist successes brought critical regions within the sphere of the Kremlin, the United States would have to shift its priorities, reorient its economy, and place greater stress on military preparedness. Prudence would dictate such a course, for recent experiences had shown that totalitarian nations, having absorbed and assimilated subordinate countries with extensive resources, might attack the United States and wage protracted war. If Germany and Japan had posed such a danger, the Soviets would be all the more formidable were they to co-opt the resources of all Europe. President Truman was advised that,

In the event of a totalitarian Europe, our foreign policy would have to be completely reoriented and a great part of what we have fought for and accomplished in the past would have been lost. The change in the power relationships involved would force us to adopt drastic domestic measures and would inevitably require great and burdensome sacrifices on the part of our citizens. . . . The sacrifices would not be simply material. With a totalitarian Europe which would have no regard for individual freedom, our spiritual loss would be incalculable.[39]

Here one can see the gradual interweaving of strategic, geopolitical, economic, and ideological considerations. The enlargement of a Soviet sphere would add to the Kremlin's military potential and compel the United States to increase its own military expenditures. Furthermore, the existence of a large economic bloc under Soviet tutelage would reshape world commercial patterns, impel the United States to turn in upon itself, and require the U.S. government to impose controls over production and trade and infringe on personal freedoms. If the Truman administration protested British discriminatory practices and European bilateralism, which it did, then the prospective absorption of the markets, raw materials, and industrial infrastructure of Western Europe into a closed Soviet orbit was much more ominous. Should this development occur, it would remove the world's most industrialized region from an open trading system where America's investment capital and comparative trade advantage afforded it the opportunity to compete economically and ideologically. Communist successes in Italy, Greece, and France as well as German alignment with the Kremlin, therefore, posed unacceptable risks to the national security and political economy of the United States.

Countermeasures

U.S. policymakers moved swiftly. They prepared a program of emergency financial relief for France and Italy, sought to ease London's exchange problems, and encouraged the British to retain their military presence in the Eastern Mediterranean and Middle East. They showed a growing disposition to consider covert operations and military force should economic aid and even military assistance prove inadequate. Furthermore, they endorsed the idea of international controls over the Ruhr and pondered the assumption of security guarantees.

As early as 10 July, Lovett foresaw the need for an emergency relief program until the administration could secure legislative passage of a comprehensive ERP. In early August, Clayton met with the most important U.S. diplomats in Europe. They agreed that "failing additional assistance by the United States this year," the situation in the United Kingdom, France, and Italy may so deteriorate that "our objectives in Western Europe and elsewhere may become unattainable." A few days later the Policy Planning Staff recommended that the administration act immediately. Secretary of State George Marshall urged Truman to convene a special session of Congress and seek passage of an interim aid program. France, Italy, Britain, and Austria required several hundred million dollars for food and fuel.[40]

While Charles Bonesteel coordinated the interdepartmental work, Clark Clifford maintained high-level collaboration with top officials in the State, Commerce, and Treasury departments and the National Military Establishment (NME). Clifford agreed with Marshall, Lovett, Harriman, and Secretary of Defense James Forrestal that the crisis was approaching monumental proportions. "The issues involved," Clifford wrote Truman, "are of such importance as to take precedence over all other questions, and the consequences of failure are too grave to permit the President to stop anywhere short of the full use of his constitutional powers in his efforts to meet the requirements of the situation."[41] After consulting with congressional leaders, Truman announced on 30 September that he was requesting key legislative committees to consider an emergency relief bill for Western Europe. Less than a month later he called Congress into special session to consider aid that would prevent the economies of France and Italy from collapsing. In December, Congress passed a $600 million emergency aid package for France, Italy, and Austria. It was designed primarily to keep these countries from sliding into chaos before Congress could consider the Marshall Plan at its regularly scheduled session in January 1948.[42]

■

However, interim aid constituted no certain palliative to the unfolding crisis. Looking at the Labour government's response to Britain's financial woes, U.S. officials feared that the British would turn increasingly to the sterling bloc, resort to bilateralism and discriminatory measures, and accelerate the trend toward autarky. They worried even more that Prime Minister Clement Attlee and Bevin might cut Britain's military presence in critical areas of the world. Mid-level officials who were negotiating with the British over the basic principles for the General Agreement on Tariffs and Trade (GATT) and the International Trade Organization (ITO) fumed at British insistence on maintaining imperial preferences. High-ranking policymakers remonstrated over the Labour government's incapacity to solve its financial problems.[43]

But the Americans nonetheless responded with restraint and constructive assistance, realizing that U.S. countermeasures had to ease Britain's way through a very difficult transition. They wanted to elicit Britain's commitment to long-term multilateralism and to sustain its presence in the Eastern Mediterranean and the Middle East. The State and Treasury departments acquiesced to British adoption of additional short-term discriminatory measures; they agreed to release the balance of $400 million on the 1945 loan; they made repeated concessions on the GATT and ITO. But in return for these actions, they secured Britain's long-term commitment to multilateralism. In addition to promoting their economic interests, multilateralism sought to bind the countries of the non-Soviet world together in a seamless economic web that could serve American geopolitical and, if necessary, military imperatives.[44]

At the very moment that British commercial and financial measures might have tempted U.S. officials to exercise a heavy hand, Marshall, Lovett, and Treasury Secretary John Snyder displayed a remarkable ability to minimize the strains on the Anglo-American relationship and to focus on shared objectives like the reconstruction of Western Europe and the containment of Soviet power in the Middle East. Bevin showed equal skill in controlling the latent friction and molding a cooperative relationship. This attempt at mutual reconciliation was evident when Marshall bitterly protested British plans to pull out of Greece and reduce their troops in Italy. The United States, Marshall insisted, was willing to launch the ERP but could not afford to supplant British military power at the same time. When Bevin realized how vexed Marshall was over this matter, he proposed that military talks take place to iron out British and U.S. roles in the Middle East. Marshall readily accepted. In November, while the European crisis was heading toward a climax, highly confidential talks took place at the Pentagon that culminated in substantial accord on British and U.S. goals and responsibilities in the Middle East.[45]

■

Marshall's great irritation with the British over Greece reflected U.S. officials' growing concern with the viability of the Greek, Italian, and French governments. The strikes, protests, public demonstrations, and insurrectionary activity (in Greece) that accompanied the announcement of the Marshall Plan and the exclusion of the Communists from governing coalitions threatened to topple the incumbent governments. U.S. policymakers now resorted to clandestine operations and military assistance and pondered the use of military force to thwart Communist efforts to take power either legally or illegally. They believed that a Communist triumph in any single country would have a bandwagon effect elsewhere. They urged middle-of-the-road politicians to refrain from collaborating not only with Communists but also with other leftists who were willing to work with Communists.[46]

The initial focus was on Greece. On 17 July, Marshall told Royall that U.S. forces might have to assist the Greek army. In August, Lovett asked the Policy Planning Staff to study what should be done in case of a Communist takeover. Marshall informed the cabinet that Lincoln MacVeagh, the U.S. ambassador in Athens, and Dwight Griswold, director of the American Mission to Aid Greece, wanted U.S. soldiers to replace British troops should the latter leave.[47] In September Loy Henderson, director of the State Department's Office of Near Eastern and African Affairs, visited Greece, and shortly thereafter, MacVeagh returned to Washington for extensive consultations. Everyone concurred that the economic situation was worsening, the insurgency growing, and the capacity of the Greek government deteriorating.[48]

On 17 September, State Department and Army officials agreed to send General S. J. Chamberlin, the director of Army intelligence, to survey the military situation. His findings had been pretty much predetermined: the Greek army had to be strengthened; reserve units had to be organized to protect the countryside; military aid had to be enlarged. Most important, the number of U.S. military advisers had to be increased substantially, and they had to be authorized to give operational advice to Greek military units. Although Chamberlin did not recommend the immediate insertion of U.S. combat troops, he emphasized that the United States had to be prepared for this contingency.

Chief of Staff Dwight Eisenhower immediately endorsed the report; so did Royall. Henderson and Lovett welcomed Chamberlin's findings. On 27 October the National Security Council (NSC) recommended the assignment of 90 additional officers to Greece. Operational advice would be provided to Greek combat units, and a Military Advisory and Planning Group would be established to assist Greek armed forces. Truman approved these measures on 4 November, and congressional leaders were secretly informed of these developments.[49]

But these steps did not allay the crisis. When the Greek insurgents declared the establishment of a "Free Democratic Greek Government" and it seemed that Communist satellite nations might recognize this entity, U.S. officials reappraised their options. Henderson pressed vigorously for a decision to insert U.S. troops, if necessary, to salvage the situation. "Greece is the test tube which the peoples of the world are watching," he wrote Marshall. Eisenhower, Chamberlin, and the Army's assistant chief of staff for plans supported Henderson's position. On 6 January the NSC staff submitted a paper to this effect. The Joint Chiefs of Staff (JCS) again endorsed the view that Greece was critical to American national security but admonished that deploying troops would raise the matter of partial mobilization.[50]

The issue was an agonizing one for top policymakers, who discussed it at meetings of the NSC on 13 January and 12 February. Although Lovett had inclined toward Henderson's view, at the January NSC meeting he voiced Marshall's reservations calling for a careful appraisal of the consequences of using force. Lovett questioned whether the mere deployment of force would compel the Communists to capitulate, as Henderson had contended. Royall pointed out that the Army did not think one U.S. division would turn the tide. Sidney Souers, executive director of the NSC, reminded everyone that the NME did not favor the use of force but sought to buttress the diplomatic posturing desired by Henderson. All agreed that the matter required more careful scrutiny of the military situation in Greece.[51]

When the question of using force arose at the next NSC meeting, policymakers were no closer to resolving the tough questions. Tension filled the meeting as Marshall outlined the problems surrounding the question of deploying U.S. troops. The outlook was "exceedingly grave." We could not "escape the dire consequences if it appears that we don't back up our policies." Acknowledging the insufficiency of U.S. forces, Marshall did not know if they should be used in Greece when they might also be needed elsewhere. Still, Marshall concluded, the United States had to be ready to deploy troops or "we will lose the game and prejudice our whole national position."[52]

Accepting Marshall's ideas, the NSC decided that all measures of an economic, political, and, if necessary, military nature should be prepared to prevent Greece from falling under Soviet domination. It was hoped that U.S. forces would not be necessary, but Marshall, Forrestal, and the NSC now sanctioned their use as a *possible* countermeasure to the Communist insurgency. Marshall was betting that the Soviets would retreat from a military showdown. Kennan, too, believed that the deployment of U.S. military forces in areas critical to Soviet security interests might impel the Kremlin to exert a restraining influence on local Communists. President Truman approved the recommendations of the NSC, thus showing his readiness to consider using U.S. military capabilities to defeat the Communists, enforce the Truman doctrine, and avert the dire consequences that might ensue from the "loss" of Greece.[53]

■

Indeed at this time U.S. officials were also examining countermeasures to a Communist seizure of power or, more likely (and more worrisomely), a Communist electoral victory in Italy. Lovett again initially solicited the views of the Policy Planning Staff. Although Kennan wished to avoid the direct use of American force in a civil war, he nevertheless stressed that "plans should now be made by the US in the event that Communist seizure of North Italy appears imminent. . . . The National interest would require that the greatest possible support be given the Italian government in its efforts to . . . regain the territory seized by the Communists." Kennan favored building up local forces of resistance and recommended military intervention "only if they show signs of failing." He preferred to delay the withdrawal of U.S. troops, as mandated by the Italian peace treaty, until the last possible day (17 December). But he also encouraged General Alfred Gruenther to expedite the contingency plans for direct military intervention.[54]

As the date for the withdrawal of U.S. troops approached and as unrest in Italy intensified, Lovett, Forrestal, and Royall scrutinized additional policy options. On 13 December, Truman publicly warned that direct or indirect threats to Italian freedom and independence would force the United States to consider additional countermeasures. At the time Eisenhower and Forrest Sherman, the deputy chief of naval operations, outlined for Forrestal the ground, air, and naval forces that could be deployed to Italy in 10–60 days. In the following weeks the United States beefed up its naval presence in the Eastern Mediterranean, sent 1,000 Marines to join the Sixth Fleet, and readied for immediate airlift a reinforced regimental combat team in Germany for quick deployment to Italy (or Greece or Palestine).[55]

At NSC meetings, officials continued to agonize over the risks of direct military intervention. Ultimately, they agreed that, if necessary, military power should be used to prevent Italy from falling under Soviet domination. The JCS kept warning that intervention would require partial mobilization and increased defense expenditures. Although Marshall, Lovett, and Kennan were entirely aware of the inadequacy of U.S. forces, they were willing to take risks because they wagered that Soviet leaders so much wanted to avoid sliding into a war that they would constrain local Communists. Manifestations of American power and assistance, meanwhile, would stiffen the will of non-Communist Italian leaders who might revert to popular front coalitions or opt for neutrality.[56]

Of course, U.S. officials hoped they would never have to intervene directly in Italy. In December 1947, the NSC authorized the CIA to carry out covert operations against the Italian Communists. The Truman administration allocated $10–20 million to pay for local election campaigns, anti-Communist propaganda, and bribes.[57] To help the government of Alcide De Gasperi to handle Communist demonstrators and to resist a possible Communist coup, U.S. officials sought to provide it with military assistance. Lovett, Forrestal, and Royall gave considerable personal attention to this matter but were hampered by legal restrictions. The Italian armed forces needed military supplies no longer defined as surplus and therefore not transferrable under existing legislation. After exploring various loopholes, the president sidestepped the legal niceties and simply authorized the shipment of munitions and supplies under his authority as commander in chief.[58]

■

U.S. officials were equally concerned about the ramifications of a Communist takeover in France. Through the CIA they promoted a schism in the French labor movement.[59] During the strikes and protests of October and November 1947, Ambassador Caffery met frequently with French leaders, established an extraordinarily supportive relationship with Premier Robert Schuman, and approved his decision to use force to disperse a mob at the St. Etienne arsenal. When the French army acted loyally and effectively, U.S. (and British) officials were exultant.[60] At the end of the London meeting of the Council of Foreign Ministers in December, Marshall and Bevin approved the idea of military aid to the French. Army officers welcomed the idea and sent General Harold R. Bull to Paris for highly confidential military talks. They wanted the French government to have the means "to cope adequately with general communist armed uprisings." [61] Marshall became a strong proponent of military aid to the French government, believing it would encourage French officials to defy protests from the left and right and induce them to cooperate with U.S. plans for rebuilding western Germany.[62]

Yet Marshall and Lovett realized that, to gain French support for the ERP, they had to allay French fears of a revitalized Germany and to guarantee France adequate supplies of fuel. The secretary and undersecretary of state had considerable sympathy for the French point of view, as did Kennan and Bonesteel, who provided key advice to Marshall and Lovett. Lovett's friends on Wall Street, like Ferdinand Eberstadt, tirelessly warned that the Ruhr must not be left in the hands of Germany alone. As a result, State Department officials decided that German production requirements should be screened by the CEEC. They were also inclined to accept Bidault's proposal for an international board to allocate Ruhr coal, coke, and steel.[63]

They faced strong opposition from General Clay, who viewed international control schemes with considerable skepticism. Either the French might use such schemes to interfere with German production or the Soviets might exploit them to gain a foothold in Germany's industrial heartland.[64] To overcome Clay's objections, Lovett met with Royall and Eisenhower. The undersecretary of state stressed the importance of taking a regional approach to European affairs.[65] Finding less opposition than anticipated from Army officials in Washington, Marshall told Bidault that, in contrast to the interwar years, "the Ruhr should not be under the exclusive control of any German government." This promise of international control was a major concession, but Marshall recognized that it would take months of negotiations to iron out the details. In the meantime, he insisted that the French cease playing an obstructionist role, agree to merge their zone with Bizonia, and cooperate in currency reform.[66]

Still more had to be done to allay French fears. The secretary of state told the Chicago Council on Foreign Relations in November that the United States should guarantee Germany's demilitarization. So long as U.S. troops still occupied Germany, there was no real threat, but Marshall acknowledged that additional steps were necessary to guarantee the security of Europe given the military potential that inhered in the resuscitation of the Ruhr coal-and-steel complex.[67] U.S. officials recognized that formal commitments would be needed both to overcome the European political crisis and to unleash the forces of production and integration.

The London Council of Foreign Ministers

U.S. plans for western Germany's participation in the ERP made four-power agreement at the November meeting of the Council of Foreign Ministers an impossibility. The Kremlin must not be given any opportunity to hamstring production in the Ruhr, obstruct the distribution of coal, orient the German economy eastward, or entice a unified Germany into the Soviet sphere. Marshall stated emphatically that he did not want a neutralized Germany that might maneuver between East and West and that might eventually align with the Kremlin.[68]

As U.S. officials prepared for the London Council of Foreign Ministers meeting on the future of Germany, their principal concern was to avoid agreements that might interfere with their plans for Western Europe and western Germany. They dreaded the possibility that Molotov might submit a deceptively appealing plan for the withdrawal of occupation troops, the economic and political unification of the four zones, and the establishment of a united Germany. In pre-conference bilateral talks with the British, they agreed they could not accept such a program lest it sabotage the Marshall Plan.[69] Ambassador Smith in Moscow warned that the mutual evacuation of troops would encourage the Soviets to capitalize on the revolutionary situation in France and Italy. Like everyone else, Smith did not expect the Kremlin to undertake aggression. The presence of U.S. occupation troops, however, constituted both a deterrent and a prospective response to insurrectionary activity in Southern and Western Europe as well as in western Germany itself. The United States, Marshall unequivocally told his cabinet colleagues, would not be duped into placing "western Germany under arrangements which would leave that country defenseless against communist penetration."[70]

Nor was the secretary of state willing to make concessions on other matters that might jeopardize western Germany's participation in the ERP. He did not want to discuss an international control regime for the Ruhr lest it afford the Soviets a pretext to wedge their way into western Germany.[71] Nor was he inclined to permit reparations from current production. The new level of German industry and the preliminary plans for German participation in the ERP did not envision any such payments. Lovett believed that the administration would have difficulty persuading Congress to appropriate additional money for Germany "if result was to make possible current reparations to Russia." [72]

Molotov railed against the ERP and U.S. policies, yet he emphasized that his government no longer insisted that reparation payments precede economic unification. He mixed his tirades with important concessions, showing a willingness to engage in tough bargaining if Marshall and Bevin reciprocated in kind. But for the Americans (and the British) an agreement with the Soviets was not nearly as desirable as implementing the ERP and integrating western Germany into a Western bloc. On 10 December, Marshall categorically rejected Soviet pleas for reparations from current production. Reparations would have to await the repayment of occupation costs and the achievement of a balanced German economy. Truman fully supported Marshall's tough stand.[73]

When the conference broke up a few days later amidst Soviet and American recriminations, the U.S. delegates breathed a sigh of relief. Now, finally, they could move forward on matters they deemed critically important. From the outset, their aim was to blame the Soviets for the collapse of the meeting. During the pre-conference bilateral talks with the British, John Hickerson, director of the State Department's Office of European Affairs, repeatedly emphasized this goal. During the conference, Smith confided to Eisenhower that "The difficulty under which we labor is that in spite of our announced position, we really do not want nor intend to accept German unification in any terms that the Russians might agree to, even though they seemed to meet most of our requirements." And after the meeting, Colonel Henry Byroade admitted that he and the other U.S. delegates had greatly feared that the Soviets might agree to numerous concessions, the effect of which would "prevent effective participation of Germany in the ERP." [74]

Resuming the Initiative

Before departing London, Marshall—along with Lewis W. Douglas, the U.S. ambassador to England, and General Clay—held extensive bilateral talks with the British and French. Bevin talked expansively and vaguely about forming a Western democratic system, not a formal alliance but a spiritual union backed by power, money, and resolute action. He stressed the importance of enhancing France's security, inaugurating military staff discussions, and providing military aid. Marshall listened, generally assenting to Bevin's inchoate, grandiose ideas, but he was much more interested in delineating the steps that had to be taken toward European economic rehabilitation. He emphasized to Bevin and to Bidault that now was the time to move swiftly toward currency reform, trizonal fusion, and the establishment of German self-government. But most of all, Marshall's attention was on the passage and implementation of the ERP, including western Germany.[75]

On 19 December, before the secretary of state returned to Washington, President

Truman submitted the ERP to Congress. For months the administration had been engaged in an intense campaign to mobilize public support for the Marshall Plan. In his address to Congress, the president explained why. After citing the program's economic and commercial advantages, Truman emphasized that

Our deepest concern with European recovery is that it is essential to the maintenance of the civilization in which the American way of life is rooted. . . . If Europe fails to recover, the people of these countries might be driven to the philosophy of despair [to totalitarianism]. Such a turn of events would constitute a shattering blow to peace and stability in the world. It might well compel us to modify our own economic system and to forgo, for the sake of our own security, the enjoyment of many of our freedoms and privileges.[76]

In their testimony before Congress, Truman's cabinet officers explicated their vision of national security that necessitated the ERP. In succession, Marshall, Douglas, Harriman, Royall, and Forrestal emphasized the huge resources, skilled labor, and industrial complex that existed in Europe. Prior to the war, the sixteen European countries composing the CEEC plus western Germany produced 37 percent of the world's steel and 40 percent of its chemicals, possessed 68 percent of the world's merchant tonnage, and sold 24 percent of its exports and purchased 39 percent of its imports. "Should that workshop," Forrestal warned, "be integrated with all of its industrial and military potential, with its great business complex, into a coalition of totalitarian states, it is possible that we in time would find ourselves isolated in a hostile world." Such a decisive shift in the world balance of power, given the *potential* warmaking capabilities of the Kremlin and the probable constriction of American access to European markets and raw materials, would force the U.S. government to increase its defense expenditures enormously and to institute comprehensive government controls over the economy. Hence, even though war might not come, U.S. perceptions of the national security threat posed by a Communist Europe would force sweeping changes in the American way of life. Passage of the Marshall Plan, therefore, was the number-one priority of the Truman administration's national security program.[77]

The opposition remained formidable. Congress took more than three months to deliberate on the Marshall Plan. The desire to economize was widespread; fear of inflation was omnipresent. Marshall and Lovett, for example, spent countless hours trying to muster the support of John Taber's House Appropriations Committee. Time and again they reiterated that the ERP would be self-liquidating.[78]

Marshall knew he had to convince Congress that the United States was not embarking on an endless giveaway. But his attitudes on so basic a question as the recovery of Germany were not shaped by congressional pressures. He and his colleagues were altogether convinced that European recovery could not occur without the increased availability of German coal, steel, fertilizer, and chemicals. Nor could it occur without the integration of the German market into a West European regional economy.[79] Transcending even this consideration, however, was the belief that, unless conditions in western Germany were ameliorated, unless the German people were allowed to govern themselves, and unless German energies were given a constructive outlet, the Germans would turn eastward to achieve their political and economic interests. The Germans, Kennan insisted, remained "sullen, bitter, unregenerate, and pathologically attached to the old chimera of German unity." Of course, the Allied occupation circumscribed what the Germans could do, but the occupation could not continue indefinitely. It was too costly, too unpopular at home and in Germany, too intrusive into German economic affairs. Preparations had to be made for a suitable transition to self-government and eventual independence. But what then would the Germans choose to do? Would they not seek to maneuver between East and West in search of German unity? Might they not align with the Kremlin, as they did at Rapallo in 1922, in pursuit of their own self-interest? "Unless western Germany during coming year is effectively associated with western European nations," Marshall and Lovett wired Caffery, "there is a real danger that whole of Germany will be drawn into eastern orbit, with obvious dire consequences for all of us." [80]

With broad authorization from Marshall, General Clay acted in great haste in the days following the London conference to boost German morale and German production. Claiming that the internal situation was worse than at any time since surrender, he and Brian Robertson, the British military governor, revised the bizonal economic council, formed an economic high court, and established a bizonal central bank. Clay also pushed vigorously for currency reform and for German self-government. Acting more peremptorily than ever, he did not consult the French and often ran roughshod over the British. He felt certain that American financing of Bizonia entitled the United States to have the decisive voice in its economic and financial affairs. Clay disliked CEEC screening of German economic plans and deeply resented the State Department's constant interference in occupation matters.[81] Undersecretary of the Army William Draper sought to restrain Clay from moving too audaciously. The challenge, Draper realized, was to seize the initiative in Germany without antagonizing the French and without provoking the Russians.[82]

Clay's peremptory behavior, however, evoked protests from the French and triggered Soviet countermeasures in eastern Germany.[83] As for the latter, Bevin realized that the Kremlin was responding to Anglo-American actions. "The initiative lies with the Western powers and the Soviet authorities have been compelled to follow this lead by establishing in the Soviet zone of Germany an imitation of the new bizonal organisation." The British foreign secretary, however, was much more solicitous of the French. No program for German rehabilitation could be taken without eliciting France's compliance. Marshall concurred. In response to Bidault's remonstrations, the British and Americans agreed to meet again in London on 23 February 1948, this time without the Russians. They would discuss, among other things, German participation in the ERP, trizonal fusion, currency reform, control of the Ruhr, reparation deliveries, German self-government, and security measures.[84]

■

French anxieties were conveyed unequivocally and persistently in numerous conversations with Ambassadors Caffery and Douglas, with General Bull, and with Admiral Richard L. Conolly, the commander in chief of U.S. naval forces in the Eastern Atlantic and Mediterranean. French leaders outlined their apprehensions about the military implications of reviving German economic power. For the long term, they worried about the possibility of a German-Soviet alignment; for the short term, they were scared that Western actions in Germany could precipitate Soviet countermeasures and accidentally trigger a war. The French feared that "should war break out, the United States will abandon Western Europe to the Soviets; that the Russian hordes will occupy the area raping women and deporting the male population for slave labor in the Soviet Union; that France and Western Europe will be occupied and devastated by the Soviet hordes and atomized by the United States." [85]

Moderate French officials like Premier Schuman and Foreign Minister Bidault encountered much domestic opposition and felt considerable hesitancy about the wisdom of augmenting German production, restoring German coal mines and steel furnaces to German management, instituting currency reform, and convening a German constituent assembly. "What is worrying French officials," Conolly wrote Forrestal, "is SECURITY. They are scared of the colossal ground forces to the eastward. They are afraid that, if Germany is resuscitated, her resources and technical proficiency would be used by the U.S.S.R. against France. They want some concrete assurances that . . . in case of attack, they could preserve part of Metropolitan France from invasion and another occupation." They wanted military aid, staff talks, a commitment to defend the Rhine, extensive international controls over the Ruhr, and guarantees to insure German demilitarization.[86]

Bevin fully grasped this reality. Since his closing talks with Marshall at the Council of Foreign Ministers meeting, he had been devising a West European bloc that would bring together, however loosely, the United States, Canada, Western Europe, and the Dominions. France, Britain, and the Benelux countries would constitute the core of the Western Union. The Treaty of Dunkirk would serve as the model. The focus, therefore, would be on Germany. The object was to thwart the growth of European communism and Soviet power by allaying French fears of a revived Germany, promoting European recovery, and eliminating the economic distress on which local Communists capitalized. On 22 January he presented his broad blueprint to Parliament. Four days later Belgium's premier, Paul-Henri Spaak, accepted Bevin's overtures for discussions. On 27 January Bevin invited the United States to discuss a separate bilateral defense arrangement that would buttress a Western Union. On 19 February, on the eve of the opening of the trilateral talks on Germany, Bevin and Bidault sent draft treaties to the Benelux governments; negotiations were scheduled to take place in Brussels in early March. Bevin was eager to keep the momentum going on Germany, including the convocation of a constituent assembly, but he anticipated persistent French intransigence if security concerns were not dealt with effectively.[87]

U.S. officials were delighted by Bevin's desire to organize Western Europe into a viable bloc. Yet Kennan and Bohlen worried that Bevin's approach might dwell too heavily on military matters, place too much responsibility on American shoulders, and address the issue of Germany inadequately. "The general adoption of a mutual assistance pact based squarely on defense against Germany," Kennan wrote Marshall, "is a poor way to prepare the ground for the eventual entry of the Germans into the concept." [88] Marshall informed President Truman that, although it was necessary for the United States to help provide security against German aggression, it was far more important to design a security system that would co-opt German power against the Soviet Union. The French and British, Marshall insisted, focused too narrowly on Germany. "Germany might possibly become threat in distant future but in meantime real threat to France seems to us to be another power which will undoubtedly seek to utilize substantial segment of German economy if unable to get control of Germany. In our opinion French security for many years to come will depend on integration of western Europe including western German economy." [89]

From Marshall's and Lovett's perspectives, it was essential to keep an eye on priorities. Bevin could go ahead with his Western Union; Washington's focus would remain on the ERP and on the co-optation of German resources into a Western bloc. Although Marshall and Lovett wished to allay French fears, they did not want the issue of U.S. strategic commitments abroad to endanger congressional passage of the ERP.[90]

At the end of February, the British and Americans were moving on a dual track, the former pioneering the organization of a political bloc, the latter pushing for West European (and German) economic union. Notwithstanding some griping about details and priorities, U.S. and British officials perceived these initiatives as complementary. The goal was to expedite Western Europe's recovery, undermine the appeal of communism, co-opt western Germany, and thwart the Kremlin. The organization of security guarantees for France constituted merely a tactical issue in the far more important struggle over who was to control and organize the industrial infrastructure, skilled labor, and resources of all of Central and Western Europe.

The Czech Coup

Stalin was worried by Western countermeasures. The Americans might intervene directly in Greece or Italy; they were prepared to pour huge sums of money into Europe's recovery; they were seeking to organize a west German government. At the same time, the British were organizing a Western alliance system and readying to negotiate a host of interlocking bilateral security treaties. All this could be seen and heard from public speeches, open diplomacy, and the West's overt actions.[91] What was not public could be learned from informants like Donald MacLean, the British chargé d'affaires in Washington, who was privy to every aspect of Anglo-American diplomacy, including Bevin's overtures for an Atlantic defense alliance and the U.S. military's desire to expand its atomic program.[92]

Not only did Stalin have to worry about a Western military bloc and U.S. atomic capabilities, but he also had to protect the Soviet periphery from the lure of the ERP, the influence of American dollars, and the centrifugal pull of nationalist forces within his own sphere. His relations with Tito were reaching the breaking point. Fearing direct U.S. intervention in Greece, Stalin told the Yugoslav government to suspend aid to the Greek Communists. He also sought to constrain Yugoslavia's influence in the Balkans and to circumscribe its autonomy in foreign policy.[93] Anticipating the implementation of the peace treaties with Hungary, Romania, and Bulgaria, Stalin proceeded to negotiate a series of bilateral defense pacts with Germany's former satellites. His aim was to restrict their ability to act independently after the official termination of the allied (Soviet) military occupation.[94]

Nothing, of course, agitated the Kremlin more than Anglo-American initiatives in western Germany. The specter of west German self-government horrified the Russians, as did the prospect of German integration into a Western economic bloc. In the Soviet view, these actions were gross violations of the Potsdam agreements. The Russians charged that German industrial recovery posed a latent military danger to the Soviet Union. Might an autonomous West Germany serve as a magnet to east Germans? Might a unified Germany challenge the Kremlin's hegemony in Eastern Europe? Once Western statesmen had seized the initiative on German matters, Stalin felt ever more compelled to tighten his grip over eastern Germany lest even this part of the former enemy slip from his control.[95]

In January and February 1948, U.S. officials and intelligence agencies scrutinized Soviet behavior and agreed that the Kremlin had been thrown on the defensive. Stalin wished to avoid war, yet the situation was fraught with danger because the Kremlin's desire to dominate the world seemed immutable, because the economic and political situation throughout Europe appeared so volatile, and because Communist parties seemed capable of winning or seizing power and orienting their countries eastward.[96] Moreover, the Kremlin was cracking down on the satellites. In Bulgaria, the opposition leader Nikola Petrov was executed; in Poland, seventeen non-Communists were accused of supplying information to the underground and tried as traitors; in Hungary, members of the Social Democratic and Smallholders' parties were expelled from the government and many were forced to flee for their lives.[97]

Kennan, Bohlen, and other analysts anticipated similar repressive acts in Czechoslovakia, but U.S. diplomats in Prague disagreed. There were signs that the Soviets might be seeking a temporary respite in their contest with the West. The Kremlin seemed to have instructed West European Communists to revert to electoral processes. Kennan and CIA analysts took note of Soviet overtures in Berlin for a possible summit meeting between Stalin and Truman. The CIA stressed the failure of Soviet satellite governments to recognize the Markos Vafiades regime in northern Greece, the "substantial concessions" in the recent Soviet proposals on Austria, the Polish announcement that the bulk of increased coal production would go to the West, and *Pravda*'s opposition to a Danubian-Balkan federation. Even Lovett could not ignore the onset of Soviet deliveries of food and raw materials to the western zones in Germany, as stipulated in the Potsdam reparation provisions.[98]

The Czech crisis surprised U.S. officials precisely because it came against a backdrop of uncertainty about Soviet intentions. Twelve ministers representing the National Socialist, People's, and Slovak Democratic parties resigned from the Czech government. Their departure allowed the Communists to take control of the government legally. They then proceeded with reckless haste and consummate brutality to crush the democratic opposition. Before 20 February, Czechoslovakia was a pluralist democratic state supportive of Soviet foreign policy yet knitted to the West economically; by 1 March it had become a Communist dictatorship, a symbol of the fate that awaited any country that accepted Communists into coalition governments.[99]

From Prague, Ambassador Laurence Steinhardt reported that democratic forces had played into the hands of the Communists by committing a series of pitiful mistakes and showing no determination to resist the Communist onslaught. He acknowledged that "there was no evidence of any Soviet troop concentrations on the borders of Czechoslovakia," "no direct evidence of Soviet interference," and fewer threats than on recent occasions in other countries when Kremlin machinations had been rebuffed. On the other hand, whereas the Czech "Communists were aggressive and bold, and were sufficiently organized to take advantage of the situation," the non-Communists "continued to place their individual party loyalties and personal ambitions ahead of their opposition to Communism."[100]

The American public was stunned by the events in Czechoslovakia, but policymakers assessed them more calmly. Because Czechoslovakia had been amenable to Soviet foreign policy leads since the end of the war, Marshall saw no substantial alteration in the balance of power. What he dreaded was that Communists elsewhere in Europe might be encouraged to emulate the Czech precedent. The ease with which the Czech Communists seized power exposed the demoralization and the impotency of European democratic forces, confirming the suspicions of U.S. officials about the fragility of democratic institutions. Soviet preponderance in Europe, they were now certain, was likely to come about as a result of local subversion, not military conquest. "The problem at present," wrote John Hickerson, "is less one of defense against overt foreign aggression than against internal fifth-column aggression supported by the threat of external force." The CIA put the matter even more bluntly: the extraordinary "psychological reaction" among West Europeans reflected their sudden awareness of their "inherent economic and military weakness" and their amazement at "the ease with which a Communist minority can seize power in a traditionally democratic state." [101]

More Countermeasures

U.S. officials had to bolster the morale and stimulate the courage of moderate European leaders like Premier De Gasperi in Italy. Policymakers in Washington wanted to enhance the ability of centrist and reformist parties to retain power and to effect the economic recovery of their nations within the parameters of a broad regional approach that included the western zones of Germany.[102] But since the Marshall Plan still had not yet been approved by Congress, U.S. efforts might come too late to prevent the Communists from winning the April elections in Italy. Even if they did not achieve a clear-cut victory, the Communists might be invited to join a coalition government or they might decide to seize power. Ambassador James Dunn reported from Rome that Czech events were having a "bandwagon" effect on the Italian electorate, with large sections of the middle class waffling in their opposition to the Communists for fear that the latter would gain power and expropriate their property.[103]

On 11 March, the NSC called for the United States to "continue its efforts to prevent Communist domination of Italy." Should this effort fail, the NSC recommended that the United States "initiate measures designed to minimize the effects of Communist domination and to facilitate continued opposition to it." [104] With the president's encouragement, Forrestal and Royall sought to expedite the secret shipment of military supplies to the Italian government. Kennan was so agitated that he wanted to prevent the Italian Communists from participating in the elections. Marshall thought the United States should do all it could to help non-Communist parties win the elections and avoid steps that might precipitate a civil war. He warned that U.S. economic aid would cease should the Italian electorate be so foolish as to elect Communists in sufficient numbers to justify their entrance into a coalition government. Such an outcome, even if legally undertaken, was unacceptable to the United States. "Following a pattern made familiar in Eastern Europe [the Communists would] take over complete control of government and transform Italy into a totalitarian state subservient to Moscow. Such a development would have a demoralizing effect throughout Western Europe, the Mediterranean, and the Middle East. Militarily, availability to the USSR of bases in Sicily and southern Italy would pose a direct threat to security of communications throughout the Mediterranean." [105]

As for France, the challenge engendered by the Czech coup for U.S. officials was somewhat different. The goal was to invigorate the French government's will to integrate a self-governing political entity in western Germany into the ERP. Events in Czechoslovakia injected a new sense of urgency into the London deliberations on Germany.[106] But Schuman and Bidault still hesitated. They feared that developments in Czechoslovakia would enliven French Communist opposition to any concessions to the Americans. They wondered whether the boldness of Communist actions in Prague might adumbrate a tough Soviet response to Western actions in Germany, which could trigger a series of reactions and countermeasures that could culminate in war. Although these were short-term constraints, the French also reiterated their apprehensions about the long-term ramifications of a powerful Germany that could act independently or in concert with Moscow. Until these fears were allayed, France would not agree to trizonal fusion, currency reform, or German self-government. France wanted extensive powers to control the production and distribution of Ruhr coal, coke, and steel in order to promote its economic self-interest and insure its security.[107]

French intransigence exasperated U.S. officials. French schemes for an international Ruhr authority that could interfere with management and production were anathema, as were French plans for an indirectly elected German government with only limited powers even to tax and to maintain internal security. Douglas warned that, if security mechanisms were punitive, Soviet bargaining power in Germany would be augmented. Clay complained even more bitterly that French plans meant international control over the German economy. He worried that, if pro-Western Germans were compelled to accept oppressive controls, they would be identified as Quislings and their leadership for the long term would be destroyed.[108]

In the immediate aftermath of the Czech coup, Marshall and Lovett were eager to break the impasse on German questions between France and the Anglo-Saxon powers at the London meetings. Marshall instructed Caffery to ascertain what Bidault really desired. The French foreign minister told Caffery he wanted a concrete military alliance. Two days later, on 4 March, he sent Marshall a rambling letter asking for political consultations. Douglas informed Washington that "if the French were assured of long-term United States defensive cooperation against German aggression, in other words, that we would fight on the Rhine in such an eventuality, the French would relax in their attitude regarding German industry and reconstruction." [109]

In response, Marshall and Lovett instructed Douglas to inform the French that the United States supported the establishment of a Military Security Board to enforce German disarmament and demilitarization. In the event of German violations, the United States was prepared to consult with the British and French. More important, the French could be informed that the Americans now anticipated a prolonged occupation. "As long as European Communism threatens US vital interests and national security we could ill afford to abandon our military position in Germany which can now likewise serve as morale element in a Europe disposed to depression by Czechoslovak submission." But if the French still proved recalcitrant about proceeding with trizonal fusion, they were warned that anticipated ERP funds for the French zone in Germany would be withheld.[110]

This combination of carrots and sticks led to some tentative progress toward an agreement regarding the fusion of the three zones, the integration of western Germany into the ERP, the establishment of a Ruhr control authority, and the formation of German political institutions. On 6 March it was announced that the London discussions would be resumed in April and that the Benelux countries would again be included.[111] Amidst Soviet protests that the Americans and British were seeking to convert the industrial potential of the Ruhr "into a strategic base for future aggression in Europe," the foreign ministers of Britain, France, and the Benelux countries then assembled in Brussels to discuss British proposals for a Western Union.[112]

As these talks got under way, Bevin learned of possible Kremlin overtures for a mutual assistance pact with Norway along the lines of those negotiated with East European countries. For the most part these agreements were aimed at Germany and appeared to be innocuous except for the article that obligated signatories not to join any alliance directed against the other party. Bevin saw this as a threat to his own plans to enlarge the Western Union. In an apocalyptic-sounding message that compared Soviet actions to "our experience with Hitler," he invited the United States to enter into talks for a North Atlantic Treaty (NAT) as part of an interlocking network of alliances that would include Western Europe and the Mediterranean.[113]

Marshall grasped the British initiative for what it was, that is, an attempt to harness American resources and power for a European security system that would satisfy the French. Bevin had already told the State Department that the Western Union alone would not suffice, and Marshall knew that it was essential to go further to stiffen morale in France and Italy. As soon as he received Bevin's message, Marshall decided to begin talks on an Atlantic security system. After consulting the president, he informed Bidault that, once the Brussels Treaty was signed, the United States would consult on what it might do to strengthen the Western Union.[114]

Tensions were sure to escalate further as U.S. policymakers decided to forsake quadripartite currency reform in Germany. Notwithstanding the blistering attacks by Soviet officials in the Allied Control Council, the Russians were making substantial concessions. But the State Department no longer wanted an agreement. After conferring with all relevant divisions, Frank G. Wisner, the influential deputy to the assistant secretary of state for occupation affairs, summed up the department's opposition to quadripartite currency reform: the Kremlin might use it to frustrate German economic recovery or to undermine the tripartite arrangements that were under discussion at London. Better to split Germany and embitter the Kremlin than to jeopardize plans for stabilizing and integrating western Germany into a Western orbit. Wisner advised that Clay cease his efforts to reach a quadripartite agreement. Lovett concurred. "Better act fast," the undersecretary instructed.[115]

At the NSC meeting on 11 March and at the cabinet meeting the next day, Marshall said nothing of Norway, lamented the absence of sufficient funds for covert operations, and cautioned against hasty action and bombastic rhetoric. The time had come to calculate American countermeasures with great care lest the United States provoke rather than deter. The aim was "to strengthen confidence of non-Communist elements and deter Soviets from further fifth column action along Czech

Model." Bevin's Western Union, appropriately enlarged and buttressed with U.S. support, constituted the most efficacious means of lifting Bidault's courage and boosting morale in France and Italy while moving ahead with Germany's integration.[116]

Marshall and his colleagues realized, however, that their diplomacy was infused with substantial risk-taking. They wanted to thwart a Communist victory in Italy, seize the initiative in Germany, and reassure France's craving for security. Any one of these goals might require the use of military force. The director of the CIA, for example, warned Truman that attempts to integrate a west German state into a West European union "might invite some form of Soviet response stronger than the mere protests received so far." [117] Yet the NME lacked the capabilities to implement the contingency war plans should conflict erupt. At meetings at the White House in February 1948, Forrestal, Royall, and Gruenther emphasized these points to the president.[118]

After the Czech crisis, there was no longer any question among top officials that they had to augment military personnel and increase defense spending. Marshall, Lovett, and Forrestal especially supported legislation calling for universal military training (UMT). It would demonstrate resolve, perhaps even to use force, and would cast shadows appropriate to support U.S. diplomacy. The enactment of UMT would hearten Europeans, especially the French, who assumed the United States would withdraw from Europe if war erupted and who were therefore reluctant to back measures that might provoke the Soviet Union or enhance Germany's power.[119] Recognizing, however, that UMT would not bolster U.S. capabilities for several years and that the United States required a "mobile striking force" of sufficient strength and size to perform its mission in Italy (or Greece or Palestine), the JCS on 10 March called for passage of Selective Service. At an NSC meeting the next day, Royall emphasized that contingency plans for military intervention in Italy made Selective Service imperative. Marshall agreed, as did Forrestal.[120]

On 17 March, in a tough speech to Congress, President Truman heaped full responsibility for the world crisis on the Soviet Union. Emphasizing the struggle between tyranny and freedom, he called for passage of the ERP, UMT, and Selective Service. He stated that U.S. occupation troops would remain in Germany "until the peace is secure in Europe." He stressed that the United States would support the Western Union. During the next few days, he authorized Forrestal to request a $3 billion supplemental military appropriation for fiscal year 1949.[121]

Rumors of war meanwhile circulated throughout Washington and in the media. Yet to grasp the dynamics of U.S. policymaking, one must realize that officials remained convinced that the Kremlin preferred to avoid conflict. U.S. military initiatives were being taken in light of possible local contingencies and in view of the need to reassure the French and not in anticipation of a Soviet military thrust. National security was defined in terms of the potential control of resources and industrial infrastructure, which were threatened in the short run not by Soviet military capabilities but by indigenous unrest and uncertainty over Germany's future alignment. Policymakers and intelligence analysts agreed that, although Soviet armies had the capability to overrun much of Europe, Stalin and his comrades wanted to avoid a military clash with the West. The men who ruled the Kremlin were not bold adventurers but domestic tyrants and prudent expansionists who knew they could not win a war against the United States. They would not jeopardize their internal power for the sake of foreign conquest.[122]

Army, Navy, State Department, and CIA reports emphasized the Kremlin's economic weaknesses, transportation bottlenecks, vulnerable petroleum industry, and unreliable allies. According to the best-informed estimate in mid-1948, it was not even considered "remotely possible" for the Kremlin to develop an atomic bomb before mid-1950. Military intelligence analysts stressed the Kremlin's incapacity to strike long range at the United States. Despite its high annual production of planes and recent addition of jet aircraft into its military arsenal, the Soviet Union still did not have transatlantic bombers that could return to the Soviet Union. Nor were its airfields capable of handling the limited number of B-29 type aircraft in its inventory. Furthermore, its air force suffered from totally inadequate supplies of aviation gas. Even if the Kremlin should conquer Western Europe militarily, it would not be able to harness its resources in wartime because of U.S. countermeasures, European resistance, and Soviet administrative deficiencies. The fundamental threat to America's national security was still the Kremlin's capacity to gain control over European resources in peacetime. Even its defense budget was not believed to be increasing at a rapid rate.[123]

However, U.S. officials did not discount the possibility of war. Marshall was extraordinarily sensitive, as were all military analysts and intelligence officers, to the possibility that American and Western initiatives could spark a sequence of Soviet reactions and American countermeasures that would culminate in war.[124] This fear, which weighed so heavily on the minds of the French, also figured prominently in U.S. calculations. Intelligence agencies continually examined prospective Soviet responses to UMT, Selective Service, and supplementary military appropriations. Royall asked Clay if the Soviets would go to war if the United States signed an Atlantic alliance or embarked on a comprehensive military assistance program to the Western Union. Lovett worried how the Kremlin might react to the London agreements on Germany if all the Western powers could reach accord.[125]

Despite their apprehensions that war could erupt from the Kremlin's miscalculation of U.S. determination, policymakers believed they had to proceed with their countermeasures. Not to proceed meant risking an eventual Soviet-German alignment or chancing Communist takeovers of key countries and their conversion into Soviet satellites. U.S. officials calculated that, when the crunch came, the Soviets would back down. Despite Clay's alarmist (and uncharacteristic) warning of 5 March that conflict might come with unanticipated suddenness, he repeatedly advocated that the United States push ahead with its German policies because he believed the Soviets would opt to avoid war. So did Truman, Marshall, and Bevin; so did Kennan and Bohlen; so did Ambassador Smith in Moscow; so did the CIA, the Office of Naval Intelligence, and the Army's Intelligence Division.[126]

U.S. officials believed they had enough power to support their diplomatic risk-taking. In March they endorsed the Brussels Treaty. Because Kennan was abroad, John Hickerson and George Butler, the acting director of the Policy Planning Staff, played leading roles in formulating the American position. Much to their satisfaction, the agreement on the Western Union between the governments of Britain, France, Holland, Belgium, and Luxembourg constituted a regional mutual-defense treaty rather than a series of bilateral pacts. Hickerson and Butler agreed that the United States should not join the Brussels Treaty but should provide it with military backing. They also urged that the Western Union should be enlarged to include most European countries, such as Norway, Denmark, Iceland, Italy, Portugal, Eire, Spain, Austria, and Germany. Scoffing at the possibility of neutrality and desiring a comprehensive anti-Soviet bloc, they called for the inclusion of Sweden and Switzerland as well as countries in the Middle East. When British and Canadian officials arrived at the Pentagon for highly secretive talks on Atlantic security, Butler, Hickerson, and their associates also discussed provisions "for countering Communist Party aggression" and for outlawing Communist parties everywhere, starting with the United States. Finally, and most important, they recommended the negotiation of a transatlantic pact of mutual assistance. Signatories would be obligated to view an act of aggression against any one of them as an attack on themselves and would agree to offer armed assistance of an unspecified nature.[127]

The talks at the Pentagon during the last ten days of March generated a consensus among the British, Canadian, and U.S. officials. The British sought a firm U.S. commitment to aid militarily in case of aggression in Europe. U.S. officials did not find this demand surprising, but they foresaw problems in securing congressional approval, especially in an election year. Although they fully endorsed the goal of a NAT, they emphasized that the U.S. government had to retain the right to determine when aggression occurred and what type of military action it would take. They argued that the NAT should model itself on the Rio Treaty, should focus on the North Atlantic area (and exclude the Middle East), and should comport with the charter of the United Nations. They agreed to an accession clause that contemplated the eventual inclusion of Germany. Upon concluding the talks, Hickerson explained to the British and Canadians that the agreement was a working paper and still required the approval of Lovett, Forrestal, and Marshall as well as the NSC, U.S. congressional leaders, and the president.[128]

No sooner had Hickerson and Butler taken this giant step toward an alliance than the State Department began to retreat. Lovett, as was his custom, met with Vandenberg, who felt that more needed to be done to safeguard American independent action, underscore European self-help, limit U.S. commitments to the North Atlantic, and associate American action with the U.N. charter. Together, Lovett and Vandenberg framed a Senate resolution that endorsed American association, by constitutional process, with regional and collective defensive arrangements based on self-help and mutual aid. But the Republican majority leader was initially uncertain whether the Senate would approve even this resolution, given the intensely partisan climate on the eve of the 1948 political conventions.[129]

The precise benefits of a defense pact seemed questionable if similar objectives could be achieved less controversially. As soon as the British and Canadians left town, Belgian premier Spaak arrived in Washington. In conversations with Lovett, Hickerson, and other high-ranking State Department officials, Spaak stressed that he did not think Soviet leaders would seek to achieve their goals through military aggression. Although he hoped the United States would extend formal guarantees, he considered it much more important to establish real military coordination.[130]

Spaak's views resonated loudly because they coincided with U.S. assessments of Soviet intentions. More important, they highlighted avenues of cooperation that might invigorate morale in Rome and Paris and elicit French cooperation at the London talks on Germany without risking political defeat at home. As the NSC staff circulated a slightly revised Policy Planning Staff document on U.S. support for the Western Union, doubts about the emphasis placed on a defense pact percolated through many of the departments dealing with national security policy. The JCS and the secretary of defense supported the idea of collective defense but questioned the wisdom of incurring new commitments prior to increasing military capabilities.[131] Kennan, too, denigrated the utility of military guarantees. He and Bohlen argued that formal commitments were superfluous, at least for the short run, because the presence of U.S. troops in Germany guaranteed American embroilment at the onset of any conflict and served as a deterrent. What Europeans needed to know was that, if American initiatives and Soviet miscalculations triggered a war, U.S. troops would stand and fight at the Rhine rather than evacuate the continent, as American war plans then envisioned.[132]

Kennan did not know it, but strategic planners and the JCS were thinking along precisely the same lines. In March General Wedemeyer, director of the Army's Plans and Operations Division, submitted a paper to his superiors calling for an alteration in U.S. strategic thinking. "The United States," Wedemeyer argued, "cannot permit the Soviet engulfment of Western Europe except as it may be willing ultimately itself to become the final victim." Although little could be done immediately to defend Europe, medium-range plans had to be revised to contemplate a defense on the continent. The Joint Strategic Plans Committee (JSPC) picked up the Army's report and ran with it. The JSPC argued that military planning could not proceed on the basis of a "strategic concept which abandons Western Europe and the Mediterranean nations without a struggle and hands over to the USSR their resources, manpower, and industrial capacity for exploitation against us." U.S. national security was bound up with the economic recovery of Western Europe, which depended on assurances of American support. Once recovery was a reality, the United States could not permit the Soviet Union to capture these resources. "An emergency war plan," the JSPC continued, "based on present capabilities will be required, but this plan should be . . . replaced rapidly and successively by plans, the strategic concepts for which hold forth an increasing measure of hope that Western Europe can be saved from Soviet conquest and occupation." At the same time, Admiral Louis Denfeld, the chief of naval operations, assailed even the short-term emergency plans for overestimating Soviet capabilities and relinquishing the continent to the adversary. "This means that the manpower, resources, and industrial capacity of these countries, plus all the augmentation of their capabilities which we hope will have been achieved by the ERP, will be handed over to the USSR for exploitation against us." [133]

In the wake of the Czech coup, U.S. military and civilian officials alike recognized that the principal threat to Europe emanated from indigenous communism and the possible co-optation of German power by the Kremlin. They were agreed that the United States had to extend some form of political and military aid in order to encourage European democratic statesmen to stand up to their Communist compatriots and to take the risks that inhered in the revival of German industry and the re-creation of a self-governing German political entity. They understood that the initiatives then being undertaken by the United States might be viewed by the Soviets as endangering their security, although the initiatives were not intended as such. The Kremlin might react in ways that could trigger a war. What divided Truman administration officials in the spring of 1948 then was simply the question of whether, taking cognizance of the domestic political context, the budgetary constraints, and the nation's existing military unpreparedness, the United States should carry on military staff talks, provide military aid, or negotiate a defense pact. By the time the London conference on Germany resumed on 20 April, everyone seemed to favor the first two and questioned only the timing of the third. The outcome of the Italian elections had much to do with how U.S. officials would proceed.

Completing the Offensive

The defeat of the left in the Italian elections on 18 April brought relief and even exultation to Washington policymakers. For almost two months they had worked diligently in behalf of a non-Communist triumph. Formally and informally, the State Department recruited labor and church leaders as well as Italian-American organizations to lend support against the Communists. The CIA poured money into democratic parties, purchased newsprint, and helped distribute leaflets. Films, documentaries, broadcasts, and radio shows, all organized by the State Department or by private groups working with the U.S. embassy in Rome, emphasized the magnitude of U.S. aid and the generosity of the Marshall Plan. In the midst of the electoral campaign, the United States, along with Britain and France, pledged the return of Trieste to Italy. Officials encouraged Italian-Americans to write letters to their relatives in Italy and the Post Office expedited shipment of this mail across the Atlantic. The Justice Department announced that anyone who voted Communist would be denied entry into the United States. Buoyed by U.S. support, De Gasperi turned the campaign into a referendum on communism. On 18–19 April, his Christian Democrats achieved a massive victory, capturing 48.5 percent of the popular vote and a clear majority in parliament.[134]

Coming just as the Greek government appeared to be turning the tide in the military struggle against the Communist guerrillas, the Italian elections seemed to represent a turning point in postwar history. The failure of the Italian Communists to win the elections and their decision not to use force to overthrow the results symbolized the success of U.S. countermeasures and demonstrated that the Communist bandwagon could be stymied. Indeed, U.S. officials hoped that De Gasperi's victory not only would invigorate spirits in the West but would accentuate malaise and disaffection in the East. Perhaps dominoes might fall in the other direction.[135] There came news, the first in a long time, of revived spirits in Eastern Europe.[136] Kennan pushed hard for the activation of covert actions. Lovett prodded his subordinates to move cautiously; he shared their assumptions and aspirations, but he did not want to provoke the Kremlin in its own sphere before completing American goals in Western Europe.[137]

As soon as the Italian results were in, Bohlen and Kennan urged Lovett and Marshall to warn Soviet leaders against taking retaliatory action. The Russians should know that, if they tried to recoup with a counterthrust, the United States would resist even to the point of going to war. Bohlen proposed that Ambassador Smith meet with Stalin and tell him that additional encroachments by the Soviet Union or by Communist parties "would almost certainly be regarded by this country as an act of Soviet aggression directly inimical to the vital interests of the United States." From Moscow, Smith retorted that this would sound like an ultimatum. He, too, favored a policy of strength, but he thought he should approach Molotov, not Stalin. He also advised that the United States focus attention on Western Europe and not vest U.S. prestige and credibility in commitments to places of secondary concern.[138]

These suggestions were accepted by Marshall, Lovett, Kennan, and Bohlen. Their primary goal now was to thwart Soviet attempts to stymie U.S. initiatives in Germany. They agreed that the Kremlin was on the defensive and did not want war, but Soviet leaders still might react in Berlin to Western initiatives. Moscow must not underestimate the West's will and must be dissuaded from taking action from which it might be unable to extricate itself. The key task for U.S. and British leaders was to find the proper mix of prudence and toughness.[139]

Yet this mix did not encompass negotiations. The Americans were outsmarted when the Soviets turned Smith's demarche into a propaganda victory. The Kremlin released the communications between the two governments. The exchanges, U.S. diplomats believed, boosted Soviet prestige by suggesting that the United States had to deal with it like a great power. Even worse, the notes appeared to show that the

Kremlin could respond reasonably to Western overtures. Kennan and Bohlen were distraught precisely because they did not want to negotiate. Neither did Marshall.[140]

For the next six weeks, virtually every American assessment of Soviet aims underscored the Kremlin's conciliatory demeanor and readiness to talk. Believing, however, that this was simply a tactical expedient, Marshall and Lovett rebuffed the overtures. With momentum in their favor, they would not diverge from their course of defeating communism in Western Europe, co-opting German power, and implementing the ERP.[141]

This attitude explains the mounting American disaffection with the French. Given the ostensible softening of Soviet policy, Schuman and Bidault tried to slow Western efforts to establish a provisional German government. At the London conference they demanded still more intrusive controls in the Ruhr. They opposed unconditional most-favored-nation treatment for Germany. Most of all they wanted security guarantees not only against the prospect of future German aggression but also against the likelihood of Soviet retaliation.[142]

The French prolonged the negotiations at London until 1 June. Then, anticipating a defeat in the Chamber of Deputies, Bidault sought to revise the agreements, pleaded for additional strategic guarantees, and tried to delay the implementation of currency reform. Even as Schuman and Bidault eked out a legislative victory on 17 June, the very narrowness of the margin compelled them to promise their supporters that in future talks they would seek additional security commitments.[143] French compliance with the Anglo-American approach to Germany was still by no means assured.

Throughout these laborious negotiations, U.S. officials refused to be diverted from their goals in respect to German recovery. Marshall informed the French that they must proceed toward German self-government. "Maximum German contribution to European recovery," he instructed Caffery, "cannot be obtained without establishment of political organization of western Germany. . . . Failure to proceed would appear to Soviets as sign of weakness. . . . While appreciating French concern, US government does not believe that western nations can permit themselves to be deterred."[144] The risks of delay—that is, of alienating the Germans and retarding reconstruction—greatly exceeded the risks of action—that is, of antagonizing the Russians and provoking war.[145] Either the French would go along, or the British and Americans would proceed without them. "Failure of French Government to approve [London] agreements," Marshall telegrammed Caffery on 7 June, "would have serious repercussions on public opinion here, would offer dangerous encouragement to Soviet Government, and would benefit no one but Communists."[146]

This tough talk, however, could not conceal U.S. sympathy for the risks they were imposing on the French. State Department officials also realized that, try as they might, Schuman and Bidault might be unable to overcome Communist and Gaullist opposition to the London accords. Hence, while standing firm on the need to proceed with German self-government, currency reform, and management of the coal mines, Marshall and Lovett sought to respond to French strategic apprehensions within the constraints imposed by a Republican Congress, the upcoming party conventions, and a presidential election in which the incumbent seemed certain to lose.[147]

Recognizing, however, that French fear of Soviet retaliation constituted a real psychological impediment to French concurrence in the London accords, Marshall, Lovett, and Forrestal agreed that the United States should provide military supplies to the French.[148] In late May 1948, they also authorized Clay to coordinate emergency plans with the French and the British.[149] Since this decision came precisely at the time when the British committed themselves to fighting at the Rhine, it marked a real turning point in postwar strategic thinking.[150] Heretofore, emergency U.S. war plans envisioned a hasty retreat from the continent. Hereafter, U.S. occupation troops would fight at the Rhine along with the French and English. The long-term goal of U.S. policy now became the augmentation of European capabilities to hold the Rhine through coordinated planning, European self-help and mutual aid, and military assistance.[151]

A revised NSC paper on American support for the Western Union incorporated this approach. It endorsed U.S. association with a European regional alliance based on self-help and cooperation. The administration would collaborate with Vandenberg to get a resolution through the Senate. Rather than work for the immediate assumption of strategic obligations abroad, however, the United States would confer with the governments of the Western Union and seek to concert military plans, coordinate military production, and proffer military supplies and assistance. U.S. participation in the Western Union consultations would be informal, and substantial military aid would not be forthcoming until the United States increased its own capabilities. Still, Marshall, Lovett, Forrestal, and the JCS viewed these actions as means to buoy French morale and encourage Bidault to take the risks that inhered in accepting the London accords on Germany.[152]

Bevin wanted the United States to do more. In May he implored Marshall not to defer formal political obligations. U.S. willingness to join a regional defensive system, the British foreign secretary argued, would do more than anything else to induce the French to go along with Anglo-American policies in Germany.[153] However appealing this logic was, Marshall and Lovett felt constrained by public attitudes and congressional sentiment. They hoped that the commitments they made to the French during the London talks, the promises they gave for coordinating military aid, and their efforts to secure Senate passage of the Vandenberg resolution (which occurred on 11 June) would suffice to reassure the French.[154]

But they did not. On the eve of the vote in the Chamber of Deputies, French diplomats flew again to London. They appealed for revisions in the London accords, for their postponement, and for a renewed demarche to secure agreement with the Kremlin.[155] Bevin again solicited Marshall's help. The French, he insisted, had to have "some additional hope of a really workable Security System if they are to be induced to accept the plan for Germany." Arguing that American delays might also give rise to a "neutral" Scandinavian system, Bevin "earnestly beg[ged]" for security talks to begin between the French, British, U.S., Canadian, and Benelux governments. Assured that these security talks would be exploratory, Marshall assented.[156]

By this time a showdown with the Kremlin was rapidly approaching. On 18 June, the day after the French Chamber finally approved the London accords, Clay announced the implementation of currency reform in the western zones of Germany but not in the western zones of Berlin. The Russians immediately responded by claiming that Berlin was within their sector and by introducing their own currency throughout the city. In turn, Clay and Robertson carried out their secret plan to circulate the new deutsche mark in western Berlin as well as in western Germany. When the Soviets began to interdict freight, barge, and passenger traffic to Berlin, much as they had done briefly at the end of March, the Americans and British also responded, much as they had in March, with an airlift of supplies to the beleaguered citizens of western Berlin.[157]

The Berlin crisis was under way. For months, the Soviets and their East European allies had been condemning Western initiatives regarding Germany and protesting developments at the London conference. They warned that they might cut off Western access to Berlin if the Western powers did not cease their efforts to pull western Germany into their sphere. But the Americans (and British) paid no heed. They would not retract the London agreements; they would not withdraw from Berlin. They had not anticipated a prolonged blockade, but rather than capitulate or retreat, they opted for the airlift. And if the Soviets interdicted air traffic, war might erupt.[158]

This showdown seemed like the ultimate test of wills, much as the French had dreaded. In a long discussion in Paris on 25 June, French minister of war Pierre Henry Teitgen summarized French apprehensions to Army Undersecretary Draper and General Wedemeyer. For the time being, he conceded, there was "no purely German danger." The threat emanated from the Kremlin. The Russians did not want war, but it could occur by accident at any time. "Much of the opposition to the London agreements," Teitgen emphasized, "stemmed from the realization that this would be interpreted by the U.S.S.R. as a gesture of provocation and that should this by any chance result in war, French opinion was deeply afraid that France, because of her geographical position, would find herself in the van [sic], unarmed and incapable of defending herself." Teitgen again inquired whether the United States would agree to fight the decisive battle for Europe as far east as possible. Over the next two years, would the United States offer the type of military assistance to make possible a defense at the Rhine? If war erupted immediately, would Clay support French defensive actions? To Caffery a few days later, Bidault reiterated the importance of providing military aid, coordinating strategic planning, and establishing a unified command. These practical measures loomed as important as formal guarantees.[159]

The Truman administration now responded with alacrity. On 23 June, Marshall had informed the French that the exploratory talks on security should proceed immediately (although final results would have to await the inauguration of a new administration in January).[160] Clay began coordinating emergency plans with his British and French counterparts for an initial defense on the Rhine, and the JCS began working on instructions for the American representatives who would be attending the London military deliberations of the Western Union.[161] On 1 July, the NSC refined and revised, and the president quickly approved, two papers outlining U.S. support for the Western Union and endorsing military aid. These actions adumbrated the formation of the North Atlantic Treaty Organization (NATO), the development of a comprehensive military assistance program, and the coordination of strategic planning. They were necessary to harmonize Anglo-American strategic thinking, allay French fears, and deter Soviet threats in the wake of U.S. efforts to revive and co-opt German power as part of the rehabilitation of Western Europe. Not by accident, NSC 9/3, the most recent draft paper on U.S. support of the Western Union, reinserted the paragraph envisioning the eventual accession of western Germany to the Brussels and NAT systems.[162]

Risk-Taking, Diplomacy, and Power

The war that the French dreaded never came. This fortunate outcome of the cycle of actions, reactions, and countermeasures owed much to U.S. (and British) perspicuity and Soviet weakness. Once U.S. officials decided to raise the level of German industry, implement currency reform, merge the three western zones, and establish self-governing institutions, they recognized the inevitability of Soviet retaliatory moves. In a memorandum that was surprising only for its candor, but which every U.S. official intuitively understood, General Omar Bradley, the Army's new chief of staff, informed Eisenhower that "the whole Berlin crisis has arisen as a result of two actions on the part of the Western Powers. These actions are (1) implementation of the decisions agreed in the London Talks on Germany and (2) institution of currency reform." [163]

U.S. officials gambled that, however much the Soviets might react to Western initiatives, they would hesitate to go to war, especially if American countermeasures showed the right combination of toughness, prudence, and imagination. "It is our view," Clay wrote Draper on 27 June, "that they are bluffing and that their hand can and should be called now. They are definitely afraid of our air might." While officials in Washington cautioned Clay not to use an armed convoy and not to be too provocative, they agreed with his appraisal. When the exploratory talks on security opened on 6 July in the midst of the Berlin crisis, Kennan and Bohlen continually emphasized that the Soviets were not likely to resort to force.[164]

Notwithstanding the Russians' superiority in conventional forces, U.S. intelligence analysts believed that the Soviets knew they could not wage war successfully against the United States. The U.S. atomic monopoly, the vast capacity of the U.S.

economy, the shortcomings of the Soviet transport system and petroleum industry, the demoralization of the Soviet people, and the unreliability of Soviet satellites were thought to be the principal deterrents to Soviet military adventurism. U.S. officials therefore assumed that the contest with the Kremlin would remain in the political, economic, and diplomatic spheres. Germany's future alignment constituted the key to victory.

Yet the focus on Germany engendered apprehension throughout Europe. The establishment of a self-governing German political entity and the reconstitution of Germany's latent industrial-military power were indeed portentous developments. No one could be certain whether Germany would remain divided. No one could predict how long it would be until the remaining constraints on German industry and political autonomy would end. No one could feel secure about Germany's future behavior or alignment. So every action regarding Germany seemed pregnant with the danger of re-creating a formidable foe or of provoking the other great power or of doing both.

In order to deal with these interlocking contingencies, U.S. officials recognized that they had to respond to Bevin's overtures and Bidault's importunings. But each countermeasure, including military aid, coordinated war planning, and prospective strategic guarantees, added to the Kremlin's perception of threat. Marshall, Lovett, and Forrestal did not wish to threaten the Soviet Union; they sought only to enhance American security. They realized, however, that the very actions they had to take to rebuild Western Europe, defeat local Communists, co-opt Germany, and reassure allies constituted potential threats, whether intended or not. "The present tension in Berlin," Marshall told the cabinet, "is brought about by loss of Russian face in Italy, France, Finland. . . . It is caused by Russian desperation in face of success of the ERP." [165]

According to U.S. analysts, Soviet leaders regarded the Marshall Plan as an economic magnet to attract the Kremlin's satellites. Supposedly, they also assumed that the United States was trying to absorb Germany into a Western bloc. Fearing reconstituted German power either as an independent entity or as part of a hostile coalition, the Russians were deterred only by their own weakness, American political-military countermeasures, and Western diplomatic determination. [166]

Deterred though they might be in the short run, U.S. officials also believed that the men in the Kremlin envisioned themselves locked in a titanic struggle with the forces of capitalism for world domination. Russian fears and Soviet aspirations meant that the Kremlin's prudence was likely to be short-lived. For the immediate future the United States had enough power to support its offensive diplomacy and gain the upper hand in the European cold war. But the United States was quickly accruing multiple commitments and worldwide responsibilities without commensurate military capabilities. As the Berlin crisis heated up and the Truman administration pondered its global interests, the country faced even more agonizing choices over priorities and expenditures.

Goals, Tactics, and the
Budgetary Conundrum,
1947-1948

As the blockade and the airlift raised tensions to unprecedented levels, Truman seized control of the decisionmaking processes. He did not want to precipitate a military conflict, nor did he wish to back down diplomatically. He concluded that the United States must not withdraw from Berlin and must not repudiate the London agreements. Either of these courses would constitute appeasement, shattering American influence in western Germany, undermining American prestige in Western Europe, and ruining his chances for reelection in the United States.[1]

Only one factor eased the strain in Washington during the summer of 1948: the Kremlin did not seem to want war. In mid-July and again in early September, when tensions were at their highest, U.S. officials found reassuring evidence that the Russians were not preparing for military hostilities. General Clay stressed this point at a critical meeting of the National Security Council (NSC) on 23 July. In September, when Ambassador Smith returned from Moscow, he emphasized that he was so sure the Soviets would not deliberately start a war that he would be willing to sit on the airfields in Germany.[2]

Yet fighting could erupt by Soviet miscalculation or U.S. provocation. If the airlift faltered, U.S. officials appeared determined to take additional steps to supply Berlin. Whether these actions would precipitate war was uncertain. Among Truman's top advisers, the military men were most cautious. They did approve the deployment of B-29's to England to boost the morale of friends and to discourage Soviet escalatory steps. But they voiced the gravest misgivings about the wisdom of holding onto Berlin. The airlift was costly. It vested U.S. prestige in a location, Berlin, that had no intrinsic strategic importance. It diverted assets from more essential military undertakings. It raised the risks of conflict when the United States was not prepared for it.[3]

The president was exasperated by the vacillation of his military advisers in Washington. He agreed with Clay: "If we move out of Berlin we have lost everything we have been fighting for." [4] The administration's entire foreign policy would be at risk; so would Truman's political career. While making his key decisions regarding Berlin and Germany, Truman launched his campaign for reelection. Political expedients and national security imperatives reinforced one another. He could make no concessions to the enemy; yet, at the same time, political considerations and domestic economic constraints dictated that he not increase military expenditures. Any action that would fuel inflation could cripple him politically.[5]

Truman was fortunate that his Republican opponent was Governor Thomas E. Dewey of New York. For the most part Dewey hesitated to play politics with foreign policy issues. His political strategy was to capitalize on public disillusionment with Truman. Supporting bipartisanship, Dewey challenged neither Truman's national security goals nor his means.[6]

The toughest questions arose within the administration. Anguishing over the widening gap between commitments and capabilities, Defense Secretary Forrestal pressed the president to increase military expenditures. But Truman would neither modify his goals nor lift his cap on military spending.[7] He continued to see the United States as locked in a fateful struggle with a totalitarian foe bent on world domination. He encouraged his advisers not only to move ahead with their European program but also to bolster U.S. interests in the Middle East and East Asia. Seeking to preserve the nation's global preponderance with limited means, Truman left his advisers with a series of agonizing decisions and excruciating trade-offs.

War Plans, Bases, and the Budget

When the National Security Act was passed in July 1947, policymakers anticipated that it would add coherence to the military budgetary process. Immediately, Forrestal decided that the fiscal year 1950 budget would be an integrated one for the entire National Military Establishment (NME). The first step was to get the military services and the Joint Chiefs of Staff (JCS) to agree on a strategic concept. Force requirements and appropriations would then be based on that strategic concept.[8]

Prior to the autumn of 1947, strategic planners had spent a great deal of time outlining the basic contours of U.S. war plans. Although these plans were crude and the information on Soviet targets inadequate, there was no doubt about what military leaders wanted to do when war erupted. They hoped to protect the Western Hemisphere, secure lines of communication across the Atlantic, evacuate occupation forces from the European continent, establish a defensive posture in Asia, safeguard Japan, and launch a bombing campaign against Soviet Russia from appropriate overseas bases. The latter undertaking constituted the core of U.S. strategic planning. Many of the key disputes among the military services revolved around the questions of which service would have primary responsibility for the strategic bombing campaign and what capabilities and bases were necessary to make it effective.[9]

Military officials generally agreed that access to the Mediterranean was critical to the success of the air campaign against the Soviet Union. General Alfred Gruenther, director of the Joint Staff, confidentially told a congressional committee that "the base that gives the planner his greatest pleasure is the one in the Middle East." The importance of bases in this region loomed ever larger as strategic planners realized that flights over the polar ice cap would not be feasible in the immediate future. Forrestal informed Truman in January 1948 that any sustained and definitive bombing campaign "would have to take place largely from the Mediterranean and its environs." Bases in this region were closest to Soviet industrial centers, petroleum fields, and refineries.[10]

A critical question was whether the United States would have the capabilities to defend the Middle East and the Mediterranean. If Forrestal could convince the president that a strategic concept based on air strikes from the Mediterranean and the Middle East (as well as from Great Britain and to a lesser extent from Okinawa) was sound, then he could justify a budget based on the force requirements that were necessary to secure this area at the onset of conflict. The Navy had a great stake in this debate because it would play the pivotal role in establishing control over the Mediterranean and protecting lines of communication to bases in North Africa and the Middle East. Moreover, from its position in the Mediterranean, the Navy could use its air power to participate in the strategic bombing campaign against the Soviet heartland. Of course, an additional attraction of this strategy was that it provided some chance to hold Middle Eastern oil.[11]

In the abstract no one contested the desirability of a strategy based on control of the Mediterranean and the Middle East. Insofar as this strategy influenced the distribution of budgetary resources, it raised profound questions. Secretary of the Air Force Stuart Symington and Chief of Air Staff Carl Spaatz, for example, agreed on the utility of bases along the North African littoral and in the Middle East. Their overriding goal, however, was to secure funding for a 70-group Air Force. In their testimony before the Finletter Commission on air policy during the autumn of 1947, Symington and his senior staff insisted that long-range strategic bombing from land bases would be effective and that 70 groups would sustain a healthy private aviation industry that could expand rapidly in wartime. Spaatz denigrated the possibility that aircraft carriers could operate safely in hostile waters and successfully launch a bombing campaign. On the other hand, naval officers questioned the efficacy of long-range bombing, sneered at the defensive weaknesses of the newly produced B-36, and maintained that transcontinental bombing was not likely to prove useful in the immediate future. Instead they wanted 14,000 aircraft of their own, and they requested funding for the new and enlarged flush-deck carriers that could accommodate planes capable of carrying atomic bombs.[12]

Forrestal was caught in the raging controversy between the Navy and Air Force.

He was not eager to embark on a large increase in defense expenditures; he remained a fiscal conservative. And he did not think that the Soviets would engage in overt aggression. The immediate threat to U.S. national security resided in the socioeconomic dislocation that beleaguered much of the world and that constituted fertile ground for the growth of Communist influence. Yet Forrestal was wed to an air/atomic strategy for waging global war, and he wanted to support a U.S. presence in the Eastern Mediterranean and Middle East in order to have access to the region's petroleum resources and air bases. His conflicting aspirations made it difficult for him to conceive of a strategic concept that might fit within budgetary constraints and not jeopardize the priority that he accorded to the Marshall Plan and economic aid. Yet even if he would have been able to solve this dilemma, it was not his style of leadership to impose a solution on his subordinates. He desperately wanted the JCS to reconcile their differences among themselves and to approve a strategic concept that would provide a convincing rationale for future force requirements and budgetary requests.[13]

Forrestal's attention, however, was not focused exclusively on planning for global war. He also believed that military capabilities had to be designed to support the nation's foreign policy. In his view the United States was defining goals and incurring commitments that might require military force it did not have. Because the State Department and the NSC tended to make policy for one country or region at a time, the same forces were often earmarked for use in more than one area. In early 1948 defense officials told the president that they had only about 29,000 troops to meet emergencies in places like Italy and Palestine. If at the same time war erupted with the Soviet Union, the Army would not have enough soldiers to seize and protect essential overseas bases.[14]

Whether force requirements were linked to war plans or to foreign policy, the NME was saying that it needed more money. Yet neither the president nor the Congress seemed inclined to increase military expenditures. In January 1948 Truman asked Congress for about $10 billion for the military services for fiscal year 1949. This sum envisioned a reduction in personnel of about 13 percent and an Air Force limited to 55 groups, leaving an overall budget surplus of almost $5 billion. The Republican-dominated House immediately went to work on a tax cut, thereby further circumscribing the sums available for the NME.[15]

The Czech crisis in late February 1948 influenced Truman's policies and altered congressional sentiment. Everyone was afraid that Communists would try to seize power in other countries, especially Italy. Secretary of State Marshall, Undersecretary Lovett, and Forrestal clamored for additional military manpower and for universal military training (UMT). Army Chief of Staff Omar Bradley called for the resumption of the draft and the development of a "mobile striking force." The Policy Planning Staff agreed that the draft would demonstrate U.S. resolve to thwart additional cases of indirect Communist aggression. In his special message to Congress on 17 March, the president called for the restoration of the draft, the passage of UMT, and the enactment of the European Recovery Program. The next day he requested a supplementary $1.5 billion primarily to cover the costs of the draft.[16]

The military services and the JCS, however, saw this as a pittance. Between 11 and 14 March, Forrestal had finally gotten the chiefs away from Washington for several days of intensive discussions at Key West, where they hammered out a vague agreement concerning roles and missions that ostensibly fit an emergency war plan named FROLIC. FROLIC was based on existing capabilities and, much to the dismay of the JCS, relinquished much of the Middle East and Eastern Mediterranean at the onset of hostilities. When the chiefs returned to the capital and realized that the president was about to denounce the Soviets and support the draft, they saw an opportunity to elicit substantial new funds. They prepared rearmament proposals of staggering proportions, requiring somewhere between $3 and $22 billion in supplemental funds. On 23 March they told Truman that $6 billion was the "rock-bottom [supplemental] figure needed to provide the strength for an initial stand against the Russian armies in case war occurred." The JCS now reverted to an emergency war plan, BROILER, which had been written in the autumn of 1947. Its ambitious aspirations for safeguarding the Middle East and using British bases at Cairo-Suez to help launch the strategic offensive had been modified previously in view of budgetary constraints.[17]

JCS demands clashed with the president's thinking. The chiefs wanted a budget based on the force requirements necessary to implement their war plan at the onset of conflict. The president reluctantly agreed to boost the supplemental request to $3 billion, a quarter of which would go to purchase additional aircraft, but he and Marshall told Forrestal that they were not planning on war.[18] Neither was the defense secretary. Forrestal did not expect the Soviets to launch a premeditated attack. Like Truman and Lovett, he sought to raise military expenditures in order to demonstrate resolve and deter the Kremlin from taking initiatives that might risk war. In fact, he thought that requests to fund a 70-group Air Force would break the budget and undermine the appropriate balance between the different services.[19]

Yet both Truman and Forrestal lost control of the legislative process. Republican leaders in the House scorned the administration's proposal for UMT and looked upon support for the Air Force as politically appealing. In the Senate, Chan Gurney, Republican chairman of the Armed Services Committee, tried but failed to mobilize support for the administration's proposals for UMT, Selective Service, and a $3 billion supplement. Isolationist senators coalesced around Robert Taft and focused on bolstering air power. During hearings, Symington broke ranks and championed 70 groups over the administration's personnel proposals. Forrestal's aides were appalled by his behavior but could not stop the House from appropriating far more funds than the defense secretary wanted for the Air Force. Envious of the latter's success, the Army and Navy now pressed Forrestal and Truman to consider a total supplement of about $3.5 billion. Truman reluctantly agreed to $3.2 billion. Congress then rebuffed the administration's request for UMT, passed a weakened

Selective Service bill, and allocated $822 million more than Truman desired for the procurement of aircraft.[20]

The fiscal year 1949 supplement added about 30 percent to military spending. The JCS now focused on defending the Mediterranean and the Middle East and on using bases there, as well as in England, for launching a bombing attack against Soviet Russia. In confidential talks with British and Canadian military planners between 12 and 21 April, the United States agreed to emergency war plan HALFMOON, which reaffirmed the importance of the Middle East but did not provide for an initial defense of the region's petroleum resources. Regretting their incapacity to defend Europe, the chiefs made this goal a primary objective of long-range war plans. For emergency planning purposes, however, they had to focus on maintaining access to the Mediterranean and the Middle East in order to exploit U.S. superiority in long-range strategic bombing and atomic weaponry. After approving HALFMOON in late May, the JCS ordered all commanders to reconcile their tactical planning with the strategy laid out in that war plan.[21]

While the chiefs were working on HALFMOON, Admiral William Leahy, still serving as a key liaison between the JCS and the White House, told the planners not to rely exclusively on atomic weapons in planning the strategic offensive. The warning came at a particularly inauspicious time because Forrestal had been trying for months to get the president to approve the transfer of the atomic stockpile from the Atomic Energy Commission (AEC) to the NME. Moreover, the admonition came immediately after the immensely successful SANDSTONE tests in the Pacific, which promised a new generation of more powerful atomic weapons that could be mass produced and tailored to the needs of each service. Even under the existing methods of production the number of implosion-type nuclear components in the stockpile had increased from 13 to 50 between June 1947 and June 1948. These atomic weapons might be of critical importance if war should erupt over Berlin. Forrestal therefore resumed his efforts to get the stockpile transferred to the NME. Army Secretary Royall pressed the NSC to study the decisionmaking machinery for the use of atomic weaponry in wartime.[22]

Budget Director James E. Webb forcefully intruded in the discussions concerning the custody of atomic weapons. Stressing the principle of civilian control and citing the astounding progress of the past year, he urged Truman not to transfer custody to the NME. He pointed to the superlative performance of the AEC in contrast to Forrestal's inept leadership at the Pentagon. Webb insisted that the transfer would obstruct, not accelerate, progress. He explained to Truman that military officials were afforded every opportunity to familiarize themselves with the bomb and to "obtain immediate possession of enough bombs for operational use." The president decided to retain civilian control. He instructed the AEC and NME to refine their arrangements for the immediate transfer of weapons when so directed by the chief executive.[23]

In September 1948, when the Berlin crisis briefly rekindled anxieties about war,

Truman assured Forrestal that, as much as he would hate to do it, he would approve the use of atomic weapons if circumstances warranted it. Soon thereafter the NSC concluded that military planning should proceed on the assumption that atomic weapons would be employed in wartime. Although Truman neither approved nor rejected this recommendation, his subordinates thereafter began to institutionalize the air/atomic strategy into their war plans.[24]

■

This orientation accentuated the need for overseas bases and intensified the penchant to define more and more places as vital to U.S. security interests. If strategic bombing were to be effective, the United States had to have forward bases. Without fighter protection from advanced bases, long-range heavy bombers were vulnerable to Soviet interdiction. "The Air Force problem," Forrestal succinctly informed the president, "would be to get a footing in North Africa and then look for bases closer to the enemy from which the war could be brought home to him. The fighter problem enters here—to get a fighter with legs long enough to gain control of the air in order to insure freedom of action for our bombers as well as for our land and sea forces." [25]

State Department officials grasped the necessity and molded U.S. foreign policy accordingly. In North Africa and the Middle East, for example, the United States increasingly aligned itself with France and Britain, often against the nationalist aspirations of Third World peoples, in order to secure access to French and British bases. It was not that U.S. officials supported colonialism or were unaware of the emerging nationalism, but countries deemed vital to U.S. interests could not be allowed to fall prey to political upheaval, Communist infiltration, and indirect Soviet control.

Kennan's Policy Planning Staff put the matter bluntly: French North Africa constituted the bridge between the Atlantic and the Mediterranean, and its strategic importance meant that it now fell under the umbrella of the Monroe Doctrine. Because of the "greatly increased potential of modern air warfare," North Africa "now lies within a logical expansion of the zones of minimum security previously maintained by this country." Hence it would be undesirable, for example, to support Moroccan independence, for a sudden break from the mother country would create a weak state, susceptible to capture by a tiny yet determined Communist party assumed to be under the control of Moscow. U.S. policy should be designed to encourage French reform in order to co-opt the forces of nationalism and to prepare Morocco for eventual independence. Meanwhile France would retain responsibility for maintaining the peace while allocating base rights to the United States. According to a top-secret agreement between French and U.S. military officers in September 1947, the United States obtained communication rights and an air station at Port Lyautey. Additional rights to stockpile fuel, aviation gas, and ammunition were secured in September 1948, at which time efforts were also made to gain access to airfields at Oran and Bizerte as well as at Port Lyautey.[26]

The U.S. approach toward the disposition of the former Italian colonies in Africa was similar. The goal was to insure that the British secured a trusteeship over Cyrenaica. With their base rights at Cairo-Suez jeopardized by Egyptian demands, the British were looking for new locations from which to launch their own strategic campaign against the Soviet Union in wartime. U.S. officials were eager for the United Kingdom to have these bases, which would be shared with the Americans in emergencies. Yet the French and Soviets supported restoration of the territory to Italy, and many Arab countries wanted immediate independence. Both options were unsatisfactory to U.S. officials. If the area were returned to Italy and if the Communists took power in that nation, they might terminate U.S. and British rights and privileges. If independence were granted, the new, weak state would be vulnerable to Communist infiltration and Soviet aggression. The only answer, therefore, was at least a brief British stewardship. Since this was unlikely to win U.N. approval, Marshall favored postponement, but, he emphasized, in any event the British must proceed with their base plans. He also acceded to the transfer of Asmara (in Eritrea) to Ethiopia once the latter government agreed to respect the U.S. communications center being built there.[27]

Safeguarding access to these prospective bases in wartime depended on adequate funding in the future. But such funding was by no means assured. Webb questioned whether international circumstances warranted a large military buildup. He was agitated by the fact that it would require $18–20 billion in subsequent years to support the forces generated by the 1949 supplement. The president's Council of Economic Advisers concurred with Webb's misgiving. Stressing that such added spending might exacerbate the inflationary spiral, the council admonished Truman that he might have to adopt comprehensive controls over prices, wages, and credit.[28]

Truman hardly needed such warnings. He wanted a slow, steady military buildup sustainable over the long run. On 3 June he sent Forrestal guidelines setting the ceilings on military personnel and on active aircraft in the Air Force and Navy. He prodded Forrestal to take charge and impose order on the services.[29]

Forrestal vacillated. He sympathized with the fiscal concerns of the White House, but he could not see how the nation's foreign policy could be supported under prevailing personnel constraints. Although prospects for intervention in Greece and Italy diminished significantly during the spring of 1948, he feared that troops might have to be sent to Palestine. He wanted the State Department to explain how policies elsewhere might be supported if deployable forces were already committed to the Middle East. Believing that the next eighteen months would be critical in U.S. relations with Russia, he also wanted to ascertain whether it made sense to base the military budget on the force requirements of the approved war plan. On 26 May, when Kennan attended a high-level meeting at the Pentagon, Forrestal asked whether the NME should be planning for a major war in the near future or whether it should assume a period of normalcy wherein no war plan would be implemented.[30]

Kennan and Lovett resented Forrestal's queries, believing that he was trying to push responsibility onto the State Department. They sniped at his hypothetical questions and his desire to clarify imponderables. In their view the gap between commitments and capabilities was perfectly natural. Policymakers simply had to accept the attendant risks and hope that goals could be accomplished without military force. They did not think that the administration should plan for a period of peak danger in the immediate future. The problems that lay ahead were mostly political, though military force was important for deterrence and for the shadows cast over diplomatic and political situations. Even in the midst of the Berlin crisis, Lovett and Kennan did not expect war. They thought it mistaken to base the military budget on the force requirements of emergency war plans.[31]

Forrestal did not find these responses very satisfactory. In his long paper on defense policy, Kennan gave scant attention to the military capabilities needed to implement policy in different parts of the globe, despite the fact that previously he had acknowledged the need for a mobile striking force. More troublesome was his inability to show how the United States could maintain a *permanent* state of "adequate military preparation" and still be capable of waging war successfully if it should erupt. Forrestal's dilemma stemmed precisely from the fact that the capabilities required to wage war were not likely to be budgeted permanently. Nor was he helped by Kennan's refusal to define national objectives and reluctance to explain what he meant by a successful war.[32]

On 10 July, Forrestal requested the NSC to prepare papers to help determine the budget for fiscal year 1950. He had already asked the JCS to catalog the commitments incurred by the administration in order to reveal the widening gap between means and ends. He now asked the NSC to spell out U.S. objectives, to assess risks, and to calculate the likely role of the military in implementing national security policy: "If the dangers are great, immediate and of a military character, this fact should be clearly reflected in our military budget and our military strength adapted accordingly. If the risks are small, if they are distant rather than immediate, or if they are primarily of a non-military character, military estimates should be adjusted to accord with this situation." Once goals, risks, and tactics were systematically elucidated, Forrestal believed that the magnitude and composition of military forces could be rationally determined.[33]

Truman was irked by Forrestal's request. Although the president admitted that the studies requested by his defense secretary were useful and should take place, he suspected Forrestal of attempting an end run around his budgetary constraints. Truman emphatically told Forrestal that he should formulate the fiscal year 1950 NME budget within the $15 billion limit decided on. He was disgusted with Forrestal's inability to resolve the differences among the services. Truman ordered him to bring together the Army, Navy, and Air Force people and establish a program within budgetary constraints: "It seems to me that is your responsibility."[34]

At this same time Truman was launching his campaign for reelection. In his acceptance of the nomination on 15 July, he acknowledged that inflation was the top campaign issue. Since the Republicans were blaming him for high prices, he called a special session of Congress and defiantly challenged them to check inflation, solve the housing shortage, and serve the needs of "ordinary people." [35] Believing in the benefits of a balanced budget and recognizing the political saliency of inflation, Truman determined that military expenditures had to be constrained.

But the president was not willing to reconsider his foreign policy goals in light of the fiscal constraints. The United States continued its efforts to establish a favorable balance of power. Europe remained the greatest foreign policy priority, but U.S. vital interests were not confined to Europe. Indeed, the success of the European Recovery Program depended on Middle Eastern oil, investment earnings from Southeast Asia, and markets and raw materials in Africa. Likewise, in Asia, Japan was potentially a great industrial power that could not be allowed to be co-opted into the Soviet orbit. But Japan needed not only markets and raw materials in Southeast Asia but also assurances that the spread of communism in China and Korea would be checked.

U.S. resources were stretched terribly thin. Miscalculation could envelop the United States in global warfare for which it was unprepared; overcommitment could entrap U.S. forces in a civil war or regional conflict for which it had inadequate capabilities. Forrestal's questions were disturbing precisely because they underscored genuine dilemmas. So long as U.S. policymakers defined their national security interests so expansively and so long as the president insisted on a balanced budget, the risks would remain high. Unable to compel obedience from his service secretaries and military chiefs, demanding precise solutions to problems with imponderable variables, and emotionally overwhelmed by the responsibilities of his office, Forrestal would pose the same questions again after the campaign.[36] Should the military budget be linked to foreign policy commitments or to the strategic concepts and basic undertakings of war plans? How much reliance should be placed on economic aid, military assistance, and skillful diplomacy? How long could one assume that the Soviets would not resort to force?

European Priorities and Titoist Opportunities

Senior officials in the Truman administration continued to give Europe top priority. Their preeminent task was to insure that the Kremlin did not seize, co-opt, or subvert the core centers of industrial power in Western Europe. If European and Soviet power were joined even for a few years, Kennan warned that the "tremendous economic and military strength from that side . . . [would] constitute a real threat to the North American continent." He reiterated, however, that the Soviets had no desire to gain control of Europe through military force. Their aim still was to capitalize on economic dislocation, political discontent, and the success of local Communist parties. Their hope was to wean western Germany from the hands of the Anglo-Americans. In contrast, the U.S. aim was to outsmart the Soviets and maneuver

"Russian power back to its natural boundaries, to a place where it can no longer threaten to seize and command the power of Europe as well as of Russia." [37]

Kennan had this goal in mind in early August 1948, when hopes were rising that the Kremlin might agree to discuss Berlin at a meeting of the Council of Foreign Ministers. This expectation prompted a thorough review of German policy. Advocating a bold new approach, Kennan maintained that western Germany could never enjoy economic viability so long as Europe was split and East-West trade circumscribed. He wanted the powers to withdraw their occupation troops, unify Germany, and establish a viable independent German government. Kennan acknowledged that his approach was infused with many risks and imponderables. But in his opinion they were outweighed by the prospect of getting the Soviets out of eastern Germany, winning over German sentiment, and ending the division of Europe. He foresaw the evolution of a federated Europe, economically stable and politically viable, that might serve as a third force in world affairs.[38]

Kennan's proposals evoked little support within the State Department. John Hickerson, director of the Office of European Affairs, insisted that the dangers Kennan himself enumerated far outweighed any benefits. Hickerson's subordinates in the Office of European Affairs fully concurred. Jack Reinstein of the economic division also ridiculed Kennan's ideas, insisting that they might jeopardize the European Recovery Program or spur the growth of communism in Germany. Charles Saltzman, director of the Office of Occupation Affairs, shared many of the same apprehensions, worrying especially that the withdrawal of U.S. troops might allow the Soviets to exert pressure on a free German government.[39]

Kennan steadfastly defended his views. The very fact that talks over the blockade failed to materialize made it all the more imperative to consider new options or face the indefinite continuation of the airlift with all its costs and uncertainties.[40] One of the greatest uncertainties related to the loyalty of the German people. German affection for the West, Kennan thought, would prove ephemeral unless the Germans experienced concrete benefits. The United States had to offer a vision of the future to Germans who longed for unification. Otherwise, they might maneuver between East and West or throw in their lot with the Soviets. To rebut his critics, Kennan also emphasized that his plan would include all of Germany in the European Recovery Program. No new concessions would be made to the Kremlin on reparations, and the Soviet Union would gain only an insignificant role in the supervisory machinery for the Ruhr. Indeed, despite all the acrimony that his ideas engendered, Kennan acknowledged that they were simply a blueprint for the future. The Kremlin would never accept his conditions.

In mid-September Kennan called in prominent consultants for two days of discussions. He briefed them on the option he had developed and the reactions to it. He felt vindicated when the group, which included former undersecretary of state Dean Acheson, supported his perspective. But they supported it precisely because it was nonnegotiable with the Kremlin. If the French and British could be convinced to endorse the proposal, it would make sense to introduce it. It would affirm the nation's striving for peace. It would constitute a major propaganda victory in Germany: ideal circumstances would be created to press more vigorously than ever for the establishment of a West German government firmly integrated into a Western European and Atlantic community.[41]

Kennan's views found no support at the top of the State Department. Marshall and Lovett had no desire to create an independent, unified Germany that might or might not constitute the core of a European third force. "Our current policy," Lovett and Hickerson reminded Harriman in December 1948, "must be to bring Western Germany into close association with the free democratic states of Western Europe and enable it to contribute to and participate in European economic recovery." Germany must not be permitted "to be drawn into the Soviet orbit or be reconstructed as an instrument of Soviet policy."[42]

Throughout the fall of 1948, U.S. policymakers focused primary attention on these goals. Notwithstanding the elusive efforts to negotiate an end to the blockade and notwithstanding the abstract debates over alternative strategies for narrowing Soviet power in Europe, day-to-day operational efforts dealt with more mundane problems. The State Department, the Economic Cooperation Administration (ECA), and the Army worked to implement the London accords, boost west German production, and reduce the trade deficit. They sought to resolve disputes among the Western allies over reparations, dismantling, and the level of industry. They tried to design acceptable arrangements for the control of Ruhr industries. They worked on rewriting the occupation statute and defining the powers of a West German government. They labored to fuse Bizonia with the French zone in Germany. All these matters were enormously complex because they affected critical economic, political, and strategic interests of European governments. U.S. officials wanted to expedite Germany's rehabilitation, reduce occupation costs, and co-opt German sentiment. At the same time they endeavored to assure their friends in Western Europe that they would have access to the resources of the Ruhr, that Germany's military strength would not be revived, and that their security would not be jeopardized.[43]

The difficult task of balancing these conflicting imperatives was made all the more onerous by the fact that large organizations and egocentric individuals had their missions and powers at stake. The State Department and the Office of Military Government in Germany were constantly at odds with one another. Clay tenaciously fought to monopolize his control over U.S. economic and financial policy inside Germany. He did not want the ECA or the State Department infringing on his prerogatives. He wanted to hold down occupation costs, minimize imports, boost production, and maximize dollar earnings from all exports. These goals, he never ceased asserting, were not his own; they were the declared objectives of the U.S. government. Because he was charged with the responsibility for reforming, democratizing, and locking bizonal Germany into a Western orientation, he could not ignore the rising discontent in Germany. Germans were unhappy with the division of their country and with the comparatively laggard recovery of their economy. The Germans, Clay realized, would soon begin to regain control over their own future. If they were unsatisfied, they might vote Communists into power or look to the East.[44]

State Department officials fumed at Clay's arrogant independence. Seeking to control the nation's foreign policy, they complained that Clay was insensitive to the larger parameters of West European recovery. Because they had no direct responsibility for developments inside Germany and because they implicitly believed that the Army's presence there vested the United States with the power to control developments, they were much more responsive to French reactions and complaints.[45]

And in the autumn of 1948 the situation in France was most distressing. Production was up, but prices were skyrocketing. Strikes flared in the coal fields, and U.S. diplomats believed that the Communists were again trying to paralyze the economy and gain power. Ambassador Caffery bluntly stated that aid would be terminated if the Communists were readmitted into a governing coalition. ECA officials said funds would be cut if the government did not take stronger action to balance the budget and control the wage-price spiral. Yet these were idle threats because U.S. officials felt compelled to work with the moderate center. The Gaullists, they realized, were more likely to gain power if Robert Schuman, Henri Queuille, and their associates faltered and unrest proliferated. This possibility frightened them because they were convinced that Charles de Gaulle would antagonize labor, unite the left, and pave the way to Communist control. De Gaulle was not capable of solving the financial crisis inside France and would prove unsympathetic to U.S. policies in Germany. "He talks about economics as a woman talks about carburetors," wrote John Hickerson.[46]

Secretary of State Marshall spent most of the autumn in France at the Paris meeting of the United Nations. He observed events with growing consternation and great sympathy for the plight of the moderate center. He was particularly attuned to the strains placed on the French government by U.S. efforts to rehabilitate German industry, curtail occupation costs, and form a viable west German political entity. The French protested American plans to retain additional industrial capacity within Germany and opposed American efforts to vest the provisional central government with substantial powers. In prolonged negotiations they sought to interpret the ambiguous London accords in ways that would enhance French economic interests, circumscribe the latitude of any provisional government in Germany, and insure French security long after occupation ended. The French were infuriated by the Anglo-American decision to allow the German government to decide the future ownership of Ruhr industries (Public Law 75). From the French perspective, this decision circumscribed the still-undefined powers of the International Authority for the Ruhr (IAR). The French feared that PL 75 meant that the industrial and military potential of the Ruhr might be turned in the future, as it had in the past, against the economic and strategic interests of France. They insisted that international supervision of the coal and steel industries must continue after the occupation. Recognizing the political sensitivity of this issue, Marshall hedged any long-term commitments. He agreed, however, that even prior to trizonal fusion France could participate on the Anglo-American control boards that oversaw operational decisions in the Ruhr.[47]

French protests and State Department compromises exasperated Clay. He claimed that PL 75 was essential to provide incentives for increased production. Attempts to extend the powers of the IAR, he warned, "would be disastrous politically in Germany."[48] Marshall and Lovett agreed. So did U.S. ambassador Lewis Douglas, who was in London doing much of the day-to-day negotiating. They, too, were distraught that France might "retard or hinder a constructive German program" when it was beginning "to offer hope that Western Germany will be able to resist Communism and attraction towards the East." Yet they felt as constrained to accommodate French fears as Clay felt impelled to allay German grievances.[49]

The dilemma was to reconcile French and German aspirations. Marshall planners were trying to achieve this task, as the historian Michael Hogan brilliantly shows, through corporatist instruments, integrationist schemes, and supranational arrangements. In this vein, Douglas suggested that French desires to control Ruhr resources could be reconciled with German pride and sovereignty if the French agreed to enlarge the area that might be under the purview of the IAR. Douglas wanted to include the Saar, Lorraine, Luxembourg, Belgium, and the Netherlands:

A body which concerned itself with the coal and steel resources of this greater area could play an important role in assuring access to those resources by all Europe, could coordinate and endorse programs for investment and development and help prevent distortions in trade with the objective of providing the necessary production of coal and steel on the most economical terms without regard for national frontiers or nationality of consumers or producers.[50]

Here was the notion of what subsequently would become the Schuman Plan and the European Coal and Steel Community. The Americans, of course, were not the originators of this concept. European integrationists and some French and German industrialists and a few politicians had been thinking about it for a generation. In the fall of 1948 French officials at the foreign ministry were discussing it, but when Douglas broached this proposal to French diplomats, they rebuffed it.[51]

Instead, French pleas for coordinated strategic planning, military assistance, and formal guarantees mounted.[52] Even U.S. officials who were normally sympathetic grew exasperated. "The French are in our hair," Hickerson wrote Caffery in late August.[53] Yet French concerns could not be dismissed. Nor could U.S. policymakers ignore the axiomatic proposition that if their policy were designed to recreate an economically viable and integrated Western Europe in peacetime, then they must not permit the Soviets to seize it in wartime.

The JCS encouraged Western Union planners to defend Europe at the Rhine if war should erupt. This strategy clashed with U.S. *short-term* war plans, which did not envision the deployment of American forces to Europe at the onset of war and which dwelled on the strategic air offensive. Nevertheless, the JCS agreed that U.S. occupation forces should stand and fight at the Rhine rather than evacuate.[54] Clay coordinated his planning with the French and British and with the newly created Western Union chiefs of staff committee. Marshall, Forrestal, and the JCS began giving serious thought to command relationships in case hostilities should eventuate. Truman agreed that American forces should be placed under the commander of Western Union forces at the onset of hostilities.[55]

Likewise, U.S. officials became increasingly committed to a program of military aid. Lovett said it would be the administration's top legislative priority at the next session of Congress.[56] Marshall, however, would not even wait this long. He approved Clay's request to reequip three French divisions on the Rhine. In the short run, this aid was designed to give France the psychological boost, "the shot in the arm," as Marshall phrased it, to support U.S. initiatives.[57] In the long run, a well-conceived program of military assistance would make the defense of Europe a realistic possibility. The Army's Plans and Operations Division now said that this goal might be accomplished by 1952. Vannevar Bush, the foremost civilian expert on military research and development, wrote Forrestal in November 1948 that the development of highly mobile and precise antitank guns could enable the Europeans "to withstand Russia on land" if the United States implemented an intelligent program of military aid.[58]

As further short-term reassurance to the French and long-term deterrent to the Soviets, the United States proceeded with the negotiation of the North Atlantic Treaty (NAT). Exploratory talks convened in Washington in July. The Western Union representatives and especially the French insisted on a firm U.S. commitment to assist signatories that were under attack. Lovett and his aides preferred to talk in general terms and stressed the principles of self-help and mutual aid. They knew nothing could be done until after the elections. They encouraged European representatives to screen their collective demands for military aid and prepare a strategic plan to include Norway, Denmark, Iceland, Ireland, and Portugal.[59]

Immediately after the election, Truman approved the work on the treaty undertaken during the summer.[60] Lovett then moved quickly to resume the exploratory talks. The draft treaty that resulted called for continuous efforts to strengthen the signatories' capacity to resist aggression. It provided for consultation whenever the security of one of the participants was threatened and whenever conditions seemed to endanger the peace. In the most important article, the draft stipulated that an armed attack against one signatory would be viewed as an attack against them all. "Consequently" each nation would "assist the party or parties attacked by taking forthwith such military or other action, individually and in concert with the other parties, as may be necessary to restore and assure the security of the North Atlantic area." Subsequent articles defined the area encompassed by the agreement and called for the establishment of a council, a defense committee, and other subsidiary bodies to implement the accord.[61]

Throughout the negotiations in December, Lovett emphasized the need for quick action. He did not dwell on the likelihood of a Soviet attack. Indeed, the importance of the treaty would be its psychological impact on the continent. The United States wanted to encourage the signatories to take the risks that inhered in rebuilding the German economy, establishing a West German republic, and accepting European integration. These risks, especially for a country like France, were domestic and foreign, short-term and long-term. The actions desired by U.S. officials threatened to exacerbate unrest within France and to accentuate the division of Europe. In the short run, the French might have to deal with a resumption of strikes or respond to additional retaliatory Soviet moves. In the long run, they might have to face a West German government that might seek greater autonomy as well as German unity and that might try to align with the Kremlin or maneuver between East and West. To encourage the French and other signatories to face these risks, to give them confidence that they could cope with the imponderables that lay ahead, and to promote economic recovery, U.S. officials pressed forward with the NAT.[62]

Lovett's negotiations did not resolve all the outstanding differences between the United States and the Western Union governments. But the commitments in the draft treaty illuminated how the logic of their assumptions about national security forced U.S. policymakers into a series of political-military actions they would have otherwise preferred to avoid. To preserve a favorable balance of power on the European continent, they had to expedite recovery and thwart Communist political successes. Assuming that recovery could not take place without German resources and that prolonged discontent in the western zones could spawn an eventual German-Soviet coalition, they decided to implement the London accords quickly. These efforts, in turn, provoked the Soviets into the blockade of Berlin and alarmed the French. To reassure the latter and deter the former, the United States then had to extend military aid, coordinate strategic planning, and offer political guarantees. As 1948 progressed and other nations cast their lot with the Americans and announced their terms of collaboration, the full costs of the U.S. vision of national security began to unfold.

■

The vision was costly because it was grandiose. It focused on creating a unified Western Europe amenable to U.S. interests and leadership but was not limited to this objective. U.S. officials also hoped to liberate Eastern Europe. In speech after speech and paper after paper during the summer and fall of 1948, Kennan emphasized that U.S. policy was designed to maneuver the Russian bear back into his cage, defined as Russia's borders prior to 1939. "Our first aim with respect to Russia in time of peace," Kennan wrote, "is to encourage and promote by means short of war the gradual retraction of undue Russian power and influence from the present satellite area." [63]

Believing that the Kremlin exaggerated its own vulnerabilities, U.S. officials moved cautiously. They did not want to trigger a war through their own miscalculations. Still, Kennan proudly acknowledged that the Marshall Plan had been designed to place the Kremlin in a dilemma. The Russians either had to allow their satellites to participate, thereby "weakening the exclusive orientation of these countries toward Russia," or had to clamp down upon them at considerable economic and political cost.[64] In configuring the NAT, Lovett and Kennan initially hoped to devise language that would not solidify the division of Europe and that might ultimately attract the countries of Eastern Europe. Later, Lovett emphasized that the Organization of European Economic Cooperation (OEEC) and the NAT must be kept entirely separate, with the former focused exclusively on European economic recovery and integration. "Any deviation from this principle," Lovett stressed, "would reduce tremendously the drawing power which the OEEC still has for Eastern European countries."[65]

To spur the disintegration of Eastern Europe, Kennan championed covert operations and organized "political warfare." Disappointed when clandestine operations were placed under the Central Intelligence Agency (CIA), not the State Department, he happily became the State Department's liaison with the newly created covert arm of the CIA, the Office of Policy Coordination. He believed that the bonds between the Communist leaders in satellite nations and the Kremlin were tenuous. Consequently, he sought to promote rifts through propaganda, aid to refugee organizations, and assistance to dissident groups "within the captured countries."[66]

The public rift between Yugoslav leader Tito and Stalin exhilarated Kennan and other U.S. policymakers. They had not foreseen it, but they were eager to capitalize on it. Averell Harriman, now the ECA's top man in Europe, Army Undersecretary Draper, and other senior military and diplomatic officials were eager to reach out to Tito, offer him some short-term aid, and provide encouragement. If Tito survived, Harriman felt certain that Soviet military options would be constrained and the United States would be able to carry through its initiatives in Western Europe.[67]

Kennan, however, was more cautious. He agreed that "a new factor of fundamental and profound significance has been introduced into the world communist movement. . . . The possibility of defection from Moscow, which has heretofore been unthinkable for foreign communist leaders, will from now on be present in one form or another in the mind of every one of them." To embrace Tito too openly, however, would undermine his credibility in Yugoslavia and among other Communist leaders. Moreover, Tito's was a Communist totalitarian state and he still defiantly opposed U.S. desires to open up the Danube to the trade of Western powers.[68]

Marshall adopted Kennan's advice. He would not fawn upon Tito; he would respond to his overtures. Aid would depend on Tito's willingness to reconcile his foreign policy goals with those of the United States. U.S. officials, for example, closely watched to see if Tito would distance himself from the Greek insurgents. Their aim was to provide the minimal assistance necessary to sustain Tito. They did not intend, however, to embrace independent Communist governments. It must be "our fixed aim," the State Department declared, and the NSC and the president concurred, to replace non-Stalinist Communist regimes with "non-totalitarian governments desirous of participating with good faith in the free world community." [69]

It is worth emphasizing, however, that although U.S. officials hoped to reduce and eliminate Soviet power in Eastern Europe, this objective was not defined as a vital national security imperative in peacetime. It was not so important as to risk war or to jeopardize more important priorities. The goal, Kennan stressed, had to be pursued discreetly and artfully over a long period. To boldly challenge the Soviets within their sphere of influence was extremely imprudent, especially in the midst of the Berlin crisis and in the context of U.S. initiatives in Western Europe. But through effective propaganda, covert operations, and skillful diplomacy, the United States might be able to score important successes. Kennan's proposal for a mutual withdrawal from Germany, for example, was prompted in part by his belief that it would dilute Soviet influence in Eastern Europe. So was his support for paramilitary activities in places like Albania that began in late 1948.[70]

If war should erupt, however, U.S. officials believed that national security interests demanded the destruction of the Soviet empire in Eastern Europe. The NSC agreed that the Kremlin's domination of any nation beyond Soviet territory could not be tolerated. Accordingly, the Cominform must also be abolished. If a remnant of the Soviet regime should continue to exist within Russian borders after a conflict, it must not be allowed to have sufficient military power to wage war again. Given the magnitude of these wartime objectives, which Kennan himself designed, and given the peacetime risks and commitments that U.S. officials were incurring in Western Europe, it was no wonder that Forrestal and his assistants wanted greater military capabilities.[71]

The Middle East

U.S. officials gave top priority to Europe, but they also defined the Middle East as vitally important. The Truman Doctrine vested U.S. prestige in the fate of Greece, Turkey, and the Eastern Mediterranean. The Marshall Plan accentuated U.S. economic interests in the Middle East. During the hearings on the European Recovery Program, administration spokesmen emphasized the importance of petroleum to the success of the Marshall Plan. Because there was a shortage of Western Hemisphere oil and the United States was becoming a net importer of oil, section 112 of the Economic Cooperation Act of 1948 mandated that European petroleum requirements should be fulfilled as much as possible from repositories outside the United States. The Middle East held the largest untapped source of oil. Its petroleum was easy to get out of the ground and could be transported to Europe more cheaply than could Western Hemisphere oil.[72]

Middle Eastern oil was also viewed as a critical resource in wartime. If war broke out in the near term, the United States and its allies would not need Middle Eastern oil until its concluding stages. But studies suggested that in wars that might occur in the mid-1950's, Middle Eastern oil would be vital to the West at the opening stages. The Soviets, moreover, would be forced to wage an "oil-starved" war if they could be denied entry into the Middle East.[73]

Even more important than the region's oil repositories were its airfields, on which U.S. and British strategic plans depended. In the fall of 1947, for example, war plan BROILER assumed that within fifteen days after the eruption of hostilities the United States would launch the air offensive from bases in the Middle East, Britain, and Okinawa. The base at Cairo-Suez was particularly attractive because a principal target was the Soviet oil-refining industry. Approximately 84 percent of this refining capacity was thought to be located within easy radius of B-29's operating out of Egypt. Believing that Soviet radar nets and air defenses in the south were weak and that launchings from Egypt might be possible for up to six months before Russian forces seized the area, U.S. policy was designed to support and to capitalize on the British presence in the region. When supplemental appropriations to the military budget were approved in the spring of 1948, the JCS formally adopted emergency war plan HALFMOON, which incorporated much of the Middle East strategy initially outlined in BROILER. [74]

Increasingly, U.S. policy in the Middle East aimed at coordinating British and American strategic interests. We "must do what we can to support the maintenance of the British . . . strategic position," Kennan emphasized to Marshall and Lovett.[75] Despite England's continuing dispute with Egypt, British military officials placed ever greater stress on "holding the Middle East for offensive purposes in the event of war with the USSR." The British war plan SPEEDWAY of December 1948 called on the defense of Egypt by British commonwealth forces while the U.S. Air Force utilized Cairo-Suez to launch an atomic offensive with scores of heavy bombers.[76]

Admiral Richard Conolly, commander of U.S. forces in the Eastern Atlantic and Mediterranean, was headquartered in London and coordinated Middle East strategy with the British. He received permission from the State Department to send planners to consult with their British counterparts in Egypt.[77] Air Force Secretary Symington wanted to expand the airstrips in the canal zone as well as enlarge the storage facilities for fuel. When, in November, Forrestal and Conolly discussed these matters with British defense officials, they were told that the British had begun work on the runways at Abu Suwair.[78] At the same time British and U.S. officials began cooperating on the development of three airfields at Dhahran that the United States could utilize in wartime.[79]

Meanwhile, U.S. officials implemented military aid to Turkey to complement the Middle East strategy envisioned in BROILER and HALFMOON. U.S. Army advisers sought to reorganize and modernize the Turkish army, augment its mobility and firepower, improve its communication and transportation infrastructure, and bolster its logistical capabilities. They wanted the Turkish army to retard the Soviet land offensive, thereby affording time for the United States and Great Britain to launch the strategic air campaign from Egyptian bases. The Turkish army was given equipment to blunt a three-pronged Soviet attack across the Bosporus, the Black Sea, and the Caucasus, to fall back gradually, and to mount a final, large-scale stand in southern Turkey in the Iskenderun pocket. During 1948 the United States also transferred over 180 F-47's, 30 B-26's, and 86 C-47's to the Turkish air force, planes that would assist Turkish ground forces inside Turkey and help interdict Soviet troops moving toward Persian Gulf oil or sweeping toward Cairo-Suez. The United States also placed a great deal of stress on reconstructing and resurfacing Turkish airfields at such places as Bandirma and Diyarbakir. As a result, Turkey began to develop the ability to attack vital Soviet petroleum resources in Romania and the Caucasus. Symington and Forrestal wanted some of the airstrips designed to handle B-29's, which, if wartime circumstances permitted, Americans would fly in. By the end of 1948 State Department officials endorsed the idea of constructing medium bomber bases in Turkey. Moreover, when Tito suspended aid to the Greek insurgents and guerrilla activity waned, U.S. officials agreed to transfer aid under the Greece-Turkey program to the latter nation, where the money could be used to bolster overall strategy for the Middle East.[80]

■

The Arab-Jewish dispute over the future of Palestine jeopardized U.S. access to Middle Eastern bases in wartime and to Middle Eastern petroleum in peacetime. In the fall of 1946, for both political and humanitarian reasons, Truman had supported the establishment of a Jewish state in Palestine. A year later the United States endorsed the U.N. majority report calling for the division of Palestine into Jewish and Arab states and the internationalization of Jerusalem. Arabs bitterly opposed this program, violence flared, and the British announced that they would not take responsibility for keeping the peace and arranging an orderly transition. U.S. defense officials and the senior policymakers in the State Department concurred that Truman's support for partition and an independent Jewish state was unwise. Arab anger might jeopardize the interests of U.S. petroleum corporations and complicate efforts to utilize Middle Eastern bases in wartime.[81]

The prospective costs of Truman's support of a Jewish state mounted during the winter of 1947–48 because it was precisely during these months that the European Recovery Program was worked out, the importance of Middle Eastern oil to European recovery acknowledged, and the rationale for strategic cooperation developed. State Department officials resolved to reverse Truman's policies. Kennan, Loy Henderson, director of the Office of Near Eastern and African Affairs, and Dean Rusk, now the chief of the Office of U.N. Affairs, told Lovett that partition was unacceptable to the Arabs and therefore unworkable. Violence would erupt and pressures to assist Israel would grow. The United States must not find itself holding "major military and economic responsibility for the indefinite maintenance by armed force of a status quo in Palestine fiercely resented by the bulk of the Arab world." [82] Nor could it entertain the possibility that the United Nations might deploy an international peacekeeping force to Palestine to enforce partition. If the Kremlin gained entry into the region in this way, Kennan proclaimed that "the whole structure of strategic and political planning which we have been building up for the Mediterranean and Middle Eastern areas would have to be reexamined and probably modified." [83]

At the end of February 1948, Marshall urged Truman to reconsider his support of partition. The president equivocated, knowing that repudiation would outrage Jewish voters. Clark Clifford, the president's trusted counsel and political adviser, stepped into the debate. Trying to refute Marshall's arguments, he explained that by changing course the United States would humiliate itself and undermine the United Nations. Conservative Arab governments, Clifford also insisted, could not afford to cut oil sales to the West. Persuasive as he was, he did not address the major concerns of Marshall, Lovett, Kennan, Rusk, and Forrestal. He did not explain how the United States could enforce partition or how it could keep Soviet forces out of the region if an international force were needed. [84]

Marshall believed that he had convinced the president to change policy. On 19 March, the U.S. representative at the United Nations announced U.S. support for a trusteeship and a truce as temporary alternatives to partition and violence. American Jews reacted with disbelief. Jews in Palestine were shocked, but they did not alter their intention to declare independence on 15 May, the announced date of Britain's withdrawal. Arabs appeared pleased but no less determined to eradicate Zionism.

Truman equivocated as he saw the reaction at home. His ambivalence infuriated Marshall, Lovett, and Forrestal. They grew more alarmed as their calls for a truce and a temporary trusteeship did not end the fighting in Palestine. On 27 March, however, Truman asked the British to retain troops in the area to keep the peace. He now acknowledged that the United States was no longer supporting partition. In fact, if troops were necessary to enforce the truce, as seemed possible, Truman said he would permit a U.S. contingent to join British and French forces. Only proposals contemplating joint intervention with the Soviets remained "preposterous." [85]

The thought of deploying troops to Palestine frayed the nerves of defense officials. Rusk presented the State Department's case to the JCS at its meeting on 4 April. "If we did nothing," Rusk insisted, "the Russians could and would take definite steps toward gaining control in Palestine." Trying to elicit the chiefs' cooperation, Rusk also noted that intervention might "give us the opportunity to construct bomber fields in the Middle East." The JCS recognized the compelling reasons for intervention. Noting, however, that it would take almost 105,000 troops to preserve order (45 percent of whom would come from the United States), the chiefs concluded that intervention would necessitate partial mobilization, overextend U.S. forces, require still additional appropriations, and erode the strength of the general reserve for the next six months.[86]

Lovett, feeling that the United States had to back up its diplomatic position, told Forrestal on 18 April that the nation must be prepared to send troops to Palestine to help maintain the peace during U.N. discussions of the truce and trusteeship.[87] Forrestal disagreed, warning that U.S. military power was not commensurate with its interests and commitments. State Department officials could not refute Forrestal's logic, yet they were exasperated by his preaching. What else could they do? All agreed that the United States had vital interests in the region, that the turmoil in Palestine jeopardized these interests by antagonizing the Arabs and offering opportunities to the Russians, and that, if the United States did not offer to keep the peace, the Soviets might happily assume the responsibility. The United States, of course, could not intervene in the Middle East and carry out all its commitments elsewhere. But this gap was nothing new; the gap had always existed.[88]

The anger of State Department officials reflected their frustration. The diplomatic options they had recommended to reconcile the nation's interests with the president's political exigencies—that is, the trusteeship and truce proposals—did not garner much support.[89] Fighting in Palestine intensified as Jewish forces received arms from Czechoslovakia, seized Haifa and parts of Jaffa, and prepared to announce the formation of an independent Israel. At a tense meeting at the White House on 12 May with the president presiding, Clifford now argued the case for recognizing Israel. The trusteeship proposal had foundered. Rusk's prediction that a truce could be arranged within two weeks had been wrong. Recognition, therefore, would reaffirm the president's earlier endorsement of partition.

Marshall and Lovett sneered at Clifford's arguments. With shocking bluntness, they stated that the rush to recognition was a transparent effort to win Jewish votes. Why move toward recognition and partition while still pressing for a truce at the United Nations and when there was no assurance that the new Jewish state would be linked to the West? Lovett pulled out a file of intelligence reports and read excerpts outlining Soviet efforts to gain influence in Israel. Marshall emphasized that on matters as important as Palestine, vital national security interests must take precedence over domestic political considerations.[90]

Truman rejected their advice and recognized Israel. Political considerations were transcendent. The truce and trusteeship proposals, however, were not likely to produce any better results diplomatically or strategically, at least not in the short run. Whether or not the United States recognized Israel, fighting would flare, the Soviets might participate in a peacekeeping force, and the United States might have to intervene. U.S. officials could not dictate developments in the region. Jewish leaders would not accept trusteeship. Arab governments would not accept a truce if it envisioned Israeli independence. Why not, then, profit politically and recognize Israel? Why not, then, fulfill one's humanitarian instincts to assist the survivors of Hitler's camps? As Clifford and Truman also knew, and as Michael Cohen has stressed in his excellent book, recognition would help the United States preempt Soviet influence in Israel.[91]

The task for U.S. policymakers was still to mold events in the area to favor fundamental American interests. The United States wanted access to bases and petroleum. Recognition, therefore, did not mean that it would defend the new Jewish state from the Arab nations. After Egypt invaded Palestine on 16 May, the U.S. embargo on the shipment of arms to Arabs and Jews continued. The United States also prepared to fend off resolutions defining the Arabs' use of violence against Israel as constituting aggression within the meaning of the U.N. charter. Kennan thus hoped to smooth relations with the Arabs and avoid a pretext for Soviet intervention in the Middle East.[92]

But protecting vital interests seemed excruciatingly difficult because Soviet diplomacy appeared wickedly clever. Soviet recognition of Israel and the shipment of arms from Czechoslovakia to the new Jewish state created manifold possibilities for the growth of Soviet influence in the region, especially within the Israeli government. Fears that Jewish immigrants from Poland and Russia might be pro-Communist, plus intelligence reports stressing Soviet influence with the Irgun and the Stern Gang, accentuated U.S. apprehensions.[93] But even if Soviet efforts in Israel were not successful, the Soviets were sure to gain if regional strife persisted and Israel's military capabilities grew. Unrest within the Arab world might topple conservative Arab governments, creating opportunities for the small Communist movements. At the very least, Arabs would demand that the United Kingdom provide them munitions to match those the Israelis were securing from Soviet satellites. British compliance would create enormous Anglo-American tension; their not complying would further undermine the Western position in the Arab world.[94]

This analysis placed a premium on securing a truce and a settlement as quickly as possible. The Truman administration fully supported U.N. mediation under Count Folke Bernadotte of Sweden. But the intermittent truces proved fragile and required enforcement. Bernadotte appealed for a U.S. Marine Corps battalion to help preserve order in Jerusalem. Marshall said no, fearing that the troops might be ensnared in the conflict and need reinforcements. But Marshall's concern for stability and desire to foreclose Soviet intervention were so intense that he did not rule out the possibility of using U.S. troops in the future.[95]

This prospect reignited the controversy that had divided the State Department and the Pentagon the previous spring. In mid-August 1948, in the midst of the Berlin crisis, the JCS forcefully argued against an international peacekeeping force for Palestine. The JCS maintained that the country did not have the troops to deploy to the Middle East. Moreover, the Soviets might use an international force to maneuver their own way into the region. Even a small number of Russian troops might lead to the Kremlin's domination of the entire area.[96]

Rusk and Joseph Satterthwaite, the new head of the Office of Near Eastern and

African Affairs, defended the State Department's position, stressing that they had not yet endorsed any plan for an international peacekeeping force. But they insisted that Soviet opportunities for maneuvering their way into the Middle East through the Stern Gang or the Irgun, on the one hand, or through the radicalization of Arab governments, on the other, were so great that the United States had to retain the option of inserting forces into the region either unilaterally or as part of an international peacekeeping force.[97] At an NSC meeting on 3 September, Marshall, Lovett, and Forrestal rehashed these views without any clear resolution of the matter, but with Lovett emphatically declaring that military options had to be maintained given the many imponderables of the situation. Most worrisome was the possibility that the Israelis might appeal for U.N. support and the Kremlin might respond by deploying several divisions to the region.[98]

The very fragility of the truce Bernadotte had arranged impelled U.S. officials to support U.N. efforts to work out a compromise settlement. Marshall was eager to coordinate U.S. and British positions. Bevin, however, was terribly agitated, believing that arms sales from the Soviet bloc to Israel during the truce had emboldened Jewish territorial claims. In his view British compliance with the arms embargo alienated Arab governments, weakened their military position, and gave the Kremlin an advantage once turmoil engulfed the Arab world. Without a settlement that was satisfactory to Arab governments, especially to Egypt and Transjordan, the West's access to bases in wartime and to oil in peacetime would be jeopardized.[99]

Although Marshall cautioned Bevin not to exaggerate the problems and to adhere to the arms embargo, he shared the British perspective. He and Bevin agreed to support a Bernadotte settlement that envisioned the recognition of an Israeli state, the incorporation of Arab Palestine into Transjordan, and the internationalization of Jerusalem. (See Map 7.) The Bernadotte plan, however, set Israeli boundaries that differed from those delineated in the November 1947 U.N. resolution. The western Galilee, which Jewish forces now occupied, would be given to Israel, but the Negev would go to Transjordan. The aim was to placate a reliable British ally, Transjordan, and thereby safeguard British bases in that country, establish the possibility for new bases in the Negev, and, most of all, protect the strategic roads passing through Palestine and Gaza toward Cairo-Suez. Bevin stated, and the Americans concurred, that the Negev was the key strategic area. It was safer if placed in the hands of Transjordan than if incorporated in a Jewish state whose long-term reliability was suspect. On 1 September, Truman endorsed the idea of a territorial settlement along these lines. Marshall supported the Bernadotte peace plan when he settled in Paris for the extended autumn meeting of the U.N. General Assembly.[100]

Yet the U.S. diplomatic position proved politically embarrassing to the president. The Democratic platform committed Truman to support an independent Israeli state with boundaries as in the November U.N. resolution: the Negev would belong to the Jewish state, but the western Galilee would go to the Arabs. Now Israeli officials insisted on having both these territories. American Zionists accused the

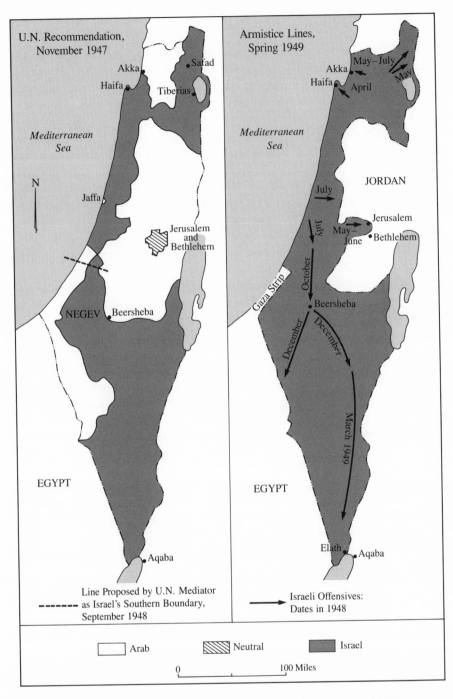

7. Partition of Palestine, 1946–49. Adapted from *The Survey of International Affairs 1939–1946*, vol. 2, *The Middle East 1945–1950* (London: Oxford University Press for the Royal Institute of International Affairs, 1954).

president of betraying his promises and Jewish voters were ready to bolt the Democratic Party—all as the president was on one of his major campaign swings. From the railroad yards in Tulsa, Oklahoma, Clifford called Lovett to explain that Truman was under intense political pressure to reaffirm his commitment to the U.N. settlement. Lovett retorted that this would constitute a "disastrous" diplomatic blunder and would humiliate Marshall. Clifford relented. The president would try to refrain from any public statements, but discussion of this issue at the General Assembly had to be postponed until after the elections.[101]

In Paris, Marshall, Rusk, and their colleagues labored with great embarrassment to gain time for the president. Rusk pleaded with John Foster Dulles, one of the delegates, to persuade Dewey not to exploit this explosive international issue for domestic political gain. But Dulles could not restrain Dewey, who indeed raised the issue. Truman responded with a forceful reaffirmation of the Democratic platform.[102] This meant that Israel should have the Negev.

Once the "silly season" was over, as Lovett contemptuously dubbed the political campaign, the administration was able to return to serious diplomacy. On the weekend following the election, Lovett and Douglas spent much time with the president recapitulating the strategic considerations behind U.S. diplomacy. For months Douglas had been trying to convey the full extent of British concerns: the Palestine issue was as significant as the Berlin crisis because Britain could not afford to lose access to the bases and oil fields of the region. Truman did not dispute this; he simply insisted that some means be found to reconcile his campaign rhetoric with the practical exigencies. Publicly he stated that he would never force Israel to relinquish that land it was entitled to as a result of the U.N. resolution on partition. But privately he was exasperated by Israel's territorial claims. He maintained that, if Israel refused to renounce the Negev, it would not have U.S. support for the western Galilee. Meanwhile, the arms embargo would continue; de jure recognition of the Israeli government would await Israeli elections; and financial aid would be promised to the entire Middle East and not to Israel alone.[103]

The settlement envisioned by U.S. policymakers was scorned by both Arabs and Jews. Given the stake that the people of the region had in any agreement, the United States could not simply impose an accord. Indeed, U.S. officials doubted whether they could even preserve the uneasy truce. Once again they and the British had to contemplate the possibility that a resumption of hostilities would lead to Jewish military successes, Arab humiliation, and Soviet opportunities. And so once again they also had to consider the prospective deployment of U.S. troops to the region.[104]

If vital interests were to be protected in peacetime and if fundamental strategic undertakings were to be performed in wartime, the gap between means and ends would have to be closed. Yet no one in administration circles talked about reducing the significance attributed to the Middle East. Indeed, its strategic importance loomed ever larger as U.S. officials placed the protection of British base rights, for example, in Egypt and Cyrenaica, ahead of other priorities like the promotion of self-determination and national sovereignty. At the same time, realizing that the prospective exclusion of Greece, Turkey, and Iran from the NAT risked their alienation, U.S. officials pondered mechanisms for satisfying these nations' demands for guarantees of their security.[105]

None of the choices before U.S. officials were very good. Whatever commitments or assistance might be offered, the United States still faced the prospect of failure. No nation could easily preserve stability half a world away in a region wracked by poverty, ethnic hatred, indigenous strife, and traditional great power rivalries. This realization, always lurking in the minds of policymakers, compounded anxieties and intensified acrimony as they continued their quest to retain the Middle East within an Anglo-American orbit.

China and Korea

China and Korea contained no vital resources and no essential bases, yet senior officials expended much more money and energy here than in the Middle East. In part this paradox was the result of the legacy of the war, for when the United States defeated Japan and repatriated Japanese troops, it committed itself to checking Soviet influence and revolutionary nationalism in Northeast Asia without calculating the costs.[106] Thereafter it was believed that any retreat would shatter U.S. credibility in more important places like Japan and Southeast Asia. Moreover, whereas in the Middle East the United States could rely on British assets, U.S. officials were operating on their own in Korea and China. And the perception of threat was much greater in these countries than in the Middle East. Yet try as they might to thwart the growth of Communist influence and Soviet power, Americans found themselves increasingly frustrated and demoralized by the gap between their desires and their capabilities.

Even while Truman, Marshall, Forrestal, and their colleagues were coming to define Western Europe as their top priority, they were unwilling to extricate the United States from China and Korea. During July and August 1947, General Wedemeyer carried out his mission, focusing most of his attention on China. In September he confidentially submitted his report to Marshall. Despite his well-known sympathies for the Nationalist regime, Wedemeyer was appalled by the incompetence, corruption, arrogance, and unpopularity of Chiang Kai-shek's government. Additional U.S. aid, he said, must be contingent on reform. Recognizing that the Nationalist military situation in Manchuria was hopeless, Wedemeyer also proposed an international trusteeship for it. Although his aim was to prevent the Kremlin from indirectly co-opting the resources of Manchuria, the suggestion invited limited Soviet intervention and was a direct assault on Chinese sovereignty. Because the report was such an indictment of Chiang and such a blow to Chinese pride, Marshall insisted on keeping it under wraps.[107]

Wedemeyer's thinking, however, was not so different from the State Department's. Practically everyone, for example, agreed that the Chinese Communists (CCP) were tools of Soviet policy and had to be contained, even if they could not be defeated. According to Philip Sprouse, the State Department expert who accompanied Wedemeyer, "the close ideological affinity between the USSR and the Chinese Communists is sufficiently clear to assure that Communist domination of China would result in a basic orientation toward the USSR rather than toward the US." American foreign service officers all over China concurred. "The Chinese Communists are a strong and effective extension of Soviet foreign policy," commented John Melby. The CCP must be considered "an arm of Soviet foreign policy," echoed Raymond Ludden, the first secretary of the embassy. Hardly anyone advocated terminating the struggle against the Communists despite the unanimous view that Chiang's regime was a travesty.[108]

U.S. military and civilian analysts were distraught by the strategic and economic advantages that would accrue to the Kremlin as a result of the Communists' domination of northern China and Manchuria. Sprouse and Melby, for example, believed that the integration of Manchuria into the Soviet Far East economy might establish a Northeast Asian economic unit that, if augmented by additional Soviet inroads into northern China and southern Korea, could significantly strengthen the Soviet economy. According to the CIA, the Kremlin might eventually be able to combine Manchurian iron ore with coal from northern China and ferro-alloys from northern Korea to create "the basis for an integrated industry." Russia might then possess "the largest industrial potential of any area in the Far East" and could exert real leverage against Japan as well.[109] In addition, Communist control of Manchuria would enable the Soviet Union to gain some defense in depth, reduce the vulnerability of its Pacific maritime provinces, and project its own power further into Asia.[110]

The real difference between Wedemeyer and some military officers, on the one hand, and the State Department China experts, on the other, was that the former still hoped to dislodge Soviet-Communist influence in Manchuria, whereas the latter had abandoned all hope that the region was recoverable. Instead, the foreign service officers wanted to focus U.S. energies on staving off the Communists in central and southern China, which they deemed even more important to U.S. interests because of their proximity to Southeast Asia. Sprouse emphasized that U.S. economic aid should be focused south of the Yangtze and contiguous to Southeast Asia "to block the further expansion of communism both in China and in other parts of Asia." It was really important, according to the China experts in the State Department, that this area had remained outside the zone of the civil war and was relatively self-sufficient. Wedemeyer's economic consultants concluded, "A reform of the government in Central and South China, with improved living standards, some industrialization and sufficient strength to hold the barrier against encroachment from the North, may be a practicable long-run policy."[111]

U.S. policy in China during late 1947 and early 1948 cannot be understood unless it is realized that, despite CCP successes in Manchuria and northern China, diplomats still believed that the CCP could and should be contained in the rest of China. In December 1947, Lewis Clark, the U.S. minister-counselor, wrote his good friend Walton Butterworth, director of the Office of Far Eastern Affairs in the State Department, that "Manchuria was gone." But a month later he still reported that it might not be too late to salvage the situation in the rest of China. Virtually no one thought that the CCP had the capacity to consolidate its hold quickly over central and southern China. A principal factor shaping Kennan's views, for example, was his conviction "that the communists will probably not take over all of China and could not make a dangerous military power out of China if they did." [112]

Notwithstanding the myriad individuals and agencies that dealt with China, one man exerted the decisive influence on the evolution of U.S. policy: Secretary of State Marshall. [113] Marshall's experiences during his mission in 1946 and his expertise in military matters meant that almost everyone deferred to his point of view when he resolved what he wanted to do. He was acutely aware of the burgeoning demands on U.S. resources in Western Europe and the possible need to insert U.S. troops in Greece, Italy, or Palestine. He agreed with Kennan that China was an area of lesser importance because it was weak, impoverished, and technologically backward. He was convinced, moreover, that Chiang could not recover Manchuria and northern China. Marshall would have liked to establish ties with other anti-Communist factions in China if their success had seemed possible. But they were disorganized, demoralized, and repressed by Chiang's increasingly dictatorial rule. Marshall concluded, therefore, that Chiang's government had "to be retained in spite of our desire to change its character." [114]

Yet Marshall carefully avoided any all-out commitment to Chiang. [115] Marshall's aim was not so much to support the Nationalist regime as it was to prevent the Soviets from gaining control over all of China. The best means was a program of limited assistance that would stymie penetration of the regions beyond Manchuria and northern China. Marshall hoped that economic aid would alleviate misery and spawn reconstruction in areas outside the war zones. If Chiang's regime disintegrated, the United States might then be able to use its remaining influence to maneuver in behalf of local leaders or political factions that might emerge. [116]

Marshall's refusal to disengage from China was not based on domestic politics. Although influential senators and congressmen pressed the administration to augment support to the Nationalists and although they linked aid to China with assistance to Europe, they did not decisively shape administration policy toward China in 1947 and 1948. Their numbers were still small and they did not have substantial public support. More and more businessmen, journalists, and missionaries, disenchanted with Chiang, were ready to contemplate accommodation with the CCP. Truman and Marshall, as the historian Nancy Bernkopf Tucker has shown, might have tapped this reservoir of opinion if they had wanted to extricate the United

States from the Chinese quagmire.[117] But they could not abide the thought of a CCP victory.

From the time Wedemeyer returned from his mission, Marshall endorsed limited aid to contain Communist influence throughout China. Even before he was confronted by Congressman Walter Judd and other supporters of Chiang during the November 1947 hearings on emergency aid to Europe, the secretary of state decided to send additional military supplies to the Nationalists.[118] Later, he supported the use of U.S. advisers to improve the Nationalist logistical supply effort.[119] In February 1948, he proposed a program of $570 million in economic aid for China. Although this was only about 10 percent of the amount earmarked for Europe, it was a staggering sum for so unimportant a country and for so ineffective a government. In fact, the administration asked for more than Congress appropriated, although Congress did mandate, against Marshall's counsel, $125 million for military aid.[120]

Marshall's position perplexed Forrestal, Royall, and the chiefs of staff. They were not staunchly in favor of continued aid to Chiang. Military officials agreed with many aspects of Marshall's appraisal. In particular, they considered China to be much less important than Western Europe and the Middle East. Royall voiced skepticism about any further aid to the Nationalists, and Forrestal wondered whether Marshall's economic aid program made any sense. Forrestal kept pressing for a much-delayed NSC study of China. When it was finally completed, it had been overtaken by events: Congress had already passed the China Aid Act.[121]

The NSC report not only was belated but also failed to resolve the differences in the executive branch. The Army, Navy, Air Force, and JCS supported a program of assistance that included military aid while the State Department and the National Security Resources Board wanted aid to be limited to the economic sphere. NME representatives could not understand how the State Department could affirm its commitment to thwarting CCP inroads into China yet oppose military aid.[122] Still, this controversy did not mean that Pentagon officials were more inclined to side with the Nationalists. At meetings in June 1948 when tensions over Berlin and fears of embroilment in Palestine were high, Royall, Bradley, and Wedemeyer expressed even more reluctance than did Marshall about placing U.S. military advisers with Nationalist units. Royall, in fact, had the strongest misgivings and insisted that the NSC look again at the nation's China policy.[123]

But during the summer of 1948 no one was willing to change policy, break completely with Chiang, or work to establish a coalition government that would include the CCP. Although some State Department officials liked to emphasize the differences between military and civilian advice, disputes were quite minor.[124] The JCS, reiterating that a CCP victory would enhance Soviet influence throughout Asia and jeopardize U.S. national security, favored limited military aid yet recognized its futility.[125] The State Department again counseled against direct military intervention but did not offer a meaningful alternative. "It is unthinkable that U.S. aid would be withdrawn," snapped Butterworth. The Policy Planning Staff agreed. On 9 August

1948, Marshall instructed Royall that China should have a higher priority than Iran in receiving military aid and that many items of equipment should go to China even before Greece.[126]

In fact, the State Department had no policy if policy is defined as reconciling tactics and goals. Marshall, Lovett, and Kennan still did not know how to stave off a Communist victory with the limited resources available. Kennan sought to make a virtue out of necessity, derided the JCS desire for a clear course of action, and insisted that the administration should wait for the dust to settle. He argued powerfully that the United States not try to prevent Chiang's demise. China, he said, was too weak and poor to warrant additional assistance. Even if the Communists consolidated their power and remained in the Soviet orbit, which he doubted, he did not think that the Kremlin would gain significantly. Yet Kennan, even at this late date, was not calling for the suspension of diplomatic relations with Chiang's government, for the recognition of a coalition government, or for any accommodation with the CCP except on terms that would clearly meet U.S. requirements. In fact, he wanted "to see the Communists defeated and replaced in the territories they now occupy by other Chinese authorities not inspired or directed by any foreign government, and not animated by any basic hostility to this country." Like many of the economic experts in the State Department and the ECA, Kennan sought distance from Chiang but did not favor rapprochement with the CCP. Instead he desired to strengthen opposition groups that might arise as the CCP foundered upon the poverty, backwardness, and regionalism that he thought would remain endemic to China.[127]

Kennan and others wrote frequently about the possibilities of Chinese Titoism. A split between the Kremlin and the CCP might occur once the latter emerged victorious in the civil war. But officials were not willing to make policy on such an expectation or to incur the risks of trying to encourage a split. Truman and Lovett decided to withdraw economic aid from areas falling under CCP control lest it strengthen their position. Lovett repeatedly ordered Ambassador John Leighton Stuart to avoid discussion of a coalition government.[128] Despite all the rhetoric at the State Department about Chinese Titoism, the much-discussed flexibility was principally designed to maintain maneuverability among the different non-Communist factions and regional leaders that were expected to emerge.[129]

In the autumn of 1948, Truman and his advisers agonized one last time over whether the United States should intervene at Tsingtao to protect the Marine Force headquarters of the western Pacific fleet. Lovett and Kennan were against intervention. So were Forrestal, Royall, and Symington. But neither Lovett nor his friends in the Pentagon wanted to abandon China to the Communists. For the time being they saw no alternative but to avoid direct embroilment. They would wait to see how events would unfold, and they expected to witness a new era of warlordism.[130]

Events impelled them to look beyond China to the rest of Asia. "The peripheral consequences of a Communist success in China are perhaps more important than the situation in China itself," concluded the CIA in December 1948. Nothing could be done immediately to ameliorate the unfavorable trend in China. "But, on the periphery of China—in Korea, in Japan, and in Southeast Asia—possibilities still exist for attempting such a reversal." [131]

■

It was surprising that in Korea, as in China, U.S. officials continued to vest such importance in a country of acknowledged weakness and marginal importance. When Soviet-U.S. talks over trusteeship, economic unification, and a provisional government languished in the summer of 1947, south Koreans clamored for their independence. Rightist and leftist factions clashed, and political assassinations were common. The national police raided the headquarters of leftist parties, arrested some of their leaders, and forced many others into hiding. But repression did not breed stability or confidence. Fifth columnists were reported to be infiltrating from the north. There were rumors that the north Korean army might attack the south or support an uprising below the 38th parallel. General MacArthur informed Washington that the situation was most precarious. General Hodge, the U.S. military governor in southern Korea, pleaded with the JCS to devise a coherent long-term policy. Meanwhile, he wanted sufficient combat troops to preserve order. His superiors in Washington were well aware that Hodge's control was tenuous, that disorders might erupt, and that additional troops might be needed.[132]

The prospect of having to deploy additional troops to Korea when conditions in Greece, Italy, and Palestine were reaching emergency levels horrified Army and State Department officials. Korea, they had concluded, was not sufficiently important to warrant a substantial investment of money or personnel. Because U.S. war plans called for the withdrawal of troops from Korea in a global conflict, it did not make sense to retain forces there in peacetime. Logic dictated that the United States extricate itself from its Korean commitment. This conclusion seemed all the more inescapable because the occupation regime was a principal source of Korean discontent and instability.[133]

Policymakers in Washington, in fact, agreed that the United States should withdraw troops from Korea. But there was a critical caveat to this conclusion. Withdrawal had to take place in a way that would foreclose Soviet control of the entire peninsula. Toward the end of July 1947, Army officials decided that the best course was to hand the matter over to the United Nations; "this would afford one means whereby the United States could withdraw from Korea without incalculable loss of prestige and influence, and without abandoning Korea to Communism." [134] State Department officials concurred. By advocating U.N. intervention and calling for unification and free elections, the administration could enhance its prestige inside Korea. In early August an interagency ad hoc committee recommended that the United States "liquidate [its] commitment of men and money," but "without abandoning Korea to Soviet domination." Otherwise, "the resulting political repercussions would seriously damage U.S. prestige in the Far East and throughout the world, and would discourage those small nations now relying on the U.S. to support them in resisting internal or external Communist pressure." A few days later virtually every agency in the U.S. government dealing with Korean issues endorsed this idea.[135]

In August and September 1947, the United States moved decisively to place Korea on the U.N. agenda. By so doing, U.S. officials hoped to break the negotiating deadlock, regain the initiative, and appear as the champion of free elections, national independence, and Korean unity. On 17 October, Warren Austin, the U.S. ambassador to the United Nations, submitted proposals to the General Assembly. These envisioned internationally supervised elections in each zone, with the freely elected representatives forming a National Assembly that would select a provisional government. The south would have preponderant influence in this assembly because U.S. plans specified proportional representation, and south Koreans outnumbered north Koreans by approximately two to one. Even though the Soviets were unlikely to accept this proposal, its submission was a shrewd maneuver. It promised to defuse tension in southern Korea, ease the task of occupation officials, and set in motion the machinery to establish a provisional government in the U.S. zone of occupation. Both Hodge and his State Department political adviser, Joseph E. Jacobs, believed that widespread repression of the left made it an auspicious time to hold elections.[136]

The Soviet proposal for a mutual withdrawal of troops accentuated the pressures on U.S. officials. This idea, Jacobs wired Washington, "had immense popular appeal among Koreans." [137] Kennan thought that the Soviet suggestion offered a means to withdraw gracefully and to leave Koreans to their own fate. Everyone recognized that the United States could not remain as occupiers once the Soviets had evacuated. Nevertheless, the consensus was that the United States could not "scuttle and run." State Department officials sneered at Army leaders who were eager to redeploy troops from Korea to areas of greater importance. Marshall emphasized that withdrawal must not damage U.S. prestige.[138]

In April 1948 the NSC concluded, and the president approved, a new study of U.S. policy toward Korea. The goal was to establish a united, self-governing Korea with a viable economy. Troop withdrawal was a "derivative objective" to be undertaken "as soon as practicable consistent with the foregoing objectives." But since the Kremlin found U.S. proposals for unification and elections to be unacceptable (because they were designed to dislodge preeminent Soviet influence in all parts of Korea), the U.S. goal was now to create an independent south Korean government capable of functioning on its own. This was no easy task because of the "political immaturity of the Korean people," the dependency of the south Korean economy on U.S.-financed imports, and the need for electric power generated above the 38th parallel. The new country would also have to face possible attack from the north. Soviet troops were departing, but, according to U.S. officials, they were leaving behind an army of 125,000 soldiers and equipment that, however worn, remained usable.[139]

Once the elections were held, the United States recognized the new government that Syngman Rhee put together in August 1948. The Truman administration also arranged for the continuation of economic aid, including electric power from specially equipped naval vessels.[140] Despite persistent Army pressure for the quick evacuation of U.S. troops, Marshall, Lovett, and Butterworth insisted that the withdrawal proceed deliberately. South Korean forces, Marshall emphasized, must be built up to at least 50,000 men. They had to be properly trained, perhaps through direct recruitment into the U.S. Army. They also had to have equipment, arms, and ammunition for at least two years of normal operations. Accordingly, on 24 August, an interim military agreement was signed.[141] Marshall also supported the most comprehensive of the economic assistance options that had been designed by the State Department's Office of Occupation Affairs in conjunction with the ECA.[142]

The growing debacle in China encouraged U.S. officials to dig in their heels in Korea. "I feel we should stand firm everywhere on the Soviet perimeter, including Korea," Jacobs informed the State Department.[143] When John J. Muccio became the first U.S. ambassador to South Korea, he immediately endorsed Rhee's appeals for the retention of some U.S. troops to shore up the new government. Despite the Soviet withdrawal from North Korea, the State Department decided to postpone the complete evacuation of U.S. troops from the south for several additional months in order to provide some additional time for training. Marshall, in fact, told the Chinese foreign minister that the United States would not withdraw if an attack from the north seemed likely. The United States had no formal commitment to defend Korea, and the JCS and the Army were willing to abandon it, but the State Department would not sever the tie.[144]

By the end of 1948 the Asia experts in the State Department were insisting that Rhee's government must survive. Utilizing Kennan's geopolitical framework to define national security interests, they emphasized that "northeast Asia is one of the four or five significant power centers of the world." If the United States did not "face up to the problems in Korea," Japan might gravitate into the Kremlin's orbit and the entire U.S. position in the Pacific would be at risk. Such apocalyptic warnings and Marshall's apparent readiness to hedge the future course of American policy toward Korea meant that the U.S. commitment was far from over.[145]

Japan and Southeast Asia

The disintegration of the Nationalist regime in China and the uncertain future of South Korea accentuated American interest in Japan and Southeast Asia. (See Map 8.) U.S. policymakers feared that if they did not successfully rehabilitate and stabilize Japan and provide markets and raw materials for its economy, then that nation, too, might eventually be co-opted into the Soviet sphere. "Our primary goal," Kennan emphasized in January 1948, is to insure that our security "must never again be threatened by the mobilization against us of the complete industrial area [in the Far East] as it was during the second world war."[146]

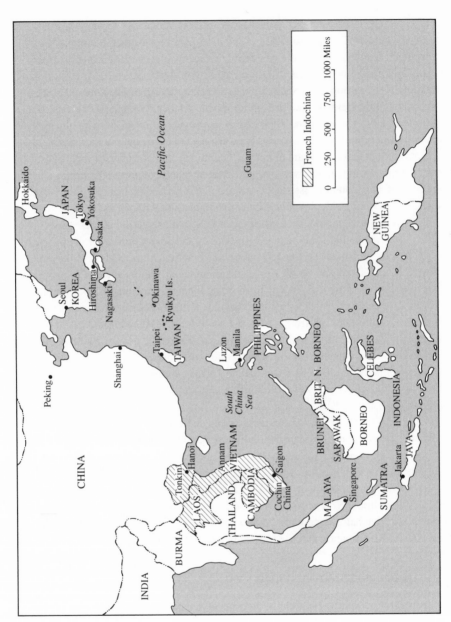

8. East and Southeast Asia, 1948

Kennan insisted that the United States must not negotiate a peace treaty with Japan until assured that a sovereign Japanese government would remain friendly. In August 1947 he and his assistant, John Paton Davies, had read a draft treaty that was being prepared in the Office of Northeast Asian Affairs. They were appalled by the emphasis on disarmament, democratization, and international supervision. When they brought this to Lovett's attention, the undersecretary authorized the Policy Planning Staff to design the criteria for the peace settlement. Lovett, however, did not rule out the possibility of an early treaty. Like many of the Far East experts in the State Department, he believed that a prompt settlement might win Japanese goodwill and unleash the forces of economic recovery.[147]

Kennan consulted with defense officials. Admiral Nimitz, chief of naval operations, doubted the wisdom of demilitarizing Japan and wanted the United States to retain forces within designated base areas. Beyond Japan, the JCS reaffirmed the importance of retaining a strategic trusteeship over the Ryukyu Islands. U.S. bases at Okinawa were still deemed essential to project American power throughout Northeast Asia. On the other hand, Army officials in the Civil Affairs Division, who were responsible for occupation policy and sensitive to internal Japanese developments, emphasized that it was most important to take steps to insure that a future autonomous Japan would choose alignment with the United States.[148]

The Policy Planning Staff considered this latter criterion to be most important: "Japan cannot possess an independent destiny. It can function only as an American or Soviet satellite." Because Japan occupied a strategically critical position between the United States and the Soviet Union and had the largest industrial plant and body of skilled workers in Asia, it was essential to prevent its co-optation by the Kremlin. The essential goal of any peace treaty must be to bring about a stable Japan amenable to U.S. leadership in foreign affairs.[149]

In mid-October, Kennan presented his conclusions to Lovett. More information was needed to determine whether Japan could survive on its own, so he suggested that someone from the State Department consult with General MacArthur. But he made clear that, although advantages might accrue from an early peace, the risks outweighed them. Once a treaty was signed, political controls would have to be lifted, and Moscow-controlled Communists would seek to dominate Japanese political life. Japan's fortunes would then depend on its political stability, which would be greatly influenced by economic conditions:

It is clear that with the loss of a certain portion of its economic substance, with the loss of its markets and raw material sources in Soviet-dominated portions of the mainland, with highly unstable conditions prevailing in China, in Indonesia, in Indochina, and in India, and with no certainty as to the resumption of certain traditional exports to the dollar area, Japan faces, even in the best of circumstances, an economic problem of extremely serious dimensions.

Before embarking on a peace settlement, Kennan wanted to determine whether Japan could successfully meet this future challenge.[150]

Undersecretary of the Army Draper and his subordinates in the Civil Affairs Division sympathized with Kennan's analysis. The Japanese economy was operating at only about 40 percent of its 1930–34 average, and the trade deficit was over $300 million annually. Draper wanted to expedite recovery and make it the main objective of occupation policy. He hoped Kennan would persuade the Far East specialists at the State Department to resist the reparation demands of Japan's former enemies. Because U.S. taxpayers and Congress would not subsidize the Japanese economy indefinitely, Army officials desired to make Japan self-supporting as soon as possible.[151]

They also wanted to stop reforming the Japanese economy. Encouraged by a small group of journalists, former Japan experts in the State Department, and big business interests, Royall and Draper vehemently opposed the industrial deconcentration ordinance that MacArthur was pushing through the Japanese Diet. They believed it would paralyze Japanese business investment and stymie recovery. When Lovett mildly defended MacArthur's program, Royall retorted that he was dissatisfied with the entire course of economic policy. At an NSC meeting on 17 December 1947, Forrestal, too, lambasted MacArthur's policies and called for a thorough reassessment of the occupation.[152]

By the end of 1947, policymakers agreed that if Japan were to be aligned with the United States, its economy had to be rehabilitated. Like in Europe, the Soviet threat was not a military one. It was based on the prospective paralysis of the Japanese economy, the destabilization of Japanese society, and the fragility of democratic institutions. The post-treaty and post-occupation Japanese government would have to be able to stifle internal subversion, preserve domestic order, and resist inducements to join the Communist economic orbit. Successful economic reconstruction, therefore, was indispensable to preserve a favorable balance of power. Although tactical decisions might be influenced by economic and financial interest groups, the objectives were primarily geopolitical and strategic.[153]

Implementation of the policy posed tough problems. MacArthur had to be coaxed into going along. The allies, who wanted large reparations and who feared the reconstitution of latent Japanese power, also had to be brought into line. Finally, Congress had to be persuaded to appropriate the additional dollars necessary to procure the foodstuffs and raw materials for the Japanese economy. Draper arranged a new legislative package. He also organized a mission under Percy Johnston to take another look at Japan's level of industry and its reparations burden. At the same time, in February 1948, Kennan traveled to Tokyo to consult with MacArthur. He wanted to gather information for the treaty he was designing and lay the basis for the reverse-course policy that he and the Army had been pressing for.[154]

Kennan's trip confirmed his predilections. When he returned, he wrote the basic paper that set the course of U.S. policy. He argued that the peace treaty should be delayed. Japan was not yet ready for independence. Its economy was too weak, its institutions too vulnerable to internal subversion. The United States should use the time afforded by Soviet and Chinese opposition to a peace settlement to prepare Japan for the future. Occupation policy should emphasize reconstruction over reform. The decartelization program should be weakened, the purges should be halted, and reparations transfers should be quickly carried out so that they no longer constrained recovery. Occupation forces should be reduced, costs cut, and responsibility relinquished to the Japanese themselves, whose police forces had to be strengthened. The treaty, when negotiated, should be nonpunitive.[155]

Japan and the Philippines, Kennan concluded, were far more critical to overall U.S. strategic interests in the Pacific than anything on the Asian mainland. Yet the United States might not need to retain bases indefinitely in these countries, either. Recapitulating much that MacArthur had said, Kennan stressed the utility of an off-shore security perimeter embracing the Aleutians, the Ryukyus, the former Japanese mandates, and Guam. Okinawa, he agreed, was critical for the deployment of American air power. Kennan advised that U.S. forces should remain in Japan at least until the peace treaty.

Kennan's general prescriptions contained several important caveats. He emphasized that Japan must be made invulnerable to economic stagnation, political subversion, and Soviet intimidation. The United States, therefore, not only had to guarantee Japanese security but also had to find markets and raw materials for its economy. Kennan knew only too well that Japan could not prosper unless its foreign trade flourished. And since that trade would have to be with the Asian mainland or with Southeast Asia, America's own security interests, in fact, gravitated beyond the so-called security perimeter.[156]

Kennan's proposals won widespread favor within the State Department, the Army, and the NME. His support for a strategic trusteeship over Okinawa and commercial facilities for the Navy at Yokosuka met the minimum demands of the military services.[157] Forrestal, Royall, and Draper wondered whether Japan needed limited defense forces to preserve order and deter aggression but tentatively concluded that they would be too great a burden on the Japanese economy, incompatible with the Japanese constitution, and unacceptable to most Far Eastern nations. Because Kennan provided for the retention of U.S. forces until the peace settlement and hedged what would occur thereafter, narrowly defined military and security issues were not nearly so pressing as were the economic ones.[158]

Throughout the spring of 1948, Draper and the State Department worked to convince Congress that the United States should infuse additional dollars into Japan, almost $500 million in fiscal year 1949, to revive its economy as well as to avert disease and unrest. Even General MacArthur, who had resisted the reverse-course policy, was now much more ready to harmonize his industrial deconcentration policies with the requirements of Japanese recovery. In August 1948, moreover, he forbade government workers from striking and encouraged the arrest of Communist agitators. Thereafter, he increasingly aligned the occupation's labor policies with the administration's stress on economic reconstruction.[159]

The Army and the State Department remained divided on one critical issue. Royall and Draper, wanting to reconcile reparations policy with the new stress on Japanese rehabilitation, pressed Marshall and Lovett to accept the recommendations of the Johnston Report. It maintained that the level of industry had to be considerably higher than anticipated and that reparation payments had to be scaled down. Kennan did not disagree, but officials in most other divisions in the State Department objected strenuously. Their opposition was tactical: a rise in Japan's level of industry would alarm and alienate allies in the Far East Commission. Royall and Draper dismissed these considerations. They were not worried about Japan's war potential. After several months of wrangling, Marshall acceded to the Army's position. In September and October 1948, the NSC and Truman approved a policy that focused on the rehabilitation of the Japanese economy, the postponement of a peace settlement, and the indefinite retention of some U.S. forces.[160]

Lovett wanted MacArthur to implement the new policy and not worry about securing the approval of the Far East Commission.[161] He was exceedingly concerned that prospective Soviet control over Manchuria, northern China, and perhaps all of Korea "might enable the USSR to tie Japan economically to the Soviet Far East, a development that would have obvious political implications." [162] In December 1948, the administration instructed MacArthur to implement a stabilization program worked out in Washington. Almost immediately, however, he remonstrated that its success depended on a U.S. aid package for Asia and on conditions in the Far East that would permit the expansion of Japanese trade.[163]

■

As historians Michael Schaller, William S. Borden, and Andrew J. Rotter have shown, policymakers recognized that a reconstruction program in East Asia depended on Japan gaining access to Far Eastern markets. "Without a market for Japanese goods in the Far East," the Army informed the NSC, "the economic recovery of Japan is most difficult—if not impossible." [164] But critical areas of Southeast Asia were wracked with instability at the same time that chunks of Northeast Asia were falling under the control of Korean and Chinese Communists. "The gravest danger to the US," concluded the CIA, "is that friction engendered by [anticolonialism and economic nationalism] may drive the so-called colonial bloc into alignment with the USSR." [165] As much as they sympathized with the goal of self-determination, U.S. officials could not allow Western influence to be excised from Southeast Asia. Their aim was to coax European governments into co-opting rather than fighting moderate nationalism. A balance had to be struck between "supporting local nationalist aspirations and maintaining the colonial economic interests of countries to whom aid has been pledged in Western Europe." [166]

There was no inclination, however, to deal with nationalist movements captured by Communists. During 1948 U.S. diplomats in Indochina reported that Ho Chi Minh's Communist-dominated Viet Minh had the overwhelming support of the local population. Ho "is the strongest and perhaps the ablest figure in Indochina," acknowledged the State Department. The French could not defeat him militarily. Yet Marshall kept inquiring whether Ho was tied to Moscow. The evidence remained inconclusive. But because Ho desired to evict the French, his triumph portended imponderables of an unacceptable kind. Marshall prodded the French to find moderate alternatives. Substantial powers should be ceded to them, rather than to Ho, in order to avert the "emergence of a state probably dominated by communists and almost certainly oriented toward Moscow." [167]

State Department officials focused on the Tito-Stalin split and speculated about Chinese Titoism, but their policy continued to be based on the assumption that the Kremlin would profit from Communist gains anywhere. Even the regional experts in the State Department who were most sympathetic to the aspirations of indigenous peoples talked about Asian nationalism and Orientalism in ways that revealed their antipathy to any development that removed Southeast Asia from its traditional subordination.[168]

■

Fear of communism also inspired U.S. officials to take an increasingly active role in mediating the struggle between the Dutch and the leaders of the Indonesian Republic, Mohammed Hatta and Sukarno. Two developments especially agitated U.S. policymakers. In the spring of 1948, the Kremlin signed an agreement to open consular relations with the Indonesian Republic, although the Dutch had still not recognized its independence.[169] Then, in September 1948, a leftist-Communist revolt against Hatta and Sukarno erupted, confirming U.S. fears that Dutch intransigence might throw Indonesian nationalism into the hands of the left. Marshall and Lovett encouraged the Dutch to strengthen Indonesian moderates by signing a political accord with them. At the same time the Americans informed Hatta and Sukarno that the insurrection provided an opportunity to crush the Communists and demonstrate their moderate credentials.[170]

U.S. concerns mounted as it became clear that Holland's failure to meet the legitimate demands of Hatta and Sukarno would destroy its reputation and credibility. The State Department designed a draft agreement and pleaded with the Dutch to accept it. The accord, in the U.S. view, provided for concessions that would bolster moderate nationalists without impairing the "essential interests" of the Dutch. Yet a political crisis in Holland thwarted progress. In December the Dutch resorted once again to military force.[171]

U.S. officials were unable to resolve the crisis. Lovett suspended transfer of almost $80 million in Marshall Plan funds earmarked for the Netherlands East Indies for fiscal year 1949, but the Dutch were unmoved; their vital interests were at risk. Besides, they knew that U.S. sanctions were circumscribed by Lovett's determination to avoid jeopardizing Dutch collaboration in the European phases of the Marshall Plan.[172]

The episode underscored the incapacity of the United States to bring about a settlement with the diplomatic and economic instruments at hand. U.S. officials had to reconsider whether they could rely on European governments to follow their enlightened self-interest and to make intelligent compromises to preserve Western control over areas of major interest. The United States itself might have to play a more assertive role, but whether it could do so with existing capabilities was questionable.[173]

The issue was by no means an academic one. "Curiously enough," Kennan wrote Marshall and Lovett in December 1948, "the most crucial issue of the moment in our struggle with the Kremlin is probably the problem of Indonesia." Failure to recognize the sovereignty of the Indonesian Republic would undermine the moderates, create chaos, and insure a Communist victory. A Communist Indonesia would consolidate Communist control over all of Indochina and Southeast Asia. "The train of events which would follow chaos in Indonesia would therefore likely lead to a bisecting of the world from Siberia to Sumatra." The East-West global communications network of the United States would be vulnerable; Australia would be exposed; "and it would be only a matter of time before the infection would sweep westward through the continent to Burma, India and Pakistan." [174]

There was no finely textured analysis here of the prospects for divisions within the Communist world and of the differences between vital and peripheral areas.[175] Kennan did occasionally say that Titoism might spread to Southeast Asia, and he did occasionally insist that nothing on the mainland was absolutely vital. But when it came to policy, Kennan was ready neither to reach out to Asian Communists nor to walk away from Southeast Asia. Although European political tutelage over the region was ending, European economies still depended on their former colonies. Furthermore, Japanese reconstruction, the fulcrum of power in Northeast Asia, appeared to depend on the retention of Southeast Asian raw materials and markets. Kennan wrote:

Indonesia is the anchor in that chain of islands stretching from Hokkaido to Sumatra which we should develop as a politico-economic counter-force to communism on the Asiatic land mass and as base areas from which, in case of necessity, we could with our air and sea power dominate continental East Asia and South Asia. If we are to hold the Malayan beachhead and the Siamese salient on a more or less unfriendly Asia, they must have at their rear a friendly Indonesia.[176]

The Dilemma of Means and Ends

From Western Europe to the Middle East to Japan and Southeast Asia, U.S. officials continued to contain the influence of Soviet-directed world communism and the appeal of revolutionary nationalism. Even in Korea the United States hesitated to withdraw, and, in China, it refused to accede to any Communist participation in a coalition government. Policymakers had made considerable headway in defining

Western Europe and Japan as priorities, for they contained great industrial and military potential that, if absorbed by the Kremlin, would add greatly to future Soviet power. But the definition of priorities did not mean that other areas became less important. In fact, the definition of priorities accentuated the importance of peripheral areas, like the Middle East and Southeast Asia, which, although not quite so crucial as the core regions, were nevertheless considered indispensable for the successful reconstruction of Western Europe and Japan.

The re-creation of power centers in Western Europe and Northeast Asia that would be viable, stable, integrated, and amenable to U.S. leadership constituted a goal of enormous proportions. But U.S. officials could pursue nothing less because they saw themselves locked in a titanic struggle with a hostile totalitarian nation that was intent on exploiting unrest for its own self-aggrandizement. Exaggerating the appeal of Marxist-Leninist doctrine, U.S. policymakers believed that the Soviet Union possessed an ideology that was attractive both to the war-weary and dispirited peoples of Europe and Asia and to the exploited and impoverished peoples of the underdeveloped world. In Washington's view, the Soviet threat still resided primarily in Stalin's capacity to control Communist parties that might capture or win power in the industrialized world and in his ability to benefit from the dislodgment of European rule in Asia and Africa. The Kremlin's penetration of the Third World, like its domination of Eastern Europe and its control over Communist parties in the Western world, rendered it capable of exerting economic leverage over core regions of industrial power and, with time, seducing them into the Kremlin's politico-economic orbit.[177]

U.S. officials, therefore, were more concerned with social, political, and economic developments outside of the Soviet Union than with events in Russia. During 1947 and 1948 factional strife within the Kremlin intensified. After launching a successful ideological crusade to cleanse the country, A. A. Zhadanov's party revivalists were themselves purged. Their close ties to Tito proved a liability as did their support for insurrectionary activity beyond the Soviet sphere. Stalin now seemed most determined to crack down on potential dissidents within his own orbit, while Zhadanov's former enemies maneuvered to recapture the influence that had eluded them during the preceding eighteen months. The meaning of this political infighting for the international configuration of power was hard to discern then and remains subject to much speculation today.[178]

However, U.S. intelligence analysts continued to monitor developments within the Soviet military establishment. They did not see anything alarming. There appeared to be no great increase in Soviet military expenditures, no startling developments in Soviet air power, and no unusual buildup of conventional forces. Soviet military progress was viewed as normal. The Kremlin, of course, strove to develop atomic capabilities but was unlikely to do so until the early 1950's. The Soviets still had no military ability to strike across the oceans, and their economic capacity to wage protracted war was incomparably less than that of the United States. Officials in the Pentagon as well as in the CIA and the State Department continued to believe that the Kremlin would not purposefully embark on military aggression and risk war with the United States.[179]

Nor was Soviet diplomatic behavior especially threatening. In fact, U.S. officials prided themselves on having taken the offensive in Europe. Efforts to implement the Marshall Plan and the London agreements on Germany had thrown the Kremlin on the defensive.[180] In the view of U.S. policymakers these initiatives had sparked discord and unrest in the Soviet orbit, as illustrated by the defection of Tito. In response, the Russians seemed to be consolidating their hold in Eastern Europe, writing off Western Europe, and reorienting their diplomatic priorities.[181]

Outside of Europe, however, Soviet actions were more timid and opportunistic than bold and adventuresome. In Japan, aside from their rhetorical campaign to restore peaceful industries, Soviet officials deferred to U.S. occupation authorities. The Russians may have hoped to lure Japan into their orbit as Communists triumphed in China and Korea.[182] Yet Americans saw scant evidence of Soviet support of the CCP during the closing phases of the civil war.[183] Moreover, while the Kremlin aided the establishment of a Communist government in North Korea and provided it with military aid, the Soviets decided to withdraw their own forces from the Korean peninsula despite its strategic proximity to their own Far Eastern provinces.[184] Elsewhere in Asia, U.S. officials deplored the establishment of consular relations between the Kremlin and several countries and ridiculed Soviet propaganda forays, espionage activities, and occasional commercial deals. But no American thought these actions were responsible for the chaos that wracked Indochina, the Dutch East Indies, Malaya, and Burma. What worried Americans was the potential of the Kremlin to capitalize on events that they really did not control.[185] The same was true in the Middle East, where the Soviets faced some of the same agonizing choices as did Western diplomats and threw in their lot initially with the Israelis, thereby sacrificing any immediate chance of capitalizing on Arab anger with the United States.[186]

Although the Soviets were not engaged in a rapid military buildup and although they acted cautiously in Asia and the Middle East, policymakers could not rule out the use of U.S. military force. State Department officials insisted that the JCS plan for the deployment of troops to the Middle East, and Marshall and Lovett delayed the withdrawal of forces from Korea. But developments in Germany most clearly illustrated the connections between political and economic initiatives and the use of military capabilities. Civilian and military officials knew that the London accords were designed to co-opt the latent economic power of western Germany for the European Recovery Program and the North Atlantic community, then in its formative stages. Although the Soviet blockade was perceived as defensive, it was nevertheless provocative because U.S. officials could not repudiate the London agreements or abandon Berlin without compromising U.S. credibility. Truman, Marshall, and Lovett, therefore, assigned additional military assets to the airlift, despite the risks and costs, because it was essential to the success of their overall diplomacy.[187]

Faced with growing commitments that might necessitate the use of force and immersed in a crisis whose resolution might depend on the application of military power, Forrestal grew increasingly agitated by the $15 billion ceiling that Truman imposed on the NME for fiscal year 1950. This limitation meant that the services would have to reduce forces from anticipated levels, and they protested bitterly. Naturally, they were protecting their institutional self-interest, but they were also raising issues of compelling importance. They did not have the capacity to insert a peacekeeping force into the Middle East, retain troops in Korea, carry on the Berlin airlift, respond to any deteriorating conditions in Greece and Italy, and implement the basic undertakings of their war plans. The JCS claimed that the emergency war plan FLEETWOOD could not be implemented because the United States could not hold the Mediterranean and launch the strategic bombing attack from the Middle East.[188]

Forrestal, the services, and the JCS were not challenging the national security objectives of the administration; nor were they questioning the State Department view that the primary threats to U.S. goals were economic and political. They were reiterating, ever more stridently, that indiscriminate commitments in unstable areas placed growing importance on deployable forces they simply did not have. They might have overcome this problem by placing more importance on readying forces for limited conflict, but, still mesmerized by the World War II experience, they considered preparations for waging total war to be essential. Conflict with the Soviet Union did seem to be more possible, although it was still improbable. The Marshall Plan, the London accords, the North Atlantic Treaty, the reverse-course policy in Japan, and the anticipated military assistance program accentuated tensions. However necessary these initiatives were, they subjected the Soviets to real strains, vested U.S. prestige in diverse areas of the globe, and increased the possibilities of an accidental war or a war by miscalculation, which the military felt the nation was unprepared to fight.

Forrestal and the JCS wanted to force the State Department and the president to face the implications of their national security conception. The defense secretary waited for months for the basic study he had requested on goals, threats, and programs. But the NSC staff was not equipped for such a comprehensive exercise, and Kennan hated to write papers of this sort, which in his view demanded an elucidation of imponderables that defied close analysis. In October, not having received any guidance from the State Department, faced with a budget deadline, and under unbearable pressures from the services, Forrestal decided to submit a basic question to Marshall and Lovett that was intended to align them with the NME against the $15 billion ceiling. Over the last few months, he inquired, had the international situation changed in ways that would warrant an actual decrease in force levels?[189]

State Department officials loathed Forrestal's effort to embroil them in the

NME's dispute with the White House. Yet they acknowledged that the international situation had not improved and that reductions in force were not warranted. Although these admissions meant that they agreed that the budget ceiling was unwise, they would not join Forrestal in a campaign to break through the limitation. Marshall felt that the military budget would be held captive to domestic fiscal priorities and internal politics. He was willing to accede to these realities and accept the inherent risks so long as the United States retained its atomic monopoly. He believed that Soviet fear of the bomb constituted a decisive deterrent, enabling the United States to carry through its major initiatives in Europe, including the airlift, without precipitating military hostilities. Moreover, he felt that a military assistance program for Europe would prove more efficacious than a buildup of U.S. military forces.[190]

Essentially, this debate was over the nature of acceptable risks and the delineation of desirable tactics, not over the conception of national security objectives or the definition of the threat. The budget constrained options and forced policymakers to make agonizing choices. Forrestal did appreciate the need to preserve a healthy domestic economy, but he more than anyone else knew about and, in case of an emergency, would be held responsible for the gap between goals and tactics. He told Truman that the $15 billion budget was incompatible with U.S. war plans and commitments. He recommended appropriations of close to $17 billion, a sum considerably less than the JCS and the services deemed appropriate. Nevertheless, he thought it might enable the United States to hold the Mediterranean, launch a bombing attack from the Middle East or North Africa, and activate FLEETWOOD. In December, Truman categorically dismissed his recommendations.[191]

Ironically, just as the State Department was rebuffing Forrestal's overtures for support and Truman was rejecting his budgetary recommendations, the NSC finally completed the study that he had requested in July. The report, "U.S. Objectives with Respect to the USSR," reiterated the now-familiar shibboleths of national security policy. The great fear pertained to "Soviet domination of the potential power of Eurasia." The aim of U.S. policy was to "reduce the power and influence of the USSR to limits which no longer constitute a threat to the peace, national independence and stability of the world family of nations." The study offered no clear definition of objectives, no lucid definition of priorities, no assessments of the attributes and weaknesses of various tactics, and no insight into the opportunities generated by prospective rifts within the Communist world. Indeed, NSC 20/4 embodied the core ingredients of U.S. national security policy: globalism and anticommunism. Despite the gap between means and ends that the budgetary conundrum compelled, Forrestal had no difficulty approving this report. He had no desire to force his colleagues to scale down objectives in order to keep them in line with capabilities.[192]

Most important, Truman himself endorsed NSC 20/4. In so doing, he reaffirmed the expansive goals he had been pursuing. In the wake of his electrifying victory against Dewey, Truman had the chance to force subordinates to reexamine basic goals and assumptions. Dewey's essential bipartisanship on foreign policy had allowed Truman to retain considerable freedom of action. Truman now might have seized the initiative before the Republican right attacked his administration for its alleged softness in fighting communism in Asia. He did not do so, for he believed in the global struggle to contain communism and found papers like NSC 20/4 compatible with his fundamental beliefs.[193]

Truman had no interest in the details of formulating national security goals and tactics. He did like to immerse himself in budgetary details. He had an abiding faith in the desirability of a balanced budget and an instinctive suspicion that the military wanted every nickel it could get without regard for the importance of fiscal priorities. So at one and the same time Truman vetoed Forrestal's budget and sanctioned NSC 20/4, perpetuating the gap between means and ends. In the future, this gap would not only beleaguer his foreign policy but would also play into the hands of his domestic opponents, whose bile was mounting as they licked their wounds from their 1948 defeat.

Acheson Takes Command,
November 1948-September 1949

President Truman had every reason to exult in his reelection. Hardly anyone but he thought victory was possible. His abiding faith in the rectitude of his policies and his competitive drive impelled him to wage his campaign with a zeal that inspired his subordinates and won the appreciation of the American electorate. Truman showed himself to be a fighter: against the special interests, against the do-nothing 80th Congress, against inflation, against the Hoover Republicans who had brought on the Depression, and against the forces of totalitarian communism. He also knew what he was for: helping ordinary farmers, workers, and blacks; balancing the budget; fostering prosperity; and containing communism. Not only did he eke out a victory for himself, but he helped restore control of both houses of Congress to the Democratic Party.

In preparing for his new administration, Truman emphasized continuity. Except for the smooth transition to new leadership in the State Department, there were no immediate shake-ups in the cabinet or the White House staff. There was an effort to inject the key themes of the campaign into the new administration. In his State of the Union message on 5 January 1949, Truman called for a Fair Deal: for continued price supports for the farmer, for higher minimum wage and social security benefits for the worker, and for fairer treatment for black Americans. The federal government, he said, should support education, improve medical care, subsidize housing, and eliminate slums. Yet it must also maintain a balanced budget and restrain inflation.[1]

Two weeks later, in his inaugural address, the president reaffirmed his global struggle against communism. Communism was a false philosophy:

[It is] based on the belief that man is so weak and inadequate that he is unable to govern himself and therefore requires the rule of strong masters. . . . Communism subjects the individual to arrest without lawful cause, punishment without trial, and forced labor as the chattel of the state. It decrees what information he shall receive, what art he shall produce, what leaders he shall follow, and what thoughts he shall think. . . . Communism maintains that social wrongs can be corrected only by violence. . . . Communism holds that the world is so widely divided into opposing classes that war is inevitable.

As the champion of the democratic world, the United States sought no territory and no privileges but was dedicated to the pursuit of peace, the liberalization of trade, the reconstruction of the international economy, and the promotion of liberty.[2]

This inaugural address was infused with the same ideological fervor that had permeated the Truman Doctrine address two years before. But now the president could speak with a buoyancy and self-confidence that had been inconceivable in March 1947. Despite the problems besetting U.S. policy in Asia and the Middle East, the most salient development in the international system was the ongoing recovery of Western Europe. Truman was not shy about taking credit for it: "Our efforts have brought new hope to all mankind. We have beaten back despair and defeatism. We have saved a number of countries from losing their liberty." [3]

And Truman was determined to move ahead, everywhere. "The initiative is ours," he declared. His administration would support the United Nations, promote world economic recovery, strengthen "freedom-loving nations against the dangers of aggression," and launch "a bold new program for making the benefits of our scientific advances and industrial progress available for the improvement and growth of underdeveloped areas." Through these four courses of action, the United States would "create the conditions that will lead eventually to personal freedom and happiness for all mankind." [4]

There was no self-restraint here. Truman saw himself as the leader of the free world, fighting evil much as the United States had done in the struggle against Nazism, fascism, and Japanese militarism during World War II. He was aware of the constraints his foreign policies placed on his Fair Deal, but this was a small price to pay when the nation's core values were at risk. Truman saw himself struggling to safeguard the nation's security and its free political economy. He implored the American people to support internationalism. For Truman, as for many of his contemporaries, isolationism had been responsible for the spread of the Depression, the rise of totalitarianism, the appeasement of the Axis powers, and the attack on Pearl Harbor. The United States, he believed, had the power to prevent the recurrence of these horrifying developments. His task was to mobilize the nation's will and to galvanize its energy. The rhetoric of anticommunism could rally the American people behind his initiatives. It also illuminated the core values of liberalism and capitalism that he hoped to preserve at home by forging a configuration of power in the international system that was preponderantly in America's favor.

If he failed he knew he would be excoriated. He would be assailed for having lost the struggle between tyranny and freedom, for this was how he liked to characterize the stakes. Had he not scorned Henry Wallace "and his Communists"? Had he not charged that a Republican victory would be welcomed by the Soviets? Had he not declared that the Democrats would never "get out of Europe or Asia" or withdraw aid from China? So Truman invited his domestic opponents to judge him by the success of his global policies.[5]

The Administrative Setup

Soon after his reelection, Truman asked former undersecretary of state Dean Acheson to return to government service and take charge of the department. George Marshall was too ill to continue, and Robert Lovett sought to return to the private sector. The president vividly recollected Acheson's personal loyalty after the Democrats' humiliating defeat in the 1946 congressional elections. Truman also knew that he could work comfortably with Acheson since he had done so when Acheson had been the number-two man in the department under James Byrnes. Truman greatly respected Acheson's intellect and competence. He also knew that Acheson would not seek to usurp his authority, as had Byrnes, or ridicule his partisanship, as had Marshall. Ironically, in view of what later occurred, Truman also hoped that Acheson would capitalize on his previous experience as the State Department's liaison with Congress and build a solid relationship with the legislative branch. Significantly, when Truman offered Acheson the position, he spent no time discussing the substance of policy. He entrusted Acheson with the conceptualization and implementation of policy, knowing full well that Acheson shared his commitment to the worldwide struggle against communism.[6]

Truman, however, did ask Acheson to take James Webb as his undersecretary of state. Shrewdly, Acheson jumped at this opportunity. Webb, having served as head of the Budget Bureau, had established a close relationship with the president and his staff. Not only was he viewed as a brilliant administrator, but White House insiders also knew that he had tried to constrain the influence of the National Military Establishment (NME) and to maintain civilian control over atomic energy.[7] With Webb's help, Acheson believed he could retain Truman's confidence, organize the State Department effectively, and institutionalize its role as leader of the competing bureaucracies dealing with international issues.[8]

Acheson recognized that Truman had little desire to control foreign policy. Having observed Byrnes's relationship with Truman, Acheson had learned that, so long as he kept the president well informed about his initiatives, Truman would give him wide discretion. From the outset, Acheson and Webb met regularly with the president. They carefully delineated major issues, submitted brief memoranda on the State Department's position, and demonstrated a willingness to harmonize their program with Truman's domestic concerns. Truman almost always followed the advice of Acheson and Webb, although occasionally his instinct was to take a much tougher attitude toward the Chinese Communists. Acheson (and Webb) almost never discussed fundamental objectives with the president. Nor did they reappraise Soviet intentions and capabilities. The discussions focused on program-matic efforts to achieve European integration, alleviate the dollar gap, and limit the negative diplomatic and political fallout from developments in China.[9]

Within the State Department, Acheson sought to clarify lines of command and to expedite decisionmaking. He relied on Webb and Deputy Undersecretary John Peurifoy to run the department. He looked to Dean Rusk to oversee the department's substantive issues. He retained George Kennan as director of the Policy Planning Staff, asked Adrian Fisher to be his legal adviser, and invited Philip C. Jessup to join the administration as an ambassador at large.[10] Below this top layer of the depart-ment, Acheson brought together an able group of assistant secretaries. George W. Perkins took over the Office of European Affairs; W. Walton Butterworth remained at the head of Far Eastern affairs; John D. Hickerson went over to U.N. affairs; George McGhee moved up to run the Office of Near Eastern and African Affairs; Willard Thorp remained at the helm of economic affairs; Edward G. Miller ran inter-American affairs; and Ernest Gross oversaw congressional relations. Acheson met daily with his top assistants. Webb, too, instituted staff meetings on Monday, Wednesday, and Friday mornings. The minutes of these initial months of meet-ings reveal the extensive influence of Rusk, Jessup, Kennan, and Counselor Charles Bohlen and the growing stature of economic experts like Thorp and Paul Nitze. So high was Acheson's regard for Jessup that he wanted Jessup treated as if he were on a level comparable to the secretary of state himself. Kennan, however, grew disaffected, believing that Acheson was downgrading the Policy Planning Staff and permitting operations officers to act independently of the planners' advice.[11]

At the onset of Acheson's stewardship, however, Kennan urged the secretary to move aggressively against bureaucratic interlopers and to improve coordination at the top rungs of the department. He deeply resented the power of occupation officials and the influence of the Economic Cooperation Administration (ECA). He wanted Acheson and Webb to gain control over the formulation, if not the imple-mentation, of German policy. He encouraged them to thwart the NME's attempts, as he interpreted them, to use the National Security Council (NSC) as a super-agency to make foreign policy.[12]

Acheson and Webb needed little prodding. They knew their subordinates had grown weary of the endless bureaucratic and tactical disputes. At the end of Janu-ary 1949, Acheson told Truman that the State Department should take charge of German policy. When formal military government ended in the spring, Truman in-structed the new high commissioner for Germany to report to the secretary of state. Top officials at Foggy Bottom also insisted that the new Military Assistance Pro-gram should not be established under a separate agency like the ECA but should be kept within the control of the State Department. In April, on the advice of Webb's former associates at the Budget Bureau, Truman decided to continue the interagency (State, NME, ECA) setup, operating as the Foreign Assistance Correlation Com-mittee, and to place it under Acheson's supervision. Webb also devised new working relationships with the NSC. The role of the NSC staff was downgraded, and the preeminent position of the State Department was recognized.[13]

So long as they were in control of policy, Acheson and Webb wanted to work out a constructive relationship with the NME. When Louis Johnson succeeded James Forrestal in March 1949, Webb asked the new secretary of defense to continue the practice of having the State Department's leading Kremlinologists brief the War Council (the secretaries of the armed services and the chiefs of staff). Acheson and Webb also tried to reduce the friction with the Army over German occupation affairs, and they instructed their subordinates to improve ties with their counterparts throughout the NME. Webb placed Rusk in charge of all high-level coordination between the Pentagon and Foggy Bottom. Despite the acrimony that quickly developed between Acheson and Johnson, Webb believed that good working relations were being forged between the Defense and State departments. Johnson's establishment of the Office of Foreign Military Affairs directly under his own purview, sometimes seen as a manifestation of hostility toward the State Department, initially was welcomed by the men at Foggy Bottom.[14]

■

The State Department's ability to control policy was greatly abetted by the dissension and demoralization within the NME. Truman's decision to hold defense spending to $15 billion in fiscal year 1950 accentuated service rivalries. Agonizing new decisions had to be made regarding force reductions. While still defense secretary, Forrestal had asked Dwight Eisenhower, now president of Columbia University, to preside temporarily over the Joint Chiefs of Staff (JCS) and to aid him on budgetary issues. But despite Eisenhower's moderating influence, tensions had flared anew between the Air Force and the Navy. Forrestal's consensual style of management proved totally ineffective, and he was increasingly irresolute. His standing at the White House plummeted. Truman's aides suspected that Forrestal had connived with Thomas Dewey to retain the defense secretaryship if the Republicans won. During the winter of 1949, Truman eased Forrestal out of his position. Thereafter, Forrestal's mental health deteriorated, and he committed suicide in May.[15]

Even before Forrestal left the Pentagon, he had come to realize that the National Security Act failed to give the defense secretary adequate authority. During January and February 1949, Marx Leva, Forrestal's special assistant, met with Charles B. Stauffacher of the Budget Bureau and George Elsey of the White House staff. Elsey and Stauffacher were even more determined than Forrestal to strengthen the office of the secretary of defense, weaken the service secretaries, and create an integrated general staff responsible to a single chief. The three men worked out proposals that Forrestal, presidential counsel Clark Clifford, and Frank Pace, the new director of the Budget Bureau, recommended to Truman. In revised form, these suggestions were passed by Congress during the summer of 1949.[16]

The amendments to the National Security Act converted the NME into a single executive department known as the Department of Defense. The Army, Navy, and Air Force departments were downgraded and their leaders placed squarely under the authority of the secretary of defense. The secretaries of the armed services no longer reported directly to the president, and they lost their seats on the NSC. The secretary of defense was given broader authority and a larger staff. He was also granted discretionary power to use agencies like the Munitions Board and the Research and Development Board. The position of chairman of the JCS was created and the Joint Staff enlarged. Truman, however, did not ask Congress for a single chief of staff and a fully integrated Joint Staff. Nor did he request authority to alter the roles and missions of the individual military services.[17]

At the end of March 1949, Louis Johnson took command of the defense establishment. He was a West Virginia lawyer who had become a leader of the American Legion in the interwar years. In the late 1930's he served as an assistant secretary of war, and he played a key role as Truman's finance chairman during the 1948 campaign. Many contemporaries believed that Johnson had huge political ambitions of his own. He certainly brought to the Pentagon a number of political cronies. Johnson's style of management was the opposite of Forrestal's. Flamboyant and outspoken, he did not hesitate to assert his leadership. He told everyone that he was in command, and those who would not defer were fired. A fiscal conservative, he intended to cut defense spending. He abruptly canceled the Navy's first supercarrier and allocated funds for intercontinental bombers, thereby confirming rumors that he was a champion of air power and atomic weapons. Secretary of the Navy John Sullivan indignantly resigned. But Johnson bore no special animus toward the Navy. Air Force Secretary Stuart Symington detested Johnson's domineering style and cost-cutting practices, and Omar Bradley, the first chairman of the JCS, considered him a liar and manipulator. Ironically, Johnson did precisely what Truman wanted of him: gain control of the Pentagon and cut costs. However, he sparked more ill will than had ever before existed.[18]

■

The disarray in the Pentagon was an embarrassment to the administration, but it abetted Acheson's efforts to make the State Department the preeminent agency dealing with national security issues. Acheson had to worry far more about his relations with Congress than he had to fear the Pentagon's interference with State Department goals. Acheson himself had little political clout; his leverage with Congress would depend on Truman's overall popularity. During his confirmation hearings, senators asked Acheson about his relationship with Alger Hiss and probed his commitment to the worldwide struggle against communism, questions that illustrated a developing penchant to blame allegedly disloyal officials for the spread of communism. The hostile queries also reflected the ephemeral nature of the bipartisan consensus Marshall and Lovett had built. Truman's blistering campaign rhetoric and the

Democrats' decision to reduce the number of Republicans on the Senate Foreign Relations Committee dampened prospects for continued bipartisanship. Acheson easily rebutted allegations of his close connections with Hiss. But he made little attempt to challenge the indiscriminate anticommunism of his inquisitors. Acheson wanted to get confirmed, not ignite new controversies. A good working relationship with the Senate Foreign Relations Committee was a key to forging a successful foreign policy. And, fundamentally, he agreed that the United States should contain communism wherever it could do so at reasonable cost.[19]

The poisonous relationship between Acheson and Congress that would evolve was not predictable in early 1949. Portents there were, and Acheson was too shrewd to be unaware of them. Because Truman both gloried in the role of leading the free world in the struggle against totalitarianism and hoped to capitalize politically on this image, he was especially vulnerable to charges that he had lost China. Yet in executive session hearings in the spring of 1949, Acheson perceived that there was no great sentiment for continued aid to Chiang Kai-shek. Republican foes of the administration, like Alexander Wiley of Wisconsin and H. Alexander Smith of New Jersey, admitted that they were woefully ignorant of developments in China. When Acheson made clear that his decision to disengage from Chiang did not reflect any change in the global crusade against communism, Senator Arthur Vandenberg begged the secretary for a persuasive statement that the Michigan senator could use to support the administration. Thereupon, Acheson concluded that he had room to maneuver even on the most volatile of questions. Not even Congress posed insuperable obstacles to his control of the nation's foreign policy.[20]

Fiscal Policy, Strategy, and Diplomacy

Acheson quickly seized command, but he did not inject the State Department into the bitter struggles over the military budget and the configuration of military forces. Truman's imposition of a $15 billion ceiling on military expenditures compelled defense officials to rethink the purposes and composition of their forces. JCS budget officers believed that force requirements had to be geared to the nation's diplomatic objectives, its assessment of risk, its strategic concepts, and its wartime goals. They repeatedly asked civilian officials to provide them with guidelines but received scant advice from the State Department. In the war plans they worked on during 1949, military planners simply incorporated the expansive generalizations from NSC 20/4. Kennan and Bohlen deplored the NME's quest for goals-and-measures papers, and they rebelled at the thought of having to elaborate and refine the administration's basic national security study. They showed little sensitivity to the baffling problems confronted by Pentagon policymakers.[21]

Left to themselves, defense officials grappled with the formidable task of designing a viable force structure within Truman's fiscal limits. About the only thing that the Army, Navy, and Air Force could agree on was that they would not be able to implement the emergency war plans drawn up during 1948. Eisenhower tried to forge a new consensus by getting the chiefs of staff to agree first on a strategic concept. Priorities could then be assigned to the tasks necessary to fulfill this concept, after which budget officers would delineate the forces required. Eisenhower anticipated that the key tasks could be accomplished within Truman's budget guidelines.[22]

The strategic concept that Eisenhower had worked out with Forrestal called for the "holding of a line containing the Western Europe complex preferably no farther to the West than the Rhine. The logical extension of this line involves the United Kingdom on the left flank and the Cairo-Suez [area] on the right flank." If this were not possible, and Eisenhower knew it was unlikely in the immediate future, he called for maintaining a "substantial bridge-head" in Western Europe. If that, too, were not feasible, he insisted that Allied armies return to the continent at the earliest possible moment lest the Kremlin gain time to communize all of Western Europe "with disastrous effects" on the United States. To accomplish this, Eisenhower enumerated, in order of priority, three key tasks: protecting the United Kingdom, controlling the Western Mediterranean, and retaining a position in the Middle East. Eisenhower downgraded the importance of the Eastern Mediterranean; strategic bombing would initially emanate primarily from bases in Great Britain. Planners concluded that deploying men and materiel to the Cairo-Suez area was not achievable with the forces available under a $15 billion ceiling. Yet Eisenhower, as will become apparent, was not willing to write off the Middle East.[23]

The JCS approved Eisenhower's strategic concept but could not agree on the composition of forces to implement it. Eisenhower requested that each service identify the forces deemed indispensable for accomplishing the strategic tasks. Each would estimate not only its own force needs but also the requirements of the other two services. Eisenhower's plan was to accept the lowest estimate offered. Service rivalries flared once again, as the Navy estimated that 48 air groups would suffice and the Air Force insisted that the Navy did not need any carrier task forces.[24]

Eisenhower found the deliberations to be excruciatingly painful. Although organizational rivalries complicated matters, he realized that he had underestimated the difficulty of his assignment. He increasingly doubted whether the United States and its allies could hold a bridgehead in Europe, retain a foothold in the Middle East, and carry out a successful strategic bombing offensive within a $15 billion budget. Moreover, his difficulties grew as Truman's budget ceiling for military spending shrunk still further during the spring of 1949. If he gave the Air Force the 63 groups that it claimed was the absolute minimum to carry out the atomic offensive, he would have to eliminate all the Navy's carriers. But he needed the carriers to maintain a foothold in the Middle East. Eisenhower did not want to abandon the British at Cairo-Suez, or forsake use of the strategic air base there, or relinquish the petroleum resources of the region. Carriers allowed for improvisation in wartime, a consideration to which he assigned great significance. Eisenhower believed the

Western Mediterranean was of unique importance because from this location U.S. forces could deploy either to the Middle East or to Western Europe.[25]

Eisenhower found himself beleaguered by conflicting impulses. He placed pre-eminent importance on the ability to launch the strategic air offensive. In peacetime, this capability had great value as a deterrent, and in war the nation had no other means to hurt the enemy at the onset of hostilities. In Eisenhower's view, strategic air power would reduce enemy capabilities and expedite victory but would not force the Soviets to surrender. He shared some of the misgivings of the Navy and Army about the efficacy of the air/atomic strategy. In particular, he agreed that it should not foreclose a determined effort to defend Western Europe.[26]

The Navy, as David Rosenberg and Floyd Kennedy have shown, presented a most persuasive critique of the air-atomic strategy. Naval officials did not think that the Air Force could effectively implement the offensive and doubted whether U.S. bombers could penetrate Soviet defenses. They were appalled by Symington's decision to procure additional B-36 aircraft, which they insisted were easy prey to enemy fighters. But most forcefully, Navy officials questioned the relationship between strategic bombing and U.S. objectives. Although an atomic blitz might disrupt a significant proportion of Russian industry, at the end of 30 days all of Europe might be in Communist hands. The Soviets might then regenerate the economic resources of Europe and the Middle East and become "the dominant power of the world." The purpose of war, emphasized Admiral D. V. Gallery, "is to gain political objectives, and a plan which results in military success and political defeat is worse than useless." [27]

The admirals emphasized that strategy should be focused on stopping Soviet ground forces from overrunning Western Europe. Gallery wrote, "Our greatest need would be for a tactical air force of fighters and dive bombers suitable for strafing railroads and highways, and for blowing up bridges and munition dumps." Rather than utilizing U.S. atomic capabilities against Soviet cities, they might be directed more profitably at enemy lines of communication, troop concentrations, and advanced stockpiles. The outcome of such a war, according to the admirals, might be decided in a few months: "When the Russian armies are stopped short of the Rhine, their leaders and people may see that they had better negotiate a peace or else they will be in for a large-scale atomic blitz. In this case, with their armies halted east of the Rhine, the threat of the blitz might have more effect than the actual blitz itself if their armies were overrunning Europe." [28]

The significance of the Navy critique of strategic bombing was obscured by its dispute with the Air Force over expenditures, roles, and missions. Because the Navy clamored for its supercarrier and for a role in strategic bombing, the larger ramifications of its concerns were often overlooked.[29] Yet the substantive points voiced by the Navy coincided with many of the ideas that Army officials also were making. Although Chief of Staff Bradley maintained that naval forces should be cut disproportionately given Soviet weakness on the seas, he nevertheless insisted that long-run strategic planning must focus greater attention on defending the home territory of prospective European allies who were about to sign the North Atlantic Treaty (NAT). Even in the short term, Army studies were showing, much could be done to slow down and perhaps blunt the Soviet conquest of Western Europe, which heretofore had been taken for granted. One study by the Transportation Corps, for example, suggested that even within present capabilities an intelligent plan for the destruction of lines of communication, particularly rail facilities, might add 90 days to the Soviet timetable: "Certain strategic areas such as Spain and Sicily can probably be held permanently and a successful defense of the Rhine may be possible if Western strength increases." [30]

Doubts about the efficacy of strategic bombing resonated not only in the Navy and Army but also in an important JCS study chaired by Air Force General H. R. Harmon. Harmon's committee, in evaluating the effect of a strategic air offensive on the Soviet war effort, stated that an atomic blitz would kill 2.7 million Russians, injure 4 million individuals, and leave another 28 million people homeless in the Soviet Union's largest 70 cities. It would cripple the Soviet petroleum industry, thereby limiting the mobility of the Russian army and significantly reducing Soviet air and naval operations. The committee concluded that "the atomic bomb . . . would constitute the only means of rapidly inflicting shock and serious damage to vital elements of the Soviet war-making capacity" but also noted that the 30–40 percent reduction in Soviet industrial capacity would not be permanent. Nor would the initial Soviet capacity to overrun areas of Western Europe, the Middle East, and the Far East be impaired. The use of atomic weapons, moreover, would increase the Soviets' incentive to employ whatever weapons of mass destruction they might be able to develop. But most disturbing was the categorical assertion, "The atomic offensive would not, per se, bring about capitulation, destroy the roots of Communism or critically weaken the power of Soviet leadership to dominate the people." [31]

■

The Harmon committee report and the Navy's concerns should have precipitated a full inquiry into the relationship of force to diplomacy. It was evident, for example, that the composition of forces needed to fulfill the wartime goals enumerated in NSC 20/4, including the elimination of Russia's influence beyond its borders, might be quite different than that needed to accomplish the purpose of the Atlantic alliance, to maintain the security of the North Atlantic area. [32] What, in fact, were the nation's most critical objectives in wartime and peacetime, and what role should the military play in the pursuit of these goals? Unfortunately, Eisenhower's task, as he defined it, was a much more limited one. His aim was to match forces to a strategic concept that could be implemented within Truman's budgetary guidelines. He recognized that force composition influenced deterrence and alliance relationships. Indeed the strategic concept itself reflected Eisenhower's grasp of the importance of

Western Europe's industrial infrastructure and of emerging alliance relationships. But in working on the budget, he was more concerned with the relationship of force structure to global war-fighting capabilities than with its relationship to deterrence and diplomacy. Johnson, moreover, unlike Forrestal, showed little interest in prodding Eisenhower or the JCS to think more deeply about the relationship of U.S. military capabilities to U.S. diplomatic goals and commitments. The secretary of defense simply demanded a military budget that would accommodate Truman's growing insistence on cutting spending.[33]

In July, Eisenhower gave Johnson what he wanted, a force structure that could be financed for $13 billion. A new emergency war plan, OFFTACKLE, that reflected the new force levels was then put together. It focused on launching the strategic bombing offensive from Great Britain and deploying U.S. forces to the Western Mediterranean at the onset of conflict. U.S. troops were not earmarked for the Middle East, but aid to the British at Cairo-Suez was not foreclosed. This was the first emergency war plan to stipulate that strategic bombing would be used to retard Soviet advances in western Eurasia and to protect areas vital to the allies. Yet OFFTACKLE did not resolve the disputes among the services, for it obfuscated the extent to which the nation would try to preserve a bridgehead in Europe or retain a presence in the Middle East. Nor was OFFTACKLE able to resolve the problems posed by inadequate base development and uncertainties about Soviet defenses. Even worse, it could not be used in discussions with continental allies because its lack of emphasis on defending Europe would have disheartened them. But planners did use their simultaneous work on a long-range war plan, DROPSHOT, to overcome some of the inadequacies of OFFTACKLE and to confirm their long-term commitment to a defense on the Rhine.[34]

State Department officials stayed aloof from all these agonizing and acrimonious deliberations within the Pentagon. Whether military forces should be configured for deterrence, support of peacetime diplomacy, waging limited war, or implementing strategic moves in time of global conflict should have been a matter of enormous concern to Acheson and his associates. But they were content to reaffirm the one paper that Kennan wrote on defense arrangements the previous year. Policy Planning Staff paper number 33 had stipulated that military force was critical for deterrence, casting shadows on the international diplomatic chessboard and influencing the psychological attitudes of the chess players. Absorbed with other concerns, Kennan and his colleagues did not care enough to study either the magnitude or the composition of forces necessary to accomplish these purposes. Truman and Budget Director Frank Pace raised occasional questions about these issues. But State Department officials, as political scientist Warner R. Schilling argued many years ago, mistakenly refrained from participating in the discussions over the size and configuration of forces. Their silence reflected their conviction that the Kremlin would seek to avoid military conflict. Confident that the ongoing contest for preponderant power was political, they continued to pursue national security goals through economic aid, military assistance, political alliances, and shrewd diplomacy.[35]

European Priorities

In one of his first appearances before the House Committee on Foreign Affairs, Acheson emphasized that West European recovery was still the administration's top priority. Western Europe, Acheson explained, "is the keystone of the world." By restoring the prosperity of Western Europe, the United States would abet the reconstruction of the international economy, diminish revolutionary nationalist unrest, contain the spread of communism, and create a balance of power compatible with national security.[36]

Appearing before the same committee, Averell Harriman argued that his primary goal was to create a "balance of power preponderantly in favor of the free countries." This task was infinitely complex. As coordinator of aid in Europe, he sought to do much more than thwart Soviet efforts to co-opt the industrial infrastructure of the Old World. He wanted to bind a united Western Europe to the United States, thereby diminishing the likelihood that a neutral third force could arise.[37]

But attempts to promote Western unity continued to founder. U.S. officials were frustrated by the difficulties of rehabilitating the western zones of Germany, creating a self-governing West German republic, and integrating it into the Atlantic community. The French insisted on a decentralized German republic and international management control of the Ruhr. They were willing to terminate formal military government, yet they wanted the allies to retain extensive residual powers over West Germany. Like the British, the French also feared the revival of German industrial competition and were eager to proceed with the dismantling of German factories.[38]

Once the Germans began writing their Basic Law and maneuvering for political advantage against one another, Allied demands simply could not ride roughshod over German sensibilities. German antipathy to such measures as the dismantling of German industry and the division of their country had to be considered carefully lest a virulent form of German nationalism reemerge. Germans with democratic sentiments and Western proclivities could become discredited. The new Germany, Kennan wrote, could turn against the West, look to the East, or play them off against one another. The Soviets would take every opportunity to attract the West Germans eastward, perhaps by calling for a withdrawal of occupation troops (as they had done in Korea), perhaps by offering trade advantages, perhaps by agreeing to revise the German-Polish border. The Kremlin might even end the blockade and assent to unification on terms that west German politicians might find irresistible.[39]

U.S. occupation authorities felt beleaguered by the conflicting pressures. General Lucius Clay's exasperation with the French reached an all-time high. "We have completely lost control of the situation," he cabled in January. "I feel certain that we are losing ground politically in Germany. . . . I cannot over-emphasize the seriousness of the present situation." [40]

Officials in Washington were also deeply worried about the long-term health of the German economy. Despite the substantial increases in German production, formidable obstacles lay ahead. "The over-all economic situation," the Central Intelligence Agency (CIA) concluded, "is unsound. Financial problems are accumulating rapidly. Investment capital is lacking and reconstruction programs are coming to a halt." Ominously, Germany still possessed a billion-dollar deficit in its balance of payments. To alleviate the need for indefinite U.S. subsidies and to pay for additional imports, Germany had to increase exports by over 400 percent. Constraints on German industry and exports, therefore, had to be relaxed; incentives to German producers had to be institutionalized. All measures had to be taken quickly because Congress might not sustain the current level of aid to Germany.[41]

No one was more concerned than high-ranking Army officials. Caught in the crossfire between Clay and the State Department, they were sensitive to congressional desires to save money yet aware of Germany's enormous financial needs. They were constrained by the limits on military spending yet conscious of the substantial costs of the Berlin airlift. When Army Secretary Kenneth Royall went to Europe in December 1948, he was appalled by the clashing interests and policies of the State Department, the ECA, and the Army. In his view, reparations, the Ruhr control plan, the occupation statute, the trizonal agreement, the program to prohibit and restrict industries, Marshall Plan aid for Germany, military assistance, and the West European security pact were all inextricably interrelated. He feared that, if policy were not better coordinated, the United States would lose leverage. He emphasized to Truman, "Because we are now approaching each of these problems piecemeal, I fear that our major objectives in Germany and perhaps in Western Europe as a whole may be threatened." Royall was willing to relinquish Army authority in Germany, but he wanted the president to form an interdepartmental committee, chaired by the secretary of state, to work out a comprehensive European program.[42]

Royall ordered the Army's Plans and Operations Division and its Civil Affairs Division to prepare papers on the relevant issues. He discussed his ideas with Chief of Staff Bradley and Deputy Chief of Staff Joseph Collins. He presented his views to Acheson within days after Acheson took office. At an NSC meeting on 27 January, Royall insisted that the French must stop obstructing the formation of a West German government, agree to changes in the program for dismantling German factories, and accept reductions in reparations. He pressed for an early meeting of the foreign ministers of Britain, France, and the United States. He thought it would be wise to withhold action on the NAT and the Ruhr control authority in order to maximize U.S. leverage.[43]

Truman sat silently while Acheson and Harriman took issue with Royall. Harriman felt too much pressure was being exerted on the French. Acheson wanted more time to study the long-term contours of policy toward Germany. The participants agreed to form an NSC subcommittee, including the secretaries of state, defense, and the Army as well as the director of the ECA. The real work would be undertaken by a steering group, including Kennan, Tracy Voorhees from the Army, Jack Ohly from the Defense Department, and George Bissell from the ECA. The State Department would retain overall coordinating authority, and the key task would be to study policy toward Germany "in light of our obligations and policy in Western Europe."[44]

Kennan was eager to embark on a comprehensive reappraisal of German policy. The challenge was to integrate a democratic and peaceful Germany into a European community it could not dominate. He feared that rapid action to form a West German government would prove counter-effective. According to Kennan, the "old defiant nationalism" was resurfacing. Germans resented the internationalization of the Ruhr, the controls over industry, and the residual powers over finances, trade, and foreign policy on which the allies were insisting. Most of all, Germans disliked the prospective long-term division of their country. A West German government, Kennan argued, not only would

become the spokesman of a resentful and defiant nationalism, but much of the edge of this resentment will inevitably be turned against the Western governments themselves. . . . Worse than that, the dominant force in Germany will become one oriented not to the integration of Germany into Europe but to the re-emergence of that unilateral German strength which has proven so impossible for Western Europe to digest in the past. Finally, it will thrust the German politicians into a position where they are almost compelled to negotiate with the Russians behind our backs for the return of the Eastern provinces.[45]

Kennan had no clear answers for these problems. The United States, he thought, should not withdraw its troops from Germany "until adequate safeguards have been established against a resurgence of German militarism and until the present tense and insecure situation in Europe has been substantially alleviated." He proposed that efforts to form a West German government be suspended. Instead, he advised that the United States establish a West German administration that would have wider discretionary authority to act than the government being contemplated. Acknowledging that his plan was not flawless, Kennan deferred to the European specialists when they rebelled at the prospect of reversing the momentum toward the formation of the West German government.[46]

Although Acheson was impressed with Kennan's illumination of the dangers ahead, he did not believe that there was any alternative to proceeding with the formation of a West German government. He could see neither how Kennan's administrative solution would work nor where it would lead. He and Webb encouraged Kennan to visit Germany, study the situation, and submit his observations and conclusions upon his return.[47]

Kennan's trip to Germany came at a critical time in the formation of policy. Acheson placed Robert Murphy at the head of a new Office of German and Austrian

Affairs. During March, Murphy worked with Army Assistant Secretary Voorhees to fashion a program acceptable to both departments.[48] The deliberations took on added importance when Jacob Malik, the Soviet U.N. representative, privately engaged Jessup in talks about the possible end of the blockade and the holding of another four-power meeting of the Council of Foreign Ministers.

Malik's overture reopened the question of whether the Western powers should suspend implementation of the London agreements and postpone establishment of a West German government.[49] But Acheson, Webb, and Rusk quickly concluded that the United States must not forfeit the diplomatic initiative by entering into another round of desultory negotiations with the Russians.[50] If the Soviets would allow eastern Germany to merge with the western zones on terms that would guarantee democratic processes and insure Germany's continued participation in the European Recovery Program, then the United States would accept a united Germany. Otherwise, it would be happy to proceed with the integration of a West German republic into Western Europe.

Risks, of course, inhered even in this approach. No one could be sure what the new West German government would do, which meant that the United States would have to play a continuous role in preserving European security. U.S. troops, Murphy and Voorhees maintained, would have to remain in Germany indefinitely. Much more would have to be done to forge a European economic and political community into which Germany could be integrated. For geopolitical reasons it was imperative to prevent a sovereign Germany from operating independently, maneuvering between East and West, or acting in conjunction with the Soviet Union.[51]

Kennan reinforced these views when he returned from Germany at the end of March. He described the incendiary political conditions: democratic forces were faltering; a new totalitarianism might emerge. The United States had to allow the Germans to govern themselves. Westerners, Kennan said, must abandon all but the most essential occupation controls or Germans would turn away from the West. "This is one of the moments," Kennan wrote, "when you can hear the garments of the Goddess of Time rustling through the course of events. Who ignores this rustling, does so at his peril."[52]

Grasping the overriding significance of the German problem, Acheson concluded that integrating a democratic Germany into a West European community could be achieved only if France felt secure. Accordingly, he thought that the North Atlantic security pact should be used as a carrot to elicit France's cooperation rather than as a stick to club that country into submission, as Royall proposed. A treaty, Acheson told influential senators, "would give France a greater sense of security against Germany as well as the Soviet Union and should materially help in the realistic consideration of the problem of Germany."[53]

As the reassessment of German policy proceeded, Acheson pushed the NAT to completion. Among the issues left unresolved by Lovett were the definition of the area and the composition of the alliance. In February, Acheson labored with great tact to lure the Norwegians and Danes into the NAT and away from a neutralist Scandinavian pact. He also opposed France's desire to include French North Africa in the treaty, settled for a provision that was limited to Algeria, and acceded to the membership of Italy, which the French championed with great vehemence. Confidentially, Acheson also told the Senate Foreign Relations Committee that someday Germany might join the pact. Papers were already being prepared in the State Department and the Army that left room for an eventual German contribution to the defense of Western Europe should the other allies assent to it.[54]

Acheson also shored up domestic support for the NAT. In February 1949 both Senator Tom Connally, the new Democratic chairman of the Foreign Relations Committee, and Senator Vandenberg expressed misgivings about assuming binding military obligations in Europe. Their statements aroused immense concern in the State Department. Article 5, the heart of the treaty, seemed in jeopardy. Thereafter, Acheson and Bohlen met frequently with members of the Senate Foreign Relations Committee to reiterate that Article 5 did not usurp Congress' right to declare war and did not dictate where and how the United States would respond to aggression. They explained that without this provision the pact's deterrent value might be diluted and European doubts about U.S. reliability would be rekindled. They agreed to cosmetic changes in the phrasing of Article 5 but did not alter the affirmation of the U.S. intention to take action immediately in response to armed aggression.[55]

Acheson and the State Department led the administration's efforts to mold congressional opinion in behalf of the NAT. Defense officials, however, were not very far behind. The JCS insisted on retaining strategic flexibility. Military leaders did not think they had the capabilities to support the commitments they were incurring and were also apprehensive about meeting Allied demands for military supplies. Yet they not only welcomed the inclusion of Italy but also called for the participation of Norway and Denmark, access to bases in Greenland, and freedom to fly over Scandinavian airspace. They valued the pact because if, on the one hand, war erupted in the near future, the alliance would facilitate the air war; if, on the other hand, the pact succeeded at deterring aggression for a few years, the alliance might help bring about the very military capabilities that would allow for a successful defense on the Rhine.[56]

State Department and Pentagon officials agreed that the NAT would bolster a favorable balance of power in Europe. When General Bradley appeared before the Senate Foreign Relations Committee, he explained how the treaty would help to co-opt the resources, skilled labor, and industrial infrastructure of Western Europe for the Atlantic community. After listening to Secretary Johnson's defense of the treaty, Senator Millard Tydings interjected that it sounded as if the United States were seeking "to put together such a preponderance of industrial plant, economic potential, financial stability, inventive genius, military equipment . . . and know-how . . . that it is almost certain to keep the peace." Acheson and Harriman maintained that this goal was precisely their objective.[57]

Acheson, Harriman, Johnson, and Bradley did not expect and were not worried about Soviet aggression. In his incisive book, Timothy Ireland correctly suggests that the Truman administration supported the Atlantic alliance primarily because it was indispensable to the promotion of European stability through German integration. Acheson believed the treaty would reassure the French and create an atmosphere of security that would encourage private capital investment, economic growth, and German rehabilitation, and he moved rapidly to get the treaty initialed. Moreover, when the foreign ministers of the North Atlantic countries gathered in Washington in early April 1949 for the signing of the historic treaty, the secretary of state quietly launched discussions with the British and French over German matters, including the occupation statute, the Basic Law, trizonal fusion, and reparations.[58]

By this time the allies were as concerned as the Americans about the mounting disaffection in western Germany. In Ernest Bevin's very first meeting with Acheson in Washington, the British foreign secretary stressed that the presence of French foreign minister Robert Schuman afforded a unique opportunity to reach an understanding on German questions. Recent reports from Kennan and Clay affirmed that Schuman had a much more positive attitude toward Germany and was much more inclined to bury past enmities. Acheson, therefore, pushed hard to get Schuman and Bevin to agree on the principles and procedures that would govern the work of a civilian High Commission. Within a few days, the three foreign ministers reconciled their differences and signed accords. Without the NAT, Acheson wrote Truman, "I doubt that we could have come to a successful conclusion of these Agreements at this time."[59]

■

Acheson was trying to create institutional mechanisms that would insure western Germany's alignment with the West. He wanted to simplify the occupation statute and specify the minimum powers that the allies would retain after formal military government ended. He sought arrangements that would discourage the use of the veto in the Allied High Commission. He believed that Germans should assume substantial responsibility for the normal functions of government and administration and that the High Commission should not intrude unnecessarily in economic, financial, and commercial matters. He wished to avoid continuous disputes with a fragile West German government that would be tempted to blame the West for its future troubles. The United States, he recognized, would retain sufficient leverage over the German economy through European Recovery Program procedures and did not have to rely on military powers. Acheson was delighted that his friend John McCloy, the former assistant secretary of war and president of the World Bank, would be willing to become the U.S. high commissioner. Clay would resign, McCloy would report to Acheson, and the Army would cede its authority to the State Department.[60]

Yet no sooner had these arrangements been reached than Acheson had to ponder their possible unraveling. On 11 April, Malik told Jessup that the Kremlin would lift the blockade if Western economic countermeasures against eastern Germany were suspended and if the United States, France, and Britain agreed to attend another four-power meeting of foreign ministers. Stalin wanted to discuss the future of Germany. A conference, however, could prove risky. The Kremlin might present an attractive plan for German unity, luring it away from the West. But if the United States rebuffed the Soviet overture, the West would be saddled with responsibility for the division of Germany. Its image would be tarnished and pro-Western German politicians would be discredited. An opportunity, moreover, would be lost to end the blockade, resolve the Berlin crisis, and terminate the costly airlift. After weighing the advantages and disadvantages, Acheson prodded Bevin and Schuman to meet with the Russians. They agreed, provided the blockade was lifted before the conference began.[61]

As U.S. policymakers prepared for the meeting, they became convinced that the Soviets might really be interested in striking a deal, unifying Germany, and ending the division of Europe. Jessup, Bohlen, Kennan, Murphy, and Nitze believed that the Soviets were hurting badly from Western economic countermeasures against eastern Germany. They suspected that the Kremlin feared the establishment of a West German government, felt overextended in Eastern Europe, and still wanted to participate in running the Ruhr. A comprehensive accord might provide for the end of the blockade, the withdrawal of Soviet troops from eastern Germany, the contraction of Soviet power in Eastern Europe, and German unification. Kennan pushed hard for a reconsideration of the ideas he had first presented in August 1948. Jessup, whom Acheson put in charge of preparations for the conference, was initially sympathetic to Kennan's desire to end the division of Germany in conjunction with ending the division of Europe.[62]

Because the stakes appeared so large, U.S. officials thoroughly reappraised their options. But as they pondered risks and benefits, they once again ruled out terms that might prove acceptable to the Russians. Their primary national security goal was not to unify Germany or ease tensions in Europe; it was to harness Germany's economic and military potential for the Atlantic community. In long, perceptive, and exhaustive studies of the trade-offs that inhered in any prospective deal, U.S. officials came to realize once again that a unified Germany posed a triple threat: it could associate with the Kremlin, maneuver between the two superpowers, or regain its independent strength. Moreover, it would be difficult to integrate into the West European economy because its prospective domination of such a grouping would impel other powers to resist its presence. They concluded, then, that although they could not overtly oppose unification lest the Soviets reap an enormous propaganda victory in Germany, the United States would accept unification only on terms that were compatible with its long-defined security interests.[63]

On 18 May the secretary of state summed up weeks of policy analysis to a meeting of the NSC. The president presided, said little, but evidently welcomed the recommendations of his top aides. Acheson stated that the United States would "go ahead with the West German government" and would agree to unification only "on the basis of consolidating the Eastern zone into ours." The State Department emphasized that "our concern is with the future of Europe and not with Germany as a problem by itself." The integration of "a greater part of Germany than we now control" would be acceptable but "only if the circumstances are right." Right circumstances meant that U.S. troops would not be pulled out of Germany even if the Soviets proposed a mutual withdrawal. Right circumstances meant that Germany must participate in the European Recovery Program. Right circumstances meant that the Soviet Union would not have a significant voice in the Ruhr control authority, would not get substantial reparations, and would not influence the level of German industry.[64]

Significantly, U.S. officials defined their interests this way at a time when they thought an accord might be negotiable with the Kremlin. Integrating the skilled labor, industrial potential, and raw materials of western Germany into an Atlantic community amenable to U.S. influence was considered more important than working out a comprehensive German settlement, averting a division of Europe, or relaxing tensions with the Kremlin. The CIA put the matter succinctly: "The real issue . . . is not the settlement of Germany, but the long-term control of German power." The French and British felt this way even more strongly, but the U.S. policy preference was *not* the result of Allied pressure. Kennan's view was a minority one. Most of his colleagues in Washington and in West European capitals were not interested in making a unified Germany the linchpin of a third force in world affairs.[65]

So uncompromising was Acheson's attitude that members of the Senate Foreign Relations Committee were stunned when he appeared before them in executive session on the eve of the foreign ministers' conference and explained the U.S. negotiating position. Vandenberg worried that it would institutionalize a permanent cold war. Acheson said his intent was not to end the cold war but to effect a preponderance of Western strength. Vandenberg kept pressing Acheson to consider an appropriate quid pro quo should the Soviets seem conciliatory. Acheson retorted that his advisers had scoured the field for possible concessions but had not found any "sugar" to offer the Russians. When Senator Claude Pepper urged Acheson to consider the possibility of treating the Soviets fairly, the secretary of state scorned the idea. Insisting that one could not trust the Soviets, he aimed to integrate west German strength into Western Europe and establish a flourishing Western community that would serve as a magnet to the Kremlin's eastern satellites.[66]

When the meeting of foreign ministers opened on 23 May, Acheson led from strength. He assailed Soviet actions and blamed the Kremlin for splitting Germany. He challenged the Soviets to accept a program of unification based on the arrangements the Western powers had designed for western Germany. These arrangements, of course, were unacceptable to the Russians because they would undermine Soviet control over their eastern zone. The Soviets would not risk either a Germany totally integrated into the West or a sovereign Germany acting as a third force. Rather than gamble for all of Germany, as U.S. officials had expected, the Kremlin opted to retain control of their own sector.[67]

Acheson and Bohlen were struck by the defensive posture of the new Soviet foreign minister, Andrei Vishinsky. The timidity of his proposals and the barrenness of his ideas confirmed the Americans' feelings that they had the Soviets on the run in Europe. The conference ended in a stalemate. But the Americans had gotten the blockade lifted (as a precondition for the conference) and avoided a Soviet propaganda victory in Germany. They had paved the way for the formation of the Federal Republic of Germany, the end of the military occupation, and the establishment of the High Commission. Acheson was elated. The Soviets "are back on the defensive. . . . They are visibly concerned and afraid of the fact that they have lost Germany." [68]

■

Acheson knew that the momentum must not be lost. He insisted that the Senate act quickly to ratify the NAT and pass the Military Assistance Program (MAP): "The most profound conviction that I got in this whole business is that the North Atlantic Treaty is the Rock of Gibraltar . . . and that the military assistance pact, or act, is absolutely vital." The French sense of security hinged on these matters. Maintaining that Schuman "is one of the greatest strokes of luck that has come along for a long time," Acheson was especially eager to bolster the French foreign minister's position.[69]

There was considerable opposition to the MAP. Legislators liked neither its cost nor the wide discretionary powers that it vested in the president. Nevertheless, Acheson pressed Truman to submit the bill to Congress so action could be taken before it adjourned. Acheson believed that the $1.4 billion in military aid, about two-thirds of which would go to Europe, was an essential component of his overall effort to shape a configuration of power favorable to the United States. This attitude was not a consequence of any fear that war was imminent. Testifying in behalf of the military assistance bill in August 1949, General Bradley emphasized that "the tide of communism is being stemmed in Europe. We are not impelled by crisis, or desperation, or fear of impending war." [70]

What did impel U.S. officials were the anticipated psychological advantages of the MAP. In the long run, State Department and Pentagon officials hoped that military assistance would augment the capabilities of the NAT signatories so that, in the event of hostilities, they could hold Soviet forces at the Rhine. For the immediate future, however, the aid was designed to complement recovery efforts and serve political and diplomatic purposes. Governments with precarious parliamentary majorities, with fractious coalitions, and with potentially rebellious minorities had to be encouraged to take the economic, social, political, and diplomatic measures that would keep them out of the Soviet orbit and aligned either formally or informally with the United States. Time and again State Department officials stressed that the primary objective of military assistance was to preserve stability and thwart internal subversion. It was supposed to assist friendly leaders to stay in power, to encourage them to take unpopular actions (combat inflation, balance budgets, rebuild Germany), and to reassure them that Soviet retaliatory steps could be deterred.[71]

Some congressmen, as historians Lawrence Kaplan and Chester Pach have shown, were not easily convinced. They forced Acheson to rewrite the bill so that specific sums were earmarked for regions or countries. They made aid to Europe contingent on the development of a satisfactory strategic plan. They compelled Acheson to accept $75 million for the general area of China. But in the end they gave Acheson virtually everything he wanted, including $1.314 billion in appropriations.[72]

Acheson and his colleagues had reason to think that they had made enormous gains in consolidating a European balance of power favorable to U.S. interests. The European Recovery Program was progressing; the NAT was ratified; the MAP was enacted; the High Commission for Germany was formed; the Federal Republic of Germany was established. And as problems were brewing across most of Eurasia and U.S. policymakers immersed themselves in the intractable problems of the Near East and Far East, they could find comfort in European developments.

The Middle East

Acheson's policies toward the Middle East and Eastern Mediterranean continued to be inspired by the conviction that "fundamental" and "critical" national security interests were at stake in the region. The task was not simply to deter Soviet aggression and to thwart the expansion of Soviet influence. Increasingly, the aim was to bring nations into a U.S.-led orbit in order to insure that they would cooperate strategically in wartime and allow Western corporations to develop and control their petroleum resources in peacetime.[73] These goals would be hard to realize because the area continued to be wracked with poverty, strife, nationalist fervor, and regional hatreds. Local leaders, no less calculating and ambitious than officials in the capitals of the great powers, sought to enhance their interests by exacting substantial financial concessions and military commitments in exchange for casting their lot with the Americans.

In early 1949, planners conceded that they would not be able to defend the Middle East with the forces then available.[74] Hence the JCS decided to work with the British in a continued effort to exploit the advantages afforded by the base at Cairo-Suez. DROPSHOT, the U.S. plan for a possible war in 1957, envisioned that two bomber groups (95 planes) would strike the Soviet Union from Egyptian airstrips.[75] The British, too, expected to attack Soviet Russia from Cairo-Suez. They even insisted that it would be more important to defend the Middle East at the onset of war than to deploy additional troops to Western Europe.[76] In April 1949, President

Truman approved the allocation of funds for lengthening the runways at Abu Suwair, Egypt.[77] In preparing the 1951 fiscal year military budget, Eisenhower supported appropriations for four carriers partly because he felt that, if war should erupt and if circumstances permitted, they could help bolster British positions in the Middle East.[78] In August 1949, after considerable wrangling with the English, the JCS also agreed that, in case of an emergency war, U.S. forces earmarked for the Western Mediterranean might be moved to the Middle East.[79]

Admiral Richard Conolly, commander in chief of U.S. naval forces in the Eastern Atlantic and Mediterranean, continued to carry on extensive theater planning with British defense officials. These discussions focused on the protection of the British base in Egypt. Conolly pleaded with his superiors for additional fighter aircraft. He planned to use them to bomb Soviet rail and road centers and destroy Soviet embarkation ports and bridges. He wanted to interdict their lines of communication, slow down the advance of Russian armies, and afford time for the British and Americans to carry out the strategic bombing offensive. He called for the development of suitable airfields, the expansion of radar facilities, the storage of aviation gas, and the stockpiling of essential equipment. He requested permission to coordinate his strategic plans with the Turks, and he looked forward to cooperating with the Egyptians and Israelis.[80]

These considerations greatly influenced the course of U.S. foreign policy in the region. To use the phrase of British undersecretary of state Michael Wright, U.S. diplomacy in the Middle East, like that of Great Britain, became the "hand-maiden" of strategic planners.[81] Herein, for example, resided the impetus for resolving the Arab-Israeli dispute. Regional strife created opportunities for Soviet maneuvering among Arabs and Israelis. "The Arab states," the State Department maintained, "presently represent a highly vulnerable area for Soviet exploitation." So, too, did Israel. Noting the Jewish state's strategic importance astride the transportation routes that Soviet forces might traverse on their way to Cairo-Suez, the JCS emphasized that Israel had to be oriented toward the West. Its forces were needed to cooperate in the defense of Egyptian airfields and Middle Eastern oil fields. Toward this goal, Anglo-Israeli military collaboration had to be encouraged.[82] Conolly, in fact, worried that Israel would oppose the deployment of British troops to Palestine and thereby complicate Anglo-American efforts to defend the Cairo-Suez base from advancing Soviet armies.[83]

During the spring of 1949, U.S. officials were particularly chagrined by Israel's defiant attitude toward the Palestinian refugees. "The presence of over 700,000 destitute, idle refugees provides the richest channel for [Soviet] exploitation," argued the State Department. Acheson told Israeli officials that they had to help solve this problem. The issue was so important that he recommended spending $120–150 million over three years to help resettle the refugees. Secretary of Defense Johnson concurred. The refugee problem, he wrote, "could have very serious repercussions on our strategic interests because those interests are bound to suffer unless the stability and friendship of the Middle East area are maintained and unless conditions there are sufficiently improved to permit Israeli and Arab reconciliation, at least to the extent that the area as a whole might reasonably be expected to resist Soviet penetration and to act in concert to oppose Soviet aggression." Heeding the advice of the State and Defense departments, Truman strongly supported the appropriation of funds for the refugees despite reports of substantial congressional resistance.[84]

Acheson's exasperation with Israel mounted as he came to believe that Israeli inflexibility on territorial issues prevented the rapid transformation of the armistice into peace agreements. He, like Lovett, maintained that Israel should offer territorial compensation to the Arabs if it wanted to hold onto the western Galilee. When Israeli foreign minister Moshe Sharrett showed no interest, Rusk, Webb, and Acheson urged the president to exert real pressure on the Israelis despite the political "heartburn" it would cause. "Disgusted" with Israel's attitude, Truman withheld aid, technical assistance, and a military mission. He also suspended the unused portion of the $100 million loan to Israel from the Export-Import Bank and refused to support Israel's position in international organizations.[85]

Although the pressure elicited no Israeli concessions, Americans hoped it would at least mollify the Arabs. Policymakers feared that Israeli peace terms would enrage the Arabs and fuel the discontent in countries like Egypt. The prospect of unrest, even revolution, worried State Department officials. They believed that the Egyptian government desired to collaborate with the West but was endangered by widespread poverty, Communist penetration, and nationalist impulses. When the British insisted on lifting the arms embargo, Acheson decided to permit the shipment of arms for internal security and defense needs. The secretary of state thought this military assistance would help the Egyptian government thwart a domestic insurrection and abet the Anglo-Egyptian base negotiations. The Americans still hoped for a friendly renegotiation of the 1936 treaty on terms that might placate Egyptian nationalist aspirations. British troops, the State Department suggested, might be removed in peacetime provided the Egyptians promised to care for the base and to permit the reentry of British forces in times of crisis. In order to avoid further irritating the Egyptians, the JCS and the State Department also decided to postpone detailed theater planning with the British inside Egypt.[86]

■

Meanwhile, officials worked diligently to prepare alternative bases in the Western Mediterranean. This option was appealing because, if war should erupt suddenly, the United States would have a greater capability to defend this area. Attention focused increasingly on Wheelus field in Tripoli, still under British control pending U.N. resolution of its status. In January 1948, the United States and Britain struck a deal providing for American access to Wheelus. The public announcement indicated that it would be used by transport planes, but in addition combat aircraft had the right to land there. In late 1948, Americans started to refurbish the housing and petroleum facilities. A few months later, Forrestal and Symington also sought funds to lengthen the runways so that the Air Force could use Wheelus for strategic operations in case of war.[87]

The Americans hoped the British would stay in Tripolitania. Yet voting patterns at the United Nations suggested that no agreement would be possible that did not envision the unification of Cyrenaica and Tripolitania and the rapid progression of the new country, Libya, from trusteeship to independence. State Department officials grudgingly acquiesced to the formation of Libya because there were no realistic alternatives. They were willing to accept Libyan independence in two or three years if they could be assured that the new country would "be so tied to the United Kingdom as to assure enjoyment of adequate strategic rights." In the interim, the United States would also seek to get behind Sayed Idriss, the emir of Cyrenaica, in order to arrange "whatever military facilities may be considered essential to our security." [88]

■

However tempting it was to look to the Western Mediterranean and North Africa, U.S. officials felt they could not abandon the Middle East. Increasingly, they found themselves willing to pay a higher price than they had initially deemed appropriate for access to the area's military bases and petroleum resources. This was most conspicuous in the case of Turkey, embittered by its exclusion from the NAT. During the winter of 1948–49, Army Secretary Royall, Admiral Conolly, and other top military leaders visited Istanbul to find that President Ismet Inönü wanted a binding commitment either through a political defense pact or through a formal association of the military staffs. "We need assurances now that we would not be abandoned should Turkey be attacked," Inönü wrote Truman.[89]

Policymakers were not eager to make new commitments to Turkey. They already faced formidable problems in working out command relationships with and supplying military aid to the founding members of the NAT.[90] Yet defense officials were more inclined than ever to use Turkey for the defense of the Middle East. Its willingness to fight the Russians continued to impress visitors from the Pentagon. Even under existing plans, the new airfields at places like Diyarbakir could accommodate U.S.-built medium-range bombers. Still not content, Forrestal and Symington asked the NSC in early 1949 to authorize the construction of additional airstrips in Turkey for U.S. use.[91]

Acheson wavered. He wanted to reap the strategic advantages without incurring new obligations or provoking the Soviets. He repeatedly tried to reassure the Turks that their exclusion from the NAT did not represent any lessening of the U.S. commitment. Yet when Foreign Minister Necmettin Sadak visited Washington in mid-April, Acheson was struck by his agitated demeanor. The peacetime military preparations undertaken by Turkey in conjunction with U.S. aid meant that, if war should erupt, the Soviet Union would attack Turkey preemptively to forestall its use as a base for U.S. operations. Why should Turkey take such risks, Sadak inquired, if the United States would not promise to defend it? Why provoke the Kremlin if the Soviets might otherwise avoid war with Turkey, as they had done during World War II?[92]

This perspective was so logical that diplomats and military officers feared that Turkey might seek a position of neutrality. The United States might then be unable to capitalize on its investments in Turkey. The officials with firsthand knowledge of the situation, like former ambassador Edwin Wilson and Admiral Conolly, pleaded for the inclusion of Turkey in the NAT or a separate pact for the Eastern Mediterranean and the Middle East.[93]

Both Truman and Acheson had to acknowledge that such a pact might be necessary, though they did not want it. They preferred strategic advantage without military obligations. But they were also convinced of the need to possess Turkey's allegiance.[94] Turkey thus held considerable bargaining power. The "situation is developing," noted the CIA, "for a harvest of claims."[95]

■

The Saudis no less than the Turks wanted firm commitments from the United States. Ambassador J. Rives Childs notified Washington that King Ibn Sa'ūd would gladly extend long-term base rights to the United States, which defense officials deemed necessary to protect oil fields and interdict advancing Soviet armies. In exchange, the king demanded help with his own defense and internal security requirements. What the Saudis really wanted, Acheson explained to Johnson, was a mutual defense pact. Though Acheson felt this request could not be met "at the present time," he noted other steps that could be taken to protect the king from domestic opponents and regional enemies. Acheson was willing to extend military aid to Saudi Arabia on a cash-reimbursable basis. He was also willing to assign military advisers to plan Saudi defense forces and to study long-term U.S. requirements at the Dhahran air base. At the end of June, an accord was completed. The protracted negotiations made it clear that U.S. strategic interests in the Persian Gulf could be advanced only in exchange for the support and protection of the Saudi monarchy.[96]

The situation was the same in Iran, where the shah stridently pressed for enormous sums of aid. He sought not only rapid economic growth but establishment of an army of 300,000 men largely equipped with U.S. arms. The army would strengthen his own position in the turmoil of Iranian politics. By constantly calling attention to the imminence of a Soviet attack, the shah hoped to extract half a billion dollars in assistance. Ambassador John Wiley was a willing accomplice.[97]

Yet Washington saw no signs of an impending Soviet invasion and considered the sums demanded by Iran to be outrageous. Acheson informed Wiley that Iran should not expect more than $12 million. He wanted to give just enough assistance to keep Iran in the American orbit and allow the shah to maintain internal order and safeguard his own authority. U.S. officials advised the shah to focus on economic and social reform.[98]

•

Indeed, Americans increasingly realized that the major threat to their strategic interests came from the Kremlin's ability to capitalize on the Middle East's enormous poverty, maldistribution of wealth, and social and political unrest.[99] To safeguard bases, protect British and U.S. oil interests, and bolster incumbent friendly governments, it was essential to generate economic growth and promote social reform. Unable to arrange an Arab-Israeli political settlement, the State Department wanted to send an economic survey mission to the region to supplement its attempt to settle the refugee problem.[100]

Economic growth in the Middle East was perceived as a key not only to U.S. strategic interests but also to sustained recovery in Western Europe. Officials were worried about the marketing and exchange problems that European nations would face after the recovery program expired. Acheson was eager to spur economic growth in the Middle East. If European surpluses could be absorbed there, allies in the Old World might not need to become dependent again on markets in the Eastern bloc. The Point Four program, showcased in Truman's 1949 inaugural address, promised to provide the technological assistance that would help to satisfy the developmental needs of the Middle East as well as the commercial and financial requirements of Western Europe. Development itself was becoming increasingly intertwined with U.S. national security thinking.[101]

China

Like leaders in Third World countries around the globe, Chiang Kai-shek continued to look to the U.S. government for support against domestic foes. But by the time of Acheson's appointment, everyone concurred that Chiang's cause was hopeless. Like Marshall, Acheson despised the Nationalists' inept leadership, corruption, and intransigence, and he yearned for a viable alternative to Chiang but could not find one. Like Marshall, Acheson was intrigued by the prospect of a rift between Stalin and Mao Tse-tung but did not reach out to the Chinese Communists or offer an attractive basis for eventual accommodation.

In January 1949, Chiang made a peace overture to the Communists. When rebuffed, he handed formal power to Vice President Li Tsung-jen. Li talked to the Chinese Communist Party (CCP) about ending the fighting and forming a coalition government. Meanwhile, the Communists consolidated their power north of the Yangtze, and, in turn, Li tried to revive the Nationalist cause in southern China and requested additional U.S. aid. But Li was hampered by the continued disintegration of Nationalist military forces, by Chiang's indirect control over the treasury and the secret police, and by the Chinese peoples' longing for peace after so many years of strife.[102]

Hardly anyone in the Truman administration believed that the Nationalist cause could be salvaged. The CIA concluded that organized resistance in mainland China would end shortly. General David Barr, the senior U.S. military officer in China, "emphatically" recommended against further military aid.[103] The State Department was split and Acheson equivocated, but Army Secretary Royall and Undersecretary Draper called for the termination of all military assistance. Recognizing that a unified, stable, friendly China was unrealizable, at least for the time being, the NSC recommended on 3 February 1949 that aid be suspended and resources be redirected to areas of greater priority.[104]

Truman was inclined to follow the advice. But Senator Vandenberg strongly dissented. He acknowledged the inevitability of a Communist victory but thought it wrong to abandon the Nationalists while they were negotiating with the CCP. It would discredit the nation in the eyes of friends abroad and people at home. He pleaded with the administration to do nothing "to seal China's doom." When the dust settled, he said, the United States could reevaluate its position. Truman agreed. He delayed shipments and opposed additional aid but did not suspend the delivery of supplies in the pipeline.[105]

Meanwhile, Acheson decided to bolster a non-Communist regime on Taiwan. The men at Foggy Bottom, especially those on the Policy Planning Staff, did not dispute military claims that Taiwan was strategically important. In peacetime Taiwan could serve as a source of food and raw materials for Japan. In wartime, enemy possession of Taiwan would jeopardize allied lines of communication between Japan and Southeast Asia and endanger U.S. bases in Okinawa and the Philippines. In the view of the JCS, however, Taiwan was not so important as to warrant the use of military force. A few small ships might be deployed to an appropriate Taiwanese port to demonstrate concern, but the JCS urged the State Department to use diplomatic finesse and economic aid to avert a CCP takeover. Acheson maintained that any show of force would backfire, yet he fully agreed with the importance that the JCS attributed to Taiwan. He hoped to deny it to the CCP by reforming the existing Chinese government on the island. If this option did not work, he favored covert action in support of an indigenous revolution by Taiwanese along with diplomatic action at the United Nations designating Taiwan as a trusteeship. The United States could thus circumvent the Cairo declaration of 1943, which called for the cession of Taiwan from Japan to China.[106]

As for developments on the mainland, Acheson was willing to wait for the dust to settle before taking any initiatives. But he foresaw a particular set of patterns. The Communists would cross the Yangtze, defeat the Nationalists, and form a government. They would have a great deal of trouble consolidating their power, and they would confront insuperable economic problems. They would beckon the West for trade and aid. Then, the United States would be able to influence affairs in China. But for the time being it was essential to be prudent and patient. Aid had to be withheld from the Nationalists and from most regional leaders because none of them showed any prospect of mobilizing indigenous support. Eventually, an effective political resistance to the CCP would emerge, and when the time was ripe, Acheson believed, the United States would support this resistance. "We shall be seeking to discover, nourish and bring to power a new revolution," he said.[107]

Unable to contain Chinese communism directly, Acheson decided to prevent China from becoming an adjunct of Soviet power. Eschewing the notion that the United States had any direct economic interests in China, Acheson believed that the goal of U.S. policy was to prevent Soviet control of Chinese resources. Like Kennan, Acheson considered it fortunate that China had neither great industrial potential nor abundant reserves of critical raw materials. Consequently, although developments there adversely affected U.S. interests, Acheson was not alarmed. China, he told the Senate Foreign Relations Committee in March 1949, could turn out to be a strategic quagmire for the Kremlin. Without squandering the nation's limited resources and without jeopardizing U.S. goals in more important places, Acheson wanted to forestall Soviet strategic use of China as a springboard to advance its influence into Southeast Asia.[108]

Acheson hoped to drive a wedge between Communist China and Soviet Russia. Analysts and diplomats often noted the potential for Sino-Soviet friction over territory, aid, and ideological leadership in Southeast Asia. They saw no immediate signs of a split and thought it premature to assume that Mao would emulate Tito's apostasy, but Acheson and his advisers nevertheless calculated that an overtly tough diplomatic and economic posture might compel Stalin and Mao to sublimate their latent differences. Because there was no immediate prospect of thwarting the CCP's acquisition of power or of toppling the party, Acheson felt it made sense to contemplate recognition of the Communist regime and to maintain some limited trade.[109]

■

The wedge strategy was not a strategy of accommodation.[110] In fact, it was infused with ideological antipathy and designed to force the Chinese Communists to appear as supplicants. It was implemented only halfheartedly and with the intention of exacting substantial concessions. The wedge strategy was encapsulated in a policy paper, NSC 41, which the president approved in early March 1949. Its principal feature was that it permitted trade in nonstrategic goods with the Communist Chinese. Immediately, however, U.S. officials hedged on its implementation, establishing a licensing system to regulate the flow of goods to China. When the British complained that it obstructed trade, Acheson retorted that licensing demonstrated Western strength and maximized U.S. leverage. The secretary of state certainly was not against all trade with China, but he made it clear that he was neither in any

hurry to enter into a trade accord with the Chinese Communists nor eager to promote commerce between Communist China and Japan, even though Japan would
benefit.[111]

Acheson assumed that economic problems would engulf the new Communist
leadership. Intelligence analysts in the State Department stressed "the contradiction
between the economic and political weakness of Chinese society and the ambitious plans of its rulers." Americans were heartened by reports of the proliferating
problems faced by the Communists as their armies crossed the Yangtze, took over
additional areas, and encountered the problems of urban and industrial China. The
Communists, they calculated, would approach the Soviets for aid and, finding that
the Kremlin had nothing to offer, would then have to turn to the West with their
heads bent low and their hands out.[112]

U.S. officials, therefore, protested only feebly when China's Nationalists blockaded the coastal cities in June 1949. The Truman administration did little to protect
American ships wanting to trade with Communist China. Privately, Truman strongly
supported the blockade; it reinforced the economic pressure that Acheson counted
on to crack the Communist monolith.[113]

Acheson contemplated recognition but took no action. In April, when Bevin
was in Washington for the signing of the NAT, Acheson acknowledged that he had
some room to maneuver. But immersed in European problems, he made little effort
to cultivate support for recognition. In fact, he "strongly" opposed hasty recognition. Rebuffing indirect Communist feelers, he seemed comfortable with the idea,
often expressed by U.S. diplomats, of utilizing recognition as a means to elicit
concessions.[114]

When the possibility arose for confidential talks in June between Chou En-lai
and Ambassador John Leighton Stuart, Truman approved. But typically, the United
States ignored Chou's appeal for a good working relationship and for aid. Truman
instructed the State Department not to soften the U.S. position. The Communists
were to be told that the United States would judge their intentions by their actions.
The president wanted the Chinese to cut the anti-American propaganda, lift the restrictions on the consul general in Mukden, and release two Marine flyers. Because
these demands were legitimate, Truman deemed it unnecessary to offer anything in
return except pious expressions of goodwill.[115] Moreover, nothing was to be said
about reversing current policies: official diplomatic relations with the Nationalist
regime, aid to the Nationalists on Taiwan, and acquiescence to Chiang's blockade.
Nor was anything to be intimated about future recognition, let alone assistance.
Mao was probably not ready for an accommodation, but Truman and Acheson made
little effort to reach out to him. Not only did they ignore the deleterious effects of
their past assistance to Chiang, but they discounted the relatively smooth transition the Communists were achieving in many cities. O. Edmund Clubb's report of
Communist actions in Peking, for example, contrasted sharply with John Cabot's
description of Nationalist revenge in Shanghai. Not even in Tito's Yugoslavia had

Cabot seen "anything quite so crude and arbitrary as the present [Nationalist] wave of executions." [116]

Truman and Acheson, however, were outraged by Peking's rhetoric and blinded by ideology. Communist Chinese speeches and articles proclaiming loyalty to Marxism and support for the Kremlin offended their sensibilities. They forbade Stuart to go to Peking, where he might have had the opportunity to meet with Communist leaders. Acheson did not want to enhance Communist prestige. Nor did he want other governments to think that the United States was veering toward recognition. He "did not intend in any way, shape, or manner to give any comfort to communism in China." [117]

The evolving political climate at home limited the administration's flexibility. Influential senators and congressmen, like Patrick McCarran, William F. Knowland, Styles Bridges, and Walter Judd, assailed the State Department for betraying Chiang. They charged that Communist fellow travelers at Foggy Bottom were responsible for the tragedy engulfing China, and they called for an investigation of the administration's Far East policy. But when Acheson stood his ground, opposing McCarran's bill for new aid to the Nationalists and championing Walton Butterworth's appointment as assistant secretary of state, he overcame the opposition. Responsible critics of the administration, like Senators Vandenberg and Smith, acknowledged that there were no simple answers to the China conundrum. They were not willing to deploy U.S. forces to China or hand additional billions to Chiang. Even the most fervent supporters of China, Senator Smith confided, "are virtually agreed that further aid to the Nationalist government would be money poured down the 'rat hole.' " [118]

Truman and Acheson had the chance to influence public opinion but lacked the determination. Only a small minority of knowledgeable Americans favored continued support of the Nationalists. Far more Americans had an unfavorable view of Chiang than a favorable view; far more wanted the United States to disengage from Chiang than to grant him additional assistance. Attitudes on China were malleable. Of those who were following developments, fewer than half opposed recognition of and trade with Communist China. Admittedly, smaller minorities favored trade (34 percent) and recognition (19 percent). But Truman's prestige was high after his victory over Dewey. If he and Acheson had tried to seek an accommodation with Communist China based on a shrewd assessment of U.S. self-interest and of nationalist rivalries within the Communist bloc, the public might have gone along. The administration's critics were not by any means confident of their appeal. According to Senator Smith, Judd's opposition was so visceral that he was largely discredited, and Bridges' was so blatantly partisan as to be suspect. [119]

For months Kennan had been urging the State Department to come out with a ringing defense of its disengagement from Chiang. The president was reluctant to do so. Acheson sheepishly told senators during confidential hearings in March that he had not developed any strategy or even given any thought to the matter. The administration relinquished the initiative to its adversaries, who were eager to claim that the Democrats were responsible for the loss of China. Only belatedly did the State Department prepare a systematic defense of its case. After he returned from the conference of foreign ministers in late June, Acheson gave substantial attention to the compilation of the famous *White Paper*. Its 400 pages of narrative and 600 pages of government documents were designed to show that the collapse of the Nationalists was beyond U.S. control. As a source for historical research, the *White Paper* was impressive; as a tool for influencing opinion, it failed.[120]

For an administration supposedly contemplating a sophisticated wedge strategy, what was most striking about the *White Paper* was its failure even to broach the idea of cracking the monolith or dividing adversaries. Much like Truman's inaugural address in January 1949, Acheson's letter of transmittal perpetuated clichés about a unified and monolithic Communist movement impervious to the national aspirations of different peoples. In the most dramatic passage, Acheson asserted:

The heart of China is in Communist hands. The Communist leaders have forsworn their Chinese heritage and have publicly announced their subservience to a foreign power, Russia. . . . We continue to believe that . . . however ruthlessly a major portion of this great people may be exploited . . . in the interest of a foreign imperialism, ultimately the profound civilization and the democratic individualism of China will reassert themselves and she will throw off the foreign yoke. I consider that we should encourage all developments in China which now and in the future work toward this end.[121]

It would be hard to design language more poorly suited to drive a wedge between Peking and Moscow or to educate the American people about the potency of nationalism. Acheson played directly into the hands of his critics. His egregious statement illustrates the extent to which he shared the ideological myopia of his adversaries. He juxtaposed communism and nationalism as if they were polar opposites. So despite his understanding of the potential for nationalist rifts within the Communist bloc, Acheson more often than not behaved as if the ideological solidarity that bound Communists together exceeded the nationalist aspirations that divided them.[122]

Throughout the summer of 1949, in fact, Acheson and most of his top advisers looked for an alternative to the Communists. They were ready to support resistance movements should they show signs of gaining indigenous support. U.S. chargé Lewis Clark made this point to Han Li-wu, the Chinese Nationalist minister of education. When Clark requested confirmation that he was correctly interpreting U.S. policy, he received a cable from Washington stressing that the United States "would welcome rallying of effective resistance which would give hope of opposition to Commie dominated China and is interested in any plans to that end."[123] Indeed at that very moment Acheson was on the brink of extending aid to Muslim generals who were still battling the Communists in northwestern China; Truman was urging the department to reconsider the whole idea of a wedge strategy; the CIA was laying plans for its initial covert aerial operations in the Far East; and Congress was inserting, and the administration accepting, a provision in the military assistance bill providing a discretionary fund of $75 million for use in the area of China.[124]

The Americans' desire to undermine Communist rule on the mainland and to forestall a Communist takeover of Taiwan persisted. But the resistance in the northwest quickly collapsed, and the Nationalists on Taiwan were repeating all the mistakes they had committed on the mainland. In late May, Livingston Merchant, a U.S. embassy official in China who had been detailed to Taipei for several months, presented a devastating critique of the Nationalists. They were doing such a horrendous job that the U.S. government needed to reconsider its policy of trying to deny Taiwan to the Communists. It "should behoove the United States," Merchant concluded, "to guard its moral position not only on Formosa and in China but throughout all Southeast Asia by minimizing its association with a governing group which has already in a larger theater demonstrated its incompetence and unpopularity." [125]

Merchant's critique precipitated another reevaluation of policy toward Taiwan. Officials were aware that support for the Kuomintang on Taiwan turned the wrath of the mainland Chinese against the United States. But it was difficult for them to cast aside their ideological predilections and accept the political, diplomatic, and strategic risks inherent in a Communist takeover of Taiwan. Even Kennan, who so incisively perceived the looming friction that would tear the Soviet and Chinese Communists apart, called for bold initiatives to prevent the loss of Taiwan. Acheson found Kennan's advice appealing, but was Taiwan important enough to warrant the use of military force? The JCS still would not make that judgment given the overall limits on U.S. military capabilities. So, rather than implement a bold policy, the State Department continued to consider turning the Taiwan problem over to the United Nations.[126]

By late summer 1949, the administration's China policy was wracked by contradictions. Officials wanted to crack the monolith but found it difficult not to oppose communism everywhere. The conflicting impulses were apparent at a key meeting of top State Department officials on 16 September. Acheson, Kennan, Jessup, Rusk, Butterworth, and their associates agreed that a recent cable from John Wesley Jones, the U.S. counselor in the embassy at Nanking, constituted the best overall guide to policy. Jones emphasized that policy had to be based on the fact that the Communists were "here to stay for some time." Successful resistance movements had to have indigenous support, and there was no anti-Communist who could lead a successful revolution against the CCP. Jones advised that the United States temporarily focus on preventing China "from becoming reinforcement to Soviet power." U.S. officials should look for the emergence of "dynamic revolutionary groups" but should not move hastily to aid them, for in the short run they could do little to hurt the CCP. Indeed, the United States should refrain from hostile acts and subversive activity until Mao and Chou learned that they would not get any tangible aid from the Kremlin. The Chinese Communists would then become disillusioned with the

Russians and would look to the West, at which time the United States could exert maximum leverage.[127]

Despite the recriminations that were beginning to poison the air in Washington, Acheson was not that far apart from his responsible critics, like Senators Vandenberg and Smith. They all believed that it was time to focus on those parts of Asia not yet in Communist hands. Acheson asked Jessup to conduct a comprehensive study of U.S. efforts in the Far East. Jessup was to assume that it was "a fundamental decision of American policy that the United States does not intend to permit any further communist domination on the continent of Asia or in Southeast Asia." Where it was still possible to thwart communism, the United States would try to do so. The wedge strategy would be used only after Communists had achieved power, and, even then, only halfheartedly.[128]

Japan and the Asian Periphery

U.S. officials did not despair over events in China because they believed that Chinese developments were important primarily insofar as they might affect trends in those parts of East Asia having much greater significance. According to policymakers, Japan was the key to Asia's future. Kennan continued to reiterate that the configuration of power on the Eurasian land mass would be decisively influenced by the alignment of Germany in Europe and Japan in Asia. "Japan," concluded the CIA in early 1949, "is the key to the development of a self-sufficient war-making complex in the Far East." Long-term U.S. security interests dictated "the denial of Japan's capacity, both economic and military, to USSR exploitation." General Douglas MacArthur in Tokyo and the JCS in Washington, despite their many differences over tactics, shared the same overriding objective to thwart the Kremlin's capacity to co-opt Japan's great industrial potential.[129]

Civilian and military officials concurred that Japan's alignment would be shaped by developments on the Asian mainland. Its economic future depended on markets and raw materials in Northeast and Southeast Asia. Soviet/Communist control over North Korea and China and prospective Communist inroads into Southeast Asia and Taiwan were thought to be portentous developments precisely because they made Japan extremely vulnerable to Communist economic pressure. If these other areas fell under Moscow's direct or indirect control, America's ability to abet Japan's industrial revival would be limited and economic conditions in Japan would further deteriorate. The Kremlin, then, could benefit either from mounting Communist influence inside Japan or from decisions by Japanese leaders to cultivate economic ties with nations already in the Soviet orbit. Japan, too, might then gravitate into the Communist sphere, since U.S. officials did not think that democratic institutions were so firmly implanted in Japan as to insure Japanese affinity for the West.[130]

The challenge, then, was to expedite Japan's rehabilitation. Although this imperative was as clear to Acheson as it had been to his predecessors, the solutions were not obvious. Even while Japan's index of production hovered below two-thirds of the 1930–34 average, inflation threatened to stifle the modest industrial recovery that had begun in 1948. In early 1949, the Japanese government, prodded by occupation authorities, unhappily concluded that earlier hopes to achieve a standard of living comparable to the 1930–34 average could not be accomplished by 1953. If Japan were to have a self-sustaining economy, it would have to be satisfied with consumption levels of about 80 percent of those of the early 1930's. But even the goal of a self-sustaining economy depended on increasing exports from approximately $600 million in 1949 to $1.5 billion in 1953.[131] Australia, New Zealand, and the Philippines, however, still frowned on Japan's industrial reconstruction, feared the revival of its latent military power, and refused to extend most-favored-nation treatment to Japanese goods.[132] And elsewhere in Southeast Asia, continuing nationalist struggles accentuated food shortages, restricted trade, and perpetuated Japan's dependence on U.S. supplies.[133]

The Army struggled with the Japanese economy. In December 1948, Treasury and Federal Reserve officials insisted that assistance for the 1950 fiscal year would be withheld unless the Japanese made a wholehearted effort to halt inflation. Army Undersecretary Draper acknowledged that the Japanese government had not made much of an attempt to control wages, stabilize the currency, or balance the budget. He also felt that MacArthur had not pushed the Japanese hard enough to accept deflationary measures. Draper invited Joseph Dodge, former president of the American Bankers Association, to take charge of economic policy and launch an austerity program in Japan. Draper knew that the Detroit banker could be relied on to crack down on government spending, constrain wages, and cut domestic consumption, all of which he thought essential to boost Japanese production, stabilize the yen, attract capital, and promote exports.[134]

Army officials were convinced that the long-term health of the Japanese economy depended on the revitalization of exports. U.S. aid financed the huge excess of imports, and Draper and Dodge knew this assistance must end. Japan had to become more competitive in international markets and find new outlets for its goods to pay for its imports. Japan also had to stop buying foodstuffs and raw materials from the United States, which required the expenditure of dollars that it was not able to earn.

Alternate sources of supply had to be found, principally in South Korea and Southeast Asia. Dodge, for example, was extremely eager to increase the production and sale of Korean rice for consumption by Japanese workers.[135] Draper prodded Acheson to secure most-favored treatment for Japanese goods in international markets. He was also extremely interested in maintaining U.S. assistance programs throughout the Far East and in promoting political stability in Southeast Asia.[136] And despite their desire to avoid direct military embroilment in South Korea, Army officials endorsed a long-term program of economic assistance to that country. Like the JCS, they refused to contemplate total disengagement from Korea lest it undermine U.S. credibility throughout the Far East and lead to a realignment of forces in favor of the Soviet Union.[137]

■

While the Army wrestled with the problems of Japanese economic stabilization, State Department officials sought to halt the spread of communism in Korea and Southeast Asia. Only belatedly, and under relentless pressure from the Army, did the State Department grudgingly acquiesce to the withdrawal of all U.S. troops from South Korea. Afterward, moreover, the men at Foggy Bottom remained extremely responsive to President Syngman Rhee's desires to build up South Korean military forces and to augment the U.S. military advisory group. Acheson, Rusk, and Butterworth also led efforts to elicit large-scale economic aid for Korea, totaling $150 million for fiscal year 1950. Although they would not guarantee South Korean territory in case of local and global conflict, U.S. diplomats constantly reassured Rhee that the troop withdrawals reflected no lessening of the U.S. commitment. They were firmly convinced that America's credibility and interests depended on bolstering the South Korean regime against its internal and external foes.[138]

More perplexing yet were the problems in Southeast Asia. Here, too, State Department officials were determined to halt the advance of communism. Regional specialists argued "that the importance of Southeast Asia to the United States economically, politically and strategically is so great that there can be no question of our making a fight to hold it. The question is simply: when do we begin, where do we begin and with what do we begin?" These questions were bedeviling because State Department officials were aware that nationalism was the most virulent force in the region and that Communists sought to place themselves at the head of the rebellion against colonial rule. But, despite their sensitivity to the nationalist impulses behind the revolutionary tide, even the Southeast Asia experts remained rigidly committed to the indiscriminate struggle against communism. As William Lacy, assistant chief in the division of Southeast Asian affairs, explained to General Albert Wedemeyer, the strategy is "to determine whether a nationalist movement was a fact of life or a figment of the imagination, and second, if it is demonstrated to be a fact of life, as in the case of Indonesia and not in Malaya, to attempt to influence it toward the American sphere of influence and to direct it wherever possible to the disadvantage of world communism, whether Kremlin directed or not." [139]

Rather than assess whether Communists were linked to, dependent on, or subservient to Moscow, State Department officials opposed revolutionary nationalist movements led by Communists like Ho Chi Minh. The State Department still possessed only meager information linking Ho to the Kremlin, but Acheson refused to take any chances. Conceding that it was a theoretical possibility for a "National Communist State on pattern Yugoslavia" to emerge, the United States would operate on such a prospect "only if every other possible avenue were closed." Although

Vietnam was beyond the reach of Soviet armies, "it will doubtless be by no means out of reach [of] Chi Commie hatchet men and armed forces." [140]

Southeast Asia, in other words, was too valuable a source of raw materials, too important a trading partner for Japan, too closely linked to West European allies, and too critical a communications crossroads to allow Communist adversaries to gain a foothold. In fact, the consolidation of Chinese Communist power in southern China accentuated the anxiety at Foggy Bottom. Mao might now be able to assist Ho in behalf of the worldwide Communist effort to gain global domination. Even Kennan, while maintaining his nuanced view of the potential for division within the world Communist movement and while displaying real sensitivity to the national-ist ferment in Indochina, could not resist thinking of Ho as Stalin's puppet. "The extension of communist authority in China," Kennan wrote, "represents a grievous political defeat for us; if [Southeast Asia] is swept by communism we shall have suffered a major political rout the repercussions of which will be felt throughout the rest of the world, especially in the Middle East and in a then critically exposed Australia." [141]

Not surprisingly, then, State Department officials supported French efforts to establish a non-Communist government in Vietnam under Bao Dai, the former emperor of Annam. The French were seeking to placate nationalist aspirations with-out relinquishing their control over Indochina. According to the accords signed in Paris on 8 March 1949 between Vincent Auriol, the president of France, and Bao Dai, France recognized the incorporation of Cochin China into Vietnam, allowed Vietnam to send diplomatic missions abroad, permitted the establishment of a Viet-namese army, and granted the Bao Dai government considerable authority over domestic finances. But France continued to exercise control over Vietnam's for-eign policies and military establishment, enjoy extraterritorial rights, and possess a privileged place in Vietnam's economy. [142]

U.S. officials did not think that the 8 March accords went far enough to co-opt Vietnamese nationalism. Experts in the Southeast Asia division, like Charlton Ogburn, advised Acheson to push hard for additional concessions if there were to be any real prospect of undercutting nationalist support for Ho. Although they were outraged when officials in the Office of West European Affairs and in the U.S. em-bassy in Paris thwarted their attempts to influence the secretary of state, their own recommendations were animated by the indiscriminate anticommunism pervading the State Department. Even the idea of approaching Ho, though designed only to "smoke" him out and entice him to leave Vietnam, was considered but momentarily and then dismissed. [143]

Acheson did not want French troops or technical advisers removed from the region. His vision of sovereignty was qualified by his fear of communism and his conviction that the West's influence had to be preserved in Southeast Asia. Believ-ing "that the paramount question in Indochina is whether the country is to be saved from Communist control," Acheson and his advisers prodded the French to placate nationalist sentiment but did not encourage them to turn real power over to the Vietnamese. Acheson was afraid that Bao Dai might flounder and that Ho Chi Minh's Viet Minh might gain control of a truly independent state.[144]

■

State Department officials employed different tactics in pursuit of the same objectives in Indonesia. After the Dutch used force in December 1948 and imprisoned Sukarno and Mohammed Hatta, Acheson threatened to withhold economic and military assistance; he worried that the nationalist movement, heretofore in the hands of moderates, might be seized by radical agitators. Yet once the Dutch accepted the reality of Indonesian independence, the United States pressed Hatta and Sukarno to yield on many other issues. U.S. officials, said Butterworth, "were particularly anxious to preserve Dutch influence in Indonesia in the economic, political, and strategic sense." [145]

Indonesian Republican leaders acceded, at least in part, to U.S. wishes. Fearing that their concessions would expose them to criticism from more radical nationalists, Sukarno and Hatta requested substantial aid from the United States. The State Department wanted to help them. Undersecretary Webb instructed subordinates to arrange financing through the ECA or through the Export-Import Bank. Officials in the division of Southeast Asian affairs needed little encouragement. They believed that the Communists might challenge the leadership of Hatta and Sukarno after full independence were granted. William Lacy pleaded with Army officials to ship military equipment that "would enable the Indonesian Republicans to liquidate their Commies." [146]

■

By the summer of 1949 all U.S. officials believed that the United States had to play a larger role in Southeast Asia. Communist gains in China caused immense disquiet because policymakers believed that Chinese minorities in Malaya, Thailand, and elsewhere would transfer their loyalty to the Communist regime. The southward march of the CCP, Webb cabled Acheson in Paris, was an ominous development that "transforms an already serious situation into an emergency." Lacy warned that "the large Chinese population in Siam is showing an alarming inclination to flop over to the Chinese Communist Government line." [147] The situation in Malaya was even more worrisome. For over a year Chinese bandits had been destroying rubber plantations and interfering with tin production. The British government banned the Communist Party and sought to contain the unrest. But now Charles S. Reed, chief of the division of Southeast Asian affairs, feared that "If China should be governed by a Communist regime then more Chinese in Malaya will support it and consequently would doubtless provide new support to the communist-led bands." [148]

The troubles in Southeast Asia intersected with and magnified the economic problems inside Japan. The conservative Democratic Liberal Party won a smashing victory in the January 1949 elections. The Socialists were routed, and the Communists increased their representation in the Diet by only 31 seats.[149] But as Dodge's austerity program took effect, U.S. worries mounted. Financial retrenchment caused unemployment and reduced domestic purchasing power. According to the CIA, the political center was being wiped out and the conservative right was tempted to return to its authoritarian past and to crush the left.[150] State Department officials anguished over the complacency of MacArthur's advisers, who appeared indifferent to the growing discontent among all shades of political opinion in Japan. Butterworth complained that occupation authorities remained too intrusive and refused to allocate responsibility to the Japanese. William J. Sebald, the State Department's political representative in Tokyo, was much more optimistic about the domestic political situation in Japan, but he was deeply concerned with the economic outlook.[151] The gap between imports and exports stayed large, and Japan's need for U.S. dollars to purchase foodstuffs and raw materials remained unchanged. Japan's economic salvation was still believed to reside in its ability to sell goods to and purchase raw materials from its non-Communist neighbors in Asia. U.S. diplomats constantly reiterated that the production of rice and raw materials throughout Southeast Asia had to be increased.[152]

The interlocking problems besetting Japan, Southeast Asia, and South Korea engendered growing dismay in Washington. Truman told Acheson that he was most concerned about the Philippines. Secretary of Defense Johnson requested a review of U.S. policy throughout Asia. Rusk and Jessup discussed the creation of a united front of non-Communist nations in the region. Butterworth called for the preparation of a Japanese peace settlement. Reed and Lacy pleaded for programs of economic and military assistance to Thailand and Indonesia. The Policy Planning Staff recommended a tripartite defense treaty with the Philippines and Australia and a theatrical propaganda campaign.[153]

Acheson was confounded. He believed that it was essential for European governments to make concessions to preserve their influence in the region, and that the United States did not have the resources to supplant European authority and assume overall responsibility. A Marshall Plan would not work because the region lacked traditions of cooperation and patterns of economic interdependence.[154] A Pacific Pact along the lines of the North Atlantic Treaty (NAT) would not be wise because the area was plagued by indigenous strife and authoritarian nationalist leaders, like Chiang Kai-shek and Syngman Rhee, who could not be trusted.[155]

Yet Acheson recognized that he needed to launch a new set of initiatives. After the loss of China, geostrategic imperatives and domestic political pressures dictated that he contain the spread of communism in Southeast Asia and South Korea, lock Japan into a Western orientation, and bolster the U.S. position in the western Pacific. He strongly favored economic aid to Korea.[156] He was prepared to move ahead and negotiate a Japanese peace treaty.[157] And he accepted a provision in the military assistance bill, sponsored by his embittered critics, authorizing $75 million of aid for the area of China. This money could be spent elsewhere in Southeast Asia, especially in Thailand and Indonesia, as his subordinates so desperately wanted.[158] Acheson, however, knew these measures would not solve the intractable regional problems. So he eagerly awaited Jessup's reappraisal of overall U.S. policy in Asia. The secretary of state realized that he would have to proceed deliberately. Although his determination to pursue containment on the periphery of Asia was increasing, the resources for doing so were becoming more constricted.[159]

The Budgetary Conundrum, Again

Throughout the spring of 1949, the U.S. economic situation deteriorated. For the first time since the war, inflation was abating and an economic contraction had begun. From mid-1948 to mid-1949, unemployment increased from about 3.5 percent to 6 percent of the civilian labor force, industrial production declined about 13 percent, and wholesale prices dropped about 9 percent.[160]

With revenues falling and expenditures growing, the Budget Bureau grew increasingly disturbed by the burgeoning deficits that loomed. In late April, Frank Pace, the new director of the bureau, informed the president of the prospect of a $3–5 billion deficit in fiscal year 1950 and $6–8 billion deficits in fiscal years 1951 and 1952. Pace believed that future spending had to be cut $2–4 billion below projected levels. Domestic programs, he felt, had been underfunded since the war, consuming only about 24 percent of the total budget, and should not be reduced. Foreign aid programs amounted to about $6.5 billion in a total budget of just under $40 billion. Although this figure was huge, as it had been in every fiscal year since the war, little could be done to scale it down because the nation was committed to European recovery and to Japanese rehabilitation. The only place where substantial cuts could be made, Pace concluded, was in the military budget. For fiscal year 1951 he recommended that new obligational authority for the NME be fixed at $13 billion. He reminded Truman that this sum was about $2.5 billion below that needed to continue the military strength, structure, and aircraft procurement planned in the 1950 budget. He therefore urged the president to reduce the new obligational authority of the NME in 1950 to no more than $13.5 billion. This figure would sustain a military establishment that could be financed with the reduced appropriations foreseen in future years. In practical terms, this meant that military spending would be reduced from $12.7 to $12.4 billion in fiscal year 1950 and from $14.1 to $13.1 billion in 1951.[161]

With Truman's apparent approval, Pace relayed the bad news to cabinet officials and to the JCS. He prepared very carefully for his meeting with Secretary Johnson on 12 May. He wanted Johnson to reevaluate the needs of the services, define their structure and missions much more precisely, and consider their requirements in relation to the "other quasi military programs of the Federal Government," like the European Recovery Program, military assistance, raw material stockpiling, and atomic energy, all designed to contribute to national security. Pace was clearly relieved when the defense secretary said he would cooperate with the bureau.[162] Yet Johnson's readiness to subordinate military spending to fiscal priorities angered military officials and complicated Eisenhower's efforts to arrange agreement among the armed services on a strategic plan. The JCS immediately protested any further declines in U.S. military strength, warning they would have an adverse effect on the international situation.[163]

Truman and Pace, however, would not be dissuaded. On 1 July, Truman convened a large meeting, including Acheson, Johnson, Pace, and John W. Snyder, secretary of the treasury. Also attending were the JCS, the three secretaries of the armed services, William C. Foster, deputy director of the ECA, Chairman Edwin Nourse of the Council of Economic Advisers, and Admiral Sidney Souers. Explaining that budget deficits would compel spending reductions and noting that considerable progress had been made toward military preparedness, Truman said the defense budget was the obvious place to make significant savings. He realized that this would mean a reduction in active-duty military strength and slower modernization for the Air Force. Yet military spending had to be compatible with the overall economic needs of the nation and set at a level that the government could sustain over the long run. The ceiling would be established at about $13 billion and might even be somewhat lower in subsequent years. The president also stressed that appropriations for the ECA would be cut by almost a billion dollars and that the State Department would have much smaller sums to work with during the next fiscal year. Indeed, Pace was now about to cut the funding for military assistance, Korean recovery, Philippine rehabilitation, and other programs from about $2 billion in fiscal year 1950 to about $200 million in fiscal year 1951.

Truman instructed the NSC to study the ramifications of these reductions. Would they entail alterations in overall strategic and diplomatic objectives? Would the consequences of lower spending for defense and foreign policy be worse than the effects of substantial deficits for the indefinite future? The president ordered his economic advisers to analyze the wisdom of the new budgetary ceilings and to examine the relationships of national security programs to a healthy, full-employment economy.[164]

Faced with a worsening but not grave economic situation, Truman decided to forgo the tax increase he had recommended earlier in the year. Instead, he would cut government spending. He did not want to tamper with his domestic programs. Heretofore they had not been adequately supported, and he could not repudiate his promises for additional aid for housing, education, and health and welfare programs without undermining the Fair Deal, the domestic base of his administration.[165]

Both Truman and Pace believed that defense spending could be cut without jeopardizing the nation's security. Despite the fall of China and the turmoil in Southeast Asia, during the past year the balance of power had shifted significantly in favor of the United States.[166] Almost all the intelligence assessments of Soviet capabilities and Soviet intentions concluded that the Kremlin could not wage war successfully against the United States and would not try to do so. State Department officials felt strongly that this was the case, even though they had been perplexed by the shifts in the leadership in the Kremlin and especially by Vishinsky's replacement of Molotov as foreign minister. Still, a long report on Soviet intentions emanating from the U.S. embassy in Moscow in April 1949 stressed that the Soviets would not resort to force in the near future and the United States could probably count on several years of peace. In fact, it appeared that the Soviet government had made a deliberate choice to weaken its near-term capabilities in order to develop its long-term economic and military strength. The Eastern Europe specialists in the State Department fully subscribed to this analysis. The European Recovery Program, the NAT, the atomic monopoly, and the growth in the atomic stockpile, they believed, would discourage any serious Soviet adventurism. The Kremlin's long-term goals might not have changed, but Soviet leaders were not likely to risk conflict in the short term. Kennan and his colleagues on the Policy Planning Staff wholeheartedly concurred.[167]

Intelligence analysts and military officials shared the same view of Soviet intentions. In May a joint ad hoc committee of all the intelligence agencies concluded that there was little evidence that the Soviets were preparing for war. Russian military preparations seemed to be precautionary and long-term. Although war from miscalculations could occur, especially in light of the Soviet perception of increased threat stemming from U.S. initiatives, the directors of all the intelligence agencies agreed that the Kremlin was likely "to exercise some care to avoid an unintentional outbreak of hostilities with the United States." Top British and U.S. military officials, including Omar Bradley, the incoming chairman of the JCS, clearly thought that under prevailing conditions the Kremlin would not risk war. The general view, from which no agency appeared to dissent, was that so long as the Soviets did not have the atomic bomb and so long as their war potential remained inferior to that of the United States, they not only would avoid a planned war but would also eschew any adventures "which would involve an obvious and real risk of precipitating a major conflict. Further, there is a strong possibility that if a dispute in an existing area of conflict should definitely threaten war, the USSR would, during the period of its inferior war potential, back down before permitting the matter to come to a test of arms, again barring the chance of miscalculation."[168]

These appraisals of Soviet intentions were largely based on assessments of Soviet capabilities. Russian military expenditures were now thought to be increasing rapidly, perhaps by as much as 30 percent between 1948 and 1949. Soviet ground forces totaling about 2.5 million were substantially larger than the forces of the NAT nations. Moreover, U.S. Army intelligence estimated that the Kremlin could mobilize 470 divisions and 12 million men within six months. Their armored vehicles, heavy mortars, and towed antitank guns were considered greatly superior to those existing in the West. Their stockpiles of armaments and munitions were thought to be large enough to equip a major armed force for the first year of war. The Soviet air force had approximately 600,000 men and 15,000 combat-type aircraft, and Russian factories were now turning out jet aircraft and B-29-type long-range bombers, the latter at a rate of about 25 per month. Soviet leaders were also assumed to have made a decision to build up their navy, especially their submarine force. As a result of all these developments, the Joint Intelligence Committee of the JCS concluded that by 1952, notwithstanding U.S. aid to Western Europe, Soviet armies would be able to overrun most of the continent within a matter of months unless they confronted U.S. forces.[169]

Despite these ostensibly formidable capabilities, policymakers and analysts were not intimidated. During the past year, Soviet military expenditures had shown a sudden jump, but the view from the U.S. embassy in Moscow was that Russian strength was only "slightly" greater. Soviet air forces were reported to be beleaguered by a shortage of trained technicians and specialists, poor air crew proficiency, and insufficient spare parts. Defectors from the air force indicated that the number of planes was much smaller than suggested in formal tables of organization. In squadrons of thirty planes, usually only six or eight were operative. The speed and ceilings of the jet aircraft almost always seemed to be exaggerated. When a Soviet jet crashed in Sweden, U.S. investigators noted the absence of any advanced electronic equipment. Moreover, Soviet pilots appeared to be inexperienced in night and all-weather flying, high-altitude bombing, and long-range navigation. The capacity of the Soviet air force to engage in anything but tactical support of Russian land armies was still severely circumscribed.[170]

Nor was the vaunted Soviet submarine force nearly as threatening as the U.S. Navy sometimes made it out to be. The Russians were thought to have 250 operational modern submarines, including the highly touted replications of the high-speed German XXI's. But information suggested that the Russians were encountering great difficulty in operating these submarines, and one source claimed that Soviet naval officers had not yet succeeded even in diving them. The British reported that Soviet attack techniques were amateurish and their evasive techniques unsophisticated. British and U.S. escort groups, they concluded, would have no difficulty handling them.[171]

But most significantly, U.S. analysts believed that Soviet industrial and logistic capabilities were too meager to risk war with the United States. The Soviet petroleum industry was technologically backward and thought incapable of producing requisite amounts of high-octane gas needed in wartime. The Soviet machine tool industry still turned out low-quality products and did not produce nearly enough spare parts. In terms of precision equipment, the Soviets suffered from a lack of instrument jewels and bearings. The transportation network was not even adequate for peacetime, let alone wartime. Rolling stock still had not been replaced fully from the devastation inflicted by the Germans. The Soviet economy also suffered from persistent shortages of certain ferro-alloys and nonferrous metals, of certain types of finished steel, and of industrial diamonds. The electronics industry was far inferior to that in the United States. Even more chronic perhaps was the inadequate supply of skilled labor, technological personnel, and competent managers. Throughout the economy, labor productivity was considered very low. As a result, the Joint Intelligence Committee of the JCS estimated that, although the Soviet armed forces would have ample equipment at the outbreak of hostilities, "Soviet and satellite industry could not meet the requirements of a long war of attrition." The State Department's Office of Intelligence and Research concluded that Soviet war potential was so inferior that in a showdown Moscow would probably "offer limited political concessions in order to prevent a seemingly certain war." [172]

Truman, therefore, had good reason to decide to scale down military expenditures. Analysts were still certain that any future war would be protracted, and the Kremlin did not have the industrial and economic capabilities to wage a long war successfully.[173] Only if the Soviets developed the atomic bomb might they take risks they had heretofore been unwilling to incur. Possession of the atomic monopoly had given U.S. officials the courage to co-opt West German power and to proceed with the NAT despite the fact that they believed the Kremlin would see these actions as threatening.[174] Not surprisingly, then, U.S. military officials agreed to focus much more of their intelligence efforts on the Soviet atomic energy program. They also proposed a substantial increase in appropriations for further development of U.S. atomic capabilities.[175]

But neither the JCS nor Secretary Johnson pressed Truman to reconsider the ceiling he placed on the defense budget. The Joint Strategic Survey Committee thoroughly reviewed the impact of a $13 billion ceiling on each of the services. The adverse consequences accentuated the strategic deficiencies in U.S. war plans. The weight and speed of the atomic air offensive would be weakened, the capacity to maintain a foothold in Western Europe would be postponed, the ability to reinforce the British at Cairo-Suez or to retain Allied control of Middle Eastern oil would be undermined, the problems of controlling the Western Mediterranean would be magnified, and assistance to the British in defending the United Kingdom would be diminished. The result would be a longer, costlier war. The JCS presented these views to Secretary Johnson but did not insist that he protest the budget cuts. Not expecting war, they deferred to his fiscal priorities.[176]

Nor did the JCS plead for any changes in national security objectives. Military officers reviewed U.S. programs around the globe. Nowhere, they concluded, should goals or commitments be terminated. Even in areas where reductions in funding might not jeopardize military plans, for example in Korea, the JCS noted that withholding assistance would adversely affect national interests and was not advisable. Reemphasizing the great gap that existed between commitments and capabilities, the JCS explicitly decided that it was better to live with the gap than to narrow national security objectives. Civilian officials had to be informed, however, of the dangers of tying down U.S. forces to a local contingency. Rather than forswear additional commitments, however, the JCS simply admonished civilians to recognize "that our military effectiveness is not now adequate for meeting even our present commitments." [177]

When the interagency group to study the implications of the budget reductions reported its findings in September 1949, it was not the Defense but the State Department that took issue with the mandated cuts. Webb and Nitze protested the reductions in many international programs. The Military Assistance Program, for example, which had been included in the miscellaneous group of $200 million, had to be placed in its own category and required funding of $1–1.5 billion in fiscal year 1951. Likewise, relief funds for Japan had to be increased by $50 million; recovery aid for Korea by $45 million; assistance to Arab refugees by $20 million; and the Point Four program needed an additional $7.5 million. Prodded by the State Department, the NSC also told Truman that additional programs, requiring about $200 million, would have to be funded. India, Pakistan, and other parts of Southeast Asia and the Middle East would need to have their dollar requirements covered by the United States, given the new financial crisis confronting the British. Indonesia would require special support now that it was on the threshold of achieving independence. New programs for other parts of the Far East would also be necessary once the current reappraisal of policy for that region was completed. [178]

These recommendations were not welcomed by the Treasury Department and the Council of Economic Advisers. The acting secretary of the treasury agreed that funding for military assistance on a substantial scale was necessary, but he opposed all other budgetary increments. Edwin Nourse, the president's chief economic adviser, excoriated the new NSC proposals. Budgetary deficits of the magnitude of $5 billion, he insisted, endangered political and economic stability at home, thwarted industrial growth, and complicated the farm surplus problem. According to Nourse, the implications for taxation, debt management, capital formation, labor relations, social services, and the fixed-income class had to be regarded as "serious, if not ominous." If these deficits continued, Nourse warned, the government would have difficulty financing another war should it come. [179]

For the moment the debate was left unresolved, and President Truman did not accept or reject the NSC report. But the NSC proposals once again underscored the global imperatives of national security policy. The threats were not military, so defense expenditures could be scaled downward. But from Western Europe to Southeast Asia, virtually every non-Communist country was now considered an object in the struggle between the Kremlin and the United States. For Acheson as for his predecessors, the key remained Western Europe because herein resided a vast potential of industrial infrastructure and skilled labor that, if co-opted, absorbed, or seized by the Soviet Union, would add greatly to the Kremlin's overall strength. The "cooperative combination of the economic potentialities of continental Europe and the USSR, under Soviet direction," warned the CIA, "might in ten years result in the creation of an industrial power equivalent to that of the United States today." [180]

To stave off this contingency, the Truman administration planned to give another $3 billion in economic aid and approximately $1 billion in military assistance to Western Europe, and the United States signed the NAT. But formidable challenges still lay ahead. Western Germany still had to be integrated into Western Europe. European productivity and commercial competitiveness still had to be restored so that U.S. Marshall Plan assistance could end in 1952 without risking a return to European autarky, economic contraction, and political turmoil.

The Near East, in contrast, possessed no potential power center of its own. Its importance, as the CIA reminded policymakers, stemmed from "its auxiliary relationship to Western Europe (with respect to petroleum resources and communications) and its potentialities as a base of air attack on the vital areas of the USSR." In this region, Acheson continued the assistance to Greece, Turkey, and Iran. But containment of the Kremlin on its periphery was not sufficient. Acheson, like Marshall and Lovett before him, feared that the Soviets would capitalize on the Arab-Israeli dispute and dislodge the British and Americans from their position of primacy in the area.[181] He wanted to mediate an Arab-Israeli settlement, offered aid to help settle the Arab refugee problem, and supported additional assistance to the region through the Point Four program and the Export-Import Bank. To preserve governments friendly to the West, Acheson approved small amounts of military aid to conservative, authoritarian regimes in key countries like Iran and Saudi Arabia. He looked favorably upon the end of the arms embargo so that the British could give similar assistance to Egypt, Iraq, and Jordan. He also endorsed covert operations in places like Syria to overthrow unfriendly governments.[182]

Whereas the tide of events seemed to be going in the West's favor in Europe and the Middle East, developments were more ominous in East Asia. Soviet actions were neither bold nor imaginative, but U.S. officials were frightened by the prospective erosion of Western influence. Communists could capture nationalist movements and capitalize on the region's massive poverty. Since "US security is global and cannot be protected in Europe alone," the CIA warned that the trend in the Far East could be profoundly important. Japan and Southeast Asia had to be denied to communism. The measures deemed necessary were primarily political and economic, with modest amounts of military assistance.[183]

With Truman's full support, Acheson continued the national security policies that were in place when he became secretary of state. Given the deficiencies in Soviet warmaking capabilities, U.S. military expenditures were still not a critical component in the struggle for predominance. So long as U.S. officials could use American dollars to satisfy the needs of other governments, so long as they were willing to incur limited strategic obligations (as in the NAT), and so long as the atomic monopoly persisted, the United States could take the risks (and could convince prospective allies to take the risks) of creating a configuration of power that favored U.S. interests. But Acheson and his aides were learning that, despite their undisputed control of the policy process and despite their ability to limit defense expenditures and oversee occupation policy, they still might not have sufficient resources to reconstruct the industrial complexes of Europe and Asia, integrate them into a multilateral world economy, and preserve Western predominance in areas of the globe wracked with poverty, revolutionary nationalist strife, ethnic hatreds, and regional rivalries. If the difficulties had not been fully apparent to Acheson during his first months in office, coming events would prove very sobering. U.S. security imperatives would require resources and commitments of a magnitude that no one had heretofore dared to contemplate.

Problems, Risk-Taking,
and NSC 68,
September 1949-June 1950

By the summer of 1949 the exultation that had accompanied Truman's electoral victory was gone. Once again the president and Congress locked horns over domestic issues. Republicans and Southern Democrats stymied many administration programs, and Truman's partisan foes accused the president's friends of influence-peddling. Truman became acerbic as he was engulfed by political controversy.[1]

The bright spots in the international picture appeared to be equally transitory. As recession at home reduced U.S. imports and accentuated the payments problems of foreign countries, U.S. officials grew apprehensive. Autarkic trends might reestablish themselves; production in Western Europe might contract; political turmoil might recur. Germans and Japanese might look to the Soviet bloc for markets and raw materials and seek accommodation with the Kremlin. The British might cut back their overseas commitments. Their retrenchment would be an alarming development at a time when Communist pressures in Asia were growing, when political stability in the Middle East remained tenuous, and when revolutionary nationalist turmoil everywhere in the Third World was mounting. The industrial core needed the Third World periphery; yet that periphery seemed more unstable than ever before. "Unless we face up to what we want, decide on how to get it, and take the necessary action," Secretary of State Acheson warned, "the whole structure of the Western World could fall apart in 1952," the year the European Recovery Program was scheduled to end.[2]

If these matters were not worrisome enough, the Soviet detonation of an atomic device forced policymakers to reexamine their strategic plans, military posture, and diplomatic assumptions. The atomic monopoly had been relied on as a chief deterrent to dangerous Soviet countermoves. Without an atomic monopoly, would it be possible to take calculated risks? Would U.S. allies go along with American wishes if they feared that American actions might invite dangerous Soviet counterthrusts that could ignite a cycle leading to war?[3]

While these questions commanded the attention of Washington officialdom, the political atmosphere in the United States became charged. Alger Hiss was convicted for perjury; Soviet espionage in the Manhattan Project was exposed; and allegations of treasonous activity within the highest echelons of the government proliferated. Senator Joseph McCarthy boldly exploited the volatile political climate and assailed the State Department for harboring Communists. Just when the complexities of the international situation demanded cool reflection and objective analysis, McCarthyism created an atmosphere that placed a premium on inflammatory rhetoric and tough action.[4]

Tensions within the administration also grew as the political climate in Washington heated up. Truman's appointment of Louis Johnson as secretary of defense exacerbated organizational rivalries and bureaucratic conflicts. Johnson's cost-cutting campaign at the Pentagon intensified the acrimony between the Navy and the Air Force. His imperious behavior alienated Omar Bradley, chairman of the JCS. Although Bradley and the chiefs of staff were inclined to defer to the leadership of the State Department on most diplomatic and political issues, Johnson felt increasingly aggrieved by the stature accorded to Acheson and even to Undersecretary of State James Webb. Occasionally, he had reason to feel incensed by Acheson's haughtiness and the State Department's machinations and aggrandizement. Nevertheless, Johnson discredited himself by his provocative behavior and nasty jibes. Cognizant that his national security advisers were warring with one another, Truman sided with Acheson yet appreciated Johnson's fiscal conservatism and aggressive leadership at the Pentagon. In the spring of 1950, the president asked Averell Harriman to return from Europe and serve as his personal assistant. Harriman's principal task, at least initially, was to coordinate policy and ease tensions between the Defense and State departments.[5]

Although the feuding among the military services received widespread attention, all was not well at Foggy Bottom either. George Kennan grew unhappy as he no longer enjoyed the special preeminence that Marshall had accorded him. Acheson still sought his advice. But Kennan's aversion to atomic weapons, preference for small mobile forces, and preoccupation with German unification did not mesh with the views of other senior State Department officers who were growing alarmed over the worsening international situation and who were determined to build situations of strength. Kennan decided to step down. In January 1950 Acheson appointed Paul Nitze to head the Policy Planning Staff.[6]

Nitze's initial task was to write a report on the impact of Soviet atomic weapons on U.S. objectives. He consulted almost daily with Acheson. He produced NSC 68, one of the most significant studies of the entire cold war era. Rather than hunt for fifth columnists in the State Department, Nitze believed that the country's attention should be riveted on containing and defeating international communism. Aside from the rhetorical flourishes and ideological fervor, NSC 68 did not establish new goals for the administration. Rather, in view of the sterling crisis, the European integration impasse, the fall of China, the threats to Southeast Asia, and the Soviet acquisition of the atomic bomb, NSC 68 laid out options and called for much larger military expenditures. Conventional rearmament and strategic superiority were now deemed indispensable for the risk-taking necessary to co-opt the industrial core of Eurasia, integrate it with the Third World periphery, and maintain America's preponderant position in the international system.[7]

The Sterling Crisis and the Dollar Gap

Despite significant advances in production and income since the inception of the Marshall Plan, Great Britain's balance of payments remained vulnerable to the vagaries of the U.S. economy. In autumn 1948, U.S. purchases of raw materials and foodstuffs from Malaya, Ceylon, Australia, and New Zealand had declined sharply. At the same time, Britain's trade deficit with the United States, Canada, and Latin America markedly increased. On 15 June 1949, Sir Stafford Cripps, the British chancellor of the exchequer, told his cabinet colleagues that there was the possibility of "a complete collapse of sterling" and the exhaustion of the country's reserves within twelve months. Three weeks later he revealed the crisis to the House of Commons and enumerated measures to cut dollar imports through quantitative restrictions and discriminatory practices.[8]

The sterling crisis raised profound apprehensions in Washington. Officials worried that British actions might divide the free world into competitive trading blocs. Harriman warned Acheson that a closed sterling area, including the continental countries, would be "politically and economically disastrous." A third force in world affairs might arise, independent of U.S. leverage and antipathetic to the U.S. vision of an open international economy. "Our ability to control events," lamented Joseph C. Satterthwaite of the State Department, might end.[9]

Americans also worried about the effects of the sterling crisis on the continent. British woes suggested that the Marshall Plan might fail to generate self-sustaining growth based on liberalized trade. Failing to see that most West European countries were not suffering as badly as was Great Britain from the impact of the American recession, U.S. officials feared that British measures might spark a new wave of bilateralism and protectionism. If this should happen, economic reverses could precipitate political instability. The American recession and the British financial crisis, warned the CIA, might adversely affect European economic conditions, "restore the subversive capabilities of local Communist parties in Western Europe, impair Western rearmament programs, accentuate the divergent economic interests of the Western powers, and weaken their hand in dealing with the USSR."[10]

But perhaps the most ominous possibility was that the British might have to cut their political and military commitments in Western Europe, the Middle East, and Southeast Asia. The worldwide "political and power consequences" would be enormous, U.S. ambassador Lewis Douglas admonished from London.[11] Jack Ohly, an assistant to Defense Secretary Johnson, prodded Undersecretary of State Webb to ascertain how "the current situation" would affect "the capacity and willingness of the British to continue existing military commitments vital to the United States. . . . Will it mean a new Greece somewhere in the world where vital U.S. interests have heretofore been protected by the U.K.?" Ohly worried that the British might have to choose between their domestic priorities and their foreign commitments.[12]

Acheson, Webb, Kennan, and Nitze wanted to help. Unlike Treasury officials who pressed the British to tackle their problems as if they were primarily financial, and unlike Economic Cooperation Administration (ECA) officials who viewed Britain's predicament mainly in terms of its impact on European economic integration, the State Department studied options in terms of their impact on the overall configuration of power between the United States and the Soviet Union. Acheson saw the British as a partner in the worldwide struggle against the forces of Soviet communism. He was cognizant of the constraints on the British, sensitive to the Labour government's antipathy to compromising its internal freedom of action, and supportive of Foreign Secretary Ernest Bevin's commitment to the British Commonwealth and its overseas territories. Throughout the summer and autumn of 1949, Acheson and Webb worked hard to iron out their differences with the Treasury Department. They tried to modify the ambitious integrationist schemes of the ECA. They endeavored to convince Truman of the need for additional U.S. measures to help check the British loss of dollars.[13]

Bevin knew that he had an ally in Acheson. Like Acheson, Bevin realized that the British and Americans should not approach the sterling crisis as if it were a technical financial issue. The geopolitical implications were enormous. Moreover, Bevin was shrewd enough to recognize that Britain's weakness bolstered his bargaining strength, for the Americans simply could not allow the British to resort to autarky or curtail their overseas ties without adding enormously to America's own costs and responsibilities abroad. By the time he arrived in Washington in early September, Bevin was willing to devalue the pound by a substantial amount, thereby meeting one of the Americans' key requirements. But Bevin demanded that the United States lower its tariffs, simplify its customs procedures, encourage the outflow of private U.S. dollars, accept discrimination against the overseas dollar sales of U.S. petroleum corporations, and increase its stockpile of tin, rubber, and other raw materials with purchases from the sterling bloc.[14]

Hearing that the Labour government was ready to devalue the pound, Acheson wanted to satisfy many of Bevin's requests. He was ready to accept British discrimination against U.S. goods so long as the British worked to increase intra-European trade and so long as multilateralism remained the long-term goal. He would try to liberalize ECA financing, simplify customs procedures, increase imports, augment tin and rubber stockpiles, encourage private investment in the sterling area, and urge the World Bank to support development projects there. But because he did not expect quick results, he emphasized the establishment of a continuing tripartite Anglo-American-Canadian organization to study ways for Britain to save and earn additional dollars.[15]

Acheson avoided undue emphasis on integrationist proposals that might seem to infringe on British sovereignty. He did not focus on a European central bank, or an interstate European commerce commission, or a European currency. Like Kennan, Nitze, and Webb, Acheson believed that the United Kingdom should not be too closely tied to European economic and political developments. It was both more feasible and more desirable to work toward a European union that excluded Britain. British payments problems would complicate the problems of European integration; British integration into Europe would make it more difficult to wean East European countries from the Kremlin's orbit, and it would distract Britain's attention from its worldwide commitments and responsibilities. Kennan felt certain that Britain's chronic financial woes would force the British to relinquish many of their responsibilities abroad. The United States had to decide whether it would cost less to assume these commitments directly or to pay the British indirectly to keep them up.[16]

Acheson and his advisers knew that in any event, despite Britain's 30 percent devaluation on 18 September, it would need additional long-term aid. They, therefore, focused more of their attention on the economic underpinnings of the nation's geopolitical requirements. At Acheson's staff meetings and at meetings of the Policy Planning Staff, which the secretary of state frequently attended during the summer and autumn of 1949, State Department officials increasingly acknowledged that some form of economic aid would have to continue after 1952. Broaching this matter with Congress, however, appeared daunting when legislators were already contemplating cuts in Marshall Plan aid for the forthcoming fiscal year. Acheson prodded Nitze to develop a program to close the dollar gap. The department's economists advocated increasing imports, but Nitze believed that it would be necessary to find new mechanisms to sustain the outflow of public and private dollars.[17]

■

Throughout these deliberations, the emphasis was on the complex relationships between international trade, West European economic stability, and U.S. political-military goals. Not much stress was placed on the relationship of U.S. exports to domestic prosperity, even at a time when the recession might have drawn more attention to the dependence of the U.S. economy on international prosperity. U.S. business periodicals appeared more concerned with how the domestic slump affected international developments than with the foreign sources of domestic economic well-being. Certainly, this was the position of the administration, which was most apprehensive that economic contraction at home would further curtail imports, exacerbate payments problems abroad, and jeopardize U.S. geopolitical goals. While Kennan occasionally wondered how the U.S. economy would fare if it had to swallow its own surpluses, Nitze maintained that the United States had to cut its exports. Domestic programs, he concluded, could take up the slack. Acheson concurred.[18]

In economic reports to the nation in July 1949 and January 1950, Truman emphasized the importance of internal measures to overcome the mild slump in the economy and to sustain future growth. He noted the need for increased imports and for promoting overseas investments but related them more to the struggle for world peace than to the quest for dynamic growth at home.[19] Similarly, Paul Hoffman, head of the ECA, and Averell Harriman explained to congressional committees in February 1950 that sustained European recovery was important not because of U.S. economic needs but because of the battle with Soviet communism. This was not simply a public relations ploy. In one of the most important memoranda written on the dollar gap, the Budget Bureau emphasized that "Foreign economic policies should not be formulated in terms primarily of economic objectives; they must be subordinated to our politico-security objectives and the priorities which the latter involve." [20]

The dollar gap did not lend itself to easy solutions. Acheson decided that the president had to take more of a personal interest in the matter. In mid-February, he warned Truman that the nation's payments surplus was assuming grave dimensions. Unless some means were found to funnel dollars abroad, U.S. exports would decrease and the domestic economy would suffer. But what gave "real urgency" to the dollar-gap problem, according to Acheson, was its prospective impact on the strength of the free world: "If nothing else is done . . . the political consequences will be a substantial shift of power from the democratic to the Soviet sphere."

Acheson wanted Truman to reappraise the nation's economic policies, continue foreign assistance beyond 1952, and designate a top staff assistant to coordinate steps to alleviate the dollar gap. The public had to be made aware of the magnitude of the problem, and Congress had to be frankly apprised of the alternatives. Although U.S. imports were surging in the last two quarters of 1949 and Britain's payments problems were improving, Acheson was still most impressed by the fact that U.S. exports exceeded imports by $5.3 billion in 1949. His plea for the president's help signified the intensity of the crisis that he saw awaiting the United States in view of Britain's chronic financial woes since the end of the war, the prospective termination of the European Recovery Program in 1952, and the ongoing failure of European allies to make progress toward European integration.[21]

The Impasse Over European Integration

The Anglo-American-Canadian talks on the sterling crisis in early September 1949 caused widespread consternation on the continent. French premier Henri Queuille told U.S. ambassador David Bruce that he was horrified by Britain's decision to devalue the pound without consultation. He was agitated by its likely impact on French economic, financial, and political conditions. He was also infuriated that the Americans had assented to a large (25 percent) devaluation of the German mark without insisting on changes in the export price of German coal. British and German devaluation, the French believed, would accentuate inflationary pressures inside France at a time when French workers anticipated an improvement in their real standard of living. The Communists were ready to exploit the rise in labor discontent, and even moderate labor leaders were allegedly discussing insurrectionary strikes. What was most exasperating to the French was that, in the midst of all this commotion emanating from sterling devaluation, the Americans continued to exert more and more pressure on the French government to cut expenditures, control credit, raise taxes, and balance the budget. Another political crisis loomed in France, raising doubts whether Communist setbacks would be lasting.[22]

Even more upsetting to the French was the apparent decision of the Anglo-Saxon powers to set up their own economic machinery to handle the dollar gap. This seemed to portend an Anglo-American withdrawal from the continent. Queuille was vexed that the Americans seemed to be showering special privileges onto the British by dealing with them separately, granting them additional assistance under new ECA guidelines, and consenting to a devaluation that went well beyond what the French considered appropriate. The handling of the matter, Queuille complained, "showed a complete lack of loyalty" to continental allies. Bruce warned his superiors in Washington that he had never seen the French premier so distraught. He urged Acheson and Webb to allay European fears that the United States was forming a separate Anglo-Saxon bloc and subordinating continental affairs. France could not be left alone to face the Germans.[23]

Acheson tried to reassure French foreign minister Robert Schuman. He insisted that the results of the Anglo-American talks would not prove inimical to French interests. The future of Europe, Acheson emphasized, depended on Franco-German cooperation. Only France had the capacity to seize the initiative; only France had the wherewithal to bring about a new Europe. The United States would not exert pressure; France would have to set the pace.[24]

Soothing rhetoric could not dispel French apprehensions. In Germany the Christian Democratic Union Party eked out a surprising electoral victory, and Konrad Adenauer was elected the first chancellor of the Federal Republic of Germany by a single vote in the Bundestag. With a tenuous parliamentary majority, he was under enormous pressure to regain for the republic a still larger measure of sovereignty than it had been accorded under the agreements negotiated in the spring of 1949. The Social Democratic opposition led by Kurt Schumacher was eager to capitalize on allegations that Adenauer was kowtowing to the allies. Adenauer declared that he wanted to cooperate with the allies and inaugurate a new relationship with the French. But politics dictated that he seek immediate concessions. He called for an end to the dismantling of factories and sought entry for Germany into international institutions like the Council of Europe, the International Monetary Fund, and the International Trade Organization. As negotiating leverage, Adenauer intimated that he might refuse to cooperate with the Military Security Board and the International Authority for the Ruhr.[25]

U.S. officials looked upon developments in Germany with great dismay. Kennan was terrified by the specter of "ugly German nationalism." Now that Germany had its own government, its demands would become more shrill and its attitude more arrogant. A democratic Germany, he thought, might not survive. Its constitution was weak; its youth frustrated; its economic prospects bleak. The only solution was to harness German energy in behalf of an integrated Europe. Otherwise, there would be a repetition of the experiences of the 1920's and 1930's, "but this time with a far stronger Russia breathing down the European neck."[26]

Henry Byroade, who now oversaw German affairs at the State Department, warned Acheson to keep the experiences of the Weimar Republic constantly in mind. Concessions should be made to liberal Germans while there was still the opportunity to co-opt German power for the West. "If we fail to inspire the Germans with a sense of confidence and faith in the Western democracies and with a genuine conviction that they are on the road to full restoration of their legitimate prerogatives as a nation, they will almost certainly turn to the East. In that event we would lose Germany by default and Russia would make a long stride toward the battle for Europe."[27]

Acheson sent a special plea to Schuman on 30 October 1949. Soviet creation of the German Democratic Republic in eastern Germany injected a dangerous new element. The Kremlin would try to use the new government "as a magnet to draw West Germany away from economic and political cooperation with Western Europe." France, therefore, had to assume a leadership role in integrating the Federal Republic into Western Europe. Long-term French security, Acheson insisted, depended on it. Now was the time to support Germans like Adenauer who appeared committed to the formation of a new Europe and a reformed Germany: "Unless we move rapidly the political atmosphere will deteriorate and we shall be faced with much more difficult and dangerous personalities in the German government. The 1920's teach us that we must give genuine and rapid support to those elements now in control of Germany if they are to be expected to retain control." Acheson beseeched Schuman to support German admission into a host of international bodies and to allow the Germans to control their own domestic affairs without unnecessary intervention by the high commissioners.[28]

So important did Acheson consider this matter that, when Bevin suggested a meeting in Paris in early November to consider the dismantling question, Acheson readily assented. Although Schuman was constrained by his parliamentary situation, Acheson and Bevin persuaded him to end much of the dismantling and to permit Germany to join a number of international organizations and to send consular representatives and commercial attachés abroad. In return, the Germans had to cooperate with the Military Security Board and with the International Authority for the Ruhr. Acheson was delighted by Schuman's goodwill and courage. He was equally pleased when he went to Bonn, met Adenauer for the first time, and found him ready to accept the agreements worked out in Paris.[29]

But the impediments toward integration remained great. The Petersberg agreements, as they came to be called, precipitated a stormy debate in the German Bundestag. Schumacher assailed Adenauer for compromising too much and for indifference to the fate of 18 million east Germans. In France, German rhetoric could easily be interpreted as ingratitude and illustrative of German aspirations to regain a position of preponderance in Europe. More ominous still was the growing talk of German rearmament, which Adenauer himself indirectly encouraged. French anxieties mounted. Seeing that the British had no interest in playing a larger role on the continent, the French felt that Acheson was asking them alone to bear the burdens of German integration.[30]

Acheson's decision to place primary responsibility on the French for Europe's integration evoked a great deal of debate among U.S. officials. Within the State Department, the Europe specialists disputed the idea that the Old World could be integrated without Great Britain playing a leading part. They believed that Kennan, whose advice Acheson was following, was naive to think that a European union without Great Britain could promote overall stability. A union devoid of British power, they insisted, would be too weak and too small to control Germany.[31]

U.S. ambassadors in Europe voiced these sentiments even more stridently at a meeting in Paris on 21 and 22 October. They feared that European integration efforts would fail. Integration, said High Commissioner John McCloy, was the best antidote to a third force movement in Germany; integration, said Bruce, was the only means of co-opting the power of a reconstructed Germany for the West. Yet without Britain's cooperation, integration seemed impossible. Lewis Douglas assailed Acheson's view that integration could be brought about through France's leadership. The British were appallingly weak financially, but their role still appeared indispensable. Bruce thought the British, and the Americans as well, could make a decisive contribution by providing binding, long-term security commitments to France. These guarantees might induce the French to welcome their traditional foe into the Western alliance as a full and equal partner. Harriman agreed. Although he spelled out a variety of economic measures that needed implementation, he placed his overwhelming emphasis on strengthening the North Atlantic Treaty (NAT). "Security," Harriman concluded, "and not economic integration or political integration, should be the point of departure of our policy."[32]

Continued British opposition to economic integration encouraged U.S. officials to place a growing emphasis on the NAT. The Americans wanted the British to strengthen the Organization of European Economic Cooperation (OEEC), liberalize intra-European trade, hold down intra-European prices, establish a clearing union for intra-European payments, and promote closer economic arrangements among smaller subgroups on the continent.[33] But the British would not go along. Bevin and Cripps did not want to inject new life into the OEEC. They did little to assist the negotiation of a customs union between France, Italy, and the Benelux nations. Their opposition to a payments union, in fact, infuriated Hoffman and Harriman.[34]

Acheson was bewildered by British intransigence. But he did not focus on *economic* integrationist schemes, nor did he abandon his keen desire to collaborate with the British. For him, integration remained primarily a means of co-opting German power for the Western alliance.[35] Like his most able advisers, Acheson concluded that the German problem should be solved in a European framework and Britain's relationship to European integration should be solved in an Atlantic (NAT) framework.[36] This way, French security needs could be met, Germany's penchant for neutrality overcome, and Britain's insistence on its economic sovereignty accommodated. At the same time, all of Western Europe and the United Kingdom would be co-opted into a U.S.-led orbit, and a favorable correlation of power vis-à-vis the Soviets would be established on the European continent.

By placing problems in a political-military context, U.S. officials hoped to make their solution easier. Such an approach did not raise the same sensitivities in London as did talk of economic union. Indeed, Bevin loved to think of himself as a partner in buttressing the free world. But even political-military cooperation was difficult. The British still placed much greater emphasis on safeguarding the Middle East than on defending Western Europe. In discussions with the French and Americans, they would not reveal how many troops they would earmark to the continent in case of conflict. Nor would they share full information on their military production or help finance NATO's military assistance program. Instead, they chastised the Americans for failing to embroil themselves more fully in the continent's political affairs and for withholding the funds to rearm Europe.[37]

British attitudes created dilemmas for U.S. officials. Could the United States do still more to allay French fears and promote European integration? Kennan and Bohlen lamented that domestic public opinion limited U.S. options. Bohlen recommended that the United States bolster the global interests of the British government so that the latter, less hamstrung by its domestic constituents, could focus on Europe.[38] But Acheson preferred to move ahead with the Military Assistance Program. Overcoming the objections of the Budget Bureau, he persuaded Truman to allocate $1 billion for military aid in the next fiscal year.[39] Seeking to be responsive to French concerns, the JCS also agreed to move beyond its observer status on the NAT's regional planning groups and to accept participation "as appropriate." The Army, too, focused more of its attention on defending territory in Western Europe.[40]

Yet these steps were meager. The military assistance envisioned by the Americans would not allow for a defense of the continent in the short run. It would take four or five years to build up 25 well-equipped divisions, and even then it would be

uncertain whether European forces themselves could hold the continent. No one believed the Soviets wanted war, but prudence demanded that officials be aware of the
consequences of a Soviet conquest of Western Europe in an accidental war. Nitze
carried around a series of charts demonstrating that, if the Kremlin gained control
of the resources and industrial infrastructure of Europe, its warmaking capabilities
would challenge those of the United States.[41]

■

The realities pointed inexorably to a greater use of German resources for the
defense of Europe. Yet open discussion of this subject was taboo. Acheson confided
to the Senate Foreign Relations Committee that the State Department was thinking
of integrating Germany for defense purposes but could not talk about it publicly because it would jeopardize efforts to bring about economic and political integration,
which were the indispensable prerequisites to military integration. When rumors circulated in the press that the United States was contemplating German rearmament,
Acheson moved quickly to crush them. Yet a careful reading of the State Department position demonstrates that Acheson and his colleagues were ruling it out only
in the near term—that is, until it was unequivocally clear that a rearmed Germany
would be firmly in the Western orbit. At Policy Planning Staff meetings, Acheson
categorically asserted, "You cannot have any sort of security in western Europe
without using German power." Kennan agreed, and so did John McCloy. When the
U.S. high commissioner testified before the Senate Foreign Relations Committee
in a closed session on 23 January 1950, he said he was for bringing Germany into
NATO and using its manpower to establish a formidable West European army.[42]

If the United States wanted to rehabilitate Europe economically in peacetime
and if France wanted to mount a successful defense at the Rhine in wartime, Germany had to be integrated into Europe as a full partner. But this prospect terrified the
French and made them question whether they wanted to proceed down the course
contemplated by the Americans. The West Germans, the French knew, would soon
be seeking to restrict further the powers of the high commissioners. They would
struggle to regain control over their foreign trade and foreign relations. The West
Germans, too, would want to lift the remaining restrictions on their industries and
would not long tolerate international regulation of production and trade in the Ruhr.
For the French, then, there were no attractive options. At best, the Germans might
dominate a Western Union; at worst, they might ally with the Russians. Yet even in
the act of co-opting German power, Soviet-U.S. rivalry might ignite a conflict that
would engulf the entire Western alliance while the Rhine remained an undefendable
frontier. So the French remained wary, not easily persuaded that they should seize
the initiative to bring about West Germany's integration.

From the U.S. perspective, however, solutions could not be postponed. McCloy
warned of the growth of German unemployment, the stagnation of German exports,
and the continuing payments deficits. Although conditions were not as bad as when

Hitler took power, McCloy considered them very worrisome. Kennan called them "bitter."[43] After the initial boom that followed the currency reform in June 1948, production gains slackened. From early 1949 through the first quarter of 1950, economic growth in West Germany was slower than anticipated. Unemployment rose to 12.2 percent of the labor force (compared with 8 percent in early 1949). The trade deficit worsened and still exceeded $1 billion in 1949. There was a steep increase in German imports from the rest of Western Europe, and the positive results of Ludwig Erhard's trade liberalization and free-market policies were not yet evident. In report after report, the CIA fretted that economic stagnation might well force the West Germans to look eastward for markets and to gravitate into the Soviet bloc.[44]

Such a prospect assumed an even more ominous character as U.S. officials began to think about the implications of the Soviet acquisition of atomic capabilities. Kennan clearly felt that it might no longer be possible for the United States to respond to a conventional Soviet attack with atomic weapons. Acheson and Nitze not only agreed but also argued that the United States and Western Europe might have to augment their conventional armaments, notwithstanding the costs that might be incurred and the reduction in living standards that might ensue.[45] Of course, these eventualities were to be deeply regretted because they might engender the social ferment and political unrest that would facilitate Communist political gains. All the more reason, therefore, to come to grips with Germany's potential contribution to the peacetime economy of Western Europe as well as to its rearmament efforts and warmaking capabilities.

The impasse over German and West European political and economic integration had to be broken. In early 1950 the ECA intensified its efforts to overcome the negative legacy of British devaluation and to eliminate the impediments to intra-European trade; the State Department resumed its assessment of the political-military mechanisms to allay French anxieties about German power; and the Army inaugurated new studies to bolster European defenses in wartime and to thwart European neutralism in peacetime.[46] But progress in all these areas appeared problematical. And meanwhile, U.S. officials had to ponder the implications of grave new developments.

The End of the Atomic Monopoly

Strategic bombing with atomic weapons had been at the core of U.S. war plans ever since the military began thinking seriously about the prospects of armed conflict with the Soviet Union. Truman was never happy with this emphasis on atomic weaponry, but he neither spent much time pondering options nor asked his subordinates to study alternatives. Comparatively, atomic weapons were cheap, and Truman accepted plans and approved budgets that made the United States dependent on their use should war erupt.[47]

In July 1949 the JCS sought again to enlarge the atomic stockpile. Although it was multiplying rapidly (from about 50 bombs in June 1948 to a little under 300 in June 1950), the military establishment wanted additional atomic weapons based on the estimated requirements of U.S. war plans.[48]

This time Truman questioned the JCS request. Military officials seemed to be trying an end run around his budgetary constraints. They were seeking additional funds not for the military budget per se but for the Atomic Energy Commission (AEC). He decided to appoint a special subcommittee of the National Security Council (NSC) to examine the matter. The president asked Acheson to chair the committee. The other members were Secretary of Defense Johnson and David Lilienthal, chairman of the AEC.[49]

Acheson put Webb in charge of the State Department review. In turn, Webb relied on the advice of Kennan and R. Gordon Arneson, his special assistant for atomic energy affairs. Kennan attended a couple of meetings with military planners and pressed them to explain the reasons for the buildup. When they responded with vague generalizations, Kennan began to articulate his own profound doubts about the merits of atomic weapons in general and the present proposals in particular. Acheson and Rusk listened, distanced themselves from his views, and decided to reserve final judgment. Arneson's advice, rather than Kennan's, impressed Webb. Arneson believed that the State Department should avoid a fight with the Pentagon over an accelerated atomic arms program. It was far more important, he thought, to elicit the Defense Department's cooperation in working out new arrangements with the British and Canadians regarding the sharing of atomic information, the distribution of fissionable material, and the production and stockpiling of atomic weapons.[50]

Under the existing agreement, the Truman administration exchanged atomic information with the British for peaceful purposes. In return the United States not only had the right (until 1950) to acquire all the newly produced uranium ore from the Belgian Congo but also had a claim to British reserves of unprocessed and unallocated atomic raw materials. The British, however, were developing their own atomic bomb. They increasingly requested information that pertained to weapons development, information that was barred under the agreement. Acheson and Lilienthal believed that the United States should face the reality of a British weapons program and should share relevant information.[51]

But Senator Brien McMahon, the Democratic chairman of the Joint Committee on Atomic Energy, and leading Republicans opposed this idea. They despised the thought of disseminating information that would allow any nation, even America's most trusted ally, to shatter the U.S. atomic monopoly.[52]

State Department officials wanted the Pentagon's help in negotiating with the British and in trying to overcome senatorial opposition. But Johnson was infuriated by the thought that the British might withdraw from the prevailing accord and thereby imperil the flow of raw materials to the United States. He attacked Webb for coddling the British and accused Lilienthal of doing an inefficient job.[53]

In Johnson's view, the only way to cut defense costs without undermining military capabilities was to strengthen the air/atomic component. Atomic weapons generated formidable striking power at relatively small cost compared with conventional weapons.[54]

Webb and Lilienthal fumed at Johnson. Big, tough, and assertive, the defense secretary was not an easy man to sympathize with.[55] But his energies were absorbed and his patience taxed by the public brawl he was having with the Navy. In August 1949 the admirals revolted when they learned that the defense secretary was about to shave the Pentagon budget by another $1 billion and that the Navy would bear the brunt of the reduction, a cut of almost $400 million. Johnson, they charged, favored the Air Force, erred in procuring additional B-36 bombers, and engaged in personal favoritism in awarding contracts.[56] The admirals claimed that U.S. war plans depended too heavily on an atomic blitz. Strategic bombing, they argued, would not force the enemy to surrender. Even if the Russians did capitulate, the civilian losses caused by atomic attacks on enemy cities would be immoral, and postwar reconstruction everywhere would be endangered.[57]

Johnson and Bradley were appalled by the admirals' accusations, many of which were voiced in open Senate hearings. They supported Francis P. Matthews, the new secretary of the Navy, when he fired Louis Denfeld, the chief of naval operations. Publicly, Johnson and Bradley sought to defend existing plans and procedures. The admirals' allegations, they insisted, distorted the importance of the B-36 in U.S. strategy and distracted attention from the balanced plans that had been decided on.[58] Privately, they continued to grapple with irreconcilable pressures. At one and the same time, they struggled to comply with the president's $13 billion budget ceiling and to formulate an integrated defense plan that met Allied demands for a defense on the Rhine. With limited funds, they attempted to match capabilities with the strategic undertakings of their war plans and with the diplomatic commitments of the State Department. In the short run, the strategic offensive, as the admirals argued, might not be able to prevent Soviet armies from overrunning Europe. But Johnson and Bradley assumed that, as the nation's air and atomic capabilities further improved and as European nations enhanced their own conventional capabilities, the Rhine would be defended. Confidentially, the Joint Chiefs of Staff (JCS) maintained that their request for an accelerated atomic weapons program stemmed from their realization that newly designed bombs could be used economically in lieu of conventional weapons to thwart the advance of Soviet forces. Army planners looked upon tactical atomic weapons as a key instrument for breaking up Soviet troop concentrations and seizing critical areas. With more and better atomic weapons, Western Europe might be held.[59]

■

Until autumn 1949, much of this discussion was of abstract importance. Officials were convinced that war was unlikely so long as the United States possessed an atomic monopoly. The bomb, in fact, served as more than a deterrent to unprovoked Russian aggression; it constituted a shield behind which the nation could pursue its diplomatic goals. So long as the Russian sphere was not directly challenged, State Department officials assumed that the Soviets would back down rather than allow a diplomatic crisis to come to a test of arms. U.S. officials, therefore, possessed the confidence to do things they might otherwise have hesitated to do if they suspected that their actions could trigger a sequence of moves that might lead to war.[60]

Then suddenly the monopoly was over. In September 1949 U.S. intelligence sources picked up traces of radioactivity over the northern Pacific and, after several weeks, concluded that the Soviets had detonated an atomic device. Truman hesitated a while before making the announcement. He feared that it would profoundly disturb the peoples of Western Europe and the United States. After a few days of bold headlines and alarmist stories, however, the public seemed to adjust. Only 5 percent of Americans said the control of atomic weapons was the most important problem facing the country. Officials were surprised by the calm reaction of people at home and abroad.[61]

In fact, U.S. policymakers were far more agitated than were the American people. Officials had known that the Soviets would soon possess the bomb. Acheson had been saying that the Kremlin would acquire atomic capabilities in mid-1950 or 1951. But the reality was shocking. U.S. officials did not fear any immediate changes in the military balance of power, but the political and psychological implications appeared enormous, coming precisely when the British were devaluing the pound and reassessing their own global capabilities.[62]

Policymakers had to rethink the place of atomic weapons in U.S. foreign and military policies. If atomic weapons had been vital to U.S. war plans, Pentagon officials would now have to reassess their strategy in light of the expectation that the Soviets would someday be able to retaliate. If the value of atomic weapons were diminished by the fact that adversaries now possessed them, it would be incumbent upon U.S. officials to reappraise their approach to the international control of atomic energy. And, most important, if atomic weapons had been central to deterrence and diplomatic risk-taking, policymakers at Foggy Bottom would have to rethink the diplomatic implications of the Soviet acquisition of atomic capabilities.[63] If Europeans concluded that the United States would not risk atomic retaliation for the defense of Europe, would they proceed with measures to integrate West Germany into Western Europe? Would they go ahead with plans to build up their military capabilities, plans that they knew the Kremlin opposed? If heretofore they had assumed that the Kremlin was deterred by the U.S. atomic monopoly, would they now choose to forgo integration and military rearmament and avoid the attendant risks? Would they seek diplomatic accommodation rather than risk diplomatic crisis and possible war? And if war came, how indeed would the United States defend Europe if, in fact, it were unwilling to use nuclear weapons and risk atomic retaliation?

At meetings with Acheson and with the Policy Planning Staff, the State Department's top officials concluded that these matters merited extremely careful study. Webb worried that countries as far away from the United States as Afghanistan might be affected by the diplomatic shadows cast by the Soviet atomic explosion. Dean Rusk felt that U.S. strategic plans now had to be reexamined. Indeed, the nation's entire foreign policy posture required a reappraisal. It was time to rethink the conclusions of NSC 20/4, ponder whether rearmament should receive greater priority than economic assistance, study whether conventional or atomic weapons should be relied on for warmaking purposes, and assess whether containment across the Eurasian land mass was desirable and practical. Rusk said he would begin exploring these matters, and Acheson agreed to broach the matter with the president.[64]

■

The Truman administration now approved the JCS request to accelerate the atomic energy program. On 10 October, Johnson, Acheson, and Lilienthal submitted their report to the president. The secretary of defense reiterated the cost effectiveness of atomic weapons. New and smaller atomic weapons would decrease the logistical and personnel requirements for certain military tasks. Although Johnson made clear that his recommendations were not directly related to the recent Soviet atomic breakthrough, he stressed that the nation now needed enough weapons to attack atomic targets in the Soviet Union as well as to fulfill the strategic undertakings already enumerated in U.S. war plans. Johnson emphasized that "when the USSR attains a stockpile of atomic weapons, overwhelming superiority of our stockpile and production rate will be necessary if our atomic weapon posture is to continue to act as a deterrent to war." Acheson agreed. Lilienthal, unhappy with the report, nevertheless acknowledged that the accelerated program was feasible, provided agreement could be reached with the United Kingdom and Canada. Truman quickly approved the subcommittee's findings. He would ask Congress to appropriate the funds during the next fiscal year.[65]

The October decision was a particularly important one for the president. It set the pattern for his support of the hydrogen bomb. As soon as news of the Soviet atomic explosion became known, champions of thermonuclear weapons stepped up their demands for money and personnel. The possibility of developing a hydrogen bomb had been discussed since the end of World War II but had not been assigned a high priority. Nevertheless, several leading scientists, including Ernest Lawrence, Edward Teller, and Luis W. Alvarez, were extremely interested in it. So were members of the Military Liaison Committee that served as the conduit between the JCS and the AEC. And in the latter agency, Commissioner Lewis L. Strauss was also a proponent of thermonuclear weapons.[66]

The appeal of a bomb based on the fusion process, a super bomb as many called it, tantalized some scientists and many military planners. For the former, the hydrogen bomb constituted a new outlet for creative talents; for the latter, weapons a hundred times more powerful than the Hiroshima bomb were irresistible. Possession of such a bomb by the United States would instantly restore its superiority. On the other hand, if the Soviets developed it, the global balance of power would be transformed. The men at the Pentagon were not alone in such thinking. Paul Nitze talked to Teller and Lawrence and learned that, in their scientific opinion, the Soviets could indeed be working on the hydrogen bomb. If this were the case and if, in fact, thermonuclear weapons could be developed, the United States had to enter the race. For if the Soviets alone had the hydrogen bomb, the psychological fallout in peacetime would be enormous. They would assume risks they had heretofore eschewed; they would capitalize on revolutionary unrest and social dislocation. According to Nitze, they "might dominate the world."[67]

A major policy review ensued, a review that has received excellent treatment by other historians. Lilienthal, a majority of the commissioners on the AEC, and all the prominent scientists on the General Advisory Committee to the AEC opposed development of a thermonuclear weapon. They contended that it was an immoral, genocidal weapon. Moreover, there was no need for it. An expanded atomic arsenal could achieve the same goals. Atomic weapons would deter the Soviets from an attack even if they possessed the hydrogen bomb. Pursuit of thermonuclear weapons would only encourage the Soviets to emulate the U.S. effort, triggering an arms race of unprecedented dimensions.[68]

Johnson, the JCS, and Strauss disagreed. The United States had to try to develop the hydrogen bomb. In wartime, thermonuclear weapons could be used profitably against large concentrations of enemy troops and against the adversary's atomic air bases. Moreover, they could prove cost effective because of their tremendous striking power. Fewer bombs would be necessary; fewer crews would have to be trained; fewer planes would be required for their delivery. But the JCS clearly thought that the psychological advantages of the hydrogen bomb outweighed its military usefulness. If the Soviets had the super bomb, it

would have grave psychological and political repercussions . . . among the nations of the Western world. . . . It would provide the Soviet leaders, people, and satellites with a tremendous psychological boost which in peacetime could lead to increased truculence in international affairs and increased political infiltration in nations of the western world. The tremendous "blackmail" potential of the thermonuclear weapon would serve the USSR well in its aims to impose its will upon the nations of Europe and to alienate these nations from the Western camp.

Knowing how important the atomic monopoly had been to U.S. diplomatic strategy and war plans, the JCS dreaded the prospective impact of thermonuclear weapons on Soviet risk-taking.[69]

These arguments drew support in the State Department. Yet Acheson initially etched out a position of neutrality between the Defense Department and the AEC. When Truman reappointed the three-man committee to advise him on whether or not to go ahead with the super bomb, Acheson stressed that he would not be hurried into a decision. He thought work on the super bomb might intensify anxieties around the world and set back economic recovery. He wanted Kennan to have the time to make his case against atomic weapons. Yet Acheson repeatedly pointed out that a no-first-use policy might undermine U.S. deterrence and hurt diplomacy.[70]

Kennan poured all his energies into convincing his colleagues to abandon their reliance on atomic weapons and settle for an imperfect system of international control. He knew his influence was waning. He would make one last concerted effort to persuade Acheson that atomic weapons were not necessary for deterrence or for war. The reliance on atomic weapons, he said, distorted clear thinking about the nature of the threat and the best means to cope with it. The contest with the Kremlin was political. Without international control, there would be a psychological penchant to use atomic weapons. But the destruction would be out of all proportion to the ends desired. Kennan preferred to rely on a few well-prepared and highly mobile divisions to implement foreign policy. He was thinking in terms of limited war and not of full-scale conflict with the Kremlin.

Kennan's position on atomic weapons was inextricably linked to his diplomatic goals. Believing that European conventional capabilities could be built up to constitute an appropriate deterrent, he argued that the conventional superiority of Soviet armies was an artifact of the war, a product of the vacuum of power in Central Europe. The most important task was to get the Kremlin out of Eastern Europe and to co-opt German strength for the West. If an agreement could be reached that would disengage the Soviets from Eastern Europe and if the rest of Europe were integrated into a third force, then a viable conventional balance could be created on the European continent. Accordingly, he opposed including Great Britain in a prospective European continental union because he thought it would accentuate the difficulties of attracting Eastern Europe into it. But if this new configuration of power could be created and if some system of international control could be devised, the world would be a much safer place, and U.S. security would be enhanced far more than it would be through a nuclear arms race. A defense posture that had atomic weapons at its core, Kennan concluded, made no sense. In wartime, their use would be disastrous; in peacetime, their presence would complicate relations with friends and foes.[71]

From September 1949 through January 1950, Kennan's views received a fair hearing at the State Department. Although few of his colleagues were inclined to think in terms of a third force, many of his other ideas were looked upon sympathetically. Acheson shared Kennan's desire to build up European conventional strength, drive a wedge into the Kremlin's sphere of influence, and lure East European governments westward. Yet atomic superiority, far from undermining the nation's diplomacy as Kennan seemed to be arguing, appeared to be an indispensable asset.[72]

Acheson gravitated toward the ideas of Nitze. Yet it must be emphasized that neither Acheson nor Nitze differed with Kennan on the nature of the Soviet threat. They differed with him primarily on the role of atomic weapons in U.S. diplomacy. The military threat, Nitze insisted, was a tertiary one. The United States was locked in a cold war with the Kremlin, and the nature of the conflict was not likely to change. Soviet leaders, Acheson and Nitze maintained, "need and want the people, industry and resources of Western Europe. . . . Success in the cold war achieves these. The hot war may lose all this and more too." The supreme task was to develop a defense posture that would thwart Soviet peacetime efforts to gain control over critical resources, industrial infrastructure, and skilled labor. "This is important," Acheson noted in the most significant memorandum dealing with the hydrogen bomb: "The loss of Western Europe or of important parts of Asia or the Middle East would be a transfer of potential from West to East, which, depending on the area, might have the gravest consequences in the long run." [73]

Soviet atomic weapons, most State Department officials believed, enhanced the Kremlin's penchant for risk-taking. The Russians were more rash, more willing to take chances, more supportive of revolutionary movements around the world. Nitze compiled an exhaustive list of recent Soviet moves and concluded that their actions bordered on recklessness, especially as they endangered the power position of the United States. "Nothing about the moves indicates that Moscow is preparing to launch in the near future an all-out military attack on the West. They do, however, suggest a greater willingness than in the past to undertake a course of action, including a possible use of force in local areas, which might lead to an accidental outbreak of general military conflict. Thus the chance of war through miscalculation is increased." [74]

If the Soviets should also develop the hydrogen bomb, they would be further emboldened. They would not want war but they would take risks and seek gains that they had heretofore not dared to contemplate. There was no immediate military threat because the Soviets were not believed to have a significant stockpile of atomic weapons or any real delivery capabilities. But in five to ten years, the Soviet stockpile might be of sufficient size to neutralize the U.S. atomic deterrent. What then would substitute for this deterrent in peacetime and for this capability in wartime? It seemed as if Europe's conventional capabilities would have to be increased and the U.S. atomic arsenal enlarged still further. But these matters were infinitely complex, and Nitze urged Acheson to undertake the comprehensive review of the nation's diplomatic and strategic posture that had been contemplated since October. Meanwhile, Nitze argued that prudence demanded that the United States proceed to develop its own super bomb. The program need not be a crash program, but it should be undertaken. [75]

When Acheson met with Johnson and Lilienthal on 31 January 1950, his mind was made up. Well aware that the president was inclined to move ahead, Acheson recognized the substantial political pressures that demanded action. Senator McMahon was pressing for the project, as were prominent Republicans who were now more enraged than ever by Acheson's refusal to disavow Alger Hiss after the latter's recent conviction for perjury. Public opinion polls in January and February overwhelmingly supported the effort to build a hydrogen bomb. Although these considerations did not prompt Lilienthal to alter his opposition to thermonuclear weapons, they reinforced the geopolitical and diplomatic influences already impelling Acheson to move in this direction.[76]

In their brief meeting with the president, Acheson and Johnson urged that the United States proceed to determine the technological feasibility of a thermonuclear weapon and that concurrent work should be undertaken on ordnance development and on a carrier program. Although Acheson and Johnson acknowledged that the Soviets probably preferred to wage a cold war and that even if the Soviets possessed the super bomb they might not use it, the United States could not take such a risk. "Sole possession by the Soviet Union of this weapon would cause severe damage not only to our military posture but to our foreign policy position." The president agreed. If the Russians could do it, so must the Americans.[77]

At a time when the international situation still seemed fluid and the accomplishments in Europe ephemeral, U.S. officials rebelled at the thought of losing superiority in atomic weapons. They did not want to forfeit the psychological edge that inspired them to take risks and afforded them significant advantages in waging the cold war. If they had to ponder the possibility that the atomic power of the Soviet Union might prevail in a conflict or neutralize their own atomic arsenal, their diplomacy might become more cautious. They assumed that, if the men in the Kremlin thought U.S. officials might hesitate to act in a crisis, lest it escalate into a global conflict, Russian diplomacy would become more aggressive. The Soviets' inclination to use force in local areas would increase, their penchant to challenge the West in its traditional spheres of influence would mount, their temptation to thwart integration efforts in Western Europe would grow, and their efforts either to intimidate or to lure Western Germany eastward would intensify. It was believed that, heretofore, America's atomic monopoly had modulated Soviet risk-taking and had enabled the United States to proceed with the establishment of a configuration of power compatible with U.S. interests. If this advantage disappeared, the cold war might be lost.

Considerations of this sort, not domestic political or exclusively military ones, drove U.S. officials into an arms race. Public opinion proved to be malleable. In February and March, American attitudes swiftly changed. The historian Barton Bernstein has shown that, once prominent senators like McMahon and Millard Tydings changed their minds and called for a renewed peace effort, the majority of Americans agreed that the government should make another attempt at the international control of atomic energy before proceeding with the development of thermonuclear weapons. But Truman and his advisers were no longer interested in international control.[78]

Instead, after the British arrested Klaus Fuchs as a Soviet spy, the U.S. government decided to accelerate work on the hydrogen bomb. Fuchs had worked on the Manhattan Project and had been deeply involved in postwar atomic research. Officials feared that the Soviets might be farther along the road to a hydrogen bomb than they had previously assumed. Major General Kenneth D. Nichols and Brigadier General Herbert B. Loper of the Military Liaison Committee, in fact, taking a worst-case scenario, warned Johnson that the Soviets might have been working on thermonuclear weapons since 1945 and that these bombs might already be in production. The Russians' stockpile of atomic weapons might be equal to or superior to that of the United States. Johnson pressured the president to authorize a crash program "if we are not to be placed in a potentially disastrous position." Swayed by this warning, Truman ordered an acceleration of the hydrogen bomb project.[79]

Once again, it is essential to emphasize that U.S. officials were not worrying about purposeful Soviet military aggression. They were worried about the diplomatic shadows cast by strategic power. In the months following the detection of the atomic explosion in the Soviet Union, analysts in the State Department, AEC, CIA, JCS, Navy, Army, and Air Force invested enormous effort in estimating Soviet atomic capabilities and their impact on Soviet goals, tactics, and behavior. The information was sketchy and there was considerable discord over some details, but only the Air Force thought the Kremlin might be tempted into an outright attack on the United States. The consensus was that real danger would emerge in the mid-1950's. And even then the danger rested not so much on the likelihood of a Soviet preemptive attack on the United States as on the possibility of a war arising from miscalculation as the Soviets reacted to U.S. efforts to establish situations of strength in Europe and Asia and as they supported insurrectionary movements in the Third World.

Soviet atomic capabilities, the intelligence analysts concurred, made the world a much more dangerous place. They estimated that the Kremlin would have 10–20 atomic bombs in mid-1950, 25–45 a year later, 45–90 in mid-1952, and 120–200 by mid-1954. Not knowing the accuracy of Soviet weapons and delivery vehicles, the analysts squabbled over the percentage of bombs that were likely to be dropped on target. But there was no doubt that, as the Soviets built up their capabilities, the U.S. capacity to strike the Soviet Union without fear of retaliation would end. Moreover, U.S. bases in the United Kingdom would be increasingly at risk, and the United States would have to devote a much greater percentage of its budget to defensive weaponry. And once the Soviets could deliver about 200 bombs to their targets in the United States, a development that was thought likely to occur in the late 1950's, it was believed that America's industrial infrastructure could be dealt a crippling blow and its ability to wage a prolonged war might be jeopardized. U.S. officials would then have to ponder whether or not to risk a nuclear war.

The Kremlin, analysts were certain, would capitalize on these doubts. According to the Joint Intelligence Committee of the JCS, the Soviets would exploit fully the opportunity to erode the influence of the Western powers throughout the world. Thinking that the Americans might back down rather than risk nuclear war, the Russians might interfere in Berlin, promote German unification, support political seizures of power in Greece, Italy, or France, encourage the Chinese to give aid to Ho Chi Minh, or interfere with the negotiation of a Japanese peace treaty. The Soviets might demand a role in the Ruhr, object to the lifting of the remaining controls over West Germany, or insist on their right to reinsert troops into Japan. Even if the United States were not bullied by such actions, the intelligence agencies agreed that America's allies might "refrain from joining this country in taking a more positive political position against the USSR." [80]

Analysts also believed that, in undertaking these types of initiatives, the Kremlin might precipitate war. The United States, of course, could choose to back down or escalate the crisis. If it backed down, its efforts to thwart Soviet preponderance would be undermined. If it escalated the crisis, the country would be subject to atomic attack if war should erupt. The dilemmas were excruciating. For good reason, therefore, Truman endorsed Acheson's desire to conduct a wide-ranging analysis of the nation's goals in light of Soviet atomic and prospective thermonuclear capabilities.[81] But before the study could be completed, problems at home and abroad would worsen still further.

The Fate of Asia

In autumn 1949, the Chinese Communists consolidated their hold in the south and southwest of China and drove the remnants of Nationalist troops into Burma and across the straits to Taiwan. In October, Mao Tse-tung established the People's Republic of China and requested foreign governments to establish formal diplomatic relations. For all intents and purposes the civil war on the mainland was over; the Communists had triumphed.

Observing the ominous trend of events, Johnson again asked Acheson to join in a comprehensive study of U.S. policy toward Asia. Acheson's assistants resented Johnson's intrusion into their bureaucratic domain. They sneered at NSC 48, the initial paper produced by the NSC staff. Instead, the Far East experts in the State Department collaborated with Philip Jessup and the two outside Republican consultants, Everett Case and Raymond Fosdick, whom Acheson had chosen to review the administration's Asian policy. Since the *White Paper* had failed to quell the accusations of the China bloc, Acheson hoped that soliciting Republican input might resuscitate bipartisanship. Although renowned for his emphasis on European priorities, Acheson nevertheless deemed Asian problems to be among his foremost concerns.[82]

■

Virtually everyone concurred in the autumn of 1949 that Japan was the most important country in Asia. Japan's significance lay in its latent manufacturing potential and trained work force. Were "Japan added to the Communist bloc," Acheson informed British ambassador Oliver Franks, "the Soviets would acquire skilled manpower and industrial potential capable of significantly altering the balance of world power." The most pressing task of policy in Asia, therefore, was to thwart the Kremlin's capacity to gain direct or indirect control over Japan's industrial potential.[83]

No one expected the Soviets to seize Japan through aggressive action. The threats were more subversive, more insidious, more long-term. The denial of Japan to the Soviet Union, said the State Department, was "a problem of combatting, not overt attack and invasion, but concealed aggression. The threat to Japan . . . comes from agitation, subversion, and coup d'état. . . . Whether it succeeds depends primarily on the political, economic, and social health of Japan itself." [84]

The State Department believed that Japanese democracy or at least a pro-Western orientation depended on bringing the occupation to an end. If it continued, the Japanese people would become increasingly disgruntled, Japanese radicals would exploit the discontent, and the Kremlin would have more room to maneuver. By mid-1949 even Kennan had come to favor a peace settlement. The risks, he conceded, would be substantial. The Japanese might on their own volition turn to the left. But Kennan thought they would more likely turn to the right. The Japanese right, however, might seek an accommodation with the Kremlin if Japan's economic needs could not be fulfilled in the West. Kennan and his colleagues saw no alternative to accepting the risks, provided action were taken to cultivate new opportunities for Japanese trade in non-Communist Asia.[85]

In September 1949, Acheson asked Bevin if the British would be willing to proceed toward a treaty. He wanted to ascertain whether the two Anglo-Saxon nations and their major partners would be able to agree on provisions that would not endanger U.S. interests. For although Acheson knew that the Japanese had to be given greater control over their own affairs if they were to remain loyal to the West, he also realized that their internal and external security depended on the retention of U.S. troops in the post-treaty period or on the establishment of Japanese forces. He also knew that, if the Japanese were to become self-sustaining, they would have to be freed of controls over their industry and permitted to trade on nondiscriminatory terms with many of their former enemies. But there was no certainty that Australia and New Zealand or the Philippines, Burma, or any Asian government would go along. Acheson did not want to attend a peace conference where the Soviets might be able to thwart U.S. objectives. He wanted the basic provisions to be worked out in advance with friends.[86]

With the president's approval, Acheson asked the JCS and General MacArthur for their views on a Japanese peace treaty. MacArthur shared the State Department's desire for an early treaty. He was eager for a peace conference to take place in Tokyo that he would chair, a glorious conclusion to his career. As for the substantive provisions, he wanted the Japanese economy to be liberated from controls and its industry to prosper. He also insisted that the Japanese should remain disarmed. More surprisingly, he contended that U.S. vital interests demanded not much more than Soviet respect for Japan's neutrality and Soviet compliance with a nonaggression treaty. If the Soviets did not agree to neutralization, then the United States would have to retain troops, at least for a while. MacArthur was inconsistent on whether the United States had to have bases in Japan once a treaty was signed. The more important consideration, thought MacArthur, was to sign a bilateral agreement that would make clear to the Russians that, if they attacked Japan, the United States would immediately go to war.[87]

MacArthur's ideas shocked most officials at the Pentagon. Tracy Voorhees, undersecretary of the Army and Johnson's personal deputy for occupation matters, was asked to take charge of the work in the Department of Defense on the Japanese peace treaty. He was intent on coordinating his efforts with MacArthur, with the JCS, and with General James H. Burns (who oversaw most political-military matters for the secretary of defense). Voorhees was familiar with MacArthur's ideas and was inclined to defer to his stature. But the Army and the JCS would not seriously consider Japan's neutralization. General Bradley emphasized that base rights must not be barred by any treaty. Army experts, moreover, concluded that Japan had to have its own armed forces and a munitions industry.[88]

Voorhees was caught in a crossfire. Siding with MacArthur, he concluded that Japan's rearmament, no matter how desirable, could not be implemented soon. America's friends in Asia, no less than its enemies, would abhor the revival of Japan's military power. But he agreed with the JCS that Japan's security and its alignment with the West could not be jeopardized by hasty withdrawal, neutralization schemes, or the renunciation of bases. This view put him at odds with MacArthur, although Voorhees did agree that quick action was needed to end the occupation. He therefore proposed the idea of an occupation statute in lieu of a peace treaty, an agreement that would grant the Japanese considerable self-government without the United States' relinquishing formal rights to retain troops and bases in Japan. Voorhees's compromise position won him no friends. MacArthur scorned it and the JCS rejected it.[89]

After three months of squabbling, the JCS decided that it was premature to negotiate a treaty. The chiefs worried that any relaxation of U.S. authority might create a vacuum of power within Japan or allow the Japanese to maneuver between East and West. Because they demanded bases and contemplated Japanese rearmament, the JCS assumed that any treaty suitable to the United States would be repugnant to the Soviets and the Communist Chinese. The Russians might respond to U.S. initiatives with countermeasures of their own, triggering a dangerous crisis. Better that nothing be done, the JCS concluded, to provoke the Soviets.[90]

Acheson was furious. On 23 December 1949, he told Bradley that it was impossible both to satisfy U.S. security requirements and to win the adherence of the Soviet Union and China. He was willing to proceed without them, provided he could line up the rest of the Far East Commission on America's side. Even this task was assuming formidable dimensions as he learned of the security guarantees demanded by other countries in exchange for the risks they would incur in accepting

Japan's rehabilitation. But now, because of the Pentagon's position, he could not even turn his attention to these matters. He would not be able to say anything to the British before their commonwealth meeting at Colombo, Ceylon. The United States, Acheson lamented, would be criticized for delaying a treaty. The Soviets would skillfully exploit this news, blaming Japan's woes on U.S. intransigence. Slowly but surely, the Communists would maneuver to capture power and place Japan within the Soviet sphere.[91]

Acheson's exasperation was compounded by the fact that he shared the JCS objectives. He rejected MacArthur's neutralization schemes and was prepared to retain U.S. forces in Japan. He approved the appropriation of funds for base development at Okinawa and a naval facility at Yokosuka. He supported the resurfacing of Japanese airfields to make them suitable for the jet fighters that were coming off U.S. assembly lines. He knew there were risks in proceeding rapidly toward a peace treaty. But the odds of provoking the Soviets were considerably smaller than the risks inherent in a strategy of delay, which, in Acheson's view, would disillusion the Japanese and create opportunities for Soviet chicanery.[92]

■

The impasse over Japanese policy was reached just as various agencies completed their review of the larger paper on Asia that the NSC staff had drafted and the State Department had revised. A new dispute erupted over Taiwan. Defense analysts thought the situation was improving and that the Nationalist administration might survive, at least for a short while. Johnson and Bradley still did not want to use U.S. forces to defend the offshore island, but they now recommended sending military assistance and advisers to supplement ongoing diplomatic support and limited economic aid.[93]

Acheson opposed this view. He felt that the Nationalists had the resources to preserve themselves on Taiwan if they had the will and determination. But believing that Chiang and his associates were rotten to the core, he no longer thought the Nationalists could salvage the situation. Although he hoped Taiwan would not fall into Communist hands, Acheson did not want the United States to get further sucked into the defense of the Nationalist government. If Taiwan were not vital to U.S. strategic interests, as the JCS again concluded, then there was no reason to do anything more than was presently being done to bolster the regime.[94]

Acheson met with the JCS on 29 December. In subsequent weeks he repeated his views and expanded upon them in executive-session testimony before the Senate. Acheson believed that the Chinese Communists were now firmly in control of the mainland. They had won because they had championed agrarian reform, capitalized on the mistakes of the Kuomintang, and captured the revolutionary impulse that was engulfing all of Asia. The most expedient thing to do was to work for a split between Soviet Russia and China. Chinese irredentism, Acheson stressed, must not be deflected onto the United States. It would be foolhardy to assume military responsibilities for protecting the Nationalists on Taiwan, because that would provoke the wrath of Chinese on the mainland, invite them to foment unrest in Indochina and Southeast Asia, and sublimate the potential for a Sino-Soviet rift.[95]

Acheson assumed that China faced a grim future. Already there were reports of mismanagement, hardship, famine, and starvation; already there were stories of Russian aggrandizement and Sino-Soviet acrimony. Acheson wanted the Chinese Communists to wallow in their own problems and to incur the blame for all the turmoil and travail that would befall China in the future. Recognition might be contemplated but not because Acheson sought to improve relations with the Chinese Communist Party (CCP). Recognition afforded opportunities to preserve contacts with potential dissidents and to promote a benign image of America among the Chinese masses. In this way, the United States would be ready to profit when the Sino-Soviet rift occurred, or when disillusionment with the Communists became widespread, or when the Communists themselves divided into factions.[96]

In other words, Acheson's ideological animus toward the Chinese Communists persisted. Acheson stressed that the Chinese Communists were true Marxists. Although they had succeeded in China by their own efforts and were therefore different than Soviet satellites in Eastern Europe, they could not be trusted. Hoping that the Chinese people would come to see that their nationalist aspirations would be crushed by their ties to the Kremlin, Acheson had little faith that their Communist leaders would develop this perspective. Repeatedly, he emphasized that the Chinese Communists were the agents of Soviet imperialism. Their influence had to be contained no less than that of the Kremlin. To focus on Taiwan, Acheson admonished, was countereffective because it allowed the Communists to embody themselves as nationalists, redounded to their popularity, and inspired them to focus their venom on the United States.[97]

Acheson despised the public controversy that arose over Taiwan when his views were leaked to the press at the end of December 1949. He saw his Republican foes either as narrow-minded partisans or as shortsighted critics.[98] He pressed Truman to issue a statement renouncing any intention to intervene militarily in the offshore island. Convinced that Chiang's followers were incorrigibly corrupt and politically incapable of holding Taiwan, Truman did as Acheson advised. Although the president's antipathy toward the Chinese Communists far exceeded Acheson's, he was persuaded that the wedge strategy was the only one that made sense in terms of U.S. hopes to contain the Moscow-Peking axis. For Truman, even more than Acheson, the wedge strategy was a policy not of accommodation but of expediency.[99]

The point that Acheson wanted to make to the president and to everyone who would listen was that U.S. interests now had to focus on Japan and the rest of non-Communist Asia. For the short run, the loss of China was irretrievable. While hoping for a Sino-Soviet split, the United States had to protect the rest of Asia from the Communist virus. "The urgent question of 1950," wrote the CIA, "is whether Soviet-oriented, China-based Communism can continue to identify itself with nationalism, exploit economic privations and anti-Western sentiment, and sweep into power by one means or another elsewhere in Asia." [100]

Acheson sought to explain the administration's position in his famous address to the National Press Club on 12 January 1950. In this speech, Acheson was not writing off the Asian mainland. He acknowledged that in time of global war the U.S. strategic defense perimeter was limited to Japan, Okinawa, and the Philippines. But the whole point of his speech was to emphasize that it was a mistake "to become obsessed with military considerations." His concern was with winning the cold war, not waging a hot war. The most salient threat to U.S. interests in the region stemmed from the opportunities for Communist subversion. This threat had to be resisted. In Japan, South Korea, and the Philippines, the Truman administration would assume primary responsibility. In the rest of Asia, the United States would work with the newly independent countries of Indonesia, India, and Pakistan as well as with the European powers—Britain, France, and Holland—that still had considerable interests in the area. [101]

From Acheson's perspective, the most significant consequence of the Nationalist defeat in China was that it enhanced Chinese Communist influence in Indochina and Southeast Asia. Mao and his comrades could now establish direct contact with Ho Chi Minh in Vietnam and provide him with assistance and, although unlikely, troops. They could foment unrest in the large Chinese communities in Thailand, Malaya, and Indonesia. They could exacerbate the chaotic conditions in Burma. They could establish diplomatic relations with their southern neighbors and infiltrate agents and saboteurs, disguised as diplomats and commercial attachés. All of Southeast Asia was now at risk. [102]

The tactical disputes over military aid to Taiwan obfuscated the consensus about safeguarding the rest of Asia from the spread of communism. Defense officials, in fact, supported military aid to Taiwan partly because it would deflect Mao's attention from Southeast Asia. [103] When Johnson and the JCS were invited by Acheson's Republican foes to testify before the Senate Foreign Relations Committee in executive session in late January, and when they had every chance to present their case for additional aid to Chiang, they reiterated that Taiwan was *not* a vital interest. Instead, they stressed that the rest of Asia, including Korea, needed U.S. support and arms. [104]

No one pressed the case for aid to Southeast Asia more stridently than did Army Undersecretary Voorhees. He was convinced that Japan would be a continuous drain on the U.S. treasury and would be susceptible to internal subversion unless it could establish prosperous commercial ties with the rest of Southeast Asia. "Japan's economic recovery," he said, "depends upon keeping Communism out of Southeast Asia, promoting economic recovery there and in further developing those countries . . . as the principal trading areas for Japan." He criticized NSC 48/2 for providing inadequate economic aid to Southeast Asia. He sent a special mission to South and Southeast Asia to determine the extent to which Japan could supply those nations with capital equipment and manufactured goods and draw on them for food and raw materials. He pressed urgently for the integration of all economic and military aid going to Japan and Southeast Asia.[105]

Voorhees was frustrated by the State Department's hostility to his proposals. He looked to the JCS for support and received it.[106] From Section 303 funds for the general area of China, the JCS wanted to allocate $10 million for Burma, $10 million for Thailand, $5 million for Indonesia, $15 million for Indochina, $5 million for Malaya, $10 million for China (including Tibet), and a reserve fund of $20 million for possible use in Taiwan. Military officers realized that their strategic perimeter— that is, the island chain of Japan, Okinawa, and the Philippines—could not survive in peacetime apart from Southeast Asia. According to the JCS, U.S. security in the Far East hinged "upon finding and securing an area to complement Japan as did Manchuria and Korea prior to World War II." If action were delayed, if the Japanese economy should unravel, and if Japan should be lured into a Communist industrial complex in the Far East, "Russia would gain, thereby, an additional war-making potential equal to 25% of her own capacity." [107]

State Department officials did not really differ. Delays in implementing policy stemmed not from any substantive differences but from tactical disputes and organizational rivalries. Acheson, Webb, Jessup, Rusk, Kennan, and Butterworth remained just as worried about Communist incursions into Southeast Asia as did Voorhees and the JCS. Notwithstanding the potential for a Sino-Soviet split, State Department leaders had little doubt that Stalin, Mao, Ho, and other Asian Communists were closely allied. The Communist drive in China and Southeast Asia, concluded Jessup, "is now the tool of traditional Russian imperialism in the Far East." Policy had to be based on the assumption that a rift would not take place within the next few years. If Japan and the other islands composing the defense perimeter were to be aligned with the United States in wartime, they had to be economically and politically stable in peacetime. Acheson told the British ambassador that U.S. interests in the area composed an arc extending from Japan through all of Southeast Asia to the Indian Ocean. Kennan emphasized that any hope "of having healthy, stable civilization in Japan" depended on reopening "some sort of empire toward the south." [108]

Despite their common goals and similar perceptions of threat, the State and Defense departments fought for the control of assistance funds, as is vividly portrayed by the historian Michael Schaller. Johnson and Acheson maneuvered to gain Truman's support; Voorhees and Butterworth feuded incessantly. Yet Butterworth and his assistants were as wed to military aid as were the JCS. Acheson simply did not want to spend any of the Section 303 funds on China, as did defense officials, especially Johnson. But the State Department believed as strongly as did Defense that non-Communist governments in Southeast Asia required additional arms and better-trained armies and police forces to insure domestic stability.[109]

Acheson also agreed with Voorhees that economic assistance had to supplement military aid. Whereas Voorhees hoped to maximize the impact of existing funds by integrating and coordinating all assistance programs for Japan and Southeast Asia, Acheson tried to elicit additional monies from Congress. When friends of China in the Senate sought to extend the China Aid Act, Acheson did not object. Pointing out that the sums available greatly exceeded the amounts that could be used effectively in Taiwan, he requested permission to use a substantial part of the money in Southeast Asia. His senatorial foes were thinking narrowly of partisan advantage while Acheson was carefully calculating the requirements of thwarting Soviet preponderance throughout Asia.[110]

The Truman administration's perception of threat intensified when the People's Republic of China recognized Ho's government in Vietnam on 8 January 1950. Three weeks later the Kremlin followed suit. The CIA estimated that Ho had the support of four-fifths of the population; a State Department Working Group said he controlled two-thirds of the country. But no Communist, in Acheson's view, could represent anyone but the rulers in the Kremlin. The Soviet recognition of Ho, Acheson declared, simply confirmed that he was the "mortal enemy" of true independence. Immediately, the United States established formal diplomatic ties with Bao Dai.[111]

■

The Kremlin's overtures to Ho were regarded in Washington as part of an aggressive campaign to seize the initiative in Asia. The Russians now supported Chinese Communist membership in all international agencies and began boycotting the United Nations in order to force China's admission. At about the same time the Soviets surprised Americans by recognizing the new government of Indonesia. In Peking, they also established a liaison office of the Communist-controlled World Federation of Trade Unions, which the CIA interpreted as an effort to exert control over Asian labor groups. Through China, as Americans long had feared, the Soviets appeared to be trying to project their influence throughout Asia.[112]

Worse yet, in mid-February Stalin and Mao signed a 30-year treaty of mutual assistance. The Kremlin would provide China with $300 million in credits over five years and would relinquish concessions it had secured over Manchurian railroads and ports.[113] Publicly, Acheson scorned the treaty and sought to humiliate Chinese Communist leaders for betraying their country. "China," the secretary of state declared, "with its long proud history, is being forced into the Soviet orbit as a dependency of the Soviet political system and the Soviet economy." [114]

The pact confirmed U.S. views that, for the time being, the Soviets and Chinese were united in their efforts to spread communism and gain a position of preponderance in Asia. Speculation, of course, persisted that Mao and Stalin were squabbling and that Moscow and Peking were competing for influence south of China's borders. But Acheson maintained he could *not* base policy on the prospect of a rift or on hopes of Chinese Titoism. The last U.S. diplomats leaving Shanghai saw no evidence of Sino-Soviet acrimony. Intelligence analysts reported that Russian military advisers and technicians were flocking into China. The State Department's China experts were shocked by the bellicosity of Communist rhetoric and apparent hatred of the United States. Dean Rusk, now the assistant secretary of state for Far Eastern affairs, concluded that the Chinese Communists were the "junior partners" of the Russians and possessed the intention not simply of taking Taiwan but of dominating all of Southeast Asia. "From our viewpoint," Acheson told America's European allies in May 1950, "the Soviet Union possesses position of domination in China which it is using to threaten Indochina, push in Malaya, stir up trouble in the Philippines, and now to start trouble in Indonesia." [115]

Although a split might still occur, Acheson could not take chances when the fate of all of Asia was at stake. Nationalist fervor and revolutionary forces were astir throughout Southeast Asia, and Japan's loyalty to the West could not be counted on. Furthermore, the Soviet acquisition of atomic weaponry might inspire the Kremlin to take risks to capitalize on favorable trends or to counter America's own initiatives. Charles Yost, director of the Office of East European Affairs, pointed out that during the apex of the Greek crisis Stalin had not recognized the Greek Communists, but now he was dealing openly with Ho. The generalists in the State Department, like Nitze, as well as the Europeanists and the Kremlinologists acknowledged that Southeast Asia had become a major theater in the cold war and was inextricably linked to developments in Western Europe and Northeast Asia.[116] But while the administration comprehensively reassessed its global objectives, its critics were reaching different conclusions about the ominous trend across the Pacific.

The Rise of McCarthy and the Demise of Bipartisanship

The sterling crisis, the European integration impasse, the Soviet acquisition of atomic capabilities, and the threat to Southeast Asia and Japan were grievous problems for the Truman administration. Until late 1949 the Democrats had largely preserved bipartisan support. Their policies had thrown the Soviets on the defensive, and Republicans had found it difficult to argue with success. Presidential candidate Thomas Dewey and Senator Arthur Vandenberg continued to identify themselves with the internationalism of the Truman administration. Those Republicans who had been tempted to challenge Truman had been kept in line by his readiness to label them appeasers, isolationists, and even friends of the Kremlin.[117]

Diplomatic setbacks now fanned the flames of the opposition. The China issue alone would not have sufficed because Chiang's friends in Congress were few. True, their ranks grew as the Nationalists fled from the mainland and as controversy whirled around the *White Paper* in August 1949. But their ability to influence legislation remained constrained and their support was limited. Only a small minority of Americans retained a favorable image of Chiang.[118]

Most Republicans had kept their distance from the China bloc. They were inclined to follow Robert A. Taft, who usually deferred to Vandenberg's leadership on foreign policy issues and who had spoken only occasionally in behalf of the Nationalist cause. Yet in 1949 Taft's aversion to Truman's domestic policies mounted and his misgivings about the benefits of bipartisanship intensified. Republicans got little credit for foreign policy successes, yet they could not take advantage of the Democrats' failures. As Taft and other Republicans contemplated strategy for the 1950 congressional elections, they yearned to launch a full assault on Truman's foreign policies. With Dewey defeated and Vandenberg dying of cancer, they took control of the party.[119]

They then struck at the Truman administration. Taft was animated by his desire to kill Truman's farm and health-insurance bills. Through the China issue, the Ohio Republican hoped to embarrass the administration. The State Department, Taft declared, was "liquidating" the Nationalists and handing China to the Communists. The U.S. Navy, he insisted, should protect Taiwan.[120]

Truman and Acheson quickly rebutted the pleas for aggressive action in East Asia. They spoke out boldly against military intervention and rallied Democrats behind them. On 5 January 1950, in one of his most brilliant performances before the Senate Foreign Relations Committee, Acheson illuminated the rationale behind his views and chastised his opponents for their shortsightedness. Most Republicans retreated. They knew that the American people did not favor using force to salvage Chiang's discredited regime, and they had no constructive alternatives to offer. The Democrats, conceded John Foster Dulles, had won the partisan battle over Taiwan.[121]

But neither Taft nor Acheson would let the matter rest. On 11 January, Taft delivered a biting speech accusing the State Department of purposely betraying Chiang. The next day, Acheson presented his views on Asia to the National Press Club. Carefully avoiding any references to Taiwan and expressing the nation's great concern with developments across the Pacific, Acheson beautifully illuminated the struggle of Asian peoples to overcome their grinding poverty and gain national independence. But then, as before, he played into the hands of his adversaries and undermined his own strategy by stressing that Communists everywhere were agents of Soviet imperialism.[122]

The reification of the ideological challenge was precisely what his enemies wanted to hear. Just over a week later, Alger Hiss was convicted of perjury. Acheson and Hiss had known one another for much of their professional careers. Like Acheson, Hiss personified the liberal, internationalist, eastern establishment that had run foreign policy for a decade. He had gone to the finest schools, clerked at the Supreme Court, identified with the New Deal, advanced rapidly in the State Department, accompanied Franklin Roosevelt to Yalta, and achieved the presidency of the Carnegie Endowment for International Peace. But now Hiss was found guilty of lying before a congressional committee and of trying to conceal his alleged Communist past and his theft of confidential documents. Although Hiss had exercised no influence on policy, his presence at Yalta and Acheson's defense of him handed the Republicans an opportunity they could not resist.[123]

They pounded away at the administration. They clamored for Acheson's resignation, assailed his legislative proposals, and even questioned the Marshall Plan. Why provide aid to foreign countries, Republicans mused, when the Hiss case had proven that the real problem rested with an administration that permitted the "enemy to guide and shape our policy"?[124]

Truman, Acheson, and their advisers were trying to regroup when they were clobbered again by news that the British had arrested Klaus Fuchs for passing atomic information to the Soviets. Fuchs "was no peripheral guy," David Lilienthal acknowledged to his congressional inquisitors, "but a scientist who knew most of the weapons stuff because he had helped work out many of the most difficult of the problems."[125] By admitting the magnitude of the problem, the outgoing chairman of the Atomic Energy Commission hoped to quell additional partisan attacks. But the Fuchs arrest, coming only weeks after the conviction of Hiss, added fuel to the fire. Republicans pummeled Democrats for their laxity on security matters and for their toleration of Communists in government. These themes resonated deeply in American minds; these themes had been used by conservative Republicans to discredit the New Deal and the Fair Deal for over a decade. Now they would be pressed with a vigor and viciousness that were unprecedented.[126]

■

On 9 February 1950 in Wheeling, West Virginia, Joseph McCarthy, the junior senator from Wisconsin, attacked Acheson, that "pompous diplomat in striped pants," for harboring 205 Communists in the Department of State. During the following days and weeks the numbers changed with dizzying rapidity, but the message remained the same. The United States was losing the cold war because Democratic officials had no desire to win, because they were sympathetic to communism, because they were betraying the "Democratic Christian World." After disregarding McCarthy's initial speech, journalists and reporters showed mounting interest in his allegations. By the time McCarthy reiterated his accusations on the Senate floor on 20 February, Senate Democrats felt they had no alternative but to appoint a subcommittee to investigate the charges. Their intent was to pull the rug out from under McCarthy before Republicans could capitalize politically on his growing publicity.[127]

The investigation began during the second week of March. The Senate caucus room was packed day after day as McCarthy named individuals and as Democrats pressed him to substantiate his charges. The Wisconsin senator's evidence was flimsy. His initial case against Dorothy Kenyon, a woman most reporters had never heard of, was appallingly weak. The Democrats now hoped to discredit McCarthy. Truman took a hard line, refusing to hand over to Senate investigators the loyalty files of individuals in the executive branch. McCarthy, faced with humiliation, raised the stakes. After casually accusing Philip Jessup, perhaps Acheson's most trusted adviser, of an "unusual affinity for Communist causes," he then went after Owen Lattimore, one of the most respected Asia scholars in the United States and an occasional private consultant to State Department officials. By pursuing Jessup and Lattimore, McCarthy linked the accusations against the administration's security measures with an indictment of its China policy, for Jessup and Lattimore were both well known for their antipathy to Chiang Kai-shek.[128]

At the end of March, the atmosphere became still more charged. Republican senator Styles Bridges requested Acheson's resignation and demanded a cleaning of the State Department's Far East division. Truman came to Acheson's defense. The attacks on his secretary of state, Truman declared, were playing into the hands of the Soviet Politburo. McCarthy, he quipped, was "the greatest asset the Kremlin had." [129]

Truman's counterattack delighted McCarthy. It gave him greater publicity and encouraged wavering Republicans to rally around him. Taft spoke out in his behalf. McCarthy was "a fighting marine who risked his life to preserve the liberties of the United States. The greatest Kremlin asset in our history," Taft continued, "has been the pro-Communist group in the State Department who surrendered to every demand of Russia at Yalta and Potsdam, and who promoted at every opportunity the Communist cause in China until today Communism threatens to take over all of Asia." [130]

Bipartisanship faded. Truman and Acheson tried to resurrect it. To palliate the opposition, Acheson named Rusk to replace Butterworth as his assistant secretary of state for Far Eastern affairs, since Butterworth had become the bête noire of the China bloc. In a still more significant gesture, Acheson asked John Foster Dulles to take charge of the preparations for a Japanese peace treaty. And finally, Truman and Acheson met with Senator Bridges, reviewed the entire range of foreign policy issues with him, and promised to hold more such chats in the future. Yet Bridges made clear that he remained unsatisfied.[131]

With the Republicans' lust for political advantage mounting, the administration found itself beset with domestic acrimony and external woes. The dynamic interaction of internal and external challenges threatened to paralyze its foreign policy. State Department officials recognized that the dollar gap, the arms race, the turmoil in Asia, and the integration impasse in Europe demanded new initiatives. These, in turn, would require congressional support, a bipartisan consensus, and a willingness to spend sums of money, lower tariffs, and assume commitments that exceeded anything the United States had done before. But the rise of McCarthy, the never-ending stream of disloyalty accusations against State Department officials, and the demise of bipartisanship meant that Acheson and his advisers had to move cautiously, plan carefully, and design a compelling case for anything they wanted to do.

Readying the Options

Gloom hung over the Department of State throughout the spring of 1950. Acheson knew the momentum had been lost. Work had to proceed on a European payments union to facilitate intra-European trade. But Acheson realized that economic measures of this sort had no popular appeal. As he explored his options and prepared for another round of talks with the British and French in May, Acheson's inclination was to look to the political realm for solutions. He wanted to strengthen the NAT and garner British help for an imaginative assault on the world's trouble spots.[132]

But his colleagues were not optimistic. They worried about labor unrest in France and the resurgence of Communist strength in Italy. They were scared that Soviet peace overtures might enliven neutralist sentiment throughout Western Europe. They were afraid that U.S. leverage would disappear after the Marshall Plan ended in 1952; even worse, the Atlantic allies might turn defeatist once they believed that the Kremlin could retaliate against the United States with atomic weapons.[133]

Worrisome as these issues were, they paled in comparison to the problem of Germany. The Federal Republic was functioning; the right was quiescent; the Communist left constituted no threat. But all was not well. Production was up, but the trade deficit was still enormous. Adenauer was cooperative, but the German chancellor governed by a slender thread. Schumacher attacked him mercilessly, insisting that Germans should regain control of their economy, foreign policy, and national destiny. The Germans, reported McCloy, were "nervous, hysterical, and uncertain." They decried the West's weakness and sought guarantees for their security yet were lured to the East by the promise of markets and unification. Accommodating their demands seemed prudent, except for the fear that "as soon as Germany recaptures her freedom of maneuver she will inevitably begin to play the West off against the East with the very real danger of coming to rest on the side of the Soviet Union. This is the nightmare of West European nations," explained Charles Bohlen, then serving as the U.S. minister in Paris, "and it should be ours as well." [134]

And it was. The immediate objective, Acheson and Nitze agreed, was to co-opt West German power for the Atlantic community. The controls over Germany had to be relaxed. But they could be relaxed only if Germany's feet were permanently grounded in the West. Then, thought Acheson, the Federal Republic could make a great contribution to the Atlantic alliance. It was too early to talk of German rearmament, for that would alarm the French, but German coal, steel, and shipbuilding could help revitalize the defenses of Western Europe.[135]

Acheson was not worried about premeditated Soviet aggression. But he believed that perceptions of Soviet military strength weakened the confidence of Europeans in the Atlantic community and jeopardized their alignment with the United States. Defense matters, therefore, now had to assume priority. The Atlantic alliance, in Acheson's view, provided a vehicle for strengthening Britain's ties to the continent, reassuring France, and facilitating German integration while allaying German anxieties about their own security. If the British still resisted greater economic ties to Europe, then they might accept a more binding political-military relationship. If the French still feared the resurrection of German productive and latent military capabilities, then their apprehensions might be allayed if they knew that German power would be balanced by a greater commitment from the Anglo-Saxon nations and a more tightly knit alliance. If Germans wanted firmer guarantees of their security and more equality, then a restructuring of NATO's floundering administrative machinery might help. Acheson acknowledged that he did not see clearly how he might go about accomplishing all these complex and contradictory tasks. But he was envisioning a permanent NAT council with a permanent staff as well as new machinery to coordinate economic and military policies. More significantly, he was contemplating the permanent deployment of up to five U.S. divisions in Europe.[136]

■

Significant though these issues were, they were not the only ones commanding Acheson's attention. The problems of Europe, Acheson emphasized, could not be solved apart from the rest of the world. Europe needed markets in and raw materials from North Africa, the Middle East, and South and Southeast Asia. The United States had to make more vigorous efforts to thwart the Communists in these areas. Acheson did *not* seek to supplant British and French power in their former colonial domains. He wanted to share the burden and divide the costs of containing communism, fostering stability, and promoting production and trade.[137]

Acheson was especially eager to talk to Bevin and Schuman about the situation in Southeast Asia. Throughout the spring of 1950, he and his aides watched conditions deteriorate in the Philippines, Malaya, and Indochina.[138] The strategic area from Japan to India, Acheson insisted, must be kept "on our side of the fence and not on the Russian side." [139] In March he and Johnson urged Truman to allocate military aid to Indochina and Thailand in addition to the amounts already earmarked for the constabulary in Indonesia and for river patrol boats in Burma. More money, Acheson and Johnson told the president, would be needed in the future.[140] Meanwhile, they expedited the shipment of scarce military supplies to Indochina and agreed to establish military advisory groups.[141] They also approved small amounts of economic assistance for the area.[142]

The one subject that Acheson did not plan to discuss with Schuman and Bevin was Japan. Defense officials would not allow him to break new ground. But here, as elsewhere, Acheson was eager to consider new options. He was convinced that the occupation had served its purposes. If the Japanese were not permitted to control their own destiny, they would become disillusioned with U.S. tutelage. The Soviets might then call for a treaty, make overtures to the Japanese, and lure them away from the U.S. orbit.[143]

To avoid this contingency, Acheson's advisers sought to link a Japanese peace treaty with a collective security pact for the Pacific. The occupation would end and Japan would regain its sovereignty. In the accompanying collective security agreement, to be signed by Japan, the United States, Australia, New Zealand, and the Philippines, Japan would be guaranteed protection from the Soviets, and Japan's former enemies would be safeguarded against the resurgence of Japanese power. The mutual security pact, State Department experts thought, might induce Japan's former adversaries to accept a liberal peace treaty. The pact would allow the United States to retain military facilities in Japan, and the treaty would not foreclose the possibility of limited Japanese rearmament. Truman said he liked these ideas. So did Dulles, who was just joining the State Department and whose help would be indispensable for garnering bipartisan support.[144]

But Johnson and the JCS objected. They doubted whether any treaty would provide adequate military facilities and fretted over the prospective retrenchment of U.S. power in East Asia and the western Pacific. But most of all, the JCS seemed genuinely worried that a peace treaty would provoke the Soviets. Should a treaty be signed without their assent and should U.S. troops depart, the Russians might claim that a state of war still legally existed between the Soviet Union and Japan. They might then deploy troops, sink Japanese shipping, or subvert Japan's economic life. Given the deteriorating situation elsewhere in Asia, the JCS did not want to incur these risks.[145]

On 24 April, Acheson met with Johnson and the JCS. The two secretaries' personal relations were now badly strained. Johnson taunted Acheson, saying the only propaganda for a peace treaty emanated from the State Department. In turn, Acheson scorned the timidity of the JCS, believing risk-taking to be essential. In his view the Soviets would not move militarily no matter what their legal rights. They were not ready for war. They might try, however, to outmaneuver the United States by issuing their own call for a peace conference. Acheson sought to mollify defense officials, reiterating that their strategic demands would be met in any agreement. But the chiefs retorted that a treaty was premature. The risks of a unilateral treaty were not warranted by the magnitude of Japanese opposition to the occupation, which they did not think was very great. Johnson requested that nothing be done until he and Bradley visited Japan in June and consulted with MacArthur. Acheson clearly wanted to discuss Japanese matters with Bevin in London, but he did not dare antagonize the military establishment, whose opposition would thwart Senate ratification of any treaty.[146]

■

When the meetings in London and Paris got under way in May, Acheson told French and British officials that he hoped for a successful holding action in Southeast Asia while the Western alliance seized the offensive in Western Europe. He reminded Schuman and Bevin that the United States would not assume primary responsibility for the fate of Southeast Asia. The British and French had to do their fair share: they had to accommodate nationalist movements but must not withdraw from the region. If they did, Ho Chi Minh would triumph because he had success-fully captured the nationalist mantle. French troops, therefore, had to stay and fight. The Truman administration would help. Acheson confided to Schuman that during May and June the United States would provide $15 million of military aid and $5 million in economic assistance. More relief would be forthcoming in the new fiscal year beginning in July.[147]

Acheson then turned his attention to European priorities. Since January the vari-ous NATO committees and regional groupings had encountered formidable prob-lems as they had turned their attention to the implementation of the strategic concept and the Medium Term Defense Plan.[148] Acheson wanted to break the logjam. He told Bevin and Schuman that European defenses had to be augmented and the insti-tutional machinery of the NAT strengthened. Economic plans had to be linked to the defense program without jeopardizing standards of living and exacerbating social unrest. Acheson said that unused industrial capacity in Germany could be geared to the military buildup and that Germany's future association with NATO should not be foreclosed. German demands for lifting the controls on its economy and sov-ereignty had to be accommodated through additional revisions of the Occupation Statute; yet its freedom to maneuver between East and West had to be circumscribed by creating a web of institutional ties with the Western alliance. Recognizing the demands that the defense effort would place on the European economy, Acheson made a significant gesture, stating that U.S. aid would continue beyond 1952. But Europeans had to integrate economically, remove trade restrictions, achieve econo-mies of scale, lower production costs, and compete more effectively in international markets. If they could agree on the European Payments Union (EPU), it would constitute an important step in this direction.[149]

Acheson's ideas were shunted aside when Schuman momentously proposed that the coal and steel industries of France and Germany be placed under a suprana-tional authority. Schuman would limit France's sovereignty as well as Germany's in order to achieve a common market, joint modernization and export programs, stan-dardization of freight rates, and the equalization of working and living conditions. Other European nations could join if they so desired. Schuman was vague on par-ticulars, but he shrewdly assessed domestic, European, and international economic and political realities. He sought to break the European integration impasse, co-opt German power, and place France in the forefront of European diplomacy before the lifting of restraints on Germany's sovereignty narrowed France's options.[150]

Officially, Acheson reserved judgment, fearing that the French might be trying to reestablish cartel-like agreements. Unofficially, he was exhilarated by the French demarche. So were other leading U.S. officials. Ambassador David Bruce consid-ered it the most constructive French action since liberation; Harriman deemed it the most important development in Europe since the Marshall Plan; Dulles said it was a "brilliantly creative" idea. By seizing the initiative, the French, in fact, had done precisely what Acheson had been urging them to do since September.[151]

U.S. officials realized that Schuman's proposals might allay French fears about Germany's productive capabilities and latent military power. If, through a supranational authority, France could achieve some permanent control over the German economy and if the French and German coal and metallurgical industries were fully integrated, Germany would not be able to wage war against the West. France might then be more willing to gear German industry to European defense needs; it might eventually even be willing to contemplate some German rearmament. If all went well, German power might be harnessed for the West, a large integrated market might be created, and Europe's dollar problems might be eased while its defense requirements might be tackled realistically.[152]

Acheson moved cautiously. Neither the French nor the British were ready to accept his emphasis on defense. Their priorities were still primarily economic. Although British thinking about Germany closely paralleled that of the United States, Acheson did not deem it prudent to push for Germany's entrance into NATO or to talk of Germany's rearmament. These issues would be greatly affected by the fate that befell the Schuman Plan.[153]

The trilateral talks in London produced general agreement along the lines of Acheson's concerns but few concrete measures to implement his ideas. The ensuing meeting of the North Atlantic Council outlined procedures for expediting and coordinating the military, economic, and financial work of the alliance. The conferees stressed the need for balanced collective rather than national forces and called for the appointment of permanent deputies to institutionalize the work of the council. Acheson was pleased, but there were no breakthroughs that might dramatically influence the overall correlation of forces that so concerned him.[154]

∎

After the meetings in Paris and London, Acheson monitored European deliberations over the Schuman Plan. Bevin had been angered by Schuman's unilateral proposals, and the British now faced a critical decision about their future role in Europe. Although Acheson subsequently was sorely disappointed that Britain decided to remain aloof from the emerging European economic community, he did not interfere in the initial European discussions.[155]

While Acheson waited, the ECA proceeded with its work on a payments union. After months of frustrating negotiations, Harriman and his assistants met British requirements for dealing with their sterling commitments and commonwealth concerns. The EPU, backed with ECA funds, liberalized European trade. The larger market, ECA officials hoped, would improve European productivity, enhance Europe's competitive position in international markets, and ease the dollar gap. Once these developments occurred, it was hoped that Europe would become self-supporting, invulnerable to Communist subversion, and capable of undertaking a significant arms buildup. In nurturing the EPU, argues political economist Robert Keohane, the United States made short-term sacrifices in order to create "a stable and prosperous international economic order in which liberal capitalism would prevail and American influence would be predominant." [156]

Defense officials, meanwhile, moved ahead in the military realm. Before resigning his position as undersecretary of the Army in April, Voorhees spearheaded a major effort to modernize the Army's research and development. He established a committee of top generals and scientists, including Alfred Gruenther and Vannevar Bush, to inquire whether Europe could be defended with conventional forces. Their assessment was extraordinarily upbeat. No one was more optimistic than Bush, who was firmly convinced that technological progress would make heavy tanks obsolete in three or four years. New, mobile guns, Bush concluded, "can destroy at a single shot—and at useful ranges—any tank whatever." He also believed that 280-mm guns could be developed to deliver atomic projectiles against heavy troop concentrations. If, along with these efforts, the Air Force would enhance its tactical air power and if the Navy could protect shipping lanes, the conventional military situation would be quickly transformed. The ability of Soviet armies to overrun Western Europe would end.[157]

JCS and Army ideas for enhancing European defenses abounded. General Joseph Collins, the Army chief of staff, instructed his subordinates to plan to stockpile equipment in France so that U.S. troops could deploy directly to Europe.[158] Voorhees proposed and Frank Pace, the incoming secretary of the Army, endorsed a variety of schemes to boost European production of military equipment.[159] Still more important, Bradley invited the French chiefs of staff to the United States. Heretofore the JCS had hesitated to share critical information with the French. Now Bradley felt that he could outline the steps that should be taken "to hold Western Europe with relatively limited means." The development of new weapons was one key ingredient. Another, of still greater portent, was Bradley's readiness to station additional U.S. forces in Europe in peacetime.[160]

At the same time, the JCS championed German rearmament. During Acheson's stay in London, Admiral Richard Conolly reminded him of the great benefits that would result from West Germany's participation in West European and North Atlantic regional defense arrangements. With Schuman's proposals hanging in the air, Acheson did not dare complicate Franco-German discussions by raising the issue of German rearmament. Although General Bradley also appreciated the significance of Schuman's initiative, noting that it "was the finest step taken since the war toward checking communism," he still pressed for a change in the existing German demilitarization policy. Bradley's position was bolstered by knowledge that Bevin supported the establishment of a West German police force and Germany's entrance into NATO.[161]

Although Truman generally stayed aloof from complex policy discussions until

Acheson brought him a recommendation he could approve, the JCS and British plans aroused his ire. He was profoundly influenced by memories of the interwar years and his distrust of Germany. He told Acheson quite plainly that German rearmament was not realistic under present conditions. Not only would it give France "a severe case of the jitters," but it might also lead to the creation of a German military machine "that can combine with Russia and ruin the rest of the world." [162]

Acheson hesitated. The integration of German forces into a European defense structure was clearly part of his long-term blueprint. He had discussed these ideas with his own advisers and had discreetly broached them with members of the Senate Foreign Relations Committee.[163] But he could also see that the time was not yet ripe for Germany's rearmament. European integration efforts had not advanced far enough to constrain a rearmed Germany, and the Germans had not yet proven that they would be reliable partners. German ties to the West, the State Department concluded, are not "so strong . . . that they might not be tempted to make a deal with the East in response to changed circumstances or a clever Soviet move." So it was prudent to wait to make certain that Germany's loyalty to the West was not transient, as Truman suspected it might be.

Meanwhile, steps would be taken to bind Germany more tightly to the West. The EPU and the Schuman Plan were two such measures. If such proposals were successful, Acheson assumed that the French would become much more receptive to altering Germany's military status. Moreover, the deployment of additional U.S. forces to Europe, which both he and Bradley were thinking about, would ease French anxieties. So would the strengthening of NATO's administrative structure, then under way. Acheson, therefore, did not reject Germany's future remilitarization; even this option was simply a matter of time and circumstance.[164]

■

So were many other initiatives around the globe. Lamenting the failure of Arabs and Israelis to advance from their armistice agreements to a peace treaty, U.S. officials encouraged direct talks between the adversaries and were distraught when secret conversations between the Jordanians and Israelis collapsed. The Americans still wanted to work with the British to stabilize pro-Western governments and thwart Soviet inroads. If new measures and additional money were necessary to achieve old goals, they would now be considered.[165]

Officials prodded Congress to allocate funds for the promotion of economic opportunity in areas settled by the Palestinian refugees. Assistant Secretary of State George McGhee and Admiral Forrest Sherman, chief of naval operations, told senators that continued refugee assistance would bring about a political settlement in the Middle East. Otherwise, the refugees would be receptive to Communist ideas, Arabs would grow more hostile to the United States, and prospects for retaining strategic access to the region would deteriorate. In June 1950, Congress allocated another $27.5 million for aid to the refugees.[166] But McGhee, Nitze, and Webb warned Acheson that refugee aid and Point Four assistance would not solve the problems of the region. Grinding poverty and seething unrest demanded that the United States consider additional options, especially long-term economic aid.[167]

U.S. policymakers also believed that leaders of countries of strategic importance who felt themselves threatened by domestic unrest or by bellicose neighbors deserved continued military assistance. The State Department pressed the Pentagon to sustain its military aid to the shah of Iran and beseeched Congress to grant reimbursable military assistance to Saudi Arabia.[168] Most significantly, Acheson supported British arms sales to Egypt once the U.N. embargo ended in August 1949. Rather than bow to domestic pressures against military aid to the Arabs, Truman and Acheson preferred to see munitions and weapons go to Jews and Arabs alike so long as they would not be used against one another.[169] Acheson proposed a tripartite Anglo-American-French declaration that would allow Middle Eastern states to acquire arms for their internal security and for the defense of the area as a whole. Prospective recipients had to renounce aggression and promise to respect frontiers. In return, the Americans, British, and French obligated themselves to stymie local aggression. In this manner, the United States hoped to buttress friendly regimes throughout the region, bind them to arms suppliers in the West, and encourage them to cooperate with Anglo-American plans to defend bases and oil fields in wartime.[170]

Of course, this policy meant that the United States aligned itself with entrenched regimes resistant to political change, social reform, and economic justice. Officials grasped the importance of co-opting Arab nationalism for the West, but they allowed themselves to become—and watched the British become—the pawns of dynastic struggles and nationalist rivalries among Arab leaders who often detested one another. The Truman administration, for example, catered to the needs of King Ibn Sa'ūd in Saudi Arabia, who lived in fear of Hashemite encirclement, and the British responded to the pleas of Jordan's King Abdullah, who wanted to incorporate Arab Palestine into his country and who considered the Egyptians and Saudis "snakes and scorpions." [171] There were risks in aligning the United States with reactionary regimes seeking their self-interest at the expense of their neighbors and their own peoples. Nonetheless, U.S. officials judged these risks more acceptable than the dangers that would ensue from the collapse of established political cliques and their replacement by younger, more liberal, and possibly more anti-Western elements.[172]

U.S. policies resulted from strategic calculations. Friendly regimes, albeit unpopular, parochial, and repressive, provided access to strategic facilities and oil repositories that were indispensable to Western global preponderance. British munition sales to Egypt might enable the British to retain and protect vital air bases in the Cairo-Suez region. U.S. arms aid to Ibn Sa'ūd would hasten the development of the air base at Dhahran and foster the protection of U.S. petroleum interests in Saudi Arabia. More aid to Iran would boost the shah's personal prestige at the expense of

Prime Minister Ali Mansur, who was suspected of being willing to strike deals with the Russians.[173]

As a result of their strategic calculations, U.S. officials also felt increasingly pressed to meet indigenous demands for formal staff talks and military pacts. In some cases these requests were based on purely regional concerns. The Saudis, for example, wanted protection against the Jordanians.[174] In other instances, however, governments escalated their demands as they sought compensation for the mounting risks they incurred by aligning themselves with the Americans or the British. For if war came, the presence of Western military facilities would act as a magnet to attract a Soviet attack. So the Turks now pressed ever more stridently for formal strategic consultations and a military pact. The British, moreover, appeared sympathetic for some alliance structure that would include Turkey and Egypt.[175]

Admiral Conolly, who was still responsible for U.S. planning in the region, resumed his advocacy of a mutual defense treaty. He feared that, if the Turks thought they could avert a Soviet attack, they might opt for neutrality in wartime and deny their facilities to the United States. Admiral Sherman, Conolly's superior, raised these matters in JCS deliberations and called for frank discussions with the Turks even if it was still premature to have formal staff conversations or a mutual defense pact. When Army Chief of Staff Collins visited Istanbul in March 1950, he talked more openly about what the Turks should do in wartime and more explicitly about what they might expect from the United States than had any previous high-level U.S. official. But the Turks still appealed for more formal guarantees.[176]

McGhee advised Acheson to reject concrete military obligations in the Middle East. The time was not ripe; European requirements demanded priority; the United States needed to retain its freedom to act unilaterally. But McGhee and his colleagues in the State Department nevertheless felt that U.S. options were limited by the strategic importance they accorded to the region. So if the Saudis or Turks or Egyptians or Iranians really threatened to realign themselves, the Americans would have to meet their needs: hence the eagerness to extend military aid and to inject economic assistance into the region; hence the proclamation of the tripartite declaration; hence the readiness to tell the Saudis that if at any time "they were menaced by aggressive action or subversive activities from any neighboring power, the United States Government will take most definite action"; hence the desire to allay Turkish disappointment with the addition of jet aircraft and new airstrips to the U.S. aid package; and hence the willingness to consider formal and reciprocal guarantees once European strength was built up.[177]

■

U.S. officials now believed that Southeast Asia, no less than the Middle East, needed U.S. economic and military assistance. When Acheson returned from London, he was determined to carry out his promises to supplement British and French efforts in the region. The Foreign Assistance Act of 1950, signed by the president on 5 June, incorporated $40 million for Southeast Asia. The money was to be used in Indochina, Thailand, Malaya, Burma, and Indonesia for agricultural assistance, health programs, and transportation infrastructure. Another section of the legislation authorized $35 million for the Point Four program of technical assistance, some of which was earmarked for Southeast Asia. At about the same time, the Export-Import Bank granted a loan of $100 million to Indonesia.[178]

The State Department placed even greater importance on its efforts to elicit another year's funding for military aid to Southeast Asia. Rusk and Jack Ohly, now the deputy director of the Mutual Defense Assistance Program in the State Department, worked closely with General Lyman L. Lemnitzer, who was in charge of the office of military assistance in the Pentagon. Together they convinced the Senate Foreign Relations Committee to allocate another $75 million for fiscal year 1951 for the "general area of China." Rusk stressed that Peking was directing and abetting Communist guerrillas in Indochina and the Philippines. When senators queried whether the United States would not be supporting French imperialism, Rusk retorted that the French had to remain in order to defeat Ho Chi Minh. Ho was popular, Rusk conceded, but could not be allowed to win because he took orders from the Kremlin. This was not a civil war in the usual sense, Rusk emphasized: "This . . . is part of an international war." If Indochina fell, Thailand would be next and all of Southeast Asia would be at risk. The senators agreed, and the legislation was ready for passage by mid-June.[179]

■

Rusk was eager for the United States to take the offensive beyond Southeast Asia. Working closely with Dulles, Rusk wanted to reverse Acheson's policy toward Taiwan. Affording protection to the offshore island, they conceded, might lead to war. But risk-taking was essential to demonstrate resolve and thwart Communist aggression. If the United States did not act to neutralize Taiwan, Rusk argued, the situation in Japan and the Philippines might "become untenable. . . . Indonesia . . . may be lost and the oil of the Middle East will be in jeopardy. If we do not act it will be everywhere interpreted that we are making another retreat because we do not dare risk war. . . . The further losses . . . would greatly increase war-making power of the Soviet Union." [180]

Rusk had no difficulty finding allies in the Pentagon. Generals Lemnitzer and Burns agreed to do all that was possible to hold Taiwan under existing policy and to augment military and economic aid. Admiral Sherman, whose influence within the JCS was growing, was eager to boost U.S. naval forces in the Pacific.[181] When Johnson and Bradley finally visited MacArthur in June, he told them that it would be strategically disastrous to allow the Communists to gain control of the offshore island. From Taiwan, MacArthur said, the Russians could attack Okinawa and bomb the Philippines. The United States, he insisted, "had to initiate measures to prevent the domination of Formosa by a Communist power." MacArthur requested permission to assess the military assistance that would be required "to hold Formosa against attack." [182]

Significantly, Truman and Acheson did not stop the study. Acheson's China experts and CIA intelligence analysts had become disheartened by the alleged rapid consolidation of Soviet influence on the mainland. They were less certain than ever of a Sino-Soviet split.[183] Oliver Franks, the British ambassador and Acheson's close friend, reported to his government that the secretary of state's views were in flux. Truman's and Acheson's contempt for Chiang Kai-shek remained unchanged. Their intent was not to salvage his regime; instead, they were now thinking of ways to deny Taiwan to Communist China. Rusk talked about trusteeship and MacArthur ruminated about transferring power to the Taiwanese. Truman liked the notion of saving China without Chiang. Moreover, both he and Acheson agreed that some dramatic initiative was imperative to restore U.S. morale and undermine the appeal of McCarthyism.[184]

■

The diplomatic offensive that was contemplated in the spring of 1950 was of enormous scope. Around the Eurasian land mass, U.S. officials hoped to regain the initiative by strengthening NATO, co-opting the power of West Germany, continuing aid after 1952, deploying additional troops to Europe, expanding military assistance to the Near East and Southeast Asia, inaugurating new programs of economic aid in the underdeveloped world, launching covert operations in the general area of China, negotiating a Japanese peace treaty, neutralizing Taiwan, and forming a Pacific alliance. But offensive diplomacy was infused with risk-taking, and risk-taking required military muscle to back it up.

NSC 68 and the Continuity of U.S. Foreign Policy

Throughout the spring of 1950, Paul Nitze devoted his time to writing the report on the impact of Soviet atomic capabilities on U.S. foreign policy goals and tactics. He conferred with prominent scientists like Robert Oppenheimer and with former officials like Robert Lovett. He coordinated his efforts with General Burns and other representatives from the Pentagon. But NSC 68 was the creation of Nitze and the Policy Planning Staff, which he now directed.[185]

Despite its hyperbolic rhetoric, NSC 68 essentially reaffirmed the assumptions that had been driving U.S. foreign policy during the Truman administration. The Soviets were animated by a "new fanatic faith, antithetical to our own." In the long run they wanted to impose their "absolute authority over the rest of the world." In the immediate future they hoped to establish "domination of the Eurasian land mass." U.S. national security was imperiled because "any substantial further extension of the area under the domination of the Kremlin would raise the possibility that no coalition adequate to confront the Kremlin with greater strength could be assembled." [186]

NSC 68, moreover, explicitly endorsed the goals that had been enumerated in NSC 20/4 of November 1948. U.S. aims, however, were not limited to deterring war, containing Soviet expansion, and thwarting internal subversion. Nitze stressed that U.S. goals were designed to reduce Soviet power on its periphery, establish independent countries in Eastern Europe, revive nationalist aspirations among subject peoples within the Soviet Union, and "foster a fundamental change in the nature of the Soviet system, a change toward which the frustration of the design is the first and perhaps most important task." [187] Although some historians have suggested that these aims diverged from earlier objectives, these goals had been frequently espoused by U.S. officials. Since the onset of the Truman administration, the object of U.S. policy had been to thwart the Kremlin's ability to gain global preponderance through its own efforts or through the machinations of its Communist allies. But once the Communists were contained, U.S. officials sought to link the power centers of Europe and Asia within an American-led orbit. From this position, the United States hoped to dislodge the Kremlin from Eastern Europe and pave the way for transformation of the system of government within Soviet Russia. [188]

Furthermore, every program alluded to in NSC 68 either had been or was in the process of being launched. Nitze called for economic assistance, military aid, covert operations, psychological warfare, and solutions to the dollar gap. He referred to the need to improve internal security and to enhance intelligence activities. He enumerated the strategic undertakings that had been laid out in dozens of war-plan exercises. [189]

What was new about NSC 68 was that Nitze simply called for more, more, and more money to implement the programs and to achieve the goals already set out. He envisioned higher taxes, and he thought that domestic social and welfare programs might have to be curtailed. Most important, he emphasized the need to build up U.S. military capabilities. More arms were needed to implement strategic undertakings; more arms were needed for military assistance; more arms were needed to support U.S. foreign policy and "to defeat local Soviet moves with local action." It was this emphasis on military means that so upset Kennan. [190]

Nitze called for a new stress on military hardware because he believed that by the mid-1950's Soviet atomic capabilities would greatly enhance Soviet risk-taking, discourage U.S. initiative, and intimidate allies. NSC 68 sought to demonstrate that the Soviets were achieving unprecedented military capabilities by allocating disproportionate amounts of the gross national product to heavy industry and arms production. The sections of the report that stressed the magnitude of the Kremlin's arms buildup received much criticism from insiders. But Nitze's key points were not disputed: the Soviets did possess a superiority in conventional arms, and they would be able to develop an arsenal of perhaps 200 atomic bombs by the mid-1950's.[191]

The real significance of these facts was *not* that the Soviets would engage in premeditated military aggression or launch an atomic assault against the United States. Nitze acknowledged that such scenarios were tertiary threats and unlikely.[192] Instead, the significance was that Soviet atomic capabilities might neutralize the diplomatic shadows heretofore cast by the U.S. atomic monopoly. Enemies and allies would both doubt U.S. willingness to risk nuclear war over limited issues; hence the United States would no longer have the means to encourage allies or to intimidate foes. Knowing this, the Soviets might show diplomatic boldness, augment their support for internal subversion, and foment local aggression. Their excessive strength, argued NSC 68, "provides the Soviet Union with great coercive power for use in time of peace in furtherance of its objectives and serves as a deterrent to the victims of its aggression from taking any action in opposition to its tactics which would risk war."[193]

U.S. officials must not equivocate or vacillate for fear of provoking the Soviets and precipitating global war, Nitze believed. Given the setbacks of late 1949, the temptation of the Soviets to engage in new forms of risk-taking, and the erosion of European influence in the Middle East and Asia, the United States had to do what was necessary to achieve its objectives. U.S. foreign policy "requires the free world to develop a successfully functioning political and economic system and a vigorous political offensive against the Soviet Union." The United States had to sign a peace treaty with Japan, link West Germany to NATO, preserve stability in the Middle East, and thwart the spread of communism in Southeast Asia. Initiatives of this sort required "an adequate military shield under which they can develop." "Without superior aggregate military strength, in being and readily mobilizeable, a policy of containment—which is in effect a policy of calculated and gradual coercion—is no more than a policy of bluff."[194]

U.S. diplomacy was imbued with an offensive spirit. In the worldview of NSC 68, there was no room for neutrality; diplomacy was a zero-sum game. The stakes were global preponderance. The risks were great. Nitze grasped it well: "Only if we had overwhelming atomic superiority and obtained command of the air might the U.S.S.R. be deterred from employing its atomic weapons *as we progressed toward the fulfillment of our objectives*."[195]

Precisely because the goals, assumptions, and arguments of NSC 68 were not new and because he placed no price tags on the programs, Nitze was able to elicit a great deal of support. Bohlen thought Nitze exaggerated Soviet intentions; Willard Thorp, head of economic affairs at the State Department, believed he overestimated Soviet economic capabilities; George Perkins, head of European affairs, and Llewellyn Thompson, his key assistant, suggested that Nitze underrated the potential efficacy of existing measures.[196] But NSC 68 was perfectly compatible with the thinking that infused all the State Department papers on Europe, the Middle East, and Southeast Asia in April and May 1950. Acheson, therefore, had no trouble accepting NSC 68. The thrust of the report, as Bohlen noted, was "unchallengeable." [197]

Defense Secretary Johnson was initially infuriated by his inadequate knowledge about the development of NSC 68. He regarded it as another effort by Acheson to circumvent normal policymaking channels, demean the Defense Department, embarrass his own cost-cutting efforts, and enhance Foggy Bottom's control of national security policy. But Nitze discreetly approached the JCS and got the chiefs to bring Johnson around. If the defense secretary had known that Nitze was thinking of tripling military spending, he would never have agreed. But hardly anyone in the Pentagon contemplated increments of this magnitude. There was no reason to oppose NSC 68, for it was obvious to everyone in official circles that U.S. policy had to be firmed up. The real issues were defining how much more should be spent on defense, how rapidly, and in what ways.[198]

Truman read NSC 68 and asked the NSC to provide him with additional information on costs and implications. An NSC ad hoc group was set up to undertake this work. It proceeded in a desultory fashion. The sums envisioned did not approach what Nitze wanted. The Budget Bureau strongly opposed large increments. The JCS equivocated. Voorhees still believed that substantial savings could be made by integrating military and economic aid. Defense planning for the next fiscal year continued on the basis of a constricted budget. In early June, Nitze grew frustrated. On 7 June he left for vacation.[199]

Top State Department officials appeared ready to raise taxes, cut domestic programs, increase imports, and accept budget deficits in pursuit of national security goals. Truman displayed no such disposition. In a series of speeches and press conferences in May and June, he passed up opportunity after opportunity to make a case for large increments in military expenditures. Yet at the same time he reaffirmed U.S. goals and supported existing policies, including the options contemplated in the spring reassessment of 1950. He hoped to achieve preponderance on the cheap.[200]

The hesitation in part emanated from the character of the threat. The Soviets now had the bomb, but hardly anyone of influence in Washington, Paris, or London expected the Kremlin to engage in overt aggression.[201] Bohlen told Nitze that he needed to do a better job substantiating his claim that the gap between Soviet and U.S. military capabilities was widening; others doubted that it was widening. The Joint Intelligence Committee at the U.S. embassy in Moscow concluded that net relative military capabilities of the Soviet bloc and the free world had changed but slightly, *and in favor of the West*, during the preceding year.[202] Moreover, there was considerable opinion in defense circles that Europe could be defended without anything resembling the increments in defense expenditures that Nitze had in mind. Bush, Voorhees, and the Army's top generals, for example, insisted that a great deal could be done through defensive weaponry and counterpart funds.[203]

Nor were Soviet actions responsible for the threats that loomed so large in American eyes. Stalin was clamping down on Eastern Europe, brutally purging foes, and preparing another reign of terror within the Soviet Union itself. But these were not the matters that preoccupied U.S. officials. Policymakers in Washington focused on the dollar gap, the European integration impasse, and the task of co-opting German and Japanese power. These problems were not caused by Soviet behavior.[204] Nor was the Soviet Union responsible for Mao's acquisition of power in China or Ho's popularity in Vietnam. Stalin's aid package to China and his recognition of the Viet Minh were neither daring nor bellicose actions, no matter how ominous they may have looked from Washington's perspective.

The problems that so perplexed and alarmed U.S. officials were not the making of the Soviet Union. But the very existence of the Soviet Union constituted a nightmare. Here was a totalitarian country with a revolutionary ideology that had great appeal to Third World peoples bent on throwing off Western rule and making rapid economic progress. Here was a totalitarian country whose domination of Eastern Europe and whose considerable influence in Northeast Asia gave it the potential to entice Germany and Japan into its orbit. Here was a totalitarian country whose developing atomic capabilities might inspire it to engage in risk-taking that it had heretofore avoided. If U.S. diplomacy were not active and vigilant, if U.S. aid were not forthcoming, and if U.S. determination were not evident to friends and foes alike, the industrial workshops of Europe and Asia and their attendant markets and raw materials could gravitate out of the U.S. orbit. The United States could become isolated in a hostile world. In such circumstances America's free and democratic system could not survive.[205]

All of this was perfectly familiar to policymakers. Hence NSC 68 provoked no great debate. It neither stirred deep emotions nor precipitated unusual controversy (except of a personal sort between Johnson and Acheson). It could not do so because it introduced no new goals and no new programs. It did not redefine the Soviet threat or claim that the Kremlin was ready to embark on outright aggression. Notwithstanding the dollar gap and the slump in the economy during 1949, it did not inject any new economic considerations into the discussion of U.S. diplomatic goals. In fact, it simply reaffirmed the geopolitical and ideological basis of U.S. foreign policy. Its major point was that Soviet atomic capabilities greatly intensified the Soviet threat by enhancing the Kremlin's penchant for risk-taking. In response, the United States had to enlarge its military capabilities if it were to fulfill its own objectives. But Nitze did not make a case for any particular level of military spending. He continued to regard military capabilities as most important for the shadows they cast, for their psychological repercussions, and for their influence on U.S. risk-taking rather than for warmaking. National security was still defined *not* in terms of numbers of troops, tanks, planes, and bombs, but in terms of control of industrial infrastructure, raw materials, and skilled labor.

NSC 68 might have made a useful contribution to policymaking had it boldly confronted the question of limited war. Heretofore U.S. officials had concluded that thwarting Soviet influence in Greece, Turkey, and Iran was vital to U.S. security; they had stressed that containing communism in Southeast Asia was critical to holding Japan. Increasingly, they were claiming that the viability of South Korea and even Taiwan was essential to U.S. credibility in the world. Such language implied that, in the absence of global war, the United States (and its friends) should be willing to fight in diverse localities to thwart internal subversion or to stymie local aggression. But much ambiguity remained, generated by the knowledge that the United States did not have the forces to wage a limited war in these areas and be prepared to fight a global war at the same time.

In NSC 68 Nitze seemed to be saying that the United States had to be ready and able to utilize force in these local situations. Superior atomic forces would provide the necessary shield for it to engage in its own risk-taking. If the United States could maintain its overwhelming lead in strategic weaponry *and* if it could bolster conventional forces in Western Europe, the Kremlin's atomic arsenal and land power could be neutralized. The United States could then move ahead to accomplish its objectives through diplomatic, economic, and, if necessary, military initiatives in disparate localities around the globe.[206] In fact, prospective neutralization of U.S. and Soviet atomic forces might make limited conventional or guerrilla wars the wave of the future.

Although the stress on limited war was an absolutely critical part of NSC 68, it was so buried in the long, rambling, and repetitive paper that it did not receive the attention it deserved. Ever since autumn 1945, U.S. military officials had wanted to know where, when, how, and in what circumstances the United States would employ force. In summer and autumn 1948, Forrestal had raised these matters stridently and forcefully. Yet in mid-1950, clear answers were still not forthcoming.

Had they been, it would have been too late anyway. North Korean forces were about to cross the 38th parallel.

Wresting the Initiative,
June-November 1950

On 25 June 1950, North Korean forces invaded South Korea. U.S. policy-makers had expected the Soviets to engage in new forms of risk-taking, but they had not anticipated "naked, deliberate, unprovoked aggression." [1]

Seeing the Democratic People's Republic of Korea and its premier, Kim Il Sung, as Soviet puppets, Truman, Dean Acheson, and their advisers had the lessons of the 1930's much on their minds. The Soviets were on the march; they were seeking world domination; they were now prepared to use tanks and heavy armor to subdue their foes. According to Truman, history taught that "aggression must be met firmly. Appeasement leads only to further aggression and ultimately to war." [2]

Truman and Acheson were determined to thwart the adversary. If necessary, they would use U.S. ground forces. But the president and the secretary of state suspected that the assault on Korea might be a ruse for even more ominous Soviet action elsewhere. Thinking that the Kremlin had higher priorities than Korea and wishing to be ready to meet force with force in areas of greater priority, policymakers in Washington were eager to avoid a wider war in Asia even while they repulsed local aggression on the Korean peninsula. [3] (See Map 9.)

From the outset, U.S. policymakers dealt with Korea in a wider cold war context. They moved rapidly to implement the plans they had been preparing the previous spring. Germany and Japan had to be economically integrated into the Western world, militarily rearmed, and pulled politically and diplomatically into the U.S. orbit. Southeast Asian nations had to be insulated from the Communist virus, defended against Chinese ambitions, and convinced that their nationalist aspirations could be fulfilled in cooperation with their former imperial masters and with the United States. Middle Eastern governments had to be protected from internal subversion and regional foes, dissuaded from pursuing neutralist options, and en-

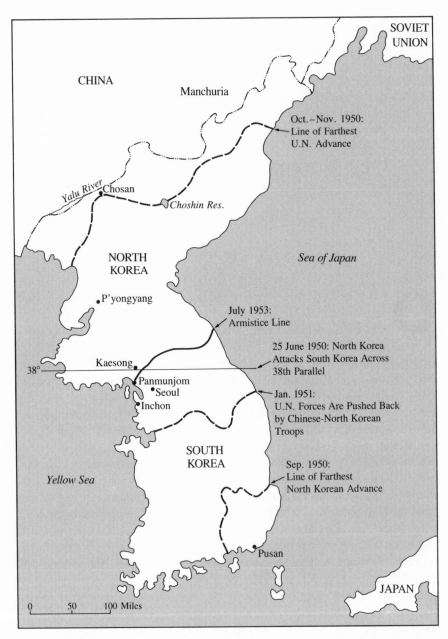

CHINA

Manchuria

SOVIET
UNION

Oct.–Nov. 1950:
Line of Farthest
U.N. Advance

Yalu River •Chosan

Choshin Res.

NORTH
KOREA

Sea of Japan

•P'yongyang

July 1953:
Armistice Line

38°   Kaesong•

25 June 1950: North Korea
Attacks South Korea Across
38th Parallel

•Panmunjom
•Seoul
•Inchon

Jan. 1951:
U.N. Forces Are Pushed Back
by Chinese-North Korean
Troops

SOUTH
KOREA

Sep. 1950:
Line of Farthest
North Korean Advance

Yellow Sea

•Pusan

JAPAN

0   50   100 Miles

9. The Korean War, 1950–53. Adapted from Richard Dean Burns, ed., *Guide to American Foreign Relations Since 1700* (Santa Barbara, Calif.: ABC-Clio, 1983), p. 818.

couraged to offer their bases and oil to the freedom-loving democracies of the West in case of global conflict.

The pursuit of these objectives required considerable risk-taking. And risk-taking without military superiority was perilous. The United States could get sucked into struggles of national liberation, embroiled in limited wars, or locked into regional disputes. If not careful, the United States could provoke Soviet reactions, perhaps against Western Europe, that might culminate in global war. Prudence dictated that U.S. officials have the military capabilities to support their foreign policy, deter war, and fulfill the basic undertakings of their war plans. In fact, without military superiority U.S. policymakers themselves might be deterred from taking the risks that inhered in the pursuit of their national objectives. Appraisals of the adversary's overall military capabilities, as the historian Marc Trachtenberg has shown, affected the Truman administration's determination to act in behalf of perceived interests. In other words, Acheson and his colleagues understood that if they could create a military shield to protect the United States and its major allies from Soviet counterthrusts, they would be able to move more safely and more expeditiously to wrest the initiative from the Kremlin. There was no alternative, then, but to increase defense expenditures for many years, well beyond the duration of the Korean conflict. America's atomic superiority would have to be maintained; its stockpile would have to be augmented, its versatility accelerated. NATO's conventional defenses would have to be strengthened, Germany rearmed, and additional U.S. troops stationed in Europe. Potential allies of the United States in Asia, the western Pacific, and the Middle East would have to receive additional grants of military aid, new commitments, or both. The significance of NSC 68 now grew.[4]

The gravity of the situation dictated a more efficient policymaking process. Truman, heretofore reluctant to participate in policy formulation, took a more hands-on approach. He urged the National Security Council (NSC) to improve its staff work and began attending its meetings on a more regular basis. He also looked to Averell Harriman, his new special assistant, to help coordinate policy within the executive branch. In view of military developments, Truman also started meeting regularly with General Omar Bradley, chairman of the Joint Chiefs of Staff (JCS). Unhappy with the functioning of the Central Intelligence Agency (CIA), the president named General Walter Bedell Smith as its director. After leaving the chairmanship of the Atomic Energy Commission vacant for almost six months, Truman appointed the hawkish N. Gordon Dean as David Lilienthal's successor. Exasperated by Defense Secretary Louis Johnson's erratic behavior, his bickering with Acheson, and his conniving with political enemies of the administration, Truman forced him to resign in early September. The president asked his former secretary of state, George Marshall, to run the Pentagon. Marshall, in poor health, reluctantly accepted and immediately called on Robert Lovett, his former undersecretary of state, to take the number-two post in the Defense Department.[5]

The personnel changes altered the dynamics of policymaking in the Truman administration. Bradley and the other chiefs of staff were able to work more effectively with and exert more influence on Marshall and Lovett than had been the case with Johnson. More important, Acheson's preeminence began to wane. The target of vitriolic attacks from conservative senators and journalists, the secretary of state was often on the defensive. Recognizing that the country faced an array of military decisions in Korea and a host of political-military decisions elsewhere, Acheson was prepared to work closely with Marshall to whom he deferred and with Lovett whom he respected. A new spirit of cooperation emerged at the top echelons of the Truman administration. Before long Acheson, Marshall, Lovett, and Bradley were meeting regularly in the JCS map room. With frankness and openness they shared their aspirations and worries. They also encouraged their subordinates to reestablish extensive lateral relationships.[6]

The improved spirit of cooperation in Washington was overshadowed by the incendiary relationship between General Douglas MacArthur and his civilian and military superiors. Truman could not abide the general's haughtiness and looked cynically upon his political aspirations. From the moment hostilities began in Korea, Truman knew he had to keep a tight rein on his Far East commander. Yet it was difficult to do so because MacArthur had so much prestige and seniority that his nominal superiors at the Pentagon hesitated to interfere with his decisions. Even after Marshall took over the secretaryship and after Bradley and his associates came to doubt MacArthur's military acumen, they remained wary of intruding into his domain. Established military tradition dictated that the commander in the field should have considerable flexibility.[7]

Domestic political considerations impelled Truman to deal cautiously with MacArthur. With elections to be held in November and with Republicans' lambasting the Democrats for their past timidity and treachery, Truman and Acheson did not seek an unnecessary squabble with the Far East commander and did not want a needless confrontation with congressmen and senators who championed an Asia-first policy. Yet they did not hesitate to challenge MacArthur when his approach to the Nationalist Chinese conflicted with their own diplomatic strategy. Nor did they shy away from their support of allies in Western Europe. Their intent, throughout, was to keep Korea in perspective. They agreed with MacArthur that opportunities had to be exploited; risks had to be taken. But for Truman, Acheson, Marshall, Lovett, and Bradley, Korea remained only a small part of their overall quest to wrest the initiative from the Kremlin and to insure Western preponderance on the land mass of Eurasia.

Intervention

The North Korean attack caught U.S. officials by surprise. Not expecting overt aggression, they had been most concerned with South Korea's spiraling inflation and President Syngman Rhee's decreasing popularity. Although Rhee's army was coping with Communist guerrillas, his regime was in disrepute. He repressed his political enemies and sought to postpone elections. However, when U.S. pressure forced him to allow his people to go to the polls on 30 May 1950, his supporters were badly beaten.[8]

North Koreans saw Rhee's electoral setback as an opportunity to launch a new political offensive. Kim Il Sung desperately wanted to unite all Koreans under his regime. He was an intense nationalist. So were many Communist leaders who fled from the south to the north when faced with imprisonment or death by Rhee's police or army. In early June 1950, North Korea called for reunification and nation-wide elections. These initiatives were regarded by U.S. officials as pure propaganda. They originated in Moscow, Ambassador John Muccio wrote Acheson, and sought to manipulate Koreans' longing for unification.[9]

Significantly, Muccio reported no major change in the military situation. For months he had been pleading for increased military aid to Rhee's Republic of Korea, especially for the procurement of military aircraft. Occasionally, he would conjure up worst-case scenarios of a North Korean conquest of South Korea in order to elicit the funding he thought appropriate. But basically, Muccio did not see any imminent military threat, nor did he dwell on the disparity of forces between the two Koreas. Despite the estimated 65 tanks and small (but growing) numbers of heavy artillery in the hands of the North, the ambassador believed that the South Korean army was its equal. According to Muccio, it was better trained and possessed superior small arms. It had higher morale and more capable leaders. If it could receive some aircraft and develop its own air force, it might even achieve superiority.[10]

Intelligence analysts were more cautious, but U.S. defense officials did not see any gaping deficiencies in South Korean military strength.[11] Only reluctantly, and in response to the State Department's *political* arguments, did they agree to transfer fighter aircraft to Rhee's air force. In general, the top men at the Pentagon did not think South Korea required additional military aid. General William L. Roberts, chief of the U.S. military advisory group to Korea, assured Bradley that the South could repel any invasion force. Roberts was an old friend of Bradley's, a soldier of experience and sound judgment, and the JCS chairman took his advice seriously.[12]

Moreover, in the days preceding the North's attack, Rhee talked to visiting dignitaries not about his fears of aggression but of his hopes to unify Korea under his own control. John Foster Dulles heard some of this on 19 June when he briefly visited Seoul in order to lift the supposedly flagging spirit of Rhee's regime. The next day, Rhee told William R. Matthews, a close friend of Dulles's, that he would launch the military offensive sometime within the next year. Surprised by the high morale of the South Korean army, Matthews thought that Rhee's claims should be taken seriously.[13]

Hence both the North's advance and the South's retreat shocked U.S. officials. Day after day, during the last week of June, the reports became more ominous. North Korean troops routed their southern brethren, seized Seoul, and poised to cross the Han River. As the news worsened, policymakers in Washington moved toward intervention by U.S. naval, air, and ground forces. Returning hurriedly from his home in Independence, Missouri, on 25 June, Truman first approved the shipment of desperately needed supplies to Rhee's army. The next day he allowed U.S. air and naval power to be used against North Korean tanks and armor. On the 27th, the United States pushed a second resolution through the Security Council of the United Nations calling for the restoration of peace and security and authorizing assistance to Korea in repelling the invasion. On the 29th, the president permitted the use of air power above the 38th parallel dividing North and South Korea. He also approved the first deployment of U.S. ground forces to hold airfields and port facilities. On that same day MacArthur visited the front, witnessed the collapse of Rhee's army, and concluded that the North would vanquish the South unless the United States committed substantial ground forces. Believing that U.S. troops should be deployed to the battle area, MacArthur wanted to send two of his four divisions to Korea. Although these divisions were understrength and short of supplies, the battle had to be joined immediately if an early counteroffensive were to be mounted. On Friday, 30 June, Truman gave the go-ahead.[14]

From the moment hostilities erupted, there was little doubt that Truman and Acheson would do what was necessary to thwart a North Korean victory. At the very first meeting with his top civilian and military advisers on Sunday night, 25 June, Truman agreed that a line must be drawn against Communist expansion. The next morning he confided that, if necessary, he was "determined to go very much further than the initial orders . . . he had approved . . . the evening before." This statement did not mean that Truman was eager to send ground troops to Korea. He certainly did not want to provoke a wider war with Soviet Russia or Communist China. But, like all of his advisers, he unquestionably believed that "If we let Korea down, the Soviet [sic] will keep right on going and swallow up one piece of Asia after another. . . . If we were to let Asia go, the Near East would collapse and no telling what would happen in Europe." U.S. inaction would destroy the credibility of U.S. commitments elsewhere, encourage neutralism, and set back hopes to wrest the initiative from the Kremlin.[15]

From the onset of the crisis, Truman's concerns were of a global nature. At meeting after meeting he prodded his subordinates to assess where the next Soviet moves might be. A key deterrent, in fact, to intervention in Korea was the thought that Stalin might divert U.S. attention to an area of tertiary significance while the Russians swiftly seized areas of greater importance. Truman instinctively believed that the Soviets wanted to overrun Iran, gain access to Middle Eastern oil, and find warm-water ports in the Persian Gulf and the Eastern Mediterranean.[16]

The idea that North Korea might be acting on its own volition to bring about a unification of the Korean people was beyond the grasp of U.S. officials. In recent years, however, illuminating studies by Robert R. Simmons, Bruce Cumings, John Merrill, and Jonathan Pollack have transformed understanding of the Korean conflict. They cast doubt on the fundamental assumption that Moscow dictated policy in Pyongyang, the North Korean capital. They demonstrate that the Korean conflict was a civil war. Notwithstanding Soviet military aid, the Kremlin did not create the conflict on the Korean peninsula. "I must stress," wrote Nikita Khrushchev, "that the war wasn't Stalin's idea, but Kim Il-song's. Kim was the initiator." [17]

Yet Truman, Acheson, and their colleagues were sure that Moscow was testing their resolve. "It was an open, clear, direct challenge," Acheson told the Senate Foreign Relations Committee in July, "and it was a challenge at about the only point in the world at which we were capable of picking it up in any way at all." Why, Acheson might have ruminated, would the Soviets pick the one spot where the Americans could react swiftly? If, in fact, the Kremlin could control the actions of its Communist puppets in Pyongyang and elsewhere, why would Stalin not test U.S. determination in more auspicious places? For Acheson, as well as for his critics, the only explanation for North Korean behavior was that Moscow calculated that the United States would not come to the defense of South Korea. [18]

Acheson claimed the Soviets had misunderstood his strategic perimeter speech of January 1950. They did not recognize that, when he and other U.S. officials excluded South Korea from America's strategic perimeter, they were referring to what the United States would do in time of global war. Supposedly, the Russians ignored Acheson's emphasis on collective action should South Korea be threatened in peacetime. They disregarded the administration's repeated efforts to win congressional aid for Rhee's regime. And they failed to grasp that U.S. officials would see local aggression as a challenge to U.S. prestige and as a test of the credibility of America's commitments. In Acheson's view, the Kremlin was calculating that, after the loss of China, it could win another easy victory in South Korea and undermine the U.S. position in Japan. The secretary of state was now determined to show the Soviets that they had erred egregiously in their estimation of U.S. resolve. They would be made to pay for their misjudgment. [19]

■

Although U.S. officials were confident that the Kremlin inspired the attack, they were equally certain that the Soviet Union was not ready for and did not want global war. If the United States demonstrated toughness, the Kremlin would back off. Korea, Truman told his aide George Elsey, "is the Greece of the Far East. If we are tough enough now, if we stand up to them like we did in Greece three years ago, they won't take any next steps." At the first meeting at the Blair House, General Bradley and Admiral Forrest Sherman told the president that they did not think the Russians were ready for global war. From the U.S. embassy in Moscow, Ambassador Alan Kirk urged Acheson to take immediate countermeasures precisely because the Soviets were not prepared for a showdown with the United States. On 29 June, Counselor George Kennan, Ambassador-at-Large Philip Jessup, Admiral Roscoe Hillenkoetter, and General James Burns concluded that the Soviets were not ready to support North Korea. By this time, Acheson was already operating on the explicit assumption that the Soviets were not inclined to risk general hostilities. The key task was to allow them a graceful means to extricate themselves from the crisis.[20]

Confident of Soviet circumspection in the face of U.S. determination and overall military superiority, Truman did not think that he was leading the country into a major war. He told the press that the United States was engaged in a police action. When Senator Kenneth Wherry, the Republican floor leader, asked the president why he had not consulted Congress before dispatching U.S. troops, Truman retorted that there was no time to consult; there was an emergency.[21] But he neither felt a great sense of danger nor expected a military confrontation with the Kremlin. When Dwight Eisenhower visited the Pentagon on 27 June and lunched with the president on 6 July, he was dismayed by the complacency he witnessed. For Truman and his key advisers, military intervention and limited war were simply new tactics to fulfill previous commitments to Korea and to thwart the expansion of Soviet-directed communism globally, much as had been the military assistance to Greece and the airlift to Berlin. As in the past, the adversary would back down and the United States would be able to seize the initiative.[22]

National security imperatives, as defined by the president and his chief advisers, were the driving force behind the administration's decisions. Truman was prepared to intervene more actively and in a variety of ways in Asia's civil wars—in Korea, China, Indochina, and the Philippines—because he saw them as part of the geopolitical and ideological struggle with the Kremlin. Domestic political concerns played a reinforcing factor. Republican partisans were quick to blame the impending debacle in Korea on the Democrats' naiveté and duplicity at Yalta and Potsdam and on their timidity and gullibility in China. Followers of Senators Joseph McCarthy and Robert Taft were willing to go further, saying that developments in Korea confirmed the treasonous actions of State Department officials and that Acheson had to resign. Truman knew that Democrats were politically vulnerable and that he had to react boldly to the unfolding crisis. Yet Republican critics did not press for the use of U.S. troops in Korea. Many Republicans, in fact, had been opposed or indifferent to aid to that country. Few of them demanded that Truman do more than safeguard Taiwan. Robert Donovan, one of the president's leading biographers, even suggests that the commitment of the Seventh Fleet to the Formosa straits was to win Republican support for direct military intervention in Korea that might not otherwise have been forthcoming.[23]

Throughout the last week in June, Truman was in control of policy. From the onset of the crisis he knew what he was prepared to do. Acheson was his leading adviser, and both men were inclined to use military force, even ground troops if necessary. When MacArthur urged the deployment of U.S. soldiers and Army Chief of Staff Joseph Collins seconded the recommendation, Truman and Acheson readily assented. They do not seem to have found this an agonizing or painful decision despite the previous reservations expressed by Johnson, Bradley, and Army Secretary Frank Pace. Truman felt no real need to consult senators and congressmen. His major concern was to see that MacArthur's behavior was monitored closely so that the Russians would not be provoked into a wider conflict. Waging limited wars, as Nitze had foreseen in NSC 68, was the necessary next step in the ongoing struggle with the Kremlin. Although he had heretofore been unwilling to face the financial implications, Truman would now have to bite the bullet. He was more inclined to do so because the intervention in Korea initially won much acclaim and created the political context to implement many of the options that had been discussed during the spring of 1950.

Wresting the Initiative

While MacArthur deployed U.S. troops to the Pusan perimeter and established a beachhead there, officials in Washington pondered the possible next moves of the Soviet Union. Would the Kremlin support a coup in Iran, inspire a satellite attack on Turkey or Yugoslavia, gamble on an East German thrust against the Federal Republic, or encourage China to intervene in Korea? With the Americans embroiled in Northeast Asia, would Soviet armies themselves make a grab for Finland or try to crush Tito's apostasy in Yugoslavia? Even more ominously, might Stalin think that conditions were propitious for a full-scale assault on Western Europe and a surprise attack on the United States?[24]

Although none of these options could be dismissed, and although the Soviet Union had the capability to launch surprise attacks along much of its periphery, U.S. officials did not think the Soviets would start a war. Stalin, reported Ambassador Kirk on 11 August, was not readying his people for battle: "What military dispositions are known are largely of a defensive nature." The Soviets had built up huge stockpiles of ammunition and equipment. They had converted manufacturing plants to the production of war materiel. CIA analysts also believed that military airfields were being rushed to completion and that satellite strength was being rapidly increased. Moreover, the Soviets' 25 divisions in East Germany and Poland were believed to be capable of marching at a moment's notice. Another 50–65 divisions could provide support, and Russia's 175 line divisions already in existence were fully mobilized. With 20,000 available aircraft and hundreds of submarines, the Kremlin could "look forward to sweeping initial successes."[25]

But the Kremlin could not defeat the United States. According to U.S. analysts, any Soviet-U.S. conflict would become a war of attrition. The Soviet economy would falter. U.S. economic strength and atomic superiority would prevail. Currently, the Soviets had fewer than 25 atomic bombs, or so it was estimated, and no effective means of delivering them. In late 1950 the United States possessed over 500 atomic bombs and at least 264 nuclear-capable aircraft. The Strategic Air Command had 22 atomic bomb assembly teams and about 500 medium- and long-distance bombers. Whereas Soviet Russia had no forward bases and nothing equivalent to the B-36, the United States had access to bases and airfields in Alaska, Canada, the Azores, the United Kingdom, Iceland, Guam, Okinawa, Libya, Saudi Arabia, and Egypt. For Truman, Acheson, and their colleagues, the conclusion was inescapable: the Kremlin would try to avoid global war, at least for the foreseeable future.[26]

Within a few years, however, the situation would become fraught with danger. In 1952 the Soviets would have about 95 atomic bombs; in 1953, 165; in 1954, 235. They would also develop and deploy medium- and long-range jet bombers. Once this occurred, the U.S. numerical superiority would not have quite the same deterrent effect because the Soviets would use their substantial, albeit inferior, stockpile to wipe out American forward bases (especially in the United Kingdom) and decimate American industry. Soviet ground forces would have the time to overrun the continent and consolidate their preponderance in Western Europe and the Middle East. From this position the Soviets would seek to harness Western Europe's manufacturing plant, assimilate its skilled workers, and utilize its air and naval bases. With U.S. strength atrophied by nuclear attack and with Soviet capabilities enormously enhanced, the United States might sue for peace. Subsequently, the correlation of forces would be to the Kremlin's advantage, the U.S. position in the world would be impaired, and U.S. security forever endangered. "If Soviet Russia ever controls the Eurasian land mass," warned General Bradley, "then the Soviet-satellite imperialism may have the broad base upon which to build the military power to rule the world." [27]

The point of maximum danger would exist in 1952, after the Soviets felt they had achieved sufficient atomic capabilities to inflict grievous damage on the U.S. economy yet prior to the buildup of formidable defensive forces in Western Europe, which would not occur until 1954. Stalin would probably want to attack when Soviet Russia's capabilities relative to the West were at their peak. For the time being, therefore—that is, until 1952—Stalin and his comrades would not want to start a war.

But this did not mean that war could not occur by miscalculation. Indeed, accidental war would become more likely as the United States sought to wrest the initiative from the Kremlin. As one CIA report after another pointed out, a military confrontation could occur as the Soviets endeavored to secure the strategic approaches to their country and tried to excise Anglo-American influence from Europe and Asia. Soviet moves of this sort would "impinge upon the vital interests of the Western powers and so incur the risk of involvement in a general war precipitated through the necessary reactions of the Western Powers." As the West sought to seize the offensive, the Kremlin might feel a need to undertake a counterthrust or might be inclined to risk a wider war—gambling, incorrectly, that the West would back down.[28]

The United States had to be able to control and to dominate the escalatory cycle in a crisis situation. It had to be able to apply force locally, had to be able to increase its intensity, and had to be able to stymie prospective counterthrusts in other regions, most conspicuously Western Europe. The United States had to have enough atomic weapons and aircraft to neutralize the Russians' atomic capabilities, retard their advance into Western Europe, and devastate their petroleum refineries, communication centers, and metallurgical and chemical industries. The United States also had to build up NATO forces so that Soviet armies would not be able to march to the Atlantic and seize the Old World's economic infrastructure. If the Kremlin knew it could not overrun Western Europe, it would respond circumspectly to U.S. initiatives elsewhere. If the Americans knew the Russians could not overrun Western Europe, they could intensify the scale of their own risk-taking on the periphery as well as in the industrial core areas of Europe and Asia. Although the aim of the United States would be to localize a crisis, it nevertheless had "to place itself in the best possible position to meet the eventuality of global war," to execute war plans, and "to enter into full-scale hostilities only at the moment and in the manner most favorable to it in the light of the situation then existing." [29]

There was no longer any alternative but to follow the strictures of NSC 68 and to augment U.S. military capabilities rapidly. State Department officials became exasperated with the Pentagon's and the CIA's laborious efforts to assess Soviet intentions. Instead of concentrating on what the adversary might or could do, Bohlen and Rusk urged that the United States move ahead with its own efforts to wrest the initiative. Acheson found their advice compelling. On 14 July, he told the cabinet that peoples around the globe were losing confidence in the United States. They were pondering neutrality and thinking of accommodating the Kremlin. It was time for action, prompt action. The action might not be perfect, but it was needed nonetheless.[30]

On 19 July, President Truman announced that U.S. military capabilities had to be built up, not simply for Korea but also for contingencies other than Korea. Secretary of Defense Johnson had already approved plans to increase Army personnel from 630,000 to 834,000, Navy combatant ships from 238 to 282, and Air Force wings from 48 to 58. Truman asked Congress for $10 billion to support this program. He also requested $260 million for the Atomic Energy Commission. Moreover, U.S. allies needed additional aid. On 1 August, the administration sought a supplementary appropriation of $4 billion in military assistance, over 80 percent of which would go to NATO governments.[31]

These actions were forerunners of a much larger buildup. Truman told the American people that a vastly increased defense effort would have to be carried out. A new emphasis would have to be placed on the production of military hardware. The economy would be strained; inflationary pressures would grow; shortages would occur. The government, therefore, required new powers to control credit, raise taxes, and restrain prices and wages. After some wrangling, Congress gave the president the authority he requested.[32]

Truman was preparing for the long haul. At an NSC meeting on 28 July, he requested departmental estimates for the implementation of NSC 68 by the first of September. The next year's budget would depend on these figures. The Atomic Energy Commission and the JCS wanted to accelerate the output of fissionable material and develop a new testing site in the continental United States. While Truman studied these recommendations, he did approve the first deployment abroad of the non-nuclear components of atomic bombs.[33]

State Department officials scoffed at these initial efforts. Sounding much like former secretary of defense James Forrestal, they now insisted that military capabilities had to be substantial enough to support U.S. foreign policy, deter Soviet aggression, and implement U.S. war plans. Military capabilities had to provide "the shield" to protect the West while the United States enacted a positive program to project American influence into the Soviet world, roll back Soviet power, and promote internal changes within the Soviet Union itself. At the very least, Western military capabilities had to deter Soviet aggression while the United States implemented "a positive political and economic program designed to win the whole-hearted support for the West of accessible non-communist-controlled regions." As the United States launched this offensive, the risks of global war would increase. But "this risk must be accepted," concluded the NSC, "since the alternative is to abandon the attempt to wrest the initiative from the USSR and accept piecemeal defeat at the hands of the Kremlin."[34]

This attitude was bold and adventurous. The strategy was particularly significant because, as will become evident shortly, it was articulated precisely when MacArthur's invasion at Inchon altered the course of the Korean War. Although U.S. officials predicted victory within weeks or months, they remained committed to a huge scaling up of military capabilities. Acheson and Nitze would brook no letdown in the military buildup. Nor would the president. From their perspective, the end of the atomic monopoly and the triumph of the Chinese Communists had whetted the Kremlin's appetite for risk-taking. Conversely, to thwart the Kremlin's penchant for risk-taking and to implement the goals that had resonated through the Clifford-Elsey report of 1946, the NSC 20 series of 1948, and NSC 68, the United States now had to possess military capabilities that the president and the State Department had once eschewed. Because Soviet atomic weapons might dissuade U.S. officials from using their own strategic forces or might cripple the U.S. economy if war should accidentally occur, the Kremlin might actually be tempted to respond in a crisis with an attack on Western Europe. America's own risk-taking, therefore, had to be supported with an ever larger array of military capabilities.[35]

At the end of September 1950, as U.S. and U.N. forces were poised to cross the 38th parallel and destroy the remnants of North Korea's battered army, the NSC approved tentative estimates to wrest the initiative from the Kremlin. National security obligations, including those for the armed forces, atomic energy, civilian defense, stockpiling, military aid, economic assistance, and psychological warfare, would total about $69.5 billion in fiscal year 1951, level off to about $56 billion for fiscal years 1952–54, and decrease to about $45 billion in 1955. The great bulk of this money would be earmarked for the U.S. military establishment. JCS plans for 1951 now called for the creation of 17 Army divisions (compared to 10 authorized in June 1950), 322 combatant ships (compared to 238 authorized in June 1950), and 70 air wings (compared to 48 authorized in June 1950). Army personnel would increase from 630,000 before the Korean War to 1,263,000; Navy personnel from 461,000 to 717,818; and Air Force personnel from 416,000 to 688,186. These figures assumed that fighting in Korea would be over by June 1951.[36]

And still, Acheson and Nitze found the sums insufficient to fulfill their ambitious foreign policy. On 22 November, Nitze urged Acheson to push for an even larger military establishment. Although spending in Korea had been less than anticipated, the United States still had to have additional capabilities to defend itself, protect Western Europe, fulfill U.N. commitments elsewhere should they arise, and undertake other responsibilities. When the NSC met the next day, Acheson expressed grave doubts about the adequacy of military preparations. He ridiculed JCS planning and dismissed the objections of the Budget Bureau. Rebuffing Marshall's and Lovett's explanations of Pentagon spending, the secretary of state "frankly did not see how we could carry out our obligations with these forces." Acheson anticipated either a continuation of the Korean conflict or additional limited wars elsewhere. He claimed that the United States might have to deploy larger forces to Europe. He wanted U.S. allies, even those in Latin America, to be militarily prepared for additional "police" actions. He desired huge stockpiles of war materiel because, if global war should come, the United States had to expect to lose some of its productive capability at the onset of conflict.[37]

Acheson put Pentagon officials on the defensive. He got support from Stuart Symington, now director of the National Security Resources Board, and Leon Keyserling, chairman of the Council of Economic Advisers. Keyserling insisted that the economy could sustain a greater defense effort than the one proposed by the JCS. But Truman worried that Congress might be hostile to the magnitude of defense appropriations called for by Acheson. As a temporary expedient, the chief executive suggested that his advisers focus strictly on the 1951 budget, ascertain whether they could get legislative approval, and try to establish a program base that would justify subsequent financial support.[38]

Meanwhile, Truman approved another huge escalation of atomic capabilities. He said he would ask Congress for $1.4 billion to construct a gaseous diffusion plant and three more heavy-water reactors. As a result, Atomic Energy Commission financing would dwarf that of the entire Manhattan Project. Within two or three years the output of fissionable material would more than double. Entire new families of atomic weapons would become available. Air Force, Navy, and Army officials would be able to choose among many delivery vehicles and would have much greater latitude to select targets. Acheson welcomed these developments because he supported the use of atomic weapons to retard the westward movement of Soviet troops should war erupt in Europe.[39]

These actions, it must be reiterated, took place prior to China's intervention in the Korean War. The plans were discussed and approved when expectations prevailed that the limited war in Korea would soon be over. Of the $54 billion that the Truman administration wanted obligated for the armed forces in 1951, only $13 billion were earmarked for Korea. No funding for combat forces in Korea was contemplated for the following fiscal years even though military obligations would be in the $45-billion range. In other words, the U.S. military buildup was designed primarily to wrest the initiative in trouble spots around the world. Indeed, State Department officials and some members of the NSC thought their requests too modest because they had not explicitly demanded funding to roll back the area of Soviet domination.[40] Yet this effort, too, was already under way.

Korea, Taiwan, and Indochina

By mid-July, MacArthur's troops were dug in and holding their own on the Pusan perimeter. From bases in Japan, U.S. air power inflicted a heavy toll on the enemy. The U.S. government welcomed the assignment of small contingents of forces from other U.N. members. Ostensibly the war would be fought in behalf of the international organization's resolution to restore peace and security to Korea. But there was never any question that U.S. civilian and military officials would control the diplomacy and strategy of the initial phases of the Korean War.

The intent of the Truman administration was to seize whatever opportunities might arise to overcome the setbacks that had been experienced the previous year and to regain the initiative in the struggle with the Soviet/Communist world. Almost immediately U.S. policymakers began to think about crossing the 38th parallel, rolling back Soviet influence, and creating a unified, independent Korea. At the same time, their readiness to use the Seventh Fleet to thwart Mao's takeover of Taiwan served as the catalyst to ponder additional moves to safeguard a non-Communist regime on the offshore island. Simultaneously, new efforts were undertaken to induce the French to persevere in their struggle to defeat Ho Chi Minh and to contain the Chinese Communists. U.S. officials understood, however, that all these initiatives were fraught with danger. Miscalculations could embroil the United States in a larger conflict on the Asian mainland or lead to global war with the Soviet Union.

■

The question of what to do when U.S. and U.N. forces reached the 38th parallel attracted attention from the early days of July. John Allison, director of the Office of Northeast Asian Affairs in the Department of State, did not want to foreclose the opportunity of going on the offensive. He and his boss, Assistant Secretary of State Dean Rusk, believed that the restoration of the status quo ante would leave South

Korea vulnerable to future attacks. The Communists, moreover, had to learn that they would pay a price for aggression. If circumstances permitted, Allison and Rusk wanted to destroy North Korean forces, eliminate Kim Il Sung's regime, and unify Korea under a government that would be friendly to U.S. interests.[41]

These objectives were hard to argue against, except that their pursuit might engender a wider war. Nitze and his assistants on the Policy Planning Staff worried that a move across the 38th parallel would frighten the Soviets and the Chinese. They would not look benignly on U.S. troops advancing toward their borders. Nor were they ready to accept an unfriendly regime in North Korea. That the Soviets and Chinese had vital interests at stake was indisputable. The great imponderable was whether they would intervene and risk a wider war with the United States in order to salvage the North Korean regime. The Policy Planning Staff urged caution but did not forswear opportunities should they arise.[42]

Truman and Acheson decided to keep their options open while the NSC studied the matter.[43] All the intelligence agencies scrutinized Soviet and Chinese intentions and capabilities. Everyone bided time, waiting to see if MacArthur's offensive in South Korea turned out to be successful. If MacArthur's bold plans for an amphibious landing at Inchon and an envelopment of North Korean troops flopped, the question of crossing the 38th parallel would be merely academic.[44]

Throughout the summer, relations between MacArthur and civilian and military authorities in Washington were strained. The JCS questioned the soundness of MacArthur's plans. "Inchon was probably the worst possible place ever selected for an amphibious landing," thought Bradley.[45] More important, Truman and Acheson were infuriated by MacArthur's overt support for Chiang Kai-shek. The Far East commander publicly expressed sympathy for the Chinese Nationalists' desire to harass and reconquer the mainland. Truman told Louis Johnson that MacArthur should withdraw his statement. When Johnson demurred, Truman ordered him to secure MacArthur's retraction. A few days later the president asked Johnson to resign and replaced him with Marshall and Lovett.[46]

■

Rather than align with Chiang to overthrow the Chinese Communists, Truman and Acheson emphasized that their goal was to neutralize Taiwan militarily. By informing Peking of their intention to defend the offshore island, U.S. officials claimed that they were seeking to deter a Chinese Communist offensive and thereby avoid an unwanted military confrontation. By stating that the Seventh Fleet would also prevent Nationalist raids on the mainland, Truman and Acheson sought to appear as if they were not taking sides.[47]

Although talk of neutralization implied impartiality, such was not the case at all. Chiang's forces could only harass the mainland. But almost all U.S. officials and intelligence analysts believed that Mao's troops could take Taiwan easily if not for U.S. protection.[48] Hence U.S. policy constituted overt intervention in behalf of one of the factions in the Chinese civil war, a point that even America's best friends understood quite clearly.[49]

The administration's public posture concealed a sophisticated yet offensive strategy in behalf of an independent Taiwan. While Acheson declared that the United States did not want the offshore island for itself, he was reconsidering the Cairo declaration, which called for the return of Taiwan to China.[50] While he said he would accept a majority decision admitting China into the United Nations, he worked actively to prevent a majority from developing.[51] While he talked publicly of deferring permanent political decisions until circumstances were more propitious, his chief advisers were privately discussing a plebiscite that might lead to an independent Taiwan.[52] And, while he scorned MacArthur's embrace of Chiang and would not tolerate his raids on the mainland, Acheson agreed to send military assistance and a military mission to the Nationalist regime.[53]

Acheson's continuing aversion to Chiang stemmed primarily from his conviction that the old Kuomintang leader had repeatedly proven himself incapable of mobilizing support. Moreover, reports indicated that Chiang was repeating the mistakes of the past. He was again appointing generals on the basis of political criteria, engaging in repressive actions, and making a mess of the economy. Nevertheless, Acheson was willing to consider a long-term relationship with the Nationalists if they created a politically stable and economically viable Taiwan.[54]

Much like the JCS, Acheson now decided that Taiwan should be protected from the Communists because, if the island were in Peking's hands, it might be used to interfere with U.S. military action either in the limited war in Korea or in a future global conflict with the Soviet Union. He assumed that if the Chinese Communists took Taiwan they would permit Soviet bases on the offshore island.[55] Although the British still talked about a wedge strategy, State Department officials scoffed at it. Repeatedly, Acheson, Jessup, Rusk, and Bohlen argued that the Red Chinese had to be seen as junior brothers and co-conspirators of the Kremlin.[56]

U.S. policy toward Taiwan outraged Chinese Communist leaders. Despite their close ties to Kim Il Sung, they had not inspired the North Korean attack. From their perspective, however, they were being held responsible for it and were being targeted for hostile U.S. action. American protection of Taiwan thwarted their desire to bring about a permanent consolidation of their power. U.S. support of a rival regime posed a long-term threat should Peking fail to win the loyalty of the Chinese masses and should a government on Taiwan attract the fealty of those who would become disillusioned with Chinese Communist rule. The anger of these officials mounted as they realized their impotence to cross the straits, watched the ominous turning of the tide on the Korean peninsula, and witnessed U.S. bombing close to their border and occasionally on their own territory.[57]

■

From Washington's perspective, Chinese reactions seemed less important than those emanating from the Kremlin. The North Koreans were believed to be the pawns of Moscow. Yet even Stalin appeared to be distancing himself from Kim Il Sung, maintaining his flexibility, and leaving himself the opportunity of a graceful exit. Soviet aid to the North Koreans was modest, and Soviet reactions to U.S. bombing in the areas of North Korea close to their own border were circumscribed. When the Soviets ended their boycott of the United Nations and returned to the Security Council in August, their initial truculence turned quickly to a more moderate posture. In September, Russian officials at the United Nations became unusually conciliatory and congenial. They talked of a cease-fire, internationally supervised elections, and a unified Korea.[58]

But Soviet moderation inspired U.S. risk-taking. As policymakers in Washington saw few signs of imminent Soviet intervention in Korea, they became bolder. The advantages of crossing the 38th parallel seemed increasingly appealing. The situation in Korea, they noted, "now provides the United States and the free world with first opportunity to regain territory from the Soviet bloc. . . . UN operations in Korea can set the stage for the non-Communist penetration into an area under Soviet control. . . . Penetration of the Soviet orbit, short of all-out war, would disturb the political, economic and military structure which the USSR is organizing between its own Far Eastern territories and the contiguous areas." Manchuria, "the pivot of this complex," might be lured away from the adversary as its products found an outlet in a free Korea and as its people had contact with the non-Communist world. The Japanese would be encouraged. "Throughout Asia, those who foresee only inevitable Soviet conquest would take hope."[59]

On 11 September, Truman approved an NSC paper authorizing MacArthur to prepare to cross the 38th parallel. His mission would be to destroy North Korean forces. But he was instructed to carry out such operations only if there had "been no entry into North Korea by major Soviet or Chinese Communist forces, no announcement of intended entry, nor a threat to counter our operations militarily in North Korea." He would also need to refrain from action along the Soviet and Chinese borders. Only Korean units could be used in close proximity to Soviet and Chinese territory. Finally, before marching into North Korea, MacArthur was told to secure the president's explicit approval.[60]

One week later MacArthur landed his troops at Inchon and smashed the Korean resistance. His success exceeded everyone's expectations. As he was heralded as a military genius for his surprise attack behind enemy lines, his forces moved rapidly forward. On 29 September, MacArthur entered Seoul. Yet tens of thousands of North Korean troops eluded his entrapment. Many of them fled above the 38th parallel. U.N. forces poised to follow suit. The time had come for the president to make his final decision.

There was little agonizing in Washington policymaking circles. The decision to cross the parallel had already been made. With no signs of imminent Soviet or Chinese intervention, Truman, Acheson, and the JCS were eager for MacArthur to go ahead. With elections less than two months away, it would have been politically foolhardy not to take advantage of a propitious military situation, especially when the risks of escalation appeared so small. Most Americans favored crossing the 38th parallel. Certainly, Senator McCarthy and his cohorts would have denounced the administration for showing any signs of weakness. But there was no reason not to appear bold when the adversary looked weak.

State Department officials focused on garnering U.N. support for the U.S. initiative. Knowing that even the British had strong misgivings about the U.S. decision, Acheson hoped to retain the support of the allies. But no one would be allowed to deflect U.S. policymakers from moving ahead to unify Korea, hold free elections, destroy the North Korean regime, and create a non-Communist government (most likely under Rhee's auspices). The Communists would pay a price for their aggression; the free world would be heartened; U.S. credibility would be vindicated; and the bandwagon effect would operate in favor of the United States.[61]

Peking warned that U.S. operations above the 38th parallel might mean war with China. Large numbers of China's best troops were moving into Manchuria. But MacArthur paid them no heed. He was eager to wipe up the remnants of North Korea's armies. CIA, JCS, and State Department analysts agreed that the Chinese were bluffing. Mao would not chance U.S. retaliation; he would not want to jeopardize his ambitious plans for modernization. Nor did the Soviets appear ready to raise the ante in Korea and gamble on a global war.[62]

U.S. officials wagered that they could move into North Korea with impunity because of the advantages afforded by their military prowess and economic capabilities. Serious risk-taking inhered in this action because policymakers knew that if they miscalculated, the conflict could widen and the United States could get embroiled in a protracted conflict with China. If they retaliated against China, as they expected to do, the Kremlin might then feel forced to intervene or might be inclined to intervene. And if the Soviets entered the fray, Moscow, anticipating a comprehensive U.S. strike, might launch an attack against Europe and precipitate the global war nobody wanted.[63]

No one was more certain than MacArthur, however, that the Chinese and the Soviets would not enter the conflict. When in mid-October he met the president at Wake Island, he reassured Truman that the war would be over by Christmas. After returning to Tokyo, MacArthur immediately ordered U.N. forces to resume the offensive. Taking liberties with his instructions, he sent U.S. forces into those most northern parts of North Korea that had previously been reserved for the operation of South Korean troops. When the JCS questioned MacArthur about his actions, the commander in chief insolently and disingenuously retorted that haste was imperative, that he could not rely on the South Koreans, and that Marshall had instructed him to feel tactically and strategically free to do what was necessary to defeat enemy forces.[64]

Chinese Communist units crossed the border at the end of October and linked up with over 100,000 North Korean troops. Quickly, they stymied MacArthur's offensive. Angered that officials in Washington had not allowed him to bomb the

Korean end of the Yalu River bridges, MacArthur sent an alarming message emphasizing that Chinese troops were pouring across the river. He again sought authority to bomb the bridges.[65]

His messages aroused immense anxiety in Washington. Perhaps the Chinese were not bluffing; perhaps the Soviets were ready to risk global war. Perhaps Stalin or Mao was betting that a show of force would cause the Americans to halt their advance. Perhaps the Kremlin was thinking that the United States, fearing a Soviet counterthrust in Western Europe, would cease its penchant for risk-taking in Northeast Asia. If ever there was a test of nerves, this was it.

Truman, Acheson, Marshall, and Bradley did not want to get bogged down in a wider war with China, but neither did they want to forgo their goals in Korea. Ignorant of Chinese–North Korean loyalties to one another and assuming the Communist Chinese were acting as Stalin's cat's-paw, they were altogether unable to comprehend Chinese anxieties as Americans approached the Manchurian border. So long as the United States did not attack China, it should not feel threatened. Truman told MacArthur to carry out the bombing, but his planes must not go into Chinese territory.[66]

But then, almost as suddenly as they appeared, Chinese Communist troops mysteriously disappeared. MacArthur's confidence soared. He planned to drive his forces quickly to the borders of China and the Soviet Union, destroy the adversary, and end the war. His intelligence analysts estimated that there were only about 30,000 Chinese troops in North Korea. Discounting the 300,000 troops that were known to be in Manchuria, MacArthur again concluded that Peking was bluffing. He would launch the final offensive on 24 November.[67]

The Pentagon had misgivings, but neither Marshall nor Bradley was prepared to overrule MacArthur. Their intelligence reports were similar to MacArthur's. The Chinese would not jeopardize their revolutionary triumph; the Soviets would not chance a global war. With victory so close and the shadows cast by U.S. military prowess so clear, risk-taking seemed wise. To question MacArthur's judgment after his success at Inchon appeared foolish and inappropriate.[68]

Acheson, too, went along. He and Truman knew there were opportunities to negotiate, but they decided to forgo them. Although most Americans had favored crossing the 38th parallel, support might have been mobilized for a negotiated settlement. Polls showed that many Americans were prepared for talks and for compromise. Despite the criticism of Acheson's judgment and patriotism, the Department of State was able to muster considerable support for the initiatives it wanted to pursue. Neither Truman nor Acheson felt overwhelmed by congressional criticism. Nor were they constrained by the prospective outcome of the off-year elections. Public opinion was not what dictated their actions; it simply reinforced their predilections.[69]

Truman and Acheson approved MacArthur's "final" offensive because they hoped to settle for nothing less than a unified, non-Communist Korea with perhaps a small demilitarized zone near the Chinese and Soviet borders. Prospects for a negotiated agreement along these lines did not appear good. To achieve their goals, they were prepared to take the necessary risks, only making an effort to reassure Peking that they would not invade Manchuria. Acheson, in fact, pleaded with the British to hold back proposals for a compromise settlement until the results of the offensive could be observed. With circumstances seemingly propitious, even the prudent secretary of state was willing to take a considerable gamble in behalf of rollback.[70]

■

The taste of victory was irresistible. For a nation locked in a global geopolitical battle, a triumph in Korea would have positive repercussions elsewhere. As the final showdown approached, the administration also sought a U.N. resolution to establish an international commission to study the Taiwan problem. In this way policymakers hoped to gain international sanction for their unilateral attempt to neutralize the offshore island. John Foster Dulles, still working as a consultant for the administration, designed this strategy. He wanted the U.N. commission to consider some form of autonomy or trusteeship for Taiwan. He insisted that any solution must take cognizance of Taiwan's strategic importance and its economic ties to Japan. Moreover, Dulles wanted representatives of the United States to participate on this commission in order to insure that U.S. concerns would be heard and that plans to hand Taiwan to China could be opposed.[71]

Allison, Jessup, and Acheson fully concurred with Dulles. They assumed that the commission's study could take at least a year to complete and perhaps much longer. The delay would buy time to make a going concern of Taiwan. In the interval, they might be able to get rid of Chiang. Perhaps some competent leadership could be found among the liberal non-Communist elements on Taiwan. With U.S. aid, the new government might be able to attract support on the mainland. Covert operations could be mounted. According to the CIA, there were over 400,000 guerrillas still operating in southern China. Even if the Communists could not be dislodged from power in Peking, China might be fragmented and Taiwan might survive. Over $200 million in military aid was now being earmarked for Taiwan for the next fiscal year. If these efforts were coupled with success in Korea, the tide of events in Asia might be reversed.[72]

■

But a great deal would also depend on developments in Indochina. Despite the increment of aid during the summer of 1950, the situation was worsening. A new mission appointed by the State and Defense departments emphasized that Ho Chi Minh still held onto the mantle of nationalism. The Vietnamese people hated the French. Bao Dai's government was faltering. Indeed Bao Dai himself spent most of the summer in France ridiculing French authorities for failing to cede sufficient power to his government.[73]

The French agreed that the situation was growing more ominous. They claimed that the Chinese Communists were training, aiding, and abetting the Viet Minh. The French remonstrated that U.S. deliveries were behind schedule. They wanted more military assistance, and they requested dollars to build up the Vietnamese army. They feared that the Chinese might cross the border, intervene directly, and fight alongside the Viet Minh. They desired military talks with the JCS and asked the United States to furnish tactical air support should a Chinese invasion occur.[74]

Acheson, Rusk, and the Southeast Asia specialists in the State Department grasped the dilemma before them. On the one hand, the French had to relinquish real power and create an indigenous army or a viable non-Communist government would never be able to win the allegiance of the Vietnamese people. On the other hand, if too much pressure were exerted on the French, they would feel no incentive to stay. They had already experienced 50,000 casualties; they were expending $500 million annually on the Indochinese war; and they were deploying 150,000 of their most experienced troops to Vietnam at a time when they were desperately needed in Europe. Acheson feared that the French might pull out. If this happened, Indochina "would probably go to pieces overnight." When he talked with Schuman in September 1950, Acheson encouraged the French to persevere. The United States could not commit tactical air support and could not supply money for local military financing. But military aid, which had already been doubled, would be increased yet again, and military talks with the JCS would be approved.[75]

But just as MacArthur's forces were landing at Inchon, the Viet Minh launched their own offensive in northern Tonkin. The French abandoned one garrison after another, lost nine battalions of men, and relinquished key positions along the Chinese frontier. The dramatic setbacks in Vietnam triggered much soul-searching among top U.S. officials. At Wake Island, Truman, MacArthur, and their colleagues discussed the gravity of the situation. "This is the most discouraging thing we face," lamented the president. "We must stiffen the backbone of the French," insisted Admiral Arthur W. Radford, commander of the Pacific fleet. Both Truman and Radford agreed that the French had to co-opt the support of the Vietnamese people, transfer power to non-Communist nationalists, and retain some vestige of their influence, much as the Dutch had done in Indonesia.[76]

Upon his return to the continental United States, Truman gave a major speech in San Francisco. Stressing that the country was locked in a global struggle with Soviet imperialism, the president declared that the battle would continue even after the impending triumph in Korea. Appealing to the nationalist aspirations of Asian peoples, Truman warned that international communism sought to enslave them. On the other hand, America represented the "endless revolutionary idea of human freedom and political equality."[77]

But what could be done in a place like Indochina, where the Communists embodied the nationalist aspirations of the Vietnamese people and where, unlike Indonesia, non-Communist nationalists were poorly organized and bereft of charismatic leadership? As Acheson so well understood, the French could not be pressed to make the same concessions as the Dutch had made because, if France should relinquish all authority and withdraw, Ho Chi Minh's Viet Minh would win or seize power easily. Only if the Americans were prepared to supplant the French and support an independent government could it survive. But Americans were immersed in so many other tasks, could they assume this responsibility? In the agonizing reassessment that went on, some officials thought the situation hopeless and advised withdrawal. Jack Ohly, deputy director of the Mutual Defense Assistance Program in the State Department, contended that Vietnam was too much of a drain, the prospects of success too slim, and the chances of becoming overcommitted too great. The CIA concurred. The loss of Southeast Asia, it contended, might not be as critical to U.S. national security interests as had been previously thought.[78]

But these ideas were rejected. The State Department, Army, Air Force, and JCS maintained that Indochina must not be written off. If the Viet Minh triumphed, all of Southeast Asia would be lost to the Communists. And not only were Southeast Asian raw materials and markets considered vital to the recovery of Japan, but the repatriation of investment earnings from Malaya was also judged indispensable to the financial health of Great Britain. Moreover, if war should erupt, the tin and oil of the region would be invaluable assets to the West and certainly had to be denied to the adversary. The Kremlin, said Acheson, was far more interested in Southeast Asia than China. "China without Indochina and Siam and Malaya," emphasized the secretary of state, "is like getting to third base and not getting to score."[79]

The decision, then, was to make yet another effort to buttress the French in Indochina. The top men at the State Department and the Pentagon were in broad agreement. The French had to reform; they had to win indigenous support; they had to create a viable Vietnamese army. But they must not withdraw. Some French controls, Acheson insisted, must remain so the French would feel an incentive to stay. Indeed, notwithstanding the growing need for French troops in Europe, the French were advised to deploy additional manpower to Indochina. They could be returned to France when local forces achieved some real strength.[80]

Meanwhile, the United States would boost its assistance. Next to Korea, aid to Indochina would have the highest priority, even higher than the priority assigned to assistance to Western Europe. Twenty-one light bombers, eight transport planes, and over 130 Navy fighters would be sent to the French as soon as possible. The U.S. military mission would assume a much larger role furnishing advice and cooperation to French and Vietnamese officers. High-level consultations between French, British, and U.S. chiefs of staff would also take place. Although Marshall insisted that U.S. forces could not be committed to the theater, he qualified even this viewpoint with the caveat "at this time." Acknowledging the worsening situation in East Asia, Acheson also concluded that U.S. forces in the Far East would not be able to be withdrawn from Korea and sent to Europe; they would be needed in East Asia for quite some time.[81]

Nobody was happy with these conclusions. But these measures were the price that had to be paid if Western preponderance were to be maintained. Wherever Communists appeared in formidable numbers, whether they were struggling to unite their country or to dislodge a colonial power, they had to be thwarted. Unless they were acting in overt defiance of Moscow's wishes, as in the case of Yugoslavia, their triumph was assumed to be of direct benefit to the Kremlin. Everywhere, then, the initiative had to be wrested. In Korea and the Formosa straits, the United States would play the key role. In Indochina, the French still had major responsibility, but the Americans would do more than ever before to help them.

Neither Taiwan nor Korea nor Indochina was part of the defense perimeter, but they had to be protected nonetheless. The defense perimeter was a wartime concept; it defined the areas that were deemed vital to waging a hot war. But U.S. officials were struggling to win the cold war. And unless the United States could demonstrate the credibility of U.S. commitments in peripheral areas and unless they could preserve essential Third World markets and raw materials, vital countries like Japan, Germany, France, Holland, and the United Kingdom might be maneuvered out of the American orbit. If this should happen, the cold war would be lost and the capacity to fight a hot war undermined. Incrementally, the Kremlin might be able to achieve sufficient power to contest U.S. preponderance. So, while U.S. officials engaged the Communists beyond the defense perimeter, their greatest attention was focused on defending Western Europe, integrating West Germany, and co-opting Japan.

West European Priorities

As soon as the initial decisions were made to intervene in Korea, U.S. officials turned their attention to Western Europe. In May and June 1950 they had been heartened by the creation of the European Payments Union and by French foreign minister Robert Schuman's proposal for a European coal and steel community. But their greatest worries related to the poor state of Europe's defenses and the uncertainty over Germany's loyalty to the West. Their intent was to tackle these interrelated problems by strengthening NATO and gradually bringing Germany into it.

The eruption of hostilities in Korea greatly magnified the anxieties of U.S. officials. No one really thought that the Soviets wanted to launch a premeditated attack against Western Europe. East German police forces, which the Soviets had been beefing up and which had assumed a quasi-military character, might attack West Germany. But the likelihood of this action also was deemed improbable. After the U.S. intervention in Korea, the Kremlin would have to assume that the United States would intercede in an intra-German war. If the Kremlin then responded, as it might have to do in such a critical area, global conflict was likely to result, for which the Soviets were believed to be unprepared. The Kremlin, therefore, would refrain from taking any provocative actions in Germany. Despite these rational calculations of Soviet intentions, Acheson, Bradley, and their civilian and military colleagues believed that the rearmament of Western Europe was now imperative.[82]

A number of compelling considerations forced the Truman administration to move hastily in Europe to wrest the initiative from the Kremlin. U.S. civilian and military officials were gravely worried that Europeans' sense of their own military weakness might incline them to opt for neutrality or capitulate to Soviet demands. Seeing that the Soviets dared to use overt military force in Korea, European governments might now decide to accommodate Soviet wishes rather than resist Soviet demands and thereby risk military confrontation. Most frightening was the thought that the West Germans might strike a deal with the Kremlin that would offset their feeling of vulnerability and at the same time satisfy their longing for unification. The spirit of defeatism in West Germany must be combatted, Acheson kept reiterating, by giving the Germans hope that they could be defended if war should come.[83]

Although, in the short run, Soviet threats were not likely to be the prelude to a Soviet military attack, that might not be the case after 1952. By that time, the Kremlin's capacity to defend against atomic attack and, more likely, its ability to drop atomic bombs on the United States might tempt it to try to conquer Western Europe. Hence it was urgent to use the available time to build up West European defenses. Within 18–24 months, State Department and Pentagon officials believed, sufficient capabilities could be developed to defend Western Europe. Antitank weapons, atomic artillery, and tactical air power, argued General Alfred Gruenther, could force Soviet armies to disperse and halt their offensive capabilities. Within a few years of intelligent effort, wrote Vannevar Bush, we "can remove much of the appalling threat of the huge Russian masses of armies." [84]

The most compelling reason for building up European defenses, however, related to the need to take risks and fight limited wars in peripheral areas like Korea. The outbreak of hostilities in Northeast Asia demonstrated that these scenarios were not purely hypothetical. The most worrisome matter was that limited wars might escalate. So long as Europe was vulnerable to Soviet attack, U.S. officials had to worry that their initiatives in one area might tempt the Russians to retaliate in the world's most important yet most vulnerable region. How much more relaxed U.S. officials would have felt all through the summer and autumn of 1950 if they had been confident that NATO were strong enough to resist a Soviet attack in Europe should U.S. actions in Korea trigger a Chinese intervention, U.S. retaliation, and Soviet counteraction. For the time being, they were willing to wager that their atomic superiority and productive potential constituted sufficient deterrent effect. But as the Soviets developed their atomic arsenal and strategic aircraft, the marginal impact of U.S. superiority might no longer be decisive. The American penchant to take risks to defend interests might decline; the Soviet penchant might increase. If there were strong forces in Western Europe, Acheson emphasized to the Senate Foreign Relations Committee, the Soviets would have to operate much more cautiously in other areas. The converse, of course, was true for the United States. Strong forces in Europe would enable the United States to take greater risks elsewhere.[85]

State Department and Pentagon officials now agreed on most of the essential steps to build up Europe's strength. Europe, Acheson maintained, would have to semi-mobilize. Allied rearmament efforts would divert raw material and capital resources away from export sectors and into the manufacture of munitions and military equipment. Britain's balance of payments position, recently improved as a result of the devaluation of 1949, might be reversed. Therefore, America's friends in Europe would need to have additional aid. Economic assistance, Harriman told the president, would have to continue beyond 1952. It would have to be used in new ways to buttress the defense buildup. Truman understood. He planned to ask Congress for supplemental appropriations of $4–6 billion, at least $4 billion of which would be earmarked for defense purposes. But the aid would be given to European countries only if they allocated more of their own revenues to defense expenditures.[86]

In addition to quadrupling U.S. military aid and to prolonging economic assistance, U.S. officials supported the deployment of additional troops to Europe. Bradley had come to favor this position even prior to the Korean War. Influential U.S. diplomats in Europe, like Lewis Douglas, supported it. On 3 August, Acheson, Harriman, and Johnson discussed the matter on the president's yacht and agreed on it, provided European governments augmented their own forces-in-being. Military officials concluded that the overall strength of U.S. forces in Europe should be four infantry divisions and the equivalent of one and a half armored divisions, eight tactical air groups, and complementary naval support. Troops should be deployed and made combat-ready as expeditiously as possible. Upon the outbreak of hostilities in Europe, additional contingents should be dispatched to the continent. Europe must not be abandoned; its economic and human resources were too valuable.[87]

NATO's institutional structure also had to be improved. Unified command was essential. A supreme commander had to be appointed as soon as sufficient troops had been earmarked for his use. The person designated should be an American, and he should have a fully integrated staff from all NATO members. This staff had to be established immediately. The United States would now participate fully in all NATO organs. U.S. troops in Europe would constitute part of a European defense force and would be subject to political and strategic guidance from NATO. The European rearmament effort also demanded much greater coordination of production and procurement. NATO's Military Production and Supply Board had to be transformed, made into an executive agency, and placed in the hands of a competent American who would have the authority to provide appropriate leadership and guidance.[88]

Everyone agreed that Germany had a critical role to play in the European rearmament effort. Europe could not be defended without German troops and German industry. Yet West Germans had little incentive to align with the West unless they were assured that their border would be protected, their economy liberated from controls, and their sovereignty fully restored. Bradley and Acheson agreed that NATO's defense goals had to be revised. No longer would it suffice, Acheson declared, to plan a defense at the Rhine. We would be "turning over to the Soviet government a tremendous asset, the whole Ruhr, the whole German industrial population; all of German military skill would be immediately in the Soviet camp. That would produce a transfer of power too great to be manageable. We just wouldn't know what to do in that case." Existing plans that sacrificed "without battle the industrial complexes of the Ruhr, one of the world's most important strategic objectives," concluded the JCS, had to be revised to insure the co-optation of German industrial and human resources in wartime and peacetime.[89]

At the same time that it came to advocate the idea of a forward defense east of the Rhine, the State Department's resistance to German rearmament faded. For the men at Foggy Bottom, the issue had always been a matter of timing and expediency, not principle. The gradualists had argued that too hasty a decision in favor of rearmament might discourage liberal forces in Germany, restore the militarists to power, and wreck the democratic experiment; too hasty a decision might ignite a destructive controversy with France, play into the hands of the French Communists, and weaken overall strength throughout Western Europe; too hasty a decision might be exploited by the Germans to augment their bargaining leverage, maneuver between East and West, or strike a deal with the Kremlin in behalf of German unification. There were still proponents of gradualism, like Henry Byroade, director of the Bureau of German Affairs. But they were overwhelmed by the views of Paul Nitze, John McCloy, David Bruce, and Lewis Douglas. "The question," Acheson wrote Truman on 31 July, "was not whether Germany should be brought into the general defensive plan but rather how this could be done without disrupting anything else that we are doing and without putting Germany into a position to act as the balance of power in Europe."[90]

The differences between the Defense and State departments, so heavily stressed in some accounts, were primarily tactical. The JCS insisted that the deployment of additional U.S. troops to Europe and the establishment of a unified command must be made contingent on European acceptance of German rearmament. Acheson and his colleagues at Foggy Bottom, no less than their counterparts at the Pentagon, wanted German rearmament. They felt, however, that it should be decoupled from the other issues. Despite this difference over a negotiating strategy, both the State and the Defense departments wanted a European army that would include contingents from the United States and Great Britain as well as from West European countries. German divisions led by German officers should compose part of this force. All national contingents would be under a central command. Germany would eventually have ten to fifteen divisions and would receive military aid under the Mutual Defense Assistance Program like other NATO recipients.

Both the State Department and the JCS were aware of the need to control German rearmament. West Germany would have no air force, no navy, and no general staff. There would be no army units above the division level; German divisions would be integrated into higher echelons. German forces would remain smaller than those in France. German industry would produce only light equipment and transportation vehicles. Germany would not be allowed to manufacture tanks, artillery, and other heavy equipment.[91]

Nevertheless, the German economy would be oriented to the European rearmament effort. For the most part, ordnance fabrication would still be barred. But Germany would be encouraged to produce more steel and more ships to be used elsewhere in Western Europe. Its factories would concentrate on the output of ball bearings, synthetic ammonia, chlorine, optics, machine tools, trucks, and electrical equipment. Within twelve or eighteen months, it could be producing these goods at an annual rate of $1 billion. Thereafter, the figures could rise. In order to promote the European rearmament effort, there would be accompanying revisions in the agreements regulating the prohibited and limited industries inside Germany. Whatever dismantling was still going on would cease.[92]

State Department officials also sought to eliminate many of the remaining controls over Germany. Acheson was prepared to be very lenient. He favored the restoration of Germany's sovereignty in order to boost the prestige of Konrad Adenauer's Christian Democratic government. He thought the allies and Germany should try to reach an agreement ending the technical state of war. As a result, Germany's ability to conduct its financial and economic affairs in the West would be promoted, its morale would be lifted, and its willingness to join in NATO's military effort would be encouraged. Defense officials advised caution because they were more wary that Germany might regain its autonomy and turn against the West.[93]

Acheson understood the reasons for the Pentagon's hesitation. He realized that the Germans would use the West's desire for German rearmament to wring as many concessions as possible. He knew that the Germans not only were bargaining tenaciously over the Schuman Plan but were also seeking larger allocations of coal from the International Authority for the Ruhr. So while Acheson wanted to offer concessions to democratic and Western-oriented Germans, he recognized the need for prudence. The Germans, he thought, should be permitted to regulate their own foreign affairs; but the allies should continue their control over Germany's political and commercial relations with the Soviet Union and the Communist bloc. Despite such qualifications, Acheson's overall view was that the need to rearm Europe justified the risks that inhered in the rearmament of Germany. An intelligent, sophisticated strategy for rearming Germany within a larger European framework, moreover, could rivet Germany in the Western camp. "At one step," McCloy wrote, and Acheson concurred, "it would fully integrate Germany into Western Europe and be the best possible insurance against further German aggression." [94]

In designing the steps to promote European rearmament, Acheson was well attuned to the president's thinking. Time and again Truman expressed his strong distrust of German militarism and his reservations about German rearmament. Nevertheless, he was eager to utilize German manpower and industry for the defense of Europe. Accordingly, so long as Acheson kept him informed about the planning under way in the administration, the president followed where his advisers wanted to go.[95]

Moreover, Truman was confident that he would be able to win legislative support for increased aid to the Old World. He was also willing to use his powers as commander in chief to assign additional troops to Europe. He made this important announcement on 9 September, conditioning the U.S. initiative on reciprocal European efforts. Neither the rise of McCarthy, nor the acerbic Republican attacks on his Far Eastern policy, nor the forthcoming elections would dissuade him from doing what he deemed necessary to wrest the initiative from the Kremlin.[96]

The president did not state publicly and Acheson did not inform the allies privately that the decision to deploy U.S. troops to the continent was contingent on their acceptance of German rearmament. So when Schuman arrived in Washington for tripartite talks with Acheson and British foreign secretary Ernest Bevin in September, he was stunned to hear the conditional nature of the U.S. commitment. Acheson, as was his custom, presented the U.S. position in a logical, persuasive manner. He emphasized that Western Europe could not be defended without German assistance. Yet German aid would not be forthcoming, indeed German loyalty to the West could not even be assumed, unless German frontiers were guaranteed. Forward defense and German rearmament were imperative for the permanent integration of West Germany into Western Europe and for the development of NATO defensive capabilities. Risks, Acheson acknowledged, inhered in these initiatives. But German rearmament would be controlled carefully, and the United States would be willing to incur another set of unprecedented responsibilities in Europe.[97]

Schuman did not contest Acheson's goals and did not rebut his reasoning, but he insisted that the timing was deplorable. Neither France nor Europe was ready for German rearmament. From a political perspective, it was unacceptable; from a diplomatic and geostrategic viewpoint, it was unwise. Before Germany rearmed, it had to be integrated into Western Europe through an unbreachable network of economic and political institutions, such as the European Coal and Steel Community and the Council of Europe, which were then being formulated by Europeans. France was willing to do its fair share to match the U.S. buildup. During the summer, France had made plans to create fifteen new divisions at a cost of about two trillion francs (or about $5.715 billion). Schuman welcomed the deployment of U.S. troops as well as the proposals for strengthening NATO's command setup. But German rearmament was beyond the pale. Circumstances did not demand such radical action, at least not right away. The Soviets were not ready for war; they should not be provoked.[98]

Notwithstanding Schuman's firm opposition, Acheson felt confident that both the British and the French would accede to U.S. wishes. He was encouraged by Bevin's response and by the reactions of the other foreign ministers at the North

Atlantic Council meeting. They would strengthen the Laender police within West Germany, improve the German labor service units (which were attached to Allied divisions), and organize German engineering formations (which could be used for mine-laying and fortification construction). The foreign ministers also agreed to revise the Occupation Statute, terminate the formal state of war, and create a German foreign ministry.[99]

Still more progress was possible if the United States acted with discretion and determination. Acheson advised against any substantive modification of the U.S. position. But he continued to think it was unwise to make the creation of an integrated European defense force contingent on German rearmament. More tact was needed in dealing with French officials like Schuman and Jules Moch, the minister of war. They faced real security dilemmas, they had tough political problems, and they had memories of travail and cruelty at the hands of the Germans that few Americans could understand. Moch's son, Acheson recalled, had been strangled by the Gestapo, and five members of Moch's family had died in concentration camps. Advances would be made, the secretary of state thought, through an astute mixture of private reassurances and financial leverage.[100]

Marshall, who was just taking command of the Pentagon, concurred fully with this approach. He had always thought that the creation of a favorable balance of power in Europe depended on reconciling France's quest for security with Germany's demands for sovereignty, equality, and economic opportunity. He, therefore, did not oppose Acheson's desire for negotiating flexibility. The French, he thought, should be allowed to make their own proposals so long as they did not delay the achievement of fundamental objectives. The incorporation of German units within a European defense force was too vital an issue to founder on the technicalities of a negotiating strategy.[101]

Like Acheson, however, Marshall was relentless in pressing for progress. As soon as Congress passed the supplementary military aid legislation, the French were told that, if they cooperated, they could expect another $200–400 million in military assistance during fiscal year 1951. Yet Schuman and Moch were also warned that, if they did not go along with U.S. wishes, Congress would cut future funding.[102]

At the end of October, the French responded with a plan of their own. Known as the Pleven Plan, after the French premier, it called for a European army of 100,000 men. Units from all participating nations, including West Germany, would make up this force. There would be a supreme commander, with vaguely defined powers, as well as a European defense minister, a European assembly, and a common European defense budget. German units would not be formed until after the negotiations on the Schuman Plan were completed. Even then, German military units would not be permitted to be larger than company or battalion size.

U.S. civilian and military officials found the Pleven Plan totally unacceptable. Publicly, they muted their criticism. Privately, they condemned it. In effect, the plan made German rearmament contingent on the creation of a new set of European institutions. References to a European defense minister, a European assembly, and a common budget presupposed the creation of a federated Europe into which the European members would merge a great deal of their sovereignty. If progress were ever to be made along these lines, it would take years. Bradley concluded that the Pleven Plan made NATO totally inoperable, precluded U.S. participation in a European defense force, and delayed German rearmament for the indefinite future.[103]

For a moment it appeared as if plans to expedite Europe's rearmament and Germany's integration were in disarray. Not surprisingly, Stalin saw an opportunity. Fearing NATO efforts to rearm West Germany and hoping to lure the latter eastward, he requested a meeting of the Council of Foreign Ministers to discuss the German problem. At the same time, Communist leaders from the Eastern bloc called for a new set of agreements that would guarantee Germany's demilitarization, terminate the state of war, lift the constraints on the German economy, bring about the withdrawal of all occupation troops, and restore German unity in conformity with the Potsdam agreements.[104]

U.S. officials were gravely worried. They feared a dangerous drift toward neutrality in West Germany at a time when the co-optation of German power seemed more imperative than ever. Anxiously awaiting MacArthur's final offensive, policymakers in Washington desperately wanted to build up Europe's military strength. Future risk-taking by both the United States and the Soviet Union would depend on perceptions of NATO's ability to mount a successful defense and prevail in a global war. Hence Acheson and Marshall agreed that the Pleven Plan must not paralyze U.S. efforts to wrest the initiative in Europe.

They decided on a two-track approach. On one track the French would explore the possibilities of a European army and a new set of political institutions. On the other track the United States would exert leadership in behalf of arrangements that would lead to the immediate strengthening of NATO and that would set the stage for the training and recruitment of German troops. Whatever happened on the first track must not be allowed to interfere with the establishment and growth of an integrated NATO defense force, eventually including German divisions, under a supreme commander and a unified staff. When the Korean fighting ended, as was expected would happen within the next few weeks, the deployment of U.S. troops to Europe could begin. Shipments of armaments, ammunition, military equipment, and machine tools to Europe would also be accelerated as the production of war materiel in the United States picked up and as the dollars appropriated by the new military assistance bill became available.[105]

The momentum ignited by the Korean War would not be lost. Neither French fears nor Soviet chicanery would be allowed to interfere with the U.S. desire to co-opt Germany, strengthen NATO, and insure Western preponderance in the global struggle for power with Soviet-directed world communism.

Japan and the Western Pacific

If it were important to move ahead in Western Europe, it was no less urgent to do so in Japan. Acheson repeatedly emphasized that progress toward a Japanese peace treaty was among his top priorities. He allowed Dulles, his Republican consultant, to carry the ball on this issue. Dulles had been in Japan when the hostilities erupted, and he returned to Washington determined to move ahead rapidly. He believed that "the Communist offensive in Korea was probably aimed at getting control over Japan, for had Korea been conquered Japan would have fallen without an open struggle." [106]

Policymakers were convinced that, once having intervened in Korea, they had a unique opportunity to make progress in Japan. According to the East Asia specialists, many Japanese would now become much more receptive to U.S. desires to retain troops and bases in Japan. They would see that America's withdrawal from Korea had invited aggression. They would realize that neutrality was not an option because they could not count on Soviet self-restraint. They would look more sympathetically upon their own rearmament. They would see that if they opted to join the free world, the United States would provide assistance. [107]

Moreover, if heretofore a key deterrent to a peace treaty had been doubts about the Japanese economy and fears of political chaos, the Korean conflict provided opportunities for the Japanese to earn dollars and become independent of U.S. assistance. Robert A. Fearey, one of the experts in the State Department's Office of Northeast Asian Affairs, estimated that as a result of the war in Korea the United States would procure about $200–300 million worth of supplies from Japan during the current fiscal year. If U.S. troops were placed on a pay-as-you-go basis after a peace treaty were signed, Japan would receive additional dollars. More important, the war and the accompanying rearmament effort meant that countries like Indonesia and Malaya would have vastly increased dollar earnings, perhaps as much as $200–300 million annually for the next few years, as a result of the accelerated demand for their rubber, tin, and other raw materials. Many of these dollars, Fearey believed, could end up in Japan if it expanded its manufactured and capital goods exports to Southeast Asia. Fortunately, Fearey thought, Japan would be able to exploit this opportunity because the rearmament effort in Europe would constrain British, French, and Dutch exports. Long-term prospects still appeared cloudy, but Dulles concluded that "for the next few years, at least, Japan's economic position will be much better than could have been imagined a short time ago." [108]

Dulles sought to reconcile the positions of the State and Defense departments regarding a Japanese peace treaty. Dulles's trip to Japan in June had coincided with the visit of Johnson and Bradley to MacArthur. They had not planned to have interdepartmental consultations on the other side of the Pacific, but Dulles talked to Johnson and Bradley as well as with MacArthur, and they came to a considerable meeting of minds on the basic security requirements for a peace treaty. Bradley, in particular, was ready to move ahead once it became evident that the State Department was prepared to accommodate the military concerns of the JCS. When they returned from Tokyo, Johnson and Bradley asked General Burns to take charge of the Defense Department's work on the peace treaty. In turn, Burns assigned the job to Major General Carter B. Magruder in the Army's office of occupation affairs. Despite the frequent carping between Johnson on the one hand and Acheson and Webb on the other, State and Defense Department officials quickly reached agreement on virtually all the essential security provisions of a peace treaty.[109]

The JCS insisted that Japan's economic potential and skilled labor had to be denied to the Soviet Union and retained within the American orbit. The Japanese could regain full sovereignty and complete economic and political autonomy provided that they permitted the United States to garrison forces inside their country. Moreover, a U.S. commander must have the right to deploy these forces in any manner he deemed necessary, provided he first informed the Japanese government of what he was going to do. Furthermore, the United States must retain a strategic trusteeship over the former Japanese mandates in the western Pacific as well as strategic control over the Ryukyu Islands, including the strategic base at Okinawa. For U.S. military officials, the Korean War underscored just how important Japan could be as a source of supply and as a forward base from which to project U.S. power onto the Asian mainland. Japanese airfields, after all, were the launching pad for U.S. planes transporting materiel to the Pusan perimeter and for U.S. fighters and bombers attacking North Korean troops, lines of supply, and industrial centers.[110]

Once the JCS agreed to proceed with a treaty, the State Department sought to fulfill the Pentagon's security requirements. Complete extraterritorial rights for Americans stationed in Japan could not be secured. But the treaty would not come into effect until the Korean War was over, and a separate bilateral accord would be negotiated laying out the details of U.S. military rights and privileges in Japan. Although other nations would not be permitted to retain forces in Japan, the United States would determine when its own troops would be withdrawn. Despite the obligatory references to the United Nations, Dulles told Johnson that military officials should not be misled by the adept language of the State Department's draft treaty. It "gave the United States the right to maintain in Japan as much force as we wanted, anywhere we wanted, for as long as wanted." [111]

Furthermore, the State Department welcomed Japanese rearmament. According to Allison, the Japanese police force and coast guard had to be beefed up immediately. A surveillance agency similar to the Federal Bureau of Investigation had to be established. These steps were prerequisite to the creation of Japanese defense forces. The Policy Planning Staff endorsed these ideas, pointing out that "The Korean conflict and the deep uncertainties regarding the future now make it imperative . . . to create Japanese forces designed to contribute to the defense of the islands." This goal could not be written into the treaty itself because the other members of the Far East Commission would never accept it. Nor was it evident that the Japanese people would alter their constitution to make it possible. Rather than spur a protracted controversy over this issue, State Department officials preferred that the treaty simply not prohibit rearmament. Meanwhile, they encouraged MacArthur to organize Japanese forces. When Marshall took over the Defense Department, General Burns informed him that MacArthur had already instructed the Japanese government to establish a centrally controlled police force of 75,000 men. It was "being organized as an army of four divisions and equipped along American lines but with some of the heavy armament omitted." The equipment for this Japanese National Police Reserve, as it was called, came from MacArthur's stocks because they were refurbished by the supplies pouring in from across the ocean in the wake of the Korean conflict.[112]

Japan needed to have sufficient forces to preserve internal security given the depletion of U.S. troops during the Korean emergency and given the prospective lifting of U.S. economic and political controls. The post-treaty Japanese government must have the means to thwart leftist unrest and resist Soviet probes. Deprived of nationalist and irredentist issues, the Japanese Communists could be checked, the strong anti-Russian sentiments of most Japanese would come to the fore, and the moderate right, like the Yoshida ministry, would prevail. Hence it was foolhardy to saddle Yoshida Shigeru with a reform program that he found distasteful. The Japanese, Kennan argued, should be permitted to jettison the reforms of the occupation period, if they so desired. Dulles concurred. If Japan were to be co-opted for the West, it must not be antagonized. "The lessons of Versailles should be remembered. . . . We must not make the same mistake with Japan." [113]

But if Japan were to have a stable and strong pro-U.S. government, its economy would have to flourish. Dulles and his aides remained acutely sensitive to this issue. They were not as worried about the power of the Japanese left as they were about the temptation of the Japanese right to look to the Asian mainland, now dominated by Communists, for the sale of Japanese goods. In prewar years as much as 20 percent of Japan's exports went to China. The Japanese, Dulles concluded, "must be assured a satisfactory livelihood, and yet from the American point of view it is essential that this be achieved without placing Japan in a position of dependence upon the Communist-dominated mainland of Asia." Dulles hoped that the Japanese capital goods industry could be enlarged and that markets for its exports might be found in the "underdeveloped areas of Southeast Asia." He and Allison wanted the United States to assume the responsibility for redirecting Japanese trade away from the Chinese mainland. "The future of the world," Dulles said over and over again, "depends largely on whether the Soviet Union will be able to get control over Western Germany and Japan by means short of war. . . . If the Soviet Union were able to add to itself the industrial capacity and trained manpower of Western Germany and Japan, the world balance of power would be profoundly altered." [114]

■

As compelling as was this geostrategic vision of international politics, not all of America's friends in the Pacific and Asia were willing to accept its implications.

Australia and New Zealand expressed their profound reservations about a liberal peace treaty that might revitalize Japanese power. Nor did they welcome renewed Japanese trade competition. They would go along with a generous treaty only if the United States offered security guarantees.[115]

Dulles had hoped that the retention of U.S. troops in Japan would reassure friends that Japan would not be allowed to resume its aggressive ways. He was not eager to offer security guarantees because he did not think the United States had the ability to safeguard all non-Communist governments in the western Pacific and East Asia. He also feared that nations that were excluded from the agreement might decide to safeguard their security by befriending the Soviets. Nevertheless, by the end of October 1950, Dulles realized that the United States would have to either offer unilateral guarantees through a presidential declaration or negotiate a Pacific Pact along the lines that State Department officials had begun thinking about the previous March. In Asia (as in Europe) a successful strategy aimed at co-opting Japanese (or German) power compelled the United States to incur commitments that would have otherwise been eschewed.[116]

■

The problems beleaguering the Philippines, however, could not be solved through a presidential declaration or a military pact. The government of President Elpidio Quirino was in total disarray. Corruption was rife; the economy was stagnating; the tax system was a monstrosity; foreign exchange reserves were dwindling; the gap between the rich and poor was widening. Agrarian discontent was widespread; labor strife was on the rise. In this environment, the Hukbalahap insurgency was flourishing. According to the JCS and the NSC, the causes of this rebellion were entirely domestic. Discontent in the agricultural provinces of central Luzon and an acquired taste for guerrilla life, developed during the Japanese occupation, inclined Filipinos to join the Huks. But whatever the indigenous sources of the insurrection, the JCS maintained that "Leadership over these lawless elements has been assumed by disciplined Communists who conduct their operations in accordance with directives from the Far Eastern Cominform." [117]

The situation endangered vital U.S. security interests. The Philippines were an integral part of the defense perimeter. The islands were deemed critical to any strategy based on defense in depth; they were useful for projecting U.S. power into Southeast Asia (especially into Indochina, where the French were beleaguered and asking for air support should the Communist Chinese aid the Viet Minh). But perhaps even more important, the Philippines were America's former colony, the symbol of the country's recognition "that nationalism in Asia is a basic reality which cannot be ignored." Failure in the Philippines, emphasized the NSC, "would discredit the United States in the eyes of the world and seriously decrease U.S. influence, particularly in Asia." [118]

The administration sent a special economic survey mission to study the situation and to make recommendations. A host of fiscal, economic, and administrative reforms were proposed; $250 million in additional aid over the next five years was earmarked for the Philippines.[119] At the same time the U.S. military mission was beefed up. Bradley and Rusk wanted U.S. officers to go into the field and act as tactical advisers to native troop commanders, much as had been done in Greece where the Communist guerrillas had been crushed.[120] If despite these measures conditions continued to deteriorate, policymakers concluded that the United States should send additional forces to the Philippines. The Soviets posed no military threat to the islands; the Huks were not believed to be receiving significant amounts of external support; and the claim that the Huks were taking orders from Moscow or were inclined to hand their country over to the Kremlin remained unsubstantiated. Yet no risks could be taken by the United States in so vital an area. "The Philippine Islands," concluded the NSC, "could be the key to Soviet control of the Far East." [121]

At a time when MacArthur was launching his "final" offensive in Korea, when the United States was buttressing the French effort in Indochina, and when the State Department was readying its peace treaty for Japan, the Philippine government could not be allowed to collapse. Although corrupt, unpopular, and inefficient, it remained one of "the instrumentalities for accomplishing our objectives." Better to work with and try to improve a regime that was friendly to U.S. interests than to push for radical change, invite political turmoil, and create a political vacuum.[122]

Strength Through Risk-Taking

As Truman administration officials maneuvered to regain the initiative, they found the Soviets ready to talk. The Kremlin, perhaps awed by the intensity of the U.S. reaction to North Korea's aggression and cognizant of the dramatic turn of events on the battlefield, invited discussions on all the most salient issues. They wanted a foreign ministers' meeting to review the German problem; they were prepared to examine Dulles's draft of a Japanese peace treaty; most of all, they showed a strong disposition to resolve the Korean conflict before it precipitated a wider war. When Truman was in New York at the end of October to address the United Nations, Soviet foreign minister Andrei Vishinsky told him that the Kremlin hoped to iron out their differences. Jacob Malik, the Soviet representative at the United Nations, repeatedly indicated to Jessup and Dulles that they could make progress on a variety of outstanding matters if they tried hard enough. These overtures, some of them quite cordial, did not mean that the Kremlin suspended its rhetorical denunciations of U.S. policy. Nor did it mean that Stalin was necessarily prepared to make large concessions. But Jessup and most observers at the United Nations had no doubt that the Soviets seriously wanted to talk, were showing malleability on key issues, and were seeking ways to end the Korean War without losing face. Moreover, intercepted radio broadcasts revealed that Moscow was telling Peking and Pyongyang that the Soviet Union wanted to stay out of the war and that aid to the North Koreans would have to come from China, if it were to come at all.[123]

U.S. officials also knew that China was not eager to get embroiled in a war with the United States. Mao chose to avoid a military showdown and did not try to take Taiwan despite the fact that this issue was of much greater importance to China than was Korea. Nor did Chinese troops intervene in Korea at the time when, in American perceptions, it would have been most propitious to do so. If they had entered the fray in June or July, MacArthur told Truman, it would have been decisive. Chinese warnings and threats did mount as U.S. troops prepared to cross the 38th parallel. But China was also careful not to foreclose all avenues for a settlement.[124]

Policymakers in Washington, however, were not looking to negotiate, at least not until more favorable conditions were established. Acheson rebuffed overtures that might have brought an end to the fighting in Korea before the enemy's forces were destroyed and unification achieved. As late as 24 November, he wrote Bevin that suggestions for a demilitarized zone along the borders separating Korea from China should be postponed until the results of MacArthur's final offensive were clear. At that time, the secretary of state continued, "we may be able to stabilize the political situation by proposals which originate from a position of strength." [125]

This attitude typified U.S. thinking in the early autumn of 1950. Negotiations with the Kremlin might be possible in the future, but not then. After the U.S. military buildup was in high gear and after U.S. efforts in Western Europe and Asia began to bear fruit, then, in the words of NSC 68/2, it might "be desirable for the United States to take an initiative in seeking negotiations in the hope that it might facilitate the process of accommodation by the Kremlin to the new situation." The objective of negotiations was to solidify U.S. preponderance. In contrast, agreements that merely confirmed prevailing realities would "be unacceptable, if not disastrous." [126]

This attitude did not mean that U.S. officials welcomed the idea of a wider war. Throughout the deliberations on whether U.S. troops should cross the 38th parallel and on whether U.S. forces should be permitted to go to the Yalu, policymakers expressed a strong preference for avoiding escalation. They suspected that the Kremlin might be trying to entrap them into a prolonged conflict on the Asian mainland. They realized that the deployment of U.S. forces to Korea put them in a less favorable position to execute emergency war plans should global war erupt. They knew that they and their allies were not ready for general hostilities, that Western Europe lay hostage to the Kremlin's whims, and that their efforts to redress the balance of forces-in-being would require 18–24 months. Hence they concluded that every effort should be made to localize the conflict. Should Soviet or Chinese Communist forces enter North Korea, substantial efforts would be made to avoid a direct confrontation.[127]

The whole point of U.S. policy, however, was to achieve certain goals, namely the unification of Korea and preponderant strength in Asia and Europe, without precipitating war. Signs of Chinese equivocation and Soviet timidity, indications of a Russian affinity for negotiations, and news of the Kremlin juxtaposing key responsibilities onto the Chinese inspired the U.S. penchant for risk-taking. The Soviets might have superior forces-in-being, but U.S. officials assumed that the Russians knew they could not win a protracted conflict. Therefore, they would seek to avoid war even more strongly than did the Americans. At the most critical NSC meeting, CIA director Walter Bedell Smith emphasized that "he saw no reason to change the previous estimate that the Soviets are not prepared themselves to bring on a general war." [128]

This perception continued to reinforce the inclination of U.S. officials to take risks to achieve their goals. The thought that they could wrest the initiative in Korea without provoking a wider war had tremendous appeal. The "decisive defeat of North Korean aggression and the successful unification of Korea," the State Department had already concluded, "would represent a victory . . . of incalculable importance in Asia and throughout the world" for the United States. The Japanese would be heartened. Sino-Soviet divisions might emerge as Communist leaders in Peking and Moscow heaped recriminations upon one another. Even Soviet satellites in Europe might feel an incentive to distance themselves from the Kremlin. [129]

General MacArthur, of course, was more willing to plunge into this risk-taking than anyone else. After Inchon, he was at the height of his prestige. He was the commander in the field, a general who defied the odds, dared to act boldly, and snatched victory from defeat. He prided himself on his grasp of the Oriental mentality and scorned his Asian adversaries. His advice aroused skepticism in the Pentagon as well as in the State Department. Bradley wavered; Acheson agonized; Marshall deferred; Truman listened and pondered. But in the end, as Clarence Lo, Barton Bernstein, and Bruce Cumings have argued, they all approved. "Defense believes, and we agree," Acheson said at the close of the most decisive meeting on 9 November, "that General MacArthur's directive should not be changed at present." [130]

Further reassessment went on in Washington during the next two weeks, but no one changed his mind. No one wanted a wider war; no one wanted to divide the allies. But everyone believed in negotiating from strength, and strength could not be achieved without risk-taking. Risks inhered in the pursuit of German rearmament and a Japanese peace treaty and an independent Taiwan. Risks inhered in a foreign policy that aimed to bring about a retraction of Soviet power, that sought to create states independent of Soviet control in Eastern Europe, and that endeavored to contain communism in the Third World. In fact, military victory in Korea was so alluring to U.S. officials precisely because it would help wrest the diplomatic initiative abroad while garnering support for those initiatives at home. [131]

Progress Amidst Anxiety,
November 1950-September 1951

On 24 November 1950, MacArthur launched his end-the-war offensive. The following night 300,000 Chinese troops entered the battle and sent U.N. forces reeling backwards. MacArthur's armies were divided and dispersed, easily susceptible to envelopment and entrapment. His local commanders went on the defensive and then flew to Tokyo for consultation. MacArthur wired the Joint Chiefs of Staff (JCS) of the dramatic reversal on the battlefield. Emphasizing the need for immediate reinforcements, he asked permission to use Chinese Nationalist troops. The war, he insisted, could no longer be localized. He wanted to bomb Manchurian bases and pursue enemy planes across the Korean-Chinese border. The constraints placed on him, he told the press, were "an enormous handicap, without precedent in history." [1]

Policymakers in Washington raged at MacArthur. The general's complaints to reporters, Undersecretary of Defense Robert Lovett said, were "among the most extraordinary things" he had ever seen. Secretary of State Dean Acheson and Chairman of the JCS Omar Bradley were embarrassed by the enormity of their misjudgment. They had gambled that the Chinese would not intervene and they had erred egregiously. As the crisis mounted, Truman accentuated everyone's fears. At a press conference on 30 November, the president stated that he was considering the use of atomic weapons. [2]

If such weapons were used or if Manchurian bases were bombed, the limited war in Korea might escalate quickly into a global war with the Soviet Union. If, however, the United States did not respond effectively and if U.N. troops were pushed off the Korean peninsula, U.S. credibility might be shattered. The courage of prospective allies in Europe and Asia might falter; resistance to Soviet demands might crumble; neutralism might flourish. Throughout Washington, grave worries about Soviet preponderance mingled with immense anxieties about global war.

As news reports dwelled on the military reversals on the battlefield, the political climate in the United States turned poisonous. Senator Joseph McCarthy and the Republican right had kept the Democrats on the defensive since the previous winter. But the president's decision to intervene in Korea had initially proved popular. The Democrats did not fare badly in the November elections. Indeed, if MacArthur's offensive had brought a rapid conclusion to the war, political developments would have taken a different turn. But the general's failure and his recriminations brought forth an avalanche of criticism. Truman's ratings in the polls plummeted once again. The Senate Republican Policy Committee requested Acheson's resignation. McCarthy and his friends accelerated their attacks. Asia, they charged, was being sacrificed by "pinkos" in the State Department, like Jessup, who lacked the guts to stand up to the Communists.[3]

The apprehensions of America's allies abroad were almost as intense as the criticisms of the administration's foes at home. In capitals everywhere, policymakers feared another world war. In London and Paris, officials lamented their failure to control U.S. leadership of the Korean War. They had had grave misgivings about crossing the 38th parallel; they had regretted the Americans' reluctance to pursue a negotiated settlement; they had agonized over the possible ramifications of MacArthur's march to the Yalu. Their failure to speak out proved disastrous. They desperately wanted U.S. aid and protection, but they also desired to monitor U.S. behavior, restrain U.S. actions, and limit the possibilities of global war. If American retaliatory action against China escalated into a wider crisis, Europe was vulnerable to Soviet conquest. Truman's talk of atomic weapons appalled them. British prime minister Clement Attlee immediately journeyed across the ocean to plead for U.S. restraint.[4]

In the midst of this turmoil, Truman and his top advisers closed ranks to face the toughest crisis of the cold war. Acheson worked harmoniously with Lovett and Secretary of Defense George Marshall. Bradley and the other chiefs of staff began meeting weekly with Philip Jessup, Paul Nitze, George McGhee, Dean Rusk, and Acheson's other top advisers. Jessup and Bradley struck up a particularly useful collaboration. There were certainly disagreements over particular tactics of waging war in Korea and over the appropriate risks that should be taken. But, faced with criticism abroad, political acrimony at home, and a defiant commander in the field, Marshall, Lovett, Bradley, and Acheson struggled to narrow their differences and support the president. In a nerve-racking and unpredictable environment, they worked tenaciously to limit the war in Korea while they progressed to solidify positions of strength everywhere else against the Communist bloc.[5]

Anxious Calculations

Truman met with his cabinet on 28 November. The atmosphere was gloomy. "The situation is very serious," the president acknowledged, "and can develop into complete involvement in total war." The Chinese would not have acted without Soviet instructions, thought Acheson. And the massive nature of China's intervention suggested that the Kremlin was prepared to take much greater risks than had been anticipated. "Time is shorter than we thought," emphasized the secretary of state. The "possibility cannot be disregarded," the Central Intelligence Agency (CIA) concluded, "that the USSR may already have decided to precipitate global war in circumstances most advantageous to itself through the development of general war in Asia." [6]

Thoughts of global war inclined some military officials to want to pull out of Korea, focus on protecting Japan, and prepare for implementing their war plans. But Acheson and his advisers in the State Department strongly urged that Korea not be abandoned. A middle course had to be found between escalating the conflict on the one hand and relinquishing Korea to the adversary on the other. Escalation was unwise because the Soviets might become embroiled and might decide to strike at Europe. Withdrawal was equally imprudent because it would invite Chinese Communist expansion into other parts of Asia. During their talks with the British, U.S. officials repeatedly stated that they did not want to retreat from Asia: they hoped to maintain their position in Korea; they did not want to jeopardize their influence in Japan and the Philippines; and they did not want to see Chinese inroads into Indochina. A strong policy had to be followed everywhere, Averell Harriman, Truman's special assistant, told Attlee. [7]

The British did not dispute the importance of maintaining the defense perimeter intact and of containing Communist expansion in Southeast Asia. Attlee, however, was immensely concerned that, in retaining a foothold in Korea, the Americans would widen the war and precipitate a global conflict. He pressed the Americans to negotiate a cease-fire. Since China was in a strong bargaining position, the British prime minister urged Truman to change U.S. policy toward Taiwan and accept Chinese Communist representation in the United Nations. Not only might such concessions bring an early end to the Korean conflict, but they might also satisfy China and drive a wedge between Moscow and Peking. [8]

Truman, Acheson, Marshall, and Bradley were not prepared to make any concessions whatsoever. The president insisted that the Communist government of China "was Russian and nothing else." Marshall declared that the Chinese and Russian Communists were "coreligionists." Acheson said that the wedge strategy was a fine theoretical construct but that it did not apply to the present situation. Throughout these discussions, Truman and Acheson freely admitted that domestic political considerations influenced their position. But with equal fervor they insisted that their views made eminent geopolitical sense and accorded with their continuous efforts to maintain a position of strength in Asia as well as in Europe. [9]

Yet U.S. officials appreciated British warnings against expanding the war. Marshall acknowledged that he was studying a variety of military options, including a blockade of Chinese ports, air strikes against the mainland, and covert action in southern China. But the risks seemed to outweigh the benefits. If the United States escalated, the enemy might invoke the Stalin-Mao treaty of February 1950. The result could be a protracted war with China or a global war with the Kremlin. Neither possibility was welcome. Embroilment with China might spur Chinese efforts to take Taiwan or Hong Kong, foment additional unrest in Malaya, or augment support to the Viet Minh. Global war with the Soviets was even more unthinkable when Europe was vulnerable to conquest. Marshall preferred to wage a limited conflict on the Korean peninsula itself, calculating that U.S. and U.N. forces could resist the Chinese onslaught. He was encouraged when, on the last day of the British-U.S. talks, Army Chief of Staff Joseph Collins returned from a quick trip to the Korean theater and reported that the military situation was not nearly so bad as had been feared.[10]

The Anglo-American talks did not delineate a clear path for terminating the war in Korea. U.S. officials concluded that they would not withdraw, would not appease, and would not escalate. Although they could not see their way out of the Korean conflict, they were determined not to allow it to distract them from more important priorities. Neither the workshops of Europe and Asia nor the areas that served as their markets and sources of raw materials must be allowed to pass into the Communist orbit. Reiterating the rationale behind U.S. thinking, the president explained in January 1951 that:

If Western Europe were to fall to Soviet Russia, it would double the Soviet supply of coal and triple the Soviet supply of steel. If the countries of Asia and Africa should fall to Soviet Russia, we would lose the sources of many of our most vital raw materials, including uranium, which is the basis of our atomic power. And Soviet command of the free nations of Europe and Asia would confront us with military forces which we could never hope to equal. In such a situation the Soviet Union could impose its demands on the world, without resort to conflict, simply through the preponderance of its economic and military power.[11]

The administration was convinced that its military tactics in Korea must complement and reinforce its larger national security strategy. The risks of a premature global war must not be magnified. A calculated policy of limited war in Korea, combined with an aggressive diplomacy and a strong rearmament effort, might enable the United States to achieve long-term goals without global war. But nothing could be taken for granted. The period ahead was perilous indeed. It could no longer be assumed that the Soviets would back down when faced with Western determination. Stalin might launch a full-scale attack as a result of a perception of threat or a decision to exploit his superior conventional forces-in-being and his growing atomic stockpile. Truman, Acheson, Marshall, Lovett, and Bradley knew they had to keep this in mind as they conducted the Korean War and simultaneously sought to build positions of strength around the Soviet periphery.

Hence the U.S. rearmament effort had to be expedited; the 1954 goals outlined in NSC 68/2 had to be fulfilled by 1952. If the United States and its allies could get beyond their present window of military vulnerability and if they could gain the time to establish positions of preponderant strength around the Soviet/Communist bloc, a hot war might never have to be waged. The Kremlin could be maneuvered to the bargaining table and forced to accept terms favorable to the United States. At a National Security Council (NSC) meeting on 14 December, Acheson offered his view of what type of strength was necessary to support his diplomacy. "It would not be too much," he said, "if we had all the troops that the military want. If we had all of the things that our European allies want it would not be too much. If we had the equipment to call out the reserves it would not be too much. If we had a system for full mobilization it would not be too much." [12]

Truman and Marshall were prepared to give Acheson most of what he wanted. On 1 December, the president asked Congress for a supplementary appropriation of $16.8 billion for the Department of Defense and $1 billion for the Atomic Energy Commission.[13] Two weeks later he approved NSC 68/4, which called for the achievement of 1954 goals by mid-1952. By that date, as contrasted with June 1950, the Army would have 1,353,000 troops rather than 655,000; the Navy would have 397 major combatant ships rather than 238; and the Air Force would have 95 wings rather than 48. Particularly noteworthy would be the rapid increase in Army divisions, medium bomber groups, and aircraft carriers.[14] The sums necessary to finance this buildup were staggering. During fiscal years 1951 and 1952, $140 billion would be needed to pay for the totality of U.S. national security programs. For fiscal year 1952 alone, Truman wanted new obligational authority totaling $60 billion for the military services, $10 billion for military and economic assistance programs, $2.9 billion for stockpiling, and $870 million for the Atomic Energy Commission.[15]

These requests, it must be emphasized, were not designed for a limited conflict in Korea. U.S. officials were creating a military posture and a mobilization base from which they would be prepared to wage global war. In their view there was nothing more important than creating the industrial base to turn out tanks, aircraft, ammunition, radar equipment, and other war materiel. Within a year their plans called for increasing the production of planes by 500 percent, combat vehicles by 400 percent, and electronics equipment by 450 percent. For the first time they would make hundreds of guided missiles, especially the Sparrow, Terrier, and Nike, which would be used for research and development purposes. They hoped to appropriate $14.4 billion so that by December 1953 the Air Force and Navy would have 10,884 new aircraft. By the end of the buildup, the Army would also be receiving 1,000 tanks per month. The overall goal was to create the capability to produce 50,000 modern military aircraft and 35,000 tanks per year. The projected rate of increase was so great that it considerably exceeded the experience of World War II. Indeed Truman, Marshall, and Lovett were extremely cognizant of comparisons to the wartime years. They found great reassurance in the thought that by June 1951 the armed forces would have substantially more personnel than in June 1942. At the NSC meeting on 14 December 1950, Marshall said he was encouraged because he could foresee the time when he would have the equivalent of 47–50 divisions. Truman, too, observed that "there is no necessity to be disturbed or alarmed." The men around him knew how to wage global war; they had done it once before; they would be prepared to do it again.[16]

The rearmament program would strain the economy and engender acrimony in Congress. Marshall urged the president to declare a national emergency. Leon Keyserling, the president's chief economic adviser, estimated the economy could handle the buildup if there were proper controls. At a White House meeting on 13 December, Truman told congressional leaders that he intended to proclaim a national emergency. Senator Robert Taft and Congressman Joseph Martin expressed reservations. Nevertheless, Truman went ahead. On 15 December he announced the creation of the Office of Defense Mobilization under Charles E. Wilson, president of General Electric. The following day Truman proclaimed the existence of a national emergency. On 18 December he asked Congress for legislation to speed defense procurement.[17]

■

The administration's strategy was clear: wage limited war in Korea; prepare for global conflict; and utilize the growing military capabilities of the United States to furnish the backdrop for an aggressive foreign policy aimed at creating a favorable balance of power in Europe, the Middle East, and Asia. But no sooner was the strategy in place than it was called into question. During the first two weeks of January 1951, the Chinese Communists and North Koreans resumed their offensive, moved south of the 38th parallel, and threatened once again to drive MacArthur's forces off the Korean peninsula. The Far East commander desperately wanted authority to expand the war.[18]

In Washington, however, military officials like Collins and Air Force Chief of Staff Hoyt Vandenberg thought it might be more advisable to evacuate U.S. troops from Korea at the earliest opportunity.[19] Proposals to withdraw resonated with the American people. In a national poll during the third week of January, 66 percent of the respondents thought the United States should pull out rather than remain. Among Republicans, the desire to withdraw was even greater than among Democrats. In his talks with members of the Armed Services Committee, Lovett found little support for the Korean venture.[20]

But after much soul-searching and after hearing Allied warnings against unnecessary escalation, Truman and his advisers decided not to depart from the course of action on which they had embarked. There were some tactical disputes among military and civilian officials regarding preparations for a naval blockade of China, air reconnaissance of Chinese coastal areas, and the magnitude of assistance to anti-Communist forces in China.[21] But during these deliberations the similarities rather than the differences among Washington officials were most striking. Truman, Acheson, Marshall, and Bradley rebuffed the calls for withdrawal. They rejected pleas for retaliatory strikes against China. They were sensitive to Allied requests for restraint. They wanted to avoid provocative actions in Korea that might bring on general war before the United States and its allies were prepared to wage it effectively. They also agreed to move steadily to co-opt German and Japanese power, contain Communist expansion in the Middle East and Southeast Asia, bolster the defense perimeter in the western Pacific, and protect Taiwan. Beyond containment, they sought to sponsor covert actions, foment unrest, and promote revolution among key satellites in the Kremlin's orbit and among ethnic groups within the Soviet Union.[22]

State Department, JCS, and CIA officials knew that the men in the Kremlin would see their vital interests threatened by America's global initiatives. At an NSC meeting on 25 January, for example, CIA director Walter Bedell Smith emphasized that a grave danger of war existed if the United States continued its effort to rearm Germany. It did not seem wise to undertake actions in Korea that might accentuate Soviet anxieties and inspire a Soviet attack when so much else was at stake in more important places. Bradley, Collins, and Admiral Forrest Sherman explained that over the next 18–24 months U.S. and Allied strength would grow enormously; Soviet abilities to overrun Western Europe would decline. Prudence and patience, therefore, were virtues. It would be most propitious to move boldly in Korea (and elsewhere) when U.S. officials could wager that a Russian thrust against Western Europe could be turned back.[23]

This perspective did not mean that risks should be forsaken while the United States and its allies built up their military strength. Everything the Truman administration was doing involved risk-taking, from modernizing airfields in Turkey to building bases in Northwest Africa, rearming Germany, negotiating the Japanese peace treaty, and supporting the French in Indochina. The United States could not build positions of strength without taking risks. The essential task was to differentiate between prudent and imprudent risk-taking. Of course these calculations were fraught with anxiety because the answers were filled with imponderables. What was clear, however, was that the capacity to take risks, even in Korea, would grow as U.S. and Allied military strength increased.

Officials concluded that, for the time being, it made no sense to take provocative actions against China and risk global war over a country as unimportant as Korea. This view prevailed throughout Washington policymaking circles once it became clear again in the latter part of January that U.N. forces would be able to thwart the Communist offensive and stabilize the military situation around the 38th parallel. Escalating the war appeared especially foolish when it would have alienated the very allies whom the United States was courting and whose airfields, labor pool, and resources were essential to wage global conflict effectively. So long as the enemy refrained from attacking U.S. bases in Japan and supply depots in South Korea, and so long as the enemy seemed unable to dislodge U.N. forces from the peninsula, it made sense for the United States to moderate its own military tactics.[24]

Of course, MacArthur disagreed with this line of reasoning. He was frustrated because most of the military buildup was not earmarked for Korea. He was being asked to hold a defensive position on the peninsula with limited manpower. He was not permitted to use U.S. air superiority to strike at Chinese bases in Manchuria. Nor was he allowed to use Chinese Nationalist troops to help offset the superior numbers of the enemy. He feared that the Chinese would use their growing air power to attack U.N. lines of communication in South Korea as well as U.S. airfields in Japan. MacArthur's frustrations and apprehensions were to be expected from a theater commander.

What was not understandable was his behavior. His constant complaining, his recriminations, his excuses, his despondency, and his failure to accept orders exasperated the JCS and jeopardized effective command relationships. Moreover, his public denunciations of administration policy violated the guidelines that Truman had laid down. MacArthur should have been more cautious. By this time his judgment had been called into question for his failure to predict the massive Chinese intervention, and his tactical ability had been criticized for his failure to concentrate his forces. No longer was he the military genius of the Inchon campaign and the preeminent expert on Oriental psychology. His luster was gone, his carping exasperating, his reliability doubtful. In early April, Truman fired him. Marshall and the JCS concurred.[25]

MacArthur returned to a tumultuous welcome in the United States. The Republican right had a hero, a general of courage and determination who had been leashed and then dumped by cowardly Democrats, the same Democrats who had appeased the Communists and had betrayed the country at Yalta and Potsdam. MacArthur was invited to the Capitol to present his views. Eloquently and forcefully, he insisted that communism had to be contained in Asia as well as Europe. Although he was against using U.S. ground troops on the Chinese mainland, he argued that waging a limited war was the equivalent of appeasement. If he had been allowed to impose a naval blockade, use Chiang Kai-shek's forces, and apply air power against targets inside China, he would have been able to force the Communist Chinese to the bargaining table. These actions, he insisted, would not have tempted the Soviets to intervene unless they had already decided to do so.[26]

Before a joint inquiry of the Senate Armed Services and Foreign Relations committees, the administration presented its case for firing MacArthur and for limiting the war. Marshall, Bradley, and Acheson testified. They did not agree with MacArthur's calculations. They did not believe that expanding the war would force China to the conference table. More important, administration officials feared that an expansion of the fighting might precipitate global conflict before the West was ready for it. These risks, said Bradley, "should not be taken unnecessarily." America's allies opposed such risk-taking, and for the time being Marshall and Bradley agreed with them. America's own forces must not be tied down in a protracted conflict with mainland China while the Kremlin could exploit divisions among the allies, maneuver for small gains elsewhere, or gamble on a quick conquest of Western Europe. "Our military mission," Bradley reminded his listeners, "is to support a policy of preventing communism from gaining the manpower, the resources, the raw materials, and the industrial capacity essential to world domination. If Soviet Russia ever controls the entire Eurasian land mass, then the Soviet-satellite imperialism may have the broad base upon which to build the military power to rule the world." [27]

The differences between MacArthur on the one hand and Acheson, Marshall, and Bradley on the other were a matter of timing. According to the latter, unnecessary risks should not be taken in Korea while the United States was rearming and trying to build strength and unity in Western Europe, the Middle East, and East Asia. Time was on the U.S. side, Acheson emphasized to his senatorial inquisitors. In the short run, war had to be avoided. But once the "shield" had been established in Western Europe and once the United States possessed the ability to implement its war plans swiftly and effectively, the time would be propitious to go on the offensive. Additional risks could then be taken because the United States would be able to dominate the escalatory process. Bradley, too, made clear that present circumspection was not likely to lead to a resolution of the Korean crisis, but it would buy time until the United States was in a better position to get decisive results. [28]

There was little question that the administration was prepared to expand the war if circumstances warranted it. Indeed, one of the reasons for removing MacArthur, the historians Roger Dingman and Michael Schaller point out, was to place a responsible officer in command who could be trusted to follow orders and escalate prudently. On the very same day that the president began the discussions with his top advisers that would culminate in MacArthur's dismissal, Truman decided to deploy atomic weapons to the Pacific theater. He instructed the Atomic Energy Commission to transfer nine atomic weapons to the custody of General Vandenberg, the Air Force chief of staff. These weapons would be available for use if the adversary's renewed offensive threatened to drive U.N. forces off the peninsula and thereby undermine the credibility of U.S. commitments throughout the rest of Asia. These weapons would be used if the Soviets entered the fighting, if their air forces struck Japan, or if their submarines interfered with the movement of supplies to Korea. By quietly informing key senators and congressmen of the deployment of these weapons, the administration also hoped to stifle allegations that it was timid and cowardly in the face of aggression. But perhaps most important, the atomic weapons could be relied on to cast diplomatic shadows and to embolden policymakers who were biding time, calculating whether to take additional risks in Korea, and working hard to establish positions of strength around the globe. [29]

European Priorities

The public controversy precipitated by MacArthur's dismissal continued the stormy debate over foreign policy that had been raging since December. Initially, Republicans had not challenged Truman's announcement that he would deploy additional troops to Europe as part of an overall NATO buildup. But the expansion of the war in Korea triggered enormous public dissatisfaction, and the Republicans sought to capitalize on it. They questioned the president's right to deploy troops abroad without congressional approval; they denounced the growing European commitments incurred by the administration; they ridiculed NATO allies for providing insufficient assistance in Korea; and they called for a reexamination of the nation's relations with the rest of the world. In the Senate, the "great debate," as it was called, centered around a resolution introduced by Kenneth Wherry. The Nebraska senator maintained that U.S. troops should not be assigned to Europe until Congress formulated its own policy and gave its concurrence.[30]

Truman and his advisers saw Wherry's resolution as a fundamental challenge to their foreign policy. They defended the president's constitutional right as commander in chief to dispatch U.S. forces as he deemed necessary. But most important, they sought to refute their critics' assumption that the United States could survive if the Kremlin gained control of Europe. In testimony before the Senate Foreign Relations and Armed Services committees, Acheson, Bradley, and Eisenhower explained yet again that the United States must not allow the Soviet Union to have the opportunity to harness the resources of the Old World for its own aggressive purposes. Secretary of State Acheson argued:

Outside of our own country, free Europe has the greatest number of scientists, the greatest industrial production, and the largest pool of skilled manpower in the world. Its resources in coal, steel, and electric power are enormous. It has a tremendous shipbuilding capacity, essential to control of the seas. Through its overseas connections, it has access to a vast supply of raw materials which are absolutely vital to American industry. As an ally, Western Europe represents more than 200,000,000 free people who can contribute their skills, their resources, and their countries to our common defense. Under the heel of an aggressor, Western Europe would represent 200,000,000 slaves, compelled to bend their energies and employ their resources for the destruction of the United States and the remainder of Western Civilization.[31]

Strategic air power and atomic weapons would not suffice to safeguard the industrial infrastructure, natural resources, and skilled labor of Western Europe from the adversary. Marshall, Bradley, and Hoyt Vandenberg emphasized that, even under prevailing conditions, wherein the United States enjoyed a large advantage in its air/atomic capabilities, ground troops were still indispensable to the defense of the Old World. Despite the devastation and suffering that U.S. bombers could inflict on Russian cities and the Russian people, Soviet troops might still be able to seize European resources and utilize them to achieve world domination. More worrisome still was the fact that, with the passage of years, the Soviets would narrow the differential in atomic capabilities. As U.S. willingness to use its own arsenal declined, lest it be subject to a retaliatory attack, the deterrent power afforded by these weapons would erode and balanced collective forces in Western Europe would become absolutely essential. If ever there was the opportunity to augment U.S. conventional strength in Europe, the time was now while the atomic shield persisted. The presence of additional U.S. troops, moreover, would deter aggression by the Kremlin's satellites and help thwart internal seizures of power like the one that had occurred in Czechoslovakia in 1948. Most important, the deployment of four more divisions to the Old World would inspire Europeans to believe that their countries could be defended. In turn, they would be encouraged to defend themselves. When their capabilities grew, perhaps in a decade, the United States could then begin to think about reducing the size of its commitment.[32]

The debate in the Senate went on throughout the winter of 1951. Most senators disliked Truman's arbitrary actions and wanted to limit his powers. But they agreed that it was in the U.S. interest to send additional troops to Europe. Their views mirrored the attitudes of the American people. Polls showed that Americans sympathized with the Republicans' stress on Congress' right to participate in the decisionmaking process. Like most senators, however, Americans did not want to retract U.S. interests to the Western Hemisphere. It was more important to contain communism in Europe and Asia than to stay out of war. If Europeans would assume their fair share of the burden, Americans said they favored beefing up U.S. forces in Europe.[33]

Final Senate action embodied the discordant constitutional and national security impulses that informed the debate. In early April, after much complex maneuvering, Senator William McClelland offered an amendment to the Wherry resolution that approved the dispatch of four additional divisions but stipulated that no further troops be deployed to the Old World without congressional authorization. The resolution passed by a 49–43 vote. It was not what Truman, Acheson, or Marshall wanted. They preferred to be free of future constraints. But because their belief in Europe's vital importance had not been repudiated and because they had no desire and no ability at that time to send more than the four divisions, they acquiesced to McClelland's compromise.[34]

■

In fact, Senate endorsement of the administration's desire to deploy four more divisions to Europe constituted an essential step toward the fulfillment of U.S. objectives around the globe. If Europe could be defended, the Soviet penchant for risk-taking elsewhere would be diminished. The opposite was also true. If there were little threat of Soviet retaliatory action in Europe, the ability of the United States to bolster the Western position in Asia and the Middle East would be enhanced. Building the appropriate NATO force structure, however, required the growth of West European military capabilities, the incorporation of German forces into an integrated European defense force, and the appointment of an American as supreme commander.

At NATO meetings in December 1950, the United States pushed ahead on these matters. Acheson reiterated that France could call a conference to discuss the creation of a European army and concomitant political institutions. In turn, France accepted a procedural course that was supposed to bring about the earliest possible recruitment of German military contingents. Instead of a German national army and a German general staff, German units would be limited to regimental combat teams and integrated into a NATO defense force or into a European army that would be under the political control of the new European institutions that the French were trying to design.[35] Once these issues were resolved, Acheson told the foreign ministers of the other NATO countries that the United States would designate Dwight Eisenhower as the new supreme commander. The French were so pleased that Defense Minister Jules Moch immediately assigned three divisions in Germany to Eisenhower's command. In order to create a more efficient and cohesive force structure, the North Atlantic Council also agreed to abolish the regional planning groups and authorized the supreme commander to configure and train the forces assigned to him as he deemed necessary.[36]

From the U.S. perspective, the most important accomplishment of the December meetings was NATO's assent to the goal of West German rearmament. Acknowledging that "the greatest military threat" before them inhered in the possibility of a West German–Soviet alignment, the Atlantic alliance decided that Western Europe must be defended not at the Rhine but as far east as possible. This forward strategy aimed to insure "that the considerable potential of Western Germany is denied to the enemy and secured for the Allies."[37]

Although U.S. officials believed that German forces were indispensable for defending Europe, they were still not confident that West Germans would align themselves permanently with the West. Many Germans still felt that they had much to gain from remaining neutral in the East-West struggle. Many Germans feared that formal association with NATO would kill prospects for the eventual unification of their country. High Commissioner John McCloy continually warned Acheson that neutralist sentiment was on the rise in West Germany. Acheson, in turn, pressed unremittingly for Germany's incorporation into the political-military institutions of the North Atlantic community. He maneuvered to avoid a new foreign ministers' meeting to discuss unification, and he rebuffed proposals for all-German talks emanating from East Germany. In Acheson's view, a united, disarmed, and neutral Germany was suicidal for West Germans, West Europeans, and Americans.[38]

The French, however, still posed a problem. At the end of January 1951, French premier René Pleven came to Washington to consult with Acheson and Marshall. Two months later, French president Vincent Auriol, accompanied by Foreign Minister Robert Schuman, made a more ceremonial visit. Pleven and Auriol talked vividly of their concerns. German rearmament remained an incendiary issue in French politics; the ruling coalition continued to be in a tenuous position; and tangible progress could not be made until after the June elections. Aside from the limitations imposed by the exigencies of French politics, Pleven expressed great fear that the Russians would see the correlation of forces turning against them. They might, therefore, launch a preemptive strike and seek to conquer all of Europe. Discreetly, Pleven sought to ascertain whether the Americans still retained the capabilities to deter this type of development.[39]

Auriol amplified these ideas. He thought the Soviets had reason to be fearful. The Germans could not be trusted; after they rearmed and regained their sovereignty, they not only would try to bring about the reunification of their country but would also aim to regain the territories they had lost. If they were stymied, they might pull their troops out of the integrated NATO defense structure. Auriol did not doubt that the Germans might again opt for war and attempt to seize East Germany with armed force. According to the French, German rearmament could provoke global war or could inaugurate a new era of chronic unrest in the center of Europe. The French wanted to be reassured that the Americans grasped the risks they were taking.[40]

Acheson, Marshall, and Harriman listened carefully to the French. No one could dispute the logic of French arguments. U.S. officials were altogether skeptical of Germany's future allegiance. All the more reason, they concluded, to meet the demands of moderate Germans like Konrad Adenauer who were inclined to align their country with the West. Risks inhered in this course of action, Harriman admitted to Auriol, but there was no alternative. It was impossible to suppress the Germans and at the same time present a strong front to the Russians. While Soviet counterthrusts could not be discounted, they might be averted if the West acted quickly. Acheson and Marshall explained to Pleven that, for the time being, the United States continued to maintain a large superiority over the Soviets in atomic weapons. They calculated that Stalin would not attack while he knew that Soviet Russia would be subject to a devastating retaliatory blow from the United States. So now was the time to build Europe's conventional shield and to rearm Germany. In a year or two the window of opportunity might close as the Soviet atomic stockpile became large enough to tempt the Russians to think that they might be able to cripple America's productive capabilities, destroy U.S. bases in England, and overrun Europe. The key task was to have a strong conventional posture in place before the benefits derived from America's atomic superiority eroded.[41]

Although U.S. officials advocated immediate German rearmament and began planning for it, they proceeded cautiously. Their circumspection related as much to German reactions as to French protests. Kurt Schumacher, the Social Democrats, and many leading figures in Germany's liberal Protestant establishment objected to their country's rearmament. As a result, Adenauer claimed that he would not be able to mobilize support for West Germany's participation in an integrated defense force unless he secured additional concessions from the occupation powers. He wanted all remnants of the occupation to end. Germany would have to be treated equally, its sovereignty fully restored, and its security guaranteed through reciprocal commitments. The Germany experts in the State Department, like Henry Byroade, sympathized with Adenauer's plight. They feared that, if the United States pressed the German chancellor to move too quickly, his proposals would be defeated in the Bundestag. The entire U.S. program for German integration into the North Atlantic community might then be jeopardized. At the same time, U.S. officials realized that strenuous efforts to accommodate West German demands would whet their former enemy's appetite for yet additional concessions. "It is important now to let them stew for a while," Acheson maintained.[42]

The secretary of state was agitated by West German dickering over the details of the Schuman Plan. He did not like the idea that the Germans might be prolonging these negotiations in order to secure a fully equal status in a European defense force. These intra-European discussions became so complex and so heated that, in mid-February, U.S. officials began to worry that the Schuman Plan might unravel.

McCloy pleaded with Adenauer to end the bargaining and sign an agreement. The U.S. high commissioner cajoled German industrialists and union leaders. Finally, in April 1951, the Europeans resolved their differences and formed the European Coal and Steel Community. Although the British remained aloof, U.S. officials regarded the Schuman Plan as a great triumph for which the French and Germans deserved major credit. Policymakers in Washington were profoundly aware that economic interdependence and supranational institutions were key instruments not only for boosting European productivity and overcoming European exchange problems but also for co-opting German power, establishing the preconditions for German rearmament, and thwarting Soviet preponderance.[43]

■

More critical, still, for the achievement of U.S. global objectives was the rearmament of America's NATO allies. This matter attracted more attention than any other European issue during the winter and spring of 1951. At NATO meetings in December 1950, Acheson urged the allies to increase their defense expenditures, boost their production of armaments, and enlarge their forces. In order to meet the requirements of the Medium Term Defense Plan, he estimated that they should double their military spending and coordinate their defense efforts. Acheson was willing to designate an American to oversee these tasks. The United States, moreover, was prepared to earmark $25.4 billion for support of the European defense effort over the next four fiscal years.[44]

Acheson hoped that Eisenhower's appointment would inspire Europeans to undertake the immense task that lay before them. The supreme commander's whirlwind tour of European capitals in January 1951 was designed to mobilize European energies behind the rearmament program. Eisenhower was not intimidated by Soviet strength, and he doubted the loyalty of the Kremlin's satellites in wartime. If he could have 40 divisions assigned to him by the end of 1952, Eisenhower believed that he could mount a formidable defense of the continent, formidable enough to deter a Soviet attack.[45]

Although Europeans complained about the emphasis that the United States attached to the defense buildup, they made a substantial effort to move ahead. As a percentage of gross national product, defense spending increased in Belgium from 2.7 percent in 1949 to 4.3 percent in 1951; in France from 5.7 to 9.7 percent; in Italy from 3.9 to 5.7 percent; in the United Kingdom from 5.9 to 8.7 percent. In about one year, national defense expenditures of all European NATO countries increased from approximately $5.3 billion to $8.2 billion. Many NATO countries extended the periods of compulsory military training; for example, in Belgium training lengthened from 12 to 18 months, and in England from 18 to 24 months. By 1951 many NATO countries had more men in the armed services than they had in 1938. The deputy director of the State Department's Office of West European Affairs called the progress "spectacular." According to Lord Ismay, the first secretary general of NATO, alliance divisions increased from 15 to 35 during 1951, and operational aircraft increased from 1,000 to 3,000. Money was allocated to create an infrastructure of airfields, pipelines, and communication centers. Eisenhower thought the changes "prodigious."[46]

Despite this impressive progress, the gap between the requirements of the Medium Term Defense Plan and the capabilities of NATO countries did not disappear. U.S. officials agonized over the persistence of this gap. At the end of February, Nitze told the JCS that, 30 days after a war began, NATO would be short 19 divisions, 3,800 planes, and 450 ships. Generals Bradley and Vandenberg seemed less worried about these deficiencies than they were about European reluctance to convert industrial production to the manufacture of war materiel, especially tactical aircraft. In June 1951, U.S. officials concluded that the commitments of NATO governments to raise ground and air forces still fell 20 and 40 percent short, respectively, of the 1954 goals. The JCS estimated that the gap would be 4 Army divisions, 85 major combatant vessels, and 3,443 aircraft. The International Security Affairs Committee (ISAC), composed of experts from the Pentagon, the State Department, and the Economic Cooperation Administration, believed that it would take an additional $25 billion to fulfill the goals of the defense plan.[47]

The slowness of U.S. military deliveries contributed to the gap. By April 1951 only 53 percent of the materiel programmed for fiscal year 1950 and only 2 percent of that earmarked for fiscal year 1951 had been shipped to Europe. State Department officials fretted over these figures. Yet little could be done in the short run because the additional production coming off assembly lines was taken by the Pentagon to meet the requirements of the U.S. buildup. In the spring, Nitze gave considerable attention to this matter. Although the existing situation was worrisome, he nevertheless calculated that the military hardware coming out of U.S. factories would increase seven-fold between June 1950 and June 1952. By the latter date, considerable supplies would be available for the allies.[48]

Throughout the spring and summer of 1951, U.S. officials prodded their NATO partners to augment their defense efforts. Progress was good, but the effort had to be even greater. The United States was willing to help. In May 1951 the president asked Congress to provide West European allies with $5.2 billion in military and $1.6 billion in economic aid. During the following month, ISAC officials started talking about the possibility of enlarging this sum by another third. Congress' willingness to approve such staggering figures remained questionable. Recognizing the impediments in the legislative branch and aware of Congress' special antipathy to economic aid, the administration accepted the strategy initially recommended the year before by Army Undersecretary Tracy Voorhees to merge all economic and military assistance into a Mutual Security Program.[49]

Yet Acheson, Marshall, and Lovett believed that Congress would be loath to act unless they saw Europeans making a greater effort of their own and moving ahead on the German rearmament issue. To impress NATO allies with the urgency of the problem and the extent to which the United States was willing to incur its fair share of the burden, Acheson and Marshall agreed that the commitment of U.S. forces to NATO should go beyond the six divisions previously committed. At the end of June, they recommended that the president approve a JCS proposal earmarking thirteen U.S. divisions to the defense of Europe by 90 days after the onset of hostilities. Some of these troops might be deployed to the continent in peacetime. In addition, the U.S. contribution to Europe's air defenses would jump from 8 to 22 air wings. And furthermore, 39 small naval vessels would be added to the 470 ships already committed to European waters. As a result, the United States would be contributing 13 percent of NATO's ground forces, 15 percent of its air forces, and 25 percent of its naval forces. Truman approved this paper on 27 June.[50]

■

Acheson was still dissatisfied. More had to be done. For most of the spring he had been monitoring the talks in Bonn between the deputy high commissioners and German officials regarding the makeup of German forces. He had also been following the discussions in Paris, where European officials were studying French proposals for a European army and defense community. He had been biding his time waiting for the French elections to take place. As soon as they were over, he decided that it was time for a real breakthrough on the German rearmament issue. Western Europe, he emphasized, could not be defended successfully without Germany's active participation. The sacrifices made and the monies expended by all NATO governments would have been wasted unless German power could be bound permanently to the Western alliance and German resources utilized in its defense.[51]

Carefully studying the interrelated issues, Acheson concluded that Germany had to be accorded real equality. The status of Germany as an occupied country had to be terminated. Existing arrangements had to be replaced with new contractual understandings wherein West Germany was treated as a sovereign nation. All rights to intervene in Germany's domestic affairs, except perhaps in an emergency, would be relinquished. The supreme authority of the allies would be limited to their ability to station troops in Germany, maintain access to Berlin, settle territorial questions, and control the final peace settlement and the unification issue. These powers would suffice to thwart any West German effort to deal with the Kremlin at the expense of Western interests. Otherwise, Acheson believed that Germany should be treated as a partner contributing to the joint defense of the West. The Federal Republic of Germany, Acheson wrote Schuman, should be admitted into NATO.

At the same time, Acheson was willing to respond to French anxieties about a sovereign and rearmed Germany. The French, Acheson thought, had legitimate concerns about what might happen if cold war tensions should diminish and the United States should choose to withdraw its troops from Europe. The West Germans might then try to reestablish a national army. They might seek to annex their brethren in East Germany and reconquer lost territories in Poland. A German crusade might once again drag all Europe into war. It was in the U.S. interest, therefore, to support institutions that would hold together NATO's defense forces after the Americans and the British departed from Europe. The European army concept made sense because it was designed to constrain the Germans from gravitating away from NATO's integrated defense structure and from forming their own national army under their own political control. Acheson urged that the United States throw its weight behind the French proposals. In return for this support, the French would have to assent to the immediate recruitment of German troops. The development of German military capabilities must not await final agreement on all the complex financial and political questions that inhered in the concept of a European defense community.

Acheson's initiative was pushed strongly by John McCloy. In late June he returned to the United States and met with Lovett, Bradley, Collins, and other key policymakers in the Pentagon. He told them great progress had been made toward reconciling German and French views. The French, McCloy thought, would accept the formation of German divisions (rather than regimental combat teams). They might also allow the Germans to have heavy armored divisions and a ministry of defense, provided that all of the above could be achieved under the rubric of the European army concept. Defense officials were not sanguine. Collins worried that the French proposal would obstruct the efficient operation of Eisenhower's forces. The Americans, British, and Europeans, he said, would have three armies, three chains of command, and three lines of communication. But after considerable discussion, Bradley suggested that these problems might be overcome if the European army was placed under Eisenhower's command.[52]

On 16 July, Acheson, Marshall, Lovett, and Bradley discussed these issues extensively. The secretary of state explained that the European allies were straining under the defense burden. They resented the U.S. insistence that they do more than they thought they were capable of doing. Therefore, if Europe were to develop the capability to defend itself, there was no alternative to the immediate recruitment of German units and the mobilization of German productive capabilities. Lovett concurred. He was especially worried that an armistice in Korea might lull Congress and European parliaments into a feeling of complacency. Acheson's ideas for simultaneous progress on the issues of German sovereignty, German rearmament, and a European army made sense. The Defense and State departments would present their views jointly to the president. Acheson hoped that the allies could agree on a new set of contractual agreements with Germany by the time the foreign ministers met in September 1951. They could then be refined and submitted to the Germans for final negotiation. These latter discussions should be concluded by the end of October, at which time Acheson hoped that the core provisions of a European army would have been agreed on. If all went well, Adenauer might be able to present the package of military and political agreements to the Bundestag in the late autumn, and steps to recruit German soldiers might begin immediately thereafter.[53]

The very next day Bradley instructed Collins and Vandenberg to assess the U.S. ability to equip German land and air units. The JCS had been planning on a German ground force of 440,000 men and an air force of 45,000. Collins estimated that equipment for the training of four divisions could be made available by January 1952. These divisions could be supplied fully by July 1952. Assuming that German factories would produce many of the general-purpose vehicles, engineering and signal equipment, and other items, Collins thought that ten divisions could be outfitted by July 1954. General Nathan Twining reported to Bradley that the Air Force could begin deliveries of fighter bomber and tactical reconnaissance aircraft in mid-1953. By the end of 1954, 750 aircraft would be available. Thereafter, U.S. factories would be in such high gear that it would be easy to fulfill rapidly the ultimate goal of 1,600–1,800 aircraft for Germany's proposed ten fighter wings.[54]

At the same time that these preparations were going on in Washington, Eisenhower presented to NATO's Standing Group his plan for the defense of Western Europe. Eisenhower called for a forward strategy based on a strong defensive zone between the Iron Curtain and the Rhine. He emphasized that German divisions must form an integral part of any defensive plan and that no time should be lost in raising German contingents. Afraid that German power might be co-opted by the enemy, Eisenhower altered his views and gave strong support to French proposals for a European army. Pending final arrangements to create a European defense ministry, as contemplated in French plans, he was also willing to oversee the recruitment and training of German units.[55]

By the time Acheson met with his French and British counterparts for a series of meetings in September 1951, a great deal of progress had been made toward resolving differences over the German rearmament issue. The high commissioners had prepared a report that spelled out the key items of the new contractual arrangements with Germany. There was still some discord over how to control Germany's rearmament, scientific research, industrial production, and civil aviation. But there was also much agreement on ending the formal status of the occupation, eliminating the office of the High Commission, and retaining supreme authority for the allies in a small number of clearly identified areas, similar to the ones previously outlined by Acheson. The U.S. secretary of state also narrowed the remaining differences, agreeing that the allies should retain the power to intervene in Germany if democratic government were threatened. Schuman, in turn, withdrew French objections to German divisions and acknowledged that the training of German units might begin under Eisenhower's jurisdiction before all the institutions of the European Defense Community were in place. He insisted, however, that the Germans must accept the European army proposals at the same time that they ratified the new set of contractual arrangements. So much accord was reached during these September talks that Herbert Morrison, the British foreign minister who had succeeded Bevin and who had never before participated in tripartite discussions with Schuman and Acheson, marveled at the rapport that had been generated.[56]

■

But not everything was settled. The British and French stated that they could not meet the rearmament guidelines set forth by the Americans. Their economies were under tremendous strain; inflationary pressures were great; labor strife was growing. Their foreign exchange problems were multiplying as the cost of raw materials spiraled under the pressures generated by the Korean War and as they converted some of their export-oriented industries to the manufacture of armaments. Hugh Gaitskill, the British chancellor of the exchequer, and René Mayer, the French finance minister, pleaded with Acheson to relax his demands and to heed their warnings that their dollar shortages were almost as bad as when the Marshall Plan had begun. Schuman, moreover, cautioned the Americans not to provoke the Soviets into attacking Europe. The Kremlin must not be led to think that NATO was contemplating aggression.[57]

Acheson responded sensitively to the financial and economic plight of his NATO allies. Marshall and Bradley also recognized the tremendous burden the rearmament program placed on all the allies. Rather than risk an open rebellion, Americans supported the appointment of a Temporary Council Committee composed of representatives of the United States, Britain, and France—"the wise men" as they came to be called—to see if ways could be found to streamline military requirements and equitably apportion financial burdens among the different NATO countries without compromising overall defense goals. After conversing with all the Allied foreign ministers, Acheson urged Truman to appoint Harriman to the committee.[58]

The secretary of state, however, would not agree to relax the military buildup. He did not expect the Soviets to launch a premeditated attack, but global war could occur by miscalculation. The Korean conflict could easily escalate. NATO forces, Acheson insisted, had to be ready as soon as possible to thwart a Soviet offensive should U.S. countermeasures in Northeast Asia or should U.S. initiatives elsewhere precipitate global war. Revolutionary nationalist fervor and neutralist sentiment abounded. Opportunities for the aggrandizement of Soviet power were widespread. Strong forces in Europe were the indispensable prerequisite for increasing America's capacity to act boldly in the defense of its national security interests in other parts of the globe.[59]

■

The need to defend Western Europe was so important that U.S. officials decided to alter existing policy and open a military relationship with Spain. The British and French strongly opposed this initiative. General Francisco Franco remained a political outcast in democratic Europe. Neither Schuman nor Morrison believed that the strategic benefits outweighed the political liabilities of dealing with a fascistic dictatorship. They feared that Americans might be enticed to defend Europe from the Pyrenees mountains rather than on the German plains. Marshall and Bradley, however, desired to bring Spain into NATO: they wanted naval and air bases; they wanted to station fighter bombers in Spain for the defense of Western Europe; and they wanted anchorage rights to help safeguard access to the Mediterranean. In exchange, they were willing to offer Spain economic and military assistance.

State Department officials worried that a bold approach to the Spanish might antagonize U.S. allies. Acheson patiently explained to defense officials that there was no possibility of negotiating Spain's entrance into NATO. Yet aware of the advantages that might accrue from bases in Spain and influenced by Marshall and Bradley, the secretary of state did agree to instruct the U.S. ambassador to open talks with the Spanish government. Franco said he would cooperate fully with U.S. wishes. Spanish facilities might be used for the defense of Europe as a whole and not for Spain alone. Prospects for an agreement were so good that Truman sent Admiral Sherman to Madrid in July 1951 to begin more concrete discussions. Sherman outlined for Franco U.S. desires to modernize airfields and ports and improve the transportation infrastructure. Again the talks went so well that the following month the JCS sent a joint military survey team to Spain. Its task was to examine Spanish air and maritime facilities and to recommend how they might be enhanced to meet U.S. wartime requirements.[60]

■

The Truman administration also struck up a cooperative military relationship with Marshal Tito's Yugoslavia. The Korean War raised anxieties that the Kremlin or its Balkan satellites might attack Yugoslavia. The modernization and growth of satellite forces accentuated these apprehensions. At the same time, Yugoslavia was hit with a terrible drought that destroyed crops, engendered economic hardship, and drained its foreign exchange reserves. Tito's domestic support, U.S. officials believed, might be undermined if he were unable to allay the unrest, secure food, purchase raw materials, and keep his factories operating.[61]

U.S. officials sought to encourage Tito's resistance to Moscow. They still regarded him as an ideological foe but could not resist the strategic and geopolitical benefits that derived from his split with Stalin. In contrast to the cases of Mao Tse-tung in China and Ho Chi Minh in Vietnam, U.S. officials did not have to offer risky inducements to promote a schism. Tito symbolized the possibility of nationalist eruptions within the Communist bloc. If he were overthrown from within or crushed from without, the psychological reverberations would be felt throughout Europe. Italy and Greece would be exposed to additional Soviet pressure. The great gains that had been made in recent years might be reversed. If Tito were assisted by the West, moreover, his 30 divisions might bulwark the defense of Southern Europe and the Eastern Mediterranean in time of global war. Acheson and Marshall were determined that he survive. In December 1950 they persuaded Congress to provide the funds for emergency relief.[62]

At the same time the JCS kept pressing the administration to offer military assistance to Tito should he ask for it. Along with their British and French counterparts, the JCS wanted to stockpile supplies in Europe for quick delivery to Yugoslavia in case of emergency. Once it was clear that Tito was ready to receive military aid from the West, the JCS leapt at the opportunity. In June 1951 the Yugoslav chief of staff came to the Pentagon and signed an accord providing for the rapid shipment of military supplies to his country. A second round of bilateral talks regarding strategic and operational matters took place in August. After protracted negotiations, a military assistance agreement was signed in November.[63]

Simultaneously, Acheson and Marshall invited the British, French, and Italians to begin joint planning for the defense of Yugoslavia. No commitments were to be incurred, but the advantages of the Tito-Stalin split were so great that support for Yugoslavia's independence would be warranted when NATO forces developed greater capabilities. Eisenhower sympathized with this goal. In September 1951 he and Bradley outlined procedures that might be taken to bring about its early realization.[64]

Providing military assistance to Yugoslavia was a risky business, as State Department analysts were well aware. There was the possibility that U.S. support might actually "stimulate a Kremlin decision in favor of an early-supported Satellite attack on Yugoslavia." Policymakers, however, were willing to gamble that, for the time being, their atomic shield would suffice to deter a Soviet assault. In a long conversation with Averell Harriman in Belgrade, Tito stressed that he did not think Stalin wanted to precipitate a conflict with the United States. Yet war could occur from miscalculation. Hence it was all the more important to act prudently in Korea while taking intelligent and necessary risks to build strength around the periphery of the Iron Curtain. With the passage of time this strength itself would supplant the atomic shield. If Europe's industrial infrastructure, resources, and skilled labor could be denied to the Kremlin in wartime, Soviet leaders would have no hope of winning a military conflict. U.S. officials could then maneuver more freely not only in Korea but also in other areas wracked with instability. Europe, therefore, remained priority number one, but the vital importance of other parts of the globe to U.S. national security could not be ignored.[65]

The Middle East

U.S. defense officials championed military collaboration with Yugoslavia because they saw it as a means of strengthening the southern flank in wartime. If Tito's 30 divisions could be arrayed on the side of the West and if Italian capabilities could be enlarged beyond treaty limits, as they were, NATO forces might be able to hold onto southern Italy. Eisenhower's plans were to apply air and sea power from the two flanks against Soviet ground forces in the center. At the very least, a strong southern flank would force the Russians to divert resources to this front and thereby lessen the pressure in the center. At a maximum, the southern flank could be used to attack Soviet oil facilities in Romania and the Caucasus and to defend the Eastern Mediterranean and the Middle East. Admiral Robert B. Carney, the new commander in chief of U.S. forces in the Eastern Atlantic and the Mediterranean and Eisenhower's choice to head Allied forces in southern Europe, was a tireless champion of collaboration with the Yugoslavs and the Turks.[66]

Turkey constituted the linchpin between Europe and the Middle East, two areas that U.S. officials saw as interdependent in peacetime and wartime. In peacetime, the importance of Middle Eastern oil was constantly mounting. U.S. analysts estimated that, during 1950–51, 70 percent of Western Europe's oil came from the Middle East. If NATO nations were denied access to the petroleum of the Middle East, European industrial recovery would be halted, British exchange problems would be exacerbated, and plans for Europe's rearmament would be jeopardized. Moreover, new studies suggested that, if war should erupt, access to Middle Eastern oil would be necessary from the onset of conflict. Turkish airfields and troops would help prevent the Soviets from seizing the Persian Gulf and the British base at Cairo-Suez. Turkish assistance would also be indispensable to contain Soviet submarines in the Black Sea and to insure Western control of the Eastern Mediterranean.[67]

Turkey's willingness to cooperate, however, became increasingly suspect. After the outbreak of the Korean War, Turkish officials again tried to ascertain what the United States would do if Turkey were attacked. These overtures agitated policymakers. State Department officials could find little evidence that the Kremlin was threatening Turkey. Lewis Jones, one of Nitze's assistants on the Policy Planning Staff, frankly told the first secretary of the Turkish embassy that "Turkey was not being made the object of a Soviet diplomatic offensive or Soviet-inspired pressures."[68]

Although Turkish officials acknowledged that domestic politics had much to do with their insistent demands, there was little doubt among U.S. policymakers that from a geopolitical and strategic perspective the neutralist option constituted a viable possibility for the Turks. Assistant Secretary of State George McGhee and his analysts in the Office of Near Eastern, South Asian, and African Affairs spent a good deal of time during the late summer and early autumn of 1950 studying the pros and cons of security guarantees. On the last day of August 1950, Acheson requested the Pentagon's views. It was essential, the secretary of state thought, to determine whether the inclusion of Turkey (and Greece) in NATO would provoke or deter the Kremlin. Would the advantages that would accrue be offset by the administrative burdens that would be imposed on NATO's fragile organizational structure? Would Turkey be reassured by the additional guarantees or frightened by the new-found knowledge that NATO lacked the capabilities to offer much concrete help should conflict erupt in the immediate future?[69]

The JCS pondered the issues. Bradley, Vandenberg, Collins, and Sherman worried that the admission of Turkey and Greece into NATO might divert arms assistance from Western Europe and complicate command relationships. Acknowledging the critical importance of the Middle East and Turkey's contribution to its protection, they nevertheless insisted that the defense of Europe must have top priority. When Western capabilities grew, it would be desirable to include Turkey and Greece in NATO. For the time being, they should be offered an associate status. In this way U.S. military officials hoped to placate Turkey and preserve the strategic advantages of cooperating with that country. But at the same time they would not be bound to deploy U.S. forces to that sector in wartime unless they judged that it was advantageous to do so.[70]

State Department officials did not like this advice, but they accepted it. They feared that it would leave the Turks dissatisfied. Acheson tried to allay Turkish disappointment by emphasizing that, after twelve or eighteen months, the United States might be able to incur new commitments. In the meantime, he believed that the Turks need not worry because an isolated Soviet attack on Turkey was most unlikely.[71]

The Turks felt aggrieved. They were contributing troops to the struggle in Korea. They were participating in the defense of freedom and the containment of Communist totalitarianism. Why should they be left in a vulnerable position? Why should they assent to the desires of the U.S. Navy to mine the straits in peacetime and why should they make commitments to allow the Americans to use their airfields in wartime if they were not guaranteed protection in return? An associated linkage to NATO was simply a sop. When McGhee visited Turkey in February 1951, President Celal Bayar bluntly expressed his personal displeasure with the existing partnership. If Turkey were not admitted into NATO, Bayar would reappraise Turkey's orientation in the cold war. McGhee wired Acheson: "There is reason to believe that Turkey will veer toward policy of neutralism, which will always have strong basic appeal. Until commitment is extended to Turkey, there is no assurance that Turkey will declare war unless attacked."[72]

■

U.S. officials were not simply worried about Turkish neutrality. Acheson, McGhee, and Nitze worried that the entire Arab world was heading in this direction. They did not believe that the Kremlin was actively stirring up trouble, nor did they think that Arab-Israeli fighting was likely to be renewed. But almost every-where in the region they saw growing instability and mounting defeatism. In view of the stalemate in Korea and their own emphasis on NATO, policymakers sus-pected that Middle Eastern governments were questioning whether the West could protect them in wartime or help them in peacetime. Many of these Arab govern-ments were beleaguered by the impoverishment of their peoples. State Department officials wanted to provide economic and technical aid. They grasped the need for social change, economic development, and political reform. The impulse for radical restructuring, however, was tempered by geopolitical imperatives. Priority number one was to keep incumbent regimes in the Western orbit. Tenuous though the sta-bility was, U.S. diplomats concluded that "it is not desirable that the present degree of stability . . . be undermined by too rapid change." The wisest course, thought Acheson and McGhee, was to bolster friendly regimes with military assistance, arms transfers, and advisory missions.[73]

Some Pentagon officials urged McGhee to move cautiously. General Collins insisted that it was a British responsibility to defend the Middle East. McGhee re-torted that his initiatives had nothing to do with a hot war; he was concerned with winning the cold war. He was talking about stability in depth, not defense in depth. In other words, he was not asking the chiefs to assume additional responsibilities in wartime; he was asking them to support new initiatives in peacetime. Bradley sympathized with McGhee's problems. British influence was waning and neutrality was growing. The JCS agreed that Congress should increase military assistance to the Middle East. A special contingency fund might be created to help preserve sta-bility in the region, thwart indigenous communism, and wean Arab governments away from the neutralist option.[74]

■

More worrisome than neutrality, however, was the rising tide of revolutionary nationalism in Egypt and Iran. In November 1950 the Egyptian prime minister opened the new session of Parliament with a speech calling for the total and im-mediate evacuation of British forces from Egypt. He also insisted that the British relinquish control over Sudan and acknowledge its unity with Egypt. Immediately, rioting erupted in the streets of Cairo. The Egyptians were no longer willing to put up with the endless rounds of negotiation that had been going on since 1946. They were angered by Britain's decision to cut off arms shipments until an acceptable agreement was reached.

As had happened so many times before, the flare-up of Egyptian nationalism forced U.S. officials to reconsider the value of the British base at Cairo-Suez. They did not think it was quite as important as did the British. They were also acutely aware of the intensity of Egyptian sentiment. Nevertheless, they were unwilling for the British to evacuate; the base still offered too many advantages. The Royal Air Force was making improvements at Abu Suwair. The airstrips could support the strategic offensive against Russia as well as help protect the refineries and oil fields of the Middle East. The most sensible thing to do, Acheson concluded, was to work out a tripartite agreement between the United States, the United Kingdom, and Egypt. By multilateralizing existing arrangements, Acheson thought, they might be made more palatable to the Egyptians. The connotations of colonialism that were present in the 1936 provisions might be eliminated without undermining the ability of the West to care for the base in peacetime and to utilize it in wartime.[75]

While the idea of a multilateral arrangement began percolating through policy-making circles in London and Washington, the United States still supported the British in their bilateral talks with the Egyptians. McGhee traveled to Cairo in April 1951 and tried to redirect Egyptian anger. He told Egyptian foreign minister Mohammed Salaheddin Bey that Soviet communism, not British imperialism, was the real threat to the region. Such comments only fueled Egyptian rancor. The British were violating their rights and affronting their sovereignty. How could Americans side with the British, the Egyptian foreign minister asked McGhee.[76]

■

McGhee had no effective response because he could see the virulence of Egyptian nationalist feeling. Moreover, the upheaval in Tehran was now complicating the negotiation of an agreement in Cairo.[77] Iranian prime minister Ali Razmara was assassinated on 7 March 1951. He had opposed the nationalization of foreign oil interests, but he died before he and the British had been able to revise the terms of the existing concession. Soon after Razmara's death, the Majlis voted to nationalize the British-owned Anglo-Iranian Oil Company. There were demonstrations in the cities and strikes in the southern oil fields. The nationalist leader Mohammed Musaddiq became prime minister. He had strong support from diverse constituencies, all of whom blamed the British and the oil company for their woes.[78]

Acheson and McGhee were terrified that the oil-rich country was heading for chaos. It had been suffering from poor harvests, financial mismanagement, and administrative corruption. The young and inexperienced shah had alienated religious leaders and traditional elites. Only among military leaders did he retain support. Moreover, he was suffering from appendicitis and thinking of going abroad for surgery. In the unfolding crisis, he appeared no match for Musaddiq, whom the British Foreign Office regarded as a lunatic. There was, then, the possibility that the British might close down their oil operations, withhold revenues from the Iranian government, or intervene with force. If the last occurred, the Iranian government might seek assistance from the Soviet Union. Yet if Musaddiq implemented the nationalization program and if the British applied economic pressure, the country might be driven to bankruptcy. Nationalist fervor might be converted to revolutionary zeal. The Tudeh Party might capitalize on the unrest, capture power, and bring Iran into the Soviet orbit.[79]

U.S. officials believed it was of "critical importance" to prevent Iran from slipping out of the Western sphere. The "loss of Iran" would expose all of the Middle East to Soviet inroads, endanger lines of communication, damage U.S. prestige, and deny the West essential supplies of petroleum. Normally Iran produced about 660,000 barrels per day, about a third of the Middle East's total output. The refinery complex at Abadan provided Western Europe with about 31 percent of its refined oil. If it were lost, it would cost another $700 million annually to find alternate sources. Moreover, the British and U.S. navies and air forces operating in the region were dependent on it for aviation gas and fuel oil.[80]

Although Acheson prodded the British to make concessions, he was not indifferent to the protection of private property rights. Pressed by the large oil corporations and solicitous of their interests, he did not want the Iranians to establish precedents that would jeopardize U.S. (as well as British) control over raw material deposits in many Third World countries.[81] But he also believed that if Iran slipped behind the Iron Curtain, the results would be far worse than nationalization. The object was to stay in Iran, work out a mutually acceptable agreement, retain access to Iranian oil, and preserve that critical country within the Western orbit. The British, Acheson thought, could relinquish the ownership of the company yet retain control of the management and reap 50 percent of the annual profits.[82]

While agreeing that the British should eschew the use of military force, McGhee desired to draw up plans to assist the shah "on a more substantial, urgent, and dramatic scale than had been possible in the past." The shah had to be convinced that he had U.S. support. The retention of his authority was absolutely critical if Iran were to be kept within the Western camp. McGhee wanted the president's physician to go to Tehran to operate on the shah so that he need not leave the country and risk a coup in his absence. More important, McGhee pushed his superiors in the State Department and persuaded the entire NSC to agree to a package of military aid, Point Four assistance, and Export-Import Bank loans. By coaxing the British into concessions and providing help to Iran, McGhee hoped to save the shah, co-opt Musaddiq, and turn Iran's intense nationalism against the Soviets rather than against the West.[83]

Accordingly, Acheson proposed that Harriman go to Tehran and mediate the dispute. The British were reluctant, but they acquiesced. During the summer of 1951, Harriman spent several weeks in Tehran and London trying to frame the terms of a settlement. He thought the British should accept the principle of nationalization and acquiesce to a 50-50 allocation of the annual profits. This division had already been agreed to by U.S. oil companies in Venezuela and Saudi Arabia. In return, Harriman maintained that the Iranians should permit the British to retain control of production and marketing. When Musaddiq refused, Harriman sided with the British. The talks collapsed at the end of August.[84]

U.S. officials fumed at the British for the tardiness of their concessions, but they were even more exasperated with Musaddiq. Harriman reported that the Iranian prime minister was impossible to deal with. Worsening economic conditions, Harriman hoped, would lead to his dismissal. Yet Harriman advised against the use of force lest it rally support behind Musaddiq and play into the hands of the Communist Tudeh Party.[85] U.S. officials grasped that it would be foolhardy to align the United States openly against the rising tide of Iranian nationalism. Economic pressure and covert action were the preferred policy instruments. McGhee, for example, encouraged private U.S. firms not to distribute Iranian oil should it be expropriated from the British. Oscar Chapman, U.S. secretary of the interior and the petroleum administrator for defense, designed a program for U.S. oil companies to collaborate with the British in supplying petroleum to traditional customers should the cutoff in Iranian oil persist. And although not all the documents have been declassified, it is safe to infer that numerous covert operations were hatched during the summer of 1951.[86]

U.S. officials looked on anxiously as the British withdrew their personnel from the oil fields, refused to resume negotiations, and reinforced their flotilla in the Persian Gulf. On 27 September 1951, Iranian troops seized the Abadan complex. Robert Lovett, who had just succeeded Marshall as secretary of defense, pleaded with Acheson to reactivate talks between the British and Iranians. A military confrontation, he feared, would play into the hands of the Tudeh Party, provoke a Soviet move into Azerbaijan, and enable the Russians to gain control of Iranian oil. If this should happen, Lovett remonstrated, the ability of the Soviet Union to wage protracted war would be greatly enhanced. Truman cautioned the British again to refrain from military intervention. Lacking U.S. support, the British reconsidered their options. Instead of fighting, they brought the matter to the United Nations and instituted a boycott of Iranian oil. Briefly, the crisis abated.[87]

■

The volatility of the situation in Egypt and Iran meant that something had to be done to firm up the Western position in the Eastern Mediterranean and the Middle East. The Kremlin's behavior in the area was not threatening. Even in Iran, the worst indictment of the Soviets was that they had negotiated a trade agreement that, notwithstanding its "perfectly normal" provisions, aroused fears that they might penetrate the country and orient its economy northward. Not Soviet action but faltering British influence and rising nationalist fervor forced the United States to fill the power vacuum in the Middle East.[88] Along with economic aid of $125 million and military assistance of $415 million, McGhee and his associates in the State Department now placed special emphasis on bringing Turkey into the Atlantic alliance. "We cannot be sure we will have Turkey as an ally," he warned the JCS on 2 May 1951, "unless we extend a security commitment." [89]

The JCS concurred. The gap between commitments and capabilities persisted. But the latter were growing quickly and the neutralist threat appeared incontrovertible. Admiral Carney pressed for action. So did Admiral Jerauld Wright, the deputy U.S. representative to NATO's Standing Group. Even General Collins, who had staunchly opposed the assumption of British responsibilities in the region, acknowledged that Turkish neutrality "would deny us access to the shortest and most expeditious routes to the nerve center of the plague that afflicts us." The money spent rehabilitating Turkish airfields, Collins insisted, must not be wasted. U.S. as well as Turkish forces could use these airstrips. Turkish ground forces, moreover, could play a key role thwarting Soviet advances toward Cairo-Suez and the Saudi oil fields. In May, the NSC concluded that the United States should work to bring Turkey and Greece into NATO.[90]

Turkey's accession to NATO could also help solve the Anglo-Egyptian impasse over British rights at Cairo-Suez. The Americans and the British now wanted to establish a Middle East Command (MECOM) that would be linked to NATO. A British officer would become Supreme Allied Commander, Middle East (SACME). His integrated command would include officers from the United States, France, and Turkey. Turkish military units would compose the core of the ground forces. In wartime they would be supplemented by reinforcements from the commonwealth nations. Egypt would be invited to participate as an equal. If it agreed, British facilities at Cairo-Suez would be returned to Egypt with the understanding that Egypt would immediately place them under the SACME. The British base, therefore, would become an Allied base. The Egyptians would help run the base as part of the multilateral force. British troops and pilots would be placed under the SACME, and their numbers would be determined in consultation with the Egyptian government.

Acheson believed that it was an ingenious scheme to palliate Egyptian nationalist sensibilities without jeopardizing British and U.S. capabilities to use the base in wartime. Of course, it was such a transparent ruse to disguise Britain's continued presence that a great deal of effort would have to be made to dress it up in acceptable garb. Acheson was prepared to help by offering Egypt a new set of special inducements, including military aid, military training, and economic assistance. But nothing could be done until Turkey joined NATO.[91]

In July 1951, Acheson called for a special meeting of the North Atlantic Council to discuss the admission of Turkey and Greece. When it convened in Ottawa, Canada, in September, he skillfully persuaded the Dutch, Danes, and Norwegians to go along with his proposal. He then immediately launched the MECOM initiative. The United States invited Turkey to become a founding member of MECOM. Action was urgent because the crisis in Egypt was heading toward a climax. U.S. officials deluded themselves into thinking that a quick overture to Cairo, coupled with promises of military and economic assistance, might stave off Egypt's determination to declare British rights at Cairo-Suez null and void.[92]

■

Summarizing developments in the Middle East, Acheson told the NSC in August 1951 that conditions were explosive. The Soviets could exploit nationalist fervor and make sizable gains. Therefore, it was all the more important to hasten the U.S.

rearmament effort. Only the shadows cast by military capabilities would allow the United States to act in local situations in ways that would deter the Kremlin. The twin crises in Iran and Egypt, occurring while the fighting in Korea still raged and while Western Europe still remained vulnerable to invasion, underscored the need for yet additional arms. More arms would afford more options in crisis situations; more arms would allow the United States to support friendly leaders, like the shah, and encourage them to act boldly. More arms would also abet diplomacy, for if incumbent Arab governments had enough of them their capacity to stay in power would be augmented, their temptation to consider neutralist options would be diminished, and their inclination to strike friendly deals with the West would be enhanced.[93]

NATO officials, however, cautioned Acheson to be sensitive to the Soviet perception of threat. The incorporation of Greece and Turkey into NATO was a significant step toward the encirclement of the adversary. The Norwegians and the Danes feared that it might provoke the Kremlin. Morrison and Schuman reminded Acheson that, at one and the same time, the United States was thinking about expanding the war in Korea, sending military supplies to Yugoslavia, modernizing airfields in Turkey, and rearming Germany. All these initiatives involved calculations of risk. Trade-offs had to be made lest the United States provoke a war before it was ready for it. Acheson understood these admonitions. As he proceeded with the co-optation of Japanese power and the assumption of new commitments in the Pacific, he carefully calculated what the traffic would bear.[94]

Japan and the Security of the Western Pacific

Chinese intervention in the Korean War convinced John Foster Dulles, Acheson's special consultant, that he had to work harder and faster to keep Japan in the U.S. orbit. If Korea were lost to the adversary, Japan would be encircled and its capacity and desire to stay linked to the Western world would diminish. Dulles was especially frightened that Japan would not be able to find markets and pay for its food and raw materials. If it were dependent economically on the Communist mainland, it would slowly be sucked into the Soviet orbit. Dulles wanted to go to Tokyo to ascertain the price that the Japanese would demand in exchange for a peace treaty that would align them permanently with the West.[95]

Like Dulles, Acheson believed the major Soviet aim in Asia was to capture, however indirectly, Japanese resources. If this occurred, the world balance of power would be altered. Acheson assumed that the Japanese would not willingly commit themselves to the free world unless their security were guaranteed and their prospects for economic advancement insured. He was ready to let them know that the United States would defend them and insure their access to food and raw materials. He would ease their exchange problems by paying for U.S. military garrisons in Japan and by procuring materiel from Japanese suppliers. Acknowledging that most nations on the Far East Commission still opposed the liberal peace he favored, Acheson also reiterated his readiness to sign mutual assistance treaties with Pacific island nations. If Marshall agreed with him, the secretary of state was prepared to send Dulles to Tokyo to discuss the terms of the peace and bilateral security treaties.[96]

Military officials demurred. The JCS once again saw nothing but potential problems in a peace treaty. Because of the Chinese offensive, they had redeployed practically all U.S. troops in the Far East to Korea. In December 1950, Japan was a military vacuum. It was vulnerable to internal subversion and external aggression. The Soviets might invade if they were provoked by a treaty they did not like and could not influence. On the other hand, the Japanese might sense U.S. weakness, bargain from a position of strength, regain their sovereignty, and withdraw U.S. and U.N. rights to use Japanese bases. With global war more of a possibility than ever before, it made no sense to jeopardize the U.S. position in Japan. The JCS preferred to defer treaty discussions until the Korean War was concluded.[97]

Acheson, however, pushed hard for his viewpoint. As in the case of the Middle East, he was ready for the United States to incur additional commitments if they were necessary to reassure potential allies and to thwart neutralist tendencies. He knew the Kremlin objected to U.S. efforts to acquire long-term base rights in Japan and the Ryukyus. He knew the Russians despised the prospect of Japan's rearmament. Unlike Generals Collins and Vandenberg, however, he did not allow apprehensions of a Soviet counterthrust into Hokkaido to dissuade him from opening talks with the Japanese on a peace treaty. If initiatives were deemed essential to align critical nations, like Japan, with the United States, he was willing to run the risk of provoking the Kremlin. To win Marshall's approval, he conceded that the talks would initially be of an exploratory nature.[98]

Dulles spent over two weeks in Japan at the end of January and the beginning of February 1951. He was eager to enlist MacArthur's support because of the supreme commander's prestige with the Japanese and because of his influence with right-wing Republicans. With memories of German repudiation of the Treaty of Versailles resonating in his mind, Dulles also wanted to talk to leaders of Japan's political opposition and with heads of labor and business organizations. Most important, Dulles wanted to ascertain whether Prime Minister Yoshida Shigeru was ready to sign a peace treaty and a bilateral security agreement that met U.S. requirements. Would the Japanese be ready to rearm to help provide for their own defense? Would they commit their forces to a regional security organization? Would they accept a strategic trusteeship for the United States in the Ryukyus? Would they allow the Americans "to station as many troops in Japan as we want where we want and for as long as we want"?[99]

At times the Japanese prime minister seemed elliptic, but he knew what he desired. Yoshida was not eager to rearm. He wanted the United States to guarantee Japan's security and to help revive its economy. Yoshida wanted to modify some of the reforms of the occupation, regain Japanese ownership of the Ryukyus, and excise the humiliating references to unconditional surrender from the peace treaty. Most of all he desired to recover the Japanese government's full sovereignty over domestic affairs; the United States should have the right to intervene only if outside powers were instigating internal chaos. In order to satisfy Japanese opinion and ease passage of the security treaty in the Japanese Diet, Yoshida advised that the two governments specify U.S. rights to retain troops in Japan in an administrative agreement that would not require parliamentary ratification.[100]

Dulles was an adroit negotiator, knowing how to be inflexible on fundamentals as well as conciliatory on matters of lesser importance. He never forgot that his most essential task was to align Japan with the United States for the long term. To accomplish this goal, he realized the Japanese had to see that their own interests were served by the agreements. He assured Yoshida that the United States would work to preserve Japan's access to raw materials and markets. He stressed that U.S. troops would intervene in Japan's domestic affairs only when there was instigation or intervention by outside powers. He was willing to rethink arrangements pertaining to the Ryukyus to see if U.S. desires for a permanent base at Okinawa might be reconciled with Japan's territorial claims. Most of these matters seemed soluble because Yoshida not only agreed to create a 50,000-man land-and-sea force but also accepted U.S. demands for unlimited rights to station troops in Japan wherever the Americans wanted and for as long as they wanted. Yoshida felt Japan would benefit from U.S. protection. Dulles, for his part, believed the retention of troops would deter Soviet aggression, discourage Communist efforts to seize power, influence the direction of Japan's post-treaty foreign policy, and reassure other allies in the region. He left Tokyo on 11 February quite encouraged.[101]

The U.S. envoy next journeyed to the Philippines, Australia, and New Zealand. In each country he encountered opposition to a liberal peace treaty and found little enthusiasm for a Pacific Pact. President Elpidio Quirino of the Philippines wanted large reparations.[102] Percy Spender and Frederick Doidge, the foreign ministers of Australia and New Zealand, respectively, sought a tripartite alliance with the United States. They wanted to establish a formal military organization, coordinate strategic planning, and create indirect linkages to NATO. Dulles worked with them on drafting a tripartite mutual security treaty. The provisions obligated each signatory to take action in case of an attack but did not specify the nature of the response or the place where it would take place. Carefully explaining that he could not commit his government, Dulles nonetheless realized that this agreement was the price that had to be paid for a liberal peace that would prevent a Japanese coalition with the Soviet Union and China.[103]

When Dulles returned to Washington, he found the Pentagon determined to build up Japanese forces. Military officials feared that either the war in Korea might spread to Japan or the negotiation of a peace treaty might incite the Soviets to assert their occupation rights and invade Japan. The four divisions (75,000 men) of the Japanese National Police Reserve, though now organized and trained along the lines of a military organization, were only partly equipped and were bereft of capable leaders. Marshall and Bradley desired to outfit them immediately with medium tanks and 155-mm howitzers and to stockpile materiel for an additional six divisions.[104] They also sought to rehabilitate Japanese former officers and to recruit them for the police reserve.[105] Furthermore, they wanted to harness Japan's industrial potential for the war effort in Korea and for the overall Western rearmament buildup. Notwithstanding the contravention of Far East Commission directives, Marshall instructed the Army, Navy, Air Force, and Munitions Board to increase their purchases of combat equipment and supplies in Japan.[106]

These initiatives threatened to block Dulles's efforts to complete a peace treaty. State Department officials feared that violations of Far East Commission directives would antagonize the allies and play into the hands of the Japanese Communists. They pleaded with Marshall, Lovett, and the JCS either to delay initiatives until the peace conference was held or to mask their violation of existing agreements.[107] Mid-level officials in the Pentagon complained, but Marshall and Lovett grasped the arguments for proper timing and acceded to State Department wishes.[108]

The JCS also realized that assurances to Spender and Doidge were necessary to win support for a lenient peace. Appropriate guarantees, moreover, might encourage Australia and New Zealand to deploy their own troops to the Middle East in times of emergency in order to defend Egyptian airstrips, the Suez Canal, and the petroleum fields of the Persian Gulf. Marshall and Bradley, however, asked Acheson and Dulles to negotiate simple, informal, and flexible arrangements that would not overly hamstring the nation's freedom of action in times of crisis. Emphasizing that some commitments were indispensable, Dulles said he would do what he could to accommodate the JCS.[109]

■

The president's decision to fire MacArthur accelerated State and Defense Department efforts to iron out their tactical differences. Acheson feared that the Japanese would interpret the dismissal of the supreme commander to mean that the United States was subordinating East Asia and disengaging from a lenient peace policy that MacArthur had consistently championed. When news of the firing was about to leak to the press, Acheson asked Dulles to return to Tokyo and reassure Japanese leaders that the Truman administration was not changing course.[110]

Dulles knew that MacArthur's dismissal would electrify the nation and spark intense controversy. His fellow Republicans might demand that he cease to implement the Democrats' East Asian policies. Consequently, he called Thomas Dewey and met with Senate Republican leaders. Acknowledging that partisanship demanded that he dissociate himself from the administration, he nevertheless emphasized that national self-interest required him to continue his efforts to co-opt Japanese power. Dulles was enormously relieved when Taft supported the latter course of action.

He was even more pleased when Truman emphatically reaffirmed his support of a lenient peace treaty and related security agreements.[111]

Dulles flew again to Tokyo. From 17 to 21 April, he consulted with Japanese officials and with General Matthew Ridgway, MacArthur's successor. Dulles stressed that the United States would go ahead with the peace treaty. He was delighted to find that Yoshida was not thinking about neutrality and not trying to elicit greater concessions. Dulles took the opportunity to explain the reactions of other governments to the proposed peace treaty. He presented the Filipinos' desire for reparations and deftly explained how ways might be found to satisfy their needs without burdening the Japanese economy. More important, he emphasized that U.S. rights to use Japanese bases must remain even if the war expanded beyond the Korean peninsula and engulfed Manchuria, China, and the Soviet Union.[112]

Despite Dulles's efforts to secure all the rights they wanted in Japan, Pentagon officials remained edgy. News that the State Department was planning to take over the nonmilitary functions of occupation authorities alarmed them. In a strongly worded memorandum to Marshall on 14 May 1951, the JCS protested any transfer of authority that would weaken control over the Japanese people, accelerate demands for additional concessions, or jeopardize the use of Japan as an essential base of operations. Emphasizing Soviet military capabilities, the joint chiefs again alluded to Soviet opposition to the United States–sponsored peace treaty and cautioned against its premature implementation lest it trigger a Soviet attack. They advised that the treaty come into effect only after the United States reestablished its garrison forces, built up Japan's capacity for self-defense, and negotiated a satisfactory bilateral Japanese-U.S. security pact. Marshall strongly endorsed the JCS conclusions.[113]

Although worried about the *implementation* of the treaty, Marshall and the JCS subscribed to the new NSC paper (NSC 48/5) outlining overall policy toward Asia and calling for the *negotiation* of the peace and security agreements with Japan.[114] Accordingly, in late May, Dulles voyaged to London and Paris to line up British and French support. Worrying that the United States might establish unfortunate precedents that would apply to Germany and fearing that Washington might provoke the Kremlin, the French pleaded for a slow relinquishment of controls. Dulles was infuriated. Delays, he said, "would be fatal and almost surely result in an eventual tie-up between Soviet Russia, Communist China, and Japan, which would be a very formidable combination which for a considerable time at least would dominate most of the entire Pacific area and Southeast Asia."[115]

Dulles's talks with the British focused on the specific provisions of the peace treaty. The British wanted to restrict Japanese commercial competition, limit their shipbuilding, and distribute their gold bullion as a form of reparations. They also wanted the Japanese to accept some sort of a war-guilt clause. Dulles was willing to make a few face-saving concessions, but on the substantive issues he remained intransigent. The purpose of the treaty, he insisted, was to co-opt Japanese power.

He did not want to pour salt on Japanese wounds or impose unnecessary obstacles in the way of Japanese recovery. The experience of interwar Germany was forever on his mind.[116]

Most emphatically, Dulles objected to British desires to have Communist China sign the treaty. Nor would he accept any language that provided for the cession of Taiwan to China. Chinese Communist participation in the peace treaty, Dulles believed, would be political dynamite in the United States and would jeopardize chances of Senate ratification. He was content to exclude both China and Taiwan, knowing that the inclusion of Chiang Kai-shek's government would affront Asian nationalists like India's Jawaharlal Nehru and Indonesia's Sukarno. But after the treaty was signed, Dulles expected Japan to establish closer links and extensive trade with the Chinese Nationalists on Taiwan.[117]

Dulles returned from Europe in mid-June. He felt that he had elicited sufficient British and French approval to put the peace and security treaties in final shape. The JCS, however, once again interjected their fundamental concerns: the United States must retain strategic control of the Ryukyus; Japan must not become dependent on the mainland; Taiwan must not be ceded to China; and the treaties must not jeopardize U.S. prosecution of the Korean War and must not come into effect until the conflict was over. These issues were again hashed out at the end of June. Acheson emphasized to Truman, Marshall, Lovett, and Bradley that U.S. interests were fully protected. The Japanese must not be antagonized. At the coming peace conference in San Francisco, they should be treated as equals and integrated into the U.S. orbit. If, at the last minute, the Soviets wanted to participate in the conference, they could do so. But the terms of the peace were not to be discussed at the conference: not with the Japanese, not with the Russians, not with anyone. The San Francisco meeting would be a ceremony, not a forum for discussion and negotiation. Thereafter, the United States could proceed toward ratification, timing its deliberations to comport with the requirements of the Korean War and U.S. self-interest.[118]

Before the conference could be held, however, the United States had to win the support of prospective allies in the Pacific. Dulles put the finishing touches on the alliance between Australia, New Zealand, and the United States (ANZUS). Complying with JCS wishes, the tripartite security treaty did not bind the United States to any particular course of action in wartime and did not create any military planning bodies. Nevertheless, the Truman administration did guarantee the security of Australia and New Zealand and did assent to the establishment of a civilian council to implement the agreement.[119] The treaty was sufficiently attractive to President Quirino of the Philippines that he, too, wanted a similar accord to placate public opinion in his country. Filipinos were angered that they would not be receiving more reparations. Recognizing how upset the Filipinos were, Acheson and Dulles pushed the JCS to accede to another bilateral security pact.[120]

Officials in the Pentagon fretted that civilians were once again extending commitments beyond capabilities. Although they deemed all of the Pacific and parts of

Southeast Asia vital to U.S. interests, they did not want to compromise the nation's freedom of action.[121] Acheson and Dulles believed, however, that precisely because countries like the Philippines had already been designated as vital, it made no sense to withhold commitments if these guarantees were necessary to get them to accede to the Japanese peace treaty. Moreover, they believed that selective alliances with the Philippines, Australia, and New Zealand now left other nations vulnerable and encouraged them to consider neutralist options and accommodationist practices. Much to the Pentagon's chagrin, Acheson insisted that the preambles to the ANZUS and Philippine treaties state that the new agreements were a prelude to more far-reaching security arrangements in the Pacific region. The president reiterated this idea publicly on 4 September 1951.[122]

U.S. officials heralded the opening of the San Francisco conference on 4 September 1951. They anticipated that the Soviets would try to obstruct its proceedings. But Acheson was determined that he would not be intimidated or outmaneuvered. When, in fact, Soviet behavior at San Francisco turned out to be less antagonistic than expected, Acheson was perplexed. He surmised that the Russians were impressed by the huge majorities that the United States mustered in support of the Japanese peace treaty. With a sense of pride and gratification, Acheson wrote Truman that the administration was about to take "a tremendous step toward changing by peaceful means the present power situation in the world in favor of the United States and its Allies." [123]

An added bonus to U.S. officials was that they had been able to incorporate language in the bilateral security treaty with Japan that permitted the United States to use Japanese bases for the preservation of peace and security throughout the entire Far East. The JCS insisted on this right because they wanted legal sanction to conduct operations from Japan against mainland China and the Soviet Union regardless of whether or not U.S. forces were operating under the aegis of the United Nations. Acquisition of this right eased their concern about what they could do should the Korean War escalate into a larger conflict. Other high-ranking policymakers, however, were contemplating post-Korean scenarios when they might want to use bases in Japan to project U.S. power elsewhere in Asia. Paul Nitze, for example, discussed such matters with Air Force officers in Tokyo in early July 1951.[124]

Amidst the progress, however, considerable anxiety remained about the future well-being of the Japanese economy. The military orders emanating from the Korean War sparked rapid increases in production and exports. But once the conflict ended, how would Japan earn the foreign exchange to purchase raw materials and foodstuffs? And where might these imports come from if Southeast Asia were lost to the Communists? Even as the peace and security treaties were signed, policymakers believed that their ultimate ability to co-opt Japanese power would depend on their capacity to convince the Japanese not to turn to the Chinese mainland or the Soviet bloc for markets and raw materials. The fate of Japan appeared as closely intertwined with that of Southeast Asia as Western Europe's was connected with the

Middle East. "Communist control of both China and Southeast Asia," concluded an NSC staff study, "would place Japan in a dangerously vulnerable position and therefore seriously affect the entire security position of the United States in the Pacific." [125]

Southeast Asia

Chinese intervention in Korea at the end of November 1950 raised profound doubts about the ability of the West to wrest the initiative from the Communists in Southeast Asia. For much of the autumn, Ho Chi Minh's forces had been bludgeoning French troops and threatening Hanoi. Increasingly, they seemed likely to receive direct support from China. Throughout December, U.S. intelligence analysts reported the movement of Chinese armies toward the Indochinese border. According to the CIA, Mao's government was purchasing drugs for the treatment of dysentery and malaria should Chinese troops be stricken with these ailments in the delta. The French situation appeared almost hopeless. [126]

Much as they pondered the prospect of China's armed intervention, U.S. officials knew Stalin and Mao bore little responsibility for the successes of the Viet Minh. The amount of aid coming from the Soviet Union remained minuscule. Until 1950, Chinese assistance was believed to have been negligible. And even during 1951, the actual amounts of Chinese assistance remained much more limited than initially anticipated. According to the National Intelligence Estimate of August 1951, the Chinese Communists gave the Viet Minh ammunition, light weapons, and some artillery. They helped train Viet Minh forces and provided military and technical advice. But the aid did not accelerate in any exponential fashion, and the hordes of Chinese "volunteers" did not materialize. [127]

The real source of Ho's success, as everyone freely acknowledged, was his nationalism. "It is ironical but . . . true," wrote Charlton Ogburn, a young foreign service officer in the Bureau of Far Eastern Affairs, "that Asians fighting on the Communist side . . . have the inspiring sense of fighting for national freedom." Bao Dai had none of the same ardor. In fact, after meeting with him on 21 January 1951, Minister Donald Heath, the State Department's top diplomat in Indochina, gathered the impression that Bao Dai was a "harassed man who could not rid himself of the sneaking feeling that the moral conviction and idealism of many Viet Minh supporters were superior to those of his own followers." And a month later, after Bao Dai reshuffled his cabinet, Heath wrote again that not a single person in it was capable of inspiring any enthusiasm. "Fact is that Ho Chi Minh is only Viet who enjoys any measure of national prestige." Privately, Acheson agreed. [128]

But Ho's communism made him an unacceptable alternative. [129] Officials in the Pentagon and at Foggy Bottom did not want to risk the loss of Indochina. They believed that it was the key to all of Southeast Asia. And if Southeast Asia fell into the hands of the adversary, it would be calamitous. Nobody made the case more eloquently than Assistant Secretary of State Dean Rusk. He was most concerned with the region's raw materials. Rice, rubber, and tin, he emphasized, "constitute the consummate prize of Southeast Asia." Denial of them to the Communists would exacerbate China's food problems in peacetime and force the Kremlin to fight with insufficient strategic materials in wartime. On the other hand, access to the tin and rubber of Malaya, Thailand, and Indonesia would enable the United States to build up its depleted stockpiles. Likewise, the region's rice would help fill Japan's 800,000-ton annual import requirement. Furthermore, Malaya's $430 million trade surplus in 1951 and its hugely favorable payments balance aided the tottering position of the entire sterling bloc.[130]

U.S. officials believed that Southeast Asia was critical to the economic health and strategic viability of the offshore defense perimeter. If Southeast Asia fell to the Communists, the transportation and communication routes from the Pacific Ocean to the Persian Gulf and Middle East would be endangered and the offshore island chain would be increasingly vulnerable to attack. Critical U.S. base areas would become isolated from one another and the entire deployment of U.S. forces in the Pacific would have to be reconsidered. To reap the advantages of the island chain in wartime, countries like Japan and the Philippines had to be co-opted and made secure in peacetime. If the Huks seized power in the Philippines or if Communist insurgencies succeeded in Southeast Asia, Japan's capacity to trade with the area on which its future economic salvation appeared to depend would be jeopardized. During 1950 and 1951, Japanese exports to Southeast Asia were soaring. In 1951, it was the one region in the world with which Japan had a large positive trade balance. Japanese plans were to purchase more and more rice, grain, sugar, and iron ore from Indochina, Malaya, and Indonesia. Between 1949 and 1951, in fact, Japanese purchases of raw materials and foodstuffs from these and other countries in the region more than tripled.[131]

State and Defense Department officials did not dispute the importance of Southeast Asia. Nor did they differ on the need to harass the Chinese Communists. The JCS, for example, hoped that military aid to Taiwan, along with numerous other measures, might "deny all of China south of the Yellow River to Communism" and might "eliminate Communist logistic support to Indochina." Acheson, Jessup, and Rusk concurred. "Our basic objective within China," they said, was "to further the development of active resistance to the Chinese Communists." Rather than escalate the Korean War, bomb Manchuria, or support Chiang, Acheson and his colleagues championed covert actions, guerrilla warfare, and economic pressure. In their view, these were the most skillful and least dangerous means of challenging Chinese Communist control of the mainland and of lifting pressure on Indochina.[132]

The State Department and the JCS also worked out agreements on what should be done within Southeast Asia. Given the demands for U.S. troops in Korea, Western Europe, and Japan, the JCS insisted that the United States could not commit any troops to the region. Except for Minister Heath in Vietnam, most State Department officials readily accepted this viewpoint. But the men at Foggy Bottom strongly favored military consultation. Acheson prodded the JCS to enter into staff talks with the French. He encouraged the military planners to devise contingency plans in case China intervened and the French requested assistance evacuating Tonkin. Marshall and Bradley agreed to follow Acheson's recommendations. Tripartite military talks with the French and British took place in May 1951 in Singapore.[133]

Both State and Defense Department officials were strong proponents of military aid. In early 1951, Rusk worked harmoniously with Pentagon officials on a new military aid package. When French premier Pleven arrived in Washington at the end of January and sought additional funds, Acheson tried to accommodate him. As the year progressed, policymakers reaffirmed that arms shipments to Indochina deserved priority over transfers to any other nation except Korea. In May, $80 million was taken from Mutual Defense Assistance Program funds earmarked for the North Atlantic area and reallocated to Indochina. Through fiscal year 1951, the administration approved funding of about $316.5 million for military supplies. Large new commitments were contemplated for 1952.[134]

More important, the equipment and ammunition started to arrive in sizable quantities. The new French commander, General Jean DeLattre de Tassigny, expressed growing pleasure at the timeliness of U.S. shipments. Particularly useful to the French were U.S. aircraft, patrol boats, napalm bombs, and ground-combat materiel. Without this aid, Rusk maintained, there was "little doubt but that Indochina would have long since been overrun by the communists and the whole of Southeast Asia might either have been absorbed by the communist forces or be in immediate peril of such absorption." In September 1951, Lovett told DeLattre that deliveries would be expedited further in the year ahead.[135]

As U.S. aid flowed into Vietnam, some officials were tempted to think that the United States should assume full responsibility for the struggle against the Communists. Economic and information officers in Washington and Vietnam were in the forefront of this movement, but their views were appreciated by foreign service officers who worked in Southeast Asia. Robert Blum, for example, was the chief of the U.S. Special Technical and Economic Mission in Vietnam. He believed that association with the French tarnished the U.S. image, impeded reforms, and set back U.S. efforts to rally support away from the Viet Minh. Blum and his colleagues believed that the French in Indochina, like the British in Egypt and Iran, were no longer reliable instruments for keeping Western control over critical Third World areas. Their inability to make timely concessions to co-opt nationalist forces was stirring unrest, creating explosive situations, and affording opportunities for Communist gains and Soviet aggrandizement.[136]

But senior officials in Washington and Saigon continued to believe that the United States maximized its interests by supplementing, supporting, and cajoling the French rather than by ridiculing and replacing them. DeLattre's ability to inspire his troops rejuvenated the spirits of influential U.S. policymakers. The bold and egocentric French general thwarted Ho's attempts to take Tonkin and reestablished French control over the Red River delta around Hanoi and Haiphong. He was building up French air strength, accelerating French amphibious operations, assembling mobile reserves, and hoping to capitalize on France's superiority in conventional arms. U.S. analysts believed that DeLattre had turned the tide and that his military success was eroding popular support for the Viet Minh. When Schuman and Acheson discussed Indochina in September 1951, they were greatly heartened by developments.[137]

Of course, U.S. officials knew that not all was well. Despite DeLattre's rhetorical commitment to working with the Vietnamese, he often acted arbitrarily to impose his will. He broke up political parties he did not like, withdrew subsidies to paramilitary groups he could not control, occasionally imprisoned critics he did not respect, and frequently fired Vietnamese bureaucrats who were not committed to his program. At the same time, the establishment of the Vietnamese army was hampered by the shortage of trained leaders, inadequate equipment, low morale, and bickering between French and Vietnamese officers. And, most important, Bao Dai's government continued to have a narrow base of support and to repel Vietnamese who were inspired with a sense of nationalism.[138]

Notwithstanding these drawbacks, Acheson in Washington and Heath in Saigon tempered their criticism of French policy. They appreciated the immense sacrifices that the French were enduring in Indochina. The French were now spending close to $1 billion a year and withstanding casualty rates of 30,000 men annually. Only the French, Heath contended, "can hold this critical pass against Communist domination and exploitation." He was most concerned, as was Acheson, that the French would get fed up with the drain on their resources and with U.S. criticism. French influence, he insisted, must not be subverted.[139]

The critical issue, as Deputy Assistant Secretary of State Livingston Merchant pointed out, was "how best do we assure the preservation of Indochina from Communism." [140] Once U.S. officials chose to define their goal this way rather than as the support of nationalism or the promotion of a wedge strategy between the Communists of different countries, they found themselves with few options but to support the French. They talked about reforms, about mobilizing indigenous support, and about buying time for the development of popular Vietnamese leaders who would choose to align with the West. But for the present, they knew no such leaders existed. If the French withdrew or free elections were held, Ho would take over. So U.S. officials had only two options: provide further aid to the French or assume the burdens themselves.

The answer was easy: provide the French with more aid. When Schuman and DeLattre visited Washington in September 1951, they were met with outstretched arms, warm smiles, and congratulatory statements. Truman met with the French general and applauded him for the job he was doing. Lovett invited him to the Pentagon and told him to regard the place as his own home. Schuman and DeLattre explained, as they had so many times before, that they needed more money, more arms, more military staff talks. Economic aid, DeLattre said, would be used to improve the transportation infrastructure. Financial aid could be used to recruit, train, and pay the newly formed armies of Vietnam and of the other Associated States (Laos and Cambodia). But most of all, DeLattre wanted military equipment: aircraft, patrol boats, combat vehicles, signal equipment, and submachine guns. If he could return to Indochina with assurances of expedited assistance, he felt he could sustain the progress he was making.

U.S. officials told Schuman and DeLattre that they would receive U.S. support. Not wanting to commit troops, they preferred to abet the French effort by rushing additional equipment to Vietnam. Of course, the nation's own rearmament effort, its assistance programs to Western Europe and the Middle East, and its plans to build up Japanese and German forces set limits on what the United States could do in Indochina. Nonetheless, Acheson agreed that Indochina deserved top priority after Korea. Rest assured, he told Schuman, that the United States had the will, if not the available means, to solve the problem. But means there were, as well. Collins pressed his subordinates to find a considerable portion of the Army materiel that DeLattre requested. The Army chief of staff also said that he would look into the possibility of shifting aid from other countries to Indochina.[141]

The reasons for accelerating assistance to the French were spelled out in a number of position papers preceding the arrival of Schuman and DeLattre. Undersecretary of State James Webb informed the president:

It is an agreed military estimate that if Indochina falls, very likely all of Southeast Asia may come under communist domination. The Philippines are less than 800 miles from Indochina, and Malaya and Indonesia furnish the majority of the Free World's rubber and tin. While the loss of these materials would seriously handicap our own defense effort, they would, if available to the communist armies of the world, enormously increase their capabilities. We are therefore most anxious that General de Lattre's continuing campaign to hold Indochina be successful.

The French general, Lovett opined, was directing America's struggle in Vietnam just as Ridgway was commanding its war in Korea.[142]

However hopeful U.S. officials were about the revitalized French effort in Vietnam, their optimism was tempered by fears of Chinese intervention. The French now appeared capable of handling the indigenous insurrection, but what would happen if the conflict escalated? U.S. intelligence analysts estimated that the Chinese Communists could invade Tonkin with a force of 100,000 field troops. There was information that the Chinese were improving road and rail networks, stockpiling supplies, and upgrading airfields. French aircraft, concentrated at three locations, were vulnerable to a surprise attack. If the Chinese Communists achieved air superiority, their capacity to carry out a large-scale ground campaign would be enhanced and their ability to transfer supplies to the Viet Minh would grow. The only comforting thought was the belief that, so long as Chinese forces were absorbed in Korea,

Mao would not invade Indochina. But if the fighting should cease in Northeast Asia, it was assumed that within two months Chinese Communist capabilities for intervention in Vietnam "could be significantly increased, while air capabilities could be greatly increased." Yet when DeLattre asked the president what the United States would do in case of a Chinese attack, he received no precise response.[143]

In truth, U.S. officials did not really know. Much would depend on progress in their own rearmament program and on building up NATO's capacity to defend Western Europe. U.S. risk-taking in Southeast Asia, as in other areas, would depend on assessments of the overall correlation of forces between the United States and the Soviet Union and on appraisals of Soviet intentions and capabilities. As DeLattre completed his round of talks in Washington, Bradley secretly called for a new appraisal of what the United States should do in Indochina.[144] With the global balance of power shifting in America's direction, the possibilities for additional action appeared to be growing. But amidst the optimistic signs, there was still need for prudence. Too much pressure at any point along the Soviet periphery, or too hasty a reaction to the adversary's initiatives, or too precipitous an effort to rearm the Germans and the Japanese could still precipitate the global war that Truman, Acheson, Marshall, Lovett, and Bradley did not want. Their aim, after all, was to win the cold war without resort to a hot war.

U.S. Risk-Taking and Soviet Capabilities and Intentions

The situation in Korea, however, remained fraught with danger. Two huge Communist offensives were turned back in April and May. U.S. and U.N. forces under the command of General Ridgway then pushed their way above the 38th parallel. Much to the chagrin of Ridgway's commanders in the field, however, policymakers in Washington restrained the northward movement of U.N. troops. The quest for a military victory in Korea risked the possible escalation of the conflict into a global war and jeopardized the pursuit of U.S. goals around the world. In June, when the Kremlin signaled that the Communist bloc welcomed cease-fire discussions, Truman, Acheson, and their advisers agreed to talk. Pressure from current and prospective allies as well as the evolving public sentiment in the United States made it impossible to rebuff Communist overtures.[145]

The intent of the Truman administration, however, was neither to relinquish the long-term goal of unifying Korea nor to endanger the military position of U.N. forces. When Chinese and North Korean negotiators at Kaesong immediately demanded withdrawal to the 38th parallel and evacuation of all foreign troops from the peninsula, Admiral Turner Joy threatened to terminate the discussions. The Communists backed down. Talks went on for about six weeks but accomplished little. The Chinese Communists continued to build up their air power and to send fresh troops to the front. U.N. forces, in turn, sought to strengthen their defensive posture and to intensify their punitive air raids. Ground fighting subsided, but both sides feared imminent escalation.[146]

The JCS acceded to State Department desires to continue the talks until the adversary's responsibility for their breakdown was clear to everyone. As inclined as defense officials were to chase enemy aircraft across the Yalu and attack Chinese airfields, they agreed that military actions in Korea should not endanger the larger objectives that the Truman administration was pursuing. They understood, moreover, that escalation could precipitate global war or frighten and alienate governments whose help the United States wanted in peacetime and wartime.[147]

In turn, State Department officials shared many of the apprehensions troubling the men at the Pentagon. They were acutely sensitive to the buildup of enemy forces. They agonized over the military and political costs of an enemy offensive that might drive U.N. forces from the Korean peninsula. All through the summer, Acheson, Rusk, and Nitze met with Marshall, Lovett, and Bradley. They pondered contingencies should the cease-fire talks fail and the war escalate. Acheson and Nitze were not ready to take the initiative and expand the war. But if the enemy renewed its ground offensive, they would permit Ridgway to move northward to the so-called neck of Korea; if the adversary bombed U.S. air and naval forces in their South Korean and Japanese sanctuaries, they would allow Ridgway to retaliate against Manchuria. If the Russians intervened or attacked Japan, Acheson and Nitze agreed that the JCS should be prepared to implement their global war plans and launch an all-out atomic blitz against the Soviet Union.[148]

For Acheson and Nitze, however, these scenarios remained worst-case possibilities. Their hope was that the United States could avoid a global war while holding its own in Korea and sustaining the momentum in all other areas of the world. They knew their actions to rearm Japan, co-opt German power, establish military ties with Yugoslavia, invite Turkey and Greece into NATO, and aid the French in Indochina were deemed provocative by the Kremlin. They knew that every move accentuated the possibilities of war. Yet they felt they had no option but to take such risks. "It was felt," said Nitze, "that the risk of provocation had to be taken, otherwise we were defeated before we started." Acheson acknowledged that he was constantly aware "of the great danger that lay in any program of build-up in the sense that the Soviet Union might feel it would be impelled to take vigorous counter-action." [149]

Acheson and Nitze were much impressed with the need for speedy action to establish a preponderance of power in which the industrial cores of Europe and Asia were integrated into a U.S. orbit. This preponderance would constitute the position of strength from which the United States could then move to reduce further the power and influence of the Kremlin and to bring about fundamental changes in Soviet conduct of international relations. State Department officials, however, did not want U.S. actions in Korea to drive the Russians to war before the United States had established this position of strength. "We in State have felt," Nitze wrote Acheson, "that there is an important interplay between our actions and those of the

Soviets. We believe that strength is the basic deterrent. We also feel that a program for building strength, prior to the time the strength has been achieved, tends to increase the likelihood of USSR counteraction. We would like to see the period of build-up and therefore of greatest sensitivity shortened as much as possible." But once the buildup was achieved, Nitze and his colleagues believed, the United States would have additional freedom of action to move in more peripheral areas, like Korea itself.[150]

■

Risk-taking, therefore, remained critical to U.S. strategy. And U.S. risk-taking was profoundly influenced by calculations of Soviet intentions and capabilities. When the Chinese intervened in Korea in November 1950, U.S. officials nearly panicked with the thought that the Kremlin was ready and eager to join the fray. But after living for several months with the nightmare that they might be on the threshold of global atomic war, U.S. assessments about Soviet intentions returned to their customary orientation. Although the international situation remained fraught with danger, there were more signs of Soviet restraint than Soviet adventurism. U.S. officials concluded that the Soviets' continued incapacity to win a protracted war would probably discourage the Kremlin from launching a premeditated attack on the West.

The Soviets, of course, continued to modernize their military forces. U.S. analysts believed that their atomic stockpile was growing more quickly than initially anticipated. In June 1950, Americans thought the Kremlin would have between 70 and 135 atomic warheads in mid-1953; in November 1950 the estimate for mid-1953 rose to 165 bombs; and in September 1951 the U.S. calculation was that the Russians would have 200 atomic bombs by 1953. The number of Soviet aircraft (TU-4's) capable of delivering these bombs on targets in the United States was expected to increase from 700 in 1951 to 1,200 in 1953.[151] The Soviet economy was also making significant gains and was in a high state of war readiness. In a long study in April 1951, the U.S. embassy in Moscow reported that the Soviet transport system was carrying 40 percent more freight than in 1940. The Soviet Union was producing 58 percent more coal, 21 percent more oil, 87 percent more electric power, 50 percent more steel, several times more aluminum, twice as much copper, three times as much synthetic rubber, and twice as much new machinery and motor vehicles.[152]

The most noteworthy development in the military capabilities of the Communist bloc in 1951, however, was said to be the rapid increase in the size and materiel of satellite armies. The Polish army, for example, was believed to have grown from 136,000 to 180,000; the Hungarian army from 28,000 to 65,000; the Bulgarian army from 87,000 to 145,000. By the spring of 1951 the total strength of East European armies had increased from 602,000 to 756,000. They now had five mechanized divisions rather than two; 52 infantry divisions rather than 51; and three tank divisions rather than two.[153]

Soviet military shortcomings, however, influenced U.S. assessments of Soviet intentions more than did Soviet military strength. Despite the increases in the Soviet atomic arsenal, the U.S. stockpile remained almost ten times the size of the Kremlin's. So long as this disparity persisted, or so long as the Russians lacked the capability to cripple U.S. industrial power, the Kremlin was likely to be deterred from a full-scale attack.[154] Of critical importance, then, was the continued absence of an effective long-range air force. U.S. analysts dwelled on the growing numbers of TU-4's, but these aircraft possessed no greater capabilities than the medium-range American B-29 bombers. Moreover, the Russians had not developed any refueling techniques. They were capable, at best, of one-way missions. At the very onset of conflict, they were not even deemed capable of launching a surprise attack on the United Kingdom let alone the United States. Their pilots lacked experience in strategic air attacks. The fragmentary evidence that existed suggested that the Soviets were still planning to use their air power not for strategic assaults on the West but for support of their ground forces or for defense of their homeland.[155]

Aside from the strategic balance, Russian capacity to win a protracted war against the United States did not seem to have greatly improved. Mechanization of Soviet land forces continued apace, but U.S. estimates suggested that the Soviets would have more and more difficulty overrunning all of Europe. "Taking account of terrain factors, Soviet logistical problems, and atomic developments," concluded the NSC in the early fall of 1951, "it is expected that areas of major strategic importance in continental Europe can be held by mid-1953." Emergency war plans for 1952 already assumed that the Soviets would have great difficulty defeating Turkish forces and getting to Cairo-Suez. Moreover, the alignment of Yugoslav forces on the side of the West generated real hopes of holding a line in Italy. Meanwhile, Soviet abilities to interfere with U.S. overseas operations were scaled downward as a result of a "drastic" revision in estimates of the numbers of Soviet high-speed, long-range submarines.[156]

The Soviet economy might have been improving, and its capacity for supporting a major war was growing. Over the long run, however, it was no match for the United States and Western Europe. The Soviet economy was geared for war but could not sustain a prolonged conflict. Striking weaknesses prevailed in the construction industry. Soviet petroleum production sufficed for peacetime purposes and for initial wartime operations, but was "insufficient to support the requirements of a large-scale war of long duration involving strategic air operations, especially if some of the refining facilities were destroyed." Furthermore, there were persistent deficiencies in the production of rubber, machine tools, precision instruments, some nonferrous metals and alloys, and some electrical equipment. The railroad links to the Baltic provinces remained in terrible shape, and the differences in the gauges between the railways in the Soviet Union and those in Poland and East Germany had not been rectified. Try as they might, intelligence analysts in Washington and the military attachés in Moscow had difficulty discerning any great speedup in military production. "There is no evidence," concluded the report from diplomats and attachés in Moscow, "that the economy is being groomed to support a full-scale aggression this year." In fact, "Red capabilities in relation to Blue will decrease progressively throughout 1951, and rapidly thereafter." [157]

Nor would the Soviet satellites compensate for chronic Soviet military and economic shortcomings. In the latter half of 1951, Soviet satellite forces were re-calculated and estimated to have reached 947,000 men. In a year and a half, they had grown by almost 50 percent. Moreover, the Soviets were resurfacing airfields throughout the region and constructing new ones. The engineering, petroleum, and chemical industries of Eastern Europe furnished almost half their output to the Soviet Union. But after elaborately detailing their potential contribution to the Russian war machine, the CIA concluded that "because of deficiencies in equipment, loyalty, and morale, the Satellite armed forces as such do not now possess the capabilities which their size would appear to indicate." [158]

The conclusions drawn from these assessments were important. In brief, U.S. officials did not think the Kremlin wanted to initiate a full-scale war. In January 1951, Admiral L. C. Stevens returned from a tour as naval attaché in Moscow and presented a detailed exposition of Soviet weaknesses. Like Stevens, Eisenhower felt confident the Soviets would not attack. Charles Bohlen, now counselor in the State Department, agreed. So did Ambassador Alan Kirk, despite his stress on the Soviet penchant for risk-taking. Illustratively, Dulles told the French not to worry about the Soviet reaction to the Japanese peace treaty; the Russians would acquiesce to it because they were afraid of global war. Despite all the talk of 1952 becoming the year of maximum danger, Acheson and Bradley agreed that they were most worried about subsequent years should West Europeans fail to rearm.[159]

Moreover, as 1951 progressed, signs of Soviet restraint were apparent to almost everyone. The atmosphere in Moscow was painfully grim, and Stalinist repression was omnipresent. But the man who ruled the Kremlin did not seem to want war. "Stalin," Khrushchev later recalled, "showed cowardice. He was afraid of the United States. . . . He developed fear, literally fear of the United States." The Soviets, in fact, invited U.S. businessmen to Moscow and reemphasized their peace campaign. Kirk reported that the Kremlin wanted to relax tensions. Ambassador Walter Gifford in London concurred. Acheson conceded that the Soviets seemed intent on stopping the fighting in Korea and were concentrating on slowing down the Western rearmament effort.[160]

Of course, all these analyses were tempered by the belief that Soviet long-term goals were immutable. War, therefore, could result from two possibilities despite the fact that the Kremlin preferred to avoid conflict. The Russians might attack before the correlation of forces changed dramatically to their disadvantage. "The outlook to them must be dim at best and promises to get dimmer," emphasized U.S. analysts in the Moscow embassy. Therefore, they might strike while they were in their best relative position. But this best position was still a bad one. Americans felt fairly confident that Stalin would not launch a premeditated attack so long as U.S. atomic capabilities greatly exceeded his own and so long as the U.S. economy remained relatively invulnerable.[161]

War from miscalculation, however, was an entirely different matter. The chances for an accidental war were alarmingly high. The instability in the Middle East, the insurgency in Indochina, the defection of Yugoslavia, and the fighting in Korea provided temptations and created pressures that the Kremlin might not be able to resist. Thus far the Kremlin had been circumspect. But if the Soviets sought to exploit opportunities in these areas, global war would result because of the likely reaction of the United States. The Kremlin might miscalculate just how important the United States regarded these matters. Likewise, if the Kremlin sought to interfere with U.S. efforts to co-opt German and Japanese strength or to stop the rearmament of these countries, they might find themselves at war with the United States.[162]

Repeatedly, U.S. officials emphasized that, if their goals were threatened, they might initiate atomic war. In other words, a premeditated Soviet assault on Western Europe might not be the only occasion for using atomic weapons. Acheson and Lovett agreed that the United States might use them in limited wars, like the one in Korea, if it were deemed propitious to do so. Certainly, the United States would retaliate with atomic weapons if the Soviets intervened directly in Korea or attacked Japan. Bradley and Nitze made this unmistakably clear to the British. They also pointed out that the United States might respond to a Soviet move against Yugoslavia with atomic weapons as well. The world was so unstable, and the United States was seeking to fill so many vacuums, that the possibilities for using atomic weapons appeared to be many, and U.S. officials were intent on keeping their options open.[163]

War, therefore, could come at any time, not because the Soviets wanted it but because the Americans would regard Soviet defensive initiatives in Germany and Japan as well as Soviet meddling, opportunism, or intervention in important Third World areas as threats to U.S. efforts to establish a preponderance of power in Europe and Asia. The NSC maintained in one of its most important papers that:

During the next two or three years, as our strength grows, spreads out from the center, and is established close to the Soviet Union and areas under its control, and as Soviet atomic resources approach possible critical dimensions, we must give increasing weight to the possibility of war. Where our vital interests overlap what the Soviet rulers regard as vital interests of their own, there will be a grave risk of Soviet action unless our ability to defend our basic position is clearly equal or superior to the Soviet ability to challenge it.

The United States, therefore, had to be able to dominate the escalatory cycle. It had to have overwhelming strategic forces so that it could either preemptively wipe out Soviet atomic capabilities or, at a minimum, persuade the Soviets that they could never neutralize America's retaliatory options. U.S. strategic forces had to be able to cast shadows to convince the Soviets that they could not "exploit their geographical position and preponderant ground and tactical air strength for local advantages without serious risk of general war." At the same time the United States had to work to build up NATO conventional forces so that the Kremlin could not make a counterthrust into the European heartland if and when the United States sought to redress a local situation.[164]

If the United States could maintain its lead in atomic weapons, and, even more important, if the United States could get NATO to mount a successful defense in Western Europe, then U.S. policymakers could go on the offensive everywhere. At NSC meetings throughout the summer of 1951, Truman and his top advisers insisted on the need to sustain the U.S. and West European rearmament effort. Neither a cease-fire nor an arms control proposal could be permitted to halt the military buildup and the worldwide offensive that the United States had launched. Acute dangers would persist so long as the United States lacked the ability to implement the goals of NSC 68/2.[165] In other words, the United States could not feel that its national security was safeguarded until it had co-opted German and Japanese power, expanded its allies and its bases around the periphery of the Soviet bloc, filled the vacuums in the Middle East, and thwarted revolutionary nationalist unrest in Asia and Africa.

Substantial progress had been made but not enough. Between June 1950 and June 1951, the Army had grown from ten to eighteen divisions, from eleven to eighteen regimental combat teams, and from 56 to 100 anti-aircraft battalions. The number of naval vessels rose from 646 to 1,037. Major combatant ships, including aircraft carriers, battleships, cruisers, destroyers, and submarines, increased from 237 to 342. Naval operating aircraft jumped from 6,177 to 7,369. Combat wings in the Air Force leapt from 48 to 87, with striking advances in the number of medium bombers and fighter bombers. Active aircraft in the inventory of the Air Force went from 8,687 to 12,870 (partly as a result of transferring planes from the Air National Guard). Yet Truman and his advisers lamented that they would not be able to fulfill their 1954 goals by 1952, a task they had set for themselves in December 1950.[166]

Despite their anxiety, they could take real pride in the progress they had made. They had thrown Chinese and North Korean troops back across the 38th parallel. They had overcome congressional objections to the deployment of four additional U.S. divisions to Europe. They had begun to establish an integrated NATO command and had appointed a supreme commander. They had pushed the Europeans to rearm, had prodded the French to negotiate a new set of contractual arrangements with Germany, and had accepted the French concept of a European Defense Community to absorb German troops. They had brought Turkey and Greece into the NATO alliance, had supported the Middle East Command in order to placate Egyptian sensibilities, and had tried to mediate the strife between Iran and the United Kingdom. In East Asia, they had consummated the peace treaty and bilateral security agreement with Japan, thereby taking big strides toward safeguarding U.S. strategic interests and co-opting Japanese power. In Southeast Asia, they had buttressed the French effort in Indochina and were encouraged by DeLattre's performance.

So much looked promising, yet it might all turn out to be ephemeral. Soviet intervention in Korea could trigger global war before the Americans and their

NATO allies were prepared for it. NATO's rearmament was under way, but its momentum was constrained by the slow delivery of U.S. equipment, by inflation, and by West European reluctance to convert consumer and export industries to the production of military hardware. The contractual agreements with Germany and the European Defense Community were on the horizon but not yet consummated, and the capacity of the Soviets to make another effort to capture German power was not yet exhausted. The specter of Turkish neutralism might have been eliminated, but the virulence of revolutionary nationalism in Iran and Egypt was not likely to be tempered by U.S. mediatory efforts or superficial changes in the command setup at the Cairo-Suez base. The San Francisco conference was a great success, but the long-term prospects of integrating Japan into a non-Communist Southeast Asia co-prosperity sphere remained bleak while the Viet Minh retained its appeal to the Vietnamese people and while Mao maintained his support of Ho.

U.S. officials believed that the Kremlin's recognition of its inability to win a global war against the United States momentarily restrained its adventurism. The United States, therefore, could take the offensive, engage in risk-taking of its own, continue its efforts to co-opt German and Japanese power, and strengthen the NATO alliance. But every move had to be carefully calibrated lest it precipitate the global war European leaders dreaded and U.S. officials hoped to avoid. Hence the war in Korea had to be waged in a prudent manner. But as the Truman administration firmed up positions of strength in the industrial heartlands of Europe and Asia, and as the U.S. rearmament program gathered additional steam, the United States would be able to move even more boldly in peripheral areas like the Middle East, Southeast Asia, and even Korea. U.S. officials now accepted the probabilities of future limited wars. They anticipated that these local conflicts could escalate to global warfare, and they began to plan for these contingencies.[167] The price of preponderance—the cost of linking Western Europe, Japan, and their dependencies to a U.S.-led orbit—was an unlimited arms race, indiscriminate commitments, constant anxiety, eternal vigilance, and a protracted cold war.

Preponderance Amidst Instability,

September 1951-January 1953

We can within the next several years gain preponderant power," Paul Nitze insisted to his State Department colleagues in the middle of 1952. That power could then be used in the pursuit of a hierarchy of objectives: first, "strength at the center"; second, "strength at the periphery"; third, "the retraction of Soviet power and a change in the Soviet system." "To seek less than preponderant power," wrote Nitze's assistants on the Policy Planning Staff, "would be to opt for defeat. Preponderant power must be the objective of U.S. policy." [1]

During their last year in office, Truman administration officials made considerable progress in strengthening the center, orienting the Federal Republic of Germany and Japan to the West, and thwarting centrifugal forces within the Western alliance. Although these achievements were not easy, the problems on the periphery were more challenging. In Southeast Asia, in the Middle East, and in Northwest Africa, the forces of revolutionary nationalism continued to gather momentum. As the British foundered in Egypt and Iran and as the French were beleaguered in Indochina, Tunisia, and Morocco, U.S. officials remonstrated over their allies' incompetence and grudgingly accepted growing responsibility for the preservation of order and the maintenance of friendly governments. "We would be in a very grave position," Averell Harriman insisted, "if we lose control of the raw material countries." [2]

Under any circumstances, preserving cohesion among the industrialized allies and linking the periphery to the center would have been formidable tasks. What made them so daunting in 1951 and 1952 was that the administration possessed so little political support at home. Savoring thoughts of revenge in the 1952 elections, Republicans savagely attacked the administration for its loss of China and for its strategy of fighting a protracted, limited war in Korea. They decried the Democrats' extravagant defense expenditures and denigrated their reliance on allegedly ungrateful European allies.[3] At the same time, Senate committee investigations discovered widespread improprieties, influence peddling, and bribery in the executive branch. Truman was not personally involved, but his loyalty to corrupt subordinates tarnished his image. In December 1951 his approval rating sank to 23 percent.[4] Yet he had to mobilize public opinion and congressional support for his military buildup at home, his assistance programs abroad, and his new initiatives regarding Japan, Germany, and the Eastern Mediterranean.

Engulfed by criticism, Truman and his top advisers continued to close ranks. After fulfilling his promise to serve as secretary of defense for a year, George Marshall, tired and sick, resigned his post in September 1951. Truman asked Robert Lovett to take his boss's job. Lovett, who had already been performing many of the most important tasks at the Defense Department, continued to labor in a spirit of harmony and friendship with Secretary of State Dean Acheson. Together, Lovett and Acheson also collaborated closely with Harriman, who was designated by the president to oversee the Mutual Security Program when Congress merged together most forms of economic and military assistance in October 1951. At the same time William Foster, who had been running the Economic Cooperation Administration during the last year of the Marshall Plan, moved to the Pentagon to become Lovett's deputy secretary. Several months later William Draper, Clay's economic chief in Germany in the early postwar years and the influential undersecretary of the Army in 1947–48, assumed Harriman's old job as special representative in Europe with responsibilities to coordinate all forms of aid. This rotation of the same men between the highest offices in the government demonstrated the commonality of purpose among top policymakers and served to unite discordant bureaucracies despite tactical differences that were bound to occur and reoccur. Acheson, Lovett, Harriman, Foster, and Draper knew one another well, shared the same objectives, and supported the president.[5]

Although Acheson and some of his assistants were under merciless attack by Senator Joseph McCarthy, the president continued to support and rely on his secretary of state. In turn, Acheson continued to be ably served by Nitze, Philip Jessup, Charles Bohlen, Dean Rusk, and Henry Byroade. Nitze and Bohlen worked on most of the critical National Security Council (NSC) papers outlining overall strategy. More often than not, they and their staffs were able to iron out differences with Joint Chiefs of Staff (JCS) and Defense Department officials. But since State Department policy now relied so heavily on the shadows cast by military power, on the actual military capabilities of the United States, and on the provision of military aid, the views of Lovett, Harriman, JCS chairman Omar Bradley, and Office of Defense Mobilization director Charles Wilson counted a great deal. When it came to matters of atomic policy, to which Acheson and Nitze attributed the highest significance, the recommendations of the JCS and of Gordon Dean's Atomic Energy Commission were also of critical importance.[6]

At the hub of U.S. national security policy in 1951–52 was the Pentagon. Lovett,

Foster, and Bradley were not the architects of policy, but they played a role in its formulation and were critical to its execution. They had to make extraordinarily tough decisions regarding the size of the atomic arsenal, the development of the mobilization base, and the allocation of funds among the services. Lovett ran a Defense Department that was undergoing enormous growth, waging a limited conflict in Korea, and preparing to fight a global war. He oversaw a bureaucracy that was tasked to support foreign policy commitments around the globe and that was helping to distribute vast amounts of military supplies to dozens of countries. Gifted with enormous administrative talent, a good sense of humor, and an unflappable disposition, Lovett worked closely with Bradley, reconciled organizational disputes among the services, and maintained cordial relations with Congress.[7]

At the top of the national security bureaucracy there remained Harry S. Truman. He now chaired most of the NSC meetings and participated in the discussions. He cajoled cabinet officers to reconcile their differences among themselves and to come to him with a united position. But rarely did he enunciate any clear-cut views or offer any suggestions on how to resolve complex problems. For the most part he approved recommendations worked out by his subordinates and gave them full responsibility for their implementation.[8]

Throughout most of his last fifteen months in office, Truman was a harassed, frustrated, irascible man. Pummeled by his domestic foes and defiant of the enemy, he supported positions that deadlocked the Korean armistice negotiations. He would not, for example, forcefully repatriate prisoners of war. But at the same time he restrained his military commanders from taking the offensive, overrunning North Korea, and bombing China. So while U.S. representatives at Panmunjom fumed at their superiors in Washington, there was no settlement and no victory—only protracted fighting in Korea and recriminations at home.[9] Truman accepted this legacy. In his view, it was the price that had to be paid for the pursuit of freedom and the containment of communism. It was a small price, he thought, compared to his successful efforts to reconstruct Western Europe, co-opt German and Japanese power, and establish a position of preponderant strength for the free world.[10]

Geopolitical Strategy, Military Planning, and the Communist Threat

By the autumn of 1951, U.S. national security goals were firmly in place. A new NSC paper, 114/2, reflected the broad consensus in the Defense and State departments. These goals were reaffirmed, even more lucidly, when preparations were made at the end of the year for the president and the secretary of state to meet with the newly elected leaders of Great Britain, Prime Minister Winston Churchill and Foreign Secretary Anthony Eden. In brief, the aims of U.S. policy were to build strength in Western Europe, Germany, and Japan, shore up the periphery in Southeast Asia and the Middle East, and pierce the Iron Curtain and roll back Soviet influence in Eastern Europe.[11]

Officials were aware that enormous risk-taking inhered in these endeavors. Their fears did not stem from thoughts that the Soviets were intending premeditated aggression. Neither Acheson nor the JCS saw evidence suggesting that the Soviets were building up forces with the intent of starting hostilities. Nor did Truman. Given the Kremlin's inadequate oil supplies, he did not think the Soviets would attack the United States.[12]

Yet the risks of war were great. "There will be grave risk of Soviet action," said one key position paper, "especially in situations in which our vital interests overlap those the Soviet rulers regard as interests vital to them." Clashes might arise over NATO's military preparations, the rearmament of Germany, or the development of overseas bases. But according to U.S. officials the greatest risks of war stemmed from instability, subversion, and local aggression in the Middle East and Southeast Asia. The Soviets, Acheson acknowledged, were not responsible for these situations, but they would seek to exploit them and to capitalize on the success of local Communist leaders. The Kremlin wanted to bleed the West, desiring to "force the maximum number of non-Communist countries to pursue a neutral policy and to deny their resources to the principal Western powers." [13]

It was the U.S. intention to make it "crystal clear to the Soviet leaders" that the United States would "resist aggression wherever it may occur." [14] The great question, of course, was whether the United States had the will and the capacity to convert this intention into practice. Throughout the Pentagon, officials complained that the United States still did not have sufficient military capabilities. Frank C. Nash, assistant to the secretary of defense for international security affairs, argued that further rearmament was essential to insure that military forces were "ready for use anywhere, at any conceivable moment, to insure the political and territorial integrity of the free nations." Karl Bendetsen, assistant secretary of the Army, acknowledged that the "bold offensive we must take [in Iran and Indochina] must be compounded of economic, political, social, psychological, and military programs." But "the decisive ingredient must be either military action or at least the will to risk the gage of battle." [15]

Nitze and his staff shared this view, and they provided Acheson with the advice he usually accepted on questions relating to military capabilities and diplomatic risk-taking. Aware that the Kremlin had recently tested two additional atomic bombs, Nitze worried that growing Soviet capabilities would influence perceptions of the military balance, which, in turn, would affect behavior during an escalatory cycle. Already this seemed to be happening in Korea, where the Truman administration hesitated to seize the offensive lest it bring on a wider war that neither the United States nor its allies were yet prepared to fight. Nitze deplored the self-deterring impact that Europe's conventional weakness exerted on the resolve of NATO nations almost as much as he remonstrated about the self-deterring impact that Soviet atomic weapons exerted on U.S. policymakers' predisposition to initiate atomic war. Would the United States, queried one member of Nitze's staff, still be able to "rely on threat, explicit or implicit, of global war to protect the periphery?"

Indeed the entire thrust of NSC 114/2 was to underscore the profound impact that Soviet atomic capabilities were likely to have on the Soviet penchant for risk-taking on the periphery: "If the Soviet rulers feel increasingly confident that their atomic capabilities may be sufficient to deter us from strategic atomic attack, they will probably feel increasingly confident about their ability to exploit their geographic position and preponderant ground and tactical air strength for local advantage without serious risk of general war." In contrast, Nitze stressed that America's ability to shore up the periphery and check Communist aggression would be immeasurably enhanced "provided we are willing to carry a war to the Chinese Communists and, if necessary, to the Soviet Union." [16]

The Soviets must not be allowed to think that U.S. officials would be self-deterred from taking the initiatives they deemed essential to achieve their objectives both at the core and on the periphery. Military planning for the United States and its allies was calculated to convince the Soviets that their armies could not overrun Western Europe and that their bombers could not cripple American industry or blunt a devastating retaliatory American attack. If the men in the Kremlin were convinced of these realities, they would have to acquiesce to U.S. initiatives to build strength at the center as well as to shore up the periphery. Moreover, if U.S. officials could convince themselves that the Soviets were convinced of these things, the United States would have the will and the determination to go on the offensive everywhere. And furthermore, if America's allies were convinced of these realities, they would have the resolve to follow the U.S. lead. [17]

Deterrence was not geared to a static and defensive national security posture but to a vigorous and forward-looking foreign policy. According to NSC 114/2, the objectives of U.S. policy were "both to develop a military shield as rapidly as practicable and to develop behind it the internal health and vitality of the free world." Nitze emphasized to Acheson that "Our relative preparedness for war must be taken into account in deciding what initiatives we can take, when we can take them, and how far we can afford to pursue them." In other words, if Western Europe could be defended, if the United States could retain a retaliatory (or second-strike) capability, and if it could possess military superiority at all levels of an escalatory cycle, then the Soviets would be deterred from interfering with the pursuit of U.S. goals. U.S. officials could proceed to rebuild, integrate, and rearm the industrial centers of Europe and Asia and safeguard critical markets and sources of raw materials on the periphery. If the Soviets proved obstreperous, if they or their satellites continued to support subversion or engaged in local aggression, then they might face a sequence of actions and reactions that could culminate in global conflict, the destruction of Soviet cities, and the eradication of the Soviet regime. [18]

■

The U.S. defense program, premised on the logic of NSC 114/2, was configured to deter an attack, support U.S. foreign policy, and wage war effectively if global conflict should erupt.[19] Toward these ends, Truman approved military expenditures totaling $51.2 billion in December 1951. His aim was not simply to maintain present strength but to build toward somewhat higher goals than had been envisioned the previous year. The new force goals contemplated an Army of 21 divisions, a Marine Corps of 3 divisions, an Air Force of 143 wings, and an active fleet of 408 combatant vessels, including 16 large aircraft carriers.[20] These objectives for fiscal year 1953 compared to forces-in-being in June 1951 of 18 Army divisions, 2.33 Marine Corps divisions, 87 Air Force wings, and 342 combatant vessels including 12 large carriers. It must be emphasized that this force structure had nothing to do with the exigencies of waging war in Korea. Fiscal year 1953 plans presupposed that the limited conflict would end by 30 June 1952.[21]

The armed services, of course, would have preferred even greater sums of money. Initial service programs called for expenditures of almost $73 billion. These sums exceeded any reasonable judgment of what Congress was likely to approve and of what Truman thought the country could afford.[22] With Lovett's hearty concurrence, the president called for a stretch-out of the full military buildup.[23] Nevertheless, Truman submitted a peacetime budget that was staggering in its military dimensions. Fully three-quarters of expenditures were earmarked for national security programs. Outlays for all other government programs were scheduled to decline from $21.2 to $20.3 billion. The government would spend approximately $11 billion more on the military services in fiscal year 1953 than in 1952. Estimating that the costs of combat operations in Korea were about $3–5 billion in 1952, non-Korean military expenditures would jump from around $35 to $51 billion. Modernization would not occur as fast as the services would have liked, but aircraft procurement would nevertheless increase from $5.8 to $11 billion, research would grow from $1 to $1.4 billion, and total expenditures on military hardware and construction would soar from $24 to $38 billion.[24]

U.S. troops were supposed to help provide a reasonable initial defense of essential Allied areas, particularly in Europe. Dwight Eisenhower sought to create a battleworthy force as quickly as possible. By the end of 1952 he wanted to have 25 combat-ready divisions and at least 25 additional divisions that could be mobilizeable within 30 days. His aim was to hold the enemy as far east as possible. Acheson and Harriman championed this forward strategy because they thought it would neutralize the 20–30 divisions that the Soviets had in East Germany. Their intent was to convince the Kremlin that it could not launch a surprise attack and conquer Western Europe. Before attacking, the adversary would have to mobilize. Even then, the Kremlin was not likely to achieve the 3:1 ratio in force levels that many analysts consider necessary to insure a successful offensive campaign.[25]

What most heartened the Defense Department was the development of new weapons that enhanced the effectiveness of NATO defense forces. Great importance was attributed to ground-fired atomic weapons, to the next generation of grenades and artillery shells, and to the nerve gas GB. This deadly gas, which would be available for "full-scale offensive" purposes in 1954, could be employed in bombs, artillery, mortar shells, rockets, or guided missile warheads. General Bradley wanted U.S. forces in Europe to be prepared to use chemical weapons on the same basis as they would use tactical atomic weapons—that is, first use would be permitted. Most encouraging as well for the overall defense of Europe was a new antitank vehicle, supposedly "armed with recoilless rifles capable of defeating any known enemy tank." [26]

Critical to the establishment of an effective European defense was U.S. air power. The Air Force was tasked to assist in the defense of the NATO area and to provide such aid to allies as was essential to the execution of their missions. Eisenhower planned to rely heavily on tactical air forces stationed in Europe as well as on naval air. Eventually he wanted sixteen carriers to operate in NATO waters. NATO infrastructure construction called for the completion of 51 airfields during 1951 and for the construction of another 53 during 1952 and 1953. U.S. Air Force plans also placed enormous importance on the rapid augmentation of tactical air wings. The total number of these wings increased from 9 to 24 during fiscal year 1951. By the end of 1952, 7 of them were deployed in Europe.[27] They were, moreover, increasingly composed of atomic-capable fighters and attack aircraft. So, too, were some of the new squadrons joining the Mediterranean fleet. The Defense Department estimated that the battlefield use of these atomic weapons would have a "devastating effect" on enemy air bases, troop concentrations, munition dumps, and transportation centers.[28]

Along with tactical air power, the Truman administration placed growing importance on the Strategic Air Command. There were 21 strategic wings on 30 June 1950, 28 on 30 June 1951, and 37 on 30 June 1952.[29] The growth of strategic air power, as Samuel F. Wells has shown, signified the emergence of the doctrine of massive retaliation. Massive retaliation in itself did not guarantee victory. If war should erupt, strategic bombing could not retard the Soviet advance into Western Europe because of the Russians' large reserves of munitions and equipment. But air attacks against Soviet oil refineries would make it virtually impossible for the Soviets to sustain a protracted conflict on many fronts. Moreover, the prospective devastation of Soviet urban-industrial centers would force the rulers of the Kremlin to question whether they really wanted to risk the destruction of the very foundations of their power.[30]

Both the defense of Europe and the capacity to retaliate massively depended on atomic warheads. In the autumn of 1951, the JCS, with Lovett's strong endorsement, called for a gigantic increment in the atomic stockpile.[31] Although the Munitions Board, the Office of Defense Mobilization, and the Atomic Energy Commission pointed out that the new program would strain the economy, Acheson endorsed the buildup of atomic weapons. The role they played in bulwarking Europe's defense, reinforcing deterrence, and inspiring future risk-taking made them irresistible.[32] On 19 January 1952, President Truman announced that the administration would increase the production of fissionable material. The new plants would cost $5–6 billion; subsequent operating costs would be about $550 million.[33] The construction program, when combined with the one launched the previous year, would generate a colossal growth in the nation's atomic stockpile from 650 warheads in 1951 to over 18,000 in the late 1950's.[34]

The military posture of the United States, focusing as it did on air/atomic capabilities, was designed to abet the defense of Europe and to support a strategy of massive retaliation. This military posture would create the shield behind which the United States could proceed with its efforts to gain strength at the center and to thwart instability on the periphery. This military posture would inspire the necessary risk-taking that inhered in a policy seeking to establish a position of preponderant power. Ultimately, this military posture might facilitate negotiations with the Russians from a position of strength. But for the present neither Truman nor Acheson wanted any such negotiations. They preferred to move forward with the initiatives they had launched in Europe, Japan, the Middle East, and Southeast Asia.[35]

Triumph and Travail in Western Europe

In the fall of 1951, U.S. policymakers wanted to rearm Western Europe, co-opt German power, and sustain the economic progress on which European political stability and social order depended. An integrated Europe, firmly implanted within an Atlantic community, would constitute a bulwark against Soviet aggression and preclude Soviet intimidation. It would inspire risk-taking on the periphery, where revolutionary nationalism and Communist subversion threatened the markets and raw materials that were deemed requisite for Europe's long-term viability. It would also foreclose the development of a third force in world affairs and perpetuate U.S. preponderance in the international arena.

After the tripartite talks in Washington in September 1951, Acheson eagerly sought to move ahead with the consummation of a new set of contractual arrangements with West Germany. Although the British, French, and Americans had agreed on the terms to be submitted to German chancellor Konrad Adenauer, they had not foreseen the obstacles that lay ahead. Adenauer himself remained strongly committed to integration with Western Europe and the Atlantic community. But many Germans did not share Adenauer's unqualified preference for integration over unification. They resented Allied efforts to control their foreign policy, oversee their relations with the Communist bloc, and intervene in their internal affairs in emergency situations. Kurt Schumacher's Social Democratic Party gave expression to their views and placed constraints on Adenauer's negotiating posture.[36] In turn, the chancellor adroitly used the domestic challenge to buttress Germany's case for equality within the European Defense Community (EDC). Germany, Adenauer insisted, must not be subjected to restrictions that did not apply to other EDC countries. Germany, he also said, must obtain explicit security guarantees from the

Americans and the British and should be entitled to membership in NATO. Furthermore, Adenauer claimed that the retention of U.S., British, and French troops in West Germany should no longer be based on the allies' wartime victory. Nor should Germany's defeat mean that it must renounce forever the right to regain lost territory beyond the Oder-Neisse. If he were to opt for the West, as he preferred to do, he had to be able to convince his domestic opponents that he was neither compromising long-term German sovereignty nor relinquishing hope for unification and territorial rectification.[37]

Adenauer's demands and German sentiment rekindled French anxieties. French foreign minister Robert Schuman was as good a European as was Adenauer. He believed that French security rested in the formation of supranational institutions, like the European Coal and Steel Community and the EDC, that would integrate Europe, limit German autonomy, and provide opportunities for French leadership. But the coalition governments to which he belonged held power as tenuously as did Adenauer's Christian Democratic Union. Schuman felt that France had to maintain some prohibitions on German paramilitary organizations, atomic research, and heavy-arms production. He worried that, after Germany rearmed, it would secede from the EDC, seek to unify Germany, and recover lost territory in the east. He believed in Adenauer's good intentions, but he had profound doubts about Adenauer's successors. He insisted that Germany must not be accepted into NATO, for once it had NATO's guarantees it would have less incentive to stay in the EDC. Within the EDC, Germany would have no general staff, no independent communications and logistics infrastructure, and no integrated air and land forces of its own. Within the EDC, Germany's military capabilities might still be monitored and constrained, its capacity for mischief and adventure circumscribed, and its ability to conduct an independent foreign policy constrained.[38]

But supranational institutions like the EDC placed constraints on the autonomy of all its prospective members. Even in France, the Gaullists could not abide the idea of an integrated European army that would dilute France's capacity to act independently. In Belgium, the Netherlands, and Luxembourg there were even more profound misgivings about the EDC. Like Britain, these countries did not like the idea that an integrated defense force might require a common budget and common taxation. Intent on maintaining their sovereignty, they seemed to prefer an Atlantic federation to a European community that might fall prey to French or German domination.[39]

The possibility that the EDC might founder before it even got started alarmed U.S. officials.[40] So, too, did the mounting financial woes of Britain and France. Rearmament drove up the cost of raw materials, created scarcities, forced European countries to increase their imports from dollar areas, and diverted resources from export industries. When Churchill and Eden visited Washington in January 1952, they acknowledged Britain's horrendous exchange situation and requested special help to overcome the shortage of steel. The French, too, faced an exchange drain and an inflationary spiral. Protesting the arms buildup, they adopted a new set of quotas and exchange restrictions, thereby jeopardizing the emerging network of liberal trade and payments agreements.[41]

A crisis of significant proportions loomed ahead. Acheson grasped the risks and opportunities. If plans for the EDC collapsed or if Britain and France retrenched on their defense expenditures, Western Europe would be susceptible to Soviet intimidation and U.S. risk-taking would be circumscribed by Europe's vulnerability. If, on the other hand, "we can get . . . things worked out in the next six to eight weeks," Acheson told the Senate Foreign Relations Committee, "I think the greatest changes are about to happen in Europe that have happened since the year 800 or the year 1000. They are really startling and dramatic changes." They amounted to the resolution of the centuries-old conflict between France and Germany and the unification of Western Europe.[42]

Acheson sought to mobilize British support for the EDC. He told Churchill and Eden that they had to use all their influence to get the Dutch and Belgian governments to join up with the French and Germans. In meetings with the ambassadors of these countries, the U.S. secretary of state patiently explained that the EDC was an instrument for locking Germany into a Western orientation. Consummation of the EDC, Acheson also emphasized, would engender even greater U.S. support for additional assistance and commitments.[43]

Acheson also sought to allay Adenauer's concerns regarding the contractual and EDC agreements. Opposing any overt discrimination against Germany, he thought the Germans should have the right to produce heavy armaments and munitions. He also wanted them to have the financial wherewithal to support the buildup of their forces. For years his policies had been heading in this direction. Although Acheson knew that progress was sometimes slow, he stressed that it was the direction that counted. Consequently, he appealed to the Germans to hold back on their desire to join NATO. This goal would eventually be realized. But to raise it now, Acheson believed, would be countereffective.[44]

Acheson was no less sensitive to French anxieties. Schuman wanted promises that the Americans would retain their troops in Germany, that the United States would not permit Germany either to secede from or to dominate the EDC, and that the United States would not champion Germany's admission into NATO. With compassion and cunning, Acheson sought to soothe Schuman's feelings, appeal to his ego, and encourage him to take the risks that inhered in a policy of German rearmament, European integration, and supranational institutions. "We have put our hands to the plow," he wrote Schuman, "and we cannot look back."[45]

At meetings in London and Lisbon in February 1952, the U.S. secretary of state made every conceivable effort to reassure Schuman without upsetting Adenauer. Acheson said that U.S. troops would remain in Germany and provide for its defense. Although these forces would no longer serve as an occupation force, the Germans would still not have the right to ask them to depart. Their continued presence would enable them to monitor developments, thwart indigenous unrest from the left or the right, deter German secession from the EDC, and forestall any German revanche.[46] At Schuman's request, Acheson also agreed that EDC military forces would be placed under NATO's supreme commander. At one and the same time this organizational setup allayed French fears about the autonomy of German units and reinforced America's leadership role within both the European and the Atlantic communities.[47] Moreover, should Germany threaten to secede from the NATO-EDC system, Acheson acknowledged that it would constitute a matter of grave concern and trigger the consultative mechanisms under Article 4 of the North Atlantic Treaty (NAT).[48]

Truman and Acheson also tried to ease the financial problems plaguing Britain and France as a result of U.S. rearmament goals. The president reminded Churchill that 1952 was an election year, that politics were ascendant, that Congress was on the warpath, and that his budgetary problems were enormous.[49] Yet he asked Congress to appropriate $6 billion for aid to Europe for fiscal year 1953. Knowing that Congress would object to economic aid, he stipulated that it be in the form of military end items and special defense assistance earmarked for the procurement of strategic raw materials. Through the offshore military procurement program and through expenditures on NATO infrastructure (like the construction of airfields), the United States also poured hundreds of millions of dollars into the continent. And at Lisbon, the Americans assented to a special assistance package for France totaling $600 million. This aid took cognizance of France's burdens in Indochina and provided assurances that France would have the capabilities to balance German power within the EDC.[50]

Simultaneously, U.S. officials agreed to relax some of the ambitious 1954 military objectives that had been established by NATO. Since the autumn of 1951, "the wise men" on the Temporary Council Committee (TCC), chaired by Harriman, had been studying whether NATO force goals fell within European political, economic, and financial capabilities. As a result of the delays in the shipments of U.S. supplies, shortages of raw materials, and inflationary pressures, the wise men decided to reduce 1954 NATO force goals by about nine divisions. Even then, the TCC realized that a $6 billion gap would exist between the anticipated four-year costs of their recommendations and the financial wherewithal and commitments of NATO members, including the United States.[51] Nevertheless, Acheson and Harriman were prepared to live with this gap. Although Bradley refused to stake his military reputation on the judgment that these Allied forces would suffice to defend Europe, he wholeheartedly agreed that the projected capabilities would constitute a real deterrent. General Alfred Gruenther, Eisenhower's chief of staff, and General Joseph McNarney, Harriman's assistant on the TCC, shared this view. U.S. defense officials realized as clearly as did their State Department counterparts that to ask the European allies to do more than they were capable of doing would be countereffective when so many diverse considerations were at stake.[52] As a result, at Lisbon the

NATO allies were able to reach agreement on force goals, defense expenditures, and levels of U.S. military assistance as well as on the reorganization of NATO's institutional mechanisms and the appointment of Britain's Lord Ismay as the first secretary general.[53]

At a cabinet meeting upon their return to Washington, Acheson, Lovett, Harriman, and Secretary of the Treasury John Snyder congratulated themselves on their performance.[54] In fact, they had capitalized on the courage, determination, and wisdom of Schuman and Adenauer, who struggled to pursue national ambitions through supranational mechanisms. Acheson's skill was in finding ways to resolve difficult issues. The U.S. contribution was in providing the marginal security guarantees and financial aid that made ultimate agreement possible. The result, U.S. officials hoped, would be the furtherance of their own goals: steady progress toward the co-optation of German power, the establishment of an effective military deterrent, and the development of a viable European economy.

■

Their optimism was short-lived. On 10 March 1952 the Kremlin presented a diplomatic note to the United States, Britain, and France asking for the early negotiation of a German peace treaty. Stalin called for the formation of an all-German government and for its direct participation in the peace negotiations. The Soviets proposed that all foreign troops be withdrawn from German territory within one year. No military bases would be permitted in Germany, and Germany would not be allowed to join an alliance that included any one of the World War II allies. No economic constraints would be imposed on Germany, and it could maintain its own limited armed forces. Its territorial boundaries would be those discussed at Potsdam. Basic freedoms and democratic rights would be guaranteed. Only those organizations inimical to democracy and peace would be barred.[55]

Whether Stalin's note offered an opportunity to unify Germany and reduce cold war tensions remains controversial. But the U.S. response is much easier to analyze. Acheson scorned the Soviet overture. In his view, Stalin had only one objective: to derail the contractual agreements and the EDC. The Kremlin dangled promises of unification, limited rearmament, unlimited economic opportunity, and free elections before the German people in order to sow distrust between them and the West. Acheson neither wanted to negotiate the status of an all-German government nor desired to discuss a peace treaty. But he realized that to dismiss the Kremlin's note completely would alienate German opinion just at the time that Adenauer needed to mobilize German sentiment in behalf of the EDC and the contractual accords.

Consequently, Acheson agreed with the British and the French that they should try to ascertain whether the Soviets would permit free elections. But he had absolutely no desire to explore whether Stalin really wanted to establish a unified, neutralized Germany. When George Kennan, the newly designated ambassador to the Soviet Union, visited the State Department on the eve of his departure, he found that no one had any interest whatsoever in talking to the Russians. Acheson wanted to co-opt German power, not haggle over German unity. A united, neutral Germany, acting as an independent entity or serving as a third force, had no appeal to the secretary of state. Such a Germany might seek to maneuver dangerously between Moscow and Washington or to dominate Europe. Even worse, it might eventually opt for a Soviet-German alliance.[56]

As Western governments exchanged notes with the Kremlin, Acheson grew impatient. From Paris, Bonn, and the Hague, he received reports of growing disillusionment.[57] He worried that the EDC and contractual agreements might unravel. Moreover, Acheson believed that the discord in Europe was weakening congressional support for his European policy, encouraging isolationist tendencies, and prompting cuts in appropriations for the president's mutual security program. If the impasse continued, Congress might adjourn before he could submit the new agreements to the Senate. With Robert Taft a likely Republican presidential candidate and the Democrats in confusion, the administration's handiwork might be undone by its successor. Acheson, therefore, urged his European counterparts to move quickly to sign the EDC and the contractuals.[58]

Throughout Western Europe, however, there was a great deal of complaining about U.S. policy. Fears abounded that U.S. actions in Asia might provoke a full-scale war. The Soviets exploited these apprehensions, declaring their own penchant for peace and portraying the Americans as bellicose. Europeans everywhere re-examined whether their own interests were being served by integrationist strategies and supranational institutions that linked their well-being and security to a transatlantic community and U.S. leadership. Many Germans still preferred unification over integration; many of the French still wanted unencumbered sovereignty and an independent army. Increasingly, the United States was criticized for advocating rearmament, championing supranationalism for others but not for itself, dividing Europe, and provoking the Kremlin. Such accusations were only half true because Schuman, Adenauer, and influential elites throughout Western Europe shared Acheson's vision of how to reconcile their sometimes divergent national interests while checking Communist advances.[59]

Acheson returned to Europe in late May 1952. When he arrived, he found that the same issues that had stymied progress during the winter had resurfaced. Several days of strenuous talks ensued. During these negotiations, Acheson sided with Adenauer's desire to end most forms of discriminatory treatment. He also readily agreed that a united Germany, if it were ever to become a reality, should have the same privileges as were accorded to the Federal Republic by the contractual agreements. In turn, the government of a united Germany would be obligated to extend the same rights to the British, French, and Americans. When the contractual agreements were signed in Bonn on 26 May, the most important of the documents was the "Convention on Relations Between the Three Powers and the FRG." It revoked the Occupation Statute and abolished the Allied High Commission. The Federal

Republic of Germany regained full control over domestic affairs, except in times of emergency, and considerable autonomy over its foreign policy, except that it could not expel Western troops, alter its territorial boundaries, conclude a peace treaty with the Kremlin, or jeopardize Western access to Berlin.[60]

More difficult than the final talks on the contractuals were the negotiations with the French. "We have gone through greater emotions than any mystery story could provide," Acheson wrote the president. At the last moment, the secretary of state recounted, the French looked directly into the eyes of their former enemy and got cold feet. The French feared that, while their own forces were tied down in Indochina, the dynamic and industrious Germans would quickly achieve a position of superiority within the EDC. Worse yet, the West Germans might establish an army and secede from the EDC. With the use of armed force, they might seek to unite their country, recover lost territory in the east, and endanger the peace of Europe. Hence, Schuman and the new French premier, Antoine Pinay, insisted on firm guarantees from the Americans (and the British); the Anglo-Saxons must not allow the Germans to secede from the EDC and embark on new adventures.[61]

Acheson doubted whether he could persuade the Senate to approve additional security guarantees. Instead, he and Eden signed a joint declaration expressing U.S. and British support of the supranational institutions that were being forged in Europe. Any action that threatened the unity of the EDC would be regarded as a threat to the security of the United States and would activate the consultative provisions of the NAT. Furthermore, the United States publicly reaffirmed its determination to keep its forces on the continent of Europe "having regard to their obligations under the North Atlantic Treaty, their interest in the integrity of the European Defense Community, and their special responsibilities in Germany." [62]

As part of the network of agreements worked out in Bonn and in Paris, the United States also signed a protocol to the NAT. This amendment obligated all members of the Atlantic alliance to guarantee the territorial integrity of the signatories of the EDC (and vice versa). In so doing the United States and Germany extended reciprocal commitments to one another without Germany formally joining NATO.[63] Adenauer would not have incurred the obligations and risks of rearming Germany and joining the EDC without such guarantees.[64] In practice, the protocol did not add a new obligation to the United States. U.S. officials had stated many times that they regarded the integrity of West German frontiers as vital to the security of the United States. Nonetheless, the formality of the guarantees underscored the price that had to be paid to co-opt German power for the Western alliance.

In a confidential meeting with the Senate Foreign Relations Committee, Acheson explained how the provisions of the contractuals and the EDC provided effective control over German power. German divisions would be raised; they would be placed under NATO's supreme commander; they would help defend the West. But German divisions would be integrated at the corps level with corresponding units from other EDC and NATO nations. Only at the corps level would there be supporting air, armor, logistics, and communications. Hence German units would not be able to leave the EDC easily and form their own national army. Moreover, the United States, Britain, and France would maintain their own troops in Germany. Under Article 5 of the convention with Germany, Acheson emphasized, these troops had the right to intervene in German domestic affairs if the democratic order were being subverted. And these rights, the secretary of state insisted, could not be altered by Germany in any treaty. According to Acheson, the critical provision was Article 7, Section 3. This provision, he said, had been modeled after the Platt amendment with Cuba. It meant that Germany's maneuverability was severely circumscribed. Unification could come only on terms acceptable to the United States and its allies; only if all of Germany were locked into the Western orbit; and only if U.S. and Western troops were permitted to remain. The purpose of the troops, moreover, was not simply to protect Germany or to fulfill commitments to NATO, but to defend the free world.[65]

Acheson hoped that the absorption of Germany into the EDC and the European Coal and Steel Community would create a European federation that would become economically viable and militarily defensible without U.S. assistance. But, for the present, West Germany remained bound by the EDC; the EDC remained subordinate to NATO; and, within NATO, U.S. influence remained preeminent. These complex arrangements, made possible by the willingness of the United States to extend its aid and incur military obligations, satisfied Adenauer's ambitions for German renewal, comforted Schuman's quest for French security, and established a configuration of power in the Old World that comported well with U.S. national security interests.

Despite the political acrimony that prevailed in the United States, and despite the rhetorical flourishes of Acheson's adversaries, the convention with Germany and the new protocol to the NATO alliance sailed through the Senate. For the Truman administration, the consummation of these agreements marked the triumph of its entire European policy. The new threat emanating from Soviet-directed world communism, Acheson wrote Truman, could now be contained with the cooperation of the former enemy.[66] As previously shown, the new threat did not stem from apprehension about an unprovoked and premeditated Soviet attack. The effective co-optation of German power, however, would advance the economic well-being of Western Europe, foster political stability, and forestall the resurgence of indigenous communism. The co-optation of German power would also mean that Germany would not be able to regain its autonomy, pursue unification, and operate independently of or contrary to the interests of the United States and its Western allies. And, the co-optation of German power would help establish an effective deterrent that would prevent Soviet intimidation or retaliatory counterthrusts should the United States choose to take provocative actions elsewhere.

■

Indeed the co-optation of German power was so important that Acheson was appalled in early June 1952 when the French and British showed signs of wanting to respond affirmatively to Stalin's follow-up note requesting a four-power conference on Germany. Acheson remonstrated that a meeting would alienate public opinion in the United States and jeopardize West German approval of the contractual agreements and the EDC. But once the U.S. Senate ratified the accords, Acheson acceded in part to the desires of Schuman and Eden. The three Western governments indicated a willingness to attend a four-power conference, but only if it focused exclusively on measures that were necessary to insure free elections in Germany. The restricted agenda evoked another burst of anger and recriminations from the Soviets. But their diplomatic notes sounded hollow. Increasingly, it seemed as if the Kremlin were acquiescing to the EDC and the contractuals. Only then did Acheson and his aides breathe a collective sigh of relief.[67]

Meanwhile, they watched West Germany's economic vitality with a mixture of awe and apprehension. Walter J. Donnelly, John McCloy's successor as high commissioner in Bonn, regarded the dynamism of Germany as the most striking development in Europe. When America's top European diplomats met in London in late September 1952, Germany's future was their first agenda item. In their view, the mounting strength of the Federal Republic posed a threat to the delicate balance with France and endangered future integration efforts. Germany, they concluded, would not remain divided forever. It would seek unification and expansion and "cast a shadow over eastern Europe." The challenge for the United States, said Leon Fuller of the Policy Planning Staff, was to use German strength to roll back Soviet power throughout the Eastern satellites without permitting the Germans themselves to establish a position of hegemony. David Bruce, now serving as deputy secretary of state, concurred: "There are risks in such a policy but any dynamic policy involves a risk."[68]

Kennan once again entered the debate, advocating negotiations with the Russians over the future of Germany. Although Soviet recriminations, contempt, and hatred were beyond anything that he had previously endured in Moscow, he nevertheless contended that the Russians felt encircled and defensive. The policy of building strength had created unbearable pressures. Now, it was time to bargain. He thought the Russians might be willing to strike a deal. And Kennan still assumed that a unified, neutralized Germany could contain Soviet power, expedite the integration of Western and Eastern Europe, and foster the dissolution of the two hostile blocs.[69]

Kennan's views received a fair hearing, but they were rejected. His colleagues in the State Department were not interested in creating a unified Europe that might fall under the hegemony of Germany and that might act as a third force between the Soviet Union and the United States. They suspected that Germany would have to be unified, but they wanted to find mechanisms to absorb all of Germany's power into the West European community. They were not certain how this could be done.[70]

They hoped, however, that by building NATO's strength they might someday be able to absorb a unified Germany and preclude the emergence of a third force. West European integration, declared the State Department, "requires concomitant evolution of well-knit larger grouping of Atlantic states within which new EUR [European] grouping can develop, thus ensuring unity of purpose of entire group and precluding possibility of EUR Union becoming third force or opposing force." In other words, the resuscitation of German strength demanded ever closer ties between the United States and the continent lest German power intimidate France and set back the very integrative mechanisms designed to co-opt that power.[71]

The specter of German power stymied French ratification of the EDC. The French did not want to join the defense community if they were to be in a position of inferiority. Because the war in Indochina had drained their strength, they called on the United States for additional assistance. But Congress cut U.S. aid by $125 million, causing the French to feel betrayed. They condemned American intrusions into their domestic affairs and fulminated against self-serving American suggestions that France rest content with a position of equality alongside the Germans in the EDC.[72]

Acheson was disappointed. He lamented the difficulties encountered by the European Coal and Steel Community and bemoaned the deferral of EDC ratification in France. But he did not place all the blame on the French. He admitted that NATO force goals were beyond French capabilities, and he realized that deliveries of U.S. military aid were greatly behind schedule.[73] At the beginning of 1953 he reacted with sadness when another reshuffling of the French government led to Schuman's departure from the foreign ministry. He was a "great Frenchman, an inspiring European, and a true friend," Acheson wrote.[74] But the U.S. secretary of state himself was about to leave office. There was little that he could do but encourage Jean Monnet and other European statesmen to persevere with their integrationist efforts and to rely on the United States to reciprocate.[75]

∎

Although Acheson was despondent, he had experienced great success in furthering U.S. goals. Western Europe's economic progress and political stability were being institutionalized. Indigenous communism was being thwarted. Thanks to Schuman, Monnet, and Adenauer, the Coal and Steel Community would overcome its initial birth pangs and transform the economic landscape of Western Europe. At the same time, the dollar gap was easing. Through offshore procurement and dollar expenditures on NATO infrastructure, Acheson and his colleagues found ways to funnel aid to European allies.[76]

Furthermore, German power was being co-opted for the West.[77] Soviet efforts to lure Germany eastward failed miserably. Adenauer demonstrated that he shared U.S. views regarding the place of Germany in a reconstructed Europe. In turn, the Americans displayed a readiness to restore Germany's rights as a sovereign power so long as it agreed to merge that sovereignty in a host of supranational institutions and bind itself to the Western alliance.

NATO was also gaining ground even though its force goals for 1954 were not to be realized and even though German troops had yet to be recruited. Worst-case scenarios, as war plans usually were, now presupposed that NATO forces could hold a position on the European continent. The Russians could no longer think that they could overrun the continent and harness European resources for a protracted war against the United States. Sufficient Western forces were in place, said Lord Ismay, to constitute a real deterrent. Bradley agreed.[78]

The shield was being created behind which Germany could be rearmed and fully integrated. When that occurred, the West would have progressed toward balancing conventional Soviet military strength in Europe. The United States could then pursue its goals elsewhere with fewer fears of Soviet counterthrusts against Eurasia's most important power center.

Success in Japan

Truman administration officials wanted to integrate Japan into the U.S. orbit almost as much as they desired to co-opt German power. When Acheson talked to Churchill and Eden in January 1952, he emphasized "the great shift in the world power situation [that would occur] if Japan with its military virtues and industrial capacity went over to the Communist side." But holding the Japanese within the Western camp seemed a formidable task because they appeared to have no ideological affinity with the West. U.S. officials were frightfully afraid that the quest for markets and the dependence on raw materials would entice the Japanese to establish commercial ties with Communist China. In pursuit of their self-interest, the Japanese might maneuver between the rival blocs. There were no legal mechanisms or quick fixes, said General Bradley, to "prevent the suicide of neutralism."[79]

At the same time, however, U.S. officials realized that they still had considerable leverage to influence Japan's long-term orientation. The United States had the money and power to help rebuild Japan's economy, finance Japan's trade deficit, and promote Japan's access to critical markets and raw materials. Moreover, the retention of bases and troops inside Japan afforded the United States great influence. As in Germany, these troops could intervene in emergencies to thwart either a leftist or rightist seizure of power. They could play a key role in training the Japanese National Police Reserve (JNPR) in peacetime and coordinating its actions in wartime. Procurements for U.S. forces could fuel the Japanese economy, establish a mobilization base, and stimulate the development of capital-export industries. But everything could backfire if the U.S. presence were overly intrusive, offended Japanese sensibilities, and constituted too overt an infringement on Japan's sovereignty.[80]

After the San Francisco conference in September 1951, the first task of U.S. officials was to secure Senate ratification of the peace and security treaties. There were significant hurdles to be overcome because Senator William Knowland convinced 56 of his colleagues to sign a resolution calling on Japan to deal exclusively with Chiang Kai-shek's regime on Taiwan. Recognizing that a tough legislative struggle lay ahead, Acheson asked John Foster Dulles to shepherd the agreements through the Senate. Dulles, in turn, maintained close ties with his Republican friends and sought to avoid Woodrow Wilson's humiliating experience with the Treaty of Versailles. By casting the agreements in terms of hard-nosed anticommunism, Dulles tried to revive the bipartisan coalition that had been so effective in 1947–48. He emphasized that the Japanese peace treaty ignored the Yalta agreements, disregarded Soviet claims to the Kuriles and southern Sakhalin, and eradicated the Kremlin's occupation rights in Japan.[81]

More important, Dulles took Senators H. Alexander Smith and John Sparkman to Japan. They were the highest-ranking Republican and Democratic members of the Senate Subcommittee on Far Eastern Affairs. Along with Dulles, they talked to Japanese prime minister Yoshida Shigeru. They warned that the reestablishment of Japanese ties with mainland China would alienate influential opinion in the United States. To ease the criticism that Yoshida was sure to face in his own country, Dulles did not insist that he acknowledge Chiang's claim to speak for all of China. But Dulles did demand that Japan abjure relations with the People's Republic of China, recognize Chiang's regime, and trade with Taiwan. Dulles crafted a letter that Yoshida was asked to sign and that Dulles used in the course of the Senate debate in the United States. The letter committed Japan to harmonizing its foreign policies with U.S. interests in Asia. The restoration of Japanese sovereignty, the historian John Dower has insightfully written, did not mean that Japan recovered "the capability of pursuing an independent foreign policy." [82]

The constraints on Japan were also evident in the negotiation of the Administrative Agreement. The purpose of the agreement was to specify all the rights, privileges, and prerogatives that were necessary to house, transport, and protect U.S. forces in Japan and to expedite military action in case of emergency. It was the indispensable complement to the broad generalizations of the security treaty. U.S. officials knew the Japanese would resent the Administrative Agreement. They wanted to delay ratification of the peace treaty and postpone the formal termination of the occupation until the Japanese agreed to it.[83]

Much of the acrimony concerning the Administrative Agreement revolved around Article 22. As originally drafted, Article 22 accorded the United States virtually unlimited authority to take action either when the international peace and security of the Far East were jeopardized or when the territorial integrity of Japan was threatened. Moreover, it provided for Japanese defense organizations, like the JNPR, to be placed under a U.S. commander when hostilities occurred or were imminent.[84] The Japanese negotiators complained that this latter provision might drive

Yoshida from office. Pleading for more ambiguity, they stated that Yoshida would assent to all the Americans wanted provided that it was not stated explicitly in the Administrative Agreement. The language sought by the United States, Yoshida's assistants maintained, would precipitate an avalanche of criticism and endanger the entire package of peace and security agreements.[85]

Dean Rusk had been put in charge of negotiating the Administrative Agreement. Taking the Japanese warnings seriously, he urged the State and Defense departments to show more sensitivity to Yoshida's political imperatives. "Japan," Rusk wrote, "has large, literate, trained industrious population, biggest industrial potential between Urals and US Midwest, and inevitable role leadership in Asia and is associate we cannot afford [to] lose by mishandling this important juncture of changing relationships." General Matthew Ridgway, commander in chief of U.S. forces in the Far East, concurred with Rusk's analysis. Rusk and Ridgway were not disagreeing with Washington's objectives. Their familiarity with public discourse in Tokyo made them conscious of the need for more adroit and ambiguous terminology. Once assured that Yoshida agreed with the substance of U.S. demands, Bradley, Lovett, and Webb accepted Rusk's suggestions.[86]

The bilateral security treaty and the more artfully crafted provision of the Administrative Agreement insured that the United States could station troops in Japan, maintain bases, and use U.S. military capabilities not only to defend Japan but to support U.S. policies throughout the Far East. In executive session hearings, Dulles stressed that, from Japan, U.S. power could be deployed against targets in Communist China or even Soviet Russia. According to General Bradley, the United States "need not wait for an actual attack on Japan to occur before taking action." U.S. forces could strike preemptively "at the source of aggression or threat to international peace and security in the Far East." Aware of these advantages and of the importance of co-opting Japanese power, the Senate in March 1952 ratified the Japanese peace treaty, the bilateral security treaty, and the two security agreements with Australia and New Zealand and with the Philippines. On 28 April, the occupation formally ended.[87]

■

Lest the accords with Japan unravel in the future, military officers continued to insist on retention of the Ryukyus and especially of Okinawa. Yet U.S. diplomats in Japan and State Department officials in Washington worried that severing the islands from Japan would be a permanent sore point in Japanese-U.S. relations. Once again, there was no fundamental dispute over goals because the State Department acknowledged that the United States must maintain strategic control over the islands, should they be returned to Japan. Disputing tactics, Ridgway and the JCS insisted that military considerations should predominate because the matter had not become politically volatile inside Japan. Military planners still assigned great importance to Okinawan airfields because their geographic location permitted U.S.

aircraft to reach targets throughout Asia and the southern Soviet Union. Bradley did not want to risk the possibility that Okinawa would be restored to Japan, Japan would opt for neutrality, and Americans would be expelled from a critical point in the defense perimeter.[88]

For U.S. military officials, however, retention of the Ryukyus was not nearly so important as the rearmament of Japan. According to the JCS, Japanese forces could buttress U.S. efforts to defend the "Japan area" and could lend support to the U.N. mission in Korea. U.S. plans called for the JNPR to be expanded into a balanced ten-division national ground force of 300,000 men. There would be complementary naval and air capabilities, with the Air Force eventually comprising 27 squadrons. Bradley hoped that in times of emergency these forces would come under U.S. command. Moreover, to the extent that they were capable of defending the home islands, U.S. troops could then be redeployed to fulfill other missions.[89]

U.S. defense officials were eager to train, recruit, equip, and finance Japanese forces. These goals conflicted with the wishes of most of America's former allies in the Pacific region as well as with the provisions of the Japanese constitution. Financing Japan's rearmament, moreover, also placed a heavy burden on the U.S. budget. Initially, in fact, the fiscal year 1953 budget did not provide for the support of Japanese forces. When informed of this fact, General Ridgway sent a blistering message to Washington. The potential consequences, he warned, would be "nothing less than catastrophic to the vital interests of our country." The rearmament of Japan, he insisted, was the most important long-range project in the Far East. "For each dollar expended . . . the United States can purchase more security through the creation of Japanese forces than can be purchased by similar expenditures in any other nation in the world, including the United States."[90]

Lovett interceded and allocated $300 million for Japan's rearmament. The appropriations were buried in the Defense Department budget. If they had come from the Mutual Security Program, as they should have, they would have attracted public notice and evoked considerable criticism.[91] In August 1952 the U.S. Army quietly turned over heavy equipment to the JNPR. At the same time the U.S. Navy made arrangements to loan 18 patrol frigates and 50 landing craft to the Japanese.[92] By the fall of 1952 the projected costs of Japan's rearmament had skyrocketed and the fiscal planners in the Budget Bureau had become agitated. They complained that anticipated expenditures for the equipment and training of Japanese forces had grown from a few hundred million dollars to over $1 billion.[93]

Yoshida was not eager to build Japanese forces. He did not think that rearmament had much public support in Japan, and he was afraid that it would constitute a heavy drain on the Japanese economy.[94] Robert Murphy, the first post-occupation ambassador, reproached Yoshida for his attitude. Yet Murphy remained sensitive to the prime minister's desires. Elections in Japan were scheduled for late 1952, and Yoshida was worried about them. The overriding goal, Murphy insisted, was to align Japan with the United States. Yoshida appeared indispensable to this objective. If Yoshida wished to focus on the development of the Japanese economy, Murphy advised that U.S. officials work with him.[95]

It was Japan's industrial potential, after all, that accounted for its vital importance in the cold war. U.S. officials looked to the Japanese economy to help maintain the West's industrial-military superiority over the Communist bloc. Office of Defense Mobilization director Charles Wilson believed that "The worsening world situation and the continuing shortage of many essential materials and supplies in this country make it essential . . . to utilize Japanese industry as a supplemental source of supply for United States requirements." Lovett and Foster wanted Japan to produce a large portion of the weapons and equipment required for the Japanese armed forces, for U.S. military assistance programs in Southeast Asia, and for U.S. armed forces in the Far East. Japanese military production, the JCS insisted, must complement that of the United States.[96]

Accordingly, Ridgway sought to establish an organization whose mission was to "integrate Japan's industrial capacity into the U.S. Industrial Mobilization Program."[97] At the end of 1951 the first orders were placed in Japan for the production of ammunition for the JNPR. Moreover, the State Department agreed that, once the peace treaty went into effect, Japan could produce military hardware not only for itself and for Korea but for export to other countries as well.[98]

Officials were altogether aware that Japan's industrial renewal required a comprehensive program. It had to be coordinated with the production of raw materials throughout Southeast Asia, the development of intraregional trade, and the provision of long-term U.S. financial and economic aid. Otherwise, Japan might be sucked into the Communist orbit and its enterprise used to strengthen Communist China.[99] After much discussion, Defense and State Department officials in the United States came up with a list of 400 items that Japan could not sell to China. Yoshida immediately assented to about 280 of them. As a result, Japanese trade with China in 1952 amounted to 0.04 percent of total exports and 0.7 percent of total imports. Yoshida accepted the controls because the possibilities of restoring a lucrative trade with Mao's China seemed uncertain at best and because it was the price that he had to pay for Japan to have access to U.S. trade, aid, and loans.[100]

The constraints placed on Japan's trade with mainland China made it all the more necessary for Japan to have access to markets and raw materials elsewhere. A new U.S. intelligence report in May 1952 reminded policymakers that, in 1941, Japan's trade with China had amounted to 17 percent of Japanese imports and to 27 percent of Japanese exports. China had supplied more than 50 percent of Japan's total coal imports, about 25 percent of its iron ore imports, and 75 percent of its soybean imports. Officials now expended enormous energy trying to discern where Japan could find alternatives for these imports and where it could earn the foreign exchange to pay for them. Japan's trade deficit for 1953 was projected to be about $575 million. Currently, this deficit was covered by the personal spending of U.S. troops in Japan as well as by the U.S. government's support for Japanese security forces, its payments for the construction of military infrastructure, and its procurement of military supplies for Southeast Asia. Through these various means, Japan would receive about $770 million. Everyone, however, acknowledged that these earnings were transitory.[101]

For U.S. officials, whether they were at Foggy Bottom, the Pentagon, or the CIA, the answer to Japan's economic dilemmas resided in Southeast Asia. U.S. goals in Japan and in Southeast Asia, Bradley insisted, were "inseparably related." If Southeast Asia were lost, Japan would have to form an "accommodation with the Communist-controlled areas in Asia." So thought Eisenhower, Lovett, Harriman, and Acheson. In fact, the Truman administration's final NSC paper on Japan was infused with the theme of integrating Japan's industrial core with the periphery in Southeast Asia. By acquiring iron ore in Malaya and the Philippines, purchasing petroleum from Indonesia, and buying rice and sugar in Thailand, Burma, Korea, and Taiwan, the Japanese would not have to spend scarce dollars for the high cost of U.S.-produced goods. These South and Southeast Asian countries might also constitute viable markets for the sale of Japanese machinery, metal products, and chemicals, which were the fastest-growing components of Japan's export sector.[102]

■

The future might still be uncertain, but by the end of 1952 U.S. officials could look with pride on their accomplishments in Japan. They had negotiated successfully for the retention of bases. They were planning for the growth of Japan's defense forces, arranging for their incorporation into a U.S. command in times of emergency, and utilizing Japan's industry to augment the free world's military buildup. Furthermore, the stationing of U.S. troops in Japan meant that the United States had the capacity to intervene in emergency situations. Should the economy falter and domestic unrest ensue, U.S. officers could consult with Yoshida and thwart insurrections from either the right or the left. U.S. officials were forever worried about leftists who might orient Japan eastward and about rightists who might maneuver Japan between the blocs. By insuring Japan's future economic prosperity, the United States hoped to establish a mutually beneficial partnership with Yoshida's Liberal Party and thereby discourage any temptation for Japan to embark on an independent foreign policy.

As in the case of Germany, U.S. officials hoped to co-opt Japan's economic potential and latent military power. If this occurred, the Communist challenge would be checked. Neither Peking nor Moscow would be able to benefit from Japan's great industrial potential. The balance of power in Asia would be insured, and U.S. preponderance in the international arena would be promoted. But just as Germany's future depended on its integration into a West European economy that was itself dependent on markets, raw materials, and dollar earnings in the Middle East, Africa, and Southeast Asia, so, too, Japan's future seemed to depend on its successful integration into a regional economy with Southeast Asia. Yet stabilizing the periphery turned out to be much more difficult than merging the industrial core into a U.S.-led capitalist economy.

Stalemate in Southeast Asia

According to U.S. policymakers, Indochina was the key to holding all of Southeast Asia. If Indochina were lost, the Communists would easily take over Burma. The Thais, in turn, would bend with the wind and reorient themselves toward the Soviet bloc. Although, from an exclusively military perspective, an effective defense might be mounted at the Isthmus of Kra in Malaya, policymakers discounted its efficacy. As the threat was not likely to be overt aggression, the significance of the loss of Indochina was not so much military as psychological. Because governments throughout the region were so fragile and because their loyalty to the West was so suspect, it was believed that a Communist victory in Indochina would have a bandwagon effect. "In the absence of effective and timely counteraction," concluded the NSC in its most important paper on Southeast Asia, "the loss of any single country [and Indochina appeared the most likely candidate] would probably lead to relatively swift submission to or an alignment with communism by the remaining countries of this group." [103]

If the Viet Minh were to be defeated, U.S. diplomats and military analysts agreed, the French had to hold Tonkin. Although the Viet Minh now controlled much of the countryside in northern Vietnam, French forces still controlled the key cities of Haiphong and Hanoi. Moreover, General Jean DeLattre's skill, tenacity, and enthusiasm had reinvigorated the morale of French troops and had generated some progress in the development of the indigenous armies of Vietnam, Laos, and Cambodia. Although there was little likelihood that the French and their allies could rapidly suppress the enemy, the prospects of a Viet Minh triumph in the near future did not seem very likely either.[104]

If, however, the Chinese Communists escalated their assistance to the Viet Minh, sent in volunteers, or invaded Indochina, the French might have to withdraw. It was precisely this scenario that worried U.S. officials in the autumn of 1951. At a meeting of the NSC on 19 December, top policymakers rehashed the many reports and rumors concerning an imminent Chinese invasion. Acheson urged the senior staff of the NSC to expedite its new study of Southeast Asia with particular attention to what the United States and its allies should do in case of Chinese intervention.[105]

The thought of engaging China in another war in Indochina impelled officials to reappraise the importance of Southeast Asia to overall U.S. national security interests. Throughout the winter of 1951–52, Acheson's most trusted assistants in the State Department and Lovett's top civilian and military advisers in the Pentagon studied this issue. Despite a great deal of friction over means and procedures, there were no organizational differences over goals. Indeed, the new assessments imbued old conclusions with greater force. Southeast Asia had to be held because it was vital to Japan's recovery, because its raw materials were vital to Western rearmament efforts, because its loss would have a terrible domino effect throughout the Middle East and North Africa, because it was vital to the security of the defense perimeter, and because its seizure or co-optation by the Communist adversary would allow for the interdiction of critical transportation routes from the Pacific to the Middle East. Loss of Southeast Asia, Bohlen categorically asserted, would mean the loss of the cold war. Nitze's charts demonstrated that the rice and raw materials of this region were absolutely indispensable to countries like Japan. Core and periphery were interdependent. If Indochina fell and if it had a domino effect on its neighbors, Japan's industrial heartland might eventually be co-opted. Indeed, all the Western industrialized nations who needed the tin, rubber, and petroleum of the region would be weakened.[106]

State and Defense Department officials agreed that Communist China had to be deterred from interfering in Southeast Asia. The idea was for the Western powers to issue a warning to Peking. If it were ignored, military action would have to be taken. The JCS insisted, however, that the United States should not join any combined command with the British and French. The French had to retain primary responsibility for the fighting in Indochina. U.S. ground forces would not be deployed there. Instead Bradley, Army Chief of Staff Joseph Collins, Air Force Chief of Staff Hoyt Vandenberg, and Admiral William M. Fechteler, the new chief of naval operations, stressed that U.S. air and naval power should be used directly against Red China itself. They knew that the British and French might object to this decision. Given the risks and complications, the JCS admonished civilian officials to decide the basic question of whether or not the United States should retaliate against Communist China should it intervene in Indochina.[107]

This JCS viewpoint exasperated Nitze and Bohlen. They wanted to defend Indochina just as much as did the men in the Pentagon. But they claimed that such an important political decision could not be made without additional JCS efforts to analyze the military costs and consequences of intervention. The chiefs retorted that they needed to know whether the administration was prepared to enlarge domestic military production, cut civilian consumption, and divert military aid from other regions of the world to Southeast Asia. They also maintained that they could not assess the costs of intervention until the State Department offered its political judgment on whether war with Communist China would precipitate conflict with the Soviet Union. And if such a contingency arose, the chiefs said they needed to know whether the United States would be able to count on the support of its NATO allies. Such inquiries infuriated Nitze because they delayed concurrence on a decision that everyone on the NSC seemed agreed on. Indochina simply had to be safeguarded; its loss would be disastrous, particularly because of its impact on Japan.[108]

While State Department and JCS officials feuded with one another, Acheson, Lovett, Bradley, Harriman, and Snyder voyaged to London and Lisbon to work out the final arrangements for the EDC, the contractual agreements with Germany, and the funding for NATO's rearmament. There, they learned that the French were far more concerned with financing the war against the Viet Minh than with defending Indochina against a Chinese invasion. In January 1952, DeLattre had died of cancer, and the war again seemed like a quagmire. The drain on French resources was becoming intolerable to French officials. If they were to maintain a position of leadership or at least equality within the EDC, they needed to have twelve divisions in Europe. They could not fulfill this goal and sustain the war in Indochina at the same time. Schuman and his colleagues hinted that they might opt to negotiate or withdraw. They could only stay if they received more aid from the United States; they could only stay if U.S. officials acknowledged that France was not waging a colonial war but undertaking its share of the worldwide struggle to defeat communism.[109]

Acheson and Lovett agreed to provide France with additional aid. Their decision was not determined by the imperatives of their European policy, as many astute writers like Robert Shaplen have claimed, but by their conviction that the West could not afford to lose Indochina. Their aim was to keep the French fighting "until the Viet Minh is liquidated and therefore no longer an effective instrument of the Kremlin and Peiping." "What we have been trying to do," Acheson explained, "is to encourage them [the French] and help them do everything we can to keep them doing what they are doing, which is taking the primary responsibility for this fight in Indochina, and not letting them in any way transfer it to us." Increased assistance to sustain the French effort made sense so long as the French would not negotiate. Nitze was willing to spend $500 million to achieve this goal; Lovett talked about $1–1.5 billion a year.[110]

Upon their return to Washington, Acheson and Lovett decided that they had to focus more attention on the threat within Indochina. The Chinese Communists could support about 150,000 troops in Indochina. But neither the intelligence analysts nor the policymakers now thought that the Chinese would intervene directly. If they did, they would be "pasted," to use Acheson's phrase. The primary task was to reassess the internal situation in Vietnam and to determine what could be done to strengthen the position of the French and the governments of the Associated States of Vietnam, Laos, and Cambodia. Yet Acheson recognized that the Chinese Communists might continually increase their aid to the Viet Minh, making it impossible for the French to restore stability. So the question of Chinese intervention could not be totally ignored. The senior staff of the NSC was instructed to determine whether a warning should be issued to the Chinese, what Chinese actions should be encompassed by the warning, and what steps should be taken to enforce the warning should it be disregarded.[111]

Closer scrutiny of conditions in Indochina provided no grounds for optimism. Bao Dai's government appeared inept, corrupt, and indifferent to the needs of the masses. But Vietnamese officials insisted that they could never capture the loyalty of their people if the French continued to control the economy and bar the establishment of representative institutions. Even the buildup of Vietnamese forces failed to enhance the reputation of the Vietnamese government. Most of the battalions were still led by French officers, and their military actions were dictated by the French high command. In March 1952, U.S. intelligence experts concluded yet once again that most Vietnamese mistrusted "French motives more than they recognize any danger from the Communists."[112]

As a result, U.S. defense officials placed ever greater stress on getting rid of the French. The secretaries of the Army, Navy, and Air Force wanted the French to cede total independence within a reasonable period of time. They called for the establishment of a broader-based government that would include genuine nationalist elements. They urged a host of political, economic, and land reforms. They wanted U.S. military advisers to play a greater role training Vietnamese forces. And they concluded that the French should remain only so long as it was necessary for the United Nations to put together an international program to end the civil war and safeguard the Associated States from Communist takeovers. Bradley and Lovett conveyed these views directly to Acheson and Truman at a White House meeting on 19 May.[113]

There may have been more sensitivity to internal developments in Indochina at the highest levels of the Pentagon than there was in the State Department. Acheson and his advisers received ample warnings from Edmund Gullion, U.S. consul general in Saigon, about the ramifications of continued French interference in the internal affairs of Vietnam. But the top men at the State Department feared that, if the French were pressed too hard, they would simply abandon their effort. In Acheson's view, moreover, the French were not to blame for the problems inside Vietnam. Emperor Bao Dai, Premier Tran Van Huu, and their associates had demonstrated their incompetence and lethargy again and again. "So far as we can see," Acheson maintained, "France has already given them [the Vietnamese] more autonomy than they have seen fit to use."[114]

The secretary of state, of course, supported reforms. But the retention of French assistance was regarded as a higher priority. In the view of Acheson and his advisers, those Pentagon officials who called for the retrenchment of French power and spoke in favor of Vietnamese independence ignored the problems of defending the area should the French pull out. The aim of the State Department was to keep both the French and their Vietnamese allies fighting. For Acheson the answer was to accelerate the buildup of the indigenous armies of the Associated States. If these forces grew quickly, the French would be able to shift their troops to Europe. At the same time, the Vietnamese armies would embody the reality of nationhood, afford prestige to Bao Dai's government, and help preserve internal security. With renewed vigor, Acheson sought additional military aid for Vietnam. Even more money was needed for native armies than had been requested, he told one senator after another.[115]

More aid alone, however, did not satisfy French concerns. When Acheson met with Pinay, Schuman, and Minister of National Defense René Pleven in May 1952, they pressed the U.S. secretary of state to acknowledge that the French effort was justified "by the political and strategic importance of that part of the world" in the contest with international communism. Acheson did not hesitate to reassure them. The war in Vietnam, he agreed, was no more self-interested than the U.S. effort in Korea and the British struggle in Malaya. All three battles were vital to the protection of the allies' mutual security.[116] Acheson then invited the French and British to issue a warning to the Chinese to deter their intervention in Indochina. The admonition would apply to forms of covert as well as overt assistance to the Viet Minh. Moreover, the warning, Acheson said, must not be a bluff. The United States was prepared to fight. Although the JCS would not deploy U.S. troops to the Indochina theater, the United States was ready to retaliate with air and naval power against China itself. Air power might be used against Chinese lines of communication; naval power might help to blockade the Communist mainland. Would the British and French cooperate?[117]

Eden and Schuman demurred. The British foreign secretary felt that he had already cautioned the Chinese not to intervene in Southeast Asia, and the French foreign minister worried that a maladroit signal might actually provoke the Chinese Communists. Whether or not they issued a warning, the British and French emphasized that any retaliatory efforts against the Chinese should be localized. Expanding the war to China proper would not necessarily prove efficacious. Moreover, they feared that their actions against China might embroil the Soviet Union and lead to global conflict.[118]

The British and French wanted more time to think through their positions regarding a warning and retaliatory action. When Acheson returned to Europe in late June, however, he was eager to reach agreement on these matters. If the Chinese attacked, or if their covert actions threatened French control of the Tonkin delta, the West had to be prepared to do something. The options, Acheson readily admitted, were not good. It would be best to warn the Chinese in order to deter them. But if they disregarded the warning, action was imperative. Moreover, the secretary of state insisted that Vietnam could not be defended in the Indochina theater. There must not be another Korea. China had to be struck where it hurt; China had to be blockaded. The object, however, was not to destroy or overthrow the Chinese government; that might trigger Soviet intervention. Instead, military force had to be used prudently in order to avoid a war with the Kremlin while compelling the Chinese to cease their aggression in Indochina or anywhere else in Southeast Asia.[119]

Eden and Schuman still had strong reservations. U.S. bombing in North Korea did not reassure them about U.S. self-discipline. Acheson emphasized that there would be no bombing in areas of acute sensitivity to the Soviets. He acknowledged, however, that the Chinese had a considerable air force that might have to be attacked wherever it was located. Eden and Schuman wanted to mitigate all risks of Soviet embroilment, yet they acknowledged that Indochina could not be abandoned to the Communists. The foreign ministers set up an ad hoc committee to define the ends and means of Allied policy should they have to use force against the Chinese. Nitze persuaded the French and British that the goal was to get the Chinese to abandon their aggression. In turn, he agreed that actions provocative to the Soviets must be avoided. Initially, the retaliatory steps would be confined to the place of aggression—for example, Indochina—and to support areas in Chinese territory.[120]

The military chiefs were angered by Nitze's deal with the British and French. They maintained that the military action envisioned by the tripartite accord was far too restrictive. The Chinese would never cease their aggression if the bombing were limited to support areas in China. The chiefs did not advocate using overt military force to overthrow Mao's regime, nor were they eager to provoke the Kremlin. But they were willing to take greater risks. Nitze, in fact, understood their misgivings. His concessions to the British and French were expedient. The important point, he emphasized, was that they had agreed to compel the Chinese to halt their aggression. They had also acknowledged that military action need not be confined to Indochina. Eventually, they would come to see that bombing China's lines of communication would not suffice to achieve the goal. Gradually, the bombing would be expanded.[121]

For the next several months, State Department and JCS officials wrangled incessantly about the terms of reference for military talks with Britain, France, New Zealand, and Australia. Bradley and his colleagues would attend such a meeting, as the State Department wished them to do, only if military officials were free to recommend whatever actions they deemed necessary to force the Chinese to cease their aggression should they attack Indochina or escalate their covert assistance. When these talks finally occurred in Washington in October 1952, the participants reaffirmed the vital importance of Indochina to Western security interests. The British, French, and U.S. military officials, however, continued to squabble over the efficacy of prospective military actions. The French wanted to mount a local defense in Indochina and requested additional deployments to achieve this task. The British did not think the allies had sufficient capabilities in the region to attack lines of communication and industrial targets inside China. Ultimately, however, the military representatives compromised with one another. They agreed that a combination of local defense, sea blockade, and air attacks against all suitable military targets in China constituted the best means of forcing the Chinese to cease their aggression.[122]

■

These deliberations, however, seemed tangential to the real threat emanating from the internal weakness of the Vietnamese government and the nationalist appeal of the Viet Minh. In June, Bao Dai appointed Nguyen Van Tam as the new prime minister. Nguyen had been minister of the interior and head of the police. He was renowned throughout Vietnam for his long-term association with the French and for his zeal in fighting Vietnamese nationalists. The "name of Tam," wrote the U.S.

consul in Hanoi, "is anathema in Tonkin." Instead of a national unity government, Gullion reported from Saigon, "we got bogus coalition headed by one whom many people regard as French hatchetman." [123]

Yet the Americans decided they had no choice but to work with Nguyen and with Jean Letourneau, the French minister of the Associated States and high commissioner in Indochina. When Letourneau visited Washington in June 1952, Assistant Secretary of State John Allison prodded him to introduce additional reforms and to relax French controls over Vietnam's economic life. He was told that in the next fiscal year the United States would further increase its aid by $150 million. The money was to be used to augment the indigenous armies. Letourneau was eager to cooperate, though he did not believe that a military victory was possible. [124]

High-ranking State Department officials were relieved that Letourneau was not about to negotiate with Ho Chi Minh. When he asked for additional transport planes and for U.S. crews to repair them, he was given what he requested. [125] Some officials still carped about French policies, but Acheson and his top advisers were now convinced that the greatest threat to U.S. interests in Southeast Asia rested in the possibility of a French pullout. If this should happen, the Viet Minh would seize power immediately. When Philip Bonsal returned from a ten-day trip to Indochina and took over the office of Philippine and Southeast Asian affairs in October 1952, he wrote that "the present Viet government depends for its existence on French armed strength. It will have no effective strength if the French depart leaving the Viet Minh militarily as strong as it is at present." Homer Byington, director of the Office of West European Affairs, shared the same view. [126]

A cruel dilemma faced Acheson and his colleagues. If the French departed, Ho and the Communists would take power. If the French stayed, there would be a protracted military conflict. A stalemate, however, worked to the advantage of the Viet Minh because the very presence of the French made it impossible for Ho's opponents to appear as nationalists. The only solution to the dilemma was to increase the U.S. commitment.

It was hard to admit that the long-established policy of relying on the European powers to decolonize in an orderly manner without losing hold of the periphery had failed. It was even more difficult to contemplate how the U.S. government could generate the cash, the forces, and the public support for a more interventionist policy in Indochina and Southeast Asia. Yet as they prepared to leave office, Acheson, Lovett, and Harriman reasserted that the United States must seek to build strength in Indochina and elsewhere in the Far East. The United States had to extend more economic and military aid; it had to train additional Vietnamese forces; it had to finance an even larger percentage of the French military effort; and, it had to be ready to retaliate against the Chinese Communists should they overtly seek to overrun Indochina or covertly abet a Viet Minh takeover of Tonkin. The United States, Acheson insisted, had to have more freedom to act militarily in the region. Truman agreed. Notwithstanding what happened in Indochina, the United States had to reserve the option to intervene in Indonesia or Malaya should indigenous unrest or external pressure make it imperative to do so.[127]

For the immediate future, the outlook in Indochina was for continued stalemate; the prospects throughout Southeast Asia were for indefinite instability. But the region could not be allowed to slip into the Communist orbit. Its resources were too valuable for Japan, for Western Europe, and for the entire free world. The Americans were not eager to assume additional responsibilities. But if the French and the British could not co-opt the region for the West, the United States would step in. Believing their country was not stigmatized by an imperial heritage, U.S. officials assumed they could do a better job rallying anti-Communist nationalists to the cause of the free world.

Instability in the Middle East and North Africa

Policymakers faced similar challenges in the Middle East and Northwest Africa. In these regions, seething unrest was translating itself into nationalist demands for control over the symbols and substance of power. The Iranians wanted to nationalize their oil resources; the Egyptians wanted to take over the British base in the Suez Canal zone; the Moroccans and Tunisians wanted to determine their own political future. U.S. officials feared neutralism and revolutionary nationalism. They suspected that the new breed of revolutionary nationalist leaders would be either outmaneuvered by local Communists or enticed into the Soviet orbit. Truman administration officials wanted to bolster British and French influence, but they felt increasingly impelled to step in and take initiatives of their own.[128]

In order to orient the Middle East westward in peacetime and to defend it in wartime, policymakers decided to bring Turkey into NATO and to establish a Middle East Command (MECOM) in Egypt. Turkey was expected to serve as the linchpin between Western Europe and the Middle East. It would belong to NATO but its forces would be placed under the Supreme Allied Commander, Middle East (SACME), who was to be a British national.[129] When General Bradley visited Turkey in October 1951, however, he found Turkish officials unalterably opposed to this scheme. They were willing to participate in MECOM, but they would not assign their forces to a British commander and they insisted on playing a role in the defense of Europe. Anything less, they believed, would affront their national prestige, endanger their internal political position, and weaken their claims for military assistance.[130]

Reconfiguring Turkey's relationship to NATO and MECOM, however, was a minor problem compared to the difficulties of eliciting Egypt's cooperation. The Egyptians showed no interest at all in MECOM. On 8 October 1951, Egypt's Wafd government unilaterally abrogated both the 1936 treaty with Britain and the 1899 Sudan Condominium Agreement. According to Egyptian law, this meant that the British presence was no longer legal. Egyptian workers refused to work for the

British, railroad lines stopped transporting British supplies, and customs officials held up British goods going to British bases. Demonstrators protested the British presence in Ismailia and Port Said. Even more ominously, Egyptian guerrilla and paramilitary forces began harassing British soldiers. In self-defense, British officers cordoned off the canal zone, seized key bridges, took over the Suez customs house, and sought control over nearby towns and cities.[131]

Washington was well apprised of the incendiary situation that was arising. Jefferson Caffery, U.S. ambassador in Cairo, grasped the pent-up frustrations of the Egyptians, their hatred of the British, and their quest for unencumbered sovereignty. He worked closely with the British ambassador, Sir Ralph Stevenson, and urged negotiations and concessions. Yet Caffery saw the entire drama unfolding in an East-West prism. The canal zone, he wrote the Department of State in a typical dispatch, may "explode with a loud bang at no distant date, an explosion with an eventual chain reaction of occupation revolution eventual Commie domination." His views and reactions were confirmed by Burton Y. Berry, the deputy assistant secretary of state for South Asian, Near Eastern, and African affairs. Berry visited Egypt in early December 1951 and was awed by the situation he witnessed. "The British are detested," he reported to a high-level meeting of State Department and military officials. "The hatred against them is general and intense. It is shared by everyone in the country. The result is that the position we desire in Egypt, the area we want for bases, and the influence of Egypt in the Arab world in support of our interests are denied to us." The Soviets, Berry concluded, were taking a low-key approach. But "Egypt is rapidly going down the drain and . . . will soon be lost unless the trend is soon reversed." [132]

Acheson cautioned the British to act prudently. But in general he supported their determination to stay in the canal zone until a viable alternative, like the MECOM proposal, had been accepted by the Egyptians. The Suez base could not be abandoned without gravely endangering Western security interests. "From both the political and military points of view," Bradley wrote to Truman, "the maintenance of efficient Allied bases in the general Suez area in peace or in war is a vital necessity." An intelligence study reevaluated the unique attributes of the Suez base: it was sufficiently removed from the Soviet orbit to be secure from a surprise attack; it could be reinforced to resist an invading force; it could support long-range bombers heading for strategic targets inside the Soviet Union; it could protect traffic through the canal; and it had an enormous infrastructure and dozens of airstrips. "No other base in the Middle East–Eastern Mediterranean area," concluded the CIA, "either individually or collectively, could compensate for the loss by the West of control of this base, even if such other bases were further developed." [133]

When Churchill and Eden came to Washington in January 1952, Acheson carefully reviewed the situation in Egypt with them. He stressed that conditions were ideal for Communist agitators: impoverished masses; a small, incompetent, and corrupt ownership class; and a foreign presence against which agitators could stir up emotions. Urging Eden to make concessions, he recommended that the British acknowledge the nominal suzerainty of the Egyptian king over Sudan if, in turn, the Egyptians promised not to intervene with the existing British setup in Sudan and not to jeopardize Sudanese self-determination. Acheson also prodded Eden to modify the MECOM concept in order to make it more palatable to the Egyptians. "What we have been trying to do," Acheson explained, "is to get to a point where we could again raise these [MECOM] proposals with the Egyptians and get them to agree to an international control of these critical areas instead of a purely British one, control in which Egypt would participate and in that way take the heat off that problem." [134]

■

Even more ominous than the situation in Egypt, however, was the mounting unrest in Iran. The British and Iranians were at an impasse. Mohammed Musaddiq had seized the Abadan refinery and expelled remaining British technicians. He wanted not only to nationalize the Anglo-Iranian Oil Company but also to remove the British from operating control. For him and his diverse followers in the National Front, these actions represented true national liberation, the recovery of national autonomy, and the expression of national independence. [135]

The British, however, did not want to negotiate with Musaddiq. They preferred either to overthrow him or to force a settlement favorable to the oil company. They continued to embargo exports to Iran. They froze Iranian dollar exchange held by the Bank of England, threatened lawsuits against any company that purchased Iranian oil, and carried on extensive covert operations. They assumed they could displace Musaddiq, install a more pliable Iranian in the prime minister's office, and then negotiate a satisfactory deal. They were firmly convinced that anything less than a favorable settlement would be "catastrophic." [136]

British intransigence alarmed U.S. officials. Musaddiq came to the United States in October 1951 to plead Iran's case before the United Nations. He chatted with the president and talked to Acheson. Musaddiq and Assistant Secretary of State George McGhee met at least twenty times to discuss the terms of a possible Anglo-Iranian agreement. [137] As a result of these conversations, U.S. officials decided that they should try to work with Musaddiq. He was not a Communist, Acheson said, not a liberal, not a reformer. He was a rich, old, Middle Eastern landowner inspired by nationalist impulses and determined to kick the British out of Iran. Moreover, he had enthusiastic support from newly emerging groups in the cities, including workers, shopkeepers, teachers, students, government employees, and some religious zealots. No matter how much pressure the British exerted and no matter how much they covertly manipulated the internal political scene, no successor would have the political freedom to sign an agreement along the lines the British demanded. The British, Acheson told Eden, had to face the facts. [138]

If they did not—if they continued their economic pressure and resisted negotiations—then two possibilities might follow. According to one scenario, Iran would
gradually collapse economically. Discontent and disillusionment would multiply.
The Communist Tudeh Party would grow in strength and seize power. The other
possibility was that Musaddiq would increase his economic ties with the East and
try to sell oil to the Soviet bloc. The Kremlin did not have the means to purchase
or transport much oil. But any sale of oil would force the Truman administration to
invoke the Battle Act, cut off military assistance, and pull out its military mission,
thereby eliminating its principal source of influence. Musaddiq would not want Iran
to become a Soviet satellite, but he would not be able to control events. He would
become the prisoner of his own actions or would be toppled by the growing strength
of his Tudeh opponents. Gradually, the Soviets would gain control over Iranian oil
and augment their capabilities to wage protracted war. Lovett and Bradley warned
Acheson of the dramatically adverse consequences that would flow from Soviet
co-optation of Iranian resources.[139]

Notwithstanding the forceful case Acheson made, the British would not budge.
They believed that the consequences of their pressure would not be as grave as
the Americans suggested. They thought they could find a successor who would be
more amenable to their interests. They wanted an agreement that left the British
with operating control over the oil and a satisfactory division of the profits. If they
could not get these terms, they wanted the Iranians to pay not only for the physical
property they seized but also for the profits that would be forfeited over the lifetime of the concession. Otherwise, other nations would move to appropriate British
investments.[140]

Acheson sympathized with these considerations. Although he agreed with
Lovett and Bradley that preventing Iran from slipping into the Soviet orbit was
the most important objective of U.S. policy, he could not ignore the impact of
an unfavorable agreement on America's worldwide investments and on the operations of the international petroleum industry. Capitulation to Musaddiq might entice
the Saudis, the Venezuelans, and the Colombians to emulate Iran's behavior. So
although Acheson discouraged military action against Musaddiq and warned of
the dire consequences of a protracted negotiating stalemate, he was not willing to
undermine British economic pressure. He told Musaddiq that U.S. financial assistance would be forthcoming only after the Iranians reached a settlement with the
British. The British, however, were given an additional $300 million to help them
deal with the indirect dollar losses they experienced as a result of the shutdown of
the Abadan refinery.[141]

Churchill and Eden, Acheson concluded, still had primary responsibility for
the fate of Iran. If they insisted on applying pressure, the United States would
defer, albeit unhappily, to their leadership. Perhaps it would lead to the peaceful replacement of Musaddiq with a more pliable Iranian leader. But should the pressure

backfire and generate mounting support for the Tudeh, U.S. officials counted on the British to have the political will and military wherewithal to stymie a Communist takeover.[142]

■

Developments in Egypt, however, continued to intensify U.S. doubts about whether the British could in fact be relied on to maintain a leadership role in the Middle East. Almost immediately after Churchill and Eden left Washington, fighting flared in the canal zone. When the local police commander in Ismailia would not surrender, the British shelled his headquarters and killed more than 50 Egyptians. As news of the massacre spread, rioting erupted in Cairo on 26 January 1952. Tacitly encouraged by some Wafd leaders, mobs burned and looted a large part of the capital city. When the violence subsided, the magnitude of the destruction appalled everyone. King Farouk quickly dismissed the Wafd ministry and named a new government to restore order.[143]

Acheson was angered. Deploring the "splutter of musketry," he monitored developments closely. In February another change in the Egyptian government caused him to worry even more about the breakdown of public order and the machinations of Communist agitators. Acheson pushed the British harder than ever to negotiate an agreement with the Egyptians. Moreover, he now realized that all foreign troops might have to be withdrawn from the canal zone. If the Egyptians cared for the bases in peacetime and promised unrestricted access to the airfields in times of emergency, Acheson thought a satisfactory deal should be struck.[144]

Eden, however, would not budge. He would not allow the Egyptians to intimidate him. He would not remove all British forces. And he would not place the defense of the great Suez base strictly in the hands of the Egyptians. Nor would he compromise the Sudanese people's right to self-determination. An ominous impasse persisted.[145]

At the same time, French reactions to Tunisian demands for self-government deeply troubled Acheson. The French offered some limited reforms. But when the followers of Habib Bourguiba rejected them, these people were arrested. "The most significant result of French policy of force," wrote U.S. intelligence analysts, "has been greatly to stimulate Tunisian nationalism. . . . The nationalists have become progressively more intransigent and have come to demand complete and immediate independence."[146]

U.S. officials wrung their hands in frustration. They did not know exactly what to do. The unrest in Tunisia, they feared, might spread to Morocco, where the U.S. Air Force was constructing a base complex that exceeded almost anything that had existed during World War II. Acheson begged Schuman to understand that timely concessions would win over local elites and co-opt the emerging nationalist movement. Home rule did not mean that the French need relinquish control over the foreign affairs and defense policies of North African states. "The U.S. Government," Acheson emphasized, "believes that continuation and strengthening of the French position in North Africa is basic and essential. Without France in North Africa that territory would disintegrate into quarreling, small, weak states, affording ideal terrain for communism and extreme nationalism. It was the U.S. desire to act in every way possible to strengthen the position of France in North Africa and that is unequivocally the policy of the Government." [147]

Much as they hoped to benefit from an orderly decolonization process in North Africa and the Middle East, U.S. officials increasingly realized that this strategy was faltering. Both the regional specialists in the State Department and the members of the Policy Planning Staff warned Acheson that the influence of Britain and France was waning. Neutralism and revolutionary nationalism were on the rise, and U.S. association with former colonial regimes was self-defeating. They thought the United States should establish linkages with local elites and indigenous military leaders in order to guide political and social change. They wanted the United States to offer military assistance. Unlike the JCS, State Department officials were willing to assign small numbers of U.S. troops to the region to demonstrate American interest. Local elites could then cooperate with the United States without having to bear the onus of collaborating with representatives of the detested former colonial powers. The overriding goal, according to the NSC staff, was "to guide, if possible, political developments in the area in ways which will involve least danger to Western interests and maximum assurance of stable non-communist governments." Acheson did not know if these recommendations would work. But he agreed that "somehow or other we must assume the leadership and manage to bring the British and French along with us on the road to a solution." [148]

Nitze, more than anyone else, insisted that U.S. goals could no longer be accomplished through close association with the British. In April 1952 he began criticizing the MECOM concept. It was linked too closely with the British, who were in disrepute everywhere in the Middle East. The Egyptians and the Turks would never put their forces under a British command. Rather than discard MECOM, Nitze wanted to redesign it. Through it, the United States might send aid to the region and deploy military advisory teams. But MECOM could not be relied on to defend the Middle East. Based on a flawed military strategy, it focused too narrowly on defending the Suez base. It sacrificed the immense advantages now afforded to the West by its alliance with Turkey. [149]

Nitze proposed a forward strategy. In addition to safeguarding the strategic air base and communications network at Suez, Nitze wanted to protect the petroleum fields in Saudi Arabia, Bahrain, and Kuwait. According to the most recent military studies, possession of this oil was necessary to wage a protracted conflict against the Soviet Union. Moreover, the forces required to defend Persian Gulf oil were not large. Some British and commonwealth divisions could be of great help; so would U.S. air and naval power. If the Turks offered six additional divisions, Nitze maintained that the West could mount an effective defense in Iran. Pakistan, as well, could be brought into the military arrangements. Over a three- or four-year period, the United States could build strength in the northern tier. This strategy would still call for the cooperation of the Arab states in a Middle East Defense Organization (MEDO), but would make the United States less dependent on British policy in Egypt.[150]

Defense officials pondered this new strategy. They acknowledged that the British could no longer be relied on to hold the region for the benefit of the West. Moreover, they liked the MEDO idea as a substitute for MECOM, and they were willing to extend direct military aid to Arab countries like Egypt. Bradley furthermore agreed that Turkish troops and Anglo-American air power might stymie Soviet attempts to seize the Persian Gulf oil fields. But he doubted whether the United States could assign any of its own troops to the region in wartime or peacetime. Collins stressed that the State Department should persuade the Australians and New Zealanders to earmark forces for the Middle East. In his view, that was the main purpose of the ANZUS alliance.[151]

■

The strategy, however, depended on maintaining Iran in a Western orbit. And developments in that country were more and more foreboding. In July 1952, the shah replaced Musaddiq with Ahmad Qavam. This action precipitated an immense outpouring of anger. Rioting flared; violence erupted. The shah's own power seemed at risk. After three days he felt compelled to reappoint Musaddiq. Musaddiq then moved against his opponents. He forced the shah's powerful twin sister to leave the country. He cut the royal budget, appointed himself war minister, and persuaded the Majlis to delegate greater powers to him than anyone in Iran had enjoyed since Reza Shah Pahlavi in the 1920's. But, aware of the rivalries within the National Front, the Tudeh Party maneuvered for power. Castigating Musaddiq's failures, the Communists prepared to capitalize on the unrest that resulted from Britain's economic pressure and Iran's inability to sell its oil in international markets.[152]

The turmoil in Iran accentuated U.S. anxieties. The CIA worked diligently to undermine Tudeh influence and to establish linkages within the National Front coalition. In collaboration with the Iranian army, U.S. military advisory teams designed plans to defend the shah and thwart a Tudeh seizure of power. But Truman, Acheson, Lovett, and Bradley realized that these actions might not overcome the deleterious consequences of British political intransigence and economic pressure. Increasingly, they now agreed that the United States might have to act independently of the British. The political current, Lovett wrote Undersecretary of State Bruce, "is running swiftly toward even more extreme and irresponsible anti-Westernism and dangers of a coup d'état, whether by the communists alone or in combination with the National Front, are more serious than had been believed." [153]

In August 1952, the secretary of defense began pressing the State Department for a change in U.S. policy. Heretofore the United States had acquiesced to British economic pressure, presupposing that the United Kingdom would be willing to intervene in the event of a seizure or threatened seizure of power by the Tudeh Party. "Since the policy was first approved," Lovett explained, "the British have been expelled from Iran; they have been compelled to concentrate in Egypt the major portion of their military forces in the Middle East; the shah has dissipated whatever independent influence he once possessed; and the climate of political opinion in Iran has become so harsh that it is doubtful that British military intervention there could be effective." Lovett argued:

The risks of continuing our present policy have become unacceptable, and . . . it must be discarded in favor of a policy of action to prevent Iran from falling to communism. Such a policy would involve a willingness, if necessary, to displace British influence and responsibility in Iran as has occurred in Greece, Turkey, and Saudi Arabia, which, it is recognized, might carry risks of damaging close relations with Britain. It would involve a willingness to accept additional political, economic, and military commitments, and to provide immediate economic assistance. It would involve measures to help Iran to secure markets for her oil and start up her oil industry, under arrangements which provide reasonable compensation to the British for the loss of their property. Every effort should be made to obtain British cooperation in this policy, but with or without British cooperation I believe we must move promptly along these lines before it is too late.[154]

Encouraged by Lovett, Acheson now urged the British to break the negotiating impasse. Between August and October, the Iranians, Americans, and British exchanged a series of notes. But Musaddiq would compensate the British only for the physical property he was expropriating, whereas Churchill and Eden demanded reimbursement for the loss of future profits as well. As the diplomatic exchanges got nowhere, the British stepped up their efforts to overthrow Musaddiq. When the Iranian leader learned of their machinations, he arrested the conspirators and severed all diplomatic relations.[155]

Lovett insisted on action: "The strategic necessities of the situation . . . require that we accept our responsibilities and act promptly and, if necessary, independently of the British in an attempt to save Iran." He wanted to provide immediate economic assistance. He called for measures to reactivate Iran's oil industry and to recover markets for its oil. By taking these political and economic initiatives, Lovett hoped to avoid outright military intervention. But he also prodded Bradley to devise contingency plans to intervene in Iran should the Communists try to take power. Furthermore, he urged Acheson and other top officials to put aside the antitrust case against the major international oil corporations. In fact, he looked to these firms for assistance in marketing Iranian oil.[156]

Acheson did not like the idea of risking a rift with the British. Yet he recognized the logic of Lovett's arguments. When he met with President-Elect Eisenhower on 18 November 1952 to discuss transition issues, he talked about the "grave disintegration" of the Iranian economy and social structure. The Tudeh Party would not be able to seize power immediately. But if nothing were done to channel events in another direction, a crisis would develop that might indeed necessitate the use of military force. The United States, therefore, had to begin to act independently of the British.[157] A few weeks later the State Department announced that it would not object if U.S. companies purchased oil from Iran. At the last NSC meetings of the Truman administration, Acheson also supported the case for dropping antitrust action against the major oil corporations.[158]

More important, Acheson approved a new NSC paper on Iran that fundamentally reoriented the U.S. position in the Middle East. Noting that "the United Kingdom no longer possesses the capability unilaterally to assure stability in the area," NSC 136/1 called on the United States to prepare to take military action to support the Iranian government against an attempted coup. High-level officials grasped that the new policy represented a reversal of the Defense Department's previous reluctance to make a major policy commitment in the Middle East because of inadequate military capabilities. Now the United States was taking from Great Britain "primary responsibility for political and military action to forestall Iran's falling to communism." The NSC also authorized plans for "the eventual inclusion of Iran in any regional defense arrangement."[159]

■

While U.S. officials were furrowing new ground in their policies toward Iran, a similar reorientation was taking place in their attitudes toward Egypt. At virtually the same time in July that demonstrators in Tehran were compelling the shah to restore Musaddiq to power, military officers in Cairo forced King Farouk to abdicate. In September 1952 a new government headed by General Mohammed Naguib informed Ambassador Caffery that it wanted to establish friendly ties with the United States, join the Middle East Defense Organization, and work out a base agreement. The U.S. and British military establishments, Naguib said, could have access to the Suez base in wartime, and their civilian technicians could maintain it in peacetime. The British only had to agree in principle to evacuate the canal zone and to begin withdrawing troops.[160]

Acheson was favorably impressed. The best hope for keeping Egypt in the Western camp, he told Harriman, was to strengthen Naguib. Seeking to break the Anglo-Egyptian impasse, Acheson volunteered to mediate the Suez base dispute. As part of a general agreement, moreover, he was willing for the United States to extend military as well as economic aid to the Egyptian government. He pressed the JCS to support a $100 million assistance program for the Arab states. Reformist military regimes seemed to be the wave of the future. By offering military aid, the United States could enhance Western influence with the new military rulers of countries like Egypt (and Syria).[161]

President Truman agreed with Acheson's overall assessment. He decided, however, to leave the matter in the lap of the incoming Eisenhower administration. Jewish groups in the United States bitterly opposed military assistance to Egypt. Let the new president, Truman thought, face the flak.[162]

■

In Egypt as well as in Iran, the United States was now prepared to take the initiative and, if necessary, act independently of the British. Although Acheson, Lovett, and Harriman agreed that the United States had to assume increased responsibility for the maintenance of internal stability throughout the Middle East, the bulk of their attention turned to Iran.[163]

The northern tier had become the new frontier of America's vital security interests. By promoting stability in Iran and championing a settlement of the oil dispute, officials hoped to accommodate the peacetime petroleum needs of Western Europe and the financial exigencies of Great Britain. By thwarting the Tudeh Party, policymakers sought to prevent their Soviet adversary from gaining opportunities to assimilate great new reservoirs of petroleum in peacetime that would enormously enhance their capabilities in wartime. By linking Turkey, Iran, and Pakistan to a regional alliance system, Nitze and his planners were aiming to protect the oil fields of the Persian Gulf and the air bases at Suez and Dhahran with only a limited use of U.S. troops.[164]

In view of the erosion of British influence in the Middle East, U.S. officials hoped to establish linkages with old and new elites in the region. Acheson would support them with military assistance and economic aid. Nitze would entangle them in a web of defense alliances bulwarked by the United States. If local leaders resisted U.S. stewardship, they might become the targets of covert action.[165] If they bolted the Western camp, their countries might be subject to military intervention.[166] In these diverse ways, Truman administration officials sought to overcome the forces of instability, co-opt revolutionary nationalist movements, and insure U.S. preponderance. But when they departed from office, in neither Iran nor Egypt had they experienced much success.

The Arms Race, the Soviet Union, and America's Strategic Vision

Throughout 1952, U.S. policymakers agonized over developments in Indochina and the Middle East. Good progress was being made in rehabilitating, integrating, and rearming the industrial heartlands of Eurasia. But long-term success in Western Europe, West Germany, and Japan would depend on their having access to the markets and raw materials in the Third World. If the periphery were lost, the industrialized West might have to augment its trade with the Eastern bloc, thereby eroding the cohesion within the U.S. orbit, indirectly benefiting the Soviet economy, and abetting the Kremlin's long-term strategic capabilities. The rearmament effort did not cause but greatly accentuated the perception of Western dependence on overseas supplies of raw materials.[167]

In their final reappraisal of overall strategy, Truman administration officials revealed their immense concern with losing parts of the periphery to the adversary. Indigenous unrest, civil wars, and regional strife raged throughout the Far East, the Middle East, and North Africa. The underdeveloped world was wracked by poverty, seething with unrest, and yearning for autonomy and independence. Nationalist leaders wanted their countries liberated from British and French control and were susceptible to the Kremlin's anti-Western propaganda. Within Third World countries, old and new elites clashed with one another as they contended for power and sought external allies. U.S. policymakers acknowledged that solutions were costly and fraught with peril; yet they could not be avoided. If one country were lost, it would supposedly have a bandwagon effect, and neighboring countries would fall outside of the Western orbit like dominoes on a playing board.[168]

Korea illustrated all the frustrations of dealing with a country on the periphery. At the end of World War II, the left had sought power, had been repressed in the south by the Americans, and had been assisted in the north by the Soviets. Two Koreas emerged, each inspired by a virulent nationalism, each intent on destroying the other and unifying the country under its own aegis. Whether deemed a civil war or a local conflict, Americans then perceived North Korean aggression as Soviet-inspired. China's intervention reinforced this view. As the armistice negotiations dragged on through the spring and summer of 1952, U.S. officials became increasingly exasperated. Although the Communist Chinese and North Koreans neither mounted a major new ground offensive nor dared assault the U.S. sanctuary in Japan, the United States expanded the bombing of North Korea, attacked hydroelectric plants, knocked out power installations on the Yalu River, and destroyed oil refineries perilously close to Soviet borders.[169]

Lovett and his military and civilian colleagues at the Pentagon wanted to do still more. So did Acheson. In September 1952, State and Defense Department officials agreed that the United States should summarize its negotiating position, suspend talks, and accelerate the pressure.[170] General Mark Clark, Ridgway's successor as commander of U.N. forces in Korea, submitted plans to strike airfields in Manchuria, bomb industrial targets in China, and impose a naval blockade.[171] Truman was not quite ready for this. Yet he, too, fantasized about issuing an ultimatum to the enemy. "You either accept our fair and just proposal," he jotted in his diary, "or you will be completely destroyed." [172]

But ruminate and remonstrate as they did, U.S. officials neither expanded the air war into China nor imposed the naval blockade. In her fine book, Rosemary Foot attributes this restraint to domestic political considerations. Other factors, however, played an even more important role, especially calculations about prospective Soviet reactions to hypothetical U.S. military initiatives. If the United States tried to blockade China, for example, intelligence analysts and policymakers believed the Soviets might respond by escorting merchant ships into Port Arthur and Dairen or by waging mine and submarine warfare. Likewise, U.S. officials assumed that the Soviets might react to U.S. attacks on lines of communication inside China by augmenting their role in defending Chinese airspace. Kennan warned that "We must not over-rate the price [the Soviets] would pay to avoid war, particularly if forced to act under threat." Other high-level career foreign service officers concurred, estimating that the Soviet reaction to attacks inside China "would undoubtedly . . . risk . . . a spiral of action and reaction which would result in world-wide conflict." [173]

Once the escalatory cycle began, the Soviets might at some point decide to overrun Europe or launch a surprise attack against the United States. Consequently, U.S. attention was riveted on the growing number of atomic bombs in the Soviet stockpile and the alleged Soviet capacity to deliver them to U.S. targets. Intelligence experts now estimated that the enemy possessed 50 atomic bombs with yields of 30–70 kilotons. It was predicted that the Kremlin would have 100 such bombs by mid-1953; 190 by mid-1954; and 300 by mid-1955. By mid-1955 the adversary might also have thermonuclear weapons. To deliver the bombs, the Soviets were believed to possess almost 900 TU-4 aircraft; by mid-1955 they might have as many as 1,100. Admittedly, the TU-4 was obsolescent and could reach the United States only on one-way missions. But according to military analysts' worst-case scenarios, the Russians could inflict 9 million casualties in 1953 (12.5 million in 1955) and paralyze 33 percent of U.S. industry (66 percent in 1955). By damaging U.S. productive capabilities and by blunting as much as a quarter of America's delivery capabilities, the Soviets could gain time to overrun Western Europe, co-opt its industrial capabilities, and create the conditions for a military stalemate.[174]

Estimates of this sort weighed heavily on U.S. officials. They knew that any Soviet preemptive attack would not destroy their ability to retaliate. They also realized that the U.S. superiority in atomic warheads would grow in future years. But policymakers increasingly suspected that:

The controlling relationship in the atomic equation appears not to be that of stockpiles to each other, but rather the relationship of one stockpile, plus its deliverability, to the number of key enemy targets, including retaliatory facilities, which must be destroyed in order to warrant an attack. If this latter relationship is controlling, then it follows that the Soviets may achieve what is, in their judgment, a level of atomic strength sufficient to warrant the risk of an all-out surprise attack, even though this level may be inferior—in absolute terms—to the then existing atomic strength of the United States.[175]

In a crisis, the Soviets might decide that they possessed enough atomic weapons to gamble on a preemptive attack. But U.S. officials did not think that the enemy wanted to make this decision. Truman, Acheson, Lovett, and Bradley accepted Bohlen's analysis of Soviet intentions. The Soviet Union, in Bohlen's view, was "fundamentally and unappeasably hostile to any society not susceptible to its control" and sought to exploit every opportunity "to weaken its enemies and increase its own power position." But Soviet rulers would not endanger "the security of the regime." Brutal, repressive, suspicious, totalitarian, the Kremlin leaders were not fools and were not bold adventurers. They would not want to risk embroilment in an atomic conflict that might destroy their home base and topple them from power.[176]

For policymakers, the supreme challenge was to exploit the Soviet fear of war and to overcome their own and their allies' penchant for self-deterrence. They had to build up military capabilities to the point where the Soviets would not dare to take an escalatory step and to the point where the United States and its allies would not hesitate to act for fear that their initiatives might precipitate dangerous Soviet reactions.[177] The self-deterrence that led to so much frustration and exasperation in Korea must not be permitted to happen elsewhere on the periphery. A basic theme, for example, of the NSC 124 series of papers on Southeast Asia was to insure that there would be greater, albeit not unrestricted, latitude for military action against China itself should U.S. officials deem it necessary to intervene in Indochina. During the course of these discussions, Nitze repeatedly emphasized that he and his colleagues "must be willing to face the danger of war with the Soviet Union." [178]

■

This thinking dominated the strategic outlook of Truman's top advisers as they concluded their tenure in office. It was a vision that called for ever more armaments. It was a strategy inspired neither by the organizational pressures of the armed services nor by the war-fighting requirements of the military planners, however much they may have welcomed it. It was a strategy championed by civilian leaders who possessed a global vision of U.S. national security interests and who believed that the raw-material-producing periphery and the industrial core of Eurasia had to be integrated and ensconced in a U.S. orbit if the Soviet/Communist adversary were not to emerge triumphant in the global struggle for power. It was also an expensive strategy. Nitze admitted that it would probably require more power to win the cold war than to fight a hot war. Acheson supported it. He believed that through military superiority the United States would wrest the initiative from the Kremlin and multiply its options for waging the cold war. "Many people," the secretary of state said, "thought that we were trying to hold a ring around Soviet Russia. In fact, we were endeavoring to see to it that freedom of choice rested with us, not the Russians." [179]

To gain this freedom of choice, Acheson, Lovett, Harriman, and Bradley recommended the continued development of U.S. strategic capabilities and the further strengthening of NATO. Hereafter the Air Force would receive favored treatment and the atomic arsenal would multiply. The 300 bombs expected to be in Soviet hands in 1955 would pale in comparison to the 2,250 warheads the United States would have in its stockpile at that time. Moreover, in 1952 the United States successfully exploded its first thermonuclear device. To deliver atomic and hydrogen bombs, the United States also began to deploy its first all-jet, medium-range B-47 bombers. By the end of 1952 the B-47's were being produced at one per day. Assembly lines in two new plants were nearing completion, and the Air Force was planning to expand the number of medium-range bomber wings from 20 in June 1952 to 30 in June 1955. At the same time, Air Force engineering teams were supervising the construction of almost 100 additional overseas installations from which the B-47's and other U.S. aircraft could fly. In 1956, the B-52 and B-60 bombers were scheduled to become operational. "The idea," said General Curtis E. LeMay, head of the Strategic Air Command, "was to have overwhelming strength." The United States would then be able "to prevail at the highest level of intensity, so that any kind of an escalation would be to the disadvantage of the enemy." [180]

But amidst the progress, a new problem began to trouble officials. They had not spent much money on early warning, jet interceptors, and civil defense. If they thought their own retaliatory capabilities and industrial infrastructure were at risk, they might hesitate to act in support of U.S. interests despite their overwhelming strategic superiority. Acheson, therefore, deemed it prudent to develop civil defense plans. On 18 June 1952, he told the NSC that it might behoove the government to evacuate certain areas when it "takes action along the lines contemplated in the recent policies on Korea, Indochina, and Berlin, which would seriously increase the possibility of global war." [181]

The Defense Department, however, did not want to divert any money from offensive forces. Accordingly, in the autumn of 1952 a major dispute erupted when the National Security Resources Board (NSRB) called for the allocation of funds for early warning and civil defense. Lovett thought such expenditures were a luxury. In his view, Soviet aircraft posed no significant danger to the continental United States. The Soviets had not developed refueling techniques for the TU-4's. Nor had they modernized the airfields on the Kola and Chukotski peninsulas, from which the planes were most likely to be launched. If the worst should happen, the TU-4's might inflict considerable damage on the American mainland, but they could not knock out U.S. industry or blunt U.S. retaliatory forces. [182]

Nitze, however, supported the NSRB. He maintained that it made eminent sense to exploit new technological advances that would enable the United States to detect Soviet planes soon after takeoff. An effective system of national defense, he insisted, would be a powerful deterrent to war: "The enemy would be reluctant to strike if its blows would not be effective against us. Furthermore, an adequate defense would increase tremendously our security, add to our power position with respect to the Soviet Union, and give us a sounder base for speaking with assurance in international affairs." [183]

Lovett grudgingly acquiesced to Nitze's arguments and the NSRB recommendation. But first he demanded, and everyone concurred, that money would not be deducted from supporting other missions. Accordingly, in their very last paper to the president, Acheson, Harriman, and Lovett stressed the importance of appropriating additional funds for continental defense: "There is an increasing danger that unless a large-scale civil defense program and measures to improve greatly our defense against air and sea attack are undertaken, the United States might find its freedom of action seriously impaired in an emergency." [184]

If the United States could retain its strategic superiority, if a viable EDC and a rearmed NATO could prevent Soviet troops from overrunning Western Europe, and if U.S. retaliatory capabilities and industrial infrastructure could survive a Soviet attack, the requirements would have been created for effective deterrence and for U.S. initiatives on the periphery. The United States could then shore up friendly regimes in the Third World, thwart Communist and revolutionary nationalist seizures of power, and retaliate against Communist China should it not halt its support of Kim Il Sung and Ho Chi Minh. It was in the Middle East and Far East, as Acheson, Harriman, and Lovett told the president, that the greatest vacuums of power now existed. The U.S. government could help overcome these vacuums by building up indigenous armies as it was in Korea and Vietnam, training and arming friendly forces as it was in Taiwan, and supporting covert actions as it was on the Chinese mainland.[185]

In other words, behind the atomic shield that served as the principal deterrent to a Soviet attack, the Truman administration was concentrating on developing the capabilities that would allow it to supplant the diminishing power of Great Britain and France in critical areas of the Middle East and Far East. The planes, tanks, and hardware pouring out of U.S. factories provided one instrument for buttressing friendly regimes. The volume of military production in January 1953 was almost seven times what it had been in June 1950. Supplies and equipment amounting to $8 billion were spewing out of U.S. factories every quarter. The mobilization base for waging total war was well along to completion. The shortage of machine tools that had strung up production in 1951 was now nearly solved. At NSC meetings, officials reported that the tough choices that had previously beleaguered Office of Defense Mobilization officials were a thing of the past. For U.S. friends abroad this was great news. They could now finally receive the equipment that had been promised to them. It also meant that additional military aid could be used to support diplomatic objectives—for example, in Egypt—and particularly to bolster the fighting capabilities of the South Koreans, Nationalist Chinese, and Indochinese armies. Acheson, Lovett, and Harriman recommended that much more military aid be sent to these countries as well as to Japan.[186]

To shore up the periphery, the United States could also use its growing covert capabilities. The State Department as well as the JCS called on the CIA's Office of Policy Coordination to spread propaganda, wage psychological warfare, support guerrilla forces, and conduct paramilitary operations particularly against the Chinese, North Korean, and Indochinese Communists. The office's total personnel strength grew from 302 in 1949 to over 6,000 in 1952; its budget jumped from $4.7 to $82 million; its overseas stations grew from 7 to 47. "Its emphasis," writes John Ranelagh, "began to shift from Europe and from crisis management to a worldwide effort to forestall and contain what was seen as communist aggression." Its covert operations increased "sixteenfold" between January 1951 and January 1953.[187]

Most important, however, State Department officials were eager for the United States to develop the mobile forces to intervene in Third World countries. Initially, the Pentagon was loath to go along with these recommendations because it continually feared it would be tied down in peripheral areas and unable to have the strength to carry out its war plans should it become necessary to wage global conflict. During the overall review of national security objectives in the summer of 1952, the Pentagon diluted State Department language calling for the development of capabilities to intervene in particular localities to stifle Communist subversion and aggression. Bohlen and Nitze finally recommended that Acheson accede to JCS wishes. But Acheson did not follow their advice. He inserted a sentence underscoring the possibility of unilateral military intervention in Southeast Asia and the Middle East. In their last report to the secretary of defense during the Truman administration, the JCS then jumped on the bandwagon. The chiefs, too, now supported the development of additional mobile forces to cope with local contingencies. In summing up, the JCS emphasized that there was need for "a flexible, efficient, and ready military force. . . . Such a force must be capable of taking early and effective action in case of war as well as in resisting shifting peripheral probes of the enemy during the cold war." [188]

The principal molders of national security policy believed that, if the United States could stave off Communist inroads on the periphery while building strength in the industrial heartland, they could eventually roll back Soviet power and undermine Communist regimes in Europe and Asia. Acheson, Nitze, and Lovett constantly reiterated that the administration's objectives were no different than they had been in 1948 when NSC 20/4 was first approved. They wanted to redraw Russia's borders to its pre-1939 status, destroy the Cominform, retract the influence of the Soviet Union, and eventually cause the Soviet system to weaken and decay. If the free world gathered enough strength, Nitze emphasized that the contradictions in the Communist system would be exposed, the satellites would be drawn to the West, and the Kremlin's control would falter. Successful containment would evolve into rollback.[189]

Until then, Truman administration officials believed they should continue to seize all opportunities "for poisoning the relations between the Kremlin and its satellites and weakening the hold of the communist regimes over the people"; "the Iron Curtain must be pierced to bring home to the Kremlin's subject peoples the fact that they have friends and allies in the free world." [190] In other words, political warfare should be conducted within the Soviet satellite system, and insurgents might be supported in both China and Eastern Europe. In 1952, for example, over 40 covert operations were under way at the same time within a single Central European country. The CIA established contact with thousands of Soviet émigrés and scores of East European liberation groups.[191] With regard to East Asia, the wedge policy was still studied, but prospects for its implementation seemed to be deferred to the future. Increasingly the State Department acquiesced to Defense Department schemes for aiding and arming the Chinese Nationalists and for harassing the Communist regime on the mainland.[192]

Truman administration officials, however, made a clear demarcation between their actions within the satellite world and their policies elsewhere. To defend, co-opt, and integrate Western Europe, West Germany, and Japan, the United States would be willing to wage atomic war; to safeguard the periphery and maintain markets and raw materials, the United States might be willing to risk a dangerous escalatory process leading to atomic war. But to pierce the satellites, there must be no such risks. Preponderance did not demand the immediate breakup of the Soviet bloc. The United States could and should be patient and prudent. All would be accomplished in time, however long it might take, so long as the industrial core and the appropriate periphery remained safe inside a U.S.-led orbit.[193]

■

Truman scorned Eisenhower's campaign in the 1952 election. Although the Republicans lambasted Democratic timidity and talked of liberation, Eisenhower and Dulles shared the geopolitical vision of the Democratic administration. Truman was right when he insisted that the Republican candidate supported all his major initiatives. The Republicans denounced Truman's policies in Korea, but they had no solutions. The Republicans preached liberation, but their commitment to it was no more and no less than that of Acheson, Nitze, Lovett, and Harriman. The Republicans said little about other problems on the periphery, but their concerns were as intense as those of their predecessors. The raw-material-producing periphery, Eisenhower wrote Dulles, must not be lost either to marching armies or to domestic political subversives.[194]

The campaign and election of 1952 left Truman feeling aggrieved and proud. In his last address to Congress on 7 January 1953, he reviewed his foreign policies: "The Second World War radically changed the power relationships of the world. Nations once great were left shattered and weak, channels of communication, routes of trade, political and economic ties of many kinds were ripped apart." The Soviets sought to exploit opportunities. They aimed "to equal or better the production levels of Western Europe and North America combined—thus shifting the balance of world economic power, and war potential, to their side." They tried "to fish in troubled waters, to seize more countries, to enslave more millions of human souls." Geography afforded them great advantages. Their military prowess and their economic power enabled them to hold out great inducements "to such widely dispersed places as Western Germany, Iran, and Japan." But the United States successfully utilized "its pre-eminent position of power to help other nations recover from the damage and dislocation of the war." The United States revitalized Western Europe and Japan, inaugurated a great military buildup, and countered the Soviet threat in the Third World. In the age-old struggle between tyranny and freedom, the United States played its decisive part.[195]

Truman's farewell address to the American people on 15 January 1953 was no less stirring. During his presidency, the U.S. role in the international arena was transformed. The United States emerged from World War II as the preponderant power in a bipolar world. By helping to reconstruct and integrate Western Europe, West Germany, and Japan into a U.S.-led orbit, Truman and his advisers averted the possibility that these core areas might slip into the Communist sphere and transform the world balance of power.[196]

But triumphant as they were in the industrial heartland of Eurasia and proud though they might be of their accomplishments, U.S. policymakers had not been able to stave off the erosion of Western influence in the Third World. And because they were convinced that the industrial world could not be safe so long as the periphery was in turmoil, they left office much more worried than Truman's words suggested. Inspired by fear, preoccupied with power, and driven by ideological fervor, they sought a preponderance that appeared elusive so long as instability wracked the periphery.[197]

—

Conclusion

I suppose," President Truman told the American people on 15 January 1953, "that history will remember my term in office as the years when the 'cold war' began to overshadow our lives. I have had hardly a day in office that has not been dominated by this all-embracing struggle—this conflict between those who love freedom and those who would lead the world back into slavery and darkness. . . . Some of you," the president continued, "may ask, when and how will the cold war end? I think I can answer that simply. The Communist world has great resources, and it looks strong. But there is a fatal flaw in their society. Theirs is a godless system, a system of slavery; there is no freedom in it, no consent."

According to the president, that system could not prevail over a free society: "As the free world grows stronger, more united, more attractive to men on both sides of the Iron Curtain—and as the Soviet hopes for easy expansion are blocked— then there will have to come a time of change in the Soviet world. Nobody can say for sure when that is going to be, or exactly how it will come about, whether by revolution, or trouble in the satellite states, or by a change inside the Kremlin." But Truman had no doubt that that change would come: "I have a deep and abiding faith in the destiny of free men. With patience and courage, we shall some day move on into a new era." [1]

Reflections

The new era that Truman foresaw is indeed dawning. And, as it does, it provides an opportunity to reflect on the national security policies of the Truman administration. On one level, those policies now appear to have been quite prescient. Truman's prediction, in fact, seems to have been borne out by the tide of history itself. Scholars, journalists, and policymakers declare U.S. victory in the cold war. Some observers, prone to Hegelian analysis and impressed by the bankruptcy of Communist ideology, go so far as to declare "the end of history." [2]

Such encomiums merit attention. They should also remind us of the transiency of events. Two decades ago, as the United States was mired in the war in Indochina and as it struggled to maintain its legitimacy and credibility, scholars and observers cast U.S. cold war policies in a very different light. Rather than shrewd and farsighted, the United States was portrayed as a "free world colossus" intent on achieving economic domination, insensitive to the security requirements of foes and friends alike, and committed to pursuing a policy of indiscriminate anticommunism everywhere. Ironically, some of those who were most critical in the 1960's are now cheerleaders for the very policies they once excoriated. [3] The swift movement of events should caution all of us to speak softly, keep our minds open, study the evidence carefully, and acknowledge that the self-evident truths of one era may become subject to heated controversy in another, especially as the Soviet side of the story has yet to be revealed.

Nevertheless, the declassification of millions of U.S. documents, the availability of scores of private manuscript collections, and the opening of the records of the military as well as the civilian branches of the U.S. government afford an opportunity to outline in bold relief the grand strategy of the Truman administration. U.S. officials defined their nation's security in terms of power relationships. In their view, power was determined by a country's industrial infrastructure, technological prowess, natural resources, and skilled labor. If necessary, these material and human resources could be converted to military purposes. Assuming that any war would be a protracted conflict, policymakers believed that economic capabilities would ultimately determine the outcome of any military struggle.

At the end of World War II, the United States possessed incomparably more power than any other nation. Aware of this, U.S. officials hoped to sustain the wartime alliance, transform vanquished enemies into democratic and capitalist friends, and persuade imperial allies in London, Paris, and the Hague to pursue orderly decolonization policies on the periphery. If friends as well as foes could be convinced of the beneficent character of a liberal capitalist multilateral order, U.S. officials believed that the world would enter a new era of peace and harmony and that the United States would recover its traditional sense of safety from external threats. All of this seemed possible because, so long as there was an open world order hospitable to the free flow of capital and goods, no nation could control sufficient resources to jeopardize U.S. security. In fact, quite the opposite was the case. America's surplus capital, comparative advantage in the production of goods, abundant supply of raw materials and foodstuffs, and huge domestic market would lure the world into a U.S.-led orbit. All the United States needed to do was to become the world's financial and economic hegemon. [4] And this role the U.S. government appeared willing to perform, as illustrated by its leadership in creating the International Monetary Fund and the World Bank, its generous lending and relief actions, and its self-professed commitment to lower tariffs and to offer most-favored-nation treatment.

The vision of a cooperative multilateral international order was an attractive one. Having learned the bitter lessons of the interwar era, the United States would join the United Nations and play a constructive role in the international economy. In so doing, policymakers would enhance U.S. security, promote its economic interests, and disseminate its ideals while serving the world community and advancing the well-being of all humankind.

It was a wonderful vision, but it was threatened by four interrelated phenomena. First, the presence of Soviet armies in Eastern Europe and Northeast Asia meant the Kremlin might absorb these areas into its own sphere in order to expedite reconstruction and enlarge its long-term military capabilities. Second, the rise of the left in Greece, Italy, France, China, Korea, and other countries meant that Communists might win or seize power, reject the liberal capitalist multilateralism espoused by the United States, and bring their nations into a Soviet orbit. Third, the demoralization and deprivation in postwar Germany and Japan suggested that leaders might arise who would seek to solve their nations' problems through statist practices, neutralist options, or a Soviet alliance. Countries like Germany and Japan with no democratic traditions might easily gravitate eastward. They could be lured by the enormous markets within the Soviet orbit or duped by hopes of regaining territory and national autonomy that the Kremlin might offer to them. And, fourth, the awakening of nationalist impulses in Southeast Asia, the Middle East, and North Africa made these areas susceptible to the appeal of Marxist ideology. The Leninist theory of imperialism explained away their backwardness while the Soviet model of development through a command economy seemed to promise rapid modernization.

The convergence of these four threats conjured up enormous apprehensions in U.S. policymaking circles. No one could dispute that in the heartland of Eurasia a brutal totalitarian state existed with the capacity to take advantage of the manifold opportunities presented by the postwar world. To what extent Stalin would choose to do so was uncertain. The signals he gave were mixed. But if he tried to exploit prevailing circumstances, Soviet Russia might gradually co-opt, either directly or indirectly, enormous industrial infrastructure, natural resources, and skilled labor. The lessons of the 1930's taught that when totalitarian powers had such resources they used them to challenge vital U.S. interests, attack the United States, and wage protracted war. Even if Stalin did not choose such an aggressive course, the United States would have to prepare for it. And as it did so, it would find itself in an unenviable situation. Increasingly, it would have to regiment its own economy in order to compete and deal with the statist regimes in Eurasia; it would have to raise taxes and boost defense expenditures; and it would have to limit dissent lest Communist sympathizers undermine the country's morale and vigor. Faced with an ominous threat in Eurasia, the United States would have to transform its own political economy and its liberal capitalist system. Even if war never came, the specter of Soviet/

Communist expansion threatened to transform the American way of life. And if war did come, Soviet domination of Eurasia might afford it the wherewithal to fight to a stalemate, perhaps even to victory. Of course, none of this would happen quickly. U.S. officials were thinking about worst-case developments over a ten-, fifteen-, or twenty-year period.

Faced with these possibilities, the United States shifted tactics. Initially content with the role of financial hegemon, U.S. officials came to believe that they had to offer economic assistance in amounts they had not anticipated; they had to establish linkages with foreign elites in ways they had not envisioned; and they had to incur strategic commitments and assume political-military responsibilities in places they had not contemplated. These new tactics were deemed essential to establish a configuration of power that safeguarded U.S. security and that institutionalized Washington's preponderant influence in the international system.

The United States moved first to integrate Western Europe, West Germany, and Japan into a U.S.-led orbit. The co-optation of these power centers, however, was considered impossible unless revolutionary nationalism on the periphery was thwarted and unless Third World markets and raw materials were linked to the industrial core areas of Eurasia. The accomplishment of all these tasks required considerable risk-taking. Conscious of their superior warmaking potential and atomic monopoly, U.S. officials initially took the attendant risks without augmenting military capabilities. They bet that the Soviets would seek to avoid a military conflict. But after the Soviets detonated their own atomic device and after the Chinese Communists intervened in the Korean War, U.S. officials felt less and less certain about the shadows cast by the existing military strength of the United States.

They came to believe that ever more weapons were necessary to support the risk-taking that inhered in co-opting the industrial core of Eurasia and in integrating its underdeveloped periphery. So long as Europe was vulnerable to Soviet counteraction and so long as there was a possibility that a Soviet preemptive strike might neutralize America's own arsenal and cripple its industrial infrastructure, the appropriate risk-taking could not proceed. So eventually rearmament became the essential prerequisite to America's diplomatic, economic, and political initiatives. As British and French power atrophied in the Third World, U.S. officials also began to assume responsibility for co-opting the periphery. They prepared to use military assistance, covert actions, and mobile forces to influence local situations while they relied on America's strategic arsenal and NATO's growing conventional capabilities to discourage any Soviet counteraction in Western Europe.

Faced with the reality of Soviet domination in Eastern Europe and the prospective growth of Soviet power throughout Eurasia, America's cold war policies took shape. Looking back, we can see that those policies were partly wise, partly prudent, and partly foolish. Given the imponderables policymakers faced in the international system and the uncertainties about Soviet aims, it is their prudence that seems most striking.

Wise Men

Truman administration officials grasped the nature of the Soviet threat. From the outset, George Kennan and Charles Bohlen believed that the Soviet Union was fundamentally weak and would not engage in premeditated aggression. Notwithstanding Soviet Russia's huge comparative military superiority over other Eurasian countries, either defeated or weakened by World War II, the men in the Kremlin were purported to have an enormous respect for America's superior warmaking capabilities as well as its atomic monopoly. Even if the latter did not intimidate Stalin, as some Soviet experts like Jonathan Haslam and Adam Ulam contend, the Soviet ruler was believed to have a healthy respect for the capacity of the United States to turn out steel, coal, and machines, all of which could be converted in wartime to the manufacture of tanks, planes, ships, munitions, and bombs.[5] It could be assumed that the Russians' awareness of their relative weakness vis-à-vis the United States would encourage them to move cautiously. When faced with U.S. determination, they would back down.

Not only did U.S. officials show a shrewd understanding of Soviet weaknesses, but they also understood Soviet strengths. The Soviet threat resided principally in the Kremlin's capacity to exploit economic vulnerabilities, capitalize on social dislocation, and take advantage of the nascent nationalism that was astir in the Third World. Communist ideology and statist solutions seemed to be alluring not only to peoples in the industrial core who, in a 30-year period, had endured two world wars and a great depression but also to peoples in the Third World who aspired to gain control over their own destiny, excise their colonial masters, and modernize their countries. Policymakers in Washington understood that their principal task was not to deal with Russian military power but to fill the vacuums of power, infuse a spirit of hope, promote economic reconstruction, and champion the principle of self-determination without compromising vital interests. By 1947 they also came to recognize that they would not have the resources to do all these things at the same time. The magnitude of the problems abroad and the intensity of the partisan struggle at home circumscribed available funds and compelled tough choices.

In selecting priorities, Washington policymakers again showed their grasp of economic and geostrategic realities. They understood that they had to turn their attention initially to the industrial core areas of Western Europe. State Department and Pentagon officials agreed that they had to thwart Communist gains and Soviet influence in France and western Germany. Revitalizing the German economy was the key to fostering economic growth and eroding Communist strength in neighboring countries. They recognized that, by providing massive economic aid designed to boost productivity, they might help the West Europeans overcome the payments deficits that encouraged statist solutions, bilateralism, and autarky. They correctly believed that open markets would fuel worldwide economic growth.[6] And though the Marshall Plan demonstrated their willingness to assume the role of hegemon, U.S. policymakers shrewdly understood that it would be self-defeating to dictate solutions. Insisting on self-help and mutual aid, they established linkages with European elites and permitted them considerable flexibility in setting priorities.[7] Europeans had only to rebuff Soviet overtures, resist indigenous Communists, and accept America's hegemonic role in the international economy.

Critical to the success of U.S. reconstruction efforts in the industrial core areas of Eurasia was occupation policy, particularly in Germany and Japan. Here again, U.S. officials wisely recognized that neither the American people nor the Germans or Japanese would be receptive to long and harsh occupations. To the chagrin of America's other wartime allies, reparations were scaled down or canceled, occupation controls lightened, and responsibilities shifted to local administrators. The emphasis on labor reform and industrial decartelization swiftly changed to economic growth, commercial expansion, and conservative fiscal practices. Instead of punishing wartime criminals and instituting progressive social reforms, occupation officials turned more of their attention to forging mutually rewarding linkages with moderate business elites and conservative reformers. The goal was to co-opt German and Japanese power by demonstrating to local elites that their national aspirations could be fulfilled within a U.S.-led orbit.[8] Dean Acheson, Robert Lovett, John McCloy, John Foster Dulles, and their friends believed that the lessons of the Versailles peace treaty and the Weimar years in Germany taught that concessions should be made to moderate leaders before demagogues on the right and left seized on the grievances of the masses to infuse their countries with a virulent nationalism.

Policymakers in Washington also shrewdly understood that the revival of German and Japanese power agitated America's other friends in Europe and Asia, endangered their security, and posed considerable risks to the international community. Once controls were lifted, autonomy restored, and sovereignty returned, no one could really be certain of what would happen. Germany and Japan might become peaceful, stable, democratic, and prosperous participants in the international system, or they might be afflicted with economic woes, social discontent, and political division. They might collaborate with the United States, or they might choose to pursue nationalist goals either alone or in combination with the Kremlin. To reassure America's allies and to maintain leverage over dangerous future scenarios, Acheson extracted promises and commitments from Konrad Adenauer and Yoshida Shigeru that they would not pursue independent foreign policies. More important, Truman administration officials decided to retain U.S. (and Allied) forces in Germany and to maintain bases in Japan. Furthermore, they helped to forge the NATO and the Australia–New Zealand–U.S. alliances, both of which were designed not simply to deter the Soviets but also to convince ambivalent allies to go ahead with the risks that accompanied Germany's and Japan's revival.

More than security guarantees were necessary to reassure wartime allies and co-opt former enemies. The Truman administration supported sophisticated supranational institutions that were designed to channel and absorb the energy and talent of the Germans and Japanese into constructive pursuits that bulwarked a U.S.-led anti-Soviet coalition. In Europe, France assumed the initiative in proposing these mechanisms, like the Organization of European Economic Cooperation, the European Coal and Steel Community, and the European Defense Community. French foreign minister Robert Schuman and Jean Monnet hoped to harness German economic and military power for the good of the larger European community. Officials in Washington warmly applauded these efforts. At the same time they worried that, in the long run, these institutions might encourage West Europeans to become a third force or to pursue policies independent of the United States. Consequently, U.S. officials focused more of their own attention on developing NATO as an institutional device to insure U.S. leadership and to preserve cohesion within an Atlantic community that periodically would be afflicted with its own centrifugal forces.[9]

Behind this sophisticated strategy rested the conviction that, if the United States could successfully co-opt the industrial core of Eurasia, it would establish a magnet to attract the Kremlin's satellites westward. Here, too, U.S. policymakers demonstrated a sagacious understanding of the intensity of nationalist feelings in Eastern Europe and of the tenuous nature of Soviet controls. The Truman administration never conceded Eastern Europe to the Russians. For the moment, it was a low priority. But these men understood that they were fashioning strategies for the long run. If they were successful in co-opting the industrial core and integrating that core with the underdeveloped periphery, they would demonstrate the superiority of Western liberal capitalist institutions, create a flourishing international economy, and demonstrate the bankruptcy of Soviet economic as well as political and ideological leadership.

The magnet, however, would only work if the industrial core prospered within the U.S.-led multilateral economy. The geopolitical configurations of power to which contemporary officials attributed such great importance depended on sound economic foundations. Western Europe, western Germany, and Japan would not long accept U.S. leadership if they did not prosper. And the split between the so-called free world and the slave world, which U.S. policies accelerated after 1947, initially made it more difficult for the industrial core areas to prosper if they accepted the multilateral norms of open trade and capital movements that U.S. officials deemed so important. Indeed the division of Europe accentuated the payments problems of European friends because they were cut off from traditional markets and raw materials in Eastern and Central Europe and had to replace them with supplies from the Western Hemisphere and markets in the Third World. Likewise, Mao's seizure of power and U.S. wariness about Japanese trade with the Chinese mainland underscored the need for the Japanese to find markets and raw materials elsewhere. Policymakers in Washington demonstrated an incisive awareness of these problems. They did not insist that their allies immediately comply with the multilateral rules they championed. While pressing their allies to boost productivity, limit domestic consumption, and welcome the economic benefits that inhered in

Germany and Japan's rehabilitation, the Americans did what they could to ease the difficult transition. The United States not only provided the dollars and the security safeguards but also encouraged the development of cheap raw materials and food-stuffs in the Third World and sought to foster the growth of markets abroad and (less successfully) to reduce tariffs at home.[10]

In understanding the nature of the Soviet threat in the early postwar years, in grasping the economic foundations of geopolitical success, in forging ties with moderate elites, in modulating the severity and duration of occupation regimes, in acquiescing to large doses of national autonomy within an overall integrationist strategy, and in supporting supranational mechanisms of control, Truman admin-istration officials manifested sagacity, sensitivity, and wisdom. Of course, none of this would have been possible if the United States did not have the wealth and power to offer economic aid and strategic guarantees. Money and security were of decisive importance to governments and peoples who were wavering in 1946–47 between alternative strategies of development and who were as wary about Germany and Japan as they were about Soviet Russia. But U.S. policymakers' judicious use of power to support farsighted objectives that had the support of people abroad as well as at home was what made them wise.

Prudent Men

Prudent officials take calculated risks. Operating on given sets of assumptions and beliefs and with finite information, they seek to advance national interests and avoid worst-case scenarios. For the prudent and powerful men who made U.S. policy in the aftermath of World War II, the worst case involved another totalitarian adversary gaining direct or indirect control of Eurasia and mobilizing its resources against the United States. To avoid this specter, Truman administration officials were willing to accept moderate costs and intermediate dangers if they were reasonably confident that short-term sacrifices could be translated into long-term gains. They were pre-pared, if necessary, to break with the Kremlin, avoid negotiations, grant financial aid and strategic guarantees to allies, and even run the risk of war so long as they thought that such initiatives would stave off a redistribution of power that would seriously jeopardize U.S. security. Ultimately, their policies were successful, but flawed assumptions and beliefs drove up the costs of their efforts. Of course, this is clearer in retrospect than it was at the time; contemporaries saw great impon-derables, felt very vulnerable, and thought they were acting prudently by building situations of strength.

All this became most apparent in late 1946 and early 1947, when Truman ad-ministration officials decided they had to seize the initiative in Western Europe, Germany, and Japan notwithstanding the prospective impact of their actions on the Soviet Union. Ever since the war ended, they had determined that Soviet power must not extend beyond the reach of Russian armies of occupation. And although

Soviet policies were not uniformly aggressive or expansionist, neither were they conciliatory and reassuring. The Soviet threat loomed ever larger because the prospective termination of U.S. assistance to Europe, the possible withdrawal of U.S. troops from Germany, and the anticipated negotiation of an early peace treaty with Japan portended a huge shift in the balance of domestic forces in those countries as well as in the international configuration of power.

From the perspective of Washington, the situation in Europe seemed especially fraught with peril. Despite impressive figures of macroeconomic growth, the persistent shortages and hardships, coupled with new retrenchment measures, created a volatile situation. On one level, the trend backwards toward bilateralism and regimentation was ominous. More frightening still was the anticipated capacity of Communists to capitalize on the expected economic slowdown and ensuing popular disillusionment. Particularly troublesome were Communist demands for labor reforms and welfare benefits in the midst of scarcity and inflation. Whether coalition governments were led by Socialists, as they were in France, or by Christian Democrats, as they were in Italy, leaders of the moderate left and center found it difficult to cope with adverse economic and financial developments when they were beset with irreconcilable demands and conflicting priorities. They increasingly realized that they could only succeed if they broke with the Communists, whom they now regarded as obstructionists, and solicited U.S. aid. U.S. officials communicated a strong desire to work with them. Should Paul Ramadier in France and Alcide De Gasperi in Italy excise the Communists from their governments, bar their reentry, and commit themselves to self-help, mutual aid, and the eventual achievement of a multilateral world order based on fixed exchange rates and the free flow of capital, goods, and labor, the United States would offer unprecedented assistance.[11]

The prudent men in Washington in 1947 wanted to stymie economic retrogression and Communist political gains. Already they had promised military assistance to Greece, fearing that a Communist victory there would have a bandwagon effect on the rest of Europe. U.S. officials believed that Communist-dominated governments would eagerly sign bilateral accords with the Kremlin and thereby orient their countries eastward. Should this occur, the political and diplomatic influence that might have otherwise emanated from the infusion of U.S. capital and the export of U.S. goods would never materialize. France and other countries might gravitate into the Soviet orbit. And once this occurred, the U.S. capacity to oversee the occupation of Germany would be nullified. The Germans, too, would join the bandwagon heading eastward. Gradually, the Kremlin would gain control, however indirectly, over the industrial core of Western Europe.

Prudent men aware of the wealth and power of the United States could not allow such worst-case scenarios to unfold. Hence, in the spring of 1947, they went on the offensive, proclaiming the Truman Doctrine and announcing the Marshall Plan. They championed increases in Germany's level of industrial production, supported the formation of a German government within the western zones, and promised to guarantee France's frontiers against future threats. These actions were intended to promote U.S. national security by thwarting bilateralism, fostering productivity, co-opting western Germany, and promoting West European integration within a U.S.-led orbit. The United States acted as hegemon: providing the aid, helping to establish the basic guidelines, and offering the security guarantees.

Substantial risks inhered in this course of action. U.S. officials were altogether aware that their initiatives would antagonize the Soviets, intensify the emerging rivalry, and probably culminate in the division of Germany and of Europe. Their intent was *not* to provoke the Kremlin, but they recognized that this result would be the logical consequence of their actions. The Americans were caught in the classic security dilemma whereby the steps deemed essential to promote their own security clashed with the security imperatives of the adversary. The Soviets, seeing Communists excised from the governing coalitions in Western and Southern Europe, fearing a loss of influence in Eastern Europe, and frightened by the specter of German reconstruction under Western auspices, would surely strike back.[12]

Truman administration officials were willing to accept a rupture in the Soviet-U.S. relationship because they were convinced that the dangers of inaction greatly exceeded the risks that inhered in provoking the Soviets. Simply stated, the cold war and the division of Europe were regrettable prospects but not nearly so ominous as the dangers that inhered in economic contraction, autarkical trends, Communist gains, and the prospective erosion of U.S. influence throughout the industrial core of western Eurasia. The Soviet response might be vile, but Soviet capabilities were limited. Soviet actions would be circumscribed if the United States acted with sufficient resolve and imagination. Surprised by the Soviet blockade of Berlin, U.S. officials momentarily feared the possibility of war and wondered whether, in fact, the Soviets would acquiesce to Western initiatives. But Truman and his advisers would not retreat from Berlin, repudiate the London agreements, or abandon their efforts to co-opt German strength. And when Stalin did not interfere with the airlift, U.S. policy triumphed. The diplomatic, economic, and political actions necessary to create a configuration of power compatible with U.S. security interests did provoke the Kremlin, but the shadows cast by U.S. warmaking capabilities and atomic monopoly also deterred the Soviets from escalating to the threshold of full-scale war.

The calculated risk-taking of the prudent men who occupied the highest offices in the Truman administration turned out to be a great success. But some of the assumptions undergirding this risk-taking were not altogether wise. In early 1947, for example, U.S. policymakers not only magnified the negative aspects of the proliferating bilateral agreements but may have also overestimated the adverse economic consequences of the exchange crisis under way.[13]

More significantly, they sometimes exaggerated the capacity and at other times the willingness of indigenous Communists to take their countries into the Soviet orbit. Until the summer of 1947, Communist parties beyond the Soviet sphere usually abided by democratic norms and, while respectful of the Communist motherland, nevertheless operated somewhat independently of Soviet control. Local Communists often feuded among themselves and could not always discern what Stalin wanted them to do (and for good reason, since he probably had not made up his own mind).[14] If they had won majority control by their own means, and if the United States had not threatened them, they would have had little incentive to keep their countries in the Soviet orbit. They would have seen, as did the Yugoslavs, that the Kremlin placed its needs ahead of their own and sought to exploit them. And when they perceived this reality, they would have probably demanded, as did Tito and his comrades, respect and equality.[15] This is because European Communists outside of Eastern Europe, despite their deference to Moscow's preeminent position, also possessed nationalist loyalties. Given their grass-roots support—for example, in France and Italy—and given their distance from Soviet occupation armies, had they won power freely it is not likely that they would have accepted the Kremlin's priorities and ensconced themselves happily in the Soviet orbit, as U.S. officials feared.

But even if local Communists took office and chose to collaborate with the Kremlin, would other countries have joined the bandwagon, as U.S. officials assumed would be the case? Kennan popularized the bandwagon concept and nobody disputed it at the time. But it was based on dubious assumptions. Governments do not fall like dominoes. Seeking national autonomy and security, they are as likely to balance perceived threats as they are inclined to bend with them, so long as there is some prospect of outside assistance.[16] This was clearly illustrated in the reaction of many West European countries to the Czech coup in February 1948. In retrospect, therefore, it seems likely that U.S. officials underestimated the resiliency of nationalist impulses throughout Western and Southern Europe while they exaggerated the appeal of Soviet communism.

The penchant to overstate the Kremlin's leverage was particularly apparent in the way U.S. policymakers dealt with Germany. They were forever fearful that the Germans would turn eastward, ally with the Soviets, or be co-opted by them. Germans did grow unhappy with the Allied occupation, but their antipathy toward the Russians and toward communism far outmatched any reservations they may have had about the Americans and their reconstruction policies. Particularly after the Berlin blockade, German sentiment against the Soviets hardened. When Germans were asked whether they preferred a West German government or a united Communist Germany, the overwhelming majority opted for the former. Even among Social Democrats a significant group of dissenters objected to Kurt Schumacher's affinity for neutralism. Much of this was apparent in 1952, when the majority of West Germans showed little enthusiasm for Stalin's unification proposal. Nor were they interested in trade with the East if it conflicted with U.S. wishes.[17] In short, U.S. analysts wildly exaggerated the prospects of a German-Soviet coalition.

Of course, we do not know what would have happened if the United States had operated according to a different set of beliefs and assumptions and had not seized the initiative in the spring and summer of 1947. Surely, the course of postwar history would have been different. But in what ways? With the power of hindsight we can see that sound foundations for economic recovery had been laid, that the left was neither so united nor so bound to Moscow as previously thought, that the lure of Eastern markets was not so great as assumed, and that the demoralization of conservative elites was not so advanced as U.S. officials thought. Yet without the marginal help offered by the United States, the worst-case scenarios in the minds of the prudent men in Washington *might* have unfolded.[18] Although their fears were exaggerated, they were not irrational. Their intent was to minimize dangers and take calculated risks. And the risks that inhered in the efforts to thwart indigenous Communists, rebuild Western Europe, and co-opt German and Japanese power seemed much smaller than the risks that existed in trying to work out cooperative solutions with a totalitarian power whose aims were unclear and whose ability to capitalize on systemic vacuums and internal weaknesses appeared substantial.

Theoretically, one could argue that a policy of reassurance might have worked. For example, Anders Stephanson has recently suggested that it might have been possible to fashion a German settlement based on reparations from current production.[19] But even the advocates of a strategy of reassurance acknowledge that it is a treacherous and high-risk policy when the overall balance of power is at stake, as it was in Central and Western Europe between 1946 and 1948.[20] Rather than take such risks, rather than seek compromise and accommodation (as Walt Rostow suggested in 1946 and General Lucius Clay advocated in 1947), the men who made the final decisions in Washington decided that it was more prudent to cultivate situations of strength.[21] However nastily the Soviets might respond in the short run, they would bow to power realities in the long run. They would learn to acclimatize themselves to a configuration of power that insured America's preponderance.

Foolish Men

But the configuration of power envisioned by U.S. officials was increasingly defined in ways that distorted the importance of the Third World, underestimated the local sources of conflict, and exaggerated the relevance of strategic arms and the conventional military balance in Europe to developments on the periphery. For all their wisdom and prudence, Truman administration officials, like policymakers everywhere, made significant errors.

They attributed excessive value to the Third World. The periphery was important because it contained valuable base sights (for example, in Egypt) and raw materials (for example, in Iran and Saudi Arabia). But far more significantly, the periphery was considered of vital importance because policymakers believed that the industrial core areas of Eurasia might be lured into the Soviet orbit if they were not effectively integrated with markets and resources on the periphery. When the

Marshall Plan was launched and the decisions to rehabilitate the German and Japanese economies were made, officials assumed that the advanced industrial countries of Eurasia would need to save dollars by procuring supplies of foodstuffs and raw materials in Africa, the Middle East, and Southeast Asia (rather than in North America). Likewise, they also assumed that the advanced industrial countries would have to earn dollars by competing more effectively in Third World countries and by repatriating profits from overseas investments in those areas. Not surprisingly, when U.S. policymakers became alarmed during 1949 that the Marshall Plan might end before European payments difficulties were solved, and when they realized how resistant Congress was to lowering barriers to foreign goods, they became ever more determined to preserve stability and thwart the rise of revolutionary nationalism on the periphery. Otherwise, Japan, West Germany, and Western Europe might be enticed to look to the Eastern bloc for the markets and raw materials they so desperately needed.

Officials assigned much too much importance to the role of the periphery in solving the payments problems of industrial core areas. Once Japanese and German industrial recovery got under way, these countries developed the capacity to earn dollars to pay for indispensable imports. Despite all the rhetoric about the critical importance of Southeast Asia to Japanese, British, French, and Dutch rehabilitation, there is little reason to think that this area played a decisive role in the economic performance of the advanced industrial core areas. U.S. officials underestimated the latent vitality of European and Japanese industrial producers and the magnitude of trade that would develop between the industrial core countries themselves. By the late 1950's, for example, trade between Japan and Western Europe was growing far more quickly than trade between Japan and Southeast Asia. In fact, neither exports to nor repatriated earnings from any particular country or specific region in the Third World was of decisive importance in solving the dollar-gap problems of industrial core countries, not nearly so important as America's invisible imports and overseas military expenditures. As it turned out, the underdeveloped periphery was only of marginal importance in sustaining the economic dynamism of advanced industrial core areas, despite the overall importance of export-led growth.[22]

Of course, imports of raw materials and especially of fossil fuels became critical to the economic well-being of European economies and particularly that of Japan. Cheap Middle Eastern oil fueled the economic resurgence of Western Europe and Northeast Asia. But U.S. fears that somehow this area would fall into the clutches of the Kremlin were exaggerated. Revolutionary nationalists like Mohammed Musaddiq had no affinity for the Russians. Nor did the Soviets have the capacity, the need, or the will to purchase and transport Persian Gulf oil. U.S. officials themselves acknowledged these facts. Musaddiq wanted to sell Iranian oil to the West. The problem was that the British did not want to purchase it unless they could be guaranteed an exaggerated price for its nationalization and future control over its marketing. British intransigence, not indigenous revolutionary nationalism or aggressive Soviet probing, endangered access to Persian Gulf oil.[23] And, elsewhere in the Third World, the Eastern bloc showed little desire to purchase raw materials or to invest capital in the modernization of underdeveloped economies.[24]

U.S. officials exaggerated the ability of the Soviet Union to capitalize on the rising tide of nationalism in the Third World and incorrectly assessed the relationships between most Third World Communists and Moscow. Although policymakers in the Truman administration did possess an acute appreciation of the intensity of nationalist feelings in Southeast Asia, the Middle East, and North Africa, they foolishly believed that Communist leaders in these areas had a greater loyalty to Moscow than to their own countries.[25] Nowhere was this more true than in Indochina, where the case for Ho Chi Minh's subservience to the Kremlin was always assumed rather than proved. Ho's popularity was acknowledged, but his initial overtures to the United States were rebuffed and his subsequent struggle against the French won no support.[26] In fact, America's growing indirect embroilment in the war against the Viet Minh was motivated not simply by the exigencies of winning French compliance with U.S. policies in Europe but also by the indiscriminate anticommunism that generally characterized U.S. policy everywhere in the Third World. While sensitive to nationalist impulses, the Truman administration desired orderly decolonization and did not want Third World areas to escape the control of the West. Acheson, for example, urged the French to reform but did not want them to withdraw from Indochina.

The effort to divide Communists from Moscow, the so-called wedge strategy, was pursued belatedly or not at all. Only after Tito broke with the Kremlin did he win any support from the Truman administration. Until the rift became public, U.S. officials had not the slightest notion of the difficulties plaguing Yugoslav-Russian relations. They exaggerated the salience of ideological ties and subordinated the importance of nationalist aspirations among Communist leaders. Of course, after the rupture, U.S. officials pondered the possibilities of a similar rift between Mao and Stalin. Much as they privately grasped the potential for such a break, they did rather little to encourage it. Worse yet, their public speeches and declarations greatly reinforced popular notions about the subservience of all Communists to the whims and commands of the Cominform's leaders in Moscow. The great bulk of available evidence suggests that, elsewhere in the Third World, U.S. officials wanted to isolate, discredit, and eliminate Communist factions rather than maneuver to loosen their alleged ties to Moscow or to convince them of the openness of U.S. policy.

So obsessed were U.S. officials about the Communist threat in Third World areas that they frequently confused revolutionary nationalism and indigenous discontent with externally supported Communist movements. A good example of this was in the Philippines. Inept and corrupt leadership inspired the resurgence and growth of the Huk insurrection in the late 1940's and early 1950's. U.S. officials correctly excoriated the government in Manila for its incompetence and corruption. Yet at the same time policymakers in Washington alleged that the Huks were the stooges of either the Russian or the Chinese Communists. Such accusations were unproven at the time and remain highly dubious to this day. The Huks did not receive aid from the Kremlin. Indeed, neither the Russians nor the Chinese showed much interest in the Huk insurrection.[27] Yet policymakers in Washington assumed the existence of such external support, feared it, and embraced repugnant and repressive regimes in order to counter it.

Throughout the Third World, the United States established linkages with discredited elites who, in the pursuit of their own ends, were willing to work with the Americans (as they had often done with the British and French). With regard to the Middle East, for example, U.S. policymakers acknowledged the rising tensions between emerging urban groups and traditional leaders. With equal understanding, analysts recognized the burgeoning unrest in the countryside where demands for agrarian reform were growing. Truman administration officials dwelled on the need for change and then concluded that they must nevertheless work with the very elites who were threatened by such reforms. Fear of upsetting the status quo that comported with Western interests exceeded the desire for progressive change, the consequences of which remained unclear. Increasingly, the Americans felt they could do a better job than the British and the French because they were not handicapped by the colonial image that tarnished their European friends. But as they moved into Third World countries, they found themselves supporting unpopular leaders like Mohammad Reza Pahlavi in Iran and Bao Dai in Vietnam.

Not only did U.S. officials align themselves with leaders of questionable popularity and with groups resistant to progressive change, but they vested these countries and these regimes with importance disproportionate to their true value. As the British and French hold on these areas eroded in the late 1940's, as their payments problems and those of Germany and Japan appeared to be insoluble, and as the U.S. Congress seemed unwilling to open American markets and to disperse additional economic aid, Truman administration officials grudgingly and foolishly concluded that the United States had to become the world's policeman as well as its financial hegemon. This thinking did not simply mean that the United States would increase its mobile forces and covert capabilities. In fact, the enormous increment in strategic weapons in the United States and the substantial buildup of conventional weapons in Europe were largely prompted by concerns with prospective Soviet gains on the periphery. The Soviets, thought Paul Nitze, wanted to fish in troubled waters. In turn, the United States had to shore up the periphery and counter Soviet probes. If necessary, Washington had to be prepared to dominate the escalatory process and to deter Soviet counteraction against Western Europe.

The eruption of hostilities in Korea and China's intervention in that conflict appeared to confirm U.S. expectations that the Soviets were intent on new and more daring forms of risk-taking. Yet after November 1950, U.S. officials hesitated to escalate the Korean conflict. They refrained from directly attacking China because they did not want to provoke the Soviets at a time when the United States was also seeking to rearm Germany and Japan and trying to integrate Turkey and Greece into NATO. Too much pressure might trigger the war that no one wanted and at a time when Western Europe was still susceptible to invasion. Yet Acheson, Nitze, and their associates were not content with their self-restraint. They were convinced that, if they multiplied the U.S. atomic arsenal and bolstered NATO's conventional defenses, they could escalate the war in Korea and engage in other forms of risk-taking on the periphery without fear that the Russians might strike out across the plains of Northern Europe.[28]

It is no accident that, subsequently, most of the nuclear alerts occurred over crises in the Third World.[29] During Truman's presidency, U.S. officials rarely, indeed almost never, expected the Kremlin to engage in premeditated aggression in Europe. A Soviet invasion might indeed occur, but most likely as a result of a cycle of action and reaction in which the Russians would misjudge the degree of the Americans' commitment to bolster their own or their allies' interests on the periphery. The Soviets, therefore, had to be convinced that they could not conquer Western Europe, preemptively cripple America's retaliatory capabilities, or fight a global war to a stalemate. Once convinced of these realities, the Kremlin would learn to defer to U.S. leadership in the Third World.

The thinking underlying this strategy was flawed. The relationships of costs to benefits and of costs to risks appear to have been totally out of proportion to the interests that were at stake.[30] A willingness to risk atomic war over the periphery misconstrued the intrinsic value of even the most important of these countries and misjudged the prospective behavior of neighboring states. For if nations tend to balance rather than band, if they tend to respond to outside threats rather than fall like dominoes, as the political scientist Stephen Walt contends, then even the "loss" of northern Iran or all of Iran would not justify the use of atomic weapons.[31] Yet Acheson, Nitze, and their associates talked as if they should be ready to run the risk of an escalatory cycle over much less significant interests—for example, those in Southeast Asia.

Of course, policymakers never intended to use atomic weapons over disputes in these peripheral areas. By multiplying the arsenal and casting huge military shadows, U.S. officials believed they would never have to employ the very military capabilities they sought to deploy. But how large did the arsenal really have to become to have this effect? Was there anything in Soviet behavior to suggest that they would run the risk of global war over interests in the Third World? Stalin was a monstrous person who treated his own people with utter brutality, yet he was anything but a large risk-taker in the international arena. Unfortunately, U.S. officials convinced themselves that the size of the nuclear balance decisively shaped the settlement of political conflicts in the Third World. Yet this assumption itself was a dubious one. Case studies suggest that the balance of strategic weapons rarely influences the outcomes of crisis situations.[32] And, in fact, there is little reason even to think that Soviet risk-taking has been primarily inspired by their growing atomic or nuclear capabilities.[33]

When the crunch came, of course, Truman administration officials themselves never dared to use atomic weapons. They were prudent men. Indeed, overall they were more prudent than wise and more prudent than foolish. So they, too, realized that it would be erroneous to the point of criminality to use atomic weapons over a Third World country. They might threaten their use, as their successors did by triggering a number of nuclear alerts, but it is hard to believe that they would have used them in rebuffing Communist inroads or Soviet gains in any Third World area.[34] John Mueller and McGeorge Bundy, therefore, are right in arguing that policymakers wasted large sums of money in building up stockpiles of offensive weapons that had little purpose.[35] For prudent men to have attributed so much importance to the periphery, for them to have possessed such exaggerated notions of Soviet capabilities in the Third World, and for them to have invested so heavily in strategic overkill was foolish indeed.[36]

Soviet Behavior

The type of risk-taking in which U.S. officials wanted to engage on the periphery and the magnitude of military capabilities they sought to deploy would have been justified only if the Russians intended to seek world domination. For the most part, Truman administration officials attributed such desires to the Kremlin. And in this respect U.S. policymakers made another significant error. Greatly fearing the appeal of Communist ideology to the war-devastated and disillusioned peoples of industrialized Eurasia and dreading the allure of Soviet propaganda to captive peoples in the colonial world, U.S. officials confused the ideological tenets of Marxist-Leninist thought with the actions and behavior of Soviet leaders in the Kremlin. Policymakers in Washington misconstrued Communist aspirations with Russian intentions and capabilities. Seeing before them a potentially strong totalitarian adversary with an apparently attractive ideology, Truman administration officials refused to acknowledge that their foe, however duplicitous and cruel, had far-reaching security requirements of its own.

Although the documents are still not available to determine the motivations and objectives of Soviet foreign policy, it is clear that Russian behavior was not consistently aggressive. At the end of the war, Soviet leaders must have been sorely tempted to exploit a uniquely favorable position. Their armies dominated Eastern Europe and much of Northeast Asia. Germany and Japan were defeated. Communist partisans were at the peak of their popularity in most of the countries formerly occupied by the Axis powers. And in important parts of the Third World, nationalist leaders were struggling to resist the reimposition of European imperial control or to throw it off. Yet Stalin and his colleagues did not avail themselves of all the opportunities that lay before them. They did consolidate their hold over their immediate periphery in Poland, Romania, and Bulgaria; they did maneuver for greater influence in Germany and request participatory control in Japan; they did probe in Iran and make demands on Turkey; and they did rhetorically support the nationalist struggles of Third World peoples. But the Soviets also demobilized their armies and withdrew from important areas. In 1945 and 1946 they pulled their troops out of northern Norway and Bornholm, Denmark, established acceptable governments in Austria and Finland, allowed free elections in Hungary and Czechoslovakia, discouraged revolutionary action in France, Italy, and Greece, endeavored to maintain acceptable relations with the Chinese Nationalists, and evacuated their forces, however belatedly, from Iran and Manchuria.

Soviet cooperative actions were not disinterested. To the extent that the Russians maintained friendly ties with the Americans (and the British), they could hope to secure loans and reparations and avoid the political and military costs of renewed rivalry with their wartime allies. Most of all, maintenance of the wartime coalition constituted the key to averting the prospective revival of an aggressive Germany and a bellicose Japan. These countries were Russia's traditional enemies. Germany, in particular, as Michael MccGwire has argued, was seen by Stalin as the foremost security danger to long-term Soviet interests. Through collaborative action with its wartime allies, the Soviet Union might be able to control Germany's resurgence by extracting reparations, regulating its industrial production, and overseeing its political reorientation. On the other hand, a rupture of the grand alliance could undermine the Kremlin's ability to monitor Germany's future position in the international arena. This development could be particularly dangerous if the Americans withdrew politically from Europe, as was expected, and if the Germans escaped from the control of the wartime victors, as they had managed to do after World War I.[37]

Yet much as they might have had incentive to cooperate with the Anglo-Saxons, the Russians could not do so at the expense of their most vital security imperatives. Hence they could not comply with U.S. conditions that they accept popular elections, self-determination, open trade, and the free flow of capital in the countries on their immediate periphery. Nor could they satisfy U.S. demands that they defer reparation payments and provide raw materials and foodstuffs to the western zones of Germany. Free elections would lead to the emergence of hostile governments on Russian borders. Open trade would draw its East European neighbors into a Western orbit. Two German invasions within a generation dictated the essential need for a buffer zone. The Poles could not be trusted; they had collaborated with the Germans during part of the 1930's, joined in the dismemberment of Czechoslovakia in 1938, seized part of Lithuania in 1939, and sought to regain territory that the Kremlin had taken for itself. Nor could the Russians count on the good faith of the Hungarians, Romanians, or Bulgarians, all of whom had collaborated directly or indirectly with the Nazis. And if Stalin had deferred to U.S. policy in Germany, he would have found himself sacrificing Russia's economic and strategic imperatives in order to reduce the burden on the U.S. and British treasuries and to expedite West European recovery. Given the devastation Soviet Russia had endured at the hands of the Nazis and given the uncertainties about Germany's future that prevailed everywhere, it was unreasonable to expect any Russian leader to comply with such priorities.[38]

Soviet actions during 1945 and 1946 were contradictory. The Russians showed some restraint but not enough to allay U.S. fears. In fact, those apprehensions grew for reasons independent of Soviet behavior. The Kremlin had rather little to do with the worsening exchange crisis in Western Europe, the growing insurrections in Greece and China, the popularity of Communist parties in France and Italy, the economic paralysis in western Germany and Japan, and the rise of nationalism in Indochina, Indonesia, Egypt, and India. Yet these phenomena portended a great erosion in the strength of the Western democracies and in the capacity of the United States (and Great Britain) to uphold a balance of power on the Eurasian land mass that was preponderantly favorable to U.S. (and British) interests. So the United States felt the need to take the initiative. The Truman Doctrine, the Marshall Plan, and the London agreements regarding Germany were the decisive steps leading to the collapse of the wartime coalition.

Soviet actions were reactive. The establishment of the Cominform, the strikes and demonstrations in France and Italy, the coup in Czechoslovakia, and the blockade of Berlin were responses to the Western offensive. U.S. and British officials acknowledged this truism at the time. The most standard work on Stalin's U.S. policy, ably written by a decidedly nonrevisionist scholar, accepts this interpretation.[39] The challenging question, therefore, is not whether U.S. actions exacerbated Soviet-U.S. relations but whether they were intelligent responses to the real and perceived dangers that existed at the time, including Stalin's maneuvering, previous Soviet gains, and the portentous developments both in the industrial core and on the periphery.

However one answers this question, and we shall return to it in a moment, it is clear that after 1947–48 the Soviets were on the defensive. They faced profound security dilemmas. At best, the revitalization of the western zones of Germany and the formation of the Federal Republic adumbrated the creation of a viable West European economic community and a formidable Atlantic alliance, spearheaded by the Americans. At worst, the restoration of German strength portended the reestablishment of an independent power in the center of Europe intent on territorial rectification and unification.[40] This threat, as has been described, was no figment of the Russians' imagination. It traumatized the French, deeply worried the British, and perplexed the Americans. Western allies dealt with this possibility through the formation of NATO, the retention of Allied troops in Germany, the establishment of supranational mechanisms of control, and the framing of provisions in the contractual agreements that maintained Western leverage over the Federal Republic's capacity to arrange for Germany's unification. The Russians responded with less imagination and more brutality. Faced at the same time with Tito's defection, Stalin consolidated his hold over repressive regimes in Eastern Europe, established the Council for Mutual Economic Aid, and created the German Democratic Republic.[41]

In Western Europe, Soviet capabilities were limited. The Kremlin tightened its relations with Communist parties and pressed them to obstruct the Marshall Plan. But rather than risk revolutionary action and provocative coups that might lead to war, the Communists sought primarily the right to reenter the coalitions from which they had been excluded. More daringly, the Soviets blockaded Berlin. But again fearing war, they did not challenge the airlift and eventually acquiesced to Western policies in western Germany. Defeated, the Soviets periodically tried to sidetrack the integration of the Federal Republic into the Atlantic community by holding out the lure of unification and neutralization and by talking about peace and coexistence. The United States, Britain, and France parried such initiatives with timely concessions to Adenauer's government and with redoubled efforts to achieve integration. In truth, after the Berlin crisis of 1948–49, it was not too difficult to overcome Soviet overtures because they were halfhearted at best. Stalin could not really take the idea of a unified, neutralized Germany very seriously because it portended a Germany that might cast its future with the West or that might boldly reestablish its own preponderance in Central and Eastern Europe. Faced with Germany's renewal and Western Europe's revitalization, the Kremlin did indeed face the specter of a mighty alliance, a resurgent Germany, and a powerful magnet drawing the Soviets' European satellites westward. While Stalin tightened controls at home and stepped up his ideological campaign abroad, his major hope was in a renewed economic crisis in the West that might undermine America's financial and commercial leadership, trigger renewed autarkic forces, splinter the non-Communist coalitions in France and Italy, and drive western Germany to seek markets in the Soviet sphere.[42]

These contingencies were precisely the ones most feared by Truman administration officials. However secretive, repressive, and inhumane Stalin's rule was inside Russia, it was not so much the internal character of the regime that frightened U.S. officials as its alleged capacity to expand its power abroad. Yet after the 1948–49 German crisis, Soviet behavior in Western Europe was quite cautious. But still, U.S. concerns did not abate. Policymakers remained uncertain whether they could preserve Western cohesion, overcome traditional Franco-German rivalries, sustain economic recovery, and solve the dollar gap. Hence they attributed enormous importance to Soviet atomic weapons and to Communist successes in the periphery. They worried that the existence of Soviet atomic capabilities might dissuade West European governments from going ahead with the risks that inhered in West Germany's rearmament and their own military buildup. The Americans also feared that Mao's victory in China and revolutionary nationalist unrest elsewhere in Asia and the Middle East would undermine the prospects for effectively integrating the industrial core with the Third World periphery. The North Korean attack on South Korea accentuated these apprehensions. But aside from Soviet acquiescence to the North Korean attack, or perhaps because of the U.S. response, Soviet actions on the periphery remained restrained. Throughout Southeast Asia, for example, Soviet policy was cautious. During these years little or no aid was given to the Viet Minh. Nor did the Soviets play an active role in the turbulent affairs of Iran and Egypt. No doubt they hoped to capitalize on the trend of events, but their behavior was circumspect.[43]

The Soviets, of course, did respond to the overall U.S. military buildup that went on during the Korean War. They, too, accelerated efforts to develop a hydrogen bomb, augmented their air/atomic capabilities, and strengthened the military establishments of their satellites in Eastern Europe. But as noted in previous chapters, the U.S. strategic buildup and the West's rearmament efforts far outpaced that of the Soviet Union during the last years of the Truman administration. A war might arise from miscalculations on the periphery or from an escalatory cycle, but few U.S. analysts thought the Soviets would launch a premeditated attack on Western Europe.

Judgments

U.S. analysts were right. Stalin preferred to concentrate on his own sphere and on developments inside the Soviet Union. He never concealed his desire to reannex territory lost at the end of World War I and to consolidate the gains obtained in the Molotov-Ribbentrop pact of 1939. These objectives were necessary to isolate his regime behind a security zone in Eastern Europe.[44] But the nature of that zone was not predetermined, nor was the magnitude of the Soviet challenge beyond that zone. Initially, Stalin probed only occasionally beyond the sphere of his occupation armies. His most provocative and heinous foreign policy actions came in the latter part of 1947 and 1948, but they were in response to Western initiatives. As we have seen, the formation of the Cominform, the coup in Czechoslovakia, the purges in Eastern Europe, and the blockade of Berlin were reactions to the Truman Doctrine, the Marshall Plan, and, most important of all, the affirmative program in western Germany.

There is, then, reason to assign as much of the responsibility for the origins of the cold war to the United States as to the Soviet Union. But it would be a mistake to carry the logic of this argument too far, because neither nation was simply reacting to the actions of the other. The causes of the cold war were more complex. The United States was responding to a matrix of perceived dangers. As ominous as Soviet behavior were the vacuums of power in Germany and Japan, the grass-roots support for Communist parties in France, Italy, Greece, and China, the stirrings of revolutionary nationalism in the Third World, and the disruptions of traditional patterns of commerce and finance. In other words, the cold war was the legacy of World War II. That conflict deranged the international system, altered the balance of power in Europe, shattered colonial empires, restructured economic and social arrangements within nations, and bequeathed a legacy of fear that preordained a period of unusual anxiety and tension. The national security policies of the Truman administration were an attempt to apply the lessons and cope with the legacies of World War II as much as they were an effort to contain the Soviet Union. Yet no one should deny that the very existence of the Soviet Union, situated in a predominant position in the center of Eurasia, with a totalitarian regime, a rival ideology, and expansive security interests of its own, cast harrowing shadows and accentuated anxieties. Prudent men with great power and wealth, like those occupying the highest offices in Washington, could not take chances.

Between 1947 and 1952 these men integrated Western Europe, West Germany, and Japan into a U.S.-led orbit. Through NATO, the contractual agreements with Germany, the security treaty with Japan, and other supranational mechanisms of control, they created a configuration of power in the industrial core of Eurasia that comported with U.S. security interests. By acting as financial hegemon, moreover, and by supporting multilateral trade, they helped promote unprecedented economic growth that reinforced the cohesion on which U.S. geopolitical preponderance depended. From the outset, U.S. officials also believed that success in the industrialized core would drive a wedge between Russia and Eastern Europe and bring freedom to the satellite countries. The Kremlin itself might eventually experience significant change and transform its behavior in the international system. The cold war, Truman and his advisers believed, could be won. And so it has been.

But it has taken longer than expected and the costs have been high, higher than necessary. U.S. officials exaggerated the importance of the periphery, misconstrued the relationships between the Kremlin and revolutionary nationalist leaders, and overestimated the gains that the Kremlin could derive from developments in the Third World. The United States needlessly aligned itself with corrupt and unpopular regimes, offered them military aid, and pursued policies that were indiscriminately anti-Communist. The ultimate tragedy was the war in Indochina. But for 40 years the United States squandered enormous sums of money on an arms race that was itself fueled by rivalries on the periphery and by fears of escalation in Western Europe. Over time, moreover, these military expenditures and overseas commitments may have eroded America's margin of economic superiority and facilitated the rise of formidable competitors.

Could the positive results have been achieved at lower cost? In 1946 and 1947 a tolerable configuration of power in Eurasia probably could not have been brought about without provoking the Soviets. The threats emanating from the postwar socioeconomic dislocation and power vacuums were too great to allow for a policy of reassurance. Although unlikely, a sequence of events *might* have ended in Communist victories in France, Italy, and Greece, *might* have led to an autonomous and revanchist Germany, and *might* have culminated in Soviet domination, however indirect, of major parts of western Eurasia. Prudent men could not take such risks when the leadership in the Kremlin was so totalitarian and repressive and when it possessed an ideology that appeared attractive to even larger numbers of people in the underdeveloped periphery. U.S. officials intelligently decided to rebuild Western Europe and to co-opt German and Japanese strength. These actions were of decisive importance in fueling the cold war, but they were prudently conceived and skillfully implemented in cooperation with indigenous elites.

Although U.S. actions necessarily engendered legitimate security apprehensions in the Soviet Union, the Russian response was neither so belligerent nor so daring as to have necessitated the huge buildup in strategic armaments, the stress on European conventional rearmament, and the endless struggles on the periphery. The Russians backed down in Berlin. Moreover, their capacity to affect developments in the Third World was severely circumscribed by their limited power-projection capabilities and their economic backwardness. Western Europe required security guarantees, not the extensive armaments that Americans wanted it to have. The Third World needed markets and capital and self-determination, not a reformed neocolonial leadership bolstered by U.S. military aid.

During 1949, the Americans distorted the ramifications of the Chinese Communist victory and exaggerated the significance of the Soviet acquisition of atomic weapons. These events, reinforced by the dollar gap, the European integration impasse, and the rise of McCarthyism, inspired U.S. officials to conjure up the scenarios and to imagine the falling dominoes that justified their huge strategic-arms buildup and their interventionist practices. No doubt it was prudent to establish a retaliatory or second-strike capability and to counter North Korean aggression in South Korea. But U.S. efforts to roll back the Communist regime in Korea, march to the Yalu, and achieve overwhelming strategic superiority showed a fundamental insensitivity to the security requirements of America's adversaries, however reprehensible they may have been, as well as an overestimation of the political and military shadows cast by atomic weapons.[45]

Just as it was logical for the Communist Chinese to block U.S. advances to their borders, it was equally natural for the Soviets to see U.S. behavior as ever more threatening. U.S. policymakers understood these facts but paid little heed to them except insofar as they influenced calculations concerning the amount of pressure the officials might bring to bear and the degree of risk-taking they could engage in. More strategic power and conventional armaments meant more risk-taking. More risk-taking meant integrating and rearming the industrial core (including Germany and Japan), shoring up the periphery, and rolling back the Iron Curtain. But did overwhelming strategic superiority coupled with relentless economic, political, and diplomatic pressure encourage or dissuade Soviet leaders, especially in the post-Stalin era, from considering the very changes that U.S. officials wanted to bring about? Did the preponderance of power engineered by the United States promote evolution in the Soviet system or did it fuel the security dilemma, inducing Soviet counterthrusts and postponing adaptation? Or did it do both, and, if so, to what extent?

■

It will be many years before we know the answers to questions of this sort. We will need to wait patiently for the opening of Soviet archival materials, and even then the information will be fragmentary and incomplete. Rather than speculate on such matters now, it is wiser to conclude with a self-evident proposition, but one well worth repeating: the geopolitical and ideological threat posed by the Soviet Union is gone. By helping to rebuild Western Europe, West Germany, and Japan, by co-opting their power within a U.S.-led orbit, and by sustaining a multilateral commercial order conducive to economic growth, the Truman administration prevented a potential adversary from gaining a dominating position in industrial Eurasia. By balancing Soviet power on the Eurasian land mass and by accepting the role of hegemon in the international economy, the United States established a position of preponderant influence in the international system. That system is now transformed from the one that existed at the end of World War II. As a result of economic and technological developments, a configuration of power has been created that mitigates against traditional geopolitical threats like the one that U.S. officials saw on the horizon in the mid-1940's.

Instability will persist, commercial rivalries will grow, regional conflicts will erupt, and the world will be messier and more complex. But the challenges that lie ahead will be different than in the recent past. This truism does not mean that the United States needs to compromise its security or relinquish its special place in the international system. In fact, there is no reason why the United States cannot retain a preponderance of power compatible with its security interests by capitalizing on past successes, promoting freer trade and price stability, eschewing wasteful military expenditures, and curtailing arms sales that fuel local rivalries and breed regional instability.[46]

The great achievement of the early cold war years was that U.S. officials helped forge a configuration of power in the industrial core of Eurasia that continues to safeguard vital U.S. interests. That triumph bequeaths a special opportunity to a new generation of U.S. officials. These men and women were reared in a cold war ethos, but regardless of what happens in the Soviet Union, they will govern in a world that is configured very differently from the one inherited by Truman administration officials in the 1940's. Western Europe is no longer weak and vulnerable; Germany and Japan are strong; Marxist-Leninist ideology and the Soviet model of development are discredited. The task for the new generation is to take advantage of the new realities. U.S. officials must not be distracted from the most intractable problems facing the United States: in its cities, its schools, its factories, its trade accounts, and its fiscal and budgetary practices. As the century enters its last decade, there may be a unique (and perhaps fleeting) conjunction of events—a reduced geopolitical threat and a wave of liberal political and economic thinking—that affords U.S. leaders a rare opportunity to renew the fundamental sources of America's greatness and power: the resourcefulness of its people; the productivity of its economy; the munificence of its environment; and the vitality of its political and economic system. The challenge lies within, and it must not be shirked.

Reference Matter

■

Notes

Complete references for the works cited in short form are given in the Bibliography, pp. 641–71.

Abbreviations

AAF	Army Air Forces
ABC	American-British Conversations
ACC	Allied Control Commission
AEC	Atomic Energy Commission
AFH	Air Force Headquarters
ANPB	Army-Navy Petroleum Board
ASPB	Armed Services Petroleum Board
BOB	Bureau of the Budget
BP	Bulky Package
CAD	Civil Affairs Division
CCS	Combined Chiefs of Staff
CEA	Council of Economic Advisers
CFM	Council of Foreign Ministers
CIA	Central Intelligence Agency
CIG	Central Intelligence Group
CNO	Chief of Naval Operations
DCNO	Deputy Chief of Naval Operations
DOD	Department of Defense
DOS	Department of State
DSB	*Department of State Bulletin*
ECA	Economic Cooperation Administration
ECAFE	Economic Commission for Asia and the Far East
ECE	Economic Commission for Europe
EDC	European Defense Community
ERP	European Recovery Program
FRUS	*Foreign Relations of the United States*

HSTL	Harry S. Truman Library
HSTP	Harry S. Truman Papers
ISAC	International Security Affairs Committee
JCS	Joint Chiefs of Staff
JIC	Joint Intelligence Committee
JIG	Joint Intelligence Group
JIS	Joint Intelligence Staff
JLPC	Joint Logistics Planning Committee
JPS	Joint Planning Staff
JSSC	Joint Strategic Survey Committee
JWPC	Joint War Plans Committee
LC	Library of Congress
MAP	Military Assistance Program
MemCon	Memorandum of Conversation
Memo	Memorandum
MID	Military Intelligence Division
MIS	Military Intelligence Staff
MSA	Mutual Security Agency
NA	National Archives
NATO	North Atlantic Treaty Organization
ND	No date
NEA	Office of Near Eastern, South Asian, and African Affairs
NFTC	National Foreign Trade Council
NHC	Naval Historical Center
NIE	National Intelligence Estimate
NME	National Military Establishment
NSC	National Security Council
NSRB	National Security Resources Board
OASW	Office of the Assistant Secretary of War
ODM	Office of Defense Mobilization
OEEC	Organization of European Economic Cooperation
ONI	Office of Naval Intelligence
OPD	Operations Division
OSS	Office of Strategic Services
P&O	Plans and Operations
PPP:HST	*Public Papers of the Presidents: Harry S. Truman*
PPS	Policy Planning Staff
PPS Papers	*State Department Policy Planning Staff Papers*
Pres	President
PSA	Philippines and Southeast Asia
PSB	Psychological Strategy Board
PSF	President's Secretary's File
RG	Record Group
SANACC	State-Army-Navy-Air Force Coordinating Committee
SecArmy	Secretary of the Army
SecDef	Secretary of Defense
SecNavy	Secretary of the Navy
SecState	Secretary of State
SecWar	Secretary of War
SPD	Strategic Plans Division
SWNCC	State-War-Navy Coordinating Committee
TCC	Temporary Council Committee

TS	Top Secret
UMT	Universal Military Training
UN	United Nations
UNRRA	UN Relief and Rehabilitation Administration
WSEG	Weapons Systems Evaluation Group

Preface

1. For important works on Soviet policy that have influenced my thinking, see Mastny, *Russia's Road to the Cold War*; Taubman, *Stalin's American Policy*; Ulam, *Rivals*; Ulam, *Stalin*; Adomeit, *Soviet Risk-Taking*; McCagg, *Stalin Embattled*; McNeal, *Stalin*; W. Hahn, *Postwar Soviet Politics*; Ra'anan, *International Policy Formation*; Dunmore, *Soviet Politics*; MccGwire, "Genesis of Soviet Threat Perceptions"; Resis, *Stalin and the Onset of the Cold War*; Haslam, "Stalin's Assessment of the Likelihood of War."

2. For threat perception, deterrence, and security, see Jervis, *Perception and Misperception*; Lebow, *Between Peace and War*; Jervis, Lebow, and Stein, *Psychology and Deterrence*; George and Smoke, *Deterrence*. For dependency, hegemony, and the world political economy, see Wallerstein, *Capitalist World Economy*; Kindleberger, *World in Depression*; Keohane, *After Hegemony*; Calleo, *Beyond American Hegemony*. Also, for relationships between economics and geopolitics, see Gilpin, *War and Change*; Kennedy, *Rise and Fall of the Great Powers*; Knorr, *Power and Wealth*.

3. On Eastern Europe, see, e.g., L. Davis, *Cold War Begins*; Lundestad, *American Non-Policy Towards Eastern Europe*; Mark, "American Policy Toward Eastern Europe." On China, see, e.g., Stueck, *Road to Confrontation*; E. May, *Truman Administration and China*; Borg and Heinrichs, *Uncertain Years*; N. Tucker, *Patterns in the Dust*. On Southeast Asia, see, e.g., McMahon, *Colonialism and Cold War*; Rotter, *Path to Vietnam*; Blum, *Drawing the Line*; Hess, *United States' Emergence as a Southeast Asian Power*; L. Gardner, *Approaching Vietnam*. On Europe, see, e.g., Gimbel, *Origins of the Marshall Plan*; Milward, *Reconstruction of Western Europe*; Hogan, *Marshall Plan*; J. Miller, *United States and Italy*; Wall, *United States and the Reshaping of Postwar France*.

4. For strategic policy, see, e.g., D. Rosenberg, "American Atomic Strategy"; Sherry, *Preparing for the Next War*; Herken, *Winning Weapon*; Bundy, *Danger and Survival*, 1–236; Borowski, *Hollow Threat*. For occupation policy, see, e.g., Gimbel, *American Occupation of Germany*; Backer, *Decision to Divide Germany*; Backer, *Winds of History*; Eisenberg, "U.S. Policy in Post-War Germany"; Dower, *Empire and Aftermath*, 273–492; Schaller, *American Occupation of Japan*; Schonberger, *Aftermath of War*; Matray, *Reluctant Crusade*; Cumings, *Origins of the Korean War*; Merrill, *Korea*.

5. Ovendale, ed., *Foreign Policy of British Labour Governments*, 43–60; Harbutt, *Iron Curtain*; Bullock, *Bevin*; Milward, *Reconstruction of Western Europe*; Best, *"Cooperation with Like-Minded Peoples"*; Louis, *British Empire in the Middle East*; Dingman, "Diplomacy of Dependency"; Lundestad, "Empire by Invitation?"

6. Leffler, *Elusive Quest*; Costigliola, *Awkward Dominion*; Hogan, *Informal Entente*; Schuker, *End of French Predominance*.

7. Acheson, "Why a Loan to England?" 25 Jan 46, Acheson Papers (Yale Univ.), series 1, box 46 (I am indebted to Bill Burr for this document); Acheson, *Morning and Noon*, 40; Block, *Origins of International Economic Disorder*, 40.

Introduction

1. Van der Wee, *Prosperity and Upheaval*, 25–29.
2. Paterson, *On Every Front*, 1–32.
3. Ibid., 2–13; Woodbridge, *UNRRA*, 2: 231–32, 371–72, 416–17.

4. UN, ECE, *Economic Survey of Europe* (1947), 11; UN, ECAFE, *Economic Survey of Asia and the Far East* (1948), 49.

5. Woodbridge, *UNRRA*, 2: 147, 214.

6. UN, ECE, *Economic Survey of Europe* (1947), 3–30; Milward, *Reconstruction of Western Europe*, 1–55.

7. Kennedy, *Rise and Fall of the Great Powers*, 357–58, 369.

8. Ibid., 353–72; Winkler, *Home Front U.S.A.*, 21–22.

9. Kennedy, *Rise and Fall of the Great Powers*.

10. See, e.g., Johnston, *America Unlimited*.

11. See, e.g., the 580-page "Report of the United States Military Mission to Moscow, October 18, 1943–October 31, 1945," in NA, RG 165, OPD, 336 TS; Sherry, *Preparing for the Next War*, 159–232; Marshall's comments, in Sherwin, *A World Destroyed*, 301.

12. *FRUS, Malta/Yalta*, 107–8.

13. "War Damage in the USSR," *USSR Information Bulletin* 7 (14 May 47): 5–6; for confirmation, see UN, ECE, *Economic Survey of Europe* (1947), 145–48; Riasanovsky, *History of Russia*, 585.

14. Kennan, "Notes on the Marshall Plan," 15 Dec 47, Kennan Papers, box 23.

15. Michael Forrestal to James V. Forrestal, 28 Apr and 22 May 47, Forrestal Papers, box 12. The quotation is from the later letter.

16. These generalizations emerge from a study of U.S. war plans and from assessments of Soviet capabilities. See RG 218, JCS, CCS 092 USSR (3-27-45) and CCS 381 USSR (3-2-46).

17. Van der Wee, *Prosperity and Upheaval*, 32–36; Milward, *War, Economy and Society*, 130–31, 339–45; Gati, *Hungary and the Soviet Bloc*, 59–65, 82–83; Bloomfield, *Passive Revolution*, 34–38; Morgan, *Labour in Power*, 44. But in Germany, the Nazi legacy made people suspicious of state power. See Prowe, "Economic Democracy in Post–World War II Germany," 456–57.

18. Acheson Testimony, 8 March 45, U.S. Senate, Banking and Currency, *Bretton Woods Agreements Act*, 1: 35.

19. See, e.g., Bloomfield, *Passive Revolution*, 60–67; Gati, *Hungary and the Soviet Bloc*, 1–99. For a brief summary of the Communist presence in European resistance movements, see Wright, *Ordeal of Total War*, 148–66.

20. Spriano, *Stalin and the European Communists*, 238; Westoby, *Communism*, 14–15.

21. For the view of Communist parties at the end of the war, see Joseph Grew to Truman, 27 June 45, *FRUS, Potsdam*, 1: 267; "Possible Resurrection of Communist International, Resumption of Extreme Leftist Activities, Possible Effect on United States," ibid., 1: 267–80.

22. "The Commodity Composition of Trade Between Eastern and Western Europe in 1948," UN, ECE, *Economic Bulletin for Europe* 1 (Oct 1949): 27–30; UN, ECE, *Economic Survey of Europe* (1947), 125–44.

23. UN, ECE, *Economic Survey of Europe* (1947), 31–74; Block, *Origins of International Economic Disorder*, 70–86; Milward, *War, Economy and Society*, 345–61.

24. Bernstein, ed., *Politics and Policies of the Truman Administration*, 78–105; Gaddis, *United States and the Origins of the Cold War*, 18–23.

25. Hirschman, *National Power and the Structure of Foreign Trade*; Gilpin, "Politics of Transnational Economic Relations"; Krasner, "State Power and the Structure of International Trade"; Kolko, *Politics of War*, esp. 242–340, 428–502.

26. Kennan, "Contemporary Problems of Foreign Policy," 17 Sep 48, Kennan Papers, box 17; Kennan remarks at CIA conference, 13 Oct 49, ibid.; Acheson to Oliver Franks, 24 Dec 49, *FRUS, 1949*, 7: 927–28; Paper prepared in the DOS, 5 Nov 49, ibid., 3: 296–99; Dulles Testimony, 5 Feb 52, Senate, Foreign Relations, *Executive Sessions*, 4: 127–28.

27. UN, ECE, *Economic Survey of Europe* (1947), 38–74; ibid. (1953), 10–20.

28. Nationalism was a continuing preoccupation of intelligence analysts and policymakers. See, e.g., CIA, "The Break-Up of the Colonial Empires and Its Implications for US Security,"

HSTP, PSF, box 253. For superb illustrations of policymakers' preoccupation with the economic viability of the industrial core countries and their needs for markets and raw materials, see Minutes of the PPS, 13 and 14 June 49, RG 59, PPS, box 32; Walter S. Salant, "Basic Studies Required to Determine Needed United States Foreign Economic Progress," 5 Apr 50, Elsey Papers, box 59.

29. For the ramifications of the Soviet atomic stockpile, see JIC 502, "Strategic Implications of Soviet Possession of Atomic Weapons," 20 Jan 50, RG 218, CCS 471.6 USSR (11-8-49), sec. 1; CIA, "Estimate of the Effects of the Soviet Possession of the Atomic Bomb Upon the Security of the United States and Upon the Probabilities of Direct Soviet Military Action," 6 Apr 50, HSTP, PSF, box 257. For the relationships between atomic weapons, overall strategic power, and risk-taking on the periphery to counter Chinese aggressiveness, see, e.g., Memo of DOS-JCS Mtg., 16 Jan 52, *FRUS, 1952–54*, 12: 22–34. For an elucidation of some of these relationships, see Trachtenberg, "Wasting Asset," 5–49. For the importance of risk-taking, I am also influenced by Lairson, "Hegemony, Credibility, and the Risk of War."

30. Gilpin, "Politics of Transnational Economic Relations," 408–19.

31. For geopolitical thinking, see MacKinder, "Round World and the Winning of the Peace"; Spykman, *America's Strategy in World Politics*; Spykman, *Geography of Peace*; Weigert, *Generals and Geographers*; Fifield and Pearcy, *Geopolitics*. For geopolitics in the popular media, see, e.g., "The Thousand Scientists Behind Hitler," *Reader's Digest* 38 (June 1941): 23–28; "The U.S. and the World," *Fortune* 22 (Sep 1940): 42–57; Strausz-Hupe, "Geopolitics"; Joseph J. Thorndike, Jr., "Geopolitics," *Life* (Dec 1942): 106–12; see also the weekly sections "World Battlefronts: Strategy," *Time* (1941–42). For recent assessments, see Gray, *Geopolitics of Super Power*; Sloan, *Geopolitics*; Haglund, *New Geopolitics of Minerals*, 3–34. For totalitarianism, see Lifka, *Totalitarianism*.

32. MacKinder, "Round World and the Winning of the Peace."

33. Lippmann, *United States Foreign Policy*; Steel, *Lippmann*, 404–6.

34. Burnham, "Lenin's Heir," 66–67; Pells, *Liberal Mind in a Conservative Age*, 76–83.

35. "A Security Policy for Postwar America," NHC, SPD, series 14, box 194, A1–2.

36. F. Kaplan, *Wizards of Armageddon*, 22.

37. For excellent books on air power, see, e.g., Sherry, *Rise of American Air Power*; Schaffer, *Wings of Judgment*.

38. JCS 1769/1, "United States Assistance to Other Countries from the Standpoint of National Security," 29 Apr 47, RG 165, ABC 400.336 (20 March 47), sec. 1-A. For overall strategic thinking, see the PINCHER war plan studies, RG 218, CCS 381 USSR (3-2-46); see also some of the strategic studies of different countries and regions, RG 218, CCS 092 USSR (3-27-45).

39. See, e.g., Charles C. Bonesteel, "Some General Security Implications of the German Settlement" [ND], RG 107, SecWar, Robert P. Patterson Papers, Safe File, box 1; OPD and CAD, "Analysis of Certain Political Problems Confronting Military Occupation Authorities in Germany," 10 Apr 46, ibid., OASW, Howard C. Petersen Papers, Classified, 091 Germany; Patterson to Byrnes, 10 June 46, *FRUS, 1946*, 2: 486–88.

40. *FRUS, 1948*, 1: 667.

41. CIA, "Review of the World Situation," 19 Jan 49, HSTP, PSF, box 250.

42. Memo by Acheson, 20 Dec 49, *FRUS, 1949*, 1: 615–16; see also, e.g., Acheson to Franks, 24 Dec 49, ibid., 7: 927; Acheson Testimony, 16 Feb 51, Senate, Armed Services and Foreign Relations, *Assignment of Ground Forces*, p. 81.

43. *PPP:HST* (1951), 8.

44. *PPP:HST* (1952–53), 194–95, 189.

45. Buzan, *People, States and Fear*, 44–53.

46. Graham, *Toward a Planned Society*, 91–114; Katzenstein, *Between Power and Plenty*, 23–25; Rosenof, "Freedom, Planning and Totalitarianism"; Brinkley, "New Deal and the Idea of the State"; R. Collins, *Business Response to Keynes*, 137–41, 204–9; Pells, *Liberal Mind in a Conservative Age*, 52–182; Hamby, *Beyond the New Deal*.

47. Acheson, "Why a Loan to England?" 25 Jan 46, Acheson Papers (Yale Univ.), series 1,

box 46. The relationship between domestic and international economic freedom was a frequent theme of Acheson's. See, e.g., Testimony, 13 March 46, Senate, Banking and Currency, *Anglo-American Financial Agreement*, 313–14; see also Statement by Clayton, 26 May 47, *DSB* 16 (6 Apr 47): 628–29; L. Gardner, *Architects of Illusion*, 113–38, 202–31.

48. Acheson, *Vast External Realm*, 19; Acheson Testimony, 14 Jan 52, Senate, Foreign Relations, *Executive Sessions*, 4: 2–3.

49. Winkler, *Home Front U.S.A.*, 10–23; Polenberg, *War and Society*, 236–37; Perrett, *Days of Sadness*, 299–309; Kolko, *Roots of American Foreign Policy*, 3–26; Ferguson, "From Normalcy to New Deal."

50. See, e.g., President's Committee on Foreign Aid, *European Recovery*, esp. 19–22; Dept. of the Interior, *National Resources and Foreign Aid*, iii, 3.

51. Yergin, *Shattered Peace*, 337–65; Schilling, Hammond, and Snyder, *Strategy, Politics, and Defense Budgets*, 5–266.

52. See, e.g., NSC 35, "Existing International Commitments Involving the Possible Use of Armed Forces," 17 Nov 48, *FRUS, 1948*, 1: 656–62; JCS 800/14, Memo for the SecDef, 8 Nov 48, RG 218, CCS 370 (8-19-45), sec. 11.

53. These themes will become clear in the chapters that follow, but it might be mentioned here that DOS officials were the major proponents of the huge military buildup called for in NSC 68. See Gaddis, *Strategies of Containment*, 92–95.

54. Buckley, "American Public Opinion"; Lifka, *Totalitarianism*, 91–286.

55. Levering, *American Opinion and the Russian Alliance*, 200–209; Paterson, *On Every Front*, 113–37; Nagai and Iriye, *Cold War in Asia*, 43–65.

56. Gaddis, *United States and the Origins of the Cold War*, 353–61.

57. Arthur Schlesinger, Jr., "The U.S. Communist Party," *Life* (29 July 46): 84–96; Gillon, *Politics and Vision*, 12; Pells, *Liberal Mind in a Conservative Age*, 52–116.

58. Kepley, *Collapse of the Middle Way*; Reichard, *Politics as Usual*.

59. Truman, *Memoirs: 1945*, 87; Vandenberg, *Private Papers*, 209.

60. This view is most clearly illustrated in the report written by Clark Clifford and George Elsey during the summer of 1946. See Krock, *Memoirs*, 422–82.

61. For an illuminating view of American attitudes toward the restoration of European influence in the Third World, see "Policy Paper Prepared in the Department of State," 22 June 45, *FRUS, 1945*, 6: 556–80. Fraser Harbutt captures (and overstates) the American reluctance to intervene in European political-military affairs; see Harbutt, *Iron Curtain*; Thomas, *Armed Truce*, 572–73.

62. R. Gardner, *Sterling-Dollar Diplomacy*; Eckes, *Search for Solvency*; Paterson, *Meeting the Communist Threat*, 18–34; Kolko, *Politics of War*, 242–66, 484–503.

63. Katzenstein, *Between Power and Plenty*, 51–78; Gilpin, "Politics of Transnational Economic Relations"; Paterson, "Abortive American Loan." For the intermingling of political and financial considerations in American loan-making, see also *FRUS, 1946*, 1: 1410–36.

64. *PPP:HST* (1945), 411; see also 431–38, 546–60.

65. Hogan, *Marshall Plan*; Schonberger, "Cold War and the American Empire in Asia."

66. Forrestal, *Diaries*, 350–51; see also Acheson, *Power and Diplomacy*, 39, 86; PPS 33, "Factors Affecting the Nature of the U.S. Defense Arrangements in the Light of Soviet Policies," 23 June 48, in *PPS Papers*, 2: 281–92.

67. Acheson Testimony, 16 Feb 51, Senate, Armed Services and Foreign Relations, *Assignment of Ground Forces*, 78; see also Acheson, *Power and Diplomacy*, 83–85. For Acheson's views regarding Japan, see Acheson to Franks, 24 Dec 49, *FRUS, 1949*, 7: 928. For the use of NATO as an integrative mechanism, see, e.g., U.S. Delegation Minutes, 10 Sep 51, *FRUS, 1951*, 3: 1230. For the importance of integrating Germany with the West, see Acheson to John McCloy, 12 Apr 52, *FRUS, 1952–54*, 7: 206. For Harriman's antipathy to the third force idea, see Harriman Testimony, 9 Feb 49, House of Representatives, International Relations, *Executive Session Hearings*, 24–25.

68. See, e.g., Wood, *From Marshall Plan to Debt Crisis*, 29–67; Schaller, *American Occupation of Japan*, 141–63.

69. These ideas will be elaborated upon in the chapters that follow, but see, e.g., McMahon, *Colonialism and Cold War*. For the importance of the Philippines as a model, see Dean Rusk to H. Freeman Matthews, 31 Jan 51, *FRUS, 1951*, 6: 24–25. For the need to establish linkages with elites, see PPS, "The Position of the US with Respect to the General Area of the Eastern Mediterranean and the Middle East," 27 Dec 51, ibid., 5: 258–63.

70. See, e.g., U.S. Minutes, 28 May 52, *FRUS, 1952–54*, 13: 161–66; Summary of NSC Discussion, 25 Sep 52, ibid., 2: 136–38; Memo by Acheson, 24 Sep 52, ibid., 2: 140.

71. Memo, DOS-JCS Mtg., 16 Jan 52, *FRUS, 1952–54*, 12: 22–34; Memo by Nitze, 12 May 52, ibid., 12: 89–91; Acheson, *Power and Diplomacy*, 50–54, 64–66, 80–81.

72. For the quotations, see Paper Drafted by the PPS, "Basic Issues Raised by Draft NSC 'Reappraisal of U.S. Objectives and Strategy for National Security,' " ND, *FRUS, 1952–54*, 2: 64–65; see also NSC 68/1 and 68/2, "United States Objectives and Programs for the Cold War," 21 and 30 Sep 50, RG 273, NSC. For Germany, see Acheson to McCloy, 12 Apr 52, *FRUS, 1952–54*, 7: 206. For breaking up the Soviet bloc, see also PPS, "Future Policy Toward the USSR," 6 Jan 52, HSTP, PSF, box 116.

73. Nitze to Matthews, 14 July 52, *FRUS, 1952–54*, 2: 58–59. Although the emphasis on military expenditures greatly increased after the acceptance of NSC 68 and the outbreak of the Korean War, there was a basic continuity of goals. This continuity was explicitly acknowledged in NSC papers. See NSC 135, "Reappraisal of United States Objectives and Strategy for National Security" [Summer 1952], ibid., 2: 144.

74. For illustrative background, see Isaacson and Thomas, *Wise Men*. Isaacson and Thomas deal with Acheson, Harriman, McCloy, and Lovett as well as Kennan and Charles Bohlen. What they have to say about the backgrounds of the first four men is reflective of the career patterns of many other individuals who assumed important positions in the government during the war years and then rose to even greater prominence and power.

75. McLellan, *Acheson*, 50–51.

76. Dallek, *Roosevelt and American Foreign Policy*, 502–29; Burns, *Roosevelt*, 564–79; Gaddis, *United States and the Origins of the Cold War*, 23–31.

77. Gaddis, *United States and the Origins of the Cold War*, 29–30; Kepley, *Collapse of the Middle Way*.

78. Acheson Testimony, 3 Feb 43, House of Representatives, Foreign Affairs, *Extension of the Lend-Lease Act*, 86–89; Address by Sumner Welles, in NFTC, *Report of the Twenty-Ninth National Foreign Trade Convention*, 360–62; Dept. of Commerce, *The United States in the World Economy*.

79. Notter, *Postwar Foreign Policy Preparation*, 128.

80. Henry Grady, "Taking Stock of Our Foreign Trade Position," in NFTC, *Report of the Twenty-Seventh National Foreign Trade Convention*, 450.

81. Acheson Testimony, 12 June 45, Senate, Banking and Currency, *Bretton Woods Agreements Act*, 2: 20–22, 33, 49.

82. Krasner, "State Power and the Structure of International Trade," 317–43; Gilpin, *War and Change*, 138–46; Paterson, *Soviet-American Confrontation*, 1–29; Joseph Coppock to Winthrop G. Brown, 30 Dec 47, *FRUS, 1947*, 1: 825–26.

83. Isaacson and Thomas, *Wise Men*, 119–30; Pruessen, *Dulles*, 76–152.

84. Ferdinand Eberstadt to Forrestal, 9 and 16 Sep 46 and 2 Nov 46, Eberstadt Papers, box 28; Forrestal to Eberstadt, 13 Sep 46, ibid.; Memo by John Foster Dulles, 26 Feb 47, Dulles Papers, box 31; Dulles, "The Problem of Germany and the Problem of Europe," 17 Jan 47, ibid., box 32.

85. See, e.g., Acheson to David Bruce, 30 Oct 49, *FRUS, 1949*, 3: 623; McCloy to Henry Byroade, 25 Apr 50, ibid., 4: 633–35; McCloy to Acheson, 25 Apr 50, ibid., 4: 682–83; Geoffrey W. Lewis and Theodore Achilles to Byroade, 2 May 50, ibid., 3: 913–14.

86. Truman, *Off the Record*, 57; Truman, *Dear Bess*, 522.

87. See Truman's eloquent summary of developments in his farewell address to Congress, 15 Jan 53, *PPP:HST* (1952–53), 1199–1202; Paterson, *Meeting the Communist Threat*, 3–17; E. May, *"Lessons" of the Past*, 19–51; Jervis, *Perception and Misperception*, 266–70. For the logic that inhered in this perspective, see Taubman, *Stalin's American Policy*.

88. For Forrestal, see Doig and Hargrove, *Leadership and Innovation*, 369–406; for Patterson, see R. E. Smith, *Army and Economic Mobilization*; for Lovett, see Fanton, "Lovett"; for Acheson, see McLellan, *Acheson*, 44–56; for Harriman, see Harriman and Abel, *Special Envoy*, 56–192; see also Catton, *War Lords*; Huntington, *Soldier and the State*.

89. Acheson, "The War, Rehabilitation, and Lasting Peace," 18 Dec 43, *DSB* 9 (18 Dec 43): 421.

90. Notter, *Postwar Foreign Policy Preparation*, 23–61; Schulzinger, *Wise Men of Foreign Affairs*, 59–112; Haglund, *Latin America and the Transformation of U.S. Strategic Thought*, 164–222; Berle, *Navigating the Rapids*, 318–47; Staley, "The Myth of the Continents," *Foreign Affairs* 19 (Apr 1941): 481–95; *FRUS, 1940*, 5: 1–257, 353–79.

91. NFTC, *Report of the Twenty-Seventh National Foreign Trade Convention*, 13–16; Lifka, *Totalitarianism*, esp. 18, 128.

92. NFTC, *Report of the Twenty-Seventh National Foreign Trade Convention*, 346–47; see also Roosevelt, *Complete Presidential Press Conferences*, 569–72.

93. Roosevelt, *Public Papers and Addresses*, 261; Lifka, *Totalitarianism*, 117.

94. Roosevelt, *Public Papers and Addresses*, 281–82, 372–75.

95. These generalizations emerge from Dallek, *Roosevelt and American Foreign Policy*, 199–313; Lash, *Roosevelt and Churchill*; Feis, *Road to Pearl Harbor*; Langer and Gleason, *Challenge to Isolation*; Langer and Gleason, *Undeclared War*; Offner, *Origins of the Second World War*; D. Reynolds, *Creation of the Anglo-American Alliance*; Matloff and Snell, *Strategic Planning for Coalition Warfare*; Watson, *Chief of Staff*.

96. Louis Domeratzky, "The Industrial Power of the Nazis," *Foreign Affairs* 19 (Apr 1941): 641–54; Joachim Joesten, "Scandinavia in the New Order," ibid., 19 (July 1941): 818–27; Murray, *Change in the European Balance of Power*; Milward, *War, Economy and Society*, 75–90, 132–65; U.S. Dept. of Commerce, *Economic Review of Foreign Countries, 1939 and Early 1940*, 9–24. John Gillingham recognizes that the Nazis co-opted the resources of conquered countries, but he highlights their inefficiency. See Gillingham, *Industry and Politics in the Third Reich*.

97. For Nazi intentions, see Weinberg, *World in the Balance*, 53–116; Herwig, *Politics of Frustration*, 175–262.

98. For Japan, see Morton, "Japanese Decision for War"; Prange, *At Dawn We Slept*; Cumings, "Origins and Development of the Northeast Asian Political Economy"; Milward, *War, Economy and Society*, 165–68; Barnhart, *Japan Prepares for Total War*.

99. For a similar argument, see the essay by Detlef Junker, in Trommler and McVeigh, *America and the Germans*, 30–43.

Chapter 1

1. Diary of Henry L. Stimson, 12 Apr 45, Stimson Papers.

2. Dallek, *Roosevelt and American Foreign Policy*, 520–28; Roosevelt, *Roosevelt and Churchill*, 657–709; Kimball, "Naked Reverse Right."

3. For the stimulating dichotomy between proponents of the Yalta and Riga axioms, see Yergin, *Shattered Peace*, 3–68.

4. For Truman's background and personality, see Truman, *Memoirs: 1945*, 131–224; Phillips, *Truman Presidency*, 28–47; McCoy, "Truman"; Offner, "Truman Myth Revealed." For wartime planning, see Notter, *Postwar Foreign Policy Preparation*.

5. For the quotations, see Truman's address to the UN Forum, 17 Jan 44, in *Appendix to the Cong. Record*, vol. 90, pt. 8 (78th Cong., 2nd sess.), A265–66; Address, 23 Oct 45, *PPP:HST*

(1945), 405–6; see also Truman's speech, 2 Nov 43, in *Cong. Record*, vol. 89, pt. 7 (78th Cong., 1st sess.), 8993; Haynes, *Awesome Power*, 1–120; Offner, "Truman Myth Revealed"; Miscamble, "Evolution of an Internationalist."

6. See joint statement by Senators Harley Kilgore, Elbert Thomas, and Truman, 7 March 44, *Cong. Record*, vol. 90, pt. 2 (78th Cong., 2nd sess.), 2299–2300.

7. Truman, *Off the Record*, 49, 58.

8. Messer, *End of an Alliance*, 31–70; Truman, *Memoirs: 1945*, 34–35; Truman, *Off the Record*, 16–18; M. Miller, *Plain Speaking*, 205.

9. Lifka, *Totalitarianism*, 305–8; Stettinius, *Diaries*, 317–21; George Elsey Oral History, 319–21; Stettinius to Stimson, 29 Nov 44, NA, RG 319, P&O, 350.05 TS (State Dept. Red File); James V. Forrestal to Stettinius, 1 Dec 44, ibid.; Grew, *Turbulent Era*, 2: 1449–50.

10. Stimson Diary, 14 and 15 Apr 45, and 7, 10, and 29 May 45, Stimson Papers; Forrestal, *Diaries*, 62–63.

11. Messer, *End of an Alliance*, 77, 64–70; Rose, *Dubious Victory*, 244–62.

12. Stimson Diary, Apr–June 1945, Stimson Papers; Truman, *Memoirs: 1945*, 20–21.

13. See, e.g., Stimson Diary, 19 Apr 45, 16 May 45, Stimson Papers. For the CAD, see Cline, *Washington Command Post*, 321–22; Zink, *American Military Government in Germany*; Stein, *American Civil-Military Decisions*, 311–460.

14. For Truman's view of Stimson, see, e.g., Truman, *Off the Record*, 25, 64; Truman, *Memoirs: 1945*, 20–21; see also Morison, *Turmoil and Tradition*, 395–414. For Truman's respect for Marshall, see M. Miller, *Plain Speaking*, 169, 203–4.

15. Cline, *Washington Command Post*, 320–32; for the organization of the War Dept., see P. Hammond, *Organizing for Defense*, 118–31.

16. For Forrestal's initial meetings with Truman on organizational matters, see Forrestal, *Diaries*, 46–47, 62–63; for Forrestal's views on bases and postwar reconstruction, see ibid., 25, 28, 44, 48, 52–53; Stimson Diary, 12–18 Apr 45, Stimson Papers; P. Hammond, *Organizing for Defense*, 135–58; for background, see Albion and Connery, *Forrestal and the Navy*.

17. For the role and influence of the JCS, see P. Hammond, *Organizing for Defense*, 159–85; Schnabel, *History of the JCS*, 1–12.

18. For Leahy, see Truman, *Off the Record*, 11; Truman, *Memoirs: 1945*, 21, 29–30; Elsey Oral History, 320–21; Adams, *Witness to Power*, 282–302; Thompson, *Truman Presidency*, 9.

19. Stoler, "From Continentalism to Globalism," 303–21; Schnabel, *History of the JCS*, 3–4; Villa, "U.S. Army," 66–70.

20. P. Hammond, *Organizing for Defense*, 159–85; Schnabel, *History of the JCS*, 1: 4–11; Notter, *Postwar Foreign Policy Preparation*, 125–26, 226–27, 248, 303–4, 347–50.

21. For Truman's initial displeasure with the administrative structure he inherited, see Truman, *Memoirs: 1945*, 22–23. The generalizations about Truman are based on the published and unpublished diaries of Stimson, Forrestal, Stettinius, Leahy, Morgenthau, Henry Wallace, and Joseph Davies. Typical was Wallace's notation on 27 Apr 45: "Everything [Truman] said was decisive. It almost seemed as though he was eager to decide in advance of thinking" (Wallace, *Price of Vision*, 437). See also Sherwin, *A World Destroyed*, 146–50.

22. DeSantis, *Diplomacy of Silence*, 1–130; Little, "Antibolshevism and American Foreign Policy"; Propas, "Creating a Hard Line Toward Russia"; Harriman and Abel, *Special Envoy*, 441–54; Stettinius, *Diaries*, 316–18; Forrestal, *Diaries*, 39–41; Weil, *A Pretty Good Club*.

23. JCS 1313, "Revision of Policy with Relation to Russia," 16 Apr 45, RG 218, JCS, CCS 092 USSR (3-27-45), sec. 1; JSSC to JCS, 5 Apr 45, ibid.; Deane, *Strange Alliance*, 255–304; Leahy Diary, 17 and 24 Apr 45, Leahy Papers.

24. Harriman and Abel, *Special Envoy*, 447–50; MemCon, by Charles Bohlen, 20 Apr 45, RG 59, Bohlen Papers, box 4; Forrestal, *Diaries*, 47; Leahy Diary, 20 Apr 45, Leahy Papers.

25. Leahy Diary, 23 Apr 45, Leahy Papers; Stimson Diary, 23 Apr 45, Stimson Papers; Harriman and Abel, *Special Envoy*, 449; Forrestal, *Diaries*, 49–51; also *FRUS, 1945*, 5: 839–46.

26. Stettinius, *Diaries*, 316–18; Truman, *Memoirs: 1945*, 85–99; MemCon, by Bohlen, 20 Apr 45, RG 59, Bohlen Papers, box 4.

27. For the San Francisco conference, see Stettinius, *Diaries*, 333–73; Harriman and Abel, *Special Envoy*, 455–56; Divine, *Second Chance*, 387–94; T. Campbell, *Masquerade Peace*, 159–75. For the suspension of lend lease, see Stettinius, *Diaries*, 357–58; Stimson Diary, 11 May 45, Stimson Papers; Memo by George A. Lincoln, 14 May 45, RG 165, OPD, 336 TS; Memo for the Chief of Staff by Lincoln, 11 May 45, RG 165, ABC, ABC 400.3295 Russia (19 Apr 42), sec. 3; Larson, *Origins of Containment*, 166–68; Herring, *Aid to Russia*, 180–211. For Trieste, see Grew, *Turbulent Era*, 2: 1474–85; Stimson Diary, 7, 10, and 15 May 45, Stimson Papers; Leahy Diary, 10, 11, 19, and 20 May 45, Leahy Papers; Truman, *Off the Record*, 32. See also the discussion in Chapter Two, p. 75.

28. Truman, *Memoirs: 1945*, 86–99; Vandenberg, *Private Papers*, 146–219; Bourke, *Congress and the Presidency*, 1–48.

29. Davies Diary, 30 Apr 45, Davies Papers, box 16; Wallace, *Price of Vision*, 448.

30. Davies Diary, Apr–June 1945, Davies Papers, boxes 16–19.

31. See esp. Davies Diary, 30 Apr 45, 13 and 26 May 45, and 4, 5, 8, 12, and 14 June 45, Davies Papers, boxes 16–17; Davies to Truman, 12 June 45, ibid., box 17.

32. Truman, *Off the Record*, 35, 45; Wallace, *Price of Vision*, 455; Stettinius, *Diaries*, 324–25. For Leahy's view of Yalta accords, see Leahy, *I Was There*, 315–16; Forrestal, *Diaries*, 51. Harriman also acknowledged that Roosevelt's concessions at Yalta could be interpreted to mean Soviet hegemony in Eastern Europe. See Forrestal, *Diaries*, 40.

33. Messer, *End of an Alliance*, 47–52, 76–80; Davies Diary, 6 June 45, Davies Papers, box 17.

34. Stimson Diary, 16 and 23 Apr 45, 13–16 May 45, Stimson Papers; Harriman and Abel, *Special Envoy*, 461–62.

35. Stimson Diary, 10–16 May 45, Stimson Papers.

36. Truman, *Off the Record*, 25.

37. For Truman's rejection of Winston Churchill's overtures, see *FRUS, Potsdam*, 1: 6–13; see also Truman, *Off the Record*, 21–22, 30–32, 35; Davies Diary, 21–23 May 45, Davies Papers, box 17.

38. For Hopkins's talks in Moscow, see *FRUS, Potsdam*, 1: 27–61; Sherwood, *Roosevelt and Hopkins*, 883–916; for Truman's reaction, see his *Off the Record*, 44–45; Davies Diary, 4–8 June 45, Davies Papers, box 17; Stettinius, *Diaries*, 378–91; Wallace, *Price of Vision*, 453–55; Messer, *End of an Alliance*, 82.

39. MemCon by Grew, 4 June 45, *FRUS, 1945*, 5: 324–25; Truman, *Dear Bess*, 521.

40. See, e.g., L. Davis, *Cold War Begins*, 202–395; Lundestad, *American Non-Policy Towards Eastern Europe*.

41. For the importance Truman accorded to complying with agreements, see J. Rosenberg, "Belief System of Harry S Truman," 229–31; Larson, *Origins of Containment*, 150–212.

42. Rose, *Dubious Victory*, 182–203.

43. See esp. Alperovitz, *Atomic Diplomacy*; Sherwin, *A World Destroyed*; Bernstein, "Roosevelt, Truman and the Atomic Bomb"; and the useful review article by Walker, "The Decision to Use the Bomb," esp. 111.

44. Byrnes to Truman, 11 June 45, Byrnes Papers, file 92; Truman to Grew, 9 June 45, *FRUS, Potsdam*, 1: 162–63; Briefing Book Paper, "Treaty for Demilitarization of Germany with Commitment to Use United States Forces," 27 June 45, ibid., 1: 450. Senator Vandenberg introduced the idea of a demilitarization treaty in Jan 1945. See Vandenberg, *Private Papers*, 124–25.

45. Briefing Book Paper, "American and Russian Economic Relationship in Countries of Eastern Europe" [late June 1945], *FRUS, Potsdam*, 1: 423.

46. For the DOS position, see esp. Briefing Book Paper, "Recommended Policy on the Question of Establishing Diplomatic Relations and Concluding Peace Treaties with the Former Axis Satellite States," 29 June 45, *FRUS, Potsdam*, 1: 359–62; see also ibid., 1: 180, 319, 357–63, 370, 382–83, 387–88, 714–16, 2: 1382–83. For U.S. reactions to developments in Eastern Europe and the Balkans, see DeSantis, *Diplomacy of Silence*, 106–54.

47. For the emphasis on markets, prosperity, and peace, see the essays by Barton J. Bernstein, Lloyd C. Gardner, and Thomas G. Paterson in Bernstein, ed., *Politics and Policies of the Truman Administration*, 15–148; Paterson, *Soviet-American Confrontation*; Kolko, *Politics of War*; Max, *Sovietization of Hungary*, 63–69. American apprehensions emerge clearly in congressional hearings on trade and financial legislation. See, e.g., Senate, Banking and Currency, *Bretton Woods Agreements Act*; Senate, Finance, *1945 Extension of the Reciprocal Trade Agreements Act*; Senate, Banking and Currency, *Export-Import Bank Act of 1945*; Senate, Finance, *To Repeal the Johnson Act*; see also documents on British-U.S. financial and commercial talks in *FRUS, 1945*, 6: 54–55, 85, 90–204.

48. See the memo by the OSS, submitted to the president by William J. Donovan, "Problems and Objectives of United States Policy," 2 Apr 45, HSTP, Conway Files, Misc. Material.

49. Stimson Diary, 19 Apr 45, Stimson Papers.

50. Acheson Testimony, 12 June 45, Senate, Banking and Currency, *Bretton Woods Agreements Act*, 1–51, esp. 19, 20, 21, 48–49 (for quotations).

51. For testimony, see the hearings listed in Note 47 above; see also Acheson, *Present at the Creation*, 91–109.

52. OPD, "U.S. Position Relative to Soviet Intentions in Turkey and the Near East," 6 July 45, RG 165, ABC 092 USSR (15 Nov 44); OSS, "Problems and Objectives of United States Policy," 2 Apr 45, HSTP, Conway Files, Misc. Material.

53. Truman, *Off the Record*, 49; Truman, *Dear Bess*, 516, 518.

54. Davies Diary, 15 and 16 July 45, Davies Papers, box 18.

55. Truman, *Dear Bess*, 519; Truman, *Off the Record*, 58; Stimson Diary, 17 and 18 July 45, Stimson Papers; Davies Diary, 18 July 45, Davies Papers, box 18.

56. Davies Diary, 16 July 45, Davies Papers, box 18; Truman, *Off the Record*, 53–54; Stimson Diary, 21, 23, and 24 July 45, Stimson Papers; Forrestal, *Diaries*, 78.

57. The quotation is from Byrnes. See Walter Brown Log, 20 July 45, Byrnes Papers.

58. Leahy Diary, 26 and 28 July 45, Leahy Papers. Marshall concurred with a detailed analysis of the situation in the Far East written by Army planners. See OPD, Memo, 4 June 45, RG 165, OPD, 336 TS; see also the many memoranda on possible revision of the terms of Japan's surrender, dated May and June 1945, Lincoln Papers, War Dept. Files. For the military irrelevance of Soviet intervention, see also Hayes, *History of the Joint Chiefs of Staff in World War II*, 720–72.

59. For U.S. policies toward Western Europe, see Chapter Two, pp. 63–71.

60. For the quotation, see Davies Diary, 28 and 29 July 45, Davies Papers, box 19; for Byrnes's feelings, see also Brown Log, 16 July–1 Aug, esp. 20 and 24 July 45, Byrnes Papers; the negotiations at Potsdam can be followed in *FRUS, Potsdam*, 2: 31–606; see also Messer, *End of an Alliance*, 93–114; Sherwin, *A World Destroyed*, 193–238; Rose, *Dubious Victory*, 270–355; L. Davis, *Cold War Begins*, 241–312; Boll, *Cold War*, 116–18, 138; Lukas, *Bitter Legacy*, 1–19.

61. For the quotations, see Truman, *Dear Bess*, 522; Stimson Diary, 30 July 45, Stimson Papers; see also Truman, *Off the Record*, 54, 57–58; Davies Diary, 30 July 45, Davies Papers, box 19.

62. For the quotation, see Stimson Diary, 10 Aug 45, Stimson Papers; see also Brown Log, 10 Aug 45, Byrnes Papers; Wallace, *Price of Vision*, 474–75; Villa, "U.S. Army." For background, see Feis, *Atomic Bomb and the End of World War II*, esp. 119–54. For a recent contrasting interpretation stressing domestic politics, see Sigal, *Fighting to a Finish*, 245–52.

63. For Byrnes's views, see Stimson Diary, 12 Aug–4 Sep 45, Stimson Papers; for Byrnes, the bomb, and the London conference, see also Messer, *End of an Alliance*, 115–36; Herken, *Winning Weapon*, 43–59; Stettinius, *Diaries*, 425–28; Ward, *Threat of Peace*, 18–49; Gormly, *Collapse of the Grand Alliance*, 1–15.

64. L. Davis, *Cold War Begins*, 313–20; Harbutt, *Iron Curtain*, 124–28.

65. For Byrnes's anger with Molotov, see Davies Diary, 9 Oct 45, Davies Papers, box 22; Wallace, *Price of Vision*, 501–2.

66. For the legality of Molotov's position, see Messer, *End of an Alliance*, 131–32; Ward,

Threat of Peace, 37-38. For Molotov's compromise on the trusteeship issue, see *FRUS, 1945*, 2: 192-93. For discussions regarding Eastern Europe and the demilitarization treaty, see esp. ibid., 2: 243-47, 266-68, 488-89. For overall Soviet restraint, see Knight, "Russia's Search for Peace," 137-63.

67. "Daily Summary of Opinion Developments," 24 Sep-15 Oct 45, RG 59, Public Opinion Studies, box 2; *Public Opinion Quarterly* 9 (Winter 1945-46): 512-13.

68. For Byrnes's speech, see "Neighboring Nations in One World," *DSB* 13 (4 Nov 45): 709-11; Wallace, *Price of Vision*, 501-2; Mtg. of Secretaries of State, War, and Navy, 6 Nov 45, RG 107, SecWar, Robert P. Patterson Papers, Safe File, box 3; Messer, *End of an Alliance*, 131-36; Mark, "Bohlen and Soviet Hegemony."

69. For the U.S. concern with the Soviet-Hungarian economic agreement, see *FRUS, 1945*, 4: 899-920; Max, *Sovietization of Hungary*, 52-75. For aid to Poland, see esp. Byrnes to Arthur Bliss Lane, 2 Nov 45, *FRUS, 1945*, 5: 398-99. For Bulgaria, see Byrnes to Maynard Barnes, 14 Nov 45, ibid., 4: 376-77; Boll, *Cold War*, 142-55. For Ethridge mission, see *FRUS, 1945*, 5: 622. For withdrawal of troops from Czechoslovakia, see Memo for the Pres by Byrnes, 29 Oct 45, HSTP, PSF, box 126. For the loan to Russia, see Paterson, "Abortive American Loan," 82-84.

70. DeSantis, *Diplomacy of Silence*, 155-97.

71. Stimson Diary, 19 July 45, Stimson Papers; Davies Diary, 21 July 45, Davies Papers, box 18; Stettinius, *Diaries*, 442; Brown Log, 10, 11, and 22 Aug 45, Byrnes Papers; Harriman and Abel, *Special Envoy*, 504; Grew, *Turbulent Era*, 2: 1521-26; Acheson, *Present at the Creation*, 169-71, 216-24; Bohlen, *Witness to History*, 256; Messer, *End of an Alliance*, 126.

72. Stettinius, *Diaries*, 430; see also Wallace, *Price of Vision*, 524-25.

73. For emerging disputes between military governors and Washington, see, e.g., Backer, *Winds of History*, 91-95; Cumings, *Origins of the Korean War*, 1: 179-93, 214-39; Schaller, "MacArthur's Japan," 1-10.

74. See the extensive materials in RG 218, CCS 381 (5-13-45), sec. 1. Particularly illustrative is JPS 633/6, "Basis for the Formulation of a Post-War Military Policy," 20 Aug 45, ibid.; see also *FRUS, 1946*, 1: 1160-63; Sherry, *Preparing for the Next War*, 198-205.

75. JPS 744/3, "Strategic Concept and Plan for the Employment of United States Armed Forces," 14 Sep 45, RG 218, CCS 381 (5-13-45), sec. 1.

76. Ibid.

77. For the reservations of Marshall, McCloy, and Lincoln, see Memo by Roberts, 2 Oct 45, RG 165, OPD, 336 TS; Marshall to McCloy, 2 Oct 45, ibid.; JPS, 216th Mtg., 29 Aug 45, RG 218, CCS 334 (8-2-45). For action by the JCS, see JCS 1496/2, "United States Military Policy," 17 Sep 45, RG 218, CCS 381 (5-13-45), sec. 1; *FRUS, 1946*, 1: 1160-63.

78. JCS 1545, "Military Position of the United States in the Light of Russian Policy," 8 Oct 45, RG 218, CCS 092 USSR (3-27-45), sec. 1.

79. JCS 1499/3, draft of letter, JCS to Pres, 5 Oct 45, RG 165, ABC 381 (1 Sep 45), sec. 1-A; Leahy to Secretaries of War and Navy, 24 Oct 45, HSTP, PSF, box 158.

80. For the quotation, see "Summary of the Report to Hon. James Forrestal" by Ferdinand Eberstadt, 18 Oct 45, Eberstadt Papers, box 29; see also Memo to the Pres by Forrestal, 8 Nov 45, HSTP, PSF, box 185; Forrestal, *Diaries*, 19, 63-65, 87.

81. For Patterson's opposition to the presidential board, see Patterson to Leahy, 2 Nov 45, RG 165, ABC 381 (1 Sep 45), sec. 1-A; for his concern with demobilization, see Patterson to Byrnes, 1 Nov 45, *FRUS, 1946*, 1: 1111-12.

82. Mtg. of the Secretary's Staff Committee, 13 Nov 45, *FRUS, 1946*, 1: 1119-28.

83. Ibid., 1: 1128-33; Mtg. of the Secretaries of State, War, and Navy, 20 and 27 Nov 45, RG 107, Patterson Papers, Safe File, box 3.

84. See the Mtgs. of the Secretaries of State, War, and Navy, Oct-Dec 1945, RG 107, Patterson Papers, Safe File, box 3. For Truman's actions, see Truman to Forrestal, 29 Nov 45, HSTP, PSF, box 158; Harold D. Smith Diary, 19 Dec 45, ibid., box 150.

85. Senate, Military Affairs, *Department of Armed Forces*, esp. 10–16, 30–34, 49–58, 97–103, 516–20; Caraley, *Politics of Military Unification*, 44–55.

86. Sherry, *Preparing for the Next War*, 193–98, 220–29.

87. Ibid., 197–98; Truman to Smith, 27 Nov 45, HSTP, PSF, box 150; Smith Diary, 19 Dec 45, 4 Jan 46, ibid.; Haynes, *Awesome Power*, 93–100; Wolk, *Planning the Postwar Air Force*, 80–100.

88. Truman, *Off the Record*, 72; Wallace, *Price of Vision*, 512–23; Minutes of Cabinet Mtgs., Oct–Dec 1945, Connelly Papers, box 1.

89. Davies Diary, 8 and 18 Dec 45, Davies Papers, box 22; Messer, *End of an Alliance*, 115–80.

90. Leahy Diary, 30 June 45, 15, 22, 25, and 27 Oct 45, 12 and 26 Dec 45, Leahy Papers. The quotation is from the entry on 27 Oct. See also Wallace, *Price of Vision*, 523.

91. "The Presidency: Power and Peace," *Time* 46 (5 Nov 45): 19–20; "Might and Majesty of the Fleet: Nation in Pursuit of Peace," *Newsweek* 26 (5 Nov 45): 33–35.

92. *PPP:HST* (1945), 428–38.

93. For key speeches, see ibid., 203, 401–13, 430–38, 546–60. For universal military training, see also Minutes of Cabinet Mtgs., 31 Aug 45, 7 Sep 45, Connelly Papers, box 1; Cunningham, "Truman and Universal Military Training," 410–12.

94. *PPP:HST* (1945), 553–54.

95. Truman to Forrestal, 29 Nov 45, HSTP, PSF, box 158; Truman to Smith, 27 Nov 45, ibid.; Wallace, *Price of Vision*, 519, 523–24, 530; Minutes of Cabinet Mtg., 26 Oct 45, Connelly Papers, box 1.

96. Donovan, *Conflict and Crisis*, 107–84; Wallace, *Price of Vision*, 519.

97. Wallace, *Price of Vision*, 489–90, 501–3, 520, 524, 530; Ayers Diary, 19 Nov 45 and 17 Dec 45, Ayers Papers, box 16; Minutes of Cabinet Mtg., 26 Oct 45, Connelly Papers, box 1; Leahy Diary, 14 Nov 45, Leahy Papers; Truman to Stalin, 12 Oct 45, *FRUS, 1945*, 2: 562–63; *PPP:HST* (1945), 435–36; Larson, *Origins of Containment*, 126–249; see also Thomas, *Armed Truce*, 117–29.

98. For Forrestal, see, e.g., "Summary of Russian Dispatches for the Secretary's Diary," 26 Nov 45, Forrestal Papers, box 101; Rogow, *Forrestal*, 122–80. For Leahy, see, e.g., Leahy Diary, 26 and 28 Dec 45, Leahy Papers. For Lincoln, see Lincoln to McCloy, 6 July 45, RG 165, ABC 093 Kiel (6 July 45), sec. 1-A; Stoler, "From Continentalism to Globalism," 315–19. For Vandenberg, see Vandenberg, *Private Papers*, 237–46. Although Daniel Yergin's categories are much too sharply drawn, Forrestal, Leahy, Lincoln, and Vandenberg fall clearly into the group subscribing to the "Riga" axioms. See Yergin, *Shattered Peace*, esp. 17–86.

99. Harriman and Abel, *Special Envoy*, 501–3; Eisenhower's comments at War Council mtg., 3 Dec 45, RG 107, Patterson Papers, Safe File, box 7; Eisenhower, *Papers*, 6: 284–87, 524–27; Backer, *Winds of History*, 87–94.

100. JIS 80/20, "Soviet Postwar Foreign Policy—General" [Jan 1946], RG 218, CCS 092 USSR (3-27-45), sec. 4; JIS 221/1, "Aims and Sequence of Soviet Political and Military Moves," 21 Jan 46, ibid.; JIS 80/10, "Russian Military Capabilities," 25 Oct 45, ibid., sec. 2; JIS 80/12, "Postwar Economic Policies and Capabilities of the USSR," 1 Nov 45, ibid.; JIS 211/1, "Military Capabilities of Great Britain and France," 13 Nov 45, RG 218, CCS 000.1 Great Britain (5-10-45), sec. 1; JLPC 35/9/RD, "Russian Capabilities," 15 Nov 45, RG 218, CCS 092 USSR (3-27-45), sec. 3; JIS 80/22, "Soviet Postwar Economic Capabilities and Policies," 8 Jan 46, ibid., sec. 4; ONI, "Basic Factors in World Relations" [Dec 1945], NHC, SPD, series 5, box 106, A8; Memo of Information by Thomas B. Inglis, 21 Jan 46, Forrestal Papers, box 24; Draft of Memo for the Secretaries of War and Navy, no signature [by Leahy?], 18 Jan 46, RG 165, ABC 381 USSR (2 March 46), sec. 2.

101. For foreign service officers abroad, see DeSantis, *Diplomacy of Silence*, 154–97. For the views of Bohlen, Geroid Robinson, and Cloyce K. Huston, see Bohlen and Robinson, "Re-

port"; Memo by Bohlen, 18 Oct 45, RG 59, Bohlen Papers, box 8; Mark, "Bohlen and Soviet Hegemony"; Mark, "American Policy Toward Eastern Europe"; Messer, "Paths Not Taken." For Harriman, see Harriman to Byrnes, 26 Oct 45, *FRUS, 1945,* 6: 796; Harriman to Byrnes, 27 Nov 45, ibid., 5: 922–23; Harriman and Abel, *Special Envoy,* 515–22. For Acheson and Cohen, see Wallace, *Price of Vision,* 532–33, 536.

102. Messer, *End of an Alliance,* 137–55; Herken, *Winning Weapon,* 66–94; Harbutt, *Iron Curtain,* 138–44; Maddox, *From War to Cold War,* 157–69.

103. Leahy Diary, 12, 26, 28, and 29 Dec 45, Leahy Papers; Davies Diary, 31 Dec 45, 8 Jan 46, Davies Papers, box 22; Vandenberg, *Private Papers,* 224–35; Acheson to Byrnes, 15 Dec 45, *FRUS, 1945,* 2: 609–10.

104. For Moscow conference, see *FRUS, 1945,* 2: 617–28, 668–70, 700–702, 728–36, 748–60, 781–94, 801–5; ibid., 7: 835–48; see also Ward, *Threat of Peace,* 50–77; Gormly, *Collapse of the Grand Alliance,* 108–32.

105. "Political Aspects of the Meetings of the Council on Foreign Ministers," by Bohlen [late 1946], RG 59, Bohlen Papers, box 6; Mark, "American Policy Toward Eastern Europe."

106. In addition to the citations in Note 103 above, see Herken, *Winning Weapon,* 77–94; Messer, *End of an Alliance,* 156–68.

107. Truman, *Off the Record,* 79–80; Messer, *End of an Alliance,* 156–66; Donovan, *Conflict and Crisis,* 155–62.

108. For the quotation, see Truman, *Off the Record,* 80; for Truman's penchant to link Soviet behavior to czarist precedents, see Clifford, "Truman and Peter the Great's Will"; for Truman's mindset and "operational code," see J. Rosenberg, "Belief System of Harry S Truman"; for psychological insights, see Larson, *Origins of Containment;* Jervis, Lebow, and Stein, *Psychology and Deterrence,* 18–27.

109. For Stalin's expectation of another war with Germany, see Djilas, *Conversations with Stalin,* 114; Sherwood, *Roosevelt and Hopkins,* 899–900; Davies Diary, 23 Apr 45, Davies Papers, box 16; MemCon by Bohlen, 23 Dec 45, *FRUS, 1945,* 2: 753–54; MccGwire, "Genesis of Soviet Threat Perceptions," 1–32.

110. Byrnes, "Neighboring Nations in One World," *DSB* 13 (4 Nov 45): 709–11; Memo by Bohlen, 1 Oct 45, RG 59, Bohlen Papers, box 8.

111. For the importance of asymmetrical motivations, see George, Hall, and Simons, *Limits of Coercive Diplomacy,* 218–20.

112. For Harriman's views, see MemCon by Bohlen, 20 Apr 45, RG 59, Bohlen Papers, box 4; Harriman and Abel, *Special Envoy,* 510–11, 517; Barnes to Grew, 23 June 45, *FRUS, Potsdam,* 1: 383–84.

113. For the quotations, see Briefing Book Paper, "Suggested US Policy RE Poland," 29 June 45, *FRUS, Potsdam,* 1: 784–85; see also other planning documents in ibid., 1: 714–16, 420–23; Grew to Truman, 1 May 45, *FRUS, 1945,* 4: 202–3; Acheson to Byrnes, 18 Sep 45, ibid., 2: 236–38.

114. JIS 80/10, "Soviet Postwar Foreign Policy," 25 Oct 45, RG 218, CCS 092 USSR (3-27-45), sec. 2; ONI, "Basic Factors in World Relations" [Dec 1945], NHC, SPD, series 5, box 106, A8. In his incisive article, "American Policy Toward Eastern Europe," Eduard Mark fails to consider the imponderables that an "open sphere" still posed to Soviet security interests. He also disregards Truman's public speeches and private remarks that called for free elections, representative governments, and open waterways and that did not show the same sensitivity to Soviet security imperatives as did Byrnes's speech of 31 Oct. Bohlen warned against "general unilateral statements which permit of various possible applications . . . and tend to promote constant uneasiness and uncertainty." But Truman did not follow this advice. See Bohlen and Robinson, "Report," 397; for some of Truman's public statements and private thoughts, see *PPP:HST* (1945), 433–34; *PPP:HST* (1946), 43; Truman to Byrnes, 5 Jan 46, Ayers Papers, box 18.

115. Ethridge to Byrnes, 26 Nov 45 and 8 Dec 45, *FRUS, 1945,* 5: 627–30, 638–41.

116. JCS 1595/2, 13 Feb 46, RG 218, CCS 388.1 Balkans (8-22-45), sec. 1.

117. Bohlen and Robinson, "Report," 393–99; for a similar DOS assessment, see "The Soviet Union in 1945—An Economic Review" by Thomas P. Whitney, 24 Dec 45, *FRUS, 1945*, 5: 933–36; see also JCS 1595/2, 13 Feb 46, RG 218, CCS 388.1 Balkans (8-22-45), sec. 1; Forrestal, *Diaries*, 106.

118. Hickerson to Byrnes, 10 Dec 45, *FRUS, 1945*, 4: 407–8; Truman to Byrnes, 5 Jan 45, Ayers Papers, box 18; "Political Aspects" by Bohlen [late 1946], RG 59, Bohlen Papers, box 6.

119. Bohlen and Robinson, "Report," 397–99; for JCS Studies of Soviet intentions and capabilities, see citations in Note 100 above.

120. Jervis, Lebow, and Stein, *Psychology and Deterrence*, 180–232; Jervis, *Perception and Misperception*, 143–282.

121. DeSantis, *Diplomacy of Silence*, 155–214.

122. These generalizations are based on the published and unpublished diaries and papers of Truman, Byrnes, Stimson, Leahy, Forrestal, Davies, Patterson, and Wallace.

123. For Truman's views and quotations, see his *Off the Record*, 44–45, 49, 53; Truman, *Dear Bess*, 520–22; Wallace, *Price of Vision*, 489–90; Ayers Diary, 7 Aug 45, Ayers Papers, box 16; Maddox, *From War to Cold War*, 168. For Harriman's quotations, see Harriman to Truman, 8 June 45, *FRUS, Potsdam*, 1: 61; see also Harriman and Abel, *Special Envoy*, 533–36; Leahy, *I Was There*, 322; Eisenhower, *Papers*, 6: 284–87. Byrnes was flattered by Stalin's compliments at Potsdam. See Brown Log, 1 Aug 45, Byrnes Papers; for Byrnes, see also Messer, *End of an Alliance*, 133–36.

124. For public opinion, see the polls in *Public Opinion Quarterly* 9 (Winter 1945–46): 512–35; Gallup, *Poll*, 1: 523, 530–35; Theoharis, *Seeds of Repression*, 194–95; Harbutt, *Iron Curtain*, 152–53.

125. Harriman and Abel, *Special Envoy*, 456–58; Briefing Book Paper, "Admission of American Press Correspondents into Eastern Europe," 29 June 45, *FRUS, Potsdam*, 1: 319; H. F. Arthur Schoenfeld to Byrnes, 31 Aug 45, *FRUS, 1945*, 4: 861–62.

126. For Acheson's remark, see Acheson, *Among Friends*, 59. For an account that stresses the importance of Vandenberg, the Polish vote, and partisan considerations, see Gaddis, *United States and the Origins of the Cold War*, esp. 138–49, 166–73, 282–96, 357–58; but for a more detailed look at the influence of Polish Americans, see Irons, "The Test Is Poland."

127. "Daily Summary of Opinion Developments," esp. 6 Dec 45, RG 59, Public Opinion Studies, box 2; "Opinion and Activities of American Private Organizations and Groups," weekly surveys, Nov 1945–Feb 1946, ibid., box 14.

128. Pruessen, *Dulles*, 280–84; John Foster Dulles, "The London Meeting of the Council of Foreign Ministers," 30 Oct 45, Council on Foreign Relations, Records of Mtgs., vol. 11; James Warburg to Acheson, 31 Oct 45, Acheson Papers, box 27.

129. Wallace, *Price of Vision*, 521–22, 526, 529, 536–38; Davies Diary, 18 and 31 Dec 45, Davies Papers; Leahy Diary, 26 Dec 45–4 Jan 46, Leahy Papers.

130. Vandenberg, *Private Papers*, 220–46; Maddox, *From War to Cold War*, 160–70.

131. These generalizations are based on the daily "Summaries of Opinion Developments," Dec 1945 and early Jan 1946, RG 59, Public Opinion Studies, boxes 2 and 3; see also "Fortnightly Survey," 8 Jan 46, ibid., box 11. If public opinion was not so anti-Soviet, then the claims of Messer, Maddox, and Woods and Jones that politics was driving the administration to a tougher line need to be reexamined. See Messer, *End of an Alliance*, 168, 190–94; Maddox, *From War to Cold War*, 169–72; Woods and Jones, *Dawning of the Cold War*, 84–85, 98–102, 128.

132. Harbutt, *Iron Curtain*; Ryan, *Vision of Anglo-America*.

133. L. Davis, *Cold War Begins*, 284–86, 313–20; Max, *Sovietization of Hungary*, 36–38, 63–70; Boll, *Cold War*, 128–55; Saiu, "Great Powers and Rumania," 130–33, 148–53.

Chapter 2

1. For a recent prize-winning account that stresses U.S. circumspection and ambiguity during 1945, see Harbutt, *Iron Curtain*; see also Harper, *America and the Reconstruction of Italy*, 37–87.

2. JSSC 9/1, "Air Routes Across the Pacific and Air Facilities for International Police Force," 15 March 43, NA, JCS, RG 218, CCS 360 (12-9-42), sec. 1; JCS, 69th and 71st mtgs., 23 and 30 March 43, ibid.; JCS 570/2, "United States Military Requirements for Air Bases, Facilities, and Operating Rights in Foreign Territories" [Nov 1943], ibid., sec. 2; Franklin D. Roosevelt to SecState, 7 Jan 44, ibid.

3. JCS 570/24, Joseph C. Grew to Stimson, 7 July 45, RG 218, CCS 360 (12-9-42), sec. 6; William L. Clayton to A. J. McFarland, 30 Aug 45, ibid., sec. 7.

4. See the studies and memoranda in RG 218, CCS 360 (12-9-42), secs. 7–9. On 25 Oct 45, the JCS approved JCS 570/40, "Overall Examination of United States Requirements for Military Bases and Base Rights," ibid., sec. 9; see also the discussions within the JPS during Sep 1945 in RG 218, CCS 334 (8-2-45).

5. See, e.g., JWPC 361/4, "Overall Examination of United States Requirements for Military Bases," 25 Aug 45, RG 218, CCS 360 (12-9-42), sec. 7; JCS 1477/1, "Over-All Effect of Atomic Bomb on Warfare and Military Organization," 30 Oct 45, RG 165, ABC 471.6 Atom (17 Aug 45), sec. 2.

6. "Extract of Conversations," 18 June 45, RG 165, OPD, 336 TS; Memo Concerning United States Post-War Pacific Bases, by Lincoln, 30 June 45, ibid.; see also Strategy Section, OPD, "Post-War Base Requirements in the Philippines," 23 Apr 45, ibid.

7. For the view of scientific administrators like Vannevar Bush, see JWPC 394/1/M, "Effect of Foreseeable New Developments and Countermeasures on a Postwar Strategic Concept and Plan," 22 Aug 45, RG 218, CCS 381 (5-13-45), sec. 1; for military thinking, see JCS 1477/1, "Over-All Effect of Atomic Bomb on Warfare and Military Organization," 30 Oct 45, RG 165, ABC 471.6 Atom (17 Aug 45), sec. 2; for Leslie Groves's assessment, see JPS, 215th mtg., 22 Aug 45, RG 218, CCS 381 (5-13-45), sec. 1.

8. JPS 781/1, "Over-All Examination of Requirements for Transit Air Bases," 20 Jan 46, RG 218, CCS 360 (10-9-42); H. S. Aurand to Patterson, 7 Feb 46, Aurand Papers, box 28.

9. McCloy to DOS, 31 Jan 45, RG 165, OPD, 336 TS; for the relationships between civilian and military air power, see also Fanton, "Lovett," 134–249; Schwarz, *Liberal: Adolf A. Berle*, 216–53; Converse, "United States Plans for a Military Base System," 3–4, 56–57, 175–76.

10. Lovett to H. H. Arnold and Ira C. Eaker, RG 107, Assistant SecWar for Air, Plans, Policies, and Agreements, box 199.

11. Forrestal to James K. Vardaman, 14 Sep 45, Forrestal Papers, box 100; V. Davis, *Postwar Defense Policy*, 157–206, 259–66. For Patterson's appraisal, see SecWar to William P. Hoge, 6 Oct 45, RG 165, OPD, 336 TS. For McCloy's opinion, see Memo for Hull by Harrison A. Gephardt, 16 June 45, ibid.; McCloy to Chief of Staff, 24 Nov 46, RG 165, ABC 471.6 Atom (17 Aug 45), sec. 2; Stettinius, *Diaries*, 429. For Patterson's and Forrestal's endorsement of JCS plans, see Patterson to SecNavy, 17 Oct 45, RG 165, OPD, 336 TS; JCS 1518, "Strategic Concept and Plan for the Employment of U.S. Armed Forces," 19 Sep 45, RG 218, CCS 381 (5-13-45), sec. 2. General Marshall was especially concerned about prospective costs. See, e.g., Memo for the Record by Lincoln, 30 June 45, Lincoln Papers, War Dept. Files; JCS 570/36, Memo by Marshall [Oct 1945], RG 218, CCS 360 (12-9-42), sec. 9.

12. *FRUS, 1945*, 6: 206–24; Mtgs. of the Secretaries of State, War, and Navy, 28 Feb 46, RG 107, SecWar, Robert P. Patterson Papers, Safe File, box 3.

13. Memo for the Pres by DOS, 19 Dec 44, RG 165, OPD, 336 TS; Memo by McCloy, 31 Jan 45, ibid.; Acheson to Truman, ND [Sep 1945], *FRUS, 1945*, 8: 956–58; Gormly, "Keeping the Door Open in Saudi Arabia."

14. For Truman's approval of the Dhahran air base, see Truman to Acheson, 28 Sep 45,

FRUS, 1945, 8: 958; for Truman's general view of overseas bases, see "Extract of Conversations," 18 June 45, RG 165, OPD, 336 TS; Forrestal, *Diaries*, 130–31; *PPP:HST* (1945), 203.

15. Truman to Stalin, 17 and 25 Aug 45, *FRUS, 1945*, 6: 670, 692; Stalin to Truman, 22 Aug 45, ibid., 6: 687–88.

16. JCS to Secretaries of War and Navy, 11 Feb 45, RG 218, CCS 092 (1-18-45), sec. 1; JCS 1419/1, "Proposed Legislation to Promote the Security of the Western Hemisphere," 8 Jan 46, ibid.; "Summary" by H. A. Craig, 5 Jan 45, RG 107, Assistant SecWar for Air, Establishment of Air Fields and Air Bases, box 216; War Dept., "Comprehensive Statement," ND [Jan 1945], ibid.; Aronsen, "American National Security and the Northern Frontier," 259–70; Child, *Unequal Alliance*, 77–95.

17. Stettinius, *Diaries*, 348–73; Vandenberg, *Private Papers*, 186–89; Leahy Diary, 6, 12, and 25 Sep 45, Leahy Papers; for Truman, see *PPP:HST* (1946), 43. See also *FRUS, 1946*, 1: 772, 780; *FRUS, 1945*, 9: 170–71; Mecham, *United States and Inter-American Security*, 246–77; Green, *Containment of Latin America*, 209–73.

18. In addition to citations in Note 16, see "Military-Political Cooperation with the Other American Republics," no signature, 24 June 46, RG 18, AAF, Air Adjutant General, 092 International Affairs, box 567; Patterson to SecState, 31 July 46, RG 353, SWNCC, box 76, 091 Great Britain.

19. For reports on Communist influence, see MIS, "Soviet-Communist Penetration in Latin America," 24 March 45, RG 165, OPD, 336 TS; Patterson to SecState, 4 Oct 45, ibid. For the quotation, see JWPC 361/10, "Attributes of United States Overseas Bases," 2 Nov 45, RG 218, CCS 360 (12-9-42), sec. 10.

20. Pach, "Containment of U.S. Military Aid to Latin America," 229–35; Rabe, "Inter-American Military Cooperation," 135–38; Eisenhower, *Papers*, 7: 821–22; Mtgs. of the Secretaries of State, War, and Navy, 20 Nov 45, 11 Dec 45, 2 Apr 46, RG 107, Patterson Papers, Safe File, box 3.

21. For the quotation, see Patterson to Byrnes, 18 Dec 46, RG 107, Patterson Papers, Safe File, box 3; see also the review of developments, in Aide-Memoire for the SecWar, 26 Nov 46, no signature, ibid., box 5; Pach, "Containment of U.S. Military Aid to Latin America," 232–33; Rabe, "Inter-American Military Cooperation," 135; Child, *Unequal Alliance*, 86–94.

22. William J. Donovan to Truman, 5 May 45, HSTP, Conway Files, box 15. The quotations are from the enclosed OSS memo, "Problems and Objectives of United States Policy," 2 Apr 45.

23. Ibid.

24. For DOS assessments, see JIS 161/4, "British Capabilities and Intentions," 5 Dec 45, RG 218, CCS 000.1 Great Britain (5-10-45), sec. 1. For DOS acknowledgment of a "global entente," see "Policy Paper Prepared in the Department of State," 22 June 45, *FRUS, 1945*, 6: 579. For Acheson's views, see Nitze Oral History (Truman Library), no. 3, 146–47. For views in the Pentagon, see OPD, "United States Position with Regard to General Soviet Intentions for Expansion," 6 July 45, RG 165, ABC 092 USSR (15 Nov 44); SecWar to SecState [July 1945], RG 165, ABC 093 Kiel (6 July 45), sec. 1-A; JIS 161/6, "Military Capabilities and Intentions of Great Britain," RG 218, CCS 000.1 Great Britain (5-10-45), sec. 1.

25. Briefing Paper, "British Plan for a Western European Bloc," 28 June 45, *FRUS, Potsdam*, 1: 256–64; DOS assessment in JIS 161/4, "British Capabilities and Intentions," 5 Dec 45, RG 218, CCS 000.1 Great Britain (5-10-45), sec. 1; Forrestal, *Diaries*, 58; Gowing, *Independence and Deterrence*, 92–123.

26. Harbutt, *Iron Curtain*, 3–150; Ryan, *Vision of Anglo-America*, 1–69; Bullock, *Bevin*, 12–15, 49–52, 121–29, 199–200.

27. JIS 161/4, "British Capabilities and Intentions," 5 Dec 45, RG 218, CCS 000.1 Great Britain (5-10-45), sec. 1; Bullock, *Bevin*, 12–15.

28. R. Gardner, *Sterling-Dollar Diplomacy*, 165–347; Woods, *Changing of the Guard*. It should be realized, however, that the British exaggerated their own capabilities. See Adamthwaite, "Britain and the World," 223–28.

29. Herring, "United States and British Bankruptcy"; Woods, *Changing of the Guard*, 312–13; Leahy Diary, 2 July 45 and 17 Aug 45, Leahy Papers.

30. R. Gardner, *Sterling-Dollar Diplomacy*, 165–87; Acheson, *Credit to Britain*, 4–9.

31. R. Gardner, *Sterling-Dollar Diplomacy*, 188–223; Woods, *Changing of the Guard*, 327–62; Pollard, *Economic Security*, 66–73.

32. Byrnes, *The British Loan*, 13–26; Statement by Vinson, 5 March 46, Senate, Banking and Currency, *Anglo-American Financial Agreement*, 2–27; Woods, *Changing of the Guard*, 188–211.

33. Acheson Testimony, 13 March 46, U.S. Senate, Banking and Currency, *Anglo-American Financial Agreement*, 306–40. The quotation is on p. 318; see also Clayton Testimony, 5 March 46, ibid., 151–62; *PPP:HST* (1946), 96–100.

34. Acheson, *Credit to Britain*, 2–4, 8–9; Radio Broadcast by Vinson and Acheson, *The British Loan and What It Means to Us*, 18–19.

35. Memo for the Pres by McCloy, 26 Apr 45, HSTP, PSF, box 178; Stimson to Truman, 16 May 45, ibid., box 157; *PPP:HST* (1945), 61.

36. Grew to Truman, 27 June 45, *FRUS, Potsdam*, 1: 267–80. The quotation is on p. 279. See also Grew, *Turbulent Era*, 2: 1445–50.

37. For the expert study, see the Report by the Potter-Hyndley Mission, 7 June 45, *FRUS, Potsdam*, 1: 620; Grew to Stimson, 8 June 45, ibid., 1: 524–25; Grew to Eisenhower, 24 June 45, ibid., 1: 613; Clayton to Edwin Pauley, 3 July 45, ibid., 1: 623.

38. Truman to Churchill, 24 June 45, ibid., 612.

39. Clay, *Papers*, 1: 38–48. The quotation is on p. 44. For the selection of Clay, see ibid., 1: xxxii–xxxiv; Backer, *Winds of History*, vii–viii. For the importance of coal, see also Kapstein, *Insecure Alliance*, 19–46.

40. Grew to Stimson, 8 June 45, *FRUS, Potsdam*, 1: 524–25; Grew to Truman, 18 June 45, ibid., 1: 178–79; Stimson to Grew, 4 July 45, ibid., 1: 628–30; Clayton to McCloy, 18 June 45, ibid., 1: 478; Stimson to Byrnes, 4 July 45, ibid., 1: 482; Byrnes to Truman, 5 July 45, ibid., 1: 491–92. For background, see Backer, *Decision to Divide Germany*, 34–40, 88–89.

41. Truman, *Off the Record*, 48–49; Rose, *Dubious Victory*, 276–77; Leahy Diary, 2 July 45, Leahy Papers. For Pauley's efforts, see, e.g., *FRUS, Potsdam*, 1: 510–11, 522–23, 530–31; Truman, *Memoirs: 1945*, 342–43; Kuklick, *American Policy and the Division of Germany*, 130–40.

42. Grew to Pauley, 2 July 45, *FRUS, Potsdam*, 1: 520; Byrnes to Pauley, 3 July 45, ibid., 1: 623; Clayton to Thomas C. Blaisdell, 4 July 45, ibid., 1: 627–28; DOS to British Embassy, 11 July 45, ibid., 1: 637; Backer, *Winds of History*, 86–88; Clay, *Papers*, 1: 37–38, 62–63, 113, 150.

43. Truman to Stalin, 27 July 45, *FRUS, Potsdam*, 2: 1028; Directive to Eisenhower, 26 July 45, ibid., 2: 1028–30.

44. For the quotations, see Briefing Book Papers, DOS, 27 and 28 June 45, *FRUS, Potsdam*, 1: 587–88, 258; Memo by the JSSC, ND, ibid., 1: 596; Kapstein, *Insecure Alliance*, 26.

45. Truman to Grew, 9 June 45, *FRUS, Potsdam*, 1: 162–63; Byrnes to Truman, 11 June 45, Byrnes Papers, file 92; see also *FRUS, Potsdam*, 1: 257, 263–64, 441, 451–52.

46. Stimson to Truman, 16 July 45, Eisenhower Papers, file 1652, box 103.

47. For the negotiations at Potsdam regarding Germany, see *FRUS, Potsdam*, 2: 141–42, 183–84, 275, 280–81, 297–98, 428–31, 472–75, 481–82, 486–91, 514–22, 921, 1000–1001; see also Davies Diary, 28 and 29 July 45, Davies Papers, box 19; Walter Brown Log, 27 July 45, Byrnes Papers; Harriman and Abel, *Special Envoy*, 484–87; Truman, *Off the Record*, 58; Truman, *Dear Bess*, 520–23. For Soviet views, see also Gromyko, *Memoirs*, 107–10.

48. Byrnes, *Speaking Frankly*, 81–86; Harriman and Abel, *Special Envoy*, 484–87. For the ambiguity of the Potsdam language, see Gimbel, *Origins of the Marshall Plan*, 60–61.

49. For French views, see MemCon Between Truman and Charles de Gaulle, 22 Aug 45, HSTP, PSF, box 177. For the high-level talks in Washington during Aug, see *FRUS, 1945*, 4: 707–25; de Gaulle, *War Memoirs*, 872–76, 904–11. For an excellent account of de Gaulle's views, see Caffery to SecState, 3 Nov 45, *FRUS, 1945*, 3: 890–91.

50. For Franco-American exchanges, see *FRUS, 1945*, 3: 861–925; for Eisenhower's quotation, see Eisenhower, *Papers*, 6: 481; see also Pollard, *Economic Security*, 74–77; Kapstein, *Insecure Alliance*, 38–39; Hill, "American Reconstruction Aid to France."

51. Djilas, *Conversations with Stalin*, 114; see also MccGwire, "Genesis of Soviet Threat Perceptions," 18–31.

52. Sandford, *From Hitler to Ulbricht*; Dunmore, *Soviet Politics*, 111–13; Slusser, *Soviet Economic Policy*; Nettl, *Eastern Zone and Soviet Policy*, 74–88; McCauley, *German Democratic Republic*, 18–26.

53. For Molotov's view, see Caffery to SecState, 18 Dec 45, *FRUS, 1945*, 3: 921–22. For references to Germany's military revival during the discussions over reparations, see ibid., 3: 1486–1501; see also Gromyko, *Memoirs*, 107–10.

54. Clay, *Papers*, 1: 62–65, 85, 88–89, 90, 92–93, 137, 141. For the Monthly Report of the Military Governor, see RG 165, ABC 387 Germany (18 Dec 43), sec. 4-E.

55. For the report by Calvin Hoover, see Hilldring to Patterson, 9 Oct 45, RG 107, Patterson Papers, Safe File, box 3; for the Byron Price report, see Byron Price to Truman, 9 Nov 45, ibid., box 4; see also Gimbel, *American Occupation of Germany*, 20–23.

56. Leahy Diary, 7 Nov 45, Leahy Papers.

57. For the quotation, see McCloy to Patterson, 24 Nov 45, RG 107, Patterson Papers, Safe File, box 4; see also SWNCC 210, "Analysis of Certain Economic Problems Confronting Military Occupation Authorities in Germany," by Lovett, 19 Oct 45, RG 165, ABC 387 Germany (18 Dec 43), sec. 4-E; Hilldring to Patterson, 3 Dec 45, RG 165, CAD, sec. 4, 014 Germany; Patterson to SecState, 10 Dec 45, *FRUS, 1945*, 3: 917. Coal deliveries to France were cut back. See Wall, *United States and the Reshaping of Postwar France*, chap. 2.

58. Rioux, *Fourth Republic*, 54–62.

59. For the French Communists, see Wall, *French Communism*, 29–51; for Truman's allusion to Caffery, see Truman, *Off the Record*, 56.

60. For Matthews's admission to Clay, see Clay, *Papers*, 1: 112; for views of professional foreign service officers, see W. Rostow, *Division of Europe After World War II*, 38–45, 58–69.

61. Harbutt, *Iron Curtain*, 104–16; Gaddis, *Long Peace*, 50.

62. *PPP:HST* (1945), 211.

63. Pollard, *Economic Security*, 63–81.

64. See, e.g., de Gaulle's impressions of Truman. De Gaulle, *War Memoirs*, 906–7.

65. Ellery W. Stone to Harold Alexander, 23 June 45, *FRUS, Potsdam*, 1: 689–90; Grew to Truman, 18 June 45, ibid., 1: 686; "Report on Military, Naval, and Air Clauses of the Treaty of Peace with Italy," by Ad Hoc Committee of SWNCC, 6 Sep 45, *FRUS, 1945*, 4: 1040.

66. Briefing Book Paper, "Italy," ND, *FRUS, Potsdam*, 1: 681; Truman to Grew, 2 July 45, *FRUS, 1945*, 4: 1265–66; for revision of armistice provisions, see ibid., 4: 991–1103. The peace treaty and reparation issues came up repeatedly at the CFM meetings. For the United States and the internal situation in Italy, see J. Miller, *United States and Italy*, 96–187; see also Serfaty and Gray, *Italian Communist Party*, 37–58; Urban, *Moscow and the Italian Communist Party*, 148–200.

67. Stone to Supreme Allied Commander, Mediterranean, 20 June 45, *FRUS, Potsdam*, 1: 706–7; Alexander C. Kirk to Grew, 7 July 45, ibid., 1: 709; Stark to King [July 1945], NHC, CNO, Double Zero Files, folder 23.

68. Ad Hoc Committee of SWNCC, "Report," 6 Sep 45, *FRUS, 1945*, 4: 1034–47, esp. 1037, 1041–42.

69. *FRUS, Potsdam*, 2: 207; *FRUS, 1945*, 2: 198–99.

70. J. Miller, *United States and Italy*, 176–83; *FRUS, 1945*, 4: 1288–1304. John Harper stresses ambiguities in goals as well as tactics. Harper, *America and the Reconstruction of Italy*, 37–87.

71. MacVeagh, *Reports*, 601–72; Iatrides, *Revolt in Athens*; Alexander, *Prelude to the Truman Doctrine*, 1–111.

72. MacVeagh, *Reports*, 670–72, 680–84; MacVeagh to SecState, 10 March 45, *FRUS,*

1945, 8: 116–17; MacVeagh to SecState, 4 July 45, *FRUS, Potsdam*, 1: 672; Kirk to SecState, 22 March 45, *FRUS, 1945*, 8: 122. For support of EAM, see Wittner, *American Intervention in Greece*, 430.

73. MacVeagh, *Reports*, 627–28, 660–61; MacVeagh to SecState, 18 June 45, *FRUS, 1945*, 8: 225–28; British Embassy to DOS, 16 June 45, ibid., 8: 126–27; John Balfour to SecState, 18 Aug 45, ibid., 8: 144–45; and esp. Kirk to SecState, 2 and 4 Nov 45, ibid., 8: 252–55.

74. Ryan, *Vision of Anglo-America*, 132–69; Wittner, *American Intervention in Greece*, 22–52.

75. MacVeagh, *Reports*, 680, 688–91; Grew to MacVeagh, 2 June 45, *FRUS, 1945*, 8: 222; MacVeagh to Grew, 7 June 45, ibid., 8: 223; Mtg. of SecState's Staff Committee, 29 June 45, ibid., 8: 128–30; Byrnes to MacVeagh, 2 Nov 45, ibid., 8: 253; Memo by Loy Henderson, 10 Nov 45, ibid., 8: 263–66; Ryan, *Vision of Anglo-America*, 163–65.

76. MacVeagh to SecState, 1 Jan 46, *FRUS, 1945*, 8: 298.

77. Byrnes to Truman, 10 Nov 45, ibid., 8: 266; Byrnes to MacVeagh, 28 Nov 45, ibid., 8: 272; Acheson to Truman, 20 Dec 45, ibid., 8: 290–92; Acheson to John G. Winant, 27 Dec 45, ibid., 8: 297.

78. JIC, Allied Force Headquarters, "JIC Standing Appreciation of Greece," 16 Jan 46, RG 319, P&O, 350.05 TS.

79. Rabel, *Between East and West*, 1–73. The quotation is on p. 62. See also Grew, *Turbulent Era*, 2: 1479–85.

80. Rabel, *Between East and West*, 55–65; J. Miller, *United States and Italy*, 162–68.

81. General Marshall and Admiral Leahy advised restraint. See, e.g., Leahy Diary, 11 and 19 May 45, Leahy Papers.

82. For discussions of Tripolitania at the London CFM, see *FRUS, 1945*, 2: 164–65, 172–73, 191–93, 200–201; Harbutt, *Iron Curtain*, 127.

83. Louis, *British Empire in the Middle East*, 3–50. The quotation is on p. 15.

84. Lewis, *Changing Direction*, 82–84, 256–75, 287–89, 311–17, 373. The quotation is on p. 384. Rahman, "British Military Planning for the Middle East," 513–17; Clark and Wheeler, *British Origins of Nuclear Strategy*, 82–111.

85. The quotation is in Grew's Memo for the Pres, 3 July 45, HSTP, PSF, box 175; see also Grew's Memos, 23 June and 4 July 45, ibid.; Memo Regarding Soviet-Turkish Relations, unsigned, 29 June 45, RG 59, 761.6711/6-1845; Stanley D. Embick to Handy, 4 July 45, RG 165, OPD, 336 TS; OPD, "U.S. Position Relative to Soviet Intentions in Turkey and the Near East," 6 July 45, RG 165, ABC 092 USSR (15 Nov 44).

86. JCS 1418/1, "United States Policy Concerning the Dardanelles and Kiel Canal" [July 1945], RG 218, CCS 092 (7-10-45); Embick to Handy, 4 July 45, RG 165, OPD, 336 TS.

87. For the quotation, see Expanded Draft of Letter from SecWar to SecState, "U.S. Position re Soviet Proposals on Kiel Canal and Dardanelles," 8 July 45, RG 165, ABC 093 Kiel (6 July 45), sec. 1-A. For the thinking of Army planners, see also Strategy and Policy Group, OPD, "U.S. Position Relative to Soviet Intentions in Turkey and the Near East," 6 July 45, RG 165, ABC 092 USSR (15 Nov 44); Lincoln to McCloy, 6 July 45, RG 165, ABC 093 Kiel (6 July 45); Memo by C. H. Bonesteel, ND, ibid.; Thomas D. Roberts to Lincoln, 16 July 45, ibid. For JCS and DOS views, see JCS 1418/1, "United States Policy Concerning the Dardanelles" [July 1945], RG 218, CCS 092 (7-10-45); Mtg. of the JCS, 17 July 45, *FRUS, Potsdam*, 2: 42; Leahy Diary, 24 July 45, Leahy Papers.

88. *FRUS, Potsdam*, 2: 303–4, 313–14, 366–67; *FRUS, 1945*, 8: 1242–45, 1265–66.

89. For reports on troop movements, see Edwin Wilson to SecState, 27 Oct 45, *FRUS, 1945*, 8: 1260–62; ibid., 8: 1263–64, 1268, 1270–71. For Truman's concerns, see Ayers Diary, 17 Dec 45, Ayers Papers, box 16. For intelligence reports, see Joint Intelligence Subcommittee, "The Russian Threat to Turkey," 6 Oct 45, RG 165, ABC 092 USSR (15 Nov 44); Report from U.S. Military Mission, Moscow [late Oct 1945], RG 165, OPD, 336 TS; MID, "Review of Europe, Russia, and the Middle East," 26 Dec 45, RG 165, OPD, 350.05 TS; JIC, Allied Force Headquarters, "JIC Standing Appreciation of Greece," 16 Jan 46, RG 319, P&O, 350.05 TS.

90. For Kennan's quotation, see Harriman to Byrnes, 23 Oct 45, *FRUS, 1945*, 5: 902.

91. Kuniholm, *Cold War in the Near East*, 214–302; Lytle, *Iranian-American Alliance*, 138–55; Ramazani, *Iran's Foreign Policy*, 110–26.

92. Harbutt understates American interest but is right in emphasizing Byrnes's restraint. See Harbutt, *Iron Curtain*, 135–45; Lytle, *Iranian-American Alliance*, 148–52.

93. Ramazani, *Iran's Foreign Policy*, 70–90, 157–60; Cottam, *Iran and the United States*, 55–75; McFarland, "Crises in Iran," 347–51.

94. Acheson to Wallace Murray, 10 Sep 45, *FRUS, 1945*, 8: 530–31; Byrnes to Patterson, 17 Oct 45, ibid., 8: 535–36.

95. MemCon by U.S. Delegation, 19 Dec 45, *FRUS, 1945*, 2: 685–87.

96. Loy Henderson to Byrnes, 11 Dec 45, ibid., 8: 489; see also Kuniholm, *Cold War in the Near East*, 270–302.

97. For the quotation, see Draft Memo to Pres Truman by Merriam [early Aug 1945], *FRUS, 1945*, 8: 45–48; see also Memos by John Loftus, 31 May 45, 1 June 45, ibid., 8: 51–55; A. Miller, *Search for Security*, 145.

98. Draft Memo to Pres Truman by Merriam [early Aug 1945], *FRUS, 1945*, 8: 45–48. For the special fund, see Acheson to Byrnes, 9 Oct 45, ibid., 8: 43–44.

99. For the Dhahran airfield, see ibid., 8: 956–58; Gormly, "Keeping the Door Open in Saudi Arabia." For support of the Saudi kingdom, see I. Anderson, *ARAMCO*, 143–44; Painter, *Oil and the American Century*, 85–95.

100. Lawson, "Iranian Crisis," 318.

101. Rahman, "British Military Planning for the Middle East," 513–14; JIS 161/6, "Military Capabilities and Intentions of Great Britain," 17 Dec 45, RG 218, CCS 000.1 Great Britain (5-10-45), sec. 1.

102. Lawson, "Iranian Crisis."

103. Cottam, *Iran and the United States*, 80–81; Lytle, *Iranian-American Alliance*, 128–35.

104. Lawson, "Iranian Crisis."

105. Levine, *Anvil of Victory*, 1–37.

106. Clemens, *Yalta*, 247–55; Snell, *Meaning of Yalta*, 127–66.

107. Grew to Stimson, "Policy Papers Prepared in the Department of State," 22 June 45, *FRUS, 1945*, 6: 564–66, 577–78; Memo by John Carter Vincent, 29 Jan 45, ibid., 7: 37–39; McCloy to Stimson, 17 Feb 45, RG 165, OPD, 336 TS; "United States Postwar Military Policies with Respect to China," by DOS, 3 Apr 45, *FRUS, 1945*, 7: 74–79; Grew to Truman, 27 Apr 45, HSTP, PSF, box 173; Gallicchio, *Cold War Begins in Asia*, 20–21. For the continuous anti-Communist thrust of U.S. policy, see the discussion provoked by Martin Sherwin's paper in Borg and Heinrichs, *Uncertain Years*, 3–9; Sherwin, "The White House, the Red Menace, and the Yellow Peril."

108. Buhite, *Hurley*, 220–21.

109. Stimson Diary, 13–16 May 45, Stimson Papers; Harriman and Abel, *Special Envoy*, 449–62; Grew to Stimson, 12 May 45, *FRUS, 1945*, 7: 869–70; Leahy Diary, 23 Apr 45, 17 and 28 July 45, Leahy Papers; Memo by Andrew J. McFarland, 18 June 45, *FRUS, Potsdam*, 1: 903–10; also ibid., 1: 930; Forrestal, *Diaries*, 69–77; Memos, May and June 1945, Lincoln Papers, War Dept. Files.

110. Gallicchio, *Cold War Begins in Asia*, 14–18; Sigal, *Fighting to a Finish*, 92–95, 121, 125–28, 280–81.

111. Truman-Stalin Mtg., 17 July 45, *FRUS, Potsdam*, 2: 43–46; Memo by Bohlen, 28 March 60, ibid., 2: 1584–87.

112. Truman, *Off the Record*, 53; Truman, *Dear Bess*, 519; Stimson Diary, 17 July 45, Stimson Papers.

113. See the documents in *FRUS, Potsdam*, 2: 1323–35.

114. Stimson Diary, 23 July 45, Stimson Papers.

115. Brown Log, 20 and 24 July 45, Byrnes Papers; Forrestal, *Diaries*, 78; Harriman and Abel, *Special Envoy*, 492; Sherwin, *A World Destroyed*, 220–31; Feis, *China Tangle*, 322–27.

116. Truman-Molotov Mtg., 29 July 45, *FRUS, Potsdam*, 2: 476; draft of letter from Truman to Stalin, 31 July 45, ibid., 2: 1333–34; Leahy, *I Was There*, 424; Davies Diary, 25, 27, and 28 July 45, Davies Papers. But Truman urged the Chinese to make no further concessions. See Truman to Hurley, 23 July 45, Byrnes Papers, File 569(2).

117. *FRUS, Potsdam*, 2: 276.

118. Khrushchev, *Remembers: The Glasnost Tapes*, 81. Soviet suspicion over the Potsdam ultimatum to Japan was evident to U.S. officials. See Davies Diary, 25–28 July 45, Davies Papers; Leahy Diary, 26–31 July 45, Leahy Papers; Brown Log, 27 July 45, Byrnes Papers. For the timing of the atomic attack, the resumption of Sino-Soviet talks, and the Russian declaration of war, see Liang Chin-tung, "Sino-Soviet Treaty," 387–93; Feis, *China Tangle*, 333–43; Tsou, *America's Failure in China*, 282–87.

119. Stimson Diary, 10 Aug 45, Stimson Papers; Brown Log, 10 and 11 Aug 45, Byrnes Papers; Wallace, *Price of Vision*, 474; Messer, *End of an Alliance*, 118–19.

120. Gallicchio, *Cold War Begins in Asia*, 73–87; Cumings, *Child of Conflict*, 86–91.

121. Harriman and Abel, *Special Envoy*, 494–98; Harriman, "Yalta Agreement Affecting China," 18 July 45, *FRUS, Potsdam*, 2: 1237–41; see also Tsou, *America's Failure in China*, 282–87.

122. Levine, *Anvil of Victory*, 38–40; Gallicchio, *Cold War Begins in Asia*, 82–83. For the economic importance of Manchuria, see Chang, *Last Chance in Manchuria*.

123. Albert Wedemeyer to War Dept., 19 Aug 45, RG 165, OPD, 336 TS; Schaller, *U.S. Crusade in China*, 260–74.

124. For the quotation, see Henry A. Byroade, "Post-War Chinese Air Force," 30 Aug 45, RG 165, OPD, 336.2 TS; see also Memo for Arnold by Vandenberg, 26 Aug 45, ibid.; Eaker to Chief of Staff, 30 Aug 45, ibid.; Hull to McCloy, 1 Sep 45, ibid.; Marshall to Wedemeyer, 10 Sep 45, ibid.

125. Byrnes to Truman, 3 Sep 45, *FRUS, 1945*, 7: 547–49; Acheson to Truman, 13 Sep 45, ibid., 7: 559–60; Leahy Diary, 14 Sep 45, Leahy Papers; Marshall to Wedemeyer, 15 Sep 45, RG 165, OPD, 336 TS.

126. Acheson Testimony, 4 June 51, Senate, Armed Services and Foreign Relations, *Military Situation in the Far East*, 1844–47; Frank and Shaw, *Victory and Occupation*, 566–79.

127. In fact, the Soviets were giving some aid to the CCP in Manchuria. But there was no information to this effect when the *initial* American decisions were made. For the absence of reports, see *FRUS, 1945*, 7: 1025–30, 531–71; see also Levine, *Anvil of Victory*, 32–33, 41–43.

128. For public opinion, see the Daily Summaries, Oct–Nov 1945, RG 59, Public Opinion Studies, box 2.

129. Levine, *Anvil of Victory*, 39–40.

130. Walton S. Robertson to SecState, 29 Sep 45, 9 Oct 45, 16 Nov 45, *FRUS, 1945*, 7: 572–73, 578–79, 1040–42; Wedemeyer to Marshall, 9 Nov 45, ibid., 7: 612–13; Chiang to Truman, 23 Nov 45, ibid., 7: 660–61; Tsou, *America's Failure in China*, 324–40; Reardon-Anderson, *Yenan and the Great Powers*, 102–9.

131. Wedemeyer to War Dept., 9, 14, 20, 23, and 26 Nov 45, *FRUS, 1945*, 7: 612–13, 627–28, 655, 662–65, 679–84.

132. Patterson and Forrestal to Byrnes, 26 Nov 45, ibid., 7: 670–78; Mtg. of the Secretaries of State, War, and Navy, 27 Nov 45, ibid., 7: 684–86; Wallace, *Price of Vision*, 520–21.

133. MemCons by Marshall, 11 and 14 Dec 45, *FRUS, 1945*, 7: 768–70; Marshall to Leahy, 30 Nov 45, ibid., 7: 747–51; Leahy Diary, 28 Nov and 11 Dec 45, Leahy Papers; Varg, *Closing of the Door*, 235–38; Buhite, *Soviet-American Relations in Asia*, 37–39.

134. JCS to Wedemeyer, 14 Dec 45, *FRUS, 1945*, 7: 698–99; Eisenhower, *Papers*, 7: 590–91.

135. For training Chinese air forces, see Byrnes to Robertson, 19 Nov 45, *FRUS, 1945*, 7: 638. For legislation regarding military assistance, see Forrestal to Sam Rayburn, 5 Dec 45, NHC, SPD, series 12, box 158, C-4(1). For relief of Chinese shipping, see Byrnes to Robertson, 19 Nov 45, *FRUS, 1945*, 7: 643–44; Byrnes to E. S. Land, 30 Nov 45, ibid., 7: 689–90.

136. Leahy Diary, 28 Nov and 12 Dec 45, Leahy Papers; Davies Diary, 8 and 18 Dec 45, Davies Papers. Subsequently, Marshall's views about the connections between the CCP and the Soviets would change.

137. Mtg. between Chiang and Marshall, 21 Dec 45, *FRUS, 1945*, 7: 795-99.

138. Robert L. Smyth to SecState, 1 Dec 45, ibid., 7: 1046-47; MemCon by Vincent, 1 Dec 45, ibid., 7: 1048; MemCon by Byrnes, 24 Nov 45, ibid., 7: 666; Levine, *Anvil of Victory*, 48-51; Reardon-Anderson, *Yenan and the Great Powers*, 119-31.

139. *FRUS, 1945*, 7: 835-50; ibid., 2: 720, 748-49, 756-58.

140. Liang Chin-tung, "Sino-Soviet Treaty," 380; Levine, *Anvil of Victory*, 28-30; Chang, *Last Chance in Manchuria*, 39-43.

141. Truman to Wallace, 25 Jan 46, HSTP, PSF, box 173.

142. The quote may be found in Cumings, *Child of Conflict*, 13-14; see also Matray, *Reluctant Crusade*, 5-27.

143. Matray, *Reluctant Crusade*, 42-45; see also Cumings, *Child of Conflict*, 88-89.

144. Nagai and Iriye, *Cold War in Asia*, 123-38; Lowe, *Korean War*, 12-15.

145. Cumings, *Origins of the Korean War*, 1: 3-100; Scalapino and Lee, *Communism in Korea*, 233-98.

146. Matray, *Reluctant Crusade*, 50.

147. Cumings, *Origins of the Korean War*, 1: 135-213; Matray, *Reluctant Crusade*, 57-58.

148. McCloy to Acheson, 13 Nov 45, RG 165, OPD 336, TS.

149. Matray, *Reluctant Crusade*, 64-68.

150. Lowe, *Korean War*, 21.

151. Memo by Eugene H. Dooman, 15 July 45, *FRUS, Potsdam*, 1: 933-34; Report by SWNCC Subcommittee on the Far East, "National Composition of Forces to Occupy Japan," 11 Aug 45, *FRUS, 1945*, 6: 604, 608; James, *MacArthur*, 12.

152. James, *MacArthur*, 3-9.

153. Ibid., 3: 26-27; see also Khrushchev, *Remembers: The Glasnost Tapes*, 82-83.

154. Memo by Soviet Delegation, 24 Sep 45, *FRUS, 1945*, 2: 357-58; see also the U.S. Delegation Minutes, 24 and 25 Sep 45, ibid., 2: 336-39, 367, 419-20.

155. Harriman to SecState, 25 and 26 Oct 45, *FRUS, 1945*, 6: 782-96.

156. Harriman to SecState, 13 Nov 45, ibid., 6: 850.

157. Leahy Diary, 24 Oct 45, Leahy Papers; Record of Conversation, for Acheson, 22 Oct 45, *FRUS, 1945*, 6: 769-71.

158. Byrnes to Harriman, 7 Nov 45, *FRUS, 1945*, 6: 834-36; MemCon by Vincent, 1 Dec 45, ibid., 6: 872. The final agreement was worked out at the Moscow conference in December. See ibid., 6: 886-88. For Byrnes's view, see Memo for the Pres by Byrnes, 27 Feb 46, HSTP, PSF, box 182.

159. Schaller, *American Occupation of Japan*, 20-51; James, *MacArthur*, 109-92; Dower, *Empire and Aftermath*, 292-368.

160. McMahon, *Colonialism and Cold War*, 27-42; Kahin, *Intervention*, 11-13; Hess, *United States' Emergence as a Southeast Asian Power*, 159-69.

161. Hess, "Franklin Roosevelt and Indochina," 353-68; LaFeber, "Roosevelt, Churchill, and Indochina"; Thorne, "Indochina and Anglo-American Relations."

162. Spector, *Advice and Support*, 165.

163. Abbot Low Moffat, "The Dependent Territories in Southeast Asia," 17 Jan 45, RG 59, PSA Division, box 5; R. Kennedy, "American Interests in Southeast Asia" [Spring 1945], ibid.; Herring, "Truman Administration and Indochina."

164. Matthews to Dunn, 20 Apr 45, RG 59, 851G.00/4-2045; "Policy Paper Prepared in the Department of State," 22 June 45, *FRUS, 1945*, 6: 557-58; Hess, *United States' Emergence as a Southeast Asian Power*, 149-63; Thorne, "Indochina and Anglo-American Relations," 93-96.

165. Herring, "Truman Administration and Indochina"; Watt, *Succeeding John Bull*, 194-219; McMahon, *Colonialism and Cold War*, 79-85.

166. Donovan to Truman, 21, 22, and 31 Aug 45, HSTP, Conway Files (OSS); Donovan

to Truman, 5, 6, 17, 25, and 27 Sep 45, HSTP, Misc. Historical Document File; L. Gardner, *Approaching Vietnam*, 63–66.

167. Kahin, *Intervention*, 14–20; McMahon, *Colonialism and Cold War*, 74–113.

168. For the quotations, see R. Emerson, "United States Policy Toward the Netherlands East Indies and Indochina," 18 Dec 45, RG 59, 856E.01/12-2045; see also "United States Prestige in Southeast Asia," no signature, 7 Feb 46, RG 59, PSA Division, box 6. For Vincent, see Gallicchio, *Cold War Begins in Asia*, 94–98. For perceptions of the United States, see Clymer, "Nehru and the United States," 159–61.

169. For the quotation, see Matthews to Dunn, 20 Apr 45, RG 59, 851G.00/4-2045; see also "Policy Paper Prepared in the Department of State," 22 June 45, *FRUS, 1945*, 6: 577; Immerman, "United States Perceptions of Its Interests in Indochina," 1–9; Gifford and Louis, *Transfer of Power in Africa*, 44–47.

170. Donovan to Truman, 5 May 45, HSTP, Conway Files.

171. McLane, *Soviet Strategies in Southeast Asia*, 249–350; Westoby, *Communism*, 30–32; McVey, *Soviet View of the Indonesian Revolution*, 1–32; Pike, *Vietnam and the Soviet Union*, 27–31.

172. For the widespread belief that the economic recovery of Europe depended on the retention of Europe's former colonies, see Kindleberger, *Marshall Plan Days*, 124.

173. Shalom, *United States and the Philippines*, 1–67; Hess, *United States' Emergence as a Southeast Asian Power*, 160–61, 217–50; Gifford and Louis, *Transfer of Power in Africa*, 1–18.

174. Harriman and Abel, *Special Envoy*, 519–21; Herken, *Winning Weapon*, 25–26; Memo for the Pres by Stimson, 11 Sep 45, *FRUS, 1945*, 2: 40–44; Memo for the Pres by Patterson, 26 Sep 45, Elsey Papers, box 88; Memo Requested by the Pres by Acheson, 25 Sep 45, HSTP, PSF, box 199; Notes on Cabinet Mtg., 21 Sep 45, Connelly Papers, box 1.

175. Memo by Forrestal, 21 Sep 45, Forrestal Papers, box 48; Memo for the Pres by Forrestal, 1 Oct 45, HSTP, PSF, box 158; Memo for the Pres by Leahy, 23 Oct 45, ibid., box 199; Leahy Diary, 17 Oct 45, Leahy Papers; JCS 1477/1, "Over-All Effect of the Atomic Bomb on Warfare and Military Organization," 30 Oct 45, RG 165, ABC 471.6 Atom (17 Aug 45), sec. 2.

176. *PPP:HST* (1945), 381–84. In addition to the memoranda listed in Note 174 above, see Vannevar Bush to Truman, 25 Sep 45, HSTP, PSF, box 199; Herken, *Winning Weapon*, 29–61.

177. *PPP:HST* (1945), 472–75.

178. Forrestal to Byrnes, 11 Dec 45, Forrestal Papers, box 2; Vandenberg, *Private Papers*, 228–33; Acheson to Byrnes, 15 Dec 45, *FRUS, 1945*, 2: 610; Herken, *Winning Weapon*, 66–94; Messer, *End of an Alliance*, 137–55; Bernstein, "Quest for Security," 1015–29.

179. Bundy, *Danger and Survival*, 141–45.

180. Rosenberg, "American Atomic Strategy," 62–67; Sherry, *Preparing for the Next War*, 205–13; Herken, *Winning Weapon*, 195–209.

181. For the quotation, see Bundy, *Danger and Survival*, 141, also 150–55. For the Soviet reaction, see Gromyko, *Memoirs*, 108–10; Holloway, *Soviet Union and the Arms Race*, 15–23; Kramish, *Atomic Energy*, 48–107. For the British, see Gowing, *Independence and Deterrence*, 72–73, 87–92, 160–89.

182. See, e.g., JIS 80/12, "Postwar Economic Policies and Capabilities of the USSR," 1 Nov 45, RG 218, CCS 092 USSR (3-27-45), sec. 2; JIS 80/22, "Soviet Postwar Economic Capabilities and Policies," Enclosure A, 8 Jan 46, ibid., sec. 4; JIS 80/24, "Soviet Postwar Military Policies and Capabilities," Enclosure B, 15 Jan 46, ibid.; Lewis, *Changing Direction*, 359–65; Gowing, *Independence and Deterrence*, 184–87, 209–20; Clark and Wheeler, *British Origins of Nuclear Strategy*, 43–65.

183. MID, "Review of Europe, Russia, and Middle East," 27 Nov 45, 26 Dec 45, RG 165, OPD, 350.05 TS.

184. Borowski, *Hollow Threat*.

185. JIS 211/1, "Military Capabilities of Great Britain and France," 13 Nov 45, RG 218, CCS 000.1 Great Britain (5-10-45), sec. 1.

186. JCS 1545, "Military Position of the United States in the Light of Russian Policy," 8 Oct 45, RG 218, CCS 092 USSR (3-27-45), sec. 1; Lincoln to Gardner et al., 28 Dec 45, ibid., sec. 4; JPS, 236th and 238th Mtgs., Jan 1946, ibid., secs. 4 and 5; JPS, 240th Mtg., 6 March 46, RG 218, CCS 381 USSR (3-2-46), sec. 1; draft letter for SecWar to SecState, 14 March 46, RG 165, ABC 336 Russia (22 Aug 43), sec. 2; ONI, "Basic Factors in World Relations," [Dec 1945], NHC, SPD, series 5, box 106, A8.

187. For the "logical illogicality" quotation, see Expanded Draft of Letter from SecWar to SecState, "U.S. Position re Soviet Proposals on Kiel Canal and Dardanelles," 8 July 45, RG 165, ABC 093 Kiel (6 July 45), sec. 1-A.

188. For the frequency of this occurrence, see Jervis, *Perception and Misperception*, 67–72.

189. For Khrushchev's quotation, see his *Remembers: The Glasnost Tapes*, 101. For Stalin's restraint and his failure to support revolutionary forces abroad, see Claudin, *Communist Movement*, 387–489; Spriano, *Stalin and the European Communists*, 269–84; Gati, *Hungary and the Soviet Bloc*, 4–5, 15–16, 21, 41–43. For the Soviet view of U.S. policy, see the report by the Soviet embassy in Washington in *Diplomatic History*, 15 (Fall 1991). For additional analysis of Soviet policy in 1945 and 1946, see Chapter Three, pp. 102–4, 130–38.

190. Jervis, *Perception and Misperception*, 66–76; Herz, "Idealist Internationalism and the Security Dilemma."

Chapter 3

1. Kennan's "long telegram," 22 Feb 46, in Kennan, *Memoirs, 1925–1950*, 583–98; H. Freeman Matthews to SWNCC, 1 Apr 46, *FRUS, 1946*, 1: 1167–71. For the report written by Clark Clifford and George Elsey, see Krock, *Memoirs*, 417–82.

2. For Truman's readiness to take a hard line, see the famous memo he prepared for his talk with Byrnes, in Truman, *Off the Record*, 79–80. For an analysis of Truman that stresses his continued desire for a cooperative relationship, see Larson, *Origins of Containment*, 250–301. Larson, however, does not look closely at the terms deemed requisite for a cooperative relationship that, as illustrated in Chapter Two, safeguarded U.S. preponderance.

3. Acheson Testimony, 13 March 46, U.S. Senate, Banking and Currency, *Anglo-American Financial Agreement*, 306.

4. James Forrestal to Harry S Truman, 28 Jan 46, Forrestal Papers, box 64; Acheson to Truman, 30 Apr 46, NA, RG 107, Petersen Papers, General Subject File, box 1. For Truman's quotation, see *PPP:HST* (1946), 106; see also Robert P. Patterson to Truman, 16 Apr 46, HSTP, PSF, box 157; Cabinet Minutes, Jan–March 1946, Connelly Papers, box 1; Harold D. Smith Diary, 15 May 46, HSTP, PSF, box 150.

5. For the quotation, see Clay, *Papers*, 1: 179; see also ibid., 1: 166–68, 180–81. For food situation, see also Patterson to Truman, 11 June 46, RG 165, Army Chief of Staff, 091 Germany.

6. Murphy to Byrnes, 24 Feb 46, *FRUS, 1946*, 5: 506; Matthews to James F. Byrnes, 28 Feb 46, ibid., 5: 508; Walter Bedell Smith to Byrnes, 2 Apr 46, ibid., 5: 535; Patterson to Byrnes, 25 Feb 46, RG 107, Patterson Papers, General Decimal File, box 8.

7. Rioux, *Fourth Republic*, 98–99.

8. Quoting Bevin in Greenwood, "Bevin, France, and 'Western Union,'" 332–33.

9. Caffery to Byrnes, 9 Feb 46, *FRUS, 1946*, 5: 413; for Clayton, see Minutes of the National Advisory Council, 25 Apr and 6 May 46, ibid., 5: 432–33, 441–46.

10. Forrestal, "French Situation," 6 May 46, Forrestal Papers, box 20; Thomas Handy to Dwight D. Eisenhower, 2 May 46, RG 319, P&O, OPD, 092 TS.

11. Although much still remains to be learned about the making of Soviet foreign policy during this period, and although it is still impossible to determine Stalin's intentions with any degree of exactitude, my characterization of the Soviet dictator is informed by Taubman, *Stalin's American Policy*; McCagg, *Stalin Embattled*; Ra'anan, *International Policy Formation*; Dunmore, *Soviet Politics*. See also Khrushchev, *Remembers: The Glasnost Tapes*, 72–73, 100–101.

12. For Stalin's speech, see *Vital Speeches of the Day* 12 (1 March 46): 300-304.

13. For the standard interpretation, see Gaddis, *United States and the Origins of the Cold War*, 300-303. For a totally revisionist view, see Resis, *Stalin and the Onset of the Cold War*. For my analysis of Stalin's policies, see pp. 130-38, 511-15 in this volume.

14. For the tendency of policymakers to dismiss conflicting evidence, see Jervis, *Perception and Misperception*, 382-406; for the conflicting evidence, see pp. 132-38 in this volume.

15. Taubman, *Stalin's American Policy*, 128-65; Levine, *Anvil of Victory*, 65-86; Kuniholm, *Cold War in the Near East*, 304-26.

16. Messer, *End of an Alliance*, 156-80; Donovan, *Conflict and Crisis*, 163-84; Thompson, *Truman Presidency*, 8-9; Elsey Oral History, 213-35.

17. Messer, *End of an Alliance*, 156-94; Ward, *Threat of Peace*, 50-84.

18. Acheson, *Present at the Creation*, 187-93, 216-24; Messer, "Paths Not Taken."

19. Generals Clay and Hodge were locked in disputes with the State Department. See, e.g., Cumings, *Origins of the Korean War*, 227-29; Clay, *Papers*, 1: 43. When General Marshall went to China, he established his own "rear echelon" with an Army officer assigned to Foggy Bottom working closely with Acheson. See Acheson, *Present at the Creation*, 199-200. For occupation policy in Japan, MacArthur's role, and the complex division of responsibility, see Gluck, "Entangling Illusions," 169-236; Schaller, *American Occupation of Japan*, 20-30. For Hilldring's move to the State Department and the Army's support of it, see Donald Russell to Connor [January 1946?], Byrnes Papers, File 569(1). For Hilldring's relations with Clay, see Clay, *Papers*, 1: 168-75.

20. Memo for the Record by H. A. Craig, 27 Feb 46, RG 319, P&O, 350.05 TS (State Dept. Red File); OPD, "Adequate Governmental Machinery to Handle Foreign Affairs," 13 March 46, ibid., 092 TS; SWNCC 270, "USSR Problems of Mutual Concern to the State, War, and Navy Departments," 27 Feb 46, RG 165, ABC 336 Russia (22 Aug 43), sec. 1-C.

21. JPS, 236th Mtg., 16 Jan 46, RG 218, CCS 334 (8-2-45).

22. JCS 1592 Series, Jan-Feb 1946, RG 218, CCS 092 United States (12-21-45); John L. Sullivan to Howard C. Petersen, 26 March 46, RG 107, Petersen Papers, Classified, 092; S. F. Giffin, "Draft of Proposed Comments for Assistant Secretary of War," ND, ibid.; R. L. Dennison to Hidalgo, 19 March 46, NHC, Records of Politico-Military Division, series 1, A-14.

23. Smith Diary, 18 Feb 46, HSTP, PSF, box 150; Memo for the Record by Handy, 27 Feb 46, RG 107, Patterson Papers, Safe File, box 7. For Air Force concerns, see Minutes of Air Staff Mtgs., 1946, Spaatz Papers, box 261.

24. Forrestal, *Diaries*, 129; Mtg. of the Secretaries of State, War, and Navy, 6 March 46, RG 107, Patterson Papers, Safe File, box 3.

25. *PPP:HST* (1946), 137-38, 140; Editorial Note, *FRUS, 1946*, 1: 1435.

26. Vandenberg, *Private Papers*, 237-51; Rourke, *Congress and the Presidency*, 1-48; Messer, "Paths Not Taken," 314-19.

27. Smith Diary, 18 and 28 Feb and 20 March 46, HSTP, PSF, box 150; Donovan, *Conflict and Crisis*, 163-84.

28. *Public Opinion Quarterly* 10 (Spring 1946): 115.

29. Almond, *American People and Foreign Policy*, 73.

30. "Daily Summary of Opinion Developments," Jan-Feb 1946, RG 59, Public Opinion Studies, box 2; "Fortnightly Survey of American Opinion of International Affairs," Jan-March 1946, ibid., box 11.

31. Forrestal to Byrnes, 8 March 46, Forrestal Papers, box 68; Forrestal, *Diaries*, 129; Draft Letter for SecWar from SecState and SecNavy, 14 March 46, RG 165, ABC 336 Russia (22 Aug 43), sec. 1-C; Harbutt, *Iron Curtain*, 152-57; Yergin, *Shattered Peace*, 171-74.

32. "Daily Summary of Opinion Developments," 28 Feb and 1 March 46, RG 59, Public Opinion Studies, box 2.

33. For the British loan, see "Daily Summary of Opinion Developments," Jan-Feb 1946, RG

59, Public Opinion Studies, box 2; for concerns about autarky and multilateral trade, see *FRUS, 1946*, 1: 1263–1369; for the Export-Import Bank, see ibid., 1: 1391–1436; for concerns about famine conditions and their repercussions, see, e.g., the citations in Notes 3 and 4 above.

34. Ayers Diary, 28 Feb 46, Ayers Papers, box 16; Address by Byrnes, 28 Feb 46, *DSB* 14 (10 March 46): 355–58.

35. Leahy Diary, 10, 20, and 21 Feb and 3 March 46, Leahy Papers; Harbutt, *Iron Curtain*, 159–65; Ryan, "Churchill's 'Iron Curtain' Speech."

36. Kennan to Durbrow, 21 Jan 46, Kennan Papers, box 28; Kennan, *Memoirs, 1925–1950*, 285–313; Mayers, *Kennan*, 97–102; Hixson, *Kennan*, 22–31.

37. The telegram is conveniently reprinted in Kennan, *Memoirs, 1925–1950*, 583–98.

38. Kennan, "Notes on the Marshall Plan," 15 Dec 47, Kennan Papers, box 23; see also Kennan to Byrnes, 20 March 46, *FRUS, 1946*, 6: 722–23.

39. For an especially incisive critique of Kennan's thinking during this period, see Stephanson, *Kennan*, 24–109.

40. Forrestal, *Diaries*, 134–40; Forrestal to Clarence Dillon, 11 Apr 46, Forrestal Papers, box 101; Harriman and Abel, *Special Envoy*, 548; Gardner, *Architects of Illusion*, 270–300.

41. Memo by R. L. Vittrup, 26 Feb 47, RG 107, Patterson Papers, Safe File, box 5. Air Force Chief of Staff Carl Spaatz also wanted to meet with Kennan. Bruce Hopper to Kennan, 29 March 46, Kennan Papers, box 28.

42. Harbutt, *Iron Curtain*, 185–91.

43. Ibid., 197–208; Woods and Jones, *Dawning of the Cold War*, 112–17.

44. Harbutt, *Iron Curtain*, 179–223; R. Gardner, *Sterling-Dollar Diplomacy*, 248–53; Yergin, *Shattered Peace*, 174–92.

45. When officials sense an impending change in the balance of power, they frequently take the offensive, even going to the brink of war. See Lebow, *Between Peace and War*, 57–97.

46. Events in Iran may be followed in *FRUS, 1946*, 7: 291–469; see also Kuniholm, *Cold War in the Near East*, 303–50; Lytle, *Iranian-American Alliance*, 146–73; Bill, *Eagle and the Lion*, 15–42.

47. For the quotation, see *FRUS, 1946*, 7: 346–48; Lytle, *Iranian-American Alliance*, 163–68; Bill, *Eagle and the Lion*, 38–39.

48. Harbutt, *Iron Curtain*, 220–21.

49. Wallace, *Price of Vision*, 556–57; Mtg. of Secretaries of State, War, and Navy, 6 March 46, RG 107, Patterson Papers, Safe File, box 3; Byrnes to Wallace Murray, 23 March 46, *FRUS, 1946*, 7: 375–76.

50. For a fine analysis of the Iranian crisis and the lessons derived from it, see Oneal, *Foreign Policy Making*, 78–127.

51. Mtg. of Secretaries of State, War, and Navy, 6 March 46, RG 107, Patterson Papers, Safe File, box 3.

52. For Byrnes's actions and ensuing developments, see Petersen to Patterson, 22 Apr 46, ibid., box 1; Lincoln to Petersen, 6 March 46, RG 165, ABC 336 Russia (22 Aug 43), sec. 1-C; Marshall Carter to Lincoln, 7 March 46, ibid. For dissatisfaction with the deplorable state of U.S. intelligence on the Soviet Union, see Smith Diary, 9 Jan 46, HSTP, PSF, box 150; Lincoln to John Hull, 22 March 46, RG 165, OPD, 350.05 TS.

53. JCS 161/4, "Political Estimate of Soviet Policy for Use in Connection with Military Studies," 5 Apr 46, RG 218, CCS 092 USSR (3-27-45), sec. 6; Matthews to SWNCC, 1 Apr 46, *FRUS, 1946*, 1: 1167–71; Memo by George Juskalian, 14 March 46, RG 165, OPD, 350.05 TS; Memo [by Deane?], "U.S. Policy with Respect to Russia," 17 March 46, RG 165, ABC Russia (22 Aug 43), sec. 1-C; Memo by Forrest Sherman, 17 March 46, Forrestal Papers, box 24.

54. JCS 161/4, "Political Estimate," 5 Apr 46, RG 218, CCS 092 USSR (3-27-45), sec. 6.

55. For Eisenhower's view of Soviet intentions and capabilities, see Eisenhower, *Papers*, 7: 1013; Lincoln to Hull, 12 March 46, RG 165, ABC 381 USSR (2 March 46), sec. 1-A; Draft Letter

for SecWar to SecState and SecNavy [no signature], 14 March 46, RG 165, ABC 336 Russia (22 Aug 43), sec. 1-C; Lincoln to Robert J. Wood, 22 May 46, RG 165, ABC 381 (1 Sep 45), sec. 1-A; JPS, 249th Mtg., 22 May 46, RG 218, CCS 381 USSR (3-2-46), sec. 2; OPD, "Adequate Governmental Machinery," 13 March 46, RG 319, P&O, 092 TS.

56. JCS 1641/5, "Estimate Based on Assumption of Occurrence of Major Hostilities," 11 Apr 46, RG 218, CCS 092 USSR (3-27-45), sec. 6; see also JWPC 453, "Disposition of Occupation Forces in Europe and the Far East in the Event of Hostilities in Europe, and the Importance of Certain Areas of Eurasia," 27 March 46, ibid.; Lincoln to Gardner and Everest, 10 Apr 46, RG 165, ABC 336 Russia (22 Aug 43), sec. 1-C.

57. JPS 789, "Concept of Operations for Pincher" [March 1946], RG 218, CCS 381 USSR (3-2-46), sec. 1.

58. Ibid.; "Air Plan for Makefast" [Autumn 1946], RG 165, ABC 381 USSR (2 March 46), sec. 3.

59. JPS 789, "Pincher" [March 1946], RG 218, CCS 381 USSR (3-2-46), sec. 1; see also JCS 1641/3, "U.S. Security Interests," 10 March 46, RG 218, CCS 092 USSR (3-27-45), sec. 6; Byrnes to JCS, 6 March 46, ibid., sec. 5.

60. For the PINCHER plans, see JWPC 432 Series, "Tentative Over-All Strategic Concept," May–June 1946, RG 218, CCS 381 USSR (3-2-46), sec. 2. For talks with the British, see Memo for Chester Nimitz [by Eisenhower?], 29 June 46, RG 319, P&O, 092 TS; Nimitz to Eisenhower and Leahy [mid-June 1946], RG 165, ABC 381 USSR (2 March 46), sec. 2; O.S.P. to Lincoln, 3 July 46, ibid.; D. Campbell, *Unsinkable Aircraft Carrier*, 27–28; Duke, *US Defence Bases*, 20–25.

61. JPS 789, "Pincher" [March 1946], RG 218, CCS 381 USSR (3-2-46), sec. 1; "Air Plan for Makefast" [Autumn 1946], RG 165, ABC 381 USSR (2 March 46), sec. 3. For the importance of the Middle East in Anglo-American strategic planning, see Clark and Wheeler, *British Origins of Nuclear Strategy*, 112–35.

62. Conolly Oral History, 302–3.

63. Base rights were a frequent topic at the mtgs. of the Secretaries of State, War, and Navy during the latter half of 1946. See RG 107, Patterson Papers, Safe File, box 3.

64. For base rights in the Azores, see *FRUS, 1946*, 5: 962–1022; Patterson to Acheson, 5 July 46, RG 319, P&O, 092 TS; "Negotiation for Military Transit Rights in the Azores" [no signature], [Jan 1947], RG 59, European Affairs, box 17. For Iceland, see "U.S. Military Bases in Countries Dealt with by Office of European Affairs" [no signature], 16 Jan 47, ibid. For Port Lyautey, see R. L. Dennison to Chester Nimitz, 14 and 15 Oct 46, NHC, CNO, Double Zero Files, folder 31. For bases in the Pacific and the former Japanese mandates, see esp. JCS 1619 Series, "Policy Concerning Trusteeship," June–Dec 1946, RG 218, CCS 360 (12-9-42), secs. 23–29. For the Navy and Japan, see Robert B. Carney to Nimitz, 2 Dec 46, NHC, CNO, Double Zero Files, folder 31.

65. Borowski, *Hollow Threat*, 3–111; D. Rosenberg, "U.S. Nuclear Stockpile," 26; Best, *"Cooperation with Like-Minded Peoples,"* 28–43, 89–91.

66. JCS 1641/5, "Estimate Based on Assumption of Occurrence of Major Hostilities," 11 Apr 46, RG 218, CCS 092 USSR (3-27-45), sec. 6.

67. Acheson to Byrnes, 17 March 46, *FRUS, 1946*, 1: 762–63. For a superb recapitulation of the policy ramifications of the plan, see David Lilienthal to Bernard Baruch, 19 May 46, Baruch Papers, box 63.

68. Truman, *Off the Record*, 187; Bundy, *Danger and Survival*, 162.

69. Baruch to Byrnes, 13 March 46, *FRUS, 1946*, 1: 757–58; Baruch to Truman, 26 March 46, ibid., 1: 767–68; Baruch to Lilienthal, 27 March 46, Baruch Papers, box 63; Fred Searls to Baruch, 31 March 46, ibid., box 64; Schwarz, *Speculator*, 490–98.

70. Lincoln to Hull, 11 Apr 46, RG 165, ABC 371.6 Atom (17 Aug 45), sec. 6-A; Memo for Chief of Staff by Hull, 12 Apr 46, ibid.; Memo for the Record by Hull, 15 Apr 46, ibid.;

Memo for the SecNavy by Thomas Blandy, ND [13 Apr 46?], NHC, CNO, Double Zero Files, folder: "Control of Atomic Energy"; Gardner to CNO, 13 Apr 46, ibid.; H. G. Bowen to Assistant SecNavy, 9 and 15 Apr 46, ibid.; Nimitz to SecNavy, 13 Apr 46, ibid. For bureaucratic rivalries, see Graybar, "1946 Atomic Bomb Tests."

71. For the quotation, see Truman to Baruch, 10 July 46, Baruch Papers, box 65; Acheson, *Present at the Creation*, 212–15.

72. Herken, *Winning Weapon*, 151–70; Gerber, "Baruch Plan"; Bundy, *Danger and Survival*, 161–96. For Soviet perceptions, see Gromyko, *Memoirs*, 138–40. At a meeting of Soviet and American historians in June 1990, Vladimir Shustov of the Soviet foreign ministry asserted that he had seen documents suggesting that Stalin was interested in an arms control plan. But the evidence was not made public.

73. Patterson to Byrnes, 17 Apr 46, *FRUS, 1946*, 1: 1231; Truman to Clement Attlee, 20 Apr 46, ibid., 1: 1236–37; Gormly, "Washington Declaration."

74. For the quotation, see Draft Reply to Letter from Mr. Baruch by Dennison, 4 June 46, NHC, CNO, Double Zero Files, folder 31; Nimitz to Baruch, 11 June 46, Baruch Papers, box 63; Leahy to Baruch, 11 June 46, ibid.; Eisenhower to Baruch, 1 June 46, ibid.; Memo for Lincoln by Bonesteel, 24 May 46, RG 165, ABC 471.6 Atom (17 Aug 45), sec. 6-A.

75. For some worst-case analyses, see JIC 342, "British Capabilities Versus the USSR," 6 Feb 46, RG 218, CCS 000.1 Great Britain (5-10-45), sec. 2; Senior Naval Member of JIS to JIC, 13 Feb 46, RG 165, ABC Russia (22 Aug 43), sec. 1-C; Inglis, "Resumé of Soviet Capabilities," 29 Aug 46, NHC, SPD, series 5, box 106, A8.

76. Quoted in Herken, *Winning Weapon*, 167.

77. The quotes are from Elbridge Durbrow to Charles W. Thayer, 11 Apr 46, RG 59, Bohlen Papers, box 1; Lincoln to Eisenhower, 20 May 46, Lincoln Papers, War Dept. Files; see also Vandenberg, *Private Papers*, 285–86. For Byrnes's self-proclaimed intention to be tough, see Notes on Cabinet Mtg., 19 Apr 46, Connelly Papers, box 1.

78. Price and Schorske, *Problem of Germany*, 57–58, 33–39. For statistics, see also UN, ECE, *Economic Survey of Europe* (1947), 15–17; "Coal Production and Trade in Europe Since the War," *Economic Bulletin for Europe* 1(Third Quarter 1949): 14–15; Murphy to Byrnes, 28 Apr and 10 Sep 46, *FRUS, 1946*, 5: 776, 791–92.

79. Krisch, *German Politics*; McCauley, *German Democratic Republic*, 6–35.

80. Price and Schorske, *Problem of Germany*, 107.

81. Eisenberg, "U.S. Policy in Post-War Germany." For labor issue, see Hilldring to Petersen, 21 Feb 46 and accompanying correspondence, RG 165, Army Chief of Staff, 091 Germany; see also Eisenberg, "Working-Class Politics and the Cold War," 283–90. For Army sensitivity to the bad press, see the letters and documents in RG 165, Army Chief of Staff, 091 Germany; see also Eisenhower to Joseph McNarney, 13 Feb 46 and accompanying documents, RG 107, Petersen Papers, Classified, 091 Germany.

82. Kennan to Byrnes, 6 March 46, *FRUS, 1946*, 5: 519–20; W. Rostow, *Division of Europe After World War II*, 38–50, 62–69.

83. Acheson and Hilldring to Byrnes, 9 May 46, *FRUS, 1946*, 5: 549–54; W. Rostow, *Division of Europe After World War II*, 3–9, 51–62, 94–133.

84. U.S. Delegation Record, 15 and 16 May 46, *FRUS, 1946*, 2: 395–402, 431–36. For demilitarization treaty, see ibid., 2: 146–47, 167–68. For suspension of reparations, see Gimbel, *Origins of the Marshall Plan*, 115–17; Harbutt, *Iron Curtain*, 270.

85. Gimbel, "On the Implementation of the Potsdam Agreement"; Lynch, "Resolving the Paradox of the Monnet Plan," 232–39; Kuisel, *Capitalism and the State*, 219–37. For Bidault, see Caffery to Byrnes, 5 June 46, RG 59, 851.00/6-546.

86. Patterson to Byrnes, 11 June 46, *FRUS, 1946*, 2: 486–88. For approval by top Army officers, see Memo by Dean Rusk, 10 June 46, RG 107, Petersen Papers, Classified, 091 Germany. For Bonesteel's quotations, see "Ultimate Disposition of the Ruhr and Rhineland," 29 Apr

46, ibid.; Bonesteel, "Some General Security Implications of the German Settlement" [ND], RG 107, Patterson Papers, Safe File, box 1; OPD and CAD, "Analysis of Certain Political Problems Confronting Military Occupation Authorities in Germany," 10 Apr 46, ibid.

87. Greenwood, "Bevin and the Division of Germany"; Deighton, "Frozen Front," 449–57.

88. U.S. Delegation Record, 9, 10, and 11 July 46, *FRUS, 1946*, 2: 842–50, 855, 869–76, 881–98; Molotov, *Problems of Foreign Policy*, 55–69; Slusser, *Soviet Economic Policy*, 14–17, 55–56.

89. Deighton, "Frozen Front," 456–57; Maier, "Analog of Empire," 7–11.

90. Clayton and Hilldring to Byrnes, 28 June 46, *FRUS, 1946*, 5: 785–86. For the onset of talks regarding Bizonia, see ibid., 5: 589–659.

91. Clay, *Papers*, 1: 336–43, 247–48, 251–60; O. P. Echols to Patterson, 24 Aug 46, RG 107, Patterson Papers, Safe File, box 4; Backer, *Winds of History*, 114–33.

92. Backer, *Winds of History*, 133–36. For Stuttgart speech, see *DSB* 15 (15 Sep 46): 496. For scrutiny of the speech at the White House, see Mtg. of the Secretaries of State, War, and Navy, 4 Sep 46, RG 107, Patterson Papers, Safe File, box 3; Clayton to Byrnes, 3 Sep 46, RG 218, Leahy Papers, box 6.

93. Maier, "Analog of Empire," 12.

94. Clay, *Papers*, 1: 256–58; Byrnes to John W. Snyder, 9 Sep 46, Byrnes Papers, folder 466(2); Byrnes to Robert Hannegan, 9 Sep 46, ibid., folder 465(1).

95. Wall, *United States and the Reshaping of Postwar France*, chaps. 2 and 3.

96. Citing public opinion polls in France, see Caffery to Byrnes, 10 July 46, RG 43, box 93.

97. Byrnes to Henri Bonnet, 18 June 46, *FRUS, 1946*, 5: 783. Of course, the $650 million credit did not satisfy French needs and desires. See Hill, "American Reconstruction Aid to France," 13–16.

98. MemCon by Matthews, 24 Sep 46, *FRUS, 1946*, 5: 607–10.

99. See, e.g., Editorial Note, ibid., 1: 1435–36.

100. For Germany's additional requirements, see, e.g., Patterson to Senator Elmer Thomas, 31 Oct 46, RG 107, Petersen Papers, Classified, 091 Germany; also the file marked "Trip to European Theater, October 8–24, 1946," ibid., General Subject File, box 1.

101. For cognitive dissonance, see Jervis, *Perception and Misperception*, 382–406.

102. Jervis, Lebow, and Stein, *Psychology and Deterrence*, 180–232.

103. Byrnes to JCS, 6 March 46, RG 218, CCS 092 USSR (3-27-45), sec. 5; OPD, "Adequate Governmental Machinery," 13 March 46, RG 319, P&O, 092 TS; Petersen to Patterson, 22 Apr 46, RG 107, Patterson Papers, Safe File, box 1.

104. Memo for the Record by Lincoln, 16 Apr 46, RG 165, ABC 336 Russia (22 Aug 43), sec. 1-C; Lincoln to Hull, 16 Apr 46, RG 165, ABC 092 USSR (15 Nov 44); Memo for Bonesteel [no signature], 20 Apr 46, ibid., ABC 093 Kiel (6 July 45), sec. 1-A.

105. For the importance of the Eastern Mediterranean and Cairo-Suez in U.S. strategic planning, see JWPC 432 Series, "Tentative Over-All Strategic Concept and Estimate of Initial Operations," Apr–June 1946, RG 218, CCS 381 USSR (3-2-46), sec. 2; JCS 1656, "U.S. Security Interests in the Disposition of Tripolitania," 15 Apr 46, RG 218, CCS 092 USSR (3-27-45), sec. 6; Memo [by Lincoln?], "Possible Soviet Demands in Eritrea and Italian Somaliland," 20 Apr 46, RG 165, ABC 336 Russia (22 Aug 43), sec. 1-C; Hull to Lincoln, 2 May 46, RG 165, P&O, 092 TS. Tripolitania, Eritrea, and Somaliland were under British military administration. See Rennell, *British Military Administration*; Louis, *British Empire in the Middle East*, 265–86.

106. Louis, *British Empire in the Middle East*, 420–38; M. Cohen, *Palestine and the Great Powers*, 122–23.

107. P. Hahn, "Strategy and Diplomacy," 45–63.

108. Ibid., 83–85; Louis, *British Empire in the Middle East*, 125, 232–38.

109. J. Miller, *United States and Italy*, 193–205.

110. Rabel, *Between East and West*, 74–101.

111. Memo for the Record by Handy, 27 Feb 46, RG 107, Patterson Papers, Safe File, box 7; Mtg. of the Secretaries of State, War, and Navy, 6 March 46, ibid., box 3; Memo for the SecWar [unsigned], 8 March 46, ibid., box 7. For a bureaucratic interpretation of the decision to send the USS *Missouri* to the Eastern Mediterranean, see Alvarez, *"Missouri* Visit to Turkey."

112. Rabel, *Between East and West*, 85–95; Best, *"Cooperation with Like-Minded Peoples,"* 81, 97; Forrestal, *Diaries*, 195–96.

113. For the note, see *FRUS, 1946*, 7: 828–29.

114. Handy to Eisenhower, with enclosure from State Dept., 15 Aug 46, RG 319, P&O, 092 TS.

115. Acheson to Byrnes, 15 Aug 46, *FRUS, 1946*, 7: 840–42, 844–50; Acheson, *Present at the Creation*, 195–96.

116. Durbrow to Byrnes, 5 Aug 46, RG 59, 761.67/8-546; Lincoln, "Possible Program in Connection with Turkey," 15 Aug 46, Lincoln Papers, War Dept. Files. For comments of State Dept. officials and reports of diplomats, see *FRUS, 1946*, 7: 832, 835, 860, 866–67. For the quotation, see Hoyt Vandenberg to Truman, 24 Aug 46, HSTP, PSF, box 249.

117. The weakness and hypocrisy of the U.S. diplomatic position were apparent in Jack Hickerson to Loy Henderson, 31 Dec 46, RG 59, 761.67/12-3146.

118. Louis, *British Empire in the Middle East*, 226–53, 265–80, 428–63.

119. For U.S. strategy, Turkey, and the PINCHER war plans, see JCS 789 and JWPC 432 Series, Apr–June 1946, RG 218, CCS 381 USSR (3-2-46), secs. 1 and 2; Patterson to Truman, 27 July 46, RG 319, P&O, 092 TS; JWPC 467/1, "GRIDDLE," 15 Aug 46, RG 218, CCS 092 USSR (3-27-45), sec. 11; see also JWPC 475/1, "Strategic Study of the Area Between the Alps and the Himalayas," 2 Nov 46, RG 218, CCS 381 USSR (3-2-46), sec. 3, pt. 1.

120. JCS 1704/1, "Military Implications of the Current Turkish Situation," 24 Aug 46, RG 218, CCS 092 (8-22-46), sec. 1; Lincoln to Lauris Norstad, 28 Aug 46, Lincoln Papers, War Dept. Files; Patterson to Acheson, 31 Aug 46, RG 319, P&O, 092 TS; Patterson to Acting SecState, 12 Sep 46, RG 107, Patterson Papers, Safe File, box 7; Clayton to Byrnes, 12 Sep 46, *FRUS, 1946*, 7: 211–13.

121. Mtgs. of the Secretaries of State, War, and Navy, 25 Sep and 6 Nov 46, RG 107, Patterson Papers, Safe File, box 3; Memo by British Embassy in Greece, 5 Nov 46, *FRUS, 1946*, 7: 913–14.

122. James McCormack to Henderson, with enclosed memo, 6 Sep 46, RG 319, P&O, 092 TS.

123. McCormack to Bonesteel, 9 Sep 46, ibid.; Clayton to Byrnes, 12 Sep 46, *FRUS, 1946*, 7: 211–13.

124. MacVeagh, *Reports*, 696; see also *FRUS, 1946*, 7: 146, 159–60, 162–63, 170, 174–75, 186–88.

125. Jacobs to Byrnes, 5 Oct 46, *FRUS, 1946*, 7: 229; see also ibid., 7: 161, 166–68, 182–83. For Bulgaria, see Barnes to Byrnes, 26 Nov 46, ibid., 7: 269–70. For different Yugoslav and Soviet behavior, not detected by U.S. officials, see Wittner, *American Intervention in Greece*, 57–60; Stavrakis, *Moscow and Greek Communism*, 127–46.

126. MacVeagh to Byrnes, 30 Sep 46, *FRUS, 1946*, 7: 226–27; Acheson to MacVeagh, 15 Oct 46, ibid., 7: 236–37; Memo Prepared in the Office of Near East and African Affairs, 21 Oct 46, ibid., 7: 241–45; Lincoln to Cohen, 22 June 46, RG 165, ABC 381 (1 Sep 45), sec. 1-A; War Dept. Intelligence Division, "Intelligence Estimate of the World Situation," 25 June 46, RG 319, P&O, 350.05 TS; H. Jones, *"A New Kind of War,"* 7–16.

127. *FRUS, 1946*, 7: 236–37, 255, 262–66, 278, 286–87.

128. Mtg. of Secretaries of State, War, and Navy, 18 Dec 46, RG 107, Patterson Papers, Safe File, box 3.

129. For Korea, see Truman to Edwin Pauley, 16 July 46, RG 107, Patterson Papers, General Decimal File, box 9; Truman to Patterson, 12 Aug 46, ibid.

130. For background, see Chapter Two, pp. 81–88.

131. For an excellent analysis, see Levine, "American Mediation in the Chinese Civil War." For a superb description of the Marshall mission, see Pogue, *Marshall*, 54–143.

132. Quoted in Varg, *Closing of the Door*, 294. For Marshall's views, see Levine, *Anvil of Victory*, esp. 54–56. For ideological affinity, see John Leighton Stuart to Byrnes, 31 Oct 46, *FRUS, 1946*, 10: 455–56.

133. Royall to Forrestal and Truman, 14 Jan 46, *FRUS, 1946*, 10: 724–26; Patterson to Byrnes, 18 Feb 46, ibid., 10: 729.

134. Thomas B. McCabe and Wm E. Vogelback to T. V. Soong, 21 Aug 46, *FRUS, 1946*, 10: 1050–51. For Petersen's role in negotiating this deal, see the documents in RG 107, Petersen Papers, Subject File, box 1.

135. Albert Wedemeyer to Eisenhower, 21 Jan 46, *FRUS, 1946*, 10: 815; L. J. Lincoln to Commanding General, AAF, 13 March 46, RG 319, P&O, 092 TS.

136. Acheson's Remarks, Notes on Cabinet Mtg., 2 Aug 46, RG 107, Patterson Papers, Safe File, box 2; Marshall to Acheson, 25 Sep 46, *FRUS, 1946*, 10: 875–76; John Carter Vincent to Acheson, 5 Nov 46, ibid., 10: 880–81; Pach, *Arming the Free World*, 82–84.

137. Marshall to Truman, 16 Oct 46, *FRUS, 1946*, 10: 383; Harding and Yuan Ming, *Sino-American Relations*, 31–47.

138. MemCon by Marshall, 14 Sep 47, *FRUS, 1946*, 6: 519.

139. Memo by Vincent, 9 Sep 46, *FRUS, 1946*, 10: 164; Marshall to Truman, 8 Nov 46, ibid., 10: 492; Mtg. Between Marshall and Chiang, 1 Dec 46, ibid., 10: 576–78; Mtg. Between Marshall and Stuart, 13 Dec 46, ibid., 10: 662; Eastman, *Seeds of Destruction*; Harding and Yuan Ming, *Sino-American Relations*, 51–55.

140. Mtg. Between Marshall and Charles Cooke, 24 July 46, *FRUS, 1946*, 10: 869; Marshall to Marshall Carter, 11 Aug 46, ibid., 10: 782; Mtg. Between Marshall and Chiang, 16 Aug 46, ibid., 10: 51–52; Marshall to Truman, 17 and 23 Aug 46, ibid., 10: 53–54, 79–80; Mtg. Between Marshall and Walton Butterworth, 18 Nov 46, ibid., 10: 1020–21.

141. Marshall to Truman, 17 and 30 Aug 46, *FRUS, 1946*, 10: 53–54, 110; Mtg. Between Marshall and Miao Yun-tai, 25 Oct 46, ibid., 10: 422; Vincent to Acheson, 5 Nov 46, ibid., 10: 880. See also Cray, *General of the Army*, 575–85.

142. Forrestal, *Diaries*, 173–80, 188–94; Mtg. of Secretaries of State, War, and Navy, 11 Sep 46, RG 107, Patterson Papers, Safe File, box 3.

143. Carter to Marshall, 14 Aug 46, *FRUS, 1946*, 10: 28; Memo, early Sep 1946, NHC, SPD, series 12, box 158, C-2(4).

144. For Vincent's views, see *FRUS, 1946*, 10: 24, 58, 116, 164, 228, 881; G. May, *China Scapegoat*, 144–52.

145. Draft Memo by Butterworth, 6 Sep 46, *FRUS, 1946*, 10: 148–50.

146. Carter to Handy, 7 Nov 46, ibid., 10: 482; Truman to Wallace, 25 Jan 46, HSTP, PSF, box 173.

147. For Marshall's views, see *FRUS, 1946*, 10: 422, 576–78, 587, 592, 600–601, 604, 622, 639–40, 653, 660, 662, 1020–23; Pogue, *Marshall*, 125–43.

148. For Vincent's miscalculation, see Vincent to Acheson, 5 Nov 46, *FRUS, 1946*, 10: 881. Marshall's belief that he had time is apparent in his discussions with Chinese officials and in his dialogue with other Americans. See citations in Note 147 above.

149. Handwritten Notes by Elsey, 12 and 15 July 46, Elsey Papers, box 63; Elsey Oral History, 261–64; Clifford to Byrnes, 18 July 46, Clifford Papers, box 15.

150. Clifford, *Counsel to the President*, 45–76, 109–29; Donovan, *Conflict and Crisis*, 24, 178.

151. Memo by Elsey, 8 Aug 46, Elsey Papers, box 63; Clifford Oral History, 184; Elsey Oral History, 261–67.

152. Handwritten Notes by Elsey, July 1946, Elsey Papers, box 63.

153. For the entire report, see Krock, *Memoirs*, 417–82 (for ominous Soviet behavior, see esp. 468–75; the quotations are on pp. 468 and 470).

154. Ibid., 430–32.

155. Ibid., 476–82.

156. These are my conclusions after four meetings with Soviet historians in 1989 and 1990.

157. For the quotation, see Krock, *Memoirs*, 445; see also JCS 1696, "Presidential Request for Certain Facts and Information Regarding the Soviet Union," 25 July 46, RG 218, CCS 092 USSR (3-27-45), sec. 9; Clay, *Papers*, 1: 243–44; Patterson to Pauley, 24 July 46, RG 319, P&O, 092 TS; Acheson to Clifford, 6 Aug 46, Clifford Papers, box 14.

158. For Korea, see Leahy Diary, 24 July 45, Leahy Papers; Cumings, *Child of Conflict*, 86–91. For Japan, see, e.g., Harriman to Byrnes, 29 Oct 45, *FRUS, 1945*, 6: 804–6. For north China, see, e.g., the discussions at the Dec 1945 meeting of the foreign ministers in Moscow, in ibid., 7: 837–38, 841–48; ibid., 2: 720, 748–49, 756–58. For Soviet-U.S. attempts at accommodation in Asia, see Iriye, *Cold War in Asia*.

159. On 26 Sep 46, John Carter Vincent wrote Acheson: "At present all reports indicate that the Russians are not interfering directly or materially in support of the Communists." See *FRUS, 1946*, 10: 228.

160. For Czechoslovakia, see esp. Laurence A. Steinhardt to Byrnes, 27 and 29 May 46, ibid., 6: 199–200. For Hungary, see Harriman and Abel, *Special Envoy*, 510–11; H. F. Arthur Schoenfeld to Byrnes, 9 Nov 45, *FRUS, 1945*, 4: 904–5. For the optimism that still existed in Hungary in the autumn of 1946, despite many ominous signs, see Kertesz, *Between Russia and the West*, 29–37. For Austria, see, e.g., *FRUS, Potsdam*, 1: 334–35. For differentiated Soviet policies in Eastern Europe, see Lundestad, *American Non-Policy Towards Eastern Europe*, 432–66. For withdrawal and demobilization of Soviet troops, see the weekly calculations by Carl Espe, May–Sep 1946, in NHC, SPD, series 5, box 106, A8; MID, "Review of Europe, Russia, and the Middle East," 26 Dec 45, RG 165, OPD, 350.05 TS; MID, "Soviet Intentions in Scandinavian Countries," 25 Apr 46, ibid.

161. For Kremlin opposition to Communist seizures of power in France and Italy, see Hoyt Vandenberg to Truman, 26 Nov 46, HSTP, PSF, box 249; JIS 263/1, "Invasion of Italy by USSR," 19 Nov 46, RG 218, CCS 092 USSR (3-27-45), sec. 14; *FRUS, 1946*, 5: 472–76; Spriano, *Stalin and the European Communists*, 250–78; Claudin, *Communist Movement*, 387–454; McLane, *Soviet Strategies in Southeast Asia*, esp. 348–49; Behbehani, *Soviet Union and Arab Nationalism*, 56–68; Levine, *Anvil of Victory*, 26–86.

162. Leffler, "Adherence to Agreements."

163. This point was reiterated in Patterson to Truman, 11 June 46, HSTP, PSF, box 157.

164. See, e.g., Murphy to Matthews, 14 Oct 46, *FRUS, 1946*, 5: 622–23; Murphy to Byrnes, 16 and 25 Oct 46, ibid., 5: 623–25, 632–33.

165. See, e.g., JCS to SWNCC, 11 Apr 46, *FRUS, 1946*, 1: 1171–74; Leffler, "Adherence to Agreements," 111–12.

166. MID, "Intelligence Estimate of the World Situation for the Next Five Years," 21 Aug 46, RG 319, P&O, 350.05 TS; JIC 250/12, "Presidential Request for Certain Facts and Information," 2 July 46, RG 218, CCS 092 USSR (3-27-45), sec. 9.

167. For emphasis on Stalin's cynical opportunism, see Taubman, *Stalin's American Policy*, 99–165; Haslam, "Stalin's Assessment of the Likelihood of War"; Mastny, "Europe in U.S.-U.S.S.R. Relations," 16–23; Bundy, *Danger and Survival*, 176–84.

168. The notion that Soviet influence meant domination or could be translated into domination characterized American thinking. Illustratively, an SWNCC report stated that, if the "peoples of the Middle East turn to Russia, this would have same impact in many respects as would military conquest of this area by Soviets." See War Department to Lincoln, 22 June 46, RG 319, P&O, 092 TS; M. Cohen, *Palestine and the Great Powers*, 122.

169. Resis, *Stalin and the Onset of the Cold War*; W. Hahn, *Postwar Soviet Politics*, 19–23; McNeal, *Stalin*, 280–82; Dunmore, *Soviet Politics*, 106–11; McCauley, *Origins of the Cold War*; Stephanson, *Kennan*, 39–53.

170. Philip Mosely to John T. Connor, 14 Oct 46, Kennan Papers, box 28; John Hazard to

Connor, 18 Oct 46, ibid.; Connor to Forrestal, 18 Sep 46, Forrestal Papers, box 68. Kennan's own interpretation of the role of ideology was ambivalent. He enthusiastically endorsed the tone of the Clifford-Elsey report, yet he did not like the emphasis on ideology in a paper written by Professor Edward Willett. See Kennan to Hill, 7 Oct 46, Kennan Papers, box 28.

171. Mark, "October or Thermidor?," 953–61; Jervis, *Perception and Misperception*, 67–76.

172. Bohlen, "Possible Points to Be Stressed in Conversation with Stalin," 13 March 46, RG 59, European Affairs, box 17; Smith to Byrnes, 5 Apr 46, *FRUS, 1946*, 6: 732–36.

173. MccGwire, "Genesis of Soviet Threat Perceptions," 1–36; McCauley, *Origins of the Cold War*.

174. For the airfields, see Ira Eaker to Stuart Symington, 8 May 46, Symington Papers, box 4. For the new fighters and bombers, see Knaack, *Post–World War II Fighters*, 1–40; Knaack, *Post–World War II Bombers*, 1–171. For Soviet view, see Gromyko, *Memoirs*, 135–40; see also the dispatch from Soviet ambassador Nikolai Novikov to the Soviet foreign ministry, 27 Sep 46, *Diplomatic History* 15 (Fall 1991).

175. See, e.g., Alan Kirk to Byrnes, 17 Apr 46, *FRUS, 1946*, 2: 63–64. Fear of a revived Germany was a constant theme of Molotov's; see, e.g., Molotov, *Problems of Foreign Policy*, 55–68.

176. See Stalin's inquiry regarding an Anglo-American alliance in his discussion with Ambassador Smith, *FRUS, 1946*, 6: 734–36.

177. Khrushchev, *Remembers: The Glasnost Tapes*, 100–101; see also Khrushchev, *Remembers*, 361–62.

178. Ra'anan, *International Policy Formation*; Dunmore, *Soviet Politics*; McCagg, *Stalin Embattled*; W. Hahn, *Postwar Soviet Politics*; Linz, *Impact of World War II*; Khrushchev, *Remembers*, 227–315.

179. Clifford Oral History, 180–84; Elsey, "CMC Instructions" [13 July 46?], Elsey Papers, box 63; see also Handwritten Notes by Elsey, 18, 24, and 27 July 46, ibid.

180. JCS 1696, "Presidential Request," 25 July 46, RG 218, CCS 092 USSR (3-27-45), sec. 9. Compare it with JIC 250/12, "Presidential Request," 22 July 46, ibid.

181. Memo by Lauris Norstad, 25 July 46, RG 319, P&O, 092 TS; Patterson to Truman, 27 July 46, ibid.; Forrestal to Truman, 23 July 46, ibid.; Lincoln to Norstad, 23 July 46, Lincoln Papers, War Dept. Files.

182. For Elsey's view, see Handwritten Note, 27 July 46, Elsey Papers, box 63. For Wallace's position, see Wallace, *Price of Vision*, 585–601.

183. For background, see Walker, *Wallace and American Foreign Policy*, 133–59; Walton, *Wallace, Truman, and the Cold War*, 33–117, esp. 97–117; Truman, *Off the Record*, 92–96.

184. In addition to the citations in the preceding note, see Forrestal, *Diaries*, 206–11; Ward, *Threat of Peace*, 141–45; Donovan, *Conflict and Crisis*, 222–28.

185. For the fate of the Clifford-Elsey report, see Clifford Oral History, 213–15; Elsey Oral History, 266–67; Messer, *End of an Alliance*, 208–10.

186. "Daily Summary of Opinion Developments," 23 Sep and 2 Oct 46, RG 59, Public Opinion Studies, box 3.

187. Vandenberg, *Private Papers*, 299–303; Clifford, *Counsel to the President*, 128–29.

188. For Dewey, see R. N. Smith, *Dewey*, 438–67, esp. 459. For Vandenberg, see Vandenberg, *Private Papers*, 126–317. For Dulles, see "Thoughts on Soviet Foreign Policy and What to Do About It," *Life* 20 (3, 10 July 46): 112–26 and 118–30.

189. Boylan, *New Deal Coalition and the Election of 1946*, 132–40, 151–72; Patterson, *Mr. Republican*, 303–14; *New York Times*, 4 Nov 46, p. 2.

190. Almond, *American People and Foreign Policy*, 92–106; Mark, "October or Thermidor?," 951–62.

Chapter 4

1. McCoy, *Presidency of Truman*, 91; Reichard, *Politics as Usual*, 16–19.

2. L. Eden, "Diplomacy of Force," 166–99.

3. Forrestal to Michael Forrestal, 19 Jan 47, Forrestal Papers, box 73; Forrestal comments at Conference of Naval District Commandants, 2 Dec 46, NHC, SPD, series 5, box 107, A19-Conferences; Forrestal, *Diaries*, 240; see also Truman's meeting with top defense officials in D. C. Ramsay to Chester Nimitz, 2 Dec 46, NHC, CNO, Double Zero Files, folder 31.

4. Pogue, *Marshall*, 112–13, 144–51; Stoler, *Marshall*, 152–58. For the response to Marshall's appointment, see "Fortnightly Survey," 22 Jan 47, NA, RG 59, Public Opinion Studies, box 11.

5. Pogue, *Marshall*, 151–60.

6. *FRUS, 1947*, 5: 17–44; Frazier, "Did Britain Start the Cold War?," 715–27.

7. See Chapter Two, pp. 76–81.

8. See Chapter Three, pp. 110–14, 121–25.

9. Rabel, *Between East and West*, 96–98.

10. *FRUS, 1946*, 7: 511–67; Pach, *Arming the Free World*, 102–4.

11. Acheson, *Present at the Creation*, 217–20; Memo by Clayton, 3 March 47, Clayton Papers. Regarding Acheson, see also Nitze Oral History (Truman Library), no. 3, 147–49.

12. Truman, *Memoirs: 1946–52*, 124–25.

13. Kennan, "Comments on the National Security Program," 28 March 47, Kennan Papers, box 17; George A. Lincoln to Patterson, 26 Feb 47, RG 319, P&O Division, 092 TS.

14. Memo of Phone Conversation Between Forrestal and Paul Shields, 20 March 47, Forrestal Papers, box 91; Forrestal to Paul Smith, 19 March 47, ibid.

15. "Summary of Costs of U.S. Assistance Program to Greece and Turkey Until 30 June 1948," no signature [Acheson?], ND [early March 1947], Elsey Papers, box 65; Edwin C. Wilson to SecState, 4 March 47, *FRUS, 1947*, 5: 90–91; Acheson to Embassy in Rome, 5 March 47, ibid., 5: 95; Senate, Foreign Relations, *Legislative Origins of the Truman Doctrine*, 56.

16. Senate, Foreign Relations, *Legislative Origins of the Truman Doctrine*, 21; see also Lincoln to Patterson, 12 March 47, RG 107, Petersen Papers, General Subject File, box 1.

17. Eisenhower, *Papers*, 8: 1581; Nimitz to JCS, 26 March 47, NHC, SPD, series 5, box 110, A16-1; Memo for SecNavy by Op-03, 4 Apr 47, NHC, CNO, Double Zero Files, 1948, box 1.

18. Kennan, *Memoirs, 1925–1950*, 334; Loy W. Henderson Oral History, 87; Mtg. of the Secretaries of State, War, and Navy, 12 March 47, *FRUS, 1947*, 5: 109–10; J. Jones, *Fifteen Weeks*, 162; Forrest P. Sherman, "Presentation to the President," 14 Jan 47, Sherman Papers, box 2.

19. For analyses of Soviet behavior, see Memo by Francis B. Stevens, 23 Dec 46, RG 59, Bohlen Papers, box 4; Eberstadt to Forrestal, 6 Jan 47, Forrestal Papers, box 73.

20. For the quotation, see "Fortnightly Survey," 7 Jan 47, RG 59, Public Opinion Studies, box 11; see also "Daily Summary," 15 Oct 46–15 Feb 47, esp. 1 and 4 Nov 46, 2–12, 17, and 27 Dec 46, and 2 Jan 47, ibid., boxes 2 and 3.

21. L. Eden, "Diplomacy of Force," 166–99; Kepley, *Collapse of the Middle Way*, 3–4.

22. Memo by Clayton, 5 March 47, Clayton Papers. For Hickerson, see *FRUS, 1947*, 5: 47; Acheson, *Present at the Creation*, 218–19; see also Mtg. of the Secretaries of State, War, and Navy, 26 Feb 47, *FRUS, 1947*, 5: 57–58; Freeland, *Truman Doctrine*, 70–102.

23. For the quotation, see Truman, *Memoirs: 1946–52*, 128. For the Truman Doctrine speech, see *PPP:HST* (1947), 176–80; see also Cabinet Mtg., 7 March 47, Connelly Papers, box 1; Memo of Phone Conversation Between Forrestal and Shields, 20 March 47, Forrestal Papers, box 91; Forrestal, *Diaries*, 250–52; J. Jones, *Fifteen Weeks*, 129–70.

24. "Daily Summary," 13 March 47, RG 59, Public Opinion Studies, box 3.

25. For a revealing poll that DOS sent to JCS, see "American Attitudes on U.S. Policy

Toward Russia," 19 Feb 47, RG 165, ABC 381 USSR (2 March 46), sec. 1-D; see also Almond, *American People and Foreign Policy*, 73; Westerfield, *Foreign Policy and Party Politics*, 203–26.

26. Senate, Foreign Relations, *Legislative Origins of the Truman Doctrine*, 46, 142; Hartmann, *Truman and the 80th Congress*, 56–66; Doenecke, *Not to the Swift*, 73–90; Foster, *Activism Replaces Isolationism*, 41–45.

27. L. Eden, "Diplomacy of Force," 166–273.

28. Mark, "Stalinism, Geopolitics, and the Intellectual Origins of the Cold War," 39–40; Doenecke, *Not to the Swift*, 73–90.

29. Senate, Foreign Relations, *Assistance to Greece and Turkey*, 74.

30. Mtg. of the Secretaries of State, War, and Navy, 26 Feb 47, *FRUS, 1947*, 5: 57; Acheson to Patterson, 5 March 47, ibid., 3: 197–98; Memo for the Pres by Acheson, 6 March 47, Elsey Papers, box 65; Cabinet Mtg., 7 March 47, Connelly Papers, box 1.

31. Edwin Nourse to Truman, 7 March 47, HSTP, PSF, box 143. For inflation, see *PPP:HST* (1947), 15.

32. Lincoln to Petersen, 20 Dec 46, RG 107, Petersen Papers, General Decimal File, TS, box 2. For Petersen's quotation, see Memo for the SecWar by Petersen, 1 March 47, RG 107, Patterson Papers, General Decimal File, box 9; Eisenhower, *Papers*, 8: 1546, 1609–10.

33. Special Ad Hoc Committee of SWNCC, "Policies, Procedures, and Costs of Assistance by the United States to Foreign Countries," 21 Apr 47, *FRUS, 1947*, 3: 204–19, esp. 209 for the quotation; see also J. Jones, *Fifteen Weeks*, 199–213.

34. JCS 1769/1, "United States Assistance to Other Countries from the Standpoint of National Security," 29 Apr 47, *FRUS, 1947*, 1: 736–40, esp. 739–41.

35. Kennan, "Russia's National Objectives," 10 Apr 47, Kennan Papers, box 17; Kennan, "Comments on the National Security Program," 28 March 47, ibid.

36. Report of the Rearmament Subcommittee to the Special Ad Hoc Committee, 10 July 47, RG 165, ABC 400.336 (20 March 47), sec. 1-B; War Dept. Intelligence Division, "Requirements for United States Military Aid," 20 June 47, RG 319, P&O, 350.05 TS; Report of the Working Group on Economic Aid to the Special Ad Hoc Committee of SWNCC, "Foreign Needs for United States Economic Assistance During the Next Three to Five Years" [July 1947], RG 353, SWNCC, box 134.

37. C. P. Hall to Lauris Norstad, 19 May 47, RG 319, P&O, 092 TS; Norstad to Hall, 2 June 47, ibid. This issue is also discussed in the JCS 1925 Series, ibid.

38. "Report to the President of the United States from the Atomic Energy Commission, 1 January–1 April 1947," 3 Apr 47, HSTP, PSF, box 200; Lilienthal, *Journals*, 165–66; D. Rosenberg, "U.S. Nuclear Stockpile," 25–28.

39. Patterson to Truman, 23 June 47, RG 107, Patterson Papers, Safe File, box 2; JPS 684/31, "Over-All Examination of U.S. Requirements for Military Bases and Base Rights," 24 June 47, RG 218, CCS 360 (12-9-42), sec. 29.

40. For plans to accelerate atomic stockpiling, develop the overseas base system, study aircraft procurement, and ready the strategic offensive, see JCS 1764/1, "Guidance on Military Aspects of United States Policy to Be Adopted in Event of Continuing Impasse in Acceptance of International Control of Atomic Energy," 14 July 47, RG 165, ABC 471.6 Atom (17 Aug 45), sec. 6-A; Leahy to Secretaries of War and Navy, 13 Aug 47, NHC, CNO, Double Zero Files, folder 13; D. Rosenberg, "U.S. Nuclear Stockpile," 27–28; Truman to Finletter, 18 July 47, Finletter Papers, box 7; Borowski, *Hollow Threat*, 72–90; Converse, "United States Plans for a Military Base System," 211–32; Moody, "United States Air Forces in Europe," 76–77.

41. For Petersen's appraisal, see Memo by Chief of Staff, ND [July 1947], RG 165, ABC 471.6 Atom (17 Aug 45), sec. 6-A. Forrestal's thinking was precisely along the same lines. See Forrestal, *Diaries*, 350–51.

42. Eberstadt to Forrestal, 12 Nov 46, Eberstadt Papers, box 28. For Montgomery's view, see Eisenhower, *Papers*, 8: 1530–31. For Eisenhower, see also Forrestal, *Diaries*, 265. For Smith's

estimate, see Memo by Munsom, 16 May 47, RG 107, Petersen Papers, General Decimal File, TS, box 1.

43. For assumptions in war plans, see, e.g., JWPC 465/1, "The Soviet Threat Against the Iberian Peninsula and the Means Required to Meet It," 8 May 47, RG 218, CCS 381 USSR (3-2-46), sec. 5; JWPC 474/1, "Strategic Study of Western and Northern Europe," 13 May 47, RG 218, CCS 092 USSR (3-27-45), sec. 20.

44. For assessments regarding the demobilization and withdrawal of Soviet troops, see, e.g., War Dept. Intelligence Division, "Estimate of the Possibility of War," 21 July 47, RG 319, P&O, 350.05 TS; War Dept. Intelligence Division, "Soviet Capabilities in Germany and Western Europe," 26 Dec 46, ibid.; Todd to Chief of Staff, 15 May 47, ibid.; Memo by Bonesteel, 13 Nov 46, ibid., 091.711 TS; JIC, Memo for Information no. 237, "Movement of Russian Troops Outside the USSR Except in the Far East," 31 Dec 46, RG 218, CCS 092 USSR (3-27-45), sec. 16; Memo for the Chief of Staff by Carter W. Clarks, 17 Feb 47, RG 165, Army Chief of Staff, 091 Russia TS; Evangelista, "Stalin's Postwar Army Reappraised." This information conflicts with Adam Ulam's contention that U.S. officials were unaware of Soviet weaknesses; see Ulam, *Rivals*, 19, 123, 137.

45. War Dept. Intelligence Division, "Estimate of the Possibility of War Between the United States and the USSR Today from a Comparison of the Soviet Situation Today with the Situation as It Existed in September 1946," 21 July 47, RG 319, P&O, 350.05 TS.

46. For the quotation, see Kennan's Answers to Questions at Air War College, 10 Apr 47, Kennan Papers, box 17; George M. Jones, "Conference with Mr. George F. Kennan," 24 Apr 47, RG 319, P&O, 092 TS; Hixson, *Kennan*, 37–38.

47. Senate, Select Committee, *Supplementary Reports on Military Intelligence*, 12–14, 26–27; Prados, *Presidents' Secret Wars*, 17–20; Barnes, "Secret Cold War: Part I," 404–5.

48. Kennan, "Russia's National Objectives," 10 Apr 47, Kennan Papers, box 17.

49. UN, ECE, *Economic Survey of Europe* (1947), 3–18, 31–39; "Coal Production and Trade in Europe Since the War," *Economic Bulletin for Europe* 1 (Third Quarter 1949): 17.

50. For Hoover's report, see Gimbel, *Origins of the Marshall Plan*, 182–84; for his views, see also Senate, Foreign Relations, *Foreign Relief Aid: 1947*, 30–43. For the public response, see "Daily Summaries," 3–5 March 47, RG 59, Public Opinion Studies, box 3; see also extensive public opinion polls taken by DOS, in RG 107, Petersen Papers, Classified, 092.

51. MemCon by Edwin A. Lightner, 24 Jan 47, *FRUS, 1947*, 2: 199–200; "Policy Paper Prepared in the Department of State" [Jan 1947], ibid., 2: 220–23.

52. Bonesteel, "Some General Security Implications of the German Settlement" [ND], RG 107, Petersen Papers, Classified, 091 Germany; see also Petersen to Hilldring, 5 March 47, ibid.

53. Memos by Dulles, 26 Feb and 7 March 47, Dulles Papers, box 31; Dulles speech, "The Problem of Germany and the Problem of Europe," 17 Jan 47, ibid., box 32.

54. Greenwood, "Return to Dunkirk," 58–62; Baylis, "Britain and the Dunkirk Treaty," 242–45; Hill, "Inflation and the Collapse of Tripartism," 6–12. For background, see also Young, *Britain, France, and the Unity of Europe*, 43–51.

55. MemCon, 6 March 47, *FRUS, 1947*, 2: 190–95; Marshall to Acheson, 11 March 47, ibid., 2: 241; Marshall to Truman and Acheson, 11 March 47, ibid., 2: 244; Mtg., 13 March 47, ibid., 2: 247–49; Auriol, *Journal*, 1: 131–32.

56. For developments at the Moscow conference, see *FRUS, 1947*, 2: 234–390. For the issue of reparations from current production and for the restrictive nature of the U.S. proposals, see esp. ibid., 2: 302–9; DOS, "An Economic Program for Germany," 5 Nov 47, HSTP, PSF, box 163; Eisenberg, "American Decision to Divide Germany."

57. In addition to citations in preceding note, see W. B. Smith, *Three Years in Moscow*, 224–25; Dulles, *War or Peace*, 100–105; Pruessen, *Dulles*, 341–46; Backer, *Decision to Divide Germany*, 161–70.

58. Clay, *Papers*, 1: 283, 330–32; Backer, *Winds of History*, 171–77.

59. For the difficult relationships between Dulles, Clay, and Marshall, see Backer, *Winds of History*, 155–80; J. Smith, *Clay*, 414–22; Pruessen, *Dulles*, 331–46; Kindleberger, *German Economy*, 157–61, 177.

60. Truman to Marshall, 1 Apr 47, *FRUS, 1947*, 2: 302; Marshall to Acheson, 2 Apr 47, ibid., 2: 306; Pogue, *Marshall*, 180–94.

61. MemCon, 15 Apr 47, *FRUS, 1947*, 2: 339–44; see also ibid., 2: 315–36.

62. For a balanced assessment of Soviet reparation demands, see Backer, *Decision to Divide Germany*, 61–72; see also Stephanson, *Kennan*, 127–30.

63. Clay, *Papers*, 1: 328, 332, 337–38; Donald R. Heath to SecState, 3 and 14 Apr 47, *FRUS, 1947*, 2: 863–64, 1144–46; Robert Murphy to SecState, 11 May 47, ibid., 2: 867–68.

64. *FRUS, 1947*, 2: 351–85, 475–76, 490; Backer, *Winds of History*, 181–89; Gimbel, *Origins of the Marshall Plan*, 187–98; Pogue, *Marshall*, 184–95.

65. For the quotation, see Petersen to Patterson, 12 June 47, RG 107, Patterson Papers, General Decimal File, box 8; see also Patterson to Marshall, 13 June 47, *FRUS, 1947*, 2: 1151–52; Hilldring to Acheson, 8 May 47, ibid., 2: 1146; Marshall to Anderson, 15 May 47, ibid., 2: 1149–50; Clay, *Papers*, 1: 359–63.

66. For the views of Kennan and the PPS, see *FRUS, 1947*, 3: 220–30; PPS 2, "Increase of European Coal Production," 2 June 47, in *PPS Papers*, 1: 12–21; Petersen to Marshall, 12 June 47, RG 107, Patterson Papers, General Decimal File, box 4; Petersen to Clay, 8 July 47, RG 107, Petersen Papers, Classified, 091 Germany; Memo for the SecWar by Petersen, 12 June 47, ibid.; Gimbel, *Origins of the Marshall Plan*, 199–206.

67. Clay to Daniel Noce, 27 and 29 Apr 47, *FRUS, 1947*, 2: 910–14; Noce to Clay, 1 May 47, ibid., 2: 914–15; Clay, *Papers*, 1: 353–63; James W. Riddleberger to Hilldring, 8 July 47, RG 107, Petersen Papers, Classified, 091 Germany; Gimbel, *Origins of the Marshall Plan*, 203–19.

68. Memo for the SecWar by Petersen, 12 June 47, RG 107, Petersen Papers, Classified, 091 Germany; Petersen to Clay, 25 June and 8 July 47, ibid.; Mtgs. of the Secretaries of State, War, and Navy, 7 May, 19 June, and 3 July 47, RG 107, Patterson Papers, Safe File, box 3; Patterson to Marshall, 13 June 47, ibid., box 4; Forrestal, *Diaries*, 273; MemCon by Avery F. Peterson, 29 June 47, *FRUS, 1947*, 3: 372–73; Memo by Clayton, 20 June 47, ibid., 2: 929; Gimbel, *Origins of the Marshall Plan*, 208–19.

69. SWNCC 371, "Revision of Level of Industry Plan for Germany," 26 May 47, RG 165, ABC 387 Germany (18 Dec 43), sec. 4-I.

70. Mtg. of the Secretaries of State, War, and Navy, 3 July 47, RG 107, Patterson Papers, Safe File, box 3; see also many of the documents in RG 107, Petersen Papers, Classified, 091 Germany.

71. DOS, *Decade of American Foreign Policy*, 331.

72. Radio Broadcast by Marshall, 28 Apr 47, *DSB* 16 (11 May 47): 919–24.

73. Memos by Caffery, 6 and 31 March and 11 Apr 47, *FRUS, 1947*, 3: 693–99; French Embassy to DOS, 8 Apr 47, ibid., 3: 696–97; Clayton to Acheson, 23 Apr 47, ibid., 3: 702; see also SWNCC, Special Ad Hoc Committee, "Study on U.S. Assistance to France," 9 Apr 47, RG 165, ABC 400.336 France (20 March 47).

74. Dunn to Marshall, 3 May 47, *FRUS, 1947*, 3: 891; see also Dunn to SecState, 13 March and 1 and 12 Apr 47, ibid., 3: 876–80; Marshall to Embassy in Italy, 1 May 47, ibid., 3: 889.

75. Marshall to Henri Bonnet, 7 May 47, ibid., 3: 707–8. For the $250 million loan to France, see ibid., 3: 709.

76. For Kennan's proposal regarding Italy, see Kennan to Acheson, 23 May 47, ibid., 3: 226. For Marshall and Italy, see MemCon by Marshall, 16 May 47, ibid., 3: 906–7; Marshall to Embassy in Italy, 20 May 47, ibid., 3: 909–10.

77. For Acheson's speech, 8 May 47, see *DSB* 16 (18 May 47): 994. For Iran, see *FRUS, 1946*, 7: 533–43. For Greece, see *FRUS, 1947*, 5: 10–11; Wittner, *American Intervention in Greece*, 46–47, 103–9. For situation in France, see Caffery to SecState, 12 May 47, *FRUS, 1947*,

3: 710–12; Auriol, *Journal*, 1: 209–33; Todd to Chief of Staff, 7 May 47, RG 319, P&O, 350.05 TS; Rice-Maximim, "United States and the French Left," 734–35. For Caffery quotation, see Dur, *Caffery*, 42. For Italy, see Dunn to SecState, 3, 17, and 28 May 47, *FRUS, 1947*, 3: 889–92, 896–901, 911; Marshall to Dunn, 20 May and 6 June 47, ibid., 3: 909–10, 919.

78. Dunn to Marshall, 3 May 47, *FRUS, 1947*, 3: 889–92; Caffery to Marshall, 12 May 47, ibid., 3: 710–13; Rice-Maximim, "United States and the French Left," 729–39; Hill, "Inflation and the Collapse of Tripartism"; Maier, "Analog of Empire," 14–30.

79. Harper, *America and the Reconstruction of Italy*, 18–21, 118–36; Wall, *United States and the Reshaping of Postwar France*, chap. 3.

80. "Daily Summary," 5 May–5 June 47, RG 59, Public Opinion Studies, box 3.

81. Memo by Kennan, 16 May 47, *FRUS, 1947*, 3: 221–23; Kennan to Acheson, 23 May 47, ibid., 3: 225–30; Mtgs. of the PPS, May 1947, RG 59, PPS, box 32.

82. Clayton to Acheson, 27 May 47, *FRUS, 1947*, 3: 230–32; "Summary of Discussion" by Ward P. Allen, 29 May 47, ibid., 3: 234–36; Acheson, *Present at the Creation*, 230–32.

83. For Marshall's speech, see *DSB* 16 (15 June 47): 1159–60.

84. Milward, *Reconstruction of Western Europe*; Milward, "Was the Marshall Plan Necessary?"

85. OEEC, *Interim Report on the ERP*, 1: 53–54; UN, ECE, *Economic Survey of Europe* (1947), 53–67; Hill, "Inflation and the Collapse of Tripartism."

86. Milward, "Was the Marshall Plan Necessary?," 242–53.

87. Quoting from the Sep 1947 report in OEEC, *ERP: Second Report*, 13–14, 30–31.

88. SWNCC 360, "Policies, Procedures, and Costs of Assistance," 24 Apr 47, RG 319, ABC 400.336 (20 March 47), sec. 1-A; Caffery to Marshall, 12 May 47, *FRUS, 1947*, 3: 712. See also, e.g., JIC 374/2, "Capabilities and Military Potential of Soviet and Non-Soviet Powers in 1956," 8 Jan 47, RG 218, CCS 092 USSR (3-27-45), sec. 16; JWPC 474/1, "Strategic Study of Western and Northern Europe," 13 May 47, ibid., sec. 20; War Dept. Intelligence Division, "Rewrite of JWPC Paper 'Political Trends in Western and Northern European Countries,' " 5 June 47, RG 319, P&O, 350.05 TS; P&O, "Strategic Study of Western and Northern Europe," 21 May 47, ibid., 092 TS.

89. Clayton to Acheson, 27 May 47, *FRUS, 1947*, 3: 230–32; Jackson, "Prologue to the Marshall Plan," 1053–54; Harriman, "World Trade Is Your Business," *Domestic Commerce* 35 (May 1947): 5–6; *PPP:HST* (1947), 37.

90. President's Committee on Foreign Aid, *European Recovery and American Aid*, 3.

91. President's First Economic Report, in *PPP:HST* (1947), 28–39.

92. UN, ECE, *Economic Survey of Europe* (1947), 61.

93. CEA, *Economic Report of the President*, 134–35.

94. *PPP:HST* (1947), 210–11, 263; President's Committee on Foreign Aid, *European Recovery*, 3–5.

95. *PPP:HST* (1947), 13–39, 55–97, 350–54; Heller, *Economics and the Truman Administration*, 25.

96. President's Committee on Foreign Aid, *European Recovery*; Dept. of the Interior, *National Resources and Foreign Aid*; CEA, *Impact of Foreign Aid*.

97. Clayton Statement Before the House Committee on Ways and Means, 26 March 47, *DSB* 16 (6 Apr 47): 627–28; Willard Thorp, "Our Domestic Economy and Foreign Affairs," *DSB* 16 (27 Apr 47): 758–63; R. Gardner, *Sterling-Dollar Diplomacy*, 348–61.

98. *PPP:HST* (1947), 170–71.

99. President's Committee on Foreign Aid, *European Recovery*, 18–19.

100. Ibid., 21–22.

101. Ibid., 22.

102. Willard Thorp, "We Have a Stake in Our Economic Foreign Policy," *Domestic Commerce* 35 (Feb 1947): 9. For Kennan's view, see PPS 4, "Certain Aspects of the European Recovery Problem from the United States' Standpoint," 23 July 47, *PPS Papers*, 1: 31–32; JCS 1769/1,

"United States Assistance to Other Countries," 29 Apr 47, RG 165, ABC 400.336 (20 March 47), sec. 1-A.

103. PPS 20, "Effect Upon the United States if the European Recovery Plan Is Not Adopted," *PPS Papers*, 2: 78–79.

104. For a contrasting view, see Gaddis, "Was the Truman Doctrine a Real Turning Point?"

105. Quote from 1947 General Report of the Committee on European Economic Cooperation, in *PPS Papers*, 3: 85.

106. Wood, *From Marshall Plan to Debt Crisis*, 49–50; Orchard, "ECA and the Dependent Territories," 67.

107. OEEC, *Interim Report on the ERP*, 1: 41–43, 49–80; UN, ECE, *Economic Survey of Europe* (1952), 85–144, esp. 113–21; Cowen and Westcott, "British Imperial Economic Policy During the War," 58–61; Hyam, "Africa and the Labour Government," 1–30.

108. Orchard, "ECA and the Dependent Territories," 66, 74–87; Wood, *From Marshall Plan to Debt Crisis*, 56–60.

109. President's Committee on Foreign Aid, *European Recovery*, 125–35, 194–95; Bonesteel to Petersen, 13 May 47, RG 107, Petersen Papers, Classified, 092; War Dept. Intelligence Division, "Positive U.S. Action Required to Restore Normal Conditions in Southeast Asia," 3 July 47, RG 319, P&O, 092 TS. For the decrease in East European supplies, see OEEC, *Interim Report on the ERP*, 1: 54; UN, ECE, *Economic Survey of Europe* (1952), 88.

110. McMahon, *Colonialism and Cold War*, 156–85; War Dept. Intelligence Division, "Positive United States Action to Restore Normal Conditions in Southeast Asia," 3 July 47, RG 319, P&O, 092 TS; SWNCC, Special Ad Hoc Committee, "Indonesia," 22 July 47, RG 353, SWNCC, box 109.

111. In addition to citations in previous note, see Marshall to Herman Baruch, 16 May 47, *FRUS, 1947*, 6: 924; War Dept. Intelligence Division, "The Situation in Southeast Asia as It Affects the Availability of Strategic Raw Materials" [July 1947], P&O, 092 TS.

112. SWNCC, Special Ad Hoc Committee, "Indochina" [Spring 1947], RG 165, ABC 400.336 (20 March 47), sec. 1-B; War Dept. Intelligence Division, "Situation in Southeast Asia" [July 1947], RG 319, P&O, 092 TS.

113. Ibid.

114. For the quotations, see Marshall to Caffery, 13 May 47, *FRUS, 1947*, 6: 95–97; Marshall to Caffery, 3 Feb 47, ibid., 6: 67–68; Acheson to Reed, 5 Dec 47, *FRUS, 1946*, 7: 67.

115. Memo for SecWar by Petersen, 1 March 47, RG 107, Patterson Papers, General Decimal File, box 9; Lincoln to Petersen, 4 March 47, RG 319, P&O, 092 TS; Memo by Lincoln, 4 March 47, ibid.; Patterson to Acheson, 2 Apr 47, *FRUS, 1947*, 6: 626–28.

116. Mtgs. of the Secretaries of State, War, and Navy, 19 March, 9 Apr, and 7 May 47, RG 107, Patterson Papers, Safe File, box 3; Statement by Acheson, 20 May 47, Senate, Foreign Relations, *Executive Sessions*, 1: 53–54; Acheson to Patterson, 28 March 47, *FRUS, 1947*, 6: 622–23; Acheson to Marshall, 11 Apr 47, ibid., 6: 630–31; see also Norstad to Patterson, 4 Jan 47, RG 107, Patterson Papers, General Decimal File, box 9; Lincoln to Petersen, 23 Jan 47, RG 319, P&O, 092 TS.

117. Matray, *Reluctant Crusade*, 116.

118. Ibid., 109–24.

119. For withdrawal of Soviet troops and repercussions, see Todd to Chief of Staff, 2 and 15 May 47, RG 319, P&O, 350.05 TS; Lincoln to Norstad, 12 May 47, ibid., 092 TS; Eisenhower, *Papers*, 8: 1708–10; Cumings, *Origins of the Korean War*, 2: 52–53.

120. Stueck, *Road to Confrontation*, 75–112; Matray, *Reluctant Crusade*, 99–124.

121. Memos by John Carter Vincent, 20 and 27 June 47, *FRUS, 1947*, 7: 849, 852–54; G. May, *China Scapegoat*, 151–60; Stueck, *Road to Confrontation*, 33–46. For developments inside China, see Eastman, *Seeds of Destruction*.

122. JCS, "United States Policy Toward China," 9 June 47, *FRUS, 1947*, 7: 838–48, esp. 840; Patterson to Marshall, 26 Feb 47, ibid., 7: 799–802; Mtgs. of the Secretaries of State, War, and Navy, 12 Feb and 20 June 47, RG 107, Patterson Papers, Safe File, box 3.

123. Todd to Director of P&O, 25 Apr 47, RG 319, P&O, 092 TS; War Dept. Intelligence Division, "Soviet Influence in China," 16 June 47, ibid., 350.05 TS; Lincoln to Petersen, 18 June 47, RG 107, Petersen Papers, General Decimal File, TS, box 1; Memo of Information by Charles Rend, 3 June 47, RG 218, Leahy Papers, box 2.

124. "Notes from Admiral Cooke," 25 July 47, NHC, CNO, Double Zero Files, folder 31; see also Forrestal to Marshall, 20 June 47, *FRUS, 1947*, 7: 968–69; JCS, "United States Policy Toward China," 9 June 47, ibid., 7: 838–48.

125. For Marshall's views and DOS decisions, see Statement by Marshall, 14 Feb 47, U.S. Senate, Foreign Relations, *Executive Sessions*, 1: 6–10; *FRUS, 1947*, 7: 811, 815–20, 832–36, 852–55, 947–50, 962–63, 966–68.

126. JCS, "United States Policy Toward China," 9 June 47, *FRUS, 1947*, 7: 838–48; Forrestal to Marshall, 20 June 47, ibid., 7: 968–69; Mtg. of the Secretaries of State, War, and Navy, 20 June 47, RG 107, Patterson Papers, Safe File, box 3.

127. Acheson to Forrestal, 28 March 47, *FRUS, 1947*, 7: 811; Acheson to Marshall, 2 April 47, ibid., 7: 815; Ringwalt to Vincent, 5 May 47, ibid., 7: 832–33; Memos by Vincent and Acheson, 27 June 47, ibid., 7: 852–55.

128. For the quotation, see Cabinet Mtg., 7 March 47, Connelly Papers, box 1; see also Lilienthal, *Journals*, 200–201; Mtgs. of Secretaries of State, War, and Navy, 20 and 26 June 47, RG 107, Patterson Papers, Safe File, box 3; Marshall to Forrestal, 23 July 47, *FRUS, 1947*, 7: 970–71; Marshall to Lovett, 2 July 47, ibid., 7: 635–36.

129. In addition to citations in previous note, see Stueck, *Wedemeyer Mission*, 7–28.

130. Eisenhower, *Papers*, 8: 1388–90; Patterson to Byrnes, 29 Nov 46, *FRUS, 1946*, 8: 934–35; Foltos, "New Pacific Barrier," 337–39.

131. Eisenhower, *Papers*, 8: 1402–4; DOS, *Decade of American Foreign Policy*, 731–39.

132. For the U.S. negotiating position, see Byrnes to Embassy in Manila, 22 Oct 46, RG 59, 811.24596/10-2246; Acheson to Embassy in Manila, 24 Oct 46, RG 59, 811.24596/10-2446. For the military assistance agreement, see DOS, *Decade of American Foreign Policy*, 740–43.

133. Shalom, *United States and the Philippines*, 13–67; Cullather, "United States Strategic and Economic Policy Toward the Philippines," 1–57.

134. For review of overseas base requirements, see esp. JPS, 247th, 283rd, and 285th Mtgs., 27 Feb, 10 July, and 7 Aug 47, RG 218, CCS 360 (12-9-42), secs. 29 and 30; William L. Ritchie to Glover et al., 23 May 47, ibid.; JPS 684/31, "Over-All Examination of . . . Bases," 24 June 47, ibid. For Greenland, see, e.g., Lincoln to Norstad, 12 June 47, RG 319, P&O, 092 TS; Matthews to Marshall, 28 May 47, RG 59, European Affairs, box 17. For Okinawa, see Eisenhower, *Papers*, 8: 1602–4; George Atcheson to Truman, 19 June 47, HSTP, PSF, box 182; Borowski, *Hollow Threat*, 77–78. For Dhahran, see ibid., 75; Spaatz to Patterson, 10 Apr 47, RG 107, Patterson Papers, Safe File, box 1; Memo by Harry R. Snyder, 15 May 47, RG 107, Assistant SecWar for Air, box 187B, 090. For evidence of the ongoing talks with the French, see Spaatz to Symington, ND [Oct 1947], ibid.; JCS 570/83, Appendix D, "Status of Negotiations," 12 Aug 47, RG 218, CCS 360 (12-9-42), sec. 30. For a somewhat different interpretation that stresses the gap between strategic and base planning, see Converse, "United States Plans for a Military Base System," 219–32. Converse's dissertation is very good, but he ignores U.S. policies and actions in Turkey and Egypt that complemented American base planning. He also minimizes the steps the United States was taking in Saudi Arabia and North Africa.

135. Sangmuah, "United States and the French Empire in North Africa," 133–76.

136. For Europe's growing dependence, particularly on North and Central American foodstuffs and raw materials, see OEEC, *Interim Report on the ERP*, 1: 15–22, 51–56; Eisenhower, *Papers*, 8: 1700–1703.

137. *PPP:HST* (1947), 429–32.

138. Matthew B. Ridgway to Petersen, 24 Feb 47, RG 107, Petersen Papers, General Subject File, box 1; Inter-American Defense Board to Secretary, Presidential Staff, 9 June 47 (and supporting documents), NHC, SPD, series 5, box 110, A16-1; Petersen to Eisenhower, 3 March 47, RG 107, Petersen Papers, Classified, 092.

139. For the views of Acheson, Patterson, Forrestal, and Marshall, see *FRUS, 1947*, 8: 105–15. For Eisenhower's quotation, see his *Papers*, 8: 1700.

140. JCS, "United States Assistance to Other Countries," 29 Apr 47, *FRUS, 1947*, 1: 744; Forrestal to Acheson, 31 March 47, ibid., 8: 109. For Patterson quotation, see Patterson to Acheson, 27 March 47, ibid., 8: 108.

141. For the Rio Treaty, see DOS, *Decade of American Foreign Policy*, 227–29.

142. MemCons by Marshall, 20 and 22 Aug 47, *FRUS, 1947*, 8: 48, 57–58; JCS, "United States Assistance to Other Countries," 29 Apr 47, ibid., 1: 743; see also Senate, Foreign Relations, *Executive Sessions*, 1: 141–42.

143. Lovett to Truman, 1 Dec 47, *FRUS, 1947*, 8: 92–93.

144. For emphasis on the core-periphery relationship, see McCormick, *America's Half-Century*; Rotter, *Path to Vietnam*.

145. Acheson, *Present at the Creation*, 213–17; Kennan, *Memoirs, 1925–1950*, 363; Bohlen, *Witness to History*, 258–73; comments by Frank Pace, in Thompson, *Truman Presidency*, 150; Pogue, *Marshall*, 144–60; Stoler, *Marshall*, 145–66; Backer, *Winds of History*, 172–85.

146. For Lovett, see Mee, *Marshall Plan*, 174–76. For Lovett's frequent talks with Forrestal, see Lovett Diaries, 1947–48; for his choice of Bonesteel, see ibid., 13 and 19 Aug 47. For Symington's affection for Lovett, see Symington to Madame T. V. Soong, 30 June 47, Symington Papers, box 11.

147. Kennan, *Memoirs, 1925–1950*, 285–329; L. Gardner, *Architects of Illusion*, 270–300; Lincoln to Petersen, 8 March 47, RG 107, Petersen Papers, General Subject File, box 1; "Conference with Mr. G. F. Kennan," 24 Apr 47, RG 319, P&O, 092 TS. For background on Kennan, see also Hixson, *Kennan*, 1–72; Stephanson, *Kennan*, 3–109.

148. Kennan's analytic brilliance emerges in the PPS papers and his speeches at the National War College. For the former, see *PPS Papers*, vols. 1–3; for the latter, see particularly the documents in Kennan Papers, box 17; see also Mayers, *Kennan*, 105–88; Gaddis, *Strategies of Containment*, 25–88; Nitze, *From Hiroshima to Glasnost*, 50–52, 85–87.

149. For the views of Forrestal and Eberstadt, see Memo for Forrestal, 5 July 45, Eberstadt Papers, box 29; Eberstadt, "Summary of Report . . . on Unification of the War and Navy Departments and Postwar Organization for National Security," 18 Oct 45, ibid.; Memo for SecNavy by Eberstadt, 11 March 46, ibid., box 30; Eberstadt to John McCloy, 27 Sep 46, ibid., box 29; Eberstadt to Kenney, 30 Sep 46, ibid.; Gates to McCloy, 6 Dec 46, ibid.; Forrestal to Truman, 8 Nov 45, HSTP, PSF, box 158; Forrestal to Clark Clifford, 7 Sep 46, Clifford Papers, box 16; Forrestal to Clayton, 24 Sep 46, RG 107, Patterson Papers, Safe File, box 3.

150. See the documents in Elsey Papers, boxes 82 and 83; "Brief: Opening Statement at First Meeting of NSC," 26 Sep 47, HSTP, PSF, box 203; Sander, "Truman and the National Security Council," 369–88; Nelson, "Truman and the National Security Council." For Webb, see Berman, *Office of Management and Budget*, 38–47; Clifford, *Counsel to the President*, 160–64.

151. Forrestal, *Diaries*, 313–17; Rearden, *Formative Years*, 118–25; Doig and Hargrove, *Leadership and Innovation*, 386–400.

152. Interview with Souers, 15 Dec 54, HSTP, Post-Presidential Papers, box 2; Rearden, *Formative Years*, 119–21; Nelson, "Truman and the National Security Council," 367–69.

153. For an excellent description of the organizational setup of the NME, see Rearden, *Formative Years*, 1–115.

154. Ibid., 16–35, 58–60; Notes by Elsey, ND [early 1947], Elsey Papers, box 82; Donald Stone, "The Organization of the Office of the Secretary of Defense," 21 Aug 47, ibid., box 83.

155. For Forrestal and his staff, see Rearden, *Formative Years*, 58–67; for his feelings upon taking office, see Forrestal, *Diaries*, 294–323. For Gruenther's role, see Mtg. of Four Secretaries, 13 Nov 47, NHC, Politico-Military Policy Division, series 24, box 164; Leva Oral History, 16; letters in Souers Papers, box 1.

156. There is a huge literature on the unification struggle and interservice rivalries. The classic work is Caraley, *Politics of Military Unification*; see also V. Davis, *Postwar Defense Policy*, 199–206. For Forrestal's selection of Ohly, see Rearden, *Formative Years*, 60. For Forrestal's reli-

ance on Eisenhower, see esp. Forrestal to Eisenhower, 21 Feb 48, Eisenhower Papers, File 1652, box 42. For the bitter feelings that persisted, see, e.g., Arthur W. Radford to Louis E. Denfeld, 22 Aug 47, NHC, Denfeld Papers, box 1. For efforts to get the chiefs of staff away from their staffs and to effect compromises, see McNeil Oral History, 61–65.

157. Hogan, *Marshall Plan*, 101–9, 136–51; Arkes, *Bureaucracy [and] the Marshall Plan*, 59–131; Harriman's comments, in Thompson, *Truman Presidency*, 169.

158. Comments by Pace and Harriman, in Thompson, *Truman Presidency*, 148, 173–74.

159. Isaacson and Thomas, *Wise Men*, 425–28; Vandenberg, *Private Papers*, 452–54; Hudson, "Vandenberg Reconsidered."

160. Vandenberg, *Private Papers*, 372.

161. Doig and Hargrove, *Leadership and Innovation*, 380; Rearden, *Formative Years*, 74–75.

162. Saltzman Oral History, 9–11, 24–25.

163. For post-unification controversies, see, e.g., Coletta, *U.S. Navy*; Schilling, Hammond, and Snyder, *Strategy, Politics, and Defense Budgets*.

164. Thompson, *Truman Presidency*, 169.

165. Rearden, *Formative Years*, 318–28.

166. Ibid., 423–56; Herken, *Winning Weapon*, 235–63.

167. Rearden, *Formative Years*, 118–27; Nelson, "Truman and the National Security Council," 370.

168. Senate, Select Committee, *Supplementary Reports on Military Intelligence*, 15–17, 24–31. Many of the excellent reports prepared by the CIA's Office of Research and Evaluation for the NSC can be found in HSTP, PSF, boxes 203, 249, 255, and 256.

169. "Brief: Opening Statement at First Meeting of NSC," 26 Sep 47, HSTP, PSF, box 203; Nelson, "Truman and the National Security Council," 366.

170. For a ringing endorsement of Truman's management style, see Acheson, *Present at the Creation*, 729–37. For Truman's penchant to delegate, see comments by Steelman, in Thompson, *Truman Presidency*, 43–47.

171. X [George F. Kennan], "Sources of Soviet Conduct"; L. Gardner, *Architects of Illusion*, 270–300; Gaddis, *Strategies of Containment*, 25–53.

172. Kennan's speeches, in Kennan Papers, esp. box 17; *PPS Papers*, vols. 1–3; Hixson, *Kennan*, 47–72.

173. Kennan, *Memoirs, 1925–1950*, 373–87.

174. As indicated in the text, U.S. officials thought that Communist ideas were very attractive to the dispirited peoples of postwar Europe (as evidenced by the strength of Communist parties) as well as to the inhabitants of the Third World who increasingly sought liberation from their colonial and neocolonial masters.

175. Report of Discussion with Robert A. Lovett, 12 May 47, Council on Foreign Relations, Records of Mtgs., vol. 12.

176. Kennan, "Russia's National Objectives," 10 Apr 47, Kennan Papers, box 17; Kennan, "Contemporary Problems of Foreign Policy," 17 Sep 48, ibid.; X [Kennan], "Sources of Soviet Conduct"; PPS 38, "United States Objectives with Respect to Russia," 18 Aug 48, *PPS Papers*, 2: 372–411. The breadth of Kennan's interests, aims, and aspirations is apparent in the PPS papers. For North Africa and Southeast Asia, e.g., see ibid., 2: 142–49, 3: 32–58.

177. Almond, *American People and Foreign Policy*; Lifka, *Totalitarianism*, 484–777; Freeland, *Truman Doctrine*; Mark, "October or Thermidor?," 937–62.

178. Kennan, *Memoirs, 1925–1950*, 330–41.

Chapter 5

1. Bullock, *Bevin*, 400–409; Young, *Britain, France, and the Unity of Europe*, 62–64; Cromwell, "The Marshall Plan, Britain and the Cold War," 233–40; MemCon by Avery F. Peterson, 24 June 47, *FRUS, 1947*, 3: 268–69.

2. Bullock, *Bevin*, 409–17; Hogan, *Marshall Plan*, 45–53. For Bevin's policies in the Middle

East, see esp. Louis, *British Empire in the Middle East*; see also Ovendale, *The English-Speaking Alliance*; Best, *"Cooperation with Like-Minded Peoples"*; Morgan, *Labour in Power*, 94–284; Weiler, "British Labour and the Cold War"; see also the conversations between Bevin and Clayton, 24–26 June 47, *FRUS, 1947*, 3: 268–93.

3. Rioux, *Fourth Republic*, 122–26; Young, *Britain, France, and the Unity of Europe*, 62–65.

4. Caffery to Marshall, 28 and 29 June and 1–3 July 47, *FRUS, 1947*, 3: 298–301, 303, 305–6, 309; Lewis W. Douglas to Marshall, 3 and 4 July 47, ibid., 3: 306, 311–12. For Molotov's speech of 2 July 47, see Carlyle, *Documents on International Affairs, 1947–1948*, 51–55.

5. For developments in Hungary, see *FRUS, 1947*, 4: 274–347. For the attacks on U.S. German policy, see *New Times*, no. 28 (11 July 47): 1–3, 11–13; no. 33 (13 Aug 47): 4–8. For the quotation, see Walter Bedell Smith to Marshall, 11 July 47, *FRUS, 1947*, 3: 327.

6. Milward, *Reconstruction of Western Europe*, 61–89; Bullock, *Bevin*, 424–67; Hogan, *Marshall Plan*, 60–76; Young, *Britain, France, and the Unity of Europe*, 62–69.

7. For Soviet perceptions of the Marshall Plan, see Taubman, *Stalin's American Policy*, 166–79; Ulam, *Stalin*, 658–61.

8. MemCon by Peterson, 26 June 47, *FRUS, 1947*, 3: 290–93; Summary of Discussion by Ward B. Allen, 29 May 47, ibid., 3: 235; Kennan to Dean Acheson, 23 May 47, ibid., 3: 228; Acheson, *Present at the Creation*, 309–10; Kennan, *Memoirs, 1925–1950*, 353–60.

9. Kennan to Robert Lovett, 30 June 47, NA, RG 59, PPS, box 33; Clayton to Lovett, 29 July 47, *FRUS, 1947*, 4: 437–38; Memo by R. L. Garner, 30 Sep 47, ibid., 4: 454–55.

10. Robert Murphy, Clay's adviser, did wish to use aid to undermine the Kremlin's political position in eastern Germany. See Murphy to Marshall, 30 June 47, *FRUS, 1947*, 2: 982. But Murphy was an exception. For more typical views, see W. Averell Harriman to Harry S. Truman, 12 Aug 47, RG 335, SecArmy, box 74; Leffler, "United States and the Strategic Dimensions of the Marshall Plan," 277–302.

11. For Kennan's explicit realization of the dilemma he was forcing the Soviets to confront, see PPS 38, "United States Objectives with Respect to Russia," 18 Aug 48, in *PPS Papers*, 2: 386.

12. Memo Prepared by the PPS, 21? July 47, *FRUS, 1947*, 3: 335.

13. For developments in Turkey, see Leffler, "Strategy, Diplomacy, and the Cold War." For the excision of Communists from the governing coalitions of France and Italy, see Rioux, *Fourth Republic*, 125; Wall, *French Communism*, 53–58; Serfaty and Gray, *Italian Communist Party*, 61–69. For the backlash against Communists in Latin America and for their imprisonment in Greece, see L. Bethell and Roxborough, "Latin America," 177–89; Wittner, *American Intervention in Greece*, 103–222.

14. Spriano, *Stalin and the European Communists*, 284–99; Claudin, *Communist Movement*, 425–79; Gati, *Hungary and the Soviet Bloc*, 73–121; Dunmore, *Soviet Politics*, 102–25; Stavrakis, *Moscow and Greek Communism*; Taubman, *Stalin's American Policy*, 171–80.

15. Murphy to Marshall, 19 Aug 47, *FRUS, 1947*, 2: 887. For the fluidity of the situation in mid-1947, see also McCauley, *German Democratic Republic*, 32–35; Nettl, *Eastern Zone and Soviet Policy*, 261–62. The eastern zone of Germany was more dependent on interzonal trade than the western zones, and this may have influenced Soviet policy. See ibid., 266.

16. Wall, *French Communism*, 53–74; Serfaty and Gray, *Italian Communist Party*, 64–74; Urban, *Moscow and the Italian Communist Party*, 184–224. For contemporary evidence, see Charles Bohlen, "Estimate of Soviet Strategy and Tactics in the Immediate Future," 24 June 47, RG 59, Bohlen Papers, box 6; Bohlen, "Memorandum," 28 June 47, ibid., box 4; Matthews to Lovett, 11 July 47, *FRUS, 1947*, 3: 117–21.

17. Kennan to Marshall, 21? July 47, *FRUS, 1947*, 3: 335–36; Memo by Bohlen, 30 Aug 47, ibid., 1: 764–65; Kennan to Lovett, 6 Oct 47, RG 59, PPS, box 33; Memo for Lovett [no signature], 30 Aug 47, RG 59, Bohlen Papers, box 6; "Preliminary Analysis of Announcement of the Revival of the European Comintern," 7 Oct 47, ibid.; see also Walter Bedell Smith to Dwight D. Eisenhower, 3 Sep 47, Eisenhower Papers, File 1652, box 101.

18. Lynch, "Resolving the Paradox of the Monnet Plan," 229–43; Milward, *Reconstruction*

of Western Europe, 90–145; Kuisel, *Capitalism and the State*, 187–237; Rioux, *Fourth Republic*, 112–15, 170–84; Kennan to Marshall, 1 July 47, RG 59, PPS, box 33.

19. Meeting of Three Secretaries, 3 July 47, RG 107, Patterson Papers, Safe File, box 3.

20. Gimbel, *Origins of the Marshall Plan*, 226–32; Milward, *Reconstruction of Western Europe*, 127–41.

21. Gimbel, *Origins of the Marshall Plan*, 220–33; Rioux, *Fourth Republic*, 122–26; Marshall to Caffery, 15 July 47, *FRUS, 1947*, 2: 987; Caffery to Marshall, 18 July 47, ibid., 3: 723; Lovett Diary, 18 July 47.

22. The quotation is in Bullock, *Bevin*, 432; see also Gimbel, *Origins of the Marshall Plan*, 241; Memos by Lovett, 3 and 5 Aug 47, *FRUS, 1947*, 2: 1015–20.

23. The quotation is Marshall's. See MemCon by Marshall, 21 July 47, *FRUS, 1947*, 2: 1003; see also Hilldring to Marshall, 24 July 47, ibid., 2: 1004–5; Royall and Marshall to Clay and Murphy, 26 July 47, ibid., 2: 1009; Marshall to Douglas, 8 and 12 Aug 47, ibid., 2: 1027–28; John D. Hickerson to Lovett and Marshall, 11 Aug 47, ibid., 3: 351–54.

24. Douglas to Lovett, 25 July 47, *FRUS, 1947*, 3: 44; Douglas to Lovett and John W. Snyder, 18 Aug 47, ibid., 3: 60–61; Caffery, Clayton, and Douglas to Marshall, 19 Aug 47, ibid., 2: 1041; Lovett to Douglas, 20 Aug 47, ibid., 3: 367–68; Marshall to Truman, 1 Aug 47, ibid., 3: 48; Lovett to Caffery, 2 Sep 47, ibid., 3: 733; Marshall to Caffery, 17 Sep 47, ibid., 3: 752; Cabinet Mtgs., July–Oct 1947, Connelly Papers, box 1; Minutes, "Inter-Departmental Committee on the Marshall Plan," 9 Sep 47, Clifford Papers, box 4.

25. For Marshall's views, see Memo by Clayton, 20 June 47, *FRUS, 1947*, 2: 929; Marshall to Douglas, 27 June 47, ibid., 2: 933; MemCons by Marshall, 21 July and 18 Sep 47, ibid., 2: 1003, 681; Memo by Hickerson, 12 Sep 47, ibid., 3: 744–47; Marshall Speech Before the Chicago Council on Foreign Relations, 18 Nov 47, *DSB* 17 (30 Nov 47): 1027–28. For War Dept. views, see esp. documents in RG 107, Assistant SecWar, Petersen Papers, Classified, 091 Germany; Clinton Anderson to Truman, 18 July 47, ibid.; Harriman to Truman, 12 Aug 47, RG 335, box 74. Cabinet Mtgs., 18 July and 15 Aug 47, Connelly Papers, box 1; Willard Thorp and William Strang, "Report on the Anglo-American Talks on Ruhr Coal Production," 10 Sep 47, *FRUS, 1947*, 2: 960–62; see also Hardach, "Marshall Plan in Germany," 446–47.

26. Royall to Truman, 21 Oct 47, Clifford Papers, box 4; Harriman to Truman, 12 Aug 47, RG 335, box 74; MemCon by Samuel Reber, 18 Nov 47, *FRUS, 1947*, 2: 722.

27. Douglas to Lovett, 25 July 47, *FRUS, 1947*, 3: 44; Douglas to Lovett and Snyder, 18 Aug 47, ibid., 3: 60–61; Lovett to Clayton, 19 Aug 47, ibid., 3: 63.

28. Kennan to Marshall, 21? July 47, ibid., 3: 336–37; Memo by PPS, 14 Aug 47, ibid., 3: 360–62; Memo by Wesley C. Haraldson, 8 Aug 47, ibid., 3: 345, 350. For apprehensions regarding Britain's withdrawal from Greece, see ibid., 5: 268, 273–75, 277–78, 287, 301–2, 308, 313.

29. Lovett to Clayton and Caffery, 14 Aug 47, *FRUS, 1947*, 3: 356–59; Lovett to Douglas, 20 Aug 47, ibid., 3: 367–68; Lovett to Marshall, 24 Aug 47, ibid., 3: 374–75; Clayton to Lovett, 25 Aug 47, ibid., 3: 378–79; Hogan, *Marshall Plan*, 60–87.

30. For the quotations, see Memo by Kennan, 4 Sep 47, *FRUS, 1947*, 3: 404–5; Minutes, "Inter-Departmental Committee on the Marshall Plan," 9 Sep 47, Clifford Papers, box 4; see also Lovett Diary, 6 Sep 47; MemCon by Woodruff Wallner, 24 Sep 47, *FRUS, 1947*, 3: 758–59; MemCon by Lovett, 16 Sep 47, ibid., 3: 970; James C. Dunn to Marshall, 17 Sep 47, ibid., 3: 975; Advisory Steering Committee, "Immediate Need for Emergency Aid to Europe," 29 Sep 47, ibid., 3: 472–77; CIG, "Imminent Crisis in Western Europe," 4 Sep 47, RG 330, SecDef, CD-271, filed in box 132 (1950).

31. For the situation in Greece, see Memo for the Pres by Roscoe H. Hillenkoetter, 6 June 47, HSTP, PSF, box 249; Naval Attaché in Athens to ComNavEastLant, 5 Aug 47, NHC, OPD, Secret and Under, series 2, box 32, EF 31; *FRUS, 1947*, 5: 211–40.

32. CIA, "Review of the World Situation as It Relates to the Security of the United States," 26 Sep 47, HSTP, PSF, box 203.

33. Handwritten Notes by Clifford, 15 Oct 47, Clifford Papers, box 4; Caffery to Marshall, 17 Oct 47, *FRUS, 1947*, 3: 780; Armour and Hickerson to Caffery, 25 Oct 47, ibid., 3: 792; Dur, *Caffery*, 47–48; Rioux, *Fourth Republic*, 126–30; Wall, *United States and the Reshaping of Postwar France*, chap. 3.

34. Gati, *Hungary and the Soviet Bloc*, 108–23; Spriano, *Stalin and the European Communists*, 284–302; Luza, "Czech Road to Socialism," 51–52.

35. Kennan to Lovett, 6 Oct 47, RG 59, PPS, box 33; Bohlen, "Preliminary Analysis of Announcement of Revival of the European Comintern," 7 Oct 47, RG 59, Bohlen Papers, box 6; PPS 13, "Resume of the World Situation," 6 Nov 47, *FRUS, 1947*, 1: 770–74; Caffery to Marshall, 30 Oct and 5 Dec 47, ibid., 3: 796, 813–14; Elbridge Durbrow to Marshall, 6 Oct and 1 Dec 47, ibid., 4: 596–97, 624–26; Smith to Marshall, 5 Nov 47, ibid., 4: 611–12; Memo for the Pres by Hillenkoetter, 7 Nov 47, HSTP, PSF, box 249.

36. CIA, "Review of the World Situation," 26 Sep 47, HSTP, PSF, box 203.

37. For the views of the JCS, see Royall and Forrestal to Marshall, 5 Sep 47, *FRUS, 1947*, 5: 328–29; Memo by the PPS, 24 Sep 47, ibid., 3: 977–81; CIA, "The Current Situation in France," 31 Dec 47, HSTP, PSF, box 254; Army P&O and Intelligence Division, "France," 16 Jan 48, RG 319, P&O, 091 France TS; Matthews to Lovett, 11 July 47, *FRUS, 1947*, 3: 717–21.

38. For Marshall's views, see House of Representatives, Foreign Affairs, *Emergency Foreign Aid*, 3–10. Marshall presented Kennan's analysis (PPS 13) to the cabinet on 7 Nov. See PPS 13, "Resume of the World Situation," 6 Nov 47, *FRUS, 1947*, 1: 770–77; Yergin, *Shattered Peace*, 330–31.

39. For the quotation, see Advisory Steering Committee, Memo, 29 Sep 47, *FRUS, 1947*, 3: 476; see also Marshall Testimony, 10 Nov 47, House of Representatives, Foreign Affairs, *Emergency Foreign Aid*, 10; President's Committee on Foreign Aid, *European Recovery*, 17–19.

40. For the quotation, see Caffery to Marshall, 6 Aug 47, *FRUS, 1947*, 3: 344; PPS 6, Memo by the PPS, 14 Aug 47, ibid., 3: 361–62; Marshall to Truman, 6 Sep 47, ibid., 3: 411.

41. Memo for the Pres by Clifford, 3 Oct 47, Clifford Papers, box 4; Handwritten Notes, "Taken to Morning Meeting," 15 Oct 47, ibid.; Cabinet Mtg., 10 Oct 47, Connelly Papers, box 1; Lovett to Truman, 13 Oct 47, *FRUS, 1947*, 3: 478–81.

42. Editorial Notes, *FRUS, 1947*, 3: 470–71; *PPP:HST* (1947), 445–48, 475–79, 492–98.

43. For developments regarding trade and tariffs, see Statement to Representatives of the British Commonwealth, by Clair Wilcox, 15 Sep 47, *FRUS, 1947*, 1: 983–93; see also *FRUS, 1948*, 1: 878–95. For complaints about Britain's financial problems, see Lovett to Marshall, 20 and 23 Aug 47, *FRUS, 1947*, 3: 66–67, 69. For Marshall's exasperation with the British over the situation in Greece, see Marshall to Bevin, 1 Aug 47, ibid., 5: 273–74; Marshall to Lovett, 25 Aug 47, ibid., 5: 313.

44. Memo by Joseph D. Coppock, 30 Dec 47, *FRUS, 1948*, 1: 825–26. For financial discussions and arrangements, see *FRUS, 1947*, 3: 68–94. For commercial discussions and compromises, see ibid., 1: 993–1019; *FRUS, 1948*, 1: 875–94.

45. Marshall to Douglas, 8 Sep 47, *FRUS, 1947*, 5: 331–32. For Bevin's proposal, see Douglas to Lovett, 1 Sep 47, ibid., 5: 321–23. For the Anglo-American talks at the Pentagon regarding the Middle East, see ibid., 5: 485–626; see also Bullock, *Bevin*, 438–75.

46. For the considerations weighing on the minds of U.S. officials, see, e.g., CIA, "Review of the World Situation," 26 Sep and 17 Dec 47, HSTP, PSF, box 203; CIA, "The Current Situation in France," 31 Dec 47, ibid., box 254; Kennan, "Preparedness as Part of Foreign Relations," 8 Jan 48, Kennan Papers, box 17; PPS 23, "Review of Current Trends," 24 Feb 48, *FRUS, 1948*, 1: 522–29. For warnings against collaborating with Communists, see Marshall to Griswold, 11 July 47, *FRUS, 1947*, 5: 221; DOS to Embassy in Rome, 4 Sep 47, ibid., 3: 965.

47. Marshall to Royall, 17 July 47, RG 107, Patterson Papers, General Decimal File, box 8; Minutes of the PPS, 7, 12, 14, 18, and 20 Aug 47, RG 59, PPS, box 32; Cabinet Mtg., 8 Aug 47, Connelly Papers, box 1. The U.S. military establishment opposed direct intervention. See H. Jones, *"New Kind of War,"* 79–94.

48. *FRUS, 1947*, 5: 272–393.

49. For Chamberlin's report and the reactions of Eisenhower and Royall, see Royall to Forrestal, with enclosures, 24 Oct 47, RG 330, box 2, CD 2-1-16; Summary by Albert C. Wedemeyer, 14 Nov 47, RG 353, SWNCC, box 76, 091 Greece; Memo for the Record by W. H. Arnold, 13 Nov 47, RG 335, box 75; H. Jones, *"New Kind of War,"* 95–102; Wittner, *American Intervention in Greece*, 233–38; Rearden, *Formative Years*, 148–52.

50. Draft Memo by Henderson, 22 Dec 47, *FRUS, 1947*, 5: 458–61; MemCon by John D. Jernegan, 26 Dec 47, ibid., 5: 466–69; Henderson to Marshall, 9 Jan 48, *FRUS, 1948*, 4: 11; NSC 5, "Position of the United States with Respect to Greece," 6 Jan 48, ibid., 4: 2–7; JCS to Forrestal, 8 Jan 48, ibid., 4: 8–9; K. L. Rankin to Henderson, 8 Jan 48, Rankin Papers, box 11. For PPS views, see *PPS Papers*, 2: 1–33.

51. Minutes of the NSC, 13 Jan 48, RG 273; K. Condit, *History of the Joint Chiefs of Staff*, 42–48.

52. Minutes of the NSC, 12 Feb 48, RG 273.

53. Ibid.; PPS 23, "Review of Current Trends," 24 Feb 48, *FRUS, 1948*, 1: 518–20; NSC 5/2, "Position of the United States with Respect to Greece," 12 Feb 48, ibid., 4: 46–51; CIA, "Possible Consequences of the Communist Control of Greece in the Absence of United States Counteraction," 9 Feb 48, HSTP, PSF, box 256. Because he did not use the NSC minutes and because he stresses the British decision to retain troops in Greece, Jones somewhat understates the option of deploying U.S. troops to Greece. See H. Jones, *"New Kind of War,"* 153–57.

54. For the quotations, see Memo by the PPS, 24 Sep 47, *FRUS, 1947*, 3: 976–81; see also Minutes of the PPS, 18, 22, and 25 Sep 47, RG 59, PPS, box 32; Kennan to Gruenther, 1 Oct 47, ibid., box 33; Kennan to Lovett, 1 Dec 47, ibid.; PPS 13, "Resume of the World Situation," 6 Nov 47, *FRUS, 1947*, 1: 776–77.

55. *PPP:HST* (1947), 510; Eisenhower to Forrestal, 9 Dec 47, RG 335, box 76; Sherman to Gruenther, 17 Dec 47, RG 330, box 20, CD 6-1-34; James B. Carter to Cato D. Glover, 17 Dec 47, NHC, SPD, series 5, box 111, A16-3(5); "Summary" by Edwards, 1 Dec 49, RG 319, P&O, 381 Europe TS; Rearden, *Formative Years*, 173; J. Miller, *United States and Italy*, 243.

56. NSC 1/2, "Position of the United States with Respect to Italy," 10 Feb 48, *FRUS, 1948*, 3: 767–69; Minutes of the NSC, 17 Dec 47, 13 Jan and 12 Feb 48, RG 273; William Leahy to Forrestal, 19 Feb 48, *FRUS, 1948*, 3: 771; K. Condit, *History of the Joint Chiefs of Staff*, 65–72; Kennan, "Preparedness as Part of Foreign Relations," 8 Jan 48, Kennan Papers, box 17; PPS 23, "Review of Current Trends," 24 Feb 48, *FRUS, 1948*, 1: 518–20; Dunn to Marshall, 7 and 21 Feb 48, ibid., 1: 829, 834–35.

57. Barnes, "Secret Cold War: Part I," 412; Senate, Select Committee, *Supplementary Reports on Military Intelligence*, 27–28; "NSC's First Covert Action," Wilson Center *Reports*, June 1988.

58. Forrestal to Marshall, 12 Dec 47, RG 335, box 36; Wedemeyer to Royall, 10 Dec 47, ibid.; Royall to Sidney Souers, 17 Dec 47, ibid.; Truman to Royall [ND], RG 335, box 76; E. M. Brannor to William Draper, 20 Feb 48, RG 335, Draper/Voorhees Files, box 18; Lovett to Forrestal, 17 Feb 48, ibid.; Lovett Diary, 19 Nov 47; see also *FRUS, 1948*, 3: 749–50, 754, 758–62.

59. Barnes, "Secret Cold War: Part I," 413; Wall, *United States and the Reshaping of Postwar France*, chap. 4.

60. Dur, *Caffery*, 46; R. L. Conolly to Forrestal, 10 Dec 47, RG 330, box 19, CD 6-1-45; Wall, *United States and the Reshaping of Postwar France*, chap. 3.

61. For the quotation, see the study by the Army P&O Division and Intelligence Division, "France," ND [late 1947], RG 319, P&O, 091 France TS; see also the extensive materials in same file, Oct–Dec 1947, ibid. For the Marshall-Bevin discussions, see MemCon by Frank K. Roberts, 17 Dec 47, *FRUS, 1948*, 3: 818–19. For the talks between Harold R. Bull and French officials, see Memo by Douglas MacArthur II, 29 Jan 48, ibid., 3: 617–22; Bull to Eisenhower, 9 Feb 48, RG 319, P&O, 091 France.

62. MemCons, 14 Oct and 5, 18, and 20 Dec 48, *FRUS, 1948*, 3: 265, 675–76, 678, 280–81; Marshall to Lovett, 8 and 11 Nov 48, ibid., 1: 654–55.

63. Memo by Marshall, 21 July 47, *FRUS, 1947*, 2: 1003; Memo by Reber, 18 Nov 47, ibid., 2: 722; Hickerson to Lovett, 23 Aug 47, ibid., 2: 1051–54; Ferdinand Eberstadt to Lovett, 11 and 18 Aug 47, Eberstadt Papers, box 37; Lovett to Eberstadt, 14 Aug 47, ibid.

64. Clay to War Dept., 25 Aug 47, *FRUS, 1947*, 2: 1061–62; see also ibid., 2: 1069–72.

65. Bonesteel to Lovett, 27 Aug 47, RG 59, Bohlen Papers, box 6; Bohlen to Lovett, 30 Aug 47, ibid.

66. For the quotation, see MemCon by Marshall, 8 Oct 47, *FRUS, 1947*, 2: 683; see also MemCon by Douglas, 17 Dec 47, ibid., 2: 812; Bohlen to Marshall, 8 Oct 47, RG 59, Bohlen Papers, box 4.

67. Marshall Speech Before the Chicago Council on Foreign Relations, 18 Nov 47, *DSB* 17 (30 Nov 47): 1024–28; MemCon by Douglas, 17 Dec 47, *FRUS, 1947*, 2: 812.

68. Marshall's meeting with the cabinet, cited in Yergin, *Shattered Peace*, 330–31; Marshall Speech Before the Chicago Council on Foreign Relations, 18 Nov 47, *DSB* 17 (30 Nov 47): 1024–28; "Summary of State Department's Proposed Position Papers for London Meeting of CFM," ND [Nov 1947], HSTP, PSF, box 163; MemCon by Reber, 18 Nov 47, *FRUS, 1947*, 2: 722.

69. "Limitation of Occupation Forces," in "State Department's Proposed Position Papers," ND [Nov 1947], HSTP, PSF, box 163.

70. For the quotation, see Yergin, *Shattered Peace*, 330–31; see also Smith to Marshall, 6 Nov and 30 Dec 47, *FRUS, 1947*, 2: 897–98, 908; MemCon by Beam, 24 Oct 47, ibid., 2: 690–91.

71. MemCon by Marshall, 28 Nov 47, *FRUS, 1947*, 2: 739.

72. Lovett to Marshall, 9 Dec 47, ibid., 2: 957; see also "An Economic Program for Germany," in "State Department's Proposed Position Papers," ND [Nov 1947], HSTP, PSF, box 163; "Reparation," ND [Nov 1947], ibid.

73. U.S. Delegation to Truman, 8 and 10 Dec 47, *FRUS, 1947*, 2: 757, 762; Marshall to Lovett, 11 Dec 47, ibid., 2: 764; Truman to Marshall, 11 Dec 47, ibid., 2: 764; Bullock, *Bevin*, 490–505.

74. For the quotations, see Smith to Eisenhower, 10 Dec 47, Eisenhower Papers, File 1652, box 101; Henry Byroade to Wedemeyer, 22 Dec 47, RG 319, P&O, 092 TS; see also MemCon of Hickerson and Strang, 30 Oct 47, *FRUS, 1947*, 2: 693–94; MemCon by Beam, 4 Nov 47, ibid., 2: 698.

75. MemCon by Marshall, 28 Nov 47, *FRUS, 1947*, 2: 739; British MemCons, 8 and 18 Dec 47, ibid., 2: 817–25; MemCon by Douglas, 17 Dec 47, ibid., 2: 811–12; Marshall to Lovett, 6 Dec 47, ibid., 2: 753; MemCon by Roberts, 17 Dec 47, ibid., 3: 818–19; Bullock, *Bevin*, 468–538; Hogan, *Marshall Plan*, 109–19; Young, *Britain, France, and the Unity of Europe*, 70–85.

76. *PPP:HST* (1947), 515–29. The quotation is on pp. 516–17.

77. Senate, Foreign Relations, *European Recovery Program*, 3–10, 77–82, 245–56, 445–59, 478–85 (for Forrestal's quotation, see p. 478); Address by Marshall, 13 Feb 48, Forrestal Papers, box 21; Kennan, "What Is Policy," 18 Dec 47, Kennan Papers, box 17; President's Committee on Foreign Aid, *European Recovery*, 18–22.

78. Nitze, *From Hiroshima to Glasnost*, 58–67; Isaacson and Thomas, *Wise Men*, 433–34; Pogue, *Marshall*, 237–57.

79. Notwithstanding many differences in interpretation, the importance of Germany in U.S. calculations is recognized in the most important works on European reconstruction. See, e.g., Gimbel, *Origins of the Marshall Plan*; Milward, *Reconstruction of Western Europe*; Hogan, *Marshall Plan*.

80. For the quotations, see PPS 23, "Review of Current Trends," 24 Feb 48, *FRUS, 1948*, 1: 516; Marshall to Embassy in France, 19 Feb 48, ibid., 2: 70–71; see also Marshall to Douglas, 20 Feb 48, ibid., 2: 71–73; MemCon by Douglas, 17 Dec 47, *FRUS, 1947*, 2: 811. German sentiment toward reconstruction policy was turning more unfavorable, but U.S. officials greatly exaggerated the proclivity of Germans to align with the Soviet Union. See the surveys in Merritt and Merritt, *Public Opinion in Occupied Germany*, esp. 161–63, 172–73, 181, 183–84, 192, 210–12.

81. Clay, *Papers*, 2: 536–37, 545–48; Backer, *Winds of History*, 202–12.

82. Clay, *Papers*, 2: 527–61.

83. When the French protested Clay's actions, Marshall supported Clay. See Marshall to Henri Bonnet, 17 and 31 Jan 48, *FRUS, 1948*, 2: 34–35, 53–54.

84. For the quotation, see British Embassy to DOS, 17 Feb 48, ibid., 2: 68; see also British Embassy to Marshall, 26 Jan 48, ibid., 2: 42; Marshall to Baron Inverchapel, 30 Jan 48, ibid., 2: 50–51; Bullock, *Bevin*, 513–38.

85. For the quotation, see Memo by MacArthur, 29 Jan 48, *FRUS, 1948*, 3: 617–22; see also Caffery to Lovett, 30 Jan 48, ibid., 3: 617; Bull to Eisenhower, 9 Feb 48, RG 319, P&O, 091 France TS.

86. Conolly to Forrestal, 19 Dec 47, RG 330, box 19, CD 6-1-45; Douglas to Marshall, 25, 26, and 28 Feb 48, *FRUS, 1948*, 2: 87–88, 92–93, 98–100.

87. Bullock, *Bevin*, 513–31; Best, *"Cooperation with Like-Minded Peoples,"* 152–54; Young, *Britain, France, and the Unity of Europe*, 77–85; Baylis, "Britain, the Brussels Pact, and the Continental Commitment"; Henderson, *Birth of NATO*, 2–8; *FRUS, 1948*, 3: 1–33; ibid., 2: 78–82, 95.

88. Kennan to Marshall, 20 Jan 48, *FRUS, 1948*, 3: 7–8; Henderson, *Birth of NATO*, 8–10; L. Kaplan, *United States and NATO*, 58–60.

89. Marshall to Truman, 11 Feb 48, *FRUS, 1948*, 2: 61–63; see also Memo by Hickerson, 21 Jan 48, ibid., 3: 9–12; Memo by Theodore Achilles, 13 Feb 48, ibid., 2: 64–65; Marshall to Embassy in France, 19 Feb 48, ibid., 2: 70–71.

90. MemCon by Hickerson, 7 Feb 48, ibid., 3: 22–23; Marshall to Caffery, 19 Feb 48, ibid., 2: 70–71; Marshall to Douglas, 20 Feb 48, ibid., 2: 71–73; Marshall to Caffery, 27 Feb 48, ibid., 3: 34.

91. Taubman, *Stalin's American Policy*, 171–79; Ulam, *Rivals*, 118–36.

92. For Donald MacLean's familiarity with the security pact negotiations and with the discussions over atomic policy, see *FRUS, 1948*, 3: 59, 115–16, 127–28, 148; ibid., 1: 680, 682, 700–701, 721, 723, 726, 767, 771, 776, 786–87; see also Cecil, *A Divided Life*, 69–90.

93. Djilas, *Conversations with Stalin*, 181–82; Stavrakis, *Moscow and Greek Communism*, 166–68; Calvocoressi, *Survey of International Affairs, 1947–1948*, 173–76.

94. For the treaties, see Carlyle, *Documents on International Affairs, 1947–1948*, 298–99.

95. For Molotov's speeches and Soviet protests regarding Germany, see ibid., 515–21, 545–54; Soviet Government to U.S. Government, 13 Feb 48, *FRUS, 1948*, 2: 338–39, 345–54; Djilas, *Conversations with Stalin*, 114–15; McNeal, *Stalin*, 283–84.

96. Memo for the Pres by Hillenkoetter, 2 Jan 48, HSTP, PSF, box 249; Kennan, Remarks Delivered Before the Armed Services Committee, 8 Jan 48, RG 330, box 8, CD 3-1-36; Kennan to Marshall, 3 Feb 48, RG 59, PPS, box 33.

97. Calvocoressi, *Survey of International Affairs, 1947–1948*, 195–96, 187, 192–93.

98. John H. Bruins to Marshall, 22 Dec 47, *FRUS, 1947*, 4: 255; CIA, "Review of the World Situation," 12 Feb 48, HSTP, PSF, box 250; PPS 23, "Review of Current Trends," 24 Feb 48, *FRUS, 1948*, 1: 523; Lovett Diary, 30 Dec 47.

99. For the Communist seizure of power in Czechoslovakia, see T. Hammond, *Anatomy of Communist Takeovers*, 398–432.

100. Steinhardt to Marshall, 30 Apr 48, *FRUS, 1948*, 4: 747–53. Steinhardt underestimated the Soviet role. See Luza, "Czech Road to Socialism," 53–54.

101. For the quotations, see Memo by Hickerson, 3 March 48, *FRUS, 1948*, 3: 40–41; CIA, "Review of the World Situation," 10 March 48, HSTP, PSF, box 205; see also Marshall to Caffery, 24 Feb 48, *FRUS, 1948*, 4: 736; Wedemeyer to Chamberlin, 26 Feb 48, RG 319, P&O, 350.05 TS; Intelligence Research Report, "Case Study of the Communist Party in Czechoslovakia," 5 Apr 48, ibid.

102. Hogan, *Marshall Plan*; J. Miller, *United States and Italy*, 213–74.

103. Dunn to Marshall, 10 March 48, *FRUS, 1948*, 3: 846.

104. NSC 1/3, "Position of the United States with Respect to Italy in the Light of the Pos-

sibility of Communist Participation in the Government by Legal Means," 8 March 48, ibid., 3: 777–78.

105. For the quotation, see ibid., 3: 775–76. For the shipment of military supplies, see ibid., 3: 779–90; Wedemeyer to Royall, 3 March 48, RG 335, box 76; see also Kennan to Marshall, 15 March 48, *FRUS, 1948*, 3: 848–49; Dunn to Marshall, 20 March 48, ibid., 3: 857; George Butler to Marshall, 16 March 48, RG 59, PPS, box 33; CIA, "Consequences of Communist Accession to Power in Italy by Legal Means," 5 March 48, HSTP, PSF, box 255.

106. Lovett to Douglas, 2 March 48, *FRUS, 1948*, 2: 113.

107. Douglas to Marshall, 25, 26, and 28 Feb and 2 March 48, ibid., 2: 87–89, 92–95, 98–100, 110–11; Caffery to Marshall, 2 March 48, ibid., 3: 34–35; Editorial Note, ibid., 3: 38; Milward, *Reconstruction of Western Europe*, 145–54; Bullock, *Bevin*, 540–43.

108. Clay, *Papers*, 2: 571, 574; Douglas to Marshall, 28 Feb 48, *FRUS, 1948*, 2: 98–100.

109. Douglas to Marshall, 2 March 48, *FRUS, 1948*, 2: 111; Caffery to Marshall, 2 March 48, ibid., 3: 34–35; Editorial Note, ibid., 3: 38.

110. Marshall to Douglas, 28 Feb and 4 March 48, ibid., 2: 101, 123; Lovett to Douglas, 2 March 48, ibid., 2: 113.

111. Ibid., 2: 141–44.

112. For the Soviet protest, see ibid., 2: 345–54.

113. British Embassy to DOS, 11 March 48, ibid., 3: 47–48; Bullock, *Bevin*, 513–30; Young, *Britain, France, and the Unity of Europe*, 79–92; Henderson, *Birth of NATO*, 1–12; Edmonds, *Setting the Mould*, 171–78. For the standard bilateral defense pact proposed by the Kremlin, see Carlyle, *Documents on International Affairs, 1947–1948*, 298–99.

114. Douglas to Marshall, 21 Feb 48, *FRUS, 1948*, 2: 78–79; Marshall to Truman, 12 March 48, ibid., 3: 49–50; Marshall to Caffery, 12 March 48, ibid., 3: 50; Marshall to Inverchapel, 12 March 48, ibid., 3: 48; Cabinet Mtg., 12 March 48, Connelly Papers, box 1.

115. Memo by Frank G. Wisner, 10 March 48, *FRUS, 1948*, 2: 879–80; Clay, *Papers*, 2: 561.

116. For the quotation, see Marshall to Dunn, 11 March 48, *FRUS, 1948*, 3: 45–46; see also Minutes of the NSC, 11 March 48, RG 273; Marshall to Forrestal, 23 March 48, *FRUS, 1948*, 1: 541–42. For Bevin's views, see Kirk to Marshall, 19 March 48, ibid., 3: 57–58; Bullock, *Bevin*, 518–19.

117. Memo for the Pres by Hillenkoetter, 16 March 48, HSTP, PSF, box 249.

118. Forrestal, *Diaries*, 374–76.

119. Ibid., 370–400; Lovett Diary, 4 March 48; Excerpt of Phone Conversation Between Forrestal and Walter Andrews, 3 March 48, Forrestal Papers, box 48; Senate, Armed Services, *Universal Military Training*, 3–60.

120. Omar Bradley to JCS, 11 March 48, *FRUS, 1948*, 1: 539–40; JCS to Forrestal, 10 March 48, ibid., 3: 783; Minutes of the NSC, 11 March 48, RG 273; K. Condit, *History of the JCS*, 191–99; Rearden, *Formative Years*, 316–20.

121. *PPP:HST* (1948), 182–86. For a discussion of budgetary issues and Truman's request for additional funds for the NME, see Chapter Six below.

122. Chamberlin to Bradley, 14 March 48, RG 319, P&O, 092 TS; JIC of the U.S. Embassy in Moscow, "Soviet Intentions," 1 Apr 48, RG 330, box 54, CD 2-2-2; CIA, "Possibility of Direct Soviet Military Action During 1948," 2 Apr 48, HSTP, PSF, box 255; CIA, "Review of the World Situation," 8 Apr 48, ibid., box 203. Even in estimating the Soviet capacity to overrun the continent, the effect of the American counteroffensive was not calculated. See, e.g., JIG, "Intelligence Presentation," 20 Apr 48, RG 319, P&O, 350.05 TS.

123. For the Soviet atomic program, see Nuclear Energy Intelligence Committee, "Estimate of the Status of the Russian Atomic Energy Project," 1 July 48, RG 330, box 61, CD 11-1-2. For Soviet petroleum resources, see CIG, "Petroleum Resources Within the USSR," 16 June 47, HSTP, PSF, box 254. For Soviet air power, see William Blandy to General Board, 3 May 48, CincLantFlt, NHC, General Board 425 (Serial 315); General Board of the Navy, "National Security and Navy Contributions Thereto for the Next Ten Years," 25 June 48, Enclosure D, pp. 38,

52–57, 79–80, Enclosure C, esp. p. 25, NHC, General Board 425 (Serial 315); Wooldridge to General Board, 30 Apr 48, ibid.; Thomas B. Inglis to General Board, 12 May 48, re items 59 and 117, ibid.; ONI, "USSR Aircraft Production, 1946–1947," 16 Feb 48, NHC, OPD, Series 1, Subject File, TS, A8. For Soviet military spending, see Memo of Information, "Soviet Defense Expenditures," 5 Jan 48, NHC, CNO, Double Zero Files, box 4, folder 31; see also CIA, "The Strategic Value to the USSR of the Conquest of Western Europe and the Near East (to Cairo) Prior to 1950," 30 July 48, HSTP, PSF, box 256; PPS 33, "Factors Affecting the Nature of the United States Defense Arrangements in the Light of Soviet Policies," 23 June 48, *PPS Papers*, 2: 281–93.

124. Minutes of the NSC, 23 March 48, RG 273; Marshall to Forrestal, 23 March 48, *FRUS, 1948*, 1: 541–42; Marshall to Lovett, 23 Apr 48, ibid., 3: 103; MemCon by Marshall, 14 June 48, ibid., 3: 137.

125. CIA, "Special Evaluation No. 27," 16 March 48, RG 319, P&O, 350.05 TS; Intelligence Staff Study, "Cumulative Effects of Contemplated United States Actions Upon USSR, Western Europe, and USA," attached to Chamberlin to Wedemeyer, 14 Apr 48, ibid., 092 TS; Memo of Information by Inglis, 16 March 48, NHC, SPD, A8; CIA, "Consequences of Certain Courses of Action with Respect to Greece," 5 Apr 48, HSTP, PSF, box 255. For Royall's concerns, see Clay, *Papers*, 2: 650; Testimony by Lovett, 3 June 48, Senate, Foreign Relations, *Vandenberg Resolution*, 76–79.

126. Clay, *Papers*, 2: 564, 568, 599, 602, 605, 613–14, 623; DOS to British Embassy, 11 May 48, *FRUS, 1948*, 4: 858; MemCon by Marshall, 11 May 48, ibid., 4: 861; Forrestal, *Diaries*, 431–32; Smith to Kennan, 11 June 48, Kennan Papers, box 28. For Bohlen's views, see DOS Transcript of Proceedings, "Russian Policy in Relation to United States Foreign Economic Policy," 15 June 48, RG 59, Bohlen Papers, box 6; Kennan, "Views of the PPS for the Revision of the UN Charter," 29 Apr 48, ibid., box 23; Address by Kennan, 3 June 48, RG 319, P&O, 091 Russia; General Board of the Navy, "National Security and Navy," 25 June 48, Enclosure D, pp. 38, 52–57, NHC, General Board 425 (Serial 315); Inglis to General Board, 28 Apr 48, NHC, General Board 425 (Serial 315); Memo for the Pres by Hillenkoetter, 9 June 48, HSTP, PSF, box 249; CIA, "Review of the World Situation," 17 June 48, ibid., box 203; Byroade to Draper, 18 June 48, RG 319, P&O, 092 TS, F/W 141 (11 July 48).

127. Minutes of the PPS, 16 March–2 Apr 48, RG 59, PPS, box 32; PPS 27, "Report Prepared by the PPS Concerning Western Union and Related Problems," 23 March 48, *FRUS, 1948*, 3: 61–64.

128. *FRUS, 1948*, 3: 61–75; Wiebes and Zeeman, "Pentagon Negotiations," 357–61.

129. Hudson, "Vandenberg Reconsidered," 46–63.

130. MemCon by Achilles, 5 Apr 48, *FRUS, 1948*, 3: 76–78; Memo by Gullion, 5 Apr 48, RG 59, PPS, box 27.

131. Ohly to Robert Blum, 15 Apr 48, RG 330, box 22, CD 6-2-48; Forrestal to NSC, 28 Apr 48, ibid., CD 6-2-49; K. Condit, *History of the JCS*, 360–61; Rearden, *Formative Years*, 461–63.

132. Kennan to Lovett, 29 Apr 48, *FRUS, 1948*, 3: 109; Wiebes and Zeeman, "Pentagon Negotiations," 362.

133. Wedemeyer to Bradley et al., "Coordination of United States–Western European Military Resources to Counter Soviet Communism," 20 March 48, RG 319, P&O, 381 Europe TS; Joint Strategic Plans Committee (JSPC) 876, "United States Military Alliances with Nations of Western Europe," ND [early Apr 1948], ibid., 092 TS; JCS 1844/2, Memo by CNO, "Planning Guidance for Medium Range Emergency Plan," 6 Apr 48, RG 218, CCS 381 USSR (3-2-46), sec. 13; Memo by Spaatz, 27 Apr 48, ibid.; Memo by Louis Denfeld, 29 March 48, NHC, SPD, War Plans, A16-3(5).

134. J. Miller, *United States and Italy*, 243–49; Harper, *America and the Reconstruction of Italy*, 155; Filippelli, *American Labor and Postwar Italy*, 118–54.

135. Bohlen to Lovett, 22 Apr 48, RG 59, Bohlen Papers, box 1; Lovett to Smith, 24 Apr 48, *FRUS, 1948*, 4: 834–35.

136. Selden Chapin to Marshall, 21 May 48, *FRUS, 1948*, 4: 336–37; Cavendish W. Cannon to Marshall, 8 June 48, ibid., 4: 1070–72.

137. Kennan to Lovett, 8, 16, and 17 June 48, RG 59, PPS, box 33; Lovett to Legation in Hungary, 2 June 48, *FRUS, 1948*, 4: 352–53.

138. Bohlen to Lovett, 22 Apr 48, RG 59, Bohlen Papers, box 1; Lovett to Smith, 24 Apr 48, *FRUS, 1948*, 4: 834–35; Marshall to Smith, 29 Apr 48, ibid., 4: 840–41; Smith to Marshall, 22 and 26 Apr 48, ibid., 4: 833, 836–38.

139. Marshall to Smith, 29 Apr 48, *FRUS, 1948*, 4: 840–41; British Embassy to DOS, 30 Apr 48, ibid., 4: 842–44; see also Kennan, "Views of the PPS for the Revision of the UN Charter," Kennan Papers, box 23.

140. Bohlen to Lovett, 22 Apr 48, RG 59, Bohlen Papers, box 1; Durbrow to Marshall, 11 and 12 May 48, *FRUS, 1948*, 4: 858–65. For Marshall's views, see DOS to British Embassy, 11 May 48, ibid., 4: 858; MemCon by Marshall, ibid., 4: 861; Marshall to Douglas, 11 May 48, ibid., 4: 863; Lovett to Norman J. O. Makin, 14 May 48, ibid., 5: 987–88; Kennan, *Memoirs, 1925–1950*, 364–65.

141. Walker, "No More Cold War," 75–91. For assessments of Soviet intentions, see draft telegram by Kennan, 10 May 48, RG 59, Bohlen Papers, box 1; untitled memo by Bohlen, 18 May 48, ibid.; Transcript of Proceedings, "Russian Policy in Relation to United States Foreign Economic Policy," 15 June 48, ibid., box 6; Memo for the Pres by Hillenkoetter, 20 May 48, HSTP, PSF, box 249; Smith to Kennan, 11 June 48, Kennan Papers, box 28.

142. Douglas to Marshall, 10, 11, and 19 May and 1, 4, 6, and 16 June 48, *FRUS, 1948*, 2: 230–33, 256–57, 331–35, 364–66; Caffery to Marshall, 24 and 25 May and 9 and 10 June 48, ibid., 2: 273–74, 281, 323, 325–26; Caffery to Bidault, 2 June 48, ibid., 2: 317; Clay, *Papers*, 2: 674–79; MemCon by Caffery, RG 335, Draper/Voorhees Files, box 12.

143. Young, *Britain, France, and the Unity of Europe*, 92–95; Caffery to Marshall, 18 June 48, *FRUS, 1948*, 3: 637; Auriol, *Journal*, 2: 255–75.

144. Marshall to Caffery, 26 May 48, *FRUS, 1948*, 2: 284; see also Draper to Forrestal, 2 June 48, RG 335, box 74.

145. For Lovett's assessment of the stakes in Germany, see Senate, Foreign Relations, *Vandenberg Resolution*, 81.

146. For the quotation, see Marshall to Caffery, 7 June 48, *FRUS, 1948*, 2: 320; see also Lovett to Douglas, 19 and 25 May 48, ibid., 2: 258, 276–77; Douglas to Marshall, 16 June 48, ibid., 2: 331–35; Memo by Lovett, 21 May 48, ibid., 2: 270–72; Marshall to Caffery, 10 June 48, ibid., 2: 326–27; Clay, *Papers*, 2: 679–86.

147. Marshall to Douglas, 11 and 14 May 48, *FRUS, 1948*, 2: 233–34, 248.

148. Marx Leva to Forrestal, 4 and 5 May 48, RG 330, box 24, CD 6-2-46; NSC Staff Study, "Position of the United States with Respect to Providing Military Assistance to Nations of the Non-Soviet World," 30 Apr 48, RG 319, P&O, 092 TS.

149. Marshall to Douglas, 26 May 48, *FRUS, 1948*, 2: 282.

150. For evolution of British strategic thinking, see Ovendale, *English-Speaking Alliance*, 68–80; Young, *Britain, France, and the Unity of Europe*, 90–91.

151. Although Americans would fight at the Rhine and strategic plans were evolving, the JCS still insisted that there be no infusions of U.S. troops at the onset of a conflict and that initial U.S. actions should focus on strategic bombing of the Soviet Union. See JCS 1868/6, "The Position of the United States with Respect to Support for Western Union and Other Related Free Countries," 17 May 48, RG 218, CCS 092 Western Europe (3-12-48), sec. 2; JCS 1868/11, "Guidance for United States Military Representatives for London Military Talks on the Western Union of Nations," 3 July 48, ibid., sec. 4; JCS 1844/4, "Brief of the Short-Range Emergency War Plan," 19 May 48, ibid., CCS 381 USSR (3-2-46). For Western Union strategic thinking, see Douglas to Marshall, 14 May 48, *FRUS, 1948*, 3: 123–26; see also K. Condit, *History of the JCS*, 357–68; S. Ross, *American War Plans*.

152. NSC 9/2, "The Position of the United States with Respect to Support for Western Union and Other Related Free Countries," 20 May 48, *FRUS, 1948*, 3: 117–18; Lovett to Caffery, 14 May 48, ibid., 3: 121; Lovett to Douglas, 11 and 14 May 48, ibid., 2: 233; Douglas to Marshall, 19 May 48, ibid., 2: 256–58.

153. British Embassy to DOS, ND, *FRUS, 1948*, 3: 122–23.

154. Lovett to John Balfour, 28 May 48, ibid., 3: 132–33.

155. Douglas to Marshall, 16 June 48, ibid., 2: 331–35; Chauvel, *Commentaire*, 199–203; Bidault, *Resistance*, 158–64.

156. MemCon by Marshall, 14 June 48, *FRUS, 1948*, 3: 136–38.

157. Shlaim, *United States and the Berlin Blockade*, 151–62.

158. For Soviet and East European reactions, see *FRUS, 1948*, 2: 338–74. For Soviet policy, see Adomeit, *Soviet Risk-Taking*, esp. 67–96; Mastny, "Stalin and the Militarization of the Cold War," 110–22. For Polish concerns, see esp. *FRUS, 1948*, 2: 368–71. For the determination of the United States to move ahead notwithstanding French concerns and Eastern threats, see, e.g., ibid., 2: 910ff; Shlaim, *United States and the Berlin Blockade*, 117–68; Backer, *Winds of History*, 232–91.

159. Caffery to Draper, 26 June 48, RG 335, Draper/Voorhees Files, box 12; Caffery to Marshall, 29 June 48, *FRUS, 1948*, 3: 142–43.

160. Marshall to Caffery, 23 June 48, *FRUS, 1948*, 3: 139.

161. JCS 1868/11, "Guidance for United States Military Representatives," 3 July 48, RG 218, CCS 092 Western Europe (3-12-48), sec. 4; Clay, *Papers*, 2: 679; K. Condit, *History of the JCS*, 368.

162. NSC 9/3, "The Position of the United States with Respect to Support for Western Union and Other Related Countries," 28 June 48, *FRUS, 1948*, 3: 140–41; NSC 14/1, "Position of the United States with Respect to Providing Military Assistance to Nations of the Non-Soviet World," ibid., 1: 585–88.

163. Bradley to Eisenhower, "NME Views on Situation in Germany," 30 June 48, RG 319, P&O, 092 TS. For a similar realization within the DOS, see DOS Policy Statement, "Germany," 26 Aug 48, *FRUS, 1948*, 2: 1317–18.

164. For Clay's quotation, see Clay, *Papers*, 2: 708. For U.S. perceptions of Soviet capabilities and intentions, see, e.g., Kennan to Norstad, 4 May 48, RG 59, PPS, box 33; Address by Kennan, 3 June 48, RG 319, P&O, 091 Russia; Byroade to Draper, 18 June 48, ibid., 092 TS, F/W 141 (11 July 48); PPS 33, "Factors Affecting U.S. Defense Arrangements," *PPS Papers*, 2: 281–92; Stuart Symington to Shlaim, 20 Feb 81, in the possession of Avi Shlaim; Memos for the Pres by Hillenkoetter, 20 May and 24 June 48, HSTP, PSF, box 249; CIA, "Review of the World Situation," 17 June 48, ibid., box 203. For the statements of Kennan and Bohlen at the exploratory talks on security, see *FRUS, 1948*, 3: 152–54, 157–58, 177, 186. For a recent assessment of Clay's views and actions that comports with the analysis herein presented, see J. Smith, *Clay*, 462–93.

165. Cabinet Mtg., 23 July 48, Connelly Papers, box 1.

166. For a similar analysis, see MccGwire, "Genesis of Soviet Threat Perceptions," 1–56.

Chapter 6

1. For excellent analysis of U.S. decisionmaking during the Berlin blockade, see Shlaim, *United States and the Berlin Blockade*; Oneal, *Foreign Policy Making*, 216–90.

2. Summary of NSC Discussion, 23 July 48, HSTP, PSF, box 220. For Smith's view, see Minutes of the PPS, 28 Sep 48, NA, RG 59, PPS, box 32; see also "Intelligence Division Daily Briefing," 18 Oct 48, RG 319, P&O, 350.05 TS; Memo of Information by Inglis, 28 Sep 48, NHC, CNO, Double Zero Files, box 4.

3. See, e.g., General Vandenberg's comments, Summary of NSC Discussion, 23 July 48, HSTP, PSF, box 220; Shlaim, *United States and the Berlin Blockade*, 227–70.

4. Summary of NSC Discussion, 23 July 48, HSTP, PSF, box 220.

5. For the relationships between foreign policy and the political campaign, see Donovan, *Conflict and Crisis*, 388–416; Divine, *Since 1945*, 16–24. For Truman's concern with inflation, see *PPP:HST* (1948), 409, 416–22. For business opposition to military expenditures, see Lo, "Military Spending as Crisis Management," 155–56.

6. R. N. Smith, *Dewey*, 503–39.

7. See, e.g., NSC 20, Forrestal to NSC, 10 July 48, *FRUS, 1948*, 1: 589–93; Rearden, *Formative Years*, 309–54; Schilling, Hammond, and Snyder, *Strategy, Politics, and Defense Budgets*, 135–213.

8. Rearden, *Formative Years*, 335–38.

9. The war plans can be found in RG 218, JCS, CCS 381 USSR (3-2-46). For background, see also S. Ross, *American War Plans*, 25–101; Herken, *Winning Weapon*, 195–280; K. Condit, *History of the JCS*, 165–355; D. Rosenberg, "American Atomic Strategy," 62–72.

10. For General Gruenther's comment, see "Remarks Delivered Before the Armed Services Committee of the House of Representatives at the National Defense Building," 8 Jan 48, RG 330, Office of the SecDef, box 8, CD 3-1-36; Forrestal to Truman, 6 Jan 48, HSTP, PSF, box 156.

11. For the Navy's criticism of war plan FROLIC, which, among other things, contemplated the relinquishment of control over the Eastern Mediterranean and the Middle East, see JCS 1844/2, Memo by the CNO, 6 Apr 48, RG 218, CCS 381 USSR (3-2-46), sec. 13.

12. Rearden, *Formative Years*, 313–16; K. Condit, *History of the JCS*, 168–70, 199–202.

13. For Forrestal's views, see, e.g., his *Diaries*, 350–51; Lovett Diary, 5 Jan 48; Forrestal to Truman, 6 Jan 48, HSTP, PSF, box 156; McNeil Oral History, 74–75; Forrestal to Dwight D. Eisenhower, 21 Feb 48, Forrestal Papers, box 93; Forrestal to Truman, 27 Feb 48, ibid.; Doig and Hargrove, *Leadership and Innovation*, 369–406.

14. Forrestal, *Diaries*, 374–77; Minutes of the NSC, 23 March 48, RG 273, NSC; Ohly to Forrestal, 28 Jan 48, RG 330, box 26, CD 6-2-13; Rearden, *Formative Years*, 316–17.

15. Rearden, *Formative Years*, 312–18.

16. Minutes of the NSC, 11 March 48, RG 273; Excerpt of Conversation Between Forrestal and Walter Andrews, 3 March 48, Forrestal Papers, box 48; Lovett Diary, 4 March 48; JCS to Forrestal, 10 March 48, *FRUS, 1948*, 3: 783; Editorial Note, 11 March 48, ibid., 1: 539–40; George Butler to Marshall, 12 March 48, RG 59, PPS, box 33. For Truman's address, see *PPP:HST* (1948), 182–86; Rearden, *Formative Years*, 318–20.

17. L. Eden, "Diplomacy of Force," 237–38. For war plan BROILER, see JSPG 496/1, 8 Nov 47, RG 218, CCS 381 USSR (3-2-46), sec. 8. For war plan FROLIC, see JCS 1844 and 1844/1, 9 and 17 March 48, ibid., sec. 12; S. Ross, *American War Plans*, 53–75.

18. Rearden, *Formative Years*, 318–20; Marshall to Forrestal, 23 March 48, *FRUS, 1948*, 1: 541–42.

19. Lovett Diary, 8 Apr 48; Excerpt of Phone Conversation Between Forrestal and Clarence Cannon, 9 Apr 48, Forrestal Papers, box 48; Minutes of NSC Mtg., 23 March 48, RG 273; L. Eden, "Diplomacy of Force," 240–50.

20. Rearden, *Formative Years*, 318–30; L. Eden, "Diplomacy of Force," 230–59; K. Condit, *History of the JCS*, 191–212; Leva Oral History, 50–55.

21. For HALFMOON, see JCS 1844/4, 19 May 48, RG 218, CCS 381 USSR (3-2-46), sec. 13; "Brief," regarding U.S., British, and Canadian talks [Apr 1948], RG 319, P&O, 092 TS; K. Condit, *History of the JCS*, 288–92; S. Ross, *American War Plans*, 89–93.

22. JCS 1844/6, Memo by William Leahy, 13 May 48, RG 218, CCS 381 USSR (3-2-46), sec. 15; D. Rosenberg, "U.S. Nuclear Stockpile," 26–30; Rearden, *Formative Years*, 439; Minutes of the NSC, 3 June and 2 July 48, RG 273; Royall to NSC, 19 May 48, *FRUS, 1948*, 1: 571–72.

23. Webb to Truman, 22 July 48, HSTP, PSF, box 200; Forrestal to Truman, ibid., box 202; David E. Lilienthal to Truman, 21 July 48, ibid.; Truman to Forrestal, 6 Aug 48, ibid.

24. Forrestal, *Diaries*, 487; NSC 30, "United States Policy on Atomic Weapons," 10 Sep 48, *FRUS, 1948*, 1: 625–28; Walton C. Butterworth to Marshall, 15 Sep 48, ibid., 1: 630–31; Rearden, *Formative Years*, 432–39; Herken, *Winning Weapon*, 256–72.

25. Forrestal to Truman, 8 Jan 48, HSTP, PSF, box 156; D. V. Gallery to Clark, 14 Nov 47, NHC, OP-23, Series 3, Cabinet 1456, Drawer 1; William H. P. Blandy to Chairman of the General Board of the Navy, 3 May 48, CincLantFlt, NHC, General Board 425 (Serial 315); Forrestal to Gurney, 26 March 48, NHC, Double Zero Files, Denfeld Papers, box 3.

26. PPS 25, "French North Africa," 22 March 48, *PPS Papers*, 2: 142–49; Memo for Op-09 by Edmond T. Wooldridge, 13 Oct 48, NHC, CNO, Double Zero Files, box 4; Memo for Op-09 by Wooldridge, 25 Oct 48, ibid., SPD, A14.

27. Minutes of the PPS, 19 May 48, RG 59, PPS, box 32; Marshall to the Embassy in the United Kingdom, 3 Aug 48, *FRUS, 1948*, 3: 931–32; Marshall to Certain American Diplomatic Offices, 26 Nov 48, ibid., 3: 961–63. For Eritrea, see ibid., 3: 935–65; Lovett to Forrestal, 26 Nov 48, RG 319, P&O, 092 TS; Gifford and Louis, *Decolonization and African Independence*, 159–73.

28. Webb to Frank Pace, Fred Lawton, and Lee Martin, 25 Feb 48, RG 51, BOB, Series 47.8A, box 47; "National Security," 30 Jan 48, ibid.; Fiscal Division, "Finletter Report," 9 Feb 48, ibid.; W. F. Schaub to Webb, 18 March 48, ibid., box 43; Felix Larkin to Forrestal, 17 March 48, RG 330, box 18, CD 5-1-12; Forrestal, *Diaries*, 429–32; Edwin G. Nourse, Leon Keyserling, and John D. Clark to Truman, 24 March 48, HSTP, PSF, box 143; Lovett Diary, 21 Apr 48; Rearden, *Formative Years*, 326–28.

29. Truman to Nourse, 25 March 48, HSTP, PSF, box 143; Cabinet Mtg., 16 Apr 48, Connelly Papers, box 1; Statement by the Pres to the SecDef, the Secretaries of the Three Depts., and the Three Chiefs of Staff, 13 May 48, Elsey Papers, box 64; Forrestal, *Diaries*, 431–32; Rearden, *Formative Years*, 326–28, 337–39.

30. Kennan to Marshall and Lovett, 27 May 48, RG 59, PPS, box 33; Forrestal, *Diaries*, 409–12, 430; Rearden, *Formative Years*, 336–39.

31. Kennan to Lovett, 22 Apr 48, RG 59, PPS, box 33; Kennan to Marshall and Lovett, 27 May 48, ibid.; Lovett to Forrestal, 23 Apr 48, ibid.; PPS 33, "Factors Affecting the Nature of the U.S. Defense Arrangements," 23 June 48, *PPS Papers*, 2: 281–93. For assessments of Soviet intentions, see also, e.g., Mtgs. of the Washington Exploratory Talks on Security, 6–12 July 48, *FRUS, 1948*, 3: 152–54, 157–58, 172, 177, 186.

32. See PPS 33, "Factors Affecting the Nature of the U.S. Defense Arrangements," 23 June 48, *PPS Papers*, 2: 281–93.

33. NSC 20, Forrestal to NSC, 10 July 48, *FRUS, 1948*, 1: 589–93.

34. Truman to Forrestal, 13 and 15 July 48, RG 330, box 18, CD 5-1-20.

35. *PPS:HST* (1948), 406–10, 416–22.

36. For Forrestal, see Rogow, *Forrestal*; Doig and Hargrove, *Leadership and Innovation*, 369–406.

37. For Kennan's views, see "Contemporary Problems of Foreign Policy," 17 Sep 48, Kennan Papers, box 17; Kennan, "United States Foreign Policy," 11 Oct 48, ibid.; Kennan, "Where We Are Today," 21 Dec 48, ibid.; see also Royall's discussion of his European trip in Forrestal's office, 4 Jan 49, Eisenhower Papers, File 1652, box 42; Hickerson to Harriman, 3 Dec 48, *FRUS, 1948*, 3: 306.

38. Minutes of the PPS, Aug–Sep 1948, RG 59, PPS, box 32; PPS 37, "Policy Questions Concerning a Possible German Settlement," 12 Aug 48, *PPS Papers*, 2: 322–35.

39. For criticisms of Kennan's proposals, see *FRUS, 1948*, 2: 1287–88, footnote 2; Kennan to Marshall and Lovett, 8 Sep 48, RG 59, PPS, box 33; Minutes of Mtgs. of the PPS, 1 Sep–13 Oct 48, ibid., box 32.

40. For anxieties regarding the airlift, see Minutes of the NSC, 7, 16, and 30 Sep 48, RG 273.

41. For the preceding two paragraphs, see Kennan to Marshall, 17 Sep and 18 Oct 48, RG 59, PPS, box 33; Minutes of the PPS, 15 Sep–2 Nov 48, ibid., box 32; Kennan, "Contemporary Problems of Foreign Policy," 17 Sep 48, Kennan Papers, box 17; Hixson, *Kennan*, 81–84.

42. Lovett and Hickerson to Harriman, 3 Dec 48, *FRUS, 1948*, 3: 308–9; see also DOS Policy Statement, "Germany," 26 Aug 48, ibid., 2: 1297–1319.

43. Ibid., 2: 1–866.

44. For Clay's desire for unrestricted authority, see, e.g., Clay to Dept. of the Army, 15 Nov 48, ibid., 2: 498. For disputes between the DOS and Clay, see DOS Policy Statement, "Germany," 26 Aug 48, ibid., 2: 1310–11; comments by Charles Kindleberger, 1 July 48, RG 59, PPS, box 32.

For Clay's concern about German discontent and the future orientation of Germany, see Clay to Draper, 28 Aug 48, *FRUS, 1948*, 2: 800; Clay to Dept. of the Army, 13 Nov 48, ibid., 2: 494–96; J. Smith, *Clay*, 525–26.

45. Lovett Diary, 16 July 48; Kindleberger's comments, Minutes of the PPS, 1 July 48, RG 59, PPS, box 32; Kennan to Lovett, 8 June 48, ibid., box 33; Kennan to Bohlen, 23 Aug 48, ibid.; Kennan to Acheson, 3 Jan 49, ibid.; DOS Policy Statement, "Germany," 12 Aug 48, *FRUS, 1948*, 2: 1308–19.

46. Hickerson to Henry R. Labouisse, 12 Oct 48, *FRUS, 1948*, 3: 667; see also David Bruce to Paul Hoffman, 14 Sep 48, ibid., 3: 649–50; Caffery to Marshall, 2 Oct 48, ibid., 3: 661; Policy Statement of the DOS, 20 Sep 48, ibid., 3: 653–59; Labouisse to Ben Moore, 16 Oct 48, ibid., 3: 672; Hickerson to Harriman, 3 Dec 48, ibid., 3: 306–7; Rice-Maximim, "United States and the French Left," 736–40; Wall, *United States and the Reshaping of Postwar France*, chap. 5.

47. Dur, *Caffery*, 52–54; Memo of a Mtg. of Foreign Ministers, 19 Nov 48, *FRUS, 1948*, 2: 517–22; Young, *Britain, France, and the Unity of Europe*, 131–34.

48. Clay to Draper, 3 Dec 48, *FRUS, 1948*, 2: 540–41; Clay to the Dept. of the Army, 22 Nov 48, ibid., 2: 527–28.

49. Lovett to Marshall, 13 Nov 48, ibid., 2: 493–94; Lovett to Marshall Carter, 18 Nov 48, ibid., 2: 513; Marshall to Schuman, 29 Nov 48, ibid., 2: 534–35.

50. Douglas to Marshall, 28 Nov 48, ibid., 2: 533–34. For the corporatist interpretation, see Hogan, *Marshall Plan*.

51. Milward, *Reconstruction of Western Europe*, 126–67; Gillingham, *Coal, Steel, and the Rebirth of Europe*; Douglas to Marshall, 28 and 30 Nov 48, *FRUS, 1948*, 2: 531–34, 537; DOS Policy Statement, 20 Sep 48, ibid., 3: 658–59.

52. Caffery to Marshall, 29 June 48, *FRUS, 1948*, 3: 142–43; see also French ambassador Henri Bonnet's comments during the exploratory talks on security, ibid., 3: 206–8, 209–12, 213, 218–20, 229; Memo by Marshall, 17 Aug 48, ibid., 3: 643; Armand Bérard to Bohlen, 9 Aug 48, RG 59, Bohlen Papers, box 8; Caffery to Draper, 26 June 48, RG 335, Draper/Voorhees Files, box 12.

53. Hickerson to Caffery, 24 Aug 48, RG 59, PPS.

54. JCS 1868/11, "Guidance for United States Military Representatives for London Military Talks on the Western Union of Nations," 8 July 48, RG 319, P&O, 092 TS; Albert Wedemeyer to Bradley, 22 July 48, ibid.; Wedemeyer to Bradley, 11 July 48, RG 218, Leahy Papers, box 5; Bradley to Clay, 16 July 48, ibid., box 6; A. Franklin Kibler to Wedemeyer, 13 Oct 48, ibid., box 5; Bradley to Clay, 23 Nov and 7 Dec 48, ibid.; S. Ross, *American War Plans*, 91.

55. Senior officials of the NME discussed command relationships extensively at the Newport meeting of the JCS. See "Agreed Final Minutes," 20–22 Aug 48, NHC, CNO, Double Zero Files, box 1; Marshall to Truman, 23 Aug 48, *FRUS, 1948*, 3: 221–22.

56. MemCon with Harriman by Draper, 19 July 48, HSTP, PSF, box 157; Royall to Forrestal, 6 Aug 48, RG 330, box 77; Lovett to Harriman, 3 Dec 48, *FRUS, 1948*, 3: 305.

57. Memo by JCS, 13 Sep 48, *FRUS, 1948*, 3: 648–49; MemCon by Marshall, 14 Oct 48, ibid., 3: 265–66; MemCon by Marshall, 5 Nov 48, ibid., 3: 675–76; Forrestal to Bradley, 19 Nov 48, NHC, SPD, A14. For the quotation, see Summary of Conversation by Forrestal, 10 Nov 48, HSTP, PSF, box 156.

58. Vannevar Bush to Forrestal, 13 Oct 48, NHC, SPD, A11; P&O to Draper, 29 Dec 48, RG 319, P&O, 092 TS.

59. For the exploratory talks on security during the summer of 1948, see *FRUS, 1948*, 3: 148–250.

60. Lovett to Bohlen and Hickerson, 9 Nov 48, *FRUS, 1948*, 3: 271.

61. Ibid., 3: 334–39.

62. Ibid., 3: 67–75, 301–32, 350; Lovett to Douglas, 13 Dec 48, ibid., 2: 563–64; Douglas to Lovett, 15 Dec 48, ibid., 2: 564–65; Harriman to Marshall, 16 Dec 48, ibid., 2: 567–68; untitled memo by Voorhees, 4 Jan 48 [1949], Voorhees Papers, box 4; "Presentation . . ." by Royall, 4 Jan 49, Eisenhower Papers, File 1652, box 42.

63. For the quotation, see NSC 20/1, "U.S. Objectives with Respect to Russia," 18 Aug 48, in Etzold and Gaddis, *Containment*, 184; see also Kennan, "Contemporary Problems of Foreign Policy," 17 Sep 48, Kennan Papers, box 17; Kennan, "United States Foreign Policy," 11 Oct 48, ibid.; Kennan to Smith, 20 Aug 48, ibid., box 28.

64. NSC 20/1, "U.S. Objectives with Respect to Russia," in Etzold and Gaddis, *Containment*, 182; Kennan, "Estimate of the International Situation," 8 Nov 48, Kennan Papers, box 17; Hixson, *Kennan*, 54–56.

65. Lovett and Hickerson to Harriman, 3 Dec 48, *FRUS, 1948*, 3: 304. For the concerns of Kennan and Lovett regarding the configuration of the NAT, see ibid., 3: 177, 216.

66. For Kennan's concern with covert actions and the CIA, see Kennan to Lovett and Marshall, 19 May 48, RG 59, PPS, box 33; Kennan to Lovett, 25 May and 8 and 17 June 48, ibid.; Lovett to Forrestal, 1 Oct 48, ibid. For the role of propaganda and aid to dissident groups, see, e.g., Robert P. Joyce to Carlton Savage, 1 Apr 49, ibid., box 32; see also Senate, Select Committee, *Supplementary Reports on Military Intelligence*, 27–30; Hixson, *Kennan*, 57–58; Mayers, *Kennan*, 152–53.

67. MemCon with Harriman, by Draper, 19 July 48, HSTP, PSF, box 157.

68. PPS 35, "The Attitude of This Government Towards Events in Yugoslavia," 30 June 48, *FRUS, 1948*, 4: 1079–81.

69. For the quotation, see NSC 58, "United States Policy Toward the Soviet Satellite States in Eastern Europe," 14 Sep 49, in Etzold and Gaddis, *Containment*, 223. For policy decisions on how to deal with Tito, see esp. Marshall to Douglas and Smith, 21 July 48, *FRUS, 1948*, 4: 1095–96; Frank Wisner to Harriman, 22 July 48, ibid., 4: 1095–96; Hickerson to Kennan, 26 Nov 48, ibid., 4: 1117–18; CIA, "Review of the World Situation," 14 July 48, HSTP, PSF, box 204. For the impact of the Tito-Stalin split on the Greek civil war, see Wittner, *American Intervention in Greece*, 264–82; Stavrakis, *Moscow and Greek Communism*.

70. For the role of the ERP in luring Eastern Europe westward, see, e.g., NSC 20/1, "U.S. Objectives with Respect to Russia," 18 Aug 48, in Etzold and Gaddis, *Containment*, 183; comments by Dean Acheson and Bohlen, 15 Feb 49, in House of Representatives, International Relations, *Executive Session Hearings*, 39–46. For Kennan's German initiative and its ramifications for Eastern Europe, see PPS 37, "Policy Questions Concerning a Possible German Settlement," 12 Aug 48, *FRUS, 1948*, 2: 1289–96; Kennan, "United States Foreign Policy," 11 Oct 48, Kennan Papers, box 17; Kennan, "Estimate of the International Situation," 8 Nov 48, ibid.; Stephanson, *Kennan*, 145. For covert actions in Albania, see N. Bethell, *Great Betrayal*; Gaddis, *Long Peace*, 160–61.

71. Until the latter part of 1948, civilian policymakers had been unwilling to specify wartime goals. But when they finally enumerated them in NSC 20/4, they were grandiose notwithstanding the renunciation of the idea of unconditional surrender. See NSC 20/4, "U.S. Objectives with Respect to the USSR to Counter Soviet Threats to U.S. Security," 23 Nov 48, in Etzold and Gaddis, *Containment*, 210–11. For Kennan's views, see NSC 20/1, "U.S. Objectives with Respect to Russia," 18 Aug 48, ibid., 190–203.

72. ANPB, "Middle East Oil," 11 Dec 47, RG 304, NSRB, Entry 1, box 3; Denfeld to John L. Sullivan, 24 Jan 48, NHC, CNO, Double Zero Files, box 2; PPS 19, "Position of the United States with Respect to Palestine," 19 Jan 48, *FRUS, 1948*, 5: 550–51; Painter, *Oil and the American Century*, 96–102, 156. I am indebted to David Painter for photocopies of numerous documents relating to petroleum policy from the NSRB, ASPB, ANPB, and the P&O Division.

73. JCS to Forrestal, 10 Oct 47, RG 330, box 20, CD 6-1-8; see also Robert Carney to Denfeld, 16 Apr 48, NHC, CNO, Double Zero Files, box 3; Schuyler to Wedemeyer, 21 Oct 48, RG 319, P&O, 463 TS; ASPB, "Availability of Liquid Hydrocarbon Fuel for Military Use in the Event of a Major War Commencing January 1956," 25 Oct 48, RG 334, Interservice Agencies, ANPB no. 38, box 7; Verbatim Minutes of 9th Mtg. of ASPB, 9 Nov 48, ibid., box 10. For Forrestal's great interest in Middle Eastern oil, see Forrestal to Hanson Baldwin, 16 June 48, Forrestal Papers, box 78; Forrestal to Arthur H. Hill, 10 July 48, ibid., box 79; McNeil Oral History, 74–75.

74. For BROILER, see JSPG 496/1, 8 Nov 47, RG 218, CCS 381 USSR (3-2-46), sec. 8; see also JCS 1725/1, "Strategic Guidance for Industrial Mobilization Planning," 1 May 47, in Etzold

and Gaddis, *Containment*, 302–11. For HALFMOON, see JCS 1844/4, 6 and 19 May 48, RG 218, CCS 381 USSR (3-2-46), sec. 13.

75. PPS 23, "Review of Current Trends: U.S. Foreign Policy," 24 Feb 48, *FRUS, 1948*, 5: 656.

76. Douglas to Lovett, 29 Oct 48, ibid., 5: 1530–31. For British emphasis on deploying forces to the Middle East, see Kibler to Bradley, 6 Oct 48, RG 218, Leahy Papers, box 5; Clark and Wheeler, *British Origins of Nuclear Strategy*, 95–111. For SPEEDWAY, see P. Hahn, "Strategy and Diplomacy," chap. 5. For use of commonwealth forces, see Devereux, "Britain and the Defence of the Middle East," 327–35.

77. Wooldridge to CNO, 21 Oct 48, NHC, CNO, Double Zero Files, box 4; Op-31, "Draft," 22 Oct 48, ibid., SPD, box 244, A16-3; Bohlen to Joseph Satterthwaite, 29 Jan 48, RG 59, Bohlen Papers, box 4.

78. Mtg. of Forrestal with British chiefs of staff, 13 Nov 48, HSTP, PSF, box 156; P. Hahn, "Strategy and Diplomacy," chap. 5.

79. R. D. Coleridge to Gruenther, 24 July 48, RG 330, box 120, CD 27-1-12; Leahy to Forrestal, 5 Nov 48, ibid.; JCS to Forrestal, 10 Aug 48, *FRUS, 1948*, 5: 244–46.

80. For an analysis of Turkey's place in U.S. strategic thinking, see Leffler, "Strategy, Diplomacy, and the Cold War," esp. 816–19. For the B-29's, see Symington to Forrestal, 9 March 48, RG 330, box 25, CD 6-2-38. For DOS concurrence with medium bomber bases, see Butler to Lovett, 15 Dec 48, RG 59, PPS, box 33. For the reapportionment of aid, see Minutes of the NSC, 3 Sep 48, RG 273.

81. M. Cohen, *Palestine and the Great Powers*, esp. 260–354.

82. Kennan to Lovett, 29 Jan 48, *FRUS, 1948*, 5: 573; PPS 19, "Position of the United States with Respect to Palestine," 19 Jan 48, ibid., 5: 547–54; Forrestal, *Diaries*, 359–61; M. Cohen, *Palestine and the Great Powers*, 345–54; Schoenbaum, *Waging Peace and War*, 167–68.

83. PPS 23, "Review of Current Trends," 24 Feb 48, *FRUS, 1948*, 5: 656; PPS 19, "Position of the United States with Respect to Palestine," 19 Jan 48, ibid., 5: 551; Hickerson to Lovett, 12 Apr 48, ibid., 5: 825–28.

84. Truman to Marshall, 22 Feb 48, ibid., 5: 645; Draft Report Prepared by the Staff of the NSC, 17 Feb 48, ibid., 5: 631–33; Robert M. McClintock to Dean Rusk, 27 Feb 48, ibid., 5: 664–65; CIA, "Possible Developments in Palestine," 28 Feb 48, ibid., 5: 667; Memos by Clark Clifford, 6 and 8 March 48, ibid., 5: 687–97.

85. For Truman's thoughts on a joint intervention with the Soviets, see ibid., 5: 987, footnote 2; Donovan, *Conflict and Crisis*, 373–79; Pogue, *Marshall*, 358–69; M. Cohen, *Palestine and the Great Powers*, 354–66.

86. For Rusk's quotation, see Diary Entry by Forrestal, 4 Apr 48, *FRUS, 1948*, 5: 797–98; see also JCS to Truman, 4 Apr 48, ibid., 5: 798–800.

87. Lovett to Douglas, 17 Apr 48, ibid., 5: 829; Diary Entry by Forrestal, 18 Apr 48, ibid., 5: 830.

88. Kennan to Lovett, 20 and 22 Apr 48, RG 59, PPS, box 33; Lovett to Forrestal, 23 Apr 48, ibid.

89. Rusk to Lovett, 4 May 48, *FRUS, 1948*, 5: 895; Jessup to Rusk, 4 May 48, ibid., 5: 897; Memo of Telephone Conversation by John C. Ross, 9 May 48, ibid., 5: 942; Transcript of Remarks by Rusk, 11 May 48, ibid., 5: 968; M. Cohen, *Palestine and the Great Powers*, 366–79; Schoenbaum, *Waging Peace and War*, 172–78.

90. MemCon by Marshall, 12 May 48, *FRUS, 1948*, 5: 972–77; MemCon by Lovett, 17 May 48, ibid., 5: 1005–7. For Clifford's view, see his *Counsel to the President*, 1–14.

91. M. Cohen, *Palestine and the Great Powers*, 379–96; Truman, *Memoirs: 1946–52*, 184–95. For political factors, see Snetsinger, *Truman*, 97–114. For the relationships between domestic political and world geopolitical factors, see Bain, *March to Zion*, 194–202. For Clifford's denial of the saliency of domestic politics, see his *Counsel to the President*, 14.

92. Kennan to Lovett and Marshall, 21 May 48, RG 59, PPS, box 33; Lovett to Marshall, 21 May 48, *FRUS, 1948*, 5: 1021–22; Marshall to Lovett, 24 May 48, ibid., 5: 1037.

93. Burdett to Marshall, 24 June 48, *FRUS, 1948*, 5: 1141–42; Jessup to Marshall, 1 July 48, ibid., 5: 1182; MemCons by Lovett, 8 and 21 July 48, ibid., 5: 1199, 1233; Summary of NSC Discussion, 3 Sep 48, RG 273. For Soviet relations with Israel, see Ra'anan, *International Policy Formation*, 80–84.

94. Jessup to Marshall, 1 July 48, *FRUS, 1948*, 5: 1180–84; Satterthwaite to Lovett [mid-July 1948], ibid., 5: 1217; CIA, "Possible Developments from the Palestine Truce," 27 July 48, ibid., 5: 1240–47; Douglas to Marshall, 2 Aug 48, ibid., 5: 1270.

95. Marshall to Consulate General at Jerusalem, 28 July and 3 Aug 48, ibid., 5: 1251, 1275.

96. For JCS views, see NSC 27, "U.S. Military Point of View for the Eventuality of United Nations Decision to Introduce Military Forces into Palestine," 19 Aug 48, ibid., 5: 1322–24.

97. "Department of State Comments on NSC 27" [late Aug 1948], ibid., 5: 1362–63.

98. Summary of NSC Discussion, 3 Sep 48, RG 273.

99. Douglas to Marshall, 25 May, 2 and 6 Aug, and 17 Sep 48, *FRUS, 1948*, 5: 1047–50, 1270, 1291–94, 1409–11; Douglas to Lovett, 26 Oct 48, ibid., 5: 1518; Marshall to Lovett, 27 Oct 48, ibid., 5: 1521.

100. For U.S. support of the Bernadotte plan, see Marshall to Truman, 31 Aug 48, ibid., 5: 1363; Marshall to MacDonald, 31 Aug and 1 Sep 48, ibid., 5: 1364, 1367–68; Lovett to Certain Diplomatic and Consular Offices, 21 and 22 Sep 48, ibid., 5: 1415, 1417; Lovett to Embassy in Egypt, 21 Oct 48, ibid., 5: 1504; Marshall to Lovett, 27 Oct 48, ibid., 5: 1521; Douglas to Lovett, 29 Oct 48, ibid., 5: 1530–32; MemCon by Lovett, 10 Nov 48, ibid., 5: 1562–63; Lovett to Marshall, 10 Nov 48, ibid., 5: 1571–72; Holmes to Marshall, 22 Dec 48, ibid., 5: 1681–84. For Bevin's support of Transjordan and concern for British strategic interests, see Pappé, *Britain and the Arab-Israeli Conflict*, 1–73.

101. For the Lovett/Clifford exchange, see 29 Sep 48, *FRUS, 1948*, 5: 1430–38. For the pressure on the U.S. delegation emanating from the political situation in the United States, see ibid., 5: 1470–71, 1490, 1505, 1507, 1509, 1535. For Israeli opposition to any territorial concessions, see Memo by Marshall, 5 Oct 48, ibid., 5: 1453; see also Pogue, *Marshall*, 370–78.

102. For the Rusk/Dulles exchanges, see Rusk to Lovett, 2 Oct 48, *FRUS, 1948*, 5: 1448–49; Rusk to Marshall, 7 Oct 48, ibid., 5: 1463. For Truman's statement, see ibid., 5: 1512–13.

103. Lovett to Marshall, 29 Oct and 10 Nov 48, ibid., 5: 1528, 1565–67; Douglas to Lovett, 12 Nov 48, ibid., 5: 1571–72; Marshall to Lovett, 15 Nov 48, ibid., 5: 1585–89; Truman to Chaim Weizmann, 29 Nov 48, ibid., 5: 1634.

104. Lovett to Forrestal, 18 Oct 48, ibid., 5: 1488–89; NSC 27/3, 16 Nov 48, ibid., 5: 1593–94; Butler to Lovett, 16 Nov 48, RG 59, PPS, box 33.

105. See, e.g., *FRUS, 1948*, 4: 172–76; ibid., 3: 197, 321–22; *FRUS, 1949*, 4: 62–63, 117–20, 270–71. For Cyrenaica, see ibid., 4: 532–38.

106. See Chapter Two, pp. 81–91.

107. Report to President Truman by Wedemeyer, 19 Sep 47, in DOS, *China White Paper*, 764–814. Wedemeyer carefully hedged his support for logistical and operational military assistance. See also Minutes of Mtg. of the Committee of Two, 3 Nov 47, *FRUS, 1947*, 4: 911. For Marshall's rejection of Wedemeyer's report, see Senate, Armed Services and Foreign Relations, *Military Situation in the Far East*, 2367–68; DOS, *China White Paper*, 260; see also Stueck, *Wedemeyer Mission*, 77, 86–92.

108. Sprouse to Wedemeyer, 23 Aug 47, *FRUS, 1947*, 7: 741–59, esp. 747, 753; Memo by Melby, 29 July 47, ibid., 7: 679; Memo by Ludden, 31 July 47, ibid., 7: 695; see also Memo by Ludden, 23 July 47, ibid., 7: 657–60.

109. For the quotation, see CIA, "Strategic Importance of Japan," 24 May 48, HSTP, PSF, box 255; see also CIA, "The Current Situation in China," 22 July 48, ibid.; U.S. Naval Attaché, "Intelligence Report," 12 Sep 47, ibid., box 173; Memo by Melby, 29 July 47, *FRUS, 1947*, 7: 681; Sprouse to Wedemeyer, 23 Aug 47, ibid., 7: 749.

110. Notes from Admiral Cooke for Wedemeyer, 25 July 47, NHC, CNO, Double Zero Files, folder 31; Wedemeyer Report, 19 Sep 47, in DOS, *China White Paper*, 809–12.

111. For the quotations, see Memo for Wedemeyer, "Conclusions on Financial Aid," 22 Aug

47, *FRUS, 1947*, 7: 739; see also Sprouse to Marshall, 23 Aug 47, ibid., 7: 749–51; Krantz to John Leighton Stuart, 20 Aug 47, ibid., 7: 736–38; Memo by O. Edmund Clubb, 3 Aug 47, ibid., 7: 706.

112. Clark to Butterworth, 10 Dec 47, ibid., 7: 397; Clark to Butterworth, 7 Jan 48, *FRUS, 1948*, 7: 12. For Kennan's statement, see Kennan to Marshall Carter, 10 Feb 48, RG 59, PPS, box 33.

113. Lovett Diary, 20 Nov 47 and 11 Feb 48; Butler to Lovett, 30 March 48, RG 59, PPS, box 33.

114. Minutes of Mtg. of the Committee of Two, 3 Nov 47, *FRUS, 1947*, 7: 911; DOS, *China White Paper*, 380–84. For Kennan's influence, see Kennan to Bohlen, 30 Jan 48, RG 59, PPS, box 33; Pogue, *Marshall*, 273–78.

115. E. May, *Truman Administration and China*, 28–33; Stoler, *Marshall*, 170–71.

116. DOS, *China White Paper*, 380–84; Marshall to Stuart, 9 Feb 48, *FRUS, 1948*, 8: 13; Marshall to Royall, 1 March 48, ibid., 8: 25.

117. This view differs with May's stress on public opinion; see E. May, *Truman Administration and China*, 24–26. For the influences bearing on Marshall and the relative importance of public opinion, see Feaver, "China Aid Bill"; Stueck, *Road to Confrontation*, 55–56. For the evolution of U.S. sentiment toward China, see N. Tucker, *Patterns in the Dust*, 154–72; Westerfield, *Foreign Policy and Party Politics*, 240–68.

118. Minutes of Mtg. of the Committee of Two, 3 Nov 47, *FRUS, 1947*, 7: 909–11; Marshall testimony, 10 Nov 47, in House of Representatives, Foreign Affairs, *Emergency Foreign Aid*, 24–26; Lovett Diary, 29 Dec 47.

119. Marshall to Stuart, 28 Nov 47, *FRUS, 1947*, 7: 923.

120. DOS, *China White Paper*, 387–90; Westerfield, *Foreign Policy and Party Politics*, 262–66; Paterson, "If Europe, Why Not China?"

121. Ohly to Forrestal, 14 and 26 Feb 48, RG 330, box 26, CD 6-2-17; Royall to Forrestal, 21 Feb 48, ibid.; Bradley and Blair, *A General's Life*, 518; Pach, *Arming the Free World*, 196.

122. NSC 6, "Position of the United States Regarding Short-Term Assistance to China," 26 March 48, *FRUS, 1948*, 8: 45–50; Marshall to Lovett, 7 Apr 48, ibid., 8: 53; Butler to Lovett, 30 March 48, RG 59, PPS, box 33.

123. Memo by Marshall, 11 June 48, *FRUS, 1948*, 8: 91–96; Royall to Bradley, Wedemeyer, and Draper, 7 June 48, RG 335, Draper/Voorhees Files, box 11; NSC 22, "Possible Courses of Action for the United States with Respect to the Critical Situation in China," 26 July 48, *FRUS, 1948*, 8: 118–22.

124. For the stress on the differences, see, e.g., Butler to Marshall and Lovett, 27 July 48, RG 59, PPS, box 33.

125. NSC 22/1, "Possible Courses of Action with Respect to the Critical Situation in China," 6 Aug 48, *FRUS, 1948*, 8: 133–34.

126. Memo by Butterworth, 2 Aug 48, ibid., 8: 128; Memo by Butler, 27 July 48, ibid., 8: 123–24; Marshall to Royall, 9 Aug 48, ibid., 1: 615, footnote 2.

127. For the quotation, see PPS 39/1, "United States Policy Toward China," 23 Nov 48, ibid., 8: 211; see also Minutes of Mtg. of PPS, 12 Aug 48, RG 59, PPS, box 32; Kennan to Marshall, 12 Aug 48, ibid., box 33; Kennan to Carter, 23 Aug 48, ibid.; PPS 39, "To Review and Define United States Policy Toward China," 7 Sep 48, *FRUS, 1948*, 8: 147–55; Kennan, "United States Foreign Policy," 11 Oct 48, Kennan Papers, box 17; Kennan, "Notes on China," 16 Nov 48, ibid., box 23; Lapham to Hoffman, 26 Nov 48, *FRUS, 1948*, 8: 655; Butterworth to Lovett, 16 Sep 48, ibid., 8: 669; Memo by Robert M. Magill and Richard E. Johnson, 1 Dec 48, ibid., 8: 681.

128. See esp. Memo by Butterworth, 30 Dec 48, *FRUS, 1948*, 8: 667–68; Lovett to Stuart, 23 Nov and 17 and 24 Dec 48, ibid., 7: 603, 659, 681–82; Minutes of Cabinet Mtg., 31 Dec 48, Connelly Papers, box 1.

129. In addition to citations in Note 127 above, see Draft Report by the NSC on U.S. Policy

Toward China, 2 Nov 48, *FRUS, 1948*, 8: 185–87; Butterworth to Lovett, 3 Nov 48, ibid., 8: 187–89; Memo by Butterworth, 30 Dec 48, ibid., 8: 667–68.

130. For discussions over the evacuation of Tsingtao, see *FRUS, 1948*, 8: 307–45; see also the extremely revealing NSC discussions, in Summary of Discussions, 1 and 8 Oct, 4 Nov, and 3 and 10 Dec 48, HSTP, PSF, box 220.

131. CIA, "Chinese Communist Capabilities for Control of All China," 10 Dec 48, HSTP, PSF, box 256.

132. MacArthur to Marshall, 2 July 47, *FRUS, 1947*, 6: 683–84; Joseph E. Jacobs to Marshall, 7 and 19 July, 14 Aug, 8 and 19 Sep, and 18 Oct 47, ibid., 6: 690–91, 709, 752–53, 783, 806–7, 841; Hodge to JCS, 18 July 47, RG 107, Petersen Papers, Classified, 091 Korea; Schuyler to Petersen, 21 July 47, ibid., General Subject File, box 1; Petersen to SWNCC, 24 July 47, ibid. For revealing accounts of developments inside Korea during 1947–48, see Merrill, *Korea*, 55–97; Cumings, *Origins of the Korean War*, 2: 185–290.

133. P&O, "Strategic Importance of Korea," 16 Sep 47, RG 319, P&O, 092 TS; SWNCC, Special Ad Hoc Committee, Country Report on Korea, 19 Aug 47, RG 353, SWNCC, box 109. For JCS views, see Forrestal to Marshall, 26 [29] Sep 47, *FRUS, 1947*, 6: 817–18; Wedemeyer to Forrestal, 30 Aug 48, RG 330, box 25, CD 6-2-41; Matray, *Reluctant Crusade*, 115–16.

134. Schuyler to Petersen, 21 July 47, RG 107, Petersen Papers, General Subject File, box 1; Petersen to SWNCC, 24 July 47, ibid.

135. Report by the Ad Hoc Committee on Korea, 4 Aug 47, *FRUS, 1947*, 6: 738–41; Memo by John M. Allison, 29 July 47, ibid., 6: 734–37; Memo by John C. Hilldring, 6 Aug 47, ibid., 6: 742–43; Matray, *Reluctant Crusade*, 119–24.

136. *FRUS, 1947*, 6: 773–74, 779, 791, 792, 824–25, 833–35, 852–53.

137. Jacobs to Marshall, 8 Oct 47, ibid., 6: 826.

138. For the "scuttle and run" expression, see Butterworth to Lovett, 1 Oct 47, ibid., 6: 820; see also MemCon by Marshall, 28 Oct 47, ibid., 6: 552–53; Kennan to Butterworth, 24 Sep 47, ibid., 6: 814; Kennan to Lovett, 1 Oct 47, RG 59, PPS, box 33; Schuyler to Blum, 2 Jan 48, RG 319, P&O, 091 Korea TS (Withdrawal from Korea); Biddle to Wedemeyer, 5 March 48, ibid.; Memo by Butterworth, 4 March 48, *FRUS, 1948*, 6: 1139; MemCon by Allison, 5 March 48, ibid., 6: 1140–41.

139. NSC 8, "Position of the United States with Respect to Korea," 2 Apr 48, *FRUS, 1948*, 6: 1164–69.

140. For recognition, see Marshall to Certain Diplomatic and Consular Officers, 10 July 48, ibid., 6: 1235–36. For economic aid, see Truman to Marshall, 25 Aug 48, ibid., 6: 1288. For electric power, see Saltzman to Draper, 24 Apr 48, ibid., 6: 1181.

141. Minutes of NSC Mtg., 11 March 48, RG 273; MemCon by Allison, 5 March 48, *FRUS, 1948*, 6: 1140–41; Lovett to Royall, 8 July 48, ibid., 6: 1235; Butterworth to Lovett, 17 Aug 48, ibid., 6: 1276–78; Marshall to Royall, 17 Sep 48, ibid., 6: 1303; Wedemeyer to Forrestal, 30 Aug 48, RG 330, box 25, CD 6-2-41.

142. Marshall to Hoffman, 17 Sep 48, *FRUS, 1948*, 6: 1303–4; see also Memo by Saltzman, 7 Sep 48, ibid., 6: 1292–98; Hoffman to Marshall, 1 Oct 48, ibid., 6: 1312–13.

143. Jacobs to Marshall, 12 Aug 48, ibid., 6: 1272.

144. Muccio to Marshall, 12 Nov 48, ibid., 6: 1325–27; Saltzman to Wedemeyer, 9 Nov 48, ibid., 6: 1324; MemCon by Marshall, 25 Oct 48, ibid., 8: 183; Matray, *Reluctant Crusade*, 151–74; Sawyer, *Military Advisors in Korea*, 35–42.

145. Bishop to Butterworth, 17 Dec 48, *FRUS, 1948*, 6: 1337–40; see also CIA, "Strategic Importance of Japan," 24 May 48, HSTP, PSF, box 255.

146. Kennan, "Problems of Our Foreign Policy," 14 Jan 48, Kennan Papers, box 17.

147. Memo by John Paton Davies, 11 Aug 47, *FRUS, 1947*, 6: 485–86; Kennan to Lovett, 12 Aug 47, ibid., 6: 486–87; Bishop to James K. Penfield, 14 Aug 47, ibid., 6: 493–94; Lovett to Marshall, 25 Aug 47, ibid., 6: 505.

148. Nimitz to Sullivan, 18 Aug 47, NHC, CNO, Double Zero Files, folder 20; Royall to

Lovett, 22 Aug 47, RG 335, box 76. For Army views, see also "Japanese Peace Treaty" [no signature], 14 Aug 47, ibid.; JCS 1619/24, "Review of U.S. Control Needed over the Japanese Islands," 26 Aug 47, RG 218, CCS 360 (12-9-42), sec. 30; Wooldridge to Hugh Borton, 18 Aug 47, *FRUS, 1947*, 6: 496; Draft Prepared in the War Dept., 29 Aug 47, ibid., 6: 506-9. For initial postwar naval thinking about bases in Japan, see Dingman, "U.S. Navy and the Cold War," 291-97.

149. Minutes of Mtgs. of the PPS, 25 Aug and 4 Sep 47, RG 59, PPS, box 32. The quotation is from the latter meeting.

150. Memo by Kennan, 14 Oct 47, *FRUS, 1947*, 6: 536-37; PPS 10, "Results of Planning Staff Study of Questions Involved in the Japanese Peace Settlement," 14 Oct 47, ibid., 6: 537-42.

151. Draper to Royall, 1 Oct 47, RG 335, box 53; Draper to Lovett, 20 Nov 47, *FRUS, 1947*, 6: 442. For Japanese trade problems, see Sebald to Marshall, 16 Sep and 30 Dec 47, ibid., 6: 293-94, 344-45. For Draper's importance, see Schonberger, "U.S. Policy in Postwar Japan."

152. Royall to Lovett, 28 Nov and 16 Dec 47, RG 335, box 76; Lovett to Royall, 25 Nov 47, ibid.; Gordon Gray to Royall, 11 Dec 47, ibid.; Minutes of NSC Mtg., 17 Dec 47, RG 273; Kennan to Lovett, 31 Oct 47, RG 59, PPS, box 33. For external pressures, see Schonberger, "Japan Lobby," 327-46. For intense friction between policymakers in Washington and MacArthur, see also Schaller, *American Occupation of Japan*, 107-21.

153. For a fine analysis of business interests, see Zimmern, "American Business Views Toward Japan."

154. Schonberger, "U.S. Policy in Postwar Japan"; Schaller, *American Occupation of Japan*, 122-37; MemCon by Kennan, 19 Feb 48, RG 59, PPS, box 33; Kennan to Lovett, 24 Feb 48, ibid.

155. PPS 28, "Recommendations with Respect to U.S. Policy Toward Japan," 25 March 48, *FRUS, 1948*, 6: 692-95.

156. Ibid.; Kennan, "Problems of Far Eastern Policy," 14 Jan 48, Kennan Papers, box 17; Kennan, "Present Situation in Japan," 19 May 48, ibid.; PPS 23, "Review of Current Trends," 24 Feb 48, *FRUS, 1948*, 1: 523-25; Kennan to Marshall, 14 March 48, ibid., 1: 531-35; Kennan to Lovett, 23 March 48, ibid., 6: 689-90; PPS 28/2, "Recommendations with Respect to U.S. Policy Toward Japan," 26 May 48, ibid., 6: 777-81; MemCon by Marshall Green, 28 May 48, ibid., 6: 788-94; MemCon Prepared in the Canadian Dept. of External Affairs, 3 June 48, ibid., 6: 802-7. For analyses of U.S. strategic interests in East Asia that stress the off-shore security perimeter concept and that disregard the links between Japan's rehabilitation and a non-Communist Southeast Asia, see Gaddis, *Long Peace*, 72-103; Dingman, "Strategic Planning."

157. For reactions to Kennan's proposals, see Memo by William I. Cargo, 5 Apr 48, *FRUS, 1948*, 6: 723-24; Thorp to Butterworth, 6 Apr 48, ibid., 6: 964-65; Saltzman to Butterworth, 9 Apr 48, ibid., 6: 727-34; Wedemeyer to Draper, 21 Apr 48, RG 335, Draper/Voorhees Files, box 18; Daniel Noce to Draper, 17 May 48, ibid.

158. Royall to Forrestal, 18 May 48, HSTP, PSF, box 182; MemCon Between MacArthur, Kennan, and Draper, 21 March 48, *FRUS, 1948*, 6: 706-8; Allison to Maxwell M. Hamilton, 30 Apr 48, ibid., 6: 743.

159. Schonberger, *Aftermath of War*, 190-97; T. Cohen and Passim, *Remaking Japan*, 401-28. For the labor issue, see Sebald to Marshall, 13 Aug and 9 Dec 48, *FRUS, 1948*, 6: 838-39, 919-21; DOS to MacArthur, 8 Oct 48, ibid., 6: 866.

160. Royall to Marshall, 26 May 48, RG 335, Draper/Voorhees Files, box 18; R. M. Cheseldine to Draper, 17 June 48, ibid.; Memo for the Record by H. O. Paxson, 15 Sep 48, ibid., SecArmy, box 77. For Kennan's views, see, e.g., MemCon Prepared in the Canadian Dept. of External Affairs, 3 June 48, *FRUS, 1948*, 6: 803. For other DOS views, see Thorp to Butterworth, 6 Apr 48, ibid., 6: 965; Saltzman to Butterworth, 9 Apr 48, ibid., 6: 733-34; Marshall to Royall, 10 Sep 48, ibid., 6: 1008-9; Saltzman to Marshall, 15 Sep 48, ibid., 6: 1015-16; Lovett to Royall, 28 Oct 48, ibid., 6: 1035-40; Kennan to Lovett, 6 and 27 Oct 48, RG 59, PPS, box 33.

161. Lovett to Royall, 10 Nov 48, *FRUS, 1948*, 6: 890; Memo for General Lincoln by J.G.K.M., 1 Dec 48, RG 335, Draper/Voorhees Files, box 18; Draper to MacArthur, 10 Dec 48, ibid.

162. For the quotation, see Memo Prepared in the DOS, 13 Oct 48, *FRUS, 1948*, 1: 641; Lovett to Marshall, 7 Oct 48, ibid., 6: 864–65.

163. Draper to Lovett, 14 Dec 48, ibid., 6: 1062–63.

164. For the quotation, see Daniel Cox Fahey to Sidney Souers, 29 July 48, RG 335, Draper/ Voorhees Files, box 18; see also Schaller, *American Occupation of Japan*; Borden, *Pacific Alliance*; Rotter, *Path to Vietnam*.

165. CIA, "Break-Up of the Colonial Empires and Its Implications for US Security," 3 Sep 48, HSTP, PSF, box 255.

166. For the quotation, see CIA, "Review of the World Situation," 16 Sep 48, ibid., box 204; see also DOS Policy Statement, "Great Britain," 11 June 48, *FRUS, 1948*, 3: 1091; Lovett to Marshall, 7 June 48, ibid., 6: 228; Minutes of Mtg. of the PPS, 7 June 48, RG 59, PPS, box 32.

167. DOS, "Policy Statement on Indochina," 27 Sep 48, *FRUS, 1948*, 6: 48–49; Marshall to Embassy in France, 3 July and 30 Aug 48, ibid., 6: 30 (quotation), 40; Marshall to Embassy in China, 2 July 48, ibid., 6: 28; Office of Far Eastern Affairs, Weekly Review Summary, "Communism in Southeast Asia," 21 July 48, RG 59, PSA, box 5; Hess, *United States' Emergence as a Southeast Asian Power*, 311–21.

168. William S. B. Lacy to Charles S. Reed, 4 Aug 48, RG 59, PSA, box 5; Reed to Butterworth, 13 Aug 48, ibid.

169. Lovett to the Consulate General at Batavia, 28 May 48, *FRUS, 1948*, 6: 192; Office of Far Eastern Affairs, Weekly Review Summary, "Communism in Southeast Asia," 21 July 48, RG 59, PSA, box 5. For the confused background to this agreement, see McVey, *Soviet View of the Indonesian Revolution*, 47–52.

170. MemCon by Marshall, 17 Sep 48, *FRUS, 1948*, 6: 343–45; MemCon by Lovett, 17 Sep 48, ibid., 6: 345–47; Lovett to Consulate General at Batavia, 27 Sep 48, ibid., 6: 378. For background, see McVey, *Soviet View of the Indonesian Revolution*, 59–76.

171. Lovett to Consulate General at Batavia, 3 Dec 48, *FRUS, 1948*, 6: 512–14; DOS to the Netherlands Embassy, 7 Dec 48, ibid., 6: 531–35.

172. Ibid., 6: 484–608, esp. 497, 531–35, 552, 578, 588, 593–600.

173. CIA, "Break-Up of the Colonial Empires," 3 Sep 48, HSTP, PSF, box 255; CIA, "Review of the World Situation," 16 Sep 48 and 19 Jan 49, ibid., boxes 204 and 250.

174. Kennan to Marshall and Lovett, 17 Dec 48, RG 59, PPS, box 33.

175. Contrast this interpretation to Gaddis's *Strategies of Containment*, 25–88; Gaddis, *Long Peace*, 147–67. My interpretation resembles Hixson, *Kennan*, 47–72.

176. Kennan to Marshall and Lovett, 17 Dec 48, RG 59, PPS, box 33; see also Kennan, "Where We Are Today," 21 Dec 48, Kennan Papers, box 17; CIA, "Review of the World Situation," 19 Jan 49, HSTP, PSF, box 250. Although the formal paper by the PPS on Southeast Asia was not yet in its final form, it was already under consideration in late 1948. See PPS 51, "United States Policy Toward Southeast Asia," 29 March 49, *PPS Papers*, 3: 32–58.

177. See NSC 20/4, "U.S. Objectives with Respect to the USSR to Counter Soviet Threats to U.S. Security," 23 Nov 48, *FRUS, 1948*, 1: 663–69; CIA, "Break-Up of Colonial Empires," 3 Sep 48, HSTP, PSF, box 255; CIA, "Threats to the Security of the United States," 28 Sep 48, ibid., box 256.

178. Ra'anan, *International Policy Formation*, 116–63; McCagg, *Stalin Embattled*, 261–307; W. Hahn, *Postwar Soviet Politics*, 102–35.

179. CIA, "Estimate of the Status of the Russian Atomic Energy Project," 1 July 48, RG 330, box 61, CD 11-1-2. For Soviet aviation, see CIA, Intelligence Memorandum No. 200, 19 July 49, HSTP, PSF, box 249; Inglis to Op-30, 1 Dec 48, NHC, SPD, A8. For Soviet defense budget, see Office of Naval Information, Memo of Information, 5 Jan 48, ibid., CNO, Double Zero Files, box 4; Bergson, "Russian Defense Expenditures." For overall Soviet capabilities, see JIG, "Intelligence Presentations," 12 and 20 Apr 48, RG 319, P&O, 350.05 TS. For the Soviet army, see Evangelista, "Stalin's Postwar Army Reappraised," 110–38. For assessments of Soviet intentions, see esp. the comments of Ambassador Smith, Minutes of Mtg. of the PPS, 28 Sep 48, RG 59, PPS, box 32; Lovett to Sullivan, 20 Dec 48, *FRUS, 1948*, 1: 673–74.

180. That the United States had taken the initiative in Germany and forced the Soviets to be on the defensive was the view of both Pentagon and DOS officials. This perspective is most clearly stated in the memo General Bradley had prepared for Eisenhower, "National Military Establishment Views on Situation in Germany," 30 June 48, RG 319, P&O, 092 TS; see also DOS Policy Statement, "Germany," 26 Aug 48, *FRUS, 1948*, 2: 1318–19.

181. Minutes of Cabinet Mtg., 23 July 48, Connelly Papers, box 1; Memo by Marshall, 20 Nov 48, *FRUS, 1948*, 3: 280–81; see also Kennan, "Contemporary Problems of Foreign Policy," 17 Sep 48, Kennan Papers, box 17.

182. Durbrow to Marshall, 2 Dec 47, *FRUS, 1947*, 6: 583–84; Smith to Marshall, 30 June 48, *FRUS, 1948*, 7: 327; Sebald to Marshall, 30 Sep 48, ibid., 6: 1026–28; Memo Prepared in the DOS, 13 Oct 48, ibid., 1: 640–41.

183. Lovett to Marshall, 19 Nov 48, ibid., 7: 591; PPS 39/1, "U.S. Policy Toward China," 23 Nov 48, ibid., 8: 209.

184. For the strategic importance of Korea to the Soviet Far Eastern provinces, see Inglis to General Board, 28 Apr 48, DCNO (Operations), "National Security and the Navy," NHC, General Board 425 (Serial 315); see also Cumings, *Origins of the Korean War*, 2: 325–49.

185. See, e.g., DOS, Office of Far Eastern Affairs, "Communism in Southeast Asia," 21 and 28 July 48, Weekly Review Summary, RG 59, PSA, box 5; CIA, "Break-Up of Colonial Empires," 3 Sep 48, HSTP, PSF, box 205. For background, see McLane, *Soviet Strategies in Southeast Asia*, 351–473; Nagai and Iriye, *Cold War in Asia*, 362–77.

186. Jessup to Marshall, 1 July 48, *FRUS, 1948*, 5: 1182–84; CIA, "Possible Developments from the Palestine Truce," 27 July 48, HSTP, PSF, box 255. For background, see Behbehani, *Soviet Union and Arab Nationalism*, 56–86.

187. Shlaim, *United States and the Berlin Blockade*, 171–280; see also Kennan, "Estimate of the International Situation," 8 Nov 48, Kennan Papers, box 17; Summary of NSC Discussion, 23 July and 15 Oct 48, HSTP, PSF, box 220.

188. Forrestal to Marshall, 31 Oct 48, *FRUS, 1948*, 1: 644–47; NSC 35, "Existing International Commitments Involving the Possible Use of Armed Forces," 2 Nov 48, ibid., 1: 656–62; see also the memos and assessments, Oct–Nov 1948, RG 330, box 16, "Draper—Budget File"; Forrestal, *Diaries*, 498–511; K. Condit, *History of the JCS*, 227–52; S. Ross, *American War Plans*, 94–98.

189. Forrestal to Marshall, 31 Oct 48, *FRUS, 1948*, 1: 645–46; Kennan to Lovett, 5 Aug 48, ibid., 1: 599–601.

190. Summary of NSC Discussion, 15 Oct 48, HSTP, PSF, box 220; Lovett to Marshall, 1 and 2 Nov 48, *FRUS, 1948*, 1: 647–50; Bohlen to Carter, 7 Nov 48, ibid., 1: 653–54; Marshall to Lovett, 8 Nov 48, ibid., 1: 654–55; Précis of Conversation Between Marshall and Alcide De Gasperi, 18 Oct 48, ibid., 3: 885–86; Forrestal, *Diaries*, 500–502, 510–11, 521; Shlaim, *United States and the Berlin Blockade*, 293–95.

191. Forrestal to Truman, 1 Dec 48, *FRUS, 1948*, 1: 671–72; Forrestal to Ralph Bard, 20 Nov 48, Forrestal Papers, box 78; Forrestal to Walter Andrews, 13 Dec 48, ibid.; Rearden, *Formative Years*, 347–53.

192. NSC 20/4, "U.S Objectives with Respect to the USSR to Counter Soviet Threats to U.S. Security," 23 Nov 48, *FRUS, 1948*, 1: 662–69.

193. For Dewey and the campaign, see Westerfield, *Foreign Policy and Party Politics*, 306–11. At the end of the campaign, Truman assailed Republican isolationism and charged that a Republican victory would facilitate Communist gains throughout Europe and Asia. See *PPP:HST* (1948), 929–30. For Truman's views, see also Donovan, *Conflict and Crisis*, 140–45.

Chapter 7

1. *PPP:HST* (1949), 1–7.
2. Ibid., 112–26.

3. Ibid., 113.

4. Ibid., 114–16.

5. For Truman's allusions to Wallace, see *PPP:HST* (1948), 189. For his campaign rhetoric against the Republicans, see, e.g., ibid., 925–30.

6. Acheson, *Present at the Creation*, 135–38, 249–53; Truman, *Memoirs: 1945*, 601–5; Truman, *Memoirs: 1946–52*, 487; Thompson, *Truman Presidency*, 117–18.

7. Berman, *Office of Management and Budget*, 38–47; Doig and Hargrove, *Leadership and Innovation*, 176–81; Nelson, "Truman and the National Security Council," 365.

8. Acheson, *Present at the Creation*, 250, 254–56.

9. MemCons with the Pres by Acheson, 1949, NA, RG 59, Executive Secretariat; Acheson, *Present at the Creation*, 135–38.

10. Acheson, *Present at the Creation*, 254–56; Statement by the Secretary Before House Committee on Foreign Affairs, 11 March 49, *FRUS, 1949*, 1: 2–3; Acheson Testimony, 11 March 49, Senate, Foreign Relations, *Executive Sessions*, 2: 95–105.

11. Kennan, *Memoirs, 1925–1950*, 450, 492–93; Summaries of Secretary's Daily Mtgs., 1949, RG 59, Executive Secretariat. For importance of Jessup, see ibid., 2 March 49. For Webb, see *FRUS, 1949*, 1: 283.

12. Kennan to Acheson, 3 Jan 49, RG 59, PPS, box 33; Kennan to Lovett, 8 June 48, ibid.; Secretary's Daily Mtg., 29 June 49, RG 59, Executive Secretariat; Kennan, "Where We Are Today," 21 Dec 48, Kennan Papers, box 17.

13. For DOS desires to take over German policy, see MemCons with the Pres by Acheson, 24 Jan and 4 Apr 49, RG 59, Executive Secretariat; Kennan to Rusk, 17 Feb 49, RG 59, PPS, box 33; Kennan to Webb, 25 Feb 49, ibid. For the decisions on placing military aid under the DOS, see Truman to Acheson, 13 Apr 49, RG 51, Series 47.3, M5-9; Frank Pace to Truman, 28 March 49, ibid. For relations between the DOS and the NSC, see Kennan to Webb and Acheson, 4, 14, and 25 Apr 49, RG 59, PPS, box 33; *FRUS, 1949*, 1: 271–75, 282–84, 298, 313, 326, 346, 382–84; Nelson, "Truman and the National Security Council," 369–72.

14. Secretary's Daily Mtg., 7 March, 11 Apr, and 10 Oct 49, RG 59, Executive Secretariat; Carlisle Humelsine to Acheson, 17 Nov 49, MemCons with the Pres, ibid.; Blum to Forrestal, 3 March 49, RG 330, box 33, CD 6-4-22; Memo by Louis Johnson, 3 Aug 49, *FRUS, 1949*, 1: 366–67; Memo by John Peurifoy, 17 Nov 49, ibid., 1: 410; Rearden, *Formative Years*, 127–29.

15. Doig and Hargrove, *Leadership and Innovation*, 391–400; Rearden, *Formative Years*, 38–47; Clifford, *Counsel to the President*, 171–74.

16. Untitled memo, 30 Nov 48, Elsey Papers, box 83; Memo for the director, unsigned [by Stauffacher?], 3 Jan 49, ibid., box 84; "Proposed Organization of the Military Establishment," unsigned [by Elsey?], 12 Jan 49, Clifford Papers, box 16.

17. Forrestal, Pace, and Clifford to Truman, 4 and 10 Feb 49, Elsey Papers, box 83; Rearden, *Formative Years*, 35–43.

18. Rearden, *Formative Years*, 47–50; Coletta, *United States Navy*, 126–45; K. McFarland, "1949 Revolt of the Admirals," 54–57; Bradley and Blair, *A General's Life*, 502–3.

19. Westerfield, *Foreign Policy and Party Politics*, 325–42; McLellan, *Acheson*, 137–43.

20. Senate, Foreign Relations, *Economic Assistance to China and Korea*, 17–45; Acheson to John Leighton Stuart, 24 March 49, *FRUS, 1949*, 8: 198–99; N. Tucker, *Patterns in the Dust*, 154–67.

21. For JCS budget planners' views and requests, see Joseph T. McNarney, Robert B. Carney, and George J. Richards to Forrestal, 14 Oct 48, RG 330, box 18, CD 5-1-25; JCS 1800/28, Memo by the Budget Advisers to the JCS, 13 Jan 49, RG 218, CCS 370 (8-19-45), sec. 13. For views of Kennan and Bohlen, see Kennan to Webb and Acheson, 4 and 14 Apr 49, RG 59, PPS, box 33; Undersecretary's Mtg., 15 Apr 49, *FRUS, 1949*, 1: 283–84; MemCon by Webb, 4 May 49, ibid., 1: 297–98. For the enumeration of NSC 20/4 goals in the war plans, see DROPSHOT, JCS 1920/1, "Long Range Plans for War with the USSR," 31 Jan 49, RG 218, CCS 381 USSR (3-2-46), sec. 28; OFFTACKLE, JCS 1844/46, "Joint Outline Emergency War Plan," 8 Nov 49, ibid., sec. 41; see also S. Ross, *American War Plans*, 111–12.

22. Eisenhower, *Papers*, 10: 497-98, 512-19.

23. K. Condit, *History of the JCS*, 295-96; Eisenhower, *Papers*, 10: 497, 515-19. For detailed information on the evolution of strategic planning from the autumn of 1948 to the spring of 1949, see the documents in RG 218, CCS 381 USSR (3-2-46), secs. 24-31.

24. Eisenhower, *Papers*, 10: 544-46, 551-52, 592-94; Rearden, *Formative Years*, 364-69.

25. Eisenhower, *Papers*, 10: 592-94, 651-55, 699-704, 831-36. For Eisenhower's concern with the Middle East, see Memo for Op-4 by T. M. Stokes, 25 June 49, NHC, SPD, box 250, A16-3. For the Air Force claim that it could penetrate Soviet defenses and Navy doubts, see JCS 1952/1, JCS to SecDef, 21 Dec 48, RG 218, CCS 373 (10-23-48), sec. 1; JCS 1952/2, CNO to JCS, 11 Jan 49, ibid. For the stress on flexibility in war plans, see Conference with British Chiefs of Staff, 3 Aug 49, RG 319, P&O, 092 EUR TS.

26. Eisenhower, *Papers*, 10: 699-704, 738.

27. For the quotations, see A. D. Struble, "Presentation on Broad Strategic Thinking," 22 March 49, NHC, SPD, box 250, A16-3; Gallery to DCNO (Air), 13 June 49, Ofstie Papers, box 4. For Navy questioning of Air Force estimates of strategic air offensive, see JCS 1952/2, CNO to JCS, 11 Jan 49, RG 218, CCS 373 (10-23-48), sec. 1; Rosenberg and Kennedy, "United States Aircraft Carriers," 102-50.

28. Gallery to DCNO (Air), 13 June 49, Ofstie Papers, box 4; Ofstie to Denfeld, ND [June 1949], ibid.; Memo for Op-05 by M. B. Gardner, 7 July 1949, NHC, SPD, box 250, A16-3.

29. Rosenberg and Kennedy, "United States Aircraft Carriers," 102-50.

30. For the quotation, see L. K. Tarrant to C. V. R. Schuyler, 22 July 49, RG 319, P&O, 381 EUR TS. For Bradley's concern with Western Europe, see JCS 1920/3, Memo by Bradley, 18 March 49, RG 218, CCS 381 USSR, (3-2-46), sec. 30. For Bradley's belief that naval expenditures had to be cut, see Bradley to Eisenhower, Denfeld, and Vandenberg, 25 May 49, Eisenhower Papers, File 1652, box 13. For the capacity to defend Western Europe, see also Schuyler to Bolte, 4 Oct 49, RG 319, P&O, 381 EUR TS.

31. JCS 1953/1, Report of the Ad Hoc Committee, "Evaluation of Effect of Soviet War Effort Resulting from the Strategic Air Offensive," 12 May 49, RG 218, CCS 373 (10-23-48), Bulky Package (BP), pt. 1.

32. For a contemporary emphasis on this point, see Ofstie to Op-05, 26 Apr 49, Ofstie Papers, box 4.

33. Eisenhower, *Papers*, 10: 699-704; Rearden, *Formative Years*, 369-76; Bradley and Blair, *A General's Life*, 502.

34. For OFFTACKLE, see JCS 1844/46, "Joint Outline Emergency War Plan," 8 Nov 49, RG 218, CCS 381 USSR (3-2-46), sec. 41; DROPSHOT, JCS 1920/1, "Long Range Plans for War with the USSR," 31 Jan 49, ibid., sec. 28. See also S. Ross, *American War Plans*, 109-32. For the very revealing talks with British strategists and much more circumspect talks with French military leaders, see "Conference with British Chiefs of Staff," 3 Aug 49, RG 319, P&O, 092 EUR TS; "Conference with French Chiefs of Staff," 5 Aug 49, ibid. One of the great problems beleaguering war planners is the complex interrelationships between short-term and long-term plans. If one focuses on an emergency war in the near future, one configures forces and places priorities in ways that differ substantially from what one would do if planning for a war at some distant date.

35. PPS 33, "Factors Affecting the Nature of the U.S. Defense Arrangements in the Light of Soviet Policies," 23 June 48, in *PPS Papers*, 2: 281-93; Kennan to Llewellyn Thompson, 3 May 49, RG 59, PPS, box 33; Memo by George Butler, 22 Apr 49, ibid.; Thompson to Kennan, 3 May 49, *FRUS, 1949*, 1: 292-93; G. Frederick Reinhardt to Kennan, 4 May 49, ibid., 1: 293-95; Memos by Butler, 31 May and 9 June 49, ibid., 1: 321-28. For Truman's concerns, see R. B. Landry to Truman, 16 Apr 49, HSTP, PSF, box 126; see also Pace to Truman, 5 Apr 49, ibid., box 200; Schilling, Hammond, and Snyder, *Strategy, Politics, and Defense Budgets*, 254-56.

36. House of Representatives, International Relations, *Executive Session Hearings*, 37-44. The quotation is on p. 43.

37. Ibid., 24-25.

38. For cogent and systematic analysis of Allied differences over German issues, see the two collections of position papers compiled by the CAD of the Dept. of the Army, 14 Jan and 16 Feb 49, RG 319, P&O, 091 Germany TS. For the differences with the British and French over reparations, see Douglas to Marshall, 7 Dec 48, *FRUS, 1948*, 2: 841–42; British Government to DOS, 4 Dec 48, ibid., 2: 840.

39. Paper prepared by Kennan, 8 March 49, *FRUS, 1949*, 3: 96–99. For background, see Gimbel, *American Occupation of Germany*, 186–257; Bark and Gress, *From Shadow to Substance*, 231–49.

40. Clay to Draper, 23 Jan 49, *FRUS, 1949*, 3: 86–87; see also Murphy to Lovett, 13 Dec 48, *FRUS, 1948*, 2: 1338–40.

41. CAD, "Western Germany's Long-Range Economic Program," 14 Jan 49, RG 319, P&O, 091 Germany TS; CIA, "Review of the World Situation," 16 Feb 49, HSTP, PSF, box 205. Queries about these matters arose during Acheson's testimony to the House Committee on International Relations on 15 Feb. See House of Representatives, International Relations, *Executive Session Hearings*, 50–54, 66–68. For background, see Hardach, *Political Economy of Germany*, 182–84.

42. See Royall's report on his European trip, 4 Jan 49, Eisenhower Papers, File 1652, box 42; Royall to Truman, 7 and 10 Jan 49, RG 330, box 33, CD 6-4-22; untitled memo by Voorhees, 4 Jan 48 [49], Voorhees Papers, box 4; see also the correspondence between Clay and Draper, Nov and Dec 1948, RG 330, box 37, CD 6-4-11.

43. Draper to P&O, 11 Jan 49, RG 319, P&O, 091 Germany TS; Ray T. Maddocks to Voorhees, 14 Jan 49, ibid.; "Opening Statement of the Secretary of the Army to the Special Committee on Germany," ND [28 Jan 49], ibid.; "Tentative Agenda: Special Committee on Germany," 28 Jan 49, ibid.; "Notes for the Secretary of the Army for Conference at 900," 28 Jan 49, ibid.; "Notes on Discussion Following Luncheon," 26 Jan 49, RG 335, Draper/Voorhees Files, box 16.

44. Minutes of the NSC, 27 Jan 49, RG 273; Memo by Geoffrey W. Lewis, 28 Jan 49, *FRUS, 1949*, 3: 87–89.

45. Untitled paper by Kennan, 8 March 49, *FRUS, 1949*, 3: 96–98.

46. Kennan, "Principles of Basic Policy Concerning Germany," 7 Feb 49, ibid., 3: 93; untitled paper by Kennan, 8 March 49, ibid., 3: 98–100; MemCon by Murphy, 9 March 49, ibid., 3: 102–3.

47. MemCon by Murphy, 9 March 49, ibid., 3: 102; Secretary's Daily Mtg., 28 Feb 49, RG 59, Executive Secretariat.

48. Clay, *Papers*, 2: 1033–36; Secretary's Daily Mtg., 9 March 49, RG 59, Executive Secretariat.

49. Mtg. in the DOS, 17 March 49, *FRUS, 1949*, 3: 699–700; Secretary's Daily Mtg., 22 March 49, ibid., 3: 706–7.

50. Secretary's Daily Mtgs., 8 and 22 March 49, RG 59, Executive Secretariat.

51. For the attitudes of top officials, see ibid., 8, 21, and 22 March 49; Murphy to Jessup, 19 March 49, RG 43, Jessup-Malik Conversations, box 304. For key papers, see *FRUS, 1949*, 3: 11–47. Contrast this emphasis on geopolitics with the Kolkos' stress on economics and the restoration of German propertied classes (Kolko and Kolko, *Limits of Power*, 428–35).

52. Draft of Kennan letter to Acheson, 29 March 49, Kennan Papers, box 23; Kennan, *Memoirs, 1925–1950*, 451–67.

53. For the quotation, see MemCon by Acheson, 14 Feb 49, *FRUS, 1949*, 4: 109. For Acheson's great concern with the German question and for his simultaneous work on the NAT, see Secretary's Daily Mtgs., Feb–Apr 1949, RG 59, Executive Secretariat. The interested reader should peruse the documents in *FRUS, 1949*, vol. 3, in conjunction with the materials in vol. 4. With the exception of Timothy Ireland, very few students of the NAT have bothered to study the materials on the German question and to ponder their interrelationships.

54. For negotiating strategy regarding Norway and Denmark, see Bohlen to Acheson, 10 Feb 49, RG 59, Bohlen Papers, box 4. For talks with Norway and concern with neutrality, see *FRUS, 1949*, 4: 71–72, 81–84, 89, 91–93; Cole, *Norway and the United States*, 135–37. For DOS

and Army papers and their references to Germany, see *FRUS, 1949*, 3: 123, 146. For Acheson's testimony regarding Germany, see Senate, Foreign Relations, *Vandenberg Resolution*, 125.

55. MemCon by Acheson, 17 Feb 49, *FRUS, 1949*, 4: 117; Bohlen to Acheson, 16, 18, and 21 Feb 49, RG 59, Bohlen Papers, box 1; Memo for Acheson by Bohlen, 15 Feb 49, ibid., box 4; Senate, Foreign Relations, *Vandenberg Resolution*, 88–126, 148–67; Secretary's Daily Mtgs., 2 and 9 March 49, RG 59, Executive Secretariat; L. Kaplan, *United States and NATO*, 111–19.

56. For JCS views, see Memo by JCS, 5 Jan 49, *FRUS, 1949*, 4: 11–13; JCS to SecDef, 10 Feb 49, ibid., 4: 98–99; Hickerson to Acheson, 17 Feb 49, ibid., 4: 121; JCS to SecDef, 31 March 49, RG 330, box 34, CD 6-4-18; K. Condit, *History of the JCS*, 371–84.

57. For the testimony of Johnson and Bradley, see Senate, Foreign Relations, *North Atlantic Treaty*, 147–55, 286–95. For Tydings's quotation, see ibid., 155. For views of Acheson and Harriman, see Senate, Foreign Relations, *Vandenberg Resolution*, 12–15, 220–22; see also the interesting comments by Senators Claude Pepper and William Fulbright (ibid., 244).

58. Ireland, *Creating the Entangling Alliance*. For Acheson's views, see Senate, Foreign Relations, *Vandenberg Resolution*, 213–15. For Acheson's haste, see L. Kaplan, *United States and NATO*, 119–20. For Harriman's recollection, see Thompson, *Truman Presidency*, 167.

59. For concerns about Germany, see Riddleberger to Acheson, 26 March and 2 Apr 49, *FRUS, 1949*, 3: 231, 234–35. For reports on Schuman and the French, see Notes by Kennan, 21 March 49, ibid., 3: 114. For Clay's assessment, see Caffery to Acheson, 22 March 49, ibid., 3: 115–18. For the talks in Washington between Bevin, Acheson, and Schuman, see 31 March–8 Apr 49, ibid., 3: 156–86; Secretary's Daily Mtgs., 4–8 Apr 49, RG 59, Executive Secretariat; Acheson, *Present at the Creation*, 286–90. For Acheson's quotation, see Acheson to Truman, 8 Apr 49, *FRUS, 1949*, 3: 175–76.

60. See the papers and documents in *FRUS, 1949*, 3: 138–55. For McCloy, see Secretary's Daily Mtg., 28 March 49, RG 59, Executive Secretariat; MemCon with the Pres by Acheson, 4 Apr 49, ibid.; Schwartz, *America's Germany*, 1–83.

61. *FRUS, 1949*, 3: 694–772; Murphy to Jessup, 19 March 49, RG 43, Jessup-Malik Conversations, box 304; Jessup to Bohlen, Murphy, and Thompson, 24 and 28 March 49, ibid.; Bohlen to Jessup, Kennan, Rusk et al., 15 Apr 49, ibid. For Army concerns about the costs of the airlift, see Royall to Acheson, 23 March 49, RG 330, box 37, CD 6-4-8.

62. Secretary's Daily Mtg., 22 March 49, *FRUS, 1949*, 3: 705–7; Ware Adams to Jessup, 15 Apr 49, ibid., 3: 856–59; Jessup to Acheson, 19 Apr 49, ibid., 3: 859–62; Nitze Oral History (HSTL), 123–25. For Clay's view, see *FRUS, 1949*, 3: 746–47; CIA, "Review of the World Situation," 17 May 49, HSTP, PSF, box 206; CIA, "The Soviet Position in Approaching the CFM," 18 May 49, ibid., box 256.

63. Jacob Beam, "U.S. Position in a CFM on Germany," 13 Apr 49, RG 43, Jessup-Malik Conversations, box 304; Office of German and Austrian Affairs, "U.S. Program for a CFM on Germany," 21 Apr 49, ibid.; Jessup to Byroade, 25 Apr 49, ibid.; Hickerson to Byroade, 26 Apr 49, ibid.; Jessup to Acheson et al., 7 May 49, ibid.

64. Summary of NSC Discussion, 18 May 49, RG 273. For the quotation, see "An Approach to the CFM," 11 May 49, *FRUS, 1949*, 3: 872–73; see also MemCon by Beam, 10 May 49, RG 43, Jessup-Malik Conversations, box 304; Johnson to Acheson, 14 May 49, RG 330, box 37, CD 6-4-8; CIA, "Review of the World Situation," 17 May 49, HSTP, PSF, box 206.

65. For the quotation, see CIA, "Review of the World Situation," 17 May 49, HSTP, PSF, box 206, p. 8; see also Office of German and Austrian Affairs, "U.S. Position at the Council of Foreign Ministers," 15 May 49, *FRUS, 1949*, 3: 900–902. For Kennan's lament, see Kennan to Acheson, 20 May 49, ibid., 3: 888–90. For the views of the British and French, see ibid., 3: 709–12, 724–28, 730–31, 748–50, 863–74, 867–72, 877–79, 881–84. Contrast my view with Gaddis's analysis stressing the significance of British and French pressure, see Gaddis, *Long Peace*, 65–66.

66. Senate, Foreign Relations, *Reviews of the World Situation*, 2–22. For Acheson's desire to lure Eastern Europe out of the Kremlin's grasp, see House of Representatives, International Relations, *Executive Session Hearings*, 39–46.

67. For developments at the meeting of foreign ministers, see *FRUS, 1949*, 3: 913–1040. For

assessments of the defensive orientation of Soviet diplomats, see Bohlen to Acheson, 9 June 49, RG 59, Bohlen Papers, box 1; CIA, "Review of the World Situation," 20 July 49, HSTP, PSF, box 250.

68. Senate, Foreign Relations, *Reviews of the World Situation*, 26–46; see also Kennan's report to the NSC, Minutes of the NSC, 2 June 49, RG 273.

69. Senate, Foreign Relations, *Reviews of the World Situation*, 41–42; Acheson to Embassy in France, 8 July 49, *FRUS, 1949*, 4: 308.

70. For Bradley's quotation, see Senate, Armed Services and Foreign Relations, *Military Assistance Program*, 89. For Acheson's great concern with the MAP, see MemCon with the Pres by Acheson, 19 Apr 49, RG 59, Executive Secretariat; Testimony by Acheson, 19 Apr 49, Senate, Foreign Relations, *Vandenberg Resolution*, 212–16; Acheson to Truman, 24 June 49, HSTP, PSF, box 145; Secretary's Daily Mtgs., 24 June–Sep 49, RG 59, Executive Secretariat.

71. See esp. the testimony of Acheson, Johnson, and Bradley, 8–10 Aug 49, Senate, Armed Services and Foreign Relations, *Military Assistance Program*, 7–23, 49–52, 91–109. For other unequivocal indications of the priority attached to thwarting internal subversion, see Butler to Reber, 23 March 49, RG 59, PPS, box 33; Testimony by Ernest Gross, 12 Apr 49, in Senate, Foreign Relations, *Vandenberg Resolution*, 188–89. For a systematic elaboration of the purposes of the MAP, see JCS 1868/62, "Program on Foreign Military Assistance," 7 March 49, RG 319, P&O, 092 TS; Lyman Lemnitzer, "Program for Foreign Military Assistance," 1 Apr 49, RG 330, box 24, CD 6-2-46; Foreign Assistance Correlation Committee, "Relationship of the MAP to U.S. Strategic Interests," 1 July 49, *FRUS, 1949*, 1: 348; NSC 52/3, "Governmental Programs in National Security and International Affairs for the Fiscal Year 1951," 29 Sep 49, ibid., 1: 389–90.

72. Pach, *Arming the Free World*, 219–26. L. Kaplan, *Community of Interests*, 41–49; *FRUS, 1949*, 1: 377–79, 398.

73. For overall statements of fundamental interests in the Eastern Mediterranean and the Middle East, see NSC 42/1, "U.S. Objectives with Respect to Greece and Turkey to Counter Soviet Threats to U.S. Security," 22 March 49, *FRUS, 1949*, 6: 269–79; DOS Policy Statement on Egypt, 5 May 49, ibid., 6: 208; Johnson to Acheson, 14 June 49, ibid., 6: 134–35.

74. For U.S. requirements and deficiencies at Cairo-Suez, see JLPC 416/36, "Correction of Deficiencies Revealed by the Limited Feasibility Test of ABC 101," 23 Dec 48, RG 218, CCS 381 USSR (3-2-46), sec. 26; JCS 1844/41, "Correction of Deficiencies . . . ," 18 June 49, ibid., sec. 33.

75. JCS 1920/1, DROPSHOT, 31 Jan 49, CCS 381 USSR (3-2-46), sec. 28; S. Ross, *American War Plans*, 122–23.

76. "Conference with British Chiefs of Staff," 3 Aug 49, RG 319, P&O, 092 EUR TS; Clark and Wheeler, *British Origins of Nuclear Strategy*, 91–122.

77. NSC 45/1, "Airfield Construction in the United Kingdom and the Cairo-Suez Area," 15 Apr 49, *FRUS, 1949*, 1: 285–87.

78. For Eisenhower's views on carriers and the Middle East, see Eisenhower, *Papers*, 10: 699–704, 831–36; Memo for Op-04 by Stokes, 25 June 49, NHC, SPD, box 250, A16-3.

79. "Conference with British Chiefs of Staff," 3 Aug 49, RG 319, P&O, 092 EUR TS.

80. CincNELM to JCS, 27 Apr 49, RG 218, CCS 381 USSR (3-2-46), sec. 31; Conolly to JCS, 13 Sep 49, NHC, SPD, box 254 (Spindles); Conolly to JCS, 23 Sep 49, ibid., box 250, A16-3.

81. For Wright's view, see *FRUS, 1949*, 6: 195, footnote 3.

82. "Policy Paper Prepared in the Department of State," 15 March 49, ibid., 6: 831–32; Webb to Truman, 27 May 49, ibid., 6: 1062–63; JCS, "Study of United States Strategic Objectives in Israel," 16 May 49, ibid., 6: 1011–12.

83. Conolly to Denfeld, 13 Sep 49, NHC, SPD, box 254 (Spindles); CIA, "Current Situation in Israel," 18 July 49, RG 330, box 132, CD 103-7-53. For similar British worries, see K. Helm to W. Strang, 11 Apr 50, in Bullen and Pelly, *Documents on British Policy Overseas*, 2: 40–43, esp. note 1.

84. For the quotations, see "Policy Paper Prepared in the Department of State," 15 March 49,

FRUS, 1949, 6: 831–32; Johnson to Acheson, 14 June 49, ibid., 6: 1134–35; see also Acheson to Johnson, 4 May 49, ibid., 6: 973; Acheson to Truman, 9 May 49, ibid., 6: 983–84; Memos by Webb, 23 and 26 May 49, ibid., 6: 1042, 1056; CIA, Intelligence Memorandum No. 180, 31 May 49, HSTP, PSF, box 145.

85. For Rusk's advice, see Secretary's Daily Mtg., 28 March 49, RG 59, Executive Secretariat. For Truman's disgust, see Truman to Mark Ethridge, 29 Apr 49, *FRUS, 1949*, 6: 957. The growing disillusionment with Israel is amply documented in ibid., 6: 881, 886, 890–92, 1072–75, 1109–10, 1124, 1146, 1237, 1307, 1312.

86. For the DOS concern with Egypt, see "Policy Statement on Egypt," 5 May 49, *FRUS, 1949*, 6: 208–16. For arms shipments and Egyptian internal security, see ibid., 6: 952–54, 1057–58, 1092, 1279, 1280, 1341–42. For DOS and Anglo-Egyptian base negotiations, see P. Hahn, "Strategy and Diplomacy," chap. 5. For the decision to carry on theater planning outside of Egypt, see *FRUS, 1949*, 6: 194–207, 218–19; documents, Apr 1949, RG 330, box 32, CD 6-4-32.

87. For the 1948 accord, see JCS 570/20, "Analysis of the Position of the U.S. with Respect to Military Rights on Foreign Territory," 31 March 49, RG 330, box 119, CD 27-1-21. For work at the base, see Symington to Ohly, 4 Feb 49, ibid., box 121, CD 27-1-2. For strategic operations, see ibid.; Forrestal to Acheson [ND], ibid.; Webb to Johnson, 15 June 49, ibid.; Halaby to Johnson, 28 June 49, ibid.

88. NSC 19/5, "U.S. Position on the Disposition of the Former Italian Colonies," 4 Aug 49, HSTP, PSF, box 206; Bolte to Bradley, 3 Aug 49, RG 319, P&O, 092 EUR TS. For background, see Gifford and Louis, *Decolonization and African Independence*, 159–84; *FRUS, 1949*, 4: 526–613.

89. Royall to Truman, including Message from President İnönü to Truman, 7 Jan 49, HSTP, PSF, box 189; Wadsworth to Acheson, 3 Feb 49, *FRUS, 1949*, 6: 1640–41; Kirk to Acheson, 12 Feb 49, RG 59, 867.20/2-1249; Radford to Conolly, 17 Jan 49, Radford Papers, Safe A, Drawer 1.

90. MemCon by Acheson, 17 Feb 49, *FRUS, 1949*, 4: 120; Butler to Theodore Achilles, 24 March 49, RG 59, PPS, box 33; Bohlen to Acheson, 31 March 49, RG 59, Bohlen Papers, box 4. For a good discussion of the organizational problems that would surround Turkish admission into various defensive pacts, see untitled memo by Craig, 26 Nov 49, RG 319, P&O, 092 TS.

91. Royall, "Presentation," 4 Jan 49, Eisenhower Papers, File 1652, box 42; NSC 42, "U.S. Objectives with Respect to Greece and Turkey to Counter Soviet Threats to U.S. Security," 4 March 49, RG 273, NSC; NSC 36/1, "Construction of Airfields and Stockpiling of Aviation Gasoline in Turkey," 15 Apr 49, *FRUS, 1949*, 6: 1655; ibid., 6: 1644–46. For Conolly's views, see Memo for the Record by J.R.D., 18 Feb 49, RG 319, P&O, 091 Turkey TS; Elliott B. Strauss to Op-30, 16 June 49, NHC, SPD, box 249, A14. For air plans, see C.V. Johnson to Op-30, 16 Sep 49, ibid., A8; Ohly to Thompson, 22 Nov 49, RG 59, Military Adviser to Near Eastern, South Asian, and African Affairs, box 1.

92. Memos by Acheson, 17 Feb, 9 March, and 12 Apr 49, *FRUS, 1949*, 4: 120, 177, 6: 1651–52; Acheson to Embassy in Turkey, 16 March 49, ibid., 4: 234–35; Acheson to Certain Diplomatic and Consular Offices, 23 March and 2 Apr 49, ibid., 4: 243–44, 270–71; NSC 36/1, "Construction of Airfields and Stockpiling of Aviation Gasoline in Turkey," 15 Apr 49, ibid., 6: 1655.

93. For Wilson's opinion, see Joseph Satterthwaite to Acheson, 31 March 49, RG 59, 711.67/3-3149. For Conolly's view, see untitled memo by Craig, 26 Nov 49, RG 319, P&O, 092 TS; see also Satterthwaite to Webb, 13 June 49, RG 59, 711.67/6-1549.

94. For Truman's views, see MemCon by Acheson, 28 Feb 49, *FRUS, 1949*, 4: 125; Truman to İnönü, 26 Apr 49, ibid., 6: 1656–57. For Acheson's feelings, see MemCon by Acheson, 12 Apr 49, ibid., 6: 1651–52; see also DOS Policy Statement, 5 May 49, ibid., 6: 1668–69.

95. CIA, "Review of the World Situation," 16 Feb 49, HSTP, PSF, box 205.

96. Acheson to Johnson, 10 May 49, RG 330, box 120, CD 27-1-12; Childs to Acheson, 23 May 49, *FRUS, 1949*, 6: 1598. For the temporary agreement, see ibid., 6: 1607–10.

97. Wiley to Acheson, 16 March, 29 Apr, and 12 July 49, *FRUS, 1949*, 6: 492–94, 514–16,

540; MemCon by Acheson, 14 March 49, ibid., 6: 489–92. For background, see Goode, *United States and Iran*, 8–57.

98. Acheson to Embassy in Iran, 8 and 18 Apr and 16 May 49, *FRUS, 1949*, 6: 501, 503, 519–21; NSC 54, "Position of the United States with Respect to Iran," 21 July 49, ibid., 6: 545–51.

99. CIA, "Review of the World Situation," 16 Feb 49, HSTP, PSF, box 205.

100. George McGhee to Webb and Rusk, 13 July 49, *FRUS, 1949*, 6: 1219–20; Acheson to Certain Diplomatic and Consular Offices, 16 Aug 49, ibid., 6: 1318.

101. MemCon by Acheson, 4 Apr 49, ibid., 6: 50–52; Secretary's Daily Mtg., 25 Apr 49, RG 59, Executive Secretariat.

102. See, e.g., John Leighton Stuart to Acheson, 16 and 28 March and 15 Apr 49, *FRUS, 1949*, 8: 183, 208, 240–41; Allison to Acheson, 30 March 49, ibid., 8: 210; Clark to Acheson, 5 and 18 May 49, ibid., 8: 293, 689–90; Harding and Yuan, *Sino-American Relations*, 59.

103. CIA, "Chinese Communist Capabilities for Control of All China," 10 Dec 48, HSTP, PSF, box 206; David Barr to Ray T. Maddocks, 18 Dec 48, RG 218, Leahy Papers, box 2.

104. Summary of NSC Discussion, 4 Feb 49, HSTP, PSF, box 220; Royall to Forrestal, 26 Jan 49, RG 319, P&O, 091 China TS; Maddocks to Royall, 2 Feb 49, ibid.; Forrestal to Souers, 2 Feb 49, ibid.; Royall to Forrestal, 3 Feb 49, RG 335, Draper/Voorhees Files, box 16 (014.1 Germany/Occupation); see also NSC 34/1, "United States Policy Toward China," 11 Jan 49, *FRUS, 1949*, 9: 474–75; see also Editorial Note, ibid., 9: 482–83.

105. Vandenberg, *Private Papers*, 530–31; Memo by Carter, 7 Feb 49, *FRUS, 1949*, 9: 486.

106. For the views of the JCS, see NSC 37 and NSC 37/3, "Strategic Importance of Formosa," 24 Nov 48 and 11 Feb 49, *FRUS, 1949*, 9: 261–62, 284–86. For Acheson's views, see Summary of NSC Discussions, 4 Feb and 4 March 49, HSTP, PSF, box 220; see also Minutes of Mtg. of PPS, 26 Jan 49, RG 59, PPS, box 32; CIA, "Probable Developments in Taiwan," 14 March 49, HSTP, PSF, box 256; Harding and Yuan, *Sino-American Relations*, 146–47.

107. For the quotation, see NSC 34/2, "United States Policy Toward China," 28 Feb 49, *FRUS, 1949*, 9: 494; see also Acheson to Ludden, 21 Feb 49, ibid., 8: 141–42; MemCon by Beam, 4 Apr 49, ibid., 7: 1140–41; Testimony by Acheson, 15 Feb 49, House of Representatives, International Relations, *Executive Session Hearings*, 43, 48, 58–59.

108. NSC 41, "United States Policy Regarding Trade with China," 28 Feb 49, *FRUS, 1949*, 9: 928–29; Acheson Testimony, 18 March 49, Senate, Foreign Relations, *Economic Assistance to China and Korea*, 30–31; Testimony by Acheson, 15 Feb 49, House of Representatives, International Relations, *Executive Session Hearings*, 58–59, 70–71.

109. NSC 34/2, "United States Policy Toward China," 28 Feb 49, *FRUS, 1949*, 9: 492–95; NSC 41, "United States Policy Regarding Trade with China," 28 Feb 49, ibid., 9: 827–33; Testimony by Acheson, 15 Feb 49, House of Representatives, International Relations, *Executive Session Hearings*, 48, 58; Testimony by Acheson and Walton Butterworth, 18 March 49, Senate, Foreign Relations, *Economic Assistance to China and Korea*, 34–36; Stuart to Acheson, 22 March and 15 June 49, *FRUS, 1949*, 8: 193, 385; Foy Kohler to Acheson, 19 Apr 49, ibid., 8: 250; CIA, "Prospects for Soviet Control of a Communist China," 15 Apr 49, HSTP, PSF, box 256; CIA, "Probable Developments in China," 16 June 49, ibid.; CIA, "Review of the World Situation," 20 July 49, ibid., box 250.

110. For different views of the wedge strategy and of the willingness of the Truman administration to accommodate the CCP, see, on the one hand, Warren Cohen's essay in Borg and Heinrichs, *Uncertain Years*, 15–32, and Gaddis, *Long Peace*, 147–94, and contrast them with Yuan Ming's essay in Harding and Yuan, *Sino-American Relations*, 143–54, and with G. Chang, *Friends and Enemies*, 5–80. My analysis coincides with the views of Yuan and Chang.

111. NSC 41, "United States Policy Regarding Trade with China," 28 Feb 49, *FRUS, 1949*, 9: 830–32; Acheson to Douglas, 22 June and 29 July 49, ibid., 9: 857, 867–68; Acheson to Cabot, 3 May 49, ibid., 9: 936–38; Robert R. West to MacArthur, 7 May 49, ibid., 9: 978; Secretary's Daily Mtg., 3 May 49, RG 59, Executive Secretariat.

112. For the quotation, see Office of Intelligence and Research, Division of Research for the Far East, "Problems of Domestic and Foreign Policy Confronting the Chinese Communists," 28 July 49, RG 330, box 73, CD 14-1-36; Cabot to Acheson, 16 July 49, *FRUS, 1949*, 8: 436–40; Clark to Acheson, 27 July 49, ibid., 8: 460; Clubb to Acheson, 11 Aug 49, ibid., 8: 482; Jones to Acheson, 16 Aug 49, ibid., 8: 500.

113. Stuart to Acheson, 24 June 49, *FRUS, 1949*, 9: 1106; Cabot to Acheson, 26 June 49, ibid., 9: 1109–10; McConaughy to Acheson, 17 July 49, ibid., 9: 952; MemCon by Webb, 1 Oct 49, ibid., 9: 1141; Blum, *Drawing the Line*, 81.

114. MemCon by Beam, 4 Apr 49, *FRUS, 1949*, 7: 1140–41; Acheson to Stuart, 13 May 49, ibid., 9: 22–23; MemCon by Acheson, 16 June 49, ibid., 9: 43; Acheson to Certain Diplomatic and Consular Offices, 22 June 49, ibid., 8: 702; MemCon by Sprouse, 6 Jan 49, ibid., 8: 5–6; Webb to Andrew B. Forster, 14 June 49, ibid., 8: 41–42.

115. Clubb to Webb, 1 June 49, ibid., 9: 359; Webb to Clubb, 14 June 49, ibid., 9: 384–85; Memo by Webb, 16 June 49, ibid., 9: 388.

116. Cabot to Butterworth, 11 May 49, ibid., 8: 309–10; Clubb to Acheson, 11 May 49, ibid., 8: 306; Barnett, *China*, 315–57. For recent assessments of the prospects for a rapprochement between the Chinese Communists and the Truman administration, see Ho, "Lost Chance"; Harding and Yuan, *Sino-American Relations*, 119–42.

117. For the quotation, see Smith to H. Kenaston Twitchell, 15 July 49, Smith Papers, box 98; see also Stuart to Acheson, 30 June 49, *FRUS, 1949*, 8: 767; Acheson to Stuart, 1 July 49, ibid., 8: 769; Stueck, *Road to Confrontation*, 121–26; Harding and Yuan, *Sino-American Relations*, 143–54.

118. For the quotation, see Smith to Twitchell, 15 Aug 49, Smith Papers, box 98. For Acheson's defense of the administration's case against McCarran's bill and the capitulation of its supporters, see Senate, Foreign Relations, *Economic Assistance to China and Korea*, 5–114; Vandenberg, *Private Papers*, 532–36.

119. For public opinion polls, see Gallup, *Poll*, 2: 818, 831, 834, 852; *Public Opinion Quarterly* 13 (Winter 1949–50): 722; see also Smith to Twitchell, 15 Aug 49, Smith Papers, box 98. For attitudes of interest groups, journalists, missionaries, etc., see N. Tucker, *Patterns in the Dust*, 80–172; Kusnitz, *Public Opinion and Foreign Policy*, 28–30.

120. Kennan to Marshall, 24 Nov 48, RG 59, PPS, box 33; Kennan to Acheson, 28 June 49, ibid.; PPS 45, "United States Policy Toward China in the Light of the Current Situation," 26 Nov 48, *FRUS, 1948*, 8: 215. For Truman's reluctance to speak out, see Marshall to Lovett, 26 Nov 48, ibid., 8: 220. For Acheson's unreadiness, see Senate, Foreign Relations, *Economic Assistance to China and Korea*, 42. For the *White Paper*, see DOS, *China White Paper*; Purifoy, *Truman's China Policy*, 125–31; Newman, "Self-Inflicted Wound."

121. DOS, *China White Paper*, xvi.

122. See, e.g., Senate, Foreign Relations, *Economic Assistance to China and Korea*, 35; Newman, "Self-Inflicted Wound"; Purifoy, *Truman's China Policy*, 135–36; Stueck, *Road to Confrontation*, 117–37; G. Chang, *Friends and Enemies*, 29–41.

123. Clark to Acheson, 9 Aug 49, *FRUS, 1949*, 8: 478; Acheson to Strong, 24 Aug 49, ibid., 8: 503. For similar statement by Acheson, see his testimony in Senate, Foreign Relations, *Economic Assistance to China and Korea*, 43.

124. For Truman's interest in providing aid to the resistance in the northwest and for his desire to abandon the wedge strategy, see Memo by Merchant, 24 Aug 49, *FRUS, 1949*, 9: 871. For Acheson's willingness to acquiesce to aid for the area of China, see MemCon with the Pres by Acheson, 18 Aug 49, RG 59, Executive Secretariat; Secretary's Daily Mtg., 17 and 29 Aug 49, ibid. For covert operations, see Leary and Stueck, "Chennault Plan." For an excellent analysis of developments in the summer of 1949, see Blum, *Drawing the Line*, 80–103, 125–42.

125. Merchant to Butterworth, 24 May 49, *FRUS, 1949*, 9: 337–41. For Acheson's response to the collapse of the resistance in the northwest, see Acheson to MacDonald, 8 Sep 49, ibid., 8: 523.

126. For reopening of the Taiwan question, see Webb to Edgar, 3 June 49, ibid., 9: 345; Draft Memo for Souers, 9 June 49, ibid., 9: 349–50. For Kennan's view, see PPS 53, "United States Policy Toward Formosa and Pescadores," 6 July 49, ibid., 9: 356–58; Kennan, "Estimate of the International Situation," 19 Sep 49, Kennan Papers, box 17; Minutes of Mtg. of PPS, 28 Sep 49, RG 59, PPS, box 32. For the views of Acheson and Rusk, see Secretary's Daily Mtgs., 11, 25, and 29 July and 31 Aug 49, ibid., Executive Secretariat. For DOS attitudes toward Taiwan issue, see DOS to NSC, 4 Aug 49, *FRUS, 1949*, 9: 369–71; MemCon by Freeman, 9 Sep 49, ibid., 9: 389; Report by Charles Yost, 16 Sep 49, ibid., 7: 1207. For JCS position, see NSC 37/7, "Position of the United States with Respect to Formosa," 22 Aug 49, ibid., 9: 378.

127. Jones to Acheson, 3 Sep 49, *FRUS, 1949*, 8: 519–21; Report by Yost, 16 Sep 49, ibid., 7: 1204–8.

128. For the quotation, see Blum, *Drawing the Line*, 92; see also Acheson to Douglas, 20 July 49, *FRUS, 1949*, 9: 51. For the views of other DOS officials, see Memo by Kennan, 8 July 49, ibid., 7: 1147; Paper Drafted by Davies, 7 July 49, ibid., 7: 1148–51; Jessup to Rusk, 12 July 49, ibid., 7: 1153–54; Draft by Rusk, 8 Sep 49, ibid., 7: 1196–97. For Smith's views, see Smith to Twitchell, 15 Aug 49, Smith Papers, box 98; Vandenberg, *Private Papers*, 536.

129. CIA, "Strategic Importance of the Far East to the US and the USSR," 4 May 49, HSTP, PSF, box 256; Kennan, "Where We Are Today," 21 Dec 48, Kennan Papers, box 17; MacArthur to JCS, 23 Dec 48, HSTP, PSF, box 182; NSC 49, "Strategic Evaluation of United States Security Needs in Japan," 9 June 49, *FRUS, 1949*, 7: 774–76.

130. CIA, "Strategic Importance of the Far East," 4 May 49, HSTP, PSF, box 256; CIA, "Relative US Security Interest in the European-Mediterranean Area and the Far East," 14 July 49, ibid., box 249; Bishop to Butterworth, 18 Feb 49, *FRUS, 1949*, 7: 660–63; Acheson to Certain Diplomatic Offices, 22 Apr and 8 May 49, ibid., 7: 713–14, 737.

131. Japanese Govt., Economic Stabilization Board, "Economic Rehabilitation Program of the Japanese Government: Summary of Report and Annexes," 6 Feb 49, RG 335, Draper/Voorhees Files, box 19; S. M. Fine to Draper, 9 Dec 48, ibid.; Memo for the Record by Lincoln, 11 Nov 48, RG 335, box 53; UN, ECAFE, *Economic Survey of Asia and the Far East* (1949), 414–17.

132. David M. Bane to Sebald [ND], *FRUS, 1948*, 6: 1051–54; Foster to Acheson, 13 May 49, *FRUS, 1949*, 7: 744–46.

133. UN, ECAFE, *Economic Survey of Asia and the Far East* (1949), 3–20, 293–313, 414–29.

134. Memo for the Record by Lincoln, 11 Nov 48, RG 335, box 53; Memo for the Record by Reid, 29 Nov 48, ibid., Draper/Voorhees Files, box 19; Memo for the Record [by Fine?], 8 Dec 48, ibid.; Joseph Dodge to Draper, 30 Dec 48, ibid.; Reid to Draper, 18 Feb 49, ibid.; Borden, *Pacific Alliance*, 88–94; T. Cohen and Passim, *Remaking Japan*, 429–39; Schonberger, *Aftermath of War*, 198–211.

135. For the U.S. interest in Japanese trade with Southeast Asia, see the important work by Schaller, *American Occupation of Japan*, 141–245; Borden, *Pacific Alliance*; Rotter, *Path to Vietnam*. For Korean rice and Japanese workers, see Dodge to Voorhees, 18 Aug 49, Voorhees Papers, box 4. For Korea and Japan, see Cumings, *Origins of the Korean War*, 2: 168–75.

136. Draper to Acheson, 11 Feb 49, RG 335, Draper/Voorhees Files, box 3; Ad Hoc Committee, "Study of United States Aid Program for the Far East," 16 Feb 49, RG 319, P&O, 092 Pacific TS.

137. For Army support of Korean aid, see the testimony of Generals W. E. Todd and T. S. Timberman, 12 July 49, Senate, Foreign Relations, *Economic Assistance to China and Korea*, 177–91. Defense officials also supported NSC 8/2, "Position of the United States with Respect to Korea," 22 March 49, *FRUS, 1949*, 7: 972–78; see also JCS 2032/3, "NSC 52—Governmental Programs in National Security and International Affairs for Fiscal Year 1951: General Instructions," 6 Aug 49, RG 319, P&O, 092 TS.

138. This paragraph is based primarily on material in *FRUS, 1949*, 7: 940–1076. For DOS desires to move cautiously regarding withdrawal, see esp. Saltzman to Draper, 25 Jan 49, ibid., 7: 944–45; Acheson to Johnson, 10 May 49, ibid., 7: 1016. For Acheson's concern with the size of

the military advisory group and with the adequacy of the transfer of military equipment, see esp. Acheson to Embassy in Korea, 28 Apr 49, ibid., 7: 997; Minutes of the NSC Mtg., 22 March 49, RG 273. For military assistance, see also Sawyer, *Military Advisors in Korea*, 34–95. For the decision on economic aid, see Secretary's Daily Mtg., 24 May 49, RG 59, Executive Secretariat. For the U.S. presence, see Halliday and Cumings, *Korea*, esp. 48–54. For the concern with credibility, see Matray, *Reluctant Crusade*, 175–99.

139. For the quotations, see Lacy to Reid, 13 May 49, RG 59, PSA Division, box 5; Lacy to Wedemeyer, 13 June 49, RG 319, P&O, 092 TS; see also Reed to Butterworth, 16 and 17 May 49, RG 59, PSA Division, box 10; "Outline of Far Eastern and Asian Policy for Review with the President" [no signature] [ND], ibid., box 5.

140. Acheson to Consulate at Hanoi, 20 May 49, *FRUS, 1949*, 7: 29–30. For the type of information that the DOS used to reach its conclusions regarding Ho, see, e.g., Webb to Embassy in India, 18 June 49, ibid., 7: 60; Acheson to Embassy in India, 30 June 49, ibid., 7: 670.

141. PPS 51, "United States Policy Toward Southeast Asia," 29 March 49, *PPS Papers*, 3: 39–42, 48–49, 52–54. For fear of the ramifications of Communist control of China, see also, e.g., MemCon by Sprouse, 18 January 49, RG 59, PSA Division, box 6; MemCon by Reed, 23 Feb 49, ibid.

142. For the U.S. interpretation of the 8 March accords, see esp. Butterworth to Webb, 2 June 49, RG 59, PSA Division, box 5.

143. Charlton Ogburn to Reed and O'Sullivan, 28 June 49, ibid.; Reed to Davies, 9 May 49, ibid.; Reed to Butterworth, 16 May 49, ibid., box 10; Blum, *Drawing the Line*, 118–23; Hess, *United States' Emergence as a Southeast Asian Power*, 322–28.

144. For the quotation, see Webb to Embassy, 6 June 49, *FRUS, 1949*, 7: 41–43. For an extremely revealing illustration of Acheson's views, see MemCon, 15 Sep 49, RG 43, Post-CFM 1949 Mtgs., box 312; see also Acheson to Consulate General at Saigon, 10 May 49, *FRUS, 1949*, 7: 24; Rotter, *Path to Vietnam*, 95–102.

145. For the quotation, see MemCon by Butterworth, 12 Sep 49, *FRUS, 1949*, 7: 1202–3; see also McMahon, *Colonialism and Cold War*, 251–303. For Acheson's application of pressure, see Acheson to Consulate General at Batavia, 2 and 7 Apr 49, *FRUS, 1949*, 7: 357, 364. For fear of the left, see, e.g., Merle Cochran to Acheson, 25 March 49, ibid., 7: 345–46.

146. For the quotation, see Lacy to Wedemeyer, 13 June 49, RG 319, P&O, 092 TS; Webb to Consulate General, 7 May and 10 June 49, *FRUS, 1949*, 7: 419, 421–22.

147. Memo by the DOS to the French Foreign Office, 6 June 49, *FRUS, 1949*, 7: 42; Lacy to Reed, 13 May 49, RG 59, PSA Division, box 5; Quarterly Military Survey by Edward R. Thorpe, 1 July 49, ibid., box 19; Reed to Butterworth, 17 May 49, ibid., box 5.

148. Reed to Bell, 6 May 49, RG 59, PSA Division, box 14 (folder dated 1947).

149. For the U.S. assessment, see Sebald to Acheson, 26 Jan 49, *FRUS, 1949*, 7: 628–30.

150. CIA, "Review of the World Situation," 20 July and 17 Aug 49, HSTP, PSF, box 250. For the impact of Dodge's program, see Schonberger, *Aftermath of War*, 211–25.

151. Bishop to Butterworth, 18 Feb 49, *FRUS, 1949*, 7: 660–63; Butterworth to Webb, 19 May 49, ibid., 7: 752; Sebald to Acheson, 20 Aug 49, ibid., 7: 832–36.

152. MemCon by H. Owen, 8 July 49, RG 59, PSA Division, box 5; Owen, "Department of State Views Concerning Certain Economic Aspects of U.S. Policy with Respect to South and East Asia," 13 Sep 49, ibid.; Butterworth to Webb, 5 May 49, ibid.

153. For Truman and the Philippines, see MemCons with the Pres by Acheson, 25 Apr and 11 July 49, RG 59, Executive Secretariat; Johnson to Souers, 10 June 49, RG 330, box 32, CD 6-4-42; Jessup to Rusk, 12 July 49, *FRUS, 1949*, 7: 1153–54; Butterworth to Webb, 19 May 49, ibid., 7: 752–53; Reed to Butterworth, 17 May 49, RG 59, PSA Division, box 5; Memo by Kennan, 8 July 49, *FRUS, 1949*, 7: 1147–51.

154. For the rejection of a Marshall Plan for Asia, see Ogburn, "Draft of . . . Instructions to American Diplomatic and Consular Officers in the Far East to Assist in Discussions of the Possi-

bilities of and Limitations upon US Financial and Economic Assistance," 21 Feb 49, RG 59, PSA Division, box 6; MemCon by Butterworth, 12 Sep 49, *FRUS, 1949*, 7: 1200–1204; Memo by O'Sullivan, 28 Sep 49, ibid., 7: 83–89.

155. Acheson to Embassy in Thailand, 25 July 49, *FRUS, 1949*, 7: 1175; Acheson to Embassy in Korea, 29 July 49, ibid., 7: 1178; Acheson to Embassy in Philippines, 19 Aug 49, ibid., 7: 1189.

156. MemCon with the Pres by Acheson, 14 July 49, RG 59, Executive Secretariat.

157. First, however, Acheson wished to ascertain the views of the JCS. See MemCon with the Pres, 16 Sep 49, ibid.

158. Reed to Butterworth, 17 May 49, RG 59, PSA Division, box 5; Blum, *Drawing the Line*, 125–220.

159. Acheson to Douglas, 20 July 49, *FRUS, 1949*, 9: 51; Blum, *Drawing the Line*, 92, 143–60.

160. "The President's Midyear Economic Report," 11 July 49, in *PPP:HST* (1949), 357–58.

161. Memo for the Pres [ND], HSTP, PSF, box 150; "Notes on 1951 Military Budget Problems" [no signature], 25 Apr 49, RG 51, BOB, Series 47.8A, box 50.

162. Pace to Johnson, 2 May 49, RG 51, BOB, Series 47.8A, box 50; National Security Branch of BOB to Pace, 11 May 49, ibid.; Report on Mtg. with the SecDef by G. E. Ramsey, 12 May 49, ibid.; McNeil to Johnson, 11 May 49, RG 330, box 16, CD 5-1-46.

163. Johnson to Pace, 19 May 49, RG 51, BOB, Series 47.8A, box 51; Rearden, *Formative Years*, 369–72.

164. Statement of the Pres [1 July 49], HSTP, PSF, box 150; Truman to Souers, 1 July 49, *FRUS, 1949*, 1: 350–52; NSC 52/1, "Governmental Programs in National Security and International Affairs for the Fiscal Year 1951," 8 July 49, ibid., 1: 352–53.

165. Truman to Souers, 1 July 49, *FRUS, 1949*, 1: 350–51; "Annual Message to Congress on the State of the Union," 5 Jan 49, *PPP:HST* (1949), 3–6; McCoy, *Presidency of Truman*, 163–80.

166. Pace to Truman, 22 and 30 June 49, RG 51, BOB, Series 47.8A, box 51; MemCon with the Pres by Acheson, 7 June 49, RG 59, Executive Secretariat.

167. Kohler to Acheson, 6 Apr 49, *FRUS, 1949*, 5: 603–9; Reinhardt to Kennan, 4 May 49, ibid., 1: 294–95; Memo by Butler, 9 June 49, ibid., 1: 327; Kennan to Thompson, 3 May 49, RG 59, PPS, box 33; Minutes of the PPS, 14 Sep 49, ibid., box 32; Kennan [?] to Bohlen, 15 March 49, RG 59, Bohlen Papers, box 4.

168. Office of Intelligence and Research, "Soviet Internal Situation," *FRUS, 1949*, 5: 624–27; CIA, "Possibility of Direct Soviet Military Action During 1949," HSTP, PSF, box 256. For Bradley's view, see Senate, Armed Services and Foreign Relations, *Military Assistance Program*, 98–99. For British intelligence, see A. Franklin Kibler to Bolte, 10 June 49, RG 319, P&O, 092 EUR TS. For Louis Johnson's view, see his address, 13 June 49, Johnson papers, box 140.

169. For Soviet military strength in 1949, see the figures in *FRUS, 1951*, 1: 494–95; Foster Adams to Johnson, 10 Aug 49, RG 330, box 132, CD 103-7-55; "Military Budgets of Selected Countries," 2 Aug 49, ibid.; Intelligence Division, "Briefing Report for General Handy," 22 Aug 49, RG 319, P&O, 319.25 TS; JIC 435/21, "Soviet Capabilities and Probable Courses of Action, 1952," 16 May 49, ibid., 350.05 TS.

170. CIA, "Soviet Air Forces," 25 July 49, HSTP, PSF, box 187; "Intelligence Presentation by Director, CIA, Before the JCS," 31 May 49, Eisenhower Papers, File 1652, box 63; JIC 435/21, "Soviet Capabilities and Probable Courses of Action, 1952," RG 319, P&O, 350.05 TS; JIC 439/5, "Intelligence Aspects of JCS 1952/1, Evaluation of Current Strategic Air Offensive Plans," 15 Feb 49, RG 218, CCS 373 (10-23-48), sec. 1; General Planners' Conference, 1 Sep 49, NHC, SPD, box 251, A19.

171. W. S. Post, Jr., to Op-302B, 25 Aug 49, NHC, SPD, box 249, A8; G. M. Slonim to Op-30, ND [Aug 1949], ibid.

172. JIC 435/21, "Soviet Capabilities and Probable Courses of Action, 1952," 16 May 49,

RG 319, P&O, 350.05 TS; Intelligence Division, "Briefing Report for General Handy," 22 Aug 49, ibid., 319.25 TS. For the full report of the DOS, see Office of Intelligence and Research, "Soviet Internal Situation," 1 July 49, RG 330, box 3, CD 2-2-38.

173. For belief in a protracted war, see, e.g., Interdepartmental Working Group, Staff Paper for the NSRB and NSC, "Basic U.S. Security Resources Assumptions," 1 June 49, *FRUS, 1949*, 1: 345.

174. CIA, "Possibility of Direct Soviet Military Action During 1949," 3 May 49, RG 330, box 132, CD 103-7-40.

175. For concern with the Soviet atomic program, see Hillenkoetter to Souers, 20 Apr 49, ibid., box 61, CD 11-1-2; Denfeld to Johnson, 30 June 49, ibid. For the proposal to increase U.S. capabilities, see Truman to Souers, 26 July 49, *FRUS, 1949*, 1: 501–2; Rearden, *Formative Years*, 440–44.

176. Memo for the Chief of Staff by Bolte, 18 Aug 49, RG 319, P&O, 092 TS; JCS 2032/4, "NSC 52—Governmental Programs in National Security," 23 Aug 49, ibid.; Rearden, *Formative Years*, 371–76.

177. JCS 2032/3 and 2032/4, "Governmental Programs in National Security," 6 and 23 Aug 49, RG 319, P&O, 092 TS. The quotation is on p. 59-e of JCS 2032/3. For the discussion over commitments, see Memo for the Chief of Staff by Bolte, 9 Aug 49, ibid.

178. NSC 52/3, "Governmental Programs in National Security," 29 Sep 49, *FRUS, 1949*, 1: 385–93; Secretary's Daily Mtg., 9 Sep 49, RG 59, Executive Secretariat.

179. Nourse to NSC, 30 Sep 49, *FRUS, 1949*, 1: 394–96; "Views of Acting Secretary of the Treasury," 29 Sep 49, ibid., 1: 393–94.

180. CIA, "Relative US Security Interest in the European-Mediterranean Area and the Far East," 14 July 49, HSTP, PSF, box 249.

181. Ibid.; CIA, "Review of the World Situation," 20 Apr 49, ibid., box 206.

182. For CIA operations in Syria, see Little, "Cold War and Covert Action."

183. CIA, "Review of the World Situation," 20 Apr 49, HSTP, PSF, box 206 (pp. 4 and 9 for the quotations); CIA, "Relative US Security Interest in the European-Mediterranean Area and the Far East," 14 July 49, ibid., box 249; CIA, "Strategic Importance of the Far East to the United States and the USSR," 4 May 49, RG 319, P&O, 350.05 TS.

Chapter 8

1. Donovan, *Conflict and Crisis*, 114–27; McCoy, *Presidency of Truman*, 163–90; Hamby, *Beyond the New Deal*, 267–402.

2. For Acheson's quotation, see Minutes of the PPS, 11 Oct 49, NA, RG 59, PPS, box 32; see also Kennan, "Estimate of the International Situation," 19 Sep 49, Kennan Papers, box 17.

3. For the realization that these issues required close scrutiny, see Minutes of the PPS, 11 Oct 49, RG 59, PPS, box 32; Secretary's Daily Mtg., 13 Oct 49, ibid., Executive Secretariat.

4. Oshinsky, *Conspiracy So Immense*, 72–157; Griffith, *Politics of Fear*, 27–114.

5. Many of these points will be elaborated on later in the chapter, but see Acheson, *Present at the Creation*, 373–74; Lilienthal, *Journals*, 576; Rearden, *Formative Years*, 526–27, 539–42, 547–48; Heller, *Truman White House*, 12.

6. Kennan, *Memoirs, 1925–1950*, 474–96; Acheson, *Present at the Creation*, 347–48; Nitze, *From Hiroshima to Glasnost*, 85–87.

7. NSC 68 may be found in *FRUS, 1950*, 1: 234–92; see also Nitze, *From Hiroshima to Glasnost*, 93–100.

8. Bullock, *Bevin*, 704–9; Hogan, *Marshall Plan*, 238–47; Milward, *Reconstruction of Western Europe*, 335–51; Dept. of Commerce, *Balance of Payments, 1949–1951*, 5–7.

9. Satterthwaite to Perkins, 9 Aug 49, *FRUS, 1949*, 4: 805; see also Harriman to Acheson, 25 June 49, ibid., 4: 792–93; Douglas to Acheson, 19 July 49, ibid., 4: 804; Memo by Leonard Weiss, 29 July 49, ibid., 1: 710–13.

10. For the quotation, see CIA, "Review of the World Situation," 20 July 49, HSTP, PSF, box 250; Harriman to Hoffman and Acheson, 12 March 49, *FRUS, 1949*, 4: 375–77; Harriman to ECA Mission, 25 June 49, ibid., 4: 403–5. For the different reactions of the United Kingdom and the rest of Western Europe to the American recession, see Milward, *Reconstruction of Western Europe*, 335–61.

11. Douglas to Acheson, 19 July 49, *FRUS, 1949*, 4: 804; Secretary's Daily Mtg., 25 Aug 49, RG 59, Executive Secretariat; CIA, "Review of the World Situation," 15 June 49, HSTP, PSF, box 206.

12. Ohly to Webb, 1 Sep 49, RG 218, CCS 091.3 Great Britain (9-1-49); Ohly to Gruenther, 1 Sep 49, ibid.

13. Secretary's Daily Mtgs., Aug–Oct 1949, RG 59, Executive Secretariat; MemCons with the Pres, 11 and 18 Aug 49, ibid.; Milward, *Reconstruction of Western Europe*, 282–98; Hogan, *Marshall Plan*, 238–92.

14. Bullock, *Bevin*, 703–20; Hogan, *Marshall Plan*, 243–55; Rotter, *Path to Vietnam*, 141–53.

15. Webb to Kennan, 26 Aug 49, *FRUS, 1949*, 4: 820–21; Joint Communiqué, 12 Sep 49, ibid., 4: 833–39; Secretary's Daily Mtgs., 29 Aug–12 Sep 49, RG 59, Executive Secretariat; Hogan, *Marshall Plan*, 262–64; Milward, *Reconstruction of Western Europe*, 292.

16. PPS 55, "Outline: Study of U.S. Stance Toward Question of European Union," 7 July 49, *PPS Papers*, 3: 82–100; Minutes of the PPS, 13 and 14 June and 2 and 12 Sep 49, RG 59, PPS, box 32; T. H. Landon to Gruenther, 2 Sep 49, RG 218, CCS 091.3 Great Britain (9-1-49); Mtg. of the Combined Policy Committee, 13 Sep 49, *FRUS, 1949*, 1: 520–21.

17. Minutes of the PPS, 7 Sep and 11 and 27 Oct 49, RG 59, PPS, box 32; Secretary's Daily Mtgs., 3 and 26 Oct 49, RG 59, Executive Secretariat.

18. For Nitze, Acheson, and Kennan, see Minutes of the PPS, 11 and 31 Oct and 1 Nov 49, RG 59, PPS, box 32. For business periodicals, see *Fortune* 38, 39, and 40 (1948–49); *Nation's Business* 36 and 37 (1948–49); Proceedings of the Annual Convention of the American Bankers Association, 1948 and 1949, in *Commercial and Financial Chronicle* 168 and 170 (7 Oct 48 and 10 Nov 49); *Federal Reserve Bulletin* 34 and 35 (1948 and 1949). The articles in *Nation's Agriculture* 23 and 24 (1948–49) placed a greater stress on the importance of foreign markets to U.S. economic well-being.

19. *PPP:HST* (1949), 356–67; ibid. (1950), 18–31.

20. Harriman Testimony, 22 Feb 50, House of Representatives, Foreign Affairs, *To Amend the Economic Cooperation Act of 1948*, 45–46; Hoffman Testimony, 21 Feb 50, ibid., 11–12; Acheson Testimony, 21 Feb 50, ibid., 13–16; Hoffman Testimony, 7 Feb 50, Senate, Foreign Relations, *Executive Sessions*, 2: 174–97. For the quotation, see BOB, "Suggestions for the Discussion with Gordon Gray," 14 Apr 50, Elsey Papers, box 59.

21. Acheson to Truman, 16 Feb 50, *FRUS, 1950*, 1: 834–41; the quotation is on p. 835. For the geopolitical and strategic ramifications of the dollar gap, see also Kennan to Acheson, 17 Feb 50, ibid., 1: 165–66; CIA, "Review of the World Situation," 18 Jan 50, HSTP, PSF, box 250. For the improvement in the United Kingdom's balance of payments, see Dept. of Commerce, *Balance of Payments, 1949–1951*, 8–9. Contrast my geopolitical interpretation with the Kolkos' more structural analysis and McCormick's world systems approach. Kolko and Kolko, *Limits of Power*, 453–76; McCormick, *America's Half-Century*, 88–98.

22. *FRUS, 1949*, 4: 651–91.

23. Bruce to Acheson, 22 and 23 Sep 49, ibid., 4: 661–65.

24. Acheson to Webb and Rusk, 26 Sep 49, ibid., 4: 339; MemCon Prepared in the DOS, 15 Sep 49, ibid., 4: 657–58.

25. Adenauer, *Memoirs*, 176–208; Prittie, *Adenauer*, 124–70; Bark and Gress, *From Shadow to Substance*, 250–57; Schwartz, *America's Germany*, 61–83.

26. Minutes of the PPS, 11 Oct 49, RG 59, PPS, box 32; Kennan, "Estimate of the International Situation," 19 Sep 49, Kennan Papers, box 17; Kennan to Bohlen, 12 Oct 49, RG 59, Bohlen Papers, box 1.

27. Paper Prepared in the DOS, 5 Nov 49, *FRUS, 1949*, 3: 297–99.

28. Acheson to Bruce, 30 Oct 49, ibid., 3: 623–24; CIA, "Review of the World Situation," 16 Nov 49, HSTP, PSF, box 207.

29. Bullock, *Bevin*, 736–39; Acheson, *Present at the Creation*, 337–43; Bruce Diary, 8–11 Nov 49, Bruce Papers; Acheson to Truman and Webb, 11 Nov 49, *FRUS, 1949*, 3: 305–6; Adenauer, *Memoirs*, 206–8; Schwartz, *America's Germany*, 75–80.

30. Adenauer, *Memoirs*, 208–31. For French concerns, see, e.g., MemCon by Perkins, 16 Nov 49, *FRUS, 1949*, 3: 318; Acheson to Truman and Webb, 11 Nov 49, ibid., 3: 306.

31. Minutes of the PPS, 12 and 17 Oct 49, RG 59, PPS, box 32; Harry Schwartz to Battle, 17 Oct 49, ibid., box 33.

32. Summary Record of a Mtg. of U.S. Ambassadors at Paris, 21–22 Oct 49, *FRUS, 1949*, 4: 472–96; the quotation is on p. 494.

33. Perkins to Acheson, Webb, and Hoffman, 22 Oct 49, ibid., 4: 343–44; Hogan, *Marshall Plan*, 273–75.

34. Harriman to Acheson, 6 Nov 49, *FRUS, 1949*, 4: 440–43; Harriman to Acheson and Perkins, 29 Nov 49, ibid., 4: 453–54; MemCon by McCloy, 20 Jan 50, ibid., 3: 1608–9; Hogan, *Marshall Plan*, 279–309; Newton, "1949 Sterling Crisis," 169–83.

35. Acheson Testimony, 10 Jan 50, Senate, Foreign Relations, *Reviews of the World Situation*, 113–17; Acheson to Douglas and Perkins, 24 Oct 49, *FRUS, 1949*, 4: 345; Acheson to Holmes, 15 Dec 49, ibid., 4: 360–62.

36. Webb to Acheson, 24 Sep 49, *FRUS, 1949*, 4: 666; PPS 55, "U.S. Stance Toward Question of European Union," 7 July 49, *PPS Papers*, 3: 97–99; Carlton Savage, "Principles Developed During Discussions on European Integration," 22 June 49, RG 59, PPS, box 32.

37. Bolte to Gruenther, 26 July 49, RG 319, P&O, 092 Europe TS; "Conference with British Chiefs of Staff," 3 Aug 49, ibid.; Kibler to Bolte, 28 Jan 50, RG 218, Bradley Papers, box 2; Holmes to Acheson, 28 Sep 49, *FRUS, 1949*, 4: 340. For overall U.S.–United Kingdom relations, see also Holmes to Acheson, 7 Jan 50, ibid., 3: 1599–1604; Perkins to Acheson, 24 Jan 50, ibid., 3: 1610–15.

38. Minutes of the PPS, 24 Jan 50, *FRUS, 1950*, 3: 617–22; see also Kennan to Bohlen, 12 Oct 49, RG 59, Bohlen Papers, box 1.

39. Secretary's Daily Mtgs., 1, 15, and 28 Dec 49, RG 59, Executive Secretariat; L. Kaplan, *Community of Interests*, 51–70.

40. JCS 1868/103, "Extent of U.S. Participation in Defense Planning for Western Europe (Western Union)," 26 Aug 49, RG 319, P&O, 381 Europe TS. For demolition planning and capabilities, see Schuyler to Bolte, 4 Oct 49, ibid. For new deployments to Europe, see "Summary" by Bolte, 18 Jan 50, ibid.

41. Minutes of the PPS, 16 Dec 49, *FRUS, 1949*, 1: 414–15; Acheson Testimony, 10 Jan 50, Senate, Foreign Relations, *Reviews of the World Situation*, 122; Bradley to Tydings, 25 Aug 49, RG 319, P&O, 092 TS; L. Kaplan, *Community of Interests*, 71–79.

42. For Acheson's quotation and Kennan's thinking, see Minutes of the PPS, 18 Oct 49, RG 59, PPS, box 32. For the testimony of Acheson and McCloy, see Senate, Foreign Relations, *Reviews of the World Situation*, 113–14, 221. For DOS concerns about public discussion of the German rearmament issue, see MemCon with the Pres, 17 Nov 49, RG 59, Executive Secretariat; Perkins to Acheson, 11 Oct 49, *FRUS, 1949*, 3: 285–86; Byroade to McCloy, 21 Nov 49, ibid., 3: 340–42.

43. McCloy Testimony, 25 Jan 50, Senate, Foreign Relations, *Reviews of the World Situation*, 204–6; Kennan to Acheson, 6 Jan 50, *FRUS, 1950*, 1: 129; Schwartz, *America's Germany*, 90–93.

44. See the tables in Wallich, *Mainsprings of the German Revival*, 80–81, 239–40; see also Mayer, *German Recovery*, 50; Hardach, "Marshall Plan in Germany," 466–77; CIA, "Reviews of the World Situation," 16 Nov and 21 Dec 49, HSTP, PSF, boxes 207 and 250.

45. Minutes of the PPS, 11 Oct 49, RG 59, PPS, box 32; Nitze, "Relationship of Strategic and Theater Nuclear Forces," 124–25.

46. For ECA, see Hogan, *Marshall Plan*, 293–335. For DOS, see Minutes of the PPS, 24 Jan 50, *FRUS, 1950*, 1: 617–22; MemCon by Wayne G. Jackson, 7 March 50, ibid., 3: 638–42. For Army, see Collins to Handy, 10 March 50, Voorhees Papers, box 4; Voorhees to Matthews, 23 March 50, ibid.

47. Herken, *Winning Weapon*; Messer, "America's 'Sacred Trust.' "

48. K. Condit, *History of the JCS*, 530–33; D. Rosenberg, "U.S. Nuclear Stockpile"; Lilienthal to Truman, 18 Nov 49, HSTP, PSF, box 182.

49. Truman to Souers, 26 July 49, *FRUS, 1949*, 1: 501–2.

50. Memos by Gordon Arneson, ND [early Aug 1949] and 10 Aug 49, ibid., 1: 507, 512; Kennan to Acheson, Webb, and Rusk, 3 Aug 49, ibid., 1: 507–9.

51. Hewlett and Duncan, *Atomic Shield*, 273–304; Gowing, *Independence and Deterrence*, 241–72.

52. MemCon by Arneson, 6 July 49, *FRUS, 1949*, 1: 471–74; Mtg. at Blair House, 14 July 49, ibid., 1: 476–80.

53. Memo by Arneson, ND [mid-Aug 1949], ibid., 1: 514; Lilienthal, *Journals*, 576.

54. For JCS stress on cost efficiency of atomic weapons, see "Report to the President by the Special Committee of the NSC on the Proposed Acceleration of the Atomic Energy Program," 10 Oct 49, *FRUS, 1949*, 1: 561.

55. Lilienthal, *Journals*, 576, 614, 615.

56. Stein, *American Civil-Military Decisions*, 496–513; K. McFarland, "1949 Revolt of the Admirals."

57. See, e.g., the testimony of Admirals W. H. P. Blandy, Arthur W. Radford, Louis E. Denfeld, and Ralph A. Ofstie, in House of Representatives, Armed Services, *National Defense Program*, 201–36, 39–107, 349–64, 183–93.

58. Testimony by Bradley and Johnson, in ibid., 515–41, 606–35.

59. "Report to the President by the Special Committee of the NSC on the Proposed Acceleration of the Atomic Energy Program," 10 Oct 49, *FRUS, 49*, 1: 561–62; WSEG, "Extract of Study on the Tactical Use of the Atomic Bomb," 8 Nov 49, RG 319, P&O, 471.6 TS.

60. See, e.g., Office of Intelligence and Research, Division of Research for Europe, "Soviet Internal Situation," 1 July 49, *FRUS, 1949*, 5: 627; PPS 58, "Political Implications of Detonation of Atomic Bomb by the USSR," 16 Aug 49, ibid., 1: 515.

61. "Elsey's Notes on Soviet Bomb Explosion," 24 Sep 49, Ayers Papers, box 4; *Public Opinion Quarterly* 14 (Spring 1950): 182; Boyer, *Bomb's Early Light*, 334–40. For comments on the calm reaction in Western Europe and the United States, see Summary Record of Mtg., 21–22 Oct 49, *FRUS, 1949*, 4: 475–76; JIC 502, "Implications of Soviet Possession of Atomic Weapons," 9 Feb 50, RG 218, CCS 471.6 USSR (11-8-49), sec. 1.

62. For Acheson's estimates, see MemCon by Arneson, 6 July 49, *FRUS, 1949*, 1: 471–72; Mtg. of the Joint Congressional Committee on Atomic Energy, 20 July 49, ibid., 1: 491. For some assessments of the impact of the atomic bomb on Soviet capabilities and intentions, see War Dept. Intelligence Division, "Comments on JCS 2084" [late Nov 1949], RG 319, P&O, 471.6 TS; CIA, "Review of the World Situation," 15 March 50, HSTP, PSF, box 250; CIA, "Estimates of the Effects of the Soviet Possession of the Atomic Bomb Upon the Security of the United States and Upon the Possibilities of Direct Soviet Military Action," 10 Feb 50, RG 330, box 61, CD 11-1-2.

63. For the importance of the atomic monopoly in U.S. thinking, note how Acheson began his most important memo on the H-bomb decision. Memo by Acheson, 20 Dec 49, *FRUS, 1949*, 1: 612; see also Nitze, "Military Power."

64. Secretary's Daily Mtgs., 30 Sep, 13 Oct, and 21 Nov 49, RG 59, Executive Secretariat; Minutes of the PPS, Oct–Dec 1949, ibid., PPS, box 32; CIA, "Review of the World Situation," 19 Oct 49, HSTP, PSF, box 206.

65. "Report to the President by the Special Committee of the NSC on the Proposed Acceleration of the Atomic Energy Program," 10 Oct 49, *FRUS, 1949*, 1: 561–64 (the quotation is on p. 562); *PPP:HST* (1949), 522.

66. Hewlett and Duncan, *Atomic Shield*, 362–409; D. Rosenberg, "American Atomic

Strategy," 77–84; Bernstein, "Truman and the H-Bomb," 12–18; Bundy, *Danger and Survival*, 199–214; York, *Advisors*, 20–28, 41–74.

67. In addition to the citations in the previous note, see Nitze Oral History (Air Force), 231–37. For his published account, see Nitze, *From Hiroshima to Glasnost*, 87–92.

68. For the excellent interpretations, see references in the previous two notes. See also the Statement Appended to the Report of the General Advisory Committee, 30 Oct 49, *FRUS, 1949*, 1: 571–72; Lilienthal to Truman, 9 Nov 49, ibid., 1: 579–84.

69. Memo Circulated by the Defense Members of the Working Group of the Special Committee of the NSC, ND [mid-Dec 1949], ibid., 1: 605–9; JCS to Johnson, 23 Nov 49, ibid., 1: 595–96.

70. Minutes of the PPS, 3 Nov 49, ibid., 1: 574–76; MemCon by Acheson, 7 Nov 49, ibid., 1: 214; Memo by Webb, 3 Dec 49, ibid., 1: 600; Minutes of the PPS, 11 Oct 49, RG 59, Bohlen Papers, box 1.

71. For Kennan's views, see Minutes of the PPS, 3 Nov and 16 Dec 49, *FRUS, 1949*, 1: 573–74, 416; Memo by Kennan, 20 Jan 50, *FRUS, 1950*, 1: 22–44; Kennan to Acheson, 17 Feb 50, ibid., 1: 161–65; PPS 55, "U.S. Stance Toward Question of European Union," 7 July 49, *PPS Papers*, 3: 82–100.

72. In addition to the references in the previous note, see Minutes of the PPS, Oct–Dec 1949, RG 59, PPS, box 32; Memos by Arneson, Rusk, and Hickerson, 29 Dec 49 and 6 and 11 Jan 50, *FRUS, 1950*, 1: 4–8, 9, 12; Kennan to Acheson, 6 Jan 50, ibid., 1: 127–28; Acheson Testimony, 10 Jan 50, Senate, Foreign Relations, *Reviews of the World Situation*, 111–22; Nitze, "Relationship of Strategic and Theater Nuclear Forces," 124–25.

73. For the quotation, see Memo by Acheson, 20 Dec 49, *FRUS, 1949*, 1: 615; Minutes of the PPS, 16 Dec 49, ibid., 1: 414–15; Memo by Nitze, 19 Dec 49, ibid., 1: 611; Nitze, *From Hiroshima to Glasnost*, 87–97.

74. For the quotation, see Study Prepared by Nitze, 8 Feb 50, *FRUS, 1950*, 1: 146–67. For the longer version of this study, see "Recent Soviet Moves," 8 Feb 50, HSTP, PSF, box 187; see also Kirk to Acheson, 4, 24, and 25 Jan 50, *FRUS, 1950*, 4: 1075–77, 1083–89; Record of Mtg. of the PPS, 2 Feb 50, ibid., 1: 142–43.

75. Memos by Nitze, 19 Dec 49 and 17 Jan 50, *FRUS, 1949*, 1: 611; *FRUS, 1950*, 1: 13–16; see also Minutes of the PPS, 11 Oct 49, RG 59, Bohlen Papers, box 1; Nitze, "Relationship of Strategic and Theater Nuclear Forces," 124–25.

76. Acheson, *Present at the Creation*, 347–49; Memo of Phone Conversation, 19 Jan 50, *FRUS, 1950*, 1: 512; Lilienthal, *Journals*, 620–33; Bernstein, "Truman and the H-Bomb," 17–18.

77. Report of the Special Committee of the NSC to Truman, 31 Jan 50, *FRUS, 1950*, 1: 513–22 (the quotation is on p. 515); Bundy, *Danger and Survival*, 210–29.

78. Bernstein, "Truman and the H-Bomb," 17–18. Bundy thinks Stalin might have responded to U.S. overtures; Bundy, *Danger and Survival*, 228.

79. For Johnson's quotation, see Johnson to Truman, 24 Feb 50, *FRUS, 1950*, 1: 539; see also Robert LeBaron to Johnson, 16 Feb 50, RG 330, box 61, CD 11-1-2; LeBaron to Johnson, 20 Feb 50, HSTP, PSF, box 201; Bradley and Blair, *A General's Life*, 516–17; D. Rosenberg, "American Atomic Strategy," 83–87.

80. For the quotation, see CIA, "Effect of the Soviet Possession of Atomic Bombs on the Security of the United States," 9 June 50, HSTP, PSF, box 257; see also CIA, "Estimates of the Effects of the Soviet Possession of the Atomic Bomb Upon the Security of the United States and Upon the Possibilities of Direct Soviet Military Action," 10 Feb 50, RG 330, box 61, CD 11-1-2. A revised draft of the 10 Feb study, dated 6 Apr 50, may be found in HSTP, PSF, box 257; JIC 502, "Implications of Soviet Possession of Atomic Weapons," 9 Feb 50, RG 218, CCS 471.6 (11-8-49), sec. 1; Memos of Information, 1 and 27 Feb 50, NHC, SPD, box 255, A8; War Dept. Intelligence Division, "Analysis of Soviet Actions Since 1 January 1949," RG 319, P&O, 381 Europe TS; War Dept. Intelligence Division, "Comments on JCS 2084," ibid., 471.6 TS; Memo

Prepared in the DOS, 8 Feb 50, *FRUS, 1950*, 4: 1099–1101; DOS, "Soviet Intentions and Capabilities," 18 Apr 50, ibid., 4: 1151–53; "Informal Summary of Bohlen's Remarks on Intentions and Capabilities of Soviets," ND [mid-Apr 1950], RG 59, Bohlen Papers, box 7.

81. Truman to Acheson, 31 Jan 50, *FRUS, 1950*, 1: 142; Nitze, *From Hiroshima to Glasnost*, 91.

82. Johnson to Acheson, 9 Sep 49, RG 330, box 32, CD 6-4-42; NSC 48, "Position of the United States with Respect to Asia," 26 Oct 49, HSTP, PSF, box 207; Schaller, *American Occupation of Japan*, 195–211. For bipartisanship, see Kepley, *Collapse of the Middle Way*, 37–51. For the ideas of Fosdick that presaged much of Acheson's thoughts, see Fosdick to Jessup, 29 Aug 49, Fosdick Papers, box 9. For Acheson's top agenda items, see Secretary's Daily Mtg., 21 Nov 49, RG 59, Executive Secretariat.

83. Acheson to Franks, 24 Dec 49, *FRUS, 1949*, 7: 927–28; NSC 48/1, "Position of the United States with Respect to Asia," 23 Dec 49, in Etzold and Gaddis, *Containment*, 263; CIA, "Relative US Security Interest in the European-Mediterranean Area and the Far East," 12 Sep 49, HSTP, PSF, box 256.

84. DOS, "Comments on NSC 49," 30 Sep 49, *FRUS, 1949*, 7: 871–72.

85. Kennan's response to questions at CIA conference, 13 Oct 49, Kennan Papers, box 17.

86. MemCons by Acheson, 13 and 17 Sep 49, *FRUS, 1949*, 7: 858–59, 861.

87. Acheson to MacArthur, 9 Sep 49, ibid., 7: 851–52. For MacArthur's views, see MemCon by Huston, 16 July 49, ibid., 7: 805–7; Sebald to Acheson, 26 July and 20 Aug 49, ibid., 7: 808–12, 830–32; MemCon by Sebald, 21 Sep 49, ibid., 7: 862–63; MemCon by Fearey, 2 Nov 49, ibid., 7: 890–94; Transcript of Mtg. by Voorhees, 14 Dec 49, RG 330, box 29, CD 6-3-33; Schaller, *MacArthur*, 165.

88. Voorhees to Johnson, 14 Oct 49, RG 330, box 29, CD 6-3-33; Voorhees to Webb, 24 Oct 49, ibid.; Bradley to Voorhees, 12 Oct 49, *FRUS, 1949*, 7: 886; Memo for Schuyler by J. J. Wagstaff, 16 Nov 49, RG 319, P&O, 091 Japan TS.

89. Wagstaff to Schuyler, 8 Nov 49, RG 319, P&O, 091 Japan TS; Memo for the Chief of Staff by Wagstaff, 3 Jan 50, ibid.

90. JCS to SecDef, 22 Dec 49, *FRUS, 1949*, 7: 923; MemCon by Hamilton, 24 Dec 49, ibid., 7: 925–26; Schuyler to Bolte, "U.S. Army Post-Treaty Requirements—Japan," 20 Dec 49, RG 319, P&O, 091 Japan TS.

91. MemCon by Hamilton, 24 Dec 49, *FRUS, 1949*, 7: 924–26; Informal Memo by Acheson to Franks, 24 Dec 49, ibid., 7: 926–29; MemCon by Acheson, 24 Dec 49, ibid., 7: 929–30; Acheson to Certain Diplomatic Offices, 27 Dec 49, ibid., 7: 932; MemCon by Allison, 27 Dec 49, ibid., 7: 933.

92. Acheson to Franks, 24 Dec 49, ibid., 7: 928–30; Acheson Testimony, 29 March 50, Senate, Foreign Relations, *Reviews of the World Situation*, 270–71. For Yokosuka, see Dingman, "U.S. Navy and the Cold War," 300–302. For similar concerns in the DOS and the Pentagon, see Minutes of the PPS, 28 Sep 49, RG 59, PPS, box 32. For Okinawa, see Rusk to Lay, 6 Feb 50, *FRUS, 1950*, 6: 1135. For the airfields in Japan, see Orem to Distribution List, 16 March 50, NHC, SPD, box 255, A14; Blum, *Drawing the Line*, 203.

93. NSC 37/9, "Possible United States Military Action Toward Taiwan Not Involving Major Military Forces," 27 Dec 49, *FRUS, 1949*, 9: 460–61; Summary of NSC Discussion, 30 Dec 49, HSTP, PSF, box 220.

94. MemCon by Acheson, 29 Dec 49, *FRUS, 1949*, 9: 464–67.

95. Ibid.; MemCon by Acheson, 5 Jan 50, *FRUS, 1950*, 6: 259–63; Acheson Testimony, 12 Oct 49 and 10 Jan and 29 March 50, Senate, Foreign Relations, *Reviews of the World Situation*, 93–101, 131–34, 274–76; Summary of NSC Discussion, 30 Dec 49, HSTP, PSF, box 220.

96. In addition to citations in the preceding note regarding relations and recognition, see Memo by Gerald Stryker, 2 Nov 49, *FRUS, 1949*, 9: 155–59; Memo by Ogburn, 2 Nov 49, ibid., 9: 161; Memo by Troy L. Perkins, 5 Nov 49, ibid., 9: 170. For reports on economic conditions in China, prospects for a Sino-Soviet rift, and the advantages of recognition, see Clubb to Acheson, 8

Oct and 21 and 24 Dec 49, ibid., 9: 113–14, 244, 598; Kirk to Acheson, 7 Oct 49, ibid., 9: 107–8; McConaughy to Acheson, 21 Jan and 1 Feb 50, *FRUS, 1950*, 6: 291, 304; Clubb to Acheson, 20 Jan 50, ibid., 6: 286–89; Memo by Davies, 2 Feb 50, ibid., 6: 306; CIA, "Review of the World Situation," 18 Jan 50, HSTP, PSF, box 250. For the pathbreaking work on Acheson's flexibility, which I think is much exaggerated, see Borg and Heinrichs, *Uncertain Years*, 13–52; N. Tucker, *Patterns in the Dust*.

97. MemCon by Acheson, 29 Dec 49, *FRUS, 1949*, 9: 464–67; Acheson Testimony, 12 Oct 49 and 10 Jan and 29 March 50, Senate, Foreign Relations, *Reviews of the World Situation*, 93–101, 131–34, 274–76; Acheson, "Crisis in Asia—An Examination of U.S. Policy," *DSB* 22 (23 Jan 50): 111–18; Acheson, "United States Policy Toward Asia," *DSB* 22 (15 March 50): 1–16. My interpretation here accords with G. Chang, *Friends and Enemies*, 63–76.

98. For Acheson's discussion with Senators William Knowland and H. Alexander Smith, see MemCon, 5 Jan 50, *FRUS, 1950*, 6: 259–63. For his remarks at a news conference on 5 Jan 50, see *DSB* 22 (16 Jan 50): 79–81; see also Secretary's Daily Mtgs., 2–5 Jan 50, RG 59, Executive Secretariat; Kepley, *Collapse of the Middle Way*, 53–61.

99. For Truman's public statement, see *DSB* 22 (16 Jan 50): 79. For Truman's attitudes, see MemCons with the Pres, 31 Oct and 14 and 17 Nov 49, RG 59, Executive Secretariat; Blum, *Drawing the Line*, 162–64; G. Chang, *Friends and Enemies*, 61–63.

100. CIA, "Review of the World Situation," 18 Jan 50, HSTP, PSF, box 250. For Acheson's thinking, see Summary of NSC Discussion, 30 Dec 49, ibid., box 220.

101. Acheson, "Crisis in Asia," *DSB* 22 (23 Jan 50): 111–18.

102. Acheson Testimony, 10 Jan 50, Senate, Foreign Relations, *Reviews of the World Situation*, 132. For the fear of Chinese Communist influence throughout Southeast Asia, see MemCon by Yost, 11 Nov 49, RG 59, PSA Division, box 6; O'Sullivan to Butterworth and Acheson, 6 and 20 Jan 50, ibid., box 10; K. P. Landon, "Military Assistance to Thailand," 1 Feb 50, RG 330, box 23, CD 6-2-46; CIA, "Review of the World Situation," 18 Jan and 15 Feb 50, HSTP, PSF, boxes 250 and 207.

103. For JCS views, see MemCon by Acheson, 29 Dec 49, *FRUS, 1949*, 9: 463–67; NSC 37/9, "Possible United States Military Action Toward Taiwan Not Involving Major Military Forces," 27 Dec 49, ibid., 9: 460–61.

104. Defense officials also criticized the early drafts of NSC 48 for failing to meet the internal security requirements of Southeast Asian nations. See the documents in RG 319, P&O, 092 Asia TS and 091 China TS, esp. Johnson to Bradley, 29 Dec 49, ibid., 092 Asia TS. For the testimony of Johnson and the JCS, see Senate, Foreign Relations, *Reviews of the World Situation*, 233–39.

105. NSC 61, "U.S. Economic Aid to Far Eastern Areas," 25 Jan 50, Voorhees Papers, box 3; Voorhees to Johnson, 29 Dec 49, ibid.; Mtg. of Voorhees, Stanley Andrews, et al., 18 Feb 50, ibid., box 4; Robert West and Andrews, "Report of Southeast and South Asia Food and Trade Mission," 13 March 50, ibid., box 3.

106. Voorhees to West, 23 Feb 50, ibid., box 3; Shohan to Merchant and Gay, 30 Dec 49, RG 59, PSA Division, box 1; Lacy to Merchant, 8 March 50, ibid.

107. JCS 1721/43, "Assistance for the General Area of China," 20 Jan 50, RG 319, P&O, 091 China TS.

108. For Jessup, see Jessup to Acheson, 16 Nov 49, *FRUS, 1949*, 7: 1210–14. For Acheson, see MemCon by Butterworth, 24 Dec 49, RG 59, PSA Division, box 6; Acheson to Bevin, 23 Dec 49, *FRUS, 1949*, 9: 241; MemCon by Acheson, 29 Dec 49, ibid., 9: 465–66. For Kennan, see his comments in the roundtable discussion with the consultants, "American Policy Toward China," 6 Oct 49, H. A. Smith Papers, box 98. For the assumption of no rift, see "Problem Paper Prepared by a Working Group in the Department," 1 Feb 50, *FRUS, 1950*, 6: 712; Butterworth to Acheson, 20 Oct 49, RG 59, PSA Division, box 10.

109. Voorhees to West, 23 Feb 50, Voorhees Papers, box 3; West and Andrews, "Food and Trade Mission," 13 March 50, ibid.; Secretary's Daily Mtgs., 23 Jan–10 Feb 50, RG 59, Executive Secretariat; DOS, "Problem Paper," 1 Feb 50, *FRUS, 1950*, 6: 711–15; R. Allen Griffith to Ache-

son, 18 March 50, ibid., 6: 762–63; Griffin and Lapham to Jessup, 14 Sep 49, Fosdick Papers, box 9; Schaller, *American Occupation of Japan*, 212–33.

110. Voorhees, "Economic Aid for Southeast Asia," 17 Oct 50, Voorhees Papers, box 3; Voorhees, "Illustrated Potential Savings . . . ," 24 Feb 50, ibid.; Testimony by Acheson, 24 Jan 50, Senate, Foreign Relations, *Economic Assistance to China and Korea*, 193–230; Senate, Foreign Relations, *Executive Sessions*, 2: 300–302.

111. CIA, "Crisis in Indochina," 10 Feb 50, HSTP, PSF, box 257; DOS, "Problem Paper," 1 Feb 50, *FRUS, 1950*, 6: 713; Acheson Statement, 1 Feb 50, ibid., 6: 711; Acheson to Truman, 2 Feb 50, ibid., 6: 716–17.

112. CIA, "Review of the World Situation," 15 Feb 50, HSTP, PSF, box 250; Yost to Perkins, 31 Jan 50, *FRUS, 1950*, 6: 710–11.

113. For the agreement, see Editorial Note, *FRUS, 1950*, 6: 311.

114. Acheson, "United States Policy Toward Asia," *DSB* 22 (27 March 50): 4.

115. For the quotation, see U.S. Delegation to Webb, 11 May 50, *FRUS, 1950*, 3: 1038; see also Acheson Testimony, 29 March and 1 May 50, Senate, Foreign Relations, *Reviews of the World Situation*, 271–85, 300–311; Jessup Testimony, 29 March 50, ibid., 283–84; Record of Conversation Between Jessup and Representatives of British Foreign Office, 11 March 50, *FRUS, 1950*, 6: 50. For the views of McConaughy, one of the last U.S. diplomats to depart Shanghai, see Memo by Ogburn, 2 June 50, ibid., 6: 352–57; Rusk to Acheson, 30 May 50, ibid., 6: 349–50; CIA, "Review of the World Situation," 18 Jan, 15 Feb, and 14 June 50, HSTP, PSF, boxes 250 and 207; CIA, "Reports of Current Soviet Military Activity in China," 21 Apr 50, ibid., box 257.

116. Study Prepared by Nitze, 8 Feb 50, *FRUS, 1950*, 1: 147; Memo by Yost, 15 Feb 50, ibid., 4: 1104–6; MemCon by John Auchincloss, 9 Feb 50, ibid., 4: 591; Kennan, "Estimate of International Situation," 17 Apr 50, Kennan Papers, box 18.

117. Kepley, *Collapse of the Middle Way*, 1–51; Westerfield, *Foreign Policy and Party Politics*, 296–342.

118. *Public Opinion Quarterly* 13 (Winter 1949–50): 722; Gallup, *Poll*, 2: 852; Kusnitz, *Public Opinion and Foreign Policy*, 28–35.

119. Kepley, *Collapse of the Middle Way*, 53–61.

120. Patterson, *Mr. Republican*, 434–42; Kepley, *Collapse of the Middle Way*, 60–61.

121. Senate, Foreign Relations, *Reviews of the World Situation*, 145–98; Dulles to Vandenberg, 6 Jan 50, Dulles Papers, box 48; Westerfield, *Foreign Policy and Party Politics*, 364–69; Stueck, *Road to Confrontation*, 143.

122. Acheson, "Crisis in Asia," *DSB* 22 (23 Jan 50): 111–18; Patterson, *Mr. Republican*, 443.

123. Griffith, *Politics of Fear*, 47–48; Oshinsky, *Conspiracy So Immense*, 104; Acheson, *Present at the Creation*, 250–52, 358–61; Weinstein, *Perjury*, 505–23.

124. For attacks on Acheson and for the impasse over Korean aid, see Blum, *Drawing the Line*, 183–86. For Taft's criticism, see Patterson, *Mr. Republican*, 443–44. For decreasing support for the Marshall Plan, see *Public Opinion Quarterly* 14 (Summer 1950): 381. For the quotation emanating from Congressman Richard M. Nixon, see Zinn, *Postwar America*, 151.

125. Lilienthal, *Journals*, 635; Williams, *Klaus Fuchs*.

126. Latham, *Communist Controversy in Washington*; Rogin, *Intellectuals and McCarthy*.

127. Oshinsky, *Conspiracy So Immense*, 108–17; Griffith, *Politics of Fear*, 58–67; Secretary's Daily Mtgs., 13, 17, and 21 Feb 50, RG 59, Executive Secretariat.

128. Oshinsky, *Conspiracy So Immense*, 119–38; Reeves, *McCarthy*, 235–85.

129. Kepley, *Collapse of the Middle Way*, 75–76.

130. Patterson, *Mr. Republican*, 446; Griffith, *Politics of Fear*, 75.

131. Kepley, *Collapse of the Middle Way*, 77–82.

132. MemCon by Jackson, 7 March 50, *FRUS, 1950*, 3: 638–40; LaFeber, "NATO and the Korean War."

133. CIA, "French Labor Unrest in 1950 and Its Implications for the Attainment of US Objectives in Western Europe," 10 Apr 50, HSTP, PSF, box 257; CIA, "Review of the World

Situation," 19 Apr, 17 May, and 14 June 50, ibid., boxes 250 and 207; Report to the Secretary of the Army, 19 Apr 50, Voorhees Papers, box 4; Summary Record, 22–24 March 50, *FRUS, 1950*, 3: 821–23.

134. For McCloy, see Memo by Jackson, 7 March 50, *FRUS, 1950*, 3: 641; see also Summary Record, 22–24 March 50, ibid., 3: 811–15; McCloy to Acheson, 12 and 14 Apr 50, ibid., 3: 624–28. For Bohlen, see ibid., 3: 816; see also Paper Prepared in the Office of the High Commission by Henry C. Ramsey [early Apr 1950], ibid., 4: 647–52; CIA, "Political Orientation of the West German State," 25 Apr 50, HSTP, PSF, box 257; Schwartz, *America's Germany*, 84–95.

135. Geoffrey Lewis and Achilles to Byroade, 2 May 50, *FRUS, 1950*, 3: 913–14; Acheson Testimony, 1 May 50, Senate, Foreign Relations, *Reviews of the World Situation*, 290–92.

136. For Acheson's thinking, see his testimony, 1 May 50, Senate, Foreign Relations, *Reviews of the World Situation*, 286–308; Summary of NSC Discussion, 5 May 50, HSTP, PSF, box 220; Acheson to McCloy, 31 March 50, *FRUS, 1950*, 3: 833–34; Acheson to Certain Diplomatic Offices, 6 Apr 50, ibid., 3: 41. The British, too, were placing their long-term hopes on NATO; see "Brief for the U.K. Delegation," 24 Apr 50, in Bullen and Pelly, *Documents on British Policy Overseas*, 2: 95–106.

137. For U.S. concerns that Britain and France retain their responsibilities in the Third World, see, e.g., MemCon by Butterworth, 24 Dec 49, RG 59, PSA Division, box 6; Butterworth to Rusk, 6 Dec 49, ibid.; Secretary's Daily Mtg., 9 Dec 49, RG 59, Executive Secretariat; Acheson Testimony, 1 May 50, Senate, Foreign Relations, *Reviews of the World Situation*, 290; Paper Prepared in the Bureau of European Affairs, 19 Apr 50, *FRUS, 1950*, 3: 842–44; Paper Prepared in the DOS, 28 Apr 50, ibid., 3: 1003–6; "U.S. Statement on Africa," 9 May 50, ibid., 3: 1097–98.

138. Acheson to Webb, 8 May 50, *FRUS, 1950*, 3: 1011; Johnson to Acheson, 14 Apr 50, ibid., 6: 780–85; CIA, "Review of the World Situation," 19 Apr 50, HSTP, PSF, box 250.

139. Acheson Testimony, 29 March 50, Senate, Foreign Relations, *Reviews of the World Situation*, 271.

140. Acheson to Truman, 9 March 50, *FRUS, 1950*, 6: 41; NSC 64, "Position of the United States with Respect to Indochina," 27 Feb 50, ibid., 6: 745–47.

141. For the shipment of supplies, see Ohly to Hamilton Twitchell and Norman Paul, 3 Apr 50, NHC, SPD, box 255, A14; Matthews to Johnson, 28 March 50, RG 330, box 23, CD 6-2-46; Acheson to Embassy in London, 3 May 50, *FRUS, 1950*, 6: 792. For military advisory groups, see Lemnitzer to James Bruce, 19 Apr 50, ibid., 6: 788; Webb to Johnson, 16 May 50, ibid., 6: 816–17. For future military aid, see Rusk to Webb, 25 Apr 50, ibid., 6: 83–84.

142. Acheson to Truman, 17 Apr 50, *FRUS, 1950*, 6: 785; Truman to Acheson, 1 May 50, ibid., 6: 791.

143. "Position of the Department of State on United States Policy Toward a Japanese Peace and Security Settlement," 9 March 50, ibid., 6: 1140–47; MemCon by John Howard, 24 Apr 50, ibid., 6: 1175–82.

144. Howard to Butterworth, 9 March 50, ibid., 6: 1139; Howard to Bohlen, 31 March 50, ibid., 6: 1157–60; Memo by Howard, 7 Apr 50, ibid., 6: 1162–65; Secretary's Daily Mtg., 10 and 11 Apr 50, RG 59, Executive Secretariat.

145. Memo by Howard, 24 Apr 50, *FRUS, 1950*, 6: 1175–82; Sherman to Bradley, 1 May 50, RG 218, Bradley Papers, box 1. For Voorhees's efforts to mediate the differences between the DOS and the JCS, see Voorhees to Johnson, 27 Feb and 21 and 22 Apr 50, RG 330, box 29, CD 6-3-33; Voorhees to Johnson, 11 Apr 50, RG 335, box 75; Voorhees to Acheson, 23 March 50, *FRUS, 1950*, 6: 1151–53.

146. Memo by Howard, 24 Apr 50, *FRUS, 1950*, 6: 1175–82.

147. Acheson to Webb, 8 May 50, ibid., 3: 1007–11. For Acheson's views, see also Senate, Foreign Relations, *Reviews of the World Situation*, 267–69, 292–97, 306–7.

148. L. Kaplan, *Community of Interests*, 85–100.

149. Acheson to Webb, 8 and 9 May 50, *FRUS, 1950*, 3: 1007–10, 1014–17, 1019–22; U.S.

Delegation to Webb, 11 and 12 May 50, ibid., 3: 1034–42, 1045–49; Hogan, *Marshall Plan*, 293–320.

150. Milward, *Reconstruction of Western Europe*, 362–407; Young, *Britain, France, and the Unity of Europe*, 141–49; Diebold, *Schuman Plan*, 1–60; Schwartz, *America's Germany*, 95–105.

151. Bruce Diary, 7, 10, and 22 May 50, Bruce Papers; Dulles to Acheson, 10 May 50, *FRUS, 1950*, 3: 695–96; Harriman to Acheson, 20 May 50, ibid., 3: 702–4; Acheson to Truman and Webb, 10 May 50, ibid., 3: 694–95; Schwartz, *America's Germany*, 105–9.

152. Webb to Acheson, 11 May 50, *FRUS, 1950*, 3: 696–97; Bruce to Webb, 12 May and 4 June 50, ibid., 3: 698–701, 715–17; Douglas to Acheson, 6 June 50, ibid., 3: 722–24; Hoffman Testimony, 23 June 50, Senate, Foreign Relations, *Executive Sessions*, 2: 546–47.

153. Riste, *Western Security*, 247–57; Bullock, *Bevin*, 770–71.

154. Acheson to Webb, 14 May 50, *FRUS, 1950*, 3: 1061–63; Acheson to Truman, 18 May 50, ibid., 3: 123–25.

155. Acheson to Certain Diplomatic Offices, 2 June 50, *FRUS, 1950*, 3: 715; Bullock, *Bevin*, 766–90.

156. Keohane, *After Hegemony*, 146; Hogan, *Marshall Plan*, 320–28.

157. Bush to Bradley, 13 Apr 50, Voorhees Papers, box 4; Voorhees, "Efforts to Obtain a Real Defense of Europe," 19 Oct 50, ibid., box 3; Report to the Secretary of the Army, 19 Apr 50, ibid., box 4; Voorhees to Johnson, 21 March 50, RG 330, box 76, CD 16-1-20; Gray to Johnson, 22 March 50, ibid.; Voorhees to Acheson, 10 Apr 50, *FRUS, 1950*, 3: 43–48; Doughty, *U.S. Army Tactical Doctrine*, 12–13. For contrasting analyses that stress the problems afflicting NATO and the hesitation of defense officials, see L. Kaplan, *Community of Interests*, 16–100; E. May, "American Commitment to Germany," 446–47.

158. Collins to Eisenhower, 26 May 50, Eisenhower Papers, File 1652, box 25; Charles R. Brown to Sherman, 3 June 50, Sherman Papers, box 1(B).

159. Pace to Johnson, 23 May 50, RG 330, box 34, CD 6-4-18; Voorhees to Pace, 8 May 50, Voorhees Papers, box 4; Voorhees, "A Proposal to Correlate Economic Aid to Europe with Military Defense," 29 May 50, ibid., box 4.

160. Bradley to Thomas Handy, 21 June 50, RG 218, Bradley Papers, box 1; Bradley to Johnson, 17 May 50, ibid., box 2.

161. Conolly to Sherman, 10 May 50, RG 218, CCS 337 (4-19-50), sec. 2; Bradley to Handy, 21 June 50, RG 218, Bradley Papers, box 1; NSC 71, "United States Policy Toward Germany," 8 June 50, HSTP, PSF, box 207.

162. Truman to Acheson, 16 June 50, *FRUS, 1950*, 4: 688–89.

163. See, e.g., Minutes of the PPS, 18 Oct 49, RG 59, PPS, box 32; Acheson Testimony, 10 Jan 50, Senate, Foreign Relations, *Reviews of the World Situation*, 112–15.

164. NSC 71/1, "Rearmament of Western Germany," 3 July 50, HSTP, PSF, box 207. Although dated after the outbreak of the Korean War, the DOS position was formulated before it erupted. See Acheson to McCloy, 21 June 50, *FRUS, 1950*, 4: 689–90. For a similar interpretation, see LaFeber, "NATO and the Korean War," 471–73.

165. For U.S. goals, see NSC 47/2, "United States Policy Toward Israel and the Arab States," 17 Oct 49, *FRUS, 1949*, 6: 1431–39; Statements by the US and UK Groups, 14 Nov 49, ibid., 6: 63–71.

166. Testimony by McGhee, Gordon Clapp, and Sherman, 31 Jan 50, Senate, Foreign Relations, *Executive Sessions*, 2: 130–62. For aid to the refugees under the Foreign Economic Assistance Act of 1950, see *FRUS, 1950*, 5: 921. For key background documents, see *FRUS, 1949*, 6: 1463–65, 1473–76, 1506–7, 1557–58.

167. McGhee to Acheson, 7 June 50, *FRUS, 1950*, 5: 170–71; Nitze to Acheson, 13 June 50, ibid., 5: 172–73.

168. JCS to Johnson, 1 Feb 50, RG 330, box 20, CD 6-1-28; Testimony by McGhee, Lemnitzer, and Ohly, 8 June 50, Senate, Foreign Relations, *Executive Sessions*, 2: 468–70.

169. For British arms supplies to Egypt, see NSC 65, "United States Policy Toward Arms Shipments to the Near East," 28 March 50, *FRUS, 1950*, 5: 131–34; Stabler to Berry, 1 June 50, ibid., 5: 290–91. For Acheson's views on arms sales, see Acheson to Jacob Javits, 12 Jan 50, ibid., 5: 685; MemCons, 10 and 28 March 50, ibid., 5: 799–802, 129–30. For the direction of U.S. policy, see McGhee to Webb [mid-May 1950], ibid., 5: 891; Webb to Johnson, 25 May 50, ibid., 5: 914.

170. Bullen and Pelly, *Documents on British Policy Overseas*, 2: 284–86, 289–91, 342–44, 365–68, 372–73; P. Hahn, "Strategy and Diplomacy," 249–57; see also Louis, *British Empire in the Middle East*, 583–85.

171. For the quotation, see Gerald A. Drew to Acheson, 27 June 50, *FRUS, 1950*, 5: 942. For Saudi attitudes, see ibid., 5: 1131–54. For background, see M. Wilson, *King Abdullah, Britain and the Making of Jordan*.

172. See Berry's comments, 24 Feb 50, *FRUS, 1950*, 5: 287, footnote 7; McGhee, "General Policy Considerations," 18 Jan 50, RG 319, P&O Division, 381 Middle East TS.

173. For overall strategic interests of the United States, of which oil was one component, see Statement by the US and UK Groups, 14 Nov 49, *FRUS, 1949*, 6: 63. For Egypt, see MemCons by Acheson, 10 and 28 March 50, *FRUS, 1950*, 5: 799–802, 125–30. For Saudi Arabia, see esp. McGhee to James Bruce, 14 Nov 49, RG 59, Military Adviser to the Office of Near Eastern, South Asian, and African Affairs, box 1. For Iran, see *FRUS, 1950*, 5: 506–63. For Iran's role in U.S. strategic thinking, see Memo by Collins, "Turkish and Iranian Military Effort in War," 25 Feb 50, RG 319, P&O Division, 381 Middle East TS.

174. Childs to Acheson, 17 Nov 49, *FRUS, 1949*, 6: 1618–20; Memo by Childs, 23 March 50, *FRUS, 1950*, 5: 1146–54.

175. For Turkey, see MemCon by Webb, 27 Apr 50, *FRUS, 1950*, 5: 1252–53; MemCon by Hare, 2 June 50, ibid., 5: 1265–66. For the British, see Jessup to Acheson, 27 Apr and 2 May 50, ibid., 3: 884, 975–76.

176. Conolly to Sherman, 9 March 50, Sherman Papers, box 6. For Sherman's views and JCS deliberations, see the JCS 2105 Series, March 1950, RG 218, CCS 337 (2-20-50), sec. 1; Memo by Collins, 26 March 50, *FRUS, 1950*, 5: 1243–47.

177. For the quotation, see MemCon by McGhee, 19 March 50, *FRUS, 1950*, 5: 1136. For strategic guarantees, see Report Prepared in the Bureau of Near Eastern, South Asian, and African Affairs, "Regional Security Arrangements in the Eastern Mediterranean and Near Eastern Areas," 11 May 50, ibid., 5: 152–56. For jet aircraft to Turkey, see Ohly to Lemnitzer, 14 June 50, ibid., 5: 1270–71.

178. Blum, *Drawing the Line*, 200–201; Brown and Opie, *American Foreign Assistance*, 408. For the loan to Indonesia, see *FRUS, 1950*, 6: 1023.

179. For the quotation, see Testimony by Rusk and Lemnitzer, 8 June 50, Senate, Foreign Relations, *Executive Sessions*, 2: 453–55; see also Francis T. Greene to Lemnitzer, 16 and 26 May 50, RG 330, box 24, CD 6-2-46. Acheson said much the same to Schuman. See Acheson to Webb, 8 May 50, *FRUS, 1950*, 3: 1007–11.

180. Draft Memo from Rusk to Acheson, 30 May 50, *FRUS, 1950*, 6: 349–51; Dulles to Acheson, 18 May 50, ibid., 1: 314–16; Schaller, *American Occupation of Japan*, 254–72; Stueck, *Road to Confrontation*, 147–52; G. Chang, *Friends and Enemies*, 72–76.

181. Burns to Rusk, 29 May 50, *FRUS, 1950*, 6: 347; Sherman to JCS, 6 June 50, NHC, SPD, box 256, A16-3(5); Sherman to JCS, 1 May 50, ibid., Double Zero Files, box 3, A16-3; Schaller, *American Occupation of Japan*, 265–67.

182. Memo by MacArthur, 14 June 50, RG 218, Bradley Papers, box 1.

183. For failure to stifle the study, see Dulles to Acheson, 22 June 50, *FRUS, 1950*, 6: 366–67, esp. footnote 2; CIA, "Review of the World Situation," 14 June 50, HSTP, PSF, box 207. For views of U.S. diplomats, see Schaller, *American Occupation of Japan*, 253–54.

184. For Franks's report, see Lowe, *Korean War*, 152–53. For Truman's thinking, see Li Tsung-jen to Truman, 3 June 50, HSTP, PSF, box 177; Truman to Acheson, 7 June 50, ibid.;

MemCon with President Truman by Dulles, 28 Apr 50, Dulles Papers, box 48; see also Howe to W. Park Strong, 31 May 50, *FRUS, 1950*, 6: 348–49; Memo by MacArthur, 14 June 50, RG 218, Bradley Papers, box 1; Cumings, *Origins of the Korean War*, 2: 508–44.

185. Nitze, *From Hiroshima to Glasnost*, 93–100; Schilling, Hammond, and Snyder, *Strategy, Politics, and Defense Budgets*, 267–378; Wells, "Sounding the Tocsin."

186. NSC 68, "United States Objectives and Programs for National Security," 14 Apr 50, *FRUS, 1950*, 1: 237–38.

187. Ibid., 1: 241, 288–90.

188. In his *Strategies of Containment* (pp. 3–126, esp. 90–92), John Gaddis treats NSC 68 as a qualitative break from the past. In terms of objectives, however, NSC 68 reiterated many of the same goals that even Kennan had been espousing for several years. Moreover, despite Kennan's stress (which was rejected by most of his colleagues) on the formation of independent power centers in Western Europe and Northeast Asia, he always realized that these power centers depended on markets and raw materials in the periphery, including Southeast Asia, the Middle East, and Africa. For Kennan, see NSC 20/1, "U.S. Objectives with Respect to Russia," 18 Aug 48, in Etzold and Gaddis, *Containment*, 173–203; PPS 23, "Review of Current Trends," 24 Feb 48, ibid., 115–16; PPS 51, "United States Policy Toward Southeast Asia," 19 May 49, *PPS Papers*, 3: 32–58; Kennan, "Contemporary Problems of Foreign Policy," 17 Sep 48, Kennan Papers, box 17.

189. NSC 68, "United States Objectives and Programs," 14 Apr 50, *FRUS, 1950*, 1: 283–87.

190. Ibid., 1: 276–79, 284. In his memoir, Nitze also stresses that there was nothing new in NSC 68, except for its plea for a "stepped-up level of effort to counter recent developments" (*From Hiroshima to Glasnost*, 97).

191. NSC 68, "United States Objectives and Programs," 14 Apr 50, *FRUS, 1950*, 1: 245–62. For criticism, see, e.g., Bohlen to Nitze, 5 Apr 50, ibid., 1: 222–23; Thorp to Acheson, 5 Apr 50, ibid., 1: 219–20.

192. Minutes of the PPS, 16 Dec 49, *FRUS, 1949*, 1: 414; NSC 68, "United States Objectives and Programs," 14 Apr 50, *FRUS, 1950*, 1: 249; Nitze, *From Hiroshima to Glasnost*, 95–97.

193. NSC 68, "United States Objectives and Programs," 14 Apr 50, *FRUS, 1950*, 1: 249; see also Nitze, "Military Power."

194. For the quotations, see *FRUS, 1950*, 1: 282, 253.

195. For the quotation (my emphasis), see ibid., 1: 268. For fear of neutrality, see ibid., 1: 265. Nitze's fear of neutrality hardly comports with Gaddis's stress on diversity. Although U.S. officials sought to promote free societies, they did not want their friends to pursue independent foreign policies. Wolfram Hanrieder nicely captures the paradox in his discussion of U.S. policy toward West Germany. The United States, he writes, wanted "to make the West Germans free and at the same time not free: free with respect to the personal liberties and constitutional safeguards that are the essence of a democratic political order, but not free to formulate and implement an independent foreign policy" (*Germany, America, Europe*, 5).

196. Thompson to Acheson, 3 Apr 50, *FRUS, 1950*, 1: 214; Perkins to Acheson, 3 Apr 50, ibid., 1: 215–16; Thorp to Acheson, 5 Apr 50, ibid., 1: 219–20; Bohlen to Nitze, 5 Apr 50, ibid., 1: 221–24.

197. Bohlen to Nitze, 5 Apr 50, ibid., 1: 221–22. For the preparations for the May meetings, see ibid., 3: 828–1001. For confirmation that NSC 68 was the framework for Acheson's talks with Bevin and Schuman in May 1950, see Summary of NSC Discussion, 5 May 50, HSTP, PSF, box 220; see also Acheson, *Present at the Creation*, 373–81.

198. Rearden, *Formative Years*, 523–26; Nitze, *From Hiroshima to Glasnost*, 94–95; Schilling, Hammond, and Snyder, *Strategy, Politics, and Defense Budgets*, 321–25; Bradley to Johnson, 5 Apr 50, RG 330, box 76, CD 16-1-17; Pace to Burns, 12 Apr 50 [?], ibid.

199. Truman to Lay, 12 Apr 50, *FRUS, 1950*, 1: 235; Memo by Schaub, 8 May 50, ibid., 1: 298–306; Secretary's Daily Mtgs., 22 May and 8 June 50, RG 59, Executive Secretariat; Rearden, *Formative Years*, 532–36.

200. *PPP:HST* (1950), 333–38, 440, 450–51, 464–68, 487.

201. DOS, "Soviet Intentions and Capabilities," 18 Apr 50, *FRUS, 1950*, 4: 1150–51; U.S. Delegation to Acheson, 24 Apr and 4 May 50, ibid., 3: 855, 962; MemCon by Allison, 19 June 50, ibid., 7: 108; CIA, "Estimates of the Effects of the Soviet Possession of the Atomic Bomb," 6 Apr 50, HSTP, PSF, box 257; Record of First Bipartite Official Mtg., 24 Apr 50, in Bullen and Pelly, *Documents on British Policy Overseas*, 2: 91–92; Johnson address, 17 Apr 50, Johnson papers, box 140.

202. Report by the JIC, "Soviet Intentions," 25 Apr 50, *FRUS, 1950*, 4: 1171.

203. Bush to Bradley, 13 Apr 50, ibid., 1: 227–33; Voorhees, "Personal Notes," 30 March 50, Voorhees Papers, box 4; Gruenther to Eisenhower, 5 Apr 50, Eisenhower Papers, File 1652, box 48; Collins to Eisenhower, 26 May 50, ibid.

204. Nitze acknowledged in NSC 68 that many of the problems facing the United States would exist even if there were no Soviet threat. See NSC 68, "United States Objectives and Programs," 14 Apr 50, *FRUS, 1950*, 1: 262–63.

205. Ibid., 1: 237–49.

206. Ibid., 1: 262–79, 282–84; see also Nitze, "Military Power."

Chapter 9

1. *PPP:HST* (1950), 527–37, 609–14; the quotation is on p. 528. See also Acheson, *Present at the Creation*, 404–5; Bradley and Blair, *A General's Life*, 534–46; CIA, "Intelligence Report No. 300," 28 June 50, HSTP, PSF, box 250.

2. *PPP:HST* (1950), 538.

3. Memos by Jessup, 25 and 26 June 50, *FRUS, 1950*, 7: 157–61, 178–83; Summaries of NSC Discussions, 29 and 30 June 50, HSTP, PSF, box 220; Acheson, *Present at the Creation*, 405.

4. *PPP:HST* (1950), 531–36; NSC 68/2, "United States Objectives and Programs for National Security," 30 Sep 50, NA, RG 273, NSC; Trachtenberg, "Wasting Asset."

5. For Truman's desire to improve the NSC, see Truman to Acheson, 19 July 50, *FRUS, 1950*, 1: 348–49. Harriman's role appears most clearly in the Summaries of the Secretary's Daily Mtgs., RG 59, Executive Secretariat. For Bradley's role, Smith's appointment, and Johnson's resignation, see also Bradley and Blair, *A General's Life*, 542, 551–53. For developments at the AEC, see Dean, *Forging the Atomic Shield*.

6. For an incisive portrayal of the changing relationship between Acheson and top officials at the Pentagon, see Stueck's essay in Cumings, *Child of Conflict*, 218–19. For DOS-DOD relationships, see also Acheson, *Present at the Creation*, 441; Stoler, *Marshall*, 181–84; Nitze to Acheson, 12 July 50, *FRUS, 1950*, 1: 342; Secretary's Daily Mtg., 10 Oct 50, RG 59, Executive Secretariat; Rearden, *Formative Years*, 71, 127–29, 138–41; D. Condit, *Test of War*, 34–39.

7. For Truman's feelings about MacArthur, see Truman, *Off the Record*, 47, 196; Bradley and Blair, *A General's Life*, 541–623; Schaller, "MacArthur's Japan."

8. See, e.g., *FRUS, 1950*, 7: 32–33, 36–37, 42–43; Lowe, *Korean War*, 157; Merrill, *Korea*, 168–72; Halliday and Cumings, *Korea*, 43–50.

9. Muccio to Acheson, 9 June 50, *FRUS, 1950*, 7: 98–101; Merrill, *Korea*, 172–77; Simmons, *Strained Alliance*, 102–10.

10. Muccio to Acheson, 14 June 50, *FRUS, 1950*, 7: 105; Drumright to Acheson, 11 May 50, ibid., 7: 94–95; Schnabel and Watson, *History of the JCS*, 48–55.

11. For intelligence assessments of the military strength of North and South Korea, see CIA, "Current Capabilities of the North Korean Regime," 19 June 50, *FRUS, 1950*, 7: 109–21; "Estimate of the Military Potential of the People's Democratic Republic of Korea (PDRK)," 20 Apr 50, RG 59, Military Adviser to the Office of Near Eastern, South Asian, and African Affairs, box 2; "Estimate of the Military Potential of the Republic of Korea," 20 Apr 50, ibid.

12. Parelman to Merchant, 12 Apr 50, *FRUS, 1950*, 7: 77; Memo by Howard Orem, 10 May 50, NHC, SPD, box 255, A14; Testimony by Lemnitzer, 8 June 50, Senate, Foreign

Relations, *Executive Sessions*, 2: 442; Bradley and Blair, *A General's Life*, 530; Halliday and Cumings, *Korea*, 48–50, 62–64.

13. MemCon by Allison, 19 June 50, *FRUS, 1950*, 7: 107–8; William R. Matthews to John Foster Dulles, 20 June 50, Dulles Papers, box 48.

14. Schnabel and Watson, *History of the JCS*, 57–125; *FRUS, 1950*, 7: 125–270; Acheson, *Present at the Creation*, 404–13; Matray, *Reluctant Crusade*, 236–52.

15. For the quotations, see Elsey's Notes, 26 June 50, Elsey Papers, box 71; MemCon with Members of Congress, 27 June 50, ibid.; see also Memo by Jessup, 25 June 50, *FRUS, 1950*, 7: 158; Summary of NSC Discussion, 29 June 50, HSTP, PSF, box 220; Bruce Diary, 27 June 50, Bruce Papers.

16. Memo by Elsey, 26 June 50, Elsey Papers, box 71; Truman, *Off the Record*, 185; Acheson, *Present at the Creation*, 405.

17. Khrushchev, *Remembers*, 368. Of course, Stalin did not try to dissuade Kim. Khrushchev, *Remembers: The Glasnost Tapes*, 144–47. See also Simmons, *Strained Alliance*, 110–30; Cumings, *Origins of the Korean War*; Merrill, *Korea*; Pollack, *Into the Vortex*. These views, once considered revisionist and controversial, are increasingly being accepted in standard histories of the Korean conflict. See, e.g., Lowe, *Korean War*, esp. 156–57; Kaufman, *Korean War*, esp. 32–33.

18. Senate, Foreign Relations, *Reviews of the World Situation*, 323–24.

19. Acheson, *Present at the Creation*, 356–57, 405; Acheson Testimony, 1 June 51, Senate, Armed Services and Foreign Relations, *Military Situation in the Far East*, 1741–42. For the fallacies (perhaps intentional) in Acheson's views, see Cumings, *Origins of the Korean War*, 2: 325–76, 408–65, 643–51.

20. Memo by Jessup, 25 June 50, *FRUS, 1950*, 7: 158; Kirk to Acheson, 26 and 27 June 50, ibid., 7: 169, 199; Memo of NSC Consultants, 29 June 50, ibid., 1: 328–30; Kennan, "Estimate of Possible Further Danger Points in Light of Korean Situation," 30 June 50, Kennan Papers, box 24; Acheson to Embassy in the Soviet Union, 26 June 50, *FRUS, 1950*, 7: 176–77.

21. *PPP:HST* (1950), 502–3; Memo by Elsey, 30 June 50, Elsey Papers, box 71.

22. Eisenhower, *Diaries*, 175–77. The interpretation here closely resembles the analysis in Stueck, *Road to Confrontation*, 185–95; Matray, *Reluctant Crusade*, 226–58.

23. For an interpretation that places a good deal of stress on domestic political considerations, see Stephen Pelz's essay in Cumings, *Child of Conflict*, 119–32. For the failure of the administration's critics to call for direct intervention, see Kepley, *Collapse of the Middle Way*, 85–90; see also Donovan, *Tumultuous Years*, 206–7. For a similar view that stresses the importance of international imperatives over domestic political expedients, see Stueck, *Road to Confrontation*, 186.

24. See NSC 73 series, "Position and Actions of the United States with Respect to Possible Future Soviet Moves in the Light of the Korean Situation," 1 July and 25 Aug 50, *FRUS, 1950*, 1: 331–38, 375–89.

25. For the quotation, see Kirk to Acheson, 11 Aug 50, ibid., 4: 1231. For additional assessments that the Kremlin did not want global war, see Testimony by Acheson, 24 July 50, Senate, Foreign Relations, *Reviews of the World Situation*, 315; U.S. Delegation Minutes, 29 Aug and 1 Sep 50, *FRUS, 1950*, 3: 1135–37, 1167; NSC 73/4, "Possible Future Soviet Moves," 25 Aug 50, ibid., 1: 378–79; *PPP:HST* (1950), 691. For estimates of Soviet capabilities, see CIA, NIE-3, "Soviet Capabilities and Intentions," 15 Nov 50, HSTP, PSF, box 253; CIA, "Intelligence Memorandum No. 323-SRC," 25 Aug 50, ibid., box 250.

26. CIA, NIE-3, "Soviet Capabilities and Intentions," 15 Nov 50, HSTP, PSF, box 253; CIA, "Intelligence Memorandum No. 323-SRC," 25 Aug 50, ibid., box 250. For U.S. strategic capabilities, see Poole, *History of the JCS*, 163–70; D. Rosenberg, "U.S. Nuclear Stockpile," 26, 30; S. Ross, *American War Plans*, 139.

27. For the quotation, see Bradley and Blair, *A General's Life*, 557–58; CIA, NIE-3, "Soviet Capabilities and Intentions," 15 Nov 50, HSTP, PSF, box 253; JCS 2143/6, HEADSTONE (or REAPER), 7 Dec 50, RG 218, CCS 381 (1-26-50), sec. 2, BP; Memo of NSC Consultants' Mtg., 29 June 50, *FRUS, 1950*, 1: 329–30; S. Ross, *American War Plans*, 142–48.

28. For the quotation, see CIA, "Conclusions Regarding a Possible Soviet Decision to Precipitate a Global War," 12 Oct 50, *FRUS, 1950*, 7: 937; see also CIA, "Review of the World Situation," 20 Sep 50, HSTP, PSF, box 250; CIA, NIE-3, "Soviet Capabilities and Intentions," 15 Nov 50, ibid., box 253. For the stress on 1952, see also Secretary's Daily Mtg., 12 Oct 50, RG 59, Executive Secretariat.

29. See the full conclusions of NSC 73/4, "Possible Further Soviet Moves," 25 Aug 50, HSTP, PSF, box 195; see also NSC 81/1, "United States Courses of Action with Respect to Korea," 9 Sep 50, *FRUS, 1950*, 7: 717.

30. Memo by Bohlen, 13 July 50, *FRUS, 1950*, 1: 344; Memo by Acheson, 14 July 50, ibid., 1: 344–46; Secretary's Daily Mtg., 13 July 50, RG 59, Executive Secretariat.

31. For the military buildup, see *PPP:HST* (1950), 531–36. For the AEC request, see ibid., 519. For the foreign aid request, see ibid., 564–66. For the military program, see Poole, *History of the JCS*, 38–44.

32. *PPP:HST* (1950), 533–36, 540–42, 589–90, 626–31.

33. Memo by Lay, 28 July 50, *FRUS, 1950*, 1: 351–52; Dean, *Forging the Atomic Shield*, 65–71; Hewlett and Duncan, *Atomic Shield*, 524–26; Bradley to Johnson, 1 Aug 50, RG 330, box 209, CD 471.6 (A-Bomb).

34. NSC 68/1 and 68/2, "United States Objectives and Programs for National Security," 21 and 30 Sep 50, RG 273.

35. The NSC approved NSC 68/2 on 29 Sep; South Korean troops crossed the 38th parallel on 30 Sep; U.S. troops did the same one week later. For the approval of NSC 68/2, see Minutes of the NSC, 29 Sep 50, RG 273. For the stress on continuing efforts to augment military capabilities, see Truman's remarks, *PPP:HST* (1950), 658–60; Memo by Acheson, 10 Oct 50, *FRUS, 1950*, 1: 401.

36. NSC 68/1, "United States Objectives and Programs," 21 Sep 50, RG 273; Poole, *History of the JCS*, 52–60.

37. Nitze to Acheson, 22 Nov 50, *FRUS, 1950*, 1: 419–20; Summary of NSC Discussion, 24 Nov 50, HSTP, PSF, box 220. JCS objectives for fiscal year 1951 were revised downward slightly in the chiefs' 19 Nov recommendation, as compared to their 22 Sep proposal. See Poole, *History of the JCS*, 63–66, 75. For background, see also D. Condit, *Test of War*, 223–40. The BOB had been exerting pressure on the Pentagon to cast its proposals more modestly. See esp. "1951 and 1952 Military Budgets," 17 Oct 50, RG 51, Series 47.8A, box 52; Ramsey to Lawton, 10 Nov 50, ibid. For the rearmament and possible use of Latin American troops in Korea and in future police actions, see Matthews to Burns, 9 Aug 50, *FRUS, 1950*, 1: 648; Matthews to Marshall, 27 Sep 50, ibid., 1: 664–65. For background paper, see ibid., 1: 642–46.

38. Summary of NSC Discussion, 24 Nov 50, HSTP, PSF, box 220.

39. Hewlett and Duncan, *Atomic Shield*, 525–29. For Acheson's view, see his testimony, 28 Nov 50, Senate, Foreign Relations, *Reviews of the World Situation*, 376.

40. For the figures and the goals, see NSC 68/1, "United States Objectives and Programs," 21 Sep 50, RG 273.

41. Allison to Rusk, 1 and 15 July 50, *FRUS, 1950*, 7: 272, 393–95.

42. Draft Memo Prepared by the PPS, 22 July 50, ibid., 7: 449–54; Cumings, *Child of Conflict*, 196–200; Lowe, *Korean War*, 181–84.

43. Acheson to Embassy in Korea, 14 July 50, *FRUS, 1950*, 7: 387; Truman Statement, 13 July 50, ibid., 7: 387; Lay to NSC, 17 July 50, ibid., 7: 410.

44. For an excellent analysis of the estimates of Soviet and Chinese intentions and capabilities as they related to the question of crossing the 38th parallel, see Foot, *Wrong War*, 67–87.

45. Bradley and Blair, *A General's Life*, 544; J. Collins, *War in Peacetime*, 118–29.

46. Memo for the File by Elsey, 26 Aug 50, Elsey Papers, box 72; *FRUS, 1950*, 6: 454–61.

47. Statement by Truman, 19 July 50, *FRUS, 1950*, 7: 430; Acheson to Douglas, 28 July 50, ibid., 6: 397; Truman to Austin, 27 Aug 50, *PPP:HST* (1950), 599–600.

48. Testimony by Acheson, 24 July 50, Senate, Foreign Relations, *Reviews of the World*

Situation, 316; CIA, "Review of the World Situation," 16 Aug 50, HSTP, PSF, box 209; Kennan to Acheson, 17 July 50, *FRUS, 1950*, 6: 380.

49. Douglas to Acheson, 14 July 50, *FRUS, 1950*, 7: 381–83; Bevin to Acheson, 15 July 50, ibid., 7: 398–99; MemCon by Perkins, 18 July 50, ibid., 7: 419.

50. Acheson to Douglas, 28 July 50, ibid., 6: 398.

51. Acheson to Embassy in India, 22 July 50, ibid., 7: 448–49; Acheson to Bruce, 15 Aug 50, ibid., 6: 856; Paper Prepared in the Bureau of UN Affairs, 24 Aug 50, ibid., 3: 1123; Bruce Diary, 10, 12, and 16 Aug 50, Bruce Papers.

52. MemCon by Merchant, 28 Aug 50, *FRUS, 1950*, 6: 466.

53. Summary of NSC Discussion, 27 July 50, HSTP, PSF, box 220.

54. Testimony by Acheson, 24 July 50, Senate, Foreign Relations, *Reviews of the World Situation*, 316; Acheson to Embassy in China, 14 Aug 50, *FRUS, 1950*, 6: 437–38; Strong to Clubb, 6 Sep 50, ibid., 6: 487.

55. Acheson to Douglas, 10 and 28 July 50, *FRUS, 1950*, 6: 350, 397–98.

56. Yost, "Agreed US-UK Memorandum of Discussions," 25 July 50, ibid., 3: 1658, 1662–63; Minutes of Mtg. of Representatives of France, the United Kingdom, and the United States, 4 Aug 50, ibid., 6: 420; Rusk to Douglas, 13 Aug 50, ibid., 6: 432–33.

57. Douglas to Acheson, 14 July 50, ibid., 6: 381–83; Bevin to Acheson, 15 July 50, ibid., 6: 398–99; Henderson to Acheson, 24 Aug 50, ibid., 6: 447–48; Simmons, *Strained Alliance*, 147–54; Whiting, *China Crosses the Yalu*, 47–91; Pollack, *Into the Vortex*; Hao Yufan and Zhai Zhihai, "China's Decision to Enter the Korean War," 99–115; Hunt, "Beijing and the Korean Crisis," 4–5; Cumings, *Origins of the Korean War*, 2: 350–76, 651–55.

58. Khrushchev, *Remembers: The Glasnost Tapes*, 145–46; Simmons, *Strained Alliance*, 119–82; Whiting, *China Crosses the Yalu*, 101–2, 112–14; Cumings, *Origins of the Korean War*, 2: 643–51, 663, 706. For Stalin's circumspection, see also Hao Yufan and Zhai Zhihai, "China's Decision to Enter the Korean War," 110–11; Hunt, "Beijing and the Korean Crisis," 7.

59. Draft Memo Prepared in the Dept. of Defense, 31 July 50, *FRUS, 1950*, 7: 506–7; Draft Memo by Allison and Emmerson, 21 Aug 50, ibid., 7: 620.

60. NSC 81/1, "United States Courses of Action with Respect to Korea," 9 Sep 50, ibid., 7: 716.

61. Bradley and Blair, *A General's Life*, 559–68; Schnabel and Watson, *History of the JCS*, 217–49; Lowe, *Korean War*, 181–93; Kaufman, *Korean War*, 82–88; Foot, *Wrong War*, 74–87.

62. CIA, "Review of the World Situation," 20 Sep 49, HSTP, PSF, box 250; CIA, "Situation Summary," 22 and 29 Aug 50, ibid.; CIA, "Critical Situations in the Far East," RG 330, box 132, CD 103-7-98; Bradley and Blair, *A General's Life*, 562–71; James, *MacArthur*, 486–500.

63. Foot correctly stresses that prior to October officials in Washington, including those in the DOS, expected to retaliate against mainland China should the latter intervene in behalf of North Korea. Foot, *Wrong War*, 86–87. Acheson even kept open the option of using Taiwan against China should the latter intervene in Korea. Acheson to Marshall, 11 Nov 50, *FRUS, 1950*, 6: 554–55.

64. Bradley and Blair, *A General's Life*, 572–80; Schnabel and Watson, *History of the JCS*, 263–77; James, *MacArthur*, 500–523.

65. James, *MacArthur*, 518–26; Cumings, *Origins of the Korean War*, 2: 733, 741–44.

66. Schnabel and Watson, *History of the JCS*, 277–99; Bradley and Blair, *A General's Life*, 583–88; Foot, *Wrong War*, 88–95. For Chinese perceptions, see Harding and Yuan, *Sino-American Relations*, 188–91, 213–22; Hunt, "Beijing and the Korean Crisis," 6–10; Cumings, *Origins of the Korean War*, 2: 733–41.

67. James, *MacArthur*, 523–35; Schnabel and Watson, *History of the JCS*, 299–332.

68. Bradley and Blair, *A General's Life*, 581–97; D. Condit, *Test of War*, 77–83.

69. See the opinion surveys, 10 Sep and 20 Oct 50, *Public Opinion Quarterly* 14 (Winter 1950–51): 804, and 15 (Spring 1951): 173; Truman's comments in *PPP:HST* (1950), 642, 713. The DOS found that 54 percent of the American people gave it a favorable rating in early Nov

1950. See Secretary's Daily Mtg., 6 Nov 50, RG 59, Executive Secretariat. For Acheson's sense of a more malleable Congress, see MemCon by Merchant, 31 Aug 50, *FRUS, 1950*, 6: 574–75; see also Cumings, *Child of Conflict*, 209–16; Kaufman, *Korean War*, 84–86; James, *MacArthur*, 531–32; Kusnitz, *Public Opinion and Foreign Policy*, 47–48.

70. See esp. Acheson to Bevin, 24 Nov 50, *FRUS, 1950*, 7: 1228–29; MemCon by Jessup, 21 Nov 50, ibid., 7: 1204–8; Acheson to Embassy in the United Kingdom, 21 Nov 50, ibid., 7: 1212; Farrar, "Britain's Proposal for a Buffer Zone," 341–46; Bernstein, "Policy of Risk."

71. MemCon by Allison, 23 Oct 50, *FRUS, 1950*, 6: 525–36; Acheson to Marshall, 11 Nov 50, ibid., 6: 554–55.

72. Minutes of the 39th and 40th Mtgs. of the U.S. Delegation to UN General Assembly, 14 and 15 Nov 50, ibid., 6: 562–63, 569–72; Marshall to Rusk, 27 Nov 50, ibid., 6: 582. For getting rid of Chiang, see also Halliday and Cumings, *Korea*, 67–68. For guerrilla activity in southern China, see CIA, "Soviet Capabilities and Intentions," 15 Nov 50, HSTP, PSF, box 253. For Acheson's monitoring for a potential insurgency, see his testimony, 28 Nov 50, Senate, Foreign Relations, *Reviews of the World Situation*, 394. For the military assistance program that was being worked up even prior to Chinese intervention in Korea, see Parelman to Rusk, 1 Dec 50, RG 59, PSA Division, box 1.

73. See esp. the reports by John Melby and Graves B. Erskine, 6 and 7 Aug 50, *FRUS, 1950*, 6: 842–48; Bruce Diary, 12 July 50, Bruce Papers.

74. Burns to Director of Naval Intelligence, 31 July 50, RG 330, box 178, CD 092 Indochina; MemCon by Acheson, 23 Aug 50, Acheson Papers, box 65; U.S. Delegation Minutes, 30 Aug 50, *FRUS, 1950*, 3: 1148–53.

75. Testimony by Acheson, 11 Sep 50, Senate, Foreign Relations, *Reviews of the World Situation*, 357–58; Rusk to Acheson, 8 Sep 50, *FRUS, 1950*, 6: 878–80; U.S. Delegation Minutes, 13 Sep 50, ibid., 3: 1227–28.

76. Substance of Statements Made at Wake Island Conference, 13 Oct 50, *FRUS, 1950*, 7: 957–58.

77. *PPP:HST* (1950), 674–79.

78. Ohly to Acheson, 20 Nov 50, *FRUS, 1950*, 6: 925–30; CIA, "Consequences to the United States of Communist Domination of Mainland Southeast Asia," 13 Oct 50, HSTP, PSF, box 257.

79. For Acheson's quotation, see his testimony, 11 Sep 50, Senate, Foreign Relations, *Reviews of the World Situation*, 357–58. For Army, Air Force, and DOS dissents to the CIA study, see the annexes to CIA, "Consequences of Communist Domination of Southeast Asia," 13 Oct 50, HSTP, PSF, box 257. For the importance of Southeast Asia, see, e.g., Paper Prepared by the Tripartite Drafting Group, 1 Sep 50, *FRUS, 1950*, 3: 1172–75; Webb to Johnson, 4 Aug 50, RG 330, box 198, CD 381 (General).

80. Acheson to Embassy in France, 11 Nov 50, *FRUS, 1950*, 6: 920; NSC 64/1, JCS to Marshall, 28 Nov 50, ibid., 6: 946–48.

81. For Marshall's caveat, see Notes on Cabinet Mtg., 20 Oct 50, Connelly Papers, box 2. For Acheson's views, see Memo by Battle, 21 Nov 50, *FRUS, 1950*, 7: 1201–3. For the importance assigned to aid to Indochina, see, e.g., Matthews to Acheson, 19 Oct 50, ibid., 6: 900–901. For the augmentation of French air power through U.S. assistance, see Carter to Marshall and Lovett, 1 Nov 50, Marshall Papers, SecDef Files, box 198. For the role of U.S. military advisers, see Robert E. Hoey to Rusk, 13 Nov 50, RG 59, PSA Division, box 8.

82. NSC 73/4, "Possible Further Soviet Moves in the Light of the Korean Situation," 25 Aug 50, *FRUS, 1950*, 1: 376–89; U.S. Delegation Minutes, 29 and 31 Aug 50, ibid., 3: 1136–37, 1167.

83. Memo by Pace, Matthews, and Finletter, 1 Aug 50, *FRUS, 1950*, 1: 356–57; Matthews to Burns, 16 Aug 50, ibid., 3: 212; U.S. Delegation Minutes, 13 Sep 50, ibid., 3: 1208; McCloy to Acheson, 27 Sep 50, ibid., 4: 727.

84. Bush to Voorhees, 11 July 50, Voorhees Papers, box 4; Gruenther to Voorhees, 9 July 50, ibid. For Acheson's confidence that defense capabilities could be built up within 18–24 months, see Minutes of a Private Conference, 14 Sep 50, *FRUS, 1950*, 3: 293–300; Acheson Testimony, 28 Nov 50, Senate, Foreign Relations, *Reviews of the World Situation*, 373–83.

85. Acheson Testimony, 11 Sep 50, Senate, Foreign Relations, *Reviews of the World Situation*, 340.

86. Memo of Telephone Conversation, 20 July 50, Acheson Papers, box 65; JCS and Pace, Matthews, and Finletter to Johnson, 13 July 50, *FRUS, 1950*, 3: 133–34; MemCon by Acheson, 21 July 50, ibid., 3: 136–37; Acheson Testimony, 24 July 50, Senate, Foreign Relations, *Reviews of the World Situation*, 320–21, 329–30, 336–37.

87. Bradley to Johnson, 30 Aug and 7 Sep 50, RG 330, box 176, CD 091.7 (Europe); Johnson to JCS, 14 Aug 50, ibid., box 206, CD 388.3 Germany; Douglas to Acheson, 12 July 50, *FRUS, 1950*, 3: 130–32; Memo by Barbara Evans, 3 [4] Aug 50, ibid., 3: 183; D. Condit, *Test of War*, 318–19.

88. Bradley to Johnson, 30 Aug 50, RG 330, box 176, CD 091.7 (Europe); JCS 2124/18, Bradley to Johnson, 1 Sep 50, RG 218, CCS 092 Germany (5-4-49), sec. 3; Acheson and Johnson to Truman, 8 Sep 50, *FRUS, 1950*, 3: 273–77.

89. Acheson Testimony, 11 Sep 50, Senate, Foreign Relations, *Reviews of the World Situation*, 343–44; U.S. Delegation Minutes, 12 Sep 50, *FRUS, 1950*, 3: 1192–94; JCS 2124/11 and 2124/18, Bradley to Johnson, 27 July and 1 Sep 50, RG 218, CCS 092 Germany (5-4-49), sec. 3.

90. For Acheson's statement, see Acheson to Truman, 31 July 50, *FRUS, 1950*, 3: 167–68; see also Byroade to Acheson, 23 July 50, ibid., 3: 699. For Nitze's view, see Secretary's Daily Mtg., 18 July 50, RG 59, Executive Secretariat; McCloy to Acheson, 3 Aug 50, *FRUS, 1950*, 3: 180–81; Douglas to Acheson, 8 Aug 50, ibid., 3: 190–92; Acheson, *Present at the Creation*, 437–40.

91. For the above two paragraphs, see Memo by Acheson, 31 July 50, *FRUS, 1950*, 3: 167–68; Matthews to Burns, 16 Aug 50, ibid., 3: 211–19; Acheson and Johnson to Truman, 8 Sep 50, ibid., 3: 273–78; JCS 2124/18, Bradley to Johnson, 1 Sep 50, RG 218, CCS 092 Germany (5-4-49), sec. 3; D. Condit, *Test of War*, 319. The JCS protested, however, when the DOS talked vaguely about ceding sovereignty to the European Defense Force. See JCS 2124/16, "Rearmament of Western Germany," 26 Aug 50, RG 218, CCS 092 Germany (5-4-49). For bureaucratic differences, see L. Kaplan, *Community of Interests*, 112; Schwartz, *America's Germany*, 130–35.

92. Acheson Testimony, 11 Sep 50, Senate, Foreign Relations, *Reviews of the World Situation*, 346–48; Intergovernmental Study Group on Germany, Report to the Foreign Ministers, 4 Sep 50, *FRUS, 1950*, 3: 1248–76; U.S. Delegation Minutes, 18 Sep 50, ibid., 3: 1235–38; Acheson to McCloy, 18 Oct 50, ibid., 3: 390–91; JCS 2124/18, Bradley to Johnson, 1 Sep 50, RG 218, CCS 092 Germany (5-4-49), sec. 3.

93. For ending the state of war, see MemCon by Acheson, 21 Aug 50, *FRUS, 1950*, 4: 653–54; Acheson Testimony, 11 Sep 50, Senate, Foreign Relations, *Reviews of the World Situation*, 348; Webb to Johnson, 10 Aug 50, RG 335, box 74; Johnson to Acheson, 12 Sep 50, ibid.

94. For the quotation, see McCloy to Acheson, 3 Aug 50, *FRUS, 1950*, 3: 181–82. For Acheson's views, see his discussions with the French and British in Sep 1950, ibid., 3: 288, 1208, 1214–16. For Germany's relations with the East, see also the Report of the Intergovernmental Group on Germany on the Occupation Statute, 1 Sep 50, ibid., 3: 1258–60. For Acheson's concern with Germany's bargaining position, see, e.g., Acheson to Webb, 17 Sep 50, ibid., 3: 320; Bruce to Acheson, 21 Sep 50, ibid., 3: 748–49. For the dispute in the International Authority for the Ruhr over coal, see Acheson to U.S. Delegation, 16 Oct 50, RG 43, IAR, box 274; Livengood to Acheson, 20 Oct 50, ibid. For the frustration over the German approach to the Schuman Plan negotiations, see Bohlen to Acheson, 25 Oct 50, *FRUS, 1950*, 3: 761.

95. MemCon by Acheson, 24 July 50, Acheson Papers, box 65; MemCon by Acheson, 31 July 50, *FRUS, 1950*, 3: 167–68; MemCon by Acheson, 21 Aug 50, ibid., 4: 653–54.

96. MemCon by Acheson, 21 July 50, *FRUS, 1950*, 3: 136–37; MemCon by Acheson, 21 Aug 50, Acheson Papers, box 65; Carpenter, "United States NATO Policy," 394–401.

97. For Acheson's presentation of the U.S. position to Schuman, Bevin, and other European statesmen, see *FRUS, 1950*, 3: 286–344, 1192–1247, 1392–93.

98. Schuman's views are recorded by Acheson in the preceding note. For French rearmament initiatives, which impressed Ambassador Bruce, see Bruce Diary, 7 Aug 50, Bruce Papers. For

French and European views that the Kremlin was not ready for and did not want global war, see U.S. Delegation Minutes, 29 Aug 50, *FRUS, 1950,* 3: 1135–37; Acheson to Embassy in France, 17 Oct 50, ibid., 3: 384; CIA, "Review of the World Situation," 18 Oct 50, RG 330, box 132, CD 103-14-8. For Acheson's special concern for undermining the contention that the Kremlin might be provoked, see Acheson to Truman, 15 Sep 50, *FRUS, 1950,* 3: 1231. For background, see Wall, *United States and the Reshaping of Postwar France,* chap. 7.

99. Notes on Cabinet Mtg., 29 Sep 50, Connelly Papers, box 2; Acheson to Truman, 20 Sep 50, *FRUS, 1950,* 3: 1245–47; Acheson to Webb, 23 Sep 50, ibid., 4: 723–24.

100. Acheson to Truman, 15 and 20 Sep 50, *FRUS, 1950,* 3: 1229–31, 1245–47; MemCon by Webb, 26 Sep 50, ibid., 3: 353–54; Acheson to Marshall, 16 Oct 50, ibid., 3: 381–82; MemCon by Acheson, 25 Oct 50, ibid., 3: 404–6; Acheson Testimony, 28 Nov 50, Senate, Foreign Relations, *Reviews of the World Situation,* 373–74.

101. Marshall to JCS, 2 Oct 50, *FRUS, 1950,* 3: 356–57; MemCon by Nitze, 9 Oct 50, ibid., 3: 364–66; D. Condit, *Test of War,* 320–25.

102. MemCon by Webb, 26 Sep 50, *FRUS, 1950,* 3: 353–54; Acheson to Bruce, 16, 17, and 31 Oct and 3 Nov 50, ibid., 3: 383, 384, 423, 429–31; MemCon by Acheson, 25 Oct 50, ibid., 3: 404.

103. Bradley to Marshall, 27 Oct 50, RG 218, Bradley Papers, box 2; Marshall to Owen Roberts, 16 Nov 50, Marshall Papers, SecDef Files, box 198; Acheson to Embassy in France, 27 Oct 50, *FRUS, 1950,* 3: 410–14; D. Condit, *Test of War,* 326–27.

104. For the statement of the foreign ministers of the Eastern bloc, 21 Oct 50, and for Acheson's response, see *FRUS, 1950,* 3: 665–67. For Germany's defense contribution, German politics, and Soviet maneuvering, see Adenauer, *Memoirs,* 271–305.

105. Acheson to Bruce, 3 and 29 Nov 50, *FRUS, 1950,* 3: 426–31, 496–98; Acheson to Embassy in the United Kingdom, 14 Nov 50, ibid., 3: 450–53; Acheson to Spofford, 18 Nov 50, ibid., 3: 471–72; Acheson Testimony, 28 Nov 50, Senate, Foreign Relations, *Reviews of the World Situation,* 373–83; Schwartz, *America's Germany,* 145–55.

106. For Dulles's view, see the mtg. of the Study Group on Japanese Peace Treaty Problems, Council on Foreign Relations, 23 Oct 50, Dulles Papers, box 48. For similar views in the DOS, see Intelligence Estimate, Office of Intelligence and Research, 25 June 50, *FRUS, 1950,* 7: 151. For the importance Acheson accorded the Japanese peace treaty, see Secretary's Daily Mtgs., 10, 21, and 22 Aug 50, RG 59, Executive Secretariat.

107. Sebald to Acheson, 27 June 50, *FRUS, 1950,* 6: 1228–29; Dulles to Acheson, 19 July 50, ibid., 6: 1243–44.

108. For Dulles's quotation, see Study Group, Council on Foreign Relations, 23 Oct 50, Dulles Papers, box 48; Fearey to Allison, 8 Aug 50, *FRUS, 1950,* 6: 1266–67.

109. Dulles to Acheson, 27 July 50, *FRUS, 1950,* 6: 1259–60; Jessup to Acheson, 24 July 50, ibid., 6: 1254; Bradley and Blair, *A General's Life,* 529–30; Burns to Marshall, 7 Nov 50, RG 330, box 205, CD 387 (Japan); D. Condit, *Test of War,* 189–90. For carping, see Unsigned Memo Prepared in the DOS, 14 Aug 50, *FRUS, 1950,* 6: 1274; Memo by W. J. Sheppard, 21 Aug 50, ibid., 6: 1276.

110. Bradley to Johnson, 22 Aug 50, *FRUS, 1950,* 6: 1279–82.

111. Memo of Phone Conversation by Dulles, ibid., 6: 1265; Allison to Acheson, 24 Aug 50, ibid., 6: 1286–88.

112. For the quotations, see Unsigned Memo by the PPS, 26 July 50, ibid., 6: 1256; Burns to Marshall, 7 Nov 50, RG 330, box 205, CD 387 (Japan); see also Memos by Allison, 24 July and 24 Aug 50, *FRUS, 1950,* 6: 1253–54, 1286–87; Douglas W. Overton to U. Alexis Johnson, 15 Sep 50, ibid., 6: 1305. At their meeting on Wake Island, MacArthur told Truman that he was organizing four divisions under a Japanese National Police Reserve. See Bradley, "Substance of Statements Made at Wake Island," 15 Oct 50, Elsey Papers, box 72.

113. Study Group, Council on Foreign Relations, 23 Oct 50, Dulles Papers, box 48; Kennan to Dulles, 20 July 50, *FRUS, 1950,* 6: 1250; U. Alexis Johnson to Sebald, 14 Sep 50, ibid., 6: 1304. For Dulles's views and role, see Schonberger, *Aftermath of War,* 250–53.

114. Study Group, Council on Foreign Relations, Dulles Papers, box 48; see also Dulles to Nitze, 20 July 50, *FRUS, 1950*, 6: 1247–48; Fearey, "Answers to Questions . . . ," 26 Oct 50, ibid., 6: 1329–30; Yasuhara, "Japan, Communist China, and Export Controls."

115. Editorial Note, *FRUS, 1950*, 6: 1308; MemCon by Stanton Babcock, 27 Sep 50, ibid., 6: 1323; Magruder to Marshall, 30 Sep 50, RG 330, box 205, CD 387 (Japan).

116. Study Group, Council on Foreign Relations, 23 Oct 50, Dulles Papers, box 48; Magruder to Marshall, 17 Oct 50, RG 330, box 205, CD 387 (Japan); Dulles to MacArthur, 15 Nov 50, *FRUS, 1950*, 6: 1351; Pruessen, *Dulles*, 463–84.

117. Bradley to Johnson, 6 Sep 50, *FRUS, 1950*, 6: 1486; NSC 84/2, "Position of the United States with Respect to the Philippines," 9 Nov 50, ibid., 6: 1515–20.

118. NSC 84/2, "Position of the United States with Respect to the Philippines," 9 Nov 50, ibid., 6: 1515–16; MemCon by Ferguson H. Clay, 22 Sep 50, ibid., 6: 1491. The utility of the Philippines in bolstering the French effort in Indochina is apparent in Bowers, *United States Air Force in Southeast Asia*, 3–11.

119. For the Bell Mission Report, 9 Oct 50, see ibid., 6: 1497–1502; Stanley, *Reappraising an Empire*, 293–99.

120. Bradley to Johnson, 6 Sep 50, *FRUS, 1950*, 6: 1488; MemCon by F. H. Clay, 22 Sep 50, ibid., 6: 1491.

121. NSC 84/2, "Position of the United States with Respect to the Philippines," 9 Nov 50, ibid., 6: 1515. For NSC discussion of NSC 84/2, see Summary of Discussion, 10 Nov 50, RG 273. For the estimate of outside aid to the Huks, see Memo by R. A. Moore, "Philippine Situation," 26 June 50, NHC, SPD, box 258, EG-52 (Philippines). For a military intelligence estimate of the situation, see also Memo of Information by Felix Johnson, 12 Sep 50, RG 330, CD 092 Philippines; CIA, "Prospects for Stability in the Philippines," 10 Aug 50, Univ. Publications of America, Microfilm Series, Reel 5.

122. Record of the Undersecretary's Mtg., 3 Nov 50, *FRUS, 1950*, 6: 1510–11; NSC 84/2, "Position of the United States with Respect to the Philippines," 9 Nov 50, ibid., 6: 1518–20; Stanley, *Reappraising an Empire*, 291–92.

123. Stueck, *Korean War*, chap. 3; MemCon by Babcock, 26–27 Oct 50, *FRUS, 1950*, 6: 1335–36; Truman, *Off the Record*, 197; Simmons, *Strained Alliance*, 155–64; Whiting, *China Crosses the Yalu*, 112–14. For the complicated and still only partially understood relationships between the Soviet Union, China, and North Korea, see Pollack, *Into the Vortex*; Hao Yufan and Zhai Zhihai, "China's Decision to Enter the Korean War," 110–11.

124. Stueck, *Korean War*, chap. 3; Hunt, "Beijing and the Korean Crisis," 7–10; Simmons, *Strained Alliance*, 137–68; Whiting, *China Crosses the Yalu*, 68–150. For MacArthur's view, see "Substance of Statements Made at Wake Island," 15 Oct 50, *FRUS, 1950*, 7: 953. Pollack, *Into the Vortex*, stresses the ambiguities and hesitation in Chinese policy.

125. Acheson to Bevin, 24 Nov 50, *FRUS, 1950*, 7: 1228–29; Farrar, "Britain's Proposal for a Buffer Zone," 341–47; Stueck, *Korean War*, chap. 3.

126. NSC 68/2, "United States Objectives and Programs for National Security," 30 Sep 50, RG 273.

127. NSC 81/1, "United States Courses of Action with Respect to Korea," 9 Sep 50, *FRUS, 1950*, 7: 712–21; Schnabel and Watson, *History of the JCS*, 217–332.

128. Summary of NSC Discussion, 10 Nov 50, RG 273. Although war plans continued to stress the Soviet capacity to seize large parts of Western Europe, U.S. officials did not think the Soviets could win a protracted war.

129. Memo Prepared in the DOS, 28 Aug 50, *FRUS, 1950*, 7: 655–56.

130. For the quotation, see Summary of NSC Discussion, 10 Nov 50, RG 273; Lo, "Civilian Policymakers and Military Objectives"; Bernstein, "Policy of Risk"; Cumings, *Origins of the Korean War*, 2: 709; see also Bradley and Blair, *A General's Life*, 581–97.

131. For decisionmaking just prior to MacArthur's final offensive, see *FRUS, 1950*, 7: 1201–24; D. Condit, *Test of War*, 78–83; Lo, "Civilian Policymakers and Military Objectives," 235–40. For the goals, somewhat understated here, see NSC 68/2, "United States Objectives and Pro-

grams," 30 Sep 50, RG 273. For the reflections of Acheson and Truman, the veracity of which should be checked against the actual documents in the *FRUS* volumes and the NSC records, see Acheson, *Present at the Creation*, 466–68; Truman, *Memoirs: 1946–52*, 423–38.

Chapter 10

1. Schnabel and Watson, *History of the JCS*, 333–47; Bradley and Blair, *A General's Life*, 595–604; James, *MacArthur*, 535–42.

2. For the statement by Lovett, see MemCon by Acheson, 2 Dec 50, Acheson Papers, box 65; see also Bradley and Blair, *A General's Life*, 581–616; Acheson, *Present at the Creation*, 461–76; *PPP:HST* (1950), 727.

3. For Truman's approval ratings, see *Public Opinion Quarterly* 15 (Spring 1951): 177–78. For Truman's view of the elections, see *PPP:HST* (1950), 713; see also Kepley, *Collapse of the Middle Way*, 85–104; Reeves, *McCarthy*, 327–46. For the impact of McCarthy's attacks, see the documents in Jessup Papers, boxes A138 and A140.

4. Foot, "Anglo-American Relations in the Korean Crisis"; Stueck, *Korean War*; Schnabel and Watson, *History of the JCS*, 347–55.

5. For efforts to coordinate policy, see, e.g., MemCon by Acheson, 16 Oct 51, Acheson Papers, box 66; Jessup to Bradley, 25 Sep 51, NA, RG 218, Bradley Papers, box 3; Secretary's Daily Mtgs., 7 Dec 50 and 18 Jan 51, RG 59, Executive Secretariat; Editorial Comment, *FRUS, 1951*, 1: 33 (footnote 1).

6. Notes of Cabinet Mtg., 28 Nov 50, Connelly Papers, box 2; Memo by Elsey, 28 Nov 50, Elsey Papers, box 72; CIA, "Soviet Intentions in the Current Situation," 2 Dec 50, *FRUS, 1950*, 7: 1310.

7. U.S. Minutes, Truman-Attlee Conversations, 4, 5, and 7 Dec 50, *FRUS, 1950*, 3: 1716–17, 1733–34, 1770–72; Kennan Notes, 6 Dec 50, Acheson Papers, box 65; Schnabel and Watson, *History of the JCS*, 347–69.

8. U.S. Minutes, Truman-Attlee Conversations, 4 and 7 Dec 50, *FRUS, 1950*, 3: 1728–30, 1762–63.

9. U.S. Minutes, Truman-Attlee Conversations, 4, 7, and 8 Dec 50, ibid., 3: 1712–15, 1733–38, 1763–68, 1773; MemCon by Jessup, 4 Dec 50, ibid., 3: 1720–22; the quotation is on p. 1768.

10. U.S. Minutes, Truman-Attlee Conversations, 7 and 8 Dec 50, ibid., 3: 1768–69, 1775–79.

11. *PPP:HST* (1951), 8; see also Notes of Cabinet Mtg., 22 Dec 50, Connelly Papers, box 2; Mtg. of the Pres with Congressional Leaders, 13 Dec 50, Elsey Papers, box 73.

12. For the quotation, see Summary of NSC Discussion, 15 Dec 50, RG 273. For the above two paragraphs, see also Memo Prepared by the PPS, 9 Dec 50, *FRUS, 1950*, 1: 462–66; NSC 68/4, "United States Objectives and Programs for National Security," 14 Dec 50, ibid., 1: 488–89; Testimony by Acheson, Senate, Foreign Relations, *Reviews of the World Situation*, 398–99; see also Trachtenberg, "Wasting Asset."

13. *PPP:HST* (1950), 728–29.

14. For figures, see Memo by the JCS, 6 Dec 50, *FRUS, 1950*, 1: 475–77; Poole, *History of the JCS*, 38–39, 77.

15. *PPP:HST* (1951), 29, 63, 70–71, 86.

16. Summary of NSC Mtg., 15 Dec 50, RG 273. For figures on the buildup, see *PPP:HST* (1950), 743; ibid. (1951), 11. For missile development, see BOB, National Security Branch, "Department of Defense Budget Estimates, Fiscal Year 1952," 10 Apr 51, RG 51, Series 47.8A, box 52; W. H. Shapley to Ramsey, 29 Jan 51, ibid., box 5.

17. *PPP:HST* (1950), 741–50; ibid. (1951), 28–44. For the mtg. with congressional leaders, see Mtg. of the Pres, 13 Dec 50, Elsey Papers, box 73; see also Notes of Cabinet Mtgs., 8 and 12 Dec 50, Connelly Papers, box 2; Minutes of NSC Mtg., 11 Dec 50, RG 273.

18. James, *MacArthur*, 546–56; Schaller, *MacArthur*, 223–27.

19. Schnabel and Watson, *History of the JCS*, 388–431.

20. For the polls, see *Public Opinion Quarterly* 15 (Summer 1951): 386–87. For the impressions of Lovett, see Kennan Notes, 6 Dec 50, Acheson Papers, box 65.

21. For key documents, see NSC 101, "Courses of Action Relative to Communist China and Korea," 12 Jan 51, *FRUS, 1951*, 7: 70–72; NSC 101/1, "U.S. Action to Counter Chinese Communist Aggression," 15 Jan 51, ibid., 7: 79–81; Rusk to Acheson, 17 Jan 51, ibid., 7: 1514–15; Memo Prepared in the DOS, 17 Jan 51, ibid., 7: 1515–17; DOS-JCS Mtg., 30 Jan 51, ibid., 7: 1536–42; Summary of NSC Discussion, 18 Jan 51, HSTP, PSF, box 220.

22. In addition to the citations in the previous note, see JCS to Marshall, 15 Jan 51, *FRUS, 1951*, 1: 61–62; JCS, "Review of the Current World Situation," 15 Jan 51, ibid., 1: 63–73; DOS-JCS Mtg., 24 Jan 51, ibid., 1: 34–37. For an especially fine account of Allied pressures, see Stueck, *Korean War*, chap. 4.

23. Summary of NSC Discussion, 25 Jan 51, HSTP, PSF, box 220; DOS-JCS Mtg., 24 Jan 51, *FRUS, 1951*, 1: 34–37; Memo by John H. Ferguson and Robert W. Tufts, 29 Jan 51, ibid., 1: 39–40; Memo by Ferguson, 8 Feb 51, ibid., 1: 43–48.

24. Schnabel and Watson, *History of the JCS*, 432–77; Foot, *Wrong War*, 128–39. For a fine discussion of the military situation in Korea, see Blair, *Forgotten War*, 633–780.

25. Bradley and Blair, *A General's Life*, 609–37; Truman, *Memoirs: 1946–52*, 490–510; James, *MacArthur*, 560–604; D. Condit, *Test of War*, 100–108; Schaller, *MacArthur*, 228–40.

26. Senate, Armed Services and Foreign Relations, *Military Situation in the Far East*, esp. 3–320; James, *MacArthur*, 607–40.

27. For the quotations, see Bradley Testimony, 7 May 51, Senate, Armed Services and Foreign Relations, *Military Situation in the Far East*, 730–31; see also Foot, *Wrong War*, 131–39.

28. Testimony by Bradley and Acheson, 15 May and 1 June 51, Senate, Armed Services and Foreign Relations, *Military Situation in the Far East*, 732–33, 745, 756, 1718–20.

29. Dingman, "Atomic Diplomacy," 69–79; Dean, *Forging the Atomic Shield*, 107–9, 136–43; Schaller, *MacArthur*, 234–38. For estimates of Soviet intentions and capabilities and for appraisals of the correlation of power that affected decisionmaking, see Foot, *Wrong War*; Trachtenberg, "Wasting Asset."

30. Carpenter, "United States NATO Policy," 394–405.

31. Acheson Testimony, 16 Feb 51, Senate, Armed Services and Foreign Relations, *Assignment of Ground Forces*, 77–105; the quotation is on p. 81. See also Testimony by Eisenhower and Bradley, ibid., 3, 145–46.

32. Ibid., 40–69, 78–81, 126–29, 139–40, 222–31; see also Nitze, "Relationship of Strategic and Theater Nuclear Forces," 124–25.

33. For polls, see *Public Opinion Quarterly* 14 (Winter 1950–51): 819; ibid., 15 (Summer 1951): 382–84. For feelings in the Senate, see Kepley, *Collapse of the Middle Way*, 101–16.

34. Kepley, *Collapse of the Middle Way*, 101–16; Carpenter, "United States NATO Policy," 405–14.

35. For key agreements, see *FRUS, 1950*, 3: 531–49; Spofford to Acheson, 3 Dec 50, ibid., 3: 513–15; Edward Fursdon's essay in Heller and Gillingham, *NATO*, chap. 10.

36. U.S. Delegation Minutes, 18 and 19 Dec 50, ibid., 3: 588–603. For U.S. thinking and interdepartmental planning, see also Bradley to Marshall, 4 Dec 50, RG 218, CCS 092 Germany (5-4-49), sec. 6; Marshall to Bradley, 5 Dec 50, RG 330, box 176, CD 091.7 (Europe); Phone Conversation, 6 Dec 50, Acheson Papers, box 66.

37. Report by the North Atlantic Military Committee, "Military Aspects of German Participation in the Defense of Western Europe," 12 Dec 50, *FRUS, 1950*, 3: 538–39.

38. Acheson to Embassy in the United Kingdom, 12 Jan 51, *FRUS, 1951*, 3: 1447–49; Acheson to Schuman, 20 Dec 50, *FRUS, 1950*, 3: 606; Testimony by Acheson, 22 Dec 50, Senate, Foreign Relations, *Reviews of the World Situation*, 445; Testimony by Acheson, 16 Feb 51, Senate, Armed Services and Foreign Relations, *Assignment of Ground Forces*, 78. For Soviet and East German proposals and the U.S. reaction, see *FRUS, 1951*, 3: 1751–1827; Acheson, *Present at the*

Creation, 551–55. For McCloy's warnings, see McCloy to Acheson, 5 and 16 Jan 51, *FRUS, 1951*, 3: 1319–20, 1452–53; Schwartz, "German Rearmament," 303–5.

39. U.S. Minutes, Truman-Pleven Mtg., 30 Jan 51, *FRUS, 1951*, 4: 319–20; Jessup to Marshall, 24 Jan 51, RG 330, box 264, CD 337 (Four Powers); Burns to Marshall, 24 Jan 51, ibid.; Acheson, *Present at the Creation*, 551–53.

40. U.S. Minutes, Truman-Auriol Mtg., 29 March 51, *FRUS, 1951*, 4: 366; Memo by Harriman, 31 March 51, ibid., 4: 378–79.

41. U.S. Minutes, Truman-Pleven Mtg., 30 Jan 51, *FRUS, 1951*, 4: 319–20; Pace, Matthews, and Finletter to Marshall, 26 Jan 51, RG 330, box 264, CD 337 (Four Powers). For fear that German rearmament might provoke a Soviet attack, see Summary of NSC Discussion, 25 Jan 51, HSTP, PSF, box 220; Robert Wampler's essay in Heller and Gillingham, *NATO*, chap. 16.

42. For the quotation, see Notes of Cabinet Mtg., 8 Dec 50, Connelly Papers, box 2; see also Secretary's Daily Mtg., 6 Feb 51, RG 59, Executive Secretariat. For Byroade's comments, see Minutes of the Undersecretary's Mtg., 23 Feb 51, ibid. See also Bark and Gress, *From Shadow to Substance*, 274–87; Schwartz, *America's Germany*, 148–55.

43. Acheson to Certain Diplomatic Offices, 8 Dec 50, *FRUS, 1950*, 3: 764; Thorp to Acheson, 14 Dec 50, ibid., 3: 766; Briefing Paper Prepared in the Office of the U.S. High Commissioner for Germany, 2 Feb 51, *FRUS, 1951*, 4: 88–90; McCloy to Acheson, 19 Feb and 3 March 51, ibid., 4: 92, 97–98; Hogan, *Marshall Plan*, 364–78. For the most recent analyses of the Schuman Plan that stress the U.S. role, see Gillingham, *Coal, Steel, and the Rebirth of Europe*; Schwartz, *America's Germany*, 154–55, 186–99. The British position can now be conveniently studied in Bullen and Pelly, *Documents on British Policy Overseas*, vol. 1.

44. U.S. Delegation Minutes, 19 Dec 50, *FRUS, 1950*, 3: 596–97; Acheson to Certain Diplomatic and ECA Missions, 15 Jan 51, *FRUS, 1951*, 3: 29–30; NSC 68/3, Annex no. 2, "Foreign and Economic Assistance Programs," 8 Dec 50, *FRUS, 1950*, 1: 434.

45. For Eisenhower's tour, see *FRUS, 1951*, 3: 392–458; Eisenhower Statement, 1 Feb 51, Senate, Armed Services and Foreign Relations, *Assignment of Ground Forces*, 15–31. For Soviet forces, see JCS 1924/49, "Estimate of the Scale and Nature of the Immediate Communist Threat to Security of the United States," 5 Feb 51, RG 218, CCS 092 USSR (3-27-45), sec. 55.

46. Cabot to Acheson, 27 March 51, *FRUS, 1951*, 3: 103–5; House of Representatives, Foreign Affairs, *Selected Executive Session Hearings*, 9: 110; Minutes of Undersecretary's Mtgs., 11 June 51, RG 59, Executive Secretariat; Ismay, *NATO*, 102; Eisenhower, *Papers*, 12: 847; see also Charles Maier's essay in Heller and Gillingham, *NATO*, chap. 15.

47. DOS-JCS Mtg., 20 Feb 51, *FRUS, 1951*, 3: 58–63; Paper Prepared by ISAC [June 1951], ibid., 3: 195–96; Poole, *History of the JCS*, 244–45.

48. NSC 114/1, Appendix A, 8 Aug 51, *FRUS, 1951*, 1: 154–55; Secretary's Daily Mtgs., 30 Apr and 4 May 51, RG 59, Executive Secretariat; Minutes of the Undersecretary's Mtgs., 9 May 51, ibid.

49. *PPP:HST* (1951), 302–8; Paper Prepared by ISAC, "North Atlantic MTDP and Related United States Assistance" [June 1951], *FRUS, 1951*, 3: 193–94; Byrne, "United States and Mutual Security," 81–113.

50. MemCon by E. M. Martin, 21 June 51, *FRUS, 1951*, 3: 197–204; "United States Forces in Defense of Western Europe," 27 June 51, RG 330, box 226, CD 091.7 (Europe); D. Condit, *Test of War*, 371–72; Poole, *History of the JCS*, 240–47.

51. For the talks in Bonn, see *FRUS, 1951*, 3: 990–1047. For the opening stages of the Paris conference on the EDC, see ibid., 3: 755–847. For Acheson's views in this and the following two paragraphs, see Memos by Acheson, 6 and 16 July 51, ibid., 3: 813–18, 836–38; Acheson and Lovett to Truman, 30 July 51, ibid., 3: 850–52; Acheson to Schuman, 9 Aug 51, ibid., 3: 1164–67.

52. MemCon by R. E. Beebe, 26 June 51, RG 330, box 226, CD 091.7 (Europe); Marshall to Eisenhower, 27 June 51, ibid.; Allied High Commissioners for Germany to the Governments of the United States, the United Kingdom, and France, 22 June 51, *FRUS, 1951*, 3: 1044–47; Schwartz, "Skeleton Key," 378–85.

53. MemCon by Beebe, 16 July 51, RG 330, box 226, CD 091.7 (Europe); Acheson and Lovett to Truman, 30 July 51, *FRUS, 1951*, 3: 850–52; Acheson to Schuman, 9 Aug 51, ibid., 3: 1164–67.

54. Bradley to Marshall, 28 Feb 51, RG 330, box 175, CD 091.7 (Europe); Bradley to Vandenberg and Collins, 17 July 51, RG 218, Bradley Papers, box 3; Collins to Bradley, 6 Aug 51, ibid.; Nathan A. Twining to Bradley, 18 Aug 51, ibid.

55. Nash to Marshall, 25 Aug 51, RG 330, box 227, CD 091.7 (Europe); Eisenhower to Marshall, 18 July 51, *FRUS, 1951*, 3: 838–39; Eisenhower, *Diaries*, 196–97; Eisenhower, *Papers*, 12: 457–63; Schwartz, *America's Germany*, 216–30.

56. Report of the Allied High Commissioners Concerning the Establishment of a New Relationship Between the Allied Powers and Germany, 9 Aug 51, *FRUS, 1951*, 3: 1501–11; U.S. Delegation Minutes, 12–14 Sep 51, ibid., 3: 1268–86, 1295.

57. U.S. Delegation Minutes, 12 and 13 Sep 51, ibid., 3: 1259, 1288–90. For French caution, see Heuser, *Western 'Containment' Policies in the Cold War*, 136–37. For a fine discussion of the problems emanating from the U.S. rearmament program, see Wall, *United States and the Reshaping of Postwar France*, chap. 7.

58. Acheson to Truman, 19 Sep 51, *FRUS, 1951*, 3: 679–80. For Marshall's and Bradley's understanding of the economic problems and pressures, see, e.g., MemCon by Martin, 21 June 51, ibid., 3: 197–204; Maier's essay in Heller and Gillingham, *NATO*, chap. 15.

59. For Acheson's views, see, e.g., MemCon by Martin, 21 June 51, ibid., 3: 201; U.S. Delegation Minutes, 11 Sep 51, ibid., 3: 1239–43; U.S. Delegation to Webb, 16 Sep 51, ibid., 3: 656–57. For background thinking of U.S. officials, see MemCon by Nitze, 13 Sep 51, ibid., 1: 889; PPS Memo, 22 Sep 51, ibid., 1: 174–75.

60. For the above two paragraphs, see ibid., 4: 771–839; U.S. Delegation Minutes, 13 Sep 51, ibid., 3: 1286; see also First Progress Report on NSC 72/4, "United States Policy Toward Spain," 5 June 51, HSTP, PSF, box 213; "NSC Progress Report on the Implementation of United States Policy Toward Spain," 7 Sep 51, ibid., box 214; "Terms of Reference for the Joint Military Survey Team (Spain)," 10 Aug 51, RG 330, box 241, CD 092.2 (Spain).

61. Much of this can be followed in *FRUS, 1950*, 4: 1441–1515.

62. The basic papers are NSC 18/4, "United States Policy Toward the Conflict Between the USSR and Yugoslavia," 17 Nov 49, ibid., 4: 1341–48; NSC 18/6, "Position of the United States with Respect to Yugoslavia," 7 March 51, RG 273; see also Acheson to Tom Connally, 31 Oct 50, *FRUS, 1950*, 4: 1491–92; Editorial Note, ibid., 4: 1507–8; Heuser, *Western 'Containment' Policies in the Cold War*, 170–83.

63. Bradley to Johnson, 23 Aug 50, *FRUS, 1950*, 4: 1441–44; *FRUS, 1951*, 4: 1677–1858; Heuser, *Western 'Containment' Policies in the Cold War*, 162–64.

64. Acheson to Spofford, 16 June 51, *FRUS, 1951*, 4: 1814; Acheson to Embassy in the United Kingdom, 14 July 51, ibid., 4: 1828; Memos by Bradley, Sep 1951, RG 218, Bradley Papers, box 3; Eisenhower to Bradley, 20 Sep 51, ibid.

65. For the quotation, see DOS, Office of Intelligence and Research, "Estimate of Probable Western and Soviet Reaction to Alternate U.S. Policies Concerning an Attack on Yugoslavia in 1951," 5 March 51, *FRUS, 1951*, 4: 1757–58, footnote 2; Harriman to Acheson, 27 Aug 51, ibid., 4: 1842–43; Nitze to Acheson, 31 July 51, ibid., 1: 110–11; PPS Memo, 22 Sep 51, ibid., 1: 174–75; Eisenhower, *Papers*, 12: 224–25.

66. For the relationship between Yugoslavia and southern Italy, see DOS-JCS Mtg., 30 Jan 51, *FRUS, 1951*, 5: 42. For Eisenhower's strategy, see Notes on a Mtg. at the White House, 31 Jan 51, ibid., 3: 454. For advantages to be derived from adding Yugoslav and Turkish strength, see MemCon by Perkins, 16 Sep 51, ibid., 3: 662; JCS 1704/49, "Analysis of Military Aid Program to Turkey," by Collins, 4 May 51, RG 218, CCS 092 (8-22-46), sec. 53. For the efforts of Carney and Eisenhower, see, e.g., Carney to Sherman, 8 Jan 51, NHC, Double Zero Files, 1950, box 1(1); Eisenhower to JCS, 6 May 51, Sherman Papers, box 7. For raising Italian armaments beyond treaty limits, see E. Smith, "From Disarmament to Rearmament," 371–82.

67. See NIE 14, "Importance of Iranian and Middle East Oil to Western Europe Under Peacetime Conditions," 8 Jan 51, *FRUS, 1951*, 5: 270–75. For the growing importance of Middle Eastern oil in wartime, see McGhee to Burns, 27 Dec 50, RG 330, box 182, CD 092 (UK); JCS 1741/46, "Need for Middle East Oil Throughout a War," 21 March 51, RG 218, CCS 463.7 (9-6-45), sec. 18. For Turkey's overall importance, see NSC 109, "Position of the United States with Respect to Turkey," *FRUS, 1951*, 5: 1148–62.

68. MemCon by Lewis Jones, 1 Sep 50, RG 59, Military Adviser to the NEA, box 1.

69. Acheson to Johnson, 31 Aug 50, *FRUS, 1950*, 3: 257–61; NEA, "Security Problems in the Near East and Africa," 29 Aug 50, RG 330, box 184, CD 092.3 (NATO–Council of Ministers).

70. Johnson to Acheson, 11 Sep 50, RG 330, box 184, CD 092.3 (NATO–Council of Ministers); see also JCS 1887/16, Memo of the JCS, 25 Oct 50, RG 218, CCS 381 Eastern Mediterranean and Middle East Area (11-19-47), sec. 2.

71. Acheson to Webb, 19 Sep 50, *FRUS, 1950*, 5: 1321–22; see also U.S. Delegation Minutes, 13 Sep 50, ibid., 3: 1218–20.

72. McGhee to Acheson, 22 Feb 51, RG 330, box 243, CD 092.3 NATO (GEN); see also Memo by Henry S. Villard, 5 Feb 51, *FRUS, 1951*, 5: 1117–18; NIE 9, "Turkey's Position in the East-West Struggle," 26 Feb 51, ibid., 5: 1119–26.

73. For the quotation and the conclusions of U.S. diplomats at a mtg. at Istanbul, see *FRUS, 1951*, 5: 62–76; see also Acheson to Marshall, 27 Jan 51, ibid., 5: 21–23; Paper by Stabler, 24 Oct 50, *FRUS, 1950*, 5: 229; NEA, "Regional Policy Statement," 28 Dec 50, ibid., 5: 272–74.

74. See esp. DOS-JCS Mtg., 30 Jan 51, *FRUS, 1951*, 5: 29–32; Paper Prepared by ISAC, 20 Feb 51, ibid., 5: 81; NSC 47/5, "Arab States and Israel," 14 March 51, ibid., 5: 95–101; Bradley to British Joint Service Mission, RG 218, Bradley Papers, box 2.

75. Approved Summary of Conclusions, U.S.-U.K. Chiefs of Staff, 23 Oct 50, *FRUS, 1950*, 3: 1686–87; U.S. Minutes, 26 Oct 50, ibid., 3: 1691–92; Paper by Stabler, 24 Oct 50, ibid., 5: 224–25; Acheson to Embassy in Egypt, 20 Nov 50, ibid., 5: 321; NSC Progress Report on the Implementation of NSC 45/1, 31 Oct 50, HSTP, PSF, box 210; JCS 2143/6, "HEADSTONE," 7 Dec 50, RG 218, CCS 381 (1-26-50), BP, pt. 1.

76. Caffery to Acheson, 1 Apr 51, *FRUS, 1951*, 5: 353–55.

77. Caffery to Acheson, 23 March 51, ibid., 5: 351, n. 4; Memo of Informal U.S.-U.K. Discussions, 2–3 Apr 51, ibid., 5: 105–8, 357–61.

78. Louis, *British Empire in the Middle East*, 632–57; Cottam, *Iran and the United States*, 90–95.

79. See esp. NSC 107/1, "Position of the United States with Respect to Iran," 6 and 20 June 51, RG 273; Acheson to McGhee, 31 March 51, *FRUS, 1951*, 5: 296–97; Minutes of Undersecretary's Mtg., 6 and 25 Apr 51, RG 59, Executive Secretariat; Louis, *British Empire in the Middle East*, 657–78; Goode, *United States and Iran*, 89–94.

80. NSC 107/1, "Position of the United States with Respect to Iran," 6 and 20 June 51, RG 273; NIE 14, "Importance of Iranian and Middle East Oil," 8 Jan 51, *FRUS, 1951*, 5: 270; Painter, "Oil and U.S. Policy," 2–9.

81. MemCon by Richard Funkhouser, 14 May 51, *FRUS, 1951*, 5: 309–14; Acheson to Certain Diplomatic and Consular Offices, 23 Aug 51, ibid., 5: 328–29; Minutes of Undersecretary's Mtg., 9 May 51, RG 59, Executive Secretariat; Painter, "Oil and U.S. Policy," 10–17.

82. For Acheson's thinking, see MemCons by Acheson, 27 Apr and 12 July 51, Acheson Papers, box 66; Notes on Cabinet Mtg., 22 June 51, Connelly Papers, box 2.

83. Minutes of Undersecretary's Mtg., 25 Apr 51, RG 59, Executive Secretariat; Secretary's Daily Mtgs., 23 and 30 Apr 51, ibid.; DOS-JCS Mtg., 2 May 51, *FRUS, 1951*, 5: 118–20. For the quotation, see DOS, "First Progress Report on NSC 107," 2 May 51, HSTP, PSF, box 212.

84. Painter, "Oil and U.S. Policy," 9–13; Louis, *British Empire in the Middle East*, 678–88; Harriman to Truman and Acheson, 17 July 51, HSTP, PSF, box 180; Memo for the Director of Central Intelligence by William L. Langer, 3 Aug 51, ibid.; Notes on Cabinet Mtg., 31 Aug 51, Connelly Papers, box 2.

85. Notes on Cabinet Mtg., 31 Aug and 14 Sep 51, Connelly Papers, box 2; Minutes of Undersecretary's Mtg., 29 Aug 51, RG 59, Executive Secretariat; Painter, *Oil and the American Century*, 176–79.

86. For McGhee, see MemCon by Funkhouser, 14 May 51, *FRUS, 1951*, 5: 311–12. For the actions of the Petroleum Administration for Defense, see Oscar Chapman to NSC, 2 Dec 51, HSTP, PSF, box 219; Painter, *Oil and the American Century*, 179–81. Suspicions about covert operations are generated by the large sections of the Annex to NSC 107/1 that still remain classified. See Annex to NSC 107/1, "Position of the United States with Respect to Iran," 20 June 51, RG 273. Moreover, beginning in spring 1951, the CIA and the DOS Near East experts began meeting on a regular basis. See Goode, *United States and Iran*, 94.

87. For Lovett, see Notes on Cabinet Mtg., 21 Sep 51, Connelly Papers, box 2; Memo of Phone Conversation, 25 Sep 51, Acheson Papers, box 66. For British policy, see Louis, *British Empire in the Middle East*, 657–66, 686–89.

88. For Soviet commercial penetration of Iran, see Matthews to Burns, 28 Nov 50, RG 330, box 175, CD 091.31 Iran. For the absence of Soviet threats, see NEA, "Regional Policy Statement," 28 Dec 50, *FRUS, 1950*, 5: 272. Also note the absence of any stress on Soviet aggressive behavior in the basic NSC paper, NSC 47/5, "Arab States and Israel," 14 March 51, ibid., 5: 95–97. Nor did U.S. diplomats, meeting in Istanbul, dwell on Soviet initiatives. See ibid., 5: 50–78, 102–4. In their comprehensive review of regional developments for their colleagues in the DOS, NEA officials said hardly a word about Soviet aggressiveness. See Minutes of the Undersecretary's Mtg., 25 May 51, RG 59, Executive Secretariat. The generalizations regarding Iran comport with Goode's recent analysis (*United States and Iran*, 84–109).

89. DOS-JCS Mtg., 2 May 51, *FRUS, 1951*, 5: 114–17; Memo by McGhee, 24 Apr 51, ibid., 3: 512–15; Acheson to Marshall, 24 March 51, ibid., 3: 501–5. For aid, see ibid., 5: 150.

90. Carney, "Summary of Strategic Implications" [15 March 51], *FRUS, 1951*, 5: 103–4; JCS 2009/12, "Inclusion of Greece and Turkey as Full Members in the North Atlantic Treaty Organization," by Jerauld Wright, 16 March 51, RG 218, CCS 370 (2-20-50), sec. 1. For the quotation, see JCS 1704/49, "Analysis of Military Aid Program to Turkey," by Collins, 1 May 51, RG 218, CCS 092 (8-22-46), sec. 53; "Summary of Views and Bases for JCS Position on Security Arrangements for Greece and Turkey" [9? Apr 51], RG 330, box 243, CD 092.3 NATO; NSC 109, "Position of the United States with Respect to Turkey," *FRUS, 1951*, 5: 1148–62.

91. For the above two paragraphs, see Acheson to Truman, 12 Sep 51, *FRUS, 1951*, 5: 185–87; Webb to Embassy in Egypt, 8 Sep 51, ibid., 5: 181–82; U.S. Delegation Minutes, 10 Sep 51, ibid., 3: 1232–34. For JCS views, see Bradley to Marshall, 29 Aug 51, ibid., 5: 378–80. For the relationship between commonwealth forces and the Middle East, see Devereux, "Britain and the Defence of the Middle East," 330–35.

92. U.S. Delegation Minutes, 12 Sep 51, *FRUS, 1951*, 3: 1260–67; MemCon by Ridgway B. Knight, 20 Sep 51, ibid., 3: 680–82; Webb to Embassy in Turkey, 20 Sep 51, ibid., 3: 576–77; Bradley to Eisenhower, 18 Sep 51, ibid., 3: 671.

93. Summary of NSC Discussion, 9 Aug 51, HSTP, PSF, box 220; Minutes of Undersecretary's Mtg., 8 Aug 51, RG 59, Executive Secretariat; see also Acheson's comments in Minutes of Tripartite Ministerial Mtg., 6 Nov 51, *FRUS, 1951*, 1: 580.

94. MemCon by Perkins, 16 Sep 51, *FRUS, 1951*, 3: 661–63; U.S. Delegation Minutes, 12 Sep 51, ibid., 3: 1260; Elmer J. Rogers to Marshall [ND], RG 330, box 245, CD 092.3 NATO.

95. Dulles to Acheson, 30 Nov 50, Dulles Papers, box 48; Dulles to Acheson, 8 Dec 50, *FRUS, 1950*, 6: 1359–60; Memos by Allison, 11 and 12 Jan 51, *FRUS, 1951*, 6: 791–92.

96. Acheson to Marshall, 13 Dec 50, *FRUS, 1950*, 6: 1363–66.

97. JCS 2180/2, "United States Policy Toward Japan," 28 Dec 50, ibid., 6: 1389–90.

98. Acheson to Sebald, 3 Jan 51, *FRUS, 1951*, 6: 778–79; Collins to MacArthur, 3 Jan 51, ibid., 6: 780; Acheson to Marshall, 9 Jan 51, ibid., 6: 789.

99. Memos by Fearey, 26, 27, and 29 Jan 51, ibid., 6: 811–13, 819–23; the quotation is on p. 812. See also Miyasato, "Dulles and the Peace Settlement with Japan," 19–26.

100. MemCon by Allison, 29 Jan 51, *FRUS, 1951*, 6: 827–30; Undated Memo by Yoshida,

ibid., 6: 833–35; Memo by Fearey, 7 Feb 51, ibid., 6: 863–64; Yoshida, *Memoirs*, 246–51; Schonberger, *Aftermath of War*, 256–59.

101. Memos by Fearey, 31 Jan and 5, 7, and 10 Feb 51, *FRUS, 1951*, 6: 835–36, 857–72; Dulles to Acheson, 10 Feb 51, ibid., 6: 874; Minutes of Undersecretary's Mtg., 28 Feb 51, RG 59, Executive Secretariat; Study Group Discussion, Council on Foreign Relations, 23 Oct 50, Dulles Papers, box 48; Pruessen, *Dulles*, 468–76.

102. Babcock to Earl D. Johnson, 26 Feb 51, RG 330, box 279, CD 387 (Japan); Memo by Allison, 12 Feb 51, *FRUS, 1951*, 6: 881–83; Schonberger, *Aftermath of War*, 261–62.

103. Memos by Fearey, 14, 16, and 17 Feb 51, *FRUS, 1951*, 6: 155–65, 169–71; Dulles to Frederick Doidge, 18 Feb 51, ibid., 6: 175; Babcock to Johnson, 26 Feb 51, RG 330, box 279, CD 387 (Japan); Pruessen, *Dulles*, 478–81.

104. Marshall to Acheson, 15 Feb 51, *FRUS, 1951*, 6: 884–85.

105. Bradley to Marshall, 2 and 11 July 51, RG 330, box 231, CD 092 (Japan).

106. Marshall to Pace et al., 28 March 51, RG 330, box 317, CD 092 (Japan); Pace to Marshall, 4 May 51, ibid., box 231.

107. Thomas Cabot to Burns, 9 March 51, RG 330, box 231, CD 092 (Japan); Webb to Lovett, 28 Sep 51, ibid.; Nash to Lovett, 2 Oct 51, ibid.; see also Rusk to Matthews, 22 Feb 51, *FRUS, 1951*, 6: 890–95; Webb to Marshall, 1 March 51, ibid., 6: 899–900; Rusk to Acheson, 20 July 51, ibid., 6: 1208–15; JCS to Marshall, 14 Sep 51, ibid., 6: 1350; Rusk to Acheson, 25 Sep 51, ibid., 6: 1358.

108. Marshall to Acheson, 20 Apr 51, RG 330, box 231, CD 092 (Japan); Marshall to Truman, 28 Aug 51, ibid.

109. DOS-JCS Mtg., 11 Apr 51, *FRUS, 1951*, 6: 194–201; Marshall to Acheson, 13 Apr 51, ibid., 6: 201–2; Dulles to Acheson, 13 Apr 51, ibid., 6: 203; Devereux, "Britain and the Defence of the Middle East," 330–35.

110. DOS-JCS Mtg., 11 Apr 51, *FRUS, 1951*, 6: 969–71; Memo by Dulles, 12 Apr 51, Dulles Papers, box 53.

111. Memo by Dulles, 12 Apr 51, Dulles Papers, box 53.

112. MemCons, 17 and 18 Apr 51, *FRUS, 1951*, 6: 980, 987–88.

113. Bradley to Marshall, 14 May 51, RG 330, box 279, CD 387 (Japan); Marshall to Acheson, 18 May 51, ibid.

114. JCS to Marshall, 17 Apr 51, *FRUS, 1951*, 6: 991–92; Dulles to Acheson, 25 Apr 51, ibid., 6: 1020; NSC 48/5, "United States Objectives, Policies and Courses of Action with Respect to Asia," 17 May 51, ibid., 6: 38–39.

115. MemCon by Dulles, 11 June 51, ibid., 6: 1113; see also Dulles to Acheson, 4 June 51, ibid., 6: 1104.

116. Dulles to Acheson, 4–8 June 51, ibid., 6: 1104–10. For background on Dulles's talks with the British, see ibid., 6: 909–26, 961–64, 1003–37, 1055–1104; Pruessen, *Dulles*, 485–88.

117. MemCons by Allison, 5 and 12 Apr 51, *FRUS, 1951*, 6: 964–66, 978; Memo by Acheson, 28 May 51, ibid., 6: 1050–51; Acheson to Sebald, 2 Aug 51, ibid., 6: 1236–37; MemCon by Sebald, 3 Sep 51, ibid., 6: 1314–16; Unsigned MemCon by H. Alexander Smith, ND [5 Sep 51], ibid., 6: 1326–27. For senatorial statement to Truman opposing relations between the Communist Chinese and the Japanese, see Editorial Note, ibid., 6: 1347.

118. Marshall to Acheson, 28 June 51, *FRUS, 1951*, 6: 1156–59; Acheson to Truman, 28 June 51, ibid., 6: 1160–61; Memo by Acheson, 29 June 51, ibid., 6: 1163–64; Memo of Mtg. on Japanese peace conference, 24 Aug 51, ibid., 6: 1293; Acheson to Truman, 29 Aug 51, ibid., 6: 1300–1302.

119. Brands, "From ANZUS to SEATO," 250–55.

120. *FRUS, 1951*, 6: 223–45; Dingman, "Diplomacy of Dependency," 314–21.

121. Nash to Lovett, 13 Aug 51, RG 330, box 279, CD 387 (Japan); Bradley to Nash, 16 Aug 51, ibid.; A. C. Davis to Nash, 27 and 29 Aug 51, ibid.

122. Draft Letter, Acheson to Marshall, ND, *FRUS, 1951*, 6: 241–42; Memo by Dulles,

10 Aug 51, ibid., 6: 242–43; Dulles to Marshall, 9 Aug 51, ibid., 6: 244–45. For Truman, see *PPP:HST* (1951), 506–8. Dulles and the DOS had wanted to bring Indonesia into the security agreements. See Dulles to Acheson, 8 Dec 50, *FRUS, 1950*, 6: 1360; Dulles, "Draft of a Possible Pacific Ocean Pact," 3 Jan 51, *FRUS, 1951*, 6: 134; Cochran to Acheson, 3 Feb 51, ibid., 6: 147. For concerns about the impact of nonexclusion and the need for a larger pact, see NSC Staff Study [May 1951], ibid., 6: 63; DOS-JCS Mtg., 11 Apr 51, ibid., 6: 197; Memo by Fearey, 17 Feb 51, ibid., 6: 164–65.

123. Acheson to Truman, 29 Aug 51, *FRUS, 1951*, 6: 1300–1302; Acheson to Webb, 6 Sep 51, ibid., 6: 1334–35.

124. Bradley to Marshall, 17 July 51, RG 330, box 279, CD 387 (Japan). For Nitze, see Minutes of Undersecretary's Mtg., 13 July 51, RG 59, Executive Secretariat; see also Pace, Kimball, and Finletter to Marshall, 17 July 51, RG 330, box 279, CD 387 (Japan); JCS to Marshall, 17 Aug 51, *FRUS, 1951*, 6: 1260–61.

125. For the quotation, see NSC Staff Study, "United States Objectives, Policies, and Courses of Action in Asia," May 1951, DOD, *United States–Vietnam Relations*, 8: 442. For a good, brief discussion of the progress made and the problems that still loomed in the future for the Japanese economy, see UN, ECAFE, *Economic Survey of Asia and the Far East* (1951), 166–82; CIA, "Probable Developments in the World Situation Through Mid-1953," 24 Sep 51, *FRUS, 1951*, 1: 204; Borden, *Pacific Alliance*, 137–65.

126. CIA, "Situation Summary," 8 and 22 Dec 50, HSTP, PSF, box 250; NIE 5, "Indochina: Current Situation and Probable Developments," 29 Dec 50, *FRUS, 1950*, 6: 959–62; Hoey to Jessup, 27 Dec 50, ibid., 6: 957–58. For background, see Duiker, *Communist Road to Power*, 139–49.

127. Compare NIE 5, "Indochina," 29 Dec 50, to NIE 35, "Probable Developments in Indochina During the Remainder of 1951," 7 Aug 51; they may be found in *FRUS, 1950*, 6: 961, and *FRUS, 1951*, 6: 470. See also Ogburn to Rusk, 15 Jan 51, ibid., 6: 7–8; Duiker, *Communist Road to Power*, 139–40; Pike, *Vietnam and the Soviet Union*, 31–35.

128. Ogburn to Rusk, 15 Jan 51, *FRUS, 1951*, 6: 7–8; Heath to Acheson, 21 Jan and 24 Feb 51, ibid., 6: 357, 384–85; MemCon by Acheson, 9 Jan 51, Acheson Papers, box 66.

129. NIE 5 is a typical U.S. assessment. See NIE 5, "Indochina," 29 Dec 50, *FRUS, 1950*, 6: 960–63.

130. Rusk to Matthews, 31 Jan 51, *FRUS, 1951*, 6: 20–26; Heath to Lacy, 20 July 51, ibid., 6: 457; UN, ECAFE, *Economic Survey of Asia and the Far East* (1951), 144, 148–52. For the special importance of Malaya, see Rotter, *Path to Vietnam*, esp. 141–56.

131. NSC Staff Study, "United States Objectives, Policies, and Courses of Action in Asia," May 1951, DOD, *United States–Vietnam Relations*, 8: 441–44. For concern with the Philippines, see, e.g., Carter to Malony, 25 Apr 51, RG 330, box 220, CD 091.3 (Philippines); Marshall to Malony, 2 May 51, ibid. For Japan's trade with Southeast Asia, see UN, ECAFE, *Economic Survey of Asia and the Far East* (1951), 167–73, 181–82, 102.

132. The quotations come from two important JCS and DOS papers. See JCS, "Courses of Action Relative to Communist China and Korea—Anti-Communist Chinese," 14 March 51, *FRUS, 1951*, 7: 1598–1605, esp. 1605; Memo Prepared in the DOS, 9 Feb 51, ibid., 7: 1574–78. The respective views of the agencies were harmonized in NSC 48/5, "United States Objectives, Policies, and Courses of Action in Asia," 17 May 51, ibid., 6: 33–39. For background, see also ibid., 7: 93–94, 1536–42, 1566–68. Acheson's strong support for covert action was apparent at the NSC meeting on 12 Jan 51. See Summary of NSC Discussion, 13 Jan 51, HSTP, PSF, box 220. For a discussion of covert actions in China during this time, see Leary, *Perilous Missions*, 124–43. For overall similarities in the approaches of U.S. officials to the Korean conflict, see Foot, *Wrong War*; Bernstein, "New Light on the Korean War."

133. Bradley to Marshall, 26 Jan 51, RG 330, box 264, CD 337 (Four Powers); Heath to Acheson, 1 Jan 51, *FRUS, 1951*, 6: 336–37; Acheson to Legation in Saigon, 30 Jan 51, ibid., 6: 369; Bradley to Marshall, 2 Feb 51, RG 218, Bradley Papers, box 2; "Conference Report on

Tripartite Military Talks on Southeast Asia," 15–18 May 51, *FRUS, 1951*, 6: 65–71; DOS-JCS Mtg., 8 June 51, ibid., 6: 72–76.

134. For preparations of the military aid package, see Rusk to Cabot, 25 Jan 51, RG 59, PSA Division, box 1. For Pleven's talks with Truman and Acheson, see *FRUS, 1951*, 4: 306–12, 334–35; ibid., 6: 366–69. For the transfer of funds in May 1951, see Editorial Note, ibid., 6: 423. For aid through fiscal year 1951, see "United States Position on Items of the Agenda for Military Staff Talks . . . Concerning . . . the Defense of Southeast Asia," May 1951, RG 330, box 230, CD 092 (Indochina). For Truman's request for additional funds, see *PPP:HST* (1951), 304, 309–11.

135. Rusk to Bonesteel, 8 June 51, RG 59, PSA Division, box 1. For the impact of U.S. aid, see NIE 35, "Probable Developments in Indochina," 7 Aug 51, *FRUS, 1951*, 6: 470. For French appreciation, see Bruce to Acheson, 18 March 51, ibid., 6: 404–6. For Lovett's views, see Record of Mtg., 20 Sep 51, ibid., 6: 517–21; Lovett to Acheson, 1 Oct 51, ibid., 6: 525.

136. Heath to Acheson, 15 May, 14, 29, and 30 June, and 20 July 51, *FRUS, 1951*, 6: 419–20, 428, 435–41, 457–59; Robert Blum to Foster, 12 July 51, ibid., 6: 450–52; Merchant to Rusk, 27 July 51, ibid., 6: 462–64; Gullion to Acheson, 18 Aug 51, ibid., 6: 480–83.

137. NIE 35, "Probable Developments in Indochina," 7 Aug 51, ibid., 6: 470–75; Gullion to Acheson, 18 Aug 51, ibid., 6: 480–82; Memo by Heath, ND [late Aug 1951], ibid., 6: 485–86; Mtg. of the Foreign Ministers, 14 Sep 51, ibid., 6: 500–501. For the real setbacks suffered by the Viet Minh, see Duiker, *Communist Road to Power*, 149–51.

138. NIE 35, "Probable Developments in Indochina," 7 Aug 51, ibid., 6: 471–73; Gullion to Acheson, 18 Aug 51, ibid., 6: 481; "First Progress Report on NSC 48/5," 25 Sep 51, ibid., 6: 95–97; Kahin, *Intervention*, 36–38.

139. Heath to Acheson, 29 June 51, and Heath to Lacy, 20 July 51, *FRUS, 1951*, 6: 433–39, 457–59; the quotation is on p. 438. For Acheson's views, see Acheson to the Embassy in France, 11 Nov 50, *FRUS, 1950*, 6: 920; U.S. Delegation Minutes, 11 and 14 Sep 51, *FRUS, 1951*, 3: 1249, 1294–95.

140. Merchant to Rusk, 27 July 51, *FRUS, 1951*, 6: 463.

141. For the above two paragraphs, see U.S. Delegation Minutes, 11 Sep 51, ibid., 3: 1249–50; Mtg. of Foreign Ministers, 14 Sep 51, ibid., 6: 500–501; MemCon by Heath, 14 Sep 51, ibid., 6: 499; MemCon by William Gibson, 14 Sep 51, ibid., 6: 502–3; Record of a Mtg. at the Pentagon by J. D. Mitchell, 20 Sep 51, ibid., 6: 517–21.

142. Webb to Truman, 13 Sep 51, ibid., 6: 496–97; Merchant to Acheson, 12 Sep 51, ibid., 6: 494–96; Record of a Mtg. at the Pentagon by Mitchell, 20 Sep 51, ibid., 6: 520; Wall, *United States and the Reshaping of Postwar France*, chap. 8.

143. NIE 35, "Probable Developments in Indochina," 7 Aug 51, *FRUS, 1951*, 6: 473–75; MemCon by Heath, 14 Sep 51, ibid., 6: 499.

144. Bradley to Lovett, 14 Sep 51, RG 330, box 230, CD 092 (Indochina).

145. Kaufman, *Korean War*, 183–97; Blair, *Forgotten War*, 817–940; Stueck, *Korean War*, chap. 6.

146. Kaufman, *Korean War*, 183–206; Blair, *Forgotten War*, 918–47; Foot, *Wrong War*, 148–50; "First Progress Report on NSC 48/5," 25 Sep 51, *FRUS, 1951*, 6: 90–93.

147. MemCon by Acheson, 27 June 51, Acheson Papers, box 66; Bradley to Ridgway, 11 Aug and 5 Sep 51, *FRUS, 1951*, 7: 811, 882–83. For the reconciliation of DOS and JCS positions, see ibid., 7: 859–64, 880–91, 911–14.

148. In addition to the documents cited in the preceding note, see *FRUS, 1951*, 7: 893–98, 914–16; MemCon by Ferguson, 6 Aug 51, ibid., 1: 876–80; MemCon by Nitze, 13 Sep 51, ibid., 1: 885–89; Foot, *Wrong War*, 147–52.

149. MemCon by Arneson, 14 June 51, *FRUS, 1951*, 1: 847.

150. For the quotation, see Nitze to Acheson, 31 July 51, ibid., 1: 111; PPS Memo by Nitze, 22 Sep 51, ibid., 1: 174–75; NSC 114/2, "United States Programs for National Security," 12 Oct 51, ibid., 1: 182–92; Trachtenberg, "Wasting Asset."

151. CIA, "Effect of Soviet Possession of Atomic Weapons on the Security of the United States," 9 June 50, HSTP, PSF, box 257; CIA, "Soviet Capabilities and Intentions," 15 Nov 50,

ibid., box 253; CIA, "Probable Developments in the World Situation Through Mid-1953," 24 Sep 51, ibid., box 215; CIA, "Status of the Soviet Atomic Energy Program," 28 July 51, ibid., box 250.

152. Kirk to Acheson, 25 Apr 51, RG 59, 661.00/4-2551; CIA, "Probable Developments in the World Situation Through Mid-1953," 24 Sep 51, HSTP, PSF, box 215.

153. Kirk to Acheson, 25 Apr 51, RG 59, 661.00/4-2551.

154. For the size of the U.S. arsenal, see Cochran, Arkin, and Hoenig, *Nuclear Weapons Databook*, 15. For the deterrent effect of the U.S. stockpile, see Acheson's comments in U.S. Minutes, 30 Jan 51, *FRUS, 1951*, 4: 318; Memo by Savage, 23 May 51, ibid., 1: 836; Nitze to Acheson, 31 July 51, ibid., 1: 110–11.

155. For the air threat to the United Kingdom, see JCS 1844/49, "IRONBARK," 3 July 51, RG 218, CCS 381 USSR (3-2-46), BP, pt. 5. For support of ground troops, see Weckerling to Robert Grow, 10 July 51, RG 319, Army—Intelligence Project File, box 193. For the critical caveat about one-way missions and air refueling techniques, see CIA, "Probable Developments in World Situation Through Mid-1953," 24 Sep 51, *FRUS, 1951*, 1: 194. For Soviet air power, see also P. Murphy, *Soviet Air Forces*, 179–80; Lee, *Soviet Air and Rocket Forces*, 107–8; Evangelista, "Evolution of the Soviet Tactical Air Forces," 452–57. Limited Soviet strategic capabilities did not mean that the Soviets could not inflict damage on the United States; it meant they could not be confident of victory and, therefore, would be inclined to take fewer risks than the United States. For an incisive analysis of these considerations, see Betts, *Nuclear Blackmail*, 144–80.

156. For the quotation, see NSC 114/2, "United States Programs for National Security," 12 Oct 51, *FRUS, 1951*, 1: 186; JCS 1844/49, "IRONBARK," 3 July 51, RG 218, CCS 381 USSR (3-2-46), BP, pt. 5. For Italy, see DOS-JCS Discussion, 6 Feb 51, *FRUS, 1951*, 5: 42. For the revised estimate of Soviet submarines, see Secretary's Daily Mtg., 12 Feb 51, RG 59, Executive Secretariat. Of course, weaknesses remained, and they were dwelled on by war planners in the Pentagon; see S. Ross, *American War Plans*, 142–48.

157. For the quotations, see NIE 22, "Vulnerability of the Soviet Bloc to Economic Warfare," 19 Feb 51, HSTP, PSF, box 211; Kirk to Acheson, 25 Apr 51, RG 59, 661.00/4-2551; see also CIA, "Probable Developments in the World Situation Through Mid-1953," 24 Sep 51, *FRUS, 1951*, 1: 196. This report plays down Soviet economic shortcomings, but note the critical caveat, a caveat that appears in most war plans as well, that the estimates disregard the impact of U.S. bombing on Soviet wartime production capabilities. For deficiencies in the Soviet transport net that U.S. military officers thought worthy of comment, see Grow to Bolling, 19 Dec 50, RG 319, Army—Intelligence Project Decimal File, box 193; JCS to SHAPE, 29 Oct 51, RG 218, CCS 092 USSR (3-27-45), sec. 60.

158. CIA, "Soviet Control of the European Satellites and Their Economic and Military Contributions to Soviet Power, Through Mid-1953," 7 Nov 51, HSTP, PSF, box 253.

159. For Admiral L. C. Stevens's speech, see Robert P. Joyce to Nitze, 2 Feb 51, *FRUS, 1951*, 1: 43–44; Eisenhower, *Papers*, 12: 90; Statement by Eisenhower, 1 Feb 51, Senate, Armed Services and Foreign Relations, *Assignment of Ground Forces*, 15–16, 25, 30–31; Memo by Bohlen, 22 Aug 51, *FRUS, 1951*, 1: 164–66; Kirk to Acheson, 25 Apr 51, ibid., 4: 1574–75, 1579; MemCon by Dulles, 11 June 51, ibid., 6: 1112–13. For Acheson and Bradley, see MemCon by Martin, 21 June 51, ibid., 3: 201.

160. For Khrushchev's quote, see his *Remembers: The Glasnost Tapes*, 147. For Stalin's view that war could be avoided, see Editorial Note, *FRUS, 1951*, 4: 1532–33; Kirk to Acheson, 19 Feb, 28 July, and 7 Aug 51, ibid., 4: 1534–35, 1620, 1633; Kennan to Acheson, 13 March 51, ibid., 4: 1557–60; Gifford to Acheson, 27 July 51, ibid., 4: 1617–18; Acheson to Morrison, 19 July 51, ibid., 7: 699.

161. Kirk to Acheson, 25 Apr 51, *FRUS, 1951*, 4: 1574–76. The quotation comes from the full report; see RG 59, 661.00/2-2551; NIE 25, "Probable Soviet Courses of Action in Mid-1952," 2 Aug 51, *FRUS, 1951*, 1: 120–22; Memo by Bohlen, 22 Aug 51, ibid., 1: 164–65; U.S. Minutes, 30 Jan 51, ibid., 4: 318–20.

162. MemCon by Arneson, 25 May and 14 June 51, *FRUS, 1951*, 1: 841, 849–51; MemCon

by Ferguson, 6 Aug 51, ibid., 1: 876–78; NSC 114/1, "Status and Timing of Current U.S. Programs for National Security," 8 Aug 51, ibid., 1: 152–53; Memo by Nitze, 13 Sep 51, ibid., 1: 885–89; CIA, "Probable Developments in the World Situation Through Mid-1953," 24 Sep 51, ibid., esp. 1: 196–202.

163. In addition to the citations in the preceding note, see Paper Prepared by the JSSC and Representatives of the DOS, "United States Position on Considerations Under Which the United States Will Accept War and on Atomic Warfare," 3 Aug 51, *FRUS, 1951*, 1: 865–72; MemCon by Jessup, 11 Sep 51, ibid., 1: 881–82. For Yugoslavia, see also Heuser, *Western 'Containment' Policies in the Cold War*, 164–70.

164. NSC 114/2, "United States Programs for National Security," 12 Oct 51, ibid., 1: 182–92; the quotations are on pp. 191, 187–88.

165. Summaries of NSC Discussions, 28 June and 2 and 9 Aug 51, HSTP, PSF, box 220; Nitze to Acheson, 31 July 51, *FRUS, 1951*, 1: 110–11; NSC 114/1, "Status and Timing of Current U.S. Programs for National Security," 8 Aug 51, ibid., 1: 130–53; NSC 114/2, "United States Programs for National Security," 12 Oct 51, ibid., 1: 182–92. For recognition that arms control initiatives must not interfere with the buildup, see, e.g., Hickerson to Acheson, 18 Oct 51, ibid., 1: 542–44; U.S. Delegation Minutes, 3 Nov 51, ibid., 1: 571–72; Tripartite Ministerial Mtg. Minutes, 6 Nov 51, ibid., 1: 579–80.

166. In addition to the NSC 114 series cited in the preceding note, see esp. Annex no. 1, "Military and Mobilization Programs," 27 July 51, RG 273, Policy Paper Files.

167. JSSC and DOS, "Considerations Under Which the United States Will Accept War," 3 Aug 51, *FRUS, 1951*, 1: 866–74.

Chapter 11

1. Nitze to Matthews, 14 July 52, *FRUS, 1952–54*, 2: 59; Paper Drafted by the PPS, "Basic Issues Raised by Draft NSC 'Reappraisal of U.S. Objectives and Strategy for National Security' " [ND], ibid., 2: 64.

2. Harriman Testimony, 17 Jan 52, Senate, Foreign Relations, *Executive Sessions*, 4: 111.

3. Caridi, *Korean War and American Politics*.

4. McCoy, *Presidency of Truman*, 276–80, 296–300.

5. For the good spirit with which these men labored together at international conferences, see, e.g., Acheson to Truman, 17 Dec 52, *FRUS, 1952–54*, 5: 353; see also Isaacson and Thomas, *Wise Men*, 504–58; D. Condit, *Test of War*, 36–39, 513–19.

6. The work of Nitze, Bohlen, and their staffs on basic national security issues is elucidated in *FRUS, 1952–54*, 2: 1–222; see esp. Bohlen to Acheson, 21 Aug 52, ibid., 2: 87–88. For Dean and the AEC, see Dean, *Forging the Atomic Shield*, 151–200; see also D. Condit, *Test of War*, esp. 514–17; J. Collins, *War in Peacetime*, 332.

7. D. Condit, *Test of War*; Poole, *History of the JCS*, 1–476. For Bradley's comments on Lovett, see Bradley and Blair, *A General's Life*, 648–51.

8. These generalizations are based on a reading of the Summaries of NSC Discussions, 1951–52, HSTP, PSF, box 220.

9. The implication here is not that the Chinese and North Koreans were any more compromising but that the U.S. negotiating position did not ease the way to a solution. For the problems of negotiating an armistice, see Bernstein's essay in Cumings, *Child of Conflict*, 261–307; Foot, *A Substitute for Victory*.

10. *PPP:HST* (1952–53), 707–10, 1114–28.

11. NSC 114/2, "United States Programs for National Security," 12 Oct 51, *FRUS, 1951*, 1: 182–91; see also the many briefing papers written in preparation for the talks with Churchill and Eden, late Dec 1951 and early Jan 1952, HSTP, PSF, box 116.

12. MemCon by Acheson, 5 Jan 52, *FRUS, 1952–54*, 6: 736–37; MemCon by Xanthaky, 22 Feb 52, ibid., 5: 129; Memo by Bohlen, 27 March 52, ibid., 2: 5–8; Acheson Testimony, 5 Feb

52, Senate, Foreign Relations, *Executive Sessions*, 4: 159–60; JCS to Bradley, 17 Nov 51, NA, RG 218, Bradley Papers, box 3; MemCon by Acheson, 23 Oct 51, Acheson Papers, box 66; NIE, "Likelihood of the Deliberate Initiation of Full-Scale War by the USSR Against the United States and Its Western Allies Prior to the End of 1952," 8 Jan 52, HSTP, PSF, box 253.

13. For the quotations, see Steering Group, "US and UK Appreciation of Probable Soviet Actions in the Near Future" [early Jan 1952], HSTP, PSF, box 116; see also MemCon by Acheson, 5 Jan 52, *FRUS, 1952–54*, 6: 736–37; MemCon by Xanthaky, 22 Feb 52, ibid., 5: 129; House of Representatives, Foreign Affairs, *Selected Executive Session Hearings*, 15: 179.

14. Steering Group, "US and UK Appreciation" [early Jan 1952], HSTP, PSF, box 116.

15. Frank C. Nash to Mrs. William Wright, 17 Dec 51, RG 330, box 256, CD 320.2; Karl R. Bendetsen to Pace, 30 March 52, RG 330, box 361, CD 381 (General).

16. The quotations are from NSC 114/2, "Programs for National Security," 12 Oct 51, *FRUS, 1951*, 1: 187–88; Schwartz to Bohlen, 12 May 52, *FRUS, 1952–54*, 2: 14; PPS to Acheson, 16 Oct 51, *FRUS, 1951*, 1: 225–27; Memo of DOS-JCS Mtg., 16 Jan 52, *FRUS, 1952–54*, 12: 31.

17. The generalizations in this paragraph have been especially influenced by NSC 114/2, "Programs for National Security," 12 Oct 51, *FRUS, 1951*, 1: 184–91; Nitze to Bruce, 21 May 52, RG 59, PPS, box 7; JCS 1953/11, "Estimate of the Over-All Effect of Air Bombing of the Industrial Capacity of the USSR on the Soviet Capability to Prosecute a Campaign in Western Europe," 28 May 52, RG 218, CCS 373 (10-23-48), sec. 7.

18. For the quotations, see NSC 114/2, "Programs for National Security," 12 Oct 51, *FRUS, 1951*, 1: 184–85; Nitze to Acheson, 17 Oct 51, ibid., 1: 233; Nitze, "Relationship of Strategic and Theater Nuclear Forces"; see also the many briefing papers written for the talks with Churchill and Eden and especially "US and UK Appreciation" [early Jan 1952], HSTP, PSF, box 116.

19. NSC 114/3, "Summary Statement No. 1—The Military Program," 10 May 52, *FRUS, 1952–54*, 2: 21–45.

20. *PPP:HST* (1952–53), 68–69.

21. Poole, *History of the JCS*, 133. For costs of the Korean War, see Lovett to Lay, 2 July 52, RG 330, box 362, CD 381 (War Plans—NSC 68).

22. Poole, *History of the JCS*, 109–11.

23. Notes on Cabinet Mtg., 4 Jan 52, Connelly Papers, box 2; Lovett to Truman, 4 Jan 52, *FRUS, 1952–54*, 2: 2.

24. *PPP:HST* (1952–53), 55, 60, 65, 68–69. For expenditures on hard goods and construction, see *FRUS, 1952–54*, 2: 28. For the costs of combat operations in Korea, see McNeil to Rosenberg, 17 June 52, RG 330, box 362, CD 381 (War Plans—NSC 68).

25. U.S. Delegation to Webb, 27 Nov 51, *FRUS, 1951*, 3: 731–32; Acheson to Truman, 30 Nov 51, ibid., 3: 748; Summary of TCC Report, 6 Feb 52, *FRUS, 1952–54*, 5: 203–4; Acheson Testimony, 15 Jan 52, House of Representatives, Foreign Affairs, *Selected Executive Session Hearings*, 15: 169, 176–77; Harriman Testimony, 17 Jan and 4 March 52, ibid., 15: 97, 101, 269–74. For provocative analyses that play down Soviet conventional capabilities, see Evangelista, "Soviet Military Capabilities," and Combs, "An Exaggerated Vulnerability?"

26. DOD to NSC, "Status of United States Military Programs as of 30 June 1952," 29 July 52, RG 330, box 361, CD 381 (General); Bradley to Ridgway, 11 Sep 52, RG 218, Bradley Papers, box 4.

27. U.S. Delegation to Webb, 27 Nov 51, *FRUS, 1951*, 3: 731–32. For NATO infrastructure, see *FRUS, 1952–54*, 5: 116, footnote 9. For the figures on tactical air wings, see Poole, *History of the JCS*, 134–35. For Air Force tasks, see *FRUS, 1952–54*, 2: 22.

28. For the quotation, see DOD to NSC, "Status of United States Military Programs," 29 July 52, RG 330, box 361, CD 381 (General). For atomic-capable aircraft, JCS 2220/4, "Information for General Eisenhower on Availability of Atomic Weapons," 31 Jan 52, Microfilm Collection, JCS, pt. 2, Strategic Issues, sec. 1, reel 3 (starting frame 1077). For pioneering work on the role of atomic weapons in Europe's defense, see Wampler, "The Die Is Cast."

29. Poole, *History of the JCS*, 168; Key Data Book [Oct 1952], *FRUS, 1952–54*, 2: 172.

30. Wells, "Origins of Massive Retaliation"; JCS 1953/11, "Estimate of the Over-All Effect of Air Bombing of the Industrial Capacity of the USSR on the Soviet Capability to Prosecute a Campaign in Western Europe," 28 May 52, RG 218, CCS 373 (10-23-48), sec. 7.

31. Lovett to H. D. Smyth, 6 Nov 51, RG 330, box 287, CD 471.6 (A-Bomb); D. Rosenberg, "Toward Armageddon," 154-82.

32. Small to Lovett, 31 Oct and 17 Nov 51, RG 330, box 282, CD 400.174 Military Agencies; Summary of NSC Discussion, 18 Oct 51, HSTP, PSF, box 220; Dean, *Forging the Atomic Shield*, 188-95; Hewlett and Duncan, *Atomic Shield*, 559-81.

33. *PPP:HST* (1952-53), 55, 59; Dean, *Forging the Atomic Shield*, 181.

34. D. Rosenberg, "Origins of Overkill," 23. For numbers of nuclear weapons, see Cochran, Arkin, and Hoenig, *Nuclear Weapons Databook*, 15.

35. For the desire *not* to negotiate, see MemCon by Kirk, 26 Oct 51, *FRUS, 1951*, 4: 1666-67; Steering Group, "Prospects for an Acceptable Settlement of Major Issues," 29 Dec 51, HSTP, PSF, box 116; Steering Group, "Big Four Meeting or Other High Level Negotiations with the U.S.S.R.," 28 Dec 51, ibid.

36. McCloy to Acheson, 23 Sep and 2 Oct 51, *FRUS, 1951*, 3: 1523-24, 1540-43; Adenauer, *Memoirs*, esp. 415-18.

37. "Report by the Allied High Commissioners . . . on the Status of the Contractual Negotiations with the FRG," 17 Nov 51, *FRUS, 1951*, 3: 1583-97; U.S. Delegation Minutes, 23 Nov 51, ibid., 3: 1598-1604; Allied High Commissioners, "Status of Contractual Relations with the Federal Republic," 12 Feb 52, *FRUS, 1952-54*, 5: 87-88; Adenauer, *Memoirs*, 360-407; Bark and Gress, *From Shadow to Substance*, 272-91; Schwartz, *America's Germany*, 243-45, 249.

38. For French views, see Schuman to Acheson, 29 Jan and 7 Feb 52, *FRUS, 1952-54*, 5: 7-11, 27-28; Bruce to Acheson, 1 and 7 Feb 52, ibid., 5: 12-13, 612-13; MemCon by Acheson, 15 Feb 52, ibid., 5: 40-43; U.S. Delegation to DOS, 18 Feb 52, ibid., 5: 56-58; Minutes by Laukhuff, 18 Feb 52, ibid., 5: 69-71; Bruce to DOS, 3 Feb 52, ibid., 7: 7-8. Public opinion polls in West Germany suggested that Schuman had good reason for his fears. See Merritt and Merritt, *Public Opinion in Semisovereign Germany*, 174-75.

39. Bruce to Acheson, 3 Jan 52, *FRUS, 1952-54*, 3: 986-89; DOS, "EDC and the German Contribution to European Defense" [early Feb 1952], ibid., 5: 598-601; Acheson to Embassy in Belgium, 11 Jan 52, ibid., 5: 582-83; Eisenhower to Truman, 4 Jan 52, HSTP, PSF, box 118; Fursdon's essay in Heller and Gillingham, *NATO*.

40. Acheson to Eden, 8 Dec 51, *FRUS, 1951*, 3: 955-56; Eisenhower to Truman, 4 Jan 52, HSTP, PSF, box 118.

41. For Britain's financial woes, see U.S. Minutes, 7 Jan 52, *FRUS, 1952-54*, 6: 747-51; Memo of Luncheon Mtg., Dept. of the Treasury, 8 Jan 52, ibid., 6: 787-89; Memo of a Mtg. at the Dept. of the Treasury, 9 Jan 52, ibid., 6: 819-20. For French difficulties, see Memo by Knight, 24 Feb 52, ibid., 6: 1178-79; Labouisse to Harlan Cleveland, 7 March 52, ibid., 6: 1181-84. For a thorough and incisive discussion of the problems plaguing Britain and France and of the impediments to monetary equilibrium, see UN, ECE, *Economic Survey of Europe* (1952), 11-20, 85-144.

42. Acheson Testimony, 14 Jan 52, Senate, Foreign Relations, *Executive Sessions*, 4: 10-12; Acheson Testimony, 15 Jan 52, House of Representatives, Foreign Affairs, *Selected Executive Session Hearings*, 15: 164-69.

43. For Acheson's talks with Churchill and Eden and his emphasis on the EDC, see *FRUS, 1952-54*, 6: 732, 761, 774, 798; see also Acheson to Embassy in the Netherlands, 11 Jan 52, ibid., 5: 581; Acheson to Embassy in Belgium, 11 Jan 52, ibid., 5: 583; MemCon by Perkins, 10 Jan 52, Acheson Papers, box 67.

44. Acheson Testimony, 8 Feb 52, Senate, Foreign Relations, *Executive Sessions*, 4: 142-47; Acheson Testimony, 8 Feb 52, House of Representatives, Foreign Affairs, *Selected Executive Session Hearings*, 15: 220-26, 234; Memo by Acheson, 15 Feb 52, *FRUS, 1952-54*, 5: 42-43; U.S. Minutes, 16 Feb 52, ibid., 5: 48-51; U.S. Delegation to DOS, 18 Feb 52, ibid., 5: 56-58; Minutes by Laukhuff, 18 Feb 52, ibid., 5: 69-71; Acheson to Truman, 21 Feb 52, ibid., 5: 82-86.

45. Acheson to Schuman, 4 Feb 52, *FRUS, 1952–54*, 5: 20–23; Schuman to Acheson, 29 Jan 52, ibid., 5: 9–13.

46. Acheson Testimony, 8 Feb and 2 June 52, Senate, Foreign Relations, *Executive Sessions*, 4: 146–47, 469–82; Memo by Acheson, 15 Feb 52, *FRUS, 1952–54*, 5: 42; U.S. Minutes, 16 Feb 52, ibid., 5: 46–47; Acheson to Truman, 16 Feb 52, ibid., 5: 79.

47. Report by the North Atlantic Council Deputies, "Relations Between EDC and NATO," 20 Feb 52, *FRUS, 1952–54*, 5: 250.

48. Memo by James K. Penfield, 17 Feb 52, ibid., 5: 53–54; Acheson to Truman, 21 Feb 52, ibid., 5: 82, 85–86.

49. U.S. Delegation Minutes, 18 Jan 52, ibid., 6: 853–55.

50. *PPP:HST* (1952–53), 180–85; Acheson to DOS, 24 Feb 52, *FRUS, 1952–54*, 5: 272–73; U.S.-French Memo of Understanding, 25 Feb 52, ibid., 5: 274–76; U.S. Delegation to DOS, 25 Feb 52, ibid., 5: 143–45; Dunn to DOS, 12 July 52, ibid., 6: 1222; Acheson, *Present at the Creation*, 623–25.

51. For comparisons of force goals, see the figures in Poole, *History of the JCS*, 246–47, 293. For projected expenditures and costs, see Summary of TCC Report, 6 Feb 52, *FRUS, 1952–54*, 5: 204–6.

52. McNarney Testimony, 16 Jan 52, House of Representatives, Foreign Affairs, *Selected Executive Session Hearings*, 15: 190–207; Harriman Testimony, 4 March 52, ibid., 15: 269–80; Harriman Testimony, 17 Jan 52, Senate, Foreign Relations, *Executive Sessions*, 4: 96–97, 104–7; Acheson, *Present at the Creation*, 623; Eisenhower to Truman, 4 Jan 52, HSTP, PSF, box 118; Memo for the Record by Pace, 3 Dec 51, RG 330, box 227, CD 091.7. For Gruenther's views, see U.S. Delegation to Webb, 27 Nov 51, *FRUS, 1951*, 3: 731–32.

53. Acheson, *Present at the Creation*, 615–27.

54. Notes of Cabinet Mtg., 29 Feb 52, Connelly Papers, box 2.

55. Soviet Ministry of Foreign Affairs to Embassy of the United States, 10 March 52, *FRUS, 1952–54*, 7: 170–72.

56. For the preceding two paragraphs, see Acheson to Embassy in the United Kingdom, 14 and 15 March and 18 Apr 52, *FRUS, 1952–54*, 7: 176, 177, 211–12; Acheson to Embassy in France, 17 March 52, ibid., 7: 184; Acheson to McCloy, 22 March and 12 Apr 52, ibid., 7: 189–90, 206; Memo by Louis Pollak, 2 Apr 52, ibid., 7: 195–98; Kennan, *Memoirs, 1950–1963*, 106–11. For a brief description of the historiographical debate, see Bark and Gress, *From Shadow to Substance*, 298–300; for a provocative interpretation, see Steininger, *German Question*.

57. Dunn to DOS, 30 March and 11 May 52, *FRUS, 1952–54*, 5: 629, 655–56; McCloy to DOS, 2, 14, and 16 May 52, ibid., 7: 46, 65, 70; Perkins to Acheson, 12 May 52, ibid., 5: 659.

58. Memo by Acheson, 8 Apr 52, ibid., 7: 24–25; Acheson to McCloy, 11 Apr 52, ibid., 7: 25–27; Acheson to Embassy in France, 11 Apr and 3 May 52, ibid., 5: 640–42, 653; Acheson to Eden, 21 May 52, ibid., 5: 666. For congressional cuts in foreign assistance, see ibid., 6: 459–60, 479.

59. For sentiment in Germany, see McCloy to DOS, 21 and 28 Apr and 2 and 9 May 52, ibid., 7: 36–37, 38, 46, 55–56; Schwartz, *America's Germany*, 260–69. For French attitudes, see Dunn to DOS, 11 May 52, *FRUS, 1952–54*, 5: 655. For overall sentiment in Europe, see Bonbright to Acheson, 21 May 52, ibid., 5: 299–300.

60. Minutes of Mtgs. of the Foreign Ministers, 24 and 25 May 52, *FRUS, 1952–54*, 7: 91–107; "Convention on Relations Between the Three Powers and the FRG," 26 May 52, ibid., 7: 112–16.

61. Acheson to Truman, 26 May 52, ibid., 5: 681–83; U.S. Minutes, 28 May 52, ibid., 13: 159, 165; Acheson Testimony, 2 June 52, Senate, Foreign Relations, *Executive Sessions*, 4: 468–69, 476–78.

62. For "Tripartite Declaration Providing Assurances to Western Europe, Germany, and Berlin," 27 May 52, see DOS, *Documents on Germany*, 384–85; see also *PPP:HST* (1952–53), 397–98.

63. See *FRUS, 1952–54*, 5: 684–85.

64. Adenauer had been emphasizing this point since 1949. See Riste, *Western Security*, 150–77.

65. Acheson Testimony, 2 June 52, Senate, Foreign Relations, *Executive Sessions*, 4: 468–89.

66. Acheson to Truman, 26 May 52, *FRUS, 1952–54*, 5: 681.

67. See esp. Acheson to Gifford and Dunn, 10, 12, and 19 June 52, ibid., 7: 264, 267, 271–73; Acheson to DOS, 28 June 52, ibid., 7: 277; McCloy to DOS, 8 July 52, ibid., 7: 287–88; Acheson to Embassy in France, 31 July 52, ibid., 7: 350–53; Bruce to Embassy in France, 25 Aug 52, ibid., 7: 298–99.

68. For the quotations, see Fuller to Nitze, 4 Sep 52, ibid., 7: 358–60; Briefing Memo for Bruce, 18 Sep 52, ibid., 6: 637; see also Walter J. Donnelly to DOS, 28 Aug 52, ibid., 7: 355–56; Summary Minutes of the Chiefs of Mission Mtg., 24–26 Sep 52, ibid., 6: 644–62.

69. Kennan to DOS, 27 Aug 52, ibid., 7: 303; Summary Minutes of the Chiefs of Mission Mtg., 24–26 Sep 52, ibid., 6: 644–46, 659–61; Ferguson to Nitze, 26 Sep 52, ibid., 7: 362–67; Kennan, *Memoirs, 1950–1963*, 105–44, 327–51; see also Kennan's long reports from the Moscow embassy, *FRUS, 1952–54*, 8: 971–1053.

70. Fuller to Nitze, 4 Sep 52, *FRUS, 1952–54*, 7: 358–61; Ferguson to Nitze, 26 Sep 52, ibid., 7: 362–67; Donnelly to DOS, 28 Aug, 14 Oct, and 5 Dec 52, ibid., 7: 355–56, 383–84, 390–91; Summary Minutes of the Chiefs of Mission Mtg., 24–26 Sep 52, ibid., 6: 653–62.

71. For the quotation, see Acheson to Embassy in France, 19 Sep 52, ibid., 5: 324; see also Psychological Strategy Board, "A National Psychological Strategy with Respect to Germany," 9 Oct 52, ibid., 7: 373; Donnelly to DOS, 15 Nov 52, ibid., 7: 388–89. For concerns about an independent third force, see also Summary Minutes of the Chiefs of Mission Mtg., 24–26 Sep 52, ibid., 6: 655–58; Memo by Achilles, 28 Nov 52, ibid., 6: 244; Mutual Security Agency, "Draft Circular Telegram," 9 Jan 53, ibid., 6: 263–64.

72. Dunn to DOS, 8, 21, and 24 Oct 52, ibid., 6: 1251–52, 1266–67, 1269, 1280–81. For a good discussion of Franco-American acrimony over financial matters, see Wall, *United States and the Reshaping of Postwar France*, chap. 7.

73. Staff Mtg., 29 July 52, *FRUS, 1952–54*, 6: 142; Acheson to Embassy in France, 8 Nov 52, ibid., 6: 1277–78; Acheson to Lovett, 19 June 52, ibid., 5: 302–8.

74. Acheson to Schuman, 19 Jan 53, ibid., 6: 1290.

75. MemCon by Acheson, 14 Dec 52, ibid., 6: 254. For the implementation of the Schuman Plan, see Gillingham, *Coal, Steel, and the Rebirth of Europe*, 299–372.

76. For the improvement in Europe's payments problems in late 1952 and 1953, see Paper Prepared in the MSA [Sep 1952], ibid., 6: 501–4; Richard Bissell to Ohly, 29 Oct 52, ibid., 6: 516–26; UN, ECE, *Economic Survey of Europe* (1953), 19–26.

77. Reber to DOS, 16 Dec 52, *FRUS, 1952–54*, 7: 392–94; see the Editorial Note, ibid., 5: 698.

78. NSC 135/1, Annex, pt. 2, 22 Aug 52, ibid., 2: 106–7; NSC 141, "Reexamination of United States Programs for National Security," 19 Jan 53, ibid., 2: 219–21; NSC 141, "Part Two—Analysis," RG 273; Draper to DOS, 22 Sep 52, *FRUS, 1952–54*, 5: 328. For Ismay's view, see Draper to DOS, 26 Aug 52, ibid., 5: 315.

79. For Acheson's quotation, see U.S. Delegation Minutes, 8 Jan 52, *FRUS, 1952–54*, 6: 783. For Bradley's assessment, see Bradley, "Security in the Pacific," 22 Jan 52, RG 218, Bradley Papers, box 4; NSC 125/2, "United States Objectives and Courses of Action with Respect to Japan," 7 Aug 52, *FRUS, 1952–54*, 14: 1303–6. For an excellent discussion of Japan's trade and its influence on Japan's political orientation, see NIE, "Probable Future Orientation of Japan," 29 May 52, HSTP, PSF, box 253.

80. Bradley, "Security in the Pacific," 22 Jan 52, RG 218, Bradley Papers, box 4; JCS to Lovett, 12 Dec 51, *FRUS, 1951*, 6: 1432–37; Webb and Lovett to Truman, 15 Feb 52, *FRUS, 1952–54*, 14: 1161–63.

81. Dulles to Senate Foreign Relations Committee, 31 Jan 52, Dulles Papers, box 61.

82. For the visit of Dulles, Smith, and Sparkman to Japan and the Yoshida letter, see *FRUS*,

1951, 6: 1437–39, 1443–50, 1466–70. For the importance Dulles attributed to the Yoshida letter, see Dulles to David Astor, 24 March 52, Dulles Papers, box 61. For the quotation, see Dower, *Empire and Aftermath*, 370–71. For a similar interpretation, see Schonberger, "Peacemaking in Asia."

83. Nash to Lovett, 19 Sep 51, RG 330, box 279, CD 387 (Japan); DOS-JCS Discussion, 6 Feb 52, *FRUS, 1952–54*, 14: 1133–34.

84. For Article 22, see *FRUS, 1952–54*, 14: 1108; Acheson and Lovett to Truman, 18 Jan 52, ibid., 14: 1095–97.

85. MemCons by Bond, 30 Jan and 18 Feb 52, ibid., 14: 1124–25, 1177–79; Allison to Acheson, 9 Feb 52, ibid., 14: 1147–49.

86. Rusk to DOS, 8 and 19 Feb 52, ibid., 14: 1144–45, 1181–84; Ridgway to DOD, 11 Feb 52, ibid., 14: 1154; Lovett to Acheson, 13 Feb 52, ibid., 14: 1157; Webb and Lovett to Truman, 15 Feb 52, ibid., 14: 1161–63; JCS to Lovett, 20 Feb 52, ibid., 14: 1187; Schonberger, *Aftermath of War*, 265–69.

87. Dulles Testimony, 5 Feb 52, Senate, Foreign Relations, *Executive Sessions*, 4: 130–31; Bradley, "Security in the Pacific," 22 Jan 52, RG 218, Bradley Papers, box 4.

88. Myron M. Cowen to Acheson, 25 Jan 52, *FRUS, 1952–54*, 14: 1117–20; Murphy to Allison, 31 March and 11 Aug 52, ibid., 14: 1223, 1311–13; Memo of DOS-JCS Discussion, 2 Apr 52, ibid., 14: 1224–26; JCS to Lovett, 15 Aug 52, ibid., 14: 1324–27; MemCon by Robert McClurkin, 22 Sep 52, ibid., 14: 1333–34.

89. JCS to Lovett, 12 Dec 52, ibid., 14: 1432–35; Bradley to Lovett, 28 July 52, ibid., 14: 1290; Bradley to Lovett, 2 June 52, RG 330, box 317, CD 092 (Japan).

90. Collins to Ridgway, 17 Dec 51, *FRUS, 1951*, 6: 1441–43; Ridgway to Dept. of the Army, 20 Dec 51, ibid., 6: 1451–53.

91. For Lovett's action, see ibid., 6: 1453, footnote 3; see also Lovett to Truman, 22 Apr 52, *FRUS, 1952–54*, 14: 1243–44.

92. MemCon by Young, 7 Aug 52, ibid., 14: 1309–10.

93. E. Bennewitz to Veatch, 15 Sep 52, RG 51, BOB, Series 47.8A, box 43. For DOS and DOD views, see Bruce to Embassy in Japan, 28 and 30 Oct 52, *FRUS, 1952–54*, 14: 1347–48, 1350; Allison to Bruce, 18 Nov 52, ibid., 14: 1360–62.

94. Dower, *Empire and Aftermath*, 377–400.

95. Murphy to DOS, 8 June and 6 Sep 52, *FRUS, 1952–54*, 14: 1268–69, 1328–29.

96. Wilson to Lovett, 15 Nov 51, RG 330, box 231, CD 092 (Japan); Foster to Ridgway, 28 Nov 51, ibid.; JCS to Lovett, 12 Dec 51, *FRUS, 1951*, 6: 1433.

97. See the report that Ridgway sent Lovett, "Continuation of Current Activity for Integration of Japanese Potential into Overall U.S. Industrial Mobilization Programs in Post-Treaty Period," 31 Dec 51, RG 330, box 317, CD 092 (Japan).

98. For the production of ammunition, see *FRUS, 1952–54*, 14: 1211, footnote 4; see also Allison to John C. Houston, 3 March 52, ibid.

99. Roger S. Nelson to Lawton, 6 March 52, RG 51, BOB, Series 47.8A, box 43; Memo by Rusk, 27 Nov 51, *FRUS, 1951*, 6: 1416–17.

100. Notes of the SecState's Staff Mtg., 5 Aug 52, *FRUS, 1952–54*, 14: 1295–96; Harold F. Linder to Bruce, 6 Aug 52, ibid., 14: 1299. For the agreement with Japan, see SecState to Certain Diplomatic and Consular Offices, 19 Sep 52, ibid., 14: 1332; see also Yasuhara, "Japan, Communist China, and Export Controls," 85–89; Dower, *Empire and Aftermath*, 410–14.

101. Nelson to Lawton, 6 March 52, RG 51, BOB, Series 47.8A, box 43; NIE, "Probable Future Orientation of Japan," *FRUS, 1952–54*, 14: 1264–65; NSC 125/2, "United States Objectives and Courses of Action with Respect to Japan," 7 Aug 52, ibid., 14: 1304–8.

102. Bradley to Lovett, 28 July 52, *FRUS, 1952–54*, 14: 1290. For Eisenhower, see MemCon by Vernon Walters, 30 Apr 52, ibid., 6: 1203. For Lovett, see MemCon by Charles A. Sullivan, 20 Aug 52, ibid., 14: 1314–15; NSC 125/2, "United States Objectives . . . with Respect to Japan," 7 Aug 52, ibid., 14: 1302–8. For trade and economic information, see NIE, "Probable Future

Orientation of Japan," ibid., 14: 1264–65; see also Dunn, *Peace-Making and the Settlement with Japan*, 144–49.

103. The quotation is from NSC 124/2, "United States Objectives and Courses of Action with Respect to Southeast Asia," 25 June 52, ibid., 12: 127; see also NSC 124, "United States Objectives . . . with Respect to Southeast Asia," 13 Feb 52, ibid., 12: 46–51.

104. Memo by Collins, 13 Nov 51, *FRUS, 1951*, 6: 544–45; Fall, *Street Without Joy*, 27–55.

105. Minutes of NSC Mtg., 19 Dec 51, RG 273; see also James Lay's comments in Summary of NSC Discussions, 6 March 52, HSTP, PSF, box 220. Chinese assistance to the Viet Minh did increase, but it was small compared to U.S. aid to the French. See Taylor, *China and Southeast Asia*, 8–9.

106. NSC 124, "United States Objectives . . . with Respect to Southeast Asia," 13 Feb 52, *FRUS, 1952–54*, 12: 46–51; DOS-JCS Mtg., 16 Jan 52, ibid., 12: 23–34.

107. DOS-JCS Mtgs., 23 Jan and 5 March 52, ibid., 12: 35–36, 55–67; Davis to JCS, 5 Feb 52, ibid., 12: 37–44; Vandenberg to Lovett, 3 March 52, in DOD, *United States–Vietnam Relations*, 8: 487–92.

108. DOS-JCS Mtg., 5 March 52, *FRUS, 1952–54*, 12: 55–67; Memo by Nitze, 5 March 52, ibid., 12: 68–69.

109. Acheson to DOS, 24 Feb 52, ibid., 5: 272–73; U.S.-French Memo of Understanding, 25 Feb 52, ibid., 5: 274–76; U.S. Delegation to DOS, 25 Feb 52, ibid., 5: 143–45; Wall, *United States and the Reshaping of Postwar France*, chap. 7.

110. For Acheson's quotation, see his testimony, 8 Feb 52, Senate, Foreign Relations, *Executive Sessions*, 4: 151. For the advice emanating from his Asia experts, see Allison to Acheson, 11 Feb 52, *FRUS, 1952–54*, 13: 32–34. For Nitze's comments, see DOS-JCS Mtg., 5 March 52, ibid., 12: 65–66; Summary of NSC Mtg., 6 March 52, ibid., 12: 70–72; Shaplen, *Lost Revolution*, 84–85.

111. Summary of NSC Discussion, 6 March 52, *FRUS, 1952–54*, 12: 70–74; Memo for Lovett, 5 March 52, in DOD, *United States–Vietnam Relations*, 8: 504–5; NIE, "Probable Developments in Indochina Through Mid-1952," 3 March 52, *FRUS, 1952–54*, 13: 53–60. For Acheson's quotation, see his testimony, 8 Feb 52, Senate, Foreign Relations, *Executive Sessions*, 4: 151.

112. NIE, "Probable Developments in Indochina Through Mid-1952," 3 March 52, *FRUS, 1952–54*, 13: 53–60.

113. Pace, Kimball, and Roswell Gilpatric to Lovett, 8 Apr 52, ibid., 13: 117–24; Memo by Battle, 19 May 52, ibid., 12: 92.

114. For the quotation, see MemCon by Acheson, 3 Apr 52, Acheson Papers, box 67. For Gullion, see Shaplen, *Lost Revolution*, 66–67, 77–91.

115. Allison to Acheson, 7 May 52, *FRUS, 1952–54*, 13: 124–29; MemCon by Nitze, 12 May 52, ibid., 13: 141–43. For Acheson's talks with senators, see MemCons by Battle, 14 May 52, Acheson Papers, box 67.

116. U.S. Minutes, 28 May 52, *FRUS, 1952–54*, 13: 161.

117. U.S. Minutes, 26 and 28 May 52, ibid., 12: 97–105; U.S. Minutes, 28 May 52, ibid., 13: 162–64.

118. U.S. Minutes, 28 May 52, ibid., 12: 103–4.

119. Memo by Battle, 17 June 52, ibid., 12: 113–14; NSC 124/2, "United States Objectives . . . with Respect to Southeast Asia," 25 June 52, ibid., 12: 130–32; Memo by Battle, 17 June 52, Acheson Papers, box 67.

120. U.S. Minutes, 26 and 27 June 52, *FRUS, 1952–54*, 12: 135–41; Gifford to DOS, 28 June 52, ibid., 12: 143–44.

121. Allison to Matthews, 15 July 52, ibid., 12: 147–48; DOS-JCS Mtg., 16 July 52, ibid., 12: 149–54. For Nitze's and Acheson's views, see also MemCon by Nitze, 12 May 52, ibid., 12: 89–91.

122. JCS to Lovett, 5 Aug and 14 Nov 52, ibid., 12: 184–85, 241–42; Report of the Five-

Power Military Conference on Southeast Asia, 17 Oct 52, ibid., 12: 231–32; J. Sladen Bradley to JCS, 23 Oct 52, ibid., 12: 235–37.

123. Sturm to DOS, 10 June 52, ibid., 13: 177–79; Gullion to DOS, 15 June 52, ibid., 13: 188–89; Hammer, *Struggle for Indochina*, 281–86.

124. U.S. Minutes, 16 and 17 June 52, *FRUS, 1952–54*, 13: 192–202; Acheson to Embassy in France, 17 June 52, ibid., 13: 203; Acheson to Legation at Saigon, 20 June 52, ibid., 13: 204–9; Unsigned Memo for Foster, 17 June 52, RG 330, box 309, CD 091.3 (Indochina).

125. Acheson to Legation in Saigon, 20 June 52, *FRUS, 1952–54*, 13: 207–8. For the transport planes and repair crews, see Heath to DOS, 5 and 20 Dec 52, ibid., 13: 308, 326–27; Lovett to Harriman, 10 Sep 52, RG 330, box 309, CD 091.3 (Indochina).

126. Bonsal to Allison, 18 Nov 52, *FRUS, 1952–54*, 13: 292–94; Memo by Bonsal, 15 Dec 52, ibid., 13: 318; Byington to Bonsal, 12 Jan 53, ibid., 13: 349–51; JCS, "Current Situation in Indochina," 5 Dec 52, ibid., 13: 312.

127. For the views of Acheson, Lovett, and Harriman, see NSC 141, "Reexamination of United States Programs for National Security," 19 Jan 53, ibid., 2: 220–22. For Acheson's desire to have more freedom of military action, see Summary of NSC Discussion, 25 Sep 52, HSTP, PSF, box 220. For overall policy toward Southeast Asia, including the possibility of using military force in Indonesia, see NSC 124/2, "United States Objectives . . . with Respect to Southeast Asia," 25 June 52, *FRUS, 1952–54*, 12: 127–34. For the readiness of the JCS to contemplate military action in Malaya and Indonesia, see also JCS to NSC Senior Staff [March 1952], in DOD, *United States–Vietnam Relations*, 8: 500–501.

128. PPS, "Position of the United States with Respect to the General Area of the Eastern Mediterranean and the Middle East," 27 Dec 51, *FRUS, 1951*, 5: 259–63; NSC 129/1, "United States Objectives and Policies with Respect to the Arab States and Israel," 24 Apr 52, *FRUS, 1952–54*, 9: 222–23; "Recommended Redraft of Letter from State to Budget to Be Concurred in by Defense," no signature, RG 330, box 310, CD 091.3 (Middle East).

129. Eisenhower to Bradley, Juin, and Slim, 9 Oct 51, RG 218, Bradley Papers, box 3.

130. Bradley to Truman, 18 Oct 51, *FRUS, 1951*, 3: 597–98; Memo of Discussion at Informal Mtg., 27 Nov 51, ibid., 3: 726–28; MemCon by Norbert L. Anschuetz, 29 Nov 51, ibid., 3: 744; Robert Carney to Bradley, Vandenberg, and Collins, 22 March 52, RG 218, Bradley Papers, box 4.

131. Vatikiotis, *History of Egypt*, 367–70.

132. Caffery to Acheson, 30 Nov 51, *FRUS, 1951*, 5: 428–29; see also Caffery to Acheson, 7 Dec 51, ibid., 5: 430. For Berry, see "Substance of Discussions," 12 Dec 51, ibid., 5: 435–37.

133. Bradley to Truman, 18 Oct 51, ibid., 3: 599; NIE, "British Position in Egypt," 15 Oct 51, HSTP, PSF, box 253; Acheson to Morrison, 17 Oct 51, *FRUS, 1951*, 5: 405.

134. Memo by Acheson, 5 Jan 52, *FRUS, 1952–54*, 6: 732, 737–38. For the Acheson-Eden talks regarding Egypt, see also Memo by Stabler, 9 Jan 52, ibid., 6: 809–12. For the quotation, see Acheson Testimony, 14 Jan 52, Senate, Foreign Relations, *Executive Sessions*, 4: 25.

135. Ramazani, *Iran's Foreign Policy*, 215; Diba, *Mossadegh*.

136. Memo by Roundtree, 9 Jan 52, *FRUS, 1952–54*, 6: 828–31. For covert operations, see Gasiorowski, "1953 Coup d'Etat in Iran," 261–68; Painter, *Oil and the American Century*, 179; Louis, *British Empire in the Middle East*, 685.

137. For the mtg. between Musaddiq, Truman, and Acheson, see MemCon by Acheson, 23 Oct 51, Acheson Papers, box 66. For the extensive talks between Musaddiq and McGhee, see McGhee, *Envoy to the Middle World*, 388–404.

138. Acheson Testimony, 14 Jan 52, Senate, Foreign Relations, *Executive Sessions*, 4: 18–27; Lovett to Eisenhower, 24 Jan 52, *FRUS, 1952–54*, 6: 861; MemCon by Roundtree, 9 Jan 52, ibid., 6: 824–31; CIA, "Possible Developments in Iran in 1952 in the Absence of an Oil Settlement," 4 Feb 52, HSTP, PSF, box 253. For the views of Musaddiq, see also Nitze, *From Hiroshima to Glasnost*, 130–35.

139. In addition to citations in Note 138, see Acheson Testimony, 15 Jan 52, House of Rep-

resentatives, Foreign Affairs, *Selected Executive Session Hearings*, 15: 182–84; Steering Group on Preparations for the Talks Between the President and Prime Minister Churchill, "Iran," 5 Jan 52, HSTP, PSF, box 116; NSC 117, "Anglo-Iranian Problem," 18 Oct 51, RG 273; see also the extremely revealing letter from Lovett to Acheson, 23 Jan 52, RG 330, box 316, CD 092 (Iran).

140. Painter, "Oil and U.S. Policy," 13–28. For contrasting Anglo-American responses, see Cottam, *Iran and the United States*, 95–104.

141. Acheson Testimony, 5 Feb 52, Senate, Foreign Relations, *Executive Sessions*, 4: 158–61. The views presented here rely heavily on Painter's insightful work. See Painter, "Oil and U.S. Policy"; Painter, *Oil and the American Century*, 176–84; Brands, "Cairo-Teheran Connection," 441–42.

142. NSC 107/2 had stated that the United States would provide political and perhaps military support if the British exercised military action to stymie a Communist takeover. Lovett, however, was beginning to doubt whether the British could be relied on. See Lovett to Acheson, 23 Jan 52, RG 330, box 316, CD 092 (Iran); see also Steering Group, "Iran," 5 Jan 52, HSTP, PSF, box 116.

143. Lapping, *End of Empire*, 244–54; Vatikiotis, *History of Egypt*, 369–71.

144. MemCon by Battle, 27 Jan 52, *FRUS, 1952–54*, 9: 1755; Acheson to Embassy in Britain, 28 Jan 52, ibid., 9: 1758; Berry to Acheson, 8 Feb and 3 March 52, ibid., 9: 1761, 1773; Matthews to Lovett, 23 Feb 52, ibid., 9: 1765–66; Acheson to Eden, 26 March 52, ibid., 9: 1779–82.

145. Eden to Acheson, 18 Apr 52, ibid., 9: 1792.

146. NIE, "Current Situation in North Africa," 12 Sep 52, ibid., 11: 133.

147. For the quotation, see U.S. Delegation Minutes, 3 June 52, ibid., 11: 767. For comments on the base complex in Morocco, see the remarks of Byroade, ibid., 11: 128–29. For the difficulty of knowing what to do, see, e.g., MemCon by Leo G. Cyr, 22 May 52, ibid., 11: 758–63.

148. The quotation comes from an NSC Staff Study, "United States Objectives and Policies with Respect to the Arab States and Israel," 24 Apr 52, RG 273. For Acheson's quotation, see Summary of NSC Discussion, 24 Apr 52, ibid.; see also Harold B. Hoskins to Byroade, 7 Apr 52, *FRUS, 1952–54*, 9: 205–12; MemCon by Alexander B. Daspit, 24 Apr 52, ibid., 9: 219–21; NSC 129/1, "United States Objectives and Policies with Respect to the Arab States and Israel," 24 Apr 52, ibid., 9: 222–25; H. P. Smith to H. R. Kreps, 10 March 52, RG 330, box 310, CD 091.3 (Middle East).

149. MemCon by Daspit, 24 Apr 52, *FRUS, 1952–54*, 9: 219–22; DOS-JCS Mtg., 18 June 52, ibid., 9: 237–44; Matthews to Lovett, 28 May 52, ibid., 9: 234–36; Acheson to Embassy in United Kingdom, 21 June 52, ibid., 9: 248; Acheson to DOS, 27 June 52, ibid., 9: 249–50; Byroade to Acheson, 21 July 52, ibid., 9: 1838–40.

150. In addition to the citations in Note 149, see Memo Prepared by the PPS, 21 May 52, ibid., 9: 232–34; Matthews to Lovett, 15 Aug 52, ibid., 9: 266–67; Memo by Nolting, 1 Oct 52, ibid., 9: 280–81. For military studies stressing the wartime need for oil from the southern Persian Gulf, see JCS 1741/59, "World-Wide Demand and Supply of Petroleum in Event of Major War," 8 Nov 51, RG 218, CCS 463.7 (9-6-45), sec. 10; JCS 1887/36, "Feasibility of Holding the Bahrein-Qatar-Saudi Arabia Area," 21 Jan 52, RG 218, CCS 381 EMMEA (11-19-47), sec. 7; JCS 1887/38, "Bahrein-Qatar-Saudi Arabia Area," 11 Feb 52, ibid., sec. 8. For the growing importance of Pakistan, see also Jalal, "Towards the Baghdad Pact," 418–27.

151. DOS-JCS Mtg., 18 June 52, *FRUS, 1952–54*, 9: 237–47; Memo by Nolting, 1 Oct 52, ibid., 9: 280–81.

152. Lapping, *End of Empire*, 213–16; Cottam, *Iran and the United States*, 98–101; Diba, *Mossadegh*, 115–76. For an insightful analysis of the links between the crises in Egypt and Iran, see Brands, "Cairo-Teheran Connection."

153. Lovett to Bruce, 16 Aug 52, RG 330, box 316, CD 092 (Iran); Bradley to Lovett, 5 Sep 52, ibid.; Mtg. with the Pres by Acheson, 21 July 52, Acheson Papers, box 67; MemCon by Byroade, 8 Aug 52, *FRUS, 1952–54*, 9: 265–66; Gasiorowski, "1953 Coup d'Etat in Iran," 267–68.

154. Lovett to Bruce, 16 Aug 52, RG 330, box 316, CD 092 (Iran).

155. Painter, "Oil and U.S. Policy," 20–30; Lapping, *End of Empire*, 215–16; Ramazani, *Iran's Foreign Policy*, 225–50.

156. Lovett to Acheson, 24 Oct 52, RG 330, box 316, CD 092 (Iran); see also Lovett to Acheson, 10 Nov 52, ibid.; MemCon by Nitze, 8 Oct 52, Acheson Papers, box 67A.

157. Acheson to Lovett, 4 Nov 52, *FRUS, 1952–54*, 10: 510–13; Memo by Acheson, 18 Nov 52, ibid., 1: 25–26.

158. Summary of NSC Discussions, 17 Dec 52 and 9 Jan 53, HSTP, PSF, box 220; Painter, *Oil and the American Century*, 183–89.

159. NSC 136/1, "United States Policy Regarding the Present Situation in Iran," 20 Nov 52, RG 273; *FRUS, 1952–54*, 10: 526–29. For the quotation regarding the assumption of "primary responsibility," see Edmond L. Taylor to Morgan, 6 Oct 52, PSB, box 7.

160. Caffery to DOS, 20 Aug, 8 Sep, and 21 Oct 52, *FRUS, 1952–54*, 9: 1851–52, 1860–61, 297–98; Matthews to Lovett, 2 Sep 52, ibid., 9: 1853; Brands, "Cairo-Teheran Connection," 446.

161. MemCon by Stabler, 15 Nov 52, ibid., 9: 1881; DOS to British Embassy, 5 Nov 52, ibid., 9: 312–13; Acheson to Lovett, 21 Nov and 12 Dec 52, ibid., 9: 1889–92, 1911–12; Mem-Con by Acheson, 7 Jan 53, ibid., 9: 1954–55; DOS-JCS Mtg., 29 Oct 52, ibid., 9: 309–10; NIE, "Conditions and Trends in the Middle East Affecting U.S. Security," 15 Jan 53, ibid., 9: 341. For the extent to which the JCS felt pressed by the DOS, see Bradley to Lovett, 5 Nov 52, RG 330, box 310, CD 091.3 (Middle East). For Syria, see Little, "Cold War and Covert Action," 54–61. For U.S. links with the new leadership in Pakistan, see Jalal, "Towards the Baghdad Pact," 420.

162. MemCon by Acheson, 7 Jan 53, *FRUS, 1952–54*, 9: 1954–55; Andrew D. Fritzlan to Hare, 16 Jan 53, ibid., 9: 2432.

163. For concern with the Arab world, see NSC 141, "Reexamination of United States Programs for National Security," 19 Jan 53, ibid., 2: 220–21.

164. NSC 136/1, "United States Policy Regarding the Present Situation in Iran," 20 Nov 52, RG 273; Lovett to Acheson, 24 Oct 52, RG 330, box 316, CD 092 (Iran); NIE, "Probable Developments in Iran Through 1953," 9 Jan 53, HSTP, PSF, box 254; NIE, "Conditions and Trends in the Middle East Affecting U.S. Security," 15 Jan 53, *FRUS, 1952–54*, 9: 334–41; Memo Prepared by the PPS, 21 May 52, ibid., 9: 232–34. These generalizations are supported by Brands, "Cairo-Teheran Connection," and by Jalal, "Towards the Baghdad Pact."

165. Gasiorowski, "1953 Coup d'Etat in Iran"; Little, "Cold War and Covert Action."

166. NSC 136/1, "United States Policy Regarding the Present Situation in Iran," 20 Nov 52, RG 273.

167. For stress on raw materials, see MSA, "Proposed Materials Development Program for Fiscal Year 1954," 16 Sep 52, *FRUS, 1952–54*, 6: 508; ODM, "Summary Statement No. 2—The Mobilization Program" [ND], ibid., 6: 36; *PPP:HST* (1952–53), 180, 192.

168. For the stress on the periphery, especially the Middle East and Southeast Asia, see NSC 135/3, "Reappraisal of United States Objectives and Strategy for National Security," 25 Sep 52, *FRUS, 1952–54*, 2: 146–47, 152–55; Statement of Policy by Nitze, 30 July 52, ibid., 2: 71–73; Summary of NSC Discussion, 25 Sep 52, ibid., 2: 136–38.

169. Foot, *Wrong War*, 176–86; Futrell, *United States Air Force in Korea*, 480–97. For the armistice negotiations, see Bernstein's essay in Cumings, *Child of Conflict*, 261–307.

170. See, e.g., MemCon by Johnson, 17 Sep 52, *FRUS, 1952–54*, 15: 522–24; Memo by Lay, 24 Sep 52, ibid., 15: 532–38; Foot, *A Substitute for Victory*, 142–50.

171. Clark to JCS, 29 Sep 52, *FRUS, 1952–54*, 15: 548–50.

172. Truman, *Off the Record*, 250–51.

173. For the quotations, see Kennan to DOS, 30 July 52, *FRUS, 1952–54*, 15: 433; PPS, "Political Annex to NSC 147," 4 June 53, ibid., 15: 1143; see also CIA, "Probable Effects of Various Possible Courses of Action with Respect to Communist China," 5 June 52, ibid., 14: 59–62; Foot, *Wrong War*, 174–203.

174. NSC 135/1 Annex, "Reappraisal of United States Objectives," 22 Aug 52, *FRUS, 1952–*

54, 2: 111; NIE, "Estimate of the World Situation Through 1954," 21 Nov 52, ibid., 2: 188; Report of the Special Evaluation Subcommittee of the NSC, "Summary Evaluation of the Net Capability of the USSR to Inflict Direct Injury on the United States Up to July 1, 1955" [Spring 1953], ibid., 2: 333–47; JIC 382/30, "JIC Presentation for the Ad Hoc Study Group on Continental Defense," 7 Jan 53, RG 218, CCS 381 US (5-23-46), sec. 23.

175. NSC 135/1 Annex, "Reappraisal of United States Objectives," 22 Aug 52, *FRUS, 1952–54*, 2: 111.

176. For Bohlen's views, see Memo by Bohlen, 27 March 52, ibid., 2: 5–8. Bohlen's views were incorporated into the administration's overall assessment of national security objectives. See NSC 135/1 Annex, "Reappraisal of United States Objectives," 22 Aug 52, ibid., 2: 89–94; Bohlen's quotation is on p. 89. For Acheson's views, see U.S. Minutes, 4 Aug 52, ibid., 12: 181–82; see also NIE, "Estimate of the World Situation Through 1954," 21 Nov 52, ibid., 2: 195–96.

177. U.S. officials were determined to overcome "the fear of our allies . . . that the overall strength of the United States is not sufficient to insure that action can be taken to counter local aggression without serious risk of global war." See Annex to NSC 135/1, "Reappraisal of United States Objectives," late Sep 1952, *FRUS, 1952–54*, 2: 108.

178. For Nitze's views, see DOS-JCS Mtg., 16 Jan 52, ibid., 12: 30–31; NSC 124/2, "United States Objectives . . . with Respect to Southeast Asia," 25 June 52, ibid., 12: 129–32.

179. For the emphasis on preponderance, see Nitze to Matthews, 14 July 52, ibid., 2: 58–59. For Acheson's quotation, see U.S. Minutes, 4 Aug 52, ibid., 12: 182–83. Among the key documents on which this interpretation is based, see also Schwartz to Bohlen, 12 May 52, ibid., 2: 12–17; Paper Drafted by the PPS [July 1952], ibid., 2: 61–68; Statement of Policy by Nitze, 30 July 52, ibid., 2: 68–73; NSC 135/3, "Reappraisal of United States Objectives," 25 Sep 52, ibid., 2: 142–56.

180. For the quotations by Generals LeMay and Jack J. Catton, see Kohn and Harahan, "U.S. Strategic Air Power," 89. For the buildup, see DOD, "Status of United States Military Programs," 29 July 52, RG 330, box 361, CD 381 (General); ODM, *New Resources Bring New Opportunities*, 10; Key Data Book [Oct 1952], *FRUS, 1952–54*, 2: 171–73. For bomber aircraft development, see Knaack, *Post–World War II Bombers*, 99–132, 205–44.

181. For the quotation, see Summary of NSC Discussion, 19 June 52, HSTP, PSF, box 220.

182. For Lovett's view, see Summary of NSC Discussion, 4 Sep 52, *FRUS, 1952–54*, 2: 122. For an excellent description of perceived Soviet capabilities, see JIC 382/30, "JIC Presentation . . . on Continental Defense," 7 Jan 53, RG 218, CCS 381 US (5-23-46), sec. 23.

183. Paper Drafted by Nitze and Savage, 11 Nov 52, *FRUS, 1952–54*, 2: 183.

184. NSC 141, "Reexamination of United States Programs for National Security," 19 Jan 53, ibid., 2: 213. For the dispute between the DOD and the NSRB, see also Summaries of NSC Discussions, 4 and 25 Sep 52, ibid., 2: 122 and 139; Paper Distributed by Gorrie at NSC Mtg., 24 Sep 52, ibid., 2: 141–42; Memo by Bruce, 14 Oct 52, ibid., 2: 164–65. For a study requested by Lovett that emphasized the needs of continental defense, see "Summary Report," 4 Dec 52, RG 218, CCS 373.24 US (9-8-49), BP, pt. 2.

185. For the recommendations of Acheson, Lovett, and Harriman, see NSC 141, "Reexamination of United States Programs," 19 Jan 53, *FRUS, 1952–54*, 2: 215–17.

186. For the progress in defense mobilization, see Summary of NSC Discussion, 25 Sep 52, ibid., 2: 137; see also ibid., 2: 157–63. For illustrative statistics, see ODM, *Job Ahead for Defense Mobilization*, 11–13. For the recommendations of Acheson, Lovett, and Harriman, see NSC 141, "Reexamination of United States Programs," 19 Jan 53, *FRUS, 1952–54*, 2: 215–17.

187. Ranelagh, *The Agency*, 219–20; Treverton, *Covert Action*, 40–42; Senate, Select Committee, *Supplementary Reports on Military Intelligence*, 31–36. For JCS support of covert operations, see JCS to Lovett, 4 March 52, *FRUS, 1952–54*, 14: 18. For covert support of Chinese Nationalist operations on the mainland, see ibid., 14: 120; Leary, *Perilous Missions*, 113–43.

188. For the quotation, see JCS to Lovett, 10 Nov 52, RG 330, box 361, CD 381 (General).

For discussions of intervention in Third World locales during the preparation of NSC 135/1, see JCS to Lovett, 29 Aug 52, *FRUS, 1952–54*, 2: 114; Walmsley to Acheson, 4 Sep 52, ibid., 2: 125–26; Bohlen to Acheson, 22 Sep 52, ibid., 2: 134–35; Summary of NSC Discussion, 25 Sep 52, ibid., 2: 136–38; Memo by Acheson, 24 Sep 52, ibid., 2: 140.

189. Paper Drafted by the PPS [July 1952], *FRUS, 1952–54*, 2: 66–68; Draft Statement of Policy by Nitze, 30 July 52, ibid., 2: 68–72; Draft Statement, 12 Aug 52, ibid., 2: 78–80. For Acheson's stress on continuities, see Summary of NSC Discussion, 4 Sep 52, ibid., 2: 119. Louis Halle, one of Nitze's bright assistants on the PPS, stressed that once the Soviet system was eliminated, the United States could champion a world of diversity. But even then the United States "as the preponderant power in the world" would play the leading role in designing the rule of law by an international authority. Memo by Halle, 29 Dec 52, ibid., 2: 201.

190. Steering Group, "Political Warfare Against USSR," 6 Jan 52, HSTP, PSF, box 116; PPS, "Future Policy Toward the USSR," 6 Jan 52, ibid. Both these papers were approved as official policy and submitted to Truman and Acheson in preparation for their talks with Churchill and Eden; see also Heuser, *Western 'Containment' Policies in the Cold War*, 138–39.

191. Senate, Select Committee, *Supplementary Reports on Military Intelligence*, 36. The Central European country was not identified.

192. NIE, "Relations Between the Chinese Communist Regime and the USSR: Their Present Character and Probable Future Courses," 10 Sep 52, *FRUS, 1952–54*, 14: 97–103; DOS-JCS Mtg., 3 Apr 52, ibid., 14: 35–41; Nash to Steering Group on NSC 128, 13 June 52, ibid., 14: 66–70; DOS-DOD Mtg., 19 Aug 52, ibid., esp. 14: 88, 90–91; Heuser, *Western 'Containment' Policies in the Cold War*, 146–47.

193. "PHN Notes on PSB," 7 Dec 51, RG 59, PPS, box 11A; Paper Drafted by the PPS [July 1952], *FRUS, 1952–54*, 2: 67–68; Statement of Policy by Nitze, 30 July 52, ibid., 2: 71–72.

194. For the 1952 election, see Caridi, *Korean War and American Politics*, 209–45; Reichard, *Politics as Usual*, 60–84. For Truman's defense of his foreign policies and his reactions to Eisenhower's accusations, see, e.g., *PPP:HST* (1952–53), 805, 813, 889–90, 945, 968. For Eisenhower's concerns with raw materials on the periphery, see esp. Eisenhower to Dulles, 20 June 52, Dulles Papers, box 60; Eisenhower, *Papers*, 10: 1098.

195. *PPP:HST* (1952–53), 1117–28.

196. Ibid., 1197–1202.

197. For the concerns of Acheson, Lovett, and Harriman, see NSC 141, "Reexamination of United States Programs," 19 Jan 53, *FRUS, 1952–54*, 2: 210–22.

Conclusion

1. *PPP:HST* (1952–53), 1201.

2. Fukuyama, "The End of History?"

3. A good example is David Horowitz. His *Free World Colossus* was one of the more popular revisionist works of the 1960's.

4. Keohane, *After Hegemony*, 31–41, 135–81.

5. Haslam, "Stalin's Assessment of the Likelihood of War"; Ulam, *Rivals*, 95.

6. Van der Wee, *Prosperity and Upheaval*, 258–77, 345–64, 421–40.

7. Lundestad, "Empire by Invitation?"; Hogan, *Marshall Plan*; Wall, *United States and the Reshaping of Postwar France*; Nau, *Myth of America's Decline*, 99–128; Esposito, "American Aid in French Economics and Politics."

8. These conclusions have been influenced by Dower, *Empire and Aftermath*; Schonberger, *Aftermath of War*; Eisenberg, "U.S. Policy in Post-War Germany"; Backer, *Winds of History*.

9. For the role of NATO, see Calleo, *Beyond American Hegemony*, 27–43.

10. Keohane, *After Hegemony*, 135–84; R. Gardner, *Sterling-Dollar Diplomacy*; Van der Wee, *Prosperity and Upheaval*, 345–86; Nau, *Myth of America's Decline*, 77–128.

11. These generalizations, suggesting a synergy between the needs of officials in Washing-

ton, Paris, and Rome, are influenced by Wall, *United States and the Reshaping of Postwar France*; Harper, *America and the Reconstruction of Italy*; Hill, "Inflation and the Collapse of Tripartism"; Esposito, "American Aid in French Economics and Politics." For an adept summary, see Van der Wee, *Prosperity and Upheaval*, 436–54.

12. MccGwire, "Genesis of Soviet Threat Perceptions." Taubman's analysis is also very useful; see his *Stalin's American Policy*, 178–79.

13. For an assessment of the bilateral agreements, showing that they were not nearly so harmful as usually thought, see Polk and Patterson, "Emerging Pattern of Bilateralism," 118–42. For the major reassessment of the economic implications of the exchange crisis, see Milward, *Reconstruction of Western Europe*, 1–125; Milward, "Was the Marshall Plan Necessary?," 237–48.

14. These generalizations about Stalin and European Communist parties are especially influenced by Spriano, *Stalin and the European Communists*, 247–78; Gati, *Hungary and the Soviet Bloc*, 1–121; Urban, *Moscow and the Italian Communist Party*, esp. 148–224; Serfaty and Gray, *Italian Communist Party*, 21–35; Wall, *French Communism*, 3–74; Bloomfield, *Passive Revolution*, 23–123; Stavrakis, *Moscow and Greek Communism*.

15. Dedijer, *Battle Stalin Lost*, 31–132; Kardelj, *Reminiscences*, 90–125.

16. Walt, "Alliance Formation and the Balance of World Power," 3–41; Jervis, *Meaning of the Nuclear Revolution*, 228–35.

17. See the polls in Merritt and Merritt, *Public Opinion in Occupied Germany*, 172–73, 181, 211–12, 250, 261; Merritt and Merritt, *Public Opinion in Semisovereign Germany*, 175; see also Deutsch and Edinger, *Germany Rejoins the Powers*, 21–22; Drummond, *German Social Democrats*, 30–33; Noelle and Neumann, *Germans*, 523, 510; Vardys, "Germany's Postwar Socialism," 239–43.

18. In her nuanced work, Chiarella Esposito emphasizes that U.S. power to influence developments in France was limited. But she also concludes that "it appears that American aid was quite necessary in France's political context and that it played a crucial role in 1948–1949 in achieving a centrist political stabilization and economic recovery" ("American Aid in French Economics and Politics," 36–37).

19. Stephanson, *Kennan*, 117–35.

20. For the problems inherent in a strategy of reassurance, see Jervis, Lebow, and Stein, *Psychology and Deterrence*, 198–99.

21. W. Rostow, *Division of Europe After World War II*; Eisenberg, "American Decision to Divide Germany"; J. Smith, *Clay*, 414–22.

22. Van der Wee, *Prosperity and Upheaval*, 450–51, 258–77. For Japanese trade with Western Europe, see UN, ECAFE, *Economic Survey of Asia and the Far East* (1962), 121–33.

23. Louis, *British Empire in the Middle East*, 632–89; Painter, *Oil and the American Century*, 172–98.

24. Van der Wee, *Prosperity and Upheaval*, 390–413; Walt, "Alliance Formation and the Balance of World Power," 39. For illustrative trade statistics, see UN, ECAFE, *Economic Survey of Asia and the Far East* (1962), 8.

25. Walt, "Alliance Formation and the Balance of World Power," 24–41; McFarlane, "Successes and Failures in Soviet Policy Toward Marxist Revolutions."

26. L. Gardner, *Approaching Vietnam*, 54–119; Hess, *United States' Emergence as a Southeast Asian Power*, 169–84, 193–208, 325–26.

27. McLane, *Soviet Strategies in Southeast Asia*, 423–32; Taruc, *He Who Rides the Tiger*, 33; Greenberg, *Hukbalahap Insurrection*, 50. The minuscule role of the Soviet Union is also evident in Kerkvliet, *Huk Rebellion*; Kessler, *Rebellion and Repression*.

28. In addition to the analysis presented in Chapters Nine, Ten, and Eleven of this volume, see Trachtenberg, "Wasting Asset."

29. For an overall analysis, see Betts, *Nuclear Blackmail*.

30. These conclusions are influenced by Jervis, *Illogic of American Nuclear Strategy*; Jervis, *Meaning of the Nuclear Revolution*; Betts, *Nuclear Blackmail*.

NOTES TO PAGES 510-18639

31. Walt, "Alliance Formation and the Balance of World Power," 3–41; Walt, "Case for Finite Containment," 16–49; see also Jervis, *Illogic of American Nuclear Strategy*, 126–46. For some indications of the balancing phenomenon, see Menon and Nelson, *Limits to Soviet Power*, 197–98; Holloway, *Soviet Union and the Arms Race*, 90–95, 105–6.

32. Blechman and Kaplan, *Force Without War*, 132; Kugler, "Terror Without Deterrence," 501.

33. Adomeit, "Soviet Crisis Prevention," esp. 42–43, 60–61; Mueller, "Irrelevance of Nuclear Weapons"; Holloway, *Soviet Union and the Arms Race*, 102, 179; Bundy, *Danger and Survival*, 587, 597; Lebow, "Windows of Opportunity"; Betts, *Nuclear Blackmail*, 214–18, 228.

34. Hence Betts concludes it is best not to bluff; see his *Nuclear Blackmail*, 212–33.

35. Mueller, "Irrelevance of Nuclear Weapons," 79; Bundy, *Danger and Survival*, 606–7.

36. These conclusions have been influenced by Walt, "Case for Finite Containment"; Johnson, "Exaggerating America's Stakes in Third World Conflicts"; McFarlane, "Successes and Failures in Soviet Policy Toward Marxist Revolutions"; Menon and Nelson, *Limits to Soviet Power*, esp. 1–23, 157–224. For the Soviets' rather prudent use of military force and military assistance, see esp. S. Kaplan, *Diplomacy of Power*; Hosmer and Wolfe, *Soviet Policy and Practice Toward Third World Conflicts*; Menon, *Soviet Power and the Third World*.

37. MccGwire, "Genesis of Soviet Threat Perceptions."

38. Ibid.

39. Taubman, *Stalin's American Policy*.

40. No one should forget the overwhelming German desire in the late 1940's and early 1950's to regain lost territory in the east. See Merritt and Merritt, *Public Opinion in Semisovereign Germany*, 167, 175; Deutsch and Edinger, *Germany Rejoins the Powers*, 25.

41. For the Soviet response to America's initial containment policies, see Mastny, "Stalin and the Militarization of the Cold War."

42. Shulman's analysis still seems pertinent; see his *Stalin's Foreign Policy Reappraised*.

43. The Soviets made contingency plans for an attack on Yugoslavia but never dared to implement them. See Mastny, "Stalin and the Militarization of the Cold War," 126–27. For Soviet restraint in Southeast Asia, see McLane, *Soviet Strategies in Southeast Asia*, 351–473. For Egypt, see Behbehani, *Soviet Union and Arab Nationalism*, 105–11. For Iran, see Ramazani, *Iran's Foreign Policy*, 231–42. For Vietnam, see Pike, *Vietnam and the Soviet Union*, 28–35.

44. These points are nicely emphasized in Hyland, *Cold War Is Over*.

45. For an interesting analysis of the perceptions of Chinese leaders and of their decision to intervene in Korea, see Hao Yufan and Zhai Zhihai, "China's Decision to Enter the Korean War."

46. This summarizes, admittedly at too high a level of generalization, some of the key points in the debate over America's decline. See Kennedy, *Rise and Fall of the Great Powers*, 347–535; Nye, *Bound to Lead*; Nau, *Myth of America's Decline*; Huntington, "U.S.—Decline or Renewal?"

Bibliography

Manuscript Collections and Oral Histories

Dean G. Acheson Papers, Harry S. Truman Library, Independence, Mo.
Henry S. Aurand Papers, Dwight D. Eisenhower Library, Abilene, Kans.
Eben A. Ayers Papers, Truman Library
Bernard Baruch Papers, Seely G. Mudd Library, Princeton University, Princeton, N.J.
David Bruce Papers, Virginia Historical Society, Richmond, Va.
James F. Byrnes Papers, Clemson University Library, Clemson, S.C.
Lucius D. Clay Oral History, Truman Library
Clark M. Clifford Oral History, Truman Library
Clark M. Clifford Papers, Truman Library
Matthew J. Connelly Papers, Truman Library
Richard Conolly Oral History, Naval Historical Center, Washington, D.C.
Council on Foreign Relations, Records of Meetings, New York City
Joseph Davies Papers, Library of Congress, Washington, D.C.
Louis E. Denfeld Papers, Naval Historical Center
Robert L. Dennison Papers, Truman Library
John F. Dulles Papers, Mudd Library
Ferdinand Eberstadt Papers, Mudd Library
Dwight D. Eisenhower Pre-Presidential Papers, Eisenhower Library
George M. Elsey Oral History, Truman Library
George M. Elsey Papers, Truman Library
Thomas Finletter Papers, Truman Library
James V. Forrestal Papers, Mudd Library
Raymond F. Fosdick Papers, Mudd Library
Gordon Gray Oral History, Truman Library
Paul H. Griffith Papers, Truman Library
Loy W. Henderson Oral History, Truman Library
John D. Hickerson Oral History, Truman Library
Harry N. Howard Papers, Truman Library
Philip C. Jessup Papers, Library of Congress
Louis Johnson Papers, Alderman Library, University of Virginia

George F. Kennan Papers, Mudd Library
W. John Kenney Papers, Truman Library
Dan A. Kimball Papers, Truman Library
William L. Leahy Papers, Library of Congress
Marx Leva Oral History, Truman Library
David Lilienthal Papers, Mudd Library
George A. Lincoln Papers, U.S. Military Academy, West Point, N.Y.
Robert A. Lovett Diaries, New York Historical Society, New York City
George G. McGhee Papers, Truman Library
Wilfrid J. McNeil Oral History, Truman Library
George C. Marshall Papers, George C. Marshall Library, Lexington, Va.
Francis P. Matthews Papers, Truman Library
National Security Council Files, Truman Library
Paul H. Nitze Oral History (for the Air Force), Nitze Office
Paul H. Nitze Oral History (for the Truman Library), Paul H. Nitze Office, Rosslyn, Va.
Ralph A. Ofstie Papers, Naval Historical Center
Frank Pace Papers, Truman Library
Floyd L. Parks Papers, Eisenhower Library
President's Air Policy Commission Files, Truman Library
Psychology Strategy Board Files, Truman Library
Arthur W. Radford Papers, Naval Historical Center
Karl Lott Rankin Papers, Mudd Library
Stuart W. Rockwell Oral History, Truman Library
Charles G. Ross Papers, Truman Library
Charles E. Saltzman Oral History, Truman Library
Forrest P. Sherman Papers, Naval Historical Center
H. Alexander Smith Papers, Mudd Library
Walter Bedell Smith Papers, Eisenhower Library
Sidney W. Souers Papers, Truman Library
Carl Spaatz Papers, Library of Congress
Henry L. Stimson Papers, Sterling Library, Yale University, New Haven, Conn.
W. Stuart Symington Papers, Truman Library
Harry S. Truman Papers, President's Official Files, Truman Library
Harry S. Truman Papers, President's Secretary's Files, Truman Library
Harry S. Truman Post-Presidential Papers, Truman Library
Harry H. Vaughan Oral History, Truman Library
Tracy Voorhees Papers, Rutgers University Library, New Brunswick, N.J.
James E. Webb Papers, Truman Library
Eugene Zuckert Oral History, Truman Library

Unpublished U.S. Government Documents

National Archives of the United States, Washington, D.C.
    Record Group 18, Records of Headquarters, Army Air Forces
        Records of the Office of Air Adjutant General
            Confidential and Secret Decimal Correspondence File, 1945–1948
    Record Group 43, Records of International Conferences, Commissions, and Expositions
        Records of the International Authority of the Ruhr
        Records of the Jessup-Malik Conversations
        Records of the Meetings of the Council of Foreign Ministers and Related Conferences,
            1945–1949
        Records of the Post-CFM Meetings

Record Group 51, Records of the Bureau of the Budget
Record Group 59, General Records of the Department of State
   Decimal Files
   Papers of Charles E. Bohlen, 1942–1952
   Records of the Military Adviser to the Office of Near Eastern, South Asian, and African
      Affairs, 1945–1950
   Records of the Office of European Affairs, 1934–1947
      (John D. Hickerson and H. Freeman Matthews Papers)
   Records of the Office of the Executive Secretariat
      Memoranda of Conversations with the President, 1949–1950
      Memoranda of Undersecretary's Meetings, 1949–1952
      Summaries of Secretary's Daily Meetings, 1949–1952
   Records of the Office of Public Opinion Studies, 1943–1965
   Records of the Philippines and Southeast Asian Division, 1944–1952
   Records of the Policy Planning Staff
Record Group 107, Records of the Office of the Secretary of War
   Records of the Office of the Assistant Secretary of War
      Howard C. Petersen Papers
   Records of the Office of the Assistant Secretary of War for Air
      Decimal Files, 1940–1946
      Establishment of Air Fields and Air Bases, 1940–1945
      Incoming and Outgoing Cablegrams, 1942–1947
      Plans, Policies, and Agreements, 1943–1947
   Robert P. Patterson Papers
Record Group 165, Records of the War Department General and Special Staffs
   Records of American-British Conversations
   Records of the Civil Affairs Division
   Records of the Office of the Chief of Staff of the Army
   Records of the Operations Division
Record Group 218, Records of the Joint Chiefs of Staff
   Omar Bradley Papers
   William Leahy Papers
Record Group 273, Records of the National Security Council
Record Group 319, Records of the Army Plans & Operations Division
Record Group 330, Records of the Office of the Secretary of Defense
Record Group 335, Records of the Office of the Secretary of the Army
   Records of the Office of the Undersecretary of the Army, 1947–1949
   Records of the Office of the Undersecretary of the Army, Draper/Voorhees Files, 1947–1950
Record Group 353, Records of the State-War-Navy Coordinating Committee
Naval Historical Center, Washington, D.C.
   Records of the Chief of Naval Operations, Double Zero Files
   Records of the General Board
   Records of the Operations Division
   Records of the Organizational Research and Policy Division
   Records of the Politico-Military Division
   Records of the Strategic Plans Division

Published U.S. Government Documents

Congress

House of Representatives

Committee on Armed Services. *The National Defense Program, Unification and Strategy.* 81st Cong., 1st sess., 1949.

Committee on Banking and Currency. *Bretton Woods Agreements Act.* 79th Cong., 1st sess., 1945.

Committee on Foreign Affairs. *Emergency Foreign Aid.* 80th Cong., 1st sess., 1947.

——. *Extension of the Lend-Lease Act.* 78th Cong., 1st sess., 1943.

——. *Selected Executive Session Hearings of the Committee, 1951–1956. Historical Series.* Vol. 9, pt. 1, *Mutual Security Program,* 1980.

——. *Selected Executive Session Hearings of the Committee, 1951–1956. Historical Series.* Vol. 15, *European Problems,* 1980.

——. *To Amend the Economic Cooperation Act of 1948.* 81st Cong., 2nd sess., 1950.

Committee on International Relations. *Selected Executive Session Hearings of the Committee, 1943–1950. Historical Series.* Vol. 4, pt. 2, *Foreign Economic Assistance Programs,* 1976.

Senate

Committee on Appropriations. *United Nations Relief and Rehabilitation Administration, 1946.* 79th Cong., 1st sess., 1945.

Committee on Armed Services. *Universal Military Training.* 80th Cong., 2nd sess., 1948.

Committee on Armed Services and Committee on Foreign Relations. *Assignment of Ground Forces of the United States to Duty in the European Area.* 82nd Cong., 1st sess., 1951.

——. *Military Assistance Program.* 81st Cong., 1st sess., 1949.

——. *Military Situation in the Far East.* 82nd Cong., 1st sess., 1951.

Committee on Banking and Currency. *Anglo-American Financial Agreement.* 79th Cong., 2nd sess., 1946.

——. *Bretton Woods Agreements Act.* 79th Cong., 1st sess., 1945.

——. *Export-Import Bank Act of 1945.* 79th Cong., 1st sess., 1945.

Committee on Finance. *1945 Extension of the Reciprocal Trade Agreements Act.* 79th Cong., 1st sess., 1945.

——. *To Repeal the Johnson Act.* 79th Cong., 1st sess., 1945.

Committee on Foreign Relations. *Assistance to Greece and Turkey.* 80th Cong., 1st sess., 1947.

——. *Economic Assistance to China and Korea: 1949–50. Historical Series.* 81st Cong., 1st and 2nd sess., 1974.

——. *European Recovery Program.* 80th Cong., 2nd sess., 1948.

——. *Executive Sessions of the Senate Foreign Relations Committee. Historical Series.* Vol. 1. 80th Cong., 1st and 2nd sess., 1976.

——. *Executive Sessions of the Senate Foreign Relations Committee. Historical Series.* Vol. 2. 81st Cong., 1st and 2nd sess., 1976.

——. *Executive Sessions of the Senate Foreign Relations Committee. Historical Series.* Vol. 4. 82nd Cong., 2nd sess., 1976.

——. *The Legislative Origins of American Foreign Policy.* Vol. 3, *Legislative Origins of the Truman Doctrine.* New York: Garland, 1979.

——. *The Legislative Origins of American Foreign Policy.* Vol. 4, *Foreign Relief Aid: 1947.* New York: Garland, 1979.

——. *The Legislative Origins of American Foreign Policy.* Vol. 5, *Foreign Relief Assistance Act of 1948.* New York: Garland, 1979.

——. *The Legislative Origins of American Foreign Policy.* Vol. 6, *The Vandenberg Resolution and the North Atlantic Treaty.* New York: Garland, 1979.

———. *The Legislative Origins of American Foreign Policy*. Vol. 9, *Military Assistance Program: 1949*. New York: Garland, 1979.
———. *The Legislative Origins of American Foreign Policy*. Vol. 10, *Extension of the European Recovery Program: 1949*. New York: Garland, 1979.
———. *The North Atlantic Treaty*. Pt. I. 80th Cong., 2nd sess., 1949.
———. *Reviews of the World Situation: 1949–50. Historical Series*. 81st Cong., 1st and 2nd sess., 1974.
Committee on Military Affairs. *Department of Armed Forces, Department of Military Security*. 79th Cong., 1st sess., 1945.
Select Committee to Study Governmental Operations with Respect to Intelligence Activities. *Supplementary Detailed Staff Reports on Foreign and Military Intelligence: Final Report, Book IV*. 94th Cong., 2nd sess., 1976.

Executive Branch

Cabinet Departments

Department of Commerce. *Balance of Payments of the United States, 1949–1951*, 1952.
———. *Economic Review of Foreign Countries, 1939 and Early 1940*, 1941.
———. *The United States in the World Economy*, 1943.
Department of Defense. *United States–Vietnam Relations, 1945–1967*, 1971.
Department of State. *Bulletin*, 1945–52.
———. *China White Paper, August 1949*. Reissue. Stanford, Calif.: Stanford Univ. Press, 1967.
———. *A Decade of American Foreign Policy, Basic Documents, 1941–1949*. Rev. ed., 1985.
———. *Documents on Germany, 1944–1985*, 1986.
———. *Foreign Relations of the United States, 1940*. Vols. 1–3, 1957–59.
———. *Foreign Relations of the United States, 1941*. Vol. 1, 1958.
———. *Foreign Relations of the United States, 1945*. 9 vols., 1967–69.
———. *Foreign Relations of the United States, 1946*. 11 vols., 1969–72.
———. *Foreign Relations of the United States, 1947*. 8 vols., 1971–77.
———. *Foreign Relations of the United States, 1948*. 9 vols., 1972–76.
———. *Foreign Relations of the United States, 1949*. 9 vols., 1974–78.
———. *Foreign Relations of the United States, 1950*. 7 vols., 1977–80.
———. *Foreign Relations of the United States, 1951*. 7 vols., 1977–85.
———. *Foreign Relations of the United States, 1952–54*. 26 vols., 1979–89.
———. *Foreign Relations of the United States. Conference of Berlin (Potsdam), 1945*. 2 vols., 1970.
———. *Foreign Relations of the United States. The Conferences at Malta and Yalta, 1945*, 1955.
———. *Policy Planning Staff Papers*. Ed. Anna Kasten Nelson. 3 vols. New York: Garland, 1983.
Department of the Interior. *National Resources and Foreign Aid*, 1947.

Central Intelligence Agency

CIA Research Reports. *Japan, Korea, and the Security of Asia*. Ed. Paul Kesaris. Frederick, Md.: Univ. Publications of America, 1983. 5 reels.

White House

Council of Economic Advisers. *Annual Report*, 1946–50.
———. *Economic Report of the President*, 1947–48.
———. *The Impact of Foreign Aid Upon the Domestic Economy*, 1947.
Office of Defense Mobilization. *The Job Ahead for Defense Mobilization*, 1953.
———. *New Resources Bring New Opportunities*, 1952.
President's Air Policy Commission. *Survival in the Air Age*, 1948.
President's Committee on Foreign Aid (Harriman). *European Recovery and American Aid*, 1947.

Contemporary Periodicals, Convention Proceedings, Newspapers

Business Week
Commercial and Financial Chronicle
Domestic Commerce
Economic Bulletin for Europe
Federal Reserve Bulletin
Foreign Affairs
Fortune
Life
National Foreign Trade Council. *Report of the Twenty-Sixth [to Thirty-Seventh] National Foreign Trade Convention.* New York: NFTC, 1939–50.
Nation's Agriculture
Nation's Business
Newsweek
New Times
New York Times
Public Opinion Quarterly
Reader's Digest
Time
U.S. News
USSR Information Bulletin
Vital Speeches of the Day

Other Cited Sources: Primary and Secondary

Acheson, Dean G. *Among Friends: Personal Letters of Dean Acheson.* Ed. David S. McLellan and David C. Acheson. New York: Dodd, Mead, 1980.
——. *The Credit to Britain and World Trade.* Washington, D.C.: GPO, 1946.
——. *Morning and Noon.* Boston, Mass.: Houghton Mifflin, 1955.
——. *Power and Diplomacy.* Cambridge, Mass.: Harvard Univ. Press, 1959.
——. *Present at the Creation: My Years at the State Department.* New York: Norton, 1969.
——. *This Vast External Realm.* New York: Norton, 1973.
Adams, Henry H. *Witness to Power: The Life of Fleet Admiral William D. Leahy.* Annapolis, Md.: Naval Institute Press, 1985.
Adamthwaite, Anthony. "Britain and the World, 1945–49: The View From the Foreign Office." *International Affairs* 61 (Spring 1985): 223–35.
Adenauer, Konrad. *Memoirs, 1945–1953.* Trans. Beate Ruhm von Oppen. Chicago, Ill.: Regnery, 1965.
Adomeit, Hannes. "Soviet Crisis Prevention and Management: Why and When Do the Soviet Leaders Take Risks?" *Orbis* 30 (Spring 1986): 42–64.
——. *Soviet Risk-Taking.* Boston, Mass.: Allen & Unwin, 1982.
Albion, Robert G., and Robert H. Connery. *Forrestal and the Navy.* New York: Columbia Univ. Press, 1962.
Alexander, G. M. *The Prelude to the Truman Doctrine: British Policy in Greece, 1944–47.* Oxford, Eng.: Clarendon, 1982.
Almond, Gabriel. *The American People and Foreign Policy.* New York: Praeger, 1960.
Alperovitz, Gar. *Atomic Diplomacy: Hiroshima and Potsdam.* New York: Vintage, 1965.
Alphand, Hervé. *L'Etonnement d'être: Journal (1939–1973).* Paris: Fayard, 1977.

Alvarez, David J. "The *Missouri* Visit to Turkey: An Alternative Perspective on Cold War Diplomacy." *Balkan Studies* 15 (1974): 225–36.

Anderson, Irvine. *ARAMCO, the United States and Saudi Arabia: A Study of the Dynamics of Foreign Oil Policy, 1933–50.* Princeton, N.J.: Princeton Univ. Press, 1981.

Arkes, Hadley. *Bureaucracy, the Marshall Plan, and the National Interest.* Princeton, N.J.: Princeton Univ. Press, 1972.

Arneson, R. Gordon. "The H-Bomb Decision." *Foreign Service Journal* 6 (May 1969): 27–29; (June 1969): 24–27, 43.

Aronsen, Lawrence R. "American National Security and the Defense of the Northern Frontier, 1945–1951." *Canadian Review of American Studies* 14 (Fall 1983): 259–77.

Auriol, Vincent. *Journal Du Septennat, 1947–1954.* Vols. 1–2. Paris: Librairie Armand Colin, 1970, 1974.

Backer, John H. *The Decision to Divide Germany: American Foreign Policy in Transition.* Durham, N.C.: Duke Univ. Press, 1978.

———. *Priming the German Economy: American Occupational Policies, 1945–1948.* Durham, N.C.: Duke Univ. Press, 1971.

———. *Winds of History: The German Years of Lucius Dubignon Clay.* New York: Van Nostrand Reinhold, 1983.

Bain, Kenneth Ray. *The March to Zion: United States Policy and the Founding of Israel.* College Station: Texas A&M Univ. Press, 1979.

Bark, Dennis L., and David R. Gress. *From Shadow to Substance, 1945–1963.* Vol. 1 of *A History of West Germany.* New York: Basil Blackwell, 1990.

Barnes, Trevor. "The Secret Cold War: The C.I.A. and American Foreign Policy in Europe, 1946–1956. Part I." *Historical Journal* 24 (June 1981): 399–415.

———. "The Secret Cold War: The C.I.A. and American Foreign Policy in Europe, 1946–1956. Part II." *Historical Journal* 25 (Sep 1982): 649–70.

Barnett, A. Doak. *China on the Eve of Communist Takeover.* New York: Praeger, 1963.

Barnhart, Michael. *Japan Prepares for Total War: The Quest for Economic Security, 1919–1941.* Ithaca, N.Y.: Cornell Univ. Press, 1987.

Baylis, John. "Britain and the Dunkirk Treaty: The Origins of NATO." *Journal of Strategic Studies* 5 (June 1982): 236–47.

———. "Britain, the Brussels Pact, and the Continental Commitment." *International Affairs* 60 (Aug 1984): 615–31.

Behbehani, Hashim S. H. *The Soviet Union and Arab Nationalism, 1917–1966.* London: KPI, 1986.

Bergson, Abram. "Russian Defense Expenditures." *Foreign Affairs* 26 (Jan 1948): 373–76.

Berle, Adolf A. *Navigating the Rapids, 1918–1971: From the Papers of Adolf A. Berle.* Ed. Beatrice Bishop Berle and Travis Beal Jacobs. New York: Harcourt Brace Jovanovich, 1973.

Berman, Larry. *The Office of Management and Budget and the Presidency, 1921–1979.* Princeton, N.J.: Princeton Univ. Press, 1979.

Bernstein, Barton J. "New Light on the Korean War." *International History Review* 3 (Apr 1981): 256–77.

———. "The Policy of Risk: Crossing the 38th Parallel and Marching to the Yalu." *Foreign Service Journal* 54 (March 1977): 16–29.

———. "The Quest for Security: American Foreign Policy and International Control of Atomic Energy, 1942–1946." *Journal of American History* 60 (March 1974): 1003–44.

———. "Roosevelt, Truman and the Atomic Bomb, 1941–1945: A Reinterpretation." *Political Science Quarterly* 90 (Spring 1975): 23–69.

———. "Truman and the H-Bomb." *Bulletin of the Atomic Scientists* 40 (March 1984): 12–20.

———, ed. *Politics and Policies of the Truman Administration.* Chicago, Ill.: Quadrangle, 1972.

Best, Richard A., Jr. *"Cooperation with Like-Minded Peoples": British Influence on American Security Policy, 1945–1949.* New York: Greenwood, 1986.

Bethell, Leslie, and Ian Roxborough. "Latin America Between the Second World War and the Cold War: Some Reflections on the 1945–48 Conjuncture." *Journal of Latin American Studies* 20 (May 1948): 167–89.

Bethell, Nicholas. *The Great Betrayal: The Untold Story of Kim Philby's Biggest Coup.* London: Hodder & Stoughton, 1984.

Betts, Richard K. *Nuclear Blackmail and Nuclear Balance.* Washington, D.C.: Brookings, 1987.

Bidault, Georges. *Resistance: The Political Autobiography of Georges Bidault.* London: Weidenfeld & Nicolson, 1967.

Bill, James A. *The Eagle and the Lion: The Tragedy of American-Iranian Relations.* New Haven, Conn.: Yale Univ. Press, 1988.

Blair, Clay. *The Forgotten War: America in Korea, 1950–1953.* New York: Time Books, 1987.

Blechman, Barry M., and Stephen S. Kaplan. *Force Without War: U.S. Armed Forces as a Political Instrument.* Washington, D.C.: Brookings, 1978.

Block, Fred L. *The Origins of International Economic Disorder: A Study of United States International Monetary Policy from World War II to the Present.* Berkeley, Calif.: Univ. of California Press, 1977.

Bloomfield, Jon. *Passive Revolution: Politics and the Czechoslovak Working Class, 1945–8.* London: Allison & Busby, 1979.

Blum, Robert M. *Drawing the Line: The Origin of American Containment Policy in East Asia.* New York: Norton, 1982.

Bohlen, Charles. *Witness to History, 1929–1969.* New York: Norton, 1973.

Bohlen, Charles, and Geroid T. Robinson. "The Bohlen-Robinson Report." *Diplomatic History* 1 (Fall 1977): 389–99.

Boll, Michael M. *Cold War in the Balkans: American Foreign Policy and the Emergence of Communist Bulgaria, 1943–1947.* Lexington: Univ. of Kentucky Press, 1984.

Borden, William S. *The Pacific Alliance: United States Foreign Economic Policy and Japanese Trade Recovery, 1947–1955.* Madison: Univ. of Wisconsin Press, 1984.

Borg, Dorothy, and Waldo Heinrichs, eds. *Uncertain Years: Chinese-American Relations, 1947–1950.* New York: Columbia Univ. Press, 1980.

Borowski, Harry R. *A Hollow Threat: Strategic Air Power and Containment Before Kennan.* Westport, Conn.: Greenwood, 1982.

Bourke, John. *Congress and the Presidency in U.S. Foreign Policymaking: A Study of Interaction and Influence, 1945–1982.* Boulder, Colo.: Westview, 1983.

Bowers, Ray L. *The United States Air Force in Southeast Asia: Tactical Airlift.* Washington, D.C.: Office of Air Force History, 1983.

Boyer, Paul. *By the Bomb's Early Light: American Thought and Culture at the Dawn of the Atomic Age.* New York: Pantheon, 1985.

Boylan, James R. *The New Deal Coalition and the Election of 1946.* New York: Garland, 1981.

Bradley, Omar N., and Clay Blair. *A General's Life: An Autobiography.* New York: Simon & Schuster, 1983.

Brands, Henry W. "The Cairo-Teheran Connection: Anglo-American Rivalry in the Middle East, 1951–1953." *International History Review* 11 (Aug 1989): 434–56.

———. "From ANZUS to SEATO: United States Strategic Policy Toward Australia and New Zealand." *International History Review* 9 (May 1987): 250–70.

Brinkley, Alan. "The New Deal and the Idea of the State." In *The Rise and Fall of the New Deal Order.* Ed. Steve Fraser and Gary Gerstle. Princeton, N.J.: Princeton Univ. Press, 1989.

Brown, L. Carl, ed. *Centerstage: American Foreign Policy Since World War II.* New York: Holmes & Meier, 1989.

Brown, William Adams, Jr., and Redvers Opie. *American Foreign Assistance.* Washington, D.C.: Brookings, 1953.

Buckley, Gary J. "American Public Opinion and the Origins of the Cold War: A Speculative Reassessment." *Mid-America* 60 (Jan 1978): 35–42.

Buhite, Russell D. *Patrick J. Hurley and American Foreign Policy*. Ithaca, N.Y.: Cornell Univ. Press, 1973.

——. *Soviet-American Relations in Asia, 1945–54*. Norman: Univ. of Oklahoma Press, 1981.

Bullen, Roger, and M. E. Pelly, eds. *Documents on British Policy Overseas*. Series 2, vols. 1–2. London: Her Majesty's Stationery Office, 1986–87.

Bullock, Allen Louis Charles. *Ernest Bevin: Foreign Secretary, 1945–1951*. New York: Oxford Univ. Press, 1983.

Bundy, McGeorge. *Danger and Survival: Choices About the Bomb in the First Fifty Years*. New York: Random House, 1988.

Burnham, James. "Lenin's Heir." *Partisan Review* 12 (Winter 1945): 61–72.

Burns, James MacGregor. *Roosevelt: The Soldier of Freedom*. New York: Harcourt Brace Jovanovich, 1979.

Buzan, Barry. *People, States and Fear: The National Security Problem in International Relations*. Sussex, Eng.: Wheatsheaf, 1983.

Byrne, Richard Dean. "The United States and Mutual Security, 1949–1952." Ph.D. diss., Univ. of Iowa, 1987.

Byrnes, James F. *All in One Lifetime*. New York: Harper & Brothers, 1958.

——. *The British Loan*. Washington, D.C.: GPO, 1946.

——. *Speaking Frankly*. New York: Harper & Brothers, 1947.

Calleo, David P. *Beyond American Hegemony*. New York: Basic, 1987.

Calleo, David P., and Benjamin M. Rowland. *America and the World Political Economy: Atlantic Dreams and National Realities*. Bloomington: Indiana Univ. Press, 1973.

Calvocoressi, Peter. *Survey of International Affairs, 1947–1948*. London: Oxford Univ. Press, 1952.

——. *Survey of International Affairs, 1949–1950*. London: Oxford Univ. Press, 1953.

Campbell, Duncan. *The Unsinkable Aircraft Carrier: American Military Power in Britain*. London: Grafton, 1984.

Campbell, Thomas M. *Masquerade Peace: America's U.N. Policy*. Tallahassee: Florida State Univ. Press, 1973.

Caraley, Demetrios. *The Politics of Military Unification: A Study of Conflict and the Policy Process*. New York: Columbia Univ. Press, 1966.

Caridi, Ronald J. *The Korean War and American Politics: The Republican Party as a Case Study*. Philadelphia: Univ. of Pennsylvania Press, 1968.

Carlyle, Margaret, ed. *Documents on International Affairs, 1947–1948*. New York: Oxford Univ. Press, 1952.

——. *Documents on International Affairs, 1949–1950*. New York: Oxford Univ. Press, 1953.

Carpenter, Ted Galen. "United States NATO Policy at the Crossroads: The Great Debate of 1950–51." *International History Review* 8 (Aug 1986): 389–414.

Catton, Bruce. *The War Lords of Washington*. New York: Harcourt, Brace, 1948.

Cecil, Robert. *A Divided Life: A Biography of Donald Maclean*. London: Bodley Head, 1988.

Chang, Gordon H. *Friends and Enemies: The United States, China, and the Soviet Union, 1948–1972*. Stanford, Calif.: Stanford Univ. Press, 1990.

Chang Kai-ngau. *Last Chance in Manchuria: The Diary of Chang Kai-ngau*. Ed. Donald G. Gillin and Ramon H. Myers. Stanford, Calif.: Hoover Institution Press, 1989.

Chauvil, Jean. *Commentaire: D'Alger A Berne (1944–1952)*. Paris: Fayard, 1972.

Child, Jack. *Unequal Alliance: The Inter-American Military System, 1938–1978*. Boulder, Colo.: Westview, 1980.

Churchill, Winston, and Franklin D. Roosevelt. *Churchill and Roosevelt: The Complete Correspondence*. 3 vols. Ed. Warren F. Kimball. Princeton, N.J.: Princeton Univ. Press, 1984.

Clark, Ian, and Nicholas J. Wheeler. *The British Origins of Nuclear Strategy, 1945–1955*. Oxford, Eng.: Clarendon, 1989.

Claudin, Fernando. *The Communist Movement: From Comintern to Cominform*. Trans. Brian Pearce and Francis MacDonagh. Middlesex, Eng.: Penguin, 1975.

Clay, Lucius D. *The Papers of General Lucius D. Clay: Germany, 1945–1949.* 2 vols. Ed. Jean Edward Smith. Bloomington: Indiana Univ. Press, 1974.

Clemens, Diane S. *Yalta.* New York: Oxford Univ. Press, 1970.

Clifford, Clark, with Richard Holbrooke. *Counsel to the President.* New York: Random House, 1991.

Clifford, J. Garry. "President Truman and Peter the Great's Will." *Diplomatic History* 4 (Fall 1980): 371–85.

Cline, Ray S. *Washington Command Post: The Operations Division.* Washington, D.C.: Dept. of the Army, 1951.

Clymer, Kenton. "Jawaharlal Nehru and the United States." *Diplomatic History* 14 (Spring 1990): 143–61.

Cochran, Thomas R., William M. Arkin, and Milton Hoenig. *Nuclear Weapons Databook.* Vol 1. Cambridge, Mass.: Ballinger, 1984.

Cohen, Michael J. *Palestine and the Great Powers, 1945–1948.* Princeton, N.J.: Princeton Univ. Press, 1982.

Cohen, Theodore, and Herbert Passim, eds. *Remaking Japan: The American Occupation as New Deal.* New York: Free Press, 1987.

Cohen, Warren I. "Conversations with Chinese Friends: Zhou Enlai's Associates Reflect on Chinese-American Relations in the 1940's and the Korean War." *Diplomatic History* 11 (Summer 1987): 283–89.

Cole, Wayne. *Norway and the United States, 1905–1955: Two Democracies in Peace and War.* Ames: Iowa State Univ. Press, 1989.

Coletta, Paolo E. *The United States Navy and Defense Unification.* Newark: Univ. of Delaware Press, 1981.

Collins, J. Lawton. *War in Peacetime: The History and Lessons of Korea.* Boston, Mass.: Houghton Mifflin, 1969.

Collins, Robert M. *The Business Response to Keynes, 1929–1964.* New York: Columbia Univ. Press, 1981.

Combs, Jerald A. "An Exaggerated Vulnerability? The United States and the Conventional Defense of Western Europe, 1948–1952." Unpublished paper, 1989.

Condit, Doris M. *History of the Office of Secretary of Defense: The Test of War, 1950–1953.* Washington, D.C.: Office of the Secretary of Defense, 1988.

Condit, Kenneth W. *The History of the Joint Chiefs of Staff: The Joint Chiefs of Staff and National Policy.* Vol. 2, *1947–1949.* Wilmington, Del.: Glazier, 1979.

Connery, Robert H. *The Navy and Industrial Mobilization in World War II.* Princeton, N.J.: Princeton Univ. Press, 1949.

Converse, Elliott V. "United States Plans for a Postwar Overseas Military Base System, 1942–1948." Ph.D. diss., Princeton Univ., 1984.

Costigliola, Frank. *Awkward Dominion: American Political, Economic, and Cultural Relations with Europe, 1919–1937.* Ithaca, N.Y.: Cornell Univ. Press, 1984.

Cottam, Richard W. *Iran and the United States: A Cold War Case Study.* Pittsburgh, Pa.: Univ. of Pittsburgh Press, 1988.

Coutouvidis, John, and Jaime Reynolds. *Poland, 1939–1947.* Leicester, Eng.: Leicester Univ. Press, 1986.

Cowen, Michael, and Nicholas Westcott. "British Imperial Economic Policy During the War." In *Africa and the Second World War.* Ed. David Killingray and Richard Rathbone. London: Macmillan, 1986.

Cray, Ed. *General of the Army: George C. Marshall, Soldier and Statesman.* New York: Norton, 1990.

Cromwell, William C. "The Marshall Plan, Britain, and the Cold War." *Review of International Studies* 8 (Oct 1982): 233–51.

Cullather, Nicholas Barry. "United States Strategic and Economic Policy Toward the Philippines: Bilateralism Versus Integration." Master's thesis, Univ. of Virginia, 1987.

Cumings, Bruce, ed. *Child of Conflict: The Korean-American Relationship, 1943–1953.* Seattle: Univ. of Washington Press, 1983.

——. "Origins and Development of the Northeast Asian Political Economy." *International Organization* 38 (Winter 1984): 1–41.

——. *The Origins of the Korean War.* 2 vols. Princeton, N.J.: Princeton Univ. Press, 1981, 1990.

Cunningham, Frank D. "Harry S. Truman and Universal Military Training, 1945." *The Historian* 46 (May 1984): 397–415.

Dallek, Robert. *Franklin D. Roosevelt and American Foreign Policy.* New York: Oxford Univ. Press, 1979.

Davis, Lynn E. *The Cold War Begins: Soviet-American Conflict over Eastern Europe.* Princeton, N.J.: Princeton Univ. Press, 1974.

Davis, Vincent. *Postwar Defense Policy and the U.S. Navy, 1943–1946.* Chapel Hill: Univ. of North Carolina Press, 1962.

Dean, Gordon E. *Forging the Atomic Shield: Excerpts from the Diary of Gordon E. Dean.* Ed. Roger M. Anders. Chapel Hill: Univ. of North Carolina Press, 1987.

Deane, John R. *The Strange Alliance: The Story of Our Efforts at Wartime Co-operation with Russia.* New York: Viking, 1947.

Dedijer, Vladimir. *The Battle Stalin Lost: Memoirs of Yugoslavia, 1948–1953.* New York: Viking, 1971.

de Gaulle, Charles. *The Complete War Memoirs of Charles DeGaulle.* Trans. Jonathan Griffin. New York: Simon & Schuster, 1955.

Deighton, Anne. "The 'Frozen Front': The Labour Government, the Division of Germany and the Origins of the Cold War, 1945–1947." *International Affairs* 63 (Summer 1987): 449–65.

DeSantis, Hugh. *The Diplomacy of Silence: The American Foreign Service, the Soviet Union and the Cold War, 1933–1947.* Chicago, Ill.: Univ. of Chicago Press, 1979.

Deutsch, Karl W., and Lewis J. Edinger. *Germany Rejoins the Powers.* Stanford, Calif.: Stanford Univ. Press, 1959.

Devereux, David R. "Britain, the Commonwealth, and the Defence of the Middle East." *Journal of Contemporary History* 24 (Apr 1989): 327–45.

Diba, Farhad. *Mohammad Mossadegh: Political Biography.* London: Croom Helm, 1986.

Diebold, William, Jr. *The Schuman Plan: A Study in Economic Cooperation, 1950–1959.* New York: Praeger, 1959.

Dingman, Roger. "Atomic Diplomacy During the Korean War." *International Security* 13 (Winter 1988–89): 50–91.

——. "The Diplomacy of Dependency: The Philippines and Peacemaking with Japan." *Journal of Southeast Asian Studies* 27 (Sep 1986): 307–21.

——. "Strategic Planning and the Policy Process: American Plans for War in East Asia, 1945–1950." *Naval War College Review* 32 (Nov–Dec 1979): 4–21.

——. "The United States Navy and the Cold War: The Japan Case." In *New Aspects of Naval History.* Ed. Craig L. Symonds. Annapolis, Md.: Naval Institute Press, 1981.

Divine, Robert A. *Second Chance: The Triumph of Internationalism in America During World War II.* New York: Atheneum, 1967.

——. *Since 1945: Politics and Diplomacy in Recent American History.* 3d ed. New York: Knopf, 1985.

Djilas, Milovan. *Conversations with Stalin.* New York: Harcourt, Brace & World, 1962.

Dobbs, Charles M. *The Unwanted Symbol: American Foreign Policy, the Cold War and Korea, 1945–1950.* Kent, Ohio: Kent State Univ. Press, 1981.

Dockrill, M. L. "The Foreign Office, Anglo-American Relations, and the Korean War, June 1950–June 1951." *International Affairs* 3 (Summer 1986): 459–76.

Doenecke, Justus D. *Not to the Swift: The Old Isolationists and the Cold War Era.* Lewisburg, Pa.: Bucknell Univ. Press, 1979.

Doig, James W., and Erwin C. Hargrove, eds. *Leadership and Innovation: A Biographical Perspective on Entrepreneurs in Government.* Baltimore, Md.: Johns Hopkins Univ. Press, 1987.
Donovan, Robert J. *Conflict and Crisis: The Presidency of Harry S. Truman, 1945–1948.* New York: Norton, 1977.
———. *Tumultuous Years: The Presidency of Harry S. Truman, 1949–1953.* New York: Norton, 1982.
Doughty, Robert A. *The Evolution of U.S. Army Tactical Doctrine, 1946–1976.* Leavenworth, Kans.: Current Studies Institute, 1979.
Dower, John W. *Empire and Aftermath: Yoshida Shigeru and the Japanese Experience, 1868–1954.* Cambridge, Mass.: Harvard Univ. Press, 1979.
Drummond, Gordon D. *The German Social Democrats in Opposition.* Norman: Univ. of Oklahoma Press, 1982.
Duiker, William J. *The Communist Road to Power in Vietnam.* Boulder, Colo.: Westview Press, 1981.
Duke, Simon. *US Defence Bases in the United Kingdom: A Matter for Joint Decision?* London: Macmillan, 1987.
Dulles, John Foster. *War or Peace.* New York: Macmillan, 1950.
Dunmore, Timothy. *Soviet Politics, 1945–1953.* London: Macmillan, 1983.
Dunn, Frederick S. *Peace-Making and the Settlement with Japan.* Princeton, N.J.: Princeton Univ. Press, 1963.
Dur, Philip F. *Jefferson Caffery of Louisiana: Ambassador of Revolutions.* Lafayette: Univ. of Southwestern Louisiana Libraries, 1982.
Eastman, Lloyd E. *Seeds of Destruction: Nationalist China in War and Revolution, 1937–1949.* Stanford, Calif.: Stanford Univ. Press, 1984.
Eckes, Alfred E., Jr. *The Search for Solvency: Bretton Woods and the International Monetary System, 1941–1947.* Austin: Univ. of Texas Press, 1975.
Eden, Anthony. *Full Circle: The Memoirs of Anthony Eden.* Boston, Mass.: Houghton Mifflin, 1962.
Eden, Lynn Rachele. "The Diplomacy of Force: Interests, the State, and the Making of American Military Policy in 1948." Ph.D. diss., Univ. of Michigan, 1985.
Edmonds, Robin. *Setting the Mould: The United States and Britain, 1945–1950.* New York: Oxford Univ. Press, 1986.
Eisenberg, Carolyn. "The American Decision to Divide Germany." Paper presented at the annual convention of the American Historical Association. Chicago, Ill., 1986.
———. "U.S. Policy in Post-War Germany: The Conservative Restoration." *Science and Society* 46 (Spring 1982): 24–38.
———. "Working-Class Politics and the Cold War: American Intervention in the German Labor Movement, 1945–49." *Diplomatic History* 7 (Fall 1983): 283–306.
Eisenhower, Dwight D. *The Eisenhower Diaries.* Ed. Robert H. Ferrell. New York: Norton, 1981.
———. *The Papers of Dwight David Eisenhower.* Vols. 6–13. Vol. 6 ed. Louis Galambos and Alfred D. Chandler; vols. 7–13 ed. Louis Galambos. Baltimore, Md.: Johns Hopkins Univ. Press, 1978–89.
Esposito, Chiarella. "The Role of American Aid in French Economics and Politics, 1948–1950." Paper presented at the annual convention of the American Historical Association. San Francisco, Calif., 1989.
Etzold, Thomas H., and John L. Gaddis, eds. *Containment: Documents on American Policy and Strategy, 1945–1950.* New York: Columbia Univ. Press, 1978.
Evangelista, Matthew A. "The Evolution of the Soviet Tactical Air Forces." *Soviet Armed Forces Review Annual* 7 (1982–83): 451–79.
———. "Soviet Military Capabilities and Objectives in the Early Postwar Period, 1945–1953." Occasional Paper, no. 1. Brookline, Mass.: Institute for Defense and Disarmament Studies, 1981.
———. "Stalin's Postwar Army Reappraised." *International Security* 7 (Winter 1982–83): 110–38.

Fall, Bernard B. *Street Without Joy: Indochina at War, 1946–54*. Harrisburg, Pa.: Stackpole, 1961.

Fanton, Jonathan Foster. "Robert A. Lovett: The War Years." Ph.D. diss., Yale Univ., 1978.

Farrar, Peter N. "Britain's Proposal for a Buffer Zone South of the Yalu in November 1950: Was it a Neglected Opportunity to End the Fighting in Korea?" *Journal of Contemporary History* 18 (Apr 1983): 327–51.

Feaver, John H. "The China Aid Bill of 1948: Limited Assistance as a Cold War Strategy." *Diplomatic History* 5 (Spring 1981): 107–20.

Feis, Herbert. *The Atomic Bomb and the End of World War II*. Princeton, N.J.: Princeton Univ. Press, 1970.

——. *The China Tangle: The American Effort in China from Pearl Harbor to the Marshall Mission*. New York: Atheneum, 1967.

——. *The Road to Pearl Harbor: The Coming of the War Between the United States and Japan*. Princeton, N.J.: Princeton Univ. Press, 1950.

Ferguson, Thomas. "From Normalcy to New Deal: Industrial Structure, Party Competition, and American Public Policy in the Great Depression." *International Organization* 38 (Winter 1984): 41–95.

Fifield, Russell H., and G. Etzel Pearcy. *Geopolitics in Principle and Practice*. Boston, Mass.: Ginn, 1944.

Filippelli, Ronald L. *American Labor and Postwar Italy, 1943–1953: A Study of Cold War Politics*. Stanford, Calif.: Stanford Univ. Press, 1989.

Foltos, Lester J. "The New Pacific Barrier: America's Search for Security in the Pacific, 1945–47." *Diplomatic History* 13 (Summer 1989): 317–42.

Foot, Rosemary. "Anglo-American Relations in the Korean Crisis: The British Effort to Avert an Expanded War, December 1950–January 1951." *Diplomatic History* 10 (Winter 1986): 43–57.

——. "Negotiating a Stalemate: U.S. Policy at the Korean Armistice Negotiations and the Factors Constraining Agreement." Paper presented at the annual meeting of the Society for Historians of American Foreign Relations. Washington, D.C., 1988.

——. *A Substitute for Victory: The Politics of Peacemaking at the Korean Armistice Talks*. Ithaca, N.Y.: Cornell Univ. Press, 1990.

——. *The Wrong War: American Policy and the Dimensions of the Korean Conflict*. Ithaca, N.Y.: Cornell Univ. Press, 1985.

Forrestal, James. *The Forrestal Diaries*. Ed. Walter Millis. New York: Viking, 1951.

Foster, H. Schuyler. *Activism Replaces Isolationism: U.S. Public Attitudes, 1940–1975*. Washington, D.C.: Foxhall, 1983.

Frank, Benis M., and Henry I. Shaw, Jr. *Victory and Occupation: History of the U.S. Marine Corps Operations in World War II*. Vol. 5. Washington, D.C.: GPO, 1968.

Frazier, Robert. "Did Britain Start the Cold War? Bevin and the Truman Doctrine." *Historical Journal* 27 (Sep 1984): 715–27.

Freeland, Richard M. *The Truman Doctrine and the Origins of McCarthyism: Foreign Policy, Domestic Politics and Internal Security, 1946–1948*. New York: New York Univ. Press, 1985.

Fukuyama, Francis. "The End of History?" *The National Interest* 16 (Summer 1989): 1–18.

Fursdon, Edward. *The European Defense Community: A History*. New York: St. Martin's, 1980.

Futrell, Robert Frank. *The United States Air Force in Korea*. New York: Duell, Sloan and Pearce, 1961.

Gaddis, John Lewis. "The Emerging Post-Revisionist Thesis on the Origins of the Cold War." *Diplomatic History* 7 (Summer 1983): 171–90.

——. *The Long Peace: Inquiries into the History of the Cold War*. New York: Oxford Univ. Press, 1987.

——. *Strategies of Containment: A Critical Appraisal of American National Security Policy*. New York: Oxford Univ. Press, 1982.

——. *The United States and the Origins of the Cold War, 1941–1947*. New York: Columbia Univ. Press, 1972.

——. "Was the Truman Doctrine a Real Turning Point?" *Foreign Affairs* 52 (Jan 1974): 386–402.

Gaitskill, Hugh. *The Diary of Hugh Gaitskill, 1945–1956.* Ed. Philip M. Williams. London: Jonathan Casse, 1983.

Gallicchio, Marc S. *The Cold War Begins in Asia: American East Asian Policy and the Fall of the Japanese Empire.* New York: Columbia Univ. Press, 1988.

Gallup, George H. *The Gallup Poll: Public Opinion, 1935–1971.* Vols. 1 and 2. New York: Random House, 1972.

Gardner, Lloyd C. *Approaching Vietnam: From World War II Through Dienbienphu, 1941–1954.* New York: Norton, 1988.

——. *Architects of Illusion: Men and Ideas in American Foreign Policy, 1941–1949.* Chicago, Ill.: Quadrangle, 1970.

Gardner, Richard N. *Sterling-Dollar Diplomacy in Current Perspective: The Origins and Prospects of Our International Economic Order.* New York: Columbia Univ. Press, 1980.

Gasiorowski, Mark J. "The 1953 Coup d'Etat in Iran." *International Journal of Middle East Studies* 19 (Aug 1987): 261–86.

Gati, Charles. *Hungary and the Soviet Bloc.* Durham, N.C.: Duke Univ. Press, 1986.

George, Alexander L., David K. Hall, and William E. Simons. *The Limits of Coercive Diplomacy: Laos, Cuba, Vietnam.* Boston, Mass.: Little, Brown, 1971.

George, Alexander L., and Richard Smoke. *Deterrence in American Foreign Policy: Theory and Practice.* New York: Columbia Univ. Press, 1974.

Gerber, Larry G. "The Baruch Plan and the Origins of the Cold War." *Diplomatic History* 6 (Winter 1982): 69–95.

Gifford, Prosser, and Wm. Roger Louis. *The Transfer of Power in Africa: Decolonization 1940–1960.* New Haven, Conn.: Yale Univ. Press, 1982.

——, eds. *Decolonization and African Independence: The Transfers of Power, 1960–1980.* New Haven, Conn.: Yale Univ. Press, 1988.

Gillingham, John R. *Coal, Steel, and the Rebirth of Europe, 1945–1955: The Germans and French from Ruhr Conflict to Economic Community.* Cambridge, Eng.: Cambridge Univ. Press, 1991.

——. *Industry and Politics in the Third Reich: Ruhr Coal, Hitler and Europe.* New York: Columbia Univ. Press, 1985.

Gillon, Steven. *Politics and Vision: The ADA and American Liberalism.* New York: Oxford Univ. Press, 1987.

Gilpin, Robert. "The Politics of Transnational Economic Relations." *International Organization* 25 (Summer 1971): 398–419.

——. *War and Change in World Politics.* New York: Cambridge Univ. Press, 1981.

Gimbel, John. *The American Occupation of Germany: Politics and the Military, 1945–1949.* Stanford, Calif.: Stanford Univ. Press, 1968.

——. "On the Implementation of the Potsdam Agreement." *Political Science Quarterly* 87 (June 1972): 242–69.

——. *The Origins of the Marshall Plan.* Stanford, Calif.: Stanford Univ. Press, 1976.

Gladwyn, Hubert Miles Gladwyn Jebb. *The Memoirs of Lord Gladwyn.* London: Weidenfeld & Nicolson, 1972.

Gluck, Carol. "Entangling Illusions: Japanese and American Views of the Occupation." In *New Frontiers in American–East Asian Relations.* Ed. Warren I. Cohen. New York: Columbia Univ. Press, 1983.

Goode, James F. *The United States and Iran, 1946–51: The Diplomacy of Neglect.* New York: St. Martin's, 1989.

Gormly, James L. *The Collapse of the Grand Alliance, 1945–1948.* Baton Rouge: Louisiana State Univ. Press, 1987.

——. "Keeping the Door Open in Saudi Arabia: The United States and the Dhahran Airfield, 1945–46." *Diplomatic History* 4 (Spring 1980): 189–206.

——. "The Washington Declaration and the 'Poor Relation': Anglo-American Atomic Diplomacy, 1945–1946." *Diplomatic History* 8 (Spring 1984): 125–44.

Gowing, Margaret. *Independence and Deterrence: Britain and Atomic Energy, 1945–1952*. London: Macmillan, 1974.

Graham, Otis L., Jr. *Toward a Planned Society: From Roosevelt to Nixon*. New York: Oxford Univ. Press, 1976.

Gray, Colin. *The Geopolitics of Super Power*. Lexington: Univ. of Kentucky Press, 1988.

Graybar, Lloyd J. "The 1946 Atomic Bomb Tests: Atomic Diplomacy or Bureaucratic Infighting." *Journal of American History* 72 (March 1986): 888–907.

Green, David. *The Containment of Latin America: A History of Myths and Realities of the Good Neighbor Policy*. Chicago, Ill.: Quadrangle, 1971.

Greenberg, Lawrence M. *The Hukbalahap Insurrection: A Case Study of a Successful Anti-Insurgency Operation in the Philippines, 1945–1955*. Washington, D.C.: U.S. Army Center of Military History, 1986.

Greenwood, Sean. "Bevin, the Ruhr, and the Division of Germany: August 1945–December 1946." *Historical Journal* 29 (March 1986): 203–12.

——. "Ernest Bevin, France, and 'Western Union,' August 1945–February 1946." *European History Quarterly* 14 (Jan 1984): 319–35.

——. "Return to Dunkirk: The Origins of the Anglo-French Treaty of March 1947." *Journal of Strategic Studies* 6 (Dec 1983): 49–65.

Grew, Joseph C. *Turbulent Era: A Diplomatic Record of Forty Years, 1904–1945*. 2 vols. Boston, Mass.: Houghton Mifflin, 1952.

Griffith, Robert S. *The Politics of Fear: Joseph R. McCarthy and the Senate*. Lexington: Univ. of Kentucky Press, 1970.

Gromyko, Andrei. *Memoirs*. New York: Doubleday, 1989.

Haglund, David G. *Latin America and the Transformation of U.S. Strategic Thought, 1936–1940*. Albuquerque: Univ. of New Mexico Press, 1984.

——, ed. *The New Geopolitics of Minerals: Canada and International Resource Trade*. Vancouver: Univ. of British Columbia Press, 1989.

Hahn, Peter. "Strategy and Diplomacy in the Early Cold War: United States Policy Toward Egypt, 1945–1956." Ph.D. diss., Vanderbilt Univ., 1987.

Hahn, Werner G. *Postwar Soviet Politics: The Fall of Zhdanov and the Defeat of Moderation*. Ithaca, N.Y.: Cornell Univ. Press, 1982.

Halliday, Jon, and Bruce Cumings. *Korea: The Unknown War*. New York: Pantheon, 1988.

Hamby, Alonzo. *Beyond the New Deal: Harry S. Truman and American Liberalism*. New York: Columbia Univ. Press, 1973.

Hammer, Ellen. *The Struggle for Indochina*. Stanford, Calif.: Stanford Univ. Press, 1954.

Hammond, Paul Y. *Organizing for Defense: The American Military Establishment in the Twentieth Century*. Princeton, N.J.: Princeton Univ. Press, 1961.

Hammond, Thomas T., ed. *The Anatomy of Communist Takeovers*. New Haven, Conn.: Yale Univ. Press, 1975.

Hanrieder, Wolfram F. *Germany, America, Europe: Forty Years of German Foreign Policy*. New Haven, Conn.: Yale Univ. Press, 1989.

Hao Yufan and Zhai Zhihai. "China's Decision to Enter the Korean War: History Revisited." *China Quarterly* 121 (March 1990): 94–115.

Harbutt, Fraser. *The Iron Curtain: Churchill, America and the Origins of the Cold War*. New York: Oxford Univ. Press, 1986.

Hardach, Karl. "The Marshall Plan in Germany, 1948–1952." *Journal of European Economic History* 16 (Winter 1987): 433–86.

——. *The Political Economy of Germany in the Twentieth Century*. Berkeley: Univ. of California Press, 1980.

Harding, Harry, and Yuan Ming, eds. *Sino-American Relations, 1945–1955: A Joint Reassessment of a Critical Decade*. Wilmington, Del.: Scholarly Resources, 1989.

Harper, John L. *America and the Reconstruction of Italy, 1945–1948*. New York: Cambridge Univ. Press, 1986.

Harriman, W. Averell, and Elie Abel. *Special Envoy to Churchill and Stalin, 1941–1946*. New York: Random House, 1975.

Hartmann, Susan M. *Truman and the 80th Congress*. Columbia: Univ. of Missouri Press, 1971.

Haslam, Jonathan. "Stalin's Assessment of the Likelihood of War." Paper presented at King's College. Cambridge, Eng., 1988.

Hathaway, Robert M. *Ambiguous Partnership: Britain and America, 1944–1947*. New York: Columbia Univ. Press, 1981.

Hayes, Grace Person. *The History of the Joint Chiefs of Staff in World War II*. Annapolis, Md.: Naval Institute Press, 1982.

Haynes, Richard F. *The Awesome Power: Harry S. Truman as Commander in Chief*. Baton Rouge: Louisiana State Univ. Press, 1973.

Heller, Francis H. *The Truman White House: The Administration of the Presidency, 1945–53*. Lawrence: Regents Press of Kansas, 1980.

——, ed. *Economics and the Truman Administration*. Lawrence: Regents Press of Kansas, 1981.

Heller, Francis H., and John R. Gillingham, eds. *NATO: The Founding of the Atlantic Alliance and the Integration of Europe*. Forthcoming.

Henderson, Nicholas. *The Birth of NATO*. Boulder, Colo.: Westview, 1983.

Henrickson, Allan K. "The Map as an 'Idea': The Role of Cartographic Imagery During the Second World War." *The American Cartographer* 2 (1975): 19–53.

Herken, Gregg. *The Winning Weapon: The Atomic Bomb in the Cold War*. New York: Knopf, 1980.

Herring, George C., Jr. *Aid to Russia, 1941–1946: Strategy, Diplomacy and the Origins of the Cold War*. New York: Columbia Univ. Press, 1973.

——. "The Truman Administration and the Restoration of French Sovereignty in Indochina." *Diplomatic History* 1 (Spring 1977): 97–117.

——. "The United States and British Bankruptcy, 1944–1945: Responsibilities Deferred." *Political Science Quarterly* 86 (June 1971): 260–80.

Herwig, Holger H. *Politics of Frustration: The United States in German Naval Planning, 1889–1941*. Boston, Mass.: Little, Brown, 1976.

Herz, John H. "Idealist Internationalism and the Security Dilemma." *World Politics* 2 (Jan 1950): 157–80.

Hess, Gary R. "Franklin Roosevelt and Indochina." *Journal of American History* 59 (Sep 1982): 359–68.

——. *The United States' Emergence as a Southeast Asian Power, 1945–1950*. New York: Columbia Univ. Press, 1987.

Heuser, Beatrice. *Western 'Containment' Policies in the Cold War: The Yugoslav Case, 1948–1953*. London: Routledge, 1989.

Hewlett, Richard G., and Francis Duncan. *Atomic Shield, 1947–52: A History of the United States Atomic Energy Commission*. University Park: Pennsylvania State Univ. Press, 1969.

Hill, John S. "American Reconstruction Aid to France before the Marshall Plan, 1944–1946." Paper presented at the annual convention of the American Historical Association. San Francisco, Calif., 1989.

——. "Inflation and the Collapse of Tripartism, 1945–1947." Paper presented at the annual convention of the American Historical Association. Chicago, Ill., 1986.

Hirschman, Albert. *National Power and the Structure of Foreign Trade*. Berkeley: Univ. of California Press, 1946.

Hixson, Walter L. *George F. Kennan: Cold War Iconoclast*. New York: Columbia Univ. Press, 1989.

Ho Zhigong. " 'Lost Chance' or 'Inevitable Hostility'? Two Contending Interpretations of the Late 1940's Chinese-American Relations." Society for Historians of American Foreign Relations *Newsletter* 20 (Sep 1989): 67–78.

Hogan, Michael J. *Informal Entente: The Private Structure of Cooperation in Anglo-American Economic Diplomacy, 1918–1928*. Columbia: Univ. of Missouri Press, 1977.

———. *The Marshall Plan: America, Britain, and the Reconstruction of Western Europe, 1947–1952*. New York: Cambridge Univ. Press, 1987.

Holloway, David. *The Soviet Union and the Arms Race*. New Haven, Conn.: Yale Univ. Press, 1983.

Horowitz, David. *The Free World Colossus: A Critique of American Foreign Policy in the Cold War*. New York: Hill & Wang, 1965.

Hosmer, Stephen T., and Thomas W. Wolfe. *Soviet Policy and Practice Toward Third World Conflicts*. Lexington, Mass.: Lexington, 1983.

Hudson, Daryl L. "Vandenberg Reconsidered: Senate Resolution 239 and American Foreign Policy." *Diplomatic History* 1 (Winter 1977): 46–63.

Hunt, Michael H. "Beijing and the Korean Crisis, June 1950–June 1951." Unpublished paper (1990).

Huntington, Samuel P. *The Soldier and the State: The Theory and Politics of Civil-Military Relations*. Cambridge, Mass.: Harvard Univ. Press, 1957.

———. "The U.S.—Decline or Renewal?" *Foreign Affairs* 67 (Winter 1988–89): 76–96.

Hyam, Ronald. "Africa and the Labour Government, 1945–1951." In *Studies in British Imperial History: Essays in Honour of A. P. Thornton*. Ed. Gordon Martel. London: Macmillan, 1985.

Hyland, William. *The Cold War Is Over*. New York: Random House, 1990.

Iatrides, John O. *Revolt in Athens: The Greek Communist Second Round, 1944–1945*. Princeton, N.J.: Princeton Univ. Press, 1972.

Immerman, Richard H. "United States Perceptions of Its Interests in Indochina." Unpublished manuscript.

Ireland, Timothy P. *Creating the Entangling Alliance: The Origins of the North Atlantic Treaty Organization*. Westport, Conn.: Greenwood, 1981.

Iriye, Akira. *The Cold War in Asia: A Historical Introduction*. Englewood Cliffs, N.J.: Prentice Hall, 1974.

Irons, Peter H. " 'The Test Is Poland': Polish-Americans and the Origins of the Cold War." *Polish-American Studies* 30 (Fall 1973): 5–63.

Isaacson, Walter, and Evan Thomas. *The Wise Men: Six Friends and the World They Made*. New York: Simon & Schuster, 1986.

Ismay, Hastings Lionel. *NATO: The First Five Years, 1949–1954*. Netherlands: Bosch-Utrecht, 1955.

Jackson, Scott. "Prologue to the Marshall Plan." *Journal of American History* 65 (March 1979): 1043–68.

Jalal, Ayesha. "Towards the Baghdad Pact: South Asia and Middle East Defence in the Cold War, 1947–1955." *International History Review* 11 (Aug 1989): 409–33.

James, D. Clayton. *The Years of MacArthur: Triumph and Disaster, 1945–1964*. Vol. 3. Boston, Mass.: Houghton Mifflin, 1985.

Jervis, Robert. "Cooperation Under the Security Dilemma." *World Politics* 30 (Jan 1978): 167–215.

———. *The Illogic of American Nuclear Strategy*. Ithaca, N.Y.: Cornell Univ. Press, 1984.

———. *The Meaning of the Nuclear Revolution*. Ithaca, N.Y.: Cornell Univ. Press, 1989.

———. *Perception and Misperception in International Politics*. Princeton, N.J.: Princeton Univ. Press, 1976.

Jervis, Robert, Richard Ned Lebow, and Janice Gross Stein. *Psychology and Deterrence*. Baltimore, Md.: Johns Hopkins Univ. Press, 1985.

Johnson, Robert H. "Exaggerating America's Stakes in Third World Conflicts." *International Security* 10 (Winter 1985–86): 32–68.

Johnston, Eric. *America Unlimited*. New York: Doubleday, Doran, 1944.

Jones, Howard. *"A New Kind of War": America's Global Strategy and the Truman Doctrine in Greece*. New York: Oxford Univ. Press, 1989.

Jones, Joseph M. *The Fifteen Weeks*. New York: Viking, 1955.

Kahin, George McT. *Intervention: How America Became Involved in Vietnam*. Garden City, N.Y.: Anchor, 1987.

Kaplan, Fred. *The Wizards of Armageddon*. New York: Simon & Schuster, 1983.

Kaplan, Lawrence S. *A Community of Interests: NATO and the Military Assistance Program, 1948–1951*. Washington, D.C.: Office of the Secretary of Defense, 1980.

———. *The United States and NATO: The Formative Years*. Lexington: Univ. of Kentucky Press, 1984.

Kaplan, Stephen S. *Diplomacy of Power: Soviet Armed Forces as a Political Instrument*. Washington, D.C.: Brookings, 1981.

Kapstein, Ethan B. *The Insecure Alliance: Energy Crisis and Western Politics Since 1944*. New York: Oxford Univ. Press, 1990.

Kardelj, Edvard. *Reminiscences: The Struggle for Recognition and Independence. The New Yugoslavia, 1944–1957*. London: Blond & Briggs, 1982.

Katzenstein, Peter J., ed. *Between Power and Plenty: Foreign Economic Policies of Advanced Industrial States*. Madison: Univ. of Wisconsin Press, 1978.

Kaufman, Burton I. *The Korean War: Challenges in Crisis, Credibility, and Command*. New York: Knopf, 1986.

Kennan, George F. *Memoirs, 1925–1950*. New York: Bantam, 1967.

———. *Memoirs, 1950–1963*. Boston, Mass.: Little, Brown, 1972.

———. "The Sources of Soviet Conduct." *Foreign Affairs* 25 (July 1947): 566–82.

Kennedy, Paul M. *The Rise and Fall of the Great Powers*. New York: Random House, 1987.

Keohane, Robert O. *After Hegemony: Cooperation and Discord in the World Political Economy*. Princeton, N.J.: Princeton Univ. Press, 1984.

Kepley, David R. *The Collapse of the Middle Way: Senate Republicans and the Bipartisan Foreign Policy, 1948–52*. New York: Greenwood, 1988.

Kerkvliet, Benedict J. *The Huk Rebellion: A Study of Peasant Revolt in the Philippines*. Berkeley: Univ. of California Press, 1977.

Kertesz, Stephen D. *Between Russia and the West: Hungary and the Illusion of Peacemaking, 1945–1947*. Notre Dame, Ind.: Univ. of Notre Dame Press, 1984.

Kessler, Richard J. *Rebellion and Repression in the Philippines*. New Haven, Conn.: Yale Univ. Press, 1989.

Khrushchev, Nikita. *Khrushchev Remembers*. Ed. Strobe Talbott. Boston, Mass.: Little, Brown, 1970.

———. *Khrushchev Remembers: The Glasnost Tapes*. Trans. and ed. Jerrold Schecter with Vyacheslav Luchkov. Boston, Mass.: Little, Brown, 1990.

Kimball, Warren F. "Naked Reverse Right: Roosevelt, Churchill and Eastern Europe from Tolstoy to Yalta—and a Little Beyond." *Diplomatic History* 9 (Winter 1985): 1–24.

Kindleberger, Charles P. *The German Economy, 1945–1947: Charles P. Kindleberger's Letters from the Field*. Westport, Conn.: Meckler, 1989.

———. *Marshall Plan Days*. Boston, Mass.: Allen & Unwin, 1987.

———. *The World in Depression, 1929–1939*. Berkeley: Univ. of California Press, 1973.

Knaack, Marcelle Size. *Post–World War II Bombers, 1945–1973*. Washington, D.C.: Office of Air Force History, 1988.

———. *Post–World War II Fighters, 1945–1973*. Washington, D.C.: Office of Air Force History, 1986.

Knight, Jonathan. "Russia's Search for Peace: The London Council of Foreign Ministers, 1945." *Journal of Contemporary History* 13 (Jan 1978): 137–63.

Knorr, Klaus. *Power and Wealth: The Political Economy of International Power*. New York: Basic, 1973.

Kohn, Richard H., and Joseph P. Harahan, eds. "U.S. Strategic Air Power, 1948–1962." *International Security* 12 (Spring 1988): 78–95.

Kolko, Gabriel. *Politics of War: The World and United States Foreign Policy 1943–1945*. New York: Random House, 1968.

——. *The Roots of American Foreign Policy*. Boston, Mass.: Beacon, 1969.

Kolko, Gabriel, and Joyce Kolko. *The Limits of Power: The World and United States Foreign Policy, 1945–1954*. New York: Harper & Row, 1972.

Kramish, Arnold. *Atomic Energy in the Soviet Union*. Stanford, Calif.: Stanford Univ. Press, 1959.

Krasner, Stephen D. *Defending the National Interest: Raw Materials Investments and U.S. Foreign Policy*. Princeton, N.J.: Princeton Univ. Press, 1978.

——. "State Power and the Structure of International Trade." *World Politics* 28 (Apr 1976): 317–47.

Krisch, Henry. *German Politics Under Soviet Occupation*. New York: Columbia Univ. Press, 1974.

Krock, Arthur. *Memoirs: Sixty Years on the Firing Line*. New York: Funk & Wagnalls, 1968.

Kugler, Jacek. "Terror Without Deterrence: Reassessing the Role of Nuclear Weapons." *Journal of Conflict Resolution* 28 (Sep 1984): 470–506.

Kuisel, Richard F. *Capitalism and the State in Modern France: Renovation and Economic Management in the Twentieth Century*. Cambridge, Eng.: Cambridge Univ. Press, 1981.

Kuklick, Bruce. *American Policy and the Division of Germany: The Clash with Russia over Reparations*. Ithaca, N.Y.: Cornell Univ. Press, 1972.

Kuniholm, Bruce R. *The Origins of the Cold War in the Near East: Great Power Conflict and Diplomacy in Iran, Turkey, and Greece*. Princeton, N.J.: Princeton Univ. Press, 1980.

Kusnitz, Leonard A. *Public Opinion and Foreign Policy: America's China Policy, 1949–1979*. Westport, Conn.: Greenwood, 1984.

LaFeber, Walter. "NATO and the Korean War: A Context." *Diplomatic History* 13 (Fall 1989): 461–78.

——. "Roosevelt, Churchill, and Indochina, 1942–45." *American Historical Review* 80 (Dec 1975): 1277–95.

Lairson, Thomas D. "Hegemony, Credibility, and the Risk of War: American Strategy, 1947–1950." Unpublished paper.

Langer, William L., and S. Everett Gleason. *The Challenge to Isolation, 1937–1940*. New York: Harper & Row, 1954.

——. *The Undeclared War, 1940–1941*. New York: Harper & Row, 1953.

Lapping, Brian. *End of Empire*. New York: St. Martin's, 1985.

Larson, Deborah Welch. *Origins of Containment: A Psychological Explanation*. Princeton, N.J.: Princeton Univ. Press, 1985.

Lash, Joseph P. *Roosevelt and Churchill, 1939–1941: The Partnership that Saved the West*. New York: Norton, 1976.

Latham, Earl. *The Communist Controversy in Washington: From the New Deal to McCarthy*. Cambridge, Mass.: Harvard Univ. Press, 1966.

Lawson, Fred H. "The Iranian Crisis of 1945–1946 and the Spiral Model of International Conflict." *International Journal of Middle East Studies* 21 (Aug 1989): 307–26.

Leahy, William. *I Was There*. New York: Whittlesey House, 1950.

Leary, William M. *Perilous Missions: Civil Air Transport and CIA Covert Operations in Asia*. Tuscaloosa: Univ. of Alabama Press, 1984.

Leary, William M., and William Stueck. "The Chennault Plan to Save China: U.S. Containment in Asia and the Origins of the CIA's Aerial Empire, 1949–1950." *Diplomatic History* 8 (Fall 1984): 349–64.

Lebow, Richard Ned. *Between Peace and War: The Nature of International Crisis*. Baltimore, Md.: Johns Hopkins Univ. Press, 1981.

——. "Windows of Opportunity: Do States Jump Through Them?" *International Security* 9 (Summer 1984): 147–86.

Lee, Asher, ed. *The Soviet Air and Rocket Forces*. New York: Praeger, 1959.

Leffler, Melvyn P. "Adherence to Agreements: Yalta and the Experiences of the Early Cold War." *International Security* 11 (Summer 1986): 88–123.

——— . *The Elusive Quest: America's Pursuit of European Stability and French Security, 1919–1933.* Chapel Hill: Univ. of North Carolina Press, 1979.

——— . "Strategy, Diplomacy, and the Cold War: The United States, Turkey, and NATO, 1945–1952." *Journal of American History* 71 (March 1985): 807–25.

——— . "The United States and the Strategic Dimensions of the Marshall Plan." *Diplomatic History* 12 (Summer 1988): 277–306.

Levering, Ralph. *American Opinion and the Russian Alliance, 1939–1945.* Chapel Hill: Univ. of North Carolina Press, 1976.

Levine, Steven I. *Anvil of Victory: The Communist Revolution in Manchuria, 1945–1948.* New York: Columbia Univ. Press, 1987.

——— . "A New Look at American Mediation in the Chinese Civil War: The Marshall Mission and Manchuria." *Diplomatic History* 3 (Fall 1979): 349–77.

Lewis, Julian. *Changing Direction: British Military Planning for Postwar Strategic Defense, 1942–1947.* London: Sherwood, 1988.

Liang Chin-tung. "The Sino-Soviet Treaty of Friendship and the Alliance of 1945." In *Nationalist China During the Sino-Japanese War, 1937–1945.* Ed. Paul K. T. Sih. Hicksville, N.Y.: Exposition Press, 1977.

Lifka, Thomas F. *The Concept of "Totalitarianism" and American Foreign Policy 1933–1949.* New York: Garland, 1988.

Lilienthal, David E. *The Journals of David E. Lilienthal: The Atomic Energy Years, 1945–1950.* Vol. 2. New York: Harper & Row, 1964.

Linz, Susan, ed. *The Impact of World War II on the Soviet Union.* Totowa, N.J.: Barnes & Noble, 1985.

Lippmann, Walter. *The Cold War: A Study in U.S. Foreign Policy.* New York: Harper, 1947.

——— . *United States Foreign Policy: Shield of the Republic.* Boston, Mass.: Little, Brown, 1943.

Little, Douglas. "Antibolshevism and American Foreign Policy, 1919–1939: The Diplomacy of Self-Delusion." *American Quarterly* 35 (Fall 1983): 376–90.

——— . "The Cold War and Covert Action: The United States and Syria, 1945–1958." *Middle East Journal* 44 (Winter 1990): 51–75.

Lo, Clarence Y. H. "Civilian Policymakers and Military Objectives: A Case Study of the U.S. Offensive to Win the Korean War." *Journal of Political and Military Sociology* 7 (Fall 1979): 229–42.

——— . "Military Spending as Crisis Management: The U.S. Response to the Berlin Blockade and the Korean War." *Berkeley Journal of Sociology* 20 (Summer 1976): 147–81.

Louis, Wm. Roger. *The British Empire in the Middle East, 1945–1951: Arab Nationalism, the United States, and Postwar Imperialism.* New York: Oxford Univ. Press, 1984.

——— . *Imperialism at Bay.* New York: Oxford Univ. Press, 1978.

Lowe, Peter. *Origins of the Korean War.* London: Longman, 1986.

Lukas, Richard C. *Bitter Legacy: Polish-American Relations in the Wake of World War II.* Lexington: Univ. of Kentucky Press, 1982.

——— . *The Strange Allies: The United States and Poland, 1941–45.* Knoxville: Univ. of Tennessee Press, 1978.

Lundestad, Geir. *The American Non-Policy Towards Eastern Europe, 1943–1947.* Tromsø, Norway: Universitetsforlaget, 1978.

——— . "Empire by Invitation? The United States and Western Europe, 1945–1952." *Journal of Peace Research* 23 (Sep 1986): 263–77.

Luza, Radomir V. "February 1948 and the Czechoslovak Road to Socialism." *East Central Europe* 4 (1977): 44–55.

Lynch, Frances M. B. "Resolving the Paradox of the Monnet Plan: National and International Planning in French Reconstruction." *Economic History Review* 37 (May 1984): 229–43.

Lytle, Mark Hamilton. *The Origins of the Iranian-American Alliance, 1941–1953*. New York: Holmes & Meier, 1987.

McCagg, William O. *Stalin Embattled 1943–1948*. Detroit, Mich.: Wayne State Univ. Press, 1978.

McCauley, Martin. *The German Democratic Republic Since 1945*. London: Macmillan, 1983.

——. *The Origins of the Cold War*. London: Longman, 1983.

MccGwire, Michael. "The Genesis of Soviet Threat Perceptions." Brookings Institution Paper, Washington, D.C., 1987.

McCormick, Thomas J. *America's Half-Century: United States Foreign Policy in the Cold War*. Baltimore, Md.: Johns Hopkins Univ. Press, 1989.

McCoy, Donald R. "Harry S. Truman: Personality, Politics, and Presidency." *Presidential Studies Quarterly* 12 (Spring 1982): 216–25.

——. *The Presidency of Harry S. Truman*. Lawrence: Univ. Press of Kansas, 1984.

McFarland, Keith. "The 1949 Revolt of the Admirals." *Parameters: Journal of the U.S. Army War College* 11 (Summer 1981): 53–63.

McFarland, Stephen L. "A Peripheral View of the Origins of the Cold War: The Crises in Iran, 1941–47." *Diplomatic History* 4 (Fall 1980): 333–51.

MacFarlane, S. Neil. "Successes and Failures in Soviet Policy Toward Marxist Revolutions in the Third World, 1917–1985." In *The USSR and Marxist Revolutions in the Third World*. Ed. Mark N. Katz. New York: Cambridge Univ. Press, 1991.

McGhee, George. *Envoy to the Middle World: Adventures in Diplomacy*. New York: Harper & Row, 1983.

MacKinder, Halford. "The Round World and the Winning of the Peace." *Foreign Affairs* 21 (July 1943): 598–605.

McLane, Charles B. *Soviet Strategies in Southeast Asia: An Exploration of Eastern Policy Under Lenin and Stalin*. Princeton, N.J.: Princeton Univ. Press, 1966.

McLellan, David S. *Dean Acheson: The State Department Years*. New York: Dodd, Mead, 1976.

McMahon, Robert J. *Colonialism and Cold War: The United States and the Struggle for Indonesian Independence, 1945–1949*. Ithaca, N.Y.: Cornell Univ. Press, 1981.

McNeal, Robert H. *Stalin: Man and Ruler*. New York: New York Univ. Press, 1988.

MacVeagh, Lincoln. *Ambassador MacVeagh Reports: Greece, 1933–1947*. Ed. John O. Iatrides. Princeton, N.J.: Princeton Univ. Press, 1980.

McVey, Ruth T. *The Soviet View of the Indonesian Revolution*. Ithaca, N.Y.: Cornell Univ. Press, 1957.

Maddox, Robert J. *From War to Cold War: The Education of Harry S. Truman*. Boulder, Colo.: Westview, 1988.

Maier, Charles S. "Analog of Empire: Constitutive Moments of United States Ascendancy After World War II." Paper presented at the Woodrow Wilson International Center. Washington, D.C., 30 May 89.

——. "The Two Postwar Eras and the Conditions for Stability in Twentieth-Century Western Europe." *American Historical Review* 86 (Apr 1981): 327–52.

Mark, Eduard. "American Policy Toward Eastern Europe and the Origins of the Cold War, 1941–46: An Alternative Interpretation." *Journal of American History* 68 (Sep 1981): 313–36.

——. "Charles E. Bohlen and the Acceptable Limits of Soviet Hegemony in Eastern Europe: A Memorandum of 18 October 1945." *Diplomatic History* 3 (Spring 1979): 201–14.

——. "October or Thermidor? Interpretations of Stalinism and the Perception of Soviet Foreign Policy in the United States, 1927–1947." *American Historical Review* 9 (Oct 1989): 937–62.

——. "Stalinism, Geopolitics, and the Intellectual Origins of the Cold War: Interpretations of Soviet Communism in the United States, 1927–1947." Unpublished manuscript.

Marshall, George C. *Marshall's Mission to China*. 2 vols. Arlington, Va.: Univ. Publications of America, 1976.

Massigli, René. *Une Comédie des Erreurs, 1943–1956: Souvenirs et Réflexions sur une Etape de la Construction Européenne*. Paris: Plon, 1978.

Mastny, Vojtech. "Europe in U.S.-U.S.S.R. Relations: A Topical Legacy." *Problems of Communism* 37 (Jan–Feb 1988): 16–29.
——. *Russia's Road to the Cold War*. New York: Columbia Univ. Press, 1979.
——. "Stalin and the Militarization of the Cold War." *International Security* 9 (Winter 1984–85): 109–29.
Matloff, Maurice, and Edwin M. Snell. *Strategic Planning for Coalition Warfare, 1941–1942*. Washington, D.C.: Dept. of the Army, 1953.
Matray, James I. *The Reluctant Crusade: American Foreign Policy in Korea, 1941–1950*. Honolulu: Univ. of Hawaii Press, 1985.
Max, Stanley M. *The United States, Great Britain, and the Sovietization of Hungary, 1945–1948*. New York: Columbia Univ. Press, 1985.
May, Ernest R. "The American Commitment to Germany, 1949–1955." *Diplomatic History* 13 (Fall 1989): 431–60.
——. *"Lessons" of the Past: The Use and Misuse of History in American Foreign Policy*. New York: Oxford Univ. Press, 1973.
——. *The Truman Administration and China, 1945–1949*. Philadelphia, Pa.: Lippincott, 1975.
May, Gary. *China Scapegoat: The Diplomatic Ordeal of John Carter Vincent*. Washington, D.C.: New Republic, 1979.
Mayer, Herbert Carleton. *German Recovery and the Marshall Plan*. New York: Edition Atlantic Forum, 1969.
Mayers, David Allan. *Cracking the Monolith: United States Policy Against the Sino-Soviet Alliance, 1948–1955*. Baton Rouge: Louisiana State Univ. Press, 1986.
——. *George Kennan and the Dilemmas of U.S. Foreign Policy*. New York: Oxford Univ. Press, 1989.
Mecham, John Lloyd. *The United States and Inter-American Security, 1899–1960*. Austin: Univ. of Texas Press, 1961.
Mee, Charles L., Jr. *The Marshall Plan*. New York: Simon & Schuster, 1984.
Menon, Rajan. *Soviet Power and the Third World*. New Haven, Conn.: Yale Univ. Press, 1986.
Menon, Rajan, and Daniel N. Nelson. *Limits to Soviet Power*. Lexington, Mass.: Lexington, 1989.
Merrill, John. *Korea: The Peninsular Origins of the War*. Newark: Univ. of Delaware Press, 1989.
Merritt, Anna J., and Richard L. Merritt, eds. *Public Opinion in Occupied Germany: The OMGUS Surveys, 1945–1949*. Urbana: Univ. of Illinois Press, 1970.
——. *Public Opinion in Semisovereign Germany: The HICOG Surveys, 1949–1955*. Urbana: Univ. of Illinois Press, 1980.
Messer, Robert L. "America's 'Sacred Trust': Truman and the Bomb, 1945–1949." Paper presented at the annual convention of the American Historical Association. Washington, D.C., 1987.
——. *The End of an Alliance: James F. Byrnes, Roosevelt, Truman, and the Origins of the Cold War*. Chapel Hill: Univ. of North Carolina Press, 1982.
——. "Paths Not Taken: The U.S. Department of State and Alternatives to Containment." *Diplomatic History* 1 (Fall 1977): 297–319.
Miller, Aaron. *Search for Security: Saudi Arabian Oil and American Foreign Policy, 1939–1949*. Chapel Hill: Univ. of North Carolina Press, 1980.
Miller, James E. *The United States and Italy: The Politics and Diplomacy of Stabilization*. Chapel Hill: Univ. of North Carolina Press, 1986.
Miller, Merle. *Plain Speaking: An Oral Biography of Harry S. Truman*. New York: Putnam's Sons, 1973.
Milward, Alan S. *The German Economy at War*. London: Univ. of London, Athlone Press, 1965.
——. *The Reconstruction of Western Europe, 1945–1951*. Berkeley: Univ. of California Press, 1984.
——. *War, Economy and Society, 1939–1945*. Berkeley: Univ. of California Press, 1977.
——. "Was the Marshall Plan Necessary?" *Diplomatic History* 13 (Spring 1989): 231–53.

Miscamble, Wilson D. "The Evolution of an Internationalist: Harry S. Truman and American Foreign Policy." *Australian Journal of Politics and History* 23 (Aug 1977): 268–83.

Miyasato, Siegen. "John Foster Dulles and the Peace Settlement with Japan." Paper presented at the John Foster Dulles Centennial Conference. Princeton, N.J., 1988.

Molotov, V. M. *Problems of Foreign Policy: Speeches and Statements, April 1945–November 1948.* Moscow: Foreign Language Publishing House, 1949.

Monnet, Jean. *Memoirs.* Garden City, N.Y.: Doubleday, 1978.

Montgomery, Bernard Law. *The Memoirs of Field-Marshal the Viscount Montgomery of Alamein.* Cleveland, Ohio: World, 1958.

Moody, Walter S. "United States Air Forces in Europe and the Beginning of the Cold War." *Aerospace Historian* 23 (June 1976): 76–84.

Morgan, Kenneth O. *Labour in Power, 1945–51.* New York: Oxford Univ. Press, 1984.

Morison, Elting E. *Turmoil and Tradition: A Study of the Life and Times of Henry L. Stimson.* New York: Atheneum, 1964.

Morton, Louis. "The Japanese Decision for War." U.S. Naval Institute *Proceedings* 80 (Dec 1954): 1325–35.

Mueller, John. "The Essential Irrelevance of Nuclear Weapons." *International Security* 13 (Fall 1988): 55–79.

Murphy, Paul J. *The Soviet Air Forces.* Jefferson, N.C.: McFarland, 1984.

Murphy, Robert. *Diplomat Among Warriors.* New York: Pyramid, 1965.

Murray, Williamson. *The Change in the European Balance of Power, 1938–1939: The Path to Ruin.* Princeton, N.J.: Princeton Univ. Press, 1984.

Nagai, Yonosuke, and Akira Iriye, eds. *The Origins of the Cold War in Asia.* New York: Columbia Univ. Press, 1977.

Nau, Henry R. *The Myth of America's Decline: Leading the World Economy into the 1990's.* New York: Oxford Univ. Press, 1990.

Nelson, Anna K. "President Truman and the Evolution of the National Security Council." *Journal of American History* 72 (Sep 1985): 360–78.

Nettl, J. P. *The Eastern Zone and Soviet Policy in Germany, 1945–1950.* New York: Octagon, 1977.

Newman, Robert P. "The Self-Inflicted Wound: The China White Paper of 1949." *Prologue* 14 (Fall 1982): 141–56.

Newton, Scott. "The 1949 Sterling Crisis and British Policy Toward European Integration." *Review of International Studies* 11 (July 1985): 169–92.

Nitze, Paul H. *From Hiroshima to Glasnost: At the Center of Decision—A Memoir.* New York: Grove Weidenfeld, 1989.

——. "Military Power: A Strategic View." *Fletcher Forum* 5 (Winter 1981): 152–62.

——. "The Relationship of Strategic and Theater Nuclear Forces." *International Security* 2 (Fall 1977): 122–31.

Noelle, Elisabeth, and Erich Peter Neumann, eds. *The Germans: Public Opinion Polls, 1947–1966.* Allensbach & Bonn: Verlag Für Demoskopie, 1967.

Notter, Harley A. *Postwar Foreign Policy Preparation, 1939–1945.* Washington, D.C.: GPO, 1950.

"NSC's First Covert Action." Wilson Center *Reports.* June 1988.

Nye, Joseph S., Jr. *Bound to Lead: The Changing Nature of American Power.* New York: Basic, 1990.

Offner, Arnold. *The Origins of the Second World War: American Foreign Policy and World Politics, 1914–1941.* New York: Praeger, 1975.

——. "The Truman Myth Revealed: From Parochial Nationalist to Cold Warrior." Paper presented at the annual meeting of the Organization of American Historians. Reno, Nev., 1988.

Oneal, John R. *Foreign Policy Making in Times of Crisis.* Columbus: Ohio State Univ. Press, 1982.

Orchard, John E. "ECA and the Dependent Territories." *Geographical Review* 41 (Jan 1951): 66–87.

Organization of European Economic Cooperation. *European Recovery Programme: Second Report of the OEEC*. Paris: OEEC, 1950.

————. *Interim Report on the European Recovery Programme*. Vols. 1–2. Paris: OEEC, 1948.

Oshinsky, David M. *A Conspiracy So Immense: The World of Joe McCarthy*. New York: Free Press, 1983.

Ovendale, Ritchie. *The English-Speaking Alliance: Britain, the United States, the Dominions, and the Cold War, 1945–1951*. Boston, Mass.: Allen & Unwin, 1985.

————, ed. *The Foreign Policy of the British Labour Governments, 1945–1951*. Leicester, Eng.: Leicester Univ. Press, 1984.

Pach, Chester J., Jr. "The Containment of U.S. Military Aid to Latin America, 1944–1949." *Diplomatic History* 6 (Summer 1982): 225–43.

————. *Arming the Free World: The Origins of the United States Military Assistance Program, 1945–1950*. Chapel Hill: Univ. of North Carolina Press, 1991.

Painter, David S. *Oil and the American Century: The Political Economy of U.S. Foreign Oil Policy, 1941–1954*. Baltimore, Md.: Johns Hopkins Univ. Press, 1986.

————. "Oil and U.S. Policy Toward Iran, 1951–1954: The Political Economy of Intervention." Paper presented at the annual meeting of the Society for Historians of American Foreign Relations. Annapolis, Md., 1987.

Papp, N. G. "The Democratic Struggle for Peace in Hungary, 1945–1946." *East Central Europe* 6 (1979): 1–19.

Pappé, Ilan. *Britain and the Arab-Israeli Conflict, 1948–51*. New York: St. Martin's, 1988.

Paterson, Thomas G. "The Abortive American Loan to Russia, and the Origins of the Cold War." *Journal of American History* 56 (June 1969): 70–92.

————. "If Europe, Why Not China? The Containment Doctrine, 1947–1949." *Prologue* 13 (Spring 1981): 19–38.

————. *Meeting the Communist Threat: America's Cold War History*. New York: Oxford Univ. Press, 1988.

————. *On Every Front: The Making of the Cold War*. New York: Norton, 1979.

————. *Soviet-American Confrontation: Postwar Reconstruction and the Origins of the Cold War*. Baltimore, Md.: Johns Hopkins Univ. Press, 1973.

Patterson, James T. *Mr. Republican: A Biography of Robert A. Taft*. Boston, Mass.: Houghton Mifflin, 1972.

Pells, Richard H. *The Liberal Mind in a Conservative Age: American Intellectuals in the 1940's and 1950's*. New York: Harper & Row, 1985.

Perrett, Geoffrey. *Days of Sadness, Years of Triumph: The American People, 1939–1945*. Baltimore, Md.: Penguin, 1973.

Petersen, Nikolaj. "Who Pulled Whom and How Much? Britain, the United States and the Making of the North Atlantic Treaty." *Millenium* 11 (Summer 1982): 93–113.

Phillips, Cabell. *The Truman Presidency: The History of a Triumphant Succession*. New York: Macmillan, 1966.

Pike, Douglas. *Vietnam and the Soviet Union*. Boulder, Colo.: Westview, 1987.

Pogue, Forrest. *George C. Marshall: Statesman, 1945–1949*. New York: Viking, 1987.

Polenberg, Richard. *War and Society: The United States, 1941–1945*. Philadelphia, Pa.: Lippincott, 1972.

Polk, Judd, and Gardner Patterson. "The Emerging Pattern of Bilateralism." *Quarterly Journal of Economics* 62 (Nov 1947): 118–42.

Pollack, Jonathan D. "Into the Vortex: China, the Sino-Soviet Alliance, and the Korean War." Prepublication draft of Rand Paper, 1990.

Pollard, Robert A. *Economic Security and the Origins of the Cold War, 1945–1950*. New York: Columbia Univ. Press, 1985.

Polonsky, Antony. "Stalin and the Poles, 1941–7." *European History Quarterly* 17 (Oct 1987): 453–92.

Polonsky, Antony, and Boleslaw Drukier, eds. *The Beginnings of Communist Rule in Poland.* London: Routledge & Kegan Paul, 1980.

Poole, Walter S. *The History of the Joint Chiefs of Staff: The Joint Chiefs of Staff and National Policy.* Vol. 4, *1950–1952.* Wilmington, Del.: Glazier, 1980.

Prados, John. *Presidents' Secret Wars: CIA and Pentagon Covert Operations from World War II Through Iranscam.* New York: William Morrow, 1986.

Prange, Gordon W. *At Dawn We Slept: The Untold Story of Pearl Harbor.* New York: Penguin, 1981.

Price, Hoyt, and Carl E. Schorske. *The Problem of Germany.* New York: Council on Foreign Relations, 1947.

Prittie, Terence. *Konrad Adenauer, 1876–1967.* London: Tom Stacey, 1972.

Propas, Frederic L. "Creating a Hard Line Toward Russia: The Training of State Department Experts, 1927–1937." *Diplomatic History* 8 (Summer 1984): 209–26.

Prowe, Diethelm. "Economic Democracy in Post–World War II Germany: Corporatist Crisis Response, 1945–1948." *Journal of Modern History* 57 (Sep 1985): 451–82.

Pruessen, Ronald W. *John Foster Dulles: The Road to Power.* New York: Free Press, 1982.

Purifoy, Lewis McCarroll. *Harry Truman's China Policy: McCarthyism and the Diplomacy of Hysteria, 1947–51.* New York: Franklin Watts, 1976.

Ra'anan, Gavriel D. *International Policy Formation in the U.S.S.R.: Factional "Debates" During the Zhdanovschina.* Hamden, Conn.: Archon, 1983.

Rabe, Stephen G. "Inter-American Military Cooperation, 1944–1951." *World Affairs* 137 (Fall 1974): 132–49.

Rabel, Roberto G. *Between East and West: Trieste, the United States and the Cold War, 1941–1954.* Durham, N.C.: Duke Univ. Press, 1988.

Rahman, Habibur. "British Post–Second World War Military Planning for the Middle East." *Journal of Strategic Studies* 5 (Dec 1982): 511–29.

Ramazani, Rouhollah K. *Iran's Foreign Policy, 1941–1973: A Study of Foreign Policy in Modernizing Nations.* Charlottesville: Univ. of Virginia Press, 1975.

Ranelagh, John. *The Agency: The Rise and Decline of the CIA.* New York: Simon & Schuster, 1986.

Rearden, Stephen L. *History of the Office of Secretary of Defense: The Formative Years, 1947–1950.* Washington, D.C.: Office of the Secretary of Defense, 1984.

Reardon-Anderson, James. *Yenan and the Great Powers: The Origins of Chinese Communist Foreign Policy, 1944–1946.* New York: Columbia Univ. Press, 1980.

Reeves, Thomas C. *The Life and Times of Joe McCarthy: A Biography.* New York: Stein & Day, 1982.

Reichard, Gary. *Politics as Usual: The Age of Truman and Eisenhower.* Arlington Heights, Ill.: Harland Davidson, 1988.

Reid, Escott. *Time of Fear and Hope: The Making of the North Atlantic Treaty, 1947–1949.* Toronto, Ont.: McClelland & Stewart, 1977.

Rennell, Francis James. *British Military Administration of Occupied Territories in Africa During the Years 1941–1947.* Westport, Conn.: Greenwood, 1970.

Resis, Albert. *Stalin, the Politburo, and the Onset of the Cold War, 1945–1946.* Pittsburgh, Pa.: Univ. of Pittsburgh Center for Russian and East European Studies, 1988.

Reynolds, David. *The Creation of the Anglo-American Alliance, 1937–1941.* Chapel Hill: Univ. of North Carolina Press, 1981.

———. "The Origins of the Cold War: The European Dimension, 1944–1951." *Historical Journal* 28 (June 1985): 497–515.

Reynolds, Jaime. "'Lublin' versus 'London': The Party and the Underground Movement in Poland, 1944–1945." *Journal of Contemporary History* 16 (Oct 1981): 617–48.

Riasanovsky, Nicholas V. *A History of Russia.* New York: Oxford Univ. Press, 1963.

Rice-Maximim, Edward. "The United States and the French Left, 1945–1949: The View from the State Department." *Journal of Contemporary History* 19 (Oct 1984): 729–47.

——. "The United States, France, and Vietnam, 1945–1950: The View from the State Department." *Contemporary French Civilization* 7 (Fall 1982): 20–40.

Rioux, Jean-Pierre. *The Fourth Republic, 1944–1958*. Trans. Godfrey Rogers. Cambridge, Eng.: Cambridge Univ. Press, 1987.

Riste, Olav, ed. *Western Security: The Formative Years, 1947–1953*. New York: Columbia Univ. Press, 1985.

Rogin, Michael Paul. *The Intellectuals and McCarthy: The Radical Specter*. Cambridge, Mass.: M.I.T. Press, 1967.

Rogow, Arnold A. *James Forrestal: A Study in Personality, Politics and Policy*. New York: Macmillan, 1963.

Roosevelt, Franklin D. *Complete Presidential Press Conferences of Franklin D. Roosevelt*. Vol. 15, *January 1940–June 1940*. New York: Da Capo, 1972.

——. *The Public Papers and Addresses of Franklin D. Roosevelt, 1940*. Ed. Samuel I. Rosenman. New York: Macmillan, 1941.

——. *Roosevelt and Churchill: Their Secret Wartime Correspondence*. Ed. Francis L. Loewenheim, Harold D. Langley, and Manfred Jonas. New York: Dutton, 1975.

Rose, Lisle. *Dubious Victory: The United States and the End of World War II*. Kent, Ohio: Kent State Univ. Press, 1973.

Rosenberg, David Alan. "American Atomic Strategy and the Hydrogen Bomb Decision." *Journal of American History* 66 (June 1979): 62–87.

——. "Origins of Overkill: Nuclear Weapons and American Strategy, 1945–1960." *International Security* 7 (Spring 1983): 3–71.

——. "Toward Armageddon: The Foundations of United States Nuclear Strategy, 1945–1961." Ph.D. diss., Univ. of Chicago, 1983.

——. "U.S. Nuclear Stockpile, 1945–1950." *Bulletin of the Atomic Scientists* 38 (May 1982): 25–30.

Rosenberg, David Alan, and Floyd D. Kennedy, Jr. "United States Aircraft Carriers in the Strategic Role: History of the Strategic Arms Competition, 1945–1972." Washington, D.C.: Lulejian, 1975.

Rosenberg, J. Philipp. "The Belief System of Harry S Truman and Its Effect on Foreign Policy Decision-Making During His Administration." *Presidential Studies Quarterly* 12 (Spring 1982): 226–38.

Rosenof, Theodore. "Freedom, Planning and Totalitarianism: The Reception of F. A. Hayek's *Road to Serfdom*." *Canadian Review of American Studies* 5 (Fall 1974): 149–65.

Ross, Steven T. *American War Plans, 1945–1950*. New York: Garland, 1988.

Rostow, Walt W. *The Division of Europe After World War II: 1946*. Austin: Univ. of Texas Press, 1981.

Rotter, Andrew J. *The Path to Vietnam: Origins of the American Commitment to Southeast Asia*. Ithaca, N.Y.: Cornell Univ. Press, 1987.

Rourke, John. *Congress and the Presidency in United States Foreign Policymaking: A Study of Interaction and Influence, 1945–1982*. Boulder, Colo.: Westview, 1983.

Ryan, Henry B. "A New Look at Churchill's 'Iron Curtain' Speech." *Historical Journal* 22 (Dec 1979): 895–920.

——. *The Vision of Anglo-America: The US-UK Alliance and the Emerging Cold War, 1943–1946*. Cambridge, Eng.: Cambridge Univ. Press, 1987.

Saiu, Liliana. "The Great Powers and Rumania, 1944–1946: A Study of the Cold War Era." Unpublished manuscript.

Sander, Alfred D. "Truman and the National Security Council, 1945–1947." *Journal of American History* 59 (Sep 1972): 347–88.

Sandford, Gregory W. *From Hitler to Ulbricht: The Communist Reconstruction of East Germany, 1945–46*. Princeton, N.J.: Princeton Univ. Press, 1983.

Sangmuah, Egya Ndayinanse. "The United States and the French Empire in North Africa: Decolonization in the Age of Containment." Ph.D. diss., Univ. of Toronto, 1989.

Sawyer, Robert K. *Military Advisors in Korea: KMAG in Peace and War*. Washington, D.C.: Dept. of the Army, 1962.

Scalapino, Robert A., and Chong-Sik Lee. *Communism in Korea, Part I: The Movement*. Berkeley: Univ. of California Press, 1972.

Schaffer, Ronald. *Wings of Judgment: American Bombing in World War II*. New York: Oxford Univ. Press, 1985.

Schaller, Michael. *The American Occupation of Japan: The Origins of the Cold War in Asia*. New York: Oxford Univ. Press, 1985.

——. *Douglas MacArthur: The Far Eastern General*. New York: Oxford Univ. Press, 1989.

——. "MacArthur's Japan: The View from Washington." *Diplomatic History* 10 (Winter 1986): 1–23.

——. *The U.S. Crusade in China, 1938–1945*. New York: Columbia Univ. Press, 1979.

Schilling, Warner R., Paul Y. Hammond, and Glenn H. Snyder. *Strategy, Politics, and Defense Budgets*. New York: Columbia Univ. Press, 1962.

Schlesinger, Arthur, Jr. "Origins of the Cold War." *Foreign Affairs* 46 (Oct 1967): 22–52.

Schnabel, James. *The History of the Joint Chiefs of Staff: The Joint Chiefs of Staff and National Policy*. Vol. 1. Wilmington, Del.: Glazier, 1979.

Schnabel, James, and Robert J. Watson. *The History of the Joint Chiefs of Staff: The Joint Chiefs of Staff and National Policy*. Vol. 3. Wilmington, Del.: Glazier, 1979.

Schoenbaum, Thomas J. *Waging Peace and War: Dean Rusk in the Truman, Kennedy, and Johnson Years*. New York: Simon & Schuster, 1988.

Schonberger, Howard B. *Aftermath of War: Americans and the Remaking of Japan, 1945–1952*. Kent, Ohio: Kent State Univ. Press, 1989.

——. "The Cold War and the American Empire in Asia." *Radical History Review* 33 (1985): 139–54.

——. "The Japan Lobby in American Diplomacy, 1947–1952." *Pacific Historical Review* 46 (Aug 1977): 327–59.

——. "Peacemaking in Asia: The United States, Great Britain, and the Japanese Decision to Recognize Nationalist China, 1951–1952." *Diplomatic History* 10 (Winter 1986): 59–73.

——. "U.S. Policy in Postwar Japan: The Retreat from Liberalism." *Science and Society* 46 (Spring 1982): 39–60.

Schuker, Stephen A. *The End of French Predominance in Europe: The Financial Crisis of 1924 and the Adoption of the Dawes Plan*. Chapel Hill: Univ. of North Carolina Press, 1976.

Schulzinger, Robert D. *The Wise Men of Foreign Affairs: The History of the Council on Foreign Relations*. New York: Columbia Univ. Press, 1984.

Schwartz, Thomas A. *America's Germany: John J. McCloy and the Federal Republic of Germany*. Cambridge, Mass.: Harvard Univ. Press, 1991.

——. "The Case of German Rearmament: Alliance Crisis in the 'Golden Age.' " *Fletcher Forum* 8 (Summer 1984): 295–309.

——. "The 'Skeleton Key': American Foreign Policy, European Unity, and German Rearmament, 1949–1954." *Central European History* 19 (Dec 1986): 369–85.

Schwarz, Jordan A. *Liberal: Adolf A. Berle and the Vision of an American Era*. New York: Free Press, 1987.

——. *The Speculator: Bernard M. Baruch in Washington, 1917–63*. Chapel Hill: Univ. of North Carolina Press, 1981.

Serfaty, Simon, and Lawrence Gray, eds. *The Italian Communist Party: Yesterday, Today and Tomorrow*. Westport, Conn.: Greenwood, 1980.

Shalom, Stephen R. *The United States and the Philippines: A Study of Neocolonialism*. Philadelphia, Pa.: Institute for the Study of Human Issues, 1981.

Shaplen, Robert. *The Lost Revolution: The United States in Vietnam, 1946–1966*. New York: Harper Colophon, 1966.

Sherry, Michael S. *Preparing for the Next War: American Plans for Postwar Defense, 1941–45*. New Haven, Conn.: Yale Univ. Press, 1977.

——. *The Rise of American Air Power: The Creation of Armageddon*. New Haven, Conn.: Yale Univ. Press, 1987.

Sherwin, Martin J. "The White House, the Red Menace, and the Yellow Peril: An Inquiry into the Relationship Between U.S. Policy Toward China During the Roosevelt-Truman Administrations and the Origins and Evolution of Containment, 1942–1950." Paper presented at the Conference on the Causes of the Cold War and Sino-American Relations. Mt. Kisco, N.Y., 1978.

——. *A World Destroyed: The Atomic Bomb and the Grand Alliance*. New York: Vintage, 1977.

Sherwood, Robert E. *Roosevelt and Hopkins: An Intimate History*. New York: Harpers, 1948.

Shlaim, Avi. *The United States and the Berlin Blockade: A Study in Crisis Decision Making*. Berkeley: Univ. of California Press, 1983.

Shulman, Marshall D. *Stalin's Foreign Policy Reappraised*. New York: Atheneum, 1965.

Sigal, Leon V. *Fighting to a Finish: The Politics of War Termination in the United States and Japan, 1945*. Ithaca, N.Y.: Cornell Univ. Press, 1988.

Simmons, Robert R. *The Strained Alliance: Peking, P'yongyang, Moscow and the Politics of the Korean Civil War*. New York: Free Press, 1975.

Sloan, G. R. *Geopolitics in United States Strategic Policy, 1890–1987*. New York: St. Martin's, 1988.

Slusser, Robert. *Soviet Economic Policy in Postwar Germany*. New York: Research Program on the USSR, 1953.

Smith, E. Timothy. "From Disarmament to Rearmament: The United States and the Revision of the Italian Peace Treaty of 1947." *Diplomatic History* 13 (Summer 1989): 359–82.

Smith, Jean Edward. *Lucius D. Clay: An American Life*. New York: Henry Holt, 1990.

Smith, R. Elberton. *The Army and Economic Mobilization*. Washington, D.C.: GPO, 1959.

Smith, Richard Norton. *Thomas E. Dewey and His Times*. New York: Simon & Schuster, 1982.

Smith, Walter Bedell. *My Three Years in Moscow*. Philadelphia, Pa.: Lippincott, 1950.

Snell, John L., ed. *The Meaning of Yalta: Big Three Diplomacy and the New Balance of Power*. Baton Rouge: Louisiana State Univ. Press, 1956.

Snetsinger, John. *Truman, the Jewish Vote, and the Creation of Israel*. Stanford, Calif.: Hoover Institution Press, 1974.

Soviet Union. Ministry of Foreign Affairs. *Stalin's Correspondence with Roosevelt and Truman, 1941–1945*. New York: Capricorn, 1965.

Spector, Ronald H. *Advice and Support: The Early Years of the United States Army in Vietnam, 1941–1960*. New York: Free Press, 1985.

Spender, Percy Claude. *Exercises in Diplomacy: The ANZUS Treaty and the Colombo Plan*. New York: New York Univ. Press, 1970.

Spriano, Paolo. *Stalin and the European Communists*. London: Verso, 1985.

Spykman, Nicholas John. *America's Strategy in World Politics: The United States and the Balance of Power*. New York: Harcourt, Brace, 1942.

——. *The Geography of Peace*. New York: Harcourt, Brace, 1944.

Stanley, Peter W. *Reappraising an Empire: New Perspectives on Philippine-American History*. Cambridge, Mass.: Harvard Univ. Press, 1984.

Stavrakis, Peter J. *Moscow and Greek Communism, 1944–1949*. Ithaca, N.Y.: Cornell Univ. Press, 1989.

Steel, Ronald. *Walter Lippmann and the American Century*. Boston, Mass.: Little, Brown, 1980.

Stein, Harold, ed. *American Civil-Military Decisions*. Birmingham: Univ. of Alabama Press, 1963.

Steininger, Rolf. *The German Question: The Stalin Note of 1952 and the Problem of Reunification*. Trans. Jane T. Hedges. Ed. Marc Cioc. New York: Columbia Univ. Press, 1990.

Stephanson, Anders. *Kennan and the Art of Foreign Policy*. Cambridge, Mass.: Harvard Univ. Press, 1989.

Stettinius, Edward R., Jr. *The Diaries of Edward R. Stettinius, Jr., 1943–1946*. Ed. Thomas M. Campbell and George Herring. New York: New Viewpoints, 1975.

Stoler, Mark. "From Continentalism to Globalism: General Stanley D. Embrick, the Joint Strategic Survey Committee, and the Military View of American National Policy During the Second World War." *Diplomatic History* 6 (Summer 1982): 303–21.

——. *George C. Marshall: Soldier-Statesman of the American Century.* Boston: Twayne, 1989.

Strausz-Hupe, Robert. "Geopolitics." *Fortune* 24 (Nov 1941): 110–19.

Stueck, William W., Jr. *The Korean War: An International History.* Forthcoming.

——. *The Road to Confrontation: American Policy Toward China and Korea, 1947–1950.* Chapel Hill: Univ. of North Carolina Press, 1981.

——. "The Soviet Union and the Origins of the Korean War." *World Politics* 28 (July 1976): 622–35.

——. *The Wedemeyer Mission.* Athens: Univ. of Georgia Press, 1984.

Taruc, Luis. *He Who Rides the Tiger.* New York: Praeger, 1967.

Taubman, William. *Stalin's American Policy: From Entente to Detente to Cold War.* New York: Norton, 1982.

Taylor, Jay. *China and Southeast Asia: Peking's Relations with Revolutionary Movements.* New York: Praeger, 1974.

Theoharis, Athan. *Seeds of Repression: Harry S. Truman and the Origins of McCarthyism.* Chicago, Ill.: Quadrangle, 1971.

Thomas, Hugh. *Armed Truce: The Beginnings of the Cold War, 1945–6.* New York: Atheneum, 1987.

Thompson, Kenneth W., ed. *The Truman Presidency: Intimate Perspectives.* Frederick, Md.: Univ. Press of America, 1984.

Thorne, Christopher. *Allies of a Kind: The United States, Britain, and the War Against Japan.* New York: Oxford Univ. Press, 1978.

——. "Indochina and Anglo-American Relations, 1942–1945." *Pacific Historical Review* 45 (Feb 1976): 73–96.

Trachtenberg, Marc. "A 'Wasting Asset': American Strategy and the Shifting Nuclear Balance, 1949–1954." *International Security* 13 (Winter 1988–89): 5–49.

Treverton, Gregory F. *Covert Action: The Limits of Intervention in the Postwar World.* New York: Basic, 1987.

Trommler, Frank, and Joseph McVeigh. *America and the Germans: An Assessment of a Three Hundred Year History.* Vol. 2, *The Relationship in the Twentieth Century.* Philadelphia: Univ. of Pennsylvania Press, 1985.

Truman, Harry S. *Dear Bess: Letters from Harry to Bess Truman.* Ed. Robert H. Ferrell. New York: Norton, 1983.

——. *Memoirs: 1945, Year of Decisions.* New York: Signet, 1955.

——. *Memoirs: Years of Trial and Hope, 1946–52.* New York: Signet, 1956.

——. *Off the Record: The Private Papers of Harry S. Truman.* Ed. Robert H. Ferrell. New York: Harper & Row, 1980.

——. *Public Papers of the Presidents.* 8 vols. Washington, D.C.: GPO, 1961–66.

Tsou, Tang. *America's Failure in China, 1941–1950.* Chicago: Univ. of Chicago Press, 1963.

Tucker, Nancy Bernkopf. *Patterns in the Dust: Chinese-American Relations and the Recognition Controversy.* New York: Columbia Univ. Press, 1983.

Tucker, Robert C. "Stalin and the Soviet Controversy over Foreign Policy, 1949–1953." Paper presented at the U.S.-USSR Seminar on United States–Soviet Relations, 1950–1955. Athens, Ohio, 1988.

Ulam, Adam. *The Rivals: America and Russia Since World War II.* New York: Viking, 1971.

——. *Stalin, the Man and His Era.* New York: Viking, 1973.

United Nations. Dept. of Economic Affairs. *Economic Report: Salient Features of the World Economic Situation, 1945–1947.* Lake Success, N.Y.: United Nations, 1948.

——. *World Economic Report, 1948.* Lake Success, N.Y.: United Nations, 1948.

United Nations. Economic Commission for Asia and the Far East. *Economic Survey of Asia and the Far East.* Annually, 1948–1953, 1962. Lake Success, N.Y.: United Nations, 1949–1954, 1963.

United Nations. Economic Commission for Europe. *Economic Bulletin for Europe, 1949–1950.* Vols. 1–2. Geneva: United Nations, 1949–51.

——. *Economic Survey of Europe.* Annually, 1947–1953. Geneva: United Nations, 1948–1954.

Urban, Joan Barth. *Moscow and the Italian Communist Party: From Togliatti to Berlinguer.* Ithaca, N.Y.: Cornell Univ. Press, 1986.

Vandenberg, Arthur H. *Private Papers of Senator Vandenberg.* Ed. Arthur H. Vandenberg, Jr. Boston, Mass.: Houghton Mifflin, 1952.

Van der Wee, Herman. *Prosperity and Upheaval: The World Economy, 1945–1980.* Berkeley: Univ. of California Press, 1987.

Vardys, V. Stanley. "Germany's Postwar Socialism: Nationalism and Kurt Schumacher." *The Review of Politics* 27 (Apr 1965): 220–45.

Varg, Paul A. *The Closing of the Door: Sino-American Relations, 1936–1946.* East Lansing: Michigan State Univ. Press, 1973.

Vatikiotis, P. J. *The History of Egypt.* Baltimore, Md.: Johns Hopkins Univ. Press, 1985.

Villa, Brian L. "The U.S. Army, Unconditional Surrender, and the Potsdam Proclamation." *Journal of American History* 63 (June 1976): 66–92.

Vinson, Fred, and Dean Acheson. *The British Loan and What It Means to Us.* Washington, D.C.: GPO, 1946.

Walker, J. Samuel. "The Decision to Use the Bomb: An Historiographical Update." *Diplomatic History* 14 (Winter 1990): 97–114.

——. *Henry A. Wallace and American Foreign Policy.* Westport, Conn.: Greenwood, 1976.

——. " 'No More Cold War': American Foreign Policy and the 1948 Soviet Peace Offensive." *Diplomatic History* 5 (Winter 1981): 75–91.

Wall, Irwin M. *French Communism in the Era of Stalin: The Quest for Unity and Integration, 1945–1962.* Westport, Conn.: Greenwood, 1983.

——. *The United States and the Reshaping of Postwar France, 1945–1954.* New York: Cambridge Univ. Press, 1991.

Wallace, Henry A. *The Price of Vision: The Diary of Henry A. Wallace, 1942–1946.* Ed. John M. Blum. Boston, Mass.: Houghton Mifflin, 1973.

Wallerstein, Immanuel. *The Capitalist World Economy.* Cambridge, Eng.: Cambridge Univ. Press, 1979.

Wallich, Henry C. *Mainsprings of the German Revival.* New Haven, Conn.: Yale Univ. Press, 1955.

Walt, Stephen M. "Alliance Formation and the Balance of World Power." *International Security* 9 (Spring 1985): 3–43.

——. "The Case for Finite Containment: Analyzing U.S. Grand Strategy." *International Security* 14 (Summer 1989): 5–49.

Walton, Richard J. *Henry Wallace, Harry Truman, and the Cold War.* New York: Viking, 1976.

Wampler, Robert A. "The Die Is Cast: The United States and NATO Nuclear Planning, 1951–1954." Unpublished paper, 1987.

Ward, Patricia Dawson. *The Threat of Peace: James F. Byrnes and the Council of Foreign Ministers.* Kent, Ohio: Kent State Univ. Press, 1979.

Watson, Mark Skinner. *Chief of Staff: Prewar Plans and Preparations.* Washington, D.C.: Dept. of the Army, 1950.

Watt, D. Cameron. *Succeeding John Bull: America in Britain's Place, 1900–1975.* Cambridge, Eng.: Cambridge Univ. Press, 1984.

Weigert, Hans W. *Generals and Geographers: The Twilight of Geopolitics.* New York: Oxford Univ. Press, 1955.

Weil, Martin. *A Pretty Good Club: The Founding Fathers of the U.S. Foreign Service.* New York: Norton, 1978.

Weiler, Peter. "British Labour and the Cold War: The Foreign Policy of the Labour Governments, 1945–1951." *Journal of British Studies* 26 (Jan 1987): 54–82.

Weinberg, Gerhard L. *World in the Balance: Behind the Scenes of World War II*. Hanover, N.H.: Univ. Press of New England, 1981.

Weinstein, Allen. *Perjury: The Hiss-Chambers Case*. New York: Knopf, 1978.

Wells, Samuel F. "The Origins of Massive Retaliation." *Political Science Quarterly* 96 (Spring 1981): 31–52.

——. "Sounding the Tocsin: NSC 68 and the Soviet Threat." *International Security* 4 (Fall 1979): 116–48.

Westerfield, H. Bradford. *Foreign Policy and Party Politics: Pearl Harbor to Korea*. New Haven, Conn.: Yale Univ. Press, 1955.

Westoby, Adam. *Communism Since World War II*. New York: St. Martin's, 1981.

Wexler, Imanuel. *The Marshall Plan Revisited: The European Recovery Program in Economic Perspective*. Westport, Conn.: Greenwood, 1983.

Whiting, Allen S. *China Crosses the Yalu: The Decision to Enter the Korean War*. Stanford, Calif.: Stanford Univ. Press, 1960.

Wiebes, Carl, and Bert Zeeman. "The Pentagon Negotiations, March 1948: The Launching of the North Atlantic Treaty." *International Affairs* 59 (Summer 1983): 351–63.

Williams, Robert Chadwell. *Klaus Fuchs, Atom Spy*. Cambridge, Mass.: Harvard Univ. Press, 1987.

Wilson, Mary C. *King Abdullah, Britain and the Making of Jordan*. Cambridge, Eng.: Cambridge Univ. Press, 1987.

Winkler, Allan M. *Home Front U.S.A.: America During World War II*. Arlington Heights, Ill.: Harland Davidson, 1986.

Wittner, Lawrence S. *American Intervention in Greece, 1943–49*. New York: Columbia Univ. Press, 1982.

Wolk, Herman S. *Planning and Organizing the Postwar Air Force, 1943–1947*. Washington, D.C.: Office of Air Force History, 1984.

Wood, Robert E. *From Marshall Plan to Debt Crisis: Foreign Aid and Development Choices in the World Economy*. Berkeley: Univ. of California Press, 1986.

Woodbridge, George. *UNRRA: The History of the United Nations Relief and Rehabilitation Administration*. 3 vols. New York: Columbia Univ. Press, 1950.

Woodhouse, C. M. *The Struggle for Greece, 1941–1949*. London: Hart-Davis, MacGibbon, 1976.

Woods, Randall B. *A Changing of the Guard: Anglo-American Relations, 1941–1946*. Chapel Hill: Univ. of North Carolina Press, 1990.

Woods, Randall B., and Howard Jones. *Dawning of the Cold War: The United States' Quest for Order*. Athens: Univ. of Georgia Press, 1991.

Wright, Gordon. *The Ordeal of Total War, 1939–1945*. New York: Harper & Row, 1968.

Yasuhara, Yoko. "Japan, Communist China, and Export Controls in Asia, 1948–1952." *Diplomatic History* 10 (Winter 1986): 75–89.

Yergin, Daniel. *Shattered Peace: The Origins of the Cold War and the National Security State*. Boston, Mass.: Houghton Mifflin, 1977.

York, Herbert. *The Advisors: Oppenheimer, Teller, and the Superbomb*. San Francisco, Calif.: Freeman, 1976.

Yoshida Shigeru. *The Yoshida Memoirs: The Story of Japan in Crisis*. Boston, Mass.: Houghton Mifflin, 1962.

Young, John W. *Britain, France, and the Unity of Europe, 1945–1951*. Leicester, Eng.: Leicester Univ. Press, 1984.

Zimmern, Emily F. "American Business Views Toward Japan During the Allied Occupation, September 1945–April 1952." Master's thesis, Vanderbilt Univ., 1978.

Zink, Harold. *American Military Government in Germany*. New York: Macmillan, 1947.

Zinn, Howard. *Postwar America, 1945–1971*. Indianapolis, Ind.: Bobbs-Merrill, 1973.

Index

In this index an "f" after a number indicates a separate reference on the next page, and an "ff" indicates separate references on the next two pages. A continuous discussion over two or more pages is indicated by a span of page numbers, e.g., "57–59." *Passim* is used for a cluster of references in close but not consecutive sequence.

Library of Congress Cataloging-in-Publication Data

Leffler, Melvyn P., 1945–
    A preponderance of power : national security, the Truman
administration, and the cold war / Melvyn P. Leffler.
        p.   cm.
    Includes bibliographical references and index.
    ISBN 0-8047-1924-1
    1. United States—Foreign relations—1945–1953.   2. United States—
National security.   3. Cold War.   I. Title.
E813.L45   1991
327.73—dc20   70 3
91-13481
    CIP

⊗ This book is printed on acid-free paper